Title 16
Commercial Practices

Parts 1000 to End

Revised as of January 1, 2013

Containing a codification of documents of general applicability and future effect

As of January 1, 2013

Published by the Office of the Federal Register
National Archives and Records Administration
as a Special Edition of the Federal Register

U.S. GOVERNMENT OFFICIAL EDITION NOTICE

Legal Status and Use of Seals and Logos

The seal of the National Archives and Records Administration (NARA) authenticates the Code of Federal Regulations (CFR) as the official codification of Federal regulations established under the Federal Register Act. Under the provisions of 44 U.S.C. 1507, the contents of the CFR, a special edition of the Federal Register, shall be judicially noticed. The CFR is prima facie evidence of the original documents published in the Federal Register (44 U.S.C. 1510).

It is prohibited to use NARA's official seal and the stylized Code of Federal Regulations logo on any republication of this material without the express, written permission of the Archivist of the United States or the Archivist's designee. Any person using NARA's official seals and logos in a manner inconsistent with the provisions of 36 CFR part 1200 is subject to the penalties specified in 18 U.S.C. 506, 701, and 1017.

Use of ISBN Prefix

This is the Official U.S. Government edition of this publication and is herein identified to certify its authenticity. Use of the 0–16 ISBN prefix is for U.S. Government Printing Office Official Editions only. The Superintendent of Documents of the U.S. Government Printing Office requests that any reprinted edition clearly be labeled as a copy of the authentic work with a new ISBN.

U.S. GOVERNMENT PRINTING OFFICE

U.S. Superintendent of Documents • Washington, DC 20402–0001

http://bookstore.gpo.gov

Phone: toll-free (866) 512-1800; DC area (202) 512-1800

Table of Contents

Cite this Code: CFR

To cite the regulations in this volume use title, part and section number. Thus, 16 CFR 1000.1 *refers to title 16, part 1000, section 1.*

Explanation

The Code of Federal Regulations is a codification of the general and permanent rules published in the Federal Register by the Executive departments and agencies of the Federal Government. The Code is divided into 50 titles which represent broad areas subject to Federal regulation. Each title is divided into chapters which usually bear the name of the issuing agency. Each chapter is further subdivided into parts covering specific regulatory areas.

Each volume of the Code is revised at least once each calendar year and issued on a quarterly basis approximately as follows:

Title 1 through Title 16 ....as of January 1
Title 17 through Title 27 ....as of April 1
Title 28 through Title 41 ....as of July 1
Title 42 through Title 50 ....as of October 1

The appropriate revision date is printed on the cover of each volume.

LEGAL STATUS

The contents of the Federal Register are required to be judicially noticed (44 U.S.C. 1507). The Code of Federal Regulations is prima facie evidence of the text of the original documents (44 U.S.C. 1510).

HOW TO USE THE CODE OF FEDERAL REGULATIONS

The Code of Federal Regulations is kept up to date by the individual issues of the Federal Register. These two publications must be used together to determine the latest version of any given rule.

To determine whether a Code volume has been amended since its revision date (in this case, January 1, 2013), consult the "List of CFR Sections Affected (LSA)," which is issued monthly, and the "Cumulative List of Parts Affected," which appears in the Reader Aids section of the daily Federal Register. These two lists will identify the Federal Register page number of the latest amendment of any given rule.

EFFECTIVE AND EXPIRATION DATES

Each volume of the Code contains amendments published in the Federal Register since the last revision of that volume of the Code. Source citations for the regulations are referred to by volume number and page number of the Federal Register and date of publication. Publication dates and effective dates are usually not the same and care must be exercised by the user in determining the actual effective date. In instances where the effective date is beyond the cut-off date for the Code a note has been inserted to reflect the future effective date. In those instances where a regulation published in the Federal Register states a date certain for expiration, an appropriate note will be inserted following the text.

OMB CONTROL NUMBERS

The Paperwork Reduction Act of 1980 (Pub. L. 96–511) requires Federal agencies to display an OMB control number with their information collection request.

Many agencies have begun publishing numerous OMB control numbers as amendments to existing regulations in the CFR. These OMB numbers are placed as close as possible to the applicable recordkeeping or reporting requirements.

PAST PROVISIONS OF THE CODE

Provisions of the Code that are no longer in force and effect as of the revision date stated on the cover of each volume are not carried. Code users may find the text of provisions in effect on any given date in the past by using the appropriate List of CFR Sections Affected (LSA). For the convenience of the reader, a "List of CFR Sections Affected" is published at the end of each CFR volume. For changes to the Code prior to the LSA listings at the end of the volume, consult previous annual editions of the LSA. For changes to the Code prior to 2001, consult the List of CFR Sections Affected compilations, published for 1949-1963, 1964-1972, 1973-1985, and 1986-2000.

"[RESERVED]" TERMINOLOGY

The term "[Reserved]" is used as a place holder within the Code of Federal Regulations. An agency may add regulatory information at a "[Reserved]" location at any time. Occasionally "[Reserved]" is used editorially to indicate that a portion of the CFR was left vacant and not accidentally dropped due to a printing or computer error.

INCORPORATION BY REFERENCE

What is incorporation by reference? Incorporation by reference was established by statute and allows Federal agencies to meet the requirement to publish regulations in the Federal Register by referring to materials already published elsewhere. For an incorporation to be valid, the Director of the Federal Register must approve it. The legal effect of incorporation by reference is that the material is treated as if it were published in full in the Federal Register (5 U.S.C. 552(a)). This material, like any other properly issued regulation, has the force of law.

What is a proper incorporation by reference? The Director of the Federal Register will approve an incorporation by reference only when the requirements of 1 CFR part 51 are met. Some of the elements on which approval is based are:

(a) The incorporation will substantially reduce the volume of material published in the Federal Register.

(b) The matter incorporated is in fact available to the extent necessary to afford fairness and uniformity in the administrative process.

(c) The incorporating document is drafted and submitted for publication in accordance with 1 CFR part 51.

What if the material incorporated by reference cannot be found? If you have any problem locating or obtaining a copy of material listed as an approved incorporation by reference, please contact the agency that issued the regulation containing that incorporation. If, after contacting the agency, you find the material is not available, please notify the Director of the Federal Register, National Archives and Records Administration, 8601 Adelphi Road, College Park, MD 20740-6001, or call 202-741-6010.

CFR INDEXES AND TABULAR GUIDES

A subject index to the Code of Federal Regulations is contained in a separate volume, revised annually as of January 1, entitled CFR INDEX AND FINDING AIDS. This volume contains the Parallel Table of Authorities and Rules. A list of CFR titles, chapters, subchapters, and parts and an alphabetical list of agencies publishing in the CFR are also included in this volume.

An index to the text of "Title 3—The President" is carried within that volume.

The Federal Register Index is issued monthly in cumulative form. This index is based on a consolidation of the "Contents" entries in the daily Federal Register.

A List of CFR Sections Affected (LSA) is published monthly, keyed to the revision dates of the 50 CFR titles.

REPUBLICATION OF MATERIAL

There are no restrictions on the republication of material appearing in the Code of Federal Regulations.

INQUIRIES

For a legal interpretation or explanation of any regulation in this volume, contact the issuing agency. The issuing agency's name appears at the top of odd-numbered pages.

For inquiries concerning CFR reference assistance, call 202–741–6000 or write to the Director, Office of the Federal Register, National Archives and Records Administration, 8601 Adelphi Road, College Park, MD 20740-6001 or e-mail *fedreg.info@nara.gov*.

SALES

The Government Printing Office (GPO) processes all sales and distribution of the CFR. For payment by credit card, call toll-free, 866-512-1800, or DC area, 202-512-1800, M-F 8 a.m. to 4 p.m. e.s.t. or fax your order to 202-512-2104, 24 hours a day. For payment by check, write to: US Government Printing Office – New Orders, P.O. Box 979050, St. Louis, MO 63197-9000.

ELECTRONIC SERVICES

The full text of the Code of Federal Regulations, the LSA (List of CFR Sections Affected), The United States Government Manual, the Federal Register, Public Laws, Public Papers of the Presidents of the United States, Compilation of Presidential Documents and the Privacy Act Compilation are available in electronic format via *www.ofr.gov*. For more information, contact the GPO Customer Contact Center, U.S. Government Printing Office. Phone 202-512-1800, or 866-512-1800 (toll-free). E-mail, *ContactCenter@gpo.gov*.

The Office of the Federal Register also offers a free service on the National Archives and Records Administration's (NARA) World Wide Web site for public law numbers, Federal Register finding aids, and related information. Connect to NARA's web site at *www.archives.gov/federal-register*.

The e-CFR is a regularly updated, unofficial editorial compilation of CFR material and Federal Register amendments, produced by the Office of the Federal Register and the Government Printing Office. It is available at *www.ecfr.gov*.

CHARLES A. BARTH,
Director,
Office of the Federal Register.
January 1, 2013.

THIS TITLE

Title 16—COMMERCIAL PRACTICES is composed of two volumes. The first volume contains parts 0–999 and comprises chapter I—Federal Trade Commission. The second volume containing part 1000 to end comprises chapter II—Consumer Product Safety Commission. The contents of these volumes represent all current regulations codified under this title of the CFR as of January 1, 2013.

For this volume, Jonn V. Lilyea was Chief Editor. The Code of Federal Regulations publication program is under the direction of Michael L. White, assisted by Ann Worley.

Title 16—Commercial Practices

(This book contains part 1000 to End)

CHAPTER II—CONSUMER PRODUCT SAFETY COMMISSION

EDITORIAL NOTES: 1. For documents affecting chapter II on rule review under the Regulatory Flexibility Act see 52 FR 5079, Feb. 19, 1987 and 54 FR 601, Jan. 9, 1989.

2. Nomenclature changes to chapter II appear at 69 FR 18803, Apr. 9, 2004.

SUBCHAPTER A—GENERAL

SUBCHAPTER A—GENERAL

PART 1000—COMMISSION ORGANIZATION AND FUNCTIONS

AUTHORITY: 5 U.S.C. 552(a).

SOURCE: 71 FR 5165, Feb. 1, 2006, unless otherwise noted.

§ 1000.1 The Commission.

(a) The Consumer Product Safety Commission is an independent regulatory agency formed on May 14, 1973, under the provisions of the Consumer Product Safety Act (Pub. L. 92–573, 86 Stat. 1207, as amended (15 U.S.C. 2051, *et seq.*)). The purposes of the Commission under the CPSA are:

(1) To protect the public against unreasonable risks of injury associated with consumer products;

(2) To assist consumers in evaluating the comparative safety of consumer products;

(3) To develop uniform safety standards for consumer products and to minimize conflicting State and local regulations; and

(4) To promote research and investigation into the causes and prevention of product-related deaths, illnesses, and injuries.

(b) The Commission is authorized to consist of five members appointed by the President, by and with the advice and consent of the Senate, for terms of seven years. However, the Departments of Veterans Affairs and Housing and Urban Development, and Independent Agencies Appropriations Act, 1993, Public Law 102–389, limited funding to that for three Commissioners for fiscal year 1993 and thereafter.

§ 1000.2 Laws administered.

The Commission administers five acts:

(a) The Consumer Product Safety Act (Pub. L. 92–573, 86 Stat. 1207, as amended (15 U.S.C. 2051, *et seq.*)).

(b) The Flammable Fabrics Act (Pub. L. 90–189, 67 Stat. 111, as amended (15 U.S.C. 1191, *et seq.*)).

(c) The Federal Hazardous Substances Act (Pub. L. 86–613, 74 Stat. 380, as amended (15 U.S.C. 1261, *et seq.*)).

(d) The Poison Prevention Packaging Act of 1970 (Pub. L. 91–601, 84 Stat. 1670, as amended (15 U.S.C. 1471, *et seq.*)).

(e) The Refrigerator Safety Act of 1956 (Pub. L. 84–930, 70 Stat. 953, (15 U.S.C. 1211, *et seq.*)).

§ 1000.3 Hotline.

(a) The Commission operates a toll-free telephone Hotline by which the public can communicate with the Commission. The number for use in all 50 states is 1–800–638–CPSC (1–800–638–2772).

(b) The Commission also operates a toll-free Hotline by which hearing or speech-impaired persons can communicate with the Commission by teletypewriter. The teletypewriter number for use in all states is 1–800–638–8270.

(c) The Commission also makes available to the public product recall information, its public calendar, and other information through its worldwide Web site at *http://www.cpsc.gov*. The public may also report product hazards or other information to the Commission at its e-mail address: *info@cpsc.gov*.

§ 1000.4 Commission address.

The principal Offices of the Commission are at 4330 East West Highway, Bethesda, Maryland 20814. All written communications with the Commission, including those sent by U.S. Postal Service, private express and messenger should be addressed to the Consumer Product Safety Commission at that address, unless otherwise specifically directed.

§ 1000.5 Petitions.

Any interested person may petition the Commission to issue, amend, or revoke a rule or regulation by submitting a written request to the Secretary, Consumer Product Safety Commission, 4330 East West Highway, Bethesda, Maryland 20814. Petitions must comply with the Commission's procedure for petitioning for rulemaking at 16 CFR part 1051.

§ 1000.6 Commission decisions and records.

(a) Each decision of the Commission, acting in an official capacity as a collegial body, is recorded in Minutes of Commission meetings or as a separate Record of Commission Action. Copies of Minutes or of a Record of Commission Action may be obtained by e-mail (*cpsc-os@cpsc.gov*) or written request to the Secretary, Consumer Product Safety Commission, 4330 East West Highway, Bethesda, Maryland 20814, or may be examined at Commission headquarters. Requests should identify the subject matter of the Commission action and the approximate date of the Commission action, if known.

(b) Other records in the custody of the Commission may be requested by e-mail (*cpsc-os@cpsc.gov*) or in writing from the Office of the Secretary pursuant to the Commission's Procedures for Disclosure or Production of Information under the Freedom of Information Act (16 CFR part 1015).

§ 1000.7 Advisory opinions and interpretations of regulations.

(a) *Advisory opinions*. Upon written request, the General Counsel provides written advisory opinions interpreting the acts and administrative regulations (*e.g.*, Freedom of Information Act regulations) the Commission administers, provided the request contains sufficient specific factual information upon which to base an opinion. Advisory opinions represent the legal opinions of the General Counsel and may be changed or superseded by the Commission. Requests for advisory opinions should be sent to the General Counsel, Consumer Product Safety Commission, 4330 East West Highway, Bethesda, Maryland 20814. Previously issued advisory opinions are available on the CPSC Web site at *http://www.cpsc.gov/library/foia/advisory/advisory.html*. A copy of a particular previously issued advisory opinion or a copy of an index of such opinions may also be obtained by written request to the Office of the Secretary, Consumer Product Safety Commission, 4330 East West Highway, Bethesda, Maryland 20814.

(b) *Interpretations of regulations*. Upon written request, the Assistant Executive Director for Compliance will issue written interpretations of Commission regulations pertaining to the safety standards and the enforcement of those standards, provided the request contains sufficient specific factual information upon which to base an interpretation. Interpretations of regulations represent the interpretations of the staff and may be changed or superseded by the Commission. Requests for such interpretations should be sent to the Assistant Executive Director for Compliance, Consumer Product Safety Commission, 4330 East West Highway, Bethesda, Maryland 20814.

§ 1000.8 Meetings and hearings; public notice.

(a) The Commission may meet and exercise all its powers in any place.

(b) Meetings of the Commission are held as ordered by the Commission and, unless otherwise ordered, are held at the principal office of the Commission at 4330 East West Highway, Bethesda, Maryland. Meetings of the Commission for the purpose of jointly conducting the formal business of the agency, including the rendering of official decisions, are generally announced in advance and open to the public, as provided by the Government in the Sunshine Act (5 U.S.C. 552b) and the Commission's Meetings Policy (16 CFR part 1012).

(c) The Commission may conduct any hearing or other inquiry necessary or appropriate to its functions anywhere in the United States. It will publish a notice of any proposed hearing in the FEDERAL REGISTER and will afford a reasonable opportunity for interested persons to present relevant testimony and data.

(d) Notices of Commission meetings, Commission hearings, and other Commission activities are published in a Public Calendar, as provided in the Commission's Meetings Policy (16 CFR part 1012). The Public Calendar is available on the Commission Web site at *http://www.cpsc.gov*.

§ 1000.9 Quorum.

Three members of the Commission constitute a quorum for the transaction of business. If there are only three members serving on the Commission, two members constitute a quorum. If there are only two members serving on the Commission because of vacancies, two members constitute a quorum, but only for six months from the time the number of members was reduced to two.

NOTE: The Departments of Veterans Affairs and Housing and Urban Development, and Independent Agencies Appropriations Act, 1993, Pub. L. 102–389, limited funding to that for three Commissioners for fiscal year 1993 and thereafter.

§ 1000.10 The Chairman and Vice Chairman.

(a) The Chairman is the principal executive officer of the Commission and, subject to the general policies of the Commission and to such regulatory decisions, findings, and determinations as the Commission is by law authorized to make, he or she exercises all of the executive and administrative functions of the Commission.

(b) The Commission shall annually elect a Vice Chairman for a term beginning on June 1. The Vice Chairman shall serve until the election of his or her successor. The Vice Chairman acts in the absence or disability of the Chairman or in case of a vacancy in the Office of the Chairman.

§ 1000.11 Delegation of functions.

Section 27(b)(9) of the Consumer Product Safety Act (15 U.S.C. 2076(b)(9)) authorizes the Commission to delegate any of its functions and powers, other than the power to issue subpoenas, to any officer or employee of the Commission. Delegations are documented in the Commission's Directives System.

§ 1000.12 Organizational structure.

The Consumer Product Safety Commission is composed of the principal units listed in this section.

(a) The following units report directly to the Chairman of the Commission:

(1) Office of the General Counsel;

(2) Office of Congressional Relations;

(3) Office of the Inspector General;

(4) Office of Equal Employment Opportunity and Minority Enterprise;

(5) Office of the Executive Director.

(b) The following units report directly to the Executive Director of the Commission:

(1) Office of Financial Management, Planning and Evaluation;

(2) Office of Hazard Identification and Reduction;

(3) Office of Information and Public Affairs;

(4) Office of Compliance and Field Operations;

(5) Office of Human Resources Management;

(6) Office of Information and Technology Services;

(7) Office of International Programs and Intergovernmental Affairs.

(c) The following units report directly to the Assistant Executive Director for Hazard Identification and Reduction:

(1) Directorate for Economic Analysis;

(2) Directorate for Epidemiology;

(3) Directorate for Health Sciences;

(4) Directorate for Engineering Sciences;

(5) Directorate for Laboratory Sciences.

§ 1000.13 Directives System.

The Commission maintains a Directives System which contains delegations of authority and descriptions of Commission programs, policies, and procedures. A complete set of directives is available for inspection in the public reading room at Commission headquarters.

§ 1000.14 Office of the General Counsel.

The Office of the General Counsel provides advice and counsel to the Commissioners and organizational components of the Commission on matters of law arising from operations of the Commission. It prepares the legal analysis of Commission legislative proposals and comments on relevant legislative proposals originating elsewhere. The Office, in conjunction with the Department of Justice, is responsible for the conduct of all Federal court litigation to which the Commission is a party. The Office also advises the Commission on administrative litigation matters. The Office provides final legal review of and makes recommendations to the Commission on proposed product safety standards, rules, regulations, petition actions, and substantial hazard actions. It also provides legal review of certain procurement, personnel, and administrative actions and drafts documents for publication in the FEDERAL REGISTER.

§ 1000.15 Office of Congressional Relations.

The Office of Congressional Relations is the principal contact with the committees and members of Congress and state legislative bodies. It performs liaison duties for the Commission, provides information and assistance to Congress on matters of Commission policy, and coordinates testimony and appearances by Commissioners and agency personnel before Congress.

§ 1000.16 Office of the Inspector General.

The Office of the Inspector General is an independent office established under the provisions of the Inspector General Act of 1978, 5 U.S.C. appendix, as amended. This Office independently initiates, conducts, supervises, and coordinates audits, operations reviews, and investigations of Commission programs, activities, and operations. The Office also makes recommendations to promote economy, efficiency, and effectiveness within the Commission's programs and operations. The Office receives and investigates complaints or information concerning possible violations of law, rules, or regulations, mismanagement, abuse of authority, and waste of funds. It reviews existing and proposed legislation concerning the economy, efficiency, and effectiveness of such legislation on Commission operations.

§ 1000.17 Office of Equal Employment Opportunity and Minority Enterprise.

The Office of Equal Employment Opportunity and Minority Enterprise is responsible for assuring compliance with all laws and regulations relating to equal employment opportunity. The Office provides advice and assistance to the Chairman and Commission staff on all EEO related issues including the agency Small and Disadvantaged Business Utilization Program. The Office develops agency EEO program policies. The Office manages the discrimination complaint process, including the adjudication of discrimination complaints, and facilitates Affirmative Employment Program (AEP) planning for women, minorities, individuals with disabilities and disabled veterans. The Office plans and executes special emphasis programs and special programs with minority colleges, and EEO, diversity, prevention of sexual harassment and related training. The Office identifies trends, personnel policies and practices that have an impact on EEO and makes recommendations to the Chairman on the effectiveness and efficiency of EEO programs and methods to enhance equal opportunity.

§ 1000.18 Office of Executive Director.

The Executive Director with the assistance of the Deputy Executive Director, under the broad direction of the Chairman and in accordance with Commission policy, acts as the chief operating manager of the agency, supporting the development of the agency's budget and operating plan before and after Commission approval, and managing the execution of those plans. The Executive Director has direct line authority over the following directorates and offices: the Office of Financial Management, Planning and Evaluation, the Office of Hazard Identification and Reduction, the Office of Information and Public Affairs, the Office of Compliance and Field Operations, the Office of Human Resources Management, the Office of Information and Technology Services, and the Office of International Programs and Intergovernmental Affairs.

§ 1000.19 Office of Financial Management, Planning and Evaluation.

The Office of Financial Management, Planning and Evaluation is responsible for developing the Commission's funds control system, long-range strategic plans, annual performance budgets and operating plans; analysis of major policy and operational issues; performing evaluations and management studies of Commission programs and activities; ensuring that Commission resources are procured and expended as planned and according to purchasing regulations; the review, control, and payment of Commission financial obligations; and, reporting on the use and performance of Commission resources. The Office recommends actions to the Executive Director to enhance the effectiveness of Commission programs and the management of budget, planning and evaluation, financial, and procurement activities. The Office serves as the staff support to the Commission Chief Financial Officer.

§ 1000.20 Office of Information and Public Affairs.

The Office of Information and Public Affairs, which is managed by the Director of the Office, is responsible for the development, implementation, and evaluation of a comprehensive national information and public affairs program designed to promote product safety. This includes responsibility for developing and maintaining relations with a wide range of national groups such as consumer organizations; business groups; trade associations; state and local government entities; labor organizations; medical, legal, scientific and other professional associations; and other Federal health, safety and consumer agencies. The Office also is responsible for implementing the Commission's media relations program nationwide. The Office serves as the Commission's spokesperson to the national print and broadcast media, develops and disseminates the Commission's news releases, and organizes Commission news conferences.

§ 1000.21 Office of Compliance and Field Operations.

The Office of Compliance and Field Operations conducts compliance and administrative enforcement activities under all administered acts, provides advice and guidance on complying with all administered acts and reviews proposed standards and rules with respect to their enforceability. The Office's responsibilities also include identifying and addressing safety hazards in consumer products already in distribution, promoting industry compliance with existing safety rules, and conducting administrative litigation. It conducts field enforcement efforts, including providing program guidance, advice, and case guidance to field staff. It enforces the Consumer Product Safety Act reporting requirements. It reviews consumer complaints, conducts inspections and in-depth investigations, and analyzes available data to identify those consumer products containing defects posing a substantial risk of injury or which do not comply with existing safety requirements. The Office negotiates and monitors corrective action plans for products that are defective or fail to comply with specific regulations. It gathers information on product hazards that may be addressed through rulemaking or voluntary standards. The Office develops surveillance strategies and programs designed to assure compliance with Commission standards and regulations. The Office of Compliance and Field Operations also assists the Office of Information and Public Affairs in implementing consumer information activities nationwide, including wide-ranging public information and education programs designed to reduce consumer product injuries and deaths, and maintaining liaison with, and providing support to, other components of the Commission and appropriate State and local government offices.

§ 1000.22 Office of Human Resources Management.

The Office of Human Resources Management, which is managed by the Director of the Office, provides human resources management support to the Commission in the areas of recruitment and placement, position classification, training and executive development, employee and labor relations, employee benefits and retirement assistance, employee assistance programs, drug testing, leave administration, disciplinary and adverse actions, grievances and appeals, and performance management.

§ 1000.23 Office of Information and Technology Services.

The Office of Information and Technology Services houses the Commission's Secretariat, which facilitates the preparation of the Commission's agenda; coordinates Commission business at official meetings; maintains the dockets and other materials for the Commission's public and non-public administrative and adjudicative meetings and hearings; prepares and publishes the Public Calendar; maintains the Commission's Injury Information Clearinghouse; issues Commission Orders; provides legal notice of Commission decisions through publication in the FEDERAL REGISTER; processes all filings that the Commission receives in paper, electronic and alternative media formats; exercises joint responsibility with the Office of the General Counsel for interpretation and application of the Privacy Act, Freedom of Information Act, and the Government in the Sunshine Act; prepares reports required by these acts; and maintains and manages all official Commission records including those pertaining to continuing guarantees of compliance with applicable standards of flammability under the Flammable Fabrics Act filed with the Commission. The Secretary is the agency's Chief Freedom of Information Act Officer. The Office of Information and Technology Services is also responsible for the general policy and planning issues related to the dissemination of information by the Commission including, but not limited to, OMB Circular A–130, the Federal Information Security Management Act, the Government Paperwork Elimination Act, Section 508 of the Americans with Disabilities Act, and the E-Government Act under the President's Management Agenda; the design, implementation and support of the Commission's information technology system needs; maintaining and/or providing access to administrative applications for the Commission's business processes such as payroll, accounting, personnel, budget, information management and work tracking; administration of the network, telephone systems, and Help Desk. The Office of Information and Technology Services also is responsible for providing the Commission with printing, mail, and copy services, library services, logistical, real and personal property management services; and addressing safety and ergonomic issues in the work place.

§ 1000.24 Office of International Programs and Intergovernmental Affairs.

The Office of International Programs and Intergovernmental Affairs provides a comprehensive and coordinated effort in consumer product safety standards development and implementation at the international, Federal, State and local level. The office conducts activities and creates strategies aimed at ensuring greater import compliance with recognized American safety standards and exportation of CPSC regulatory policies, technologies and methodologies into other jurisdictions. The office also works to harmonize the use of standards worldwide.

§ 1000.25 Office of Hazard Identification and Reduction.

The Office of Hazard Identification and Reduction, under the direction of the Assistant Executive Director for Hazard Identification and Reduction, is responsible for managing the Commission's Hazard Identification and Analysis Program and its Hazard Assessment and Reduction Program. The Office reports to the Executive Director, and has line authority over the Directorates for Epidemiology and Health Sciences, Economic Analysis, Engineering Sciences, and Laboratory Sciences. The Office develops strategies for and implements the agency's operating plans for these two hazard programs. This includes the collection and analysis of data to identify hazards and hazard patterns, the implementation of the Commission's safety standards development projects, the coordination of voluntary standards activities, and providing overall direction and evaluation of projects involving hazard analysis, data collection, emerging hazards, mandatory and voluntary standards, petitions, and labeling rules. The Office assures that relevant technical, environmental, economic, and social impacts of projects are comprehensively and objectively presented to the Commission for decision.

§ 1000.26 Directorate for Epidemiology.

The Directorate for Epidemiology, managed by the Associate Executive Director for Epidemiology, is responsible for the collection and analysis of data on injuries and deaths associated with consumer products. The Directorate has two divisions: the Data Systems Division and the Hazard Analysis Division. The Data Systems Division operates the national data collection systems which provide the data that serve as the basis for the Commission's estimates of the numbers of deaths and injuries associated with consumer products. These data systems include the National Electronic Injury Surveillance System, a nationally representative sample of hospital emergency departments; a death certificate file, which contains data obtained from death certificates on deaths associated with consumer products; and the Injury and Potential Injury Incident file, which contains information on, among other things, incidents associated with consumer products, based on news clips, medical examiner reports, hotline reports, Internet complaints, and referrals. The Hazard Analysis Division conducts statistical analysis of these data and conducts epidemiologic studies to estimate the numbers of injuries and deaths associated with various consumer products and to examine factors associated with these injuries and deaths. In addition, staff in the Hazard Analysis Division design special studies, design and analyze data from experiments for testing of consumer products, and provide statistical expertise and advice to Commission staff in support of regulation development.

§ 1000.27 Directorate for Health Sciences.

The Directorate for Health Sciences is managed by the Associate Executive Director for Health Sciences and is responsible for reviewing and evaluating the human health effects and hazards related to consumer products and assessing exposure, uptake and metabolism, including information on population segments at risk. Directorate staff conducts health studies and research in the field of consumer product-related injuries. The Directorate performs risk assessments for chemical, physiological and physical hazards based on methods such as medical injury modeling, and on injury and incident data for mechanical, thermal, chemical and electrical hazards in consumer products. It provides the Commission's primary source of scientific expertise for implementation of the Poison Prevention Packaging Act and the Federal Hazardous Substances Act. The Directorate assists in the development and evaluation of product safety standards and test methods based on scientific and public health principles. It provides support to the Commission's regulatory development and enforcement activities. It manages hazard identification and analysis, and hazard assessment and reduction projects as assigned. The Directorate provides liaison with the National Toxicology Program, the Department of Health and Human Services (including the Food and Drug Administration, the Centers for Disease Control and Prevention, the National Institutes of Health), the Occupational Health and Safety Administration, the Environmental Protection Agency, other Federal agencies and programs, and other organizations concerned with reducing the risk to consumers from exposure to consumer product hazards.

§ 1000.28 Directorate for Economic Analysis.

The Directorate for Economic Analysis, which is managed by the Associate Executive Director for Economic Analysis, is responsible for providing the Commission with advice and information on economic and environmental matters and on the economic, social and environmental effects of Commission actions. It analyzes the potential effects of CPSC actions on consumers and on industries, including effects on competitive structure and commercial practices. The Directorate acquires, compiles, and maintains economic data on movements and trends in the general economy and on the production, distribution, and sales of consumer products and their components to assist in the analysis of CPSC priorities, policies, actions, and rules. It plans and carries out economic surveys of consumers and industries. It studies the costs of accidents and injuries. It evaluates the economic, societal, and environmental impact of product safety rules and standards. It performs regulatory analyses and studies of costs and benefits of CPSC actions as required by the Consumer Product Safety Act, The National Environmental Policy Act, the Regulatory Flexibility Act and other Acts, and by policies established by the Consumer Product Safety Commission. The Directorate manages hazard assessment and reduction projects as assigned.

§ 1000.29 Directorate for Engineering Sciences.

The Directorate for Engineering Sciences, which is managed by the Associate Executive Director for Engineering Sciences, is responsible for developing technical policy for and implementing the Commission's engineering programs. The Directorate manages hazard assessment and reduction projects as assigned by the Office of Hazard Identification and Reduction; provides engineering technical support and product safety assessments for the Office of Compliance and Field Operations; provides engineering, scientific, and technical expertise to the Commission and Commission staff as requested; and provides engineering technical support to other Commission organizations, activities, and programs as needed. The Directorate develops and evaluates product safety standards, product safety tests and test methods, performance criteria, design specifications, and quality control standards for consumer products, based on engineering and scientific methods. It conducts engineering analysis and testing of the safety of consumer products, and evaluates and participates in the development of mandatory and voluntary standards for consumer products including engineering and human factors analyses in support of standards development and product compliance testing. The Directorate performs or monitors research for consumer products in a broad array of engineering disciplines including chemical, electrical, fire protection, human factors, and mechanical engineering. It conducts and coordinates engineering research, testing, and evaluation activities with other Federal agencies, private industry, and consumer interest groups. The Directorate conducts human factors studies and research of consumer product related injuries, including evaluations of labels, signs and symbols, instructions, and other measures intended to address the human component of injury prevention. The Directorate provides technical supervision and direction of engineering activities including tests and analyses conducted in the field.

§ 1000.30 Directorate for Laboratory Sciences.

The Directorate for Laboratory Sciences, which is managed by the Associate Executive Director for Laboratory Sciences, is responsible for conducting engineering analyses and testing of consumer products, supporting the development of voluntary and mandatory standards, and supporting the Agency's compliance activities through product safety assessments. A wide variety of products are tested and evaluated to determine the causes of failure and the hazards presented. Product safety tests involve mechanical, electrical, and combustion engineering, as well as thermal and chemical analyses. Test protocols are developed, test fixtures and setups are designed and fabricated, and tests are conducted following the requirements and guidance of voluntary and mandatory standards and/or using sound engineering and scientific judgment. The Laboratory participates with and supports other agency directorates on multi-disciplinary teams in the development of voluntary and mandatory standards. The Laboratory coordinates and cooperates with other Federal agencies, private industry, and consumer interest groups by sharing engineering and scientific research, test, and evaluation expertise. Additionally, Corrective Action Plans, proposed by manufacturers to correct a product defect, are tested and evaluated to assure that the proposed changes adequately resolve the problem. Regulated products, such as children's products, sleepwear, and bicycle helmets, are routinely tested and evaluated for compliance with the Consumer Product Safety Act, the Federal Hazardous Substances Act, the Flammable Fabrics Act, and the Poison Prevention Packaging Act. The Directorate is composed of the Mechanical Engineering Division, the Electrical Engineering Division (which includes flammable fabrics), and the Chemical Division. Overall, the directorate provides engineering, scientific, and other technical expertise to all entities within the Consumer Product Safety Commission.

PART 1009—GENERAL STATEMENTS OF POLICY OR INTERPRETATION

§ 1009.3 Policy on imported products, importers, and foreign manufacturers.

(a) This policy states the Commission's views as to imported products subject to the Consumer Product Safety Act (15 U.S.C. 2051) and the other Acts the Commission administers: The Federal Hazardous Substances Act (15 U.S.C. 1261), the Flammable Fabrics Act (15 U.S.C. 1191), the Poison Prevention Packaging Act (15 U.S.C. 1471), and the Refrigerator Safety Act (15 U.S.C. 1211). Basically, the Policy states that in order to fully protect the American consumer from hazardous consumer products the Commission will seek to ensure that importers and foreign manufacturers, as well as domestic manufacturers, distributors, and retailers, carry out their obligations and responsibilities under the five Acts. The Commission will also seek to establish, to the maximum extent possible, uniform import procedures for products subject to the Acts the Commission administers.

(b) The Consumer Product Safety Act recognizes the critical position of importers in protecting American consumers from unreasonably hazardous products made abroad and accordingly, under that Act, importers are made subject to the same responsibilities as domestic manufacturers. This is explicitly stated in the definition of "manufacturer" as any person who manufacturers or imports a consumer product (Section 3(a)(4); 15 U.S.C. 2052(a)(4)).

(c) The Federal Hazardous Substances Act (15 U.S.C. 1261 *et seq.*), the Flammable Fabrics Act (15 U.S.C. 1191 *et seq.*), the Poison Prevention Packaging Act (15 U.S.C. 1471 *et seq.*), which were transferred to the jurisdiction of the Consumer Product Safety Commission under its enabling act, all assign responsibilities to importers comparable to those of manufacturers and distributors.

(d) Historically, foreign-made products entering the United States were "cleared" by those agencies with particular jurisdiction over them. Products so cleared were limited in number relative to total imports. The Consumer Product Safety Commission has jurisdiction over a far larger number of products entering the United States through over 300 ports of entry. In addition, the total number of imports has dramatically increased over the years and modern technology has brought air transport and containerized freight for rapid handling and distribution of consumer and other products. For the Commission to effectively "clear" such products through ports of entry could seriously impede and delay the transport of consumer products and impose additional costs to both the consumer and the importer.

(e) The Consumer Product Safety Act provides alternative means to both assure the consumer safe products and facilitate the free movement of consumer products in commerce. For example, it requires certification by manufacturers (foreign and domestic), importers and private labelers of products that are subject to a consumer product safety standard. Such certification must be based on a test of each product or upon a reasonable testing program. The other acts enforced by the Commission do not specifically require certificates; however, both the Flammable Fabrics Act and the Federal Hazardous Substances Act encourage guarantees of compliance by protecting from criminal prosecution persons who have in good faith received such guarantees (15 U.S.C. 1197(a); 16 CFR 302.11; 15 U.S.C. 1264(b)).

(f) In the interest of giving the American consumer the full measure of protection from hazardous products anticipated by the Congress, it is the Commission's policy to assure that importers and foreign manufacturers carry out their responsibilities under all laws administered by this Commission. Specifically:

(1) Importers have responsibilities and obligations comparable to those of domestic manufacturers. Rules and regulations promulgated by the Commission will reflect these responsibilities and obligations.

(2) In promulgating its rules and regulations, the Commission encourages the participation and comments of the import community, including importers and foreign manufacturers.

(3) All imported products under the jurisdiction of the Consumer Product Safety Commission shall, to the maximum extent possible, be subject to uniform import procedures. The Commission recognizes the need to establish and implement procedures that minimize delay and expense involved in inspecting cargo at a port of entry. The Commission encourages cooperation between importers, foreign manufacturers and foreign governments, which increases the safety of the consumer and facilitates the free movement of goods between countries.

(4) When enforcement actions are appropriate, they will be directed toward the responsible officials of any import organization and will not be restricted to action solely against the product.

(5) Legal actions sought by the Commission will usually be primarily directed toward the owner or consignee of imported goods rather than against the customs broker even though his or her name may appear as the importer of record. However, the Commissioner believes it will not serve the public interest to impede the Commission's rights of investigation and enforcement by exempting a customs broker from the coverage of the law merely because of his or her title or usual form of business. It may be relevant that a customs broker, who does not have an ownership interest in the goods but who is acting as an agent for the actual owner or consignee, signs the entry documents as importer of record. What effect and possible need for inclusion this will have in a particular case can be judged by the Commission on a case-by-case basis.

(6) Commission procedures on imports shall be developed in the context of the overall responsibilities, authorities, priorities, resources, and compliance philosophy of this Commission. Any existing procedures which have been inherited from predecessor agencies will be reviewed and revised, if necessary, to be consistent with the authority and philosophy of this Commission.

(g) The Commission recognizes that the importer may not be the only person to be held responsible for protecting American Consumers from unreasonably hazardous products made abroad, but the importer is, at least, in a strategic position to guarantee the safety of imported products.

(h) Whenever, in the application of this policy, it appears that barriers to free trade may arise, the Commission may consider exceptions to this policy insofar as it can be done without compromising the Commission's responsibilities to assure safe products to the consumer.

(i) Whenever, in the application of this policy, it appears that administrative or procedural aspects of the Commission's regulations are unduly burdening the free flow of goods, the Commission may consider modifications which alleviate such burdens. However, the Commission cannot consider any modifications which do not assure the consumer the same protection from unsafe foreign goods as from unsafe domestic goods.

(Sec. 9, 15 U.S.C. 1198, 67 Stat. 114; Sec. 14, 15 U.S.C. 1273, 74 Stat. 379; 80 Stat. 1304, 1305; Sec. 17, 15 U.S.C. 2066, 86 Stat. 1223)

[40 FR 47486, Oct. 9, 1975, as amended at 41 FR 47915, Nov. 1, 1976]

§ 1009.8 Policy on establishing priorities for Commission action.

(a) This document states the Consumer Product Safety Commission's policy on establishing priorities for action under the five acts the Commission administers. The policy is issued pursuant to sections 4(f)(2) and 4(f)(3) of the Consumer Product Safety Act, as amended, and in further implementation of the Commission's statement of policy dated September 21, 1973.

(b) It is the general policy of the Commission that priorities for Commission action will be established by a majority vote of its members. The policy will be reflected by votes on all requests for appropriations, an annual operating plan, and any revisions thereof. Recognizing that these documents are the result of a lengthy planning process, during which many decisions are made that substantially determine the content of the final documents, the Chairman shall continually keep the Commission apprised of, and seek its guidance concerning, significant problems, policy questions and alternative solutions throughout the planning cycle leading to the development of budget requests and operating plans.

(1) *Requests for appropriations.* Requests for appropriations are submitted concurrently to the President or the Office of Management and Budget and to the Congress pursuant to section 27(k)(1) of the Consumer Product Safety Act.

(2) *Annual operating plan.* The operating plan shall be as specific as possible with regard to products, groups of products, or generic hazards to be addressed. It shall be submitted to the Commission for approval at least 30 days prior to the beginning of the fiscal year.

(c) In establishing and revising its priorities, the Commission will endeavor to fulfill each of its purposes as set forth in section 2(b) of the Consumer Product Safety Act. In so doing, it will apply the following general criteria:

(1) *Frequency and severity of injuries.* Two major criteria in determining priorities are the frequency and severity of injuries associated with consumer products. All available data including the NEISS hazard index and supplementary data collection systems, such as fire surveys and death certificate collection, shall be used to attempt to identify the frequency and severity of injuries. Consideration shall also be given to areas known to be undercounted by NEISS and a judgment reached as to the probable frequency and severity of injuries in such areas. The judgment as to severity shall include an evaluation of the seriousness of the injury.

(2) *Causality of injuries.* Consideration shall then be given to the amenability of a product hazard to injury reduction through standard setting, information and education, or other Commission action. This step involves an analysis of the extent to which the product and other factors such as consumer behavior are causally related to the injury pattern. Priority shall be assigned to products according to the extent of product causality involvement and the extent of injuries that can reasonably be expected to be reduced or eliminated through commission action.

(3) *Chronic illness and future injuries.* Certain products, although not presently associated with large numbers of

frequent or severe injuries, deserve priority attention if there is reason to believe that the products will in the future be associated with many such injuries. Although not as susceptible to measurements as other product related injuries and illnesses, these risks shall be evaluated on the basis of the best information available and given priority on the basis of the predicted future illnesses and injuries and the effectiveness of Commission action in reducing or eliminating them.

(4) *Cost and benefit of CPSC action.* Consideration shall be given on a preliminary basis to the prospective cost of Commission action to consumers and producers, and to the benefits expected to accrue to society from the resulting reduction of injuries. Consideration of product cost increases will be supplemented to the extent feasible and necessary by assessments of effects on utility or convenience of the product; product sales and shifts to substitutes; and industry supply factors, competitive structure, or employment. While all these facets of potential social "cost" cannot be subsumed in a single, quantitative cost measure, they will be weighed, to the extent they are available, against injury reduction benefits. The benefit estimates will be based on (i) explicitly stated expectations as to the effectiveness of regulatory options (derived from criterion (2), "causality of injuries"); (ii) costs of injuries and deaths based on the latest injury cost data and analyses available to the Commission; (iii) explicit estimates or assumptions as to average product lives; and (iv) such other factors as may be relevant in particular cases. The Commission recognizes that in analyzing benefits as well as costs there will frequently be modifying factors—e.g., criteria (5) and (6)—or analytical uncertainties that complicate matters and militate against reliance on single numerical expressions. Hence the Commission cannot commit itself to priorities based solely on the preliminary cost/benefit comparisons that will be available at the stage of priority setting, nor to any one form of comparison such as net benefits or cost-benefit ratios. Commission costs will also be considered. The Commission has a responsibility to insure that its resources are utilized efficiently. Assuming other factors to be equal, a higher priority will be assigned to those products which can be addressed using fewer Commission resources.

(5) *Unforeseen nature of the risk.* Other things being equal, consideration should be to the degree of consumer awareness both of the hazard and of its consequences. Priority could then be given to unforeseen and unforeseeable risks arising from the ordinary use of a product.

(6) *Vulnerability of the population at risk.* Children, the elderly, and the handicapped are often less able to judge or escape certain dangers in a consumer product or in the home environment. Because these consumers are, therefore, more vulnerable to danger in products designed for their special use or frequently used by them, the Commission will usually place a higher priority, assuming other factors are equal, on preventing product related injury to children, the handicapped, and senior citizens.

(7) *Probability of exposure to hazard.* The Commission may also consider several other things which can help to determine the likelihood that a consumer would be injured by a product thought to be hazardous. These are the number of units of the product that are being used by consumers, the frequency with which such use occurs, and the likelihood that in the course of typical use the consumer would be exposed to the identified risk of injury.

(8) *Additional criteria.* Additional criteria may arise that the staff believes warrant the Commission's attention. The Commission encourages the inclusion of such criteria for its consideration in establishing priorities. The Commission recognizes that incontrovertible data related to the criteria identified in this policy statement may be difficult to locate or develop on a timely basis. Therefore, the Commission may not require extensive documentation on each and every criterion before making a decision. In addition, the Commission emphasizes that the order of listing of the criteria in this policy is not intended to indicate either the order in which they are to be considered or their relative importance. The Commission will consider

all the criteria to the extent feasible in each case, and as interactively or jointly as possible.

(Sec. 4, 15 U.S.C. 2053, 86 Stat. 1210; as amended by sec. 4, Pub. L. 94–284)

[42 FR 53953, Oct. 4, 1977]

§ 1009.9 Policy regarding the granting of emergency exemptions from Commission regulations.

(a) This document states the Consumer Product Safety Commission's policy with respect to emergency requests for exemptions for companies which inadvertently produce products that do not conform to Commission regulations issued under the five acts the Commission administers. These acts are the Consumer Product Safety Act, the Federal Hazardous Substances Act, the Flammable Fabrics Act, the Poison Prevention Packaging Act of 1970 and the Refrigerator Safety Act. While the Commission is reluctant to grant such requests, it believes that the public should be apprised of the manner in which it rules on exemption requests and therefore is publishing the policy to provide guidance to industry and others making such requests. The publication of the policy will also serve to inform the public of the criteria that the Commission uses in ruling upon such requests. This policy is intended to cover emergency requests for exemptions and, while relevant, is not intended to limit the discretion of CPSC staff to close or not to open cases in the routine enforcement of CPSC regulations.

(b) The policy governs requests for exemption from any regulation under any act the Commission administers. The policy lists criteria the Commission considers in deciding whether to grant or deny an exemption request and therefore, should provide guidance to companies on the types of information to be submitted with requests. In addition, published Commission procedures regarding petitioning for amendments to regulations may assist companies in determining what supporting data to submit with a request. (See, for example, existing Commission procedures at 16 CFR 1110, 16 CFR 1607.14, 16 CFR 1500.82 and 16 CFR 1500.201). The exemption requests themselves should be filed with the Office of the Secretary of the Commission.

(c) It is the general policy of the Commission that when a particular exemption request is made and granted, all similarly situated persons are accorded the same relief as the person who requested the exemption. Therefore, when any amendment to a Commission regulation is proposed or a statement of enforcement policy is issued, the document to the extent practicable will be phrased in objective terms so that all similarly situated persons will be able to determine whether their products would fall within the relief.

(d) In deciding whether to grant or deny an exemption request, the Commission considers the following general criteria:

(1) *The degree to which the exemption if granted would expose consumers to an increased risk of injury:* The Commission does not believe it should exempt products which would present a significantly greater risk to consumers than complying products. Therefore, the Commission will not grant exemption requests in such cases.

(2) *The cost to the Commission of granting emergency requests:* Granting emergency exemption requests will in most cases require drafting a proposed and a final amendment or a statement of enforcement policy for publication in the FEDERAL REGISTER. Such action may also require the Commission to monitor the sale or distribution of the products. These activities consume scarce Commission resources. In some instances, the costs to the Commission may exceed the benefit to be derived by a company and similarly situated companies. If so, the Commission may deny the request on this ground.

(3) *The precedential effect of exempting some products:* The Commission recognizes that decisions to exempt some products set precedents in at least two ways. First, they indicate to companies that the CPSC will permit deviations to a given regulation. Second, they indicate to companies that the CPSC will permit deviations to regulations in general. Both precedents, if set carelessly by the CPSC, could result in many requests for exemption and could

undermine the stability and integrity of the Commission's regulations.

(e) In deciding whether to grant or deny an exemption request, the Commission also considers the following factors which relate specifically to the company making the request: (If the request is granted, all similarly situated companies, however, will be accorded the same relief).

(1) *The nature of the emergency exemption request:* The Commission will not reward bad quality control or faulty design work by permitting companies to market their mistakes. Although it is difficult to detail specific instances, the Commission is sympathetic to companies that produced noncomplying products due to factors beyond their immediate control or despite their best efforts.

(2) *The economic loss which a company will suffer if its emergency request is denied:* The greater the loss a company may suffer the more likely the Commission will favorably consider an exemption. However, the Commission does not believe economic loss alone should be determinative of an emergency exemption request.

(3) *The fairness to competitors:* The Commission is reluctant to grant relief if it could place the company at an unfair competitive advantage over other companies which have successfully complied with the same regulation. Therefore, the Commission will afford the same relief to similarly situated companies, and will decline to grant a request where unfair competitive advantage may result.

(15 U.S.C. 1191, 1261, 1471, 2051, 2111)

[44 FR 40639, July 12, 1979]

PART 1010 [RESERVED]

PART 1011—NOTICE OF AGENCY ACTIVITIES

Sec.

AUTHORITY: 5 U.S.C. 552b(g); Pub. L. 92–573, 86 Stat. 1207 (15 U.S.C. 2051–81) as amended by Pub. L. 94–284, 90 Stat. 503, Pub. L. 95–319, 92 Stat. 386, Pub. L. 95–631, 92 Stat. 3742; Pub. L. 90–189, 81 Stat. 568 (15 U.S.C. 1191–1204); Pub. L. 86–613, 74 Stat. 372, as amended by Pub. L. 89–756, 80 Stat. 1303, and Pub. L. 91–113, 83 Stat. 187 (15 U.S.C. 1261–74); Pub. L. 91–601, 84 Stat. 1670 (15 U.S.C. 1471–76) and the Act of Aug. 7, 1956, 70 Stat. 953 (15 U.S.C. 1211–14).

SOURCE: 46 FR 38322, July 24, 1981, unless otherwise noted.

§ 1011.1 General policy considerations; scope.

(a) In order for the Consumer Product Safety Commission to properly carry out its mandate to protect the public from unreasonable risks of injury associated with consumer products, the Commission has determined that it must involve the public in its activities to the fullest possible extent.

(b) To ensure public confidence in the integrity of Commission decision-making, the Agency, to the fullest possible extent, will conduct its business in an open manner free from any actual or apparent impropriety.

(c) This part 1011 presents general provisions concerning public notice for various types of Agency activities.

§ 1011.2 Definitions.

As used in this part 1011, the following terms shall have the meanings set forth:

(a) *Agency.* The entire organization which bears the title Consumer Product Safety Commission (CPSC).

(b) *Agency staff.* Employees of the Agency other than the five Commissioners.

(c) *Commissioner.* An individual who belongs to the collegial body heading the CPSC.

(d) *Commission.* The Commissioners of the Consumer Product Safety Commission acting in an official capacity.

(e) *Commission Meeting.* A meeting of the Commissioners subject to the Government in the Sunshine Act, 5 U.S.C. 552b. This term is more fully defined in the Commission's regulations under the Government in the Sunshine Act, 16 CFR part 1013.

(f) *Agency meeting.* A meeting between Agency personnel, including individual Commissioners, and outside parties. This term and the term "outside party" are more fully defined in the Commission's Meeting Policy, 16 CFR part 1012.

§ 1011.3 General requirements for various kinds of meetings.

Meetings which involve Agency staff or the Commissioners, other than Commission meetings, are classified in the following categories and shall be held according to the procedures outlined within each category.

(a) *Hearings.* Hearings are public inquiries held by direction of the Commission for the purpose of fact finding or to comply with statutory requirements. The Office of the Secretary is responsible for providing transcription services at the hearings. Where possible, notice of forthcoming hearings will be published in the Public Calendar and the FEDERAL REGISTER at least 30 days before the date of the hearings.

(b) *Meetings between Commissioners or Agency staff and outside parties.* The requirements for Agency meetings between Commissioners or Agency staff and outside parties involving substantial interest matters are contained in 16 CFR part 1012.

(c) *Commission meetings.* The requirements for Commission meetings under the Government in the Sunshine Act, 5 U.S.C. 552b are contained in 16 CFR part 1013.

(d) *Staff meetings.* As a general rule, only Agency employees attend staff meetings. At the discretion of the participants, Staff meetings may be listed on the Public Calendar and attendance by the public may be permitted. Recordkeeping is at the discretion of the participants.

(e) *Advisory committee meetings.* Meetings of the Agency's advisory committees are scheduled by the Commission. Advance notice will be given in both the Public Calendar and the FEDERAL REGISTER. Advisory committee meetings serve as a forum for discussion of matters relevant to the Agency's statutory responsibilities with the objective of providing advice and recommendations to the Commission. The Agency's advisory committees are the National Advisory Committee for the Flammable Fabrics Act, the Product Safety Advisory Council, the Technical Advisory Committee on Poison Prevention Packaging and the Toxicological Advisory Board. The Office of the Secretary is responsible for the recordkeeping for such meetings. The Commission's regulation for the management of its advisory committees is set out in 16 CFR part 1018.

§ 1011.4 Forms of advance public notice of meetings; Public Calendar/ Master Calendar and Federal Register.

Advance notice of Agency activities is provided so that members of the public may know of and participate in these activities to the fullest extent possible. Where appropriate, the Commission uses the following types of notice for both Agency meetings subject to 16 CFR part 1012 and Commission meetings subject to 16 CFR part 1013:

(a) *Public Calendar/Master Calendar.* (1) The printed Public Calendar and the Master Calendar maintained in the Office of the Secretary are the principal means by which the Agency notifies the public of its day-to-day activities. The Public Calendar and/or Master Calendar provide advance notice of public hearings, Commission meetings, Agency meetings with outside parties involving substantial interest matters, other Agency meetings, selected staff meetings, advisory committee meetings, and other activities such as speeches and participation in panel discussions, regardless of the location. The Public Calendar also lists recent CPSC FEDERAL REGISTER issuances and Advisory Opinions of the Office of the General Counsel.

(2) Upon request in writing to the Office of the Secretary, Consumer Product Safety Commission, Washington, D.C. 20207, any person or organization will be sent the Public Calendar on a regular basis free of charge. In addition, interested persons may contact the Office of the Secretary to obtain information from the Master Calendar which is kept current on a daily basis.

(3) The Public Calendar and the Master Calendar, supplemented by meeting summaries, are intended to serve the requirements of section 27(j)(8) of the Consumer Product Safety Act (15 U.S.C. 2076(j)(8)).

(b) *Federal Register*. FEDERAL REGISTER is the publication through which official notifications, including formal rules and regulations of the Agency, are made. Because the Public Calendar and/or Master Calendar are the primary devices through which the Agency notifies the public of its routine, daily activities, the FEDERAL REGISTER will be utilized only when required by the Government in the Sunshine Act (as provided in 16 CFR part 1013) or other applicable law, or when the Agency believes that the additional coverage which the FEDERAL REGISTER can provide is necessary to assist in notification to the public of important meetings.

PART 1012—MEETINGS POLICY—MEETINGS BETWEEN AGENCY PERSONNEL AND OUTSIDE PARTIES

Sec.

AUTHORITY: Pub. L. 92–573, 86 Stat. 1207 (15 U.S.C. 2051–81) as amended by Pub. L. 94–284, 90 Stat. 503, Pub. L. 95–319, 92 Stat. 386, Pub. L. 95–631, 92 Stat. 3742; Pub. L. 90–189, 81 Stat. 568 (15 U.S.C. 1191–1204); Pub. L. 86–613, 74 Stat. 372, as amended by Pub. L. 89–756, 80 Stat. 1303, and Pub. L. 91–113, 83 Stat. 187 (15 U.S.C. 1261–74); Pub. L. 91–601, 84 Stat. 1670 (15 U.S.C. 1471–76) and the Act of Aug. 7, 1956, 70 Stat. 953 (15 U.S.C. 1211–14).

SOURCE: 46 FR 38323, July 24, 1981, unless otherwise noted.

§ 1012.1 General policy considerations; scope.

(a) To achieve its goals of involving the public in its activities and conducting its business in an open manner, the Agency, whenever practicable, shall notify the public in advance of all meetings involving matters of substantial interest held or attended by its personnel, and shall permit the public to attend such meetings. Furthermore, to ensure the widest possible exposure of the details of such meetings, the Agency will keep records of them freely available for inspection by the public.

(b) This part 1012, the Agency's Meetings Policy, sets forth requirements for advance public notice, public attendance, and recordkeeping for Agency meetings.

§ 1012.2 Definitions.

(a) As used in this part 1012, the following terms have the respective meanings set forth in paragraphs (a)–(d) of § 1011.2 of this subchapter: "Agency," "Agency staff," "Commissioner," "Commission."

(b) *Agency meeting*. Any face-to-face encounter, other than a Commission meeting subject to the Government in the Sunshine Act, 5 U.S.C. 552b, and part 1013, in which one or more employees, including Commissioners, discusses with an outside party any subject relating to the Agency or any subject under its jurisdiction. The term Agency meeting does not include telephone conversations, but see § 1012.8 which relates to telephone conversations.

(c) *Outside party*. Any person not an employee, not under contract to do work for the Agency, or not acting in an official capacity as a consultant to the Consumer Product Safety Commission, such as advisory committee members or offeror personnel. Examples of persons falling within this definition are representatives from industry and consumer groups. Members of the news media when acting in a newsgathering capacity are not outside parties. (See also § 1012.7.) Officers and employees of the Federal Government when acting in their official capacities (except when advocating a particular course of action on behalf of an outside party) are not outside parties.

(d) *Substantial interest matter*. Any matter, other than that of a trivial nature, that pertains in whole or in part to any issue that is likely to be the subject of a regulatory or policy decision by the Commission. Pending matters, i.e., matters before the Agency in which the Agency is legally obligated to make a decision, automatically constitute substantial interest matters. Examples of pending matters are: Scheduled administrative hearings;

matters published for public comments; petitions under consideration; and mandatory standard development activities. The following are some examples of matters that do not constitute substantial interest matters: Inquiries concerning the status of a pending matter; discussions relative to general interpretations of existing laws, rules, and regulations; inspection of nonconfidential CPSC documents by the public; negotiations for contractual services; and routine CPSC activities such as recruitment, training, meetings involving consumer deputies, or meetings with hospital staff and other personnel involved in the National Electronic Injury Surveillance System.

§ 1012.3 Advance public notice of agency meetings.

(a) Commissioners and Agency employees are responsible for reporting meeting arrangements for Agency meetings to the Office of the Secretary so that they may be published in the Public Calendar or entered on the Master Calendar at least seven days before a meeting, except as provided in paragraph (d) of this section. These reports shall include the following information:

(1) Probable participants and their affiliations;

(2) Date, time and place of the meeting;

(3) Subject of the meeting (as fully and precisely described as possible);

(4) Who requested the meeting;

(5) Whether the meeting involves matters of substantial interest;

(6) Notice that the meeting is open or reason why the meeting or any portion of the meeting is closed (e.g., discussion of trade secrets); and

(7) Names and telephone number of the CPSC host or CPSC contact person.

(b) Once a report has been made to the Office of the Secretary, Agency employees subsequently desiring to attend the meeting need not notify the Office of the Secretary.

(c) When there is no opportunity to give seven days advance notice of a meeting, Agency employees (other than the Commissioners or their personal staff) who desire to hold or attend such a meeting must obtain the approval of the General Counsel or his or her designee. Requests for waiver of the seven-day advance notice requirement by members of the staff who report to the Executive Director may only be submitted to the General Counsel or his or her designee in writing by the Executive Director or his or her designee. Personal staff of Commissioners must obtain the approval of their respective Commissioners. If the short notice is approved, the Agency employee must notify the Office of the Secretary in advance of the meeting to record the meeting on the Master Calendar. The Office of the Secretary shall publish notice of the meeting as an addendum to the next Public Calendar.

(d) Exceptions. The notice requirement shall not apply to:

(1) Meetings with outside parties not involving substantial interest matters (although such meetings should be limited where the public interest would be served);

(2) Meetings with outside parties held during the normal course of surveillance, inspection, or investigation under any of the Acts administered by the Commission, including informal citation hearings under the Federal Hazardous Substance Act or the Poison Prevention Packaging Act;

(3) Meetings with outside parties concerning the settlement or negotiation of an individual case, including proposed remedial action, or meetings concerning any administrative or judicial action in which the outside party is a participant, party, or *amicus curiae;*

(4) Routine speeches given by CPSC personnel before outside parties. However, for information purposes, personnel are encouraged to submit advance notice of these speeches to the Office of the Secretary for inclusion in the Public Calendar;

(5) Meetings with other Federal personnel that are also attended by outside parties except where a specific matter to be discussed is also pending before the Commission or its staff;

(6) Meetings with state, local or foreign government personnel concerning intergovernmental cooperative efforts and not the advocacy of a particular course of action on behalf of a constituency of the governmental entity;

(7) Meetings or discussions with or at the request of either members of Congress and their staffs relating to legislation, appropriation or oversight matters, or Management and Budget personnel relating to legislation or appropriation matters;

(8) Pre-proposal conferences involving confidential contracts made pursuant to 41 U.S.C. 252(c)(12) in connection with potential litigation matters.

§ 1012.4 Public attendance at agency meetings.

(a) Any person may attend any meeting involving a substantial interest matter unless that meeting has been listed as a closed meeting. For meetings not involving substantial interest matters, the chairperson of the meeting may exercise his or her discretion to allow attendance by a member of the public.

(b) When meetings between Agency employees and outside parties are open to the public, attendance may be limited by space. When feasible, a person or organization desiring to attend such a meeting should give at least one day advance notice to one of the employees holding or attending the meeting so that sufficient space can be arranged for all those wishing to attend.

(c) Members of the public attending Agency meetings generally may observe only. The chairperson of the meeting may exercise his or her discretion to permit members of the public to participate as well.

(d) The following Agency meetings are not open to the public:

(1) Meetings, or, if possible, portions of meetings where the General Counsel or his or her designee has determined that proprietary data are to be discussed in such a manner as to imperil their confidentiality;

(2) Meetings held by outside parties at which limits on attendance are imposed by lack of space, provided that such meetings are open to the news media;

(3) Meetings with outside parties held during the normal course of surveillance, inspection, or investigation under any of the Acts administered by the Commission, including informal citation hearings under the Federal Hazardous Substances Act or the Poison Prevention Packaging Act;

(4) Meetings with outside parties concerning the settlement or negotiation of an individual case, including proposed remedial action, or meetings concerning any administrative or judicial action in which the outside party is a participant, party, or *amicus curiae;*

(5) Meetings with other Federal personnel that are attended by outside parties except where a specific matter to be discussed is also pending before the Commission or its staff;

(6) Meetings with state, local or foreign government personnel concerning intergovernmental cooperative efforts and not the advocacy of a particular course of action on behalf of a constituency of the governmental entity;

(7)(i) Meetings between Agency staff (other than Commissioners and their personal staff) and an outside party when the General Counsel or his or her designee determines that extraordinary circumstances require that the meeting be closed. Requests for exemption by members of the staff who report to the Executive Director may be submitted to the General Counsel or his or her designee in writing only by the Executive Director or his or her designee. In such a case, the reasons for closing the meeting or a portion of the meeting shall be stated in the Public Calendar notice announcing the meeting;

(ii) Meetings between a Commissioner (or his or her personal staff) and an outside party when, in the opinion of the Commissioner, extraordinary circumstances require that the meeting be closed. In such a case, the reasons for closing the meeting or a portion of the meeting must be stated in the Public Calendar notice announcing the meeting;

(8) Meetings or discussions with or at the request of either members of Congress and their staffs relating to legislation, appropriation or oversight matters, or Management and Budget personnel relating to legislation or appropriation matters; and

(9) Pre-proposal conferences involving confidential contracts made pursuant to 41 U.S.C. 252(c)(12), in connection with the potential litigation matters.

§ 1012.5 Recordkeeping for agency meetings.

(a) This section describes and establishes requirements for the two types of records maintained for Agency meetings, Agency meeting summaries and transcripts.

(b) *Agency meeting summaries.* Agency meeting summaries are written records settling forth the issues discussed at all Agency meetings with outside parties involving substantial interest matters. Any Commission employee who holds or attends an Agency meeting involving a substantial interest matter must prepare a meeting summary. However, only one agency meeting summary is required for each meeting even if more than one CPSC employee holds or attends the meeting. Agency meeting summaries are generally available to the public in the Agency's Public Reading Room in the Office of the Secretary as described in paragraph (b)(2) of this section.

(1) An agency meeting summary should state the essence of all substantive matters relevant to the Agency, especially any matter discussed which was not listed on the Public Calendar, and should describe any decisions made or conclusions reached regarding substantial interest matters. An agency meeting summary should also indicate the date of the meeting and the identity of persons who attended.

(2) An agency meeting summary or a notice of cancellation of the meeting must be submitted to the Office of the Secretary within twenty (20) calendar days after the meeting for which the summary is required. The Office of the Secretary shall maintain a file of the meeting summaries in chronological order, which shall be available to the public to the extent permitted by law.

(c) *Transcripts.* Transcripts are generally taken at public hearings and certain Agency meetings when complex subjects indicate *verbatim* records are desirable. The transcript may also include exhibits submitted to be part of the formal record of an Agency meeting. Copies of such transcripts are placed on file for public inspection in the Office of the Secretary.

§ 1012.6 The news media.

The Agency recognizes that the news media occupy a unique position in informing the public of the Agency's activities. The Commission believes that the inherently public nature of the news media allows their activities to be exempt from the requirements of this part whenever Agency meetings are held with the news media for the purpose of informing them about Agency activities. Such Agency meetings are not exempt in the event that any representative of the news media attempts to influence any Agency employee on a substantial interest matter.

§ 1012.7 Telephone conversations.

(a) Telephone conversations present special problems regarding Agency meetings. The Commission recognizes that persons outside the Agency have a legitimate right to receive information and to present their views regarding Agency activities. The Commission also recognizes that such persons may not have the financial means to travel to meet with Agency employees. However, because telephone conversations, by their very nature, are not susceptible to public attendance, or participation, Agency employees must take care to ensure that telephone conversations are not utilized to circumvent the provisions of this part.

(b) Two basic rules apply to telephone conversations:

(1) Any Agency employee holding a telephone conversation in which substantial interest matters are discussed with an outside party must prepare a telephone call summary of the conversation. The summary must meet the requirements of § 1012.5(b), and must be submitted to the Office of the Secretary within twenty (20) calendar days of the conversation. The Office of the Secretary shall maintain file of telephone call summaries in chronological order which shall be available to the public to the extent permitted by law.

(2) All Agency employees must exercise sound judgment in discussing substsantial interest matters during a telephone conversation. In the exercise of such discretion Agency employees should not hesitate to terminate a telephone conversation and insist that the

matters being discussed be postponed until an Agency meeting with appropriate advance public notice may be scheduled, or, if the outside party is financially or otherwise unable to meet with the Agency employee, until the matter is presented to the Agency in writing.

PART 1013—GOVERNMENT IN THE SUNSHINE ACT, RULES FOR COMMISSION MEETINGS

Sec.

AUTHORITY: 5 U.S.C. 552b(g).

SOURCE: 46 FR 38326, July 24, 1981, unless otherwise noted.

§ 1013.1 General policy considerations; scope.

(a) In enacting the Government in the Sunshine Act, 5 U.S.C. 552b, the Congress stated the policy that, to the fullest practicable extent, the public is entitled to information regarding the decisionmaking processes of the Federal Government. The purpose of the Government in the Sunshine Act is to provide the public with such information while protecting both the rights of individuals and the ability of the Government to carry out its responsibilities. When the Commissioners of the Consumer Product Safety Commission hold meetings for the purpose of jointly conducting or disposing of Commission business they will conduct these meetings in accordance with the provisions of the Government in the Sunshine Act.

(b) This part 1013 prescribes rules the Commission follows in carrying out the Government in the Sunshine Act.

§ 1013.2 Definitions.

(a) As used in this part 1013, the following terms shall have the respective meanings set forth in paragraphs (a), (c) and (d) of § 1011.2 of this subchapter: "Agency," "Commissioner," "Commission."

(b) *Majority of the Commission.* Three or more of the Commissioners.

(c) *Commission meeting.* The joint deliberations of at least a majority of the Commission where such deliberations determine or result in the joint conduct or disposition of official Agency business. This term does not include meetings required or permitted by § 1013.4(b) (to determine whether a meeting will be open or closed), meetings required or permitted by § 1013.3(e) (to change the subject matter of a meeting or the determination to open or close a meeting after the public announcement) or meetings required or permitted by 1013.3(c) (to dispense with the one week advance notice of a meeting).

§ 1013.3 Announcement of Commission meetings and changes after announcement.

(a) The Secretary of the Commission is responsible for preparing and making public the announcements and notices relating to Commission meetings that are required in this part.

(b) The Agency shall announce each Commission meeting in the Public Calendar or Master Calendar at least one week (seven calendar days) before the meeting. The Agency shall concurrently submit the announcement for publication in the FEDERAL REGISTER. The announcement and the FEDERAL REGISTER notice shall contain the following information:

(1) The date, time, and place of the meeting;

(2) The subject matter of the meeting;

(3) Whether the meeting will be open or closed to the public;

(4) The name and phone number of the official who responds to requests for information about the meeting.

(c) If a majority of the Commission determines by recorded vote that Agency business requires calling a meeting without seven calendar days advance public notice, the Office of the Secretary shall announce this determination in the Public Calendar or Master Calendar at the earliest practicable time and shall concurrently transmit the announcement for publication in the FEDERAL REGISTER.

(d) When necessary and at the direction of the Chairman, the Secretary shall change the time of a Commission meeting after the announcement in the Public Calendar or Master Calendar. Any such change shall be entered on the Master Calendar and such other notice shall be given as is practicable.

(e) After announcement of a Commission meeting in the Public Calendar or Master Calendar, the Commission may change the subject matter of a Commission meeting or the decision to open or close a Commission meeting or portion thereof to the public, only if a majority of the Commission determines by recorded vote that Agency business so requires, and only if a majority of the Commission determines by recorded vote that no earlier announcement of the change was possible. The Commission shall announce the change in the Public Calendar or Master Calendar at the earliest practicable time before the meeting and shall concurrently transmit the announcement for publication in the FEDERAL REGISTER. Announcement of the change shall include the vote of each Commissioner upon the change. (See also § 1013.4(d) for requirements for Commission reconsideration of a decision to open or close a meeting to the public.)

§ 1013.4 Public attendance at Commission meetings.

(a) *Attendance by the public.* Every portion of every Commission meeting shall be open to public observation except as provided in paragraph (b) of this section. Notwithstanding the applicability of the exemptions contained in paragraph (b) of this section, a Commission meeting or portions thereof shall be open to public observation when the Commission determines that the public interest so requires. The Commission shall take into account in all cases the relative advantages and disadvantages to the public of conducting the Commission meeting in open session. The number of public observers shall be limited only by availability of space. Attendance by the public shall usually be limited to observation and shall not include participation except where, by majority vote, the Commission determines that data or views from certain members of the public will be permitted. To the extent their use does not interfere with the conduct of open meetings, cameras and sound-recording equipment may be used at open Commission meetings. The Chairman or presiding Commissioner shall insure that use of such equipment does not disrupt the meeting.

(b) *Exemptions to the requirement of openness.* The requirement in paragraph (a) of this section that all Commission meetings be open to public observation shall not apply to any Commission meeting or portion thereof for which the Commission has determined in accordance with the procedures for closing meetings set forth in paragraph (c) of this section, that such meeting or portion thereof is likely to:

(1) Disclose matters that are specifically authorized under criteria established by an Executive Order to be kept secret in the interest of national defense or foreign policy and in fact are properly classified pursuant to such Executive Order;

(2) Relate solely to the internal personnel rules and practices of the Agency;

(3) Disclose matters specifically exempted from disclosure by statute (other than 5 U.S.C. 552): *Provided*, That such statute (i) requires that the matters be withheld from the public in such a manner as to leave no discretion on the issue, or (ii) establishes particular criteria for withholding or refers to particular types of matters to be withheld;

(4) Disclose trade secrets and commercial or financial information obtained from a person and privileged or confidential;

(5) Involve accusing any person of a crime, or formally censuring any person;

(6) Disclose information of a personal nature where disclosure would constitute a clearly unwarranted invasion of personal privacy;

(7) Disclose investigatory records compiled for law enforcement purposes or information which if written would be contained in such records, but only

to the extent that the production of such records or information would,

(i) Interfere with enforcement proceedings,

(ii) Deprive a person of a right to a fair trial or an impartial adjudication,

(iii) Constitute an unwarranted invasion of personal privacy,

(iv) Disclose the identity of a confidential source and, in the case of a record compiled by a criminal law enforcement authority in the course of a criminal investigation, or by an agency conducting a lawful national security intelligence investigation, confidential information furnished only by the confidential source,

(v) Disclose investigative techniques and procedures or,

(vi) Endanger the life or physical safety of law enforcement personnel;

(8) Disclose information contained in or related to examination, operating or condition reports prepared by, on behalf of, or for the use of an agency responsible for the regulation or supervision of financial institutions;

(9) Disclose information the premature disclosure of which would be likely to significantly frustrate implementation of a proposed Agency action. This provision does not apply in any instance where the Agency has already disclosed to the public the content or nature of its proposed action, or where the Agency is required by law to make such disclosure on its own initiative prior to taking final agency action on such proposal; or

(10) Specifically concern the Agency's issuance of a subpoena, or the Agency's participation in a civil action or proceeding, an action in a foreign court or international tribunal, or an arbitration, or the initiation, conduct, or disposition by the Agency of a particular case of formal agency adjudication pursuant to the procedures in 5 U.S.C. 554 or otherwise involving a determination on the record after opportunity for a hearing.

(c) *Procedure for closing Commission Meetings.* The following procedure shall be followed in closing a Commission meeting or portion thereof to public observation:

(1) A majority of the Commission must vote to close a meeting or portion thereof to public observation pursuant to paragraph (b) of this section. A separate vote of the Commission shall be taken for each matter with respect to which a Commission meeting is proposed to be closed to public observation. Each such vote may, at the discretion of the Commission, apply to that portion of any meeting held within the following thirty days in which such matter is to be discussed. The vote of each Commissioner participating in such vote shall be recorded and no proxies shall be allowed.

(2) Any person whose interest may be directly affected if a portion of a Commission meeting is open may request in writing to the Office of the Secretary that the Commission close that portion of the meeting on the basis of paragraph (b) (5), (6), or (7) of this section. The Commission shall vote on such requests if at least one Commissioner desires to do so.

(3) Before the Commission may hold a closed meeting the General Counsel must certify that in his or her opinion, the meeting may properly be closed to the public. Such certification shall be in writing and shall state each relevant exemptive provision.

(4) Within one day of a vote in accordance with paragraph (c) (1) or (2) of this section to close a Commission meeting or portion thereof, the Secretary shall make available to the public a notice setting forth:

(i) The results of the vote reflecting the vote of each Commissioner;

(ii) A full explanation of the action of the Commission closing the meeting or portion thereof, including reference to the specific basis for such closing (see paragraph (b) of this section) and an explanation, (without disclosing exempt information), of why the Commission concludes on balance, taking into account the relative advantages and disadvantages to the public of conducting the meeting in open or closed session, that the public interest would best be served by closing the meeting;

(iii) A list of all non-Agency personnel expected to attend the meeting and their affiliations; and

(iv) A certification by the General Counsel that in his or her opinion, the meeting may properly be closed to the public. If a vote to close a Commission meeting takes place on the same day as the meeting, the certification must be made available to the public before the meeting is convened.

(5) The public release of the portion of the written statement required by paragraph (c)(4)(ii) of this section may be delayed upon a determination by the Commission, by recorded vote, that such a notice, or portion thereof, would disclose information which may be withheld in accordance with paragraphs (b) (1) through (10) of this section.

(d) *Reconsideration of a decision to open or close a Commission meeting.* The Commission may, in accordance with the procedures in § 1013.3(3) or paragraph (c)(2) of this section, reconsider its decision to open or close a Commission meeting when it finds that the public interest so requires.

[46 FR 38326, July 24, 1981, as amended at 48 FR 36566, Aug. 12, 1983]

§ 1013.5 Recordkeeping requirements.

(a) Commission meetings, transcripts, recordings, or minutes.

(1) The Agency shall maintain a complete transcript or electronic recording of each Commission meeting, whether open or closed, except that in the case of a Commission meeting or portion thereof closed to the public pursuant to paragraph (b)(10) of § 1013.4, the Agency may elect to maintain a set of meeting minutes instead of a transcript or a recording. Minutes of such closed Commission meetings shall:

(i) Fully and clearly describe all matters discussed, and

(ii) Provide a full and accurate summary of any actions taken and the reasons therefor, including a description of each of the views expressed on any item and the record of any roll call vote (reflecting the vote of each Commissioner on the question). All documents considered in connection with any action shall be identified in the meeting minutes.

(2) The transcript, recording or minutes of closed Commission meetings shall include the certification by the General Counsel or by his or her designee, required by § 1013.4(c)(3) and a statement by the presiding Commissioner setting forth the date, time and place of the meeting and the persons present.

(3) The transcript, recording, or minutes of any Commission meeting may include attachments such as Commission opinions, briefing papers, or other documents presented at the meeting.

(4) The transcript and accompanying material shall be maintained by the Secretary for a period of at least two years after the meeting, or until one year after the conclusion of any Agency proceeding with respect to which the meeting, or portion thereof, was held, whichever occurs later.

(b) Minutes of Commission Decisions. Minutes of Commission Decisions summarizing the issues presented to the Commission for decision and indicating the vote of each Commissioner document the decisions of the Commission, whether made at open or closed meetings or by ballot vote. The Commission's final Minutes of Commission Decisions, issued by the Office of the Secretary, constitute the official means of recording the decisions of the Commission and the votes of individual Commissioners.

§ 1013.6 Public availability of transcripts, recordings and minutes of Commission meetings.

(a) Availability of transcripts, recordings or minutes. The Agency shall make available to the public the transcript, recording or minutes of Commission meetings. However, unless the Commission finds that the public interest requires otherwise, any portion of the transcript, recording or minutes of a closed Commission meeting which is determined to contain information which may properly be withheld from the public on the basis of paragraphs (b) (1) through (10) of § 1013.4 need not be made available to the public.

(b) Procedures for making available transcripts, recordings or meeting minutes. Meeting records will be made available for inspection, or copies will be furnished, as requested, in accordance with the following procedures.

(1) *Requests.* Requests for inspection or copies shall be in writing addressed to the Secretary, Consumer Product Safety Commission, Washington, D.C. 20207. A request must reasonably describe the Commission meeting, or portion thereof, including the date and

subject matter or any other information which may help to identify the requested material.

(2) *Responses to requests.* The responsibility for responding to requests for meeting records is vested in the Secretary of the Commission. In any case where the Secretary or his or her designee, in his or her discretion, determines that a request for an identifiable meeting record should be initially determined by the Commission, the Secretary or his or her designee may certify the matter to the Commission for decision. In that event, the Commission decision shall be made within the time limits set forth in paragraph (b)(5)(iii) of this section and shall be final.

(3) *Time limitations on responses to requests.* The Secretary or his or her designee shall respond to all written requests for copies of meeting records within ten (10) working days. The time limitations on responses to requests shall begin to run as of the time a request for records is received and date stamped by the Office of the Secretary.

(4) *Responses. Form and content.* When a requested meeting record has been identified and is available for disclosure the requester shall either be informed as to where and when the records will be made available for inspection or be supplied with a copy. A response denying a written request for a meeting record of a closed Commission meeting shall be in writing signed by the Secretary and shall include:

(i) A reference to the specific exemptions under the Government in the Sunshine Act (5 U.S.C. 552b(c)) authorizing the denial; and

(ii) A statement that the denial may be appealed to the Commission pursuant to paragraph (b)(5) of this section.

(5) *Appeals to the Commissioners.* (i) When the Secretary or his or her designee has denied a request for records in whole or in part, the requester may, within 30 days of its receipt, appeal the denial to the Commissioners of the Consumer Product Safety Commission by writing to the attention of the Chairman, Consumer Product Safety Commission, Washington, D.C. 20207.

(ii) The Commission will act upon an appeal within 20 working days of its receipt. The time limitations on an appeal begin to run as of the time an appeal is received by the Office of the Chairman and date stamped.

(iii) The Commission's action on appeal shall be in writing, signed by the Chairman of the Commission if the appeal is denied and shall identify the Commissioners who voted for a denial. A denial in whole or in part of a request on appeal for records of a closed meeting shall set forth the exemption relied on and a brief explanation (without disclosing exempt information) of how the exemption applies to the records withheld. A denial in whole or in part shall also inform the requester of his or her right to seek judicial review as specified in 5 U.S.C. 552b(h).

(6) *Fees.* (i) Fees shall be charged for copies of transcriptions of recording or minutes in accordance with the schedule contained in paragraph (b)(6)(iii) of this section.

(ii) There shall be no fee charged for services rendered in connection with production or disclosure of meeting records unless the charges, calculated according to the schedule below, exceed the sum of $25.00. Where the charges are calculated to be an amount in excess of $25.00, the fee charged shall be the difference between $25.00 and the calculated charges.

(iii) The schedule of charges for furnishing copies of meeting records is as follows:

(A) Reproduction, duplication or copying of transcripts or minutes: 10 cents per page.

(B) Reproduction of recordings: actual cost basis.

(C) Transcription (where meeting records are in the form of a recording only): actual cost basis.

(D) Postage: actual cost basis.

PART 1014—POLICIES AND PROCEDURES IMPLEMENTING THE PRIVACY ACT OF 1974

Sec.

AUTHORITY: Privacy Act of 1974 (5 U.S.C. 552a).

SOURCE: 40 FR 53381, Nov. 18, 1975, unless otherwise noted.

§ 1014.1 Purpose and scope.

This part sets forth the regulations of the Consumer Product Safety Commission implementing the Privacy Act of 1974 (Pub. L. 93–579). The purpose of these regulations is to inform the public about records maintained by the Commission which contain personal information about individuals, and to inform those individuals how they may seek access to and correct records concerning themselves. These regulations do not apply to requests for information made pursuant to the Freedom of Information Act (except where such disclosures would constitute an invasion of privacy of an individual).

§ 1014.2 Definitions.

As used in this part:

(a) *Individual* means a person who is a citizen of the United States or an alien lawfully admitted for permanent residence.

(b) *Privacy Act* means the Privacy Act of 1974 (Pub. L. 93–579).

(c) *Record* means any item of personal information relating to an individual, such as educational, employment, financial or medical information.

(d) *Statistical record* means a record in a system of records maintained for statistical research or reporting purposes only and not used in whole or in part in making any determination about an identifiable individual.

(e) *System of records* or *records systems* means a group of records maintained by the Commission from which information may be retrieved by the name of an individual or some other individual identifier.

(f) *Maintain* includes the collection, use, storage, and dissemination of information.

§ 1014.3 Procedures for requests pertaining to individual records.

(a) Any individual may request the Commission to inform him or her whether a particular record system named by the individual contains a record pertaining to him or her. The request may be made by mail or in person during business hours (8:30 a.m. to 5 p.m.) to the Freedom of Information/Privacy Act Officer, Office of the Secretary, Consumer Product Safety Commission, 4330 East West Highway, Bethesda, Maryland (mailing address: Consumer Product Safety Commission, Washington, DC 20207).

(b) An individual who believes that the Commission maintains a record pertaining to him or her but who cannot determine which record system may contain the record, may request assistance by mail or in person at the Office of the Secretary during business hours.

(c) A Commission officer or employee or former employee who desires to review or obtain a copy of a personnel record pertaining to him or her may make a request by mail or in person at the Office of Human Resources Management, Room 523, 4330 East West Highway, Bethesda, Maryland (mailing address: Consumer Product Safety Commission, Washington, DC 20207).

(d) Each individual requesting the disclosure of a record or a copy of a record shall furnish the following information to the extent known with the request to the Freedom of Information/Privacy Act Officer or to the Division of Personnel's Processing Unit, as applicable:

(1) A description of the record sought;

(2) The approximate date of the record;

(3) The name or other description of the record system containing the record;

(4) Proof as required in § 1014.4 that he or she is the individual to whom the requested record relates; and

(5) Any other information required by the notice describing the record system.

(e) An individual personally inspecting his or her records may be accompanied by other persons of his or her own choosing. The individual shall sign a written statement authorizing disclosure of the record in the other person's presence.

(f) Any individual who desires to have a record concerning himself or herself disclosed to or mailed to another person may authorize that person to act as his or her agent for that specific purpose. The authorization shall be in writing, signed by the individual, and shall be notarized. An agent requesting the review or copy of another's record shall submit with the request the authorization and proof of his or her identify as required by § 1014.4(c).

(g) The parent of any minor individual or the legal guardian of any individual who has been declared by a court of competent jurisdiction to be incompetent, due to physical or mental incapacity or age, may act on behalf of that individual in any matter covered by this part. A parent or guardian who desires to act on behalf of such individual shall present suitable evidence of parentage or guardianship, by birth certificate, certified copy of a court order, or similar documents, and proof of the individual's identity in a form that complies with § 1014.4(c).

(h) An individual may request an accounting of all disclosures made to other persons or agencies of his or her record, except those disclosures made to law enforcement agencies pursuant to section (b)(7) of the Privacy Act (5 U.S.C. 552a(b)(7)). A request for accounting, whenever made, shall be treated as a request for disclosure of records.

[40 FR 53381, Nov. 18, 1975, as amended at 53 FR 52404, Dec. 28, 1988; 62 FR 46667, Sept. 4, 1997]

§ 1014.4 Requirements for identification of individuals making requests.

The following proof of identity is required for requests for records made pursuant to § 1014.3:

(a) An individual seeking a record about himself or herself in person may establish his or her identity by the presentation of a single document bearing a photograph (such as a passport or driver's license) or by a presentation of two items of identification which do not bear a photograph but do bear both a name and address. An individual who cannot provide documentation of his or her identity may provide a written statement affirming his or her identity and the fact that he or she understands the penalties for making false statements (18 U.S.C. 1001 and 5 U.S.C. 552a(i)(3)).

(b) An individual seeking a record by mail shall include a statement signed by the individual and properly notarized, that he or she appeared before a notary public and submitted proof of identity acceptable to the notary public.

(c) Requests made by an agent, parent, or guardian shall, in addition to establishing the identity of the minor or other person he or she represents as required by paragraphs (a) and (b), establish his or her agency, parentage, or guardianship by documentation.

(d) In any case in which the Commission determines that the proof of identity is not adequate, it may request the individual to submit additional proof of identity.

§ 1014.5 Disclosure of requested information to individuals.

(a) Upon submission of proof of identity, the Office of the Secretary or the Director of Resource Utilization, as applicable, shall promptly forward the request to the system manager who will promptly allow the individual to see and/or have a copy of the requested record or send a copy of the record to the individual by mail, as requested by the individual. If the individual asks to see the record, the record should be made available for review and/or copying at the location where the record is maintained, in the Office of the Secretary, or the Director of Resource Utilization, or at the nearest Area Office.

(b) If the system manager should determine, for any reason, that the requested records are exempt from the right of access, a notice of denial shall be sent to the requester stating the reasons for denial, and the requester's right to appeal the denial in accordance with the procedures set forth in § 1014.8 of these regulations.

§ 1014.6 Request for correction or amendment to a record.

(a) Any individual who has reviewed a record pertaining to himself or herself may request the Executive Director to correct or amend all or any part of the record.

(b) Each request for a correction or amendment of a record shall be in writing and shall contain the following information:

(1) The name of the individual requesting the correction or amendment;

(2) The name or other description of the system of records in which the record sought to be amended is maintained;

(3) The location of that record in the system of records to the extent that it is known;

(4) A copy of the record sought to be amended or a description of that record;

(5) A statement of the material in the record that should be corrected or amended;

(6) A statement of the specific wording of the correction or amendment sought; and

(7) A statement of the basis for the requested correction or amendment including any material that the individual can furnish to substantiate the reasons for the amendment sought.

[40 FR 53381, Nov. 18, 1975, as amended at 42 FR 22878, May 5, 1977]

§ 1014.7 Agency review of request for correction or amendment of a record.

(a) Not later than 10 working days after the receipt of the request for the correction or amendment of a record under § 1014.6, the responsible Commission official shall acknowledge receipt of the request and inform the individual whether further information is required before the correction or amendment can be considered.

(b) The responsible Commission official will promptly review the request and either make the requested correction or amendment or notify the individual of his or her refusal to do so, including in the notification the reasons for the refusal, and the appeal procedures provided by § 1014.8.

(c) The responsible Commission official will make each requested correction or amendment to a record if that correction or amendment will correct anything within the record that is not accurate, relevant, timely, or complete. A copy of each corrected or amended record shall be furnished to the individual who requested the action. If an accounting of disclosure has been kept, all previous recipients of the record shall be notified of the correction and its substance.

§ 1014.8 Appeal of initial denial of access, correction or amendment.

(a) Any individual whose request for access, correction or amendment to a record is denied, in whole or in part, may appeal that decision within 30 working days to the Chairman, Consumer Product Safety Commission, Washington, D.C. 20207.

(b) The appeal shall be in writing and shall:

(1) Name the individual making the appeal;

(2) Identify the record to which access is sought or which is sought to be corrected or amended;

(3) Name or describe the record system in which the record is contained;

(4) Contain a short statement describing the correction of amendment sought;

(5) State the name and location of the Commission official who initially denied the correction or amendment; and

(6) State the date of the initial denial.

(c) Not later than 30 working days after the date on which the appeal is received, the Chairman shall complete a review of the appeal and make a final decision thereon. However, for good cause shown, the Chairman of the Commission may extend the 30-day period. If the Chairman so extends the period, he or she shall promptly notify the individual requesting the review that the extension has been made.

(d) If after review of an appeal request, the Chairman also refuses to amend the record or grant access to the record in accordance with the request, he or she shall send a written notice to the requester containing the following information:

(1) The decision and the reasons for the decision;

(2) The right of the requester to institute a civil action in a Federal District Court for judicial review of the decision; and

(3) The right of the requester to file with the Chairman a concise statement setting forth the reasons for his or her disagreement with the denial of the correction or amendment. A copy of the statement of disagreement shall be filed with the record in issue, and the record in issue shall be so marked as to indicate that there is a disagreement. The system manager shall make the statement of disagreement available to prior recipients of the disputed record to the extent that an accounting of disclosures was maintained, and to any person to whom the record is later disclosed, together with a brief statement, if deemed appropriate, of the reasons for denying the requested correction or amendment.

[40 FR 53381, Nov. 18, 1975, as amended at 42 FR 22878, May 5, 1977]

§ 1014.9 Disclosure of record to person other than the individual to whom it pertains.

(a) Any person or agency (other than an officer or employee of the Commission who has a need for individual records in the performance of his or her duty) seeking disclosure of personal records of another individual which are contained in a system of records shall submit a request in accordance with the Commission's Procedures for Disclosure of Production of Information under the Freedom of Information Act (16 CFR part 1015, subpart A).

(b) The determination of whether or not the requested disclosure is proper will be made in accordance with the provisions of the Freedom of Information Act, as amended (5 U.S.C. 552) and the Commission's policies and procedures issued thereunder (16 CFR part 1015).

[41 FR 30324, July 23, 1976]

§ 1014.10 Fees.

The Commission shall not charge an individual for the costs of making a search for a record, the costs of reviewing or copying a record, or the cost of correcting or amending a record.

§ 1014.11 Penalties.

Any person who makes a false statement in connection with any request for a record, or an amendment thereto, under this part, is subject to the penalties prescribed in 18 U.S.C. 494, 495, and 1001; and 5 U.S.C. 552a(i)(3).

§ 1014.12 Specific exemptions.

(a) *Injury information.* (1) The Bureau of Epidemiology maintains a file of Accident Reports (In-Depth Investigations) which are conducted on a sample of product related injuries reported to the Commission by selected hospital emergency rooms, by consumers through the Commission's "Hot-Line" telephone service and through written consumer complaints and by other means such as newspaper reports. The purpose of this record system is to compile accident statistics for analyzing the incidence and severity of product related injuries.

(2) Inasmuch as the maintenance of the record system listed in paragraph (a)(1) of this section is authorized by section 5 of the Consumer Product Safety Act (15 U.S.C. 2054) and the data are used solely as statistical records, the system is exempted from the requirements of the Privacy Act relating to making available the accounting of disclosures, correction or amendment of the record and the application of these rules to the system of records. Specifically, the system is exempt from 5 U.S.C. 552a(c)(3); (d) (2) and (3); (e)(1); (e)(4) (G), (H) and (I); and (f). However, Accident Reports made by Commission employees are disclosable in accordance with paragraph (a)(3) of this section.

(3) Section 25(c) of the Consumer Product Safety Act (15 U.S.C. 2074(c)) provides that accident or investigation reports made by an officer or employee of the Commission shall be made available to the public in a manner which will not identify any injured person or any person treating him or her, without the consent of the person identified. Consequently, an accident or investigation report which identifies individuals is available to the injured party or the person treating him or her

but would not be available for disclosure to a third party without the consent of the injured party or person treating him or her.

(4) Since accident or investigation reports are compiled only for statistical purposes and are not used in whole or in part in making any determination about an individual, they are exempted from the requirement to correct or amend a record as provided by subsection (d)(2) of the Privacy Act (5 U.S.C. 552a (d)(2)). Exceptions from this paragraph, insofar as they relate to amendments or additions, may be allowed by the Executive Director.

(b) *Inspector General Investigative Files—CPSC–6*. All portions of this system of records which fall within 5 U.S.C. 552a(k)(2) (investigatory materials compiled for law enforcement purposes) and 5 U.S.C. 552a(k)(5) (investigatory materials solely compiled for suitability determinations) are exempt from 5 U.S.C. 552a(c)(3) (mandatory accounting of disclosures); 5 U.S.C. 552a(d) (access by individuals to records that pertain to them); 5 U.S.C. 552a(e)(1) (requirement to maintain only such information as is relevant and necessary to accomplish an authorized agency purpose); 5 U.S.C. 552a(e)(4)(G) (mandatory procedures to notify individuals of the existence of records pertaining to them); 5 U.S.C. 552a(e)(4)(H) (mandatory procedures to notify individuals how they can obtain access to and contest records pertaining to them); 5 U.S.C. 552a(e)(4)(I) (mandatory disclosure of records source categories); and the Commission's regulations in 16 CFR part 1014 which implement these statutory provisions.

(c) *Enforcement and Litigation Files—CPSC–7*. All portions of this system of records that fall within 5 U.S.C. 552a(k)(2) (investigatory materials compiled for law enforcement purposes) are exempt from 5 U.S.C. 552a(c)(3) (mandatory accounting of disclosures); 5 U.S.C. 552a(d) (access by individuals to records that pertain to them); 5 U.S.C. 552a(e)(1) (requirement to maintain only such information as is relevant and necessary to accomplish an authorized agency purpose); 5 U.S.C. 552a(e)(4)(G) (mandatory procedures to notify individuals of the existence of records pertaining to them); 5 U.S.C. 552a(e)(4)(H) (mandatory procedures to notify individuals how they can obtain access to and contest records pertaining to them); 5 U.S.C. 552a(e)(4)(I) (mandatory disclosure of records source categories); and the Commission's regulations in 16 CFR part 1014 that implement these statutory provisions.

[40 FR 53381, Nov. 18, 1975, as amended at 42 FR 9161, Feb. 15, 1977; 59 FR 32078, June 22, 1994; 62 FR 48756, Sept. 17, 1997]

PART 1015—PROCEDURES FOR DISCLOSURE OR PRODUCTION OF INFORMATION UNDER THE FREEDOM OF INFORMATION ACT

Subpart A—Production or Disclosure Under 5 U.S.C. 552(a)

Sec.

Subpart B—Exemptions From Production and Disclosure Under 5 U.S.C. 552(b)

Subpart C—Disclosure of Commission Accident or Investigation Reports Under 15 U.S.C. 2074(c)

AUTHORITY: 15 U.S.C. 2051–2084; 15 U.S.C. 1261–1278; 15 U.S.C. 1471–1476; 15 U.S.C. 1211–1214; 15 U.S.C. 1191–1204; 5 U.S.C. 552.

SOURCE: 42 FR 10490, Feb. 22, 1977, unless otherwise noted.

Subpart A—Production or Disclosure Under 5 U.S.C. 552(a)

§ 1015.1 Purpose and scope.

(a) The regulations of this subpart provide information concerning the procedures by which Consumer Product Safety Commission records may be made available for inspection and the procedures for obtaining copies of records from the Consumer Product Safety Commission. Official records of the Consumer Product Safety Commission consist of all documentary material maintained by the Commission in any format, including an electronic format. These records include those maintained in connection with the Commission's responsibilities and functions under the Consumer Product Safety Act, as well as those responsibilities and functions transferred to the Commission under the Federal Hazardous Substances Act, Poison Prevention Packaging Act of 1970, Refrigerator Safety Act, and Flammable Fabrics Act, and those maintained under any other authorized activity. Official records do not, however, include objects or articles such as tangible exhibits, samples, models, equipment, or other items of valuable property; books, magazines, or other reference material; or documents routinely distributed by the Commission in the normal course of business such as copies of FEDERAL REGISTER notices, pamphlets, and laws. Official records include only existing records. Official records of the Commission made available under the requirements of the Freedom of Information Act (5 U.S.C. 552) shall be furnished to the public as prescribed by this part 1015. A request by an individual for records about himself or herself that are contained in the Commission's system of records under the Privacy Act (5 U.S.C. 552a) will be processed under the Privacy Act. A request by a third party for records that are contained in the Commission's system of records under the Privacy Act will be processed administratively under these regulations with respect to the time limits and appeals rights (§§ 1015.5 and 1015.7), but substantively under the applicable provisions of first the Freedom of Information Act and then the Privacy Act. Documents routinely distributed to the public in the normal course of business will continue to be furnished to the public by employees of the Commission informally and without compliance with the procedures prescribed herein.

(b) The Commission's policy with respect to requests for records is that disclosure is the rule and withholding is the exception. All records not exempt from disclosure will be made available. Moreover, records which may be exempted from disclosure will be made available as a matter of discretion when disclosure is not prohibited by law or is not against the public interest. See, § 1015.15(b). Section 6(a)(2) of the Consumer Product Safety Act, 15 U.S.C. 2055(a)(2), prohibits the disclosure of trade secrets or other matters referred to in 18 U.S.C. 1905.

(c) The Attorney General's Memorandum on the 1974 Amendments to the Freedom of Information Act published in February, 1975 is available from the Superintendent of Documents and may be consulted in considering questions arising under the Freedom of Information Act.

[42 FR 10490, Feb. 22, 1997, as amended at 62 FR 46196, Sept. 2, 1997]

§ 1015.2 Public reference facilities.

(a) The Consumer Product Safety Commission will maintain in a public reference room or area the materials relating to the Consumer Product Safety Commission that are required by 5 U.S.C. 552(a)(2) and 552(a)(5) to be made available for public inspection and copying. The principal location will be in the Office of the Secretary of the Commission. The address of this office is:

Office of the Secretary, Consumer Product Safety Commission, Room 502, 4330 East West Highway, Bethesda, MD 20814.

(b) This public reference facility will maintain and make available for public inspection and copying a current index of the materials available at that facility which are required to be indexed by 5 U.S.C. 552(a)(2). For the purpose of providing the opportunity for greater public access to records of the Consumer Product Safety Commission, the Commission may establish additional public reference facilities. Each such additional reference facility will also maintain and make available for public inspection and copying a current index of the materials available at that facility which are required to be indexed by 5 U.S.C. 552(a)(2).

(c) The Consumer Product Safety Commission will maintain an "electronic reading room" on the World-Wide Web for those records that are required by 5 U.S.C. 552(a)(2) to be available by "computer telecommunications."

[42 FR 10490, Feb. 22, 1997, as amended at 62 FR 46197, Sept. 2, 1997]

§ 1015.3 Requests for records and copies.

(a) A request for access to records of the Commission shall be in writing addressed to the Secretary, Consumer Product Safety Commission, Washington, DC 20207. Any written request for records covered by this part shall be deemed to be a request for records pursuant to the Freedom of Information Act, whether or not the Freedom of Information Act is mentioned in the request. An oral request for records will not be considered a request for records pursuant to the Freedom of Information Act. Responses to oral requests for records shall be made as promptly as resources and time restraints permit.

(b) A request for access to records must reasonably describe the records requested. Where possible, specific information regarding dates, title, file designations, and other information which may help identify the records should be supplied by the requester. If the request relates to a matter in pending litigation, where the Commission is a party, the court and its location should be identified. Where the information supplied by the requester is not sufficient to permit identification and location of the records by Commission personnel without an unreasonable amount of effort, the requester will be contacted and asked to supply the necessary information. Every reasonable effort shall be made by Commission personnel to assist in the identification and location of requested records.

(c) If it is determined that a request would unduly burden or interfere with the operations of the Commission, the response shall so state and shall extend to the requester an opportunity to confer with appropriate Commission personnel in an attempt to reduce the request to manageable proportions by reformulation and by agreeing on an orderly procedure for the production of the records.

(d) If a requested record cannot be located from the information supplied, or is known to have been destroyed or otherwise disposed of, the requester shall be so notified by the Secretary or delegate of the Secretary.

(e) The Consumer Product Safety Commission uses a multitrack system to process requests under the Freedom of Information Act that is based on the amount of work and/or time involved in processing requests. Requests for records are processed in the order they are received within each track. Upon receipt of a request for records, the Secretary or delegate of the Secretary will determine which track is appropriate for the request. The Secretary or delegate of the Secretary may contact requesters whose requests do not appear to qualify for the fastest tracks and provide such requesters the opportunity to limit their requests so as to qualify for a faster track. Requesters who believe that their requests qualify for the fastest tracks and who wish to be notified if the Secretary or delegate of the Secretary disagrees may so indicate in the request and, where appropriate and feasible, will also be given an opportunity to limit their requests.

[42 FR 10490, Feb. 22, 1997, as amended at 62 FR 46197, Sept. 2, 1997]

§ 1015.4 Responses to requests for records; responsibility.

The ultimate responsibility for responding to requests for records is vested in the Secretary of the Consumer Product Safety Commission. The Secretary or delegate of the Secretary may respond directly or forward the request to any other office of the Commission for response. In any case where the Secretary or delegate of the

Secretary in his/her discretion determines that a request for an identifiable record should be initially determined by the Commission, the Secretary, or the delegate of the Secretary, may certify the matter to the Commission for a decision. In that event the Commission decision shall be made within the time limits set forth in § 1015.5 and shall be final. The Commission response shall be in the form set forth in § 1015.7(d) for action on appeal. If no response is made by the Commission within twenty working days, or any extension thereof, the requester and the Commission may take the action specified in § 1015.7(e).

[42 FR 10490, Feb. 22, 1997, as amended at 62 FR 46197, Sept. 2, 1997]

§ 1015.5 Time limitation on responses to requests for records and requests for expedited processing.

(a) The Secretary or delegate of the Secretary shall respond to all written requests for records within twenty (20) working days (excepting Saturdays, Sundays, and legal public holidays). The time limitations on responses to requests for records shall begin to run as of the time a request for records is received by the Office of the Secretary and a date stamp notation placed directly on the request.

(b) The time for responding to requests for records may be extended by the Secretary at the initial stage or by the General Counsel of the Commission at the appellate stage up to an additional ten (10) working days under the following unusual circumstances:

(1) The need to search for and collect the requested records from field facilities or other establishments that are separate from the Office of the Secretary.

(2) The need to search for, collect and appropriately examine a voluminous amount of separate and distinct records which are demanded in a single request.

(3) The need for consultation, which shall be conducted with all practicable speed, with another agency having a substantial interest in the determination of the request or among two or more components of the Commission having substantial subject matter interest therein.

(c) Any extension of time must be accompanied by written notice to the person making the request setting forth the reason(s) for such extension and the time within which a response is expected to be made.

(d) If the Secretary at the initial stage or the General Counsel at the appellate stage determines that an extension of time greater than ten (10) working days is necessary to respond to a request satisfying the "unusual circumstances" specified in paragraph (b) of this section, the Secretary or the General Counsel shall so notify the requester and give the requester the opportunity to:

(1) Limit the scope of the request so that it may be processed within the time limit prescribed in paragraph (b); or

(2) Arrange with the Secretary or the General Counsel an alternative time frame for processing the request or a modified request.

(e) The Secretary or delegate of the Secretary may aggregate and process as a single request requests by the same requester, or a group of requesters acting in concert, if the Secretary or delegate reasonably believes that the requests actually constitute a single request which would otherwise satisfy the unusual circumstances specified in paragraph (b) of this section, and the requests involve clearly related matters.

(f) The Secretary or delegate of the Secretary will provide expedited processing of requests in cases where the requester demonstrates a compelling need for such processing.

(1) The term "compelling need" means:

(i) That a failure to obtain requested records on an expedited basis could reasonably be expected to pose an imminent threat to the life or physical safety of an individual; or

(ii) With respect to a request made by a person primarily engaged in disseminating information, that there is an urgency to inform the public concerning actual or alleged Federal Government activity.

(2) Requesters for expedited processing must include in their requests a statement setting forth the basis for

the claim that a "compelling need" exists for the requested information, certified by the requester to be true and correct to the best of his or her knowledge and belief.

(3) The Secretary or delegate of the Secretary will determine whether to grant a request for expedited processing and will notify the requester of such determination within ten (10) days of receipt of the request.

(4) Denials of requests for expedited processing may be appealed to the Office of the General Counsel as set forth in § 1015.7 of this part. The General Counsel will expeditiously determine any such appeal.

(5) The Secretary or delegate of the Secretary will process as soon as practicable the documents responsive to a request for which expedited processing is granted.

(g) The Secretary may be unable to comply with the time limits set forth in this § 1015.5 when disclosure of documents responsive to a request under this part is subject to the requirements of section 6(b) of the Consumer Product Safety Act, 15 U.S.C. 2055(b), and the regulations implementing that section, 16 CFR part 1101. The Secretary or delegate of the Secretary will notify requesters whose requests will be delayed for this reason.

[42 FR 10490, Feb. 22, 1997, as amended at 62 FR 46197, Sept. 2, 1997]

§ 1015.6 Responses: Form and content.

(a) When a requested record has been identified and is available for disclosure, the requester shall either be supplied with a copy or notified as to where and when the record will be made available for inspection. If a requester desires to inspect records at one of the regional offices of the Commission, the Secretary will ordinarily make the records available at the requested regional office. If the payment of fees is required the requester shall be advised by the Secretary in writing of any applicable fees under § 1015.9 hereof.

(b) A response denying a written request for a record shall be in writing signed by the Secretary or delegate of the Secretary and shall include:

(1) The identity of each person responsible for the denial.

(2) A reference to the specific exemption or exemptions under the Freedom of Information Act authorizing the withholding of the record with a brief explanation of how the exemption applies to the record withheld; and

(3) An estimation of the volume of requested material withheld. When only a portion or portions of a document are withheld, the amount of information deleted shall be indicated on the released portion(s) of the record. When technically feasible, the indication of the amount of material withheld will appear at the place in the document where any deletion is made. Neither an estimation of the volume of requested material nor an indication of the amount of information deleted shall be included in a response if doing so would harm an interest protected by the exemption in 5 U.S.C. 552(b) pursuant to which the material is withheld.

(4) A statement that the denial may be appealed to the Commissioners of the Consumer Product Safety Commission. Any such appeal must be made within 30 calendar days of receipt of the denial by the requester.

(c) If no response is made within twenty (20) working days or any extension thereof, the requester can consider his or her administrative remedies exhausted and seek judicial relief in a United States District Court as specified in 5 U.S.C. 552(a)(4)(B). When it appears that no response can be made to the requester within the applicable time limit, the Secretary or delegate of the Secretary may ask the requester to forego judicial relief until a response can be made. The Secretary or delegate of the Secretary shall inform the requester of the reason for the delay, of the date on which a response may be expected and of his/her right to seek judicial review as specified in 5 U.S.C. 552(a)(4)(B).

[42 FR 10490, Feb. 22, 1997, as amended at 62 FR 46197, Sept. 2, 1997]

§ 1015.7 Appeals from initial denials; reconsideration by the Secretary.

(a) When the Secretary or delegate of the Secretary has denied a request for records in whole or in part, the requester may, within 30 days of its receipt, appeal the denial to the General

Counsel of the Consumer Product Safety Commission, attention of the Secretary, Washington, DC 20207.

(b) The General Counsel, or the Secretary upon reconsideration, will act upon an appeal within 20 working days of its receipt. The time limitations on an appeal begin to run as of the time an appeal is received by the Office of the Secretary and date stamped.

(c) After reviewing the appeal, the Secretary will reconsider his/her initial denial. If the Secretary upon reconsideration decides to release any or all of the information requested on appeal, an appeal as to the information released will be considered moot; and the Secretary will so inform the requester and submitter of the information in accordance with §§ 1015.6(a) and 1015.18(b). If the Secretary decides to affirm the initial denial, in whole or in part, the General Counsel will decide the appeal within the 20-day time limit or any extension thereof in accordance with § 1015.5.

(d) The General Counsel shall have the authority to grant or deny all appeals and, as an exercise of discretion, to disclose records exempt from mandatory disclosure under 5 U.S.C. 552(b). In unusual or difficult cases the General Counsel may, in his/her discretion, refer an appeal to the Commissioners for determination.

(e) The General Counsel's action on appeal shall be in writing, shall be signed by the General Counsel, and shall constitute final agency action. A denial in whole or in part of a request on appeal shall set forth the exemption relied upon; a brief explanation, consistent with the purpose of the exemption, of how the exemption applies to the records withheld; and the reasons for asserting it. A denial in whole or in part shall also inform the requester of his/her right to seek judicial review of the Commission's final determination in a United States district court, as specified in 5 U.S.C. 552(a)(4)(B).

(f) If no response is made to the requester within 20 working days or any extension thereof, the requester may consider his/her administrative remedies exhausted and seek judicial relief in a United States district court. When no response can be made within the applicable time limit, the General Counsel shall inform the requester of the reason for the delay, of the date by which a response may be expected, and of the requester's right to seek judicial review as specified in 5 U.S.C. 552(a)(4)(B).

(g) Copies of all appeals and copies of all actions on appeal shall be furnished to and maintained in a public file by the Secretary.

(5 U.S.C. 552(a)(6)(A); 5 U.S.C. 553; 15 U.S.C. 2076(b)(9))

[50 FR 7753, Feb. 26, 1985]

§ 1015.8 Requests received during the course of administrative hearings. [Reserved]

§ 1015.9 Fees for production of records.

(a) The Commission will provide, at no charge, certain routine information. For other Commission responses to information requests, the Secretary shall determine and levy fees for duplication, search, review, and other services, in accordance with this section.

(b) Fees shall be paid by check or money order, payable to the Treasury of the United States and sent to the Commission.

(c) The following definitions shall apply under this section:

(1) *Direct costs* means those expenditures which an agency actually incurs in searching for and duplicating (and in the case of commercial requesters, reviewing) documents to respond to a FOIA request.

(2) *Search* includes all time spent looking for material that is responsive to a request, including page-by-page or line-by-line identification of material within documents.

(3) *Duplication* refers to the process of making a copy of a document necessary to respond to a FOIA request.

(4) *Review* refers to the process of examining documents located in response to a commercial use request to determine whether any portion of any document located is permitted to be withheld.

(5) *Commercial use request* refers to a request that seeks information for a use or purpose that furthers commercial, trade, or profit interests.

(6) *Educational institution* refers to an entity organized and operated exclusively for educational purposes, whose purpose is scholarly.

(7) *Non-commercial scientific institution* refers to an entity organized and operated exclusively for the purpose of conducting scientific research, the results of which are not intended to promote any particular product or industry.

(8) *Representative of the news media* refers to any person or organization which regularly publishes or disseminates news to the public, in print or electronically.

(d) A commercial use request may incur charges for duplication, search, and review. The following requests may incur charges only for duplication: A request from an educational institution for records not sought for commercial use; a request from a non-commercial scientific institution for records not sought for commercial use; a request from a representative of the news media. Any other request may incur charges for duplication and search.

(e) The following fee schedule will apply:

(1) Copies of documents reproduced on a standard photocopying machine: $0.10 per page.

(2) File searches conducted by clerical personnel: $3.00 for each one-quarter hour (a fraction thereof to be counted as one-quarter hour). Any special costs of sending records from field locations to headquarters for review will be included in search fees, billed at the clerical personnel rate.

(3) File searches conducted by non-clerical or professional or managerial personnel: $4.90 for each one-quarter hour (a fraction thereof to be counted as one-quarter hour).

(4) Review of records: $4.90 for each one-quarter hour (a fraction thereof to be counted as one-quarter hour).

(5) Computerized records: $0.10 per page of computer printouts or, for central processing, $0.32 per second of central processing unit (CPU) time; for printer, $10.00 per 1,000 lines; and for computer magnetic tapes or discs, direct costs.

(6) Postage: Direct-cost basis for mailing requested materials, if the requester wants special handling or if the volume or dimensions of the materials requires special handling.

(7) Microfiche: $0.35 for each frame.

(8) Other charges for materials requiring special reproducing or handling, such as photographs, slides, blueprints, video and audio tape recordings, or other unusual materials: direct-cost basis.

(9) Any other service: An appropriate fee established by the Secretary, based on direct costs.

(f) Fees shall be waived as follows:

(1) No automatic fee waiver shall apply to commercial use requests.

(2) The first $10.00 of duplication costs shall be waived for requests from educational institutions, non-commercial scientific institutions, and representatives of the news media.

(3) For all other requests, the first $10.00 of duplication costs and the first $40 of search costs shall be waived.

(4) The Secretary shall waive or reduce fees whenever disclosure of the requested information is in the public interest because it is likely to contribute significantly to public understanding of the operations or activities of the government and disclosure of the requested information is not primarily in the commercial interest of the requester.

(5) In making a determination under paragraph (f)(4) of this section, the Secretary shall consider the following factors:

(i) The subject of the request: Whether the subject of the requested records concerns the operations or activities of the government.

(ii) The informative value of the information to be disclosed: Whether the disclosure is likely to contribute to an understanding of government operations or activities.

(iii) The contribution to an understanding of the subject by the general public likely to result from disclosure: Whether disclosure of the requested information will contribute to public understanding.

(iv) The significance of the contribution to public understanding: Whether the disclosure is likely to contribute significantly to public understanding of government operations or activities.

(v) The existence and magnitude of a commercial interest: Whether the requester has a commercial interest that would be furthered by the requested disclosure; and, if so

(vi) The primary interest in disclosure: Whether the magnitude of the identified commercial interest of the requester is sufficiently large, in comparison with the public interest in disclosure, that disclosure is primarily in the commercial interest of the requester.

(6) Any determination made by the Secretary concerning fee waivers may be appealed by the requester to the Commission's General Counsel in the manner described at §1015.7.

(g) Collection of fees shall be in accordance with the following:

(1) Interest will be charged on amounts billed, starting on the 31st day following the day on which the requester received the bill. Interest will be at the rate prescribed in 31 U.S.C. 3717.

(2) Search fees will be imposed (on requesters charged for search time) even if no responsive documents are located or if the search leads to responsive documents that are withheld under an exemption to the Freedom of Information Act. Such fees shall not exceed $25.00, unless the requester has authorized a higher amount.

(3) Before the Commission begins processing a request or discloses any information, it will require advance payment if:

(i) Charges are estimated to exceed $250.00 and the requester has no history of payment and cannot provide satisfactory assurance that payment will be made; or

(ii) A requester failed to pay the Commission for a previous Freedom of Information Act request within 30 days of the billing date.

(4) The Commission will aggregate requests, for the purposes of billing, whenever it reasonably believes that a requester or group of requesters is attempting to separate a request into more than one request for the purpose of evading fees.

(5) If a requester's total bill is less than $9.00, the Commission will not request payment.

[52 FR 28979, Aug. 5, 1987, as amended at 62 FR 46198, Sept. 2, 1997]

§ 1015.10 Commission report of actions to Congress.

On or before February 1 of each year, the Commission shall submit a report of its activities with regard to freedom of information requests during the preceding fiscal year to the Attorney General of the United States. This report shall include:

(a) The number of determinations made by the Commission not to comply with requests for records made to the Commission under the provisions of this part and the reasons for each such determination.

(b)(1) The number of appeals made by persons under such provisions, the result of such appeals, and the reason for the action upon each appeal that results in a denial of information; and

(2) A complete list of all statutes that the Commission relies upon to withhold information under such provisions, a description of whether a court has upheld the decision of the Commission to withhold information under each such statute, and a concise description of the scope of any information withheld.

(c) The number of requests for records pending before the Commission as of September 30 of the preceding year, and the median number of days that such requests had been pending before the Commission as of that date.

(d) The number of requests for records received by the Commission and the number of requests which the Commission processed.

(e) The median number of days taken by the Commission to process different types of requests.

(f) The total amount of fees collected by the Commission for processing requests.

(g) The number of full-time staff of the Commission devoted to processing requests for records under such provisions, and the total amount expended by the Commission for processing such requests.

[42 FR 10490, Feb. 22, 1997, as amended at 62 FR 46198, Sept. 2, 1997]

§ 1015.11 Disclosure of trade secrets to consultants and contractors; nondisclosure to advisory committees and other government agencies.

(a) In accordance with section 6(a)(2) of the CPSA, the Commission may disclose information which it has determined to be a trade secret under 5 U.S.C. 552(b)(4) to Commission consultants and contractors for use only in their work for the Commission. Such persons are subject to the same restrictions with respect to disclosure of such information as any Commission employee.

(b) In accordance with section 6(a)(2) of the CPSA, the Commission is prohibited from disclosing information which it has determined to be a trade secret under 5 U.S.C. 552(b)(4) to advisory committees, except when required in the official conduct of their business, or to other Federal agencies and state and local governments.

§ 1015.12 Disclosure to Congress.

(a) All records of the Commission shall be disclosed to Congress upon a request made by the chairman or ranking minority member of a committee or subcommittee of Congress acting pursuant to committee business and having jurisdiction over the matter about which information is requested.

(b) An individual member of Congress who requests a record for his or her personal use or on behalf of any constituent shall be subject to the same rules that apply to members of the general public.

[42 FR 10490, Feb. 22, 1977, as amended at 52 FR 45632, Dec. 1, 1987; 53 FR 3868, Feb. 10, 1988]

Subpart B—Exemptions From Production and Disclosure Under 5 U.S.C. 552(b)

§ 1015.15 Purpose and scope.

(a) The regulations of this subpart provide information concerning the types of records which may be withheld from production and disclosure by the Consumer Product Safety Commission and the internal Commission procedure for withholding exempt records. These regulations also provide information on the method whereby persons submitting information to the Commission may request that the information be considered exempt from disclosure, and information concerning the Commission's treatment of documents submitted with a request that they be treated as exempt from disclosure.

(b) No identifiable record requested in accordance with the procedures contained in this part shall be withheld from disclosure unless it falls within one of the classes of records exempt under 5 U.S.C 552(b). The Commission will make available, to the extent permitted by law, records authorized to be withheld under 5 U.S.C. 552(b) unless the Commission determines that disclosure is contrary to the public interest. In this regard the Commission will not ordinarily release documents that provide legal advice to the Commission concerning pending or prospective litigation where the release of such documents would significantly interfere with the Commission's regulatory or enforcement proceedings.

(c) Draft documents that are agency records are subject to release upon request in accordance with this regulation. However, in order to avoid any misunderstanding of the preliminary nature of a draft document, each draft document released will be marked to indicate its tentative nature. Similarly, staff briefing packages, which have been completed but not yet transmitted to the Commission by the Office of the Secretary are subject to release upon request in accordance with this regulation. Each briefing package or portion thereof released will be marked to indicate that it has not been transmitted to or acted upon by the Commission. In addition, briefing packages, or portions thereof, which the Secretary upon the advice of the Office of the General Counsel has determined would be released upon request in accordance with this regulation, will be publicly available in the public reference facility established under § 1015.2 promptly after the briefing package has been transmitted to the Commissioners by the Office of the Secretary. Such packages will be marked to indicate that they have not been acted upon by the Commission.

(d) The exceptions contained in § 1015.16 are as contained in 5 U.S.C.

552(b). These exemptions will be interpreted in accordance with the applicable law at the time a request for production or disclosure is considered.

[42 FR 10490, Feb. 22, 1977, as amended at 45 FR 22022, Apr. 3, 1980]

§ 1015.16 Exemptions (5 U.S.C. 552(b)).

(a) Records specifically authorized under criteria established by an Executive Order to be kept secret in the interest of national defense or foreign policy and are in fact properly classified pursuant to such Executive Order.

(b) Records related solely to the internal personnel rules and practices of the Commission.

(c) Records specifically exempted from disclosure by statute (other than section 552b of Title 5, United States Code), provided that such statute either requires that the matters be withheld from the public in such a manner as to leave no discretion on the issue, or establishes particular criteria for withholding or refers to particular types of matters to be withheld.

(d) Trade secrets and commercial or financial information obtained from a person and privileged or confidential.

(e) Interagency or intra-agency memoranda or letters which would not be available by law to a party other than an agency in litigation with the agency.

(f) Personnel and medical files and similar files the disclosure of which would consititute a clearly unwarranted invasion of personal privacy.

(g) Records or information compiled for law enforcement purposes, but only to the extent that the production of such law enforcement records or information:

(1) Could reasonably be expected to interfere with enforcement proceedings,

(2) Would deprive a person of a right to a fair trial or an impartial adjudication,

(3) Could reasonably be expected to constitute an unwarranted invasion of personal privacy,

(4) Could reasonably be expected to disclose the identity of a confidential source, including a State, local, or foreign agency or authority or any private institution which furnished information on a confidential basis, and, in the case of a record or information compiled by criminal law enforcement authority in the course of a criminal investigation or by an agency conducting a lawful national security intelligence investigation, information furnished by a confidential source,

(5) Would disclose techniques and procedures for law enforcement investigations or prosecutions, or would disclose guidelines for law enforcement investigations or prosecutions if such disclosure could reasonably be expected to risk circumvention of the law, or

(6) Could reasonably be expected to endanger the life or physical safety of any individual.

(h) Records contained in or related to examinations, operating, or condition reports prepared by, on behalf of, or for the use of an agency responsible for the regulation or supervision of financial institutions.

(i) Records of geological and geophysical information and data, including maps, concerning wells.

[42 FR 10490, Feb. 22, 1977, as amended at 52 FR 44597, Nov. 20, 1987]

§ 1015.17 Internal Commission procedure for withholding exempt records.

Paragraphs (a) and (b) of this section describe the internal Commission procedure to be followed for requesting that a record exempt from disclosure under the inter- intra-agency memorandum exemption, 5 U.S.C. 552(b)(5), or the investigatory file exemption, 5 U.S.C. 552(b)(7), not be disclosed.

(a) If a bureau or office director believes that it is against the public interest to disclose a Commission record prepared by his/her bureau or office, he/she may request in writing that the Secretary withhold the document. The request must specify why the release would be against the public interest.

(1) If the Secretary agrees to withhold the document, the requester shall be notified in writing of the denial and of his/her right to appeal in accordance with § 1015.6(b).

(2) If the Secretary decides to release the document, the bureau or office director shall be notified and given two working days within which to appeal to

the Commissioners. An appeal by a bureau or office director shall be in writing addressed to the Chairman. If an appeal is taken by a bureau or office director, the Secretary will not disclose the document. The Commissioner's action on appeal shall be in accordance with §1015.7(d).

(b) If a Commissioner believes that it is not in the public interest to disclose a Commission record prepared by himself/herself or by his/her office personnel, the Commissioner shall so inform the Secretary and shall specify in writing why the release would be against the public interest. The Secretary shall notify the requester in writing of the denial in accordance with §1015.6(b). Any appeal by a requester shall be in accordance with §1015.7 except the provisions for reconsideration by the Secretary is not applicable. On appeal, the Commissioner who withheld the document shall not participate in the decision.

[42 FR 10490, Feb. 22, 1977, as amended at 45 FR 22023, Apr. 3, 1980]

§1015.18 Information submitted to the Commission; request for treatment as exempt material.

(a) A person who is submitting information to the Commission, after being notified by the Commission of his/her opportunity to request confidential treatment for information, must accompany the submission with a request that the information be considered exempt from disclosure or indicate that a request will be submitted within 10 working days of the submission. The failure to make a request within the prescribed time limit will be considered an acknowledgment that the submitter does not wish to claim exempt status.

(b) A person who has previously submitted information to the Commission, that is now the subject of a Freedom of Information request, after being notified by the Commission of his/her opportunity to request confidential treatment for the information, must submit a request that the information be considered exempt from disclosure within 5 working days from receipt of notification. The failure to make a request within the prescribed time limit will be considered an acknowledgment that the submitter does not wish to claim exempt status.

(c) Each request for exemption from disclosure under 5 U.S.C. 552(b)(4) as a trade secret or privileged or confidential commercial or financial information must:

(1) Specifically identify the exact portion(s) of the document claimed to be confidential;

(2) State whether the information claimed to be confidential has ever been released in any manner to a person who was not an employee or in a confidential relationship with the company;

(3) State whether the information so specified is commonly known within the industry or is readily ascertainable by outside persons with a minimum of time and effort;

(4) State how release of the information so specified would be likely to cause substantial harm to the company's competitive position; and

(5) State whether the submitter is authorized to make claims of confidentiality on behalf of the person or organization concerned.

(d) Material received with a request that it be considered exempt shall not be maintained in a public file. If, in complying with a request for the disclosure of records, it is determined that some or all of the material relative to the request has been claimed to be exempt from disclosure, the requester will be supplied with a list of this material and informed that those portions found not to be exempt will be made available as soon as possible.

(e) No request for exemption from disclosure under 5 U.S.C. 552(b)(4) should be made by any person who does not intend in good faith to assist the Commission in the defense of any judicial proceeding that might thereafter be brought to compel the disclosure of information which the Commission has determined to be a trade secret or privileged or confidential commercial or financial information.

§1015.19 Decisions on requests for exemption from disclosure under 5 U.S.C. 552(b)(4).

(a) The Commission generally will not decide whether material received with a request for exemption from disclosure under 5 U.S.C. 552(b)(4) is entitled to be withheld until a request for production or disclosure is made for that information. The determination will be based on the most authoritative judicial interpretations available at the time a request for disclosure or production is considered. Any reasonably segregable portion of a record will be disclosed to any person requesting such record after deletion of any portions determined to be exempt under 5 U.S.C. 552(b)(4). The requester will be given a brief description of any information found to be exempt.

(b) If material received with a request for exemption from disclosure under 5 U.S.C. 552(b)(4) is found to be disclosable, in whole or in part, the person submitting the material will be notified in writing and given 10 calendar days from the receipt of the letter to seek judicial relief. In no event, however, will the material be returned to the person submitting it.

Subpart C—Disclosure of Commission Accident or Investigation Reports Under 15 U.S.C. 2074(c)

§ 1015.20 Public availability of accident or investigation reports.

(a) Accident or investigation reports made by an officer, employee, or agent of the Commission are available to the public under the procedures set forth in subpart A of this part 1015. No portion of such report are subject to the investigatory file exemption contained in the Freedom of Information Act (as restated in § 1015.16) except that portions identifying any injured person or any person treating such injured person will be deleted in accordance with section 25(c)(1) of the CPSA. Where disclosure of an accident or investigation report is requested by supplying the name of the person injured or other details of a specific accident (other than cases where the report is requested by the injured person or the injured person's legal representative), the Commission will offer to obtain the written consent of the injured party or the injured party's representative to the disclosure of the report without deleting the party's identity. No deletion of identifying portions of such reports or refusal to disclose without the Commission having first obtained written consent shall be considered as a denial by the Commission of disclosure of Commission records.

(b) Research reports, demonstration reports, and reports of other related activities of the Commission are available to the public under the procedures set forth in subpart A of this part 1015.

PART 1016—POLICIES AND PROCEDURES FOR INFORMATION DISCLOSURE AND COMMISSION EMPLOYEE TESTIMONY IN PRIVATE LITIGATION

AUTHORITY: 15 U.S.C. 2051–81; 15 U.S.C. 1261–74; 15 U.S.C. 1191–1204; 15 U.S.C. 1471–76; 15 U.S.C. 1211–14; 5 U.S.C. 552; and 5 U.S.C. 552a.

SOURCE: 53 FR 6594, Mar. 2, 1988, unless otherwise noted.

§ 1016.1 Purpose and policy.

(a) The Commission's policy is to make official records available to private litigants, to the fullest extent possible.

(b) The Commission's policy and responsibility is to conserve the time of its employees for work on Commission projects and activities. Participation of Commission employees in private litigation, in their official capacities, is generally contrary to this policy and responsibility. In addition, such participation could impair the effectiveness of Commission employees as witness in litigation in which the Commission is directly involved.

§ 1016.2 Definition.

Private litigation refers to any legal proceeding which does not involve the United States government, or any department or agency of the U.S. government, as a party.

§ 1016.3 Disclosure and certification of information and records.

(a) Identifiable information and records in the Commission's possession will be made available to private litigants in accordance with the Commission's Procedures for Disclosure or Production of Information under the Freedom of Information Act (16 CFR part 1015), the Freedom of Information Act (5 U.S.C. 552), sections 6 and 25(c) of the Consumer Product Safety Act (15 U.S.C. 2055 and 2074(c)), and any other applicable statutes or regulations.

(b) The Secretary of the Commission shall certify the authenticity of copies of Commission records. Requests must be in writing and must include the records to be certified. Requests should be sent to: Secretary, Consumer Product Safety Commission, Washington, DC 20207.

(c) Any subpoena duces tecum served on a Commission employee will be handled by the Office of the Secretary in conjunction with the Office of the General Counsel. Whenever necessary to prevent the improper disclosure of documents, the General Counsel will take steps, in conjunction with the Department of Justice, to quash such subpoenas or seek protective orders.

§ 1016.4 Testimony of Commission employees in private litigation.

(a) No Commission employee shall testify in his or her official capacity in any private litigation, without express authorization from the Commission's General Counsel. The Commission may, in its discretion, review a decision by the General Counsel to authorize such employee testimony. The General Counsel shall in such instances, where time permits, advise the Commission, on a no objection basis, of the authorization of such employee testimony.

(b) If any Commission employee is served with a subpoena seeking testimony in private litigation, he or she must immediately notify the Office of the General Counsel. The Office of the General Counsel, in conjunction with the Department of Justice, will (1) take steps to quash the subpoena or (2) direct the employee to appear in response to the subpoena but refuse to testify on the ground that it is prohibited by this section.

(c) If the General Counsel becomes aware of private litigation in which testimony by a Commission employee would be in the interests of the Commission, he or she may authorize such testimony, notwithstanding paragraph (b) of this section. The Commission may, in its discretion, review a decision by the General Counsel to authorize such employee testimony. The General Counsel shall in such instances, where time permits, advise the Commission, on a no objection basis, of the authorization of such employee testimony. Any such testimony must be provided in a way that minimizes the use of Commission resources as much as possible.

PART 1017 [RESERVED]

PART 1018—ADVISORY COMMITTEE MANAGEMENT

Subpart A—General Provisions

Sec.

Subpart B—Establishment of Advisory Committees

Subpart C—Operation of Advisory Committees

Subpart D—Administration of Advisory Committees

AUTHORITY: Sec. 8, Pub. L. 92–463, 86 Stat. 770 (5 U.S.C. App. I).

SOURCE: 41 FR 45882, Oct. 18, 1976, unless otherwise noted.

Subpart A—General Provisions

§ 1018.1 Purpose.

This part contains the Consumer Product Safety Commission's regulations governing the establishment, operations and administration of advisory committees under its jurisdiction. These regulations are issued pursuant to section 8(a) of the Federal Advisory Committee Act (Pub. L. 92–463, 5 U.S.C. App. I), and supplement Executive Order No. 11769 (39 FR 7125 (1974)) and Office of Management and Budget Circular No. A–63 (Rev.) (39 FR 12369 (1974)).

§ 1018.2 Definitions.

(a) *Advisory Committee Act* or *Act* means the Federal Advisory Committee Act (Pub. L. 92–463, 5 U.S.C. App. I (1974)).

(b) *OMB Circular No. A–63* means Office of Management and Budget Circular No. A–63 (Rev.), entitled "Advisory Committee Management" (39 FR 12369, April 5, 1974), as amended.

(c) *Advisory Committee* means any committee, board, commission, council, conference, panel, task force or other similar group, or any subcommittee or other subgroup, thereof, which is established or used by the Commission in the interest of obtaining advice or recommendations and which is not composed wholly of full-time officers or employees of the Federal Government.

(d) *Statutory advisory committee* means an advisory committee established or directed to be established by Congress.

(e) *Non-statutory advisory committee* means an advisory committee established by the Commission, including a committee which was authorized, but not established by Congress.

(f) *Ad hoc advisory committee* means a non-continuing, non-statutory advisory committee established by the Commission for the stated purpose of providing advice or recommendations regarding a particular problem which must be resolved immediately or within a limited period of time.

(g) *Non-Commission established advisory committee* means an advisory committee established by a Federal, State, or local instrumentality other than the Commission, or by a private organization or group and utilized by the Commission for advisory services.

(h) *GSA Secretariat* means the Committee Management Secretariat of the General Services Administration.

(i) *Chairman* means the Chairman of the Consumer Product Safety Commission.

[41 FR 45882, Oct. 18, 1976, as amended at 46 FR 63248, Dec. 31, 1981]

§ 1018.3 Policy.

In application of this part, Commission officials shall be guided by the Advisory Committee Act, the statutes creating the Commission's advisory committees, and by the directives in Executive Order No. 11769 and OMB Circular No. A–63. Principles to be followed include:

(a) Limiting the number of advisory committees to those that are essential and terminating any committee not fulfilling its purpose;

(b) Insuring effective use of advisory committees and their recommendations, while assuring that decisional authority is retained by the responsible Commission officers;

(c) Providing clear goals, standards, and uniform procedures with respect to the establishment, operation, and administration of advisory committees;

(d) Ensuring that adequate information is provided to the public regarding advisory committees; and

(e) Ensuring adequate opportunities for access by the public to advisory committee meetings and information.

§1018.4 Applicability.

(a) This part shall apply to all advisory committees (whether statutory or non-statutory) subject to the jurisdiction of the Commission. This part also shall apply to ad hoc advisory committees and non-Commission established advisory committees when they are performing advisory services for the Commission.

(b) Nothing in this part shall apply to any of the following types of organizations:

(1) Any local civic group whose primary function is that of rendering a public service with respect to a Federal program;

(2) Any state or local government committee, council, board, commission, or similar group established to advise or make recommendations to State or local officials or agencies;

(3) Any committee whether advisory, interagency, or intraagency which is composed wholly of full-time officers or employees of the Federal Government;

(4) Persons or organizations having contractual relationships with the Commission; and

(5) Persons or organizations developing consumer product safety standards under section 7 of the Consumer Product Safety Act (15 U.S.C. 2056).

(c) This part shall not apply to a committee or other group to the extent that it is specifically exempted by statute from the Federal Advisory Committee Act.

[41 FR 45882, Oct. 18, 1976, as amended at 46 FR 63248, Dec. 31, 1981]

§1018.5 Advisory Committee Management Officer.

The Chairman shall designate an Advisory Committee Management Officer who shall:

(a) Exercise control and supervision over the establishment, procedures, and accomplishments of all advisory committees established or utilized by the Commission;

(b) Assemble and maintain the reports, records, and other papers of any such committee during its existence, and carry out, on behalf of the Secretary of the Commission, the provisions of section 552 of Title 5, United States Code (Freedom of Information Act) and the Commission's Procedures for Disclosure or Production of Information Under the Freedom of Information Act (16 CFR part 1015) with respect to such reports, records, and other papers; and

(c) Perform such other functions as specified in this part.

Subpart B—Establishment of Advisory Committees

§1018.11 Charters.

(a) No advisory committee shall meet or take any action until its charter has been filed with the GSA Secretariat in accordance with the requirements of section 9(c) of the Federal Advisory Committee Act.

(b) The Advisory Committee Management officer shall have responsibility for the preparation and filing of charters.

[41 FR 45882, Oct. 18, 1976, as amended at 46 FR 63249, Dec. 31, 1981]

§1018.12 Statutory advisory committees.

The Commission has one statutory advisory committee subject to the Federal Advisory Committee Act. The Toxicological Advisory Board was established by the Commission on December 22, 1978, pursuant to section 20 of the Federal Hazardous Substances Act, as amended (Pub. L. 95–631, 92 Stat. 3747, 15 U.S.C. 1275).

[46 FR 63248, Dec. 31, 1981]

§1018.13 Non-statutory advisory committees.

(a) In proposing to establish a non-statutory advisory committee, the Commission shall follow the procedural requirements of section 9(a)(2) of the Advisory Committee Act and section 6(a) of OMB Circular No. A–63.

(b) A non-statutory advisory committee shall not be established if the proposed function can be performed effectively by Commission personnel, by an existing advisory committee, or by another Federal agency.

§ 1018.14 Non-Commission established advisory committees.

(a) To the extent practicable, the Commission shall utilize advisory committees already established by Federal, State, or local government or by private organizations, rather than establish a new advisory committee or expand the functions of an existing Commission advisory committee.

(b) In utilizing a non-Commission established advisory committee, Commission officials shall follow the applicable provisions of this part and the requirements of the Advisory Committee Act.

§ 1018.15 Membership composition.

The Toxicological Advisory Board, as specified in section 20 of the Federal Hazardous Substances Act, as amended (Pub. L. 95–631, 92 Stat. 3747, 15 U.S.C. 1275), shall be composed of nine members appointed by the Commission. Each member of the Board shall be qualified by training and experience in one or more fields applicable to the duties of the Board, and at least three of the members of the Board shall be members of the American Board of Medical Toxicology. The Commission will seek a balanced membership, including individuals representative of consumers, government and industry.

[46 FR 63248, Dec. 31, 1981]

§ 1018.16 Membership selection.

(a) Whenever new applicants are required for a Commission advisory committee, public notice will be issued in the FEDERAL REGISTER inviting individuals to submit, on or before a specified date, applications or nominations for membership.

(b) An applicant for membership on an advisory committee shall disclose all affiliations, either paid or as a volunteer, that bear any relationship to the subject area of product safety or to membership on the advisory committee. This disclosure shall include both current affiliations and relevant past affiliations.

(c) The Secretary of the Commission shall, from time to time, appoint a Candidate Evaluation Panel consisting of qualified, staff members of the Commission, including the Advisory Committee Management Officer.

(d) The Candidate Evaluation Panel, using selection criteria established by the Commission, shall evaluate all candidates and submit to the Commissioners the names of those candidates it recommends for membership. Where possible, at least three candidates shall be recommended for each appointment to be made. Final selection for membership shall be made by the Commissioners.

(e) The membership of each Commission Advisory Committee shall be fairly balanced in terms of geographic location, age, sex, and race.

§ 1018.17 Appointments.

(a) The Chairman shall appoint as members to advisory committees those persons selected by the Commissioners.

(b) The term of appointment to an advisory committee shall be for two years, unless otherwise specified by the Commission. To promote maximum participation, an advisory committee member may serve for only one consecutive full term. This subsection shall not be deemed to affect the term of appointment of any present member of an advisory committee in effect on the original effective date of this part, September 24, 1975.

(c) A vacancy that occurs during the term of an appointment normally will be filled by the Commission from the applications or nominations on file. Appointment to any such vacancy will be for the unexpired portion of the original appointment. Appointees to such an unexpired term may be reappointed for a full two-year term.

(d) Notwithstanding paragraphs (b) and (c) above, members of the Toxicological Advisory Board shall be appointed for terms of three years. Members may be reappointed for a subsequent three-year term. Any vacancy on the Board shall be filled in the same manner in which the original appointment was made. Any person appointed to fill a vacancy occurring before the expiration of the term for which his or her predecessor was appointed shall serve only for the remainder of such term.

[41 FR 45882, Oct. 18, 1976, as amended at 43 FR 60876, Dec. 29, 1978]

Subpart C—Operation of Advisory Committees

§ 1018.21 Calling of meetings.

Advisory committees shall, as a general rule, meet four times per year, except that, as provided by statute, the Toxicological Advisory Board shall meet not less than two times each year. No advisory committee shall hold a meeting without advance approval of the Chairman or the Commission official designated under § 1018.23(a). Before giving such advance approval, the Chairman or Commission official shall notify the Commission of the date of the proposed meeting.

[41 FR 45822, Oct. 18, 1976, as amended at 43 FR 60876, Dec. 29, 1978]

§ 1018.22 Notice of meetings.

(a) Meetings shall be called by written and/or oral notice to all members of the advisory committee.

(b) Notice of each advisory committee meeting shall be published in the FEDERAL REGISTER as well as other means to give widespread public notice, at least 15 calendar days before the date of the meeting, except that shorter notice may be provided in emergency situations. Reasons for such emergency exceptions shall be made part of the meeting notice.

(c) A meeting notice shall include:

(1) The official designation of the committee;

(2) The address and site of the meeting;

(3) The time of the meeting;

(4) The purpose of the meeting, including where appropriate, a summary of the agenda;

(5) Whether, or the extent to which, the public will be permitted to attend or participate;

(6) An explanation of how any person who wishes to do so may file a written statement with the committee before, during, or after the meeting; and

(7) The procedure by which a public attendee may present an oral statement or question to members of the committee.

§ 1018.23 Designated Commission employee.

(a) The Chairman shall designate a member of the Commission or other Commission officer or employee to chair or attend each meeting of each advisory committee.

(b) Unless otherwise provided in the statute creating a statutory advisory committee, the committee normally will be chaired, on a rotating basis, by a member of the Commission.

(c) No advisory committee shall conduct any meeting in the absence of the officer or employee designated under paragraph (a) of this section.

(d) The officer or employee designated under paragraph (a) of this section is authorized to adjourn any advisory committee meeting whenever he or she determines adjournment to be in the public interest.

§ 1018.24 Agenda.

Prior to each advisory committee meeting, the Advisory Committee Management Officer shall prepare and, after approval by the officer or employee designated under § 1018.23 (a), shall distribute to each committee member the agenda for that meeting. The agenda for a meeting shall list the matters to be discussed at the meeting and shall indicate whether and when any part of the meeting will concern matters which are exempt from public disclosure under the Freedom of Information Act (5 U.S.C. 552(b) or section 6(a)(2) of the Consumer Product Safety Act (15 U.S.C. 2045(a)(2)).

§ 1018.25 Minutes and meeting reports.

(a) The Advisory Committee Management Officer shall be responsible for the preparation of detailed minutes of each meeting of each advisory committee. The minutes shall include at least the following:

(1) The time and place of the meeting;

(2) A list of advisory committee members and staff and Commission employees present at the meeting;

(3) A complete summary of all matters discussed and conclusions reached;

(4) Copies of all reports received, issued, or approved by the advisory committee; and

(5) A description of public participation, including a list of members of the public who presented oral or written statements and an estimate of the number of members of the public who attended the meeting.

(b) The chairman of the advisory committee shall certify the accuracy of the minutes.

(c) Whenever a non-Commission established committee convenes and, at the request of the Commission, a portion of the session is allocated to the rendering of advisory services to the Commission, the Advisory Committee Management Officer shall attend and prepare minutes for that portion of the meeting in accordance with this section.

(d) In addition to the information required by subsection (a) of this section, the minutes of the Toxicological Advisory Board shall specify the reasons for all conclusions reached and, where conclusions are not unanimous, the Board is encouraged to submit minority or dissenting opinions.

[41 FR 45882, Oct. 18, 1976, as amended at 43 FR 60876, Dec. 29, 1978]

§ 1018.26 Advisory functions.

(a) Unless otherwise specifically provided by statute, advisory committees shall be utilized solely for advisory functions.

(b) The Commission shall ensure that the advice and recommendations of advisory committees shall not be inappropriately influenced by the Commission, its staff, or by any special interest, but will be the result of the advisory committee's independent judgment.

§ 1018.27 Public participation.

(a) The Commission is committed to a policy of encouraging public participation in its activities and will hold all advisory committee meetings open to the public.

(b) The guidelines in section 8(c) of OMB Circular A–63 shall be followed in providing public access to advisory committee meetings.

§ 1018.28 Records and transcripts.

(a) Subject to section 552 of title 5, United States Code (Freedom of Information Act) and 16 CFR part 1015 (Commission's Procedures for Disclosure or Production of Information under the Freedom of Information Act), the records, reports, transcripts, minutes, appendices, working papers, drafts, studies, agendas or other documents which were made available to or prepared for or by an advisory committee shall be made available for public inspection and copying in the Commission's Office of the Secretary.

(b) Advisory Committee documents shall be made available until the advisory committee ceases to exist. Disposition of the advisory committee documents shall be determined by the Secretary of the Commission at that time.

§ 1018.29 Appeals under the Freedom of Information Act.

Appeals from the denial of access to advisory committee documents shall be considered in accordance with the Commission's Procedures for Disclosure or Production of Information under the Freedom of Information Act (16 CFR part 1015).

Subpart D—Administration of Advisory Committees

§ 1018.31 Support services.

Unless the statutory authority for a particular advisory committee provides otherwise, the Advisory Committee Management Officer shall be responsible for providing and overseeing all necessary support services for each advisory committee established by or reporting to the Commission. Support services include providing committee staff, meeting rooms, supplies, and funds, including funds for the publication of reports.

§ 1018.32 Compensation and travel expenses.

(a) A single rate of compensation will be offered to members of all advisory committees with the exception of government employees and those individuals whose company or organization prohibits such payment. This rate shall be $100 per day for each day in attendance at the meeting and for each day of travel.

(b) The Commission shall determine per diem and travel expenses for members, staffs, and consultants in accordance with section 7(d) of the Advisory Committee Act and section 11 of OMB Circular No. A–63.

(c) Members of advisory committees, while engaged in the performance of their duties away from their homes or regular place of business, may be allowed travel expenses including per diem in lieu of expenses as authorized by 5 U.S.C. 5703.

§ 1018.33 Change of status.

Any advisory committee member who changes his or her affiliation or who assumes an additional affiliation, so as to actually or potentially affect his or her representational capacity on an advisory committee (upon which the member's application was based), shall immediately notify, in writing, the Advisory Committee Management Officer. Such notification shall include all relevant information concerning the change in affiliation and a statement by the member expressing his or her opinion regarding the implications of such change. The notification and any other relevant information shall be evaluated by the Commissioners to determine the appropriateness of the member's continued membership on the advisory committee.

§ 1018.34 Conflict of interest.

Members of the Commission's statutory advisory committees are not legally subject to the standards of conduct and conflict of interest statutes and regulations applicable to Commission employees. However, it is important to avoid situations in which a member of an advisory committee has an actual or apparent conflict of interest between the member's private interests (or the interests of the member's organization) and the member's interest in properly performing his or her duties as an advisory committee member. To preclude any such actual or apparent conflict of interest, committee members shall be subject to the following guidelines:

(a) Committee members should not personally participate, either for themselves or on behalf of an organization, in negotiations, or the preparation of negotiations, for contracts with or grants from the Commission. Nor should committee members, either as an individual or on behalf of an organization, become personally involved in the performance of work under such a negotiated contract or grant awarded by the Commission. Committee members may participate in preparing bids for and performing work under advertised contracts where price is the single factor in the determination of award.

(b) Committee members should not become personally involved in the preparation or submission of a proposal to develop a safety standard or regulation under any of the Acts administered by the Commission.

(c) Committee members representing anyone in a professional capacity in a proceeding before the Commission should, pursuant to paragraph (e) and (f) of this section, advise the committee chairperson and the other members of the committee on which he or she serves of the representation prior to the committee's discussion regarding that proceeding. Where the chairperson of the committee determines that the representation involves a conflict or the appearance of a conflict of interest, the member will be asked to withdraw from the discussion of the proceeding. In circumstances where withdrawal from the committee's discussion or consideration of the matter is determined by the Commission to be insufficient to avoid a conflict or apparent conflict of interest, continued representation may be considered incompatible with membership on the committee.

(d) Committee members should exercise caution to ensure that their public statements are not interpreted to be official policy statements of the Commission.

(e) Committee members shall disclose to the committee chairperson and to the other members of the committee on which he or she serves, any special interest in a particular proceeding or matter then pending before the committee which in any way may affect that member's position, views or arguments on the particular proceeding or matter. The disclosure shall be made orally prior to the commencement of the discussion. "Special interest" is not intended to include a member's general interest in presenting a position, views, or arguments in his or her representational capacity.

(f) Where the chairperson of the committee determines that the disclosure referred to in paragraph (e) of this section reveals a conflict or apparent conflict of interest with respect to a member's involvement in the committee's consideration or discussion of a particular matter, the member will be asked to withdraw from the discussion of the matter.

(g) The provisions of paragraphs (a) and (b) of this section do not apply to state and local government officers and employees.

§ 1018.35 Termination of membership.

Advisory committee membership may be terminated at any time upon a determination by the Commission that such action is appropriate.

Subpart E—Records, Annual Reports and Audits

§ 1018.41 Agency records on advisory committees.

(a) In accordance with section 12(a) of the Advisory Committee Act, the Advisory Committee Management Officer shall maintain, in the Office of the Secretary, records which will fully disclose the nature and extent of the activities of each advisory committee established or utilized by the Commission.

(b) The records shall include a current financial report itemizing expenditures and disclosing all funds available for each advisory committee during the current fiscal year.

(c) The records shall also include a complete set of the charters of the Commission's advisory committee and copies of the annual reports on advisory committees.

§ 1018.42 Annual report.

(a) The Advisory Committee Management Officer shall prepare an annual report on the Commission's advisory committees for inclusion in the President's annual report to Congress as required by section 6(c) of the Advisory Committee Act. This report shall be prepared and submitted in accordance with General Services Administration guidelines (39 FR 44814, December 27, 1974).

(b) Results of the annual comprehensive review of advisory committee made under § 1018.43 shall be included in the annual report.

§ 1018.43 Comprehensive review.

A comprehensive review of all Commission established or utilized advisory committees shall be made annually in accordance with section 10 of the GSA Circular No. A–63, as amended, and shall be submitted to the GSA Secretariat by November 30 of each year.

[41 FR 45882, Oct. 18, 1976, as amended at 46 FR 63249, Dec. 31, 1981]

Subpart F—Termination and Renewal

§ 1018.61 Statutory advisory committees.

A new charter shall be filed for each statutory advisory committee in accordance with section 9(c) of the Advisory Committee Act and § 1018.11 upon the expiration of each successive two-year period following the date of enactment of the statute establishing or requiring the establishment of the committee.

§ 1018.62 Non-statutory advisory committees.

(a) Each non-statutory advisory committee established by the Commission after the effective date of this part shall terminate not later than two years after its establishment unless prior to that time it is renewed in accordance with paragraph (c) of this section.

(b) Each non-statutory advisory committee which is renewed by the Commission shall terminate not later than two years after its renewal unless prior to that time it is again renewed in accordance with paragraph (c) of this section.

(c) Before a non-statutory advisory committee can be renewed by the Commission, the chairman shall inform the GSA Secretariat by letter not more than 60 days nor less than 30 days before the committee expires of the following:

(1) His or her determination that renewal is necessary and is in the public interest;

(2) The reasons for his or her determination;

(3) The Commission's plan to attain balanced membership of the committee, and;

(4) An explanation of why the committee's functions cannot be performed by the Commission or by another existing advisory committee.

(d) If the GSA Secretariat concurs, the Chairman shall certify in writing that the renewal of the advisory committee is in the public interest and shall publish notice of the renewal in the FEDERAL REGISTER and shall file a new charter.

[41 FR 45882, Oct. 18, 1976, as amended at 46 FR 63249, Dec. 31, 1981]

PART 1019—EXPORT OF NONCOMPLYING, MISBRANDED, OR BANNED PRODUCTS

Subpart A—Procedures for Export of Noncomplying, Misbranded, or Banned Products

Subpart B—Statement of Policy and Interpretation Concerning Export of Noncomplying, Misbranded, or Banned Products

AUTHORITY: 15 U.S.C. 1196, 1202, 1263, 1264, 1273, 2067, 2068.

SOURCE: 61 FR 29647, June 12, 1996, unless otherwise noted.

Subpart A—Procedures for Export of Noncomplying, Misbranded, or Banned Products

§ 1019.1 Purpose, applicability, and exemptions.

(a) *Purpose.* The regulations in this subpart A of this part 1019 establish the procedures exporters must use to notify the Consumer Product Safety Commission of their intent to export from the United States products which are banned or fail to comply with an applicable safety standard, regulation, or statute. These regulations also set forth the procedures the Commission uses in transmitting the notification of export of noncomplying products to the country to which those products will be sent. The Consumer Product Safety Act Authorization Act of 1978 (Pub. L. 95–631), which became effective November 10, 1978, established these notification requirements and authorizes the Commission to issue regulations to implement them.

(b) *Applicability.* These regulations apply to any person or firm which exports from the United States and item which is:

(1) A consumer product that does not conform to an applicable consumer product safety rule issued under sections 7 and 9 of the Consumer Product Safety Act (15 U.S.C. 2056, 2058), or which has been declared to be a banned hazardous product under provisions of sections 8 and 9 of that Act (15 U.S.C. 2057, 2058); or

(2) A misbranded hazardous substance or a banned hazardous substance within the meaning of sections 2(p) and 2(q) of the Federal Hazardous Substances Act (15 U.S.C. 1261); or

(3) A fabric or related material or an item of wearing apparel or interior furnishing made of fabric or related material which fails to conform with an applicable flammability standard or regulations issued under section 4 of the Flammable Fabrics Act (15 U.S.C. 1191, 1193).

(c) *Exemption for certain items with noncomplying labeling.* The exporter of an item that fails to comply with a standard or regulation only because it is labeled in a language other than

English need not notify the Commission prior to export if the product is labeled with the required information in the language of the country to which the product will be sent.

(d) *Exemption for samples.* The exporter of an item that fails to comply with a standard or regulation, but which is intended for use only as a sample and not for resale, need not notify the Commission prior to export, if the item is conspicuously and labeled in English with the statement: "Sample only. Not for resale." (The Commission encourages exporters to provide this label, in addition, in the language of the importing country, but does not require the foreign language labeling.) To qualify as a sample shipment under this exemption, the quantity of goods involved must be consistent with prevalent trade practices with respect to the specific product.

(e) *Exemption for items not in child-resistant packaging.* The exporter of an item which is a "misbranded hazardous substance" within the meaning of section 2(p) of the Federal Hazardous Substances Act (15 U.S.C. 1261(p)) only because it fails to comply with an applicable requirement for child-resistant packaging under the Poison Prevention Packaging Act of 1970 (15 U.S.C. 1471 *et seq.*) need not notify the Commission prior to export.

§ 1019.2 Definitions.

As used in this subpart A of this part 1019:

(a) *Consignee* means the person, partnership, corporation or entity in a foreign country to whom noncomplying goods are sent;

(b) *Export* means to send goods outside the United States or United States possessions for purposes of trade, except the term does not apply to sending goods to United States installations located outside the United States or its possessions;

(c) *Exporter* means the person, partnership, corporation or entity that initiates the export of noncomplying goods;

(d) *Noncomplying goods* means any item described in § 1019.1(b), except for those items excluded from the requirements of these regulations by § 1019.1 (c), (d), and (e).

§ 1019.3 General requirements for notifying the Commission.

Not less than 30 days before exporting any noncomplying goods described in § 1019.1(b), the exporter must file a statement with the Consumer Product Safety Commission, as described in §§ 1019.4 and 1019.5 of this subpart A. The exporter need not notify the Commission about the export of items described in § 1019.1 (c), (d), or (e). As described in § 1019.5, the exporter may request the Commission to allow the statement to be filed between 10 and 29 days before the intended export, and the request may be granted for good cause.

§ 1019.4 Procedures for notifying the Commission; content of the notification.

(a) *Where notification must be filed.* The notification of intent to export shall be addressed to the Assistant Executive Director for Compliance, Consumer Product Safety Commission, Washington, DC 20207.

(b) *Coverage of notification.* An exporter must file a separate notification for each country to which noncomplying goods are to be exported. Each notification may include a variety of noncomplying goods being shipped to one country. The notification may include goods intended to be shipped to one country in any one year, unless the Assistant Executive Director of Compliance directs otherwise in writing.

(c) *Form of notification.* The notification of intent to export must be in writing and must be entitled: "Notification of Intent to Export Noncomplying Goods to [indicate name of country]." The Commission has no notification forms, but encourages exporters to provide the required information in the order listed in paragraphs (d) and (e) of this section.

(d) *Content of notification; required information.* The notification of intent to export shall contain the information required by this subsection. If the notification covers a variety of noncomplying goods the exporter intends to export to one country, the information required below must be clearly provided for each class of goods, and may include an estimate of the information required in paragraphs (d) (3) and (5) of this section. The required information is:

(1) Name, address and telephone number of the exporter;

(2) Name and address of each consignee;

(3) Quantity and description of the goods to be exported to each consignee, including brand or trade names or model or other identifying numbers;

(4) Identification of the standards, bans, regulations and statutory provisions applicable to the goods being exported, and an accurate description of the manner in which the goods fail to comply with applicable requirements; and

(5) Anticipated date of shipment and port of destination.

(e) *Optional information.* In addition to the information required by paragraph (d) of this section, the notification of intent to export may contain, at the exporter's option, the following information:

(1) Copies of any correspondence from the government of the country of destination of the goods indicating whether the noncomplying goods may be imported into that country; and

(2) Any other safety-related information that the exporter believes is relevant or useful to the Commission or to the government of the country of intended destination.

(f) *Signature.* The notification of intent to export shall be signed by the owner of the exporting firm if the exporter is a sole-proprietorship, by a partner if the exporter is a partnership, or by a corporate officer if the exporter is a corporation.

§ 1019.5 Time notification must be made to Commission; reductions of time.

(a) *Time of notification.* The notification of intent to export must be received by the Commission's Assistant Executive Director for Compliance at least 30 days before the noncomplying goods are to leave the customs territory of the United States. If the notification of intent to export includes more than one shipment of noncomplying goods to a foreign country, the Assistant Executive Director for Compliance must receive the notification at least 30 days before the first shipment of noncomplying goods is to leave the customs territory of the United States.

(b) *Incomplete notification.* Promptly after receiving notification of intent to export, the Assistant Executive Director will inform the exporter if the notification of intent to export is incomplete and will described which requirements of § 1019.4 are not satisfied. The Assistant Executive Director may inform the exporter that the 30-day advance notification period will not begin until the Assistant Executive Director receives all the required information.

(c) *Requests for reduction in 30-day notification requirement.* Any exporter may request an exemption from the requirement of 30-day advance notification of intent to export by filing with the Commission's Assistant Executive Director for Compliance (Washington, DC 20207) a written request that the time be reduced to a time between 10 and 30 days before the intended export. The request for reduction in time must be received by the Assistant Executive Director for Compliance at least 3 working days before the exporter wishes the reduced time period to begin. The request must:

(1) Be in writing;

(2) Be entitled "Request for Reduction of Time to File Notification of Intent to Export Noncomplying Goods to [indicate name of country]";

(3) Contain a specific request for the time reduction requested to a time between 10 and 30 days before the intended export); and

(4) Provide reasons for the request for reduction in time.

(d) *Response to requests for reduction of time.* The Assistant Executive Director for Compliance has the authority to approve or disapprove requests for reduction of time. The Assistant Executive Director shall indicate the amount of time before export that the exporter must provide the notification. If the request is not granted, the Assistant Executive Director shall explain the reasons in writing.

§ 1019.6 Changes to notification.

If the exporter causes any change to any of the information required by § 1019.4, or learns of any change to any of that information, at any time before the noncomplying goods reach the country of destination, the exporter must notify the Assistant Executive Director for Compliance within two working days after causing or learning of such change, and must state the reason for any such change. The Assistant Executive Director will promptly inform the exporter whether the 30-day advance notification period will be discontinued, and whether the exporter must take any other steps to comply with the advance notification requirement.

§ 1019.7 Commission notification of foreign governments.

After receiving notification from the exporter, or any changes in notification, the Assistant Executive Director for Compliance shall inform on a priority basis the appropriate government agency of the country to which the noncomplying goods are to be sent of the exportation and the basis on which the goods are banned or fail to comply with Commission standards, regulations, or statutes, and shall send all information supplied by the exporter in accordance with § 1019.4(d). The Assistant Executive Director shall also enclose any information supplied in accordance with § 1019.4(e), but he or she may also state that the Commission disagrees with or takes no position on its content, including its relevance or accuracy. The Assistant Executive Director shall take whatever other action is necessary to provide full information to foreign countries and shall also work with and inform the U.S. State Department and foreign embassies and international organizations, as appropriate. The Assistant Executive Director shall also seek acknowledgment of the notification from the foreign government. Foreign governments intending to prohibit entry of goods that are the subject of a notification from the Commission should initiate action to prevent such entry and should notify the exporter directly of that intent.

§ 1019.8 Confidentiality.

If the exporter believes any of the information submitted should be considered trade secret or confidential commercial or financial information, the exporter must request confidential treatment, in writing, at the time the information is submitted or must indicate that a request will be made within 10 working days. The Commission's regulations under the Freedom of Information Act, 16 CFR part 1015, govern confidential treatment of information submitted to the Commission.

Subpart B—Statement of Policy and Interpretation Concerning Export of Noncomplying, Misbranded, or Banned Products

§ 1019.31 Purpose and scope.

(a) This subpart B of this part 1019 states the policy of the Consumer Product Safety Commission and its interpretation of the Consumer Product Safety Act and the Federal Hazardous Substances Act with regard to exportation of products which have been sold, offered for sale, or distributed in commerce for use in the United States which:

(1) Fail to comply with an applicable consumer product safety standard or banning rule issued under provisions of the Consumer Product Safety Act (15 U.S.C. 2051 *et seq.*); or

(2) Are "misbranded hazardous substances" or "banned hazardous substances" as those terms are used in the Federal Hazardous Substances Act (15 U.S.C. 1261 *et seq.*).

(b) The policy expressed in this subpart B of part 1019 does not apply to any of the following products:

(1) Products which could be regulated only under provisions of the Consumer Product Safety Act but which are not subject to a consumer product safety standard or banning rule issued under that Act.

(2) Consumer products which are subject to and fail to comply with an applicable standard or banning rule issued under provisions of the Consumer Product Safety Act but which have never been distributed in commerce for use in the United States. See section 18(b) of the Consumer Product Safety Act 15, U.S.C. 2067(b), and subpart A of this part 1019 for requirements governing export of such products.)

(3) Products which could be regulated under one or more sections of the Federal Hazardous Substances Act but which are neither "misbranded hazardous substances" nor "banned hazardous substances" as those terms are used in the Act.

(4) Products which are "misbranded hazardous substances" or "banned hazardous substances" as those terms are used in the Federal Hazardous Substances Act but which have never been sold or offered for sale in domestic commerce. (See sections 5(b) and 14(d) of the Federal Hazardous Substances Act (15 U.S.C. 1264(b) and 1273(d) and subpart A of this part 1019 for requirements governing export of such products.)

(5) Products for which the Commission has granted an exemption from an applicable standard, ban, or labeling requirement under the CPSA, FHSA, or FFA, in accordance with provisions of 16 CFR 1009.9. (These products remain subject to the notification requirements of subpart A of this part 1019.)

(6) Products which fail to comply with an applicable standard of flammability issued under provisions of the Flammable Fabrics Act (15 U.S.C. 1191 *et seq.*). The Commission's policy regarding export of such products is set forth in the Commission's Memorandum Decision and Order *In the Matter of Imperial Carpet Mills, Inc.*, CPSC Docket No. 80–2, July 7, 1983, and allows export without regard to whether the products have been distributed in domestic commerce. (See section 15 of the Flammable Fabrics Act, 15 U.S.C. 1202, and subpart A of this part 1019 for requirements governing export of such products.)

§ 1019.32 Statutory provisions.

(a) Section 18(a) of the Consumer Product Safety Act (15 U.S.C. 2057(a)) states:

This Act [the Consumer Product Safety Act] shall not apply to any consumer product if: (1) It can be shown that such product is manufactured, sold, or held for sale for export from the United States (or that such product was imported for export), unless (A) such consumer product is in fact distributed in commerce for use in the United States, or (B) the Commission determines that exportation of such product presents an unreasonable risk of injury to consumers within the United States, and (2) such consumer product when distributed in commerce, or any container in which it is enclosed when so distributed, bears a stamp or label stating that such consumer product is intended for export; except that this Act shall apply to any consumer product manufactured for sale, offered for sale, or sold for shipment to any installation of the United States located outside of the United States.

(b) Section 4 of the Federal Hazardous Substances Act (15 U.S.C. 1263) states in part:

The following acts and the causing thereof are hereby prohibited: (a) The introduction or delivery for introduction into interstate commerce of any misbranded hazardous substance or banned hazardous substance. * * * (c) The receipt in interstate commerce of any misbranded hazardous substance or banned hazardous substance and the delivery or proffered delivery thereof for pay or otherwise.

(c) Section 5(b) of the Federal Hazardous Substances Act (15 U.S.C. 1264(b)) provides in part:

No person shall be subject to the penalties of this section * * * (3) for having violated subsection (a) or (c) of section 4 with respect to any hazardous substance shipped or delivered for shipment for export to any foreign country, in a package marked for export on the outside of the shipping container and labeled in accordance with the specifications of the foreign purchaser and in accordance with the laws of the foreign country, but if such hazardous substance is sold or offered for sale in domestic commerce, or if the Consumer Product Safety Commission determines that exportation of such substance presents an unreasonable risk of injury to persons residing within the United States, this clause shall not apply.

§ 1019.33 Statement of policy and interpretation.

(a) In its enforcement of the Consumer Product Safety Act, the Commission interprets the provisions of that Act to prohibit the export of products which fail to comply with an applicable consumer product safety standard or banning rule issued under that Act if those products have at any time been distributed in commerce for use in the United States.

(b) In its enforcement of the Federal Hazardous Substances Act, the Commission interprets the provisions of the Act to prohibit the export of products which are misbranded substances or banned hazardous substances as those terms are used in that Act if those products have at any time been sold or offered for sale in domestic commerce.

PART 1020—SMALL BUSINESS

AUTHORITY: 5 U.S.C. 601 note.

SOURCE: 61 FR 52878, Oct. 9, 1996, unless otherwise noted.

§ 1020.1 Why is the Commission issuing this rule?

(a) To state the Commission's policies on small businesses;

(b) To assure that the Commission continues to treat small businesses fairly;

(c) To assure that small businesses do not bear a disproportionate share of any burden or cost created by a Commission regulatory, enforcement, or other action; and

(d) To assure that small businesses are given every opportunity to participate fully in the Commission's regulatory process.

§ 1020.2 What is the definition of "small business"?

As used in this part, the term *small business* means any entity that is either a *small business, small organization*, or *small governmental jurisdiction*, as those terms are defined at 5 U.S.C. 601(3), (4), and (5), respectively.

§ 1020.3 What are the qualifications and duties of the Small Business Ombudsman?

(a) The Chairman will appoint a senior, full-time Commission employee as Small Business Ombudsman. The Ombudsman must:

(1) Have a working knowledge of the Commission's statutes and regulations;

(2) Be familiar with the industries and products that the Commission regulates;

(3) Develop a working knowledge of the regulatory problems that small businesses experience;

(4) Perform the Ombudsman duties in addition to, and consistently with, other Commission responsibilities; and

(5) Not work in the Office of Compliance or Office of Hazard Identification and Reduction.

(b) The duties of the Small Business Ombudsman will include, but not be limited to, the following:

(1) Developing and implementing a program to assist small businesses that is consistent with § 1020.4;

(2) Working to expedite Commission responses to small businesses and providing information, guidance, and technical assistance to small businesses;

(3) Performing a review, at least twice a year, of the Commission's regulatory agenda for actions likely to have a significant impact on small businesses; and

(4) Pursuing the interests of small businesses by maintaining a working relationship with appropriate officials in the Small Business Administration, in national trade associations that represent small businesses, and in the Commission.

§ 1020.4 What is the Small Business Program?

(a) Whenever the Commission is aware of the interests of small businesses, it will consider those interests before taking any action that will likely have a significant effect on small businesses.

(b) Small businesses may request and receive special assistance from the Commission, as appropriate and consistent with Commission resources. Examples of such assistance are:

(1) Small businesses may contact the Small Business Ombudsman to obtain information about Commission statutes, regulations, or programs; to obtain technical assistance; to determine who in the agency has particular expertise that might be helpful to the small business; or to help expedite a small business's request.

(2) Small businesses may request assistance from the Commission by using the small business extension on the Commission's hotline telephone system. The number is 1–800–638–2772, extension 234.

(3) The Small Business Ombudsman will directly provide small businesses

with the requested assistance, or will direct the small business to the appropriate Commission staff for help.

(c) Whenever the Commission issues a final regulatory flexibility analysis for a rule, under the Regulatory Flexibility Act (5 U.S.C. 604), the Commission will publish a compliance guide for small businesses. The guide will explain in easy-to-understand language what action a small business must take to comply with the rule.

(d) The Commission may take other appropriate actions to assist small businesses, but such actions will not treat any other Commission constituent unfairly.

§ 1020.5 What is the Small Business Enforcement Policy?

(a) When appropriate, the Commission will, subject to all applicable statutes and regulations and paragraph (b) of this section:

(1) Waive or reduce civil penalties for violations of a statutory or regulatory requirement by a small business and/or

(2) Consider a small business's ability to pay in determining a penalty assessment against that small business,

(b) The Commission may decline to waive civil penalties or consider a small business's ability to pay, under paragraph (a) of this section, when one or more of the following circumstances applies:

(1) The small business's violations posed serious health or safety threats.

(2) The small business was subject to multiple enforcement actions by the Commission.

(3) The small business's violations involved willful or criminal conduct.

(4) The small business failed to correct violations within a reasonable time.

(5) The small business failed to make a good faith effort to comply with the law.

(6) The small business acted in any other way that would make it unfair or inappropriate for the Commission to provide a benefit under paragraph (a) of this section.

PART 1021—ENVIRONMENTAL REVIEW

Subpart A—General

Subpart B—Procedures

Subpart C—Contents of Environmental Review Documents

AUTHORITY: 42 U.S.C 4321–4347; 40 CFR part 1500 *et seq.*

SOURCE: 45 FR 69434, Oct. 21, 1980, unless otherwise noted.

Subpart A—General

§ 1021.1 Purpose.

This part contains Consumer Product Safety Commission procedures for review of environmental effects of Commission actions and for preparation of environmental impact statements (EIS) and related documents. These procedures supersede any Commission procedures previously applicable. The procedures provide for identification of effects of a proposed action and its alternatives on the environment; for assessment of the significance of these effects; for consideration of effects at the appropriate points in the Commission's decision-making process; and for preparation of environmental impact statements for major actions significantly affecting the environment. These procedures are intended to implement the Council on Environmental Quality's final regulations of November 29, 1978 (43 FR 55978; 40 CFR part 1500, et seq.) concerning agency compliance with the National Environmental Policy Act, as amended (NEPA) (15 U.S.C. 4321–4347 as amended by Pub. L. 94–83, August 8, 1975).

§ 1021.2 Policy.

It is the policy of the Commission to weigh and consider the effects upon the human environment of a proposed action and its reasonable alternatives. Actions will be designed to avoid or minimize adverse effects upon the quality of the human environment wherever practicable.

§ 1021.3 Definitions.

(a) The term *CPSC actions* means rulemaking actions; enforcement actions; adjudications; legislative proposals or reports; construction, relocation, or renovation of CPSC facilities; decisions on petitions; and any other agency activity designated by the Executive Director as one necessitating environmental review.

(b) The term *Commission* means the five Commissioners of the Consumer Product Safety Commission.

(c) The term *CPSC* means the entire organization which bears the title Consumer Product Safety Commission.

(d) The term *NEPA regulations* means the Council of Environmental Quality regulations of November 29, 1978 (43 FR 55978) for implementing the provisions of the National Environmental Policy Act, as amended (42 U.S.C 4321, et. seq).

(e) The term *environmental review process* refers to all activities associated with decisions to prepare an environmental assessment, a finding of no significant impact, or an environmental impact statement.

(f) The definitions given in part 1508 of the Council's NEPA regulations are applicable to this part 1021 and are not repeated here.

§ 1021.4 Overview of environmental review process for CPSC actions.

The environmental review process normally begins during the staff development of a proposed action and progresses through the following steps:

(a) *Environmental assessment.* (Section 1508.9 of the NEPA regulations). The assessment is initiated along with the staff development of a proposal and the identification of realistic alternatives. The assessment shall be available to the Commission before the Commission votes on a proposal and its alternatives. Its purpose is to identify and describe foreseeable effects on the environment, if any, of the action and its alternatives. The assessment culminates in a written report. This report generally contains analyses of the same categories of information as would an EIS, but in a much less detailed fashion. (See § 1021.10(a), below.) It contains sufficient information to form a basis for deciding whether effects on the environment are likely to be "significant." (See § 1508.27 of the NEPA regulations.).

(b) *Decision as to significance of effects on the environment.* This decision is made by the Executive Director of the CPSC and is based upon the results of the environmental assessment as well as any other pertinent information. If the effects are significant, CPSC publishes in the FEDERAL REGISTER a notice of intent to prepare an environmental impact statement. (See § 1508.22 of the NEPA regulations.) If not, a finding of no significant impact is prepared. (Section 1508.13 of the NEPA regulations.)

(c) *Finding of no significant impact.* This is a written document which gives reasons for concluding that the effects of a proposed action, or its alternatives, on the environment will not be significant. Together with the environmental assessment, it explains the basis for not preparing an EIS. The finding of no significant impact is signed by the Executive Director. The finding of no significant impact and the environmental assessment accompany the proposed action throughout the Commission decision-making process.

(d) *Draft environmental impact statement.* The content of a draft EIS is described in § 1021.12, below. For a particular proposal, the breadth of issues to be discussed is determined by using the scoping process described in § 1501.7 of the NEPA regulations. The draft EIS pertaining to a proposed rule is before the Commission at the time it considers the proposed action and is available to the public when the notice of proposed rulemaking is published or as soon as possible thereafter. In appropriate instances, the FEDERAL REGISTER preamble for a proposed rule may serve as the draft EIS. The draft EIS shall accompany the proposed action throughout the remainder of the Commission decision-making process.

(e) *Final EIS*. The content of this document is described in § 1021.12. A final EIS responds to all substantive comments on the draft statement. It is before the Commission when it considers a final action.

(f) *Supplemental statements*. When CPSC makes changes in the proposed action that are important to environmental issues or when there is significant new environmental information, the Executive Director instructs CPSC staff to prepare supplements to either the draft or final EIS (See § 1502.9(c) of the NEPA regulations).

(g) *Record of decision*. (Sections 1505.2 and 1506.1 of the NEPA regulations.) At the time of a decision on a proposed action which involves an EIS, CPSC prepares a written record of decision explaining the decision and why any alternatives discussed in the EIS were rejected. This written record is signed by the Secretary of the Commission for the Commission. No action going forward on the proposal may be taken until the record of decision is signed and filed in the Office of the Secretary of the Commission.

§ 1021.5 Categories of CPSC actions.

(a) There are no CPSC actions which ordinarily produce significant environmental effects. Therefore, there are no actions for which an environmental impact statement is normally required.

(b) The following categories of CPSC actions have the potential of producing environmental effects and therefore, normally require environmental assessments but not necessarily environmental impact statements:

(1) Regulatory actions dealing with health risks.

(2) Actions requiring the destruction or disposal of large quantities of products or components of products.

(3) Construction, relocation, or major renovation of CPSC facilities.

(4) Recommendations or reports to Congress on proposed legislation that will substantially affect the scope of CPSC authority or the use of CPSC resources, authorize construction or razing of facilities, or dislocate large numbers of employees.

(5) Enforcement actions which result in the widespread use of substitute products, which may present health risks.

(c) The following categories of CPSC actions normally have little or no potential for affecting the human environment; and therefore, neither an environmental assessment nor an environmental impact statement is required. (These categories are termed "categorical exclusions" in the NEPA regulations; see §§ 1507.3(b)(2) and 1508.4):

(1) Rules or safety standards to provide design or performance requirements for products, or revision, amendment, or revocation of such standards.

(2) Product certification or labeling rules.

(3) Rules requiring poison prevention packaging of products or exempting products from poison prevention packaging rules.

(4) Administrative proceedings to require individual manufacturers to give notice of and/or to correct, repair, replace, or refund the purchase price of banned or hazardous products. Other administrative adjudications which are primarily law enforcement proceedings.

(5) Recommendations or reports to Congress on proposed legislation to amend, delete or add procedural provisions to existing CPSC statutory authority.

(6) Decisions on petitions for rulemaking.

(7) Issuance of subpoenas, general orders, and special orders.

(d) In exceptional circumstances, actions within category in paragraph (c) of this section ("categorical exclusions") may produce effects on the human environment. Upon a determination by the Executive Director that a normally excluded proposed action may have such an effect, an environmental assessment and a finding of no significant impact or an environmental impact statement shall be prepared.

Subpart B—Procedures

§ 1021.6 Responsible official.

(a) The Executive Director of the CPSC shall have the responsibility to ensure that the Commission's policies and procedures set forth in this part are carried out. He or she shall have the following specific powers and duties:

(1) To ensure that CPSC environmental review is conducted in accordance with the NEPA regulations as well as this part 1021.

(2) To evaluate the significance of effects of a CPSC action on the environment and to determine whether a finding of no significant impact or an EIS should be prepared.

(3) To determine when a categorical exclusion requires environmental review because of exceptional circumstances indicating that the otherwise excluded action may produce an environmental effect.

(4) To instruct CPSC staff to prepare supplements to either draft or final EIS's where there is new environmental information or when CPSC makes changes in a proposed action that are important to environmental issues.

(5) To ensure that environmental documents are before the Commission at all stages of review of proposed action.

(6) To make provisions for soliciting public comment on the anticipated effects on the environment of proposed CPSC actions and their reasonable alternatives at any stage of the environmental review process, whenever he or she decides that such comment will be helpful. The Executive Director, for example, shall have the power to require that provision for soliciting such comments, written or oral, be included in any announcement of a public hearing on proposed rulemaking or on the merits of a petition for rulemaking.

(7) To call upon all resources and expertise available to CPSC to ensure that environmental review is accomplished through an interdisciplinary effort.

(8) To delegate any of his or her powers and duties, other than paragraphs (a) (2) and (3) of this section, to any officer or employee of the CPSC.

§ 1021.7 Coordination of environmental review with CPSC procedures.

(a) The Commission shall consider all relevant environmental documents in evaluating proposals for Commission action. The preparation and completion of assessments and statements required by this part shall be scheduled to assure that available environmental information is before the Commission at all appropriate stages of development of CPSC actions along with technical and economic information otherwise required. The range of alternatives discussed in appropriate environmental documents shall be encompassed by the range of alternatives considered by the Commission for an action.

(b) An environmental assessment on a proposed rulemaking action requiring environmental review shall be available to the commission before the Commission votes on a proposed rule, and its alternatives. If the Executive Director determines that an EIS is needed, the draft EIS shall normally be before the Commission at the time it votes to publish a proposed rule. A final EIS shall be before the Commission when it considers final action on a proposed rule. Relevant environmental documents shall accompany the proposed rulemaking action throughout the Commission's decisionmaking process.

(c) Draft EISs or findings of no significant impact together with environmental assessments shall be made available to the public for comment at the time of publication in the FEDERAL REGISTER of CPSC proposals for regulatory action requiring environmental review or promptly thereafter. Pursuant to § 1506.10 of the NEPA regulations, no decision on a proposed action shall be made by the Commission until the later of 90 days after the Environmental Protection Agency (EPA) has published a notice announcing receipt of the draft EIS or 30 days after EPA announces receipt of the final EIS. These time periods may run concurrently. In addition, with regard to rulemaking for the purpose of protecting the public health and safety, the Commission may waive the 30 day period and publish a decision on a final rule simultaneously with publication by EPA of the notice of availability.

(d) Whenever the Commission decides to solicit offers by an outside person or organization to develop a proposed consumer product safety standard in accordance with section 7 of the Consumer Product Safety Act (15 U.S.C. 2056) and the Executive Director has determined that environmental review is needed, the Executive Director shall recommend to the Commission whether the "offeror" should perform an environmental assessment during development of the proposed standard. In making this recommendation, the Executive Director shall take into account the resources of the "offeror", including the expertise and money available to it. If the Commission decides that the "offeror" should perform an assessment, the agreement between the Commission and the offeror shall so provide. CPSC, however, shall independently evaluate any assessment prepared and shall take responsibility for the scope and content of the assessment.

(e) CPSC adjudications are primarily law enforcement proceedings and therefore are not agency actions within the meaning of NEPA. (See § 1508.18(8) of the NEPA regulations.) However, in CPSC formal rulemaking proceedings, all available environmental information, including any supplements to a draft or final EIS, shall be filed in the Office of the Secretary and shall be made part of the formal record of the proceeding.

§ 1021.8 Legislative proposals.

Draft EISs on legislative proposals which may significantly affect the environment shall be prepared as described in § 1506.8 of the NEPA regulations. The draft EIS, where feasible, shall accompany the legislative proposal or report to Congress and shall be available in time for Congressional hearings and deliberations. The draft EIS shall be forwarded to the Environmental Protection Agency in accordance with § 1506.9 of the NEPA regulations. Comments on the legislative statement and CPSC's responses shall be forwarded to the appropriate Congressional committees.

§ 1021.9 Public participation, notice, and comment.

(a) Information and comments are solicited from and provided to the public on anticipated environmental effects of CPSC actions as follows:

(1) Promptly after a decision is made to prepare a draft EIS, a notice of intent to prepare the draft EIS shall be published in the CPSC Public Calendar and in the FEDERAL REGISTER. The notice shall state the nature of the proposed action and available alternatives and shall describe the planned scoping process. The notice shall solicit information and comment by other governmental agencies and the public.

(2) As soon as practicable after a finding of no significant impact is completed, a copy of the finding together with the environmental assessment report shall be forwarded to the Office of the Secretary of the Commission to be made available to the public. Any information and comments received from the public on the documents will be considered and will accompany the documents throughout the CPSC decisionmaking process, but comments will not ordinarily be answered individually.

(3)(i) Upon completion of a draft EIS, a notice of its availability for comment should be published in the CPSC Public Calendar and in the FEDERAL REGISTER. Copies of the draft EIS shall be filed with the Environmental Protection Agency (EPA) in accordance with § 1506.9 of the NEPA regulations. The length of the comment period on the draft EIS shall be stated in the notice of availability and on the cover of the draft EIS. The comment period, in accordance with § 1506.10 of the NEPA regulations, shall be a minimum of 45 days from the date the notice of receipt of the draft EIS is published in the FEDERAL REGISTER by EPA. It should also be stated in the CPSC notice that comments received during the comment period will be addressed in the final EIS, whereas late comments will be considered to the extent practicable, and that all comments will be appended to the final EIS.

(ii) Copies of the draft EIS shall be sent to public and private organizations known by CPSC to have special expertise with respect to the environmental effects involved, those who are known to have an interest in the action, and those who request an opportunity to comment. Also, copies shall be circulated for comment to Federal, State, and local agencies with jurisdiction by law and special expertise with respect to environmental effects involved. Part 1503 of the NEPA regulations shall be consulted for further details of this procedure.

(iii) Draft EIS's shall be available to the public in the Office of the Secretary at Commission headquarters.

(4) Upon completion of a final EIS, a notice of its availability in the Office of the Secretary, shall be published in the CPSC Public Calendar and if deemed appropriate, in the FEDERAL REGISTER. Copies of the final EIS shall be forwarded to EPA and one copy shall be sent to each entity or person who commented on the draft EIS.

(5) A list of EIS's under preparation and of EIS's or findings of no significant impact and environmental assessments completed shall be available to the public in the Office of the Secretary, at Commission headquarters. The list shall be continuously updated.

(6) In addition to publication in the CPSC Public Calendar and the FEDERAL REGISTER, notices called for by this section may also be publicized through press releases or local newspapers, whenever appropriate.

§ 1021.10 Emergencies.

Where emergency circumstances make it necessary to take an action without observing all the provisions of these implementing procedures or the NEPA regulations, CPSC will consult with the Council on Environmental Quality about alternative arrangements.

§ 1021.11 Information regarding NEPA compliance.

Interested persons may contact the Commission's Office of the Executive Director (301–504–0550) for information regarding CPSC NEPA compliance.

[45 FR 69434, Oct. 21, 1980, as amended at 62 FR 46667, Sept. 4, 1997]

Subpart C—Contents of Environmental Review Documents

§ 1021.12 Environmental assessment.

(a) An environmental assessment shall first briefly describe the proposed action and realistic alternative actions. Next, it shall identify all effects on the environment that can be expected to result from the proposed and alternative actions. After each anticipated effect is identified, it shall be described as fully as can be done with available data in order to show its magnitude and significance. Sources of information for assessment include CPSC staff studies and research reports, information gathered at hearings or meetings held to obtain the views of the public on the proposed action, and other information received from members of the public and from governmental entities.

(b) The assessment shall identify and describe any methods or approaches which would avoid or minimize adverse effects on the environment.

§ 1021.13 Finding of no significant impact.

(a) A finding of no significant impact shall cite and be attached to the environmental assessment upon which it is based. It shall refer to anticipated effects upon the environment identified in the environmental assessment and give the reason(s) why those effects will not be significant. The final paragraph of the finding shall give the reasons why the overall impact on the environment is not regarded as significant.

(b) The signature of the Executive Director shall appear at the end of the finding of no significant impact.

§ 1021.14 Environmental impact statement.

(a) Draft and final EIS's, unless there is a compelling reason to do otherwise, shall conform to the recommended format specified in § 1502.10 of the NEPA regulations and shall contain the material required by §§ 1502.11 through 1502.18 of those regulations.

(b) It may be necessary to include in an EIS a description of effects which are not effects on the natural or physical environment, but rather are, for example, purely economic or health effects. For this reason, an EIS may include issues and facts that are thoroughly analyzed in other comprehensive CPSC documents such as hazard analyses, economic impact analyses, or analyses of impact on particular age groups among consumers. In such cases, the EIS shall not duplicate the other documents, but rather shall cite and summarize from them. A list of background documents and sources of data cited in the EIS shall appear at the end of every EIS.

PART 1025—RULES OF PRACTICE FOR ADJUDICATIVE PROCEEDINGS

Subpart A—Scope of Rules, Nature of Adjudicative Proceedings, Definitions

Subpart B—Pleadings, Form, Execution, Service of Documents

Subpart C—Prehearing Procedures, Motions, Interlocutory Appeals, Summary Judgments, Settlements

Subpart D—Discovery, Compulsory Process

Subpart E—Hearings

Subpart F—Decision

Subpart G—Appearances, Standards of Conduct

Subpart H—Implementation of the Equal Access to Justice Act in Adjudicative Proceedings With the Commission

AUTHORITY: Consumer Product Safety Act (secs. 15, 20, 27 (15 U.S.C. 2064, 2069, 2076), the Flammable Fabrics Act (sec. 5, 15 U.S.C. 1194), the Federal Trade Commission Act (15 U.S.C. 45)), unless otherwise noted.

SOURCE: 45 FR 29215, May 1, 1980, unless otherwise noted.

Subpart A—Scope of Rules, Nature of Adjudicative Proceedings, Definitions

§ 1025.1 Scope of rules.

The rules in this part govern procedures in adjudicative proceedings relating to the provisions of section 15 (c), (d), and (f) and 17(b) of the Consumer Product Safety Act (15 U.S.C. 2064 (c), (d), (f); 2066(b)), section 15 of the Federal Hazardous Substances Act (15 U.S.C. 1274), and sections 3 and 8(b) of the Flammable Fabrics Act (15 U.S.C. 1192, 1197(b)), which are required by statute to be determined on the record after opportunity for a public hearing. These rules will also govern adjudicative proceedings for the assessment of civil penalties under section 20(a) of the Consumer Product Safety Act (15 U.S.C. 2068(a)), except in those instances where the matter of a civil penalty is presented to a United States District Court in conjunction with an action by the Commission for injunctive or other appropriate relief. These Rules may also be used for such other adjudicative proceedings as the Commission, by order, shall designate. A basic intent of the Commission in the development of these rules has been to promulgate a single set of procedural rules which can accommodate both simple matters and complex matters in adjudication. To accomplish this objective, broad discretion has been vested in the Presiding Officer who will hear a matter being adjudicated to allow him/her to alter time limitations and other procedural aspects of a case, as required by the complexity of the particular matter involved. A major concern of the Commission is that all matters in adjudication move forward in a timely manner, consistent with the Constitutional due process rights of all parties. It is anticipated that in any adjudicative proceedings for the assessment of civil penalties there will be less need for discovery since most factual matters will already be known by the parties. Therefore, the Presiding Officer should, whenever appropriate, expedite the proceedings by setting shorter time limitations than those time limitations generally applicable under these Rules. For example, the 150-day limitation for discovery, as provided in § 1025.31(g), should be shortened, consistent with the extent of discovery reasonably necessary to prepare for the hearing.

[45 FR 29215, May 1, 1980, as amended at 47 FR 46846, Oct. 21, 1982]

§ 1025.2 Nature of adjudicative proceedings.

Adjudicative proceedings shall be conducted in accordance with Title 5, United States Code, sections 551 through 559, and these Rules. It is the policy of the Commission that adjudicative proceedings shall be conducted expeditiously and with due regard to the rights and interests of all persons affected and in locations chosen with due regard to the convenience of all parties. Therefore, the Presiding Officer and all parties shall make every effort at each stage of any proceedings to avoid unnecessary delay.

§ 1025.3 Definitions.

As used in this part:

(a) *Application* means an *ex parte* request by a party for an order that may be granted or denied without opportunity for response by any other party.

(b) *Commission* means the Consumer Product Safety Commission or a quorum thereof.

(c) *Commissioner* means a Commissioner of the Consumer Product Safety Commission.

(d) *Complaint Counsel* means counsel for the Commission's staff.

(e) *Motion* means a request by a party for a ruling or order that may be granted or denied only after opportunity for responses by all other parties.

(f) *Party* means any named person or any intervenor in any proceedings governed by these Rules.

(g) *Person* means any individual, partnership, corporation, unincorporated association, public or private organization, or a federal, state or municipal governmental entity.

(h) *Petition* means a written request, addressed to the Commission or the Presiding Officer, for some affirmative action.

(i) *Presiding Officer* means a person who conducts any adjudicative proceedings under this part, and may include an administrative law judge qualified under Title 5, United States

Code, section 3105, but shall not include a Commissioner.

(j) *Respondent* means any person against whom a complaint has been issued.

(k) *Secretary* means the Secretary of the Consumer Product Safety Commission.

(l) *Staff* means the staff of the Consumer Product Safety Commission.

Additional definitions relating to prohibited communications are in §1025.68.

Subpart B—Pleadings, Form, Execution, Service of Documents

§1025.11 Commencement of proceedings.

(a) *Notice of institution of enforcement proceedings.* Any adjudicative proceedings under this part shall be commenced by the issuance of a complaint, authorized by the Commission, and signed by the Associate Executive Director for Compliance and Enforcement.

(b) *Form and content of complaint.* The complaint shall contain the following:

(1) A statement of the legal authority for instituting the proceedings, including the specific sections of statutes, rules and regulations involved in each allegation.

(2) Identification of each respondent or class of respondents.

(3) A clear and concise statement of the charges, sufficient to inform each respondent with reasonable definiteness of the factual basis or bases of the allegations of violation or hazard. A list and summary of documentary evidence supporting the charges shall be attached.

(4) A request for the relief which the staff believes is in the public interest.

(c) *Notice to the public.* Once issued, the complaint shall be submitted without delay to the FEDERAL REGISTER for publication.

§1025.12 Answer.

(a) *Time for filing.* A respondent shall have twenty (20) days after service of a complaint to file an answer.

(b) *Contents of answer.* The answer shall contain the following:

(1) A specific admission or denial of each allegation in the complaint. If a respondent is without knowledge or information sufficient to form a belief as to the truth of an allegation, the respondent shall so state. Such statement shall have the effect of a denial. Allegations that are not denied shall be deemed to have been admitted.

(2) A concise statement of the factual or legal defenses to each allegation of the complaint.

(c) *Default.* Failure of a respondent to file an answer within the time provided, unless extended, shall constitute a waiver of the right to appear and contest the allegations in the complaint, and the Presiding Officer may make such findings of fact and conclusions of law as are just and reasonable under the circumstances.

§1025.13 Amendments and supplemental pleadings.

The Presiding Officer may allow appropriate amendments and supplemental pleadings which do not unduly broaden the issues in the proceedings or cause undue delay.

§1025.14 Form and filing of documents.

(a) *Filing.* Except as otherwise provided in these Rules, all documents submitted to the Commission or the Presiding Officer shall be addressed to, and filed with, the Secretary. Documents may be filed in person or by mail and shall be deemed filed on the day of filing or mailing.

(b) *Caption.* Every document shall contain a caption setting forth the name of the action, the docket number, and the title of the document.

(c) *Copies.* An original and three (3) copies of all documents shall be filed. Each copy must be clear and legible.

(d) *Signature.* (1) The original of each document filed shall be signed by a representative of record for the party or participant; or in the case of parties or participants not represented, by the party or participant; or by a partner, officer or other appropriate official of any corporation, partnership, or unincorporated association, who files an appearance on behalf of the party or participant.

(2) By signing a document, the signer represents that the signer has read it and that to the best of the signer's knowledge, information and belief, the

statements made in it are true and that it is not filed for purposes of delay.

(e) *Form.* (1) All documents shall be dated and shall contain the address and telephone number of the signer.

(2) Documents shall be on paper approximately 8½ × 11 inches in size. Print shall not be less than standard elite or 12 point type. Pages shall be fastened in the upper left corner or along the left margin.

(3) Documents that fail to comply with this section may be returned by the Secretary.

§ 1025.15 Time.

(a) *Computation.* In computing any period of time prescribed or allowed by these rules, the day of the act, event, or default from which the designated period of time begins to run shall not be included. The last day of the period so computed shall be included, unless it is a Saturday, a Sunday, or a legal holiday, in which event the period runs until the end of the next day which is not a Saturday, a Sunday, or a legal holiday. When the period of time prescribed or allowed is less than seven (7) days, intermediate Saturdays, Sundays, and legal holidays shall be excluded in the computation. As used in this rule, "legal holiday" includes New Year's Day, Washington's Birthday, Memorial Day, Independence Day, Labor Day, Columbus Day, Veterans' Day, Thanksgiving Day, Christmas Day, and any other day declared as a holiday by the President or the Congress of the United States.

(b) *Additional time after service by mail.* Whenever a party is required or permitted to do an act within a prescribed period after service of a document and the document is served by mail, three (3) days shall be added to the prescribed period.

(c) *Extensions.* For good cause shown, the Presiding Officer may extend any time limit prescribed or allowed by these rules or by order of the Commission or the Presiding Officer, except for those sections governing the filing of interlocutory appeals and appeals from Initial Decisions and those sections expressly requiring Commission action. Except as otherwise provided by law, the Commission, for good cause shown, may extend any time limit prescribed by these rules or by order of the Commission or the Presiding Officer.

§ 1025.16 Service.

(a) *Mandatory service.* Every document filed with the Secretary shall be served upon all parties to any proceedings, i.e., Complaint Counsel, respondent(s), and party intervenors, as well as the Presiding Officer. Every document filed with the Secretary shall also be served upon each participant, if the Presiding Officer or the Commission so directs.

(b) *Service of complaint, ruling, petition for interlocutory appeal, order, decision, or subpoena.* A complaint, ruling, petition for interlocutory appeal, order, decision, or subpoena shall be served in one of the following ways:

(1) *By registered or certified mail.* A copy of the document shall be addressed to the person, partnership, corporation or unincorporated association to be served at his/her/its residence or principal office or place of business and sent by registered or certified mail; or

(2) *By delivery to an individual.* A copy of the document may be delivered to the person to be served; or to a member of the partnership to be served; or to the president, secretary, or other executive officer, or a director of the corporation or unincorporated association to be served; or to an agent authorized by appointment or by law to receive service; or

(3) *By delivery to an address.* If the document cannot be served in person or by mail as provided in paragraph (b)(1) or (b)(2) of this section, a copy of the document may be left at the principal office or place of business of the person, partnership, corporation, unincorporated association, or authorized agent with an officer or a managing or general agent; or it may be left with a person of suitable age and discretion residing therein, at the residence of the person or of a member of the partnership or of an executive officer, director, or agent of the corporation or unincorporated association to be served; or

(4) By publication in the FEDERAL REGISTER. A respondent that cannot be served by any of the methods already described in this section may be served

by publication in the FEDERAL REGISTER and such other notice as may be directed by the Presiding Officer or the Commission, where a complaint has issued in a class action pursuant to § 1025.18.

(c) *Service of other documents*. Except as otherwise provided in paragraph (b) of this section, when service of a document starts the running of a prescribed period of time for the submission of a responsive document or the occurrence of an event, the document may be served as provided in paragraph (b) of this section or by ordinary first-class mail, properly addressed, postage prepaid.

(d) *Service on a representative*. When a party has appeared by an attorney or other representative, service upon that attorney or other representative shall constitute service upon the party.

(e) *Certificate of service*. The original of every document filed with the Commission and required to be served upon all parties to any proceedings, as well as participants if so directed by the Presiding Officer, shall be accompanied by a certificate of service signed by the party making service, stating that such service has been made upon each party and participant to the proceedings. Certificates of service may be in substantially the following form:

I hereby certify that I have served the attached document upon all parties and participants of record in these proceedings by mailing, postage prepaid, (or by delivering in person) a copy to each on

____

____

(Signature)

For ______________________________

(f) *Date of service*. The date of service of a document shall be the date on which the document is deposited with the United States Postal Service, postage prepaid, or is delivered in person.

§ 1025.17 Intervention.

(a) *Participation as an intervenor*. Any person who desires to participate as a party in any proceedings subject to these rules shall file a written petition for leave to intervene with the Secretary and shall serve a copy of the petition on each party.

(1) A petition shall ordinarily be filed not later than the convening of the first prehearing conference. A petition filed after that time will not be granted unless the Presiding Officer determines that the petitioner has made a substantial showing of good cause for failure to file on time.

(2) A petition shall:

(i) Identify the specific aspect or aspects of the proceedings as to which the petitioner wishes to intervene,

(ii) Set forth the interest of the petitioner in the proceedings,

(iii) State how the petitioner's interest may be affected by the results of the proceedings, and

(iv) State any other reasons why the petitioner should be permitted to intervene as a party, with particular reference to the factors set forth in paragraph (d) of this section. Any petition relating only to matters outside the jurisdiction of the Commission shall be denied.

(3) Any person whose petition for leave to intervene is granted by the Presiding Officer shall be known as an "intervenor" and as such shall have the full range of litigating rights afforded to any other party.

(b) *Participation by a person not an intervenor*. Any person who desires to participate in the proceedings as a nonparty shall file with the Secretary a request to participate in the proceedings and shall serve a copy of such request on each party to the proceedings.

(1) A request shall ordinarily be filed not later than the commencement of the hearing. A petition filed after that time will not be granted unless the Presiding Officer determines that the person making the request has made a substantial showing of good cause for failure to file on time.

(2) A request shall set forth the nature and extent of the person's alleged interest in the proceedings. Any request relating only to matters outside the jurisdiction of the Commission shall be denied.

(3) Any person who files a request to participate in the proceedings as a nonparty and whose request is granted by the Presiding Officer shall be known as a "Participant" and shall have the right to participate in the proceedings to the extent of making a written or oral statement of position, filing proposed findings of fact, conclusions of law and a post hearing brief with the

Presiding Officer, and filing an appellate brief before the Commission if an appeal is taken by a party or review is ordered by the Commission in accordance with § 1025.53 or § 1025.54, as applicable, of these rules.

(c) *Response to petition to intervene.* Any party may file a response to a petition for leave to intervene after the petition is filed with the Secretary, with particular reference to the factors set forth in paragraph (d) of this section.

(d) *Ruling by Presiding Officer on petition.* In ruling on a petition for leave to intervene, the Presiding Officer shall consider, in addition to all other relevant matters, the following factors:

(1) The nature of the petitioner's interest, under the applicable statute governing the proceedings, to be made a party to the proceedings;

(2) The nature and extent of the petitioner's interest in protecting himself/herself/itself or the public against unreasonable risks of injury associated with consumer products;

(3) The nature and extent of the petitioner's property, financial or other substantial interest in the proceedings;

(4) Whether the petitioner would be aggrieved by any final order which may be entered in the proceedings;

(5) The extent to which the peititioner's intervention may reasonably be expected to assist in developing a sound record;

(6) The extent to which the petitioner's interest will be represented by existing parties;

(7) The extent to which the petitioner's intervention may broaden the issues or delay the proceedings; and

(8) The extent to which the petitioner's interest can be protected by other available means.

If the Presiding Officer determines that a petitioner has failed to make a sufficient showing to be allowed to intervene as a party, the Presiding Officer shall view such petition to intervene as if it had been timely filed as a request to participate in the proceedings as a participant pursuant to paragraph (b) of this section.

(e) *Ruling by Presiding Officer on request.* In ruling on a request to participate as a participant, the Presiding Officer, in the exercise of his/her discretion, shall be mindful of the Commission's mandate under its enabling legislation (see 15 U.S.C. 2051 *et seq.*) and its affirmative desire to afford interested persons, including consumers and consumer organizations, as well as governmental entities, an opportunity to participate in the agency's regulatory processes, including adjudicative proceedings. The Presiding Officer shall consider, in addition to all other relevant matters, the following factors:

(1) The nature and extent of the person's alleged interest in the proceedings;

(2) The possible effect of any final order which may be entered in the proceedings on the person's interest; and

(3) The extent to which the person's participation can be expected to assist the Presiding Officer and the Commission in rendering a fair and equitable resolution of all matters in controversy in the proceedings.

The Presiding Officer may deny a request to participate if he/she determines that the person's participation cannot reasonably be expected to assist the Presiding Officer or the Commission in rendering a fair and equitable resolution of matters in controversy in the proceedings or if he/she determines that the person's participation would unduly broaden the issues in controversy or unduly delay the proceedings.

(f) *Designation of single representative.* If the Presiding Officer determines that a petitioner pursuant to paragraph (a) of this section or a person requesting to participate pursuant to paragraph (b) of this section is a member of a class of prospective intervenors or participants, as applicable, who share an identity of interest, the Presiding Officer may limit such intervention or participation, as applicable, through designation of a single representative by the prospective intervenors or participants, as applicable, or, if they are unable to agree, by designation of the Presiding Officer.

§ 1025.18 Class actions.

(a) *Prerequisites to a class action.* One or more members of a class of respondents may be proceeded against as representative parties on behalf of all respondents if:

(1) The class is so numerous or geographically dispersed that joinder of all members is impracticable;

(2) There are questions of fact or issues of law common to the class;

(3) The defenses of the representative parties are typical of the defenses of the class; and

(4) The representative parties will fairly and adequately protect the interests of the class.

(b) *Composition of class.* A class may be composed of:

(1) Manufacturers, distributors, or retailers, or a combination of them, of products which allegedly have the same defect, or

(2) Manufacturers, distributors, or retailers, or a combination of them, of products which allegedly fail to conform to an applicable standard, regulation, or consumer product safety rule, or

(3) Manufacturers, distributors, or retailers, or a combination of them, who have themselves allegedly failed to conform to an applicable standard, regulation, or consumer product safety rule.

When appropriate, a class may be divided into subclasses and each subclass shall be treated as a class.

(c) *Notice of commencement.* A complaint issued under this section shall identify the class, the named respondents considered to be representative of the class, and the alleged defect or nonconformity common to the products manufactured, imported, distributed or sold by the members of the class. The complaint shall be served upon the parties in accordance with §1025.16.

(d) *Proper class action determination.* Upon motion of Complaint Counsel and as soon as practicable after the commencement of any proceedings brought as a class action, the Presiding Officer shall determine by order whether the action is a proper class action. It is a proper class action if the prerequisites of paragraph (a) of this section are met and if the Presiding Officer finds that:

(1) The prosecution of separate actions against individual members of the respondent class might result in (i) inconsistent or varying determinations with respect to individual members of the class which might produce incompatible or conflicting results, or (ii) determinations with respect to individual members of the class which would, as a practical matter, be dispositive of the interests of the other members who are not parties to the proceedings or would substantially impair or impede the ability of the absent members to protect their interests; or

(2) The Commission has acted on grounds generally applicable to the class, thereby making appropriate an order directed to the class as a whole.

In reaching a decision, the Presiding Officer shall consider the interests of members of the class in individually controlling the defense of separate actions, the extent and nature of any proceedings concerning the controversy already commenced against members of the class, the desirability or undesirability of concentrating the litigation in one adjudication, and the difficulties likely to be encountered in the management of a class action, as well as the benefits expected to result from the maintenance of a class action.

(e) *Revision of class membership.* Upon motion of any party or any member of the class, or upon the Presiding Officer's own initiative, the Presiding Officer may revise the membership of the class.

(f) *Orders in conduct of class actions.* In proceedings to which this section applies, the Presiding Officer may make appropriate orders:

(1) Determining the course of the proceedings or prescribing measures to prevent undue repetition and promote the efficient presentation of evidence or argument;

(2) Requiring (for the protection of the members of the class, or otherwise for the fair conduct of the action) that notice be given, in such manner as the Presiding Officer may direct, of any step in the action, of the extent of the proposed order, or of the opportunity for members to inform the Presiding Officer whether they consider the representation to be fair and adequate, or of the opportunity for class members to intervene and present defenses;

(3) Requiring that the pleadings be amended to eliminate allegations concerning the representation of absent persons; or

(4) Dealing with other procedural matters.

The orders may be combined with a prehearing order under § 1025.21 of these rules and may be altered or amended as may be necessary.

(g) *Scope of final order*. In any proceedings maintained as a class action, any Decision and Order of the Presiding Officer or the Commission under § 1025.51 or § 1025.55, as applicable, whether or not favorable to the class, shall include and describe those respondents whom the Presiding Officer or the Commission finds to be members of the class.

(h) *Notice of results*. Upon the termination of any adjudication that has been maintained as a class action, the best notice practicable of the results of the adjudication shall be given to all members of the class in such manner as the Presiding Officer or the Commission directs.

§ 1025.19 Joinder of proceedings.

Two or more matters which have been scheduled for adjudicative proceedings and which involve similar issues may be consolidated for the purpose of hearing or Commission review. A motion for consolidation may be filed by any party to such proceedings not later than thirty (30) days prior to the hearing and served upon all parties to all proceedings in which joinder is contemplated. The motion may include a request that the consolidated proceedings be maintained as a class action in accordance with § 1025.18 of these rules. The proceedings may be consolidated to such extent and upon such terms as may be proper. Such consolidation may also be ordered upon the initiative of the Presiding Officer or the Commission. Single representatives may be designated by represented parties, intervenors, and participants with an identity of interests.

Subpart C—Prehearing Procedures, Motions, Interlocutory Appeals, Summary Judgments, Settlements

§ 1025.21 Prehearing conferences.

(a) *When held*. Except when the presiding officer determines that unusual circumstances would render it impractical or valueless, a prehearing conference shall be held in person or by conference telephone call within fifty (50) days after publication of the complaint in the FEDERAL REGISTER and upon ten (10) days' notice to all parties and participants. At the prehearing conference any or all of the following shall be considered:

(1) Petitions for leave to intervene;

(2) Motions, including motions for consolidation of proceedings and for certification of class actions;

(3) Identification, simplification and clarification of the issues;

(4) Necessity or desirability of amending the pleadings;

(5) Stipulations and admissions of fact and of the content and authenticity of documents;

(6) Oppositions to notices of depositions;

(7) Motions for protective orders to limit or modify discovery;

(8) Issuance of subpoenas to compel the appearance of witnesses and the production of documents;

(9) Limitation of the number of witnesses, particularly to avoid duplicate expert witnesses;

(10) Matters of which official notice should be taken and matters which may be resolved by reliance upon the laws administered by the Commission or upon the Commission's substantive standards, regulations, and consumer product safety rules;

(11) Disclosure of the names of witnesses and of documents or other physical exhibits which are intended to be introduced into evidence;

(12) Consideration of offers of settlement;

(13) Establishment of a schedule for the exchange of final witness lists, prepared testimony and documents, and for the date, time and place of the hearing, with due regard to the convenience of the parties; and

(14) Such other matters as may aid in the efficient presentation or disposition of the proceedings.

(b) *Public notice*. The Presiding Officer shall cause a notice of the first prehearing conference, including a statement of the issues, to be published in the FEDERAL REGISTER at least ten (10) days prior to the date scheduled for the conference.

(c) *Additional conferences*. Additional prehearing conferences may be convened at the discretion of the Presiding Officer, upon notice to the parties, any participants, and to the public.

(d) *Reporting*. Prehearing conferences shall be stenographically reported as provided in § 1025.47 of these rules and shall be open to the public, unless otherwise ordered by the Presiding Officer or the Commission.

(e) *Prehearing orders*. The Presiding Officer shall issue a final prehearing order in each case after the conclusion of the final prehearing conference. The final prehearing order should contain, to the fullest extent possible at that time, all information which is necessary for controlling the course of the hearing. The Presiding Officer may require the parties to submit a jointly proposed final prehearing order, such as in the format set forth in appendix I.

§ 1025.22 Prehearing briefs.

Not later than ten (10) days prior to the hearing, unless otherwise ordered by the Presiding Officer, the parties may simultaneously serve and file prehearing briefs which should set forth:

(a) A statement of the facts expected to be proved and of the anticipated order of proof;

(b) A statement of the issues and the legal arguments in support of the party's contentions with respect to each issue; and

(c) A table of authorities relied upon.

§ 1025.23 Motions.

(a) *Presentation and disposition*. During the time a matter in adjudication is before the Presiding Officer, all motions, whether oral or written, except those filed under § 1025.42(e), shall be addressed to the Presiding Officer, who shall rule upon them promptly, after affording an opportunity for response.

(b) *Written motions*. All written motions shall state with particularity the order, ruling, or action desired and the reasons why the action should be granted. Memoranda, affidavits, or other documents supporting a motion shall be served and filed with the motion. All motions shall contain a proposed order setting forth the relief sought. All written motions shall be filed with the Secretary and served upon all parties, and all motions addressed to the Commission shall be in writing.

(c) *Opposition to motions*. Within ten (10) days after service of any written motion or petition or within such longer or shorter time as may be designated by these Rules or by the Presiding Officer or the Commission, any party who opposes the granting of the requested order, ruling or action may file a written response to the motion. Failure to respond to a written motion may, in the discretion of the Presiding Officer, be considered as consent to the granting of the relief sought in the motion. Unless otherwise permitted by the Presiding Officer or the Commission, there shall be no reply to the response expressing opposition to the motion.

(d) *Rulings on motions for dismissal*. When a motion to dismiss a complaint or a motion for other relief is granted, with the result that the proceedings before the Presiding Officer are terminated, the Presiding Officer shall issue an Initial Decision and Order in accordance with the provisions of § 1025.51. If such a motion is granted as to all issues alleged in the complaint in regard to some, but not all, respondents or is granted as to any part of the allegations in regard to any or all respondents, the Presiding Officer shall enter an order on the record and consider the remaining issues in the Initial Decision. The Presiding Officer may elect to defer ruling on a motion to dismiss until the close of the case.

§ 1025.24 Interlocutory appeals.

(a) *General*. Rulings of the Presiding Officer may not be appealed to the Commission prior to the Initial Decision, except as provided in this section.

(b) *Exceptions*. (1) Interlocutory appeals to Commission. The Commission may, in its discretion, consider interlocutory appeals where a ruling of the Presiding Officer:

(i) Requires the production of records claimed to be confidential;

(ii) Requires the testimony of a supervisory official of the Commission other than one especially knowledgeable of the facts of the matter in adjudication;

(iii) Excludes an attorney from participation in any proceedings pursuant to § 1025.42(b);

(iv) Denies or unduly limits a petition for intervention pursuant to the provisions of § 1025.17.

(2) Procedure for interlocutory appeals. Within ten (10) days of issuance of a ruling other than one ordering the production of records claimed to be confidential, any party may petition the Commission to consider an interlocutory appeal of a ruling in the categories enumerated above. The petition shall not exceed fifteen (15) pages. Any other party may file a response to the petition within ten (10) days of its service except where the order appealed from requires the production of records claimed to be confidential. The response shall not exceed fifteen (15) pages. The Commission shall decide the petition or may request such further briefing or oral presentation as it deems necessary.

(3) If the Presiding Officer orders the production of records claimed to be confidential a petition for interlocutory appeal shall be filed within five (5) days of the entry of the order. Any opposition to the petition shall be filed within five (5) days of service of the petition. The order of the Presiding Officer shall be automatically stayed until five (5) days following the date of entry of the order to allow an affected party the opportunity to file a petition with the Commission for an interlocutory appeal pursuant to § 1025.24(b)(2). If an affected party files a petition with the Commission pursuant to § 1025.24(b)(2) within the 5-day period, the stay of the Presiding Officer's order is automatically extended until the Commission decides the petition.

(4) *Interlocutory appeals from all other rulings*—(i) *Grounds*. Interlocutory appeals from all other rulings by the Presiding Officer may proceed only upon motion to the Presiding Officer and a determination by the Presiding Officer in writing that the ruling involves a controlling question of law or policy as to which there is substantial ground for differences of opinion and that an immediate appeal from the ruling may materially advance the ultimate termination of the litigation, or that subsequent review will be an inadequate remedy. The Presiding Officer's certification shall state the reasons for the determination.

(ii) *Form*. If the Presiding Officer makes the determination described in paragraph (b)(4)(i) of this section, a petition for interlocutory appeal under this subparagraph may be filed in accordance with paragraph (b)(2) of this section.

(c) *Proceedings not stayed*. Except as otherwise provided under this section, a petition for interlocutory appeal shall not stay the proceedings before the Presiding Officer unless the Presiding Officer or the Commission so orders.

§ 1025.25 Summary decisions and orders.

(a) *Motion*. Any party may file a motion, with a supporting memorandum, for a Summary Decision and Order in its favor upon all or any of the issues in controversy. Complaint Counsel may file such a motion at any time after thirty (30) days following issuance of a complaint, and any other party may file a motion at any time after issuance of a complaint. Any such motion by any party shall be filed at least twenty (20) days before the date fixed for the adjudicative hearing.

(b) *Response to motion*. Any other party may, within twenty (20) days after service of the motion, file a response with a supporting memorandum.

(c) *Grounds*. A Summary Decision and Order shall be granted if the pleadings and any depositions, answers to interrogatories, admissions, or affidavits show that there is no genuine issue as to any material fact and that the moving party is entitled to a Summary Decision and Order as a matter of law.

(d) *Legal effect*. A Summary Decision and Order upon all the issues being adjudicated shall constitute the Initial Decision of the Presiding Officer and may be appealed to the Commission in accordance with § 1025.53 of these rules. A Summary Decision, interlocutory in character, may be rendered on fewer than all issues and may not be appealed prior to issuance of the Initial Decision.

(e) *Case not fully adjudicated on motion*. A Summary Decision and order that does not dispose of all issues shall include a statement of those material facts about which there is no substantial controversy and of those material facts that are actually and in good faith controverted. The Summary Order shall direct such further proceedings as are appropriate.

§ 1025.26 Settlements.

(a) *Availability*. Any party shall have the opportunity to submit an offer of settlement to the Presiding Officer.

(b) *Form*. Offers of settlement shall be filed *in camera* and the form of a consent agreement and order, shall be signed by the respondent or respondent's representative, and may be signed by any other party. Each offer of settlement shall be accompanied by a motion to transmit the proposed agreement and order to the Commission. The motion shall outline the substantive provisions of the agreement and state reasons why it should be accepted by the Commission.

(c) *Contents*. The proposed consent agreement and order which constitute the offer of settlement shall contain the following:

(1) An admission of all jurisdictional facts;

(2) An express waiver of further procedural steps and of all rights to seek judicial review or otherwise to contest the validity of the Commission order;

(3) Provisions that the allegations of the complaint are resolved by the consent agreement and order;

(4) A description of the alleged hazard, noncompliance, or violation;

(5) If appropriate, a listing of the acts or practices from which the respondent shall refrain; and

(6) If appropriate, a detailed statement of the corrective action(s) which the respondent shall undertake. In proceedings arising under Section 15 of the Consumer Product Safety Act, 15 U.S.C. 2064, this statement shall contain all the elements of a "Corrective Action Plan," as outlined in the Commission's Interpretation, Policy, and Procedure for Substantial Product Hazards, 16 CFR part 1115.

(d) *Transmittal*. The Presiding Officer may transmit to the Commission for decision all offers of settlement and accompanying memoranda that meet the requirements enumerated in paragraph (c) of this section. The Presiding Officer shall consider whether an offer of settlement is clearly frivolous, duplicative of offers previously made and rejected by the Commission or contrary to establish Commission policy. The Presiding Officer may, but need not, recommend acceptance of offers. Any party may object to the transmittal to the Commission of a proposed consent agreement by filing a response opposing the motion.

(e) *Stay of proceedings*. When an offer of settlement has been agreed to by all parties and has been transmitted to the Commission, the proceedings shall be stayed until the Commission has ruled on the offer. When an offer of settlement has been made and transmitted to the Commission but has not been agreed to by all parties, the proceedings shall not be stayed pending Commission decision on the offer, unless otherwise ordered by the Presiding Officer or the Commission.

(f) *Commission ruling*. The Commission shall rule upon all transmitted offers of settlement. If the Commission accepts the offer, the Commission shall issue an appropriate order, which shall become effective upon issuance.

(g) *Commission rejection*. If the Commission rejects an offer of settlement, the Secretary, in writing, shall give notice of the Commission's decision to the parties and the Presiding Officer. If the proceedings have been stayed, the Presiding Officer shall promptly issue an order notifying the parties of the resumption of the proceedings, including any modifications to the schedule resulting from the stay of the proceedings.

(h) *Effect of rejected offer*. Neither rejected offers of settlement, nor the fact of the proposal of offers of settlement are admissible in evidence.

Subpart D—Discovery, Compulsory Process

§ 1025.31 General provisions governing discovery.

(a) *Applicability*. The discovery rules established in this subpart are applicable to the discovery of information among the parties in any proceedings.

Parties seeking information from persons not parties may do so by subpoena in accordance with § 1025.38 of these rules.

(b) *Discovery methods.* Parties may obtain discovery by one or more of the following methods:

(1) Written interrogatories;

(2) Requests for production of documents or things;

(3) Requests for admission; or

(4) Depositions upon oral examination.

Unless the Presiding Officer otherwise orders under paragraph (d) of this section, the frequency of use of these methods is not limited.

(c) *Scope of discovery.* The scope of discovery is as follows:

(1) *In general.* Parties may obtain discovery regarding any matter, not privileged, which is within the Commission's statutory authority and is relevant to the subject matter involved in the proceedings, whether it relates to the claim or defense of the party seeking discovery or to the claim or defense of any other party, including the existence, description, nature, custody, condition and location of any books, documents, or other tangible things and the identity and location of persons having knowledge of any discoverable matter. It is not ground for objection that the information sought will be inadmissible at the hearing if the information sought appears reasonably calculated to lead to the discovery of admissible evidence.

(2) *Privilege.* Discovery may be denied or limited, or a protective order may be entered, to preserve the privilege of a witness, person, or governmental agency as governed by the Constitution, any applicable Act of Congress, or the principles of the common law as they may be interpreted by the Commission in the light of reason and experience.

(3) *Hearing preparation: materials.* Subject to the provisions of paragraph (c)(4) of this section, a party may obtain discovery of documents and tangible things otherwise discoverable under paragraph (c)(1) of this section and prepared in anticipation of litigation or for hearing by or for another party or by or for that other party's representative (including his attorney or consultant) only upon a showing that the party seeking discovery has substantial need of the materials in the preparation of his case and that he is unable without unique hardship to obtain the substantial equivalent of the materials by other means. In ordering discovery of such materials when the required showing has been made, the Presiding Officer shall protect against disclosure of the mental impressions, conclusions, opinions, or legal theories of an attorney or other representative of a party.

(4) *Hearing preparation: experts.* Discovery of facts known and opinions held by experts, otherwise discoverable under the provisions of paragraph (c)(1) of this section and acquired or developed in anticipation of litigation or for trial, may be obtained only as follows:

(i)(A) A party may through interrogatories require any other party to identify each person whom the other party expects to call as an expert witness at trial, to state the subject matter on which the expert is expected to testify, to state the substance of the facts and opinions to which the expert is expected to testify, and to provide a summary of the grounds for each opinion.

(B) Upon motion, the Presiding Officer may order further discovery by other means upon a showing of substantial cause and may exercise discretion to impose such conditions, if any, as are appropriate in the case.

(ii) A party may discover facts known or opinions held by an expert who has been retained or specially employed by another party in anticipation of litigation or preparation for trial and who is not expected to be called as a witness at trial only upon a showing of exceptional circumstances under which it is impracticable for the party seeking discovery to obtain facts or opinions on the same subject by other means.

(iii) The Presiding Officer may require as a condition of discovery that the party seeking discovery pay the expert a reasonable fee, but not more than the maximum specified in 5 U.S.C. 3109 for the time spent in responding to discovery.

(d) *Protective orders.* Upon motion by a party and for good cause shown, the Presiding Officer may make any order which justice requires to protect a party or person from annoyance, embarrassment, competitive disadvantage, oppression, or undue burden or expense, including one or more of the following:

(1) That the discovery shall not be had;

(2) That the discovery may be had only on specified terms and conditions, including a designation of the time or place;

(3) That the discovery shall be had only by a method of discovery other than that selected by the party seeking discovery;

(4) That certain matters shall not be inquired into or that the scope of discovery shall be limited to certain matters;

(5) That discovery shall be conducted with no one present except persons designated by the Presiding Officer;

(6) That a trade secret or other confidential research, development, or commercial information shall not be disclosed or shall be disclosed only in a designated way or only to designated parties; and

(7) That responses to discovery shall be placed *in camera* in accordance with § 1025.45 of these rules.

If a motion for a protective order is denied in whole or in part, the Presiding Officer may, on such terms or conditions as are appropriate, order that any party provide or permit discovery.

(e) *Sequence and timing of discovery.* Discovery may commence at any time after filing of the answer. Unless otherwise provided in these Rules or by order of the Presiding Officer, methods of discovery may be used in any sequence and the fact that a party is conducting discovery, whether by deposition or otherwise, shall not operate to delay any other party's discovery.

(f) *Supplementation of responses.* A party who has responded to a request for discovery with a response that was complete when made is under a duty to supplement that response to include information later obtained.

(g) *Completion of discovery.* All discovery shall be completed as soon as practical but in no case longer than one hundred fifty (150) days after issuance of a complaint, unless otherwise ordered by the Presiding Officer in exceptional circumstances and for good cause shown. All discovery shall be commenced by a date which affords the party from whom discovery is sought the full response period provided by these Rules.

(h) *Service and filing of discovery.* All discovery requests and written responses, and all notices of deposition, shall be filed with the Secretary and served on all parties and the Presiding Officer.

(i) *Control of discovery.* The use of these discovery procedures is subject to the control of the Presiding Officer, who may issue any just and appropriate order for the purpose of ensuring their timely completion.

§ 1025.32 Written interrogatories to parties.

(a) *Availability; procedures for use.* Any party may serve upon any other party written interrogatories to be answered by the party served or, if the party served is a public or private corporation or a partnership or unincorporated association or governmental entity, by any officer or agent, who shall furnish such information as is available to the party. Interrogatories may, without leave of the Presiding Officer, be served upon any party after the filing of an answer.

(b) *Procedures for response.* Each interrogatory shall be answered separately and fully in writing under oath, unless it is objected to, in which event the reasons for objection shall be stated in lieu of an answer. Each answer shall be submitted in double-spaced typewritten form and shall be immediately preceded by the interrogatory, in single-spaced typewritten form, to which the answer is responsive. The answers are to be signed by the person making them, and the objections signed by the person or representative making them. The party upon whom the interrogatories have been served shall serve a copy of the answers, and objections if any, within 30 days after service of the interrogatories. The Presiding Officer may allow a shorter or longer time for response. The party submitting the interrogatories may move for an order under § 1025.36 of these rules with respect to any objection to, or other failure to answer fully, an interrogatory.

(c) *Scope of interrogatories.* Interrogatories may relate to any matters which can be inquired into under § 1025.31(c), and the answers may be used to any extent permitted under these rules. An interrogatory otherwise proper is not objectionable merely because an answer to the interrogatory would involve an opinion or contention which relates to fact or to the application of law to fact, but the Presiding Officer may order that such an interrogatory need not be answered until a later time.

(d) *Option to produce business records.* Where the answer to an interrogatory may be derived or ascertained from the business records of the party upon whom the interrogatory has been served, or from an examination, audit, or inspection of such business records, or from a compilation, abstract, or summary of those records, and the burden of deriving the answer is substantially the same for the party serving the interrogatory as for the party served, it is a sufficient answer to the interrogatory to specify the records from which the answer may be derived or ascertained and to afford to the party serving the interrogatory reasonable opportunity to examine, audit, or inspect such records and to make copies, compilations, abstracts, or summaries.

§ 1025.33 Production of documents and things.

(a) *Scope.* Any party may serve upon any other party a request:

(1) To produce and permit the party making the request, or someone acting on behalf of that party, to inspect and copy any designated documents (including writings, drawings, graphs, charts, photographs, phono-records, and any other data compilation from which information can be obtained, translated, if necessary, by the party in possession through detection devices into reasonably usable form), or to inspect and copy, test, or sample any tangible things which constitute or contain matters within the scope of § 1025.31(c) and which are in the possession, custody, or control of the party upon whom the request is served, or

(2) To permit entry upon designated land or other property in the possession or control of the party upon whom the request is served for the purpose of inspection (including photographing), or sampling any designated object or operation within the scope of § 1025.31(c).

(b) *Procedure for request.* The request may be served at any time after the filing of an answer without leave of the Presiding Officer. The request shall set forth the items to be inspected, either by individual item or by category, and shall describe each item or category with reasonable particularity. The request shall specify a reasonable time, place, and manner for making the inspection and performing the related acts.

(c) *Procedure for response.* The party upon whom the request is served shall respond in writing within thirty (30) days after service of the request. The Presiding Officer may allow a shorter or longer time for response. The response shall state, with respect to each item or category requested, that inspection and related activities will be permitted as requested, unless the request is objected to, in which event the reasons for objection shall be stated. If objection is made to only part of an item or category, that part shall be specified. The party submitting the request may move for an order under § 1025.36 with respect to any objection to or other failure to respond to the request or any part thereof, or to any failure to permit inspection as requested.

(d) *Persons not parties.* This section does not preclude an independent action against a person not a party for production of documents and things.

§ 1025.34 Requests for admission.

(a) *Procedure for request.* A party may serve upon any other party a written request for the admission, for the purposes of the pending proceedings only, of the truth of any matters within the scope of § 1025.31(c) set forth in the request that relate to statements of fact or of the application of law to fact, including the genuineness of any documents described in the request. Copies of documents shall be served with the request unless they have been or are otherwise furnished or made available for inspection and copying. The request may, without leave of the Presiding Officer, be served upon any party after filing of the answer. Each matter about which an admission is requested shall be separately set forth.

(b) *Procedure for response.* The matter about which an admission is requested will be deemed admitted unless within thirty (30) days after service of the request, or within such shorter or longer time as the Presiding Officer may allow, the party to whom the request is directed serves upon the party requesting the admission a written answer or objection addressed to the matter, signed by the party or the party's representative and stating the reasons for the objections. The answer shall specifically admit or deny the matter or set forth in detail the reasons why the answering party cannot truthfully admit or deny the matter. A denial shall fairly meet the substance of the requested admission. When good faith requires that a party qualify an answer or deny only a part of the matter to which an admission is requested, the party shall specify the portion that is true and qualify or deny the remainder. An answering party may not give lack of information or knowledge as a reason for failure to admit or deny a fact unless the party states that he/she has made reasonable inquiry and that the information known or readily available to him/her is insufficient to enable him/her to admit or deny a fact. A party who considers that a matter to which an admission has been requested presents a genuine issue for hearing may not, on that ground alone, object to the request but may deny the matter or set forth reasons why the party cannot admit or deny it. The party who has requested an admission may move to determine the sufficiency of any answer or objection in accordance with §1025.36 of these Rules. If the Presiding Officer determines that an answer does not comply with the requirements of this section, he/she may order that the matter be deemed admitted or that an amended answer be served.

(c) *Effect of admission.* Any matter admitted under this section is conclusively established unless the Presiding Officer on motion permits withdrawal or amendment of such admission. The Presiding Officer may permit withdrawal or amendment when the presentation of the merits of the action will be served thereby and the party who obtained the admission fails to satisfy the Presiding Officer that withdrawal or amendment will prejudice that party in maintaining an action or defense on the merits. Any admission made by a party under this section is for the purposes of the pending adjudication only and is not an admission by that party for any other purposes, nor may it be used against that party in any other proceedings.

§ 1025.35 Depositions upon oral examination.

(a) *When depositions may be taken.* At any time after the first prehearing conference, upon leave of the Presiding Officer and under such terms and conditions as the Presiding Officer may prescribe, any party may take the deposition of any other party, including the agents, employees, consultants, or prospective witnesses of that party at a place convenient to the deponent. The attendance of witnesses and the production of documents and things at the deposition may be compelled by subpoena as provided in §1025.38 of these rules.

(b) *Notice of deposition*—(1) *Deposition of a party.* A party desiring to take a deposition of another party to the proceedings shall, after obtaining leave from the Presiding Officer, serve written notice of the deposition on all other parties and the Presiding Officer at least ten (10) days before the date noticed for the deposition. The notice shall state:

(i) The time and place for the taking of the deposition;

(ii) The name and address of each person to be deposed, if known, or if the name is not known, a general description sufficient to identify him/her; and

(iii) The subject matter of the expected testimony. If a subpoena *duces tecum* is to be served on the person to be deposed, the designation of the materials to be produced, as set forth in the subpoena, shall be attached to or included in the notice of deposition.

(2) *Deposition of a non-party.* A party desiring to take a deposition of a person who is not a party to the proceedings shall make application for the issuance of a subpoena, in accordance with § 1025.38 of these rules, to compel the attendance, testimony, and/or production of documents by such non-party. The paty desiring such deposition shall serve written notice of the deposition on all other parties to the proceedings, after issuance of the subpoena. The date specified in the subpoena for the deposition shall be at least twenty (20) days after the date on which the application for the subpoena is made to the Presiding Officer.

(3) *Opposition to notice.* A person served with a notice of deposition may oppose, in writing, the taking of the deposition within five (5) days of service of the notice. The Presiding Officer shall rule on the notice and any opposition and may order the taking of all noticed depositions upon a showing of good cause. The Presiding Officer may, for good cause shown, enlarge or shorten the time for the taking of a deposition.

(c) *Persons before whom depositions may be taken.* Depositions may be taken before any person who is authorized to administer oaths by the laws of the United States or of the place where the examination is held. No deposition shall be taken before a person who is a relative, employee, attorney, or representative of any party, or who is a relative or employee of such attorney or representative, or who is financially interested in the action.

(d) *Taking of deposition*—(1) *Examination.* Each deponent shall testify under oath, and all testimony shall be recorded. All parties or their representatives may be present and participate in the examination. Evidence objected to shall be taken subject to any objection. Objections shall include the grounds relied upon. The questions and answers, together with all objections made, shall be recorded by the official reporter before whom the deposition is taken. The original or a verified copy of all documents and things produced for inspection during the examination of the deponent shall, upon a request of any party present, be marked for identification and made a part of the record of the deposition.

(2) *Motion to terminate or limit examination.* At any time during the deposition, upon motion of any party or of the deponent, and upon a showing that the examination is being conducted in bad faith or in such manner as unreasonably to annoy, embarrass or oppress the deponent or party, the Presiding Officer may order the party conducting the examination to stop the deposition or may limit the scope and manner of taking the deposition as provided in § 1025.31(d) of these rules.

(3) *Participation by parties not present.* In lieu of attending a deposition, any party may serve written questions in a sealed envelope on the party conducting the deposition. That party shall transmit the envelope to the official reporter, who shall unseal it and read the questions to the deponent.

(e) *Transcription and filing of depositions*—(1) *Transcription.* Upon request by any party, the testimony recorded at a deposition shall be transcribed. When the testimony is fully transcribed, the deposition shall be submitted to the deponent for examination and signature and shall be read to or by the deponent, unless such examination and signature are waived by the deponent. Any change in form or substance which the deponent desires to make shall be entered upon the deposition by the official reporter with a statement of the reasons given by the deponent for making them. The deposition shall then be signed by the deponent, unless the deponent waives signature or is ill or cannot be found or refuses to sign. If the deposition is not signed by the deponent within thirty (30) days of its submission to him/her, the official reporter shall sign the deposition and state on the record the fact of the waiver of signature or of the illness or absence of the deponent or of the refusal to sign, together with a statement of the reasons therefor. The deposition may then be used as fully as though signed, in accordance with paragraph (i) of this section.

(2) *Certification and filing.* The official reporter shall certify on the deposition that it was taken under oath and that the deposition is a true record of the

testimony given and corrections made by the deponent. The official reporter shall then seal the deposition in an envelope endorsed with the title and docket number of the action and marked "Deposition of [name of deponent]" and shall promptly file the deposition with the Secretary. The Secretary shall notify all parties of the filing of the deposition and shall furnish a copy of the deposition to any party or to the deponent upon payment of reasonable charges.

(f) *Costs of deposition.* The party who notices the deposition shall pay for the deposition. The party who requests transcription of the deposition shall pay for the transcription.

(g) *Failure to attend or to serve subpoena; expenses.* If a party who notices a deposition fails to attend or conduct the deposition, and another party attends in person or by a representative pursuant to the notice, the Presiding Officer may order the party who gave the notice to pay to the attending party the reasonable expenses incurred. If a party who notices a deposition fails to serve a subpoena upon the deponent and as a result the deponent does not attend, and if another party attends in person or by a representative because that party expects the deposition to be taken, the Presiding Officer may order the party who gave notice to pay to the attending party the reasonable expenses incurred.

(h) *Deposition to preserve testimony*—(1) *When available.* By leave of the Presiding Officer, a party may take the deposition of his/her own witness for the purpose of perpetuating the testimony of that witness. A party who wishes to conduct such a deposition shall obtain prior leave of the Presiding Officer by filing a motion. The motion shall include a showing of substantial reason to believe that the testimony could not be presented at the hearing. If the Presiding Officer is satisfied that the perpetuation of the testimony may prevent a failure of justice or is otherwise reasonably necessary, he/she shall order that the deposition be taken.

(2) *Procedure.* Notice of a deposition to preserve testimony shall be served at least fifteen (15) days prior to the deposition unless the Presiding Officer authorizes less notice when warranted by extraordinary circumstances. The deposition shall be taken in accordance with the provisions of paragraph (d) of this section. Any deposition taken to preserve testimony shall be transcribed and filed in accordance with paragraph (e) of this section.

(i) *Use of depositions.* At the hearing or upon a petition for interlocutory appeal, any part or all of a deposition may be used against any party who was present or represented at the deposition or who had reasonable notice of the deposition, in accordance with any of the following:

(1) Any deposition may be used by any party for the purpose of contradicting or impeaching the testimony of the deponent as a witness.

(2) The deposition of anyone who at the time of the taking of the deposition was an officer, director, managing agent, or person otherwise designated to testify on behalf of a public or private corporation, partnership or unincorporated association or governmental entity which is a party to the proceedings, may be used by any adverse party for any purpose.

(3) The deposition of a witness may be used by any party for any purpose if the Presiding Officer finds:

(i) That the witness is dead; or

(ii) That the witness is out of the United States, unless it appears that the absence of the witness was procured by the party offering the deposition; or

(iii) That the witness is unable to attend or testify because of age, illness, infirmity, or imprisonment; or

(iv) That the party offering the depostion has been unable to procure the attendance of the witness by subpoena; or

(v) That such exceptional circumstances exist as to make it desirable, in the interest of justice and with due regard for the importance of presenting the testimony of witnesses orally during the hearing, to allow the deposition to be used.

(4) If only part of a deposition is offered in evidence by a party, any other party may move to introduce any other part of the deposition.

§ 1025.36 Motions to compel discovery.

If a party fails to respond to discovery, in whole or in part, the party seeking discovery may move within twenty (20) days for an order compelling an answer, or compelling inspection or production of documents, or otherwise compelling discovery. For purposes of this section, an evasive or incomplete response is to be treated as a failure to respond. When taking depositions, the discovering party shall continue the examination to the extent possible with respect to other areas of inquiry before moving to compel discovery.

§ 1025.37 Sanctions for failure to comply with discovery orders.

If a party fails to obey an order to provide or permit discovery, the Presiding Officer may take such action as is just, including but not limited to the following:

(a) Infer that the admission, testimony, document or other evidence would have been adverse to the party;

(b) Order that for the purposes of the proceedings, the matters regarding which the order was made or any other designated facts shall be taken to be established in accordance with the claim of the party obtaining the order;

(c) Order that the party withholding discovery not introduce into evidence or otherwise rely, in support of any claim or defense, upon the documents or other evidence withheld;

(d) Order that the party withholding discovery not introduce into evidence, or otherwise use at the hearing, information obtained in discovery;

(e) Order that the party withholding discovery forfeit its right to object to introduction and use of secondary evidence to show what the withheld admission, testimony, documents, or other evidence would have shown;

(f) Order that a pleading, or part of a pleading, or a motion or other submission by the party, concerning which the order was issued, be stricken, or that decision on the pleadings be rendered against the party, or both; and

(g) Exclude the party or representative from the proceedings, in accordance with § 1025.42(b) of these rules.

Any such action may be taken by order at any point in the proceedings.

§ 1025.38 Subpoenas.

(a) *Availability.* A subpoena shall be addressed to any person not a party for the purpose of compelling attendance, testimony, and production of documents at a hearing or deposition, and may be addressed to any party for the same purposes.

(b) *Form.* A subpoena shall identify the action with which it is connected; shall specify the person to whom it is addressed and the date, time, and place for compliance with its provisions; and shall be issued by order of the Commission and signed by the Secretary or by the Presiding Officer. A subpoena *duces tecum* shall specify the books, papers, documents, or other materials or data-compilations to be produced.

(c) *How obtained*—(1) *Content of application.* An application for the issuance of a subpoena, stating reasons, shall be submitted in triplicate to the Presiding Officer. The Presiding Officer shall bring the application to the attention of the Commission by forwarding it or by communicating its contents by any other means, e.g., by telephone, to the Commission.

(2) *Procedure for application.* The original and two copies of the subpoena, marked "original," "duplicate" and "triplicate," shall accompany the application. The Commission shall rule upon an application for a subpoena *ex parte,* by issuing the subpoena or by issuing an order denying the application.

(d) *Issuance of a subpoena.* The Commission shall issue a subpoena by authorizing the Secretary or the Presiding Officer to sign and date each copy in the lower right-hand corner. The "duplicate" and "triplicate" copies of the subpoena shall be transmitted to the applicant for service in accordance with these Rules; the "original" shall be retained by, or be forwarded to, the Secretary for retention in the docket of the proceedings.

(e) *Service of a subpoena.* A subpoena may be served in person or by registered or certified mail, return receipt requested, as provided in § 1025.16(b) of these rules. Service shall be made by delivery of the signed "duplicate" copy to the person named therein.

(f) *Return of service.* A person serving a subpoena shall promptly execute a return of service, stating the date, time, and manner of service. If service is effected by mail, the signed return receipt shall accompany the return of service. In case of failure to make service, a statement of the reasons for the failure shall be made. The "triplicate" copy of the subpoena, bearing or accompanied by the return of service, shall be returned without delay to the Secretary after service has been completed.

(g) *Motion to quash or limit subpoena.* Within five (5) days of receipt of a subpoena, the person to whom it is directed may file a motion to quash or limit the subpoena, setting forth the reasons why the subpoena should be withdrawn or why it should be limited in scope. Any such motion shall be answered within five (5) days of service and shall be ruled on immediately. The order shall specify the date, if any, for compliance with the specifications of the subpoena.

(h) *Consequences of failure to comply.* In the event of failure by a person to comply with a subpoena, the Presiding Officer may take any of the actions enumerated in § 1025.37 of these rules, or may order any other appropriate relief to compensate for the withheld testimony, documents, or other materials. If in the opinion of the Presiding Officer such relief is insufficient, the Presiding Officer shall certify to the Commission a request for judicial enforcement of the subpoena.

§ 1025.39 Orders requiring witnesses to testify or provide other information and granting immunity.

(a) *Applicability to Flammable Fabrics Act only.* This section applies only to proceedings arising under the Flammable Fabrics Act.

(b) *Procedure.* A party who desires the issuance of an order requiring a witness or deponent to testify or provide other information upon being granted immunity from prosecution under title 18, United States Code, section 6002, may make a motion to that effect. The motion shall be made and ruled on in accordance with § 1025.23 of these rules and shall include a showing:

(1) That the testimony or other information sought from a witness or deponent, or prospective witness or deponent, may be necessary to the public interest; and

(2) That such individual has refused or is likely to refuse to testify or provide such information on the basis of that individual's privilege against self-incrimination.

(c) *Approval of the Attorney General.* If the Presiding Officer determines that the witness' testimony appears necessary and that the privilege against self-incrimination may be invoked, he/she may certify to the Commission a request that it obtain the approval of the Attorney General of the United States for the issuance of an order granting immunity.

(d) *Issuance of order granting immunity.* Upon application to and approval by the Attorney General of the United States, and after the witness has invoked the privilege against self-incrimination, the Presiding Officer shall issue the order granting immunity unless he/she determines that the privilege was improperly invoked.

(e) *Sanctions for failure to testify.* Failure of a witness to testify after a grant of immunity or after a denial of a motion for the issuance of an order granting immunity shall result in the imposition of appropriate sanctions as provided in § 1025.37 of these rules.

Subpart E—Hearings

§ 1025.41 General rules.

(a) *Public hearings.* All hearings conducted pursuant to these Rules shall be public unless otherwise ordered by the Commission or the Presiding Officer.

(b) *Prompt completion.* Hearings shall proceed with all reasonable speed and, insofar as practicable and with due regard to the convenience of the parties, shall continue without suspension until concluded, except in unusual circumstances or as otherwise provided in these Rules.

(c) *Rights of parties.* Every party shall have the right of timely notice and all other rights essential to a fair hearing, including, but not limited to, the rights to present evidence, to conduct such cross-examination as may be necessary for a full and complete disclosure of the facts, and to be heard by objection, motion, brief, and argument.

(d) *Rights of participants.* Every participant shall have the right to make a written or oral statement of position and to file proposed findings of fact, conclusions of law, and a post hearing brief, in accordance with §1025.17(b) of these Rules.

(e) *Rights of witnesses.* Any person compelled to testify in any proceedings in response to a subpoena may be accompanied, represented, and advised by legal counsel or other representative, and may purchase a transcript of his/her testimony.

§ 1025.42 Powers and duties of Presiding Officer.

(a) *General.* A Presiding Officer shall have the duty to conduct full, fair, and impartial hearings, to take appropriate action to avoid unnecessary delay in the disposition of proceedings, and to maintain order. He/she shall have all powers necessary to that end, including the following powers:

(1) To administer oaths and affirmations;

(2) To compel discovery and to impose appropriate sanctions for failure to make discovery;

(3) To rule upon offers of proof and receive relevant, competent, and probative evidence;

(4) To regulate the course of the proceedings and the conduct of the parties and their representatives;

(5) To hold conferences for simplification of the issues, settlement of the proceedings, or any other proper purposes;

(6) To consider and rule, orally or in writing, upon all procedural and other motions appropriate in adjudicative proceedings;

(7) To issue Summary Decisions, Initial Decisions, Recommended Decisions, rulings, and orders, as appropriate;

(8) To certify questions to the Commission for its determination; and

(9) To take any action authorized by these Rules or the provisions of title 5, United States Code, sections 551–559.

(b) *Exclusion of parties by Presiding Officer.* A Presiding Officer shall have the authority, for good cause stated on the record, to exclude from participation in any proceedings any party, participant, or representative who violates the requirements of §1025.66 of these rules. Any party, participant or representative so excluded may appeal to the Commission in accordance with the provisions of §1025.24 of these rules. If the representative of a party or participant is excluded, the hearing may be suspended for a reasonable time so that the party or participant may obtain another representative.

(c) *Substitution of Presiding Officer.* In the event of the substitution of a new Presiding Officer for the one originally designated, any motion predicated upon such substitution shall be made within five (5) days.

(d) *Interference.* In the performance of adjudicative functions, a Presiding Officer shall not be responsible to or subject to the supervision or direction of any Commissioner or of any officer, employee, or agent engaged in the performance of investigative or prosecuting functions for the Commission. All directions by the Commission to a Presiding Officer concerning any adjudicative proceedings shall appear on and be made a part of the record.

(e) *Disqualification of Presiding Officer.* (1) When a Presiding Officer considers himself/herself disqualified to preside in any adjudicative proceedings, he/she shall withdraw by notice on the record and shall notify the Chief Administrative Law Judge and the Secretary of such withdrawal.

(2) Whenever, for good and reasonable cause, any party considers the Presiding Officer to be disqualified to preside, or to continue to preside, in any adjudicative proceedings, that party may file with the Secretary a motion to disqualify and remove, supported by affidavit(s) setting forth the alleged grounds for disqualification. A copy of the motion and supporting affidavit(s) shall be served by the Secretary on the Presiding Officer whose removal is sought. The Presiding Officer shall have ten (10) days to respond in writing to such motion. However, the motion shall not stay the proceedings unless otherwise ordered by the Presiding Officer or the Commission. If the Presiding Officer does not disqualify himself/herself, the Commission shall determine the validity of the grounds alleged, either directly or on the report of another Presiding Officer appointed

to conduct a hearing for that purpose and, in the event of disqualification, shall take appropriate action by assigning another Presiding Officer or requesting loan of another Administrative Law Judge through the U.S. Office of Personnel Management.

§ 1025.43 Evidence.

(a) *Applicability of Federal Rules of Evidence.* Unless otherwise provided by statute or these rules, the Federal Rules of Evidence shall apply to all proceedings held pursuant to these Rules. However, the Federal Rules of Evidence may be relaxed by the Presiding Officer if the ends of justice will be better served by so doing.

(b) *Burden of proof.* (1) Complaint counsel shall have the burden of sustaining the allegations of any complaint.

(2) Any party who is the proponent of a legal or factual proposition shall have the burden of sustaining that proposition.

(c) *Admissibility.* All relevant and reliable evidence is admissible, but may be excluded by the Presiding Officer if its probative value is substantially outweighed by unfair prejudice or confusion of the issues, or by considerations of undue delay, waste of time, immateriality, or needless presentation of cumulative evidence.

(d) *Official notice*—(1) *Definition.* Official notice means use by the Presiding Officer or the Commission of facts not appearing on the record and legal conclusions drawn from those facts. An officially noticed fact or legal conclusion must be one not subject to reasonable dispute in that it is either:

(i) Generally known within the jurisdiction of the Commission or

(ii) Capable of accurate and ready determination by resort to sources whose accuracy cannot reasonably be questioned.

(2) *Method of taking official notice.* The Presiding Officer and/or the Commission may at any time take official notice upon motion of any party or upon its own initiative. The record shall reflect the facts and conclusions which have been officially noticed.

(e) [Reserved]

(f) *Offer of proof.* When an objection to proffered testimony or documentary evidence is sustained, the sponsoring party may make a specific offer, either in writing or orally, of what the party expects to prove by the testimony or the document. When an offer of proof is made, any other party may make a specific offer, either in writing or orally, of what the party expects to present to rebut or contradict the offer of proof. Written offers of proof or of rebuttal, adequately marked for identification, shall accompany the record and be available for consideration by any reviewing authority.

§ 1025.44 Expert witnesses.

(a) *Definition.* An expert witness is one who, by reason of education, training, experience, or profession, has peculiar knowledge concerning the subject matter to which his/her testimony relates and from which he/she may draw inferences based upon hypothetically stated facts or offer opinions from facts involving scientific or technical knowledge.

(b) *Method of presenting testimony of expert witness.* Except as may otherwise be ordered by the Presiding Officer, the direct testimony of an expert witness shall be in writing and shall be filed on the record and exchanged between the parties no later than ten (10) days preceding the commencement of the hearing. The written testimony of an expert witness shall be incorporated into the record and shall constitute the direct testimony of that witness. Upon a showing of good cause, the party sponsoring the expert witness may be permitted to amplify the written direct testimony during the hearing.

(c) *Cross-examination and redirect examination of expert witness.* Cross-examination, redirect examination, and recross-examination of an expert witness shall proceed in due course based upon the written testimony and any amplifying oral testimony.

(d) *Failure to file or exchange written testimony.* Failure to file or exchange written testimony of expert witnesses as provided in this section shall deprive the sponsoring party of the use of the expert witness and of the conclusions which that witness would have presented, unless the opposing parties consent or the Presiding Officer otherwise orders in unusual circumstances.

§ 1025.45 *In camera* materials.

(a) *Definition. In camera* materials are documents, testimony, or other data which by order of the Presiding Officer or the Commission are kept confidential and excluded from the public record.

(b) *In camera treatment of documents and testimony.* The Presiding Officer or the Commission shall have authority, when good cause is found on the record, to order documents or testimony offered in evidence, whether admitted or rejected, to be received and preserve *in camera.* The order shall specify the length of time for *in camera* treatment and shall include:

(1) A description of the documents or testimony;

(2) The reasons for granting *in camera* treatment for the specified length of time; and

(3) The terms and conditions imposed by the Presiding Official, if any, limiting access to or use of the *in camera* material.

(c) *Access and disclosure to parties.* (1) Commissioners and their staffs, Presiding Officers and their staffs, and Commission staff members concerned with judicial review shall have complete access to *in camera* materials. Any party to the proceedings may seek access only in accordance with paragraph (c)(2) of this section.

(2) Any party desiring access to, or disclosure of, *in camera* materials for the preparation and presentation of that party's case shall make a motion which sets forth its justification. The Presiding Officer or the Commission may grant such motion for good cause shown and shall enter a protective order prohibiting unnecessary disclosure and requiring any other necessary safeguards. The Presiding Officer or the Commission may examine the *in camera* materials and excise any portions prior to disclosure of the materials to the moving party.

(d) *Segregation of in camera materials. In camera* materials shall be segregated from the public record and protected from public view.

(e) *Public release of in camera materials. In camera* materials constitute a part of the confidential records of the Commission and shall not be released to the public until the expiration of *in camera* treatment.

(f) *Reference to in camera materials.* In the submission of proposed findings, conclusions, briefs, or other documents, all parties shall refrain from disclosing specific details of *in camera* materials. However, such refraining shall not preclude general references to such materials. To the extent that parties consider necessary the inclusion of specific details of *in camera* materials, those references shall be incorporated into separate proposed findings, conclusions, briefs, or other documents marked "Confidential, Contains *In Camera* Material," which shall be placed *in camera* and become part of the *in camera* record. Those documents shall be served only on parties accorded access to the *in camera* materials by these rules, the Presiding Officer, or the Commission.

§ 1025.46 Proposed findings, conclusions, and order.

Within a reasonable time after the closing of the record and receipt of the transcript, all parties and participants may file, simultaneously unless otherwise directed by the Presiding Officer, post-hearing briefs, including proposed findings of fact and conclusions of law, as well as a proposed order. The Presiding Officer shall establish a date certain for the filing of the briefs, which shall not exceed fifty (50) days after the closing of the record except in unusual circumstances. The briefs shall be in writing and shall be served upon all parties. The briefs of all parties shall contain adequate references to the record and authorities relied upon. Replies shall be filed within fifteen (15) days of the date for the filing of briefs unless otherwise established by the Presiding Officer. The parties and participants may waive either or both submissions.

§ 1025.47 Record.

(a) *Reporting and transcription.* Hearings shall be recorded and transcribed by the official reporter of the Commission under the supervision of the Presiding Officer. The original transcript shall be a part of the record of proceedings. Copies of transcripts are available from the reporter at a cost not to exceed the maximum rates fixed by contract between the Commission and the reporter. In accordance with Section 11 of the Federal Advisory Committee Act (Pub. L. 92–463, 5 U.S.C. appendix I), copies of transcripts may be made by members of the public or by Commission personnel, when available, at the Office of the Secretary at reproduction costs as provided in §1025.49.

(b) *Corrections.* Corrections of the official transcript may be made only when they involve errors affecting substance and then only in the manner described in this section. The Presiding Officer may order corrections, either on his/her own motion or on motion of any party. The Presiding Officer shall determine the corrections to be made and shall so order. Corrections shall be interlineated or otherwise inserted in the official transcript so as not to obliterate the original text.

§ 1025.48 Official docket.

The official docket in any adjudicatory proceedings shall be maintained in the Office of the Secretary and be available for public inspection during normal business hours of the Commission.

§ 1025.49 Fees.

(a) *Fees for deponents and witnesses.* Any person compelled to appear in person in response to a subpoena or notice of deposition shall be paid the same attendance and mileage fees as are paid witnesses in the courts of the United States, in accordance with title 28, United States Code, section 1821. The fees and mileage referred to in this paragraph shall be paid by the party at whose instance deponents or witnesses appear.

(b) *Fees for production of records.* Fees charged for production or disclosure of records contained in the official docket shall be in accordance with the Commission's "Procedures for Disclosures or Production of Information Under the Freedom of Information Act," title 16, Code of Federal Regulations, §1015.9.

Subpart F—Decision

§ 1025.51 Initial decision.

(a) *When filed.* The Presiding Officer shall endeavor to file an Initial Decision with the Commission within sixty (60) days after the closing of the record or the filing of post-hearing briefs, whichever is later.

(b) *Content.* The Initial Decision shall be based upon a consideration of the entire record and shall be supported by reliable, probative, and substantial evidence. The Initial Decision shall include:

(1) Findings and conclusions, as well as the reasons or bases for such findings and conclusions, upon the material questions of fact, material issues of law, or discretion presented on the record, and should, where practicable, be accompanied by specific page citations to the record and to legal and other materials relied upon; and

(2) An appropriate order.

(c) *By whom made.* The Initial Decision shall be made and filed by the Presiding Officer who presided over the hearing, unless otherwise ordered by the Commission.

(d) *Reopening of proceedings by Presiding Officer; termination of jurisdiction.* (1) At any time prior to, or concomitant with, the filing of the Initial Decision, the Presiding Officer may reopen the proceedings for the reception of further evidence.

(2) Except for the correction of clerical errors, or where the proceeding is reopened by an order under paragraph (d)(1) of this section, the jurisdiction of the Presiding Officer is terminated upon the filing of the Initial Decision, unless and until such time as the matter may be remanded to the Presiding Officer by the Commission.

§ 1025.52 Adoption of initial decision.

The Initial Decision and Order shall become the Final Decision and Order of the Commission forty (40) days after issuance unless an appeal is noted and perfected or unless review is ordered by the Commission. Upon the expiration of the fortieth day, the Secretary shall prepare, sign, and enter an order adopting the Initial Decision and Order, unless otherwise directed by the Commission.

§ 1025.53 Appeal from initial decision.

(a) *Who may file notice of intention.* Any party may appeal an Initial Decision to the Commission, provided that within ten (10) days after issuance of the Initial Decision such party files and serves a notice of intention to appeal.

(b) *Appeal brief.* An appeal is perfected by filing a brief within forty (40) days after service of the Initial Decision. The appeal brief must be served upon all parties. The appeal brief shall contain, in the order indicated, the following:

(1) A subject index of the matters in the brief, with page references, and a table of cases (alphabetically arranged), textbooks, statutes, and other material cited, with page references thereto;

(2) A concise statement of the case;

(3) A statement containing the reasons why the party believes the Initial Decision is incorrect;

(4) The argument, presenting clearly the points of fact and law relied upon to support each reason why the Initial Decision is incorrect, with specific page references to the record and the legal or other material relied upon; and

(5) A proposed form of order for the Commission's consideration in lieu of the order contained in the Initial Decision.

(c) *Answering brief.* Within thirty (30) days after service of the appeal brief upon all parties, any party may file an answering brief which shall contain a subject index, with page references, and a table of cases (alphabetically arranged), textbooks, statutes, and other material cited, with page references thereto. Such brief shall present clearly the points of fact and law relied upon in support of the reasons the party has for each position urged, with specific page references to the record and legal or other materials relied upon.

(d) *Participant's brief.* Within thirty (30) days after service of the appeal brief upon all parties, any participant may file a brief on appeal, presenting clearly the position urged.

(e) *Cross appeal.* If a timely notice of appeal is filed by a party, any other party may file a notice of cross appeal within ten (10) days of the date on which the first notice of appeal was filed. Cross appeals shall be included in the answering brief and shall conform to the requirements for form, content, and filing specified in paragraph (b) of this section for an appeal brief. If an appeal is noticed but not perfected, no cross appeal shall be permitted and the notice of cross appeal shall be deemed void.

(f) *Reply brief.* A reply brief shall be limited to rebuttal of matters presented in answering briefs, including matters raised in cross-appeals. A reply brief shall be filed and served within fourteen (14) days after service of an answering brief, or on the day preceding the oral argument, whichever comes first.

(g) *Oral argument.* The purpose of an oral argument is to emphasize and clarify the issues. The Commission may order oral argument upon request of any party or upon its own initiative. A transcript of oral arguments shall be prepared. A Commissioner absent from an oral argument may participate in the consideration of and decision on the appeal.

§ 1025.54 Review of initial decision in absence of appeal.

The Commission may, by order, review a case not otherwise appealed by a party. Should the Commission so order, the parties shall, and participants may, file briefs in accordance with § 1025.53, except that the Commission may, in its discretion, establish a different briefing schedule in its order. The Commission shall issue its order within forty (40) days after issuance of the Initial Decision. The order shall set forth the issues which the Commission will review and may make provision for the filing of briefs. If the filing of briefs is scheduled by the Commission, the order shall designate which party or parties shall file the initial brief and which party or parties may thereafter file an answering brief, or the order may designate the simultaneous filing of briefs by the parties.

§ 1025.55 Final decision on appeal or review.

(a) *Consideration of record.* Upon appeal from or review of an Initial Decision, the Commission shall consider the record as a whole or such parts of the record as are cited or as may be necessary to resolve the issues presented and, in addition, shall, to the extent necessary or desirable, exercise all the powers which it could have exercised if it had made the Initial Decision.

(b) *Rendering of final decision.* In rendering its decision, the Commission shall adopt, modify, or set aside the findings, conclusions, and order contained in the Initial Decision, and shall include in its Final Decision a statement of the reasons for its action and any concurring or dissenting opinions. The Commission shall issue an order reflecting its Final Decision.

(c) Except as otherwise ordered by the Commission, the Commission shall endeavor to file its Decision within ninety (90) days after the filing of all briefs or after receipt of transcript of the oral argument, whichever is later.

§ 1025.56 Reconsideration.

Within twenty (20) days after issuance of a Final Decision and Order by the Commission, any party may file a petition for reconsideration of such decision or order, setting forth the relief desired and the grounds in support of the petition. Any petition filed under this section must be confined to new questions raised by the decision or order upon which the petitioner had no previous opportunity to argue. Any party desiring to oppose such a petition shall file an opposition to the petition within ten (10) days after sevice of the petition. The filing of a petition for reconsideration shall not stay the effective date of the Final Decision and Order or toll the running of any statutory time period affecting the Decision or Order unless specifically ordered by the Commission.

§ 1025.57 Effective date of order.

(a) *Orders in proceedings arising under the Consumer Product Safety Act.* An order of the Commission in proceedings arising under the Consumer Product Safety Act becomes effective upon receipt, unless otherwise ordered by the Commission.

(b) *Orders in proceedings arising under the Flammable Fabrics Act*—(1) *Consent orders.* An order in proceedings arising under the Flammable Fabrics Act, which has been issued following the Commission's acceptance of an offer of settlement in accordance with § 1025.26 of these rules, becomes effective upon receipt of notice of Commission acceptance, unless otherwise ordered by the Commission.

(2) *Litigated orders.* All other orders in proceedings arising under the Flammable Fabrics Act become effective upon the expiration of the statutory period for court review specified in Section 5(c) of the Federal Trade Commission Act, title 15, United States Code, section 45(c), or, if a petition for review has been filed, upon a court's affirmance of the Commission's order.

(c) *Consequences of failure to comply with effective order.* A respondent against whom an order has been issued who is not in compliance with such order on or after the date the order becomes effective is in violation of such order and is subject to an immediate action for the civil or criminal penalties provided for in the applicable statute.

§ 1025.58 Reopening of proceedings.

(a) *General.* Any proceedings may be reopened by the Commission at any time, either on its own initiative or upon petition of any party to the proceedings.

(b) *Exception.* Proceedings arising under the Flammable Fabrics Act shall not be reopened while pending in a United States court of appeals on a petition for review after the transcript of the record has been filed, or while pending in the Supreme Court of the United States.

(c) *Commission-originated reopening*—(1) *Before effective date of order.* At any time before the effective date of a Commission order, the Commission may, upon its own initiative and without prior notice to the parties, reopen any proceedings and enter a new decision or order to modify or set aside, in whole or in part, the decision or order previously issued.

(2) *After effective date of order.* Whenever the Commission is of the opinion that changed conditions of fact or law or the public interest may require that a Commission decision or order be altered, modified, or set aside in whole or

in part, the Commission shall serve upon all parties to the original proceedings an order to show cause, stating the changes the Commission proposes to make in the decision or order and the reasons such changes are deemed necessary. Within thirty (30) days after service of an order to show cause, any party to the original proceedings, may file a response. Any party not responding to the order to show cause within the time allowed shall be considered to have consented to the proposed changes.

(d) *Petition for reopening.* Whenever any person subject to a final order is of the opinion that changed conditions of fact or law require that the decision or order be altered, modified, or set aside, or that the public interest so requires, that person may petition the Commission to reopen the proceedings. The petition shall state the changes desired and the reasons those changes should be made, and shall include such supporting evidence and argument as will, in the absence of any opposition, provide the basis for a Commission decision on the petition. The petition shall be served upon all parties to the original proceedings. Within thirty (30) days after service of the petition, Complaint Counsel shall file a response. Any other party to the original proceedings also may file a response within that period.

(e) *Hearings*—(1) *Unopposed.* Where an order to show cause or petition to reopen is not opposed, or is opposed but the pleadings do not raise issues of fact to be resolved, the Commission, in its discretion, may decide the matter on the order to show cause or petition and responses, or it may serve upon the parties a notice of hearing containing the date when the matter will be heard. The proceedings normally will be limited to the filing of briefs but may include oral argument when deemed necessary by the Commission.

(2) *Factual issues.* When the pleadings raise substantial factual issues, the Commission may direct such hearings as it deems appropriate. Upon conclusion of the hearings, and after opportunity for the parties to file post-hearing briefs containing proposed findings of fact and conclusions of law, as well as a proposed order, the Presiding Officer shall issue a Recommended Decision, including proposed findings and conclusions, and the reasons, as well as a proposed Commission order. If the Presiding Officer recommends that the Commission's original order be reopened, the proposed order shall include appropriate provisions for the alteration, modification or setting aside of the original order. The record and the Presiding Officer's Recommended Decision shall be certified to the Commission for final disposition of the matter.

(f) *Commission disposition.* Where the Commission has ordered a hearing, upon receipt of the Presiding Officer's Recommended Decision, the Commission shall make a decision and issue an order based on the hearing record as a whole. If the Commission determines that changed conditions of fact or law or the public interest requires, it shall reopen the order previously issued; alter, modify, or set aside the order's provisions in whole or in part; and issue an amended order reflecting the alterations, modifications, or deletions. If the Commission determines that the original order should not be reopened, it shall issue an order affirming the original order. A decision stating the reasons for the Commission's order shall accompany the order.

Subpart G—Appearances, Standards of Conduct

§ 1025.61 Who may make appearances.

A party or participant may appear in person, or by a duly authorized officer, partner, regular employee, or other agent of the party or participant, or by counsel or other duly qualified representative, in accordance with § 1025.65.

§ 1025.62 Authority for representation.

Any individual acting in a representative capacity in any adjudicative proceedings may be required by the Presiding Officer or the Commission to show his/her authority to act in such capacity. A regular employee of a party who appears on behalf of the party may be required by the Presiding Officer or the Commission to show his/her authority to so appear.

§ 1025.63 Written appearances.

(a) *Filing*. Any person who appears in any proceedings shall file a written notice of appearance with the Secretary or deliver a written notice of appearance to the Presiding Officer at the hearing, stating for whom the appearance is made and the name, address, and telephone number (including area code) of the person making the appearance and the date of the commencement of the appearance. The written appearance shall be made a part of the record.

(b) *Withdrawal*. Any person who has previously appeared in any proceedings may withdraw his/her appearance by filing a written notice of withdrawal of appearance with the Secretary. The notice of withdrawal of appearance shall state the name, address, and telephone number (including area code) of the person withdrawing the appearance, for whom the appearance was made, and the effective date of the withdrawal of the appearance. Such notice of withdrawal shall be filed within five (5) days of the effective date of the withdrawal of the appearance.

§ 1025.64 Attorneys.

Any attorney at law who is admitted to practice before any United States court or before the highest court of any State, the District of Columbia, or any territory or commonwealth of the United States, may practice before the Commission. An attorney's own representation that he/she is in good standing before any of such courts shall be sufficient proof thereof, unless otherwise directed by the Presiding Officer or the Commission.

§ 1025.65 Persons not attorneys.

(a) *Filing and approval of proof of qualifications*. Any person who is not an attorney at law may be admitted to appear in any adjudicative proceedings as a representative of any party or participant if that person files proof to the satisfaction of the Presiding Officer that he/she possesses the necessary knowledge of administrative procedures, technical, or other qualifications to render valuable service in the proceedings and is otherwise competent to advise and assist in the presentation of matters in the proceedings. An application by a person not an attorney at law for admission to appear in any proceedings shall be submitted in writing to the Secretary, not later than thirty (30) days prior to the hearing. The application shall set forth in detail the applicant's qualifications to appear in the proceedings.

(b) *Exception*. Any person who is not an attorney at law and whose application has not been approved shall not be permitted to appear in Commission proceedings. However, this provision shall not apply to any person who appears before the Commission on his/her own behalf or on behalf of any corporation, partnership, or unincorporated association of which the person is a partner or general officer.

§ 1025.66 Qualifications and standards of conduct.

(a) *Good faith transactions*. The Commission expects all persons appearing in proceedings before the Commission or the Presiding Officer to act with integrity, with respect, and in an ethical manner. Business transacted before and with the Commission or the Presiding Officer shall be conducted in good faith.

(b) *Exclusion of parties, participants, or their representatives*. To maintain orderly proceedings, the Commission or the Presiding Officer may exclude parties, participants, or their representatives for refusal to comply with directions, continued use of dilatory tactics, refusal to adhere to reasonable standards of orderly and ethical conduct, failure to act in good faith, or violation of the prohibition in § 1025.68 against certain *ex parte* communications.

(c) *Exclusions from the record*. The Presiding Officer or the Commission may disregard and order the exclusion from the record of any written or oral submissions or representations which are not made in good faith or which are unfair, incomplete, or inaccurate.

(d) *Appeal by excluded party*. An excluded party, participant, or representative may petition the Commission to entertain an interlocutory appeal in accordance with § 1025.24 of these rules. If, after such appeal, the representative of a party or participant is excluded, the hearing shall, at the request of the party or participant, be suspended for a reasonable time so that the party or participant may obtain another representative.

§ 1025.67 Restrictions as to former members and employees.

(a) *Generally.* Except as otherwise provided in paragraph (b) of this section, the post-employee restrictions applicable to former Commission members and employees, as set forth in the Commission's "Post Employment Restrictions Applicable to Former Commission Officers and Employees", 16 CFR part 1030, subpart L, shall govern the activities of former Commission members and employees in matters connected with their former duties and responsibilities.

(b) *Participation as witness.* A former member or employee of the Commission may testify in any proceeding subject to these Rules concerning his/her participation in any Commission activity. This section does not constitute a waiver by the Commission of any objection provided by law to testimony that would disclose privileged or confidential material. The provisions of 18 U.S.C. 1905 prohibiting the disclosure of trade secrets also applies to testimony by former members and employees.

(c) *Procedure for requesting authorization to appear.* In cases to which paragraph (a) of this section is applicable, a former member or employee of the Commission may request authorization to appear or participate in any proceedings or investigation by filing with the Secretary a written application disclosing the following information:

(1) The nature and extent of the former member's or employee's participation in, knowledge of, and connection with the proceedings or investigation during his/her service with the Commission;

(2) Whether the files of the proceedings or investigation came to his/her attention;

(3) Whether he/she was employed in the directorate, division, or other organizational unit within the Commission in which the proceedings or investigation is or has been pending;

(4) Whether he/she worked directly or in close association with Commission personnel assigned to the proceedings or investigation and, if so, with whom and in what capacity; and

(5) Whether during service with the Commission, he/she was engaged in any matter concerning the person involved in the proceedings or investigation.

(d) *Denial of request to appear.* The requested authorization shall not be given in any case:

(1) Where it appears that the former member or employee, during service with the Commission, participated personally and substantially in the proceedings or investigation; or

(2) Where the Commission is not satisfied that the appearance or participation will not involve any actual or apparent impropriety; or

(3) In any case which would result in a violation of title 18, United States Code, section 207.

§ 1025.68 Prohibited communications.

(a) *Applicability.* This section is applicable during the period commencing with the date of issuance of a complaint and ending upon final Commission action in the matter.

(b) *Definitions*—(1) *Decision-maker.* Those Commission personnel who render decisions in adjudicative proceedings under these rules, or who advise officials who render such decisions, including:

(i) The Commissioners and their staffs;

(ii) The Administrative Law Judges and their staffs;

(iii) The General Counsel and his/her staff, unless otherwise designated by the General Counsel.

(2) *Ex parte communication.* (i) Any written communication concerning a matter in adjudication which is made to a decision-maker by any person subject to these Rules, which is not served on all parties; or

(ii) Any oral communication concerning a matter in adjudication which is made to a decision-maker by any person subject to these Rules, without advance notice to all parties to the proceedings and opportunity for them to be present.

(c) *Prohibited ex parte communications.* Any oral or written *ex parte* communication relative to the merits of any proceedings under these Rules is a prohibited *ex parte* communication, except as otherwise provided in paragraph (d) of this section.

(d) *Permissible ex parte communications.* The following communications shall not be prohibited under this section.

(1) *Ex parte* communications authorized by statute or by these rules. (See, for example, § 1025.38 which governs applications for the issuance of subpoenas.)

(2) Any staff communication concerning judicial review or judicial enforcement in any matter pending before or decided by the Commission.

(e) *Procedures for handling prohibited ex parte communication*—(1) *Prohibited written ex parte communication.* To the extent possible, a prohibited written *ex parte* communication received by any Commission employee shall be forwarded to the Secretary rather than to a decision-maker. A prohibited written *ex parte* communication which reaches a decision-maker shall be forwarded by the decision-maker to the Secretary. If the circumstances in which a prohibited *ex parte* written communication was made are not apparent from the communication itself, a statement describing those circumstances shall be forwarded with the communication.

(2) *Prohibited oral ex parte communication.* (i) If a prohibited oral *ex parte* communication is made to a decision-maker, he/she shall advise the person making the communication that the communication is prohibited and shall terminate the discussion; and

(ii) In the event of a prohibited oral *ex parte* communication, the decision-maker shall forward to the Secretary a signed and dated statement containing such of the following information as is known to him/her.

(A) The title and docket number of the proceedings;

(B) The name and address of the person making the communication and his/her relationship (if any) to the parties and/or participants to the proceedings;

(C) The date and time of the communication, its duration, and the circumstances (e.g., telephone call, personal interview, etc.) under which it was made;

(D) A brief statement of the substance of the matters discussed; and

(E) Whether the person making the communication persisted in doing so after being advised that the communication was prohibited.

(3) *Filing.* All communications and statements forwarded to the Secretary under this section shall be placed in a public file which shall be associated with, but not made a part of, the record of the proceedings to which the communication or statement pertains.

(4) *Service on parties.* The Secretary shall serve a copy of each communication and statement forwarded under this section on all parties to the proceedings. However, if the parties are numerous, or if other circumstances satisfy the Secretary that service of the communication or statement would be unduly burdensome, he/she, in lieu of service, may notify all parties in writing that the communication or statement has been made and filed and that it is available for insection and copying.

(5) *Service on maker.* The Secretary shall forward to the person who made the prohibited *ex parte* communication a copy of each communication or statement filed under this section.

(f) *Effect of ex parte communications.* No prohibited *ex parte* communication shall be considered as part of the record for decision unless introduced into evidence by a party to the proceedings.

(g) *Sanctions.* A person subject to these Rules who make, a prohibited *ex parte* communication, or who encourages or solicits another to make any such communication, may be subject to any appropriate sanction or sanctions, including but not limited to, exclusion from the proceedings and an adverse ruling on the issue which is the subject of the prohibited communication.

Subpart H—Implementation of the Equal Access to Justice Act in Adjudicative Proceedings With the Commission

AUTHORITY: Equal Access to Justice Act, Pub. L. 96–481, 94 Stat. 2325, 5 U.S.C. 504 and the Administrative Procedure Act, 5 U.S.C. 551 *et seq.*

SOURCE: 47 FR 25513, June 14, 1982, unless otherwise noted.

§ 1025.70 General provisions.

(a) *Purpose of this rule.* The Equal Access to Justice Act, 5 U.S.C. 504 (called "the EAJA" in this subpart), provides for the award of attorney fees and other expenses to eligible persons who are parties to certain adversary adjudicative proceedings before the Commission. An eligible party may receive an award when it prevails over Commission complaint counsel, unless complaint counsel's position in the proceeding was substantially justified or special circumstances make an award unjust. This subpart describes the parties eligible for awards and the proceedings covered. The rules also explain how to apply for awards and the procedures and standards that the Commission will use to make them.

(b) *When the EAJA applies.* The EAJA applies to any adversary adjudicative proceeding pending before the Commission at any time between October 1, 1981 and September 30, 1984. This includes proceedings commenced before October 1, 1981, if final Commission action has not been taken before that date, and proceedings pending on September 30, 1984, regardless of when they were initiated or when final Commission action occurs.

(c) *Proceedings covered.* (1) The EAJA and this rule apply to adversary adjudicative proceedings conducted by the Commission. These are adjudications under 5 U.S.C. 554 in which the position of the Commission or any component of the Commission is represented by an attorney or other representative who enters an appearance and participates in the proceeding. The rules in this subpart govern adversary adjudicative proceedings relating to the provisions of sections 15 (c), (d) and (f) and 17(b) of the Consumer Product Safety Act (15 U.S.C. 2064 (c) (d) and (f); 2066(b)), sections 3 and 8(b) of the Flammable Fabrics Act (15 U.S.C. 1192, 1197(b)), and section 15 of the Federal Hazardous Substances Act (15 U.S.C. 1274), which are required by statute to be determined on the record after opportunity for a public hearing. These rules will also govern administrative adjudicative proceedings for the assessment of civil penalties under section 20(a) of the Consumer Product Safety Act (15 U.S.C. 2068(a)). *See* 16 CFR 1025.1.

(2) The Commission may designate a proceeding not listed in paragraph (c)(1) of this section as an adversary adjudicative proceeding for purposes of the EAJA by so stating in an order initiating the proceeding or designating the matter for hearing. The Commission's failure to designate a proceeding as an adversary adjudicative proceeding shall not preclude the filing of an application by a party who believes the proceeding is covered by the EAJA. Whether the proceeding is covered will then be an issue for resolution in proceedings on the application.

(3) If a proceeding includes both matters covered by the EAJA and matters specifically excluded from coverage, any award made will include only fees and expenses related to covered issues.

(d) *Eligibility of applicants.* (1) To be eligible for an award of attorney fees and other expenses under the EAJA, the applicant must be a party to the adversary adjudication for which it seeks an award. The term "party" is defined in 5 U.S.C. 551(3) and 16 CFR 1025.3(f). The applicant must show that it meets all conditions of eligibility set out in this paragraph and in § 1025.71.

(2) The types of eligible applicants are:

(i) Individuals with a net worth of not more than $1 million;

(ii) Sole owners of unincorporated businesses who have a net worth of not more than $5 million including both personal and business interests, and not more than 500 employees;

(iii) Charitable or other tax-exempt organizations described in section 501(c)(3) of the Internal Revenue Code (26 U.S.C. 501(c)(3)) which have not more than 500 employees;

(iv) Any other partnership, corporation, association, or public or private organization with a net worth of not more than $5 million and which have not more than 500 employees.

(3) For the purpose of eligibility, the net worth and number of employees of an applicant shall be determined as of the date the proceeding was initiated.

(4) An applicant who owns an unincorporated business will be considered as an "individual" rather than as a "sole owner of an unincorporated business" if the issues on which the applicant prevails are related primarily to

personal interests rather than to business interests.

(5) The number of employees of an applicant include all persons who regularly perform services for remuneration for the applicant, under the applicant's direction and control. Part-time employees shall be included on a proportional basis.

(6) The net worth and number of employees of the applicant and all of its affiliates shall be aggregated to determine eligibility. For this purpose, *affiliate* means (i) An individual, corporation or other entity that directly or indirectly controls or owns a majority of the voting shares or other interest of the applicant, or (ii) Any corporation or other entity of which the applicant directly or indirectly owns or controls a majority of the voting shares or other interest. However, the presiding officer may determine that such treatment would be unjust and contrary to the purposes of the EAJA in light of the actual relationship between the affiliated entities. In addition, the presiding officer may determine that financial relationships of the applicant other than those described in this paragraph constitute special circumstances that would make an award unjust.

(7) An applicant that participates in a proceeding primarily on behalf of one or more other persons or entities that would be ineligible is not itself eligible for an award.

(8) An applicant that represents himself/herself regardless of whether he is licensed to practice law may be awarded all such expenses and fees available to other prevailing eligible parties. *See* 16 CFR 1025.61 and 1025.65 of the Commission's rules.

(e) *Standards for awards.* (1) An eligible prevailing applicant may receive an award for fees and expenses incurred in connection with a proceeding, or in a significant and discrete substantive portion of the proceeding, unless the position of Commission complaint counsel over which the applicant has prevailed was substantially justified. Complaint counsel bear the burden of proof that an award should not be made to an eligible prevailing applicant. Complaint counsel may avoid the granting of an award by showing that its position was reasonable in law and fact.

(2) An award will be reduced or denied if the applicant has unduly or unreasonably protracted the proceeding or if special circumstances make the award sought unjust.

(f) *Allowable fees and expenses.* (1) Awards will be based on rates customarily charged by persons engaged in the business of acting as attorneys, agents and expert witnesses, even if the services were made available without charge or at a reduced rate to the applicant.

(2) No award for the fee of an attorney or agent under these rules may exceed $75 per hour. No award to compensate an expert witness may exceed the highest rate at which the Commission is authorized to pay expert witnesses. However, an award may also include the reasonable expenses of the attorney, agent, or witness as a separate item, if the attorney, agent or witness ordinarily charges clients separately for such expenses.

(3) In determining the reasonableness of the fee sought for an attorney, agent or expert witness, the presiding officer shall consider the following:

(i) If the attorney, agent or witness is in private practice, his or her customary fee for similar services, or, if an employee of the applicant, the fully allocated cost of the services;

(ii) The prevailing rate for similar services in the community in which the attorney, agent or witness ordinarily performs services;

(iii) The time actually spent in the representation of the applicant;

(iv) The time reasonably spent in light of the difficulty or complexity of the issues in the proceeding; and

(v) Such other factors as may bear on the value of the services provided.

(4) The reasonable cost of any study, analysis, engineering report, test, project or similar matter prepared on behalf of a party may be awarded, to the extent that the charge for the service does not exceed the prevailing rate for similar services, and the study or other matter was necessary for preparation of the applicant's case.

(5) Fees may be awarded to eligible applicants only for service performed after the issuance of a complaint and

the commencement of the adjudicative proceeding in accordance with 16 CFR 1025.11(a).

(g) *Rulemaking on maximum rates for attorney fees.* (1) If warranted by an increase in the cost of living or by special circumstances, the Commission may adopt regulations providing that attorney fees may be awarded at a rate higher than $75 per hour in some or all of the types of proceedings covered by this subpart. The Commission will conduct any rulemaking proceedings for this purpose under the informal rulemaking procedures of the Administrative Procedure Act, 5 U.S.C. 533.

(2) Any person may file with the Commission a petition for rulemaking to increase the maximum rate for attorney fees, in accordance with the Administrative Procedure Act, 5 U.S.C. 553(e). The petition should identify the rate the petitioner believes the Commission should establish and the types of proceedings in which the rate should be used. The petition should also explain fully the reasons why the higher rate is warranted. The Commission will respond to the petition within a reasonable time after it is filed, by initiating a rulemaking proceeding, denying the petition, or taking other appropriate action.

(h) *Presiding officer.* The presiding oficer in a proceeding covered by this regulation is a person as defined in the Commission's Rules, 16 CFR 1025.3(i), who conducts an adversary adjudicative proceeding.

§ 1025.71 Information required from applicant.

(a) *Contents of application.* (1) An application for an award of fees and expenses under the EAJA shall identify the applicant and the proceeding for which an award is sought. The application shall show that the applicant has prevailed and identify the position of complaint counsel in the adjudicative proceeding that the applicant alleges was not substantially justified. Unless the applicant is an individual, the application shall also state the number of employees of the applicant and describe briefly the type and purpose of its organization or business.

(2) The application shall also include a verified statement that the applicant's net worth does not exceed $1 million (if an individual) or $5 million (for all other applicants, including their affiliates). However, an applicant may omit this statement if it attaches a copy of a ruling by the Internal Revenue Service that it qualifies as an organization described in section 501(c)(3) of the Internal Revenue Code or, in the case of a tax-exempt organization not required to obtain a ruling from the Internal Revenue Service on its exempt status, a statement that describes the basis for the applicant's belief that it qualifies under such section.

(3) The application shall state the amount of fees and expenses for which an award is sought.

(4) The application may also include any other matters that the applicant wishes the Commission to consider in determining whether and in what amount an award should be made.

(5) The application shall be signed by the applicant or an authorized officer or attorney of the applicant. It shall also contain or be accompanied by a written verification under oath or under penalty of perjury that the information provided in the application is true and correct.

(b) *Net worth exhibit; confidential treatment.* (1) Each applicant except a qualified tax-exempt organization or cooperative association must provide with its application a detailed exhibit showing the net worth of the applicant and any affiliates (as defined in § 1025.70(d)(6) of this subpart) when the proceeding was initiated. The exhibit may be in any form convenient to the applicant that provides full disclosure of the applicant's and its affiliates' assets and liabilities and is sufficient to determine whether the applicant qualifies under the standards in this subpart. The presiding officer may require an applicant to file additional information to determine its eligibility for an award.

(2) Ordinarily, the net worth exhibit will be included in the public record of the proceeding. However, an applicant that objects to public disclosure of information in any portion of the exhibit or to public disclosure of any other information submitted, and believes there are legal grounds for withholding it from disclosure, may move to have that information kept confidential and

excluded from public disclosure in accordance with §1025.45 of the Commission rules for *in camera* materials, 16 CFR 1025.45. This motion shall describe the information sought to be withheld and explain, in detail, why it falls within one or more of the specific exemptions from mandatory disclosure under the Freedom of Information Act, 5 U.S.C. 552(b)(1)–(9).

(3) Section 6(a)(2) of the Consumer Product Safety Act, 15 U.S.C. 2055(a)(2), provides that certain information which contains or relates to a trade secret or other matter referred to in section 1905 of title 18, United States Code, or subject to 5 U.S.C. 552(b)(4) shall not be disclosed. This prohibition is an Exemption 3 statute under the Freedom of Information Act, 5 U.S.C. 552(b)(3). Material submitted as part of an application for which *in camera* treatment is granted shall be available to other parties only in accordance with 16 CFR 1025.45(c) of the Commission Rules and, if applicable, section 6(a)(2) of the CPSA. If the presiding officer determines that the information should not be withheld from disclosure because it does not fall within section 6(a)(2) of the CPSA, he shall place the information in the public record but only after notifying the submitter of the information in writing of the intention to disclose such document at a date not less than 10 days after the date of receipt of notification. Otherwise, any request to inspect or copy the exhibit shall be disposed of in accordance with the Commission's established procedures under the Freedom of Information Act (*see* 16 CFR part 1015).

(c) *Documentation of fees and expenses.* The application shall be accompanied by full documentation of the fees and expenses, including the cost of any study, analysis, engineering report, test, project or similar matter, for which an award is sought. A separate itemized statement shall be submitted for each professional firm or individual whose services are covered by the application, showing the hours spent in connection with the proceeding by each individual, a description of the specific services performed, the rate at which each fee has been computed, any expenses for which reimbursement is sought, the total amount claimed, and the total amount paid or payable by the applicant or by any other person or entity for the services provided. The presiding officer may require the applicant to provide vouchers, receipts; or other substantiation for any expenses claimed.

(d) *When an application may be filed.* (1) An application may be filed whenever the applicant has prevailed in a proceeding covered by this subpart or in a significant and discrete substantive portion of the proceeding. However, an application must be filed no later than 30 days after the Commission's final disposition of such a proceeding.

(2) If review or reconsideration is sought or taken of a decision as to which an applicant believes it has prevailed, proceedings for the award of fees shall be stayed pending final disposition of the underlying controversy.

(3) If review or reconsideration is sought or taken of a decision as to which an applicant believes it has prevailed, proceedings for the award of fees shall be stayed pending final disposition of the underlying controversy.

(4) For purposes of this subpart, final disposition means the later of:

(i) The date on which an initial decision by the presiding officer becomes final, *see* 16 CFR 1025.52;

(ii) The date on which the Commission issues a final decision (*See* 16 CFR 1025.55);

(iii) The date on which the Commission issues an order disposing of any petitions for reconsideration of the Commission's final order in the proceeding (*See* 16 CFR 1025.56; or

(iv) Issuance of a final order or any other final resolution of a proceeding, such as a settlement or voluntary dismissal, which is not subject to a petition for reconsideration.

(e) *Where an application must be filed.* The application for award and expenses must be submitted to the Office of the Secretary, Consumer Product Safety Commission, Washington, D.C. 20207 in accordance with the application requirements of this section.

§ 1025.72 Procedures for considering applications.

(a) *Filing and service of documents.* Any application for an award or other pleading or document related to an application shall be filed and served on all parties to the proceeding in the same manner as provided in the Commission's Rules of Practice, 16 CFR 1025.11–1025.19.

(b) *Answer to application.* (1) Within 30 days after service of an application for an award of fees and expenses, complaint counsel in the underlying administrative proceeding upon which the application is based may file an answer to the application. Unless complaint counsel requests an extension of time for filing or files a statement of intent to negotiate under paragraph (b)(2) of this section, failure to file an answer within the 30-day period may be treated as a consent to the award requested.

(2) If complaint counsel and the applicant believe that the issues in the fee application can be settled, they may jointly file a statement of their intent to negotiate a settlement. The filing of this statement shall extend the time for filing an answer for an additional 30 days, and further extensions may be granted by the presiding officer upon request by complaint counsel and the applicant.

(3) The answer shall explain in detail any objections to the award requested and identify the facts relied on in support of Commission counsel's position. If the answer is based on any alleged facts not already in the record of the proceeding, complaint counsel shall include with the answer either supporting affidavits or a request for further proceedings under paragraph (f) of this section.

(c) *Reply.* Within 15 days after service of an answer, the applicant may file a reply. If the reply is based on any alleged facts not already in the record of the proceeding, the applicant shall include with the reply either supporting affidavits or a request for further proceedings under paragraph (f) of this section.

(d) *Comments by other parties.* Any party to a proceeding other than the applicant and complaint counsel may file comments on an application within 30 days after it is served or on an answer within 15 days after it is served. A commenting party may not participate further in proceedings on the application unless the presiding officer determines that the public interest requires such participation in order to permit full exploration of matters raised in the comments.

(e) *Settlement.* The applicant and complaint counsel may agree on a proposed settlement of the award before final action on the application, either in connection with a settlement of the underlying proceeding, or after the underlying proceeding has been concluded, in accordance with the Commission's standard settlement procedure (*See* 16 CFR 1115.20(b), 1118.20, 1025.26, and 1605.3). If a prevailing party and complaint counsel agree on a proposed settlement of an award before an application has been filed, the application shall be filed with the proposed settlement.

(f) *Further proceedings.* (1) Ordinarily, the determination of an award will be made on the basis of the written record. However, on request of either the applicant or complaint counsel, or on his or her own initiative, the presiding officer may order further proceedings. Such further proceedings shall be held only when necessary for full and fair resolution of the issues arising from the application, and shall be conducted as promptly as possible.

(2) A request that the presiding officer order further proceedings under this paragraph shall specifically identify the information sought or the disputed issues and shall explain why the additional proceedings are necessary to resolve the issues.

(g) *Initial decision.* The presiding officer shall endeavor to issue an initial decision on the application within 30 days after completion of proceedings on the application. The decision shall include written findings and conclusions on the applicant's eligibility and status as a prevailing party, and an explanation of the reasons for any difference between the amount requested and the amount awarded. The decision shall also include, if at issue, findings on whether the complaint counsel's position was substantially justified, whether the applicant unduly protracted the proceedings, or whether special circumstances make an award unjust. If the applicant has sought an award against more than one agency, the decision of this Commission will only address the allocable portion for which this Commission is responsible to the eligible prevailing party.

(h) *Agency review.* (1) Either the applicant or complaint counsel may seek review of the initial decision on the fee application, or the Commission may decide to review the decision on its own initiative, in accordance with 16 CFR 1025.54, 1025.55 and 1025.56.

(2) If neither the applicant nor Commission complaint counsel seeks review and the Commission does not take review on its own initiative, the initial decision on the application shall become a final decision of the Commission 30 days after it is issued.

(3) If an appeal from or review of an initial decision under this subpart is taken, the Commission shall endeavor to issue a decision on the application within 90 days after the filing of all briefs or after receipt of transcripts of the oral argument, whichever is later, or remand the application to the presiding officer for further proceedings.

(i) *Judicial review.* Judicial review of final Commission decisions on awards may be sought as provided in 5 U.S.C. 504(c)(2).

(j) *Payment of award.* An applicant seeking payment of an award shall submit to the Secretary of the Commission a copy of the Commission's final decision granting the award, accompanied by a verified statement that the applicant will not seek review of the decision in the United States courts. (Office of the Secretary, Consumer Product Safety Commission, Washington, D.C. 20207.) The Commission will pay the amount awarded to the applicant within 60 days, unless judicial review of the award or of the underlying decision of the adversary adjudication has been sought by the applicant or any other party to the proceeding. Comments and accompanying material may be seen in or copies obtained from the Office of the Secretary, Consumer Product Safety Commission, Washington, D.C. 20207, during working hours Monday through Friday.

APPENDIX I TO PART 1025—SUGGESTED FORM OF FINAL PREHEARING ORDER

Case Caption

A final prehearing conference was held in this matter, pursuant to Rule 21 of the Commission's Rules of Practice for Adjudicative Proceedings (16 CFR 1025.21), on the ____ day of ____, 19__, at ____ o'clock, __ stm.

Counsel appeared as follows:

For the Commission staff:

For the Respondent(s):

Others:

1. Nature of Action and Jurisdiction. This is an action for ____ and the jurisdiction of the Commission is invoked under United States Code, Title ____, Section ____ and under the Code of Federal Regulations, Title ____, Section ____. The jurisdiction of the Commission is (not) disputed. The question of jurisdiction was decided as follows:

2. Stipulations and Statements. The following stipulation(s) and statement(s) were submitted, attached to, and made a part of this order:

(a) A comprehensive written stipulation or statement of all uncontested facts;

(b) A concise summary of the ultimate facts as claimed by each party. (Complaint Counsel must set forth the claimed facts, specifically; for example, if a violation is claimed, Complaint Counsel must assert specifically the acts of violation complained of; each respondent must reply with equal clarity and detail.)

(c) Written stipulation(s) or statement(s) setting forth the qualifications of the expert witnesses to be called by each party;

(d) Written list(s) of the witnesses whom each party *will* call, written list(s) of the additional witnesses whom each party *may* call, and a statement of the subject matter on which each witness will testify;

(e) An agreed statement of the contested issues of fact and of law, or separate statements by each party of any contested issues of fact and law not agreed to;

(f) A list of all depositions to be read into evidence and statements of any objections thereto;

(g) A list and brief description of any charts, graphs, models, schematic diagrams, and similar objects that will be used in opening statements or closing arguments but will not be offered in evidence. If any other such objects are to be used by any party, those objects will be submitted to opposing counsel at least three days prior to the hearing. If there is then any objection to their use, the dispute will be submitted to the Presiding Officer at least one day prior to the hearing;

(h) Written waivers of claims or defenses which have been abandoned by the parties.

The foregoing were modified at the pretrial conference as follows:
(To be completed at the conference itself. If none, recite "none".)

3. Complaint Counsel's Evidence. 3.1 The following exhibits were offered by Complaint Counsel, received in evidence, and marked as follows:
(Identification number and brief description of each exhibit)

The authenticity of these exhibits has been stipulated.

3.2 The following exhibits were offered by Complaint Counsel and marked for identification. There was reserved to the respondent(s) (and party intervenors) the right to object to their receipt in evidence on the grounds stated:
(Identification number and brief description of each exhibit. State briefly ground of objection, e.g., competency, relevancy, materiality)

4. Respondent's Evidence. 4.1 The following exhibits were offered by the respondent(s), received in evidence, and marked as herein indicated:
(Identification number and brief description of each exhibit)

The authenticity of these exhibits has been stipulated.

4.2 The following exhibits were offered by the respondent(s) and marked for identification. There was reserved to Complaint Counsel (and party intervenors) the right to object to their receipt in evidence on the grounds stated:
(Identification number and brief description of each exhibit. State briefly ground of objection, e.g., competency, relevancy, materiality)

5. Party Intervenor's Evidence. 5.1 The following exhibits were offered by the party intervenor(s), received in evidence, and marked as herein indicated:
(Identification number and brief description of each exhibit)

The authenticity of these exhibits has been stipulated.

5.2 The following exhibits were offered by the party intervenor(s) and marked for identification. There was reserved to Complaint Counsel and respondent(s) the right to object to their receipt in evidence on the grounds stated:
(Identification number and brief description of each exhibit. State briefly ground of objection, e.g., competency, relevancy, materiality)

NOTE: If any other exhibits are to be offered by any party, such exhibits will be submitted to opposing counsel at least ten (10) days prior to hearing, and a supplemental note of evidence filed into this record.

6. Additional Actions. The following additional action(s) were taken:
(Amendments to pleadings, agreements of the parties, disposition of motions, separation of issues of liability and remedy, etc., if necessary)

7. Limitations and Reservations. 7.1 Each of the parties has the right to further supplement the list of witnesses not later than ten (10) days prior to commencement of the hearing by furnishing opposing counsel with the name and address of the witness and general subject matter of his/her testimony and by filing a supplement to this pretrial order. Thereafter, additional witnesses may be added only after application to the Presiding Officer, for good cause shown.

7.2 Rebuttal witnesses not listed in the exhibits to this order may be called only if the necessity of their testimony could not reasonably be foreseen ten (10) days prior to trial. If it appears to counsel at any time before trial that such rebuttal witnesses will be called, notice will immediately be given to opposing counsel and the Presiding Officer.

7.3 The probable length of hearing is ____ days. The hearing will commence on the ________ day of ________, 19___, at ___ o'clock __ m. at _______.

7.4 Prehearing briefs will be filed not later than 5:00 p.m. on ________
(Insert date not later than ten (10) days prior to the hearing.) All anticipated legal questions, including those relating to the admissibility of evidence, must be covered by prehearing briefs.

This prehearing order has been formulated after a conference at which counsel for the respective parties appeared. Reasonable opportunity has been afforded counsel for corrections or additions prior to signing. It will control the course of the hearing, and it may not be amended except by consent of the parties and the Presiding Officer, or by order of the Presiding Officer to prevent manifest injustice.

____
Presiding Officer.
Dated: ________________
Approved as to Form and Substance
Date: ________________

____
Complaint Counsel.

____
Attorney for Respondent(s)

____
*Attorney for Intervenors

*NOTE: Where intervenors appear pursuant to §1025.17 of these Rules, the prehearing order may be suitably modified; the initial page may be modified to reflect the intervention.

PART 1027—SALARY OFFSET

AUTHORITY: 5 U.S.C. 5514, E.O. 11809 (redesignated E.O. 12107), and 5 CFR part 550, subpart K.

SOURCE: 55 FR 34904, Aug. 27, 1990, unless otherwise noted.

§ 1027.1 Purpose and scope.

(a) This regulation provides procedures for the collection by administrative offset of a Federal employee's salary without his/her consent to satisfy certain debts owed to the Federal government. These regulations apply to all Federal employees who owe debts to the Consumer Product Safety Commission (CPSC) and to current employees of CPSC who owe debts to other Federal agencies. This regulation does not apply when the employee consents to recovery from his/her current pay account.

(b) This regulation does not apply to debts or claims arising under:

(1) The Internal Revenue Code of 1954, as amended, 26 U.S.C. 1 *et seq.*;

(2) The Social Security Act, 42 U.S.C. 301 *et seq.*;

(3) The tariff laws of the United States; or

(4) Any case where a collection of a debt by salary offset is explicitly provided for or prohibited by another statute.

(c) This regulation does not apply to any adjustment to pay arising out of an employee's selection of coverage or a change in coverage under a Federal benefits program requiring periodic deductions from pay if the amount to be recovered was accumulated over four pay periods or less.

(d) This regulation does not preclude the compromise, suspension, or termination of collection action where appropriate under the standards implementing the Federal Claims Collection Act, 31 U.S.C. 3711 *et seq.*, and 4 CFR parts 101 through 105.

(e) This regulation does not preclude an employee from requesting waiver of an overpayment under 5 U.S.C. 5584, 10 U.S.C. 2774, or 32 U.S.C. 716, or in any way questioning the amount or validity of the debt by submitting a subsequent claim to the General Accounting Office. This regulation does not preclude an employee from requesting a waiver pursuant to other statutory provisions applicable to the particular debt being collected.

(f) Matters not addressed in these regulations should be reviewed in accordance with the Federal Claims Collection Standards at 4 CFR 101.1 *et seq.*

§ 1027.2 Definitions.

For the purposes of this part the following definitions will apply:

Agency means an executive agency as defined at 5 U.S.C. 105, including the U.S. Postal Service and the U.S. Postal Rate Commission; a military department as defined at 5 U.S.C. 102; an agency or court in the judicial branch; an agency of the legislative branch, including the U.S. Senate and House of Representatives; and other independent establishments that are entities of the Federal government.

Certification means a written debt claim received from a creditor agency which requests the paying agency to offset the salary of an employee.

CPSC or *Commission* means the Consumer Product Safety Commission.

Creditor agency means an agency of the Federal Government to which the debt is owed.

Debt means an amount owed by a Federal employee to the United States from sources which include loans insured or guaranteed by the United States and all other amounts due the United States from fees, leases, rents, royalties, services, sales of real or personal property, overpayments, penalties, damages, interests, fines, forfeitures (except those arising under the Uniform Code of Military Justice), and all other similar sources.

Disposable pay means the amount that remains from an employee's Federal pay after required deductions for social security, Federal, State or local income tax, health insurance premiums, retirement contributions, life insurance premiums, Federal employment taxes, and any other deductions that are required to be withheld by law.

Executive Director means the Executive Director of the Consumer Product Safety Commission, who is the person designated by the Chairman to determine whether an employee is indebted to the United States and to take action to collect such debts.

Hearing official means an individual responsible for conducting a hearing with respect to the existence or amount of a debt claimed, or the repayment schedule of a debt, and who renders a decision on the basis of such hearing. A hearing official may not be under the supervision or control of the Chairman of the Commission.

Paying agency means the agency that employs the individual who owes the debt and authorizes the payments of his/her current pay.

Salary offset means an administrative offset to collect a debt pursuant to 5 U.S.C. 5514 by deduction(s) at one or more officially established pay intervals from the current pay account of an employee without his/her consent.

§ 1027.3 Applicability.

(a) These regulations are to be followed when:

(1) The Commission is owed a debt by an individual who is a current employee of the CPSC; or

(2) The Commission is owed a debt by an individual currently employed by another Federal agency; or

(3) The Commission employs an individual who owes a debt to another federal agency.

§ 1027.4 Notice requirements before offset.

(a) Salary offset shall not be made against an employee's pay unless the employee is provided with written notice signed by the Executive Director of the debt at least 30 days before salary offset commences.

(b) The written notice shall contain:

(1) A statement that the debt is owed and an explanation of its nature and amount;

(2) The agency's intention to collect the debt by deducting from the employee's current disposable pay account;

(3) The amount, frequency, proposed beginning date, and duration of the intended deduction(s);

(4) An explanation of interest, penalties, and administrative charges, including a statement that such charges will be assessed unless excused in accordance with the Federal Claims Collections Standards at 4 CFR 101.1 *et seq.*;

(5) The employee's right to inspect, request, and receive a copy of government records relating to the debt;

(6) The employee's opportunity to establish a written schedule for the voluntary repayment of the debt in lieu of offset;

(7) The employee's right to an oral hearing or a determination based on a review of the written record ("paper hearing") conducted by an impartial hearing official concerning the existence or the amount of the debt, or the terms of the repayment schedule;

(8) The procedures and time period for petitioning for a hearing;

(9) A statement that a timely filing of a petition for a hearing will stay the commencement of collection proceedings;

(10) A statement that a final decision on the hearing (if requested) will be issued by the hearing official not later than 60 days after the filing of the petition requesting the hearing unless the employee requests and the hearing official grants a delay in the proceedings;

(11) A statement that knowingly false or frivolous statements, representations, or evidence may subject the employee to appropriate disciplinary procedures and/or statutory penalties;

(12) A statement of other rights and remedies available to the employee under statutes or regulations governing the program for which the collection is being made;

(13) Unless there are contractual or statutory provisions to the contrary, a statement that amounts paid on or deducted for the debt which are later waived or found not owed to the United States will be promptly refunded to the employee; and

(14) A statement that the proceedings regarding such debt are governed by

section 5 of the Debt Collection Act of 1982 (5 U.S.C. 5514).

§ 1027.5 Hearing.

(a) *Request for hearing.* (1) An employee may file a petition for an oral or paper hearing in accordance with the instructions outlined in the agency's notice to offset.

(2) A hearing may be requested by filing a written petition addressed to the Executive Director stating why the employee disputes the existence or amount of the debt or, in the case of an individual whose repayment schedule has been established other than by a written agreement, concerning the terms of the repayment schedule. The petition for a hearing must be received by the Executive Director not later than fifteen (15) calendar days after the employee's receipt of the offset notice, or notice of the terms of the payment schedule, unless the employee can show good cause for failing to meet the filing deadline.

(b) *Hearing procedures.* (1) The hearing will be presided over by an impartial hearing official.

(2) The hearing shall conform to procedures contained in the Federal Claims Collection Standards, 4 CFR 102.3(c). The burden shall be on the employee to demonstrate that the existence or the amount of the debt is in error.

§ 1027.6 Written decision.

(a) The hearing official shall issue a final written opinion no later than 60 days after the filing of the petition.

(b) The written opinion will include: A statement of the facts presented to demonstrate the nature and origin of the alleged debt; the hearing official's analysis, findings, and conclusions; the amount and validity of the debt; and the repayment schedule.

§ 1027.7 Coordinating offset with another Federal agency.

(a) *The CPSC as the creditor agency.* (1) When the Executive Director determines that an employee of another agency (i.e., the paying agency) owes a debt to the CPSC, the Executive Director shall, as appropriate:

(i) Certify in writing to the paying agency that the employee owes the debt, the amount and basis of the debt, the date on which payment was due, and the date the Government's right to collect the debt accrued, and that this part 1027 has been approved by the Office of Personnel Management.

(ii) Unless the employee has consented to salary offset in writing or signed a statement acknowledging receipt of the required procedures, and the written consent is sent to the paying agency, the Executive Director must advise the paying agency of the action(s) taken under this part 1027, and the date(s) they were taken.

(iii) Request the paying agency to collect the debt by salary offset. If deductions must be made in installments, the Executive Director may recommend to the paying agency the amount or percentage of disposable pay to be collected in each installment;

(iv) Arrange for a hearing upon the proper petitioning by the employee;

(v) If the employee is in the process of separating from the Federal service, the CPSC must submit its debt claim to the paying agency as provided in this part. The paying agency must certify the total amount collected, give a copy of the certification to the employee, and send a copy of the certification and notice of the employee's separation to the CPSC. If the paying agency is aware that the employee is entitled to Civil Service Retirement and Disability Fund or other similar payments, it must certify to the agency responsible for making such payments that the debtor owes a debt, including the amount of the debt, and that the provisions of 5 CFR 550.1108 have been followed; and

(vi) If the employee has already separated from federal service and all payments due from the paying agency have been paid, the Executive Director may request, unless otherwise prohibited, that money payable to the employee from the Civil Service Retirement and Disability Fund or other similar funds be collected by administrative offset.

(2) [Reserved]

(b) *The CPSC as the paying agency.* (1) Upon receipt of a properly certified debt claim from another agency, deductions will be scheduled to begin at the next established pay interval. The employee must receive written notice that CPSC has received a certified debt claim from the creditor agency, the amount of the debt, the date salary offset will begin, and the amount of the deduction(s). CPSC shall not review the merits of the creditor agency's determination of the validity or the amount of the certified claim.

(2) If the employee transfers to another agency after the creditor agency has submitted its debt claim to CPSC and before the debt is collected completely, CPSC must certify the amount collected. One copy of the certification must be furnished to the employee. A copy must be furnished to the creditor agency with notice of the employee's transfer.

§ 1027.8 Procedures for salary offset.

(a) Deductions to liquidate an employee's debt will be by the method and in the amount stated in the Executive Director's notice of intention to offset as provided in § 1027.4. Debts will be collected in one lump sum where possible. If the employee is financially unable to pay in one lump sum, collection must be made in installments.

(b) Debts will be collected by deduction at officially established pay intervals from an employee's current pay account unless alternative arrangements for repayment are made.

(c) Installment deductions will be made over a period not greater than the anticipated period of employment. The size of installment deductions must bear a reasonable relationship to the size of the debt and the employee's ability to pay. The deduction for the pay intervals for any period must not exceed 15% of disposable pay unless the employee has agreed in writing to a deduction of a greater amount.

(d) Unliquidated debts may be offset against any financial payment due to a separated employee including but not limited to final salary or leave payment in accordance with 31 U.S.C. 3716.

§ 1027.9 Refunds.

(a) CPSC will promptly refund to an employee any amounts deducted to satisfy debts owed to CPSC when the debt is waived, found not owed to CPSC, or when directed by an administrative or judicial order.

(b) Another creditor agency will promptly return to CPSC any amounts deducted by CPSC to satisfy debts owed to the creditor agency when the debt is waived, found not owed, or when directed by an administrative or judicial order.

(c) Unless required by law, refunds under this paragraph shall not bear interest.

§ 1027.10 Statute of limitations.

(a) If a debt has been outstanding for more than 10 years after CPSC's right to collect the debt first accrued, the agency may not collect by salary offset unless facts material to the Government's right to collect were not known and could not reasonably have been known by the official or officials who were charged with the responsibility for discovery and collection of such debts.

(b) [Reserved]

§ 1027.11 Non-waiver of rights.

An employee's involuntary payment of all or any part of a debt collected under these regulations will not be construed as a waiver of any rights that the employee may have under 5 U.S.C. 5514 or any other provision of law.

§ 1027.12 Interest, penalties, and administrative costs.

Charges may be assessed on a debt for interest, penalties, and administrative costs in accordance with 31 U.S.C. 3717 and the Federal Claims Collection Standards, 4 CFR 101.1 *et seq.*

PART 1028—PROTECTION OF HUMAN SUBJECTS

Sec.

AUTHORITY: 5 U.S.C. 301; 42 U.S.C. 300v–1(b).

SOURCE: 56 FR 28012, 28019, June 18, 1991, unless otherwise noted.

§ 1028.101 To what does this policy apply?

(a) Except as provided in paragraph (b) of this section, this policy applies to all research involving human subjects conducted, supported or otherwise subject to regulation by any federal department or agency which takes appropriate administrative action to make the policy applicable to such research. This includes research conducted by federal civilian employees or military personnel, except that each department or agency head may adopt such procedural modifications as may be appropriate from an administrative standpoint. It also includes research conducted, supported, or otherwise subject to regulation by the federal government outside the United States.

(1) Research that is conducted or supported by a federal department or agency, whether or not it is regulated as defined in § 1028.102(e), must comply with all sections of this policy.

(2) Research that is neither conducted nor supported by a federal department or agency but is subject to regulation as defined in § 1028.102(e) must be reviewed and approved, in compliance with §§ 1028.101, 1028.102, and 1028.107 through 1028.117 of this policy, by an institutional review board (IRB) that operates in accordance with the pertinent requirements of this policy.

(b) Unless otherwise required by department or agency heads, research activities in which the only involvement of human subjects will be in one or more of the following categories are exempt from this policy:

(1) Research conducted in established or commonly accepted educational settings, involving normal educational practices, such as (i) research on regular and special education instructional strategies, or (ii) research on the effectiveness of or the comparison among instructional techniques, curricula, or classroom management methods.

(2) Research involving the use of educational tests (cognitive, diagnostic, aptitude, achievement), survey procedures, interview procedures or observation of public behavior, unless:

(i) Information obtained is recorded in such a manner that human subjects can be identified, directly or through identifiers linked to the subjects; and

(ii) Any disclosure of the human subjects' responses outside the research could reasonably place the subjects at risk of criminal or civil liability or be damaging to the subjects' financial standing, employability, or reputation.

(3) Research involving the use of educational tests (cognitive, diagnostic, aptitude, achievement), survey procedures, interview procedures, or observation of public behavior that is not exempt under paragraph (b)(2) of this section, if:

(i) The human subjects are elected or appointed public officials or candidates for public office; or

(ii) Federal statute(s) require(s) without exception that the confidentiality of the personally identifiable information will be maintained throughout the research and thereafter.

(4) Research, involving the collection or study of existing data, documents, records, pathological specimens, or diagnostic specimens, if these sources are publicly available or if the information is recorded by the investigator in such a manner that subjects cannot be identified, directly or through identifiers linked to the subjects.

(5) Research and demonstration projects which are conducted by or subject to the approval of department or agency heads, and which are designed to study, evaluate, or otherwise examine:

(i) Public benefit or service programs;

(ii) Procedures for obtaining benefits or services under those programs;

(iii) Possible changes in or alternatives to those programs or procedures; or

(iv) Possible changes in methods or levels of payment for benefits or services under those programs.

(6) Taste and food quality evaluation and consumer acceptance studies, (i) if wholesome foods without additives are consumed or (ii) if a food is consumed that contains a food ingredient at or below the level and for a use found to be safe, or agricultural chemical or environmental contaminant at or below the level found to be safe, by the Food and Drug Administration or approved by the Environmental Protection Agency or the Food Safety and Inspection Service of the U.S. Department of Agriculture.

(c) Department or agency heads retain final judgment as to whether a particular activity is covered by this policy.

(d) Department or agency heads may require that specific research activities or classes of research activities conducted, supported, or otherwise subject to regulation by the department or agency but not otherwise covered by this policy, comply with some or all of the requirements of this policy.

(e) Compliance with this policy requires compliance with pertinent federal laws or regulations which provide additional protections for human subjects.

(f) This policy does not affect any state or local laws or regulations which may otherwise be applicable and which provide additional protections for human subjects.

(g) This policy does not affect any foreign laws or regulations which may otherwise be applicable and which provide additional protections to human subjects of research.

(h) When research covered by this policy takes place in foreign countries, procedures normally followed in the foreign countries to protect human subjects may differ from those set forth in this policy. (An example is a foreign institution which complies with guidelines consistent with the World Medical Assembly Declaration (Declaration of Helsinki amended 1989) issued either by sovereign states or by an organization whose function for the protection of human research subjects is internationally recognized.) In these circumstances, if a department or agency head determines that the procedures prescribed by the institution afford protections that are at least equivalent to those provided in this policy, the department or agency head may approve the substitution of the foreign procedures in lieu of the procedural requirements provided in this policy. Except when otherwise required by statute, Executive Order, or the department or agency head, notices of these actions as they occur will be published in the FEDERAL REGISTER or will be otherwise published as provided in department or agency procedures.

(i) Unless otherwise required by law, department or agency heads may waive the applicability of some or all of the provisions of this policy to specific research activities or classes of research activities otherwise covered by this policy. Except when otherwise required by statute or Executive Order, the department or agency head shall forward advance notices of these actions to the Office for Human Research Protections, Department of Health and Human Services (HHS), or any successor office, and shall also publish them in the FEDERAL REGISTER or in such other manner as provided in department or agency procedures.[1]

[56 FR 28012, 28019, June 18, 1991; 56 FR 29756, June 28, 1991, as amended at 70 FR 36328, June 23, 2005]

[1] Institutions with HHS-approved assurances on file will abide by provisions of title 45 CFR part 46, subparts A-D. Some of the other Departments and Agencies have incorporated all provisions of title 45 CFR part 46 into their policies and procedures as well. However, the exemptions at 45 CFR 46.101(b) do not apply to research involving prisoners, subpart C. The exemption at 45 CFR 46.101(b)(2), for research involving survey or interview procedures or observation of public

§ 1028.102 Definitions.

(a) *Department or agency head* means the head of any federal department or agency and any other officer or employee of any department or agency to whom authority has been delegated.

(b) *Institution* means any public or private entity or agency (including federal, state, and other agencies).

(c) *Legally authorized representative* means an individual or judicial or other body authorized under applicable law to consent on behalf of a prospective subject to the subject's participation in the procedure(s) involved in the research.

(d) *Research* means a systematic investigation, including research development, testing and evaluation, designed to develop or contribute to generalizable knowledge. Activities which meet this definition constitute research for purposes of this policy, whether or not they are conducted or supported under a program which is considered research for other purposes. For example, some demonstration and service programs may include research activities.

(e) *Research subject to regulation,* and similar terms are intended to encompass those research activities for which a federal department or agency has specific responsibility for regulating as a research activity, (for example, Investigational New Drug requirements administered by the Food and Drug Administration). It does not include research activities which are incidentally regulated by a federal department or agency solely as part of the department's or agency's broader responsibility to regulate certain types of activities whether research or non-research in nature (for example, Wage and Hour requirements administered by the Department of Labor).

(f) *Human subject* means a living individual about whom an investigator (whether professional or student) conducting research obtains:

(1) Data through intervention or interaction with the individual, or

behavior, does not apply to research with children, subpart D, except for research involving observations of public behavior when the investigator(s) do not participate in the activities being observed.

(2) Identifiable private information.

Intervention includes both physical procedures by which data are gathered (for example, venipuncture) and manipulations of the subject or the subject's environment that are performed for research purposes. Interaction includes communication or interpersonal contact between investigator and subject. "Private information" includes information about behavior that occurs in a context in which an individual can reasonably expect that no observation or recording is taking place, and information which has been provided for specific purposes by an individual and which the individual can reasonably expect will not be made public (for example, a medical record). Private information must be individually identifiable (i.e., the identity of the subject is or may readily be ascertained by the investigator or associated with the information) in order for obtaining the information to constitute research involving human subjects.

(g) *IRB* means an institutional review board established in accord with and for the purposes expressed in this policy.

(h) *IRB approval* means the determination of the IRB that the research has been reviewed and may be conducted at an institution within the constraints set forth by the IRB and by other institutional and federal requirements.

(i) *Minimal risk* means that the probability and magnitude of harm or discomfort anticipated in the research are not greater in and of themselves than those ordinarily encountered in daily life or during the performance of routine physical or psychological examinations or tests.

(j) *Certification* means the official notification by the institution to the supporting department or agency, in accordance with the requirements of this policy, that a research project or activity involving human subjects has been reviewed and approved by an IRB in accordance with an approved assurance.

§ 1028.103 Assuring compliance with this policy—research conducted or supported by any Federal Department or Agency.

(a) Each institution engaged in research which is covered by this policy and which is conducted or supported by a Federal department or agency shall provide written assurance satisfactory to the department or agency head that it will comply with the requirements set forth in this policy. In lieu of requiring submission of an assurance, individual department or agency heads shall accept the existence of a current assurance, appropriate for the research in question, on file with the Office for Human Research Protections, HHS, or any successor office, and approved for federalwide use by that office. When the existence of an HHS-approved assurance is accepted in lieu of requiring submission of an assurance, reports (except certification) required by this policy to be made to department and agency heads shall also be made to the Office for Human Research Protections, HHS, or any successor office.

(b) Departments and agencies will conduct or support research covered by this policy only if the institution has an assurance approved as provided in this section, and only if the institution has certified to the department or agency head that the research has been reviewed and approved by an IRB provided for in the assurance, and will be subject to continuing review by the IRB. Assurances applicable to federally supported or conducted research shall at a minimum include:

(1) A statement of principles governing the institution in the discharge of its responsibilities for protecting the rights and welfare of human subjects of research conducted at or sponsored by the institution, regardless of whether the research is subject to federal regulation. This may include an appropriate existing code, declaration, or statement of ethical principles, or a statement formulated by the institution itself. This requirement does not preempt provisions of this policy applicable to department- or agency-supported or regulated research and need not be applicable to any research exempted or waived under § 1028.101 (b) or (i).

(2) Designation of one or more IRBs established in accordance with the requirements of this policy, and for which provisions are made for meeting space and sufficient staff to support the IRB's review and recordkeeping duties.

(3) A list of IRB members identified by name; earned degrees; representative capacity; indications of experience such as board certifications, licenses, etc., sufficient to describe each member's chief anticipated contributions to IRB deliberations; and any employment or other relationship between each member and the institution; for example: full-time employee, part-time employee, member of governing panel or board, stockholder, paid or unpaid consultant. Changes in IRB membership shall be reported to the department or agency head, unless in accord with § 1028.103(a) of this policy, the existence of an HHS-approved assurance is accepted. In this case, change in IRB membership shall be reported to the Office for Human Research Protections, HHS, or any successor office.

(4) Written procedures which the IRB will follow:

(i) For conducting its initial and continuing review of research and for reporting its findings and actions to the investigator and the institution;

(ii) For determining which projects require review more often than annually and which projects need verification from sources other than the investigators that no material changes have occurred since previous IRB review; and

(iii) For ensuring prompt reporting to the IRB of proposed changes in a research activity, and for ensuring that such changes in approved research, during the period for which IRB approval has already been given, may not be initiated without IRB review and approval except when necessary to eliminate apparent immediate hazards to the subject.

(5) Written procedures for ensuring prompt reporting to the IRB, appropriate institutional officials, and the department or agency head of (i) any unanticipated problems involving risks to subjects or others or any serious or continuing noncompliance with this

policy or the requirements or determinations of the IRB and (ii) any suspension or termination of IRB approval.

(c) The assurance shall be executed by an individual authorized to act for the institution and to assume on behalf of the institution the obligations imposed by this policy and shall be filed in such form and manner as the department or agency head prescribes.

(d) The department or agency head will evaluate all assurances submitted in accordance with this policy through such officers and employees of the department or agency and such experts or consultants engaged for this purpose as the department or agency head determines to be appropriate. The department or agency head's evaluation will take into consideration the adequacy of the proposed IRB in light of the anticipated scope of the institution's research activities and the types of subject populations likely to be involved, the appropriateness of the proposed initial and continuing review procedures in light of the probable risks, and the size and complexity of the institution.

(e) On the basis of this evaluation, the department or agency head may approve or disapprove the assurance, or enter into negotiations to develop an approvable one. The department or agency head may limit the period during which any particular approved assurance or class of approved assurances shall remain effective or otherwise condition or restrict approval.

(f) Certification is required when the research is supported by a federal department or agency and not otherwise exempted or waived under §1028.101 (b) or (i). An institution with an approved assurance shall certify that each application or proposal for research covered by the assurance and by §1028.103 of this Policy has been reviewed and approved by the IRB. Such certification must be submitted with the application or proposal or by such later date as may be prescribed by the department or agency to which the application or proposal is submitted. Under no condition shall research covered by §1028.103 of the Policy be supported prior to receipt of the certification that the research has been reviewed and approved by the IRB. Institutions without an approved assurance covering the research shall certify within 30 days after receipt of a request for such a certification from the department or agency, that the application or proposal has been approved by the IRB. If the certification is not submitted within these time limits, the application or proposal may be returned to the institution.

(Approved by the Office of Management and Budget under Control Number 0990–0260)

[56 FR 28012, 28019, June 18, 1991; 56 FR 29756, June 28, 1991, as amended at 70 FR 36328, June 23, 2005]

§§ 1028.104–1028.106 [Reserved]

§ 1028.107 IRB membership.

(a) Each IRB shall have at least five members, with varying backgrounds to promote complete and adequate review of research activities commonly conducted by the institution. The IRB shall be sufficiently qualified through the experience and expertise of its members, and the diversity of the members, including consideration of race, gender, and cultural backgrounds and sensitivity to such issues as community attitudes, to promote respect for its advice and counsel in safeguarding the rights and welfare of human subjects. In addition to possessing the professional competence necessary to review specific research activities, the IRB shall be able to ascertain the acceptability of proposed research in terms of institutional commitments and regulations, applicable law, and standards of professional conduct and practice. The IRB shall therefore include persons knowledgeable in these areas. If an IRB regularly reviews research that involves a vulnerable category of subjects, such as children, prisoners, pregnant women, or handicapped or mentally disabled persons, consideration shall be given to the inclusion of one or more individuals who are knowledgeable about and experienced in working with these subjects.

(b) Every nondiscriminatory effort will be made to ensure that no IRB consists entirely of men or entirely of women, including the institution's consideration of qualified persons of both sexes, so long as no selection is made to the IRB on the basis of gender. No

IRB may consist entirely of members of one profession.

(c) Each IRB shall include at least one member whose primary concerns are in scientific areas and at least one member whose primary concerns are in nonscientific areas.

(d) Each IRB shall include at least one member who is not otherwise affiliated with the institution and who is not part of the immediate family of a person who is affiliated with the institution.

(e) No IRB may have a member participate in the IRB's initial or continuing review of any project in which the member has a conflicting interest, except to provide information requested by the IRB.

(f) An IRB may, in its discretion, invite individuals with competence in special areas to assist in the review of issues which require expertise beyond or in addition to that available on the IRB. These individuals may not vote with the IRB.

§ 1028.108 IRB functions and operations.

In order to fulfill the requirements of this policy each IRB shall:

(a) Follow written procedures in the same detail as described in § 1028.103(b)(4) and, to the extent required by, § 1028.103(b)(5).

(b) Except when an expedited review procedure is used (see § 1028.110), review proposed research at convened meetings at which a majority of the members of the IRB are present, including at least one member whose primary concerns are in nonscientific areas. In order for the research to be approved, it shall receive the approval of a majority of those members present at the meeting.

§ 1028.109 IRB review of research.

(a) An IRB shall review and have authority to approve, require modifications in (to secure approval), or disapprove all research activities covered by this policy.

(b) An IRB shall require that information given to subjects as part of informed consent is in accordance with § 1028.116. The IRB may require that information, in addition to that specifically mentioned in § 1028.116, be given to the subjects when in the IRB's judgment the information would meaningfully add to the protection of the rights and welfare of subjects.

(c) An IRB shall require documentation of informed consent or may waive documentation in accordance with § 1028.117.

(d) An IRB shall notify investigators and the institution in writing of its decision to approve or disapprove the proposed research activity, or of modifications required to secure IRB approval of the research activity. If the IRB decides to disapprove a research activity, it shall include in its written notification a statement of the reasons for its decision and give the investigator an opportunity to respond in person or in writing.

(e) An IRB shall conduct continuing review of research covered by this policy at intervals appropriate to the degree of risk, but not less than once per year, and shall have authority to observe or have a third party observe the consent process and the research.

(Approved by the Office of Management and Budget under Control Number 0990–0260)

[56 FR 28012, 28019, June 18, 1991, as amended at 70 FR 36328, June 23, 2005]

§ 1028.110 Expedited review procedures for certain kinds of research involving no more than minimal risk, and for minor changes in approved research.

(a) The Secretary, HHS, has established, and published as a Notice in the FEDERAL REGISTER, a list of categories of research that may be reviewed by the IRB through an expedited review procedure. The list will be amended, as appropriate after consultation with other departments and agencies, through periodic republication by the Secretary, HHS, in the FEDERAL REGISTER. A copy of the list is available from the Office for Human Research Protections, HHS, or any successor office.

(b) An IRB may use the expedited review procedure to review either or both of the following:

(1) Some or all of the research appearing on the list and found by the reviewer(s) to involve no more than minimal risk,

(2) Minor changes in previously approved research during the period (of one year or less) for which approval is authorized.

Under an expedited review procedure, the review may be carried out by the IRB chairperson or by one or more experienced reviewers designated by the chairperson from among members of the IRB. In reviewing the research, the reviewers may exercise all of the authorities of the IRB except that the reviewers may not disapprove the research. A research activity may be disapproved only after review in accordance with the non-expedited procedure set forth in §1028.108(b).

(c) Each IRB which uses an expedited review procedure shall adopt a method for keeping all members advised of research proposals which have been approved under the procedure.

(d) The department or agency head may restrict, suspend, terminate, or choose not to authorize an institution's or IRB's use of the expedited review procedure.

[56 FR 28012, 28019, June 18, 1991, as amended at 70 FR 36328, June 23, 2005]

§1028.111 Criteria for IRB approval of research.

(a) In order to approve research covered by this policy the IRB shall determine that all of the following requirements are satisfied:

(1) Risks to subjects are minimized:

(i) By using procedures which are consistent with sound research design and which do not unnecessarily expose subjects to risk, and

(ii) Whenever appropriate, by using procedures already being performed on the subjects for diagnostic or treatment purposes.

(2) Risks to subjects are reasonable in relation to anticipated benefits, if any, to subjects, and the importance of the knowledge that may reasonably be expected to result. In evaluating risks and benefits, the IRB should consider only those risks and benefits that may result from the research (as distinguished from risks and benefits of therapies subjects would receive even if not participating in the research). The IRB should not consider possible long-range effects of applying knowledge gained in the research (for example, the possible effects of the research on public policy) as among those research risks that fall within the purview of its responsibility.

(3) Selection of subjects is equitable. In making this assessment the IRB should take into account the purposes of the research and the setting in which the research will be conducted and should be particularly cognizant of the special problems of research involving vulnerable populations, such as children, prisoners, pregnant women, mentally disabled persons, or economically or educationally disadvantaged persons.

(4) Informed consent will be sought from each prospective subject or the subject's legally authorized representative, in accordance with, and to the extent required by §1028.116.

(5) Informed consent will be appropriately documented, in accordance with, and to the extent required by §1028.117.

(6) When appropriate, the research plan makes adequate provision for monitoring the data collected to ensure the safety of subjects.

(7) When appropriate, there are adequate provisions to protect the privacy of subjects and to maintain the confidentiality of data.

(b) When some or all of the subjects are likely to be vulnerable to coercion or undue influence, such as children, prisoners, pregnant women, mentally disabled persons, or economically or educationally disadvantaged persons, additional safeguards have been included in the study to protect the rights and welfare of these subjects.

§1028.112 Review by institution.

Research covered by this policy that has been approved by an IRB may be subject to further appropriate review and approval or disapproval by officials of the institution. However, those officials may not approve the research if it has not been approved by an IRB.

§1028.113 Suspension or termination of IRB approval of research.

An IRB shall have authority to suspend or terminate approval of research that is not being conducted in accordance with the IRB's requirements or that has been associated with unexpected serious harm to subjects. Any suspension or termination of approval shall include a statement of the reasons for the IRB's action and shall be reported promptly to the investigator, appropriate institutional officials, and the department or agency head.

(Approved by the Office of Management and Budget under Control Number 0990–0260)

[56 FR 28012, 28019, June 18, 1991, as amended at 70 FR 36328, June 23, 2005]

§ 1028.114 Cooperative research.

Cooperative research projects are those projects covered by this policy which involve more than one institution. In the conduct of cooperative research projects, each institution is responsible for safeguarding the rights and welfare of human subjects and for complying with this policy. With the approval of the department or agency head, an institution participating in a cooperative project may enter into a joint review arrangement, rely upon the review of another qualified IRB, or make similar arrangements for avoiding duplication of effort.

§ 1028.115 IRB records.

(a) An institution, or when appropriate an IRB, shall prepare and maintain adequate documentation of IRB activities, including the following:

(1) Copies of all research proposals reviewed, scientific evaluations, if any, that accompany the proposals, approved sample consent documents, progress reports submitted by investigators, and reports of injuries to subjects.

(2) Minutes of IRB meetings which shall be in sufficient detail to show attendance at the meetings; actions taken by the IRB; the vote on these actions including the number of members voting for, against, and abstaining; the basis for requiring changes in or disapproving research; and a written summary of the discussion of controverted issues and their resolution.

(3) Records of continuing review activities.

(4) Copies of all correspondence between the IRB and the investigators.

(5) A list of IRB members in the same detail as described is § 1028.103(b)(3).

(6) Written procedures for the IRB in the same detail as described in §§ 1028.103(b)(4) and 1028.103(b)(5).

(7) Statements of significant new findings provided to subjects, as required by § 1028.116(b)(5).

(b) The records required by this policy shall be retained for at least 3 years, and records relating to research which is conducted shall be retained for at least 3 years after completion of the research. All records shall be accessible for inspection and copying by authorized representatives of the department or agency at reasonable times and in a reasonable manner.

(Approved by the Office of Management and Budget under Control Number 0990–0260)

[56 FR 28012, 28019, June 18, 1991, as amended at 70 FR 36328, June 23, 2005]

§ 1028.116 General requirements for informed consent.

Except as provided elsewhere in this policy, no investigator may involve a human being as a subject in research covered by this policy unless the investigator has obtained the legally effective informed consent of the subject or the subject's legally authorized representative. An investigator shall seek such consent only under circumstances that provide the prospective subject or the representative sufficient opportunity to consider whether or not to participate and that minimize the possibility of coercion or undue influence. The information that is given to the subject or the representative shall be in language understandable to the subject or the representative. No informed consent, whether oral or written, may include any exculpatory language through which the subject or the representative is made to waive or appear to waive any of the subject's legal rights, or releases or appears to release the investigator, the sponsor, the institution or its agents from liability for negligence.

(a) Basic elements of informed consent. Except as provided in paragraph (c) or (d) of this section, in seeking informed consent the following information shall be provided to each subject:

(1) A statement that the study involves research, an explanation of the

purposes of the research and the expected duration of the subject's participation, a description of the procedures to be followed, and identification of any procedures which are experimental;

(2) A description of any reasonably foreseeable risks or discomforts to the subject;

(3) A description of any benefits to the subject or to others which may reasonably be expected from the research;

(4) A disclosure of appropriate alternative procedures or courses of treatment, if any, that might be advantageous to the subject;

(5) A statement describing the extent, if any, to which confidentiality of records identifying the subject will be maintained;

(6) For research involving more than minimal risk, an explanation as to whether any compensation and an explanation as to whether any medical treatments are available if injury occurs and, if so, what they consist of, or where further information may be obtained;

(7) An explanation of whom to contact for answers to pertinent questions about the research and research subjects' rights, and whom to contact in the event of a research-related injury to the subject; and

(8) A statement that participation is voluntary, refusal to participate will involve no penalty or loss of benefits to which the subject is otherwise entitled, and the subject may discontinue participation at any time without penalty or loss of benefits to which the subject is otherwise entitled.

(b) Additional elements of informed consent. When appropriate, one or more of the following elements of information shall also be provided to each subject:

(1) A statement that the particular treatment or procedure may involve risks to the subject (or to the embryo or fetus, if the subject is or may become pregnant) which are currently unforeseeable;

(2) Anticipated circumstances under which the subject's participation may be terminated by the investigator without regard to the subject's consent;

(3) Any additional costs to the subject that may result from participation in the research;

(4) The consequences of a subject's decision to withdraw from the research and procedures for orderly termination of participation by the subject;

(5) A statement that significant new findings developed during the course of the research which may relate to the subject's willingness to continue participation will be provided to the subject; and

(6) The approximate number of subjects involved in the study.

(c) An IRB may approve a consent procedure which does not include, or which alters, some or all of the elements of informed consent set forth above, or waive the requirement to obtain informed consent provided the IRB finds and documents that:

(1) The research or demonstration project is to be conducted by or subject to the approval of state or local government officials and is designed to study, evaluate, or otherwise examine:

(i) Public benefit of service programs;

(ii) Procedures for obtaining benefits or services under those programs;

(iii) Possible changes in or alternatives to those programs or procedures; or

(iv) Possible changes in methods or levels of payment for benefits or services under those programs; and

(2) The research could not practicably be carried out without the waiver or alteration.

(d) An IRB may approve a consent procedure which does not include, or which alters, some or all of the elements of informed consent set forth in this section, or waive the requirements to obtain informed consent provided the IRB finds and documents that:

(1) The research involves no more than minimal risk to the subjects;

(2) The waiver or alteration will not adversely affect the rights and welfare of the subjects;

(3) The research could not practicably be carried out without the waiver or alteration; and

(4) Whenever appropriate, the subjects will be provided with additional pertinent information after participation.

(e) The informed consent requirements in this policy are not intended to preempt any applicable federal, state, or local laws which require additional information to be disclosed in order for informed consent to be legally effective.

(f) Nothing in this policy is intended to limit the authority of a physician to provide emergency medical care, to the extent the physician is permitted to do so under applicable federal, state, or local law.

(Approved by the Office of Management and Budget under Control Number 0990–0260)

[56 FR 28012, 28019, June 18, 1991, as amended at 70 FR 36328, June 23, 2005]

§ 1028.117 Documentation of informed consent.

(a) Except as provided in paragraph (c) of this section, informed consent shall be documented by the use of a written consent form approved by the IRB and signed by the subject or the subject's legally authorized representative. A copy shall be given to the person signing the form.

(b) Except as provided in paragraph (c) of this section, the consent form may be either of the following:

(1) A written consent document that embodies the elements of informed consent required by § 1028.116. This form may be read to the subject or the subject's legally authorized representative, but in any event, the investigator shall give either the subject or the representative adequate opportunity to read it before it is signed; or

(2) A short form written consent document stating that the elements of informed consent required by § 1028.116 have been presented orally to the subject or the subject's legally authorized representative. When this method is used, there shall be a witness to the oral presentation. Also, the IRB shall approve a written summary of what is to be said to the subject or the representative. Only the short form itself is to be signed by the subject or the representative. However, the witness shall sign both the short form and a copy of the summary, and the person actually obtaining consent shall sign a copy of the summary. A copy of the summary shall be given to the subject or the representative, in addition to a copy of the short form.

(c) An IRB may waive the requirement for the investigator to obtain a signed consent form for some or all subjects if it finds either:

(1) That the only record linking the subject and the research would be the consent document and the principal risk would be potential harm resulting from a breach of confidentiality. Each subject will be asked whether the subject wants documentation linking the subject with the research, and the subject's wishes will govern; or

(2) That the research presents no more than minimal risk of harm to subjects and involves no procedures for which written consent is normally required outside of the research context.

In cases in which the documentation requirement is waived, the IRB may require the investigator to provide subjects with a written statement regarding the research.

(Approved by the Office of Management and Budget under Control Number 0990–0260)

[56 FR 28012, 28019, June 18, 1991, as amended at 70 FR 36328, June 23, 2005]

§ 1028.118 Applications and proposals lacking definite plans for involvement of human subjects.

Certain types of applications for grants, cooperative agreements, or contracts are submitted to departments or agencies with the knowledge that subjects may be involved within the period of support, but definite plans would not normally be set forth in the application or proposal. These include activities such as institutional type grants when selection of specific projects is the institution's responsibility; research training grants in which the activities involving subjects remain to be selected; and projects in which human subjects' involvement will depend upon completion of instruments, prior animal studies, or purification of compounds. These applications need not be reviewed by an IRB before an award may be made. However, except for research exempted or waived under § 1028.101 (b) or (i), no human subjects may be involved in any project supported by these awards until the project has been reviewed and approved by the IRB, as provided in this policy, and certification submitted, by the institution, to the department or agency.

§ 1028.119 Research undertaken without the intention of involving human subjects.

In the event research is undertaken without the intention of involving human subjects, but it is later proposed to involve human subjects in the research, the research shall first be reviewed and approved by an IRB, as provided in this policy, a certification submitted, by the institution, to the department or agency, and final approval given to the proposed change by the department or agency.

§ 1028.120 Evaluation and disposition of applications and proposals for research to be conducted or supported by a Federal Department or Agency.

(a) The department or agency head will evaluate all applications and proposals involving human subjects submitted to the department or agency through such officers and employees of the department or agency and such experts and consultants as the department or agency head determines to be appropriate. This evaluation will take into consideration the risks to the subjects, the adequacy of protection against these risks, the potential benefits of the research to the subjects and others, and the importance of the knowledge gained or to be gained.

(b) On the basis of this evaluation, the department or agency head may approve or disapprove the application or proposal, or enter into negotiations to develop an approvable one.

§ 1028.121 [Reserved]

§ 1028.122 Use of Federal funds.

Federal funds administered by a department or agency may not be expended for research involving human subjects unless the requirements of this policy have been satisfied.

§ 1028.123 Early termination of research support: Evaluation of applications and proposals.

(a) The department or agency head may require that department or agency support for any project be terminated or suspended in the manner prescribed in applicable program requirements, when the department or agency head finds an institution has materially failed to comply with the terms of this policy.

(b) In making decisions about supporting or approving applications or proposals covered by this policy the department or agency head may take into account, in addition to all other eligibility requirements and program criteria, factors such as whether the applicant has been subject to a termination or suspension under paragarph (a) of this section and whether the applicant or the person or persons who would direct or has have directed the scientific and technical aspects of an activity has have, in the judgment of the department or agency head, materially failed to discharge responsibility for the protection of the rights and welfare of human subjects (whether or not the research was subject to federal regulation).

§ 1028.124 Conditions.

With respect to any research project or any class of research projects the department or agency head may impose additional conditions prior to or at the time of approval when in the judgment of the department or agency head additional conditions are necessary for the protection of human subjects.

PART 1030—EMPLOYEE STANDARDS OF CONDUCT

Subpart A—General

AUTHORITY: 5 U.S.C. 552a, 7301; 15 U.S.C. 2053(c).

SOURCE: 61 FR 65458, Dec. 13, 1996, unless otherwise noted.

Subpart A—General

§ 1030.101 Cross-references to employee ethical conduct standards and financial disclosure regulations.

Employees of the Consumer Product Safety Commission are subject to the Standards of Ethical Conduct, 5 CFR part 2635, which are applicable to all executive branch personnel; the CPSC regulations at 5 CFR part 8101, which supplement the executive branch standards; the Office of Personnel Management regulations on employee conduct at 5 CFR part 735; and the financial disclosure regulations at 5 CFR part 2634, which are applicable to all executive branch personnel. In addition, the Commissioners of the CPSC are subject to the statutory provisions of 15 U.S.C. 2053(c).

Subparts B–D [Reserved]

PART 1031—COMMISSION PARTICIPATION AND COMMISSION EMPLOYEE INVOLVEMENT IN VOLUNTARY STANDARDS ACTIVITIES

Subpart A—General Policies

Sec.

Subpart B—Employee Involvement

Subpart C—Public Participation and Comment

AUTHORITY: 15 U.S.C. 2051–2083; 15 U.S.C. 1261–1276; 15 U.S.C. 1191–1204.

SOURCE: 71 FR 38755, July 10, 2006, unless otherwise noted.

Subpart A—General Policies

§ 1031.1 Purpose and scope.

(a) This part 1031 sets forth the Consumer Product Safety Commission's guidelines and requirements on participating in the activities of voluntary standards bodies. Subpart A sets forth general policies on Commission involvement, and subpart B sets forth policies and guidelines on employee involvement in voluntary standards activities. Subpart C sets forth the criteria governing public review and comment on staff involvement in voluntary standards activities.

(b) For purposes of both subpart A and subpart B of this part 1031, voluntary standards bodies are private sector domestic or multinational organizations or groups, or combinations thereof, such as, but not limited to, all non-profit organizations, industry associations, professional and technical societies, institutes, and test laboratories, that are involved in the planning, development, establishment, revision, review or coordination of voluntary standards. Voluntary standards development bodies are voluntary standards bodies, or their sub-groups, that are devoted to developing or establishing voluntary standards.

§ 1031.2 Background.

(a) Congress enacted the Consumer Product Safety Act in 1972 to protect consumers against unreasonable risks of injury associated with consumer products. In order to achieve that goal, Congress established the Consumer Product Safety Commission as an independent regulatory agency and granted it broad authority to promulgate mandatory safety standards for consumer products as a necessary alternative to industry self regulation.

(b) In 1981, the Congress amended the Consumer Product Safety Act, the Federal Hazardous Substances Act, and the Flammable Fabrics Act, to require the Commission to rely on voluntary standards rather than promulgate a mandatory standard when voluntary standards would eliminate or adequately reduce the risk of injury addressed and it is likely that there will be substantial compliance with the voluntary standards. (15 U.S.C. 2056(b), 15 U.S.C. 1262(g)(2), 15 U.S.C. 1193(h)(2)). The 1981 Amendments also require the Commission, after any notice or advance notice of proposed rulemaking, to provide technical and administrative assistance to persons or groups who propose to develop or modify an appropriate voluntary standard. (15 U.S.C. 2054(a)(3)). Additionally, the amendments encourage the Commission to provide technical and administrative assistance to groups developing product safety standards and test methods, taking into account Commission resources and priorities (15 U.S.C. 2054(a)(4)). Although the Commission is required to provide assistance to such groups, it may determine the level of assistance in accordance with the level of its own administrative and technical resources and in accordance with its assessment of the likelihood that the groups being assisted will successfully develop a voluntary standard that will preclude the need for a mandatory standard.

(c) In 1990, Congress passed the Consumer Product Safety Improvement Act (CPSIA), amending section 15(b) of the CPSA to require that manufacturers, distributors, and retailers notify the Commission about products that fail to comply with an applicable voluntary standard upon which the Commission has relied under section 9 of the CPSA. CPSIA also amended section 9(b)(2) of the CPSA to require that the CPSC afford interested persons the opportunity to comment regarding any voluntary standard prior to CPSC termination and reliance.

§ 1031.3 Consumer Product Safety Act amendments.

The Consumer Product Safety Act, as amended, contains several sections pertaining to the Commission's participation in the development and use of voluntary standards.

(a) Section 7(b) provides that the Commission shall rely on voluntary consumer product safety standards prescribing requirements described in subsection (a) whenever compliance with such voluntary standards would eliminate or adequately reduce the risk of injury addressed and it is likely that there will be substantial compliance with such voluntary standards. (15 U.S.C. 2056(b)).

(b) Section 5(a)(3) provides that the Commission shall, following publication of an advance notice of proposed rulemaking or a notice of proposed rulemaking for a product safety rule under any rulemaking authority administered by the Commission, assist public and private organizations or groups of manufacturers, administratively and technically, in the development of safety standards addressing the risk of injury identified in such notice. (15 U.S.C. 2054(a)(3)).

(c) Section 5(a)(4) provides that the Commission shall, to the extent practicable and appropriate (taking into account the resources and priorities of the Commission), assist public and private organizations or groups of manufacturers, administratively and technically, in the development of product safety standards and test methods. (15 U.S.C. 2054(a)(4)).

§ 1031.4 Effect of voluntary standards activities on Commission activities.

(a)(1) The Commission, in determining whether to begin proceedings to develop mandatory standards under the acts it administers, considers whether mandatory regulation is necessary or whether there is an existing voluntary standard that adequately addresses the problem and the extent to which that voluntary standard is complied with by the affected industry.

(2) The Commission acknowledges that there are situations in which adequate voluntary standards, in combination with appropriate certification programs, may be appropriate to support a conclusion that a mandatory standard is not necessary. The Commission may find that a mandatory standard is not necessary where compliance with an existing voluntary standard would

eliminate or adequately reduce the risk of injury associated with the product, contains requirements and test methods that have been evaluated and found acceptable by the Commission, and it is likely that there will be substantial and timely compliance with the voluntary standard. Under such circumstances, the Commission may agree to encourage industry compliance with the voluntary standard and subsequently evaluate the effectiveness of the standard in terms of accident and injury reduction for products produced in compliance with the standard.

(3) In evaluating voluntary standards, the Commission will relate the requirements of the standard to the identified risks of injury and evaluate the requirements in terms of their effectiveness in eliminating or reducing the risks of injury. The evaluation of voluntary standards will be conducted by Commission staff members, including representatives of legal, economics, engineering, epidemiological, health sciences, human factors, other appropriate interests, and the Voluntary Standards Coordinator. The staff evaluation will be conducted in a manner similar to evaluations of standards being considered for promulgation as mandatory standards.

(4) In the event that the Commission has evaluated an existing voluntary standard and found it to be adequate in all but a few areas, the Commission may defer the initiation of a mandatory rulemaking proceeding and request the voluntary standards organization to revise the standard to address the identified inadequacies expeditiously.

(b) In the event the Commission determines that there is no existing voluntary standard that will eliminate or adequately reduce a risk of injury the Commission may commence a proceeding for the development of a consumer product safety rule or a regulation in accordance with section 9 of the Consumer Product Safety Act, 15 U.S.C. 2058, section 3(f) of the Federal Hazardous Substances Act, 15 U.S.C. 1262(f), or section 4(a) of the Flammable Fabrics Act, 15 U.S.C. 1193(g), as may be applicable. In commencing such a proceeding, the Commission will publish an advance notice of proposed rulemaking which shall, among other things, invite any person to submit to the Commission an existing standard or portion of an existing standard, or to submit a statement of intention to modify or develop, within a reasonable period of time, a voluntary standard to address the risk of injury.

(c) The Commission will consider those provisions of a voluntary standard that have been reviewed, evaluated, and deemed to be adequate in addressing the specified risks of injury when initiating a mandatory consumer product safety rule or regulation under the Consumer Product Safety Act, the Federal Hazardous Substances Act, or the Flammable Fabrics Act, as may be applicable. Comments will be requested in the advance notice of proposed rulemaking on the adequacy of such voluntary standard provisions.

§ 1031.5 Criteria for Commission involvement in voluntary standards activities.

The Commission will consider the extent to which the following criteria are met in considering Commission involvement in the development of voluntary safety standards for consumer products:

(a) The likelihood the voluntary standard will eliminate or adequately reduce the risk of injury addressed and that there will be substantial and timely compliance with the voluntary standard.

(b) The likelihood that the voluntary standard will be developed within a reasonable period of time.

(c) Exclusion, to the maximum extent possible, from the voluntary standard being developed, of requirements which will create anticompetitive effects or promote restraint of trade.

(d) Provisions for periodic and timely review of the standard, including review for anticompetitive effects, and revision or amendment as the need arises.

(e) Performance-oriented and not design-restrictive requirements, to the maximum practical extent, in any standard developed.

(f) Industry arrangements for achieving substantial and timely industry compliance with the voluntary standard once it is issued, and the means of ascertaining such compliance based on overall market share of product production.

(g) Provisions in the standard for marking products conforming to the standard so that future Commission investigation can indicate the involvement of such products in accidents and patterns of injury.

(h) Provisions for insuring that products identified as conforming to such standards will be subjected to a testing and certification (including self-certification) procedure, which will provide assurance that the products comply with the standard.

(i) The openness to all interested parties, and the establishment of procedures which will provide for meaningful participation in the development of such standards by representatives of producers, suppliers, distributors, retailers, consumers, small business, public interests and other individuals having knowledge or expertise in the areas under consideration, and procedures for affording other due process considerations.

§ 1031.6 Extent and form of Commission involvement in the development of voluntary standards.

(a) The extent of Commission involvement will be dependent upon the Commission's interest in the particular standards development activity and the Commission's priorities and resources.

(b) The Commission's interest in a specific voluntary standards activity will be based in part on the frequency and severity of injuries associated with the product, the involvement of the product in accidents, the susceptibility of the hazard to correction through standards, and the overall resources and priorities of the Commission. Commission involvement in voluntary standards activities generally will be guided by the Commission's operating plan and performance budget.

(c) Commission involvement in voluntary standards activities varies.

(1) The Commission staff may maintain an awareness of the voluntary standards development process through oral or written inquiries, receiving and reviewing minutes of meetings and copies of draft standards, or attending meetings for the purpose of observing and commenting during the standards development process in accordance with subpart B of this part. For example, Commission staff may respond to requests from voluntary standards organizations, standards development committees, trade associations and consumer organizations; by providing information concerning the risks of injury associated with particular products, National Electronic Injury Surveillance System (NEISS) data, death, injury, and incident data, summaries and analyses of in-depth investigation reports; discussing Commission goals and objectives with regard to voluntary standards and improved consumer product safety; responding to requests for information concerning Commission programs; and initiating contacts with voluntary standards organizations to discuss cooperative voluntary standards activities.

(2) Employee involvement may include membership as defined in § 1031.10(a). Commission staff may regularly attend meetings of a standard development committee or group and take an active part in the discussions of the committee and in developing the standard, in accordance with subpart B of this part. The Commission may contribute to the deliberations of the committee by expending resources to provide technical assistance (e.g., research, engineering support, and information and education programs) and administrative assistance (e.g., travel costs, hosting meetings, and secretarial functions) in support of the development and implementation of those voluntary standards referenced in the Commission's operating plan, performance budget, mid-year review, or other official Commission document. The Commission may also support voluntary standards activities as described in § 1031.7. Employee involvement may include observation as defined in § 1031.10(c).

(d) Normally, the total amount of Commission support given to a voluntary standards activity shall be no greater than that of all non-Federal participants in that activity, except where it is in the public interest to do so.

(e) In the event of duplication of effort by two or more groups (either inside or outside the Commission) in developing a voluntary standard for the same product or class of products, the Commission shall encourage the several groups to cooperate in the development of a single voluntary standard.

§ 1031.7 Commission support of voluntary standards activities.

(a) The Commission's support of voluntary safety standards development activities may include any one or a combination of the following actions:

(1) Providing epidemiological and health science information and explanations of hazards for consumer products.

(2) Encouraging the initiation of the development of voluntary standards for specific consumer products.

(3) Identifying specific risks of injury to be addressed in a voluntary standard.

(4) Performing or subsidizing technical assistance, including research, health science data, and engineering support, in the development of a voluntary standard activity in which the Commission staff is participating.

(5) Providing assistance on methods of disseminating information and education about the voluntary standard or its use.

(6) Performing a staff evaluation of a voluntary standard to determine its adequacy and efficacy in reducing the risks of injury that have been identified by the Commission as being associated with the use of the product.

(7) Encouraging state and local governments to reference or incorporate the provisions of a voluntary standard in their regulations or ordinances and to participate in government or industrial model code development activities, so as to develop uniformity and minimize conflicting State and local regulations.

(8) Monitoring the number and market share of products conforming to a voluntary safety standard.

(9) Providing for the involvement of agency personnel in voluntary standards activities as described in subpart B of this part.

(10) Providing administrative assistance, such as hosting meetings and secretarial assistance.

(11) Providing funding support for voluntary standards development, as permitted by the operating plan, performance budget, mid-year review, or other official Commission document.

(12) Taking other actions that the Commission believes appropriate in a particular situation.

(b) [Reserved]

§ 1031.8 Voluntary Standards Coordinator.

(a) The Executive Director shall appoint a Voluntary Standards Coordinator to coordinate agency participation in voluntary standards bodies so that:

(1) The most effective use is made of agency personnel and resources, and

(2) The views expressed by such personnel are in the public interest and, at a minimum, do not conflict with the interests and established views of the agency.

(b) The Voluntary Standards Coordinator is responsible for managing the Commission's voluntary standards program, as well as preparing and submitting to the Commission a semiannual summary of staff's voluntary standards activities. The summary shall set forth, among other things, the goals of each voluntary standard under development, the extent of CPSC staff activity, the current status of standards development and implementation, and, if any, recommendations for additional Commission action. The Voluntary Standards Coordinator shall also compile information on the Commission's voluntary standards activities for the Commission's annual report.

Subpart B—Employee Involvement

§ 1031.9 Purpose and scope.

(a) This subpart sets forth the Consumer Product Safety Commission's criteria and requirements governing membership and involvement by Commission officials and employees in the activities of voluntary standards development bodies.

(b) The Commission realizes there are advantages and benefits afforded by greater involvement of Commission personnel in the standards activities of domestic and international voluntary standards organizations. However, such involvement might present an appearance or possibility of the Commission giving preferential treatment to an organization or group or of the Commission losing its independence or impartiality. Also, such involvement may present real or apparent conflict of interest situations.

(c) The purpose of this subpart is to further the objectives and programs of the Commission and to do so in a manner that ensures that such involvement:

(1) Is consistent with the intent of the Consumer Product Safety Act and the other acts administered by the Commission;

(2) Is not contrary to the public interest;

(3) Presents no real or apparent conflict of interest, and does not result in or create the appearance of the Commission giving preferential treatment to an organization or group or the Commission compromising its independence or impartiality; and

(4) Takes into account Commission resources and priorities.

(d) Commission employees must obtain approval from their supervisor and the Office of the Executive Director to be involved in voluntary standards activities. They must regularly report to the Voluntary Standards Coordinator regarding their involvement in standards activities, and provide copies of all official correspondence and other communications between the CPSC and the standards developing entities.

(e) All Commission employees involved in voluntary standards activities are subject to any restrictions for avoiding conflicts of interest and for avoiding situations that would present an appearance of bias.

§ 1031.10 Definitions.

For purposes of describing the level of involvement in voluntary standards activities for which Commission employees may be authorized, the following definitions apply:

(a) *Membership*. Membership is the status of an employee who joins a voluntary standards development or advisory organization or subgroup and is listed as a member. It includes all oral and written communications which are incidental to such membership.

(b) *Employee involvement*. Employee involvement may include the active, ongoing involvement of an official or employee in the development of a new or revised voluntary standard pertaining to a particular consumer product or to a group of products that is the subject of a Commission voluntary standards project. These projects should be those that are approved by the Commission, either by virtue of the agency's annual budget or operating plan, or by other specific agency authorization or decision, and are in accord with subpart A. Employee involvement may include regularly attending meetings of a standards development committee or group, taking an active part in discussions and technical debates, expressing opinions and expending other resources in support of a voluntary standard development activity. It includes all oral and written communications which are part of the process. Employee involvement may also involve maintaining an awareness related to general voluntary standards projects set forth in the agency's annual budget or operating plan or otherwise approved by the agency.

(c) *Observation*. Observation is the attendance by an official or employee at a meeting of a voluntary standards development group for the purpose of observing and gathering information.

§ 1031.11 Procedural safeguards.

(a) Subject to the provisions of this subpart and budgetary and time constraints, Commission employees may be involved in voluntary standards activities that will further the objectives and programs of the Commission, are consistent with ongoing and anticipated Commission regulatory programs as set forth in the agency's operating plan, and are in accord with the Commission's policy statement on involvement in voluntary standards activities set forth in subpart A of this part.

(b) Commission employees who are involved in the development of a voluntary standard and who later participate in an official evaluation of that standard for the Commission shall describe in any information, oral or written, presented to the Commission, the extent of their involvement in the development of the standard. Any evaluation or recommendation for Commission actions by such employee shall strive to be as objective as possible and be reviewed by higher-level Commission officials or employees prior to submission to the Commission.

(c) Involvement of a Commission official or employee in a voluntary standards committee shall be predicated on an understanding by the voluntary standards group that such involvement by Commission officials and employees is on a non-voting basis.

(d) In no case shall Commission employees or officials vote or otherwise formally indicate approval or disapproval of a voluntary standard during the course of a voluntary standard development process.

(e) Commission employees and officials who are involved in the development of voluntary standards may not accept voluntary standards committee leadership positions, e.g., committee chairman or secretary. Subject to prior approval by the Executive Director, the Voluntary Standards Coordinator may accept leadership positions with the governing bodies of standards making entities.

(f) Attendance of Commission personnel at voluntary standards meetings shall be noted in the public calendar and meeting summaries shall be submitted to the Office of the Secretary as required by the Commission's meetings policy, 16 CFR part 1012.

§ 1031.12 Membership criteria.

(a) The Commissioners, their special assistants, and Commission officials and employees holding the positions listed below, may not become members of a voluntary standards group because they either have the responsibility for making final decisions, or advise those who make final decisions, on whether to rely on a voluntary standard, promulgate a consumer product safety standard, or to take other action to prevent or reduce an unreasonable risk of injury associated with a product.

(1) The Commissioners;

(2) The Commissioners' Special Assistants;

(3) The General Counsel and General Counsel Staff;

(4) The Executive Director, the Deputy Executive Director, and Special Assistants to the Executive Director;

(5) The Associate Executive Directors and Office Directors;

(6) The Assistant Executive Director of the Office of Hazard Identification and Reduction, the Deputy Assistant Executive Director of the Office of Hazard Identification and Reduction and any Special Assistants to the Assistant Executive Director of that office.

(b) All other officials and employees not covered under § 1031.12(a) may be advisory, non-voting members of voluntary standards development and advisory groups with the advance approval of the Executive Director. In particular, the Commission's Voluntary Standards Coordinator may accept such membership.

(c) Commission employees or officials who have the approval of the Executive Director to accept membership in a voluntary standards organization or group pursuant to paragraph (b) of this section shall apprise the General Counsel and the Voluntary Standards Coordinator prior to their acceptance.

(d) Commission officials or employees who desire to become a member of a voluntary standards body or group in their individual capacity must obtain prior approval of the Commission's Ethics Counselor for an outside activity pursuant to the Commission's Employee Standards of Conduct, 16 CFR part 1030.

§ 1031.13 Criteria for employee involvement.

(a) Commission officials, other than those positions listed in § 1031.12(a), may be involved in the development of voluntary safety standards for consumer products, but only in their official capacity as employees of the Commission and if permitted to do so by their supervisor and any other person designated by agency management procedures. Such involvement shall be in accordance with Commission procedures.

(b) Employees in positions listed in § 1031.12(a)(4), (5), and (6) may be involved, on a case-by-case basis, in the development of a voluntary standard provided that they have the specific advance approval of the Commission.

(c) Except in extraordinary circumstances and when approved in advance by the Executive Director in accordance with the provisions of the Commission's meetings policy, 16 CFR part 1012, Commission personnel shall not become involved in meetings concerning the development of voluntary standards that are not open to the public for attendance and observation. Attendance of Commission personnel at a voluntary standard meeting shall be noted in the public calendar and meeting logs filed with the Office of the Secretary in accordance with the Commission's meetings policy.

(d) Generally, Commission employees may become involved in the development of voluntary standards only if they are made available for comment by all interested parties prior to their use or adoption.

(e) Involvement by Commission officials and employees in voluntary standards bodies or standards-developing groups does not, of itself, connote Commission agreement with, or endorsement of, decisions reached, approved or published by such bodies or groups.

§ 1031.14 Observation criteria.

A Commission official or employee may, on occasion, attend voluntary standards meetings for the sole purpose of observation, with the advance approval of his or her supervisor and any other person designated by agency management procedures. Commission officials and employees shall notify the Voluntary Standard Coordinator, for information purposes, prior to observing a voluntary standards meeting.

§ 1031.15 Communication criteria.

(a) Commission officials and employees, who are not in the positions listed in § 1031.12(a), or who are not already authorized to communicate with a voluntary standards group or representative incidental to their approved membership in a voluntary standard organization or group or as part of a voluntary standard, may:

(1) Communicate, within the scope of their duties, with a voluntary standard group, representative, or other committee member, on voluntary standards matters which are substantive in nature, i.e., matters that pertain to the formulation of the technical aspects of a specific voluntary standard or the course of conduct for developing the standard, only with the specific advance approval from the person or persons to whom they apply to obtain approval for involvement pursuant to § 1031.13. The approval may indicate the duration of the approval and any other conditions.

(2) Communicate, within the scope of their duties, with a voluntary standard group, representative, or other committee member, concerning voluntary standards activities which are not substantive in nature.

(b) Commission employees may communicate with voluntary standards organizations only in accordance with Commission procedures.

(c) Commissioners can engage in substantive and non-substantive written communications with voluntary standards bodies or representatives, provided a disclaimer in such communications indicates that any substantive views expressed are only their individual views and are not necessarily those of the Commission. Where a previous official Commission vote has taken place, that vote should also be noted in any such communication. Copies of such communications shall thereafter be provided to the other Commissioners, the Office of the Secretary, and the Voluntary Standards Coordinator.

(d) The Voluntary Standards Coordinator shall be furnished a copy of each written communication of a substantive nature and a report of each oral communication of a substantive nature between a Commission official or employee and a voluntary standards organization or representative which pertains to a voluntary standards activity. The information shall be provided to the Voluntary Standards Coordinator as soon as practicable after the communication has taken place.

Subpart C—Public Participation and Comment

§ 1031.16 Purpose and scope.

(a) This subpart sets forth the Consumer Product Safety Commission's criteria and requirements governing public review and comment on staff involvement in the activities of voluntary standards development bodies.

(b) The Commission realizes there are advantages and benefits afforded by greater public awareness of staff involvement in standards development activities. Furthermore, the Commission recognizes public comment and input as an important part of the voluntary standards development process.

(c) The purpose of this subpart is to further the objectives and programs of the Commission and to do so in a manner that ensures openness and transparency.

§ 1031.17 Background.

(a) In a FEDERAL REGISTER Notice (Vol. 69, No. 200) dated October 18, 2004, the CPSC announced that it was launching a pilot program to open CPSC staff activities for public review and comment. The pilot program covered information on CPSC staff participation with respect to a cross-section of voluntary standards, including advance notice of proposed staff positions on issues to be considered by voluntary standards organizations. The program was based on the premise that increased public awareness and participation would enhance the quality and conclusions of the proposed recommendations made by CPSC staff.

(b) The pilot program ended on April 18, 2005, after a 6-month period. CPSC invited general comments on whether to continue the programs beyond the pilot period and solicited suggestions for improving the program.

(c) On July 28, 2005, the CPSC staff submitted to the Commission an assessment of the pilot program's results, including data that indicated the voluntary standards site ranked among the top 20 directories visited on the CPSC Web site. Further, the report included the staff's recommendation that the voluntary standards Web site be expanded to include information on all standards activities.

(d) On August 4, 2005, in accordance with the staff's recommendation, the Commission voted unanimously to continue the voluntary standards program and expand it to include all voluntary standards activities.

§ 1031.18 Method of review and comment.

(a) Each of the voluntary standards activities in which Commission staff is involved shall have a unique Web link on the Commission Web site with relevant information regarding CPSC activity, including:

(1) The name(s) of CPSC staff working on the activity; and

(2) The e-mail and mailing addresses of the CPSC Office of the Secretary, to which any interested party may communicate their particular interest.

(b) E-mail and written comments on voluntary standards from the public to the CPSC shall be managed by the Office of the Secretary. Such communication shall be forwarded to appropriate staff for consideration and/or response.

(c) On the voluntary standards Web site, consumers shall have the opportunity to register for periodic e-mail notices from the Commission with respect to their standard of interest. Such notices shall be issued by the CPSC each time a voluntary standard site has been updated and no less than once every calendar year.

PART 1033—DISPLAY OF CONTROL NUMBERS FOR COLLECTION OF INFORMATION REQUIREMENTS UNDER THE PAPERWORK REDUCTION ACT

AUTHORITY: 44 U.S.C. 3506(c)(1); 5 U.S.C. 553.

§ 1033.1 Purpose.

The purpose of this part 1033 is to display all control numbers assigned by the Office of Management and Budget (OMB) to collection of information requirements contained in rules enforced by the Consumer Product Safety Commission. Display of OMB control numbers is required by provisions of the Paperwork Reduction Act at 44 U.S.C.

3507(f) and by regulations issued by OMB to implement that act at 5 CFR 1320.7(f)(2), 1320.12(d), 1320.13(j), and 1320.14(e).

[48 FR 57478, Dec. 30, 1983]

§ 1033.2 Display of control numbers.

The following rules enforced by the Consumer Product Safety Commission containing collections of information are listed with the control numbers assigned by the Office of Management and Budget:

Part or section of title 16 Code of Federal Regulations	Currently assigned OMB control No.
Part 1019	3041–0003
Part 1204	3041–0006
Part 1509	3041–0012
Part 1508	3041–0013
Part 1632	3041–0014
Part 1210	3041–0016
Part 1630, 1631	3041–0017
Sections 1500.18(a)(6), 1500.86(a)(4)	3041–0019
Part 1209	3041–0022
Parts 1610, 1611	3041–0024
Parts 1615, 1616	3041–0027
Part 1505	3041–0035
Part 1406	3041–0040
Part 1205	3041–0091
Part 1211	3041–0125

(44 U.S.C. 3506(c)(1); 5 U.S.C. 553)

[62 FR 42397, Aug. 7, 1997]

PART 1034—ENFORCEMENT OF NONDISCRIMINATION ON THE BASIS OF HANDICAP IN PROGRAMS OR ACTIVITIES CONDUCTED BY THE CONSUMER PRODUCT SAFETY COMMISSION

AUTHORITY: 29 U.S.C. 794.

SOURCE: 51 FR 4575, 4579, Feb. 5, 1986; 52 FR 405, Jan. 6, 1987, unless otherwise noted.

§ 1034.101 Purpose.

This part effectuates section 119 of the Rehabilitation, Comprehensive Services, and Developmental Disabilities Amendments of 1978, which amended section 504 of the Rehabilitation Act of 1973 to prohibit discrimination on the basis of handicap in programs or activities conducted by Executive agencies or the United States Postal Service.

§ 1034.102 Application.

This part applies to all programs or activities conducted by the agency.

§ 1034.103 Definitions.

For purposes of this part, the term—

Assistant Attorney General means the Assistant Attorney General, Civil Rights Division, United States Department of Justice.

Auxiliary aids means services or devices that enable persons with impaired sensory, manual, or speaking skills to have an equal opportunity to participate in, and enjoy the benefits of, programs or activities conducted by the agency. For example, auxiliary aids useful for persons with impaired vision include readers, Brailled materials, audio recordings, telecommunications devices and other similar services and devices. Auxiliary aids useful for persons with impaired hearing include telephone handset amplifiers, telephones compatible with hearing aids, telecommunication devices for deaf persons (TDD's), interpreters, notetakers, written materials, and other similar services and devices.

Complete complaint means a written statement that contains the complainant's name and address and describes the agency's alleged discriminatory action in sufficient detail to inform the agency of the nature and date of the alleged violation of section 504. It shall be signed by the complainant or by someone authorized to do so on his or her behalf. Complaints filed on behalf of classes or third parties shall describe or identify (by name, if possible) the alleged victims of discrimination.

Facility means all or any portion of buildings, structures, equipment, roads, walks, parking lots, rolling stock or other conveyances, or other real or personal property.

Handicapped person means any person who has a physical or mental impairment that substantially limits one or more major life activities, has a record of such an impairment, or is regarded as having such an impairment.

As used in this definition, the phrase:

(1) *Physical or mental impairment* includes—

(i) Any physiological disorder or condition, cosmetic disfigurement, or anatomical loss affecting one of more of the following body systems: Neurological; musculoskeletal; special sense organs; respiratory, including speech organs; cardiovascular; reproductive; digestive; genitourinary; hemic and lymphatic; skin; and endocrine; or

(ii) Any mental or psychological disorder, such as mental retardation, organic brain syndrome, emotional or mental illness, and specific learning disabilities. The term *physical or mental impairment* includes, but is not limited to, such diseases and conditions as orthopedic, visual, speech, and hearing impairments, cerebral palsy, epilepsy, muscular dystrophy, multiple sclerosis, cancer, heart disease, diabetes, mental retardation, emotional illness, and drug addition and alcholism.

(2) *Major life activities* includes functions such as caring for one's self, performing manual tasks, walking, seeing, hearing, speaking, breathing, learning, and working.

(3) *Has a record of such an impairment* means has a history of, or has been misclassified as having, a mental or physical impairment that substantially limits one or more major life activities.

(4) *Is regarded as having an impairment* means—

(i) Has a physical or mental impairment that does not substantially limit major life activities but is treated by the agency as constituting such a limitation;

(ii) Has a physical or mental impairment that substantially limits major life activities only as a result of the attitudes of others toward such impairment; or

(iii) Has none of the impairments defined in subparagraph (1) of this definition but is treated by the agency as having such an impairment.

Qualified handicapped person means—

(1) With respect to any agency program or activity under which a person is required to perform services or to achieve a level of accomplishment, a handicapped person who meets the essential eligibility requirements and who can achieve the purpose of the program or activity without modifications in the program or activity that the agency can demonstrate would result in a fundamental alteration in its nature; or

(2) With respect to any other program or activity, a handicapped person who meets the essential eligibility requirements for participation in, or receipt of benefits from, that program or activity.

(3) *Qualified handicapped person* is defined for purposes of employment in 29 CFR 1613.702(f), which is made applicable to this part by § 1034.140.

Section 504 means section 504 of the Rehabilitation Act of 1973 (Pub. L. 93–112, 87 Stat. 394 (29 U.S.C. 794)), as amended by the Rehabilitation Act Amendments of 1974 (Pub. L. 93–516, 88 Stat. 1617), and the Rehabilitation, Comprehensive Services, and Developmental Disabilities Amendments of 1978 (Pub. L. 95–602, 92 Stat. 2955). As used in this part, section 504 applies only to programs or activities conducted by Executive agencies and not to federally assisted programs.

[51 FR 4575, 4579, Feb. 5, 1986; 51 FR 7543, Mar. 5, 1986]

§§ 1034.104–1034.109 [Reserved]

§ 1034.110 Self-evaluation.

(a) The agency shall, by April 9, 1987, evaluate its current policies and practices, and the effects thereof, that do not or may not meet the requirements of this part, and, to the extent modification of any such policies and practices is required, the agency shall proceed to make the necessary modifications.

(b) The agency shall provide an opportunity to interested persons, including handicapped persons or organizations representing handicapped persons, to participate in the self-evaluation process by submitting comments (both oral and written).

(c) The agency shall, until three years following the completion of the self-evaluation, maintain on file and make available for public inspections:

(1) A description of areas examined and any problems identified, and

(2) A description of any modifications made.

§ 1034.111 Notice.

The agency shall make available to employees, applicants, participants, beneficiaries, and other interested persons such information regarding the provisions of this part and its applicability to the programs or activities conducted by the agency, and make such information available to them in such manner as the head of the agency finds necessary to apprise such persons of the protections against discrimination assured them by section 504 and this regulation.

§§ 1034.112–1034.129 [Reserved]

§ 1034.130 General prohibitions against discrimination.

(a) No qualified handicapped person shall, on the basis of handicap, be excluded from participation in, be denied the benefits of, or otherwise be subjected to discrimination under any program or activity conducted by the agency.

(b)(1) The agency, in providing any aid, benefit, or service, may not, directly or through contractual, licensing, or other arrangements, on the basis of handicap—

(i) Deny a qualified handicapped person the opportunity to participate in or benefit from the aid, benefit, or service;

(ii) Afford a qualified handicapped person an opportunity to participate in or benefit from the aid, benefit, or service that is not equal to that afforded others;

(iii) Provide a qualified handicapped person with an aid, benefit, or service that is not as effective in affording equal opportunity to obtain the same result, to gain the same benefit, or to reach the same level of achievement as that provided to others;

(iv) Provide different or separate aid, benefits, or services to handicapped persons or to any class of handicapped persons than is provided to others unless such action is necessary to provide qualified handicapped persons with aid, benefits, or services that are as effective as those provided to others;

(v) Deny a qualified handicapped person the opportunity to participate as a member of planning or advisory boards; or

(vi) Otherwise limit a qualified handicapped person in the enjoyment of any right, privilege, advantage, or opportunity enjoyed by others receiving the aid, benefit, or service.

(2) The agency may not deny a qualified handicapped person the opportunity to participate in programs or activities that are not separate or different, despite the existence of permissibly separate or different programs or activities.

(3) The agency may not, directly or through contractual or other arrangements, utilize criteria or methods of administration the purpose or effect of which would—

(i) Subject qualified handicapped persons to discrimination on the basis of handicap; or

(ii) Defeat or substantially impair accomplishment of the objectives of a program or activity with respect to handicapped persons.

(4) The agency may not, in determining the site or location of a facility, make selections the purpose or effect of which would—

(i) Exclude handicapped persons from, deny them the benefits of, or otherwise subject them to discrimination under any program or activity conducted by the agency; or

(ii) Defeat or substantially impair the accomplishment of the objectives of a program or activity with respect to handicapped persons.

(5) The agency, in the selection of procurement contractors, may not use criteria that subject qualified handicapped persons to discrimination on the basis of handicap.

(c) The exclusion of nonhandicapped persons from the benefits of a program limited by Federal statute or Executive order to handicapped persons or the exclusion of a specific class of handicapped persons from a program limited by Federal statute or Executive order to a different class of handicapped persons is not prohibited by this part.

(d) The agency shall administer programs and activities in the most integrated setting appropriate to the needs of qualified handicapped persons.

§§ 1034.131–1034.139 [Reserved]

§ 1034.140 Employment.

No qualified handicapped person shall, on the basis of handicap, be subjected to discrimination in employment under any program or activity conducted by the agency. The definitions, requirements, and procedures of section 501 of the Rehabilitation Act of 1973 (29 U.S.C. 791), as established by the Equal Employment Opportunity Commission in 29 CFR part 1613, shall apply to employment in federally conducted programs or activities.

§§ 1034.141–1034.148 [Reserved]

§ 1034.149 Program accessibility: Discrimination prohibited.

Except as otherwise provided in § 1034.150, no qualified handicapped person shall, because the agency's facilities are inaccessible to or unusable by handicapped persons, be denied the benefits of, be excluded from participation in, or otherwise be subjected to discrimination under any program or activity conducted by the agency.

§ 1034.150 Program accessibility: Existing facilities.

(a) *General.* The agency shall operate each program or activity so that the program or activity, when viewed in its entirety, is readily accessible to and usable by handicapped persons. This paragraph does not—

(1) Necessarily require the agency to make each of its existing facilities accessible to and usable by handicapped persons; or

(2) Require the agency to take any action that it can demonstrate would result in a fundamental alteration in the nature of a program or activity or in undue financial and administrative burdens. In those circumstances where agency personnel believe that the proposed action would fundamentally alter the program or activity or would result in undue financial and administrative burdens, the agency has the burden of proving that compliance with § 1034.150(a) would result in such alteration or burdens. The decision that compliance would result in such alteration or burdens must be made by the agency head or his or her designee after considering all agency resources available for use in the funding and operation of the conducted program or activity, and must be accompanied by a written statement of the reasons for reaching that conclusion. If an action would result in such an alteration or such burdens, the agency shall take any other action that would not result in such an alteration or such burdens but would nevertheless ensure that handicapped persons receive the benefits and services of the program or activity.

(b) *Methods.* The agency may comply with the requirements of this section through such means as redesign of equipment, reassignment of services to accessible buildings, assignment of aides to beneficiaries, home visits, delivery of services at alternate accessible sites, alteration of existing facilities and construction of new facilities, use of accessible rolling stock, or any other methods that result in making its programs or activities readily accessible to and usable by handicapped persons. The agency is not required to make structural changes in existing facilities where other methods are effective in achieving compliance with this section. The agency, in making alterations to existing buildings, shall meet accessibility requirements to the extent compelled by the Architectural Barriers Act of 1968, as amended (42 U.S.C. 4151–4157), and any regulations implementing it. In choosing among available methods for meeting the requirements of this section, the agency shall give priority to those methods that offer programs and activities to qualified handicapped persons in the most integrated setting appropriate.

(c) *Time period for compliance.* The agency shall comply with the obligations established under this section by June 6, 1986, except that where structural changes in facilities are undertaken, such changes shall be made by April 7, 1989, but in any event as expeditiously as possible.

(d) *Transition plan.* In the event that structural changes to facilities will be undertaken to achieve program accessibility, the agency shall develop, by October 7, 1986, a transition plan setting forth the steps necessary to complete such changes. The agency shall provide an opportunity to interested persons, including handicapped persons or organizations representing handicapped persons, to participate in the development of the transition plan by submitting comments (both oral and written). A copy of the transition plan shall be made available for public inspection. The plan shall, at a minimum—

(1) Identify physical obstacles in the agency's facilities that limit the accessibility of its programs or activities to handicapped persons;

(2) Describe in detail the methods that will be used to make the facilities accessible;

(3) Specify the schedule for taking the steps necessary to achieve compliance with this section and, if the time period of the transition plan is longer than one year, identify steps that will be taken during each year of the transition period; and

(4) Indicate the official responsible for implementation of the plan.

[51 FR 4575, 4579, Feb. 5, 1986; 51 FR 7543, Mar. 5, 1986]

§ 1034.151 Program accessibility: New construction and alterations.

Each building or part of a building that is constructed or altered by, on behalf of, or for the use of the agency shall be designed, constructed, or altered so as to be readily accessible to and usable by handicapped persons. The definitions, requirements, and standards of the Architectural Barriers Act (42 U.S.C. 4151–4157), as established in 41 CFR 101–19.600 to 101–19.607, apply to buildings covered by this section.

§§ 1034.152–1034.159 [Reserved]

§ 1034.160 Communications.

(a) The agency shall take appropriate steps to ensure effective communication with applicants, participants, personnel of other Federal entities, and members of the public.

(1) The agency shall furnish appropriate auxiliary aids where necessary to afford a handicapped person an equal opportunity to participate in, and enjoy the benefits of, a program or activity conducted by the agency.

(i) In determining what type of auxiliary aid is necessary, the agency shall give primary consideration to the requests of the handicapped person.

(ii) The agency need not provide individually prescribed devices, readers for personal use or study, or other devices of a personal nature.

(2) Where the agency communicates with applicants and beneficiaries by telephone, telecommunication devices for deaf persons (TDD's) or equally effective telecommunication systems shall be used.

(b) The agency shall ensure that interested persons, including persons with impaired vision or hearing, can obtain information as to the existence and location of accessible services, activities, and facilities.

(c) The agency shall provide signage at a primary entrance to each of its inaccessible facilities, directing users to a location at which they can obtain information about accessible facilities. The international symbol for accessibility shall be used at each primary entrance of an accessible facility.

(d) This section does not require the agency to take any action that it can demonstrate would result in a fundamental alteration in the nature of a program or activity or in undue financial and administrative burdens. In those circumstances where agency personnel believe that the proposed action would fundamentally alter the program or activity or would result in undue financial and administrative burdens, the agency has the burden of proving that compliance with § 1034.160 would result in such alteration or burdens. The decision that compliance would result in such alteration or burdens must be made by the agency head or his or her designee after considering all agency resources available for use in the funding and operation of the conducted program or activity, and must be accompanied by a written statement of the reasons for reaching that conclusion. If an action required to comply with this section would result in such an alteration or such burdens, the agency shall take any other action that would not result in such an alteration or such burdens but would nevertheless ensure that, to the maximum extent possible, handicapped persons receive the benefits and services of the program or activity.

§§ 1034.161–1034.169 [Reserved]

§ 1034.170 Compliance procedures.

(a) Except as provided in paragraph (b) of this section, this section applies to all allegations of discrimination on the basis of handicap in programs or activities conducted by the agency.

(b) The agency shall process complaints alleging violations of section 504 with respect to employment according to the procedures established by the Equal Employment Opportunity Commission in 29 CFR part 1613 pursuant to section 501 of the Rehabilitation Act of 1973 (29 U.S.C. 791).

(c) The Office of Equal Employment Opportunity and Minority Enterprise shall be responsible for coordinating implementation of this section. Complaints may be sent to the Director, Office of Equal Employment Opportunity and Minority Enterprise, Consumer Product Safety Commission, Washington, D.C. 20207.

(d) The agency shall accept and investigate all complete complaints for which it has jurisdiction. All complete complaints must be filed within 180 days of the alleged act of discrimination. The agency may extend this time period for good cause.

(e) If the agency receives a complaint over which it does not have jurisdiction, it shall promptly notify the complainant and shall make reasonable efforts to refer the complaint to the appropriate government entity.

(f) The agency shall notify the Architectural and Transportation Barriers Compliance Board upon receipt of any complaint alleging that a building or facility that is subject to the Architectural Barriers Act of 1968, as amended (42 U.S.C. 4151–4157), or section 502 of the Rehabilitation Act of 1973, as amended (29 U.S.C. 792), is not readily accessible to and usable by handicapped persons.

(g) Within 180 days of the receipt of a complete complaint for which it has jurisdiction, the agency shall notify the complainant of the results of the investigation in a letter containing—

(1) Findings of fact and conclusions of law;

(2) A description of a remedy for each violation found; and

(3) A notice of the right to appeal.

(h) Appeals of the findings of fact and conclusions of law or remedies must be filed by the complainant within 90 days of receipt from the agency of the letter required by § 1034.170(g). The agency may extend this time for good cause.

(i) Timely appeals shall be accepted and processed by the head of the agency.

(j) The head of the agency shall notify the complainant of the results of the appeal within 60 days of the receipt of the request. If the head of the agency determines that additional information is needed from the complainant, he or she shall have 60 days from the date of receipt of the additional information to make his or her determination on the appeal.

(k) The time limits cited in paragraphs (g) and (j) of this section may be extended with the permission of the Assistant Attorney General.

(l) The agency may delegate its authority for conducting complaint investigations to other Federal agencies, except that the authority for making the final determination may not be delegated to another agency.

[51 FR 4575, 4579, Feb. 5, 1986, as amended at 51 FR 4575, Feb. 5, 1986]

§§ 1034.171–1034.999 [Reserved]

PART 1051—PROCEDURE FOR PETITIONING FOR RULEMAKING

AUTHORITY: 5 U.S.C. 553(e), 5 U.S.C. 555(e).

SOURCE: 48 FR 57123, Dec. 28, 1983, unless otherwise noted.

§ 1051.1 Scope.

(a) This part establishes procedures for the submission and disposition of petitions for the issuance, amendment or revocation of rules under the Consumer Product Safety Act (CPSA) (15 U.S.C. 2051 *et seq.*) or other statutes administered by the Consumer Product Safety Commission.

(b) Persons filing petitions for rulemaking shall follow as closely as possible the requirements and are encouraged to follow as closely as possible the recommendations for filing petitions under § 1051.5.

(c) Petitions regarding products regulated under the Federal Hazardous Substances Act (FHSA) (15 U.S.C. 1261 *et seq.*) are governed by existing Commission procedures at 16 CFR 1500.82. Petitions regarding the exemption of products regulated under the Poison Prevention Packaging Act of 1970 (PPPA) (15 U.S.C. 1471 *et seq.*) are governed by existing Commission procedures at 16 CFR part 1702. In addition, however, persons filing such petitions shall follow the requirements and are encouraged to follow the recommendations for filing petitions as set forth in § 1051.5.

[48 FR 57123, Dec. 28, 1983 as amended at 64 FR 48704, Sept. 8, 1999]

§ 1051.2 General.

(a) Any person may file with the Commission a petition requesting the Commission to begin a proceeding to issue, amend or revoke a regulation under any of the statutes it administers.

(b) A petition which addresses a risk of injury associated with a product which could be eliminated or reduced to a sufficient extent by action taken under the Federal Hazardous Substances Act, the Poison Prevention Packaging Act of 1970, or the Flammable Fabrics Act may be considered by the Commission under those Acts. However, if the Commission finds by rule, in accordance with section 30(d) of the CPSA, as amended by Public Law 94–284, that it is in the public interest to regulate such risk of injury under the CPSA, it may do so. Upon determination by the Office of the General Counsel that a petition should be considered under one of these acts rather than the CPSA, the Office of the Secretary shall docket and process the petition under the appropriate act and inform the petitioner of this determination. Such docketing, however, shall not preclude the Commission from proceeding to regulate the product under the CPSA after making the necessary findings.

§ 1051.3 Place of filing.

A petition should be mailed to: Office of the Secretary, Consumer Product Safety Commission, Washington, DC 20207. Persons wishing to file a petition in person may do so in the Office of the Secretary, at 4330 East West Highway, Bethesda, Maryland.

[48 FR 57123, Dec. 28, 1983, as amended at 62 FR 46667, Sept. 4, 1997]

§ 1051.4 Time of filing.

For purposes of computing time periods under this part, a petition shall be considered filed when time-date stamped by the Office of the Secretary. A document is time-date stamped when it is received in the Office of the Secretary.

§ 1051.5 Requirements and recommendations for petitions.

(a) *Requirements.* To be considered a petition under this part, any request to issue, amend or revoke a rule shall meet the requirements of this paragraph (a). A petition shall:

(1) Be written in the English language;

(2) Contain the name and address of the petitioner;

(3) Indicate the product (or products) regulated under the Consumer Product

Safety Act or other statute the Commission administers for which a rule is sought or for which there is an existing rule sought to be modified or revoked. (If the petition regards a procedural or other rule not involving a specific product, the type of rule involved must be indicated.)

(4) Set forth facts which establish the claim that the issuance, amendment, or revocation of the rule is necessary (for example, such facts may include personal experience; medical, engineering or injury data; or a research study); and

(5) Contain an explicit request to initiate Commission rulemaking and set forth a brief description of the substance of the proposed rule or amendment or revocation thereof which it is claimed should be issued by the Commission. (A general request for regulatory action which does not reasonably specify the type of action requested shall not be sufficient for purposes of this subsection.)

(b) *Recommendations.* The Commission encourages the submission of as much information as possible related to the petition. Thus, to assist the Commission in its evaluation of a petition, to the extent the information is known and available to the petitioner, the petitioner is encouraged to supply the following information or any other information relating to the petition. The petition will be considered by the Commission even if the petitioner is unable to supply the information recommended in this paragraph (b). However, as applicable, and to the extent possible, the petitioner is encouraged to:

(1) Describe the specific risk(s) of injury to which the petition is addressed, including the degree (severity) and the nature of the risk(s) of injury associated with the product and possible reasons for the existence of the risk of injury (for example, product defect, poor design, faulty workmanship, or intentional or unintentional misuse);

(2) State why a consumer product safety standard would not be feasible if the petition requests the issuance of a rule declaring the product to be a banned hazardous product; and

(3) Supply or reference any known documentation, engineering studies, technical studies, reports of injuries, medical findings, legal analyses, economic analyses and environmental impact analyses relating to the petition.

(c) *Procedural recommendations.* The following are procedural recommendations to help the Commission in its consideration of petitions. The Commission requests, but does not require, that a petition filed under this part:

(1) Be typewritten,

(2) Include the word "petition" in a heading preceding the text,

(3) Specify what section of the statute administered by the Commission authorizes the requested rulemaking,

(4) Include the telephone number of the petitioner, and

(5) Be accompanied by at least five (5) copies of the petition.

§ 1051.6 Documents not considered petitions.

(a) A document filed with the Commission which addresses a topic or involves a product outside the jurisdiction of the Commission will not be considered to be a petition. After consultation with the Office of the General Counsel, the Office of the Secretary, if appropriate, will forward to the appropriate agency documents which address products or topics within the jurisdiction of other agencies. The Office of the Secretary shall notify the sender of the document that it has been forwarded to the appropriate agency.

(b) Any other documents filed with the Office of the Secretary that are determined by the Office of the General Counsel not to be petitions shall be evaluated for possible staff action. The Office of the General Counsel shall notify the writer of the manner in which the Commission staff is treating the document. If the writer has indicated an intention to petition the Commission, the Office of the General Counsel shall inform the writer of the procedure to be followed for petitioning.

§ 1051.7 Statement in support of or in opposition to petitions; Duty of petitioners to remain apprised of developments regarding petitions.

(a) Any person may file a statement with the Office of the Secretary in support of or in opposition to a petition prior to Commission action on the petition. Persons submitting statements in opposition to a petition are encouraged to provide copies of such statements to the petitioner.

(b) It is the duty of the petitioner, or any person submitting a statement in support of or in opposition to a petition, to keep himself or herself apprised of developments regarding the petition. Information regarding the status of petitions is available from the Office of the Secretary of the Commission.

(c) The Office of the Secretary shall send to the petitioner a copy of the staff briefing package on his or her petition at the same time the package is transmitted to the Commissioners for decision.

§ 1051.8 Public hearings on petitions.

(a) The Commission may hold a public hearing or may conduct such investigation or proceeding, including a public meeting, as it deems appropriate to determine whether a petition should be granted.

(b) If the Commission decides that a public hearing on a petition, or any portion thereof, would contribute to its determination of whether to grant or deny the petition, it shall publish in the FEDERAL REGISTER a notice of a hearing on the petition and invite interested persons to submit their views through an oral or written presentation or both. The hearings shall be informal, nonadversary, legislative-type proceedings in accordance with 16 CFR part 1052.

§ 1051.9 Factors the Commission considers in granting or denying petitions.

(a) The major factors the Commission considers in deciding whether to grant or deny a petition regarding a product include the following items:

(1) Whether the product involved presents an unreasonable risk of injury.

(2) Whether a rule is reasonably necessary to eliminate or reduce the risk of injury.

(3) Whether failure of the Commission to initiate the rulemaking proceeding requested would unreasonably expose the petitioner or other consumers to the risk of injury which the petitioner alleges is presented by the product.

(4) Whether, in the case of a petition to declare a consumer product a "banned hazardous product" under section 8 of the CPSA, the product is being or will be distributed in commerce and whether a feasible consumer product safety standard would adequately protect the public from the unreasonable risk of injury associated with such product.

(b) In considering these factors, the Commission will treat as an important component of each one the relative priority of the risk of injury associated with the product about which the petition has been filed and the Commission's resources available for rulemaking activities with respect to that risk of injury. The CPSC Policy on Establishing Priorities for Commission Action, 16 CFR 1009.8, sets forth the criteria upon which Commission priorities are based.

§ 1051.10 Granting petitions.

(a) The Commission shall either grant or deny a petition within a reasonable time after it is filed, taking into account the resources available for processing the petition. The Commission may also grant a petition in part or deny it in part. If the Commission grants a petition, it shall begin proceedings to issue, amend or revoke the rule under the appropriate provisions of the statutes under its administration. Beginning a proceeding means taking the first step in the rulemaking process (issuance of an advance notice of proposed rulemaking or a notice of proposed rulemaking, whichever is applicable).

(b) Granting a petition and beginning a proceeding does not necessarily mean that the Commission will issue, amend or revoke the rule as requested in the petition. The Commission must make a final decision as to the issuance, amendment, or revocation of a rule on the basis of all available relevant information developed in the course of the rulemaking proceeding. Should later information indicate that the action is unwarranted or not necessary, the Commission may terminate the proceeding.

§ 1051.11 Denial of petitions.

(a) If the Commission denies a petition it shall promptly notify the petitioner in writing of its reasons for such denial as required by the Administrative Procedure Act, 5 U.S.C. 555(e).

(b) If the Commission denies a petition, the petitioner (or another party) can refile the petition if the party can demonstrate that new or changed circumstances or additional information justify reconsideration by the Commission.

(c) A Commission denial of a petition shall not preclude the Commission from continuing to consider matters raised in the petition.

PART 1052—PROCEDURAL REGULATIONS FOR INFORMAL ORAL PRESENTATIONS IN PROCEEDINGS BEFORE THE CONSUMER PRODUCT SAFETY COMMISSION

AUTHORITY: 15 U.S.C. 1193(d), 15 U.S.C. 2058(d)(2), 15 U.S.C. 2076(a), and 5 U.S.C. 553(c).

SOURCE: 48 FR 57122, Dec. 28, 1983, unless otherwise noted.

§ 1052.1 Scope and purpose.

(a) Section 9(d)(2) of the Consumer Product Safety Act, 15 U.S.C. 2058(d)(2), and section 4(d) of the Flammable Fabrics Act, 15 U.S.C. 1193(d), provide that certain rules under those statutes shall be promulgated pursuant to section 4 of the Administrative Procedure Act, 5 U.S.C. 553, except that the Commission shall give interested persons an opportunity for the oral presentation of data, views or arguments in addition to the opportunity to make written submissions. Several rulemaking provisions of the statutes administered by the Commission are subject only to the rulemaking procedures of the Administrative Procedure Act. Section 4(c) of the Administrative Procedure Act provides that the opportunity for oral presentations may or may not be granted in rulemaking under that section. In addition, section 27(a) of the Consumer Product Safety Act, 15 U.S.C. 2076(a), authorizes informal proceedings that can be conducted in nonrulemaking investigatory situations.

(b) This part sets forth rules of procedure for the oral presentation of data, views or arguments in the informal rulemaking or investigatory situations described in subsection (a) of this section. In situations where the opportunity for an oral presentation is not required by statute, the Commission will determine whether to provide the opportunity on a case-by-case basis.

§ 1052.2 Notice of opportunity for oral presentation.

The Commission will publish in the FEDERAL REGISTER notice of opportunity for an oral presentation in each instance. The notice shall be sufficiently in advance of the oral presentation to allow interested persons to participate. If the oral presentation involves a proposed rule, the notice of opportunity may be in the notice proposing the rule or in a later, separate FEDERAL REGISTER notice.

§ 1052.3 Conduct of oral presentation.

(a) The purpose of the oral presentation is to afford interested persons an opportunity to participate in person in the Commission's rulemaking or other proceedings and to help inform the Commission of relevant data, views and arguments.

(b) The oral presentation, which shall be taped or transcribed, shall be an informal, non-adversarial legislative-type proceeding at which there will be no formal pleadings or adverse parties.

(c) The proceedings for the oral presentation shall be conducted impartially, thoroughly, and expeditiously to allow interested persons an opportunity for oral presentation of data, views or arguments.

§ 1052.4 Presiding officer; appointment, duties, powers.

(a) For oral presentations, the presiding officer shall either be the Chairman of the Commission or a presiding officer shall be appointed by the Chairman with the concurrence of the Commission.

(b) The presiding officer shall chair the proceedings, shall make appropriate provision for testimony, comments and questions, and shall be responsible for the orderly conduct of the proceedings. The presiding officer shall have all the powers necessary or appropriate to contribute to the equitable and efficient conduct of the oral proceedings including the following:

(1) The right to apportion the time of persons making presentations in an equitable manner in order to complete the presentations within the time period allotted for the proceedings.

(2) The right to terminate or shorten the presentation of any party when, in the view of the presiding officer, such presentation is repetitive or is not relevant to the purpose of the proceedings.

(3) The right to confine the presentations to the issues specified in the notice of oral proceeding or, where no issues are specified, to matters pertinent to the proposed rule or other proceeding.

(4) The right to require a single representative to present the views of two or more persons or groups who have the same or similar interests. The presiding officer shall have the authority to identify groups or persons with the same or similar interests in the proceedings.

(c) The presiding officer and Commission representatives shall have the right to question persons making an oral presentation as to their testimony and any other relevant matter.

PART 1061—APPLICATIONS FOR EXEMPTION FROM PREEMPTION

Sec.

AUTHORITY: 15 U.S.C. 2075; 15 U.S.C. 1261n; 15 U.S.C. 1203; 15 U.S.C. 1476.

SOURCE: 56 FR 3416, Jan. 30, 1991, unless otherwise noted.

§ 1061.1 Scope and purpose.

(a) This part applies to the submission and consideration of applications by State and local governments for exemption from preemption by statutes, standards, and regulations of the Consumer Product Safety Commission.

(b) This part implements section 26 of the Consumer Product Safety Act (CPSA) (15 U.S.C. 2075), section 18 of the Federal Hazardous Substances Act (FHSA) (15 U.S.C. 1261n), section 16 of the Flammable Fabrics Act (FFA) (15 U.S.C. 1203), and section 7 of the Poison Prevention Packaging Act (PPPA) (15 U.S.C. 1476), all as amended.

§ 1061.2 Definitions.

For the purposes of this part:

(a) *Commission* means the Consumer Product Safety Commission.

(b) *Commission's statutory preemption provisions* and *statutory preemption provisions* means section 26 of the CPSA (15 U.S.C. 2075), section 18 of the FHSA (15 U.S.C. 1261n), section 16 of the FFA (15 U.S.C. 1203) and section 7 of the PPPA (15 U.S.C. 1476).

(c) *Commission statute, standard, or regulation* means a statute, standard, regulation, or requirement that is designated as having a preemptive effect by the Commission's statutory preemption provisions.

(d) *State* means a State, the District of Columbia, the Commonwealth of Puerto Rico, the Virgin Islands, Guam, Wake Island, Midway Island, Kingman Reef, Johnston Island, the Canal Zone, American Samoa, or the Trust Territory of the Pacific Islands.

(e) *Local government* means any political subdivision of a State having the authority to establish or continue in effect any standard, regulation, or requirement that has the force of law and is applicable to a consumer product.

(f) *State or local requirement* means any statute, standard, regulation, ordinance, or other requirement that applies to a product regulated by the Commission, that is issued by a State or local government, and that is intended to have the force of law when in effect.

§ 1061.3 Statutory considerations.

(a) The Commission's statutory preemption provisions provide, generally, that whenever consumer products are subject to certain Commission statutes, standards, or regulations, a State or local requirement applicable to the same product is preempted, i.e., superseded and made unenforceable, if both are designed to protect against the same risk of injury or illness, unless the State or local requirement is identical to the Commission's statutory requirement, standard, or regulation. A State or local requirement is not preempted if the product it is applicable to is for the State or local government's own use and the requirement provides a higher degree of protection than the Commission's statutory requirement, standard, or regulation.

(b) The Commission's statutory preemption provisions provide, generally, that if a State or local government wants to enforce its own requirement that is preempted, the State or local government must seek an exemption from the Commission before any such enforcement. The Commission may, by regulation, exempt a State or local requirement from preemption if it finds that the State or local requirement affords a significantly higher degree of protection than the Commission's statute, standard, or regulation, and that it does not unduly burden interstate commerce. Such findings must be included in any exemption regulation.

§ 1061.4 Threshold requirements for applications for exemption.

(a) The Commission will consider an application for preemption on its merits, only if the application demonstrates all of the following:

(1) The State or local requirement has been enacted or issued in final form by an authorized official or instrumentality of the State or local government. For purposes of this section, a State or local requirement may be considered to have been enacted or issued in final form even though it is preempted by a Commission standard or regulation.

(2) The applicant is an official or instrumentality of a State or local government having authority to act for, or on behalf of, that government in applying for an exemption from preemption for the safety requirement referred to in the application.

(3) The State or local requirement is preempted under a Commission statutory preemption provision by a Commission statute, standard, or regulation. A State or local requirement is preempted if the following tests are met:

(i) There is a Commission statute, standard, or regulation in effect that is applicable to the product covered by the State or local requirement.

(ii) The Commission statute, standard, or regulation is designated as having a preemptive effect under a statutory preemption provision.

(iii) The State or local requirement is designed to protect against the same risk of injury or illness as that addressed by the Commission statute, standard, or regulation.

(iv) The State or local requirement is not identical to the Commission statute, standard, or regulation.

(b) State and local governments may contact the Commission's Office of the General Counsel to obtain informal advice on whether a State or local requirement meets the threshold requirements of paragraph (a) of this section.

§ 1061.5 Form of applications for exemption.

An application for exemption shall:

(a) Be written in the English language.

(b) Clearly indicate that it is an application for an exemption from preemption by a Commission statute, standard, or regulation.

(c) Identify the State or local requirement that is the subject of the application and give the date it was enacted or issued in final form.

(d) Identify the specific Commission statute, standard, or regulation that is believed to preempt the State or local requirement.

(e) Contain the name and address of the person, branch, department, agency, or other instrumentality of the State or local government that should be notified of the Commission's actions concerning the application.

(f) Document the applicant's authority to act for, or on behalf of, the State or local government in applying for an exemption from preemption for the particular safety requirement in question.

(g) Be signed by an individual having authority to apply for the exemption from federal preemption on behalf of the applicant.

(h) Be submitted, in five copies, to the Secretary, Consumer Product Safety Commission, Washington, DC 20207.

§1061.6 Contents of applications for exemption.

Applications for exemption shall include the information specified in §§1061.7 through 1061.10. More generally, a State or local government seeking an exemption should provide the Commission with the most complete information possible in support of the findings the Commission is required to make in issuing an exemption regulation. If any of the specified information is omitted because it is unavailable or not relevent, such omission should be explained in the application.

§1061.7 Documentation of the State or local requirement.

An application for an exemption from preemption shall contain the following information:

(a) A copy of the State or local requirement that is the subject of the application. Where available, the application shall also include copies of any legislative history or background materials used in issuing the requirement, including hearing reports or studies concerning the development or consideration of the requirement.

(b) A written explanation of why compliance with the State or local requirement would not cause the product to be in violation of the applicable Commission statute, standard, or regulation.

§1061.8 Information on the heightened degree of protection afforded.

An application for an exemption from preemption shall also contain information demonstrating that the State or local requirement provides a significantly higher degree of protection from the risk of injury or illness than the preempting Commission statute, standard, or regulation. More specifically, an application shall contain:

(a) A description of the risk of injury or illness addressed by the State or local requirement.

(b) A detailed explanation of the State or local requirement and its rationale.

(c) An analysis of differences between the State or local requirement and the Commission statute, standard, or regulation.

(d) A detailed explanation of the State or local test method and its rationale.

(e) Information comparing available test results for the Commission statute, standard, or regulation and the State or local requirement.

(f) Information to show hazard reduction as a result of the State or local requirement, including injury data and results of accident simulation.

(g) Any other information that is relevant to applicant's contention that the State or local requirement provides a significantly higher degree of protection than does the Commission statute, standard, or regulation.

(h) Information regarding enforcement of the State or local requirement and sanctions that could be imposed for noncompliance.

§1061.9 Information about the effect on interstate commerce.

An application for exemption from preemption shall provide information on the effect on interstate commerce a granting of the requested exemption would be expected to cause, including the extent of the burden and the benefit to public health and safety that would be provided by the State or local requirement. More specifically, applications for exemption shall include, where available, information showing:

(a) That it is technologically feasible to comply with the State or local requirement. Evidence of technological feasibility could take the form of:

(1) Statements by affected persons indicating ability to comply with the State or local government requirement.

(2) Statements indicating that other jurisdictions have established similar requirements that have been, or could be, met by persons affected by the requirement that is the subject of the application.

(3) Information as to technological product or process modifications necessary to achieve compliance with the State or local requirement.

(4) Any other information indicating the technological feasibility of compliance with the State or local requirement.

(b) That it is economically feasible to comply with the State or local requirement, i.e., that there would not be significant adverse effects on the production and distribution of the regulated products. Evidence of economic feasibility could take the form of:

(1) Information showing that the State or local requirement would not result in the unavailability (or result in a significant decline in the availability) of the product, either in the interstate market or within the geographic boundary of the State or local government imposing the requirement.

(2) Statements from persons likely to be affected by the State or local requirement concerning the anticipated effect of the requirement on the availability or continued marketing of the product.

(3) Any other information indicating the economic impact of compliance with the State or local requirement, such as projections of the anticipated effect of the State or local requirement on the sales and prices of the product, both in interstate commerce and within the geographic area of the State or local government.

(c) The present geographic distribution of the product to which the State or local requirement would apply, and projections of future geographic distribution. Evidence of the geographic distribution could take the form of governmental or private information or data (including statements from manufacturers, distributors, or retailers of the product) showing advertising in the interstate market, interstate retailing, or interstate distribution.

(d) The probability of other States or local governments applying for an exemption for a similar requirement. Evidence of the probability that other States or local governments would apply for an exemption could take the form of statements from other States or local governments indicating their intentions.

(e) That specified local conditions require the State or local government to apply with the exemption in order to adequately protect the public health or safety of the State or local area.

§ 1061.10 Information on affected parties.

An application for an exemption from preemption shall include a statement which identifies in general terms, parties potentially affected by the State or local requirement, especially small businesses, including manufacturers, distributors, retailers, consumers, and consumer groups.

§ 1061.11 Incomplete or insufficient applications.

(a) If an application fails to meet the threshold requirements of § 1061.4(a) of this part, the Office of General Counsel will inform the applicant and return the application without prejudice to its being resubmitted.

(b) If an application fails to provide all the information specified in §§ 1061.5 through 1061.10 of this part, and fails to fully explain why it has not been provided, the Office of General Counsel will either:

(1) Return it to the applicant without prejudice to its being resubmitted,

(2) Notify the applicant and allow it to provide the missing information, or

(3) If the deficiencies are minor and the applicant concurs, forward it to the Commission for consideration on its merits.

(c) If the Commission or the Commission staff believes that additional information is necessary or useful for a proper evaluation of the application, the Commission or Commission staff will promptly request the applicant to furnish such additional information.

(d) If an application is not returned under paragraphs (a) or (b) of this section, the Commission will consider it on its merits.

§ 1061.12 Commission consideration on merits.

(a) If the Commission proposes to grant an application for exemption it will, in accordance with 5 U.S.C. 553, publish a notice of that fact in the FEDERAL REGISTER, including a proposed exemption regulation, and provide an opportunity for written and oral comments on the proposed exemption by any interested party.

(b) The Commission will evaluate all timely written and oral submissions received from interested parties, as well as any other available and relevant information on the proposal.

(c) The Commission's evaluation will focus on:

(1) Whether the State or local requirement provides a significantly higher degree of protection than the Commission statute or regulation from the risk of injury or illness that they both address.

(2) Whether the State or local requirement would unduly burden interstate commerce if the grant of the exemption from preemption allows it to go into effect. The Commission will evaluate these factors in accordance with the Commission's statutory preemption provisions and their legislative history.

(3) Whether compliance with the State or local requirements would not cause the product to be in violation of the applicable Commission statute, standard, or regulation.

(d) If, after evaluating the record, the Commission determines to grant an exemption, it will publish a final exemption regulation, including the findings required by the statutory preemption provisions, in the FEDERAL REGISTER.

(e) If the Commission denies an application, whether or not published for comment, it will publish its reasons for doing so in the FEDERAL REGISTER.

SUBCHAPTER B—CONSUMER PRODUCT SAFETY ACT REGULATIONS

PART 1101—INFORMATION DISCLOSURE UNDER SECTION 6(b) OF THE CONSUMER PRODUCT SAFETY ACT

AUTHORITY: Section 6(b) of Public Law 92–573, as amended by Section 211 of Public Law 110–314, 122 Stat. 3016, 15 U.S.C. 2055(b), 5 U.S.C. 553(b).

SOURCE: 48 FR 57430, Dec. 29, 1983, unless otherwise noted.

Subpart A—Background

§ 1101.1 General background.

(a) *Basic purpose.* This rule sets forth the Consumer Product Safety Commission's policy and procedure under sections 6(b)(1)–(5) of the Consumer Product Safety Act (CPSA) (15 U.S.C. 2055(b)(1)–(5)) which relate to public disclosure of information from which the identity of a manufacturer or private labeler of a product can be readily ascertained. In addition, these rules provide for retraction of inaccurate or misleading information the Commission has disclosed that reflects adversely on the safety of a consumer product or class of products or on the practices of any manufacturer, private labeler, distributor or retailer of consumer products as required by section 6(b)(7) of the CPSA (15 U.S.C. 2055(b)(7)).

(b) *Statutory requirements.* Section 6(b) establishes procedures that the

Commission must follow when it releases certain firm specific information to the public and when it retracts certain information it has released.

(1) Generally, section 6(b)(1) requires the Commission to provide manufacturers or private labelers with advance notice and opportunity to comment on information the Commission proposes to release, if the public can readily ascertain the identity of the firm from the information. Section 6(b)(1) also requires the Commission to take reasonable steps to assure that the information is accurate and that disclosure is fair in the circumstances and reasonably related to effectuating the purposes of the Acts administered by the Commission. Disclosure of information may not occur in fewer than 15 days after notice to the manufacturer or private labeler unless the Commission publishes a finding that the public health and safety requires a lesser period of notice. Exceptions to these requirements are established in section 6(b)(4). Additional limitations on the disclosure of information reported to the Commission under section 15(b) of the CPSA are established in section 6(b)(5).

(2) Section 6(b)(2) requires the Commission to provide further notice to manufacturers or private labelers where the Commission proposes to disclose product-specific information the firms have claimed to be inaccurate.

(3) Section 6(b)(3) authorizes manufacturers and private labelers to bring lawsuits against the Commission to prevent disclosure of product-specific information after the firms have received the notice specified.

(c) *Internal clearance procedures.* Section 6(b)(6) requires the Commission to establish internal clearance procedures for Commission initiated disclosures of information that reflect on the safety of a consumer product or class of products, even if the information is not product specific. This rule does not address section 6(b)(6) because the Commission has internal clearance procedures in its directives system. (Directive 1450.2 "Clearance Procedures for Commission Staff to Use in Providing Information to the Public." April 27, 1983.

[48 FR 57430, Dec. 29, 1983, as amended at 73 FR 72334, Nov. 28, 2008]

§1101.2. Scope.

Section 6(b) and these rules apply to information concerning products subject to the CPSA (15 U.S.C. 2051–2085), and to the four other acts the Commission administers (transferred acts). These transferred acts are the Flammable Fabrics Act, 15 U.S.C. 1191–1204 (FFA); the Poison Prevention Packaging Act of 1970, 15 U.S.C. 1471–1476 (PPPA); the Federal Hazardous Substances Act, 15 U.S.C. 1261–1276 (FHSA); and the Refrigerator Safety Act, 15 U.S.C. 1211–1214 (RSA). These provisions are now applicable to the Virginia Graeme Baker Pool and Spa Safety Act, 15 U.S.C. 8003(a); and the Children's Gasoline Burn Prevention Act §2(a), Public Law 110–278, 122 Stat. 2602 (July 17, 2008).

[73 FR 72334, Nov. 28, 2008]

Subpart B—Information Subject to Notice and Analysis Provisions of Section 6(b)(1)

§1101.11 General application of provisions of section 6(b)(1).

(a) *Information subject to section 6(b)(1).* To be subject to the notice and analysis provisions of section 6(b)(1), information must meet all the following criteria:

(1) The information must pertain to a specific product which is either designated or described in a manner which permits its identity to be ascertained readily by the public.

(2) The information must be obtained, generated or received by the Commission as an entity or by individual members, employees, agents, contractors or representatives of the Commission acting in their official capacities.

(3) The Commission or its members, employees, agents or representatives must propose to disclose the information to the public (see §1101.12).

(4) The manner in which the product is designated or described in the information must permit the public to ascertain readily the identity of the manufacturer or private labeler. [See § 1101.13.]

(b) *Information not subject to section 6(b)(1).* The requirements of section 6(b)(1) do not apply to:

(1) Information described in the exclusions contained in section 6(b)(4) of the CPSA (see subpart E of this rule).

(2) Information the Commission is required by law to make publicly available. This information includes, for example, Commission notifications to foreign governments regarding certain products to be exported, as required by section 18(b) of the CPSA, 15 U.S.C. 2068(b); section 14(d) of the FHSA, 15 U.S.C. 1273(d); and section 15(c) of the FFA, 15 U.S.C. 1202(c). (See the Commission's Export Policy Statement, 16 CFR part 1017.)

(3) Information required to be disclosed to the President and Congress pursuant to section 27(j) of the CPSA, 15 U.S.C. 2076(j).

(4) Press releases issued by firms.

(5) Information filed or presented in administrative proceedings or litigation to which the Commission is a party and which is not expressly subject to the section 6(b)(4) exceptions.

§ 1101.12 Commission must disclose information to the public.

Public. For the purposes of section 6(b)(1), the public includes any person except:

(a) Members, employees, agents, representatives and contractors of the Commission, in their official capacity.

(b) State officials who are commissioned officers under section 29(a)(2) of the CPSA, 15 U.S.C. 2078(a)(2), to the extent that the Commission furnishes them information necessary for them to perform their duties under that section. Such officials may not release to the public copies of such information unless the Commission has complied with section 6(b) or the information falls within an exception to section 6(b).

(c) Members of a Commission Chronic Hazard Advisory Panel established under section 28 of the CPSA (15 U.S.C. 2077). However, disclosures of information by such a Panel are subject to section 6(b).

(d) The persons or firms to whom the information to be disclosed pertains, or their legal representatives.

(e) The persons or firms who provided the information to the Commission, or their legal representatives.

(f) Other Federal agencies or state or local governments to whom accident and investigation reports are provided pursuant to section 29(e) of the CPSA (15 U.S.C. 2078(e)). However, as required by that section, employees of Federal agencies or state or local governments may not release to the public copies of any accident or investigation report made under the CPSA by an officer, employee or agent of the Commission unless CPSC has complied with the applicable requirements of section 6(b).

(g) The Chairman or ranking minority member of a committee or subcommittee of Congress acting pursuant to committee business and having jurisdiction over the matter which is the subject of the information requested.

(h) Any federal, state, local, or foreign government agency pursuant to, and in accordance with, section 29(f) of the Consumer Product Safety Improvement Act of 2008 (Pub. L. 110–314, 122 Stat. 3016 (August 14, 2008)).

[48 FR 57430, Dec. 29, 1983, as amended at 73 FR 72335, Nov. 28, 2008]

§ 1101.13 Public ability to ascertain readily identity of manufacturer or private labeler.

The advance notice and analysis provisions of section 6(b)(1) apply only when a reasonable person receiving the information in the form in which it is to be disclosed and lacking specialized expertise can readily ascertain from the information itself the identity of the manufacturer or private labeler of a particular product. The Commission will provide the advance notice and opportunity to comment if there is a question whether the public could readily ascertain the identity of a manufacturer or private labeler.

Subpart C—Procedure for Providing Notice and Opportunity To Comment Under Section 6(b)(1)

§ 1101.21 Form of notice and opportunity to comment.

(a) *Notice may be oral or written.* The Commission will generally provide to manufacturers or private labelers written notice and opportunity to comment on information subject to section 6(b)(1). However, when the Commission publishes a finding that the public health and safety requires a lesser period of notice pursuant to section 6(b)(1) of the CPSA, the Commission may determine that it is necessary to provide the notice and opportunity to comment orally, either in person or by telephone.

(b) *Content of notice.* The Commission will provide the manufacturer or private labeler with:

(1) Either the actual text of the information to be disclosed or, if appropriate, a summary of the information.

(2) A general description of the manner in which the Commission will disclose the information, including any other relevant information the Commission intends to include with the disclosure. If the Commission advises that the form of disclosure will be by press release, for example, the Commission need not provide further notice to disclose a summary of the press release.

(3) A request for comment with respect to the information, including a request for explanatory data or other relevant information for the Commission's consideration.

(4) A statement that, in the absence of a specific request by a firm that its comments be withheld from disclosure, the Commission will release to the public the firm's comments (or a summary thereof prepared by the firm or, if the firm declines to do so, by the Commission).

(5) A statement that a request that comments be withheld from disclosure will be honored.

(6) Notice that the firm may request confidential treatment for the information, in accordance with section 6(a)(3) of the Consumer Product Safety Act, 15 U.S.C. 2055(a)(3) (*see* § 1101.24(b)).

(7) A statement that no further request for comment will be sought by the Commission if it intends to disclose the identical information in the same format, unless the firm specifically requests the opportunity to comment on subsequent information disclosures.

(8) The name, address, and telephone number of the person to whom comments should be sent and the time when any comments are due (*see* § 1101.22).

[48 FR 57430, Dec. 29, 1983, as amended at 73 FR 72335, Nov. 28, 2008]

§ 1101.22 Timing: request for time extensions.

(a) *Time for comment.* (1) Generally firms will receive ten (10) calendar days from the date of the letter in which the Commission transmits the notice to furnish comments to the Commission. Firms that receive requests for comments by mail will receive an additional three (3) days to comment to account for time in the mail.

(2) Upon his or her own initiative or upon request, the Freedom of Information Officer may provide a different amount of time for comment, particularly for firms that receive voluminous or complex material. In addition, the Commission may publish a finding that the public health and safety requires a lesser period of notice and may require a response in a shorter period of time (*see* § 1101.24).

(b) *No response submitted.* (1) If the Commission has not received a response within the time specified and if it has received no request for extension of time, the Commission will analyze the information as provided in subpart D. If no comments are submitted the Commission will not give the further notice provided in section 6(b)(2).

(2) Unless the Commission publishes a finding that the public health and safety requires a lesser period of notice (see § 1101.23), the Commission will not disclose the information in fewer than 15 days after providing a manufacturer or private labeler notice and opportunity to comment.

(c) *Requests for time extension.* (1) Requests for extension of time to comment on information to be disclosed must be made to the person who provided the Commission's notice and opportunity to comment. The request for time extension may be either oral or written. An oral request for a time extension must be promptly confirmed in writing.

(2) Requests for extension of time must explain with specificity why the extension is needed and how much additional time is required.

(3) The Commission will promptly respond to requests for extension of time.

[48 FR 57430, Dec. 29, 1983, as amended at 73 FR 72335, Nov. 28, 2008]

§ 1101.23 Providing less than 15 days notice before disclosing information.

There are two circumstances in which the Commission may disclose to the public information subject to section 6(b)(1) in a time less than 15 days after providing notice to the manufacturer or private labeler.

(a) *Firm agrees to lesser period or does not object to disclosure.* The Commission may disclose to the public information subject to section 6(b)(1) before the 15-day period expires when, after receiving the Commission's notice and opportunity to comment, the firm involved agrees to the earlier disclosure; notifies the Commission that it has no comment; or notifies the Commission that it does not object to disclosure.

(b) *Commission finding a lesser period is required.* Section 6(b)(1) provides that the Commission may publish a finding that the public health and safety requires a lesser period of notice than the 15 days advance notice that section 6(b)(1) generally requires. The Commission may find that the public health and safety requires less than 15 days advance notice, for example, to warn the public quickly because individuals may be in danger from a product hazard or a potential hazard, or to correct product safety information released by third persons, which mischaracterizes statements made by the Commission about the product or which attributes to the Commission statements about the product which the Commission did not make.

(c) *Notice of finding.* The Commission will inform a manufacturer or private labeler of a product which is the subject of a public health and safety finding that the public health and safety requires less than 15 days advance notice either orally or in writing, depending on the immediacy of the need for quick action. Where applicable, before releasing information, the Commission will comply with the requirements of section 6(b) (1) and (2) by giving the firm the opportunity to comment on the information, either orally or in writing depending on the immediacy of the need for quick action, and by giving the firm advance notice before disclosing information claimed by a manufacturer or private labeler to be inaccurate (see § 1101.25).

[48 FR 57430, Dec. 29, 1983, as amended at 73 FR 72335, Nov. 28, 2008]

§ 1101.24 Scope of comments Commission seeks.

(a) *Comment in regard to the information.* The section 6(b) opportunity to comment on information is intended to permit firms to furnish information and data to the Commission to assist the agency in its evaluation of the accuracy of the information. A firm's submission, therefore, must be specific and should be accompanied by documentation, where available, if the comments are to assist the Commission in its evaluation of the information. Comments of a general nature, such as general suggestions or allegations that a document is inaccurate or that the Commission has not taken reasonable steps to assure accuracy, are not sufficient to assist the Commission in its evaluation of the information or to justify a claim of inaccuracy. The weight accorded a firm's comments on the accuracy of information and the degree of scrutiny which the Commission will exercise in evaluating the information will depend on the specificity and completeness of the firm's comments and of the accompanying documentation. In general, specific comments which are accompanied by documentation will be given more weight than those which are undocumented and general in nature.

(b) *Claims of confidentiality.* If the manufacturer or private labeler believes the information involved cannot be disclosed because of section 6(a)(2) of the CPSA (15 U.S.C. 2055(a)(2)), which pertains to trade secret or other confidential material, the firm may make claims of confidentiality at the time it submits its comments to the Commission under this section. Such claims must identify the specific information which the firm believes to be confidential or trade secret material and must state with specificity the grounds on which the firm bases it claims. (See Commission's Freedom of Information Act regulation, 16 CFR part 1015, particularly 16 CFR 1015.18.)

(c) *Requests for nondisclosure of comments.* If a firm objects to disclosure of its comments or a portion thereof, it must notify the Commission at the time it submits its comments. If the firm objects to the disclosure of a portion of its comments, it must identify those portions which should be withheld.

§ 1101.25 Notice of intent to disclose.

(a) *Notice to manufacturer or private labeler.* In accordance with section 6(b)(2) of the CPSA, if the Commission, after following the notice provisions of section 6(b)(1), determines that information claimed to be inaccurate by a manufacturer or private labeler in comments submitted under section 6(b)(1) should be disclosed because the Commission believes it has complied with section 6(b)(1), the Commission shall notify the manufacturer or private labeler that it intends to disclose the information not less than 5 days after the date of the receipt of notification by the firm. The notice of intent to disclose will include an explanation of the reason for the Commission's decision, copies of any additional materials, such as explanatory statements and letters to Freedom of Information Act requesters, which were not previously sent to the firm.

(b) *Commission finding a lesser period is required.* The Commission may determine that the public health and safety requires less than 5 days advance notice of its intent to disclose information claimed to be inaccurate. For example, the Commission may determine it is necessary to warn the public quickly because individuals may be in danger from a product hazard or a potential hazard, or to correct product safety information released by third persons, which mischaracterized statements made by the Commission about the product or which attributes to the Commission statements about the product which the Commission did not make.

(c) *Notice of findings.* The Commission will inform a manufacturer or private labeler of a product which is the subject of a public health and safety finding that the public health and safety requires less than 5 days advance notice either orally or in writing, depending on the immediacy of the need for quick action.

[48 FR 57430, Dec. 29, 1983, as amended at 73 FR 72335, Nov. 28, 2008]

§ 1101.26 Circumstances when the Commission does not provide notice and opportunity to comment.

(a) *Notice to the extent practicable.* Section 6(b)(1) requires that "to the extent practicable" the Commission must provide manufacturers and private labelers notice and opportunity to comment before disclosing information from which the public can ascertain readily their identity.

(b) *Circumstances when notice and opportunity to comment is not practicable.* The Commission has determined that there are various circumstances when notice and opportunity to comment is *not* practicable. Examples include the following:

(1) When the Commission has taken reasonable steps to assure that the company to which the information pertains is out of business and has no identifiable successor.

(2) When the information is disclosed in testimony in response to an order of the court during litigation to which the Commission is not a party.

Subpart D—Reasonable Steps Commission Will Take To Assure Information It Discloses Is Accurate, and That Disclosure Is Fair in the Circumstances and Reasonably Related to Effectuating the Purposes of the Acts It Administers

§ 1101.31 General requirements.

(a) *Timing of decisions.* The Commission will attempt to make its decision on disclosure so that it can disclose information in accordance with section 6(b) as soon as is reasonably possible after expiration of the statutory fifteen day moratorium on disclosure.

(b) *Inclusion of comments.* In disclosing any information under this section, the Commission will include any comments or other information submitted by the manufacturer or private labeler unless the manufacturer or private labeler at the time it submits its section 6(b) comments specifically requests the Commission not to include the comments or to include only a designated portion of the comments and disclosure of the comments on such a designated portion is not necessary to assure that the disclosure of the information which is the subject of the comments is fair in the circumstances.

(c) *Explanatory statements.* Where appropriate, the Commission will accompany the disclosure of information subject to this subpart with an explanatory statement that makes the nature of the information disclosed clear to the public. Inclusion of an explanatory statement is in addition to, and not a substitute for, taking reasonable steps to assure the accuracy of information. To the extent it is practical the Commission will also accompany the disclosure with any other relevant information in its possession that places the released information in context.

(d) *Information previously disclosed.* If the Commission has previously disclosed, in accordance with section 6(b)(1), the identical information it intends to disclose again in the same format, it will not customarily take any additional steps to assure accuracy unless the Commission has some reason to question its accuracy or unless the firm, in its comments responding to the Commission's initial section 6(b) notice, specifically requests the opportunity to comment on subsequent disclosures, or unless the Commission determines that sufficient time has passed to warrant seeking section 6(b) comment again. Before disclosing the information the Commission will again review the information to see if accuracy is called into question and will further look to whether disclosure is fair in the circumstances and reasonably related to effectuating the purposes of the Acts the Commission administers.

[48 FR 57430, Dec. 29, 1983, as amended at 73 FR 72335, Nov. 28, 2008]

§ 1101.32 Reasonable steps to assure information is accurate.

(a) The Commission considers that the following types of actions are reasonable steps to assure the accuracy of information it proposes to release to the public:

(1) The Commission staff or a qualified person or entity outside the Commission (e.g., someone with requisite training or experience, such as a fire marshal, a fire investigator, an electrical engineer, or an attending physician) conducts an investigation or an inspection which yields or corroborates the product information to be disclosed; or

(2) The Commission staff conducts a technical, scientific, or other evaluation which yields or corroborates the product information to be disclosed or the staff obtains a copy of such an evaluation conducted by a qualified person or entity; or

(3) The Commission staff provides the information to be disclosed to the person who submitted it to the Commission for review and, if necessary, correction, and the submitter confirms the information as accurate to the best of the submitter's knowledge and belief, provided that:

(i) The confirmation is made by the person injured or nearly injured in an incident involving the product; or

(ii) The confirmation is made by a person who, on the basis of his or her own observation or experience, identifies an alleged safety-related defect in or problem with such a product even though no incident or injury associated with the defect or problem may have occurred; or

(iii) The confirmation is made by an eyewitness to an injury or safety-related incident involving such a product; or

(iv) The confirmation is made by an individual with requisite training or experience who has investigated and/or determined the cause of deaths, injuries or safety-related incidents involving such a product. Such persons would include, for example, a fire marshal, a fire investigator, an electrical engineer, an ambulance attendant, or an attending physician; or

(v) The confirmation is made by a parent or guardian of a child involved in an incident involving such a product, or by a person to whom a child is entrusted on a temporary basis.

(b) The steps set forth below are the steps the Commission will take to analyze the accuracy of information which it proposes to release to the public.

(1) The Commission will review each proposed disclosure of information which is susceptible of factual verification to assure that reasonable steps have been taken to assure accuracy in accordance with § 1101.32(a).

(2) As described in subpart C, the Commission will provide a manufacturer or private labeler with a summary or text of the information the Commission proposes to disclose and will invite comment with respect to that information.

(3) If the Commission receives no comments or only general, undocumented comments claiming inaccuracy, the Commission will review the information in accordance with § 1101.32(a) and release it, generally without further investigating its accuracy if there is nothing on the face of the information that calls its accuracy into question.

(4) If a firm comments on the accuracy of the information the Commission proposes to disclose, the Commission will review the information in light of the comments. The degree of review by the Commission and the weight accorded a firm's comments will be directly related to the specificity and completeness of the firm's comments on accuracy and the accompanying documentation. Documented comments will be given more weight than undocumented comments. Specific comments will be given more weight than general comments. Further steps may be taken to determine the accuracy of the information if the Commission determines such action appropriate.

§ 1101.33 Reasonable steps to assure information release is fair in the circumstances.

(a) The steps set forth below are the steps the Commission has determined are reasonable to take to assure disclosure of information to the public is fair in the circumstances:

(1) The Commission will accompany information disclosed to the public with the manufacturer's or private labeler's comments unless the manufacturer or private labeler asks in its section 6(b) comments that its comments or a designated portion thereof not accompany the information.

(2) The Commission generally will accompany the disclosure of information with an explanatory statement that makes the nature of the information disclosed clear to the public. The Commission will also take reasonable steps to disclose any other relevant information it its possession that will assure disclosure is fair in the circumstances.

(3) The Commission will limit the form of disclosure to that which it considers appropriate in the circumstances. For example, the Commission may determine it is not appropriate to issue a nationwide press release in a particular situation and rather will issue a press release directed at certain localities, regions, or user populations.

(4) The Commission may delay disclosure of information in some circumstances. For example, the Commission may elect to postpone an information release until an investigation, analysis or test of a product is complete, rather than releasing information piecemeal.

(b) The Commission will not disclose information when it determines that disclosure would not be fair in the circumstances. The following are examples of disclosures which generally would not be fair in the circumstances.

(1) Disclosure of information furnished by a firm to facilitate prompt remedial action or settlement of a case when the firm has a reasonable expectation that the information will be maintained by the Commission in concidence.

(2) Disclosure of notes or minutes of meetings to discuss or negotiate settlement agreements and of drafts of documents prepared during settlement negotiations, where the firm has a reasonable expectation that such written materials will be maintained by the Commission in confidence.

(3) Disclosure of the work-product of attorneys employed by a firm and information subject to an attorney/client privilege, if the Commission has obtained the information from the client or the attorney, the attorney or client advises the Commission of the confidential nature of the information at the time it is submitted to the Commission, and the information has been maintained in confidence by the client and the attorney.

(4) Disclosure of a firm's comments (or a portion thereof) submitted under section 6(b)(1) over the firm's objection.

§ 1101.34 Reasonable steps to assure information release is "reasonably related to effectuating the purposes of the Acts" the Commission administers.

(a) The steps set forth below are the steps the Commission has determined are reasonable to take to assure that the disclosure of information to the public effectuates the purposes of the Acts it administers.

(1) *Purposes of the CPSA.* The Commission will review information to determine whether disclosure would be reasonably related to effectuating one or more of the specific purposes of the CPSA, as set forth in sections 2(b) and 5, 15 U.S.C. 2051(b) and 2054.

(2) *Purposes of the FHSA, FFA, PPPA and RSA.* The Commission will also review information concerning products subject to the transferred acts it administers and to the Commission's specific functions under those acts to determine whether disclosure of information would be reasonably related to effectuating the purposes of those acts.

(3) *Purposes of the FOIA.* FOIA requests will be reviewed to determine whether disclosure of the information is reasonably related to effectuating one or more of the purposes of the acts administered by the Commission. In the event of a close question on this issue, the Commission will defer to the purposes of the FOIA. The FOIA establishes a general right of the public to have access to information in the Commission's possession, particularly information that reveals whether the Commission is meeting its statutory responsibilities or information upon which the Commission bases a decision that affects the public health and safety.

(b) In reviewing proposed information disclosures, the Commission will consider disclosing the material on the basis of whether release of the information, when taken as a whole, was prepared or is maintained in the course of or to support an activity of the Commission designed to accomplish one or more of the statutory purposes.

Subpart E—Statutory Exceptions of Section 6(b)(4)

§ 1101.41 Generally.

(a) *Scope.* This subpart describes and interprets the exceptions to the requirements of section 6(b)(1)–(b)(3) that are set forth in section 6(b)(4). These exceptions apply to:

(1) Information about a product reasonably related to the subject matter of an imminent hazard action in federal court;

(2) Information about a product which the Commission has reasonable cause to believe is in violation of any consumer product safety rule or provision under the Consumer Product Safety Act (15 U.S.C. 2051, *et seq.*) or similar rule or provision of any other act enforced by the Commission;

(3) Information in the course of or concerning a rulemaking proceeding; or

(4) information in the course of or concerning an adjudicatory, administrative or judicial proceeding.

(b) *Application to transferred act.* The Commission will apply the exceptions contained in section 6(b)(4) to those provisions in the transferred acts, comparable to the specific provisions in the CPSA to which section 6(b)(4) applies.

[48 FR 57430, Dec. 29, 1983, as amended at 73 FR 72335, Nov. 28, 2008]

§ 1101.42 Imminent hazard exception.

(a) *Statutory provision.* Section 6(b)(4)(A) provides that the requirements of section 6(b)(1) do not apply to public disclosure of "information about any consumer product with respect to which product the Commission has filed an action under section 12 (relating to imminently hazardous products)."

(b) *Scope of exception.* This exception applies once the Commission has filed an action under section 12 of the CPSA (15 U.S.C. 2061), in a United States district court. Once the exception applies, information may be disclosed to the public while the proceeding is pending without following the requirements of section 6(b)(1) if the information concerns or relates to the product alleged to be imminently hazardous. Upon termination of the proceeding, information filed with the court or otherwise made public is not subject to section 6(b). Information in the Commission's possession which has not been made public is subject to section 6(b).

§ 1101.43 Section 6(b)(4)(A) exception.

(a) *Statutory provision.* Section (6)(b)(4)(A) provides that the requirements of section 6(b)(1) do not apply to public disclosure of information about any consumer product which the Commission has reasonable cause to believe is in violation of any consumer product safety rule or provision under the Consumer Product Safety Act (15 U.S.C. 2051 *et seq.*) or similar rule or provision of any other act enforced by the Commission.

(b) *Scope of exception.* This exception applies once the Commission has "reasonable cause to believe" there has occurred a violation of any consumer product safety rule or provision under the Consumer Product Safety Act (15 U.S.C. 2051 *et seq.*) or similar rule or provision of any other act enforced by the Commission. Once the exception applies, the Commission may disclose information to the public without following the requirements of section 6(b)(1) if the information concerning the product is reasonably related to the violation.

[73 FR 72335, Nov. 28, 2008]

§ 1101.44 Rulemaking proceeding exception.

(a) *Statutory provision.* Section 6(b)(4)(B) provides that the requirements of section 6(b)(1) do not apply to public disclosure of information "in the course of or concerning a rulemaking proceeding (which shall commence upon the publication of an advance notice of proposed rulemaking or a notice of proposed rulemaking) * * * under this Act."

(b) *Scope of exception.* This exception applies upon publication in the FEDERAL REGISTER of an advance notice of proposed rulemaking or, if no advance notice of proposed rulemaking is issued, upon publication in the FEDERAL REGISTER of a notice of proposed rulemaking, under any of the acts the Commission administers. Once the exception applies, the Commission may publicly disclose information in the course of the rulemaking proceeding which is presented during the proceeding or which is contained or referenced in the public record of the proceeding and or which concerns the proceeding without following the requirements of section 6(b)(1). Documentation supporting the public record is also excepted from section 6(b). A rulemaking proceeding includes a proceeding either to issue, to amend, or to revoke a rule.

(c) The phrase "in the course of" refers to information disclosed as part of the proceeding and may, therefore, include information generated before the proceeding began and later presented as part of the proceeding. A rulemaking proceeding ends once the Commission has published the final rule or a notice of termination of the rulemaking in the FEDERAL REGISTER.

(d) The phrase "concerning" refers to information about the proceeding itself both after the proceeding has begun and indefinitely thereafter. Therefore, the Commission may publicly disclose information that describes the substance, process and outcome of the proceeding. By issuing opinions and public statements, the Commissioners, and the presiding official, who act as decisionmakers, may also publicly explain their individual votes and any decision rendered.

§ 1101.45 Adjudicatory proceeding exception.

(a) *Statutory provision.* Section 6(b)(4)(B) provides that the requirements of section 6(b)(1) do not apply to public disclosure of "information in the course of or concerning * * * [an] adjudicatory proceeding * * * under this Act."

(b) *Scope of exception.* This exception applies once the Commission begins an administrative adjudication under the CPSA. The Commission will also apply the exception to any administrative adjudicatory proceeding under FHSA, FAA, or PPPA. An adjudicatory proceeding begins with the filing of a complaint under section 15(c) or (d), 17(a)(1) or (3), or 20 of the CPSA (15 U.S.C. 2064(c) or (d), 2066(a)(1), or (3), or 2069); section 15 of the FHSA (15 U.S.C. 1274); section 5(b) of the FFA, (15 U.S.C. 1194(b)); or section 4(c) of the PPPA (15 U.S.C. 1473(c)). An adjudicatory proceeding ends when the Commission issues a final order, 16 CFR 1025.51–1025.58.

(c) The phrase "in the course of" refers to information disclosed as part of the adjudication, whether in documents filed or exchanged during discovery, or in testimony given in such proceedings, and may therefore, include information generated before the adjudication began.

(d) The phrase "concerning" refers to information about the administrative adjudication itself, both once it begins and indefinitely thereafter. Therefore, the Commission may publicly disclose information that describes the substance, process and outcome of the proceeding including, for example, the effectiveness of any corrective action such as information on the number of products corrected as a result of a remedial action. By issuing opinions and public statements, the Commissioners and the presiding official, who act as decisionmakers, may publicly explain their individual votes and any decision rendered.

[48 FR 57430, Dec. 29, 1983, as amended at 49 FR 8428, Mar 7, 1984]

§ 1101.46 Other administrative or judicial proceeding exception.

(a) *Statutory provision.* Section 6(b)(4)(B) provides that the requirements of section 6(b)(1) do not apply to public disclosure of "information in the course of or concerning any * * * other administrative or judicial proceeding under this Act."

(b) *Scope of exception.* This exception applies to an administrative or judicial proceeding, other than a rulemaking or administrative adjudicatory proceeding, under the CPSA, FHSA, FFA, or PPPA. Proceedings within this exception include:

(1) A proceeding to act on a petition to start a rulemaking proceeding. This proceeding begins with the filing of a petition and ends when the petition is denied or, if granted, when the rulemaking proceeding begins. Information subject to the exception for petition proceedings is the petition itself and the supporting documentation, and information subsequently compiled by the staff and incorporated or referenced in the staff briefing papers for and recommendation to the Commission.

(2) A proceeding to act on a request for exemption from a rule or regulation. This proceeding begins with the filing of a request for exemption and ends when the request is denied or, if granted, when the Commission takes the first step to implement the exemption, e.g., when an amendment to the rule or regulation is proposed.

(3) A proceeding to issue a subpoena or general or special order. This proceeding begins with a staff request to the Commission to issue a subpoena or general or special order and ends once the request is granted or denied.

(4) A proceeding to act on a motion to quash or to limit a subpoena or general or special order. This proceeding begins with the filing with the Commission of a motion to quash or to limit and ends when the motion is granted or denied.

(5) Any judicial proceeding to which the Commission is a party. This proceeding begins when a complaint is filed and ends when a final decision (including appeal) is rendered with respect to the Commission.

(6) Any administrative proceeding to which the Commission is a party, such as an administrative proceeding before the Merit Systems Protection Board or the Federal Labor Relations Authority.

This proceeding begins and ends in accordance with the applicable regulations or procedures of the administrative body before which the proceeding is heard.

(7) A proceeding to obtain a retraction from the Commission pursuant to subpart F of these rules. This proceeding begins with the filing with the Secretary of the Commission of a request for retraction and ends when the request is denied or, if granted, when the information is retracted.

(c) *In the course of or concerning.* The phrase "in the course of or concerning" shall have the same meaning as set forth in either § 1101.44 (c) and (d) or § 1101.45 (c) and (d), whichever is applicable.

Subpart F—Retraction

§ 1101.51 Commission interpretation.

(a) *Statutory provisions.* Section 6(b)(7) of the CPSA provides: If the Commission finds that, in the administration of this Act, it has made public disclosure of inaccurate or misleading information which reflects adversely upon the safety of any consumer product or class of consumer products, or the practices of any manufacturer, private labeler, distributor, or retailer of consumer products, it shall, in a manner equivalent to that in which such disclosure was made, take reasonable steps to publish a retraction of such inaccurate or misleading information.

(b) *Scope.* Section 6(b)(7) applies to inaccurate or misleading information only if it is *adverse—i.e.*, if it reflects adversely either on the safety of a consumer product or on the practices of a manufacturer, private labeler, distributor or retailer. In addition, the Commission will apply section 6(b)(7) to information about products, and about manufacturers and private labelers of products, the Commission may regulate under any of the statutes it administers. Section 6(b)(7) applies to information already disclosed by the Commission, members of the Commission, or the Commission employees, agents, contractors or representatives in their official capacities.

§ 1101.52 Procedure for retraction.

(a) *Initiative.* The Commission may retract information under section 6(b)(7) on the initiative of the Commission, upon the request of a manufacturer, private labeler, distributor, or retailer of a consumer product, or upon the request of any other person in accordance with the procedures provided in this section.

(b) *Request for retraction.* Any manufacturer, private labeler, distributor or retailer of a consumer product or any other person may request a retraction if he/she believes the Commission or an individual member, employee, agent, contractor or representative of the Commission has made public disclosure of inaccurate or misleading information, which reflects adversely either on the safety of a product with which the firm deals or on the practices of the firm. The request must be in writing and addressed to the Secretary, CPSC. Washington, D.C. 20207.

(c) *Content of request.* A request for retraction must include the following information to the extent it is reasonably available:

(1) The information disclosed for which retraction is requested, the date on which the information was disclosed, the manner in which it was disclosed, who disclosed it, the type of document (e.g., letter, memorandum, news release) and any other relevant information the firm has to assist the Commission in identifying the information. A photocopy of the disclosure should accompany the request.

(2) A statement of the specific aspects of the information the firm believes are inaccurate or misleading and reflect adversely either on the safety of a consumer product with which the firm deals or on the firm's practices.

(3) A statement of the reasons the firm believes the information is inaccurate or misleading and reflects adversely either on the safety of a consumer product with which the firm deals or on the firm's practices.

(4) A statement of the action the firm requests the Commission to take in publishing a retraction in a manner equivalent to that in which disclosure was made.

(5) Any additional data or information the firm believes is relevant.

(d) *Commission action on request.* The Commission will act expeditiously on any request for retraction within 30 working days unless the Commission determines, for good cause, that a longer time period is appropriate. If the Commission finds that the Commission or any individual member, employee, agent contractor or representative of the Commission has made public disclosure of inaccurate or misleading information that reflects adversely either on the safety of the firm's product or the practices of the firm, the Commission will publish a retraction of information in a manner equivalent to that in which the disclosure was made. If the Commission finds that fuller disclosure is necessary, it will publish a retraction in the manner it determines appropriate under the circumstances.

(e) *Notification to requester.* The Commission will promptly notify the requester in writing of its decision on request for retraction. Notification shall set forth the reasons for the Commission's decision.

Subpart G—Information Submitted Pursuant to Section 15(b) of the CPSA

§ 1101.61 Generally.

(a) *Generally.* In addition to the requirements of section 6(b)(1), section 6(b)(5) of the CPSA imposes further limitations on the disclosure of information submitted to the Commission pursuant to section 15(b) of the CPSA, 15 U.S.C. 2064(b).

(b) *Criteria for disclosure.* Under section 6(b)(5) the Commission shall not disclose to the public information which is identified as being submitted pursuant to section 15(b) or which is treated by the Commission staff as being submitted pursuant to section 15(b). Section 6(b)(5) also applies to information voluntarily submitted after a firm's initial report to assist the Commission in its evaluation of the section 15 report. However, the Commission may disclose information submitted pursuant to section 15(b) in accordance with section 6(b)(1)–(3) if:

(1) The Commission has issued a complaint under section 15 (c) or (d) of the CPSA alleging that such product presents a substantial product hazard; or

(2) In lieu of proceeding against such product under section 15 (c) or (d), the Commission has accepted in writing a remedial settlement agreement dealing with such product; or

(3) The person who submitted the information under section 15(b) agrees to its public disclosure.

(4) The Commission publishes a finding that the public health and safety requires public disclosure with a lesser period of notice than is required by section 6(b)(1).

[48 FR 57430, Dec. 29, 1983, as amended at 73 FR 72335, Nov. 28, 2008]

§ 1101.62 Statutory exceptions to section 6(b)(5) requirements.

(a) *Scope.* The limitations established by section 6(b)(5) do not apply to the public disclosure of:

(1) Information with respect to a consumer product which is the subject of an action brought under section 12 (*see* § 1101.42);

(2) Information with respect to a consumer product which the Commission has reasonable cause to believe is in violation of any consumer product safety rule or provision under the Consumer Product Safety Act (Pub. L. 92–573, 86 Stat. 1207, as amended (15 U.S.C. 2051, *et seq.*)) or similar rule or provision of any other act enforced by the Commission; or

(3) Information in the course of or concerning a judicial proceeding (*see* § 1101.45).

[48 FR 57430, Dec. 29, 1983, as amended at 73 FR 72335, Nov. 28, 2008]

§ 1101.63 Information submitted pursuant to section 15(b) of the CPSA.

(a) Section 6(b)(5) applies only to information provided to the Commission by a manufacturer, distributor, or retailer which is identified by the manufacturer, distributor or retailer, or treated by the Commission staff as being submitted pursuant to section 15(b).

(b) Section 6(b)(5)'s limitation also applies to the portions of staff generated documents that contain, summarize or analyze such information submitted pursuant to section 15(b).

(c) Section 6(b)(5) does not apply to information independently obtained or prepared by the Commission staff.

Subpart H—Delegation of Authority to Information Group

§ 1101.71 Delegation of authority.

(a) *Delegation.* Pursuant to section 27(b)(9) of the CPSA 15 U.S.C. 2076(b)(9) the Commission delegates to the General Counsel or his or her senior staff designees, the authority to render all decisions under this part concerning the release of information subject to section 6(b) when firms have furnished section 6(b) comment except as provided in paragraph (b). The Commission also delegates to the Secretary of the Commission, or his or her senior staff designee, authority to make all decisions under this part concerning the release of information under section 6(b) when firms have failed to furnish section 6(b) comment or have consented to disclosure except as provided in paragraph (b) of this section. The General Counsel shall have authority to establish an Information Group composed of the General Counsel and the Secretary of the Commission or their designees who shall be senior staff members.

(b) *Findings not deleted.* The Commission does not delegate its authority—

(1) To find, pursuant to section 6(b)(1) and § 1101.23(b) of this part, that the public health and safety requires less than 15 days advance notice of proposed disclosures of information.

(2) To find, pursuant to section 6(b)(2) and § 1101.25(b) of this part, that the public health and safety requires less than five (5) days advance notice of its intent to disclose information claimed to be inaccurate;

(3) To decide whether it should take reasonable steps to publish a retraction of information in accordance with section 6(b)(7) and § 1101.52 of this part.

(c) *Final agency action; Commission decision.* A decision of the General Counsel or the Secretary or their designees shall be a final agency decision and shall not be appealable as of right to the Commission. However, the General Counsel or the Secretary may in his or her discretion refer an issue to the Commission for decision.

[48 FR 57430, Dec. 29, 1983, as amended at 73 FR 72335, Nov. 28, 2008]

PART 1102—PUBLICLY AVAILABLE CONSUMER PRODUCT SAFETY INFORMATION DATABASE

AUTHORITY: 15 U.S.C. 2051, 2051 note, 2052, 2055, 2055a, 2065, 2068, 2070, 2071, 2072, 2076, 2078, 2080, 2087.

SOURCE: 75 FR 76867, Dec. 9, 2010, unless otherwise noted.

Subpart A—Background and Definitions

§ 1102.2 Purpose.

This part sets forth the Commission's interpretation, policy, and procedures with regard to the establishment and maintenance of a Publicly Available Consumer Product Safety Information Database (also referred to as the "Database") on the safety of consumer products and other products or substances regulated by the Commission.

§ 1102.4 Scope.

This part applies to the content, procedure, notice, and disclosure requirements of the Publicly Available Consumer Product Safety Information Database, including all information published therein.

§ 1102.6 Definitions.

(a) Except as specified in paragraph (b) of this section, the definitions in section 3 of the Consumer Product Safety Act (CPSA) (15 U.S.C. 2052) apply to this part.

(b) For purposes of this part, the following definitions apply:

(1) *Additional information* means any information that the Commission determines is in the public interest to include in the Publicly Available Consumer Product Safety Information Database.

(2) *Commission or CPSC* means the Consumer Product Safety Commission.

(3) *Consumer product* means a consumer product as defined in section 3(a)(5) of the CPSA, and also includes any other products or substances regulated by the Commission under any other act it administers.

(4) *Harm* means injury, illness, or death; or risk of injury, illness, or death, as determined by the Commission.

(5) *Mandatory recall notice* means any notice to the public required of a firm pursuant to an order issued by the Commission under section 15(c) of the CPSA.

(6) *Manufacturer comment* means a comment made by a manufacturer or private labeler of a consumer product in response to a report of harm transmitted to such manufacturer or private labeler.

(7) *Publicly Available Consumer Product Safety Information Database*, also referred to as the Database, means the database on the safety of consumer products established and maintained by the CPSC as described in section 6A of the CPSA.

(8) *Report of harm* means any information submitted to the Commission through the manner described in § 1102.10(b), regarding any injury, illness, or death; or any risk of injury, illness, or death, as determined by the Commission, relating to the use of a consumer product.

(9) *Submitter of a report of harm* means any person or entity that submits a report of harm.

(10) *Voluntary recall notice* means any notice to the public by the Commission relating to a voluntary corrective action, including a voluntary recall of a consumer product, taken by a manufacturer in consultation with the Commission.

Subpart B—Content Requirements

§ 1102.10 Reports of harm.

(a) *Who may submit.* The following persons or entities may submit reports of harm:

(1) *Consumers* including, but not limited to, users of consumer products, family members, relatives, parents, guardians, friends, attorneys, investigators, professional engineers, agents of a user of a consumer product, and observers of the consumer products being used;

(2) *Local, state, or federal government agencies* including, but not limited to, local government agencies, school systems, social services, child protective services, state attorneys general, state agencies, and all executive and independent federal agencies as defined in Title 5 of the United States Code;

(3) *Health care professionals* including, but not limited to, medical examiners, coroners, physicians, nurses, physician's assistants, hospitals, chiropractors, and acupuncturists;

(4) *Child service providers* including, but not limited to, child care centers, child care providers, and prekindergarten schools; and

(5) *Public safety entities* including, but not limited to, police, fire, ambulance, emergency medical services, federal, state, and local law enforcement entities, and other public safety officials and professionals, including consumer advocates or individuals who work for nongovernmental organizations, consumer advocacy organizations, and trade associations, so long as they have a public safety purpose.

(b) *Manner of submission.* To be entered into the Database, reports of harm must be submitted to the CPSC using one of the following methods:

(1) Internet submissions through the CPSC's Internet Web site on an electronic incident report form specifically developed to collect such information.

(2) Telephonic submissions through a CPSC call center, where the information is entered on the electronic incident form.

(3) Electronic mail directed to the Office of the Secretary at *info@cpsc.gov*, or by facsimile at 301–504–0127, provided that the submitter completes the incident report form available for download on the CPSC's Internet Web site specifically developed to collect such information.

(4) Written submissions to the Office of the Secretary, Consumer Product Safety Commission, 4330 East West Highway, Bethesda, MD 20814–4408. The Commission will accept only those written reports of harm that use the incident report form developed for the CPSC's Internet Web site; or

(5) Other means the Commission subsequently makes available.

(c) *Size limit of reports of harm.* The Commission may, in its discretion, limit the data size of reports of harm, which may include attachments submitted, where such reports of harm and attachments may negatively impact the technological or operational performance of the system.

(d) *Minimum requirements for publication.* Subject to §§ 1102.24 and 1102.26, the Commission will publish in the Publicly Available Consumer Product Safety Information Database reports of harm containing all of the following information:

(1) *Description of the consumer product.* The description of the consumer product must, at a minimum, include a word or phrase sufficient to distinguish the product as a consumer product, a component part of a consumer product, or a product or substance regulated by the Commission. In addition to a word or phrase sufficient to distinguish the product as a consumer product, a description of a consumer product may include, but is not limited to, the name, including the brand name of the consumer product, model, serial number, date of manufacture (if known) or date code, date of purchase, price paid, retailer, or any other descriptive information about the product.

(2) *Identity of the manufacturer or private labeler.* The name of one or more manufacturers or private labelers of the consumer product. In addition to a firm name, identification of a manufacturer or private labeler may include, but is not limited to, a mailing address, phone number, or electronic mail address.

(3) *Description of the harm.* A brief narrative description of illness, injury, or death; or risk of illness, injury, or death related to use of the consumer product. Examples of a description of harm or risk of harm include, but are not limited to: Death, asphyxiation, lacerations, burns, abrasions, contusions, fractures, choking, poisoning, suffocation, amputation, or any other narrative description relating to a bodily harm or risk of bodily harm. Incident reports that relate solely to the cost or quality of a consumer product, with no discernable bodily harm or risk of bodily harm, do not constitute "harm" for purposes of this part. A description of harm may, but need not, include the severity of any injury and whether any medical treatment was received.

(4) *Incident date.* The date, or an approximate date, on which the incident occurred.

(5) *Category of submitter.* Indication of which category the submitter is in (*i.e.*, consumers, government agencies, *etc.*) from § 1102.10(a).

(6) *Contact information.* The submitter's first name, last name, and complete mailing address. Although this information will not be published in the Database, it is required information for the report of harm. Submitters also may, but are not required to, provide an electronic mail address and a phone number to allow for efficient and timely contact regarding a report of harm, when necessary.

(7) *Verification.* A submitter of a report of harm must affirmatively verify that he or she has reviewed the report of harm, and that the information contained therein is true and accurate to the best of the submitter's knowledge, information, and belief. Verification procedures for each method of submission will be specified.

(8) *Consent.* A submitter of a report of harm must consent to publication of

the report of harm in the Database if he or she wants the information to be included in the Database.

(e) *Additional information requested on report of harm.* The minimum requirements (at § 1102.10(d)) for publication of a report of harm in the Database do not restrict the Commission from choosing to seek other categories of voluntary information in the future.

(f) *Information not published.* The Commission will exclude the following information provided on a report of harm from publication in the Database:

(1) Name and contact information of the submitter of a report of harm;

(2) Victim's name and contact information, if the victim or the victim's parent, guardian, or appropriate legally authorized representative, has not provided appropriate legal consent;

(3) Photographs that in the determination of the Commission are not in the public interest, including photographs that could be used to identify a person or photographs that would constitute an invasion of personal privacy based on the Privacy Act of 1974, Public Law 93–579 as amended;

(4) Medical records without the consent of the person about whom such records pertain or without the consent of his or her parent, guardian, or appropriate legally authorized representative;

(5) Confidential information as set forth in § 1102.24;

(6) Information determined to be materially inaccurate as set forth in § 1102.26;

(7) Reports of harm retracted at any time by the submitters of those reports, if they indicate in writing to the Commission that they supplied materially inaccurate information;

(8) Consents and verifications associated with a report of harm; and

(9) Any other information submitted on or with a report of harm, the inclusion of which in the Database, the Commission determines is not in the public interest. The Commission shall consider whether the information is related to a product safety purpose served by the Database, including whether or not the information helps Database users to:

(i) Identify a consumer product;

(ii) Identify a manufacturer or private labeler of a consumer product;

(iii) Understand a harm or risk of harm related to the use of a consumer product; or

(iv) Understand the relationship between a submitter of a report of harm and the victim.

(g) *Reports of harm from persons under the age of 18.* The Commission will not accept any report of harm when the report of harm is or was submitted by anyone under the age of 18 without consent of the parent or guardian of that person.

(h) *Incomplete reports of harm.* Any information received by the Commission related to a report of harm that does not meet the requirements for submission or publication will not be published, but will be maintained for internal use.

(i) *Official records of the Commission.* All reports of harm that are submitted to the Commission become official records of the Commission in accordance with 16 CFR 1015.1. Alteration (or disposition) of any such records will only be in accordance with the procedures specified in this part.

§ 1102.12 Manufacturer comments.

(a) *Who may submit.* A manufacturer or private labeler may submit a comment related to a report of harm if the report of harm identifies such manufacturer or private labeler.

(b) *How to submit.* A manufacturer or private labeler may submit comments to the CPSC using one of the following methods:

(1) A manufacturer or private labeler who registers with the Commission as described in § 1102.20(f) may submit comments through a manufacturer portal maintained on the CPSC's Internet Web site;

(2) A manufacturer or private labeler may submit comments by electronic mail, directed to the Office of the Secretary at *info@cpsc.gov;* or

(3) A manufacturer or private labeler may submit written comments directed to the Office of the Secretary, Consumer Product Safety Commission, 4330 East West Highway, Bethesda, MD 20814–4408.

(c) *What must be submitted.* Subject to §§ 1102.24 and 1102.26, the Commission will publish manufacturer comments related to a report of harm transmitted to a manufacturer or private labeler in the Database if such manufacturer comment meets the following requirements:

(1) *Manufacturer comment relates to report of harm.* The manufacturer or private labeler's comment must relate to information contained in a specific report of harm that identifies such manufacturer or private labeler and that is submitted for publication in the Database.

(2) *Unique identifier.* A manufacturer comment must state the unique identifier provided by the CPSC.

(3) *Verification.* A manufacturer or private labeler must verify that it has reviewed the report of harm and the comment related to the report of harm and that the information contained in the comment is true and accurate to the best of the firm's knowledge, information, and belief.

(4) *Request for publication.* When a manufacturer or private labeler submits a comment regarding a report of harm, it may request that the Commission publish such comment in the Database. A manufacturer or private labeler must affirmatively request publication of the comment, and consent to such publication in the Database, for each comment submitted to the CPSC.

(d) *Information published.* Subject to §§1102.24 and 1102.26, the Commission will publish a manufacturer comment and the date of its submission to the CPSC in the Database if the comment meets the minimum requirements for publication as described in paragraph (c) of this section.

(e) *Information not published.* The Commission will not publish in the Database consents and verifications associated with a manufacturer comment.

§1102.14 Recall notices.

All information presented in a voluntary or mandatory recall notice that has been made available to the public shall be accessible and searchable in the Database.

§1102.16 Additional information.

In addition to reports of harm, manufacturer comments, and recall notices, the CPSC shall include in the Database any additional information it determines to be in the public interest, consistent with the requirements of section 6(a) and (b) of the CPSA.

Subpart C—Procedural Requirements

§1102.20 Transmission of reports of harm to the identified manufacturer or private labeler.

(a) *Information transmitted.* Except as provided in paragraphs (a)(1) through (a)(3) of this section, the Commission will transmit all information provided in a report of harm, provided such report meets the minimum requirements for publication in the Database, to the manufacturer or private labeler identified in a report of harm. The following information will not be transmitted to a manufacturer or private labeler:

(1) Name and contact information for the submitter of the report of harm, unless such submitter provides express written consent (for example, by checking a box on the report of harm) to provide such information to the manufacturer or private labeler;

(2) Photographs that could be used to identify a person; and

(3) Medical records, unless the person about whom such records pertain, or his or her parent, guardian, or appropriate legally authorized representative, consents to providing such records to the manufacturer or private labeler.

(b) *Limitation on use of contact information.* A manufacturer or private labeler who receives name and contact information for the submitter of a report of harm and/or a victim must not use or disseminate such information to any other party for any other purpose other than verification of information contained in a report of harm. Verification of information contained in a report of harm must not include activities such as sales, promotion, marketing, warranty, or any other commercial purpose. Verification of information contained in a report of harm may include verification of the:

(1) Identity of the submitter and/or the victim, including name, location, age, and gender;

(2) Consumer product, including serial or model number, date code, color, or size;

(3) Harm or risk of harm related to the use of the consumer product;

(4) Description of the incident related to use of the consumer product;

(5) Date or approximate date of the incident; and/or

(6) Category of submitter.

(c) *Timing.* To the extent practicable, the Commission will transmit a report of harm to the manufacturer or private labeler within five business days of submission of the completed report of harm. If the Commission cannot determine whom the manufacturer or private labeler is from the report of harm, or otherwise, then it will not post the report of harm on the Database but will maintain the report for internal agency use. Examples of circumstances that may arise that may make transmission of the report of harm impracticable within five business days include, but are not limited to:

(1) The manufacturer or private labeler is out of business with no identifiable successor;

(2) The submitter misidentified a manufacturer or private labeler;

(3) The report of harm contained inaccurate or insufficient contact information for a manufacturer or private labeler; or

(4) The Commission cannot locate valid contact information for a manufacturer or private labeler.

(d) *Method of transmission.* The Commission will use the method of transmission and contact information provided by the manufacturer or private labeler. The Commission will transmit reports of harm to a manufacturer or private labeler who has registered with the Commission as described in paragraph (f) of this section. If a manufacturer or private labeler has not registered with the Commission, the Commission will send reports of harm through the United States mail to the firm's principal place of business, unless the Commission selects another equally effective method of transmission.

(e) *Size limits of manufacturer comments.* The Commission may, in its discretion, limit the data size of comments, which may include attachments submitted, where such comments and attachments may negatively impact the technological or operational performance of the system.

(f) *Manufacturer registration.* Manufacturers and private labelers may register with the Commission to select a preferred method for receiving reports of harm that identify such firm as the manufacturer or private labeler. Manufacturers and private labelers that choose to register with the Commission must:

(1) Register with the Commission through a process identified for such registration;

(2) Provide and maintain updated contact information for the firm, including the name of the firm, title of a person to whom reports of harm should be directed, complete mailing address, telephone number, electronic mail address, and Web site address (if any); and

(3) Select a specified method to receive reports of harm that identify the firm as the manufacturer or private labeler of a consumer product.

(g) *Manufacturer comments.* A manufacturer or private labeler who receives a report of harm from the CPSC may comment on the information contained in such report of harm. The Commission, in its discretion, where it determines it is in the public interest, may choose not to publish a manufacturer comment in the Database. For example, it may not be in the public interest for the Commission to publish comments that, in the unlikely event, contain language reasonably described as lewd, lascivious, or obscene.

§ 1102.24 Designation of confidential information.

(a) For purposes of this section, "confidential information" is considered to be information that contains or relates to a trade secret or other matter referred to in 18 U.S.C. 1905 or that is subject to 5 U.S.C. 552(b)(4).

(b) A manufacturer or private labeler identified in a report of harm and who receives a report of harm from the CPSC may review such report of harm for confidential information and request that portions of the report of harm be designated as confidential information. Each requester seeking such a designation of confidential information bears the burden of proof and must:

(1) Specifically identify the exact portion(s) of the report of harm claimed to be confidential;

(2) State whether the information claimed to be confidential has ever been released in any manner to a person who was not an employee or in a confidential relationship with the company;

(3) State whether the information so specified is commonly known within the industry or is readily ascertainable by outside persons with a minimum of time and effort;

(4) If known, state the company's relationship with the victim and/or submitter of the report of harm and how the victim and/or submitter of the report of harm came to be in possession of such allegedly confidential information;

(5) State how the release of the information would be likely to cause substantial harm to the company's competitive position; and

(6) State whether the person submitting the request for treatment as confidential information is authorized to make claims of confidentiality on behalf of the person or organization concerned.

(c) *Manner of submission*. Requests for designation of confidential information may be submitted in the same manner as manufacturer comments as described in §1102.12(b). A request for designation of confidential treatment must be conspicuously marked.

(d) *Timing of submission*. In order to ensure that the allegedly confidential information is not placed in the database, a request for designation of confidential information must be received by the Commission in a timely manner prior to the 10th business day after the date on which the Commission transmits the report to the manufacturer or private labeler. If a request for confidential treatment is submitted in a timely fashion, the Commission will either make a determination on the claim prior to posting on the 10th business day after transmittal to the manufacturer or, as a matter of policy, redact the allegedly confidential information from a report of harm before publication in the Database until it makes a determination regarding confidential treatment.

(e) *Assistance with defense*. No request to redact confidential information from a report of harm pursuant to 5 U.S.C. 552(b)(4) should be made by any person who does not intend in good faith, and so certifies in writing, to assist the Commission in the defense of any judicial proceeding that thereafter might be brought to compel the disclosure of information that the Commission has determined to be a trade secret or privileged or confidential commercial or financial information.

(f) *Commission determination of confidentiality*. If the Commission determines that information in a report of harm is confidential, the Commission shall:

(1) Notify the manufacturer or private labeler;

(2) Redact such confidential information in the report of harm; and

(3) Publish the report of harm in the Database without such confidential information.

(g) *Commission determination of no confidentiality*. If the Commission determines that a report of harm does not contain confidential information, the Commission shall:

(1) Notify the manufacturer or private labeler; and

(2) Publish the report of harm, if not already published, in the Database.

(h) *Removal of confidential information*. As stated at 6A(c)(1)(C)(iii) of the CPSA, to seek removal of alleged confidential information that has been published in the Database, a manufacturer or private labeler may bring an action in the district court of the United States in the district in which the complainant resides, or has its principal place of business, or in the U.S. District Court for the District of Columbia.

§ 1102.26 Determination of materially inaccurate information.

(a) For purposes of this section, the following definitions apply:

(1) *Materially inaccurate information in a report of harm* means information that is false or misleading, and which is so substantial and important as to affect a reasonable consumer's decision making about the product, including:

(i) The identification of a consumer product;

(ii) The identification of a manufacturer or private labeler;

(iii) The harm or risk of harm related to use of the consumer product; or

(iv) The date, or approximate date on which the incident occurred.

(2) *Materially inaccurate information in a manufacturer comment* means information that is false or misleading, and which is so substantial and important as to affect a reasonable consumer's decision making about the product, including:

(i) The description of the consumer product;

(ii) The identity of the firm or firms responsible for the importation, manufacture, distribution, sale, or holding for sale of a consumer product;

(iii) The harm or risk of harm related to the use of a consumer product;

(iv) The status of a Commission, manufacturer, or private labeler investigation;

(v) Whether the manufacturer or private labeler is engaging in a corrective action and whether such action has not been approved by the Commission; or

(vi) Whether the manufacturer has taken, or promised to take, any other action with regard to the product.

(b) *Request for determination of materially inaccurate information.* Any person or entity reviewing a report of harm or manufacturer comment, either before or after publication in the Database, may request that the report of harm or manufacturer comment, or portions of such report of harm or manufacturer comment, be excluded from the Database or corrected by the Commission because it contains materially inaccurate information. Each requester seeking an exclusion or correction bears the burden of proof and must:

(1) State the unique identifier of the report of harm or manufacturer comment to which the request for a determination of materially inaccurate information pertains;

(2) Specifically identify the exact portion(s) of the report of harm or the manufacturer comment claimed to be materially inaccurate;

(3) State the basis for the allegation that such information is materially inaccurate;

(4) Provide evidence, which may include documents, statements, electronic mail, Internet links, photographs, or any other evidence, sufficient for the Commission to make a determination that the designated information is materially inaccurate;

(5) State what relief the requester is seeking: Exclusion of the entire report of harm or manufacturer comment; redaction of specific information; correction of specific information; or the addition of information to correct the material inaccuracy;

(6) State whether and how an alleged material inaccuracy may be corrected without removing or excluding an entire report of harm or manufacturer comment; and

(7) State whether the person submitting the allegation of material inaccuracy is authorized to make claims of material inaccuracy on behalf of the person or organization concerned.

(c) *Manner of submission*—

(1) *Length of request and expedited review.* The Commission strongly recommends requesters seeking an expedited review of claims of materially inaccurate information to limit the length of the request described in §1102.26(b) to no more than five pages, including attachments, to allow for the expedited review of the request. Regardless of length, all submissions will be reviewed.

(2) *Manufacturers and private labelers.* A manufacturer or private labeler may request a Commission determination of materially inaccurate information related to a report of harm in the same manner as described in §1102.12(b). Such requests should be conspicuously marked.

(3) *All other requests.* All other requests for a Commission determination of materially inaccurate information contained in a report of harm or manufacturer comment made by any other person or firm must be submitted to the CPSC using one of the methods listed below. The request seeking a

Commission determination of materially inaccurate information may be made through:

(i) *Electronic mail*. By electronic mail directed to the Office of the Secretary at *info@cpsc.gov;* or

(ii) *Paper-based*. Written submission directed to the Office of the Secretary, Consumer Product Safety Commission, 4330 East West Highway, Bethesda, MD 20814–4408.

(d) *Timing of submission*. A request for a Commission determination regarding materially inaccurate information may be submitted at any time. If a request for determination of materially inaccurate information is submitted prior to publication of a report of harm in the Database, the Commission cannot withhold the report of harm from publication in the Database until it makes a determination. Absent a determination, the Commission will publish reports of harm on the tenth business day after transmitting a report of harm to the manufacturer or private labeler.

(e) *Assistance with defense*. No request for a determination of materially inaccurate information should be made by any person who does not intend in good faith, and so certifies in writing, to assist the Commission in the defense of any judicial proceeding that thereafter might be brought to compel the disclosure of information that the Commission has determined to be materially inaccurate information.

(f) *Notice*. The Commission shall notify the person or firm requesting a determination regarding materially inaccurate information of its determination and method of resolution after resolving such request.

(g) *Commission determination of material inaccuracy before publication*. If the Commission determines that information in a report of harm or manufacturer comment is materially inaccurate information before it is published in the Database, the Commission shall:

(1) Decline to add the materially inaccurate information to the Database;

(2) Correct the materially inaccurate information, and, if the minimum requirements for publication as set forth in §§ 1102.10(d) and 1102.12(c) are met, publish the report of harm or manufacturer comment in the Database; or

(3) Add information to the report of harm or the manufacturer comment to correct the materially inaccurate information, and, if the minimum requirements for publication as set forth in §§ 1102.10(d) and 1102.12(c) are met, publish the report of harm or manufacturer comment in the Database.

(h) *Commission determination of material inaccuracy after publication*. If the Commission determines, after an investigation, that the requested designated information in a report of harm or manufacturer comment contains materially inaccurate information after the report of harm or manufacturer comment has been published in the Database, the Commission shall, no later than seven business days after such determination:

(1) Remove the information determined to be materially inaccurate from the Database, including any associated documents, photographs, or comments;

(2) Correct the information, and, if the minimum requirements for publication as set forth in §§ 1102.10(d) and 1102.12(c) are met, maintain the report of harm or manufacturer comment in the Database; or

(3) Add information to the report of harm or the manufacturer comment to correct the materially inaccurate information, and, if the minimum requirements for publication as set forth in §§ 1102.10(d) and 1102.12(c) are met, maintain the report of harm or manufacturer comment in the Database.

(i) *Commission discretion*.

(1) In exercising its discretion to remove, correct, or add information to correct materially inaccurate information contained in a report of harm or manufacturer comment, the Commission shall preserve the integrity of information received for publication in the Database whenever possible. Subject to §§ 1102.10(d) and 1102.12(c), the Commission shall favor correction, and the addition of information to correct, over exclusion of entire reports of harm and manufacturer comments, where possible.

(2) *Expedited determinations*. Where a manufacturer has filed a request for a

correction or exclusion within the recommended page limit in § 1102.26(c)(1), the Commission shall attempt, where practicable, to make an expedited determination of a claim of material inaccuracy. Given the requirement of section 6A of the CPSA that reports of harm be published, the Commission will publish reports of harm on the tenth business day after transmitting a report of harm, where the Commission has been unable to make a determination regarding a claim of material inaccuracy prior to the statutorily mandated publication date. In such instances, the Commission will make any necessary correction, exclusion, or addition not later than seven business days after making a determination that there is materially inaccurate information in the report of harm. Manufacturer comments will be published at the same time as the report of harm is published, or as soon thereafter as practicable.

(j) *Commission determination of no material inaccuracy.* If the Commission determines that the requested information in a report of harm or manufacturer comment does not contain materially inaccurate information, the Commission will:

(1) Notify the requester of its determination; and

(2) Publish the report of harm or manufacturer comment, if not already published, in the Database if it meets the minimum requirements set forth in §§ 1102.10(d) and 1102.12(c).

(k) *Commission action in absence of request.* The Commission may review a report of harm or manufacturer comment for materially inaccurate information on its own initiative, following the same notice and procedural requirements set forth in paragraphs (g) through (j) of this section.

§ 1102.28 Publication of reports of harm.

(a) *Timing.* Subject to §§ 1102.10, 1102.24, and 1102.26, the Commission will publish reports of harm that meet the requirements for publication in the Database. The Commission will publish reports of harm as soon as practicable, but not later than the tenth business day after such report of harm is transmitted to the manufacturer or private labeler by the CPSC.

(b) *Exceptions.* The Commission may publish a report of harm that meets the requirements of § 1102.10(d) in the Database beyond the 10-business-day time frame set forth in paragraph (a) of this section if the Commission determines that a report of harm misidentifies or fails to identify all manufacturers or private labelers. Such information must be corrected through the procedures set forth in § 1102.26 for materially inaccurate information in a report of harm. Once a manufacturer or a private labeler has been identified correctly, the time frame set forth in paragraph (a) of this section shall apply.

§ 1102.30 Publication of manufacturer comments.

Timing. Subject to §§ 1102.12, 1102.24, and 1102.26, the Commission will publish in the Database manufacturer comments submitted in response to a report of harm that meet the minimum requirements set forth in § 1102.12(c). This publication will occur at the same time as the report of harm is published or as soon thereafter as practicable. An example of a circumstance that may make it impracticable to publish a manufacturer comment at the same time as a report of harm includes when the Commission did not receive the comment until on or after the publication date of the report of harm.

Subpart D—Notice and Disclosure Requirements

§ 1102.42 Disclaimers.

The Commission does not guarantee the accuracy, completeness, or adequacy of the contents of the Consumer Product Safety Information Database, particularly with respect to the accuracy, completeness, or adequacy of information submitted by persons outside of the CPSC. The Database will contain a notice to this effect that will be prominently and conspicuously displayed on the Database and on any documents that are printed from the Database.

§ 1102.44 Applicability of sections 6(a) and (b) of the CPSA.

(a) *Generally*. Sections 6(a) and 6(b) of the CPSA shall not apply to the submission, disclosure, and publication of information provided in a report of harm that meets the minimum requirements for publication in § 1102.10(d) in the Database.

(b) *Limitation on construction*. Section 1102.44(a) shall not be construed to exempt from the requirements of sections 6(a) and 6(b) of the CPSA information received by the Commission pursuant to:

(1) Section 15(b) of the CPSA; or

(2) Any other mandatory or voluntary reporting program established between a retailer, manufacturer, or private labeler and the Commission.

PART 1105—CONTRIBUTIONS TO COSTS OF PARTICIPANTS IN DEVELOPMENT OF CONSUMER PRODUCT SAFETY STANDARDS

Sec.

AUTHORITY: Sec. 7(c), Pub. L. 97–35, 95 Stat. 704 (15 U.S.C. 2056(c)).

SOURCE: 48 FR 57121, Dec. 28, 1983, unless otherwise noted.

§ 1105.1 Purpose.

The purpose of this part is to describe the factors the Commission considers when determining whether or not to contribute to the cost of an individual, a group of individuals, a public or private organization or association, partnership or corporation (hereinafter "participant") who participates with the Commission in developing standards. The provisions of this part do not apply to and do not affect the Commission's ability and authority to contract with persons or groups outside the Commission to aid the Commission in developing proposed standards.

§ 1105.2 Factors.

The Commission may agree to contribute to the cost of a participant who participates with the Commission in developing a standard in any case in which the Commission determines:

(a) That a contribution is likely to result in a more satisfactory standard than would be developed without a contribution; and

(b) That the participant to whom a contribution is made is financially responsible.

§ 1105.3 A more satisfactory standard.

In considering whether a contribution is likely to result in a more satisfactory standard, the Commission shall consider:

(a) The need for representation of one or more particular interests, expertise, or points of view in the development proceeding; and

(b) The extent to which particular interests, points of view, or expertise can reasonably be expected to be represented if the Commission does not provide any financial contribution.

§ 1105.4 Eligibility.

In order to be eligible to receive a financial contribution, a participant must request in advance a specific contribution with an explanation as to why the contribution is likely to result in a more satisfactory standard than would be developed without a contribution. The request for a contribution shall contain, to the fullest extent possible and appropriate, the following information:

(a) A description of the point of view, interest and/or expertise that the participant intends to bring to the proceeding;

(b) The reason(s) that representation of the participant's interest, point of view, or expertise can reasonably be expected to contribute substantially to a full and fair determination of the issues involved in the proceeding;

(c) An explanation of the economic interest, if any, that the participant has (and individuals or groups comprising the participant have) in any

Commission determination related to the proceeding;

(d) A discussion, with supporting documentation, of the reason(s) a participant is unable to participate effectively in the proceeding without a financial contribution;

(e) A description of the participant's employment or organization, as appropriate; and

(f) A specific and itemized estimate of the costs for which the contribution is sought.

§ 1105.5 Applications.

Applications must be submitted to the Office of the Secretary, Consumer Product Safety Commission, Washington, D.C. 20207, within the time specified by the Commission in its FEDERAL REGISTER notice beginning the development proceeding.

§ 1105.6 Criteria.

The Commission may authorize a financial contribution only for participants who meet all of the following criteria:

(a) The participant represents particular interest, expertise or point of view that can reasonably be expected to contribute substantially to a full and fair determination of the issues involved in the proceeding;

(b) The economic interest of the participant in any Commission determination related to the proceeding is small in comparison to the participant's costs of effective participation in the proceeding. If the participant consists of more than one individual or group, the economic interest of each of the individuals or groups comprising the participant shall also be considered, if practicable and appropriate; and

(c) The participant does not have sufficient financial resources available for effective participation in the proceeding, in the absence of a financial contribution.

§ 1105.7 Limits on compensation.

The Commission may establish a limit on the total amount of financial compensation to be made to all participants in a particular proceeding and may establish a limit on the total amount of compensation to be made to any one participant in a particular proceeding.

§ 1105.8 Costs must be authorized and incurred.

The Commission shall compensate participants only for costs that have been authorized and only for such costs actually incurred for participation in a proceeding.

§ 1105.9 Itemized vouchers.

The participant shall be paid upon submission of an itemized voucher listing each item of expense. Each item of expense exceeding $15 must be substantiated by a copy of a receipt, invoice, or appropriate document evidencing the fact that the cost was incurred.

§ 1105.10 Reasonable costs.

The Commission shall compensate participants only for costs that it determines are reasonable. As guidelines in these determinations, the Commission shall consider market rates and rates normally paid by the Commission for comparable goods and services, as appropriate.

§ 1105.11 Compensable costs.

The Commission may compensate participants for any or all of the following costs:

(a) Salaries for participants or employees of participants;

(b) Fees for consultants, experts, contractural services, and attorneys that are incurred by participants;

(c) Transportation costs;

(d) Travel-related costs such as lodging, meals, tipping, telephone calls; and

(e) All other reasonable costs incurred, such as document reproduction, postage, baby-sitting, and the like.

§ 1105.12 Advance contributions.

The Commission may make its contribution in advance upon specific request, and the contribution may be made without regard to section 3648 of the Revised States of the United States (31 U.S.C. 529).

§ 1105.13 Noncompensable costs.

The items of cost toward which the Commission will not contribute include:

(a) Costs for the acquisition of any interest in land or buildings;

(b) Costs for the payment of items in excess of the participant's actual cost; and

(c) Costs determined not to be allowable under generally accepted accounting principles and practices or part 1–15, Federal Procurement Regulations (41 CFR part 1–15).

§ 1105.14 Audit and examination.

The Commission and the Comptroller General of the United States, or their duly authorized representatives, shall have access for the purpose of audit and examination to any pertinent books, documents, papers and records of a participant receiving compensation under this section. The Commission may establish additional guidelines for accounting, recordkeeping, and other administrative procedures with which participants must comply as a condition of receiving a contribution.

PART 1107—TESTING AND LABELING PERTAINING TO PRODUCT CERTIFICATION

Subpart A—General Provisions

AUTHORITY: 15 U.S.C. 2063, Sec. 3, 102 Pub. L. 110–314, 122 Stat. 3016, 3017, 3022.

SOURCE: 76 FR 69541, Nov. 8, 2011, unless otherwise noted.

EFFECTIVE DATE NOTE: At 76 FR 69541, Nov. 8, 2011, part 1107 was added, effective Feb. 13, 2013.

Subpart A—General Provisions

§ 1107.1 Purpose.

This part establishes the protocols and standards for ensuring continued testing of children's products periodically and when there has been a material change in the product's design or manufacturing process and safeguarding against the exercise of undue influence by a manufacturer on a third party conformity assessment body. It also establishes a program for labeling of consumer products to indicate that the certification requirements have been met pursuant to sections 14(a)(2) and (i)(2)(B) of the Consumer Product Safety Act (CPSA) (15 U.S.C. 2063(a)(2) and (i)(2)(B)).

§ 1107.2 Definitions.

Unless otherwise stated, the definitions of the Consumer Product Safety Act and the Consumer Product Safety Improvement Act of 2008 apply to this part. The following definitions apply for purposes of this part:

CPSA means the Consumer Product Safety Act.

CPSC means the Consumer Product Safety Commission.

Due care means the degree of care that a prudent and competent person engaged in the same line of business or endeavor would exercise under similar circumstances. Due care does not permit willful ignorance.

High degree of assurance means an evidence-based demonstration of consistent performance of a product regarding compliance based on knowledge of a product and its manufacture.

Identical in all material respects means there is no difference with respect to compliance to the applicable rules, bans, standards, or regulations between the samples to be tested for compliance and the finished product distributed in commerce.

Manufacturer means the parties responsible for certification of a consumer product pursuant to 16 CFR part 1110.

Manufacturing process means the techniques, fixtures, tools, materials, and personnel used to create the component parts and assemble a finished product.

Material change means any change in the product's design, manufacturing process, or sourcing of component parts that a manufacturer exercising due care knows, or should know, could affect the product's ability to comply with the applicable rules, bans, standards, or regulations.

Third party conformity assessment body means a testing laboratory whose accreditation has been accepted by the CPSC to conduct certification testing on children's products. Only third party conformity assessment bodies whose scope of accreditation includes the applicable required tests can be used for children's product certification or periodic testing purposes.

Subpart B [Reserved]

Subpart C—Certification of Children's Products

§ 1107.20 General requirements.

(a) Manufacturers must submit a sufficient number of samples of a children's product, or samples that are identical in all material respects to the children's product, to a third party conformity assessment body for testing to support certification. The number of samples selected must be sufficient to provide a high degree of assurance that the tests conducted for certification purposes accurately demonstrate the ability of the children's product to meet all applicable children's product safety rules.

(b) If the manufacturing process for a children's product consistently creates finished products that are uniform in composition and quality, a manufacturer may submit fewer samples to provide a high degree of assurance that the finished product complies with the applicable children's product safety rules. If the manufacturing process for a children's product results in variability in the composition or quality of children's products, a manufacturer may need to submit more samples to provide a high degree of assurance that the finished product complies with the applicable children's product safety rules.

(c) Except where otherwise specified by a children's product safety rule, component part testing pursuant to 16 CFR part 1109 may be used to support the certification testing requirements of this section.

(d) If a product sample fails certification testing to the applicable children's product safety rule(s), even if other samples have passed the same certification test, the manufacturer must investigate the reasons for the failure and take the necessary steps to address the reasons for the failure. A manufacturer cannot certify the children's product until the manufacturer establishes, with a high degree of assurance that the finished product does comply with all applicable children's product safety rules.

§ 1107.21 Periodic testing.

(a) *General requirements for all manufacturers*. All manufacturers of children's products must conduct periodic testing. All periodic testing must be conducted by a third party conformity assessment body. Periodic testing must be conducted pursuant to either paragraph (b), (c), or (d) of this section or as provided in regulations under this title. The testing interval selected for periodic testing may be based on a fixed production interval, a set number of units produced, or another method chosen by the manufacturer based on the product produced and its manufacturing process, so long as the applicable maximum testing interval specified in paragraph (b), (c), or (d) of this section is not exceeded. Component part testing pursuant to 16 CFR part 1109 may be used to support the periodic testing requirements of this section.

(b) A manufacturer must conduct periodic testing to ensure compliance with the applicable children's product safety rules at least once a year, except as otherwise provided in paragraphs (c), and (d) of this section or as provided in regulations under this title. If a manufacturer does not conduct production testing under paragraph (c) of this section, or testing by a testing laboratory under paragraph (d) of this section, the manufacturer must conduct periodic testing as follows:

(1) *Periodic Testing Plan*. Manufacturers must develop a periodic testing

plan to ensure with a high degree of assurance that children's products manufactured after the issuance of a Children's Product Certificate, or since the previous periodic testing was conducted, continue to comply with all applicable children's product safety rules. The periodic testing plan must include the tests to be conducted, the intervals at which the tests will be conducted, and the number of samples tested. At each manufacturing site, the manufacturer must have a periodic testing plan specific to each children's product manufactured at that site.

(2) *Testing Interval.* The testing interval selected must be short enough to ensure that, if the samples selected for testing pass the test, there is a high degree of assurance that the other untested children's products manufactured during the testing interval comply with the applicable children's product safety rules. The testing interval may vary depending upon the specific children's product safety rules that apply to the children's product, but may not exceed one year. Factors to be considered when determining the testing interval include, but are not limited to, the following:

(i) High variability in test results, as indicated by a relatively large sample standard deviation in quantitative tests;

(ii) Measurements that are close to the allowable numerical limit for quantitative tests;

(iii) Known manufacturing process factors which could affect compliance with a rule. For example, if the manufacturer knows that a casting die wears down as the die nears the end of its useful life, the manufacturer may wish to test more often as the casting die wears down;

(iv) Consumer complaints or warranty claims;

(v) Introduction of a new set of component parts into the assembly process;

(vi) The manufacture of a fixed number of products;

(vii) Potential for serious injury or death resulting from a noncompliant children's product;

(viii) The number of children's products produced annually, such that a manufacturer should consider testing a children's product more frequently if the product is produced in very large numbers or distributed widely throughout the United States;

(ix) The children's product's similarity to other children's products with which the manufacturer is familiar and/or whether the children's product has many different component parts compared to other children's products of a similar type; or

(x) Inability to determine the children's product's noncompliance easily through means such as visual inspection.

(c)(1) If a manufacturer implements a production testing plan as described in paragraph (c)(2) of this section to ensure continued compliance of the children's product with a high degree of assurance to the applicable children's product safety rules, the manufacturer must submit samples of its children's product to a third party conformity assessment body for periodic testing to the applicable children's product safety rules at least once every two years. A manufacturer may consider the information obtained from production testing when determining the appropriate testing interval and the number of samples needed for periodic testing to ensure that there is a high degree of assurance that the other untested children's products manufactured during the testing interval comply with the applicable children's product safety rules.

(2) *Production Testing Plan.* A production testing plan describes the production management techniques and tests that must be performed to provide a high degree of assurance that the products manufactured after certification continue to meet all the applicable children's product safety rules. A production testing plan may include recurring testing or the use of process management techniques, such as control charts, statistical process control programs, or failure modes and effects analyses (FMEAs) designed to control potential variations in product manufacturing that could affect the product's ability to comply with the applicable children's product safety rules. A manufacturer may use measurement techniques that are nondestructive and tailored to the needs of an individual

product to ensure that a product complies with all applicable children's product safety rules. Any production test method used to conduct production testing must be effective in determining compliance. Production testing cannot consist solely of mathematical methods (such as an FMEA, with no additional components, or computer simulations). Production testing must include some testing, although it is not required that the test methods employed be the test methods used for certification. A manufacturer must document the production testing methods used to ensure continuing compliance and the basis for determining that the production testing plan provides a high degree of assurance that the product being manufactured continues to comply with all applicable children's product safety rules. A production testing plan must contain the following elements:

(i) A description of the production testing plan, including, but not limited to, a description of the process management techniques used, the tests to be conducted, or the measurements to be taken; the intervals at which the tests or measurements will be made; the number of samples tested; and the basis for determining that the combination of process management techniques and tests provide a high degree of assurance of compliance if they are not the tests prescribed for the applicable children's product safety rule;

(ii) At each manufacturing site, the manufacturer must have a production testing plan specific to each children's product manufactured at that site;

(iii) The production testing interval selected for tests must ensure that, if the samples selected for production testing comply with an applicable children's product safety rule, there is a high degree of assurance that the untested products manufactured during that testing interval also will comply with the applicable children's product safety rule. Production testing intervals should be appropriate for the specific testing or alternative measurements being conducted.

(3) If a production testing plan as described in this paragraph (c) fails to provide a high degree of assurance of compliance with all applicable children's product safety rules, the CPSC may require the manufacturer to meet the requirements of paragraph (b) of this section or modify its production testing plan to ensure a high degree of assurance of compliance.

(d)(1) For manufacturers conducting testing to ensure continued compliance with the applicable children's product safety rules using a testing laboratory accredited to ISO/IEC 17025:2005(E), "General requirements for the competence of testing and calibration laboratories," periodic tests by a third party conformity assessment body must be conducted at least once every three years. Any ISO/IEC 17025:2005(E)-accredited testing laboratory used for ensuring continued compliance must be accredited by an accreditation body that is accredited to ISO/IEC 17011:2004(E), "Conformity assessment—General requirements for accreditation bodies accrediting conformity assessment bodies." The test method(s) used by an ISO/IEC 17025:2005(E)-accredited testing laboratory when conducting testing to ensure continued compliance must be the same test method(s) used for certification to the applicable children's product safety rules. Manufacturers must conduct testing using the ISO/IEC 17025:2005(E)-accredited testing laboratory frequently enough to provide a high degree of assurance that the children's product continues to comply with the applicable children's product safety rules. A manufacturer may consider the information obtained from testing conducted by an ISO/IEC 17025:2005(E)-accredited testing laboratory when determining the appropriate testing interval and the number of samples for periodic testing that are needed to ensure that there is a high degree of assurance that the other untested children's products manufactured during the testing interval comply with the applicable children's product safety rules.

(2) If the continued testing described in paragraph (d)(1) of this section fails to provide a high degree of assurance of compliance with all applicable children's product safety rules, the CPSC may require the manufacturer to meet the requirements of paragraph (b) of

this section or modify the testing frequency or number of samples required to ensure a high degree of assurance of continued compliance.

(e) [Reserved]

(f) [Reserved]

(g) The Director of the Federal Register approves the incorporations by reference of the standards in this section in accordance with 5 U.S.C. 552(a) and 1 CFR part 51. You may inspect a copy of the standards at the Office of the Secretary, U.S. Consumer Product Safety Commission, Room 820, 4330 East West Highway, Bethesda, MD 20814, telephone (301) 504–7923, or at the National Archives and Records Administration (NARA). For information on the availability of this material at NARA, call (202) 741–6030, or go to: *http://www.archives.gov/federal_register/code_of_federal_regulations/ibr_locations.html.*

(1) International Organization for Standardization (ISO), 1, ch. de la Voie-Creuse, Case postale 56, CH–1211 Geneva 20, Switzerland; Telephone +41 22 749 01 11, Fax +41 22 733 34 30; *http://www.iso.org/iso/home.html.*

(i) ISO/IEC 17011:2004(E), "Conformity assessment—General requirements for accreditation bodies accrediting conformity assessment bodies," First Edition, September 1, 2004 (Corrected version February 15, 2005);

(ii) ISO/IEC 17025:2005(E), "General requirements for the competence of testing and calibration laboratories," Second Edition, May 15, 2005.

(2) [Reserved]

EFFECTIVE DATE NOTE: At 77 FR 72219, Dec. 5, 2012, §1107.21 was amended by adding paragraph (f), effective February 8, 2013. For the convenience of the user, the added text is set forth as follows:

§ 1107.21 Periodic testing.

* * * * *

(f) A manufacturer must select representative product samples to be submitted to the third party conformity assessment body for periodic testing. The procedure used to select representative product samples for periodic testing must provide a basis for inferring compliance about the population of untested products produced during the applicable periodic testing interval. The number of samples selected for the sampling procedure must be sufficient to ensure continuing compliance with all applicable children's product safety rules. The manufacturer must document the procedure used to select the product samples for periodic testing and the basis for inferring the compliance of the product manufactured during the periodic testing interval from the results of the tested samples.

* * * * *

§ 1107.23 Material change.

(a) *General Requirements.* If a children's product undergoes a material change in product design or manufacturing process, including the sourcing of component parts, which a manufacturer exercising due care knows, or should know, could affect the product's ability to comply with the applicable children's product safety rules, the manufacturer must submit a sufficient number of samples of the materially changed children's product for testing by a third party conformity assessment body and issue a new Children's Product Certificate. The number of samples submitted must be sufficient to provide a high degree of assurance that the materially changed component part or finished product complies with the applicable children's product safety rules. A manufacturer of a children's product that undergoes a material change cannot issue a new Children's Product Certificate for the product until the product meets the requirements of the applicable children's product safety rules. The extent of such testing may depend on the nature of the material change. When a material change is limited to a component part of the finished children's product and does not affect the ability of other component parts of the children's product or the finished children's product to comply with other applicable children's product safety rules, a manufacturer may issue a new Children's Product Certificate based on the earlier third party certification tests and on test results of the changed component part conducted by a third party conformity assessment body. A manufacturer must exercise due care to ensure that any component part undergoing component part-level testing is identical in all material respects to the component part on the finished children's product. Changes that cause a children's product safety rule to no longer apply to a children's product are not considered to be material changes.

(b) *Product Design*. For purposes of this subpart, the term "product design" includes all component parts, their composition, and their interaction and functionality when assembled. To determine which children's product safety rules apply to a children's product, a manufacturer should examine the product design for the children's product as received or assembled by the consumer.

(c) *Manufacturing Process*. A material change in the manufacturing process is a change in how the children's product is made that could affect the finished children's product's ability to comply with the applicable children's product safety rules. For each change in the manufacturing process, a manufacturer should exercise due care to determine if compliance to an existing applicable children's product safety rule could be affected, or if the change results in a newly applicable children's product safety rule.

(d) *Sourcing of Component Parts*. A material change in the sourcing of component parts results when the replacement of one component part of a children's product with another component part could affect compliance with the applicable children's product safety rule. This includes, but is not limited to, changes in component part composition, component part supplier, or the use of a different component part from the same supplier who provided the initial component part.

§ 1107.24 Undue influence.

(a) Each manufacturer must establish procedures to safeguard against the exercise of undue influence by a manufacturer on a third party conformity assessment body.

(b) The procedures required in paragraph (a) of this section, at a minimum, must include:

(1) Safeguards to prevent attempts by the manufacturer to exercise undue influence on a third party conformity assessment body, including a written policy statement from company officials that the exercise of undue influence is not acceptable, and directing that every appropriate staff member receive training on avoiding undue influence, and sign a statement attesting to participation in such training;

(2) A requirement that upon substantive changes to the requirements in this section regarding avoiding undue influence, the appropriate staff must be retrained regarding those changed requirements.

(3) A requirement to notify the CPSC immediately of any attempt by the manufacturer to hide or exert undue influence over test results; and

(4) A requirement to inform employees that allegations of undue influence may be reported confidentially to the CPSC and a description of the manner in which such a report can be made.

§ 1107.26 Recordkeeping.

(a) A manufacturer of a children's product subject to an applicable children's product safety rule must maintain the following records:

(1) A copy of the Children's Product Certificate for each product. The children's product covered by the certificate must be clearly identifiable and distinguishable from other products;

(2) Records of each third party certification test. The manufacturer must have separate certification tests records for each manufacturing site;

(3) Records of one of the following for periodic tests of a children's product:

(i) A periodic test plan and periodic test results;

(ii) A production testing plan, production test results, and periodic test results; or

(iii) Testing results of tests conducted by a testing laboratory accredited to ISO/IEC 17025:2005(E) and periodic test results.

(4) [Reserved];

(5) Records of descriptions of all material changes in product design, manufacturing process, and sourcing of component parts, and the certification tests run and the test values; and

(6) Records of the undue influence procedures, including training materials and training records of all employees trained on these procedures, including attestations described at § 1107.24(b)(1).

(b) A manufacturer must maintain the records specified in paragraph (a) of this section for five years. The manufacturer must make these records available, either in hard copy or electronically, such as through an Internet Web site, for inspection by the CPSC upon request. Records may be maintained in languages other than English if they can be:

(1) Provided immediately by the manufacturer to the CPSC; and

(2) Translated accurately into English by the manufacturer within 48 hours of a request by the CPSC, or any longer period negotiated with CPSC staff.

EFFECTIVE DATE NOTE: At 77 FR 72219, Dec. 5, 2012, §1107.26 was amended by adding paragraph (a)(4), effective Feb. 8, 2013. For the convenience of the user, the added and revised text is set forth as follows:

§1107.26 Recordkeeping.

(a) * * *

(4) Records documenting the testing of representative samples, as set forth in §1107.21(f), including the number of representative samples selected and the procedure used to select representative samples. Records also must include the basis for inferring compliance of the product manufactured during the periodic testing interval from the results of the tested samples;

* * * * *

Subpart D—Consumer Product Labeling Program

§1107.30 Labeling consumer products to indicate that the certification requirements of section 14 of the CPSA have been met.

(a) Manufacturers and private labelers of a consumer product may indicate, by a uniform label on, or provided with the product, that the product complies with any consumer product safety rule under the CPSA, or with any similar rule, ban, standard or regulation under any other act enforced by the CPSC.

(b) The label must be visible and legible, and consist of the following statement:

MEETS CPSC SAFETY REQUIREMENTS

(c) A consumer product may bear the label if the manufacturer or private labeler has certified, pursuant to section 14 of the CPSA, that the consumer product complies with all applicable consumer product safety rules under the CPSA and with all rules, bans, standards, or regulations applicable to the product under any other act enforced by the Consumer Product Safety Commission.

(d) A manufacturer or private labeler may use a label in addition to the label described in paragraph (b) on the consumer product, as long as such label does not alter or mislead consumers as to the meaning of the label described in paragraph (b) of this section. A manufacturer or private labeler must not imply that the CPSC has tested, approved, or endorsed the product.

PART 1109—CONDITIONS AND REQUIREMENTS FOR RELYING ON COMPONENT PART TESTING OR CERTIFICATION, OR ANOTHER PARTY'S FINISHED PRODUCT TESTING OR CERTIFICATION, TO MEET TESTING AND CERTIFICATION REQUIREMENTS

Subpart A—General Conditions and Requirements

Sec.

Subpart B—Conditions and Requirements for Specific Consumer Products, Component Parts, and Chemicals

Subpart C—Conditions and Requirements for Composite Testing

AUTHORITY: Secs. 3 and 102, Pub. L. 110–314, 122 Stat. 3016; 15 U.S.C. 2063.

SOURCE: 76 FR 69580, Nov. 8, 2011, unless otherwise noted.

Subpart A—General Conditions and Requirements

§ 1109.1 Scope.

(a) This part applies to tests or certifications of the following when such testing or certification is used to support a certificate of compliance pursuant to section 14(a) of the Consumer Product Safety Act (CPSA) or to meet continued testing requirements pursuant to section 14(i) of the CPSA:

(1) Component parts of consumer products; and

(2) Finished products when conducted by a party that is not required to test or certify products pursuant to part 1110 of this chapter.

(b) Component part manufacturers and suppliers may certify or test their component parts, but are not required to do so. Also, parties that are not required to test finished products, or to issue finished product certificates pursuant to part 1110 of this chapter, may do so voluntarily.

(c) Subpart A establishes general requirements for component part testing and certification, and relying on component part testing or certification, or another party's finished product certification or testing, to support a certificate of compliance issued pursuant to section 14(a) of the Consumer Product Safety Act (CPSA) or to meet continued testing requirements pursuant to section 14(i) of the CPSA. Subpart B sets forth additional requirements for component part testing of chemical content. Subpart C describes the conditions and requirements for composite testing.

§ 1109.2 Purpose.

The purpose of this part is to set forth the conditions and requirements under which passing component part test reports, certification of component parts of consumer products, or finished product testing or certification procured or issued by another party, can be used to meet, in whole or in part, the testing and certification requirements of sections 14(a) and 14(i) of the CPSA.

§ 1109.3 Applicability.

The provisions of this part apply to all manufacturers and importers who are required to issue finished product certifications pursuant to section 14(a) of the CPSA and part 1110 of this chapter and to procure tests to ensure continued compliance pursuant to section 14(i) of the CPSA. This part also applies to manufacturers and suppliers of component parts or finished products who are not required to test or certify consumer products pursuant to part 1110 of this chapter, but who voluntarily choose to undertake testing or certification.

§ 1109.4 Definitions.

The following definitions apply to this part:

(a) *Certifier* means a party that is either a finished product certifier or a component part certifier as defined in this section.

(b) *Component part* means any part of a consumer product, including a children's product that either must or may be tested separately from a finished consumer product to assess the consumer product's ability to comply with a specific rule, ban, standard, or regulation enforced by the CPSC. Within the same consumer product, the component parts to be tested and the tests to be conducted may vary, depending on the applicable regulations and required test methods, if any.

(c) *Component part certifier* means a party who, although not required to do so pursuant to part 1110 of this chapter, voluntarily certifies the following as complying with one or more rules, bans, standards, or regulations enforced by the CPSC, consistent with the content requirements for certifications in part 1110 of this chapter:

(1) Component parts to be used in consumer products; or

(2) Finished products.

(d) *CPSA* means the Consumer Product Safety Act.

(e) *CPSC* means the Consumer Product Safety Commission.

(f) *CPSIA* means the Consumer Product Safety Improvement Act of 2008.

(g) *Due care* means the degree of care that a prudent and competent person engaged in the same line of business or endeavor would exercise under similar circumstances. Due care does not permit willful ignorance.

(h) *Finished product certifier* means a party responsible for certifying compliance of a finished consumer product pursuant to part 1110 of this chapter with all applicable rules, bans, standards, and regulations enforced by the CPSC.

(i) *Identical in all material respects* means there is no difference with respect to compliance to the applicable rules, bans, standards, or regulations, between the samples to be tested for compliance and the component part or finished product distributed in commerce.

(j) *Paint* means any type of surface coating that is subject to part 1303 of this chapter or section 4.3.5.2 of ASTM F 963–08 (or any successor standard of section 4.3.5.2 of ASTM F 963–08 accepted by the Commission).

(k) *Testing party* means a party (including, but not limited to, domestic manufacturers, foreign manufacturers, importers, private labelers, or component part suppliers) who procures tests (either by conducting the tests themselves, when this is allowed, or by arranging for another party to conduct the tests), of a consumer product, or any component part thereof, for compliance, in whole or in part, with any applicable rule, ban, standard, or regulation enforced by the CPSC. Testing laboratories and third party conformity assessment bodies are not testing parties under this definition.

(*l*) *Third party conformity assessment body* means a testing laboratory whose accreditation has been accepted by the CPSC to conduct certification testing on children's products. Only third party conformity assessment bodies whose scope of accreditation includes the applicable required tests can be used to test children's products for purposes of supporting certification pursuant to section 14(a) of the CPSA and testing to ensure continued compliance pursuant to section 14(i) of the CPSA.

(m) *Traceable* means the ability of a certifier to identify all testing parties of a component part of a consumer product or a finished product, including the name and address of each testing party and any party that conducted testing on the component part or finished product. Parties that conduct testing may include a manufacturer, a supplier, a testing laboratory, or a third party conformity assessment body. Traceability extends to the component part of the product that was tested for compliance, such that if a subassembly is tested, that subassembly must be traceable, not each component part of the subassembly, if those parts were not individually tested for other rules, bans, standards, or regulations.

§ 1109.5 Conditions, requirements, and effects generally.

(a) *Component part testing allowed.* Any party, including a component part manufacturer, a component part supplier, a component part certifier, or a finished product certifier, may procure component part testing as long as it complies with the requirements in this section and subparts B and C of this part. A finished product certifier may certify compliance of a consumer product with all applicable rules, bans, standards, and regulations as required by section 14(a) of the CPSA, and may ensure continued compliance of children's products pursuant to section 14(i) of the CPSA, based, in whole or in part, on passing component part test reports or certification of one or more component parts of a consumer product if the following requirements are met:

(1) Testing of the component part is required or sufficient to assess compliance, in whole or in part, of the consumer product with the applicable rule, ban, standard, or regulation. Any doubts about whether testing one or more component parts of a consumer product is sufficient to assess whether the finished product complies with applicable rules, bans, standards, and regulations should be resolved in favor of testing the finished product; and

(2) The component part tested is identical in all material respects to the component parts used in the finished consumer product. To be identical in all material respects to a component part for purposes of supporting a certification of a children's product, a sample need not necessarily be of the same size, shape, or finish condition as the component part of the finished product; rather, it may consist of any quantity that is sufficient for testing purposes and be in any form that has

the same content as the component part of the finished product.

(b) *Test Result Integrity*. A certifier or testing party must exercise due care to ensure that while a component part or finished product is in its custody:

(1) Proper management and control of all raw materials, component parts, subassemblies, and finished products is established and maintained for any factor that could affect the finished product's compliance with all applicable rules;

(2) The manufacturing process does not add or result in a prohibited level of a chemical from any source, such as the material hopper, regrind equipment, or other equipment used in the assembly of the finished product; and

(3) No action or inaction subsequent to testing and before distribution in commerce has occurred that would affect compliance, including contamination or degradation.

(c) *Limitation*. A certifier must not use tests of a component part of a consumer product for any rule, ban, standard, or regulation that requires testing the finished product to assess compliance with that rule, ban, standard, or regulation.

(d) *Test method and sampling protocol*. Each certifier and testing party must exercise due care to ensure that when it procures a test for use in meeting the requirements of sections 14(a) or 14(i) of the CPSA:

(1) All testing is done using required test methods, if any;

(2) Required sampling protocols are followed, if any; and

(3) Testing and certification follows the applicable requirements in sections 14(a) and 14(i) of the CPSA, and part 1107 of this chapter or any more specific rules, bans, standards, or regulations, used to assess compliance of the component part or finished product.

(e) *Timing*. Subject to any more specific rule, ban, standard, or regulation, component part testing may occur before final assembly of a consumer product, provided that nothing in the final assembly of the consumer product can cause the component part or the final consumer product to become noncompliant.

(f) *Traceability*. A certifier must not rely on component part or finished product testing procured by a testing party or another certifier unless such component parts or finished products are traceable.

(g) *Documentation by certifiers and testing parties*. Each certifier and testing party must provide the following documentation, either in hard copy or electronically, to a certifier relying on such documentation as a basis for issuing a certificate:

(1) Identification of the component part or the finished product tested;

(2) Identification of a lot or batch number, or other information sufficient to identify the component parts or finished products to which the testing applies;

(3) Identification of the applicable rules, bans, standards, and regulations for which each component part or finished product was tested;

(4) Identification of the testing method(s) and sampling protocol(s) used;

(5) The date or date range when the component part or finished product was tested;

(6) Test reports that provide the results of each test on a component part or finished product, and the test values, if any;

(7) Identification of the party that conducted each test (including testing conducted by a manufacturer, testing laboratory, or third party conformity assessment body), and an attestation by the party conducting the testing that all testing of a component part or finished product by that party was performed in compliance with applicable provisions of section 14 of the CPSA, part 1107 of this chapter, or any more specific rules, bans, standards, or regulations;

(8) Component part certificate(s) or finished product certificate(s), if any;

(9) Records to support traceability as defined in § 1109.4(m); and

(10) An attestation by each certifier and testing party that while the component part or finished product was in its custody, it exercised due care to ensure compliance with the requirements set forth in subparagraph (b) of this section.

(h) *Effect of voluntary certification*. (1) The Commission will consider any certificate issued by a component part certifier in accordance with this part to be a certificate issued in accordance with section 14(a) of the CPSA. All certificates must contain all of the information required by part 1110 of this chapter.

(2) Any party who elects to certify compliance of a component part or a finished product with applicable rules, standards, bans, or regulations, must assume all responsibilities of a manufacturer under sections 14(a) and 14(i) of the CPSA and part 1107 of this chapter with respect to that component part or finished product's compliance to the applicable rules, standards, bans, or regulations.

(i) *Certification by finished product certifiers.* (1) A finished product certifier must exercise due care in order to rely, in whole or in part, on one or more of the following as a basis for issuing a finished product certificate:

(i) Finished product certificate(s) issued by another party;

(ii) Finished product test report(s) provided by another party;

(iii) Component part certificate(s); or

(iv) Component part test report(s).

(2) If a finished product certifier fails to exercise due care in its reliance on another party's certifications or test reports, then the Commission will not consider the finished product certifier to hold a certificate issued in accordance with section 14(a) of the CPSA. Exercising due care in this context means taking the steps that a prudent and competent person in the same line of business would take to conduct a reasonable review of another party's certification or test reports, and to address any concern over their validity, before relying on such documents to issue a finished product certificate. Due care does not permit willful ignorance. Such steps may vary according to the circumstances.

(3) A finished product certifier must not rely on another party's certifications or test reports unless the finished product certifier receives the documentation under paragraph (g) of this section from the certifier or testing party. The finished product certifier may receive such documentation either in hard copy or electronically, or access the documentation through an Internet Web site. The Commission may consider a finished product certifier who does not obtain such documentation before certifying a consumer product to have failed to exercise due care.

(j) *Recordkeeping requirements.* Each certifier or testing party must maintain the documentation required in paragraph (g) of this section for five years, and must make such documentation available for inspection by the CPSC upon request, either in hard copy or electronically, such as through an Internet Web site. Records may be maintained in languages other than English if they can be:

(1) Provided immediately by the certifier or testing party to the CPSC; and

(2) Translated accurately into English by the certifier or testing party within 48 hours of a request by the CPSC or any longer period negotiated with CPSC staff.

Subpart B—Conditions and Requirements for Specific Consumer Products, Component Parts, and Chemicals

§1109.11 Component part testing for paint.

(a) *Generally.* The Commission will permit certification of a consumer product, or a component part of a consumer product, as being in compliance with the lead paint limit of part 1303 of this chapter or the content limits for paint on toys of section 4.3.5.2 of ASTM F 963–08 or any successor standard of section 4.3.5.2 of ASTM F 963–08 accepted by the Commission if, for each paint used on the product, the requirements in §1109.5 and paragraph (b) of this section are met.

(b) *Requirement.* For each paint used on the product:

(1) Unless using the test method ASTM F 2853–10 to test for lead in paint, all testing must be performed on dry paint that is scraped off of a substrate for testing. The substrate used need not be of the same material as the material used in the finished product or have the same shape or other characteristics as the part of the finished product to which the paint will be applied; and

(2) The tested paint is identical in all material respects to that used in production of the consumer product. The

paint samples to be tested must have the same composition as the paint used on the finished product. However, a larger quantity of the paint may be tested than is used on the consumer product in order to generate a sufficient sample size. The paint may be supplied to the testing laboratory for testing either in liquid form or in the form of a dried film of the paint on any suitable substrate.

§ 1109.12 Component part testing for lead content of children's products.

A certifier may rely on component part testing of each accessible component part of a children's product for lead content, where such component part testing is performed by a third party conformity assessment body, provided that the requirements in § 1109.5 are met, and the determination of which, if any, parts are inaccessible pursuant to section 101(b)(2) of the Consumer Product Safety Improvement Act of 2008 (CPSIA) and part 1500.87 of this chapter is based on an evaluation of the finished product.

§ 1109.13 Component part testing for phthalates in children's toys and child care articles.

A certifier may rely on component part testing of appropriate component parts of a children's toy or child care article for phthalate content provided that the requirements in § 1109.5 are met.

Subpart C—Conditions and Requirements for Composite Testing

§ 1109.21 Composite testing.

(a) *Paint.* In testing paint for compliance with chemical content limits, certifiers and testing parties may procure tests conducted on a combination of different paint samples so long as test procedures are followed to ensure that no failure to comply with the lead limits will go undetected (see paragraph (c) of this section). A certificate may be based on testing each component part of the paint according to the requirements of § 1109.11 and certifying that each component part in the mixture individually complies with the lead in paint limit or other paint limit. Testing and certification of composite paints must also comply with §§ 1109.5 and 1109.11.

(b) *Component parts.* A certifier or testing party may procure tests conducted on a combination of component parts for compliance with chemical content limits so long as test procedures are followed to ensure that no failure to comply with the content limits will go undetected (see paragraph (c) of this section). Testing and certification of composite component parts for lead content must also comply with §§ 1109.5 and 1109.12. Testing and certification of composite component parts for phthalate content must also comply with §§ 1109.5 and 1109.13.

(c) *How to evaluate composite testing.* When using composite testing, only the total amount or percentage of the target chemical is determined, not how much was in each individual paint or component part. Therefore, to determine that each paint or component part is within the applicable limit, the entire amount of the target chemical in the composite is attributed to each paint or component part. If this method yields an amount of the target chemical that exceeds the limit applicable to any paint or component part in the composite sample, additional testing would be required to determine which of the paints or component parts, if any, fail to meet the applicable limit.

PART 1110—CERTIFICATES OF COMPLIANCE

Sec.

AUTHORITY: Pub. L. No. 110–314, § 3, 122 Stat. 3016, 3017 (2008); 15 U.S.C. 14.

SOURCE: 73 FR 68331, Nov. 18, 2008, unless otherwise noted.

§ 1110.1 Purpose and scope.

(a) This part 1110:

(1) Limits the entities required to provide certificates in accordance with section 14(a) of the Consumer Product Safety Act, as amended (CPSA), 15 U.S.C. 2063(a), to importers and U.S. domestic manufacturers;

(2) Specifies the content, form, and availability requirements of the CPSA that must be met for a certificate to satisfy the certificate requirements of section 14(a); and

(3) Specifies means by which an electronic certificate shall meet those requirements.

(b) This part 1110 does not address issues related to type or frequency of testing necessary to satisfy the certification requirements of CPSA section 14(a). It does not address issues related to CPSA section 14(g)(4) concerning advance filing of electronic certificates of compliance with the Commission and/or the Commissioner of Customs.

§ 1110.3 Definitions.

The following definitions apply for purposes of this part 1110.

(a) *Electronic certificate* means, for purposes of this part 1110, a set of information available in, and accessible by, electronic means that sets forth the information required by CPSA section 14(a) and section 14(g) and that meets the availability requirements of CPSA section 14(g)(3).

(b) Unless otherwise stated, the definitions of section 3 of the CPSA and additional definitions in the Consumer Product Safety Improvement Act of 2008 (CPSIA), Pub. L. 110–314, apply for purposes of this part 1110.

§ 1110.5 Acceptable certificates.

A certificate that is in hard copy or electronic form and complies with all applicable requirements of this part 1110 meets the certificate requirements of section 14 of the CPSA. This does not relieve the importer or domestic manufacturer from the underlying statutory requirements concerning the supporting testing and/or other bases to support certification and issuance of certificates.

§ 1110.7 Who must certify and provide a certificate.

(a) *Imports.* Except as otherwise provided in a specific standard, in the case of a product manufactured outside the United States, only the importer must certify in accordance with, and provide the certificate required by, CPSA section 14(a) as applicable, that the product or shipment in question complies with all applicable CPSA rules and all similar rules, bans, standards, and regulations applicable to the product or shipment under any other Act enforced by the Commission.

(b) *Domestic products.* Except as otherwise provided in a specific standard, in the case of a product manufactured in the United States, only the manufacturer must certify in accordance with, and provide the certificate required by, CPSA section 14(a) as applicable, that the product or shipment in question complies with all applicable CPSA rules and all similar rules, bans, standards, and regulations applicable to the product or shipment under any other Act enforced by the Commission.

(c) *Availability of certificates*—(1) *Imports.* In the case of imports, the certificate required by CPSA section 14(a) must be available to the Commission from the importer as soon as the product or shipment itself is available for inspection in the United States.

(2) *Domestic products.* In the case of domestic products, the certificate required by CPSA section 14(a) must be available to the Commission from the manufacturer prior to introduction of the product or shipment in question into domestic commerce.

§ 1110.9 Form of certificate.

As required by CPSA section 14(g)(2), the information on a hard copy or electronic certificate must be provided in English and may be provided in any other language.

§ 1110.11 Content of certificate.

As required by CPSA sections 14(a) and 14(g), a certificate must contain the following information:

(a) Identification of the product covered by the certificate.

(b) Citation to each CPSC product safety regulation or statutory requirement to which the product is being certified. Specifically, the certificate shall identify separately each applicable consumer product safety rule under the Consumer Product Safety Act and any similar rule, ban, standard or regulation under any other Act enforced by the Commission that is applicable to the product.

(c) Identification of the importer or domestic manufacturer certifying compliance of the product, including the importer or domestic manufacturer's name, full mailing address, and telephone number.

(d) Contact information for the individual maintaining records of test results, including the custodian's name, e-mail address, full mailing address, and telephone number. (CPSC suggests that each issuer maintain test records supporting the certification for at least three years as is currently required by certain consumer product specific CPSC standards, for example at 16 CFR 1508.10 for full-size baby cribs.)

(e) Date (month and year at a minimum) and place (including city and state, country, or administrative region) where the product was manufactured. If the same manufacturer operates more than one location in the same city, the street address of the factory in question should be provided.

(f) Date and place (including city and state, country or administrative region) where the product was tested for compliance with the regulation(s) cited above in subsection (b).

(g) Identification of any third-party laboratory on whose testing the certificate depends, including name, full mailing address and telephone number of the laboratory.

§ 1110.13 Availability of electronic certificate.

(a) CPSA section 14(g)(3) requires that the certificates required by section 14(a) "accompany" each product or product shipment and be "furnished" to each distributor and retailer of the product in question.

(1) An electronic certificate satisfies the "accompany" requirement if the certificate is identified by a unique identifier and can be accessed via a World Wide Web URL or other electronic means, provided the URL or other electronic means and the unique identifier are created in advance and are available, along with access to the electronic certificate itself, to the Commission or to the Customs authorities as soon as the product or shipment itself is available for inspection.

(2) An electronic certificate satisfies the "furnish" requirement if the distributor(s) and retailer(s) of the product are provided a reasonable means to access the certificate.

(b) An electronic certificate shall have a means to verify the date of its creation or last modification.

§ 1110.15 Legal responsibility for certificate information.

Any entity or entities may maintain an electronic certificate platform and may enter the requisite data. However, the entity or entities required by CPSA section 14(a) to issue the certificate remain legally responsible for the accuracy and completeness of the certificate information required by statute and its availability in timely fashion.

PART 1112—REQUIREMENTS PERTAINING TO THIRD PARTY CONFORMITY ASSESSMENT BODIES

Subpart A—Purpose and Definitions

Subpart B [Reserved]

Subpart C—Audit Requirements for Third Party Conformity Assessment Bodies

AUTHORITY: Pub. L. 110–314, section 3, 122 Stat. 3016, 3017 (2008); 15 U.S.C. 2063.

SOURCE: 77 FR 31084, May 24, 2012, unless otherwise noted.

Subpart A—Purpose and Definitions

§1112.1 [Reserved]

§1112.3 Definitions.

Unless otherwise stated, the definitions of section 3 of the CPSA and additional definitions in the Consumer Product Safety Improvement Act of 2008, Public Law 110–314, apply for purposes of this part. The following definitions apply for purposes of this subpart:

Accreditation means a procedure by which an authoritative body gives formal recognition that a third party conformity assessment body meets competence requirements to perform specific tasks. Accreditation recognizes a third party conformity assessment body's technical capability and is usually specific for tests of the systems, products, components, or materials for which the third party conformity assessment body claims proficiency.

Accreditation body means an entity that:

(1) Accredits or has accredited a third party conformity assessment body as meeting, at a minimum, the International Organization for Standardization (ISO)/International Electrotechnical Commission (IEC) Standard ISO/IEC 17025:2005, "General Requirements for the Competence of Testing and Calibration Laboratories," and any test methods or consumer product safety requirements specified in the relevant notice of requirements issued by the Commission; and

(2) Is a signatory to the International Laboratory Accreditation Cooperation–Mutual Recognition Arrangement.

Audit means a systematic, independent, documented process for obtaining records, statements of fact, or other relevant information, and assessing them objectively to determine the extent to which specified requirements are fulfilled. An audit, for purposes of this part, consists of two parts:

(1) An examination by an accreditation body to determine whether the third party conformity assessment body meets or continues to meet the conditions for accreditation (a process known more commonly as a "reassessment"); and

(2) The resubmission of the "Consumer Product Conformity Assessment Body Acceptance Registration Form" (CPSC Form 223) by the third party conformity assessment body and the Consumer Product Safety Commission's ("CPSC's") examination of the resubmitted CPSC Form 223. If the third party conformity assessment body is owned, managed, or controlled by a manufacturer or private labeler (also known as a "firewalled" conformity assessment body) or is a government-owned or government-controlled conformity assessment body, the CPSC's examination may include verification to ensure that the entity continues to meet the appropriate statutory criteria pertaining to such conformity assessment bodies.

CPSC means the Consumer Product Safety Commission.

Quality manager means an individual (however named) who, irrespective of other duties and responsibilities, has defined responsibility and authority for ensuring that the management system related to quality is implemented and followed at all times and has direct access to the highest level of management at which decisions are made on the conformity assessment body's policy or resources.

Subpart B [Reserved]

Subpart C—Audit Requirements for Third Party Conformity Assessment Bodies

§1112.30 What is the purpose of this subpart?

This subpart establishes the audit requirements for third party conformity assessment bodies pursuant to section 14(i)(1) of the Consumer Product Safety Act (CPSA) (15 U.S.C. 2063(i)(1)). Compliance with these requirements is a condition of the continuing accreditation of such third party conformity assessment bodies pursuant to section 14(a)(3)(C) of the CPSA. However, this subpart does not apply to certifying organizations under the Labeling of Hazardous Art Materials Act, even if such organizations are third party conformity assessment bodies.

§ 1112.31 Who is subject to these audit requirements?

Except for certifying organizations described in 16 CFR 1500.14(b)(8), these audit requirements apply to third party conformity assessment bodies operating pursuant to section 14(a)(2) of the CPSA. Third party conformity assessment bodies must comply with the audit requirements as a continuing condition of the CPSC's acceptance of their accreditation.

§ 1112.33 What must an audit address or cover and who conducts the audit?

(a) The reassessment portion of an audit must cover management requirements and technical requirements. Each reassessment portion of an audit also must examine the third party conformity assessment body's management systems to ensure that the third party conformity assessment body is free from any undue influence regarding its technical judgment.

(b) The third party conformity assessment body must have the reassessment portion of the audit conducted by the same accreditation body that accredited the third party conformity assessment body. For example, if a third party conformity assessment body was accredited by an accreditation body named AB–1, then AB–1 would conduct the reassessment. If, however, the same third party conformity assessment body changes its accreditation so that it becomes accredited by a different accreditation body named AB–2, then AB–2 would conduct the reassessment.

(c) The third party conformity assessment body must have the examination portion of the audit conducted by the CPSC. The examination portion of the audit will consist of resubmission of the "Consumer Product Conformity Assessment Body Acceptance Registration Form" (CPSC Form 223) by the third party conformity assessment body and the CPSC's examination of the resubmitted CPSC Form 223.

(1) For "firewalled" conformity assessment bodies, the CPSC's examination may include verification to ensure that the "firewalled" conformity assessment body continues to meet the criteria set forth in section 14(f)(2)(D) of the CPSA.

(2) For government-owned or government-controlled conformity assessment bodies, the CPSC's examination may include verification to ensure that the government-owned or government-controlled conformity assessment body continues to meet the criteria set forth in section 14(f)(2)(B) of the CPSA.

§ 1112.35 When must an audit be conducted?

(a) At a minimum, each third party conformity assessment body must be reassessed at the frequency established by its accreditation body.

(b) [Reserved]

§ 1112.37 What must a third party conformity assessment body do after an audit?

(a) When the accreditation body presents its findings to the third party conformity assessment body, the third party conformity assessment body's quality manager must receive the findings and, if necessary, initiate corrective action in response to the findings.

(b) The quality manager must prepare a resolution report identifying the corrective actions taken and any follow-up activities. If findings indicate that immediate corrective action is necessary, the quality manager must document that they notified the relevant parties within the third party conformity assessment body to take immediate corrective action and also document the action(s) taken.

(c) If the accreditation body decides to reduce, suspend, or withdraw the third party conformity assessment body's accreditation, and the reduction, suspension, or withdrawal of accreditation is relevant to the third party conformity assessment body's activities pertaining to a CPSC regulation or test method, the quality manager must notify the CPSC. Such notification must be sent to the Assistant Executive Director, Office of Hazard Identification and Reduction, Consumer Product Safety Commission, 4330 East West Highway, Bethesda, MD 20814, within five business days of the accreditation body's notification to the third party conformity assessment body.

(d) If the CPSC finds that the third party conformity assessment body no longer meets the conditions specified in CPSC Form 223, or in the relevant statutory provisions applicable to that third party conformity assessment body, the CPSC will notify the third party conformity assessment body, identify the condition or statutory provision that is no longer met, and specify a time by which the third party conformity assessment body shall notify the CPSC of the steps it intends to take to correct the deficiency, and indicate when it will complete such steps. The quality manager must document that they notified the relevant parties within the third party conformity assessment body to take corrective action and also document the action(s) taken.

(e) If the third party conformity assessment body fails to remedy the deficiency in a timely fashion, the CPSC shall take whatever action it deems appropriate under the circumstances, up to and including withdrawing the CPSC's accreditation of the third party conformity assessment body or the CPSC's acceptance of the third party conformity assessment body's accreditation.

§ 1112.39 What records should a third party conformity assessment body retain regarding an audit?

A third party conformity assessment body must retain all records related to an audit that it receives from an accreditation body regarding a reassessment and all records pertaining to the third party conformity assessment body's resolution of, or plans for, resolving nonconformities identified through a reassessment by an accreditation body or through an examination by the CPSC. A third party conformity assessment body also must retain such records related to the last three reassessments (or however many reassessments have been conducted, if the third party conformity assessment body has been reassessed less than three times) and make such records available to the CPSC, upon request.

PART 1115—SUBSTANTIAL PRODUCT HAZARD REPORTS

Subpart A—General Interpretation

Subpart B—Remedial Actions and Sanctions

Subpart C—Guidelines and Requirements for Mandatory Recall Notices

AUTHORITY: 15 U.S.C. 2061, 2064, 2065, 2066(a), 2068, 2069, 2070, 2071, 2073, 2076, 2079 and 2084.

SOURCE: 43 FR 34998, Aug. 7, 1978, unless otherwise noted.

Subpart A—General Interpretation

§ 1115.1 Purpose.

The purpose of this part 1115 is to set forth the Consumer Product Safety Commission's (Commission's) interpretation of the reporting requirements imposed on manufacturers (including importers), distributors, and retailers by section 15(b) of the Consumer Product Safety Act, as amended (CPSA) (15 U.S.C. 2064(b)) and to indicate the actions and sanctions which the Commission may require or impose to protect the public from substantial product hazards, as that term is defined in section 15(a) of the CPSA.

§ 1115.2 Scope and finding.

(a) Section 15(a) of the CPSA (15 U.S.C. 2064(a)) defines *substantial product hazard* as either:

(1) A failure to comply with an applicable consumer product safety rule, which failure creates a substantial risk of injury to the public, or

(2) A product defect which (because of the pattern of defect, the number of defective products distributed in commerce, the severity of the risk, or otherwise) creates a substantial risk of injury to the public.

(b) Section 15(b) of the CPSA requires every manufacturer (including an importer), distributor, and retailer of a consumer product distributed in commerce who obtains information which reasonably supports the conclusion that the product fails to comply with an applicable consumer product safety rule, fails to comply with a voluntary consumer product safety standard upon which the Commission has relied under section 9 of the CPSA, contains a defect which could create a substantial product hazard described in subsection 15(a)(2) of the CPSA, or creates an unreasonable risk of serious injury or death, immediately to inform the Commission, unless the manufacturer (including an importer), distributor or retailer has actual knowledge that the Commission has been adequately informed of such failure to comply, defect, or risk. This provision indicates that a broad spectrum of safety related information should be reported under section 15(b) of the CPSA.

(c) Sections 15 (c) and (d) of the CPSA, (15 U.S.C. 2064(c) and (d)), empower the Commission to order a manufacturer (including an importer), distributor, or retailer of a consumer product distributed in commerce that presents a substantial product hazard to give various forms of notice to the public of the defect or the failure to comply and/or to order the subject firm to elect either to repair, to replace, or to refund the purchase price of such product. However, information which should be reported under section 15(b) of the CPSA does not automatically indicate the presence of a substantial product hazard, because what must be reported under section 15(b) are failures to comply with consumer product safety rules or voluntary standards upon which the Commission has relied under section 9, defects that could create a substantial product hazard, and products which create an unreasonable risk of serious injury or death. (See § 1115.12.)

(d) The provisions of this part 1115 deal with all consumer products (including imports) subject to regulation under the Consumer Product Safety Act, as amended (15 U.S.C. 2051–2081) (CPSA), and the Refrigerator Safety Act (15 U.S.C. 1211–1214) (RSA). In addition, the Commission has found that risks of injury to the public from consumer products subject to regulation under the Flammable Fabrics Act (15 U.S.C. 1191–1204) (FFA), the Federal Hazardous Substances Act (15 U.S.C. 1261–1274) (FHSA), and the Poison Prevention Packaging Act of 1970 (15 U.S.C. 1471–1476) (PPPA) cannot be eliminated or reduced to a sufficient extent in a timely fashion under those acts. Therefore, pursuant to section 30(d) of the CPSA (15 U.S.C. 2079(d)), manufacturers (including importers), distributors, and retailers of consumer products which are subject to regulation under provisions of the FFA, FHSA, and PPPA must comply with the reporting requirements of section 15(b).

[43 FR 34998, Aug. 7, 1978, as amended at 57 FR 34227, Aug. 4, 1992]

§ 1115.3 Definitions.

In addition to the definitions given in section 3 of the CPSA (15 U.S.C. 2052), the following definitions apply:

(a) *Adequately informed* under section 15(b) of the CPSA means that the Commission staff has received the information requested under §§ 1115.12 and/or 1115.13 of this part insofar as it is reasonably available and applicable or that the staff has informed the subject firm that the staff is adequately informed.

(b) *Commission meeting* means the joint deliberations of at least a majority of the Commission where such deliberations determine or result in the conduct or disposition of official Commission business. This term is synonymous with "Commission meeting" as defined in the Commission's regulation issued under the Government in the Sunshine Act, 16 CFR part 1012.

(c) *Noncompliance* means the failure of a consumer product to comply with an applicable consumer product safety rule or with a voluntary consumer product safety standard upon which the Commission has relied under section 9 of the CPSA.

(d) A *person* means a corporation, company, association, firm, partnership, society, joint stock company, or individual.

(e) *Staff* means the staff of the Consumer Product Safety Commission unless otherwise stated.

(f) *Subject firm* means any manufacturer (including an importer), distributor, or retailer of a consumer product.

[43 FR 34998, Aug. 7, 1978, as amended at 57 FR 34227, Aug. 4, 1992]

§ 1115.4 Defect.

Section 15(b)(2) of the CPSA requires every manufacturer (including an importer), distributor, and retailer of a consumer product who obtains information which reasonably supports the conclusion that the product contains a defect which could create a substantial product hazard to inform the Commission of such defect. Thus, whether the information available reasonably suggests a defect is the first determination which a subject firm must make in deciding whether it has obtained information which must be reported to the Commission. In determining whether it has obtained information which reasonably supports the conclusion that its consumer product contains a defect, a subject firm may be guided by the criteria the Commission and staff use in determining whether a defect exists. At a minimum, defect includes the dictionary or commonly accepted meaning of the word. Thus, a defect is a fault, flaw, or irregularity that causes weakness, failure, or inadequacy in form or function. A defect, for example, may be the result of a manufacturing or production error; that is, the consumer product as manufactured is not in the form intended by, or fails to perform in accordance with, its design. In addition, the design of and the materials used in a consumer product may also result in a defect. Thus, a product may contain a defect even if the product is manufactured exactly in accordance with its design and specifications, if the design presents a risk of injury to the public. A design defect may also be present if the risk of injury occurs as a result of the operation or use of the product or the failure of the product to operate as intended. A defect can also occur in a product's contents, construction, finish, packaging, warnings, and/or instructions. With respect to instructions, a consumer product may contain a defect if the instructions for assembly or use could allow the product, otherwise safely designed and manufactured, to present a risk of injury. To assist subject firms in understanding the concept of defect as used in the CPSA, the following examples are offered:

(a) An electric appliance presents a shock hazard because, through a manufacturing error, its casing can be electrically charged by full-line voltage. This product contains a defect as a result of manufacturing or production error.

(b) Shoes labeled and marketed for long-distance running are so designed that they might cause or contribute to the causing of muscle or tendon injury if used for long-distance running. The shoes are defective due to the labeling and marketing.

(c) A kite made of electrically conductive material presents a risk of electrocution if it is long enough to become entangled in power lines and be within reach from the ground. The electrically conductive material contributes both to the beauty of the kite and the hazard it presents. The kite contains a design defect.

(d) A power tool is not accompanied by adequate instructions and safety warnings. Reasonably foreseeable consumer use or misuse, based in part on the lack of adequate instructions and safety warnings, could result in injury. Although there are no reports of injury, the product contains a defect because of the inadequate warnings and instructions.

(e) An exhaust fan for home garages is advertised as activating when carbon monoxide fumes reach a dangerous level but does not exhaust when fumes have reached the dangerous level. Although the cause of the failure to exhaust is not known, the exhaust fan is defective because users rely on the fan to remove the fumes and the fan does not do so.

However, not all products which present a risk of injury are defective. For example, a knife has a sharp blade and is capable of seriously injuring someone. This very sharpness, however, is necessary if the knife is to function adequately. The knife does not contain a defect insofar as the sharpness of its blade is concerned, despite its potential for causing injury, because the risk of injury is outweighed by the usefulness of the product which is made possible by the same aspect which presents the risk of injury. In determining whether the risk of injury associated with a product is the type of risk which will render the product defective, the Commission and staff will consider, as appropriate: The utility of the product involved; the nature of the risk of injury which the product presents; the necessity for the product; the population exposed to the product and its risk of injury; the obviousness of such risk; the adequacy of warnings and instructions to mitigate such risk; the role of consumer misuse of the product and the foreseeability of such misuse; the Commission's own experience and expertise; the case law interpreting Federal and State public health and safety statutes; the case law in the area of products liability; and other factors relevant to the determination. If the information available to a subject firm does not reasonably support the conclusion that a defect exists, the subject firm need not report. However, if the information does reasonably support the conclusion that a defect exists, the subject firm must then consider whether that defect could create a substantial product hazard. (See § 1115.12(f) for factors to be assessed in determining whether a substantial product hazard could exist.) If the subject firm determines that the defect could create a substantial product hazard, the subject firm must report to the Commission. Most defects could present a substantial product hazard if the public is exposed to significant numbers of defective products or if the possible injury is serious or is likely to occur. Since the extent of public exposure and/or the likelihood or seriousness of injury are ordinarily not known at the time a defect first manifests itself, subject firms are urged to report if in doubt as to whether a defect could present a substantial product hazard. On a case-by-case basis the Commission and the staff will determine whether a defect within the meaning of section 15 of the CPSA does, in fact, exist and whether that defect presents a substantial product hazard. Since a consumer product may be defective even if it is designed, manufactured, and marketed exactly as intended by a subject firm, subject firms should report if in doubt as to whether a defect exists. Defect, as discussed in this section and as used by the Commission and staff, pertains only to interpreting and enforcing the Consumer Product Safety Act. The criteria and discussion in this section are not intended to apply to any other area of the law.

[43 FR 34998, Aug. 7, 1978, as amended at 71 FR 42030, July 25, 2006]

§ 1115.5 Reporting of failures to comply with a voluntary consumer product safety standard relied upon by the Commission under section 9 of the CPSA.

(a) *General provision.* Under the CPSA, the Commission may rely on voluntary standards in lieu of developing mandatory ones. In recognition of the role of voluntary standards under the CPSA, section 15(b)(1) requires reports if a product fails to comply with a voluntary standard "upon which the Commission has relied under section 9" of the CPSA. The Commission has relied upon a voluntary consumer product safety standard under section 9 of the CPSA if, since August 13, 1981 it has terminated a rulemaking proceeding or withdrawn an existing consumer product safety rule because it explicitly determined that an existing voluntary standard, or portion(s) thereof, is likely to result in an adequate reduction of the risk of injury and it is likely there will be substantial compliance with that voluntary standard. (See appendix to this part 1115 for a list of such voluntary standards.) This provision applies only when the Commission relies upon a voluntary standard in a rulemaking proceeding under section 9 of the CPSA. In evaluating whether or not to rely upon an existing voluntary standard, the Commission shall adhere to all the procedural safeguards currently required under the provisions of the CPSA, including publication in the FEDERAL REGISTER of the Commission's intent to rely upon a voluntary standard in order to provide the public with a fair opportunity to comment upon such proposed action.

(b) *Reporting requirement.* A firm must report under this section if it has distributed in commerce, subsequent to the effective date of the Consumer Product Safety Improvement Act of 1990 (November 16, 1990), a product that does not conform to a voluntary standard or portion(s) of a voluntary standard relied upon by the Commission since August 13, 1981. If the Commission relied upon only a portion(s) of a voluntary standard, a firm must report under this section only nonconformance with the portion(s) of the voluntary standard relied upon by the Commission. Pursuant to section 7(b)(2) of the CPSA, the Commission shall monitor any modifications of a voluntary standard upon which it has relied and determine, as a matter of policy, at the time any substantive safety related modification is adopted, whether it shall continue to rely upon the former standard or whether it shall rely, subsequently, upon the modified standard. The Commission shall publish such decisions in the FEDERAL REGISTER. Until the Commission makes such a decision, subject firms need not report under this provision a product which complies with either the original version of the voluntary standard relied upon by the Commission or the new version of the standard. A firm must continue to evaluate whether deviations from other portions of a voluntary standard, or other voluntary standards not relied upon by the Commission, either constitute a defect which could create a substantial product hazard or create an unreasonable risk of serious injury or death.

[57 FR 34228, Aug. 4, 1992; 57 FR 39597, Sept. 1, 1992]

§1115.6 Reporting of unreasonable risk of serious injury or death.

(a) *General provision.* Every manufacturer, distributor, and retailer of a consumer product distributed in commerce who obtains information which reasonably supports the conclusion that its product creates an unreasonable risk of serious injury or death is required to notify the Commission immediately. 15 U.S.C. 2064(b)(3). The requirement that notification occur when a responsible party "obtains information which reasonably supports the conclusion that" its product creates an unreasonable risk of serious injury or death is intended to require firms to report even when no final determination of the risk is possible. Firms must carefully analyze the information they obtain to determine whether such information "reasonably supports" a determination that the product creates an unreasonable risk of serious injury or death. (See §1115.12(f) for a discussion of the kinds of information that firms must study and evaluate to determine whether they have an obligation to report.) Firms that obtain information indicating that their products present an unreasonable risk of serious injury or death should not wait for such serious injury or death to actually occur before reporting. Such information can include reports from experts, test reports, product liability lawsuits or claims, consumer or customer complaints, quality control data, scientific or epidemiological studies, reports of injury, information from other firms or governmental entities, and other relevant information. While such information shall not trigger a *per se* reporting requirement, in its evaluation of whether a subject firm is required to file a report under the provisions of section 15 of the CPSA, the Commission shall attach considerable significance if such firm learns that a court or jury has determined that one of its products has caused a serious injury or death and a reasonable person could conclude based on the lawsuit and other information obtained by the firm that the product creates an unreasonable risk of serious injury or death.

(b) *Unreasonable risk.* The use of the term "unreasonable risk" suggests that the risk of injury presented by a product should be evaluated to determine if that risk is a reasonable one. In determining whether a product presents an unreasonable risk, the firm should examine the utility of the product, or the utility of the aspect of the product that causes the risk, the level of exposure of consumers to the risk, the nature and severity of the hazard presented, and the likelihood of resulting serious injury or death. In its analysis, the firm should also evaluate the state of the manufacturing or scientific art, the availability of alternative designs or products, and the feasibility of eliminating the risk. The Commission expects firms to report if a reasonable person could conclude given the information available that a product creates an unreasonable risk of serious injury or death. In its evaluation of whether a subject firm is required to file a report under the provisions of section 15 of the CPSA the Commission shall, as a practical matter, attach considerable significance if such firm obtains information which reasonably supports the conclusion that its product violates a standard or ban promulgated under the FHSA, FFA, PPPA or RSA and the violation could result in serious injury or death.

(c) *Serious injury or death.* The term "serious injury" is not defined in the CPSA. The Commission believes that the term includes not only the concept of "grievous bodily injury," defined at § 1115.12(d), but also any other significant injury. Injuries necessitating hospitalization which require actual medical or surgical treatment, fractures, lacerations requiring sutures, concussions, injuries to the eye, ear, or internal organs requiring medical treatment, and injuries necessitating absence from school or work of more than one day are examples of situations in which the Commission shall presume that such a serious injury has occurred. To determine whether an unreasonable risk of serious injury or death exists, the firm should evaluate chronic or long term health effects as well as immediate injuries.

[57 FR 34228, Aug. 4, 1992]

§ 1115.7 Relation to other provisions.

The reporting requirements of section 37 of the CPSA (15 U.S.C. 2084) are in addition to the requirement in section 15 of the CPSA. Section 37 requires a product manufacturer to report certain kinds of lawsuit information. It is intended as a supplement to, not a substitute for, the requirements of section 15(b) of the CPSA. Whether or not a firm has an obligation to provide information under section 37, it must consider whether it has obtained information which reasonably supports the conclusion that its product violates a consumer product safety rule, does not comply with a voluntary safety standard upon which the Commission has relied under section 9, contains a defect which could create a substantial product hazard, or creates an unreasonable risk of serious injury or death. If a firm has obtained such information, it must report under section 15(b) of the CPSA, whether or not it is required to report under section 37. Further, in many cases the Commission would expect to receive reports under section 15(b) long before the obligation to report under section 37 arises since firms have frequently obtained reportable information before settlements or judgments in their product liability lawsuits.

[57 FR 34229, Aug. 4, 1992]

§1115.8 Compliance with product safety standards.

(a) *Voluntary standards.* The CPSA and other federal statutes administered by the Commission generally encourage the private sector development of, and compliance with voluntary consumer product safety standards to help protect the public from unreasonable risks of injury associated with consumer products. To support the development of such consensus standards, Commission staff participates in many voluntary standards committees and other activities. The Commission also strongly encourages all firms to comply with voluntary consumer product safety standards and considers, where appropriate, compliance or non-compliance with such standards in exercising its authorities under the CPSA and other federal statutes, including when making determinations under section 15 of the CPSA. Thus, for example, whether a product is in compliance with applicable voluntary safety standards may be relevant to the Commission staff's preliminary determination of whether that product presents a substantial product hazard under section 15 of the CPSA.

(b) *Mandatory standards.* The CPSA requires that firms comply with all applicable mandatory consumer product safety standards and to report to the Commission any products which do not comply with either mandatory standards or voluntary standards upon which the Commission has relied. As is the case with voluntary consumer product safety standards, compliance or non-compliance with applicable mandatory safety standards may be considered by the Commission and staff in making relevant determinations and exercising relevant authorities under the CPSA and other federal statutes. Thus, for example, while compliance with a relevant mandatory product safety standard does not, of itself, relieve a firm from the need to report to the Commission a product defect that creates a substantial product hazard under section 15 of the CPSA, it will be considered by staff in making the determination of whether and what type of corrective action may be required.

[71 FR 42030, July 25, 2006]

§1115.9 [Reserved]

§1115.10 Persons who must report and where to report.

(a) Every manufacturer (including importer), distributor, or retailer of a consumer product that has been distributed in commerce who obtains information that such consumer product contains a defect which could create a substantial risk of injury to the public shall immediately notify the Office of Compliance, Division of Corrective Actions, Consumer Product Safety Commission, Washington, DC 20207 (telephone: 301–504–0608), or such other persons as may be designated. Manufacturers (including importers), distributors, and retailers of consumer products subject to regulation by the Commission under provisions of the FFA, FHSA, PPPA, as well as consumer products subject to regulation under the CPSA and RSA, must comply with this requirement.

(b) Every manufacturer (including importer), distributor, or retailer of a consumer product that has been distributed in commerce who obtains information that such consumer product fails to comply with an applicable consumer product safety standard or ban issued under the CPSA shall immediately notify the Commission's Office of Compliance and Enforcement, Division of Corrective Actions or such other persons as may be designated. A subject firm need not report a failure to comply with a standard or regulation issued under the provisions of the RSA, FFA, FHSA, or PPPA unless it can be reasonably concluded that the failure to comply results in a defect which could create a substantial product hazard. (See paragraph (a) of this section.)

(c) Every manufacturer (including importer), distributor, and retailer of a consumer product that has been distributed in commerce who obtains information that such consumer product fails to comply with a voluntary consumer product safety standard upon which the Commission has relied under section 9 of the CPSA, shall immediately notify the Commission's Office of Compliance and Enforcement, Division of Corrective Actions or such other persons as may be designated.

(d) Every manufacturer (including importer), distributor, and retailer of a consumer product that has been distributed in commerce who obtains information that such consumer product creates an unreasonable risk of serious injury or death shall immediately notify the Commission's Office of Compliance and Enforcement, Division of Corrective Actions or such other persons as may be designated. This obligation applies to manufacturers, distributors and retailers of consumer products subject to regulation by the Commission under the Flammable Fabrics Act, Federal Hazardous Substances Act, Poison Prevention Packaging Act, and Refrigerator Safety Act as well as products subject to regulation under the CPSA.

(e) A distributor or retailer of a consumer product (who is neither a manufacturer nor an importer of that product) is subject to the reporting requirements of section 15(b) of the CPSA but may satisfy them by following the procedure detailed in § 1115.13(b).

(f) A manufacturer (including an importer), distributor, or retailer need not inform the Commission under section 15(b) of the CPSA if that person has actual knowledge that the Commission has been adequately informed of the defect or failure to comply. (See section 15(b) of the CPSA.)

[43 FR 34998, Aug. 7, 1978, as amended at 57 FR 34229, Aug. 4, 1992; 62 FR 46667, Sept. 4, 1997]

§ 1115.11 Imputed knowledge.

(a) In evaluating whether or when a subject firm should have reported, the Commission will deem a subject firm to have obtained reportable information when the information has been received by an official or employee who may reasonably be expected to be capable of appreciating the significance of the information. (See § 1115.14(b).)

(b) In evaluating whether or when a subject firm should have reported, the Commission will deem a subject firm to know what a reasonable person acting in the circumstances in which the firm finds itself would know. Thus, the subject firm shall be deemed to know what it would have known if it had exercised due care to ascertain the truth of complaints or other representations. This includes the knowledge a firm would have if it conducted a reasonably expeditious investigation in order to evaluate the reportability of a death or grievous bodily injury or other information. (See § 1115.14.)

§ 1115.12 Information which should be reported; evaluating substantial product hazard.

(a) *General.* Subject firms should not delay reporting in order to determine to a certainty the existence of a reportable noncompliance, defect or unreasonable risk. The obligation to report arises upon receipt of information from which one could reasonably conclude the existence of a reportable noncompliance, defect which could create a substantial product hazard, or unreasonable risk of serious injury or death. Thus, an obligation to report may arise when a subject firm received the first information regarding a potential hazard, noncompliance or risk. (See § 1115.14(c).) A subject firm in its report to the Commission need not admit, or may specifically deny, that the information it submits reasonably supports the conclusion that its consumer product is noncomplying, contains a defect which could create a substantial product hazard within the meaning of section 15(b) of the CPSA, or creates an unreasonable risk of serious injury or death. After receiving the report, the staff may conduct further investigation and will preliminarily determine whether the product reported upon presents a substantial product hazard. This determination can be based on information supplied by a subject firm or from any other source. If the matter is adjudicated, the Commission will ultimately make the decision as to substantial product hazard or will seek to have a court make the decision as to imminent product hazard.

(b) *Failure to comply.* A subject firm must report information indicating that a consumer product which it has distributed in commerce does not comply with an applicable consumer product safety standard or ban issued under the CPSA, or a voluntary consumer product safety standard upon which the Commission has relied under section 9 of the CPSA.

(c) *Unreasonable risk of serious injury or death.* A subject firm must report when it obtains information indicating that a consumer product which it has distributed in commerce creates an unreasonable risk of serious injury or death.

(d) *Death or grievous bodily injury.* Information indicating that a noncompliance or a defect in a consumer product has caused, may have caused, or contributed to the causing, or could cause or contribute to the causing of a death or grievous bodily injury (e.g., mutilation, amputation/dismemberment, disfigurement, loss of important bodily functions, debilitating internal disorders, severe burns, severe electrical shocks, and injuries likely to require extended hospitalization) must be reported, unless the subject firm has investigated and determined that the information is not reportable.

(e) *Other information indicating a defect or noncompliance.* Even if there are no reports of a potential for or an actual death or grievous bodily injury, other information may indicate a reportable defect or noncompliance. In evaluating whether or when a subject firm should have reported, the Commission will deem a subject firm to know what a reasonable and prudent manufacturer (including an importer), distributor, or retailer would know. (See §1115.11.)

(f) *Information which should be studied and evaluated.* Paragraphs (f)(1) through (7) of this section are examples of information which a subject firm should study and evaluate in order to determine whether it is obligated to report under section 15(b) of the CPSA. Such information may include information that a firm has obtained, or reasonably should have obtained in accordance with §1115.11, about product use, experience, performance, design, or manufacture outside the United States that is relevant to products sold or distributed in the United States. All information should be evaluated to determine whether it suggests the existence of a noncompliance, a defect, or an unreasonable risk of serious injury or death:

(1) Information about engineering, quality control, or production data.

(2) Information about safety-related production or design change(s).

(3) Product liability suits and/or claims for personal injury or damage.

(4) Information from an independent testing laboratory.

(5) Complaints from a consumer or consumer group.

(6) Information received from the Commission or other governmental agency.

(7) Information received from other firms, including requests to return a product or for replacement or credit. This includes both requests made by distributors and retailers to the manufacturer and requests from the manufacturer that products be returned.

(g) *Evaluating substantial risk of injury.* Information which should be or has been reported under section 15(b) of the CPSA does not automatically indicate the presence of a substantial product hazard. On a case-by-case basis the Commission and the staff will determine whether a defect or noncompliance exists and whether it results in a substantial risk of injury to the public. In deciding whether to report, subject firms may be guided by the following criteria the staff and the Commission use in determining whether a substantial product hazard exists:

(1) *Hazard created by defect.* Section 15(a)(2) of the CPSA lists factors to be considered in determining whether a defect creates a substantial risk of injury. These factors are set forth in the disjunctive. Therefore, the exist- ence of any one of the factors could create a substantial product hazard. The Commission and the staff will consider some or all of the following factors, as appropriate, in determining the substantiality of a hazard created by a product defect:

(i) *Pattern of defect.* The Commission and the staff will consider whether the defect arises from the design, composition, contents, construction, finish, packaging, warnings, or instructions of the product or from some other cause and will consider the conditions under which the defect manifests itself.

(ii) *Number of defective products distributed in commerce.* Even one defective product can present a substantial risk of injury and provide a basis for a substantial product hazard determination under section 15 of the CPSA if the injury which might occur is serious and/

or if the injury is likely to occur. However, a few defective products with no potential for causing serious injury and little likelihood of injuring even in a minor way will not ordinarily provide a proper basis for a substantial product hazard determination. The Commission also recognizes that the number of products remaining with consumers is a relevant consideration.

(iii) *Severity of the risk*. A risk is severe if the injury which might occur is serious and/or if the injury is likely to occur. In considering the likelihood of any injury the Commission and the staff will consider the number of injuries reported to have occurred, the intended or reasonably foreseeable use or misuse of the product, and the population group exposed to the product (e.g., children, elderly, handicapped).

(iv) *Other considerations*. The Commission and the staff will consider all other relevant factors.

(2) *Hazard presented by noncompliance*. Section 15(a)(1) of the CPSA states that a substantial product hazard exists when a failure to comply with an applicable consumer product safety rule creates a substantial risk of injury to the public. Therefore, the Commission and staff will consider whether the noncompliance is likely to result in injury when determining whether the noncompliance creates a substantial product hazard. As appropriate, the Commission and staff may consider some or all of the factors set forth in paragraph (f)(1) of this section in reaching the substantial product hazard determination.

[43 FR 34998, Aug. 7, 1978, as amended at 57 FR 34229, Aug. 4, 1992; 66 FR 54925, Oct. 31, 2001; 71 FR 42031, July 25, 2006]

§ 1115.13 Content and form of reports; delegations of authority.

(a) *Written reports*. The chief executive officer of the subject firm should sign any written reports to the Commission under section 15(b) of the CPSA unless this responsibility has been delegated by filing a written delegation of authority with the Commission's Office of Compliance and Enforcement, Division of Corrective Actions. Delegations of authority filed with the Commission under § 1115.9 of the previous regulations interpreting section 15 of the CPSA will remain in effect until revoked by the chief executive officer of the subject firm. The delegation may be in the following form:

DELEGATION OF AUTHORITY

(Name of company) ____________.

I ____________ hereby certify that I am Chief Executive Officer of the above-named company and that as such I am authorized to sign documents and to certify on behalf of said company the accuracy and completeness of information in such documents.

Pursuant to the power vested in me, I hereby delegate all or, to the extent indicated below, a portion of that authority to the person listed below.

This delegation is effective until revoked in writing. Authority delegated to:

(Name) ____________

(Address) ____________

(Title) ____________

Extent of authority: ____________

Signed:

(Name) ____________

(Address) ____________

(Title) ____________

(b) *Distributors and retailers*. A distributor or retailer of a product (who is neither a manufacturer nor an importer of that product) satisfies the initial reporting requirements either by telephoning or writing the Office of Compliance and Enforcement, Division of Corrective Actions, Consumer Product Safety Commission, Washington, DC 20207, phone 301–504–0608; by sending a letter describing the noncompliance, defect or risk of injury to the manufacturer (or importer) of the product and sending a copy of the letter to the Commission's Division of Corrective Actions; or by forwarding to the Commission's Division of Corrective Actions reportable information received from another firm. A distributor or retailer who receives reportable information from a manufacturer (or importer) shall report to the Commission unless the manufacturer (or importer) informs the distributor or retailer that a report has been made to the Commission. A report under this paragraph should contain the information detailed in paragraph (c) of this section insofar as it is known to the distributor or retailer. Unless further information is requested by the staff, this action will constitute a sufficient report insofar as the distributor or retailer is concerned.

(c) *Initial report*. Immediately after a subject firm has obtained information which reasonably supports the conclusion that a product fails to comply with an applicable consumer product safety rule or a voluntary standard, contains a defecat which could create a substantial risk of serious injury or death, the subject firm should provide the Division of Corrective Actions, Office of Compliance, Consumer Product Safety Commission, Washington, DC 20207 (telephone: 301–504–0608), with an initial report containing the information listed in paragraphs (c) (1) through (6) of this section. This initial report may be made by any means, but if it is not in writing, it should be confirmed in writing within 48 hours of the initial report. (See § 1115.14 for time computations.) The initial report should contain, insofar as is reasonably available and/or applicable:

(1) An identification and description of the product.

(2) The name and address of the manufacturer (or importer) or, if the manufacturer or importer is not known, the names and addresses of all known distributors and retailers of the product.

(3) The nature and extent of the possible defect, the failure to comply, or the risk.

(4) The nature and extent of the injury or risk of injury associated with the product.

(5) The name and address of the person informing the Commission.

(6) To the extent such information is then reasonably available, the data specified in § 1115.13(d).

(d) *Full report.* Subject firms which file initial reports are required to file full reports in accordance with this paragraph. Retailers and distributors may satisfy their reporting obligations in accordance with § 1115.13(b). At any time after an initial report, the staff may modify the requirements detailed in this section with respect to any subject firm. If the staff preliminarily determines that there is no substantial product hazard, it may inform the firm that its reporting obligation has been fulfilled. However, a subject firm would be required to report if it later became aware of new information indicating a reportable defect, noncompliance, or risk, whether the new information related to the same or another consumer product. Unless modified by staff action, the following information, to the extent that it is reasonably available and/or applicable, constitutes a "full report," must be submitted to the staff, and must be supplemented or corrected as new or different information becomes known:

(1) The name, address, and title of the person submitting the "full report" to the Commission.

(2) The name and address of the manufacturer (or importer) of the product and the addresses of the manufacturing plants for that product.

(3) An identification and description of the product(s). Give retail prices, model numbers, serial numbers, and date codes. Describe any identifying marks and their location on the product. Provide a picture or a sample of the product.

(4) A description of the nature of the defect, failure to comply, or risk. If technical drawings, test results, schematics, diagrams, blueprints, or other graphic depictions are available, attach copies.

(5) The nature of the injury or the possible injury associated with the product defect, failure to comply, or risk.

(6) The manner in which and the date when the information about the defect, noncompliance, or risk (e.g., complaints, reported injuries, quality control testing) was obtained. If any complaints related to the safety of the product or any allegations or reports of injuries associated with the product have been received, copies of such complaints or reports (or a summary thereof) shall be attached. Give a chronological account of facts or events leading to the report under section 15(b) of the CPSA, beginning with receipt of the first information which ultimately led to the report. Also included may be an analysis of these facts or events.

(7) The total number of products and units involved.

(8) The dates when products and units were manufactured, imported, distributed, and sold at retail.

(9) The number of products and units in each of the following: in the possession of the manufacturer or importer, in the possession of private labelers, in the possession of distributors, in the

possession of retailers, and in the possession of consumers.

(10) An explanation of any changes (e.g., designs, adjustments, and additional parts, quality control, testing) that have been or will be effected to correct the defect, failure to comply, or risk and of the steps that have been or will be taken to prevent similar occurrences in the future together with the timetable for implementing such changes and steps.

(11) Information that has been or will be given to purchasers, including consumers, about the defect, noncompliance, or risk with a description of how this information has been or will be communicated. This shall include copies or drafts of any letters, press releases, warning labels, or other written information that has been or will be given to purchasers, including consumers.

(12) The details of and schedule for any contemplated refund, replacement, or repair actions, including plans for disposing of returned products (e.g., repair, destroy, return to foreign manufacturer).

(13) A detailed explanation and description of the marketing and distribution of the product from the manufacturer (including importer) to the consumer (e.g., use of sales representatives, independent contractors, and/or jobbers; installation of the product, if any, and by whom).

(14) Upon request, the names and addresses of all distributors, retailers, and purchasers, including consumers.

(15) Such further information necessary or appropriate to the functions of the Commission as is requested by the staff.

[43 FR 34998, Aug. 7, 1978, as amended at 57 FR 34229, Aug. 4, 1992]

§ 1115.14 Time computations.

(a) *General.* Weekends and holidays are excluded from the computation of the time periods in this part.

(b) *Imputing knowledge.* In evaluating whether or when a firm should have reported, the Commission shall impute to the subject firm knowledge of product safety related information received by an official or employee of a subject firm capable of appreciating the significance of the information. Under ordinary circumstances, 5 days should be the maximum reasonable time for information to reach the Chief Executive Officer or the official or employee responsible for complying with the reporting requirements of section 15(b) of the CPSA. The Commission will impute knowledge possessed by the Chief Executive Officer or by the official or employee responsible for complying with the reporting requirements of section 15(b) of the CPSA simultaneously to the subject firm.

(c) *Time when obligation to report arises.* The obligation to report under section 15(b) of the CPSA may arise upon receipt by a subject firm of the first information regarding a noncompliance, or a potential hazard presented by a product defect, or an unreasonable risk. Information giving rise to a reporting obligation may include, but is not limited to, complaints, injury reports, quality control and engineering data. A subject firm should not await complete or accurate risk estimates before reporting under section 15(b) of CPSA. However, if information is not clearly reportable, a subject firm may spend a reasonable time for investigation and evaluation. (See § 1115.14(d).)

(d) *Time for investigation and evaluation.* A subject firm may conduct a reasonably expeditious investigation in order to evaluate the reportability of a death or grievous bodily injury or other information. This investigation and evaluation should not exceed 10 days unless a firm can demonstrate that a longer period is reasonable. The Commission will deem that, at the end of 10 days, a subject firm has received and considered all information which would have been available to it had a reasonable, expeditious, and diligent investigation been undertaken.

(e) *Time to report.* Immediately, that is, within 24 hours, after a subject firm has obtained information which reasonably supports the conclusion that its consumer product fails to comply with an applicable consumer product safety rule or voluntary consumer product safety standard, contains a defect which could create a substantial risk of injury to the public, or creates an unreasonable risk of serious injury or death, the firm should report. (See

§1115.13.) If a firm elects to conduct an investigation in order to evaluate the existence of reportable information, the 24-hour period begins when the firm has information which reasonably supports the conclusion that its consumer product fails to comply with an applicable consumer product safety rule or voluntary consumer product safety standard upon which the Commission has relied under section 9, contains a defect which could create a substantial product hazard, or creates an unreasonable risk of serious injury or death. Thus, a firm could report to the Commission before the conclusion of a reasonably expeditious investigation and evaluation if the reportable information becomes known during the course of the investigation. In lieu of the investigation, the firm may report the information immediately.

[43 FR 34998, Aug. 7, 1978, as amended at 57 FR 34230, Aug. 4, 1992]

§1115.15 Confidentiality and disclosure of data.

(a) *General.* The Commission does not routinely make reports available to the public until the staff has made a preliminary hazard determination. Copies of reports will not be available to the public in the Commission's public reading room, and information contained in reports will not ordinarily be disclosed to the public in the absence of a formal request.

(b) *Freedom of Information Act.* Any person who submits information to the Commission who believes that any portion of the information is entitled to exemption from public disclosure under the provisions of the Freedom of Information Act, as amended (15 U.S.C. 552(b)), of the CPSA, as amended, or of another Federal statute must accompany the submission with a written request that the information be considered exempt from disclosure or indicate that a written request will be submitted within 10 working days of the submission. The request shall (1) identify the portions of the information for which exemption is claimed, which may include the identity of the reporting firm and the fact that it is making a report, and (2) state the facts and reasons which support the claimed exemption. After the staff has made its preliminary hazard determination, and regardless of whether or not the staff preliminarily determines that a product presents a substantial product hazard, the Commission will no longer honor requests for exempt status for the identity of the reporting firm, the identity of the consumer product, and the nature of the reported alleged defect or noncompliance. This information, together with the staff's preliminary hazard determination, will be made available to the public in the Commission's public reading room. Information for which exempt status is claimed (such as alleged trade secrets, confidential commercial or financial information, or information the disclosure of which would constitute an unwarranted invasion of personal privacy) shall not be released to the public except in accordance with the applicable statute or the Commission's Freedom of Information Act regulations (16 CFR part 1015).

(c) *Section 6(b) of the CPSA.* The Commission believes that the first two sentences in section 6(b)(1) of the CPSA (15 U.S.C. 2055(b)(1)) apply to affirmative dissemination of information by the Commission (such as press releases or fact sheets distributed to the public) from which the public may ascertain readily the identity of the product's manufacturer and/or private labeler. Manufacturers and private labelers will ordinarily be given 30 days' notice before the Commission makes such affirmative disseminations. However, this 30-day notice will not apply if the Commission finds that a lesser notice period is required in the interest of public health and safety.

Subpart B—Remedial Actions and Sanctions

§1115.20 Voluntary remedial actions.

As appropriate, the Commission will attempt to protect the public from substantial product hazards by seeking one or more of the following voluntary remedies:

(a) *Corrective action plans.* A corrective action plan is a document, signed by a subject firm, which sets forth the remedial action which the firm will voluntarily undertake to protect the public, but which has no legally binding effect. The Commission reserves the right to seek broader corrective action if it becomes aware of new facts or if the corrective action plan does not sufficiently protect the public.

(1) Corrective action plans shall include, as appropriate:

(i) A statement of the nature of the alleged hazard associated with the product, including the nature of the alleged defect or noncompliance and type(s) of injury or potential injury presented.

(ii) A detailed statement of the means to be employed to notify the public of the alleged product hazard (e.g., letter, press release, advertising), including an identification of the classes of persons who will receive such notice and a copy or copies of the notice or notices to be used.

(iii) A specification of model number and/or other appropriate descriptions of the product.

(iv) Any necessary instructions regarding use or handling of the product pending correction.

(v) An explanation of the specific cause of the alleged substantial product hazard, if known.

(vi) A statement of the corrective action which will be or has been taken to eliminate the alleged substantial product hazard. The firm should indicate whether it is repairing or replacing the product or refunding its purchase price. If products are to be returned to a subject firm, the corrective action plan should indicate their disposition (e.g., reworked, destroyed, returned to foreign manufacturer). Samples of replacement products and relevant drawings and test data for repairs or replacements should be available.

(vii) A statement of the steps that will be, or have been, taken to reasonably prevent recurrence of the alleged substantial product hazard in the future.

(viii) A statement of the action which will be undertaken to correct product units in the distribution chain, including a timetable and specific information about the number and location of such units.

(ix) The signatures of representatives of the subject firm.

(x) An acknowledgment by the subject firm that the Commission may monitor the corrective action and that the firm will furnish necessary information, including customer lists.

(xi) An agreement that the Commission may publicize the terms of the plan to the extent necessary to inform the public of the nature and extent of the alleged substantial product hazard and of the actions being undertaken to correct the alleged hazard presented.

(xii) Additional points of agreement, as appropriate.

(xiii) If desired by the subject firm, the following statement or its equivalent: "The submission of this corrective action plan does not constitute an admission by (the subject firm) that either reportable information or a substantial product hazard exists."

(xiv) An acknowledgment that the corrective action plan becomes effective only upon its final acceptance by the Commission.

(2) In determining whether to recommend to the Commission acceptance of a corrective action plan, the staff shall consider favorably both the promptness of the subject firm's reporting and any remedial actions taken by the subject firm in the interest of public safety. The staff also shall consider, insofar as possible, prior involvement by the subject firm in corrective action plans and Commission orders if such involvement bears on the likelihood that the firm will comply fully with the terms of the corrective action plan.

(3) Upon receipt of a corrective action plan and staff recommendation, the Commission may:

(i) Approve the plan;

(ii) Reject the plan and issue a complaint (in which case an administrative and/or judicial proceeding will be commenced); or

(iii) Take any other action necessary to insure that the plan is adequate.

(4) When time permits and where practicable in the interest of protecting the public, a summary of the plan shall be published in the Commission's Public Calendar. Those portions of the plan that are not restricted will be made available to the public in the Commission's public reading room as much in advance of the Commission

meeting as practicable. Any interested person wishing to comment on the plan must file a Notice of Intent to Comment at least forty-eight (48) hours prior to the commencement of the Commission meeting during which the plan will be discussed. If no notices of intent are received, the Commission may take final action on the plan. If such notice is received within the time limits detailed above, the plan will, if practicable, be docketed for the following week's agenda. All comments must be in writing, and final written comments must be submitted at least forty-eight (48) hours before that session.

(b) *Consent order agreements under section 15 of CPSA.* The consent order agreement (agreement) is a document executed by a subject firm (Consenting Party) and a Commission staff representative which incorporates both a proposed complaint setting forth the staff's charges and a proposed order by which such charges are resolved.

(1) Consent order agreements shall include, as appropriate:

(i) An admission of all jurisdictional facts by the Consenting Party.

(ii) A waiver of any rights to an administrative or judicial hearing and of any other procedural steps, including any rights to seek judicial review or otherwise challenge or contest the validity of the Commission's Order.

(iii) A statement that the agreement is in settlement of the staff's charges.

(iv) A statement that the Commission's Order is issued under section 15 of the CPSA (15 U.S.C. 2064) and that a violation is a prohibited act within the meaning of section 19(a)(5) of the CPSA (15 U.S.C. 2068(a)(5)) and may subject a violator to civil and/or criminal penalties under sections 20 and 21 of the CPSA (15 U.S.C. 2069 and 2070).

(v) An acknowledgment that the Commission reserves its right to seek sanctions for any violations of the reporting obligations of section 15(b) of CPSA (15 U.S.C. 2064(b)) and its right to take other appropriate legal action.

(vi) An acknowledgment that the agreement becomes effective only upon its final acceptance by the Commission and its service upon the Consenting Party.

(vii) An acknowledgment that the Commission may disclose terms of the consent order agreement to the public.

(viii) A listing of the acts or practices from which the Consenting Party will refrain.

(ix) A statement that the Consenting Party shall perform certain acts and practices pursuant to the agreement.

(x) An acknowledgment that any interested person may bring an action pursuant to section 24 of the CPSA (15 U.S.C. 2073) in any U.S. district court for the district in which the Consenting Party is found or transacts business to enforce the order and to obtain appropriate injunctive relief.

(xi) A description of the alleged substantial product hazard.

(xii) If desired by the Consenting Party, the following statement or its equivalent: "The signing of this consent order agreement does not constitute an admission by (the Consenting Party) that either reportable information or a substantial product hazard exists."

(xiii) The elements of a corrective action plan as set forth in §1115.20(a).

(2) At any time in the course of an investigation, the staff may propose to a subject firm which is being investigated that some or all of the allegations be resolved by a consent order agreement. Additionally, such a proposal may be made to the staff by a subject firm.

(3) Upon receiving an executed agreement, the Commission may:

(i) Provisionally accept it;

(ii) Reject it and issue a complaint (in which case an administrative and/or judicial proceeding will be commenced); or

(iii) Take such other action as it may deem appropriate.

(4) If the consent order agreement is provisionally accepted, the Commission shall place the agreement on the public record and shall announce provisional acceptance of the agreement in the Commission's public calendar and in the FEDERAL REGISTER. Any interested person may request the Commission not to accept the agreement by filing a written request in the Office of the Secretary. Such written request must be received in the Office of the Secretary no later than the close of

business of the fifteenth (15th) calendar day following the date of announcement in the FEDERAL REGISTER.

(5) If the Commission does not receive any requests not to accept the agreement within the time period specified above, the consent order agreement shall be deemed finally accepted by the Commission on the twentieth (20th) calendar day after the date of announcement in the FEDERAL REGISTER, unless the Commission determines otherwise. However, if the Commission does receive a request not to accept the consent order agreement, then it will consider such request and vote on the acceptability of such agreement or the desirability of further action. After the consent order agreement is finally accepted, the Commission may then issue its complaint and order in such form as the circumstances may require. The order is a final order in disposition of the proceeding and is effective immediately upon its service upon the Consenting Party pursuant to the Commission's Rules of Practice for Adjudicative Proceedings (16 CFR part 1025). The Consenting Party shall thereafter be bound by and take immediate action in accordance with such final order.

(6) If the Commission does not accept the consent order agreement on a final basis, it shall so notify the Consenting Party. Such notification constitutes withdrawal of the Commission's provisional acceptance unless the Commission orders otherwise. The Commission then may:

(i) Issue a complaint, in which case an administrative and/or judicial proceeding will be commenced;

(ii) Order further investigation; or

(iii) Take such other action as it may deem appropriate.

§ 1115.21 Compulsory remedial actions.

As appropriate, the Commission will attempt to protect the public from hazards presented by consumer products by seeking one or more of the following:

(a) *Adjudicated Commission Order.* An adjudicated Commission Order under section 15 (c) or (d) of the CPSA may be issued after parties and interested persons have had an opportunity for a hearing in accordance with section 554 of title 5, United States Code, and with section 15(f) of the CPSA. This hearing is governed by the Commission's Rules of Practice for Adjudicative Proceedings (16 CFR part 1025).

(b) *Injunctive relief.* The Commission may apply to a U.S. district court in accordance with the provisions of section 15(g) of the CPSA for a preliminary injunction to restrain the distribution in commerce of a product it has reason to believe presents a substantial product hazard. The Commission may seek enforcement of its orders issued under sections 15 (c) and (d) of the CPSA in accordance with provisions of sections 22 and 27(b)(7) of the CPSA (15 U.S.C. 2071 and 2076(b)(7)).

(c) *Judicial determination of imminent hazard.* The Commission may file a complaint in a U.S. district court in accordance with the provisions of section 12 of the CPSA (15 U.S.C. 2061).

(d) *Orders of the Secretary of the Treasury.* The Commission staff may inform the Secretary of the Treasury that a consumer product offered for importation into the customs territory of the United States fails to comply with an applicable consumer product safety rule and/or has a product defect which constitutes a substantial product hazard. The Commission may request the Secretary of the Treasury under section 17 of the CPSA (15 U.S.C. 2066) to refuse admission to any such consumer product.

§ 1115.22 Prohibited acts and sanctions.

(a) *Statements generally.* Whoever knowingly and willfully falsifies, or conceals a material fact in a report under the CPSA and rules thereunder, is subject to criminal penalties under 18 U.S.C. 1001.

(b) *Timeliness and adequacy of reporting.* A failure to inform the Commission immediately and adequately, as required by section 15(b) of the CPSA, is a prohibited act within section 19(a)(4) of the CPSA (15 U.S.C. 2068(a)(4)).

(c) *Failure to make reports.* The failure or refusal to make reports or provide information as required under the CPSA is a prohibited act within the meaning of section 19(a)(3) of the CPSA (15 U.S.C. 2068(a)(3)).

(d) *Noncomplying products.* The manufacture for sale, offering for sale, distribution in commerce, and/or importation into the United States of a consumer product which is not in conformity with an applicable consumer product safety rule under CPSA is a prohibited act within the meaning of sections 19 (a)(1) and (a)(2) of the CPSA (15 U.S.C. 2068 (a)(1) and (a)(2)).

(e) *Orders issued under section 15 (c) and/or (d).* The failure to comply with an order issued under section 15 (c) and/or (d) of the CPSA is a prohibited act within the meaning of section 19(a)(5) of the CPSA (15 U.S.C. 2068(a)(5)).

(f) *Consequences of engaging in prohibited acts.* A knowing violation of section 19(a) of the CPSA subjects the violator to a civil penalty in accordance with section 20 of the CPSA (15 U.S.C. 2069). "Knowing," as defined in section 20(c) of the CPSA (15 U.S.C. 2069(c)), means the having of actual knowledge or the presumed having of knowledge deemed to be possessed by a reasonable person who acts in the circumstances, including knowledge obtainable upon the exercise of due care to ascertain the truth of representations. A knowing and willful violation of section 19(a), after the violator has received notice of noncompliance, subjects the violator to criminal penalties in accordance with section 21 of the CPSA (15 U.S.C. 2070).

Subpart C—Guidelines and Requirements for Mandatory Recall Notices

SOURCE: 75 FR 3371, Jan. 21, 2010, unless otherwise noted.

§ 1115.23 Purpose.

(a) The Commission establishes these guidelines and requirements for recall notices as required by section 15(i) of the Consumer Product Safety Act, as amended (CPSA) (15 U.S.C. 2064(i)). The guidelines and requirements set forth the information to be included in a notice required by an order under sections 12, 15(c), or 15(d) of the CPSA (15 U.S.C. 2061, 2064(c), or 2064(d)). Unless otherwise ordered by the Commission under section 15(c) or (d) of the CPSA (15 U.S.C. 2064(c) or (d)), or by a United States district court under section 12 of the CPSA (15 U.S.C. 2061), the content information required in this subpart must be included in every such notice.

(b) The Commission establishes these guidelines and requirements to ensure that every recall notice effectively helps consumers and other persons to:

(1) Identify the specific product to which the recall notice pertains;

(2) Understand the product's actual or potential hazards to which the recall notice pertains, and information relating to such hazards; and

(3) Understand all remedies available to consumers concerning the product to which the recall notice pertains.

§ 1115.24 Applicability.

This subpart applies to manufacturers (including importers), retailers, and distributors of consumer products as those terms are defined herein and in the CPSA.

§ 1115.25 Definitions.

In addition to the definitions given in section 3 of the CPSA (15 U.S.C. 2052), the following definitions apply:

(a) *Recall* means any one or more of the actions required by an order under sections 12, 15(c), or 15(d) of the CPSA (15 U.S.C. 2061, 2064(c), or 2064(d)).

(b) *Recall notice* means a notification required by an order under sections 12, 15(c), or 15(d) of the CPSA (15 U.S.C. 2061, 2064(c), or 2064(d)).

(c) *Direct recall notice* means a notification required by an order under sections 12, 15(c), or 15(d) of the CPSA (15 U.S.C. 2061, 2064(c), or 2064(d)), that is sent directly to specifically-identified consumers.

(d) *Firm* means a manufacturer (including an importer), retailer, or distributor as those terms are defined in the CPSA.

(e) *Other persons* means, but is not limited to, consumer safety advocacy organizations, public interest groups, trade associations, industry advocacy organizations, other State, local, and Federal government agencies, and the media.

§ 1115.26 Guidelines and policies.

(a) *General.* (1) A recall notice should provide sufficient information and motivation for consumers and other persons to identify the product and its actual or potential hazards, and to respond and take the stated action. A recall notice should clearly and concisely state the potential for injury or death.

(2) A recall notice should be written in language designed for, and readily understood by, the targeted consumers or other persons. The language should be simple and should avoid or minimize the use of highly technical or legal terminology.

(3) A recall notice should be targeted and tailored to the specific product and circumstances. In determining the form and content of a recall notice, the manner in which the product was advertised and marketed should be considered.

(4) A direct recall notice is the most effective form of a recall notice.

(5) At least two of the recall notice forms listed in subsection (b) should be used.

(b) Form of recall notice—(1) Possible forms. A recall notice may be written, electronic, audio, visual, or in any other form ordered by the Commission in an order under section 15(c) or (d) of the CPSA (15 U.S.C. 2064(c) or (d)), or by a United States district court under section 12 of the CPSA (15 U.S.C. 2061). The forms of, and means for communicating, recall notices include, but are not limited to:

(i) Letter, Web site posting, electronic mail, RSS feed, or text message;

(ii) Computer, radio, television, or other electronic transmission or medium;

(iii) Video news release, press release, recall alert, Web stream, or other form of news release;

(iv) Newspaper, magazine, catalog, or other publication; and

(v) Advertisement, newsletter, and service bulletin.

(2) *Direct recall notice.* A direct recall notice should be used for each consumer for whom a firm has direct contact information, or when such information is obtainable, regardless of whether the information was collected for product registration, sales records, catalog orders, billing records, marketing purposes, warranty information, loyal purchaser clubs, or other such purposes. Direct contact information includes, but is not limited to, name and address, telephone number, and electronic mail address. Forms of direct recall notice include, but are not limited to, United States mail, electronic mail, and telephone calls. A direct recall notice should prominently show its importance over other consumer notices or mail by including "Safety Recall" or other appropriate terms in an electronic mail subject line, and, in large bold red typeface, on the front of an envelope and in the body of a recall notice.

(3) *Web site recall notice.* A Web site recall notice should be on a Web site's first entry point such as a home page, should be clear and prominent, and should be interactive by permitting consumers and other persons to obtain recall information and request a remedy directly on the Web site.

(c) *Languages.* Where the Commission for purposes of an order under section 15(c) or (d) of the CPSA (15 U.S.C. 2064(c) or (d)), or a United States district court for purposes of an order under section 12 of the CPSA (15 U.S.C. 2061), determines that it is necessary or appropriate to adequately inform and protect the public, a recall notice may be required to be in languages in addition to English. For example, it may be necessary or appropriate to require a recall notice be in a language in addition to English when a product label is in a language in addition to English, when a product is marketed in a language in addition to English, or when a product is marketed or available in a geographic location where English is not the predominant language.

§ 1115.27 Recall notice content requirements.

Except as provided in § 1115.29, every recall notice must include the information set forth below:

(a) *Terms.* A recall notice must include the word "recall" in the heading and text.

(b) *Date.* A recall notice must include its date of release, issuance, posting, or publication.

(c) *Description of product.* A recall notice must include a clear and concise statement of the information that will enable consumers and other persons to readily and accurately identify the specific product and distinguish it from similar products. The information must enable consumers to readily determine whether or not they have, or may be exposed to, the product. To the extent applicable to a product, descriptive information that must appear on a recall notice includes, but is not limited to:

(1) The product's names, including informal and abbreviated names, by which consumers and other persons should know or recognize the product;

(2) The product's intended or targeted use population (*e.g.*, infants, children, or adults);

(3) The product's colors and sizes;

(4) The product's model numbers, serial numbers, date codes, stock keeping unit (SKU) numbers, and tracking labels, including their exact locations on the product;

(5) Identification and exact locations of product tags, labels, and other identifying parts, and a statement of the specific identifying information found on each part; and

(6) Product photographs. A firm must provide photographs. Each photograph must be electronic or digital, in color, of high resolution and quality, and in a format readily transferable with high quality to a Web site or other appropriate medium. As needed for effective notification, multiple photographs and photograph angles may be required.

(d) *Description of action being taken.* A recall notice must contain a clear and concise statement of the actions that a firm is taking concerning the product. These actions may include, but are not limited to, one or more of the following: Stop sale and distribution in commerce; recall to the distributor, retailer, or consumer level; repair; request return and provide a replacement; and request return and provide a refund.

(e) *Statement of number of product units.* A recall notice must state the approximate number of product units covered by the recall, including all product units manufactured, imported, and/or distributed in commerce.

(f) *Description of substantial product hazard.* A recall notice must contain a clear and concise description of the product's actual or potential hazards that result from the product condition or circumstances giving rise to the recall. The description must enable consumers and other persons to readily identify the reasons that a firm is conducting a recall. The description must also enable consumers and other persons to readily identify and understand the risks and potential injuries or deaths associated with the product conditions and circumstances giving rise to the recall. The description must include:

(1) The product defect, fault, failure, flaw, and/or problem giving rise to the recall; and

(2) The type of hazard or risk, including, by way of example only, burn, fall, choking, laceration, entrapment, and/or death.

(g) *Identification of recalling firm.* A recall notice must identify the firm conducting the recall by stating the firm's legal name and commonly known trade name, and the city and state of its headquarters. The notice must state whether the recalling firm is a manufacturer (including importer), retailer, or distributor.

(h) *Identification of manufacturers.* A recall notice must identify each manufacturer (including importer) of the product and the country of manufacture. Under the definition in section 3(a)(11) of the CPSA (15 U.S.C. 2052(a)(11)), a manufacturer means "any person who manufactures or imports a consumer product." If a product has been manufactured outside of the United States, a recall notice must identify the foreign manufacturer and the United States importer. A recall notice must identify the manufacturer by stating the manufacturer's legal name and the city and state of its headquarters, or, if a foreign manufacturer, the foreign manufacturer's legal name and the city and country of its headquarters.

(i) *Identification of significant retailers.* A recall notice must identify each significant retailer of the product. A recall notice must identify such a retailer by stating the retailer's commonly known trade name. Under the definition in section 3(a)(13) of the CPSA (15 U.S.C. 2052(a)(13)), a retailer means "a person to whom a consumer product is delivered or sold for purposes of sale or distribution by such person to a consumer." A product's retailer is "significant" if, upon the Commission's information and belief, and in the sole discretion of the Commission for purposes of an order under section 15(c) or (d) of the CPSA (15 U.S.C. 2064(c) or (d)), or in the sole discretion of a United States district court for purposes of an order under section 12 of the CPSA (15 U.S.C. 2061), any one or more of the circumstances set forth below is present (the Commission may require manufacturers (including importers), retailers, and distributors to provide information relating to these circumstances):

(1) The retailer was the exclusive retailer of the product;

(2) The retailer was an importer of the product;

(3) The retailer has stores nationwide or regionally-located;

(4) The retailer sold, or held for purposes of sale or distribution in commerce, a significant number of the total manufactured, imported, or distributed units of the product; or

(5) Identification of the retailer is in the public interest.

(j) *Region.* Where necessary or appropriate to assist consumers in determining whether they have the product at issue, a description of the region where the product was sold, or held for purposes of sale or distribution in commerce, must be provided.

(k) *Dates of manufacture and sale.* A recall notice must state the month and year in which the manufacture of the product began and ended, and the month and year in which the retail sales of the product began and ended. These dates must be included for each make and model of the product.

(l) *Price.* A recall notice must state the approximate retail price or price range of the product.

(m) *Description of incidents, injuries, and deaths.* A recall notice must contain a clear and concise summary description of all incidents (including, but not limited to, property damage), injuries, and deaths associated with the product conditions or circumstances giving rise to the recall, as well as a statement of the number of such incidents, injuries, and deaths. The description must enable consumers and other persons to readily understand the nature and extent of the incidents and injuries. A recall notice must state the ages of all persons injured and killed. A recall notice must state the dates or range of dates on which the Commission received information about injuries and deaths.

(n) *Description of remedy.* A recall notice must contain a clear and concise statement, readily understandable by consumers and other persons, of:

(1) Each remedy available to a consumer for the product conditions or circumstances giving rise to the recall. Remedies include, but are not limited to, refunds, product repairs, product replacements, rebates, coupons, gifts, premiums, and other incentives.

(2) All specific actions that a consumer must take to obtain each remedy, including, but not limited to, instructions on how to participate in the recall. These actions may include, but are not limited to, contacting a firm, removing the product from use, discarding the product, returning part or all of the product, or removing or disabling part of the product.

(3) All specific information that a consumer needs in order to obtain each remedy and to obtain all information about each remedy. This information may include, but is not limited to, the following: Manufacturer, retailer, and distributor contact information (such as name, address, telephone and facsimile numbers, e-mail address, and Web site address); whether telephone calls will be toll-free or collect; and telephone number days and hours of operation including time zone.

(o) *Other information.* A recall notice must contain such other information as the Commission for purposes of an order under section 15(c) or (d) of the CPSA (15 U.S.C. 2064(c) or (d)), or a United States district court for purposes of an order under section 12 of the CPSA (15 U.S.C. 2061), deems appropriate and orders.

§ 1115.28 Multiple products or models.

For each product or model covered by a recall notice, the notice must meet the requirements of this subpart.

§ 1115.29 Final determination regarding form and content.

(a) *Commission or court discretion.* The recall notice content required by this subpart must be included in a recall notice whether or not the firm admits the existence of a defect or of an actual or potential hazard, and whether or not the firm concedes the accuracy or applicability of all of the information contained in the recall notice. The Commission will make the final determination as to the form and content of the recall notice for purposes of an order under section 15(c) or (d) of the CPSA (15 U.S.C. 2064(c) or (d)), and a United States district court will make the final determination as to the form and content of a recall notice for purposes of an order under section 12 of the CPSA (15 U.S.C. 2061).

(b) *Recall notice exceptions.* The Commission for purposes of an order under section 15(c) or (d) of the CPSA (15 U.S.C. 2064(c) or (d)), or a United States district court for purposes of an order under section 12 of the CPSA (15 U.S.C. 2061), may determine that one or more of the recall notice requirements set forth in this subpart is not required, and will not be included, in a recall notice.

(c) *Commission approval.* Before a firm may publish, broadcast, or otherwise disseminate a recall notice to be issued pursuant to an order under section 15(c) or (d) of the CPSA (15 U.S.C. 2064(c) or (d)), the Commission must review and agree in writing to all aspects of the notice.

Appendix to Part 1115—Voluntary Standards on Which the Commission Has Relied Under Section 9 of the Consumer Product Safety Act

The following are the voluntary standards on which the Commission has relied under section 9 of the Consumer Product Safety Act:

1. American National Standard for Power Tools—Gasoline-Powered Chain Saws—Safety Regulations, ANSI B175.1–1985 sections 4.9.4, 4.12, 4.15, 7 and 8, or the current version: ANSI B175.1–1991 sections 5.9.4, 5.12, 5.15, 8 and 9.

2. American National Standard for Gas-Fired Room Heaters, Volume II, Unvented Room Heaters, ANSI Z21.11.2–1989 and addenda ANSI Z21.11.2 a and b- 1991), sections 1.8, 1.20.9, and 2.9.

[57 FR 34230, Aug. 4, 1992]

PART 1116—REPORTS SUBMITTED PURSUANT TO SECTION 37 OF THE CONSUMER PRODUCT SAFETY ACT

Sec.

AUTHORITY: 15 U.S.C. 2055(e), 2084.

SOURCE: 57 FR 34239, Aug. 4, 1992, unless otherwise noted.

§ 1116.1 Purpose.

The purpose of this part 1116 is to establish procedures for filing with the Consumer Product Safety Commission ("the Commission") reports required by section 37 of the Consumer Product Safety Act (CPSA) (15 U.S.C. 2084) and to set forth the Commission's interpretation of the provisions of section 37.

§ 1116.2 Definitions.

(a) A *24-month period(s)* means the 24-month period beginning on January 1, 1991, and each subsequent 24-month period beginning on January 1 of the calendar year that is two years following the beginning of the previous 24-month period. The first statutory two year period ends on December 31, 1992. The second begins on January 1, 1993 and ends on December 31, 1994, and so forth.

(b) *Grievous bodily injury* includes, but is not limited to, any of the following categories of injury:

(1) Mutilation or disfigurement. Disfigurement includes permanent facial disfigurement or non-facial scarring that results in permanent restriction of motion;

(2) Dismemberment or amputation, including the removal of a limb or other appendage of the body;

(3) The loss of important bodily functions or debilitating internal disorder. These terms include:

(i) Permanent injury to a vital organ, in any degree;

(ii) The total loss or loss of use of any internal organ,

(iii) Injury, temporary or permanent, to more than one internal organ;

(iv) Permanent brain injury to any degree or with any residual disorder (e.g. epilepsy), and brain or brain stem injury including coma and spinal cord injuries;

(v) Paraplegia, quadriplegia, or permanent paralysis or paresis, to any degree;

(vi) Blindness or permanent loss, to any degree, of vision, hearing, or sense of smell, touch, or taste;

(vii) Any back or neck injury requiring surgery, or any injury requiring joint replacement or any form of prosthesis, or;

(viii) Compound fracture of any long bone, or multiple fractures that result in permanent or significant temporary loss of the function of an important part of the body;

(4) Injuries likely to require extended hospitalization, including any injury requiring 30 or more consecutive days of in-patient care in an acute care facility, or 60 or more consecutive days of in-patient care in a rehabilitation facility;

(5) Severe burns, including any third degree burn over ten percent of the body or more, or any second degree burn over thirty percent of the body or more;

(6) Severe electric shock, including ventricular fibrillation, neurological damage, or thermal damage to internal tissue caused by electric shock.

(7) Other grievous injuries, including any allegation of traumatically induced disease.

Manufacturers may wish to consult with the Commission staff to determine whether injuries not included in the examples above are regarded as grievous bodily injury.

(c) A *particular model* of a consumer product is one that is distinctive in functional design, construction, warnings or instructions related to safety, function, user population, or other characteristics which could affect the product's safety related performance. (15 U.S.C. 2084(e)(2))

(1) The *functional design* of a product refers to those design features that directly affect the ability of the product to perform its intended use or purpose.

(2) The *construction* of a product refers to its finished assembly or fabrication, its materials, and its components.

(3) *Warnings or instructions related to safety* include statements of the principal hazards associated with a product, and statements of precautionary or affirmative measures to take during the use, handling, or storage of a product, to the extent that a reasonable person would understand such statements to be related to the safety of the product. Warnings or instructions may be written or graphically depicted and may be attached to the product or appear on the product itself, in operating manuals, or in other literature that accompanies or describes the product.

(4) The *function* of a product refers to its intended use or purpose.

(5) *User population* refers to the group or class of people by whom a product is principally used. While the manufacturer's stated intent may be relevant to an inquiry concerning the nature of the user population, the method of distribution, the availability of the product to the public and to specific groups, and the identity of purchasers or users of the product should be considered.

(6) *Other characteristics which could affect a product's safety related performance* include safety features incorporated into the product to protect against foreseeable risks that might arise during the use, handling, or storage of a product.

(d) The term *manufacturer* means any person who manufactures or imports a consumer product. (15 U.S.C. 2052(a)(4)).

[57 FR 34239, Aug. 4, 1992, as amended at 58 FR 16121, Mar. 25, 1993]

§ 1116.3 Persons who must report under section 37.

A manufacturer of a consumer product must report if:

(a) A particular model of the product is the subject of at least 3 civil actions filed in Federal or State Court;

(b) Each suit alleges the involvement of that particular model in death or grievous bodily injury;

(c) The manufacturer is—

(1) A party to, or

(2) Is involved in the defense of or has notice of each action prior to entry of a final order, and is involved in the discharge of any obligation owed to plaintiff under the settlement of or in satisfaction of the judgment after adjudication in each of the suits; and

(d) During one of the 24-month periods defined in §1116.2(a), each of the three actions results in either a final settlement involving the manufacturer or in a court judgment in favor of the plaintiff.

For reporting purposes, a multiple plaintiff suit for death or grievous bodily injury is reportable if the suit involves three or more separate incidents of injury. The reporting obligation arises when at least three plaintiffs have settled their claims or when a combination of settled claims and adjudications favorable to plaintiffs reaches three. Multiple lawsuits arising from one incident involving the same product only count as one lawsuit for the purposes of section 37.

§ 1116.4 Where to report.

Reports must be sent in writing to the Commission's Office of Compliance and Enforcement, Division of Corrective Actions, Washington, DC 20207, telephone (301) 504–0608).

§ 1116.5 When must a report be made.

(a) A manufacturer must report to the Commission within 30 days after the final settlement or court judgment in the last of the three civil actions referenced in §1116.3.

(b) If a manufacturer has filed a section 37 report within one of the 24-month periods defined in §1116.2(a), the manufacturer must also report the information required by section 37(c)(1) for any subsequent settlement or judgment in a civil action that alleges that the same particular model of the product was involved in death or grievous bodily injury and that takes place during the same 24-month period. Each such supplemental report must be filed within 30 days of the settlement or final judgment in the reportable civil action.

§ 1116.6 Contents of section 37 reports.

(a) *Required information.* With respect to each of the civil actions that is the subject of a report under section 37, the report must contain the following information:

(1) The name and address of the manufacturer of the product that was the subject of each civil action;

(2) The model and model number or designation of the consumer product subject to each action;

(3) A statement as to whether the civil action alleged death or grievous bodily injury, and, in the case of an allegation of grievous bodily injury, a statement of the category of such injury;

(4) A statement as to whether the civil action resulted in a final settlement or a judgment in favor of the plaintiff; and

(5) In the case of a judgment in favor of the plaintiff, the name of the civil action, the number assigned to the civil action, and the court in which the civil action was filed.

(b) *Optional information.* A manufacturer furnishing a report may include:

(1) A statement as to whether any judgment in favor of the plaintiff is under appeal or is expected to be appealed (section 15 U.S.C. 2084(c)(2)(A));

(2) Any other information that the manufacturer chooses to provide (15 U.S.C. 2084(c)(2)(B)), including the dates on which final orders were entered in the reported lawsuits, and, where appropriate, an explanation why the manufacturer has not previously filed a report under section 15(b) of the CPSA covering the same particular product model that is the subject of the section 37 report; and

(3) A specific denial that the information it submits reasonably supports the conclusion that its consumer product caused a death or grievous bodily injury.

(c) *Statement of amount not required.* A manufacturer submitting a section 37 report is not required by section 37 or any other provision of the Consumer

Product Safety Act to provide a statement of any amount paid in final settlement of any civil action that is the subject of the report.

(d) *Admission of liability not required.* A manufacturer reporting to the Commission under section 37 need not admit that the information it reports supports the conclusion that its consumer product caused a death or grievous bodily injury.

§ 1116.7 Scope of section 37 and its relationship to section 15(b) of the CPSA.

(a) According to the legislative history of the Consumer Product Safety Improvement Act of 1990, the purpose of section 37 is to increase the reporting of information to the Commission that will assist it in carrying out its responsibilities.

(b) Section 37(c)(1) requires a manufacturer or importer (hereinafter "manufacturer") to include in a section 37 report a statement as to whether a civil action that is the subject of the report alleged death or grievous bodily injury. Furthermore, under section 37(c)(2), a manufacturer may specifically deny that the information it submits pursuant to section 37 reasonably supports the conclusion that its consumer product caused a death or grievous bodily injury, and may also include any additional information that it chooses to provide. In view of the foregoing, the reporting obligation is not limited to those cases in which a product has been adjudicated as the cause of death or grievous injury or to those settled or adjudicated cases in which the manufacturer has satisfied itself that the product was the cause of such trauma. Rather, when the specific injury alleged by the plaintiff meets the definition of "grievous bodily injury" contained in § 1116.2(b) of this part, the lawsuit falls within the scope of section 37 after settlement or adjudication. The manufacturer's opinion as to the validity of the allegation is irrelevant for reporting purposes. The category of injury alleged may be clear from the face of an original or amended complaint in a case or may reasonably be determined during pre-complaint investigation, post-complaint discovery, or informal settlement negotiation. Conclusory language in a complaint that the plaintiff suffered grievous bodily injury without further elaboration raises a presumption that the injury falls within one of the statutory categories, but is insufficient in itself to bring the suit within the ambit of the statute, unless the defendant manufacturer elects to settle such a matter without any investigation of the underlying facts. A case alleging the occurrence of grievous bodily injury in which a litigated verdict contains express findings that the injury suffered by the plaintiff did not meet the statutory criteria is also not reportable. Should a manufacturer believe that its product is wrongly implicated in an action, the statute expressly incorporates the mechanism for the manufacturer to communicate that belief to the Commission by denying in the report the involvement of the product or that the injury in fact suffered by the plaintiff was not grievous bodily injury, despite the plaintiff's allegations to the contrary. In addition, the statute imposes stringent confidentiality requirements on the disclosure by the Commission or the Department of Justice of information submitted pursuant to sections 37(c)(1) and 37(c)(2)(A). Moreover, it specifies that the reporting of a civil action shall not constitute an admission of liability under any statute or common law or under the relevant provisions of the Consumer Product Safety Act. In view of these safeguards, the reporting of lawsuits alleging the occurrence of death or grievous injury should have little adverse effect on manufacturers.

(c) Section 37 applies to judgments and "final settlements". Accordingly, the date on which a civil action is filed or the date on which the product that is the subject of such an action was manufactured is irrelevant to the obligation to report. A settlement is final upon the entry by a court of an order disposing of a civil action with respect to the manufacturer of the product that is the subject of the action, even through the case may continue with respect to other defendants.

(d) A judgment becomes reportable upon the entry of a final order by the trial court disposing of the matter in favor of the plaintiff and from which an appeal lies. Because section 37(c)(2) specifies that a reporting manufacturer may include a statement that a judgment in favor of a plaintiff is under appeal or is expected to be appealed, Congress clearly intended section 37 to apply prior to the exhaustion of or even the initiation of action to seek appellate remedies.

(e) No language in section 37 limits the reporting obligation to those litigated cases in which the plaintiff prevails completely. Therefore, if a court enters a partial judgment in favor of the plaintiff, the judgment is reportable, unless it is unrelated to the product that is the subject of the suit. For example, if a manufacturer's product is exonerated during a suit, but liability is assessed against another defendant, the manufacturer need not report under section 37.

(f)(1) Section 37 applies to civil actions that allege the involvement of a particular model of a consumer product in death or grievous bodily injury. Section 3(a) of the Consumer Product Safety Act (15 U.S.C. 2052(a)) defines a "consumer product" as any article, or component part thereof, produced or distributed for sale to a consumer for use in or around a permanent or temporary household or residence, a school, in recreation, or otherwise, or for the personal use, consumption, or enjoyment of a consumer in or around a permanent or temporary household or residence, a school, in recreation, or otherwise. The term "consumer product" does not include any article which is not customarily produced or distributed for sale to, or use or consumption by, or enjoyment of, a consumer.

(2) Since section 37 focuses on consumer products, it is the responsibility of the manufacturer of a product implicated in a civil action to determine whether the production or distribution of the product satisfies the statutory criteria of section 3(a). If it does, the action falls within the ambit of section 37. True industrial products are beyond the scope of section 37. However, if a lawsuit is based on an allegation of injury involving a consumer product, that suit falls within the scope of section 37, even though the injury may have occurred during the use of the product in employment. By the same token, occupational injuries arising during the fabrication of a consumer product are not reportable if the entity involved in the injury is not a consumer product at the time the injury occurs. In determining whether a product meets the statutory definition, manufacturers may wish to consult the relevant case law and the advisory opinions issued by the Commission's Office of the General Counsel. The unique circumstances surrounding litigation involving asbestos-containing products warrant one exception to this analysis. The Commission, as a matter of agency discretion, will require manufacturers of such products to report under section 37 only those lawsuits that allege the occurrence of death or grievous bodily injury as the result of exposure to asbestos from a particular model of a consumer product purchased by a consumer for personal use. Such lawsuits would include not only injury to the purchaser, but also to other consumers including family, subsequent property owners, and visitors. The Commission may consider granting similar relief to manufacturers of other products that present a risk of chronic injury similar to that presented by asbestos. Any such request must contain documented evidence demonstrating that compliance with the reporting requirements will be unduly burdensome and will be unlikely to produce information that will assist the Commission in carrying out its obligations under the statutes it administers.

(g) The definition of "consumer product" also encompasses a variety of products that are subject to regulation under the Federal Hazardous Substances Act (15 U.S.C. 1261 *et seq.*), the Poison Prevention Packaging Act (15 U.S.C. 1471 *et seq.*), the Flammable Fabrics Act (15 U.S.C. 1191 *et seq.*), and the Refrigerator Safety Act (15 U.S.C. 1211 *et seq.*). Lawsuits involving such products are also subject to section 37, notwithstanding the fact that the products may be regulated or subject to regulation under one of the other statutes.

(h) Relationship of Section 37 to Section 15 of the CPSA. (1) Section 37 plays a complementary role to the reporting requirements of section 15(b) of the CPSA (15 U.S.C. 2064(b)). Section 15(b) establishes a substantial obligation for firms to review information as it becomes available to determine whether an obligation to report exists. Accordingly, the responsibility to report under section 15(b) may arise long before enough lawsuits involving a product are resolved to create the obligation to report under section 37. The enactment of section 15(b)(3) in the Consumer Product Safety Improvement Act of 1990 reinforces this expectation. Under this amendment, manufacturers must report to the Commission when they obtain information that reasonably supports the conclusion that a product creates an unreasonable risk of serious injury or death. Previously, the reporting obligation for unregulated products only arose when available information indicated that the product in question was defective and created a substantial product hazard because of the pattern of the defect, the severity of the risk of injury, the number of products distributed in commerce, etc. The effect of the 1990 amendment is discussed in detail in the Commission's interpretative rule relating to the reporting of substantial product hazards at 16 CFR part 1115.

(2) The new substantive reporting requirements of section 15(b)(3) support the conclusion that Congress intended section 37 to capture product-related accident information that has not been reported under section 15(b). Between the time a firm learns of an incident or problem involving a product that raises safety-related concerns and the time that a lawsuit involving that product is resolved by settlement or adjudication, the firm generally has numerous opportunities to evaluate whether a section 15 report is appropriate. Such evaluation might be appropriate, for example, after an analysis of product returns, the receipt of an insurance investigator's report, a physical examination of the product, the interview or deposition of an injured party or an eyewitness to the event that gave rise to the lawsuit, or even preparation of the firm's responses to plaintiff's discovery requests. Even if a manufacturer does not believe that a report is required prior to the resolution of a single lawsuit, an obligation to investigate whether a report is appropriate may arise if, for example, a verdict in favor of the plaintiff raises the issue of whether the product in question creates an unreasonable risk of death or serious injury.

(3) In contrast, the application of section 37 does not involve the discretionary judgment and subjective analyses of hazard and causation associated with section 15 reports. Once the statutory criteria of three settled or adjudicated civil actions alleging grievous injury or death in a two year period are met, the obligation to report under section 37 is automatic. For this reason, the Commission regards section 37 as a ''safety net'' to surface product hazards that remain unreported either intentionally or by inadvertence. The provisions in the law limiting such reports to cases in which three or more lawsuits alleging grievous injury or death are settled or adjudicated in favor of plaintiffs during a two year period provide assurance that the product involved presents a sufficiently grave risk of injury to warrant consideration by the Commission. Indeed, once the obligation to report under section 37 arises, the obligation to file a section 15 report concurrently may exist if the information available to the manufacturer meets the criteria established in section 15(b) for reporting.

(4) Section 37 contains no specific record keeping requirements. However, to track and catalog lawsuits to determine whether they are reportable, prudent manufacturers will develop and maintain information systems to index and retain lawsuit data. In the absence of a prior section 15 report, once such systems are in place, such manufacturers will be in a position to perform a two-fold analysis to determine whether the information contained in such systems is reportable under either section 15(b) or 37. A manufacturer might conclude, for example, that the differences between products that are the subject of different lawsuits make them different models or that the type of injury alleged in one or more of the suits is not grievous bodily injury. Based on this analysis, the manufacturer might also conclude that the suits are thus

not reportable under section 37. However, a reporting obligation under section 15 may exist in any event if the same information reasonably supports the conclusion that the product(s) contain a defect which could create a substantial product hazard or create an unreasonable risk of serious injury or death.

§ 1116.8 Determination of particular model.

(a) The obligation rests with the manufacturer of a product to determine whether a reasonable basis exists to conclude that a product that is the subject of a settled or adjudicated lawsuit is sufficiently different from other similar products to be regarded as a "particular model" under section 37 because it is "distinctive." To determine whether a product is "distinctive", the proper inquiry should be directed toward the degree to which a product differs from other comparable products in one or more of the characteristics enumerated in section 37(e)(2) and § 1116.2(c) of this part. A product is "distinctive" if, after an analysis of information relating to one or more of the statutory characteristics, a manufacturer, acting in accordance with the customs and practices of the trade of which it is a member, could reasonably conclude that the difference between that product and other items of the same product class manufactured or imported by the same manufacturer is substantial and material. Information relevant to the determination of whether a product is a "particular model" includes:

(1) The description of the features and uses of the products in question in written material such as instruction manuals, description brochures, marketing or promotional programs, reports of certification of products, specification sheets, and product drawings.

(2) The differences or similarities between products in their observable physical characteristics and in components or features that are not readily observable and that are incorporated in those products for safety-related purposes;

(3) The customs and practices of the trade of which the manufacturer is a member in marketing, designating, or evaluating similar products.

(4) Information on how consumers use the products and on consumer need or demand for different products, such as products of different size. In analyzing whether products are different models, differences in size or calibration afford the basis for distinguishing between products only if those differences make the products distinctive in functional design or function.

(5) The history of the manufacturer's model identification and marketing of the products in question;

(6) Whether variations between products relate solely to appearance, ornamentation, color, or other cosmetic features; such variations are not ordinarily sufficient to differentiate between models.

(7) Whether component parts used in a product are interchangeable with or perform substantially the same function as comparable components in other units; if they are, the use of such components does not afford a basis for distinguishing between models.

(8) Retail price. Substantial variations in price arising directly from the characteristics enumerated in section 37(e)(2) for evaluating product models may be evidence that products are different models because their differences are distinctive. Price variations imposed to accommodate different markets or vendors are not sufficient to draw such a distinction.

(9) Manufacturer's designation, model number, or private label designation. These factors are not controlling in identifying "particular models".

(10) Expert evaluation of the characteristics of the products in question, and surveys of consumer users or a manufacturer's retail customers.

(b) The definition of "consumer product" expressly applies to components of consumer products. Should a component manufacturer be joined in a civil action against a manufacturer of a consumer product, the section 37 reporting requirements may apply to that manufacturer after a combination of three judgments or settlements involving the same component model during a two year period, even though the manufacturer of the finished product is exempt from such reporting because the lawsuits do not involve the same particular model of the finished consumer product. The same proposition holds true for common components used in different consumer products. If the manufacturer of such a component is a defendant in three suits and the requisite statutory criteria are met, the reporting obligations apply.

(c) Section 37 expressly defines the reporting obligation in terms of the particular model of a product rather than the manner in which a product was involved in an accident. Accordingly, even if the characteristic of a product that caused or resulted in the deaths of grievous injuries alleged in three or more civil actions is the same in all of the suits, the requirement to report under section 37 would arise only if the same particular model was involved in at least three of the suits. However, the existence of such a pattern would strongly suggest that the obligation to file a report under section 15(b) (2) or (3) (15 U.S.C. 2064(b) (2) or (3)) exists because the information reasonably supports the conclusion that the product contains a defect that could present a substantial risk of injury to the public or creates an unreasonable risk of serious injury or death.

(d) Section 37 does not require that the same category of injury be involved in multiple lawsuits for the reporting obligation to arise. As long as a particular model of a consumer product is the subject of at least three civil actions that are settled or adjudicated in favor of the plaintiff in one of the statutory two year periods, the manufacturer must report, even though the alleged category of injury and the alleged causal relationship of the product to the injury in each suit may differ.

§ 1116.9 Confidentiality of reports.

(a) Pursuant to section 6(e) of the Consumer Product Safety Act (15 U.S.C. 2055(e)) no member of the Commission, no officer or employee of the Commission, and no officer or employee of the Department of Justice may publicly disclose information furnished to the Commission under section 37(c)(1) and section 37(c)(2)(A) of the Act, except that:

(1) An authenticated copy of a section 37 report furnished to the Commission by or on behalf of a manufacturer may, upon written request, be furnished to the manufacturer or its authorized agent after payment of the actual or estimated cost of searching the records and furnishing such copies; or

(2) Any information furnished to the Commission under section 37 shall, upon written request of the Chairman or Ranking Minority Member of the Committee on Commerce, Science, and Transportation of the Senate or the Committee on Energy and Commerce of the House of Representatives or any subcommittee of such committee, be provided to the Chairman or Ranking Minority Member for purposes that are related to the jurisdiction of such committee or subcommittee.

(b) The prohibition contained in section 6(e) (15 U.S.C. 2055(e)) against the disclosure of information submitted pursuant to section 37 only applies to the specific items of information that a manufacturer is required to submit under section 37(c)(1) and to statements under section 37(c)(2)(A) relating to the possibility or existence of an appeal of a reported judgment adverse to a manufacturer. Section 6(e)(1) does not, by its terms, apply to information that the manufacturer voluntarily chooses to submit pursuant to section 37(c)(2)(B). Thus, disclosure of such information is governed by the other provisions of section 6 of the CPSA (15 U.S.C. 2055) and by the interpretative rules issued by the Commission (16 CFR parts 1101 and 1015). For example, if a manufacturer includes information otherwise reportable under section 15 as part of a section 37 report, the Commission will treat the information reported pursuant to section 15 as "additional information" submitted pursuant to section 37(c)(2)(B). Generally, any issue of the public disclosure of that information will be controlled by the relevant provisions of section 6(b), including section 6(b)(5) relating to the disclosure of substantial product hazard reports, and section 6(a) relating to the disclosure of confidential or trade secret information. However, to the extent the section 15 report reiterates or references information reported under section 37, the confidentiality provisions of section 6(e) still apply to the reiteration or reference. In addition, interpretative regulations issued under section 6(b) of the Act establish that disclosure of certain information may be barred if the disclosure would not be fair in the circumstances. 16 CFR 1101.33. Accordingly, issues of releasing additional information submitted pursuant to section 37 will also be evaluated under the fairness provisions of section 6(b). Should the Commission receive a request for such information or contemplate disclosure on its own initiative, the manufacturer will be given an opportunity to present arguments to the Commission why the information should not be disclosed, including, if appropriate, why disclosure of the information would be unfair in the circumstances. Among the factors the Commission will consider in evaluating the fairness of releasing the information are the nature of the information, the fact that it is an adjunct to a Congressional protected report, and whether the information in question supports the conclusion that a section 37 or 15(b), CPSA, report should have been filed earlier.

(c) Section 6(e) imposes no confidentiality requirements on information obtained by the Commission independently of a report pursuant to section 37. The provisions of section 6(b) govern the disclosure of such information.

§ 1116.10 Restrictions on use of reports.

No member of the Commission, no officer or employee of the Commission, and no officer or employee of the Department of Justice may use information provided to the Commission under section 37 for any purpose other than to carry out the responsibilities of the Commission.

§ 1116.11 Reports of civil actions under section 37 not admissions.

Pursuant to section 37(d), 15 U.S.C. 2084(d), the reporting of a civil action under section 37 shall not constitute an admission of—

(a) An unreasonable risk of injury;

(b) A defect in the consumer product which was the subject of the civil action;

(c) A substantial product hazard;

(d) An imminent hazard; or

(e) Any other liability under any statute or any common law.

§ 1116.12 Commission response to section 37 reports.

Upon receipt of a section 37 report, the Commission will evaluate the information contained in the report and any relevant information contained in its files or data bases to determine what, if any, follow-up or remedial action by the Commission is appropriate. If the Commission requires additional information, it will notify the manufacturer in writing of the specific information to provide. In addition, the Commission will routinely review section 37 reports to determine whether the reporting manufacturers have fulfilled their obligations under both sections 37 and 15(b) in a timely manner. Such a review may also engender a request for additional information, including the dates on which final orders were entered in each of the lawsuits reported under section 37. The Commission will treat any subsequent submission of information by the manufacturer as a submission under section 37(c)(2)(B) subject to the restrictions on public disclosure contained in sections 6(a) and (b) of the Consumer Product Safety Act.

PART 1117—REPORTING OF CHOKING INCIDENTS INVOLVING MARBLES, SMALL BALLS, LATEX BALLOONS AND OTHER SMALL PARTS

Sec.

AUTHORITY: Section 102 of the Child Safety Protection Act (Pub. L. No. 103–267), section 16(b), 15 U.S.C. 2065(b) and 5 U.S.C. 553.

SOURCE: 60 FR 10493, Feb. 27, 1995, unless otherwise noted.

§ 1117.1 Purpose.

The purpose of this part is to set forth the Commission's interpretative regulations for reporting of choking incidents required by the Child Safety Protection Act. The statute requires that each manufacturer, distributor, retailer, and importer of a marble, small ball, or latex balloon, or a toy or a game that contains a marble, small ball, latex balloon, or other small part, shall report to the Commission any information obtained by such manufacturer, distributor, retailer, or importer which reasonably supports the conclusion that an incident occurred in which a child (regardless of age) choked on such a marble, small ball, or latex balloon or on a marble, small ball, latex balloon, or other small part contained in such toy or game and, as a result of that incident the child died, suffered serious injury, ceased breathing for any length of time, or was treated by a medical professional.

§ 1117.2 Definitions.

(a) *Small part* means any part, component, or piece of a toy or game, which, when tested in accordance with the procedures in 16 CFR 1501.4(a) and 1501.4(b)(1), fits entirely within the cylinder shown in Figure 1 appended to 16 CFR 1501.

(b) *Small ball* means any ball that under the influence of its own weight, passes, in any orientation, entirely through a circular hole with a diameter of 1.75 inches (4.445 cm) in a rigid template .25 inches (6 mm.) thick. For purposes of this designation, the term "ball" includes any spherical, ovoid, or ellipsoidal object that is designed or intended to be thrown, hit, kicked, rolled, or bounced, and is either not permanently attached to another toy or article, or is attached to such a toy or article by means of a string, elastic cord, or similar tether. The term *ball* includes any multi-sided object formed by connecting planes into a generally spherical, ovoid, or ellipsoidal shape that is designated or intended to be used as a ball, and any novelty item of a generally spherical, ovoid, or ellipsoidal shape that is designated or intended to be used as a ball.

(c) *Choked* means suffered an obstruction of the airways.

(d) A *latex balloon* is a toy or decorative item consisting of a latex bag that is designed to be inflated by air or gas. The term does not include inflatable children's toys that are used in aquatic activities, such as rafts, water wings, life rings, etc.

(e) A *marble* is a ball made of a hard material, such as glass, agate, marble or plastic, that is used in various children's games, generally as a playing piece or marker.

(f) *Serious injury* includes not only the concept of "grievous bodily injury" defined in the Commission's rule for Substantial Hazard Reports at 16 CFR 1115.12(d), but also any other significant injury. Injuries necessitating hospitalization which require actual medical or surgical treatment and injuries necessitating absence from school or work of more than one day are examples of situations in which the Commission shall presume that such a serious injury has occurred.

(g) *Subject firm* means any manufacturer, distributor, retailer or importer of marbles, small balls, latex balloons, or a toy or game that contains a marble, small ball, latex balloon, or other small part.

(h) *Toy or game* includes any toy or game, including those exempt under 16 CFR 1501.3 from the small parts banning provisions of 16 CFR 1500.18(a)(9).

[60 FR 10493, Feb. 27, 1995, as amended at 60 FR 41801, Aug. 14, 1995]

§ 1117.3 Reportable information.

A subject firm shall report any information it obtains which reasonably supports the conclusion that a reportable incident occurred. Generally, firms should report any information provided to the company, orally or in writing, which states that a child choked on a marble, small ball, latex balloon, or on a marble, small ball, latex balloon or other small part contained in a toy or game *and,* as a result of that incident the child died, suffered serious injury, ceased breathing for any length of time, or was treated by a medical professional. Subject firms must not wait until they have investigated the incident or conclusively resolved whether the information is accurate or whether their product was involved in the incident. Firms shall not wait to determine conclusively the cause of the death, injury, cessation of breathing or necessity for treatment. An allegation that such a result followed the choking incident is sufficient to require a report.

§ 1117.4 Time for filing a report.

(a) A subject firm must report within 24 hours of obtaining information which reasonably supports the conclusion that an incident occurred in which a child (regardless of age) choked on a marble, small ball, or latex balloon or on a marble, small ball, latex balloon, or other small part contained in a toy or game and, as a result of that incident the child died, suffered serious injury, ceased breathing for any length of time, or was treated by a medical professional. Section 1117.5 of this part sets forth the information that must be reported.

(b) The Commission will deem a subject firm to have obtained reportable information when the information has been received by an official or employee who may reasonably be expected to be capable of appreciating the significance of the information. Under ordinary circumstances, 5 days shall be the maximum reasonable time for information to reach such an employee, the Chief Executive Officer or the official or employee responsible for complying with the reporting requirements of section 102 of the Child Safety Protection Act.

§ 1117.5 Information that must be reported and to whom.

(a) Reports shall be directed to the Division of Corrective Actions, Consumer Product Safety Commission, 4330 East West Highway, Bethesda, Maryland 20815 (Mailing Address: Washington, D.C. 20207) (Phone: 301–504–0608, facsimile: 301–504–0359).

(b) Subject firms must report as much of the following information as is known when the report is made:

(1) The name, address, and title of the person submitting the report to the Commission,

(2) The name and address of the subject firm,

(3) The name and address of the child who choked and the person(s) who notified the subject firm of the choking incident,

(4) Identification of the product involved including the date(s) of distribution, model or style number, a description of the product (including any labeling and warnings), a description of the marble, small ball, latex balloon or other small part involved, and pictures or sample if available,

(5) A description of the choking incident and any injuries that resulted or medical treatment that was necessary,

(6) Copies of any information obtained about the choking incident,

(7) Any information about changes made to the product or its labeling or warnings with the intention of avoiding such choking incidents, including, but not limited to, the date(s) of the change and its implementation, and a description of the change. Copies of any engineering drawings or product and label samples that depict the change(s).

(8) The details of any public notice or other corrective action planned by the firm,

(9) Such other information as appropriate.

(c) Retailers or distributors should supply as much of the information required in paragraph (b) of this section as is available to them but are not required to obtain information about product design changes or recall activities from the product manufacturer.

(d) Within ten days of their initial report, subject firms must supplement their reports to supply any of the information required by paragraph (b) of this section that was not available at the time of the initial report.

§ 1117.6 Relation to section 15(b) of the CPSA.

Section 15(b) of the CPSA requires subject firms to report when they obtain information which reasonably supports the conclusion that products they distributed in commerce fail to comply with an applicable consumer product safety rule or with a voluntary consumer product safety standard upon which the Commission has relied under section 9 of the CPSA, contain a defect which could create a substantial product hazard, or create an unreasonable risk of serious injury or death. The

Commission's rules interpreting this provision are set forth at 16 CFR part 1115. The requirements of section 102 of the CSPA and this part are in addition to, but not to the exclusion of, the requirements in section 15(b) and part 1115. To comply with section 15(b), subject firms must continue to evaluate safety information they obtain about their products. Subject firms may have an obligation to report under section 15(b) of the CPSA whether or not they obtain information about choking incidents. Firms must also comply with the lawsuit-reporting provisions of section 37 of the CPSA, interpreted at 16 CFR part 1116.

§ 1117.7 Confidentiality of reports.

The confidentiality provisions of section 6 of the CPSA, 15 U.S.C. 2055, apply to reports submitted under this part. The Commission shall afford information submitted under this part the protection afforded to information submitted under section 15(b), in accordance with section 6(b)(5) of the CPSA and subpart G of part 1101 of title 16 of the CFR.

§ 1117.8 Effect of reports on liability.

A report by a manufacturer, distributor, retailer, or importer under this part shall not be interpreted, for any purpose, as an admission of liability or of the truth of the information contained in the report.

§ 1117.9 Prohibited acts and sanctions.

(a) Whoever knowingly and willfully falsifies or conceals a material fact in a report submitted under this part is subject to criminal penalties under 18 U.S.C. 1001.

(b) A failure to report to the Commission in a timely fashion as required by this part is a prohibited act under section 19(a)(3) of the CPSA, 15 U.S.C. 2068(a)(3).

(c) A subject firm that knowingly fails to report is subject to civil penalties under section 20 of the CPSA, 15 U.S.C. 2069. *Knowing* means the having of actual knowledge or the presumed having of knowledge deemed to be possessed by a reasonable person who acts in the circumstances, including knowledge obtainable upon the exercise of due care to ascertain the truth of representations. Section 20(d) of the CPSA, 15 U.S.C. 2069(d).

(d) Any person who knowingly and willfully violates section 19 of this Act after having received notice of noncompliance from the Commission may be subject to criminal penalties under section 21 of the CPSA, 15 U.S.C. 2070.

PART 1118—INVESTIGATIONS, INSPECTIONS AND INQUIRIES UNDER THE CONSUMER PRODUCT SAFETY ACT

Subpart A—Procedures for Investigations, Inspections, and Inquiries

Subpart B—Consent Order Agreements

AUTHORITY: Sec. 16, Pub. L. 92–573, 86 Stat. 1222 (15 U.S.C. 2065); sec. 19, Pub. L. 92–573, 86 Stat. 1224 (15 U.S.C. 2068); sec. 27, Pub. L. 92–573, 86 Stat. 1227 (15 U.S.C. 2076); as amended by Pub. L. 94–284, 90 Stat. 509.

SOURCE: 44 FR 34929, June 18, 1979, unless otherwise noted.

Subpart A—Procedures for Investigations, Inspections, and Inquiries

§ 1118.1 Definitions, initiation of investigations, inspections, and inquiries and delegations.

(a) *Definitions.* For the purpose of these rules, the following definitions apply:

(1) *Act* means the Consumer Product Safety Act (15 U.S.C. 2051, et seq.).

(2) *Commission* means the Consumer Product Safety Commission.

(3) *Firm* means a manufacturer, private labeler, distributor, or retailer of a consumer product, except as otherwise provided by section 16(b) of the Act.

(4) *Investigation* is an undertaking by the Commission to obtain information for implementing, enforcing, or determining compliance with the Consumer Product Safety Act and the regulations, rules, and orders issued under the Act. The term investigation includes, but is not limited to, inspections (§ 1118.2), investigational hearings (§ 1118.5), and inquiries; employing subpoenas (§ 1118.4), depositions (§ 1118.6), and general or special orders (§ 1118.9).

(5) The definition of the terms set forth in section 3 of the Consumer Product Safety Act (15 U.S.C. 2052) shall apply to this part 1118.

(b) *Initiation of Investigations and Inquiries.* Investigations and inquiries will be initiated by the Commission in any manner authorized by law.

(c) *Initiation of Inspections.* An inspection as described in § 1118.2 is initiated when the Commission or its delegate authorizes the issuance of a written notice of inspection, described in § 1118.2(c).

(d) *Delegations of Authority.* The Commission hereby delegates to the Associate Executive Director for Compliance and Enforcement; the Solicitor, the Directors of the Divisions of Enforcement; the Solicitor, the Directors of the Divisions of Enforcement, Product Defect Correction, and Regulatory Management; and the directors of area offices, the power to initiate inspections in the same manner as the Commission.

§ 1118.2 Conduct and scope of inspections.

(a) After an inspection is initiated as set forth in § 1118.1, an officer or employee duly designated by the Commission shall issue the notice of inspection (hereinafter: notice). Upon presenting the notice, along with appropriate credentials, to the person or agent in charge of the firm to be inspected, the Commission officer or employee is authorized for the purposes set forth in § 1118.1(a):

(1) To enter, at reasonable times, any factory, warehouse, or establishment in which consumer products are manufactured or held, in connection with distribution in commerce, or any conveyance being used to transport consumer products in connection with distribution in commerce; and

(2) To inspect, at reasonable times and in a reasonable manner, any conveyance or those areas of the factory, warehouse, or establishment where consumer products are manufactured, held, or transported and which may relate to the safety of those products; and

(3) To have access to and to copy all relevant records, books, documents, papers, packaging or labeling which:

(i) Are required by the Commission to be established, made or maintained, or

(ii) Show or relate to the production, inventory, testing, distribution, sale, transportation, importation, or receipt of any consumer product, or that are otherwise relevant to determining whether any person or firm has acted or is acting in compliance with the Act and regulations, rules and orders promulgated under the Act, and

(4) To obtain:

(i) Information, both oral and written, concerning the production, inventory, testing, distribution, sale, transportation, importation, or receipt of any consumer product, and the organization, business, conduct, practices, and management of any person or firm being inspected and its relation to any other person or firm;

(ii) Samples of items, materials, substances, products, containers, packages and packaging, and labels and labeling, or any component at manufacturer's, distributor's or retailer's cost unless voluntarily provided; and

(iii) Information, both oral and written, concerning any matter referred to in the Act and these rules.

(b) A separate notice shall be given for each inspection, but a notice is not required for each entry made during the course of the same inspection. Each inspection shall be commenced at and completed within a reasonable period of time.

(c) The notice of inspection shall include the name and address of the person or firm being inspected; the name and title of the Commission officer or employee; the date and time of the anticipated entry; pertinent extracts from the statutory provisions upon which the right to access is based; pertinent extracts from § 1118.2 of these rules setting forth the authority of Commission officers or employees and the types of information and items they are authorized to obtain; a statement that the inspection will be conducted and the information will be provided with the cooperation of the person or firm being inspected; a statement which sets forth the purposes of the inspection and the nature of the information and items to be obtained and/or copied; and a statement that those from whom information is requested should state in writing whether any of the information submitted is believed to contain or relate to a trade secret or other matter which should be considered by the Commission to be confidential in accordance with section 6(a)(2) of the Act (15 U.S.C. 2055(a)(2)) and whether any of the information is believed to be entitled to exemption from disclosure by the Commission under the provisions of the Freedom of Information Act (5 U.S.C. 552) and the Commission's regulations under that Act, 16 CFR part 1015 (42 FR 10496, February 22, 1977) or as amended. Any statement asserting this claim of confidentiality must be in writing, and any request for exemption of the information from disclosure must be made in accordance with the Commission's Freedom of Information Act regulations, 16 CFR part 1015 (42 FR 10490, February 22, 1977) or as amended.

(d) If upon being presented with a notice by an officer or employee duly designated by the Commission, the person or agent-in-charge of the firm being inspected refuses to allow entry or inspection, the Commission may then seek a search warrant or take other appropriate legal action. If the person refuses to provide information, to allow access to or the copying of records, or to supply samples as provided in these rules, the officer or employee of the Commission shall complete the investigation to the extent that voluntary cooperation is provided. The Commission may take such additional action, including but not limited to seeking an ex parte search warrant, employing the compulsory process provided for in these rules, and/or taking other suitable legal action. If the person or agent in charge refuses to accept the notice upon its presentation, the officer or employee may affix the notice to a public entrance way on the premises and this shall constitute presentation of the notice.

§ 1118.3 Compulsory processes and service.

(a) In addition to or in lieu of authorizing the issuance of a notice, the Commission may elect either to seek an ex parte search warrant and/or use any other reasonable means authorized by law to initiate investigations, inspections, or inquires to obtain information for the purposes set forth in § 1118.1(a), including but not limited to the following compulsory processes:

(1) Subpoenas;

(2) Investigational hearings;

(3) Depositions; and

(4) General or special orders.

(b) Service in connection with any of the compulsory processes in § 1118.3(a) shall be effected:

(1) By personal service upon the person or agent in charge of the firm being investigated, inspected or inquired of; or

(2) By certified mail or delivery to the last known residence or business address of anyone being investigated, inspected or inquired of; or

(3) In the case of general or special orders where personal service, mailing or delivery has been unsuccessful, service may also be effected by publication in the FEDERAL REGISTER.

(c) The date of service of any form of compulsory process shall be the date on which the document is received by mail, delivered in person or published in the FEDERAL REGISTER. In computing a period of time in which a party is required or permitted to act, the day from which the time begins to run shall not be included. The last day of the period shall be included, unless it is a Saturday, Sunday or legal holiday, in which event the period runs until the end of the next day that is not a Saturday, Sunday or legal holiday.

(d) These rules shall be referred to in any notice of compulsory process served upon a person or firm.

(e) Anyone submitting information in response to any of the compulsory processes referred to in § 1118.3(a) should state whether any of the information submitted is believed to contain or relate to a trade secret or other matter which should be considered by the Commission to be confidential in accordance with section 6(a)(2) of the Consumer Product Safety Act (15 U.S.C. 2055(a)(2)) and whether any of the information is believed to be exempt from disclosure by the Commission under the provisions of the Freedom of Information Act (5 U.S.C. 552) and the Commission's regulations under that Act, 16 CFR part 1015 (42 FR 10490, February 22, 1977) or as amended. Any claim of confidentiality must be in writing, and any request for exemption from disclosure must be made in accordance with the Commission's Freedom of Information Act regulations, 16 CFR part 1015 (42 FR 10490, February 22, 1977), or as amended.

§ 1118.4 Subpoenas.

The Commission may issue to any person or firm a subpoena requiring the production of documentary evidence (subpoena duces tecum) and/or attendance and testimony of witnesses (subpoena ad testificandum) relating to any matter under investigation. Procedures regarding compliance with subpoenas and motions to limit or quash subpoenas are provided for in § 1118.9.

§ 1118.5 Investigational hearings.

(a) The Commission by subpoena may require any person or firm to provide information at an investigational hearing. These hearings shall be for the purpose of taking the testimony, under oath, of witnesses and receiving documents and other data relating to any subject under investigation. The hearings shall be presided over by the Commission, by one or more of the Commissioners, by an administrative law judge, or by a duly designated officer or employee, who shall be referred to as the presiding official. The hearings shall be stenographically reported, and the transcript shall be made a part of the record.

(b) A Commissioner who participates in a hearing or other investigation, inspection, or inquiry shall not be disqualified solely by reason of that participation from subsequently participating in a Commission decision in the same matter.

(c) Investigational hearings shall be closed to the public, unless otherwise ordered by the Commission.

(d) The release of the record of the hearing shall be governed by the Freedom of Information Act (5 U.S.C. 552), the Commission's regulations under that Act, 16 CFR part 1015 (42 FR 10490, February 22, 1977) or as amended and/or other applicable laws or regulations, except that a person required to give testimony or a deposition may, in accordance with § 1118.7(d), obtain a copy of his or her testimony or deposition.

§ 1118.6 Depositions.

(a) The Commission by subpoena may require testimony to be taken by deposition at any stage of any investigation. Depositions may be taken before any person who is designated by the Commission and has the power to administer oaths. The person before whom the deposition is taken shall put the deponent under oath. The testimony given shall be reduced to writing by the person taking the deposition or under that person's direction and shall then be submitted to the deponent for signature unless the deponent waives the right to sign the deposition. All depositions shall be closed to the public, unless otherwise ordered by the Commission. The release of the record of such depositions shall be governed by the Freedom of Information Act (5 U.S.C. 552), the Commission's regulations under that Act, 16 CFR part 1015 (42 FR 10490, February 22, 1977) or as amended and/or other applicable laws or regulations, except that the deponent may, in accordance with § 1118.7(d), obtain a copy of his or her deposition.

(b) Any changes which the deponent desires to make shall be entered on the face of the deposition and shall state the reasons for such changes. The deposition shall then be signed by the deponent, unless the deponent waives the right to sign, cannot be found, or is unable or refuses to sign. The deponent must sign the deposition within 30 days of its submission to him or her, or within such shorter time period as the Commission may designate. Whenever a deponent is required to sign in less than ten days, the Commission shall notify the deponent of the reasons for such shorter time period.

If the deponent does not sign the deposition within the prescribed time period, the Commission designee shall sign it and state on the record the fact of the waiver of the right to sign or of the illness or absence of the deponent, or the deponent's inability or refusal to sign, together with the reason if any is given. The deposition may be used in any administrative proceeding, as provided by these rules, or any other proceeding, as allowed by applicable rules.

§ 1118.7 Rights of witnesses at investigational hearings and of deponents at depositions.

(a) Any person, agent, or officer of a firm, who is required to produce documentary evidence or give testimony as a witness at an investigational hearing conducted under provisions of § 1118.5 or as a deponent at a deposition taken under provisions of § 1118.6 may be accompanied by an attorney, or an officer or partner of the firm, who may act as representative for the witness or the deponent. However, a person who is subpoenaed to produce documentary evidence or give testimony at an investigational hearing or deposition cannot act as attorney or representative for another witness or deponent at the same proceeding. The term attorney refers to members of the bar of a Federal court or the courts of any State or Territory of the United States, the Commonwealth of Puerto Rico, or the District of Columbia. The witness or deponent and his or her attorney or representative may act as follows during the course of an investigational hearing or deposition:

(1) A witness or deponent may confer, in confidence, with his or her attorney or representative concerning any questions asked of the witness or deponent. If the witness, deponent, or his or her attorney or representative objects to a question or any other matter relevant to the investigational hearing or deposition, the objection and basis for it shall be stated on the record. In the case of an objection based upon self-incrimination, the privilege must be asserted by the witness or deponent. If a witness at an investigational hearing refuses to answer a question or provide other information, the presiding official shall have the authority to immediately order the witness to answer the question or provide the information requested, except in circumstances where, in the discretion of the presiding official an immediate ruling would be unwarranted and except where a refusal is based upon the privilege against self-incrimination. Otherwise all objections shall be ruled upon by presiding official at the time the objection is made.

(2) Objections timely made under the provisions of § 1118.7(a) shall be noted on the record, shall be treated as continuing, and shall be preserved throughout the proceeding without the necessity of repetition during similar lines of inquiry.

(3) Except as provided by § 1118.7(a), counsel for a witness or deponent may not interrupt the examination of the witness or the deponent by making objections or statements on the record.

(4) Upon completion of the examination, any witness at an investigational hearing may clarify on the record any of his or her answers, or, if the witness is accompanied by an attorney or representative, the attorney or representative may examine the witness on the record as to answers previously given. In addition, the witness or his or her attorney or representative may make a brief statement at the conclusion of the hearing giving his, her or the firm's position with regard to matters under investigation. In order to prevent abuse of the investigational process, the presiding official shall have the authority to impose reasonable limitations on the period of time allowed for objections, clarification of answers, and statements of position.

(5) Upon completion of all testimony, a deponent may clarify on the record any of his or her answers. The attorney or representative for a deponent may examine that deponent on the record to clarify answers previously given.

(b) Any person, agent, or officer who is required to appear in person at an investigational hearing or at a deposition shall testify as to matters and information known and/or reasonably available to the person or firm involved.

(c) Any person, agent or officer who is compelled by subpoena to appear in person at an investigational hearing or at a deposition shall receive the same fees and mileage allowances as are paid witnesses in the courts of the United States.

(d) Any person, agent, or officer who is required to appear at an investigational hearing or at a deposition shall be entitled to retain a copy of any document submitted by him or her and, upon payment of lawfully prescribed costs, in accordance with the Commission's regulations under the Freedom of Information Act, shall be entitled to procure a copy of his or her own testimony as recorded.

(e) The presiding official shall take all necessary action to regulate the course of the hearing, to avoid delay and to assure that reasonable standards of orderly and ethical conduct are maintained. The presiding official, for reasons stated on the record, shall immediately report to the Commission any instance in which a witness or his or her attorney or representative has refused to comply with the presiding official's directions or to adhere to reasonable standards of orderly and ethical conduct in the course of the hearing. The Commission shall take whatever action is appropriate under the circumstances.

§1118.8 General or special orders seeking information.

The Commission may require by the issuance of general or special orders any person or firm to submit in writing any reports and answers to questions as the Commission may prescribe. The reports or answers shall be made under oath, and shall be filed within the time prescribed by the Commission. Procedures regarding compliance with general or special orders and motions to limit or quash such orders are provided for in §1118.9.

§1118.9 Motions to limit or quash subpoenas and general or special orders and delegation to modify terms for compliance.

(a) The Commission hereby delegates to the Associate Executive Director for Compliance and Enforcement; the Solicitor; the Directors of Divisions of Enforcement, Product Defect Correction, and Regulatory Management; and the General Counsel the authority:

(1) To negotiate and approve the terms of satisfactory compliance with subpoenas and general or special orders;

(2) To impose conditions upon compliance with such compulsory processes; and

(3) To extend the time for compliance and the time for filing motions to limit or quash.

(b) The person or firm served with a subpoena or general or special order may file a motion to limit or quash the subpoena or order. Any motion to limit or quash shall set forth the reasons why the subpoena or order should be limited or quashed and may be accompanied by memoranda, affidavits, or other documents submitted in support of the motion. The motion must be received in the Office of the Secretary of the Commission within 10 calendar days of receipt of the subpoena or order unless:

(1) The subpoena or order provides for a different time; or

(2) The Commission, for good cause shown, grants an extension of time to file a motion.

(c) Upon receipt of a motion to limit or quash, the Office of the Secretary shall immediately notify and transmit a copy to the appropriate staff member. Unless a different period of time is specified in the subpoena or order, the staff shall file an answer with the Office of the Secretary within 10 calendar days after receipt of the motion. A copy of the answer shall be served upon the moving party or the counsel of the moving party. No reply to the answer will be permitted.

(d) All motions to limit or quash shall be ruled upon by the Commision. The Office of the Secretary shall serve the decision on a motion to limit or quash upon the moving party or the counsel for the moving party and shall furnish a copy of the decision to the appropriate staff member. The Commission's decision is a final decision. Motions for reconsideration will not be received.

§ 1118.10 Remedies for failure to permit authorized investigations.

In the event a person or firm fails to comply with any investigative process authorized by these rules, the Commission may seek appropriate action within its authority under the Consumer Product Safety Act (15 U.S.C. 2051, et seq.)

§ 1118.11 Nonexclusive delegation of power.

No provision contained herein delegating any of the Commission's powers shall be construed as limiting the authority of the Commission to exercise the same powers.

Subpart B—Consent Order Agreements

§ 1118.20 Procedures for consent order agreements.

(a) For the procedure to be followed regarding consent order agreements involving section 15 of the Act (15 U.S.C. 2064), refer to the Commission's regulations relating to substantial product hazards (16 CFR part 1115). For all other consent order agreements under the Consumer Product Safety Act, the provisions set forth below are applicable.

(b) The consent order agreement is a document executed by a person, or firm (consenting party) and a Commission staff representative which incorporates both a proposed complaint setting forth the staff's charges and a proposed order by which such charges are resolved. A consent order agreement shall contain the following provisions, as appropriate:

(1) An admission of all jurisdictional facts by the consenting parties;

(2) A waiver of any rights to an administrative or judicial hearing and of any other procedural steps including any rights to seek judicial review or otherwise challenge or contest the validity of the Commission's order;

(3) A statement that the agreement is in settlement of the staff's charges and does not constitute an admission by the consenting party that the law has been violated;

(4) A statement describing the alleged hazard, non-compliance or violation.

(5) A statement that the Commission's order is issued under the provisions of the Act (15 U.S.C. 2051, et seq.); and that a violation of such order may subject the consenting party to appropriate legal action.

(6) An acknowledgment that the consent order agreement only becomes effective upon its final acceptance by the Commission and its service upon the consenting party;

(7) An acknowledgment that the Commission may disclose terms of the consent order agreement to the public;

(8) A statement that the consenting party shall comply with the provisions of the agreement and order;

(9) A statement that the requirements of the order are in addition to and not to the exclusion of other remedies under the Act.

(c) At any time in the course of an investigation, the staff, with the approval of the Commission, may propose to the person or firm being investigated that any alleged violation be resolved by an agreement containing a consent order. Additionally, such a proposal may be made to the Commission staff by such person or firm.

(d) Upon receiving an executed agreement, the Commission may:

(1) Provisionally accept it;

(2) Reject it and issue the complaint (in which case the matter will be scheduled for hearing in accordance with the Commission's Rules of Practice for Adjudicative Proceedings, 16 CFR part 1025, June 21, 1977 or as amended) and/or

(3) Take such other action as it may deem appropriate.

(e) If the agreement is provisionally accepted, the Commission shall place the agreement on the public record and shall announce provisional acceptance of the agreement in the FEDERAL REGISTER. Any interested person may ask the Commission not to accept the agreement by filing a written request in the Office of the Secretary. Any request must be received in the Office of the Secretary no later than the close of business of the 15th calendar day following the date of announcement in the FEDERAL REGISTER.

(f) If no requests are received, the agreement shall be deemed finally accepted by the Commission on the 16th calendar day after the date of the announcement in the FEDERAL REGISTER. Notice of final acceptance will be given and the order issued within a reasonable time.

(g) If the Commission receives one or more requests that it not finally accept an agreement, it shall, within a reasonable time, either finally accept or reject the agreement after considering the requests. The Commission shall promptly issue and serve an order indicating its decision.

(1) If the agreement is accepted, the Commission shall issue the complaint and order. The order is a final order in disposition of the proceeding and is effective immediately upon its service on the consenting party under these rules. The consenting party shall thereafter be bound by and take immediate action in accordance with the final order.

(2) If the agreement is rejected, the order so notifying the consenting party shall constitute withdrawal of the Commission's provisional acceptance. The Commission may then issue its complaint, may order further investigation, or may take any action it considers appropriate.

(h) An agreement that has been finally accepted may be vacated or modified upon petition of any party or the Commission's own initiative. The petition shall state the proposed changes in the agreement and the reasons for granting the petition. The Commission may modify or vacate where (1) false statements were relied upon in accepting the agreement or (2) there are changed conditions of fact or law. In deciding whether to grant a petition, the Commission shall consider the public interest. A petitioner, or the Commission when acting on its own initiative, shall serve a copy of the petition or notice of reconsideration, respectively, on all parties. Parties affected by the petition or notice of reconsideration may file a response within 10 calendar days. No replies shall be accepted. The Commission shall decide the petition or notice of reconsideration within a reasonable time and, by order, shall indicate its decision and its reasons.

PART 1119—CIVIL PENALTY FACTORS

Sec.

AUTHORITY: 15 U.S.C. 2058, 2063, 2064, 2067(b), 2068, 2069, 2076(e), 2084, 1261, 1263, 1264, 1270, 1273, 1278, 1191, 1192, 1193, 1194, 1195, 1196.

SOURCE: 75 FR 15998, Mar. 31, 2010, unless otherwise noted.

§ 1119.1 Purpose.

This part sets forth the Consumer Product Safety Commission's (Commission) interpretation of the statutory factors considered in determining the amount of civil penalties that the Commission may seek or compromise. The policies behind, and purposes of, civil penalties include the following: Deterring violations; providing just punishment; promoting respect for the law; promoting full compliance with the law; reflecting the seriousness of the violation; and protecting the public.

§ 1119.2 Applicability.

This part applies to all civil penalty determinations the Commission may seek or compromise under the Consumer Product Safety Act (CPSA) (15 U.S.C. 2051–2089), the Federal Hazardous Substances Act (FHSA) (15 U.S.C. 1261–1278), and the Flammable Fabrics Act (FFA) (15 U.S.C. 1191–1204). Any person who knowingly violates section 19 of the CPSA, section 4 of the FHSA, or section 5(e) of the FFA, is subject to a civil penalty.

§ 1119.3 Definitions.

For purposes of this rule, the following definitions apply:

(a) *Product defect* means a defect as referenced in the CPSA and defined in Commission regulations at 16 CFR 1115.4.

(b) *Violation* means a violation committed knowingly, as the term "knowingly" is defined in section 19 of the CPSA, section 4 of the FHSA, or section 5 of the FFA.

(c) *Person* means any manufacturer (including importer), distributor, or retailer, as those terms are defined in the CPSA, FHSA, or FFA, and any other legally responsible party.

§ 1119.4 Factors considered in determining civil penalties.

(a) *Statutory Factors.* (1) Section 20(b) of the CPSA, section 5(c)(3) of the FHSA, and section 5(e)(2) of the FFA, specify factors considered by the Commission in determining the amount of a civil penalty to be sought upon commencing an action for knowing violations of each act. These factors are:

(i) *CPSA (15 U.S.C. 2069(b)).* The nature, circumstances, extent, and gravity of the violation, including:

(A) The nature of the product defect;

(B) The severity of the risk of injury;

(C) The occurrence or absence of injury;

(D) The number of defective products distributed;

(E) The appropriateness of such penalty in relation to the size of the business of the person charged, including how to mitigate undue adverse economic impacts on small businesses; and

(F) Such other factors as appropriate.

(ii) *FHSA (15 U.S.C. 1264 (c)(3)).* The nature, circumstances, extent, and gravity of the violation, including:

(A) The nature of the substance;

(B) Severity of the risk of injury;

(C) The occurrence or absence of injury;

(D) The amount of substance distributed;

(E) The appropriateness of such penalty in relation to the size of the business of the person charged, including how to mitigate undue adverse economic impacts on small businesses; and

(F) Such other factors as appropriate.

(iii) *FFA (15 U.S.C. 1194 (e)(2)).* The nature, circumstances, extent, and gravity of the violations:

(A) The severity of the risk of injury;

(B) The occurrence or absence of injury;

(C) The appropriateness of such penalty in relation to the size of the business of the person charged; and

(D) Such other factors as appropriate.

(2) *The nature, circumstances, extent, and gravity of the violation.* Under this factor, the Commission will consider the totality of the circumstances and all other facts concerning a violation. The Commission will consider the enumerated statutory factors, as well as the factors described in paragraph (b) of this section.

(3) *Nature of the product defect.* The Commission will consider the nature of the product defect associated with a CPSA violation. This consideration will include, for example, whether the defect arises from the product's design, composition, contents, construction, manufacture, packaging, warnings, or instructions, and will include consideration of conditions or circumstances in which the defect arises. The Commission will also consider the nature of the substance associated with an FHSA violation. Two of the statutory factors in the CPSA civil penalty factors include the terms "product defect" or "defective products." However, certain violations of the CPSA, for example, failing to supply a required certificate that the product complies with an applicable consumer product safety rule, do not necessarily require that there be a product defect or defective product. The terms "product defect" or "defective products" would not apply to such situation. In such cases, however, the other civil penalty factors would still be considered.

(4) *Severity of the risk of injury.* Consistent with its discussion of severity of the risk at 16 CFR 1115.12, the Commission will consider, among other factors, the potential for serious injury, illness, or death (and whether any injury or illness required medical treatment including hospitalization or surgery); the likelihood of injury; the intended or reasonably foreseeable use or misuse of the product; and the population at risk (including vulnerable populations such as children, the elderly, or those with disabilities).

(5) *The occurrence or absence of injury.* The Commission will consider whether injuries, illnesses, or deaths have or

have not occurred with respect to any product or substance associated with a violation, and, if so, the number and nature of injuries, illnesses, or deaths. Both acute illnesses and the likelihood of chronic illnesses will be considered.

(6) *The number of defective products distributed.* The Commission will consider the number of defective products or amount of substance distributed in commerce. The statutory language makes no distinction between those defective products distributed in commerce that consumers received and those defective products distributed in commerce that consumers have not received. Therefore both could be considered in appropriate cases. This factor will not be used to penalize a person's decision to conduct a wider-than-necessary recall out of an abundance of caution. This would not include situations where such a recall is conducted due to a person's uncertainty concerning how many or which products may need to be recalled.

(7) The appropriateness of such penalty in relation to the size of the business of the person charged, including how to mitigate undue adverse economic impacts on small businesses.

(i) The Commission is required to consider the size of the business of the person charged in relation to the amount of the penalty. This factor reflects the relationship between the size of a business and the policies behind, and purposes of, a penalty (as noted above in § 1119.1). In considering business size, the Commission may look to several factors including, but not limited to, the number of employees, net worth, and annual sales. A business's size and a business's ability to pay a penalty are separate considerations. In some cases for small businesses, however, these two considerations may relate to each other. The Commission will be guided, where appropriate, by relevant financial factors to determine a small business's ability to pay a penalty, including, but not limited to, liquidity, solvency, and profitability. The burden to present clear, reliable, relevant, and sufficient evidence relating to a business's size and ability to pay rests on the business.

(ii) The statute requires the Commission to consider how to mitigate the adverse economic impacts on small businesses only if those impacts would be undue. What the Commission considers in determining what is undue may include, but is not limited to, the business's size and financial factors relating to its ability to pay. When considering how to mitigate undue adverse economic impacts, the Commission will, as appropriate, also follow its Small Business Enforcement Policy set forth at § 1020.5.

(b) *Other factors as appropriate.* In determining the amount of any civil penalty to be sought for a violation of the CPSA, FHSA, or FFA, the Commission may consider, as appropriate, such other factors in addition to those listed in the statutes. Both the Commission and a person may raise any factors they believe are relevant in determining an appropriate penalty amount. A person will be notified of any factors beyond those enumerated in the statutes that the Commission relies on as aggravating factors for purposes of determining a civil penalty amount. Additional factors that may be considered in a case include, but are not limited to, the following:

(1) *Safety/compliance program and/or system relating to a violation.* The Commission may consider, when a safety/compliance program and/or system as established is relevant to a violation, whether a person had at the time of the violation a reasonable and effective program or system for collecting and analyzing information related to safety issues. Examples of such information would include incident reports, lawsuits, warranty claims, and safety-related issues related to repairs or returns. The Commission may also consider whether a person conducted adequate and relevant premarket and production testing of the product at issue; had a program in place for continued compliance with all relevant mandatory and voluntary safety standards; and other factors as the Commission deems appropriate. The burden to present clear, reliable, relevant, and sufficient evidence of such program, system, or testing rests on the person seeking consideration of this factor.

(2) *History of noncompliance.* The Commission may consider whether or not a person's history of noncompliance with

the CPSA, FHSA, FFA, and other laws that the CPSC enforces, and the regulations thereunder, should increase the amount of the penalty. A person's history of noncompliance may be indicated by, for example, multiple violations of one or more laws or regulations that the CPSC enforces, including repeated violations of the same law or regulation. History of noncompliance may include the number of previous violations or how recently a previous violation occurred.

(3) *Economic gain from noncompliance.* The Commission may consider whether a person benefitted economically from a failure to comply, including a delay in complying, with the CPSA, FHSA, FFA, and other laws that the CPSC enforces, and the regulations thereunder.

(4) *Failure to respond in a timely and complete fashion to the Commission's requests for information or remedial action.* The Commission may consider whether a person's failure to respond in a timely and complete fashion to requests from the Commission for information or for remedial action should increase a penalty. This factor is intended to address a person's dilatory and egregious conduct in responding to written requests for information or remedial action sought by the Commission, but not to impede any person's lawful rights.

§ 1119.5 Enforcement notification.

A person will be informed in writing if it is believed that the person has violated the law and if the Commission intends to seek a civil penalty. Any person who receives such a writing will have an opportunity to submit evidence and arguments that it should not pay a penalty or should not pay a penalty in the amount sought by the Commission.

PART 1120—SUBSTANTIAL PRODUCT HAZARD LIST

AUTHORITY: 15 U.S.C. 2064(j).

SOURCE: 76 FR 37640, June 28, 2011, unless otherwise noted.

§ 1120.1 Authority.

Under the authority of section 15(j) of the Consumer Product Safety Act (CPSA), the Commission determines that consumer products or classes of consumer products listed in § 1120.3 of this part have characteristics whose existence or absence present a substantial product hazard under section 15(a)(2) of the CPSA. The Commission has determined that the listed products have characteristics that are readily observable and have been addressed by a voluntary standard, that the voluntary standard has been effective, and that there is substantial compliance with the voluntary standard. The listed products are subject to the reporting requirements of section 15(b) of the CPSA and to the recall provisions of section 15(c) and (d) of the CPSA, and shall be refused entry into the United States under section 17(a)(4) of the CPSA.

§ 1120.2 Definitions.

The definitions in section 3 of the Consumer Product Safety Act (15 U.S.C. 2052) apply to this part 1120.

(a) *Substantial product hazard* means a product defect which (because of the pattern of defect, the number of defective products distributed in commerce, the severity of the risk, or otherwise) creates a substantial risk of injury to the public.

(b) *Hand-supported hair dryer* means an electrical appliance, intended to be held with one hand during use, which creates a flow of air over or through a self-contained heating element for the purpose of drying hair.

(c) *Drawstring* means a non-retractable cord, ribbon, or tape of any material to pull together parts of upper outerwear to provide for closure.

[76 FR 37640, June 28, 2011, as amended at 76 FR 42507, July 19, 2011]

§ 1120.3 Products deemed to be substantial product hazards.

The following products or class of products shall be deemed to be substantial product hazards under section 15(a)(2) of the CPSA:

(a) Hand-supported hair dryers that do not provide integral immersion protection in compliance with the requirements of section 5 of Underwriters Laboratories (UL) *Standard for Safety for Household Electric Personal Grooming Appliances*, UL 859, 10th Edition, approved August 30, 2002, and revised through June 3, 2010, or section 6 of *UL Standard for Safety for Commercial Electric Personal Grooming Appliances*, UL 1727, 4th Edition, approved March 25, 1999, and revised through June 25, 2010. The Director of the Federal Register approves these incorporations by reference in accordance with 5 U.S.C. 552(a) and 1 CFR part 51. You may obtain a copy from UL, Inc., 333 Pfingsten Road, Northbrook, IL 60062; telephone 888–853–3503; *http://*www.comm-2000.com . You may inspect a copy at the Office of the Secretary, U.S. Consumer Product Safety Commission, Room 820, 4330 East West Highway, Bethesda, MD 20814, telephone 301–504–7923, or at the National Archives and Records Administration (NARA). For information on the availability of this material at NARA, call 202–741–6030, or go to: *http://www.archives.gov/federal_register/code_of_federal_regulations/ibr_locations.html.*

(b) (1) Children's upper outerwear in sizes 2T to 16 or the equivalent, and having one or more drawstrings, that is subject to, but not in conformance with, the requirements of ASTM F 1816–97, *Standard Safety Specification for Drawstrings on Children's Upper Outerwear*, approved June 10, 1997, published August 1998. The Director of the Federal Register approves this incorporation by reference in accordance with 5 U.S.C. 552(a) and 1 CFR part 51. You may obtain a copy from ASTM International, 100 Barr Harbor Drive, PO Box C700, West Conshohocken, PA 19428–2959 USA, telephone: 610–832–9585; *http://www2.astm.org/*. You may inspect a copy at the Office of the Secretary, U.S. Consumer Product Safety Commission, Room 502, 4330 East West Highway, Bethesda, MD 20814, telephone 301–504–7923, or at the National Archives and Records Administration (NARA). For information on the availability of this material at NARA, call 202–741–6030, or go to: *http://www.archives.gov/federal_register/code_of_federal_regulations/ibr_locations.html.*

(2) At its option, the Commission may use one or more of the following methods to determine what sizes of children's upper outerwear are equivalent to sizes 2T to 16:

(i) Garments in girls' size Large (L) and boys' size Large (L) are equivalent to girls' or boys' size 12, respectively. Garments in girls' and boys' sizes smaller than Large (L), including Extra-Small (XS), Small (S), and Medium (M), are equivalent to sizes smaller than size 12. The fact that an item of children's upper outerwear with a hood and neck drawstring is labeled as being larger than a size Large (L) does not necessarily mean that the item is not equivalent to a size in the range of 2T to 12.

(ii) Garments in girls' size Extra-Large (XL) and boys' size Extra-Large (XL) are equivalent to size 16. The fact that an item of children's upper outerwear with a waist or bottom drawstring is labeled as being larger than size Extra-Large (XL) does not necessarily mean that the item is not equivalent to a size in the range of 2T to 16.

(iii) In cases where garment labels give a range of sizes, if the range includes any size that is subject to a requirement in ASTM F 1816–97, the garment will be considered subject, even if other sizes in the stated range, taken alone, would not be subject to the requirement. For example, a coat sized 12 through 14 remains subject to the prohibition of hood and neck area drawstrings, even though this requirement of ASTM F 1816–97 only applies to garments up to size 12. A coat size 13 through 15 would not be considered within the scope of ASTM F 1816–97's prohibition of neck and hood drawstrings, but would be subject to the requirements for waist or bottom drawstrings.

(iv) To fall within the scope of paragraphs (b)(2)(i) through (2)(iii) of this section, a garment need not state anywhere on it, or on its tags, labels, package, or any other materials accompanying it, the term "girls," the term "boys," or whether the garment is designed or intended for girls or boys.

(v) The Commission may use any other evidence that would tend to show that an item of children's upper outerwear is a size that is equivalent to sizes 2T to 16.

[76 FR 37640, June 28, 2011, as amended at 76 FR 42507, July 19, 2011]

PART 1130—REQUIREMENTS FOR CONSUMER REGISTRATION OF DURABLE INFANT OR TODDLER PRODUCTS

Sec.

AUTHORITY: 15 U.S.C. 2056a, 2065(b).

SOURCE: 74 FR 68676, Dec. 29, 2009, unless otherwise noted.

§ 1130.1 Purpose, scope, and effective date.

(a) *Purpose.* This part prescribes a consumer product safety rule establishing requirements for consumer registration of durable infant or toddler products. These requirements are intended to improve the effectiveness of recalls of, and safety alerts regarding, such products.

(b) *Scope.* Part 1130 applies to manufacturers, including importers, of durable infant or toddler products, as defined in § 1130.2(a). It does not apply to infant or child restraint systems intended for use in automobiles that are covered by the registration program of the National Highway Traffic and Safety Administration (NHTSA) at 49 CFR 571.213, or to products that comprise a travel system, and are sold with a child restraint system that is covered by the NHTSA registration program at 49 CFR 571.213.

(c) *Compliance Date.* Compliance with this part 1130 shall be required on June 28, 2010 for the following products: full-size cribs and nonfull-size cribs; toddler beds; high chairs, booster chairs, and hook-on chairs; bath seats; gates and other enclosures for confining a child; play yards; stationary activity centers; infant carriers; strollers; walkers; swings; and bassinets and cradles. Compliance with this part 1130 shall be required on December 29, 2010 for the following products: Children's folding chairs, changing tables, infant bouncers, infant bath tubs, bed rails and infant slings. The rule shall apply to durable infant or toddler products, as defined in § 1130.2(a), that are manufactured on or after those dates.

§ 1130.2 Definitions.

In addition to the definitions given in section 3 of the Consumer Product Safety Act (15 U.S.C. 2052), the following definitions apply:

(a) *Durable infant or toddler product* means the following products, including combinations thereof:

(1) Full-size cribs and non-full-size cribs;

(2) Toddler beds;

(3) High chairs, booster seats, and hook-on chairs;

(4) Bath seats;

(5) Gates and other enclosures for confining a child;

(6) Play yards;

(7) Stationary activity centers;

(8) Infant carriers;

(9) Strollers;

(10) Walkers;

(11) Swings; and

(12) Bassinets and cradles;

(13) Children's folding chairs;

(14) Changing tables;

(15) Infant bouncers;

(16) Infant bathtubs;

(17) Bed rails;

(18) Infant slings.

(b) *Manufacturer*, for purposes of this part, in the case of a product produced within the United States, means the domestic manufacturer of the product, and in the case of an imported product, means the importer of the product.

(c) *Product recall* means action taken pursuant to sections 12, 15(c) or 15(d) of the CPSA (15 U.S.C. 2061, 2054(c), or 2064(d)), and action taken pursuant to a corrective action plan implemented by a company in cooperation with the Commission, where the firm is conducting one or more of the following: repair of the product; replacement of the product; or refund of the purchase price of the product.

(d) *Safety alert* means notice or warning of a potential problem with an individual product or class of products so that consumers and other users of the affected products respond accordingly to reduce or eliminate the potential for injury.

§ 1130.3 General requirements.

(a) Each manufacturer of a durable infant or toddler product shall:

(1) Provide consumers with a postage-paid consumer registration form that meets the requirements of this part 1130 with each such product;

(2) Maintain a record in accordance with the requirements set forth in § 1130.9 of the contact information (names, addresses, e-mail addresses, and telephone numbers) of consumers who register their products with the manufacturer under this part 1130;

(3) Permanently place the manufacturer name and contact information, model name and number, and the date of manufacture on each durable infant or toddler product in accordance with the requirements set forth in § 1130.4.

(b) Consumer information collected by a manufacturer pursuant to the requirements of this part 1130 shall not be used by the manufacturer, nor disseminated by the manufacturer to any other party, for any purpose other than notification to such consumer in the event of a product recall or safety alert.

EFFECTIVE DATE NOTE: At 77 FR 9524, Feb. 17, 2012, § 1130.3 was amended by removing "§ 1130.9" and add in its place "§ 1130.8", effective Feb. 18, 2013.

§ 1130.4 Identification on the product.

(a) Each durable infant or toddler product shall be permanently marked with the manufacturer name, and contact information (U.S. address and telephone number, toll free if available) model name and number, and date of manufacture.

(1) If the manufacturer regularly uses only a model name or a model number, but not both, to identify the product, he/she may provide only the model name or number rather than creating a model name or number for the sole purpose of this part 1130.

(2) If the manufacturer regularly identifies the product by a product identification number ("PIN") or other similar identifying number rather than a model number, he/she may provide that identifying number instead of a model number.

(3) The date referred to in paragraph (a) of this section shall include the month and year of manufacture and can be stated in code.

(4) A permanent mark is one that can reasonably be expected to remain on the product during the useful life of the product.

(b) The information required by this section shall be in English, legible, and in a location that is conspicuous to the consumer.

(c) The information required by this section may be combined with other information marked on the product.

§ 1130.5 Requirements for registration forms.

The registration form required under § 1130.3(a)(1) shall:

(a) Comply with the format and text requirements set forth in §§ 1130.6 and 1130.7 as shown in figures 1 and 2 of this part;

(b) State all information required by this part 1130 in the English language;

(c) Be attached to the surface of each durable infant or toddler product so that, as a practical matter, the consumer must notice and handle the form after purchasing the product;

(d) Include the manufacturer's name, model name and number for the product, and the date of manufacture;

(e) Include an option for consumers to register through the Internet;

(f) Include the statement required in § 1130.7(a) that information provided by the consumer shall not be used for any purpose other than to facilitate a recall of or safety alert regarding that product.

EFFECTIVE DATE NOTE: At 77 FR 9524, Feb. 17, 2012, § 1130.5 was amended in paragraph (a), by removing "and 1130.7"; and in paragraph (f), remove "1130.7(a)" and add, in its place "1130.6(c)(1)", effective Feb. 18, 2013.

§ 1130.6 Requirements for format of registration forms.

(a) *Size of form.* The form shall be at least the size of two standard post cards connected with perforation for later separation, so that each of the two portions is at least 3½ inches high by 5 inches wide by 0.007 inches thick.

(b) *Layout of form.* (1) General. The form shall consist of four parts: Top and bottom, divided by perforations for easy separation, and front and back.

(2) *Top of form.* The top portion of the form is to be retained by the consumer. The front top portion shall provide the purpose statement set forth in § 1130.7(a). The back of the top portion shall provide the manufacturer's contact information as required in § 1130.7(b).

(3) *Bottom of form.* The bottom portion of the form is to be returned to the manufacturer. The bottom back panel of the form shall have blocks for the consumer to provide his/her contact information as required in § 1130.7(c). Below the consumer contact information shall be product information as required in § 1130.7(d) which may be printed on the form or provided on a pre-printed label placed on the form by the manufacturer. The front of the bottom portion of the form shall be pre-addressed and postage-paid with the manufacturer's name and mailing address where registration information is to be collected.

(c) *Font size and typeface.* The registration form shall use bold black typeface. The size of the type shall be at least 12-point for the purpose statement required in § 1130.7(a) and no less than 10-point for the other information in the registration form. The title of the purpose statement shall be in all capitals. All other information shall be in capital and lower case type.

[74 FR 68676, Dec. 12, 2009, as amended at 75 FR 7551, Feb. 22, 2010]

EFFECTIVE DATE NOTE: At 77 FR 9524, Feb. 17, 2012, § 1130.6 was revised, effective Feb. 18, 2013. For the convenience of the user, the revised text is set forth as follows:

§ 1130.6 Requirements for format and text of registration forms.

(a) *Size of form.* The form shall be at least the size of two standard post cards, connected with perforation for later separation, so that each of the two portions is at least 3½ inches high x 5 inches wide x 0.007 inches thick.

(b) *Layout of form.* (1) *General.* The form shall consist of four parts: top and bottom, divided by perforations for easy separation, and front and back.

(2) *Font size and typeface.* The registration form shall use bold black typeface. The size of the type shall be at least 0.12 in (3.0 mm) for the purpose statement required in paragraph (c)(1) of this section, and no less than 0.10 in (2.5 mm) for the other information in the registration form. The title of the purpose statement and the retention statement required in paragraph (d)(2) of this section shall be in all capitals. All other information shall be in capital and lowercase type.

(c) *Front of form.* (1) *Top front of form: Purpose statement.* The top portion of the front of each form shall state: "PRODUCT REGISTRATION FOR SAFETY ALERT OR RECALL ONLY. We will use the information provided on this card to contact you only if there is a safety alert or recall for this product. We will not sell, rent, or share your personal information. To register your product, please complete and mail the bottom part of this card, or visit our online registration at: *www.Web sitename.com.*" Manufacturers that do not have a Web site may provide an email address and state at the end of the purpose statement: "To register your product, please complete and mail the bottom part of this card, or email your contact information, the model name and number, and date of manufacture of the product, as provided on this card, to: *name@firmname.com.*"

(2) *Bottom front of form: Manufacturer's mailing address.* The bottom portion of the front of each form shall be pre-addressed and postage-paid with the manufacturer's name and mailing address where registration information is to be collected. A manufacturer may list a brand name in addition to the manufacturer's name. If a manufacturer uses a third party to process registration forms, the third party's name may be included as a "c/o" ("in care of") in the address on the form.

(d) *Back of the form.* (1) *Top back of form.* (i) *Product information and manufacturer's identification.* The top portion of the back of each form shall state: "Manufacturer's Contact Information" and provide the manufacturer's name and contact information (a U.S. mailing address displayed in sentence format, Web site address, a telephone number, toll-free, if available); product model name and number (or other identifier as described in § 1130.4(a)(1) and (2)); and manufacture date of the product. A rectangular box shall be placed around the model name, model number, and manufacture date. A manufacturer may list the brand name in addition to the manufacturer's name.

(ii) *Retention statement.* On the back of each form, just above the perforation line, the form shall state: "KEEP THIS TOP PART FOR YOUR RECORDS. FILL OUT AND RETURN BOTTOM PART."

(2) *Bottom back of form.* (i) *Consumer information.* The bottom portion of the back of each form shall have blocks for the consumer to provide his/her name, address, telephone number, and email address. These blocks shall be 5 mm wide and 7 mm high, with as many blocks as possible to fill the width of the card allowing for normal printing practices.

(ii) *Product information.* The following product information shall be provided on the bottom portion of the back of each form below the blocks for consumer information printed directly on the form or on a pre-printed label that is applied to the form: the model name and number (or other identifier as described in §1130.4(a)(1) and (2)), and the date of manufacture of the product. A rectangular box shall be placed around the model name, model number, and manufacture date. A manufacturer may include its name on the bottom portion of the back of the form if they choose to do so..

§1130.7 Requirements for text of registration form.

(a) *Purpose statement.* The front top portion of each form shall state: "PRODUCT REGISTRATION FOR SAFETY ALERT OR RECALL. We will use the information provided on this card to contact you only if there is a safety alert or recall for this product. We will not sell, rent, or share your personal information. To register your product, please complete and mail this card or visit our online registration at *http://www.websitename.com.*" Manufacturers that do not have a Web site may provide an email address and state at the end of the purpose statement: "To register your product, please complete and mail this card or email your contact information, the model name and number and date of manufacture of the product as provided on this card to: *name@firmname.com*".

(b) *Manufacturer and product information.* The back of the top portion of the form shall state the manufacturer's name and contact information (a U.S. mailing address, a telephone number, toll free if available), Web site address, product model name and number (or other identifier as described in §1130.4(a)(1) and (2)), and manufacture date of the product.

(c) *Consumer information.* The bottom front portion of the form shall have blocks for the consumer to provide his/her name, address, telephone number, and email address. These blocks shall be 5 mm wide and 7 mm high, with as many blocks as possible to fill the width of the card allowing for normal printing practices.

(d) *Product information.* The following product information shall be provided on the back of the bottom portion of the form below the blocks for customer information printed directly on the form or on a pre-printed label that is applied to the form: The manufacturer's name, the model name and number (or other identifier as described in §1130.4(a)(1) and (2)), and the date of manufacture of the product. A rectangular box shall be placed around the model name, model number and manufacture date.

EFFECTIVE DATE NOTE: At 77 FR 9524, Feb. 17, 2012, §1130.7 was removed, effective Feb. 18, 2013.

§1130.8 Requirements for Web site registration or alternative e-mail registration.

(a) *Link to registration page.* The manufacturer's Web site, or other Web site established for the purpose of registration under this part 1130, shall be designed with a link clearly identified on the main web page that goes directly to "Product Registration."

(b) *Purpose statement.* The registration page shall have the following statement at the top of the page: "PRODUCT REGISTRATION FOR SAFETY ALERT OR RECALL ONLY. We will use the information provided on this page only to contact you if there is a safety alert or recall for this product. We will not sell, rent, or share your personal information. If you register on this Web site you do not need to fill out the card that came with your product."

(c) *Content of registration page.* The Web site registration page shall request only the consumer's name, address, telephone number, e-mail address, product model name and number, and the date of manufacture. The consumer's telephone number and e-mail address shall not be required for the consumer to submit the registration form. No other information shall appear on the electronic registration form, except for identification of the manufacturer or a link to the manufacturer's home page, a field to confirm submission, and a prompt to indicate any incomplete or invalid fields before submission. Accessing the electronic registration form shall not cause additional screens or electronic banners to appear.

(d) *Alternative for manufacturers without a Web site.* A manufacturer that lacks a Web site shall provide for consumers to register their product through e-mail. Such e-mail addresses shall be set up to provide an automatic reply to confirm receipt of the consumer's registration information.

EFFECTIVE DATE NOTES: 1. At 77 FR 9525, Feb. 17, 2012, § 1130.8 was redesignated as § 1130.7, effective Feb. 18, 2013.

2. At 77 FR 9525, Feb. 17, 2012, § 1130.8 was amended by adding paragraphs (d) and (e), effective Feb. 18, 2013. For the convenience of the user, the added text is set forth as follows:

§ 1130.8 Requirements for Web site registration or alternative email registration.

* * * * *

(d) Records required under this section shall be made available within 24 hours, upon the request of any officer, employee, or agent acting on behalf of the U.S. Consumer Product Safety Commission.

(e) *Optional barcode.* (1) A manufacturer may include a barcode, or other machine readable data, that when scanned would provide a direct link for the consumer to register the product.

(2) Such a link must comply with all the requirements of this part 1130, including those in § 1130.7 and the restriction that the manufacturer shall not use or disseminate the consumer registration information for any purpose other than notifying the consumer of a safety alert or recall.

§ 1130.9 Recordkeeping and notification requirements.

(a) Each manufacturer of a durable infant or toddler product shall maintain a record of registrants for each product manufactured that includes all of the information provided by each consumer registered.

(b) Each manufacturer of a durable infant or toddler product shall use the information provided by the registrant to notify the registrant in the event of a voluntary or involuntary recall of, or safety alert regarding, such product.

(c) Each manufacturer of a durable infant or toddler product shall maintain a record of the information provided by the registrant for a period of not less than 6 years after the date of manufacture of the product.

EFFECTIVE DATE NOTE: At 77 FR 9525, Feb. 17, 2012, § 1130.9 was redesignated as § 1130.8, effective Feb. 18, 2013.

FIGURE 1 TO PART 1130—FRONT OF REGISTRATION FORM

PRODUCT REGISTRATION FOR SAFETY ALERT OR RECALL ONLY

We will use the information provided on this card to contact you only if there is a safety alert or recall for this product. We will not sell, rent, or share your personal information. To register your product, please complete and mail this card or visit our on-line registration at www.websitename.com.

NO POSTAGE
NECESSARY
IF MAILED
IN THE
UNITED STATES

BUSINESS REPLY MAIL
FIRST-CLASS MAIL PERMIT NO. 1234 ALEXANDRIA, VA

POSTAGE WILL BE PAID BY ADDRESSEE

MANUFACTURER'S NAME
POST OFFICE BOX 0000
ANYTOWN, ST 12345-6789

FIGURE 1 TO PART 1130 - FRONT OF REGISTRATION FORM

EFFECTIVE DATE NOTE: At 77 FR 9525, Feb. 17, 2012, figure 1 to part 1130 was revised, effective Feb. 18, 2013. For the convenience of the user, the added and revised text is set forth as follows:

FIGURE 1 TO PART 1130—FRONT OF REGISTRATION FORM

PRODUCT REGISTRATION FOR SAFETY ALERT OR RECALL ONLY

We will use the information provided on this card to contact you only if there is a safety alert or recall for this product. We will not sell, rent, or share your personal information. To register your product, please complete and mail the bottom part of this card, or visit our online registration at: www.website.com.

NO POSTAGE NECESSARY IF MAILED IN THE UNITED STATES

BUSINESS REPLY MAIL

FIRST-CLASS MAIL PERMIT NO.

POSTAGE WILL BE PAID BY ADDRESSEE

Manufacturer's Name
Post Office Box 0000
Anytown, ST 01234

FIGURE 1 TO PART 1130 – FRONT OF REGISTRATION FORM

FIGURE 2 TO PART 1130—BACK OF REGISTRATION FORM

Model Name :

Model Number :

Manufacture Date :

Manufacturer's Name

www.websitename.com

Phone Number - Toll Free (if available) :

Tear off and mail this part.
Please print clearly in the spaces below.

Name

Mailing address

City **State** **Zip Code**

Telephone number

E-mail address

Model Name :

Model Number :

Manufacture Date :

FIGURE 2 TO PART 1130 - BACK OF REGISTRATION FORM

EFFECTIVE DATE NOTE: At 77 FR 9525, Feb. 17, 2012, figure 2 to part 1130 was revised, effective Feb. 18, 2013. For the convenience of the user, the added and revised text is set forth as follows:

FIGURE 2 TO PART 1130—FRONT OF REGISTRATION FORM

Manufacturer's Contact Information

Manufacturer's Name • 111 Main St • Anytown, ST 01234
www.website.com
Phone Number – Toll-Free (if available)

Model Name:

Model Number:

Manufacture Date:

KEEP THIS TOP PART FOR YOUR RECORDS.
FILL OUT AND RETURN BOTTOM PART.

Name

Mailing Address

City State Zip Code

Telephone Number
- -

E-mail address

Model Name:

Model Number:

Manufacture Date:

FIGURE 2 TO PART 1130 – BACK OF REGISTRATION FORM

PART 1145—REGULATION OF PRODUCTS SUBJECT TO OTHER ACTS UNDER THE CONSUMER PRODUCT SAFETY ACT

AUTHORITY: 15 U.S.C. 2079(d).

§ 1145.1 Scope.

In this part 1145, the Commission establishes rules which provide that risks of injury associated with consumer products that could be eliminated or reduced to a sufficient extent by action under the Federal Hazardous Substances Act (FHSA) (15 U.S.C. 1261–1274), the Poison Prevention Packaging Act of 1970 (PPPA) (15 U.S.C. 1471–1476), or the Flammable Fabrics Act (FFA) (15 U.S.C. 1191–1204) will be regulated under the Consumer Product Safety Act (CPSA) (15 U.S.C. 2051–2081). Section 30(d) of the CPSA, as amended, provides that a risk of injury which is associated with a consumer product and which could be eliminated or reduced to a sufficient extent by action under the FHSA, PPPA, or the FFA may be regulated under this act only if the Commission by rule finds it is in the public interest to regulate such risk of injury under this act.

[42 FR 44192, Sept. 1, 1977]

§ 1145.2 Paint (and other similar surface-coating materials) containing lead; toys, children's articles, and articles of furniture bearing such paint (or similar surface-coating materials); risk of lead poisoning.

(a) The Commission finds that it is in the public interest to reduce the risk of lead poisoning to young children from the ingestion of paint and other similar surface-coating materials by action under the Consumer Product Safety Act rather than under the Federal Hazardous Substances Act because of the desirability of consolidating the public procedures related to such regulation with the proceeding to determine a safe level of lead under the Lead-Based Paint Poisoning Prevention Act (42 U.S.C. 4801–4846), as amended by the National Consumer Health Information and Health Promotion Act of 1976 (Pub. L. 94–317; 90 Stat. 705–706). Consolidation of these proceedings facilitates greater public participation and a more expeditious resolution of the issues.

(b) Paint and other similar surface-coating materials containing lead and toys, children's articles, and articles of furniture bearing such paint or other similar surface-coating materials that present a risk of lead poisoning to young children by ingestion shall therefore be regulated under the Consumer Product Safety Act. Such regulation shall include all directly related pending and future rulemaking, as well as all directly related pending and future action on petitions.

[42 FR 44192, Sept. 1, 1977]

§ 1145.3 Extremely flammable contact adhesives; risk of burns from explosive vapor ignition and flashback fire.

(a) The Commission finds that it is in the public interest to regulate the risk of burns from explosive vapor ignition and flashback fire associated with certain extremely flammable contact adhesives under the Consumer Product Safety Act rather than under the Federal Hazardous Substances Act because of the desirability of avoiding possibly lengthy, resource consuming, and inefficient rulemaking proceedings under the Federal Hazardous Substances Act and because of the availability of civil penalties under the CPSA. The Commission also believes that the complexity and formality of the rulemaking proceedings under the FHSA, in contrast to rulemaking proceedings under the CPSA may make it difficult for interested persons to participate.

(b) Extremely flammable contact adhesives and other similar liquid or semi-liquid products in containers over one-half pint that present a risk of burns from explosive vapor ignition and flashback fire shall therefore be regulated under the Consumer Product Safety Act. Such regulation shall include all directly related pending and future rulemaking, as well as all directly related future action on petitions. However, such action shall not include labeling that may be required under the Federal Hazardous Substances Act to address flammability hazards associated with other adhesives not subject to the ban.

[42 FR 63731, Dec. 19, 1977]

§ 1145.4 Consumer patching compounds containing respirable free-form asbestos; risk of cancer associated with inhalation of asbestos fibers.

(a) The Commission finds that it is in the public interest to regulate the risk of cancer associated with inhalation of asbestos fibers from consumer patching compounds containing respirable free-form asbestos under the Consumer Product Safety Act (CPSA) rather than under the Federal Hazardous Substances Act (FHSA) because of the desirability of avoiding possibly lengthy resource-consuming, inefficient rulemaking proceedings under the FHSA and because of the availability of civil penalties under the CPSA for knowing noncompliance.

(b) Therefore, consumer patching compounds containing respirable free-form asbestos are regulated under CPSA.

[42 FR 63354, Dec. 15, 1977]

§ 1145.5 Emberizing materials (embers and ash) containing respirable free-form asbestos; risk of cancer associated with inhalation of asbestos fibers.

(a) The Commission finds that it is in the public interest to regulate the risk of cancer associated with inhalation of asbestos fibers from artificial emberizing materials (embers and ash) containing respirable free-form asbestos under the Consumer Product Safety Act (CPSA) rather than under the Federal Hazardous Substances Act (FHSA) because of the desirability of avoiding possibly lengthy, resource-consuming, inefficient rulemaking proceedings under the FHSA, and because of the availability of civil penalties under the CPSA for knowing noncompliance.

(b) Therefore, artificial emberizing materials (embers and ash) containing respirable free-form asbestos are regulated under the CPSA.

[42 FR 63354, Dec. 15, 1977]

§§ 1145.9–1145.15 [Reserved]

§ 1145.16 Lighters that are intended for igniting smoking materials and that can be operated by children; risks of death or injury.

(a) The Commission finds that it is in the public interest to regulate under the Consumer Product Safety Act any risks of injury associated with the fact that lighters intended for igniting smoking materials can be operated by young children, rather than regulate such risks under the Federal Hazardous Substances Act or the Poison Prevention Packaging Act of 1970.

(b) Therefore, if the Commission finds regulation to be necessary, risks of death or injury that are associated with lighters that are intended for igniting smoking materials, where such risks exist because the lighters can be operated by young children, shall be regulated under one or more provisions of the Consumer Product Safety Act. Other risks associated with such lighters, and that are based solely on the fact that the lighters contain a hazardous substance, shall continue to be regulated under the Federal Hazardous Substances Act.

[58 FR 37556, July 12, 1993]

§ 1145.17 Multi-purpose lighters that can be operated by children; risks of death or injury.

(a) The Commission finds that it is in the public interest to regulate under the Consumer Product Safety Act any risks of injury associated with the fact that multi-purpose lighters can be operated by young children, rather than to regulate such risks under the Federal Hazardous Substances Act or the Poison Prevention Packaging Act of 1970.

(b) Therefore, if the Commission finds regulation to be necessary, risks of death or injury that are associated with multi-purpose lighters because the lighters can be operated by young children shall be regulated under one or more provisions of the Consumer Product Safety Act. Other risks that are associated with such lighters, and that are based solely on the fact that the lighters contain a hazardous substance, shall continue to be regulated under the Federal Hazardous Substances Act.

[64 FR 71884, Dec. 22, 1999]

PART 1200—DEFINITION OF CHILDREN'S PRODUCT UNDER THE CONSUMER PRODUCT SAFETY ACT

AUTHORITY: 15 U.S.C. 2052(2).

SOURCE: 75 FR 63077, Oct. 14, 2010, unless otherwise noted.

§ 1200.1 Purpose.

This part provides guidance on the definition of children's product and the factors the Commission will consider when making determinations regarding children's products as set forth under 15 U.S.C. 2052(2).

§ 1200.2 Definition of children's product.

(a) *Definition of "Children's Product"*—(1) Under section 3(a)(2) of the Consumer Product Safety Act (CPSA), a children's product means a consumer product designed or intended primarily for children 12 years of age or younger. The term "designed or intended primarily" applies to those consumer products mainly for children 12 years old or younger. Whether a product is primarily intended for children 12 years of age or younger is determined by considering the four specified statutory factors. These factors are:

(i) A statement by a manufacturer about the intended use of such product, including a label on such product if such statement is reasonable.

(ii) Whether the product is represented in its packaging, display, promotion, or advertising as appropriate for use by children 12 years of age or younger.

(iii) Whether the product is commonly recognized by consumers as being intended for use by a child 12 years of age or younger.

(iv) The Age Determination Guidelines issued by the Commission staff in September 2002 and any successor to such guidelines.

(2) The examples discussed herein may also be illustrative in making such determinations; however, the determination of whether a product meets the definition of a children's product depends on factual information that may be unique to each product and, therefore, would need to be made on a case-by-case basis. The term "for use" by children 12 years or younger generally means that children will physically interact with such products based on the reasonably foreseeable use of such product. Toys and articles that are subject to the small parts regulations at 16 CFR Part 1501 and in ASTM F963 would fall within the definition of children's product since they are intended for children 12 years of age or younger. Toys and other articles intended for children up to 96 months (8 years old) that are subject to the requirements at 16 CFR 1500.48 through 1500.49 and 16 CFR 1500.50 through 1500.53 would similarly fall within the definition of children's product given their age grading for these other regulations. Therefore, a manufacturer could reasonably conclude on the basis of the age grading for these other regulations that its product also must comply with all requirements applicable to children's products including, but not limited to, those under the Federal Hazardous Substances Act, ASTM F963, "Standard Consumer Safety Specification for Toy Safety," and the Consumer Product Safety Improvement Act of 2008.

(b) *Definition of "General Use Product"*—(1) A general use product means a consumer product that is not designed or intended primarily for use by children 12 years old or younger. General use products are those consumer products designed or intended primarily for consumers older than age 12. Some products may be designed or intended for use by consumers of all ages, including children 12 years old or younger, but are intended mainly for consumers older than 12 years of age. Examples of general use products may include products with which a child would not likely interact, or products with which consumers older than 12 would be as likely, or more likely to interact. Products used by children 12 years of age or younger that have a declining appeal for teenagers are likely to be considered children's products.

(2) Other products are specifically not intended for children 12 years of age or younger. These products, such as cigarette lighters, candles, and fireworks, which the Commission has traditionally warned adults to keep away from children, are not subject to the CPSIA's lead limits, tracking label requirement, and third-party testing and certification provisions. Similarly, products that incorporate performance requirements for child resistance are not children's products as they are designed specifically to ensure that children cannot access the contents. This would include products such as portable gasoline containers and special packaging under the Poison Prevention Packaging Act.

(c) *Factors Considered*—To determine whether a consumer product is primarily intended for a child 12 years of age or younger the four specified statutory factors must be considered together as a whole. The following four factors must be considered:

(1) A statement by a manufacturer about the intended use of such product, including a label on such product if such statement is reasonable. A manufacturer's statement about the product's intended use, including the product's label, should be reasonably consistent with the expected use patterns for a product. A manufacturer's statement that the product is not intended for children does not preclude a product from being regulated as a children's product if the primary appeal of the product is to children 12 years of age or younger, as indicated, for example, by decorations or embellishments that invite use by the child, being sized for a child or being marketed to appeal primarily to children. Similarly, a label indicating that a product is for ages 9 and up does not necessarily make it a children's product if it is a general use product. Such a label may recommend 9 years old as the earliest age for a prospective user, but may or may not indicate the age for which the product is primarily intended. The manufacturer's label, in and of itself, is not considered to be determinative.

(2) Whether the product is represented in its packaging, display, promotion, or advertising as appropriate for use by children 12 years of age or younger.

(i) These representations may be express or implied. For example, advertising by the manufacturer expressly declaring that the product is intended for children 12 years of age or younger will support a determination that a product is a children's product. While, for example advertising by the manufacturer showing children 12 years of age or younger using the product may support a determination that the product is a children's product. These representations may be found in packaging, text, illustrations and/or photographs depicting consumers using the product, instructions, assembly manuals, or advertising media used to market the product.

(ii) The product's physical location near, or visual association with, children's products may be a factor in making an age determination, but is not determinative. For example, a product displayed in a children's toy section of a store may support a determination that the product is a children's product. However, where that same product is also sold in department stores and marketed for general use, further evaluation would be necessary. The Commission recognizes that manufacturers do not necessarily control where a product will be placed in a retail establishment and such lack of control will be considered. The Commission evaluates products more broadly than on a shelf-by-shelf or store-by-store basis.

(iii) The product's association or marketing in conjunction with nonchildren's products may not be determinative as to whether the product is a children's product. For example, packaging and selling a stuffed animal with a candle would not preclude a determination that the stuffed animal is a children's product since stuffed animals are commonly recognized as being primarily intended for children.

(3) Whether the product is commonly recognized by consumers as being intended for use by children 12 years of age or younger. Consumer perception of the product's use by children, including its reasonably foreseeable use, will be evaluated. Sales data, market analyses, focus group testing, and other marketing studies may help support an analysis regarding this factor.

(i) Features and Characteristics—additional considerations that may help distinguish children's products from nonchildren's products include:

(A) Small sizes that would not be comfortable for the average adult;

(B) Exaggerated features (large buttons, bright indicators) that simplify the product's use;

(C) Safety features that are not found on similar products intended for adults;

(D) Colors commonly associated with childhood (pinks, blues, bright primary colors);

(E) Decorative motifs commonly associated with childhood (such as animals, insects, small vehicles, alphabets, dolls, clowns, and puppets);

(F) Features that do not enhance the product's utility (such as cartoons) but contribute to its attractiveness to children 12 years of age or younger; and

(G) Play value, *i.e.*, features primarily attractive to children 12 years of age or younger that promote interactive exploration and imagination for fanciful purposes (whimsical activities lacking utility for accomplishing mundane tasks; actions performed for entertainment and amusement).

(ii) Principal use of the product—the principal uses of a product take precedence over other actions that are less likely to be performed with a product. For example, when a child pretends that a broom is a horse, that does not mean the item is a children's product because the broom's principal use is for sweeping;

(iii) Cost—the cost of a given product may influence the determination of the age of intended users; and

(iv) Children's interactions, if any, with the product—products for use in a child's environment by the caregiver but not for use by the child would not be considered to be primarily intended for a child 12 years of age or younger.

(4) The Age Determination Guidelines issued by the Consumer Product Safety Commission staff in September 2002, and any successor to such guidelines. The product's appeal to different age groups and the capabilities of those age groups may be considered when making determinations about the appropriate user groups for products.

(d) *Examples*—To help manufacturers understand what constitutes a children's product under the CPSA, the following additional examples regarding specific product categories are offered:

(1) Furnishings and Fixtures—General home furnishings and fixtures (including, but not limited to: Rocking chairs, shelving units, televisions, digital music players, ceiling fans, humidifiers, air purifiers, window curtains, tissue boxes, rugs, carpets, lamps, clothing hooks and racks) that often are found in children's rooms or schools would not be considered children's products unless they are decorated or embellished with a childish theme and invite use by a child 12 years of age or younger, are sized for a child, or are marketed to appeal primarily to children. Examples of home or school furnishings that are designed or intended primarily for use by children and considered children's products include: Infant tubs, bath seats, small bean bag chairs with childish decorations, beds with children's themes, child-sized desks, and child-sized chairs. Decorative items, such as holiday decorations and household seasonal items that are intended only for display, with which children are not likely to interact, are generally not considered children's products, since they are intended to be used by adults.

(2) Collectibles—Adult collectibles may be distinguished from children's collectibles by themes that are inappropriate for children 12 years of age or

younger, have features that preclude use by children during play, such as high cost, limited production, fragile features, display features (such as hooks or pedestals), and are not marketed alongside children's products (for example, in a children's department) in ways that make them indistinguishable from children's products. For example, collectible plush bears have high cost, are highly detailed, with fragile accessories, display cases, and platforms on which to pose and hold the bears. Children's bears have lower costs and simple accessories that can be handled without fear of damage to the product. Another example of collectible items includes model railways and trains made for hobbyists.

(3) Jewelry—Jewelry intended for children is generally sized, themed, and marketed to children. The following characteristics may cause a piece of jewelry to be considered a children's product: Size; very low cost; play value; childish themes on the jewelry; sale with children's products (such as a child's dress); sale with a child's book, a toy, or party favors; sale with children's cereal or snacks; sale at an entertainment or educational event attended primarily by children; sale in a store that contains mostly children's products; and sale in a vending machine. In addition, many aspects of an item's design and marketing are considered when determining the age of consumers for whom the product is intended and will be purchased including: Advertising; promotional materials; packaging graphics and text; dexterity requirements for wearing; appearance (coloring, textures, materials, design themes, licensing, and level of realism); and cost. These characteristics will help jewelry manufacturers and consumers determine whether a particular piece of jewelry is designed or intended primarily for children 12 years of age or younger.

(4) DVDs, Video Games, and Computer Products—Most computer products and electronic media, such as CDs, DVDs, and video games, are considered general use products. However, CDs and DVDs with encoded content that is intended for and marketed to children, such as children's movies, games, or educational software may be determined to be children's products. CPSC staff may consider ratings given by entertainment industries and software rating systems when making an age determination. In addition, electronic media players and devices that are embellished or decorated with childish themes that are intended to attract children 12 years of age or younger, are sized for children, or are marketed to appeal primarily to children, are not likely to fall under the general use category where children 12 years or younger likely would be the primary users of such devices. However, electronic devices such as CD players, DVD players, game consoles, book readers, digital media players, cell phones, digital assistant communication devices, and accessories to such devices that are intended mainly for children older than 12 years of age or adults are products for general use.

(5) Art Materials—Materials sized, decorated, and marketed to children 12 years of age or younger, such as crayons, finger paints, and modeling dough, would be considered children's products. Crafting kits and supplies that are not specifically marketed to children 12 years of age or younger likely would be considered products intended for general use. Consideration of the marketing and labeling of raw materials and art tools (such as modeling clay, paint, and paint brushes) may often be given high priority in an age determination because the appeal and utility of these raw materials has such a wide audience. If a distributor or retailer sells or rents a general use product in bulk (such as a raw art materials or art tools) through distribution channels that target children 12 years of age or younger in educational settings, such as schools, summer camps, or child care facilities, this type of a distribution strategy would not necessarily convert a general use product into a children's product. However, if the product is packaged in such a manner that either expressly states or implies with graphics, themes, labeling, or instructions that the product is designed or intended primarily for children 12 years of age or younger, then it may be considered a children's product if the required consideration of all four

statutory factors supports that determination. The requirements of the Labeling of Hazardous Art Materials Act are similar to the labeling requirements of the FHSA, of which it is a part. Therefore, third party testing to LHAMA is not required. An art material designed or intended primarily for children 12 years of age or younger would have to be tested by a third party laboratory to demonstrate compliance with CPSIA, but it would not require third party testing and certification to the LHAMA requirements. For the same reasons, no general conformity certificate is required for general use art materials.

(6) Books—The content of a book can determine its intended audience. Children's books have themes, vocabularies, illustrations, and covers that match the interests and cognitive capabilities of children 12 years of age or younger. The age guidelines provided by librarians, education professionals, and publishers may be dispositive for determining the intended audience. Some children's books have a wide appeal to the general public, and in those instances, further analysis may be necessary to assess who the primary intended audience is based on consideration of relevant additional factors, such as product design, packaging, marketing, and sales data.

(7) Science Equipment—Microscopes, telescopes, and other scientific equipment that would be used by an adult, as well as a child, are considered general use products. Equipment that is intended by the manufacturer for use primarily by adults, although there may be use by children through such programs, is a general use product. Toy versions of such items are considered children's products. If a distributor or retailer sells or rents a general use product in bulk through distribution channels that target children 12 years of age or younger in educational settings, such as schools or summer camps, this type of a distribution strategy would not necessarily convert a general use product into a children's product. However, if the product is packaged in such a manner that either expressly states or implies with graphics, themes, labeling, or instructions that the product is designed or intended primarily for children 12 years of age or younger, then it may be considered a children's product if the required consideration of all four statutory factors supports that determination. Products mainly intended for use by the instructor would not be considered children's products. In general, scientific equipment that is specifically sized for children, such as protective gear, eyewear, gloves, or aprons and/or has childish themes or decorations and invites use by a child 12 years of age or younger or is marketed to appeal primarily to children is considered a children's product.

(8) Sporting Goods and Recreational Equipment—Sporting goods that are intended primarily for consumers older than 12 years of age are considered general use items. Sporting equipment, sized for adults, are general use items even though some children 12 years of age or younger will use them. Unless such items are specifically marketed to children 12 years of age or younger, or have extra features that make them more suitable for children 12 years of age or younger than for adults, they would be considered general use products. If children 12 years or younger would mainly use the product because it would be too small or inappropriate for older children to use, then it likely would be considered a children's product. Likewise, recreational equipment, such as roller blades, skateboards, bicycles, camping gear, and fitness equipment are considered general use products unless they are sized to fit children 12 years of age or younger and/or are decorated with childish features by the manufacturer.

(9) Musical Instruments—Musical instruments, including electronically-aided instruments suited for an adult musician, are general use products. Instruments intended primarily for children can be distinguished from adult instruments by their size and marketing themes. The Commission notes that if a distributor or retailer sells or rents in bulk, a general use musical instrument through distribution channels that target children 12 years of age or younger in educational settings, such as schools or summer camps, this type of a distribution strategy would not necessarily convert a general use

product into a children's product. However, if the product is packaged in such a manner that either expressly states or implies with graphics, themes, labeling, or instructions that the product is designed or intended primarily for children 12 years of age or younger, then it may be considered a children's product if the required consideration of all four statutory factors supports that determination.

PART 1201—SAFETY STANDARD FOR ARCHITECTURAL GLAZING MATERIALS

Subpart A—The Standard

Subpart B [Reserved]

Subpart C—Statements of Policy and Interpretation

AUTHORITY: Secs. 2, 3, 7, 9, 14, 19, Pub. L. 92–573, 86 Stat. 1212–17; (15 U.S.C. 2051, 2052, 2056, 2058, 2063, 2068).

SOURCE: 42 FR 1441, Jan. 6, 1977, unless otherwise noted.

Subpart A—The Standard

§ 1201.1 Scope, application and findings.

(a) *Scope.* This part 1201, a consumer product safety standard, prescribes the safety requirements for glazing materials used or intended for use in any of the following architectural products:

(1) Storm doors or combination doors.

(2) Doors.

(3) Bathtub doors and enclosures.

(4) Shower doors and enclosures.

(5) [Reserved]

(6) Sliding glass doors (patio-type).

It also requires that these architectural products which incorporate glazing materials be constructed with glazing materials that meet the requirements of this part. The safety requirements are designed to reduce or eliminate unreasonable risks of death or serious injury to consumers when glazing material is broken by human contact.

(b) *Application.* This part 1201 shall apply to glazing materials, as that term is defined in § 1201.2(a)(11), for use in the architectural products listed in paragraph (a) of this section; and to those architectural products listed in paragraph (a) of this section if they are made with, or incorporate glazing materials as that term is defined in § 1201.2(a)(11). The standard applies to glazing materials and architectural products incorporating glazing materials that are produced or distributed for sale to or for the personal use, consumption or enjoyment of consumers in or around a permanent or temporary household or residence or in recreational, school, public, or other buildings or parts thereof. This part 1201 applies only to those glazing materials manufactured after the effective date of the standard; and to those architectural products identified in paragraph (a) of this section that are manufactured after the effective date of the standard. Thus, architectural products identified in paragraph (a) of this section manufactured after the effective date of the standard must incorporate glazing materials that comply with the standard. For purposes of this standard, fabricators are considered to be manufacturers of the architectural products listed in paragraph (a) of this section. Architectural glazing materials used in the products listed in paragraph (a) of this section and used in mobile homes are not subject to the provisions of this part 1201. While this part 1201 prescribes a test method to determine whether glazing materials subject to this part 1201 standard meet the requirements of the standard, the standard itself does not require that a manufacturer test any glazing materials or products subject to the standard. All obligations of manufacturers to perform testing are imposed by section 14 of the Consumer Product Safety Act and certification regulations which will be established by a separate rulemaking proceeding. However, the Commission intends to use the test procedures set forth in this part 1201 to determine whether materials and products subject to the standard meet the requirements of the standard.

(c) *Exemptions.* The following products, materials and uses are exempt from this part 1201:

(1) Wired glass used in doors or other assemblies to retard the passage of fire, where such door or assembly is required by a federal, state, local, or municipal fire ordinance.

(2) Louvers of jalousie doors;

(3) Openings in doors through which a 3 inch diameter sphere is unable to pass;

(4) Carved glass (as defined in § 1201.2(a)(36)), dalle glass (as defined in § 1201.2(a)(37)), or leaded glass (as defined in § 1201.2(a)(14)), which is used in doors and glazed panels (as defined in §§ 1201.2(a)(7) and (a)(10)) if the glazing material meets all of the following criteria:

(i) The coloring, texturing, or other design qualities or components of the glazing material cannot be removed without destroying the material; and

(ii) The primary purpose of such glazing is decorative or artistic; and

(iii) The glazing material is conspicuously colored or textured so as to be plainly visible and plainly identifiable as aesthetic or decorative rather than functional (other than for the purpose of admitting or controlliing admission of light components or heat and cold); and

(iv) The glazing material, or assembly into which it is incorporated, is divided into segments by conspicuous and plainly visible lines.

(5) Glazing materials used as curved glazed panels in revolving doors;

(6) Commercial refrigerated cabinet glazed doors.

(d) *Findings*[1]—(1) *The degree and nature of the risk of injury the rule is designed to eliminate or reduce.* The Commission finds that the nature of the risks of injury this standard is designed to eliminate or reduce are as follows:

(i) Lacerations, contusions, abrasions, and other injury or death resulting from walking or running into glazed doors or sliding glass doors believed to be open or glazed panels mistaken as a means of ingress or egress, or pushing against glazing material in doors or glazed panels in an attempt to open a door.

(ii) Lacerations, contusions, abrasions, and other injury or death resulting from accidentally falling into or through glazed doors, sliding glass doors, glazed panels, bathtub doors and enclosures and shower doors and enclosures.

(iii) Lacerations, contusions, abrasions, and other injury or death resulting from the act of installing, replacing, storing or otherwise manipulating glazing material in doors, sliding glass doors, glazed panels, bathtub doors and enclosures and shower doors and enclosures, or from broken glazing material in doors, sliding glass doors, glazed panels, bathtub doors and enclosures and shower doors and enclosures. The Commission estimates that 73,000 injuries associated with architectural glazing materials in the architectural products within the scope of this standard were treated in hospital emergency rooms during 1975, and that about 2,400 of these injuries required the patients to be hospitalized. Extrapolating to total injuries in the United States the Commission further estimates that approximately 190,000 injuries were associated with architectural glazing products covered by this standard. Although injuries occur at any age, children aged 14 and under appear to be at particular risk of injury since as a

---

[1] The Commission's findings apply to the architectural glazing standard as issued at 42 FR 1426, on January 6, 1977. Since that date, the Commission has revoked portions of the standard which prescribed requirements for "glazed panels" (45 FR 57383, August 28, 1980); an accelerated environmental durability test for plastic glazing materials intended for outdoor exposure (45 FR 66002, October 6, 1980); and a modulus of elasticity test, a hardness test, and an indoor aging test applicable to plastic glazing materials (47 FR 27856, June 28, 1982). However, the findings have not been revised and they are therefore, not fully applicable to the remaining requirements of the standard.

group they represent approximately half the injuries while comprising less than 30 percent of the population. Lacerations are the most common injuries associated with architectural glazing materials and account for 72 percent to 93 percent of the injuries associated with the architectural products identified in paragraph (a) of this section. These lacerative injuries span a broad spectrum of severity and extent of body part affected. During 1975, an estimated 200 injuries were treated in emergency rooms for lacerations over 25 to 50 percent of the victims' bodies and over 7,000 persons were treated for lacerations to the head or face. On the basis of all injury information available to the Commission, it is apparent that the severity of the injuries associated with architectural glazing materials ranges from minor cuts to damage to tendons, nerves, muscles, and blood vessels resulting in extensive surgery. Peripheral nerve injuries result in varying degres of loss in sensation and motion which may never be restored completely. Tendon and muscle injuries may involve loss of movement. Some victims of architectural glazing material incidents are disfigured, and sustain emotional trauma as well. Severing of arteries and veins has led to death. One way of quantifying the extent of the public health problem relating to injuries associated with products is to estimate the total number of disability days resulting from the injuries. Using average days of restricted activity by age for specific injuries and body parts (Vital and Health Statistics, Series 10, Number 57, National Center for Health Statistics, U.S. Department of Health, Education, and Welfare), it is estimated that about 230,000 days of restricted activity resulted from injuries associated with architectural products which were treated in emergency rooms alone.

(2) *The approximate number of consumer products, or types or classes thereof, subject to the standard.* The types of glazing materials affected by or subject to the standard are laminated glass, tempered glass, wired glass, organic-coated glass, annealed glass, and plastics. Architectural products that incorporate the aforementioned glazing materials that are also affected by or subject to the standard are: storm doors or combination doors, doors, bathtub doors, and enclosures, shower doors and enclosures, glazed panels and sliding glass doors (patio-type) (see paragraph (a) of this section). The Commission has estimated that 13 to 16 percent of the total market for glazing material incorporated in products within the scope of the standard will be affected by the standard. Most of the glazing subject to the standard is currently covered by state safety glazing legislation. To date, more than 30 states have enacted safety glazing legislation, but this legislation is neither consistent nor completely uniform among states. Annual markets for the architectural products which incorporate glazing material and that are within the scope of the standard have been estimated by the Commission in terms of square feet of glazed area and number of units. The market for glazing material incorporated in products within the scope of the standard was estimated to be 234.8 million square feet in 1975. These figures are discussed in the Economic Impact Statement, pp. 3–7, and appendix A to the Economic Impact Statement, pp. 18–30, which are available for review in the Office of the Secretary of the Commission, Washington, D.C. 20207.

(3) *The need of the public for the architectural glazing material and products incorporating that glazing material subject to the standard, and the probable effect of the standard upon the utility, cost or availability of those products to meet the need of the public*—(i) *The need of the public for the architectural glazing materials and products incorporating that glazing material.* The need of the public for architectural products within the scope of the standard incorporating glazing material is substantial since these products serve such functions as transmission of light, visual communication, protection from weather, ventilation, and indoor climate control, and since reasonable substitutes for these products do not exist as a group. Each of the types of glazing material subject to the standard has individual properties which meet public needs, although one type of glazing material is often an acceptable substitute for another.

(ii) *Probable effect of the standard upon the cost of architectural glazing materials and architectural products incorporating the glazing material to meet the need of the public for the products.* The probable cost effects of the standard for architectural glazing materials are listed below.

(A) The cost impact of the standard on consumers will be concentrated in those states with no present state safety glazing legislation. In those states, the average increase in cost per housing start resulting from the standard is estimated to range from $30 to $50, or approximately one-tenth of one percent of the price of a typical new house; and the cost for residential remodeling and replacement is expected to be in the range of $0.25 to $0.30 per household annually.

(B) The increased cost of glazing material for nonresidential uses will be paid ultimately by consumers through higher prices of goods and services. Generally, the increased cost of glazing is not passed to consumers immediately, but is spread over the life of the nonresidential structure. Therefore, the increased cost to consumers for glazing material in nonresidential structures will probably rise slowly over time to an annual level of approximately $1.10 per household in states with no safety glazing legislation and $0.20 to $0.50 per household in the other states. In many of the states with state regulations, the impact of the standard on residential construction and new housing prices will be near zero, since most of the glazing is currently covered by the state glazing legislation.

(C) The probable effect of the standard on the various glazing materials within the scope of the standard will differ. The retail price of laminated glass used in some Category II applications will probably increase by 10 to 15 percent per square foot. The incremental cost to consumers for ungraded laminated glass is estimated to be approximately $0.14 per household, annually. The cost to consumers for tempered glass, organic-coated glass, and plastics is not expected to increase because of the standard. Information available to the Commission indicates that the technology needed for producing wired glass which can comply with the standard is not readily available. See appendix A of the Economic Impact Statement, pp. 45–56, for the incremental cost calculation by product category and application.

(iii) *Probable effect of the standard upon the utility of architectural glazing materials and architectural products incorporating the glazing materials to meet the need of the public for the products.* The probable effect of the standard in regard to the utility of architectural glazing materials and the architectural products incorporating glazing material should be to increase the utility of the products. The basic effect of the standard would be the substitution of certain safer glazing materials for annealed glass in certain architectural products. The Commission believes that such a substitution would increase utility for most consumers because of the usually increased durability of the glazing material that complies with the Commission's standard, and the knowledge that the product incorporating the glazing material is safer. There will be disutility for those consumers who prefer non-complying wired glass and organic-coated glass when these materials become unavailable for certain applications due to their likely inability to comply with the standard. However, the share of the glazing material market claimed by organic-coated and wired glass is small.

(iv) *Probable effect of the standard upon the availability of architectural glazing materials and architectural products incorporating the glazing materials to meet the need of the public for the products.* The Commission finds that the proposed standard should not have impacts of significant magnitude on the availability of architectural products within the scope of the standard, since domestic production capacity appears to be sufficient to handle any increased demand for glazing material to be used in those products. In addition, an increased demand for raw materials necessary to manufacture glazing materials that comply with the standard will be small in comparison to the volume of raw materials currently used for glazing for the products that will be subject to the standard. Furthermore, no major change in demand for the architectural products subject to the standard incorporating glazing materials which would affect production is expected. The Commission finds that, in the absence of technological advances, certain glazing materials will no longer be available for particular applications. Unless technological advances are made, wired glass will be unavailable for use in the architectural products within the scope of the standard with the exception of fire door applications where special provisions of the standard apply. Similarly, organic-coated glass which has the film applied to annealed glass at the factory may no longer be available for Category II products due to an inability to pass those impact test provisions of the standard. The availability of glass replacement glazing in residential applications may be reduced, since plastic glazing often will be the only economical material available to consumers when immediate replacement is needed.

(4) *Any means of achieving the objectives of the standard while minimizing adverse effects on competition or disruption or dislocation of manufacturing and other commercial practices consistent with the public health and safety.* The Commission has considered other means of achieving the objective of the standard, but has found none that it believes would have fewer adverse effects on competition or that would cause less disruption or dislocation of manufacturing and other commercial practices, consistent with the public health and safety. For the glazing industry in general, the disruptions and dislocations of existing manufacturing and commercial practices due to the standard are expected to be minor. However, it is possible that individual segments of the glazing materials industry are likely to be adversely affected by the standard. Specifically, there is likely to be disruption to the wired glass market, the organic-coated glass market and, to a lesser extent, to the laminated glass market. Manufacturers of wired glass will face a serious problem because technological improvements in the product will need to be made before wired glass can be used in Category I applications and because it probably will not be usable at all in Category II applications (see § 1201.2(a) (3) and (4) of the standard), since there appears to be little prospect at this time of developing a wired glass product capable of withstanding the Category II, 400 foot pound impact test prescribed in § 1201.4 of the standard. Laminated glass currently used for Category I applications can meet the 150 foot pound impact test requirements, but not all laminated glass currently used for Category II applications can meet the 400 foot pound impact test requirements. The price increase for technologically upgrading laminated glass will be borne by consumers. The Commission believes, however, that the competitive impact of the proposed changes would not severely weaken the position of laminated glass in the market place. The wired glass, organic-coated glass, and laminated glass markets affected by the standard are small in relation to the entire industry. The standard is not expected to have an appreciable impact on foreign or domestic competition. Increased competition is expected between primary glass temperers and regional temperers, with primary temperers taking an increased share of the original storm door, sliding door, bathtub enclosure and shower door markets. Sales of nonresidential glazing for major nonresidential buildings will remain with the primary glass companies. The regional temperers are expected to handle almost all the tempering of glazing for smaller nonresidential buildings. Thus, they will gain some of this market at the expense of local dealers and distributors. However, the distributors and dealers probably will operate as order takers for the smallest jobs. It is expected that glazing distributors and dealers will experience reduced market shares in both the residential and nonresidential new glazing markets. This will occur as a result of the transfer of business to the primary glass manufacturers and regional temperers, since tempered glass must be produced to size and it is not feasible to keep in inventory all sizes which might be needed.

(5) *Summary finding.* The Commission finds that there are unreasonable risks of injury associated with architectural glazing materials used in the architectural products listed in paragraph (a)

of this section. In assessing the question of whether unreasonable risks of injury or injury potential are associated with architectural glazing materials, the Commission has balanced the degree, nature and frequency of injury against the potential effect of the standard on the ability of architectural glazing materials to meet the need of the public and the effect of the standard on the cost, utility, and availability of architectural glazing materials to meet that need. The Commission finds that this standard, including its effective date, is reasonably necessary to eliminate or reduce the unreasonable risks of injury associated with architectural glazing materials and that promulgation of the standard is in the public interest.

(Sec. 9(e), Pub. L. 92–573, 86 Stat. 1215 (15 U.S.C. 2058(e)) (5 U.S.C. 553)

[42 FR 1441, Jan. 6, 1977, as amended at 43 FR 57246 Dec. 7, 1978; 45 FR 57389, Aug. 28, 1980; 47 FR 27856, June 28, 1982; 49 FR 7107, Feb. 27, 1984]

§ 1201.2 Definitions.

(a) As used in this part 1201:

(1) *Annealed glass* means glass that has been subjected to a slow, controlled cooling process during manufacture to control residual stresses so that it can be cut or subjected to other fabrication. Regular polished plate, float, sheet, rolled, and some patterned surface glasses are examples of annealed glass.

(2) *Bathtub doors and enclosures* means assemblies of panels and/or doors that are installed on the lip of or immediately surrounding a bathtub.

(3) *Category I products* means any of the following architectural products:

(i) Storm doors or combination doors that contain no single piece of glazing material greater than 9 square feet (0.83 square meters) in surface area of one side of the piece of glazing material.

(ii) Doors that contain no single piece of glazing material greater than 9 square feet (0.83 square meters) in surface area of one side of the piece of glazing material.

(4) *Category II products* means any of the following architectural products:

(i) Shower doors and enclosures.

(ii) Bathtub doors and enclosures.

(iii) Sliding glass doors (patio type).

(iv) Storm doors or combination doors that contain any piece of glazing material greater than 9 square feet (0.83 square meters) in surface area of one side of the piece of glazing material.

(v) Doors that contain any piece of glazing material greater than 9 square feet (0.83 square meters) in surface area of one side of the piece of glazing material.

(5) *Distributor* means a person to whom a consumer product is delivered or sold for purposes of distribution in commerce, including persons cutting glazing material to size, except that such term does not include a manufacturer or retailer of such product.

(6) *Distribution in commerce* means to sell in commerce, to introduce or deliver for introduction into commerce, or to hold for sale or distribution after introduction into commerce.

(7) *Door* means an assembly that is installed in an interior or exterior wall; that is movable in a sliding, pivoting, hinged, or revolving manner of movement; and that is used by consumers to produce or close off an opening for use as a means of human passage.

(8) *Fabricator* means any person who assembles or otherwise incorporates glazing materials into an architectural product listed in § 1201.1(a). A fabricator is considered a manufacturer as defined in paragraph (a)(16) of this section.

(9) *Glass* means a hard, brittle, amorphous substance produced by fusion, usually consisting of mutually dissolved silica and silicates that also contains sods and lime. It may be transparent, translucent, or opaque.

(10) [Reserved]

(11) *Glazing material* means glass, including annealed glass, organic coated glass, tempered glass, laminated glass, wired glass; or combinations thereof where these are used:

(i) In openings through the architectural products listed in § 1201.1(a), or

(ii) As the architectural products themselves, e.g. unframed doors.

(12) *Jalousie door* means a door (as "door" is defined in paragraph (a)(7) of this section) having an opening glazed with operable, overlapping louvers.

Each louver is one of a series of overlapping pieces of glazing material designed to admit ventilation and light but exclude rain and is typically operated by a crank and gear mechanism.

(13) *Laminated glass* means glazing material composed of two or more pieces of glass, each piece being either tempered glass, heat strengthened glass, annealed glass or wired glass, bonded to an intervening layer or layers of resilient plastic material.

(14) *Leaded glass* means a decorative composite glazing material made of individual pieces of glass whose perimeter is enclosed by lengths of durable metal such as lead or zinc and the pieces of glass are completely held together and supported by such metal. Such pieces of glass can be clear, colored, beveled, painted, or flashed and etched.

(15) *Manufacture* means to manufacture, produce or assemble.

(16) *Manufacturer* means any person who manufactures, fabricates or imports a glazing material or architectural product listed in § 1201.1(a) that incorporates glazing material.

(17) *Mirror* means a treated, polished or smooth glazing material that forms images by the reflection of light.

(18) *Mobile home* means a structure transportable in one or more sections, which is eight body feet (2.4 body meters) or more in width and is thirty-two body feet (9.7 body meters) or more in length, and which is built on a permanent chassis and designed to be used as a dwelling with or without a permanent foundation when connected to the required utilities.

(19) *Other buildings or parts thereof* means buildings or parts thereof (other than residential, school, public, or recreational buildings) in which all or part of the building is open to the public with or without specific invitation. Included are buildings or parts thereof such as banks and recreational or retail facilities in a building and multiuse buildings that contain residential units.

(20) *Organic-coated glass* means a glazing material consisting of a piece of glass, coated and bonded on one or both sides with an applied polymeric coating, sheeting, or film.

(21) *Patio door* (See "sliding glass doors (patio-type)" in paragraph (a)(31) of this section).

(22) *Permanent label* means a label that will remain permanently legible and visible after installation of the glazing material and that would be destroyed in attempts to remove it from the glazing material and includes (but is not limited to) sandblast, acid etch, hot-stamp, and destructible polyester labels.

(23) [Reserved]

(24) *Private labeler* means an owner of a brand or trademark on the label of a consumer product which bears a private label, and includes any fabricator, distributor, or installer who cuts certified and permanently labeled glazing materials into smaller pieces.

(25) *Public building* means a building of public assembly or meeting including (but not limited to) a museum, place of worship, or restaurant.

(26) *Recreational building* means a building used for recreational purposes including (but not limited to) a theater, stadium, gymnasium, amusement park building or library.

(27) *Residential building* means a building, permanent or temporary, such as a single or multifamily residence, including (but not limited to) a house, apartment building, lodging home, dormitory, hotel, motel, hospital, sanitarium, and nursing home, used as a dwelling for one or more persons or families and any structure which is attached to, a part of, or appurtenant to such a building. Public areas of all residential buildings, such as lobbies and other common facilities, are included within the definition of "other buildings or parts thereof" in paragraph (a)(19) of this section. For purposes of this part 1201, a mobile home as defined in paragraph (a)(18) of this section is not considered to be a residential building.

(28) *Retailer* means a person to whom a consumer product is delivered or sold for purposes of sale or distribution by such person to a consumer; the term retailer includes a person who cuts glazing material to size for consumers.

(29) *School building* means a building designed primarily for the conduct of educational instruction and includes

the classrooms, libraries, administrative offices, auditoriums, eating and sanitary facilities, stadiums, gymnasiums and all other structures associated with such buildings.

(30) *Shower door and enclosure* means an assembly of one or more panels installed to form all or part of the wall and or door of a shower stall.

(31) *Sliding glass door (patio-type)* means an assembly of one or more panels, at least one of which is suitably movable for use as a means of human ingress or egress. The term includes the nonmovable and movable panels of such assembly.

(32) *Storm door (or combination door)* means a movable assembly, used in tandem with an exterior door to protect the exterior door against weather elements and/or to improve indoor climate control.

(33) *Tempered glass* means a piece of specially heat treated or chemically treated glass that cannot be cut, drilled, ground, or polished after treatment without fracture. When fractured at any point, if highly tempered, the entire piece breaks into small particles.

(34) *Wired glass* means a single piece of annealed glass that contains wire embedded in the body of the glass.

(35) *Commission* means the Consumer Product Safety Commission.

(36) *Carved glass* means a decoration glazing material in which a permanent visible design has been produced by polishing, grinding, or otherwise removing portions of the surface.

(37) *Dalle glass* or dalle de verre (including faceted glass) means a decorative composite glazing material made of individual pieces of glass which are imbedded in a cast matrix of concrete or epoxy.

(b) Definitions given in the Consumer Product Safety Act, and not repeated in this section, are applicable to this part.

(c) Test methods and recommended practices published by the American Society for Testing and Materials (ASTM)[1], and referred to in this part 1201, are hereby incorporated by reference into this part.

(d) Test methods and recommended practices published by the American National Standards Institute (ANSI) and referred to in this part 1201, are hereby incorporated by reference into this part.

(Sec. 9(e), Pub. L. 92–573, 86 Stat. 1215; (15 U.S.C. 2058(e); (5 U.S.C. 553))

[42 FR 1441, Jan. 6, 1977, as amended at 42 FR 61860, Dec. 7, 1977; 43 FR 50422, Oct. 30, 1978; 43 FR 57247, Dec. 7, 1978; 45 FR 57389, Aug. 28, 1980; 47 FR 27856, June 28, 1982]

§ 1201.3 General requirements.

(a) All glazing materials to which this standard applies, as described in § 1201.1, shall meet the impact and environmental test requirements in § 1201.4, and shall be labeled by manufacturers in accordance with § 1201.5.

(b) Glazing materials used in architectural products not listed in § 1201.1(a) are not subject to this part. Any material not listed in the definition of "glazing material" in § 1201.2(a)(11) is not subject to this part 1201.

[42 FR 1441, Jan. 6, 1977, as amended at 47 FR 27856, June 28, 1982]

§ 1201.4 Test procedures.

(a) *Types of tests*—(1) *Impact test*. Specimens shall be struck as prescribed by paragraph (d)(1) of this section using equipment specified by paragraphs (b) (1) and (2) of this section. Results of the impact test are to be interpreted in accordance with paragraph (e)(1) of this section. The test specimens shall be selected in accordance with paragraphs (c) (1) and (2) of this section.

(2) *Accelerated environmental durability tests*. Each specimen of glazing material subject to this part 1201 shall be tested in accordance with the accelerated tests referenced in table 1, "Accelerated Tests" of this section. However, tempered glass, wired glass, and annealed glass are not required to be subjected to the accelerated environmental durability tests.

[1] ASTM test methods and recommended practices are approved by, published by, and available for purchase from the American Society for Testing and Materials, 1916 Race Street, Philadelphia, Pennsylvania 19103.

TABLE 1—ACCELERATED TEST (APPLICABLE PARAGRAPHS)

Glazing materials	Specimen	Test equipment	Exposure	Criteria for passing
Laminated glass	§ 1201.4(c)(1) and (c)(3)(i)	§ 1201.4(b)(3)(i)	§ 1201.4(d)(2)(i)	§ 1201.4(e)(2)(i)
Organic coated glass	§ 1201.4(c)(1) and (c)(3)(ii)(B)	§ 1201.4(b)(3)(ii)	§ 1201.4(d)(2)(ii)(B)	§ 1201.4(e)(2)(ii)(B)
Tempered glass	Exempt			
Wired glass	Exempt			
Annealed glass	Exempt			

(3) Separate testing is required for different glazing materials or for differences within a type of glazing material that could noticeably affect performance in the impact or environmental durability tests. Such differences could include (but are not limited to): Nominal thickness or thicknesses, method of manufacture (in appropriate cases), types and amounts of additives, and composition of base materials and adhesives.

(b) *Test equipment*—(1) *Impact test frame and subframe.* (See figures 1, 2, 3, and 4.) (i) The impact test frame shall be constructed to minimize movement and deflection of its members during testing. For this purpose, the structural framing and bracing members shall be steel angles 3 inches by 5 inches by ¼ inch (7.7 centimeters by 12.7 centimeters by 0.7 centimeters) or other sections and materials of equal or greater rigidity.

(ii) The structural framing shall be welded or securely bolted at the corners and braced by one of the alternate methods shown in figure 1 and shall be securely bolted to the floor.

(iii) The inner subframe (see figures 2, 3, and 4) for securing the test specimen on all four edges shall be reinforced at each corner. The material is shown as wood in figure 3, but other materials may be used: *Provided,* The test specimen will contact only the neoprene strips, which shall have a shore A durometer hardness of 30 to 50.

(iv) Any reasonable means may be used to secure the subframe to the test frame so long as the mounting is secure and the pressure on the glazing in the subframe is not significantly altered when the subframe is removed.

(v) Pressures on the test specimen shall be controlled, and the compression of the neoprene strips shall be between 10 and 15 percent of the original thickness of the neoprene. Securing methods such as wing bolts and clamps shall be uniformly spaced no greater than 18 inches (45 centimeters) apart with no fewer than two on any edge. To limit the compression of the neoprene and prevent distortion of the subframe, metal shims of an appropriate thickness shall be used as shown in figures 3 and 4.

(2) *Impactor.* (i) The impactor shall be a leather punching bag as shown in figure 5 on this section. The bag shall be filled with No. 7½ chilled lead shot to a total weight of completed assembly as shown in figure 5, of 100 pounds ±4 ounces (45.36±0.11 kilograms). The rubber bladder shall be left in place and filled through a hole cut into the upper part. After filling the rubber bladder, the top should be either twisted around the threaded metal rod below the metal sleeve or pulled over the metal sleeve and tied with a cord or leather thong. Note that the hanging strap must be removed. The bag should be laced in the normal manner. The exterior of the bag shall be completely covered by ½ inch (1.3 centimeters) wide glass filament reinforced pressure sensitive tape. (Figure 5.)

(ii) Provisions shall be made for raising the impactor or to drop heights of up to 48 inches (1.22 meters). At its release it shall have been supported so that the rod going through its center was in line with the steel support cable in a manner designed to minimize wobble or oscillation after its release.

(3) *Environmental durability test equipment*—(i) *Boil test.* Two containers of water shall be provided with means to maintain one at 150° ±5 °F (66° ±2 °C) and the second at a slow boil at atmospheric pressure. The containers shall be large enough to accept a rack holding three specimens, each 12 inches (30 centimeters) square, of the glazing material in a vertical position. The rack shall be positioned so that each specimen is surrounded by at least one inch (2.5 centimeters) of water.

(ii) *Simulated weathering test.* The equipment shall be a xenon arc (water-cooled) Weather-Ometer employing a lamp rated at 6500 watts and automatic light monitoring and control systems. Borosilicate inner and outer filters shall be used. An appropriate water spray cycle shall be used. Operating procedures shall be in accordance with ASTM G 26–70, "Standard Recommended Practice for Operating Light—and Water-Exposure Apparatus (Xenon-Arc Type) for Exposure of Nonmetallic Materials," April 13, 1970, as augmented for plastics by ASTM D 2565–70, "Standard Recommended Practice for Operating Xenon-Arc Type (Water-Cooled) Light- and Water-Exposure Apparatus for Exposure of Plastics," Procedure B, June 12, 1970, which are incorporated by reference. Copies of both documents are available from the American Society for Testing and Materials, 1916 Race Street, Philadelphia, Pennsylvania 19103. They are also available for inspection at the National Archives and Records Administration (NARA). For information on the availability of this material at NARA, call 202–741–6030, or go to: *http://www.archives.gov/federal_register/code_of_federal_regulations/ibr_locations.html.* This incorporation by reference was approved by the Director of the Federal Register. These materials are incorporated as they exist in the edition which has been approved by the Director of the Federal Register and which has been filed with the Office of the Federal Register.

(c) *Test specimens*—(1) *Condition of specimens.* All specimens shall be tested as supplied by the manufacturer, following removal of any temporary protective masking materials. No tests shall be commenced before the specimens have been stored in the laboratory for 4 hours. Specimens shall be arranged to permit free circulation of air to all surfaces during this period.

(2) *Impact specimens.* Impact specimens shall be of the largest size manufactured up to a maximum width of 34 inches (86 centimeters) and a maximum height of 76 inches (1.9 meters). Specimens shall be tested for each nominal thickness offered by the manufacturer.

(3) *Environmental durability specimens*—(i) *Boil test.* Three pieces 12 inches by 12 inches (30 centimeters by 30 centimeters) with nominal thickness identical to those submitted for the impact test shall be used.

(ii) *Weathering tests*—(A) [Reserved]

(B) *Organic-coated glass*—(*1*) *Orientation specified.* Six organic-coated glass specimens 2 inches by 6 inches (5 centimeters by 15 centimeters) by nominal thickness identical to those submitted for the impact test shall be used.

(*2*) *Orientation unspecified.* Nine organic-coated glass specimens, 2 inches by 6 inches (5 centimeters by 15 centimeters) by nominal thickness identical to those submitted for the impact test shall be used except that when the glazing material is symmetric across its thickness, six specimens may be used.

(iii) *Indoor service.* Four additional samples identical to those submitted for the impact test.

(d) *Test procedures*—(1) *Impact test procedure.* Each specimen shall be struck within 2 inches (5 centimeters) of its geometric center with the impactor dropped from a single height, designated according to the product category. Specimens for Category I shall be impacted one time from a drop height of 18 to 18½ inches (458 to 470 millimeters). Specimens for Category II shall be impacted one time from drop height of 48 to 48½ inches (1.22 to 1.23 meters). For all specimens that are not symmetric from surface to surface, an equal number of specimens shall be impacted on each side. For glazing materials which will be evaluated by paragraph (e)(1)(iii) of this section, this impact test procedure is not required.

(2) *Environmental durability test procedures*—(i) *Boil test.* The specimens shall be immersed in the 150 F (66 °C) water for 3 minutes. They shall then be quickly removed and immersed in the boiling water and left there for 2 hours. The specimens shall then be removed, cooled, and dried for examination as specified in paragraph (e)(2)(i) of this section.

(ii) *Accelerated weathering test.* The specimens shall be retained in the Weather-Ometer (paragraph (b)(3)(ii) of this section) for a period of 1200±1 hours, and exposed to a radiant flux of 50 microwatts per square centimeter

(12 calories per second per square centimeter) while monitoring at a wavelength of 340 nanometers.

(A) [Reserved]

(B) *Organic-coated glass*—(*1*) *Orientation specified.* Three specimens shall be mounted with the surface that is intended to be oriented indoors faced away from the radiation source; the other three specimens shall be kept in darkness at 73 °F (23 °C) for use as controls. Materials so tested shall be labeled according to § 1201.5(c) of this part 1201.

(*2*) *Orientation unspecified.* Three specimens shall be mounted with one of the surfaces toward the radiation; three specimens shall be mounted with the other surface toward the radiation, and three specimens shall be kept in darkness at 73 °F (23 °C) for use as controls. When the glazing material is symmetric across its thickness, three specimens shall be irradiated.

(e) *Interpretation of results*—(1) *Impact test.* A glazing material may be qualified for use in both Category I and Category II products if it meets the impact requirements for Category II. A glazing material shall be judged to pass the impact test if the specimen tested meets any one of the criteria listed in paragraphs (e)(1) (i) through (v) of this section:

(i) When breakage occurs (numerous cracks and fissures may occur) no opening shall develop in the test sample through which a 3 inch (76 millimeter) diameter solid steel sphere, weighing 4 pounds ±3 oz (1.81±0.08 kilograms), passes when placed (not dropped) in the opening and permitted to remain for a period of one second. For this criterion, the sample after being impacted shall be placed, while remaining in the subframe, in a horizontal, impact side up position with a minimum of one foot (31 centimeters) of free space immediately beneath the specimen.

(ii) When breakage occurs, what appear to be the 10 largest particles shall be selected within 5 minutes subsequent to the test and shall weigh no more than the equivalent weight of 10 square inches (64 square centimeters) of the original specimen. For the purposes of this section *particle* means a portion of a broken test specimen which is determined by identifying the smallest possible perimeter around all points in the portion of the broken test specimen, always passing along cracks or exposed surfaces.

(iii) [Reserved]

(iv) The specimen does not remain within the subframe and no breakage is caused by the impactor.

(v) The specimen does not break.

(2) *Environmental durability tests*— (i) *Boil test.* The glass itself may crack in this test, but no bubbles or other defects shall develop more than ½ inch (12 millimeters) from the outer edge of the specimen or from any crack that may develop. Any specimen in which the glass cracks to an extent that confuses the interpretation of the results shall be discarded, and another specimen shall be tested in its stead.

(ii) *Accelerated weathering test*—(A) [Reserved]

(B) *Organic-coated glass.* Specimens shall be judged satisfactory if they pass both the adhesion test and the tensile test described below in paragraph (e)(ii)(B) (*1*) and (*2*) of this section.

(*1*) *Adhesion test* (*organic-coated glass only*)—(*i*) *Specimens.* The specimens for this test are the 2 inch by 6 inch (5 centimeters by 15 centimeters) weathered specimens and the control specimens. The specimens shall be conditioned just prior to the performance of the adhesion test at 73° ±6 °F (23° ±3 °C) and 50±5 percent relative humidity for 24 hours.

(*ii*) *Apparatus.* The test apparatus shall consist of a constant-rate-of-extension-type (CRE) tensile tester with the moving crosshead set to move at 12 inches per minute (5 millimeters per second) and load range such that the average pull force will fall at 30 to 50 percent of full scale. A cutter shall be used containing new razor blades for cutting 1 inch (25 millimeter) wide specimens of the organic coating on the glass. The razor blades shall be used one time only.

(*iii*) *Procedure.* Using the razor cutter, cut a straight, 1 inch (25 millimeter) wide strip of the organic coating in the lengthwise direction of the glass specimen along and within ¼ inch (6 millimeters) of one edge. Peel back, cleanly and evenly, about 2 inches (50 millimeters) of one end of the 1 inch (25 millimeters) wide organic strip. Attach a strip of reinforced pressure sensitive tape to the side of the organic strip opposite the adhesive, to extend this free end to about 8 inches (200 millimeters) in length. Place the end of the glass panel from which the organic strip was removed in the lower clamp of the tensile tester and the free end of the tape in the upper clamp. Peel the remainder of the organic strip from the glass mechanically and obtain a record of the pull force value. Determine and record the average pull force value for each specimen from the chart. Weathered and control specimens are to be tested alternately.

(*iv*) *Interpretation of results.* The organic-coated glass adhesion shall be judged satisfactory if the average pull force for the weathered specimens is no less than 90 percent of the average pull force for the control specimens.

(*2*) *Tensile strength test* (*organic-coated glass only*). (*i*) The specimens for this test are the same 2 inch by 6 inch (5 centimeter by 15 centimeter) specimens used in the adhesion test.

(*ii*) *Apparatus.* The CRE tensile tester shall be used with the moving crosshead set to move at 2 inches per minute (0.8 millimeter per second) and the load range such that the specimens will break at 30 to 60% of full scale. A cutter shall be used containing new razor blades for cutting ½ inch (12 millimeter) wide specimens of the organic coating on the glass. The razor blades shall be used one time only.

(*iii*) *Procedure.* Using the ½ inch (12 millimeter) razor cutter, cut a straight strip of the organic coating in the lengthwise direction of the glass specimen for the full 6 inch (15 centimeter) length. Carefully peel this strip from the glass panel and test it for breaking strength in the tensile tester.

(*iv*) *Interpretation of results.* The organic coating tensile strength shall be judged satisfactory if the average tensile value of the weathered specimens is no less than 75 percent of the average of the control specimens. Weathered and control specimens are to be tested alternately.

(Sec. 9(e) Pub. L. 92–573, 86 Stat. 1215; (15 U.S.C. 2058(e)); (5 U.S.C. 553); sec. 9(h), Consumer Product Safety Act, as amended by the Consumer Product Safety Amendments of 1981 (Pub. L. 92–673, as amended by Pub. L. 97–35, 15 U.S.C. 2057(h)) and 5 U.S.C. 553)

[42 FR 1441, Jan. 6, 1977, as amended at 43 FR 43708, Sept. 27, 1978; 43 FR 57594, Dec. 8, 1978; 45 FR 66007, Oct. 6, 1980; 46 FR 63250, Dec. 31, 1981; 47 FR 27857, June 28, 1982]

§ 1201.5 Certification and labeling requirements.

(a) Manufacturers and private labelers of glazing materials covered by this part 1201 shall comply with the requirements of section 14 CPSA (15 U.S.C. 2063) and regulations issued under section 14.

(b) [Reserved]

(c) Organic-coated glass that has been tested for environmental exposure from one side only must bear a permanent label on the coating stating "GLAZE THIS SIDE IN" and shall bear in the central 50 percent of the surface area the following message in letters at least ¼ inch (7 millimeters) high: "SEE PERMANENT LABEL FOR IMPORTANT MOUNTING INSTRUCTION." The latter message shall be attached to either side of the glazing by any means which shall ensure the message will remain in place until installation.

[42 FR 1441, Jan. 6, 1977, as amended at 45 FR 66007, Oct. 6, 1980]

§ 1201.6 Prohibited stockpiling.

(a) *Stockpiling.* For the purposes of this section, the term *stockpiling* means manufacturing or importing the affected products between the date of issuance of this part in the FEDERAL REGISTER and the effective date set out below in § 1201.7 at a rate significantly greater (prescribed in paragraph (b) of this section) than the rate at which the affected products were produced or imported during a base period (prescribed in paragraph (c)(2) of this section).

(b) *Prohibited acts.* Manufacturers and importers of glazing materials, fabricators, and manufacturers or importers of architectural products specified in § 1201.1(a) who incorporate glazing material shall not incorporate glazing materials which do not comply with the requirements of this part 1201 into such products between the date of issuance of this part in the FEDERAL REGISTER and the effective date set out in § 1201.7 below at a rate greater than the rate of production or importation during the base period (defined in paragraph (c)(2) of this section) plus ten percent. For wired glass used in doors or other assemblies subject to this part 1201 and intended to retard the passage of fire, when such doors or other assemblies are required by a Federal, State, local or municipal fire ordinance, the rate of production during the base period may be increased annually by no more than 10 percent.

(c) *Definitions.* As used in this section:

(1) *Rate of production (or importation)* means the total number of affected architectural products incorporating glazing material not complying with this part manufactured or imported during a stated base period.

(2) *Base period* means, at the option of the manufacturer or importer, any period of 180 consecutive days prior to January 6, 1977, said period to be selected within an interval which begins July 6, 1975.

§ 1201.7 Effective date.

The effective date of this part 1201 shall be July 6, 1977 except:

(a) For glazing materials used in doors or other assemblies subject to this part and intended to retard the passage of fire when such doors or other assemblies are required by a Federal, State, or local or municipal fire ordinance, the effective date shall be January 6, 1980.

(b) Architectural glazing materials manufactured before July 6, 1977 may be incorporated into architectural products listed in § 1201.1(a) through July 5, 1978 if:

(1) The architectural glazing material conforms to ANSI Standard Z97.1–1972 or 1975, "Performance Specifications and Methods of Test for Safety Glazing Material Used in Buildings," 1972 or 1975[2], which is incorporated by reference, and

(2) The architectural glazing material is permanently labeled to indicate it conforms to ANSI Z97.1–1972 or 1975 or is accompanied by a certificate certifying conformance to ANSI Z97.1 1972 or 1975.

(c) Tempered glass manufactured before July 6, 1977 may be incorporated into architectural products listed in § 1201.1(a) through July 5, 1981 if:

(1) The tempered glass conforms to ANSI Z97.1–1972 or 1975; and

(2) The tempered glass is permanently labeled to indicate it conforms to ANSI Z97.1–1972 or 1975 or is accompanied by a certificate certifying conformance to ANSI Z97.1–1972 or 1975.

(d) Laminated glass manufactured on or after July 6, 1977 through December 3, 1977 may be incorporated into category II products as defined in § 1201.2(a)(4) through July 5, 1978 if:

(1) The laminated glass conforms to ANSI Z97.1–1972 or 1975; and

(2) The laminated glass is permanently labeled to indicate that it conforms to ANSI Z97.1–1972 or 1975 or is accompanied by a certificate in accordance with section 14(a) of the CPSA certifying conformance to ANSI Z97.1–1972 or 1975.

(e) Architectural products manufactured between July 6, 1977 and July 5, 1978 incorporating glazing material in accordance with paragraph (b) of this section, may be distributed and sold without restriction.

(f) Architectural products manufactured between July 6, 1977 and July 5, 1981 incorporating tempered glass in accordance with paragraph (c) of this section, may be distributed and sold without restriction.

(g) Architectural products identified in § 1201.2(a)(4) manufactured between

---

[2] Copies of ANSI Standard Z97.1–1972 or 1975 are available from the American National Standards Institute, 1430 Broadway, New York, New York 10018. They are also available for inspection at the National Archives and Records Administration (NARA). For information on the availability of this material at NARA, call 202–741–6030, or go to: *http://www.archives.gov/federal_register/code_of_federal_regulations/ibr_locations.html.* This incorporation by reference was approved by the Director of the Federal Register. These materials are incorporated as they exist in the editions which have been approved by the Director of the Federal Register and which have been filed with the Office of the Federal Register.

July 6, 1977 and July 5, 1978 incorporating laminated glass in accordance with § 1201.7(d) may be distributed and sold without restriction.

(h) Patinaed glass manufactured between July 6, 1977 and January 8, 1979, in accordance with the Commission's stay order published in the FEDERAL REGISTER of August 9, 1977 (42 FR 40188), may be sold without restriction. Architectural products incorporating such glazing may also be sold without restriction.

[43 FR 50422, Oct. 30, 1978, as amended at 43 FR 57247, Dec. 7, 1978; 46 FR 63250, Dec. 31, 1981]

FIGURE 1 TO SUBPART A OF PART 1201—GLASS IMPACT TEST STRUCTURE

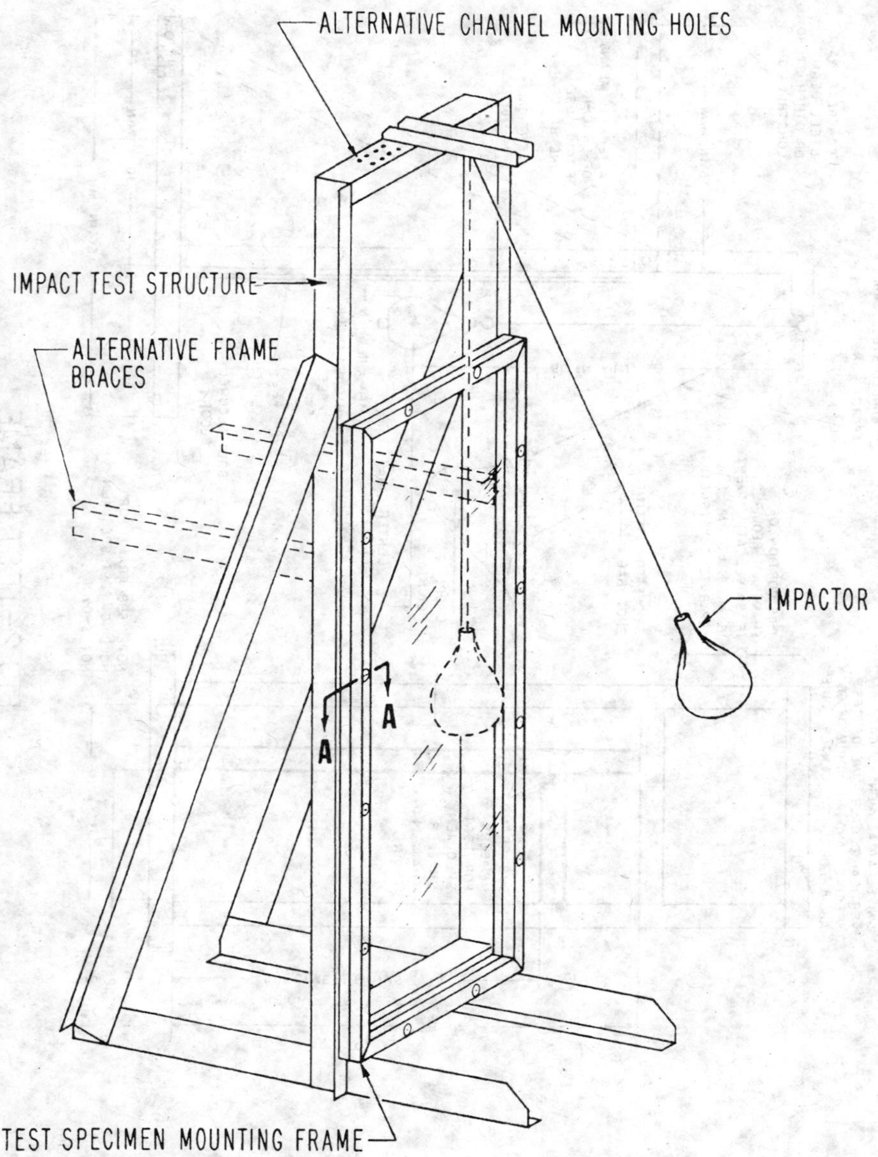

FIG I-GLASS IMPACT TEST STRUCTURE

FIGURE 2 TO SUBPART A OF PART 1201—TEST FRAME

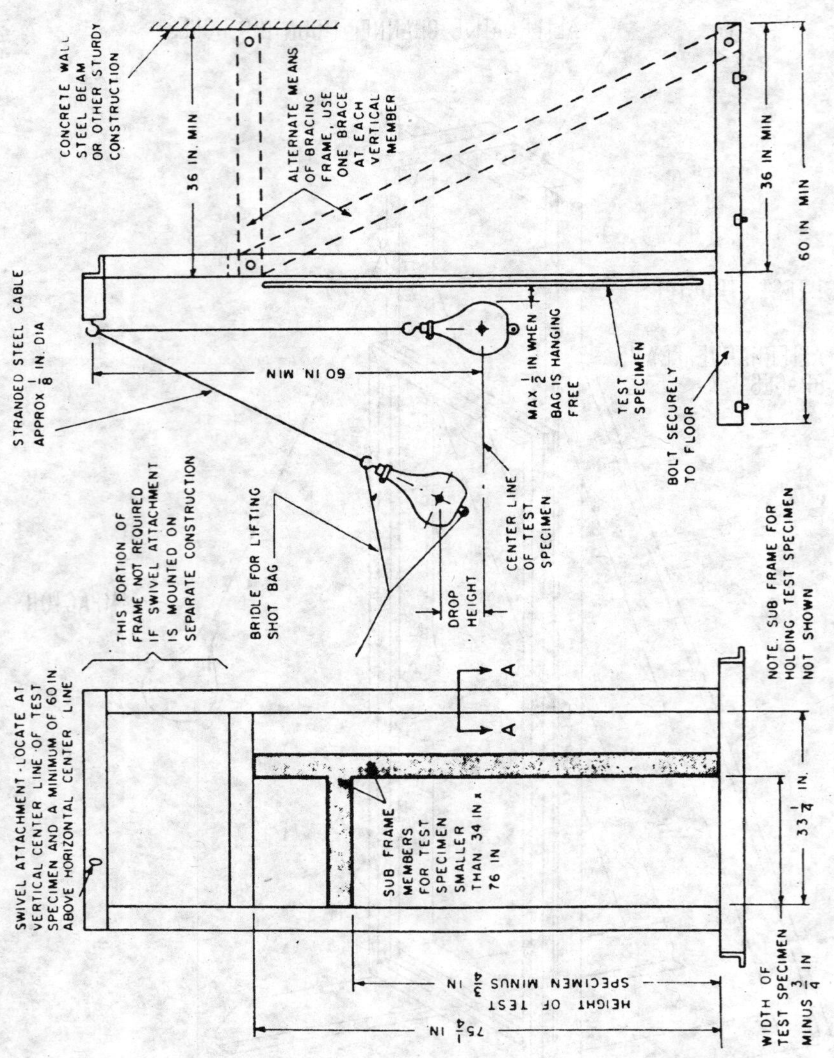

FIGURES 3 AND 4 TO SUBPART A OF PART 1201—TEST SPECIMENS

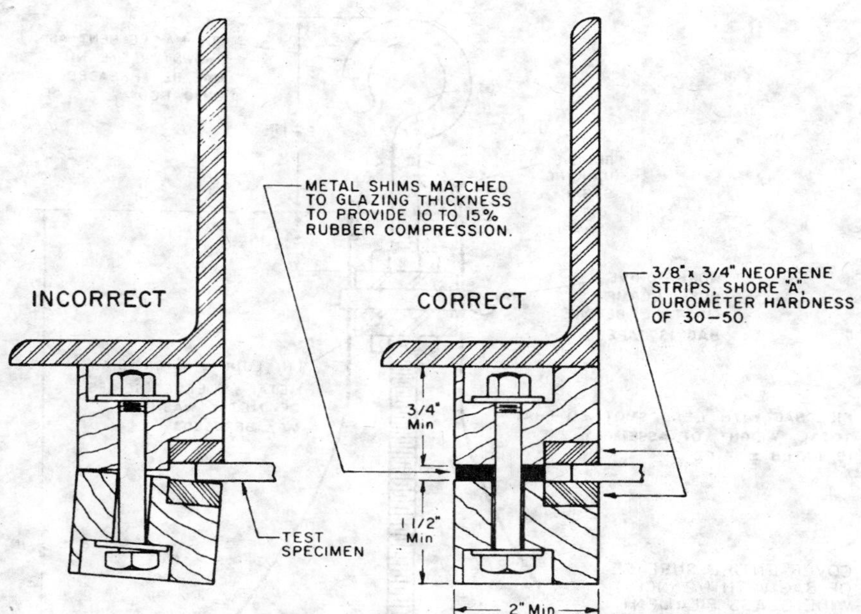

FIG 3—PROPERLY & IMPROPERLY CLAMPED TEST SPECIMEN (>1/8" THICK)

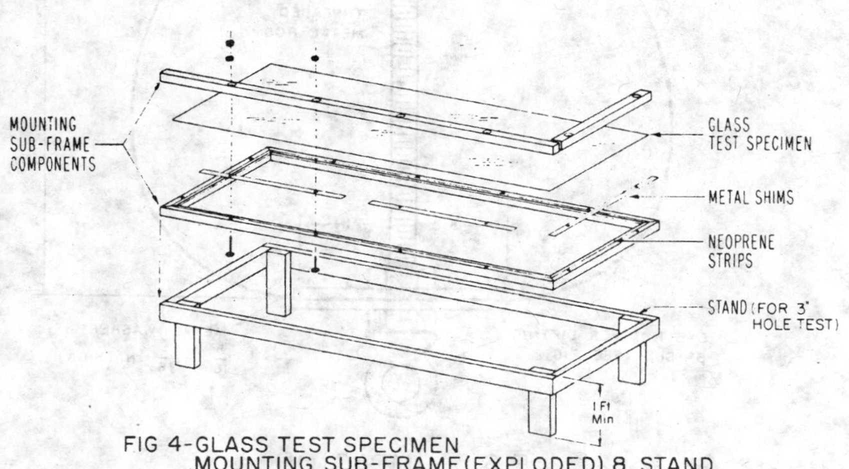

FIG 4-GLASS TEST SPECIMEN MOUNTING SUB-FRAME (EXPLODED) & STAND

FIGURE 5 TO SUBPART A OF PART 1201—IMPACTOR

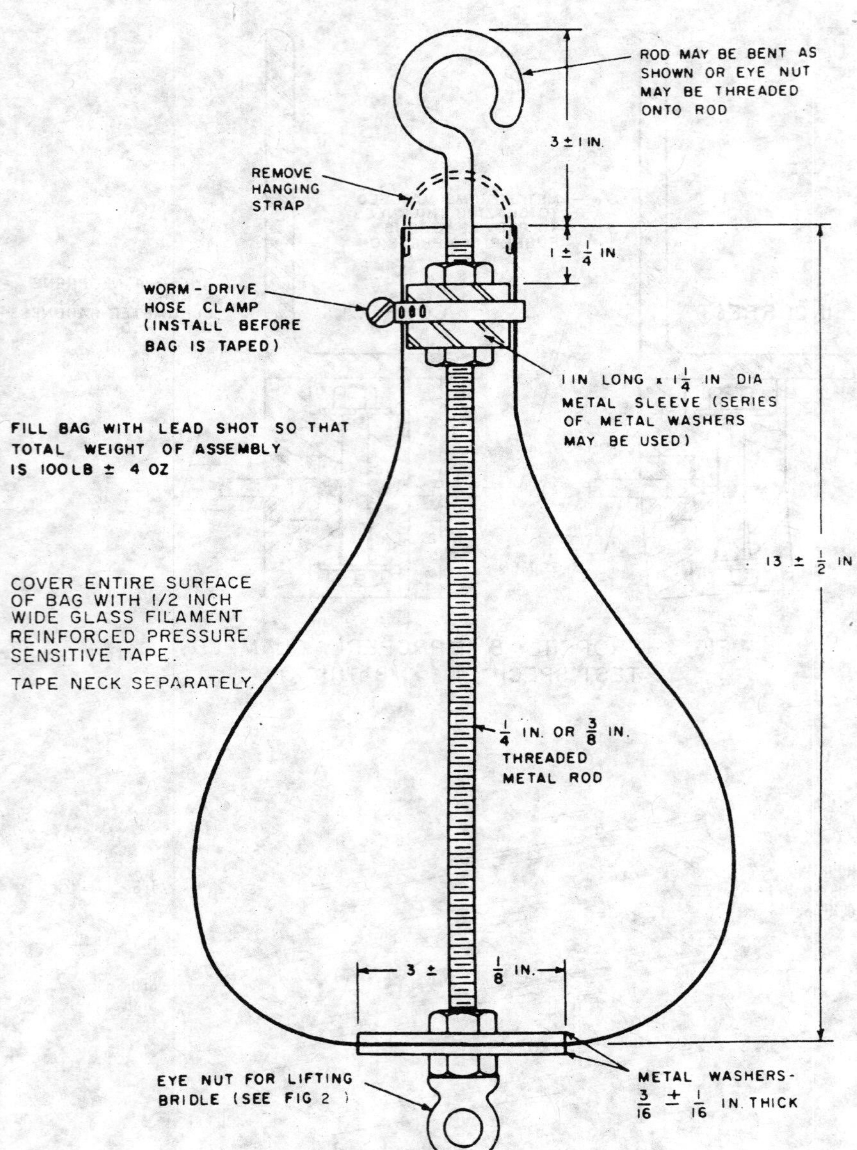

FIG 5—IMPACTOR

Subpart B [Reserved]

Subpart C—Statements of Policy and Interpretation

§ 1201.40 Interpretation concerning bathtub and shower doors and enclosures.

(a) *Purpose and background.* The purpose of this section is to clarify the scope of the terms "bathtub doors and enclosures" and "shower door and enclosure" as they are used in the Standard in subpart A. The Standard lists the products that are subject to it (§ 1201.1(a)). This list includes *bathtub doors and enclosures,* a term defined in the Standard to mean "assemblies of panels and/or doors that are installed on the lip of or immediately surrounding a bathtub" (§ 1201.2(a)(2)). The list also includes *shower doors and enclosures,* a term defined to mean "(assemblies) of one or more panels installed to form all or part of the wall and/or door of a shower stall" (§ 1201.2(a)(30)). Since the Standard became effective on July 6, 1977, the question has arisen whether the definitions of these products include glazing materials in a window that is located over a bathtub or within a shower stall and in the exterior wall of a building. The definitions of the terms "bathtub doors and enclosures" and "shower door and enclosure" contain no specific exemption for glazing materials in such windows. If read literally, the Standard could include glazing materials in an exterior wall window located above a bathtub because that window could be interpreted as being "immediately surrounding" the bathtub. Similarly, the Standard, if read literally, could include glazing materials in an exterior wall window because that window could be interpreted as forming "all or part of the wall * * * of a shower stall."

(b) *Interpretation.* When the Consumer Product Safety Commission issued the Standard, it did not intend the standard to apply to any item of glazing material in a window that is located over a bathtub or within a shower stall and in the exterior wall of a building. The Commission clarifies that the Standard does not apply to such items of glazing material or such windows. This interpretation applies only to the term "bathtub doors and enclosures" and "shower door and enclosure" and does not affect the applicability of the Standard to any other product.

[46 FR 45751, Sept. 15, 1981]

PART 1202—SAFETY STANDARD FOR MATCHBOOKS

AUTHORITY: Secs. 2, 3, 7, 9, 14, 16, and 19. Pub. L. 92–573, 86 Stat. 1212–17 (15 U.S.C. 2051, 2052, 2056, 2058, 2063, 2065, and 2068).

SOURCE: 43 FR 53709, Nov. 17, 1978, unless otherwise noted.

§ 1202.1 Scope and effective date.

(a) *Scope.* This part 1202, a consumer product safety standard, prescribes the safety requirements, including labeling requirements, for the matchbook. This part 1202 applies to all matchbooks manufactured in or imported into the United States after its effective date.

(b) *Effective date.* The effective date shall be May 4, 1978.

§ 1202.2 Findings. [1]

(a) *Risk of injury.* The Commission finds that unreasonable risks of injury from accidents are associated with matchbooks. These unreasonable risks,

[1] The Commission's findings apply to the matchbook standard that it published on May 4, 1977 (42 FR 22656–70). On Mar. 31, 1978, the U.S. Court of Appeals for the First Circuit set aside portions of that standard (*D. D. Bean & Sons, Co.* v. *CPSC,* 574 F. 2d 643). On Nov. 17, 1978, the Commission published a revised version of the standard which reflects the court's decision. However, the findings have not been revised and they are therefore not fully applicable to the revised matchbook requirements. For example, the revised standard does not address the unreasonable risk of injury of "[b]urn injuries that have been sustained by persons from fires that have been set by the afterglow of extinguished bookmatches" (§ 1202.2(a)(6)) because the court set aside the afterglow performance requirement.

which this part 1202 is intended to reduce or eliminate, are:

(1) Burn injuries, sustained by children and others, including mentally or physically impaired persons, who play with or otherwise improperly use bookmatches.

(2) Burn injuries sustained by persons who use bookmatches that fragment or have delayed ignition.

(3) Eye injuries sustained by persons who use bookmatches that fragment and cause particles from such matches to lodge in a person's eye.

(4) Burn injuries sustained by persons who use bookmatches that, when struck, ignite the remaining matches in the matchbook.

(5) Burn injuries sustained by persons from fires that have resulted from unexpected ignition of bookmatches with no deliberate action by the user.

(6) Burn injuries that have been sustained by persons from fires that have been set by the afterglow of extinguished bookmatches.

(b) *Products subject to this standard.* (1) The products subject to this standard are those kinds of manufactured ignition devices known as matchbooks. The matchbook consists of a group of bookmatches joined together and fastened within a cover. Although matchbooks are commonly referred to as paper matches or paper-stem matches to distinguish them from individual stick matches such as wooden stem matches packaged in boxes, all matchbooks, regardless of the materials of manufacture of the covers or of the bookmatches fastened within, are subject to this standard.

(2) Matchbooks subject to this standard can be divided into two basic categories: Resale matchbooks and special reproduction matchbooks. Resale matchbooks can be subdivided into advertising and nonadvertising matchbooks. Nonadvertising matchbooks are generally sold by large chain stores, and constitute a small portion of the total resale matchbook volume. Resale matchbooks with advertising are generally given away by tobacco shops, drug stores, vending firms, and other mass distribution outlets. Special reproduction matchbooks, characterized by their distinctive and unique cover designs, are purchased and distributed for promotional purposes by hotels, restaurants, financial institutions, and other business enterprises, and are given free to users.

(3) The Commission estimates that resale matchbooks accounted for almost 75 percent of the volume of matchbooks in 1975, or about 15 billion matchbooks, while special reproduction matchbooks accounted for just over 25 percent, or about 5.5 billion matchbooks.

(c) *Effects on utility, cost, and availability.* (1) The Commission finds that the public need for ignition devices which are small, portable, and can be used to provide a source of fire, is substantial since such products meet basic requirements for a source of fire to ignite tobacco products, fires, candles, or other products, and are also used for miscellaneous other purposes such as providing short term illumination. Three types of products: Matchbooks, individual stick matches, and lighters, predominantly supply the source of fire to meet these requirements.

(i) The Commission estimates that in 1976 U.S. consumers required approximately 645 billion such fire sources or "lights," as they are known, with almost 98 percent of this total required for tobacco products. In the aggregate, the requirements by U.S. consumers for a source of fire has been growing at an annual rate of approximately 3 percent. Matchbooks, the products regulated in this standard, are estimated to have supplied about 65 percent of the source of lights, lighters accounted for about 25 percent, and individual stick matches (primarily wooden-stem type) accounted for the remainder.

(ii) The Commission also finds that matchbooks fulfill a need by institutions and business enterprises for a particular form of specialty advertising that is both relatively inexpensive and effective in reaching a specified audience or population segment with the advertiser's message. Various studies of matchbooks as a form of advertising have found that readership can average 3 to 15 times higher than average readership, listenership, and viewership figures from competing media such as magazines, newspapers, radio, and television, and that readership retention of the matchbook advertising message was extremely high, about 45 percent. In addition, matchbooks tend to be considerably less expensive than other forms of specialty advertising, including those competing advertising items such as address books, key cases, litterbags, and the like, which are themselves relatively inexpensive.

(2) The Commission finds that the standard will have no adverse effects on the utility that consumers derive from matchbooks. To the extent that injuries and property damage associated with the use of matchbooks is reduced or eliminated as a result of this standard, the utility of matchbooks as a source of fire will be increased.

(3) The Commission estimates that manufacturing cost increases as a direct or indirect effect of this standard will be modest for the industry as a whole. Such increases will tend to be concentrated in one-time costs to complete changeover to reverse friction, and in costs to establish and implement testing programs and certification procedures.

(i) Because some 80–90 percent of the matchbooks produced annually are given free to consumers, there is not likely to be any direct cost impact on the consumer as a result of the standard. Some proportion of increased manufacturing costs will be passed on to the institutions and business enterprises that purchase matchbooks for promotional purposes. To the extent that increases in advertising and promotional costs may be reflected in higher prices for goods and services sold by these businesses, there may be indirect cost effects on consumers. If so, such impacts would likely be small, if not imperceptible.

(ii) For the 12–20 percent of matchbooks that are purchases at retail by consumers, some proportion of any manufacturing cost increases may be passed on to the consumer. A resulting increase in retail prices for such matchbooks will be small, no more than a few cents per box of 50 matchbooks.

(4) The Commission finds that the standard will not have impacts of significant magnitude on the availability of matchbooks. Although some institutions and business enterprises may reduce their matchbook purchases or eliminate them in response to any increased price of matchbooks, the large number of such purchasers, and the large volume purchased annually, are such that curtailment of purchases by some businesses is likely to have very small effects on the total number of matchbooks available to U.S. consumers.

(d) *Alternatives.* (1) The Commission has considered other means of achieving the objective of the standard throughout the course of its development. Certain other more elaborate test requirements were considered and were shown to have the potential for severe adverse effects on competition and estimated to result in disruptions and dislocations of manufacturing and commercial practices. Therefore, having considered and rejected such other means of achieving the objective of the standard, the Commission has found none that would cause less disruption or dislocation of manufacturing and other commercial practices, consistent with the public health and safety than this standard.

(2) Because of competition from substitute products such as inexpensive disposable butane lighters and because of other prevailing business and economic conditions, the industry manufacturing matchbooks has been in a state of contraction in recent years. This contraction, marked by the exit of some firms and by plant closings or consolidations, is likely to continue in the future; but this will neither be the result of, nor significantly accelerated by, effects of the standard. Currently, aggressive price and service competition prevails among firms vying for customer accounts. It is anticipated that this competition for sales may increase as an indirect effect of the standard. To the extent that this occurs, there may be some disruption or dislocation of manufacturing, sales, or distribution practices in certain matchbook product categories and market segments. Marginal firms and firms producing limited product categories or for limited market segments may be affected to a greater degree

than multiproduct category or multimarket firms.

(e) *Conclusion.* The Commission finds that this standard, including its effective date, is reasonably necessary to eliminate or reduce the unreasonable risks of injury associated with matchbooks and that the issuance of the standard is in the public interest.

§ 1202.3 Definitions.

In addition to the definitions given in section 3 of the Consumer Product Safety Act (15 U.S.C. 2052), the following definitions apply for the purpose of this standard:

(a) *Bookmatch* means a single splint, with a matchhead attached, that comes from a matchbook.

(b) *Bridge* means the matchhead material held in common by two or more splints.

(c) *Broken bridge* means a bridge that has become separated.

(d) *Caddy* means a package of two or more matchbooks wrapped or boxed together at a production plant.

(e) *Comb* means a piece of wood, paper, or other suitable material that has been formed into splints, that remain joined at their base, and that are designed to have matchheads attached to their tips.

(f) *Cover* means the paperboard or other suitable material that is wrapped around and fastened to the comb(s).

(g) *Friction* means the dried chemical mixture on the matchbook cover used to ignite the bookmatch.

(h) *Match* means a single splint with matchhead attached.

(i) *Matchbook* means one or more combs with matchheads attached and a cover that is wrapped around and fastened to those combs.

(j) *Matchhead* means the dried chemical mixture on the end of a splint.

(k) *Splint* means the support for the matchhead or that portion normally held when using the bookmatch.

§ 1202.4 Matchbook general requirements.

A matchbook shall meet the following general requirements:

(a) The friction shall be located on the outside back cover near the bottom of the matchbook.

(b) The cover shall remain closed without external force.

(c) No friction material shall be located on the inside of the cover where possible contact with the matchheads may occur during ordinary use.

(d) There shall be no bridge(s) or broken bridge(s).

(e) No matchhead in the matchbook shall be split, chipped, cracked, or crumbled.

(f) No portion of any matchhead shall be outside the matchbook cover when the cover is closed.

(g) No part of a staple or other assembly device for securing the cover and combs shall be within or touching the friction area.

(h) A staple used as an assembly device for securing the cover and combs shall be fully clinched so that the ends are flattened or turned into the cover.

§ 1202.5 Certification.

Certification shall be in accordance with section 14(a) of the Consumer Product Safety Act (15 U.S.C. 2063(a)). Under this provision, manufacturers and private labelers of products subject to safety standards must certify that their products conform to the standard, based on either a test of each product or on a reasonable testing program.

§ 1202.6 Marking.

(a) The manufacturer's or private labeler's name and city or a symbol which will identify the name and city shall appear on the matchbook. In addition, every private labeler must label the matchbook with a code which enables it to identify, if requested, the manufacturer of the product.

(b) Boxes or cartons in which two or more caddies are shipped shall be marked "For safety, store in a cool, dry place."

§ 1202.7 Prohibited stockpiling.

Section 9(d)(2) of the Consumer Product Safety Act (15 U.S.C. 2058(d)(2)) authorizes the Commission to prohibit manufacturers and importers from stockpiling a product subject to a consumer product safety standard between its date of issuance and its effective date. A manufacturer or importer is in violation of Section 9(d)(2) and of this section if it fails to comply with the following:

(a) *Definitions.* (1) *Base period* means, at the option of the manufacturer or importer concerned, any period of 365 consecutive days beginning on or after January 1, 1973, and ending on or before December 31, 1975.

(2) *Rate of production (or importation)* means the total number of matchbooks manufactured (or imported) during a stated time period. In determining whether a matchbook was manufactured during a stated time period, the date on which the cover and combs were assembled to form a matchbook shall be used. In the event that a manufacturer currently operates a matchbook manufacturing plant that it did not operate during the base period, or that it did not operate for an entire base period, that manufacturer shall use, as the rate of production during the base period for that plant, either (i) the average daily rate of production (including nonproduction days such as Sundays, holidays, and vacations) for the part of the base period he did operate that plant, multiplied by 365 or (ii) the rate of production during the base period of his most nearly similar matchbook manufacturing plant.

(b) *Prohibited act.* Manufacturers and importers of matchbooks, as these products are defined in §1202.3(i), shall not manufacture or import matchbooks that do not comply with the requirements of this part between the date that this part is issued and the date that it becomes effective at a rate that is greater than the rate of production or importation during the base period plus 15 percent of that rate.

(c) *Documentation.* Manufacturers and importers shall maintain, for a period of six (6) months after the effective date specified in §1202.1(b), appropriate documentation to be able to substantiate to the Commission that they are in compliance with the provisions of this section.

PART 1203—SAFETY STANDARD FOR BICYCLE HELMETS

Subpart A—The Standard

Sec.

Subpart B—Certification

Subpart C—Recordkeeping

Subpart D—Requirements for Bicycle Helmets Manufactured From March 17, 1995, Through March 10, 1999

AUTHORITY: 15 U.S.C. 2056, 2058, and 6001–6006. Subpart B is also issued under 15 U.S.C. 2063. Subpart C is also issued under 15 U.S.C. 2065.

SOURCE: 63 FR 11729, Mar. 10, 1998, unless otherwise noted.

Subpart A—The Standard

§ 1203.1 Scope, general requirements, and effective date.

(a) *Scope.* The standard in this subpart describes test methods and defines minimum performance criteria for all bicycle helmets, as defined in § 1203.4(b).

(b) *General requirements*—(1) *Projections.* All projections on bicycle helmets must meet the construction requirements of § 1203.5.

(2) *Labeling and instructions.* All bicycle helmets must have the labeling and instructions required by § 1203.6.

(3) *Performance tests.* All bicycle helmets must be capable of meeting the peripheral vision, positional stability, dynamic strength of retention system, and impact-attenuation tests described in §§ 1203.7 through 1203.17.

(4) *Units.* The values stated in International System of Units ("SI") measurements are the standard. The inch-pound values stated in parentheses are for information only.

(c) *Effective date.* The standard shall become effective March 10, 1999 and shall apply to all bicycle helmets manufactured after that date. Bicycle helmets manufactured from March 17, 1995 through March 10, 1999, inclusive, are subject to the requirements of Subpart D, rather than this subpart A.

§ 1203.2 Purpose and basis.

The purpose and basis of this standard is to reduce the likelihood of serious injury and death to bicyclists resulting from impacts to the head, pursuant to 15 U.S.C. 6001–6006.

§ 1203.3 Referenced documents.

(a) The following documents are incorporated by reference in this standard. (1) Draft ISO/DIS Standard 6220–1983—Headforms for Use in the Testing of Protective Helmets.[1]

(2) SAE Recommended Practice SAE J211 OCT88, Instrumentation for Impact Tests.

(b) This incorporation by reference was approved by the Director of the Federal Register in accordance with 5 U.S.C. 552(a) and 1 CFR Part 51. Copies of the standards may be obtained as follows. Copies of the draft ISO/DIS Standard 6220–1983 are available from American National Standards Institute, 11 W. 42nd St., 13th Floor, New York, NY 10036. Copies of the SAE Recommended Practice SAE J211 OCT88, Instrumentation for Impact Tests, are available from Society of Automotive Engineers, 400 Commonwealth Dr., Warrendale, PA 15096. Copies may be inspected at the Office of the Secretary, Consumer Product Safety Commission, 4330 East-West Highway, Bethesda, Maryland 20814, or at the National Archives and Records Administration (NARA). For information on the availability of this material at NARA, call 202–741–6030, or go to: *http://www.archives.gov/federal_register/code_of_federal_regulations/ibr_locations.html.*

§ 1203.4 Definitions.

(a) *Basic plane* means an anatomical plane that includes the auditory meatuses (the external ear openings) and the inferior orbital rims (the bottom edges of the eye sockets). The ISO headforms are marked with a plane corresponding to this basic plane (see Figures 1 and 2 of this part).

(b) *Bicycle helmet* means any headgear that either is marketed as, or implied through marketing or promotion to be, a device intended to provide protection from head injuries while riding a bicycle.[2]

---

[1] Although the draft ISO/DIS 6220–1983 standard was never adopted as an international standard, it has become a consensus national standard because all recent major voluntary standards used in the United States for testing bicycle helmets establish their headform dimensions by referring to the draft ISO standard.

[2] Helmets specifically marketed for exclusive use in a designated activity, such as skateboarding, rollerblading, baseball, roller hockey, etc., would be excluded from this definition because the specific focus of their marketing makes it unlikely that such helmets would be purchased for other than their stated use. However, a multi-purpose helmet—one marketed or represented as providing protection either during general use or in a variety of specific activities other

(c) *Comfort or fit padding* means resilient lining material used to configure the helmet for a range of different head sizes.

(d) *Coronal plane* is an anatomical plane perpendicular to both the basic and midsagittal planes and containing the midpoint of a line connecting the right and left auditory meatuses. The ISO headforms are marked with a transverse plane corresponding to this coronal plane (see Figures 1 and 2 of this part).

(e) *Field of vision* is the angle of peripheral vision allowed by the helmet when positioned on the reference headform.

(f) *Helmet positioning index ("HPI")* is the vertical distance from the brow of the helmet to the reference plane, when placed on a reference headform. This vertical distance shall be specified by the manufacturer for each size of each model of the manufacturer's helmets, for the appropriate size of headform for each helmet, as described in § 1203.10.

(g) *Midsagittal plane* is an anatomical plane perpendicular to the basic plane and containing the midpoint of the line connecting the notches of the right and left inferior orbital ridges and the midpoint of the line connecting the superior rims of the right and left auditory meatuses. The ISO headforms are marked with a longitudinal plane corresponding to the midsagittal plane (see Figures 1 and 2 of this part).

(h) *Modular elastomer programmer ("MEP")* is a cylindrical pad, typically consisting of a polyurethane rubber, used as a consistent impact medium for the systems check procedure. The MEP shall be 152 mm (6 in) in diameter, and 25 mm (1 in) thick and shall have a durometer of 60±2 Shore A. The MEP shall be affixed to the top surface of a flat 6.35 mm (¼ in) thick aluminum plate. See § 1203.17(b)(1).

(i) *Preload ballast* is a "bean bag" filled with lead shot that is placed on the helmet to secure its position on the headform. The mass of the preload ballast is 5 kg (11 lb).

(j) *Projection* is any part of the helmet, internal or external, that extends beyond the faired surface.

(k) *Reference headform* is a headform used as a measuring device and contoured in the same configuration as one of the test headforms A, E, J, M, and O defined in draft ISO DIS 6220–1983. The reference headform shall include surface markings corresponding to the basic, coronal, midsagittal, and reference planes (see Figures 1 and 2 of this part).

(l) *Reference plane* is a plane marked on the ISO headforms at a specified distance above and parallel to the basic plane (see Figure 3 of this part).

(m) *Retention system* is the complete assembly that secures the helmet in a stable position on the wearer's head.

(n) *Shield* means optional equipment for helmets that is used in place of goggles to protect the eyes.

(o) *Spherical impactor* is an impact fixture used in the instrument system check of § 1203.17(b)(1) to test the impact-attenuation test equipment for precision and accuracy. The spherical impactor shall be a 146 mm (5.75 in) diameter aluminum sphere mounted on the ball-arm connector of the drop assembly. The total mass of the spherical-impactor drop assembly shall be 5.0±0.1 kg (11.0±0.22 lb).

(p) *Test headform* is a solid model in the shape of a human head of sizes A, E, J, M, and O as defined in draft ISO/DIS 6220–1983. Headforms used for the impact-attenuation test shall be constructed of low-resonance K–1A magnesium alloy. The test headforms shall

---

than bicycling—would fall within the definition of bicycle helmet if a reasonable consumer could conclude, based on the helmet's marketing or representations, that bicycling is among the activities in which the helmet is intended to be used. In making this determination, the Commission will consider the types of specific activities, if any, for which the helmet is marketed, the similarity of the appearance, design, and construction of the helmet to other helmets marketed or recognized as bicycle helmets, and the presence, prominence, and clarity of any warnings, on the helmet or its packaging or promotional materials, against the use of the helmet as a bicycle helmet. A multi-purpose helmet marketed without specific reference to the activities in which the helmet is to be used will be presumed to be a bicycle helmet. The presence of warnings or disclaimers advising against the use of a multi-purpose helmet during bicycling is a relevant, but not necessarily controlling, factor in the determination of whether a multi-purpose helmet is a bicycle helmet.

include surface markings corresponding to the basic, coronal, midsagittal, and reference planes (see Figure 2 of this part).

(q) *Test region* is the area of the helmet, on and above a specified impact test line, that is subject to impact testing.

§ 1203.5 Construction requirements—projections.

Any unfaired projection extending more than 7 mm (0.28 in.) from the helmet's outer surface shall break away or collapse when impacted with forces equivalent to those produced by the applicable impact-attenuation tests in § 1203.17 of this standard. There shall be no fixture on the helmet's inner surface projecting more than 2 mm into the helmet interior.

§ 1203.6 Labeling and instructions.

(a) *Labeling.* Each helmet shall be marked with durable labeling so that the following information is legible and easily visible to the user:

(1) Model designation.

(2) A warning to the user that no helmet can protect against all possible impacts and that serious injury or death could occur.

(3) A warning on both the helmet and the packaging that for maximum protection the helmet must be fitted and attached properly to the wearer's head in accordance with the manufacturer's fitting instructions.

(4) A warning to the user that the helmet may, after receiving an impact, be damaged to the point that it is no longer adequate to protect the head against further impacts, and that this damage may not be visible to the user. This label shall also state that a helmet that has sustained an impact should be returned to the manufacturer for inspection, or be destroyed and replaced.

(5) A warning to the user that the helmet can be damaged by contact with common substances (for example, certain solvents [ammonia], cleaners [bleach], etc.), and that this damage may not be visible to the user. This label shall state in generic terms some recommended cleaning agents and procedures (for example, wipe with mild soap and water), list the most common substances that damage the helmet, warn against contacting the helmet with these substances, and refer users to the instruction manual for more specific care and cleaning information.

(6) *Signal word.* The labels required by paragraphs (a) (2) through (5) of this section shall include the signal word "WARNING" at the beginning of each statement, unless two or more of the statements appear together on the same label. In that case, the signal word need only appear once, at the beginning of the warnings. The signal word "WARNING" shall be in all capital letters, bold print, and a type size equal to or greater than the other text on the label.

(b) *Instructions.* Each helmet shall have fitting and positioning instructions, including a graphic representation of proper positioning.

§ 1203.7 Samples for testing.

(a) *General.* Helmets shall be tested in the condition in which they are offered for sale. To meet the standard, the helmets must be able to pass all tests, both with and without any attachments that may be offered by the helmet's manufacturer and with all possible combinations of such attachments.

(b) *Number of samples.* To test conformance to this standard, eight samples of each helmet size for each helmet model offered for sale are required.

§ 1203.8 Conditioning environments.

Helmets shall be conditioned to one of the following environments prior to testing in accordance with the test schedule at § 1203.13. The barometric pressure in all conditioning environments shall be 75 to 110 kPa (22.2 to 32.6 in of Hg). All test helmets shall be stabilized within the ambient condition for at least 4 hours prior to further conditioning and testing. Storage or shipment within this ambient range satisfies this requirement.

(a) *Ambient condition.* The ambient condition of the test laboratory shall be within 17 °C to 27 °C (63 °F to 81 °F), and 20 to 80% relative humidity. The ambient test helmet does not need further conditioning.

(b) *Low temperature.* The helmet shall be kept at a temperature of −17 °C to

−13 °C (1 °F to 9 °F) for 4 to 24 hours prior to testing.

(c) *High temperature.* The helmet shall be kept at a temperature of 47 °C to 53 °C (117 °F to 127 °F) for 4 to 24 hours prior to testing.

(d) *Water immersion.* The helmet shall be fully immersed "crown" down in potable water at a temperature of 17 °C to 27 °C (63 °F to 81 °F) to a crown depth of 305 mm ±25 mm (12 in. ±1 in.) for 4 to 24 hours prior to testing.

§ 1203.9 Test headforms.

The headforms used for testing shall be selected from sizes A, E, J, M, and O, as defined by DRAFT ISO/DIS 6220–1983, in accordance with § 1203.10. Headforms used for impact testing shall be rigid and be constructed of low-resonance K–1A magnesium alloy.

§ 1203.10 Selecting the test headform.

A helmet shall be tested on the smallest of the headforms appropriate for the helmet sample. A headform size is appropriate for a helmet if all of the helmet's sizing pads are partially compressed when the helmet is equipped with its thickest sizing pads and positioned correctly on the reference headform.

§ 1203.11 Marking the impact test line.

Prior to testing, the impact test line shall be determined for each helmet in the following manner.

(a) Position the helmet on the appropriate headform as specified by the manufacturer's helmet positioning index (HPI), with the brow parallel to the basic plane. Place a 5-kg (11-lb) preload ballast on top of the helmet to set the comfort or fit padding.

(b) Draw the impact test line on the outer surface of the helmet coinciding with the intersection of the surface of the helmet with the impact line planes defined from the reference headform as shown in:

(1) Figure 4 of this part for helmets intended only for persons 5 years of age and older.

(2) Figure 5 of this part for helmets intended for persons age 1 and older.

(c) The center of the impact sites shall be selected at any point on the helmet on or above the impact test line.

§ 1203.12 Test requirements.

(a) *Peripheral vision.* All bicycle helmets shall allow unobstructed vision through a minimum of 105° to the left and right sides of the midsagittal plane when measured in accordance with § 1203.14 of this standard.

(b) *Positional stability.* No bicycle helmet shall come off of the test headform when tested in accordance with § 1203.15 of this standard.

(c) *Dynamic strength of retention system.* All bicycle helmets shall have a retention system that will remain intact without elongating more than 30 mm (1.2 in.) when tested in accordance with § 1203.16 of this standard.

(d) *Impact attenuation criteria*—(1) *General.* A helmet fails the impact attenuation performance test of this standard if a failure under paragraph (d)(2) of this section can be induced under any combination of impact site, anvil type, anvil impact order, or conditioning environment permissible under the standard, either with or without any attachments, or combinations of attachments, that are provided with the helmet. Thus, the Commission will test for a "worst case" combination of test parameters. What constitutes a worst case may vary, depending on the particular helmet involved.

(2) *Peak acceleration.* The peak acceleration of any impact shall not exceed 300 g when the helmet is tested in accordance with § 1203.17 of this standard.

§ 1203.13 Test schedule.

(a) Helmet sample 1 of the set of eight helmets, as designated in Table 1203.13, shall be tested for peripheral vision in accordance with § 1203.14 of this standard.

(b) Helmet samples 1 through 8, as designated in Table 1203.13, shall be conditioned in the ambient, high temperature, low temperature, and water immersion environments as follows: helmets 1 and 5—ambient; helmets 2 and 7—high temperature; helmets 3 and 6—low temperature; and helmets 4 and 8—water immersion.

(c) Testing must begin within 2 minutes after the helmet is removed from the conditioning environment. The helmet shall be returned to the conditioning environment within 3 minutes after it was removed, and shall remain in the conditioning environment for a minimum of 2 minutes before testing is resumed. If the helmet is out of the conditioning environment beyond 3 minutes, testing shall not resume until the helmet has been reconditioned for a period equal to at least 5 minutes for each minute the helmet was out of the conditioning environment beyond the first 3 minutes, or for 4 hours, (whichever reconditioning time is shorter) before testing is resumed.

(d) Prior to being tested for impact attenuation, helmets 1–4 (conditioned in ambient, high temperature, low temperature, and water immersion environments, respectively) shall be tested in accordance with the dynamic retention system strength test at § 1203.16. Helmets 1–4 shall then be tested in accordance with the impact attenuation tests on the flat and hemispherical anvils in accordance with the procedure at § 1203.17. Helmet 5 (ambient-conditioned) shall be tested in accordance with the positional stability tests at § 1203.15 prior to impact testing. Helmets 5–8 shall then be tested in accordance with the impact attenuation tests on the curbstone anvil in accordance with § 1203.17. Table 1203.13 summarizes the test schedule.

TABLE 1203.13—TEST SCHEDULE

	§ 1203.14 Peripheral vision	§ 1203.15 Positional stability	§ 1203.16 Retention system strength	§ 1203.17 Impact tests	
				Anvil	Number of Impacts
Helmet 1, Ambient	X		X	X Flat	2
				X Hemi	2
Helmet 2, High Temperature			X	X Flat	2
				X Hemi	2
Helmet 3, Low Temperature			X	X Flat	2
				X Hemi	2
Helmet 4, Water Immersion			X	X Flat	2
				X Hemi	2
Helmet 5, Ambient		X		X Curb	1
Helmet 6, Low Temperature				X Curb	1
Helmet 7, High Temperature				X Curb	1
Helmet 8, Water Immersion				X Curb	1

§ 1203.14 Peripheral vision test.

Position the helmet on a reference headform in accordance with the HPI and place a 5-kg (11-lb) preload ballast on top of the helmet to set the comfort or fit padding. (NOTE: Peripheral vision clearance may be determined when the helmet is positioned for marking the test lines.) Peripheral vision is measured horizontally from each side of the midsagittal plane around the point K (see Figure 6 of this part). Point K is located on the front surface of the reference headform at the intersection of the basic and midsagittal planes. The vision shall not be obstructed within 105 degrees from point K on each side of the midsagittal plane.

§ 1203.15 Positional stability test (roll-off resistance).

(a) *Test equipment.*

(1) *Headforms.* The test headforms shall comply with the dimensions of the full chin ISO reference headforms sizes A, E, J, M, and O.

(2) *Test fixture.* The headform shall be secured in a test fixture with the headform's vertical axis pointing downward and 45 degrees to the direction of gravity (see Figure 7 of this part). The test fixture shall permit rotation of the headform about its vertical axis and include means to lock the headform in the face up and face down positions.

(3) *Dynamic impact apparatus.* A dynamic impact apparatus shall be used to apply a shock load to a helmet secured to the test headform. The dynamic impact apparatus shall allow a 4-kg (8.8-lb) drop weight to slide in a guided free fall to impact a rigid stop anvil (see Figure 7 of this part). The entire mass of the dynamic impact assembly, including the drop weight, shall be no more than 5 kg (11 lb).

(4) *Strap or cable.* A hook and flexible strap or cable shall be used to connect the dynamic impact apparatus to the

helmet. The strap or cable shall be of a material having an elongation of no more than 5 mm (0.20 in.) per 300 mm (11.8 in.) when loaded with a 22-kg (48.5 lb) weight in a free hanging position.

(b) *Test procedure.*

(1) Orient the headform so that its face is down, and lock it in that orientation.

(2) Place the helmet on the appropriate size full chin headform in accordance with the HPI and fasten the retention system in accordance with the manufacturer's instructions. Adjust the straps to remove any slack.

(3) Suspend the dynamic impact system from the helmet by positioning the flexible strap over the helmet along the midsagittal plane and attaching the hook over the edge of the helmet as shown in Figure 7 of this part.

(4) Raise the drop weight to a height of 0.6 m (2 ft) from the stop anvil and release it, so that it impacts the stop anvil.

(5) The test shall be repeated with the headform's face pointing upwards, so that the helmet is pulled from front to rear.

§ 1203.16 Dynamic strength of retention system test.

(a) *Test equipment.* (1) ISO headforms without the lower chin portion shall be used.

(2) The retention system strength test equipment shall consist of a dynamic impact apparatus that allows a 4-kg (8.8-lb) drop weight to slide in a guided free fall to impact a rigid stop anvil (see Figure 8 of this part). Two cylindrical rollers that spin freely, with a diameter of 12.5±0.5 mm (0.49 in.±0.02 in.) and a center-to-center distance of 76.0±1 mm (3.0±0.04 in.), shall make up a stirrup that represents the bone structure of the lower jaw. The entire dynamic test apparatus hangs freely on the retention system. The entire mass of the support assembly, including the 4-kg (8.8-lb) drop weight, shall be 11 kg±0.5 kg (24.2 lb±1.1 lb).

(b) *Test procedure.* (1) Place the helmet on the appropriate size headform on the test device according to the HPI. Fasten the strap of the retention system under the stirrup.

(2) Mark the pre-test position of the retention system, with the entire dynamic test apparatus hanging freely on the retention system.

(3) Raise the 4-kg (8.8-lb) drop weight to a height of 0.6 m (2 ft) from the stop anvil and release it, so that it impacts the stop anvil.

(4) Record the maximum elongation of the retention system during the impact. A marker system or a displacement transducer, as shown in Figure 8 of this part, are two methods of measuring the elongation.

§ 1203.17 Impact attenuation test.

(a) *Impact test instruments and equipment*—(1) *Measurement of impact attenuation.* Impact attenuation is determined by measuring the acceleration of the test headform during impact. Acceleration is measured with a uniaxial accelerometer that is capable of withstanding a shock of at least 1000 g. The helmet is secured onto the headform and dropped in a guided free fall, using a monorail or guidewire test apparatus (see Figure 9 of this part), onto an anvil fixed to a rigid base. The center of the anvil shall be aligned with the center vertical axis of the accelerometer. The base shall consist of a solid mass of at least 135 kg (298 lb), the upper surface of which shall consist of a steel plate at least 12 mm (0.47 in.) thick and having a surface area of at least 0.10 m^2 (1.08 ft^2).

(2) *Accelerometer.* A uniaxial accelerometer shall be mounted at the center of gravity of the test headform, with the sensitive axis aligned within 5 degrees of vertical when the test headform is in the impact position. The acceleration data channel and filtering shall comply with SAE Recommended Practice J211 OCT88, Instrumentation for Impact Tests, Requirements for Channel Class 1000.

(3) *Headform and drop assembly—centers of gravity.* The center of gravity of the test headform shall be at the center of the mounting ball on the support assembly and within an inverted cone having its axis vertical and a 10-degree included angle with the vertex at the point of impact. The location of the center of gravity of the drop assembly (combined test headform and support assembly) must meet the specifications of Federal Motor Vehicle Safety Standard No. 218, Motorcycle Helmets, 49

CFR 571.218 (S7.1.8). The center of gravity of the drop assembly shall lie within the rectangular volume bounded by x=−6.4 mm (−0.25 in.), x=21.6 mm (0.85 in.), y=6.4 mm (0.25 in.), and y=−6.4 mm (−0.25 in.), with the origin located at the center of gravity of the test headform. The origin of the coordinate axes is at the center of the mounting ball on the support assembly. The rectangular volume has no boundary along the z-axis. The positive z-axis is downward. The x-y-z axes are mutually perpendicular and have positive or negative designations as shown in Figure 10 of this part. Figure 10 shows an overhead view of the x-y boundary of the drop assembly center of gravity.

(4) *Drop assembly*. The combined mass of the drop assembly, which consists of instrumented test headform and support assembly (excluding the test helmet), shall be 5.0±0.1 kg (11.00±0.22 lb).

(5) *Impact anvils*. Impact tests shall be performed against the three different solid (*i.e.*, without internal cavities) steel anvils described in this paragraph (a)(5).

(i) *Flat anvil*. The flat anvil shall have a flat surface with an impact face having a minimum diameter of 125 mm (4.92 in.). It shall be at least 24 mm (0.94 in.) thick (see Figure 11 of this part).

(ii) *Hemispherical anvil*. The hemispherical anvil shall have a hemispherical impact surface with a radius of 48±1 mm (1.89±0.04 in.) (see Figure 12 of this part).

(iii) *Curbstone anvil*. The curbstone anvil shall have two flat faces making an angle of 105 degrees and meeting along a striking edge having a radius of 15 mm±0.5 mm (0.59±0.02 in.). The height of the curbstone anvil shall not be less than 50 mm (1.97 in.), and the length shall not be less than 200 mm (7.87 in.) (see Figure 13 of this part).

(b) *Test Procedure*—(1) *Instrument system check (precision and accuracy)*. The impact-attenuation test instrumentation shall be checked before and after each series of tests (at least at the beginning and end of each test day) by dropping a spherical impactor onto an elastomeric test medium (MEP). The spherical impactor shall be a 146 mm (5.75 in.) diameter aluminum sphere that is mounted on the ball-arm connector of the drop assembly. The total mass of the spherical-impactor drop assembly shall be 5.0±0.1 kg (11.0±0.22 lb). The MEP shall be 152 mm (6 in.) in diameter and 25 mm (1 in.) thick, and shall have a durometer of 60±2 Shore A. The MEP shall be affixed to the top surface of a flat 6.35 mm (¼ in.) thick aluminum plate. The geometric center of the MEP pad shall be aligned with the center vertical axis of the accelerometer (see paragraph (a)(2) of this section). The impactor shall be dropped onto the MEP at an impact velocity of 5.44 m/s±2%. (Typically, this requires a minimum drop height of 1.50 meters (4.9 ft) plus a height adjustment to account for friction losses.) Six impacts, at intervals of 75±15 seconds, shall be performed at the beginning and end of the test series (at a minimum at the beginning and end of each test day). The first three of six impacts shall be considered warm-up drops, and their impact values shall be discarded from the series. The second three impacts shall be recorded. All recorded impacts shall fall within the range of 380 g to 425 g. In addition, the difference between the high and low values of the three recorded impacts shall not be greater than 20 g.

(2) *Impact sites*. Each of helmets 1 through 4 (one helmet for each conditioning environment) shall impact at four different sites, with two impacts on the flat anvil and two impacts on the hemispherical anvil. The center of any impact may be anywhere on or above the test line, provided it is at least 120 mm (4.72 in), measured on the surface of the helmet, from any prior impact center. Each of helmets 5 through 8 (one helmet for each conditioning environment) shall impact at one site on the curbstone anvil. The center of the curbstone impacts may be on or anywhere above the test line. The curbstone anvil may be placed in any orientation as long as the center of the anvil is aligned with the axis of the accelerometer. As noted in § 1203.12(d)(1), impact sites, the order of anvil use (flat and hemispherical), and curbstone anvil sites and orientation shall be chosen by the test personnel to provide the most severe test for the helmet. Rivets and other mechanical fasteners, vents, and any other helmet feature

within the test region are valid test sites.

(3) *Impact velocity*. The helmet shall be dropped onto the flat anvil with an impact velocity of 6.2 m/s±3% (20.34 ft/s±3%). (Typically, this requires a minimum drop height of 2 meters (6.56 ft), plus a height adjustment to account for friction losses.) The helmet shall be dropped onto the hemispherical and curbstone anvils with an impact velocity of 4.8 m/s±3% (15.75 ft/s±3%). (Typically, this requires a minimum drop height of 1.2 meters (3.94 ft), plus a height adjustment to account for friction losses.) The impact velocity shall be measured during the last 40 mm (1.57 in) of free-fall for each test.

(4) *Helmet position*. Prior to each test, the helmet shall be positioned on the test headform in accordance with the HPI. The helmet shall be secured so that it does not shift position prior to impact. The helmet retention system shall be secured in a manner that does not interfere with free-fall or impact.

(5) *Data*. Record the maximum acceleration in g's during impact. See Subpart C, § 1203.41(b).

Subpart B—Certification

§ 1203.30 Purpose, basis, and scope.

(a) *Purpose*. The purpose of this subpart is to establish requirements that manufacturers and importers of bicycle helmets subject to the Safety Standard for Bicycle Helmets (subpart A of this part 1203) shall issue certificates of compliance in the form specified.

(b) *Basis*. Section 14(a)(1) of the Consumer Product Safety Act (CPSA), 15 U.S.C. 2063(a)(1), requires every manufacturer (including importers) and private labeler of a product which is subject to a consumer product safety standard to issue a certificate that the product conforms to the applicable standard. Section 14(a)(1) further requires that the certificate be based either on a test of each product or on a "reasonable testing program." The Commission may, by rule, designate one or more of the manufacturers and private labelers as the persons who shall issue the required certificate. 15 U.S.C. 2063(a)(2).

(c) *Scope*. The provisions of this subpart apply to all bicycle helmets that are subject to the requirements of the Safety Standard for Bicycle Helmets, subpart A of this part 1203.

§ 1203.31 Applicability date.

All bicycle helmets manufactured on or after March 11, 1999, must meet the standard and must be certified as complying with the standard in accordance with this subpart B.

§ 1203.32 Definitions.

The following definitions shall apply to this subpart:

(a) *Foreign manufacturer* means an entity that manufactured a bicycle helmet outside the United States, as defined in 15 2052(a)(10) and (14).

(b) *Manufacturer* means the entity that either manufactured a helmet in the United States or imported a helmet manufactured outside the United States.

(c) *Private labeler* means an owner of a brand or trademark that is used on a bicycle helmet subject to the standard and that is not the brand or trademark of the manufacturer of the bicycle helmet, provided the owner of the brand or trademark caused, authorized, or approved its use.

(d) *Production lot* means a quantity of bicycle helmets from which certain bicycle helmets are selected for testing prior to certifying the lot. All bicycle helmets in a lot must be essentially identical in those design, construction, and material features that relate to the ability of a bicycle helmet to comply with the standard.

(e) *Reasonable testing program* means any tests which are identical or equivalent to, or more stringent than, the tests defined in the standard and which are performed on one or more bicycle helmets selected from the production lot to determine whether there is reasonable assurance that all of the bicycle helmets in that lot comply with the requirements of the standard.

§ 1203.33 Certification testing.

(a) *General*. Manufacturers, as defined in § 1203.32(b) to include importers, shall conduct a reasonable testing program to demonstrate that their bicycle helmets comply with the requirements of the standard.

(b) *Reasonable testing program.* This paragraph provides guidance for establishing a reasonable testing program.

(1) Within the requirements set forth in this paragraph (b), manufacturers and importers may define their own reasonable testing programs. Reasonable testing programs may, at the option of manufacturers and importers, be conducted by an independent third party qualified to perform such testing programs. However, manufacturers and importers are responsible for ensuring compliance with all requirements of the standard in subpart A of this part.

(2) As part of the reasonable testing program, the bicycle helmets shall be divided into production lots, and sample bicycle helmets from each production lot shall be tested. Whenever there is a change in parts, suppliers of parts, or production methods, and the change could affect the ability of the bicycle helmet to comply with the requirements of the standard, the manufacturer shall establish a new production lot for testing.

(3) The Commission will test for compliance with the standard by using the standard's test procedures. However, a reasonable testing program need not be identical to the tests prescribed in the standard.

(4) If the reasonable testing program shows that a bicycle helmet may not comply with one or more requirements of the standard, no bicycle helmet in the production lot can be certified as complying until sufficient actions are taken that it is reasonably likely that no noncomplying bicycle helmets remain in the production lot. All identified noncomplying helmets in the lot must be destroyed or altered by repair, redesign, or use of a different material or component, to the extent necessary to make them conform to the standard.

(5) The sale or offering for sale of a bicycle helmet that does not comply with the standard is a prohibited act and a violation of section 19(a) of the CPSA (15 U.S.C. 2068(a)), regardless of whether the bicycle helmet has been validly certified.

§ 1203.34 Product certification and labeling by manufacturers (including importers).

(a) *Form of permanent label of certification.* Manufacturers, as defined in § 1203.32(a), shall issue certificates of compliance for bicycle helmets manufactured after March 11, 1999, in the form of a durable, legible, and readily visible label meeting the requirements of this section. This label is the helmet's certificate of compliance, as that term is used in section 14 of the CPSA, 15 U.S.C. 2063.

(b) *Contents of certification label.* The certification labels required by this section shall contain the following:

(1) The statement "Complies with U.S. CPSC Safety Standard for Bicycle Helmets for Persons Age 5 and Older" or "Complies with U.S. CPSC Safety Standard for Bicycle Helmets for Persons Age 1 and Older (Extended Head Coverage)", as appropriate; this label may spell out "U.S. Consumer Product Safety Commission" instead of "U.S. CPSC";

(2) The name of the U.S. manufacturer or importer responsible for issuing the certificate or the name of a private labeler;

(3) The address of the U.S. manufacturer or importer responsible for issuing the certificate or, if the name of a private labeler is on the label, the address of the private labeler;

(4) The name and address of the foreign manufacturer, if the helmet was manufactured outside the United States;

(5) The telephone number of the U.S. manufacturer or importer responsible for issuing the certificate or, if the name of a private labeler is on the label, the telephone number of the private labeler;

(6) An identification of the production lot; and

(7) The uncoded month and year the product was manufactured.

(c) *Coding.* (1) The information required by paragraphs (b)(4) and (b)(6) of this section, and the information referred to in paragraph (c)(2) of this section, may be in code, provided:

(i) The person or firm issuing the certificate maintains a written record of the meaning of each symbol used in the code, and

(ii) The record shall be made available to the distributor, retailer, consumer, and Commission upon request.

(2) A serial number may be used in place of a production lot identification on the helmet if it can serve as a code to identify the production lot. If a bicycle helmet is manufactured for sale by a private labeler, and if the name of the private labeler is on the certification label, the name of the manufacturer or importer issuing the certificate, and the name and address of any foreign manufacturer, may also be in code.

(d) *Placement of the label(s).* The information required by paragraphs (b)(2), (b)(3), and (b)(5) of this section must be on one label. The other required information may be on separate labels. The label(s) required by this section must be affixed to the bicycle helmet. If the label(s) are not immediately visible to the ultimate purchaser of the bicycle helmet prior to purchase because of packaging or other marketing practices, a second label is required. That label shall state, as appropriate, "Complies with U.S. CPSC Safety Standard for Bicycle Helmets for Persons Age 5 and Older", or "Complies with U.S. CPSC Safety Standard for Bicycle Helmets for Persons Age 1 and Older (Extended Head Coverage)". The label shall be legible, readily visible, and placed on the main display panel of the packaging or, if the packaging is not visible before purchase (e.g., catalog sales), on the promotional material used with the sale of the bicycle helmet. This label may spell out "U.S. Consumer Product Safety Commission" instead of "U.S. CPSC."

(e) *Additional provisions for importers*—(1) *General.* The importer of any bicycle helmet subject to the standard in subpart A of this part 1203 must issue the certificate of compliance required by section 14(a) of the CPSA and this section. If a reasonable testing program meeting the requirements of this subpart has been performed by or for the foreign manufacturer of the product, the importer may rely in good faith on such tests to support the certificate of compliance, provided:

(i) The importer is a resident of the United States or has a resident agent in the United States,

(ii) There are records of such tests required by § 1203.41 of subpart C of this part, and

(iii) Such records are available to the Commission within 48 hours of a request to the importer.

(2) *Responsibility of importers.* Importers that rely on tests by the foreign manufacturer to support the certificate of compliance shall—in addition to complying with paragraph (e)(1) of this section—examine the records supplied by the manufacturer to determine that they comply with § 1203.41 of subpart C of this part.

Subpart C—Recordkeeping

§ 1203.40 Effective date.

This subpart is effective March 10, 1999, and applies to bicycle helmets manufactured after that date.

§ 1203.41 Recordkeeping requirements.

(a) *General.* Every person issuing certificates of compliance for bicycle helmets subject to the standard in subpart A of this part shall maintain records which show that the certificates are based on a reasonable testing program. The records shall be maintained for a period of at least 3 years from the date of certification of the last bicycle helmet in each production lot. These records shall be available, upon request, to any designated officer or employee of the Commission, in accordance with section 16(b) of the CPSA, 15 U.S.C. 2065(b). If the records are not physically available during the inspection because they are maintained at another location, the firm must provide them to the staff within 48 hours.

(b) *Records of helmet tests.* Complete test records shall be maintained. These records shall contain the following information.

(1) An identification of the bicycle helmets tested;

(2) An identification of the production lot;

(3) The results of the tests, including the precise nature of any failures;

(4) A description of the specific actions taken to address any failures;

(5) A detailed description of the tests, including the helmet positioning index (HPI) used to define the proper position of the helmet on the headform;

(6) The manufacturer's name and address;

(7) The model and size of each helmet tested;

(8) Identifying information for each helmet tested, including the production lot for each helmet;

(9) The environmental condition under which each helmet was tested, the duration of the helmet's conditioning, the temperatures in each conditioning environment, and the relative humidity and temperature of the laboratory;

(10) The peripheral vision clearance;

(11) A description of any failures to conform to any of the labeling and instruction requirements;

(12) Performance impact results, stating the precise location of impact, type of anvil used, velocity prior to impact, and maximum acceleration measured in g's;

(13) The results of the positional stability test;

(14) The results of the dynamic strength of retention system test;

(15) The name and location of the test laboratory;

(16) The name of the person(s) who performed the test;

(17) The date of the test; and

(18) The system check results.

(c) *Format for records.* The records required to be maintained by this section may be in any appropriate form or format that clearly provides the required information. Certification test results may be kept on paper, microfiche, computer disk, or other retrievable media. Where records are kept on computer disk or other retrievable media, the records shall be made available to the Commission on paper copies, or via electronic mail in the same format as paper copies, upon request.

Subpart D—Requirements For Bicycle Helmets Manufactured From March 17, 1995, Through March 10, 1999

§ 1203.51 Purpose and basis.

The purpose and basis of this subpart is to protect bicyclists from head injuries by ensuring that bicycle helmets comply with the requirements of appropriate existing voluntary standards, as provided in 15 U.S.C. 6004(a).

§ 1203.52 Scope and effective date.

(a) This subpart D is effective March 17, 1995, except for § 1203.53(a)(8), which is effective March 10, 1998. This subpart D shall apply to bicycle helmets manufactured from March 17, 1995, through March 10, 1999, inclusive. Such bicycle helmets shall comply with the requirements of one of the standards specified in § 1203.53. This subpart shall be considered a consumer product safety standard issued under the Consumer Product Safety Act.

(b) The term "bicycle helmet" is defined at § 1203.4(b).

(c) These interim mandatory safety standards will not apply to bicycle helmets manufactured after March 10, 1999. Those helmets are subject to the requirements of Subparts A through C of this part 1203.

§ 1203.53 Interim safety standards.

(a) Bicycle helmets must comply with one or more of the following standards. The standards in paragraphs (a)(1) through (a)(7) of this section are incorporated herein by reference:

(1) American National Standards Institute (ANSI) standard Z90.4–1984, Protective Headgear for Bicyclists,

(2) ASTM standards F 1447–93 or F 1447–94, Standard Specification for Protective Headgear Used in Bicycling, incorporating the relevant provisions of ASTM F 1446–93 or ASTM F 1446–94, Standard Test Methods for Equipment and Procedures Used in Evaluating the Performance Characteristics of Protective Headgear, respectively,

(3) Canadian Standards Association standard, Cycling Helmets—CAN/CSA-D113.2-M89,

(4) Snell Memorial Foundation (Snell) 1990 Standard for Protective Headgear for Use in Bicycling (designation B–90),

(5) Snell 1990 Standard for Protective Headgear for Use in Bicycling, including March 9, 1994 Supplement (designation B–90S),

(6) Snell 1994 Standard for Protective Headgear for Use in Non-Motorized Sports (designation N–94), or

(7) Snell 1995 standard for Protective Headgear for Use with Bicycles B–95.

(8) Subparts A through C of this part 1203.

(b) The incorporation by reference of the standards listed in paragraphs (a)(1) through (a)(7) are approved by the Director of the Federal Register in accordance with 5 U.S.C. 552(a) and 1 CFR part 51. Copies of the standards may be obtained as follows. Copies of the ANSI Z90.4 standard are available from: American National Standards Institute, 11 W. 42nd Street, 13th Floor, New York, NY 10036. Copies of the ASTM standards are available from: ASTM, 100 Barr Harbor Drive, West Conshohocken, PA 19428–2959. Copies of the Canadian Standards Association CAN/CSA-D113.2-M89 standard are available from: CSA, 178 Rexdale Boulevard, Rexdale (Toronto), Ontario, Canada, M9W 1R3. Copies of the Snell standards are available from: Snell Memorial Foundation, Inc., 6731–A 32nd Street, North Highlands, CA 95660. Copies may be inspected at the Office of the Secretary, Consumer Product Safety Commission, 4330 East-West Highway, Bethesda, Maryland 20814, or at the National Archives and Records Administration (NARA). For information on the availability of this material at NARA, call 202–741–6030, or go to: *http://www.archives.gov/federal_register/code_of_federal_regulations/ibr_locations.html.*

FIGURE 1 TO PART 1203—ANATOMICAL PLANES

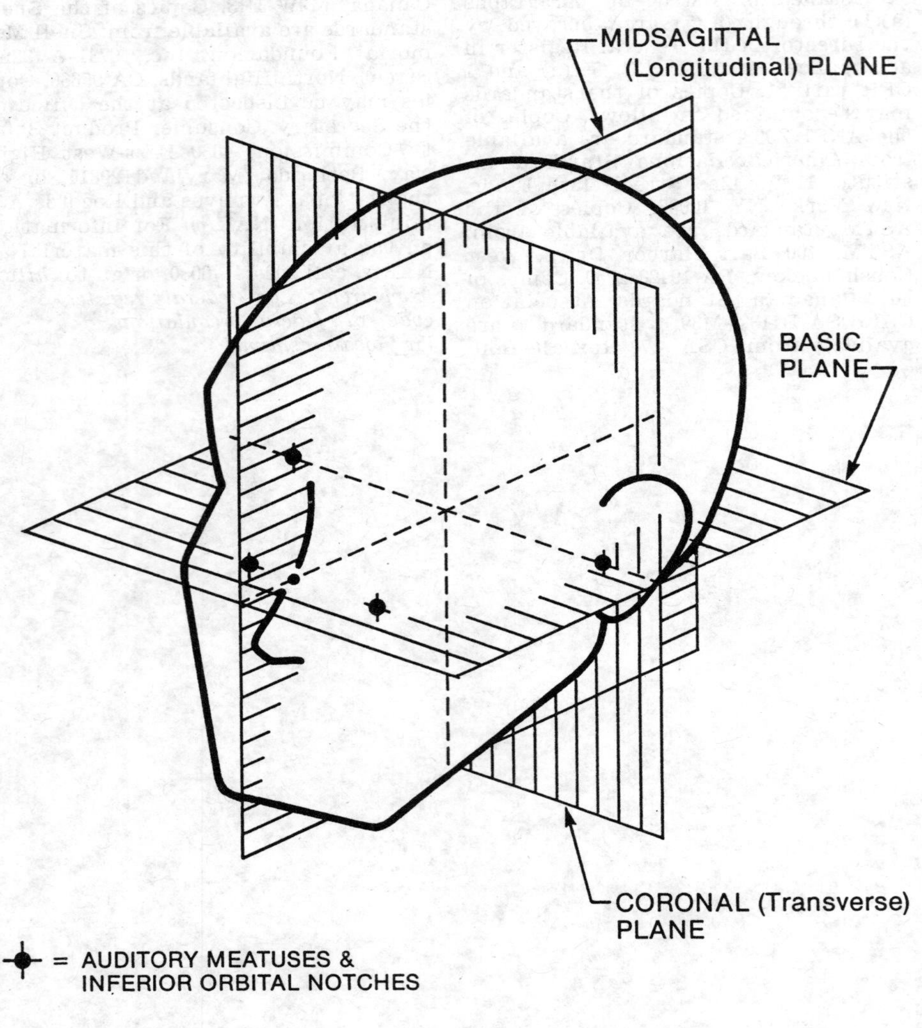

Figure 1. Anatomical Planes

FIGURE 2 TO PART 1203—ISO HEADFORM-BASIC, REFERENCE, AND MEDIAN PLANES

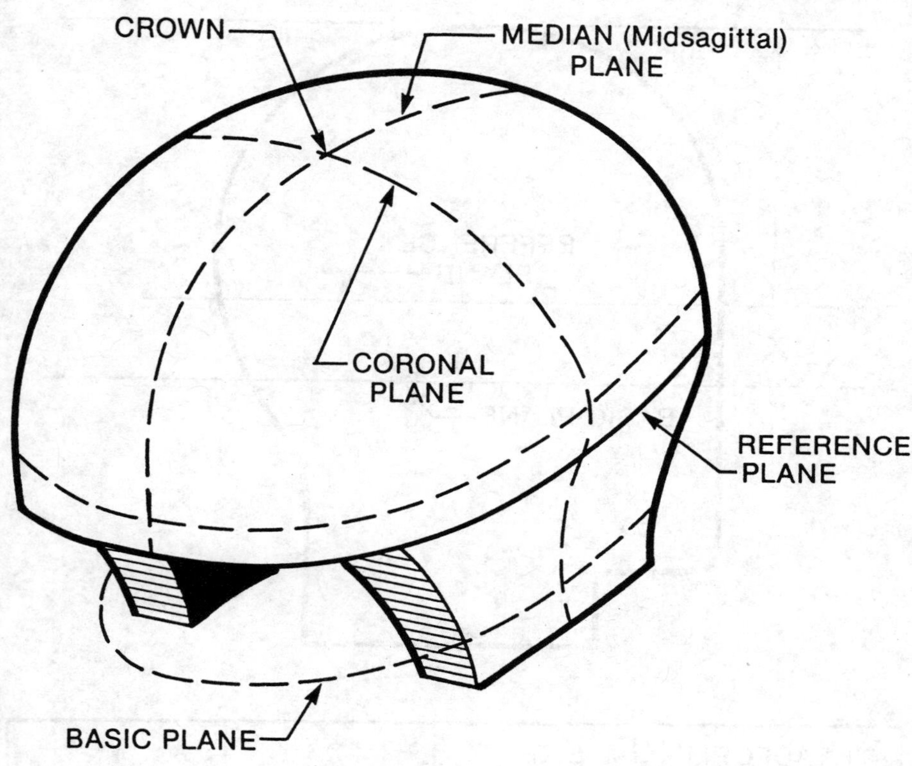

Figure 2. ISO Headform-Basic, Reference, and Median Planes

FIGURE 3 TO PART 1203—LOCATION OF REFERENCE PLANE

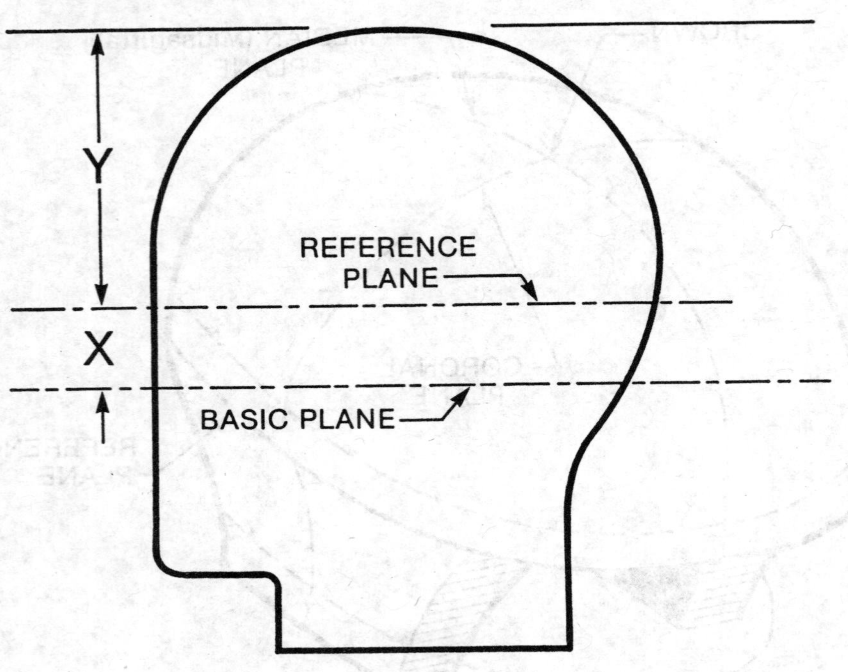

HEADFORM	SIZE	X	Y
A	500	24	90
E	540	26	96
J	570	27.5	102.5
M	600	29	107
O	620	30	110

DIMENSIONS IN MILLIMETERS

Figure 3. Location of Reference Plane

FIGURE 4 TO PART 1203—LOCATION OF TEST LINES FOR HELMETS INTENDED FOR PERSONS FIVE (5) YEARS OF AGE AND OLDER

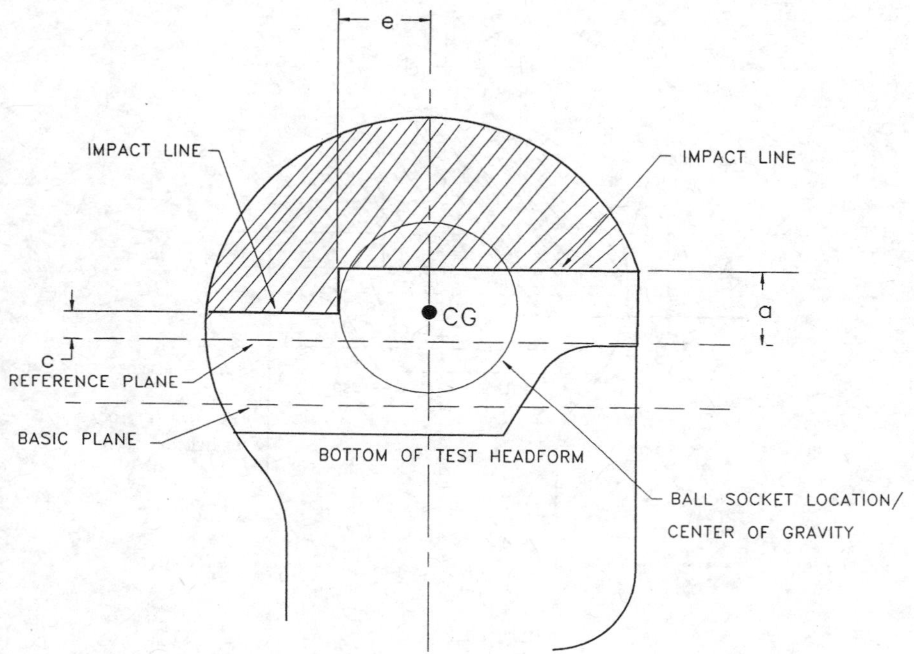

HEADFORM	DIMENSIONS mm(in)		
	a	c	e
ISO A	38 (1.49)	27 (1.06)	49 (1.93)
ISO E	39 (1.54)	27 (1.06)	52 (2.05)
ISO J	41 (1.61)	27 (1.06)	54 (2.13)
ISO M	41 (1.61)	27 (1.06)	55 (2.16)
ISO O	42 (1.65)	27 (1.06)	56 (2.20)

Figure 4. Location of Test Lines for Helmets Intended for Persons Five (5) Years of Age and Older.

FIGURE 5 TO PART 1203—LOCATION OF TEST LINES FOR HELMETS INTENDED FOR PERSONS AGES 1 AND OLDER

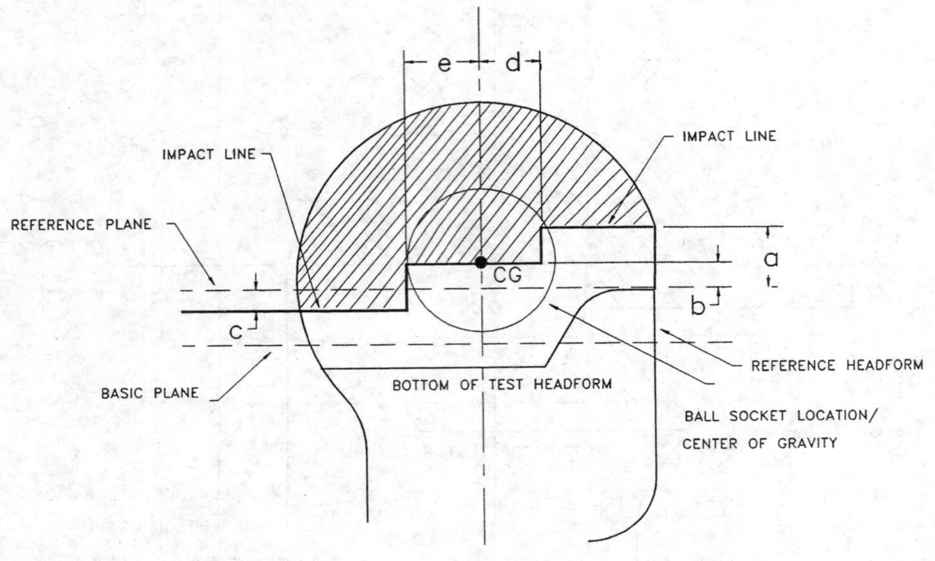

HEADFORM	DIMENSIONS mm (in)				
	a	b	c	d	e
ISO A	30 (1.18)	12.7 (0.50)	15 (0.59)	25 (0.98)	30 (1.18)
ISO E	32 (1.26)	12.7 (0.50)	16 (0.63)	27 (1.06)	32 (1.26)

Figure 5. Location of Test Lines for Helmets Intended for Persons Ages 1 and Older

FIGURE 6 TO PART 1203—FIELD OF VISION

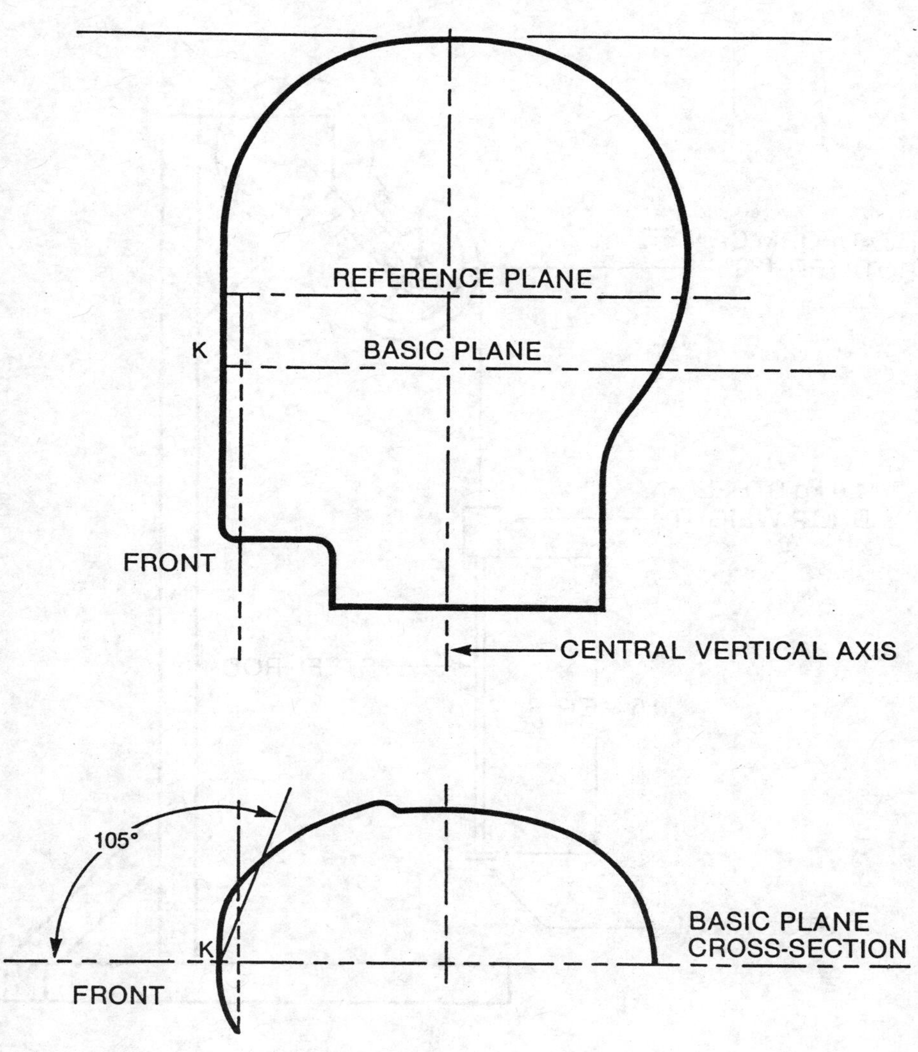

Figure 6. Field of Vision

FIGURE 7 TO PART 1203—TYPICAL TEST APPARATUS FOR POSITIONAL STABILITY TEST

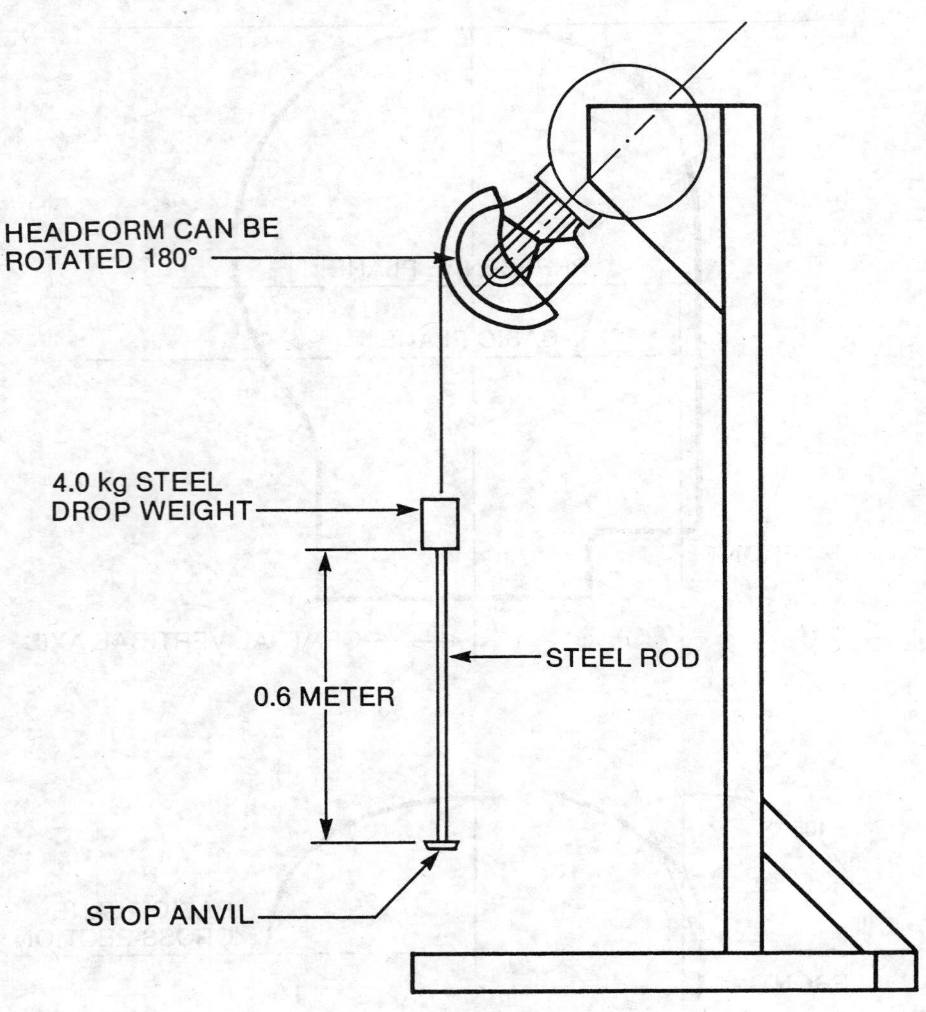

Figure 7. Typical Test Apparatus for Positional Stability Test

FIGURE 8 TO PART 1203—APPARATUS FOR TEST OF RETENTION SYSTEM STRENGTH

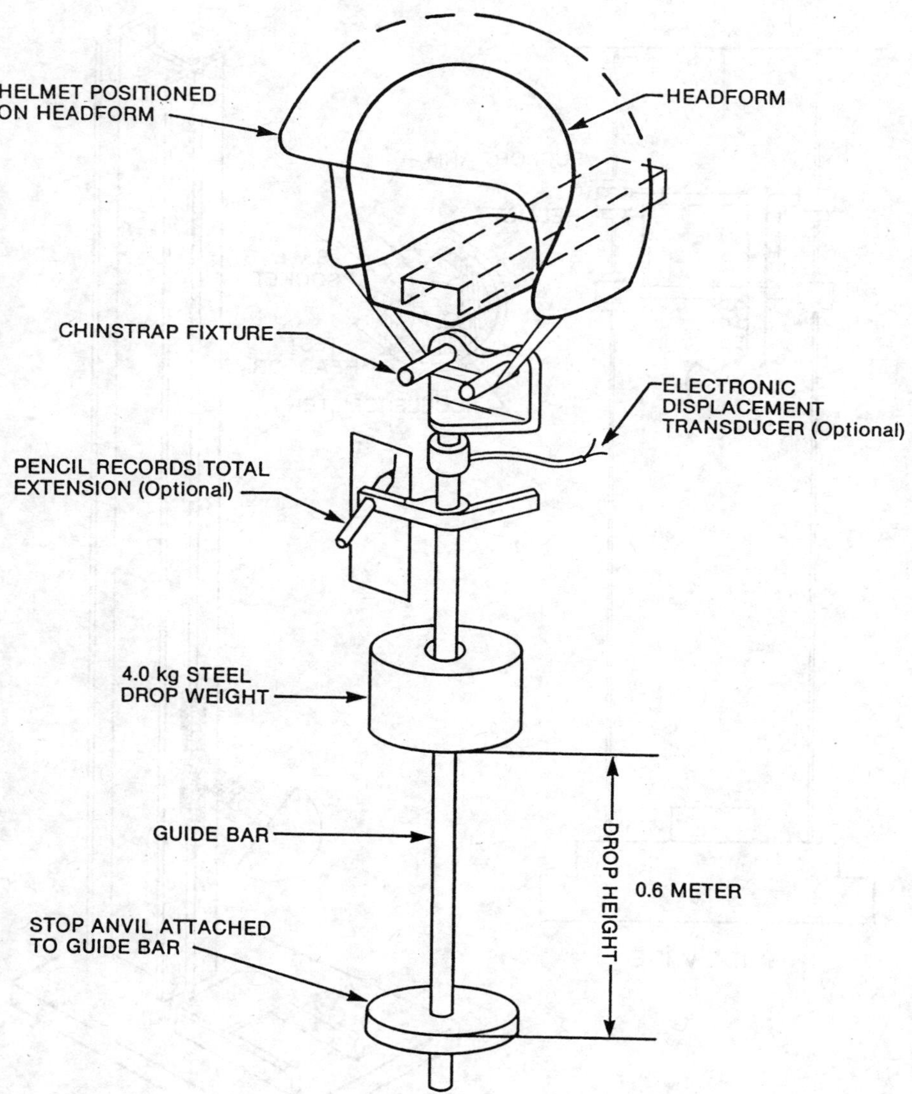

Figure 8. Apparatus for Test of Retention System Strength

FIGURE 9 TO PART 1203—IMPACT TEST APPARATUS

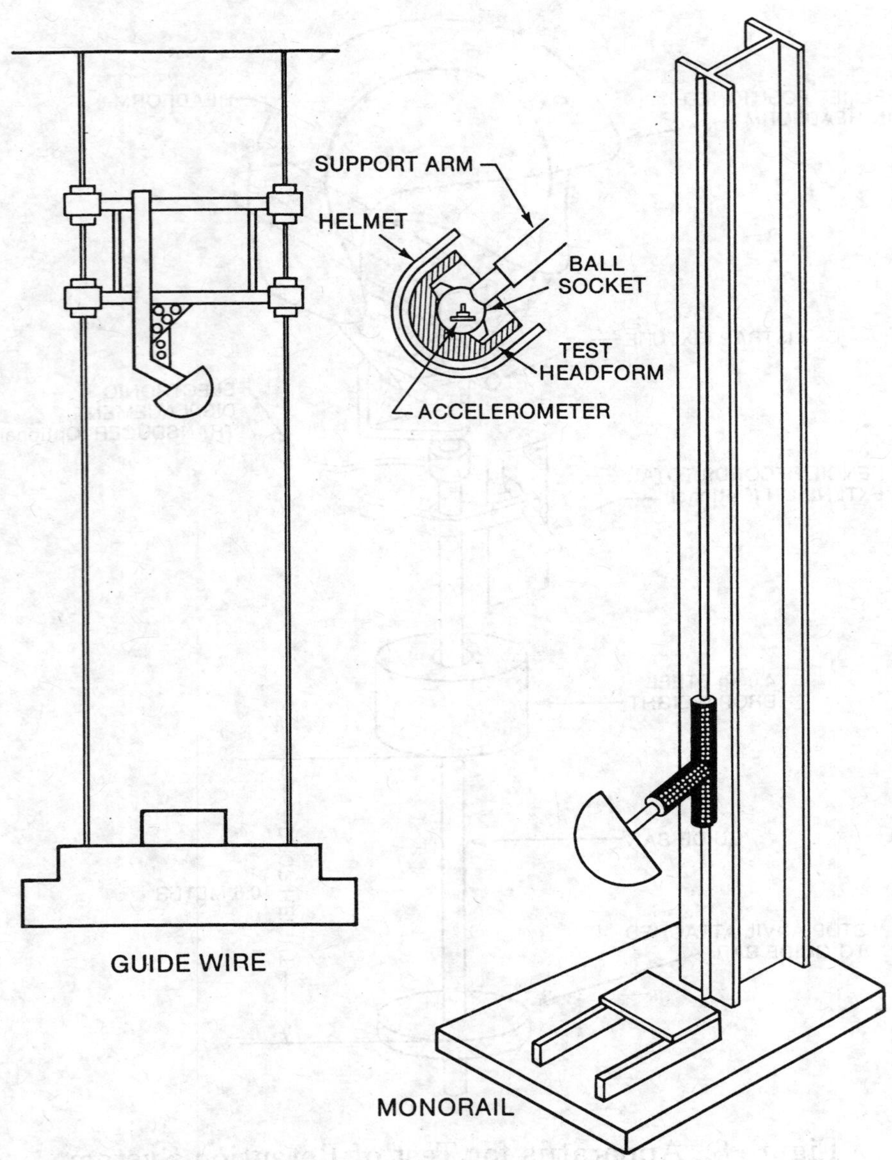

Figure 9. Impact Test Apparatus

FIGURE 10 TO PART 1203—CENTER OF GRAVITY FOR DROP ASSEMBLY

Overhead View of Ball-Arm as Installed on Impact Test Apparatus

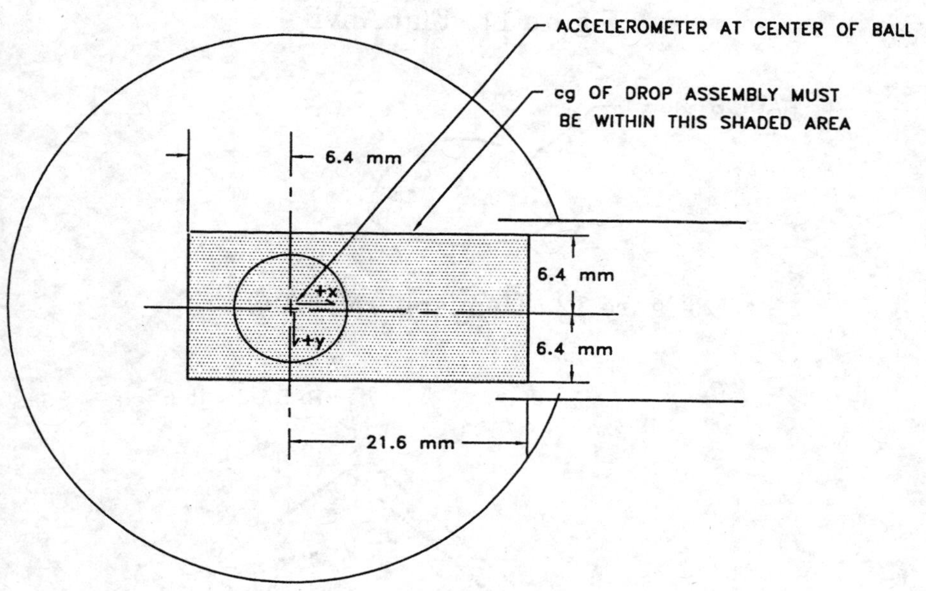

Figure 10. Center of Gravity for Drop Assembly

FIGURES 11, 12 AND 13 TO PART 1203—HEMISPHERICAL ANVIL AND CURBSTONE ANVIL

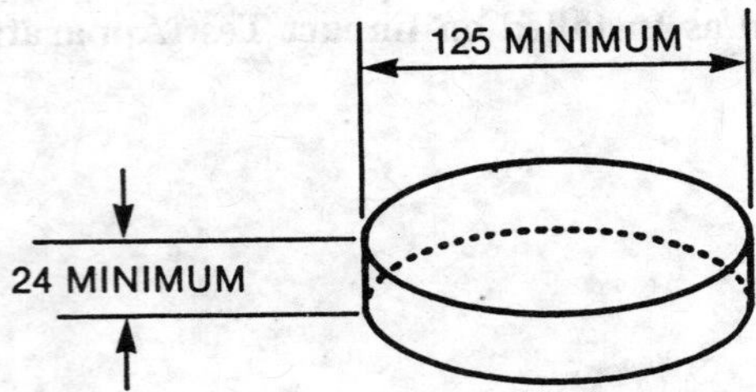

Figure 11. Flat Anvil

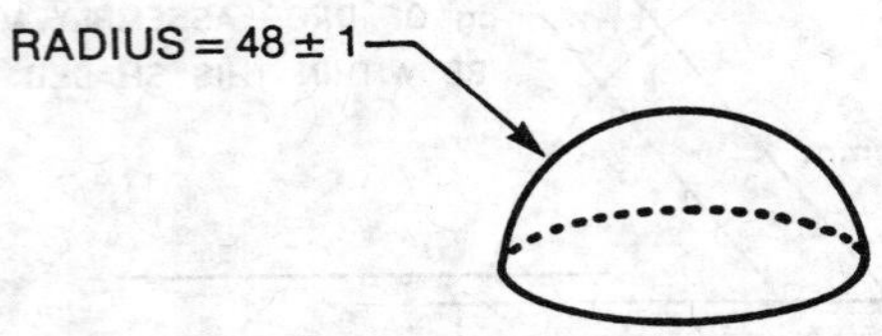

Figure 12. Hemispherical Anvil

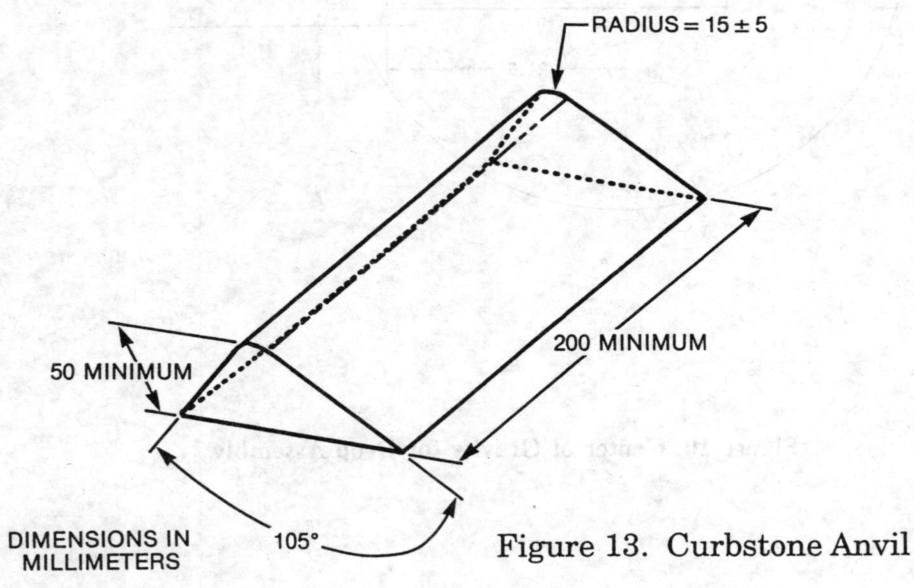

Figure 13. Curbstone Anvil

PART 1204—SAFETY STANDARD FOR OMNIDIRECTIONAL CITIZENS BAND BASE STATION ANTENNAS

AUTHORITY: Secs. 2, 3, 5, 7, 9, 14, 16, 19, 25, Pub. L. 92–573, 86 Stat. 1207, 1208, 1211–17, 1220, as amended Pub. L. 95–319, sec. 1, 92 Stat. 386, Pub. L. 94–284, 90 Stat. 503; 15 U.S.C. 2051, 2052, 2054, 2056, 2058, 2063, 2065, 2068, 2074.

SOURCE: 47 FR 36201, Aug. 19, 1982, unless otherwise noted.

Subpart A—The Standard

§ 1204.1 Scope of the standard.

(a) *General.* This subpart A of part 1204 is a consumer product safety standard which prescribes safety requirements for Citizens Band omnidirectional base station antennas. The standard is intended to reduce the risk of electrocution or serious injuries occurring if the antenna contacts an electric power line while the antenna is being put up or taken down. One way that this can be accomplished is to insulate the antenna so that if it contacts the power line, there is less of a likelihood that a harmful electric current will be transmitted from the power line through the antenna and mast and ultimately through a person holding the antenna mast. Another possible way to provide this protection is to incorporate an insulating barrier between the antenna and the mast or other supporting structure, so that a harmful electric current will not pass from the antenna to a person in contact with the mast. (If this alternative were chosen, the feed cable from the antenna would have to be insulated or otherwise protected so that it would not provide an electrical path to the mast or a person touching the cable.)

(b) *Description of the standard*—(1) *Performance tests.* The standard describes two performance tests to determine if the means chosen by the manufacturer to protect against the shock hazard will provide adequate protection.

(i) First, there is an Insulating Material Effectiveness Test (§ 1204.4(d) of this subpart) in which a high voltage electrode or test rod is brought into contact with the antenna at any point within the protection zone established by § 1204.2(k) of this subpart to ensure that the insulation can withstand the voltage for 5 minutes without transmitting more than 5 milliamperes (mA) root-mean-square (rms) of electric current.

(ii) The other test is an Antenna-Mast System Test (§ 1204.4(e) of this subpart) which is intended to determine whether the means provided to protect against electrocution will withstand the stress imposed when an antenna-mast system falls onto a power line. This test consists of mounting the antenna to be tested on a specified mast and allowing the assembled antenna and mast to fall onto a power line of 14,500 volts rms phase to ground.

(2) *Recommended materials.* (i) Since a substantial portion of the accidents addressed by this standard occur when the antenna is being taken down after it has been installed in an outdoor environment for a number of years, the materials selected to provide protection from shock should be weather resistant.

(ii) Although other materials may also be suitable, materials meeting the following criteria should be reasonably weather resistant:

(A) Material composition includes an ultraviolet stabilizer or screen.

(B) Heat resistance of 212 °F (100 °C) without loss of elasticity (ANSI/ASTM D 746–79).

(C) Moisture absorption of not more than 0.2 percent (ANSI/ASTM D 570–77).

(D) For heat shrinkable sleeving, temperature flexibility to −40 °F (−40 °C) with no cracks (Mil Spec. MIL-I-23053C, 20 May 1976).

(3) *Warning:* Section 1204.5 of this subpart requires a statement in the instructions that the standard will not protect in every instance against electrocution caused by contact with power lines. This is because the standard is intended to provide protection for power line voltages of up to 14,500 volts. Some power lines carry more voltage than this. In addition, not all portions of the antenna are required to be insulated, and the antenna's mast is not required to be insulated. If the power line were to contact one of these uninsulated areas, an electrocution could occur. Furthermore, when the antenna was manufactured it may not in fact have complied with the standard, or the insulation may have deteriorated or been damaged since the antenna was manufactured. In addition, the insulation cannot withstand high voltages indefinitely, and, after a period of time, the current may penetrate the insulation. Therefore, even if a harmful amount of current is not transmitted immediately, the user should not attempt to remove an antenna that falls into electric power lines, since the insulation could break down while the antenna is being removed. For these reasons, persons handling these antennas should ensure that the antennas are kept away from power lines so that the antenna cannot contact the line while being transported, installed, or removed, even if the antenna is dropped. The Commission recommends that antennas be located at least twice the combined length of the antenna and mast from the nearest power line.

(c) *Scope.* (1) Except as noted below, the standard applies to all omnidirectional CB base station antennas that are consumer products and are manufactured or imported on or after May 24, 1983.

(2) The Commission may extend the effective date of the standard for as long as an additional 90 days for any firm which has 750 employees or fewer and, is not a subsidiary or division of a firm having more than 750 employees, and which manufactures or imports products subject to the standard, upon written application, addressed to the Associate Executive Director for Compliance and Administrative litigation, Consumer Product Safety Commission, Washington, D.C. 20207, received not later than January 17, 1983. An application for extension of the effective date shall:

(i) Identify the requesting firm as a manufacturer or importer of products subject to the standard.

(ii) State the total number of employees of the firm, including all employees of any subsidiary or division, and all employees of any firm of which the requesting firm is a subsidiary or division.

(iii) Request extension of the effective date to a specific date not later than May 27, 1983.

(iv) Explain why the requested extension of the effective date is needed.

(v) Describe all activities undertaken by the requesting firm to achieve compliance with the requirements of the standard.

(vi) State that the requesting firm will market complying products after the extended effective date.

(3) The Associate Executive Director for Compliance and Administrative Litigation will evaluate each request for extension of the effective date. The following criteria will be used in determining whether to grant an application for extension of the effective date:

(i) Does the application demonstrate that the requesting firm cannot meet the general effective date,

(ii) Does the application demonstrate that the requesting firm has made a good faith effort to achieve compliance with the requirements of the standard by the general effective date.

(iii) Does the application demonstrate that the firm is likely to produce or market complying products if the requested extension is granted.

(4) The Associate Executive Director will advise each requesting firm in writing if the requested extension is granted or denied. If the Associate Executive Director for Compliance and Administrative Litigation denies a request for extension of the effective

date, the firm may request the Commission to reconsider the denial.

(5) Section 3(a)(1) of the Consumer Product Safety Act (CPSA, 15 U.S.C. 2052(a)(1) defines the term *consumer product* as an "article, or component part thereof, produced or distributed (i) for sale to a consumer for use in or around a permanent or temporary household or residence, a school, in recreation, or otherwise, or (ii) for the personal use, consumption or enjoyment of a consumer in or around a permanent or temporary household or residence, a school, in recreation, or otherwise." The term does not include products that are not customarily produced or distributed for sale to, or for the use or consumption by, or enjoyment of, a consumer. A limited exception from coverage of the standard is provided by section 18(a) of the CPSA, 15 U.S.C. 2067, for certain products intended for export and meeting the requirements of section 18(b) of the CPSA.

(d) *Prohibited acts.* It is unlawful to manufacture for sale, offer for sale, distribute in commerce, or import into the United States any product subject to this standard that does not conform with the standard.

(Sec. 9(h), Pub. L. 92–573, 86 Stat. 1207, as amended, Pub. L. 95–319, 92 Stat. 386, Pub. L. 95–631, 92 Stat. 3742, Pub. L. 96–373, 94 Stat. 1366, Pub. L. 97–35, 95 Stat. 703, 15 U.S.C. 2058(h))

[47 FR 36201, Aug. 19, 1982, as amended at 48 FR 29683, June 28, 1983]

§ 1204.2 Definitions.

In addition to the definitions given in section 3 of the Consumer Product Safety Act (15 U.S.C. 2052), the following definitions apply for the purposes of this standard.

(a) *Antenna system* means a device for radiating and/or receiving radio waves. Where they are present, the antenna system includes active elements, ground plane elements, matching networks, element-connecting hardware, mounting hardware, feed cable, and other functional or non-functional elements.

(b) *Antenna-mast system* means the completed assembly of the antenna system and the mast.

(c) *Base station* means a transmitter and/or receiver in a fixed location.

(d) *Citizens Band (CB)* means the frequency band allocated for citizen's band radio service.

(e) *Current* means the total rate at which electrical charge is transported through the antenna-mast system in response to the applied test voltage, including both capacitive and resistive components.

(f) *Electrical breakdown* means a failure of the insulating material used with the antenna, such that in the Antenna-Mast System Test of § 1204.4(e) of this subpart, the current flowing through the antenna-mast system is sufficient to actuate the automatic internal cut-off of the high voltage source or exceeds the current that can be measured by the current monitoring device.

(g) *Feed cable* means the electrical cable that connects the antenna system to the transmitter and/or receiver.

(h) *Field joint* means any joint between antenna system sections or parts, or between the antenna system and the mast, that is not assembled by the antenna manufacturer.

(i) *Insulating material and insulation* mean a material that has a very small electric conductivity.

(j) *Omnidirectional antenna* means an antenna system designed or intended primarily to exhibit approximately equal signal transmission or reception capabilities in all horizontal directions simultaneously.

(k) *Protection zone* means that portion of an antenna system which can contact the test rod during the Insulating Material Effectiveness Test or can contact the power line during the Antenna-Mast System Test. This zone consists of those elements of the antenna system extending from the uppermost tip of an upright antenna downward to a point that is 12.0 inches (30.5 cm) above the top of the mast when the antenna system is mounted according to the manufacturer's instructions.

(l) *Voltage, phase to ground,* means that voltage which exists between a single phase of a three phase power system and ground.

§ 1204.3 Requirements.

All omnidirectional CB base station antennas are required to comply with the following requirements.

(a) *Field joints.* Parts or accessories intended to protect a field joint so that it will meet any other requirement of this standard, and that must be put into place by the person assembling the antenna system, shall be integral with, or not readily removable from, at least one of the antenna sections or parts involved in the joint or shall be necessary in order to complete the joint.

(b) *Feed cable.* When compliance with the requirements of this standard depends on the insulating or other properties of the feed cable, at least 50 feet of the cable shall be supplied by the manufacturer with the antenna system.

(c) *Electrical protection.* Antenna systems shall be manufactured so that if all points within the protection zone of an antenna system were tested by the Insulating Material Effectiveness Test of § 1204.4(d) of this subpart, and the Antenna-Mast System Test of § 1204.4(e) of this subpart, the current measured by the current monitoring device connected to the mast would be no greater than 5.0 milliamperes rms and no electrical breakdown of the antenna system's insulating material would occur.

§ 1204.4 Electric shock protection tests.

(a) *Safety precautions.* For tests involving high voltage, the following recommended minimum safety precautions should be followed:

(1) At least one test operator and one test observer (preferably one with cardiopulmonary resusitation (CPR) training) should be present at every test.

(2) The test area (outdoors or indoors) should secure against accidental intrusion by other persons during tests.

(3) Test areas located indoors should be ventilated to avoid buildup of potentially hazardous concentrations of gaseous byproducts which may result from the tests.

(4) Fire extinguishers should be easily accessible in case materials on the test specimen ignite.

(5) "High Voltage Test" warning devices should be activated before start of a test.

(6) Emergency phone numbers should be posted.

(b) *Test conditions*—(1) *Specimens.* All specimens shall be tested as supplied by the manufacturer, following assembly in accordance with the manufacturer's instructions except as provided in paragraph (e)(2) of this section.

(2) *Temperature.* Ambient temperature shall be in the range from 32 °F (0 °C) to 104 °F (40 °C)

(3) *Relative humidity.* Ambient relative humidity shall be in the range of from 10 to 90 percent.

(4) *Voltage.* Voltage, phase to ground, of the power line or test probe shall be 14.5 kilovolts rms, 60 hertz.

(5) *Conditioning.* Prior to testing, all specimens shall be exposed for at least 4 hours to the ambient test area environment.

(c) *Test equipment.* (1) High voltage source capable of delivering at least 15 mA rms at 14.5 kV rms, 60 Hz. The source should have an automatic internal cut-off actuated by a preset current level.

(2) Instrumentation to measure the rms voltage applied to the antenna system.

(3) Current monitoring device to indicate hazardous components of the total rms current flowing to ground through the mast. One configuration of the circuitry for the current monitoring device (shown in Figure 1) consists of three parallel branches as follows. One branch consists of a resistor in series with a true-rms milliammeter with a maximum error of 5% of the reading in the frequency range of 50Hz to 10MHz (the total of the resistor and the internal resistance of the milliammeter is to be 1000 ohms). A parallel branch consists of a 1000 ohm resistor in series with a 0.08 microfarad capacitor. Another parallel branch should consist of a spark gap rated at 50 to 100 volts as a meter protection device. A different current monitoring device may be used if the measured value of the rms current corresponds to that indicated by the configuration described above.

(4) For the Insulating Material Effectiveness Test:

(i) High voltage electrode or test rod consisting of ¼ in. (6.4 mm) diameter aluminum rod.

(ii) Support jig, structure, or hanger made of insulating material which is capable of holding antenna system test specimens electrically isolated from all surrounding structures or ground.

(5) For the Antenna-Mast System Test, a high voltage test facility, as shown in Figures 2 and 3, which includes a single power line spanning between two poles 95 to 105 feet (29 to 32 meters) apart, a tensioning device to adjust the cable sag to from 9 to 12 inches (23 to 30 cm), and a pivot fixture (Figure 2), for holding the base of an antenna-mast system, which can be moved horizontally to adjust the distance to the cable. The cable consists of ¼ in. diameter 7 by 19 galvanized steel aircraft cable. The low point of the cable shall be between 28 and 29 feet (8.5 to 8.8 meters) above a horizontal plane through the pivot axis of the pivot fixture.

(d) *Insulating Material Effectiveness Test procedure.* (1) A short piece of typical tubular mast shall be attached to the antenna system to be tested, in accordance with mounting instructions provided with the antenna system by the manufacturer.

(2) If a feed cable is provided with the antenna system, it shall be used in the test. If no cable is provided with the antenna system, a RG–213 cable shall be used in the test (Mil Spec. MIL-C-17/75C, 15 March 1977). In either case, the cable shall be connected to the antenna system, installed parallel to the mast, and secured by taping or similar means at one point on the mast. The side of the bottom end of the cable also shall be secured to the mast.

(3) With the antenna system properly supported and isolated from ground and with the current monitoring device connected to the mast, the test rod shall be connected to the high voltage source and brought into contact with the antenna system at any point within the protection zone (see §1204.2(k) of this subpart). For each contact point, the voltage shall be increased from 0 to 14.5 kV at a rate of at least 2 kV per second and held at 14.5 kV for 5.0 minutes. Current shall be monitored and the maximum recorded.

(e) *Antenna-Mast System Test procedure.* (1) The antenna system to be tested shall be attached to a mast in accordance with mounting instructions provided by the manufacturer. The mast shall be assembled of commercially available 1¼ inch outside diameter 16 gauge tubular steel sections, commonly sold for antenna-mast installations in 5 and 10 feet lengths. The slip joints between the mast sections shall be secured (as with screws) to prohibit rotational or longitudinal movement at the joint. The length of the mast shall be such that when it is mounted in the pivot fixture of the high voltage test facility, the distance from the pivot to the uppermost point on the antenna system is 41.75 to 42.25 feet (12.7 to 12.9 meters).

(2) If a feed cable is provided with the antenna system, it shall be used in the test. If no cable is provided with the antenna system, a RG–213 feed cable shall be used in the test for specification of an RG–213 cable see (Mil. Spec. MIL-C-17/75C, 15 March 1977). In either case, the cable shall be connected to the antenna system, installed parallel to the mast, and secured by taping or similar means every two feet along the length of the mast. The side of the bottom end of the cable also shall be secured to the mast.

(3) The antenna-mast system shall be mounted in the pivot fixture. The pivot fixture shall be adjusted so that the point of impact between the antenna and the power line takes place at any desired point within the antenna's protection zone. The antenna-mast system shall then be erected to a position of up to 5° from the vertical, leaning toward the simulated power line (see Figure 4). The antenna-mast system shall then be released and allowed to fall against the power line. The test may be performed with different test positions such that the antenna system flexes after impact and slides off the power line and or so that it remains in contact with the power line for 5.0 minutes. Current flow from the antenna-mast system to ground shall be monitored and recorded for each test.

(f) *Interpretation of Results.* An antenna shall pass the Insulating Material Effectiveness Test or the Antenna-Mast System Test if no electrical breakdown occurs and if no current reading exceeds 5 mA rms.

§ 1204.5 Manufacturer's instructions.

(a) For all antennas covered under this part 1204, the following statement shall be included in the manufacturer's instructions, in addition to the material required by 16 CFR 1402.4(a)(1)(ii):

Under some conditions, this antenna may not prevent electrocution. Users should keep antenna away from any overhead wires. If antenna contacts a power line, any initial protection could fail at any time. IF ANTENNA NEARS ANY OVERHEAD WIRES, IMMEDIATELY LET GO, STAY AWAY, AND CALL UTILITY COMPANY.

(b) This warning statement shall be in a separate paragraph immediately following the warning statement required by 16 CFR 1402.4(a)(1)(ii)(A).

(c) This warning statement shall be legible and conspicuous and shall be in type that is at least as large as the largest type used on the remainder of the page, with the exception of the logo and any identification of the manufacturer, brand, model, or similar designations, and that is preferably no smaller than 10 point type.

§ 1204.6 Findings.

As required by section 9 (b) and (c) of the Consumer Product Safety Act, 15 U.S.C. 2058 (b) and (c), the Commission makes the following findings:

(a) *The degree and nature of the risk of injury the rule is designed to reduce.* (1) The rule addresses the risk of injury or death caused by electric shock occuring when the antenna comes into contact with electrical power lines while the antenna is being put up or taken down.

(2) About 175 fatalities were estimated to be associated with omnidirectional CB antennas in 1976. The estimated number of fatalities declined to about 125 in 1977 and to about 55 in 1978. Since then, the number of fatalities appears to have leveled off at about 45–50 each year. In addition to the 45–50 deaths, it is estimated that a somewhat greater number of injuries occur annually and that about half of them are serious enough to require surgery, amputation, skin grafts, etc. It is common for multiple deaths or injuries to occur in a single accident.

(3) The Commission's staff has estimated that since 1979 about 20 percent of the accidents involved antennas less than a year old, resulting in about 8 deaths in 1980.

(4) Since a substantial portion of the accidents associated with these antennas occur when the antenna is being taken down after it has been installed in an outdoor environment for a number of years, the standard recommends that materials selected to provide protection from shock be weather resistant.

(5) The standard specifies that protection shall be provided against voltages of 14,500 volts phase-to-ground. Voltages of this level or less are involved in 98 percent of the accidents and 95 percent of the total circuit mileage of distribution circuits.

(b) *The approximate number of consumer products, or types or classes thereof, subject to the rule.* (1) The standard applies to omnidirectional CB base station antennas. The Commission estimates that there were approximately 5 million omnidirectional base station antennas in use in 1981, and at that time as many as 75,000 of these antennas were expected to be sold each year for the next several years.

(2) [Reserved]

(c)(1) *The need of the public for the consumer products subject to the rule.* Omnidirectional CB base station antennas are used in non-mobile applications to obtain essentially uniform receiving and transmitting capabilities in all directions simultaneously. Although directional antennas can obtain greater reception and transmitting capabilities in one or more directions than can omnidirectionals, directionals are generally more expensive and must be oriented so that they point in the desired direction. Therefore, omnidirectional antennas are preferred by many base station operators, and they can also be used in conjunction with a directional antenna to locate another station to which the directional antenna can then be oriented.

(2) CB stations are used by individuals as a communications device for both practical and personal enjoyment purposes. Some operators volunteer to monitor the commonly used and/or emergency channels for distress calls

and summon aid where appropriate, relay messages, and aid local authorities and motorists in monitoring traffic conditions and accidents.

(3) Although operators can fabricate their own antennas, and antennas made for other purposes can be adapted for CB use, for most operators there is no adequate substitute for the commercial CB base station antennas subject to this rule.

(d) *The probable effect of the rule upon the utility, cost, and availability of the product*—(1) *Utility*. Tests performed for the Commission have shown that an external layer of insulation that will enable the antenna to comply with this standard can be provided that will have no significant effect on the performance of the antenna that cannot be compensated for by minor changes in the antenna. It is also likely that an insulated antenna's useful life would be somewhat longer than that of an uninsulated antenna. To the extent that manufacturers minimize the number of antenna elements in the protection zone, antennas should become less complex and bulky, and installation may also be eased. This may tend to make installation and removal of the antenna somewhat safer as well. If the isolation technique were used to comply with the standard, there should be no effect on the performance of the antenna.

(2) *Cost*. For the simpler designs of omnidirectional CB base station antennas, the manufacturers' production costs will be increased by approximately 20 percent, or $4 per antenna. For a few models, the production cost increase could be as much as 50 percent. Some models of antennas for which cost increases could be expected to be substantially greater will likely be discontinued. Some manufacturers already make antennas that either comply with the standard or can be made to do so with changes that involve no significant cost increases. The average rise in retail prices due to the standard is expected to be from 20 percent, or about $10 per antenna.

(3) *Availability*. The 30 or more different models of omnidirectional CB base station antennas available to consumers in 1981 are expected to be reduced in number substantially, perhaps by as much as half, after product line changes are made to meet the standard. The difference among some of the models likely to be discontinued are small (often relating only to primarily cosmetic features that provide a certain degree of product differentiation but do not significantly affect performance). Changes in product lines may be discernible to some consumers, however, since different brands and models of antennas will tend to look more alike (i.e., without upper radials, "hats" or other physical appendages previously incorporated). The availability of replacement components for older antennas may also be restricted somewhat if new, complying components are not compatible with some older models. Production of complying antennas is expected to be sufficient to satisfy demand; no overall "shortage" of antennas is anticipated as a result of the standard. Sales will, instead, shift from relatively low levels for each of many models to relatively higher levels for fewer models.

(e) *Means of achieving the objective of the order while minimizing adverse effects on competition or disruption or dislocation of manufacturing and other commercial practices consistent with the public health and safety*. (1) The standard may have significant adverse effects on competition among antenna producers. The additional costs associated with the standard, coupled with the recent history of decreasing sales, may cause a number of manufacturers, including one or two of the major producers, to abandon production of omnidirectional CB base station antennas. The standard is likely to impact most heavily on smaller manufacturers, which may have smaller and fewer capital sources from which to draw funds for product design and production changes and for product testing.

(2) Concentration of sales among the two largest manufacturers will probably increase as a result of the standard. However, the shrinking size of the market itself may prompt some major firms to drop this product line. Companies currently making antennas that substantially comply with the standard will probably gain a significant short-run competitive advantage over other

producers whose products do not already comply with the standard's basic provisions.

(3) Compliance with the standard may be relatively more burdensome for the smaller firms in the producing industry. Several small firms which entered the market in the early- and mid-1970's have already left the market due to the overall decrease in demand for the product. Those that remain account for less than 10 percent of annual unit shipments. None of these small firms is expected to go out of business as a result of issuance of the standard because most also produce directional CB and other base and mobile communications antennas and equipment. However, the Commission anticipates that most of these small firms will probably discontinue omnidirectional CB base station antenna production, at least temporarily, until a supplier of complying components is found, or until a decision can be made about long-term prospects.

(4) In order to minimize the adverse effects on competition and manufacturing and other commercial practices, the standard is a performance standard defined in terms of the factors the Commission determined to be significant for the protection of consumers. Thus, manufacturers have a maximum degree of flexibility in how to meet the standard, since the standard does not specify how the protection performance is to be obtained.

(5) The Commission also considered alternative technical approaches to reducing or eliminating unreasonable risks of injury associated with omnidirectional CB base station antennas, including incorporation of provisions in the standard which would allow the antenna to meet its requirements by grounding. The Commission rejected this approach because of the absence of any practical means for a consumer to ensure that the ground system will be adequate to dissipate the large amounts of power involved in a powerline contact accident. Additionally, the Commission considered the possibility that the standard might require CB base station antennas to incorporate a device to sense the electromagnetic field of a powerline. The Commission rejected this alternative because of the cost involved in such an approach, and because consumers could install an antenna even though the presence of a powerline is indicated.

(6) The Commission considered making the provisions of the standard less stringent and eliminating requirements applicable to the antenna's feed cable, in order to lessen the adverse impact of the standard on competition and manufacturing practices. However, it was determined that such changes to the standard would reduce the effectiveness of the standard and thus were not consistent with the public health and safety. Furthermore, these changes would not significantly reduce the adverse effects on competition and manufacturing practices. The elimination of requirements applicable to the feed cable would, with known technology, result in almost completely negating the benefits of the standard and is thus not consistent with the public health and safety.

(7) The Commission also considered the possibility of issuing the requirements of the standard as a voluntary test method rather than as a mandatory standard. The Commission estimated that if the provisions of the standard were issued as a voluntary test method, the total cost of such a voluntary test method to consumers during the first year after issuance would be about 30 percent of the total cost to consumers expected to result from promulgation of a mandatory standard. However, the Commission estimated that a voluntary test method would prevent only about 25 percent of the deaths and injuries which may be avoided by issuance of a mandatory standard. The Commission declined to issue the provisions of the standard as a voluntary test method because it concluded that such an approach would not only prevent fewer deaths and injuries each year than a mandatory standard, but would also have a less favorable ratio of benefits to costs than a mandatory standard.

(8) The Commission also considered the possibility of undertaking a joint effort with a trade association to inform all users of CB antennas of the dangers which can result from contact with overhead powerlines as an alternative to issuance of a mandatory

standard. The Commission observed that this alternative would have a relatively small economic impact on the industry. The Commission also observed that extensive efforts to promote public awareness of the dangers of contacting overhead powerlines have been conducted in the past by the Commission, antenna manufacturers, and utility companies, and that electrocutions and serious injuries continue to occur during installation and removal of CB base station antennas. For this reason, the Commission concluded that a public information campaign would prevent fewer deaths and injuries than issuance of a mandatory standard, and rejected such a campaign as an alternative to issuance of the standard.

(f) *The rule, including its effective date, is reasonably necessary to eliminate or reduce an unreasonable risk of injury associated with the product.* (1) The provisions of the standard constitute a related system of performance parameters which are needed as a group to ensure that the performance of new antennas will provide the degree of safety which the Commission has determined is reasonably necessary. Minor changes in the value of each parameter would not significantly reduce the costs of the standard, although in some cases they could substantially reduce the standard's effectiveness.

(2) The Commission estimates that increased retail prices due to the standard will cost consumers up to about $750,000 per year. The Commission also estimates that the standard will prevent approximately 8 deaths and 8 or more injuries during the first year the standard is in effect. Thus, if the standard saves 8 lives per year, the cost of the standard will be about $94,000 for each life saved.[1]

(3) As to the benefits from reduced injuries, the Commission estimates that, if 8 injuries are prevented during the first year the standard is in effect, the actual costs saved by the accidents prevented by the standard will amount to up to $21,000 to $37,000, exclusive of pain, suffering, or disability. If a monetary factor for these less quantifiable components is included, annual injury reduction benefits could be about $288,000 to $1,680,000.

(4) The effective date of the standard was selected after balancing the increased costs to manufacturers and consumers that are associated with shorter effective dates against the benefits to the public that would be caused by having the effective date as soon as possible.

(5) The requirement for the cautionary statement in the instructions for the antenna is intended to ensure the effectiveness of the standard by discouraging any relaxation of present safety practices involving staying away from powerlines. Since instructions for this product are already required by 16 CFR part 1402, the additional statement should have little or no adverse economic impact.

(6) After considering the costs and benefits associated with the standard, the Commission concludes that the standard, including its effective date, is reasonably necessary to eliminate or reduce an unreasonable risk of electric shock injury associated with omnidirectional CB base station antennas and that promulgation of the rule is in the public interest.

Subpart B—Certification

§ 1204.11 General.

Section 14(a) of the Consumer Product Safety Act ("the act"), 15 U.S.C. 2063(a), requires each manufacturer, private labeler, or importer of a product which is subject to a Consumer Product Safety Standard and which is distributed in commerce to issue a certificate of compliance with the applicable standard and to base that certificate upon a test of each item or upon

[1] The Commission believes that, in the area of consumer product safety, it is not generally necessary or appropriate to assign a specific monetary value to human life. However, several studies on the costs of injuries and deaths have been conducted in recent years. Value-of-life estimates based on discounted future earnings and the willingness-to-pay approach range from about $200,000 to about $3 million. The estimated costs of the CB antenna standard per life saved fall below or within the range suggested by these value-of-life estimating methodologies.

a reasonable testing program. The purpose of this subpart B of part 1204 is to establish requirements that manufacturers and importers must follow to certify that their products comply with the Safety Standard for Omnidirectional CB base Station Antennas (16 CFR part 1204, subpart A). Private labelers of CB antennas subject to the standard need not issue a certificate of compliance if they have been furnished a certificate issued by the manufacturer or importer of the antennas. This subpart B describes the minimum features of a reasonable testing program and includes requirements for recordkeeping.

§ 1204.12 Definitions.

In addition to the definitions set forth in section 3 of the act, and in § 1204.2 of the standard, the following definitions shall apply to this subpart B of part 1204:

(a) *Private labeler* means an owner of a brand or trademark which is used on the label of a CB antenna subject to the standard, which bears a private label as defined in section 3(a)(7) of the act, 15 U.S.C. 2052(a)(7).

(b) *Production interval* means a period of time determined by the manufacturer or importer that is appropriate for conducting a test on one or more samples of the CB antennas produced during that period in order to provide a high degree of assurance that all of the products manufactured during that period meet the requirements of the standard. An appropriate production interval may vary depending on the construction of the antenna, the likelihood of variations in the production process, and the severity of the test that is used. The time period for a production interval shall be short enough to provide a high degree of assurance that if the samples selected for testing pass the test, all other CB antennas produced during the period will meet the standard.

§ 1204.13 Certificate of compliance.

(a) The manufacturer or importer of any product subject to the standard must issue the certificate of compliance required by section 14(a) of the act. If the testing required by this subpart B of part 1204 has been performed by or for the foreign manufacturer of a product, the importer may rely on such tests to support the certificate of compliance if the importer is a resident of the United States or has a resident agent in the U.S., and the records are maintained in the U.S. The importer is responsible for ensuring that the foreign manufacturer's records show that all testing used to support the certificate of compliance has been performed properly with passing or acceptable results and that the records provide a reasonable assurance that all antennas imported comply with the standard.

(b) A certificate of compliance must accompany each product or otherwise be furnished to any distributor or retailer to whom the product is delivered by the manufacturer or importer.

(c) The certificate shall state:

(1) That the product "complies with all applicable consumer product safety standards (16 CFR part 1204)",

(2) The name and address of the manufacturer or importer issuing the certificate, and

(3) The date of manufacture and, if different from the address in paragraph (c)(2) of this section, the place of manufacture.

§ 1204.14 Certification tests.

(a) *General.* As explained in § 1204.11 of this subpart, certificates of compliance required by section 14(a) of the act must be based on either a test of each item or on a reasonable testing program.

(b) *Tests of each item.* If the certificate is based on tests of each item, the tests may be either those prescribed by the standard or any other test procedure that will determine that the item tested will comply with the standard.

(c) *Reasonable testing programs*—(1) *Requirements.* (i) A reasonable testing program for a particular model of CB antennas is one which demonstrates with a high degree of assurance that all the antennas of that model will meet all requirements of the standard. Manufacturers and importers shall determine the types and frequency of testing for their own reasonable testing programs. A reasonable testing program which does not test each item produced should be sufficiently stringent that any variations in production, etc., over the production interval would not cause any antenna to fail if tested according to the requirements of the standard.

(ii) All reasonable testing programs shall include qualification tests, which must be performed on one or more samples of the CB antennas representative of each model produced, or to be produced, to demonstrate that the product is capable of passing the tests prescribed by the standard and shall also include production tests, which must be performed during appropriate production intervals as long as the product is being manufactured.

(iii) Corrective action and/or additional testing must be performed whenever certification tests of samples of the product give results that do not provide a high degree of assurance that all antennas manufactured during the applicable production interval will pass the tests of the standard.

(2) *Testing by third parties.* At the option of the manufacturer or importer, some or all of the testing of each item or of the reasonable testing program may be performed by a commercial testing laboratory or other third party. However, the manufacturer or importer is responsible for ensuring that all certification testing has been properly performed with passing or acceptable results and for maintaining all records of such tests in accordance with §1204.17 of this subpart.

§ 1204.15 Qualification testing.

(a) *Testing.* Before any manufacturer or importer of CB antennas which are subject to the standard distributes them in commerce, one or more samples of each model shall be tested to determine that all such antennas manufactured after the effective date of the standard will comply with the standard. The type of tests and the manner of selecting samples shall be determined by the manufacturer or importer to provide a reasonable assurance that all antennas subject to the standard will comply with the standard. Any or all of the qualification testing required by this paragraph may be performed before the effective date of the standard.

(b) *Product modifications.* If any changes are made to a product, after initial qualification testing, that could affect the ability of the product to meet the requirements of the standard, additional qualification tests must be made before the changed antennas are manufactured for sale or distributed in commerce.

§ 1204.16 Production testing.

(a) *General.* Manufacturers and importers shall test antennas subject to the standard periodically as they are manufactured, to demonstrate that the antennas meet the requirements of the standard.

(b) *Types and frequency of testing.* Manufacturers and importers shall determine the types of tests for production testing. Each production test shall be conducted at a production interval short enough to provide a high degree of assurance that, if the samples selected for testing pass the production tests, all other antennas produced during the interval will meet the standard.

(c) *Test failure*—(1) *Sale of antennas.* If any test yields results which do not indicate that all antennas manufactured during the production interval will meet the standard, production must cease and the faulty manufacturing process or design must be corrected. In addition, products manufactured before the appropriate corrective action is taken may not be distributed in commerce unless they meet the standard. It may be necessary to modify the antennas or perform additional tests to ensure that only complying antennas are distributed in commerce. Antennas which are subject to the standard but do not comply with the requirements of the standard cannot be offered for sale, distributed in commerce, or imported in the United States.

(2) *Corrective actions.* When any production test fails to provide a high degree of assurance that all antennas comply with the standard, corrective action must be taken. Corrective action may include changes in the manufacturing and/or assembly process, equipment adjustment, repair or replacement, or other action deemed appropriate by the manufacturer or importer to achieve passing production test results.

§ 1204.17 Records.

Each manufacturer or importer of CB antennas subject to the standard shall maintain the following records, which shall be maintained for 3 years after the creation of the records and shall be available to any designated officer or employee of the Commission in accordance with section 16(b) of the Consumer Product Safety Act (15 U.S.C. 2065(b)):

(a) Records of the qualification and production testing required by this subpart B, including a description of the types of tests conducted, the dates and results of the tests, and the production interval selected for the performance of the production testing.

(b) Records of all corrective actions taken, including the specific actions taken to improve the design or manufacture and to correct any noncomplying antenna produced during the period, the date the action was taken, and the test failure which necessitated the action.

(Information collection requirements contained in paragraph (a) were approved by the Office of Management and Budget under control number 3041–0006)

FIGURES 1 AND 2 TO PART 1204—SUGGESTED INSTRUMENTATION FOR CURRENT MONITORING DEVICE AND HIGH VOLTAGE FACILITY

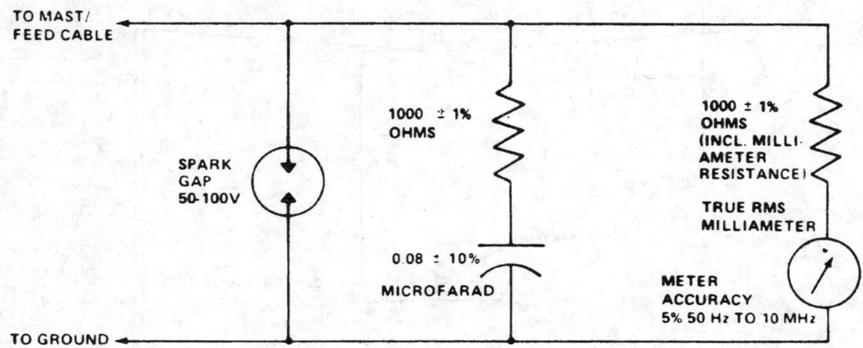

SUGGESTED INSTRUMENTATION FOR CURRENT MONITORING DEVICE

FIGURE 1

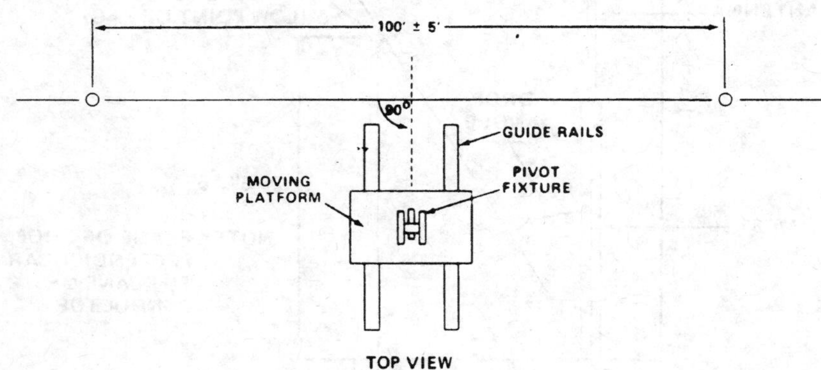

HIGH VOLTAGE TEST FACILITY

FIGURE 2

FIGURES 3 AND 4 TO PART 1204—HIGH VOLTAGE TEST FACILITY AND ANTENNA SYSTEM TEST SETUP

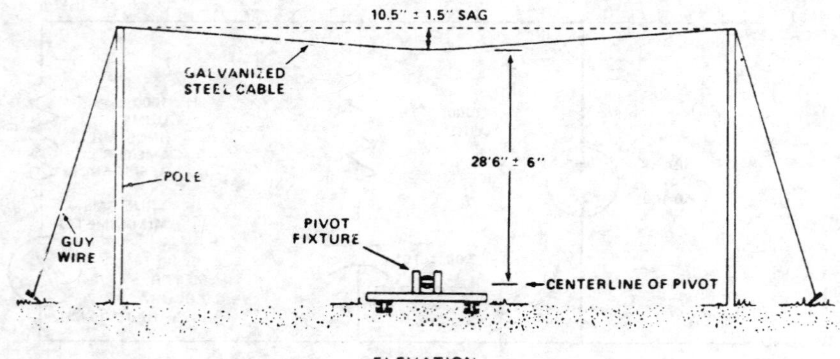

FIGURE 3

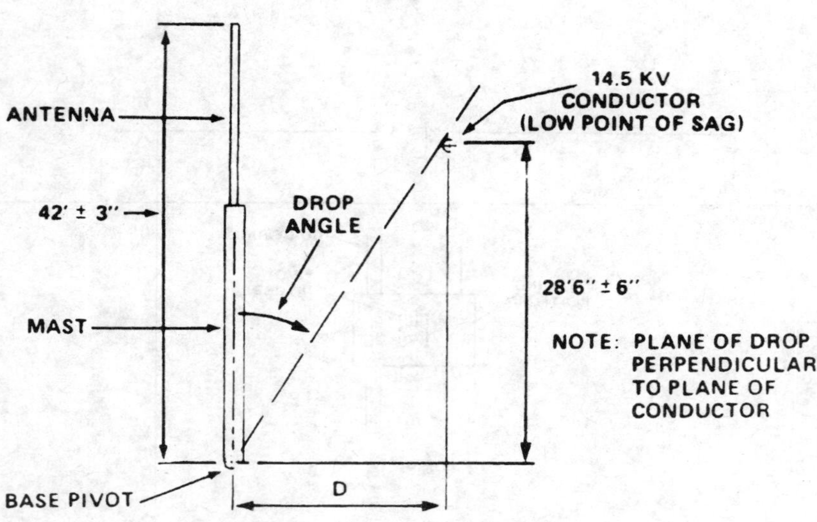

FIGURE 4

[47 FR 36201, Aug. 19, 1982; 48 FR 57125, Dec. 28, 1983]

PART 1205—SAFETY STANDARD FOR WALK-BEHIND POWER LAWN MOWERS

Subpart A—The Standard

Subpart B—Certification

AUTHORITY: Secs. 2, 3, 7, 9, 14, 19, Pub. L. 92–573, 86 Stat. 1207, 1208, 1212–1217, 1220, 1224; 15 U.S.C. 2051, 2052, 2056, 2058, 2063, 2068; sec. 1212, Pub. L. 97–35, 95 Stat. 357.

SOURCE: 44 FR 10024, Feb. 15, 1979, unless otherwise noted.

Subpart A—The Standard

§ 1205.1 Scope of the standard.

(a) *General.* This subpart A of part 1205 is a consumer product safety standard which prescribes safety requirements for certain walk-behind power lawn mowers, including labeling and performance requirements. The performance requirements of the standard apply to rotary mowers. The labeling requirements apply to both rotary and reel-type mowers. The standard is intended to reduce the risk of injury to consumers caused by contact, primarily of the foot and hand, with the rotating blade of the mower. A detailed discussion of the risk of injury and of the anticipated costs, benefits, and other factors associated with the standard is contained in § 1205.8 *Findings*.

(b) *Scope.* (1) Except as provided in paragraph (c) of this section, all walk-behind rotary and reel-type power lawn mowers manufactured or imported on or after the effective date of the standard are subject to the requirements of this standard if they are "consumer products". "Walk behind power lawn mower" is defined as a grass cutting machine with a minimum cutting width of 12 in (305 mm) that employs an engine or motor as a power source. Section 3(a)(1) of the Consumer Product Safety Act ("CPSA"), 15 U.S.C. 2052(a)(1), defines the term *consumer product* as an "article, or component part thereof, produced or distributed (i) for sale to a consumer for use in or around a permanent or temporary household or residence, a school, in recreation, or otherwise, or (ii) for the personal use, consumption or enjoyment of a consumer in or around a permanent or temporary household or residence, a school, in recreation, or otherwise." The term does not include products that are not customarily produced or distributed for sale to, or for the use or consumption by, or enjoyment of, a consumer.

(2) It is unlawful to manufacture for sale, offer for sale, distribute in commerce, or import into the United States any product subject to this standard that is not in conformity with the standard. The Commission is not applying the standard to rental transactions or to the ultimate sale of used rental mowers by rental firms.

(c) *Exclusions*—(1) *General.* Mowers that have all three of the following characteristics are not covered by the standard:

(i) A cutting width of 30 in (762 mm) or greater,

(ii) A weight of 200 lb (90.7 kg) or more, and

(iii) For engine-powered mowers, an engine of 8 horsepower (6 kw) or more.

(2) *Reel-type mowers.* Reel-type power lawn mowers need not meet the performance requirements of the standard but they must be labeled as required by § 1205.6.

§ 1205.2 Effective date.

This standard applies to all rotary walk behind power lawn mowers manufactured after June 30, 1982, except § 1205.6 *Warning labels*, applies to rotary and reel-type walk-behind power lawn mowers manufactured after December 31, 1979.

[44 FR 10024, Feb. 15, 1979, as amended 45 FR 86417, Dec. 31, 1980]

§ 1205.3 Definitions.

(a) As used in this part 1205:

(1) *Blade* means any rigid or semi-rigid device or means that is intended to cut grass during mowing operations and includes all blades of a multi-bladed mower.

(2) *Blade tip circle* means the path described by the outermost point of the blade as it moves about its axis.

(3) *Crack* means a visible external fissure in a solid body caused by tensile, compressive, or shear forces.

(4) *Cutting width* means the blade tip circle diameter or, for a multi-bladed mower, the width, measured perpendicular to the forward direction, of a composite of all blade tip circles.

(5) *Deform* means any visible alteration of shape or dimension of a body caused by stresses induced by external forces.

(6) *Engine* means a power producing device which converts thermal energy from a fuel into mechanical energy.

(7) *Manual starting* means starting the mower engine with power obtained from the physical efforts of the operator.

(8) *Maximum operating speed* means the maximum revolutions per minute (rpm) obtainable by the engine or motor under the conditions of the particular test where the term is used. For an electrically powered mower, it is the speed attained when the mower is energized from a 60 Hz alternating current source that delivers a voltage no greater than 120 V and no less than 115 V at the power input to the mower, with the mower running. For a battery-powered mower, it is the speed attained after the battery has been fully charged in accordance with the mower manufacturer's instructions.

(9) *Motor* means a power producing device that converts electrical energy into mechanical energy.

(10) *Normal starting means* is the primary mechanism intended to be actuated by the operator to start a mower's engine or motor (e.g., the cord mechanism of a manual start engine, the switch of an electric motor, or a power start mechanism).

(11) *Operating control zone* means the space enclosed by a cylinder with a radius of 15 in (381 mm) having a horizontal axis that is (1) perpendicular to the fore-aft centerline of the mower and (2) tangent to the rearmost part of the mower handle, extending 4 in (102 mm) beyond the outermost portion of each side of the handle (See Fig. 1).

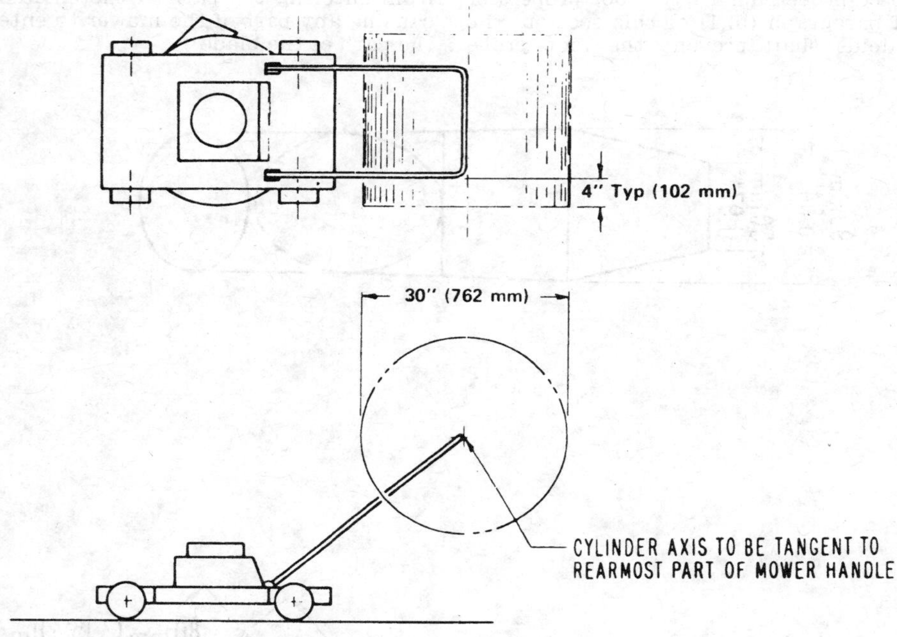

FIGURE 1 – OPERATING CONTROL ZONE

(12) *Power source* means an engine or motor.

(13) *Reel-type mower* means a lawn mower which cuts grass by rotating one or more helically formed blades about a horizontal axis to provide a shearing action with a stationary cutter bar or bed knife.

(14) *Rotary mower* means a power lawn mower in which one or more cutting blades rotate in essentially a horizontal plane about at least one vertical axis.

(15) *Separate* means to cause to have any apparent relative displacement induced by external forces.

(16) *Shield* means a part or an assembly which restricts access to a hazardous area. For the purposes of this part 1205, the blade housing is considered a shield.

(17) *Stress* means a force acting across a unit area in a solid material in resisting separation, compacting, or sliding that tends to be induced by external forces.

(18) *Top of the mower's handles* means the uppermost portion(s) of the handle that would be gripped by an operator in the normal operating position.

(19) *Walk-behind power lawn mower* means a grass cutting machine either pushed or self-propelled, with a minimum cutting width of 12 in (305 mm) that employs an engine or a motor as a power source and is normally controlled by an operator walking behind the mower.

(b) Where applicable, the definitions in section 3 of the Consumer Product Safety Act (15 U.S.C. 2052) apply to this part 1205.

[44 FR 10024, Feb. 15, 1979, as amended at 46 FR 54934, Nov. 5, 1981]

§ 1205.4 Walk-behind rotary power mower protective shields.

(a) *General requirements.* Walk-behind rotary power mowers shall meet the following requirements:

(1) When the foot probe of Fig. 2 is inserted under any point within the areas

to be probed during the foot probe test of paragraph (b)(1) of this section, the shields shall prevent the foot probe from entering the path of the blade or causing any part of the mower to enter the path of the blade.

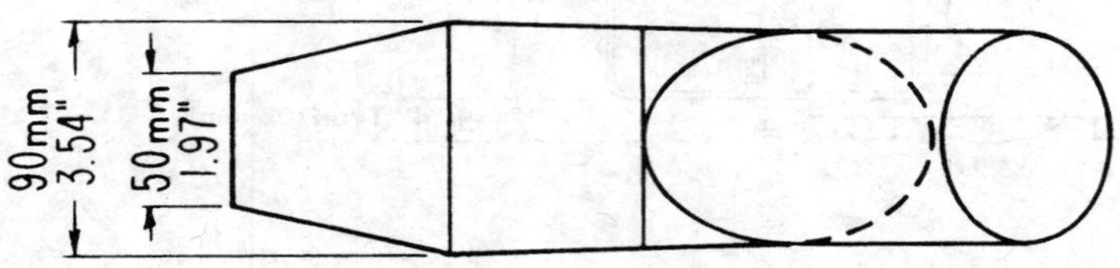

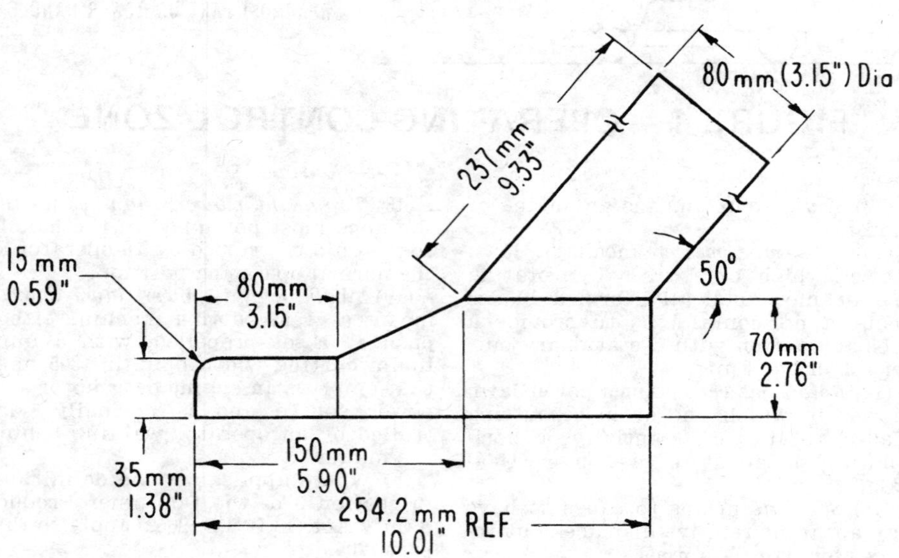

FIG 2—FOOT PROBE

(2) Any shield located totally or partly within the areas to be probed, as defined in paragraph (b)(1)(ii) of this section, shall not permanently separate, crack, or deform when the shield is subjected to a 50 lb (222 N) static tensile force, uniformly distributed over not less than half the length of the

shield. The force shall be applied for at least 10 seconds in the direction which produces the maximum stress on the shield. While being tested, a shield shall be attached to the mower in the manner in which it is intended to be used. (This requirement does not apply to the housing.)

(3) During the obstruction test of paragraph (b)(2) of this section, shields shall not:

(i) Stop the mower as a result of contact with the raised obstacle,

(ii) Enter the path of the blade, or

(iii) Cause more than one wheel at a time to be lifted from the fixture surface.

(b) *Shield tests—general*—(1) *Foot probe test.* (i) The following test conditions shall be observed:

(A) The test shall be performed on a smooth level surface.

(B) Pneumatic tires, when present, shall be inflated to the cold pressures recommended by the mower manufacturer.

(C) The mower housing shall be adjusted to its highest setting relative to the ground.

(D) The blade shall be adjusted to its lowest position relative to the blade housing.

(E) The mower shall be secured so that the mower may not move horizontally but is free to move vertically.

(ii) *Areas to be probed.* (A)(*1*) The minimum area to be probed shall include an area both 60 degrees to the right and 60 degrees to the left of the rear of the fore-aft centerline of the cutting width. For single-blade mowers, these angles shall be measured from a point on this fore-aft centerline which is at the center of the blade tip circle (see Fig. 3). For multi-blade mowers, these angles shall be measured from a point on the fore-aft centerline of the cutting width which is one half of the cutting width forward of the rearmost point of the composite of all the blade tip circles (See Fig. 4).

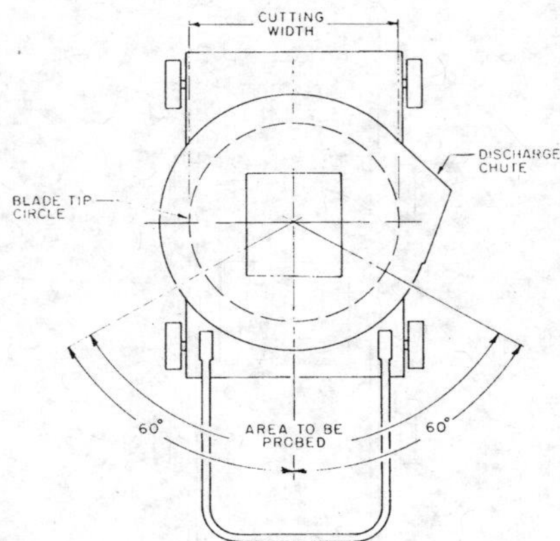

FIGURE 3 - AREA TO BE PROBED

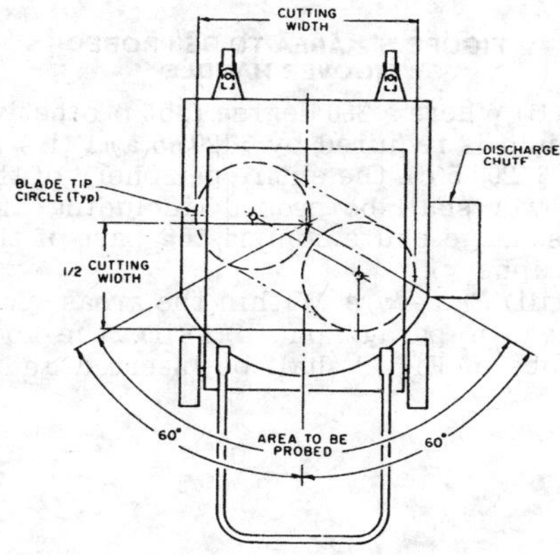

FIGURE 4 - AREA TO BE PROBED MULTI-BLADE MOWERS

(*2*) For a mower with a swing-over handle, the areas to be probed shall be determined as in paragraph (b)(1)(ii)(A)(*1*) of this section from both possible rear positions. (See Fig. 5.)

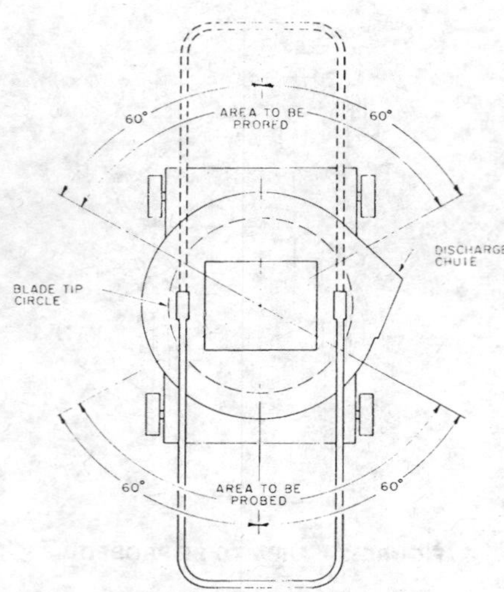

FIGURE 5 - AREA TO BE PROBED SWINGOVER HANDLE

(B) Where a 360 degree foot protective shield is required by § 1205.5(a)(1)(iv)(B) or § 1205.5(c), the entire periphery of the mower shall be probed (including any discharge chute comprising part of the periphery).

(iii) *Procedure.* Within the areas specified in paragraph (b)(1)(ii), the foot probe of Fig. 2 shall be inserted under the bottom edge of the blade housing and shields. During each insertion, the "sole" of the probe shall be kept in contact with the supporting surface. Insertion shall stop when the mower housing lifts or the horizontal force used to insert the probe reaches 4 lb (17.8 N), whichever occurs first. As the foot probe is withdrawn after each insertion, the "toe" shall be pivoted upward around the "heel" as much as possible without lifing the mower.

(2) *Obstruction test.* (i) The following test conditions shall be observed:

(A) Pneumatic tires, when present, shall be inflated to the cold pressure recommended by the mower manufacturer.

(B) The mower housing shall be at its highest setting relative to the ground.

(ii) The test shall be performed on the fixture of Fig. 6, which consists of a level surface having (A) a 0.99 in (25 mm) deep depression with a 5.90 in (150 mm) radius of curvature and (B) a raised obstacle 0.60 in (15 mm) square, each extending the full width of the fixture. The depression shall be lined with a material having a surface equivalent to a 16- to 36-grit abrasive. The depression and the obstacle shall be located a sufficient distance apart so that the mower contacts only one at a time.

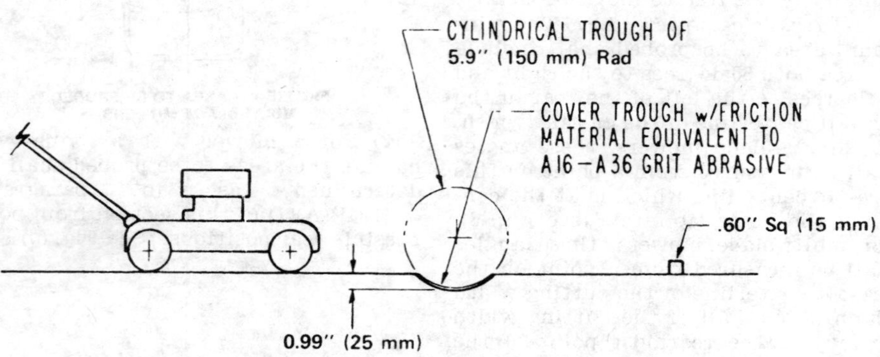

FIGURE 6 – OBSTRUCTION TEST FIXTURE

(iii) The test fixture may be relieved, only to the extent necessary, to prevent interference with any blade retaining device.

(iv) The mower shall be pushed forward and pulled rearward perpendicular to and across the depression and the raised obstacle on the fixture. The mower shall be pulled and pushed, without lifting, with a horizontal force sufficient to transit the obstruction fixture at a speed not to exceed 2.2 ft/sec (0.7 m/sec).

(c) *Movable shields*—(1) *General.* Movable shields must meet the general shield requirements of paragraph (a) of this section. In addition, movable shields which are in any of the areas to be probed defined in paragraph (b)(1)(ii) of this section and which are intended to be movable for the purpose of attaching auxiliary equipment, when deflected to their extreme open position in the manner intended by the manufacturer and released, shall either:

(i) Return automatically to a position that meets the requirements of subpart A of this part 1205 when the attached equipment is not present, or

(ii) Prevent operation of the blade(s) unless the attached equipment is present or the movable shield is returned to a position that meets the requirements of subpart A of this part 1205.

(2) *Tests.* (i) Automatic return of a movable shield shall be determined by manually deflecting the shield to its extreme open position, then releasing the shield and visually observing that it immediately returns to the closed position.

(ii) Prevention of operation of the blade(s) shall be determined, first by manually deflecting the shield to its extreme open position, then, following the appropriate manufacturer's instructions, completing the procedures necessary to operate the blade. Observe, using any safe method, that the blade(s) has been prevented from operating.

[44 FR 10024, Feb. 15, 1979, as amended at 45 FR 86417, 86418, Dec. 31, 1980; 46 FR 54934, Nov. 5, 1981; 48 FR 6328, Feb. 11, 1983]

§ 1205.5 Walk-behind rotary power mower controls.

(a) *Blade control systems*—(1) *Requirements for blade control.* A walk-behind rotary power mower shall have a blade control system that will perform the following functions:

(i) Prevent the blade from operating unless the operator actuates the control.

(ii) Require continuous contact with the control in order for the blade to continue to be driven.

(iii) Cause the blade motion in the normal direction of travel to come to a complete stop within 3.0 seconds after release of the control.

(iv) For a mower with an engine and with only manual starting controls, this blade control shall stop the blade without stopping the engine, unless:

(A) The engine starting controls for the lawn mower are located within 24 inches from the top of the mower's handles, or

(B) The mower has a protective foot shield which extends 360 degrees around the mower housing (see § 1205.4 (b)(1)(ii)(B)).[1]

(2) All walk-behind rotary power mowers shall have, in addition to any blade control required by paragraph (a)(1) of this section, another means which must be manually actuated before a stopped blade can be restarted. This additional means may be either a control which is separate from the control required by paragraph (a)(1) of this section, or may be incorporated into the control required by paragraph (a)(1) of this section as a double-action device requiring two distinct actions to restart the blade.

(b) *Blade stopping test*—(1) *General.* Any test method that will determine the time between the release of the blade control and the complete stop of the blade motion in the normal direction of travel may be used.

(2) *Conditions.* (i) The mower shall be operated at maximum operating speed

[1] Paragraphs (A) and (B) of § 1205.5(a)(1)(iv), permitting mowers that stop the blade by stopping the engine but that do not have power restart, were added to the standard as directed by Sec. 1212 of the Omnibus Budget Reconciliation Act of 1981, Pub. L. 97–35, 95 Stat. 357.

for at least 6 minutes immediately prior to the test.

(ii) The blade must be at maximum operating speed when the blade control is released.

(c) *Starting controls location.* Walk-behind mowers with blades that begin operation when the power source starts shall have their normal starting means located within the operating control zone unless the requirements of paragraphs (a)(1)(iv) (A) or (B) of this section apply to the mowers.

[44 FR 10024, Feb. 15, 1979, as amended at 46 FR 54934, Nov. 5, 1978]

§ 1205.6 Warning label for reel-type and rotary power mowers.

(a) *General.* Walk-behind power lawn mowers shall be labeled on the blade housing or, in the absence of a blade housing, on other blade shielding or on an adjacent supporting structure or assembly, with the warning label shown in Fig. 7. The label shall be at least 3.25 in (82.5 mm) high and 4 in (102 mm) wide, and the lettering and symbol shall retain the same size relation to each other and to the label as shown in Fig. 7.

FIGURE 7

(b) *Rotary mowers.* Walk-behind rotary mowers shall have one label as shown in Fig. 7, on the blade housing. The label shall be located as close as possible to any discharge opening, or, if there is no discharge opening, in a position that is conspicuous to an operator in the normal operating position.

(c) *Reel-type mowers.* Walk-behind power reel-type mowers shall have one label as shown in Fig. 7, located as close to the center of the cutting width of the blade as possible. However, in the absence of a suitable mounting surface near the center of the cutting width, the label shall be placed on the nearest suitable mounting surface to the center of the cutting width.

[44 FR 10024, Feb. 15, 1979, as amended at 45 FR 86417, Dec. 31, 1980]

§ 1205.7 Prohibited stockpiling.

(a) *Stockpiling. Stockpiling* means manufacturing or importing a product which is the subject of a consumer product safety rule between the date of issuance of the rule and its effective date at a rate that is significantly greater than the rate at which such product was produced or imported during a base period prescribed by the Consumer Product Safety Commission.

(b) *Prohibited acts.* Stockpiling of power lawn mowers that do not comply with this subpart A of part 1205 at a rate that exceeds by 20% the rate at which the product was produced or imported during the base period described in paragraph (c) of this section is prohibited.

(c) *Base period.* The base period for power lawn mowers is, at the option of each manufacturer or importer, any period of 365 consecutive days beginning on or after September 1, 1971, and ending on or before August 31, 1978.

§ 1205.8 Findings.

(a) *General.* In order to issue a rule such as part 1205, the Consumer Product Safety Act requires the Commission to consider and make appropriate findings with respect to a number of topics. These findings are discussed below.

(b) *The degree and nature of the risk of injury part 1205 is designed to eliminate or reduce.* (1) The Commission estimates that there are approximately 77,000 injuries to consumers each year caused by contact with the blades of power lawn mowers. From 1977 data, the Commission estimates that each year there are approximately 7,300 finger amputations, 2,600 toe amputations, 2,400 avulsions (the tearing of flesh or a body part), 11,450 fractures, 51,400 lacerations, and 2,300 contusions. Among the lacerations and avulsions, 35,800 were to hands and fingers and 18,000 were to toes and feet. The estimated costs caused by these injuries are $253 million, not counting any monetary damages for pain and suffering. These injuries are caused when consumers accidentally contact the blade, either inadvertently while in the vicinity of the mower, or while intentionally performing some task which they erroneously believe will not bring their hand or foot into the path of the blade.

(2) Part 1205 is expected to eliminate or reduce the severity of about 60,000 blade contact injuries per year, or 77% of all such injuries. The Commission estimates that if all mowers had been in compliance with the standard in 1977, about 6,800 finger amputations, 1,500 toe amputations, 11,000 fractures, 1,800 avulsions, 38,400 lacerations, and several hundred contusions would not have occurred. Of the lacerations and avulsions, 28,300 were finger injuries and 9,400 were toe injuries.

(c) *Consumer products subject to the rule.* The products subject to this standard are walk-behind power mowers. Power mowers with rigid or semi-rigid rotary blades are subject to all the provisions of the standard while reel-type and rotary mowers are subject to the labeling requirements. Mowers that in combination have engines of 8 hp or greater, weigh 200 lb or more, and have a cutting width of 30 in or more are excluded from the standard. The Commission estimates that at least 98% of the total annual market (by unit volume) for walk-behind mowers will be affected by the standard, and the Commission estimates that in 1978 this market was 5.4 million units.

(d) *Need of the public for the products subject to the rule.* The Commission finds that the public need for walk-behind power mowers, which provide a relatively quick and effective way to cut grass, is substantial. Riding mowers, lawn and garden tractors, hand reel mowers, trimmers and edgers, and sickle-bar mowers also provide grass-cutting services, but walk-behind power rotary mowers are by far the most commonly used devices for maintaining household lawns. There are no devices that can completely substitute for walk-behind power mowers as a group, since they have applications for which other products are not as suitable. Each type of walk-behind power mower has individual properties which meet public needs, although one type of walk-behind is often an acceptable substitute for another. The newly developed monofilament line mower is not included within the scope of the standard and could be a substitute for mowers using rigid or semi-rigid blades under some conditions.

(e) *Probable effect of the rule upon the utility of the product.* (1) The Commission finds that the probable overall effect of the standard on the utility of mowers should be to increase their utility. In the first place, consumers are likely to experience an increased sense of security from having a safer mower. A study of brake-clutch mowers conducted by the Federal Supply Service (GSA) shows that almost all users appreciated the safety features on brake-clutch mowers. In addition, by releasing the blade control and stopping the blade, the operator can then travel over gravel or other surfaces without fear of thrown objects or of the blade striking objects that might damage the mower. Brake-clutch type mowers would also give an increase in utility by virtue of enabling the operator to use the clutch to prevent stalling when the mower bogs down in heavy grass. On the other hand, there may be some minor adverse effects on utility caused by some aspects of complying mowers. For example, in very heavy mowing conditions, there may be some difficulty in engaging the blade in a blade-clutch mower. (However, mowers that are currently on the market that are not equipped with a blade clutch may have difficulty in starting the engine in heavy grass.) Complying mowers may require slightly more time and a few additional actions to operate. Since complying mowers may have more electrical and mechanical parts than current mowers, they may weigh more and require more maintenance than current mowers. No significant increase in mowing time is expected if a brake-clutch device is used to comply with the standard since each engagement of the blade would require only a few seconds. The amount of additional time and expense required for maintenance, if any, will be dependent on the design solution used. Such disutilities are expected to be slight and to be more than balanced by the increased sense of security consumers are likely to experience from having a safer mower.

(2) During the development of the rule, questions were raised about whether changes in the shields necessitated by the foot probe requirements would adversely affect utility by causing mowers to be hard to push in grass or to be unable to mow close to walls. At the time of issuance of this rule, mowers are available that will pass a 360° foot probe and others are available that will pass rear and side foot probing without any significant loss of utility caused by shielding. Therefore, the Commission concludes that this requirement will not adversely affect the utility of mowers. Mowers with swing-over handles, however, may be more difficult to design in this regard, since 120° at each end of the mower are subject to the foot probe requirement. However, since mowers meeting this requirement have already been built without apparent loss of utility, the Commission concludes that shielding can be designed so that there should be no loss of utility even for mowers with swing-over handles.

(3) As required by section 9(b) of the CPSA, the Commission, in considering the issues involved in issuing a power lawn mower safety standard, has considered and taken into account the special needs of elderly and handicapped persons to determine the extent to which such persons may be adversely affected by the rule. The Commission has determined that there will be no significant adverse effect on such persons as a result of this part 1205. In the first place, the rule can affect only those persons who are physically capable of using a power lawn mower. None of the rule's provisions will make it more difficult to operate a mower that complies with the standard. On the contrary, complying mowers should be easier to use because the need for manually restarting the mower will be less and because, if the mower uses a brake-clutch to comply with the blade control requirement, use of the brake-clutch can reduce the tendency of the engine to stall in heavy grass. Although a person's ability to hold a device such as a blade control for a long period of time will decline with age, the force required to hold the blade control can be made low enough that it will not be a problem during the length of time that it takes for consumers to mow a lawn.

(4) After considering the possible adverse effects on mowers that could be caused by the standard and balancing

them against the increase in utility that is expected, the Commission concludes that, for a typical consumer, the increases in utility should more than offset any decreases.

(f) *Probable effect of the rule upon the cost of the product.* The Commission estimates that the retail price impact of the standard will be about $35 for the average walk-behind mower. Based on an average useful mower-life of about 8 years, the additional annual cost to the purchaser is expected to average about $4.40. The probable effect of the standard will differ on the various types of mowers within its scope. Percentage increases in price will vary from about a 7 percent increase for power-restart self-propelled mowers to about a 30 percent increase for gasoline-powered manual start push mowers. The costs attributable to individual requirements of the standard are discussed in paragraph (i) of this section.

(g) *Probable effect of the rule upon the availability of the product.* (1) The Commission finds that the standard is not expected to have a significant impact on the availability of walk-behind rotary mowers, since domestic production capacity appears to be sufficient to handle any increased demand for safety-related components or materials. Although adapting some types of power mowers to the standard may be more costly than others, the effects of the standard on the price or utility of a particular category of power mowers are not expected to cause radical shifts in demand among types of mowers. The Commission finds that all types of power mowers subject to the standard will be available, although some, such as house-current-powered mowers, may increase their market shares becauses they can be brought into compliance with the standard at a lesser cost.

(2) Because some manufacturers may not revise their entire product line before the effective date of the standard, individual mower manufacturers may initially have less varied lines than at present, but there should be no decrease in the overall types and features of mowers available to consumers.

(h) *Alternative methods.* (1) The Commission has considered other means of achieving the objective of the standard. For example, alternatives were considered such as hand probes, ''blade harmless'' tests, and blade control by engine kill but allowing manual restart. These alternatives have been rejected by the Commission as being either unfeasible or not as effective as the rule which is being issued.

(2) Similarly, the Commission has found no alternative means of achieving the objective of the standard that it believes would have fewer adverse effects on competition or that would cause less disruption or dislocation of manufacturing and other commercial practices, consistent with the public health and safety.

(i) *Unreasonable risk of injury.* (1) The determination of whether a consumer product safety rule is reasonably necessary to reduce an unreasonable risk of injury involves a balancing of the degree and nature of risk of injury addressed by the rule against the probable effect of the rule on the utility, cost, or availability of the product. The factors of utility and availability of the products, adverse effects on competition, and disruption or dislocation of manufacturing and other commercial practices have been discussed above. The following discussion concerns the relationship of anticipated injury reduction and costs for various requirements of the standard. (See the report, *Economic Impact of Blade Contact Requirements for Power Mowers*, January 1979, for a detailed analysis of the possible effects of discounting and inflation on the computation of the quantifiable benefits associated with this regulation.)

(2) The foot probe and related requirements are expected to reduce the number of blade contact injuries to the foot by 13,000 each year. It is not possible to apportion this injury reduction among the respective requirements. The cost of these requirements is estimated to be about $4.00 per mower, mostly for redesign of the shields. The shield strength requirement is similar to a requirement in the existing voluntary standard that is almost universally complied with, and should comprise only a small portion of the $4.00 retail cost increase compared to prestandard mowers that is attributable to this related group of requirements.

Also, shields complying with the movable shield requirement are featured in some currently produced mowers.

(3) The foot probe and related requirements should result in a cost increase of about $22,000,000 and undiscounted injury savings of about $46,000,000, exclusive of any allowance for pain and suffering.

(4) The starting location control requirement would apply only to mowers with a power restart capability using engine kill to stop the blade. The cost for relocating the power restart switch, if necessary, should be very minor, and more than offset by the elimination of a clutch, as discussed below.

(5) The requirement that the blade stop within 3 seconds of the release of the blade control is supported by (i) the requirement that those mowers that stop the blade by stopping the engine must have a power restart (to remove the motivation to disable the blade control because of the inconven- ience of manually starting the mower each time the control is released) and by (ii) the requirement for an additional control that must be actuated before the blade can resume operation (to prevent accidental starting of the blade). Together, these requirements are expected to reduce the number of blade contact injuries by 46,500 per year for an undiscounted savings in injury costs of about $165,000,000 per year, exclusive of pain and suffering.

(6) Virtually all mowers will be subjected to a cost increase of about $3 for the blade control actuating means and $1 for the second control required to restart the blade. (The $1 cost could be eliminated for power restart-engine kill mowers that do not start when the blade control is actuated.)

(7) Also, most mowers would require a brake for the blade in order to achieve a 3 second stop time. This would add another $6.50–$8.50, depending on the type of mower. Mowers with power restart capability could stop the blade by killing the engine and thus would not need to provide a clutch to disconnect the engine from the blade. Mowers using manual restart would have to provide a clutch or other blade disengagement devices, which would probably be combined with the brake in a unitary brake-clutch mechanism.

(8) The following are the Commission's estimates of the probable retail price increases associated with certain types of currently produced mowers that will be caused by the blade control requirements.

Type of mower	Blade control retail price increases
Electric mowers (house current or battery powered)	$15.00
Present Electric start gasoline mowers	13.00–19.50
Present Manual start gasoline mowers brake clutch approach	32.50
Power restart approach	29.00–39.50

(9) The weighted average retail price increase of the blade stop requirements is expected to be about $31 per mower for a total retail cost increase of $167,000,000.

(10) The foot probe and blade stop requirements of the standard will obviously not completely protect the users of mowers under all circumstances. It is still essential for consumers to be aware of the hazard of blade contact and take the proper precautions to protect themselves. It is especially important that users not become complacent with the knowledge that the mower incorporates blade contact safety requirements. Accordingly, the Commission has determined that it is desirable that mowers complying with the standard bear a label warning of the danger of blade contact. Such a requirement would result in practically no effect on the retail price of mowers since labels are very inexpensive and practically all currently produced mowers bear some type of warning label. In view of the hazard that will be associated with power mowers even after the effective date of the standard, and the low cost of the label, the Commission concludes there is an unreasonable risk of injury that can be addressed by the label requirements in this part 1205.

(j) *Conclusion*. Therefore, after considering the anticipated costs and benefits of part 1205 and the other factors discussed above, and having taken into account the special needs of elderly and handicapped persons to determine the extent to which such persons may be adversely affected by the rule, the Commission finds that part 1205 (including the effective dates) is reasonably necessary to eliminate or reduce the unreasonable risk of injury associated with walk-behind power lawn mowers and that promulgation of the rule is in the public interest.

[44 FR 10024, Feb. 15, 1979, as amended at 45 FR 86417, Dec. 31, 1980]

Subpart B—Certification

SOURCE: 44 FR 70386, Dec. 6, 1979, unless otherwise noted.

§ 1205.30 Purpose, scope, and application.

(a) *Purpose.* Section 14(a) of the Consumer Product Safety Act, 15 U.S.C. 2063(a), requires every manufacturer (including importer) and private labeler of a product which is subject to a consumer product safety standard to issue a certificate that the product conforms to the applicable standard, and to base that certificate either on a test of each product or on a "reasonable testing program." The purpose of this subpart B of part 1205 is to establish requirements that manufacturers and importers of walk-behind rotary power lawn mowers subject to the Safety Standard for Walk-Behind Power Lawn Mowers (16 CFR part 1205, subpart A), shall issue certificates of compliance in the form of specified labeling and shall keep records of the testing program on which the certificates are based.

(b) *Scope and application.* (1) The provisions of this rule apply to all rotary walk-behind power lawn mowers which are subject to the requirements of the Safety Standard for Walk-Behind Power Lawn Mowers. This rule does not apply to reel-type mowers, which are subject only to the labeling requirements of the standard.

(2) As authorized by section 14(a)(2) of the act, the Commission exempts manufacturers who manufacture or import only component parts, and private labelers, from the requirement to issue certificates. (Private labelers who are also importers must still certify.)

§ 1205.31 Effective date.

Any walk-behind rotary power mower manufactured after December 31, 1981, must meet the standard and must be certified as complying with the standard in accordance with this rule.

§ 1205.32 Definitions.

In addition to the definitions set forth in section 3 of the act (15 U.S.C. 2052) and in § 1205.3 of the standard, the following definitions shall apply to this subpart B of part 1205:

(a) *Manufacturer* means any person or firm that manufactures or imports power lawn mowers subject to this standard, and includes those that assemble power lawn mowers from parts manufactured by other firms.

(b) *Manufactured* means the earliest point at which the mower is in the form in which it will be sold or offered for sale to the consumer or is in the form in which it will be shipped to a distributor or retailer. In these forms, a "manufactured" mower may still require partial assembly by the consumer or the lawn mower dealer.

(c) *Private labeler* means an owner of a brand or trademark which is used on a power lawn mower subject to the standard and which is not the brand or trademark of the manufacturer of the mower, provided the owner of the brand or trademark has caused or authorized the mower to be so labeled and the brand or trademark of the manufacturer of such mower does not appear on the label.

(d) *Production lot* means a quantity of mowers from which certain mowers are selected for testing prior to certifying the lot. All mowers in a lot must be essentially identical in those design, construction, and material features which relate to the ability of a mower to comply with the standard.

(e) *Reasonable testing program* means any test or series of tests which are identical or equivalent to, or more stringent than, the tests defined in the standard and which are performed on one or more mowers of the production lot for the purpose of determining whether there is reasonable assurance that the mowers in that lot comply with the requirements of the standard.

§ 1205.33 Certification testing.

(a) *General.* Manufacturers and importers shall either test each individual rotary walk-behind power lawn mower (or have it tested) or shall rely upon a reasonable testing program to demonstrate compliance with the requirements of the standard.

(b) *Reasonable testing program.* (1) A reasonable testing program for rotary walk-behind power mowers is one that provides reasonable assurance that the mowers comply with the standard. Manufacturers and importers may define their own reasonable testing programs. Such reasonable testing programs may, at the option of manufacturers and importers, be conducted by an independent third party qualified to perform such testing programs.

(2) To conduct a reasonable testing program, the mowers shall be divided into production lots. Sample mowers from each production lot shall be tested in accordance with the reasonable testing program so that there is a reasonable assurance that if the mowers selected for testing meet the standard, all mowers in the lot will meet the standard. Where there is a change in parts, suppliers of parts, or production methods that could affect the ability of the mower to comply with the requirements of the standard, the manufacturer should establish a new production lot for testing.

(3) The Commission will test for compliance with the standard by using the test procedures contained in the standard. However, a manufacturer's reasonable testing program may include either tests prescribed in the standard or any other reasonable test procedures. (For example, in the shield strength test (§ 1205.4), the manufacturer might choose to use a force higher than the 50 lb force specified in the standard.)

(4) If the reasonable testing program shows that a mower does not comply with one or more requirements of the standard, no mower in the production lot can be certified as complying until the noncomplying mowers in the lot have been identified and destroyed or altered by repair, redesign, or use of a different material or components to the extent necessary to make them conform to the standard. The sale or offering for sale of mowers that do not comply with the standard is a prohibited act and a violation of section 19(a)(1) of the CPSA, regardless of whether the mower has been validly certified.

§ 1205.34 Recordkeeping requirements.

(a) *General.* Every person issuing certificates of compliance for walk-behind rotary power lawn mowers subject to the standard shall maintain written records which show that the certificates are based on a test of each mower or on a reasonable testing program. The records shall be maintained for a period of at least 3 years from the date of certification of each mower or each production lot. These records shall be available to any designated officer or employee of the Commission upon request in accordance with section 16(b) of the act (15 U.S.C. 2065(b)).

(b) *Content of records.* Records shall identify the mower tested and the production lot and describe the tests the mowers have been subjected to and the results of the tests.

(c) *Format for records.* The records required to be maintained by this section may be in any appropriate form or format that clearly provides the required information.

§ 1205.35 Product certification and labeling by manufacturers.

(a) *Form of permanent label of certification.* Manufacturers (including importers) shall issue certificates of compliance for walk-behind rotary power lawn mowers manufactured after the effective date of the mower standard in the form of a label which can reasonably be expected to remain on the mower during the period the mower is capable of being used. Such labeling shall be deemed to be a "certificate" of compliance as that term is used in section 14 of the act. (15 U.S.C. 2063.)

(b) *Contents of certification label.* The certification labels required by this section shall clearly and legibly contain the following information:

(1) The statement "Meets CPSC blade safety requirements."

(2) An identification of the production lot.

(3) The name of the person or firm issuing the certificate.

(4) The location where the product was principally assembled.

(5) The month and year the product was manufactured.

(c) *Coding.* Except for the requirements of paragraphs (b)(1) and (b)(3) of this section, all of the information required by § 1205.35 may be in code, provided the person or firm issuing the certificate maintains a written record of the meaning of each symbol used in the code that will be made available to the distributor, retailer, consumer, and the Commission upon request. If a mower is manufactured for sale by a private labeler, and if the name of the private labeler is also on the certification label, the name of the manufacturer or importer issuing the certificate may also be in such a code.

(d) *Placement of label.* The label required by this section must be visible and legible to the ultimate purchaser of the lawn mower. For mowers manufactured before January 1, 1984, where the label is not visible to the consumer at the time of sale because of packaging or marketing practices, an additional label or notice, which may be temporary, stating "Meets CPSC blade safety requirements" shall also appear on the container, or, if the container is not so visible, the promotional material, used in connection with the sale of the mowers.

[44 FR 70386, Dec. 6, 1979, as amended at 49 FR 28241, July 11, 1984]

§ 1205.36 Product certification and labeling by importers.

(a) *General.* The importer of any rotary walk-behind power lawn mower subject to the standard must issue the certificate of compliance required by section 14(a) of the Act and § 1205.35 of this regulation. If testing of each mower, or a reasonable testing program, meeting the requirements of this subpart B of part 1205 has been performed by or for the foreign manufacturer of the product, the importer may rely in good faith on such tests to support the certificate of compliance provided the importer is a resident of the United States or has a resident agent in the United States and the records of such tests required by § 1205.34 of this part are maintained in the United States.

(b) *Responsibility of importer.* If the importer relies on tests by the foreign manufacturer to support the certificate of compliance, the importer bears the responsibility for examining the records supplied by the manufacturer to determine that the records of such tests appear to comply with § 1205.34 of this part.

PART 1207—SAFETY STANDARD FOR SWIMMING POOL SLIDES

AUTHORITY: Secs. 2, 7, 9, 14, 30, Pub. L. 92–573; 86 Stat. 1207, 1212, 1215, 1220, 1236; (15 U.S.C. 2051, 2056, 2058, 2063, 2079).

SOURCE: 41 FR 2751, Jan. 19, 1976, unless otherwise noted.

§ 1207.1 Scope, purpose, and findings.

(a) *Scope and purpose.* This part 1207 sets forth the consumer product safety standard issued by the Consumer Product Safety Commission for the manufacture and construction of slides for use in swimming pools. The requirements of this standard are designed to reduce or eliminate the unreasonable risks of death or injury associated with swimming pool slides. This standard also makes certain recommendations regarding the installation, maintenance, and intended use of swimming pool slides that supplement its mandatory requirements. This standard is applicable to all swimming pool slides manufactured after July 17, 1976. Paragraph (b) of this section sets forth the findings which the Commission is required to make by section 9(c) of the Consumer Product Safety Act (15 U.S.C. 2058(c)).

(b) *Findings.*[1] (1) The Commission finds that unreasonable risks of death

[1] The Commission's findings apply to the swimming pool slide standard that it published on January 19, 1976 (42 FR 2751). On March 3, 1978 the U.S. Court of Appeals for the Fifth Circuit set aside portions of that standard (*Aqua Slide 'N' Drive Corporation* v. *CPSC*, 569 F.2d 831 (5th Cir. 1978)). On December 18, 1978, the Commission published revisions to the standard which reflect the *Continued*

or injury from accidents are associated with swimming pool slides. These risks are (i) quadriplegia and paraplegia resulting from users (primarily adults using the swimming pool slide for the first time) sliding down the slide in a head first position and striking the bottom of the pool, (ii) leg fractures resulting from feet first entry, (iii) impact of sliders with other people in the pool, and (iv) falls from the slide ladder.

(2) The Commission finds that the types or classes of products that are subject to this standard are those swimming pool slides manufactured, constructed, or imported for use in connection with all swimming pools, whether in-ground, on-ground, or above-ground, regardless of the materials of manufacture or structural characteristics of the slides. It is estimated that 350,000 of these slides are currently in service and that each year the number of slides in use may increase by 5 to 10 percent.

(3) The Commission finds that the public uses swimming pool slides in recreation at both public and private swimming pools, and it is estimated that 75% of these slides are located at residential pools. It is anticipated that public demand for the products will decline slightly for a time following issuance of this standard as a result of consumer awareness of hazards associated with the product caused by the mandatory signs placed on the slides and as a result of recommendations regarding the installation and intended use of the products. The decline in demand is expected to be short-term. It is anticipated that the utility of the slides as a recreational device will be increased to the extent that injury or death associated with the use of the product is eliminated or reduced.

(4) The Commission also finds that manufacturing cost increases as a direct result of this standard and promotional cost increases as an indirect result of this standard are expected to be modest for the industry as a whole. Any resulting increase in the cost of slides to consumers attributable directly or indirectly to the requirements of this standard will be small. No adverse effect on the availability of the product to consumers is expected.

(5) The Commission has considered other means of achieving the objective of the standard, but has found none that would have fewer adverse effects on competition or that would cause less disruption or dislocation of manufacturing and other commercial practices, consistent with the public health and safety.

(6) The Commission also finds that this standard, including its effective date, is reasonably necessary to eliminate or reduce the unreasonable risks of injury associated with swimming pool slides and that promulgation of the standard is in the public interest.

[41 FR 2751, Jan. 19, 1976; 41 FR 9307, Mar. 4, 1976, as amended at 41 FR 23187, June 9, 1976; 43 FR 58813, Dec. 18, 1978]

§ 1207.2 Effective date.

This part 1207 shall become effective July 17, 1976. All swimming pool slides manufactured after that date must meet the requirements of this part 1207.

[41 FR 23187, June 9, 1976]

§ 1207.3 Definitions.

(a) As used in this part 1207:

(1) *Aboveground pool slide ladder* means a slide ladder that is not anchored in the ground or support deck and that can be removed from the slide or hinged and locked so that unauthorized or unsupervised use of the slide is prevented.

(2) *Abrasion hazard* means a sharp or rough surface of a swimming pool slide that would scrape the skin upon casual contact.

(3) *Assembled product* means all parts, components, and fasteners as defined in and assembled according to the manufacturer's assembly and installation instructions.

court's decision. However, the findings have not been revised and they are therefore not fully applicable to the revised swimming pool slide requirements. For example, the revised standard does not address the risk of quadriplegia and paraplegia (except insofar as the standard specifies a low angle of attack of the slider into the water) because the court set aside the provisions concerning installation instructions and warning signs.

(4) *Bracing* means members providing structural support to the assembled, installed slide.

(5) *Casual contact* means contact of any body part with the slide occurring by chance or nonchalant encounters.

(6) *Center of gravity* means the point that represents the mean position of the concentrated mass of a body.

(7) *Curved slide* means a slide whose runway curves out of the vertical plane at any point along the slide path.

(8) *Cutting hazard* means a slide surface that would cut the skin under casual contact.

(9) *Designated waterline* means the horizontal line through whichever of the following is applicable: (i) The midpoint of the operating range of the skimmers, or (ii) on pools with overflow systems, the height of the overflow rim.

(10) *Edge guards* means shields designed to cover sharp edges on slides.

(11) [Reserved]

(12) *Freestanding slide* means a slide designed for aboveground pools that is not fastened to the pool deck or the ground. This slide may have attachments to the aboveground pool to prevent misalignment.

(13) *Friction* means the force tending to reduce the velocity of the slider on the slide.

(14) [Reserved]

(15) *Intended use* means behavior on swimming pool slides as disclosed by the manufacturer, as specified in this part 1207, or to which the slide may be subjected by a reasonable user (including reasonably foreseeable misuse).

(16) *Ladder angle* means the angle of the ladder measured from a plumbline.

(17) *Ladder platform* means a platform built into the slide ladder.

(18) *Operational strength* means the strength of the slide and/or its components after installation according to the manufacturer's instructions.

(19) *Performance test* means a test to measure the functional or structural characteristics of the slide and may include:

(i) Observations and measurements of the slide's functioning in the "intended use" mode, installed according to the manufacturer's installation instructions, and/or

(ii) Observations and measurements of the slide's response to dynamic and static loads.

(20) [Reserved]

(21) *Pinching hazard* means any configuration of slide components that would pinch or entrap the fingers or toes of a child or an adult.

(22) *Puncture hazard* means any slide surface or protrusion that would puncture a child's skin under casual contact.

(23) *Runway* means the surface on which the user slides in the intended use of a slide.

(24) *Runway rail* means a raised edge or guard that keeps the slider on the runway.

(25) *Runway length* means the length of the runway measured along its centerline.

(26) *Slide width* means the width of the slide runway measured between the inside of the left and right runway rails.

(27) *Straight slide* means a slide whose runway curves only in the vertical plane.

(28) *Swimming pool slide* means any device used to enter a swimming pool by sliding down an inclined plane.

(29) *Tamperproof* means that tools are required to alter or remove portions of the slide such as guards, treads, etc.

(30) *Trajectory* means the path of a slider's center of gravity from start to finish.

(31) [Reserved]

(32) *Tread contact surface* means foot contact surfaces of ladder, step, stair, or ramp.

[41 FR 2751, Jan. 19, 1976, as amended at 43 FR 58813, Dec. 18, 1978]

§ 1207.4 Recommended standards for materials of manufacture.

(a) *General.* The materials used in swimming pool slides should be compatible with man and compatible with the environment in which they are installed. These materials should be capable of fulfilling the design requirements prescribed by § 1207.5.

(b) *Effects of environment.* The choice of materials for swimming pool slides should be such that the operational strength of the entire slide assembly, as defined by the performance tests in

§ 1207.5, should not be adversely affected by exposure to rain, snow, ice, sunlight, local, normal temperature extremes, local normal wind variations, expected local air pollution products, and the mechanical, electrical, and chemical environment in and around swimming pools. For purposes of this part 1207, "local normal" temperature extremes and wind variations are defined as the average annual record limits for the past 10 years at any slide installation point in the U.S.A. where such statistical information exists (see reference (a) in § 1207.11)

(c) *Materials selection*. The selection of all materials for swimming pool slides should be such that all surfaces and edges that may come in contact with the user are assembled, arranged, and/or finished (deburred, polished, etc.) so that they will not constitute a cutting, pinching, puncturing, or abrasion hazard under casual contact and intended use by children or adults.

(d) *Toxicity*. The selection of materials used in swimming pool slides should be such that the assembled and installed products should not be toxic to man or harmful to the environment under intended use and reasonably foreseeable abuse or disposal. All paints and finishes used on swimming pool slides shall comply with 16 CFR 1303.2(b)(2) and 1303.4(a).

(e) *Chemical compatibility*. The selection of materials for swimming pool slides should be such that the assembled and installed product, and the parts, are chemically compatible with the materials and environment contacted under intended use and reasonably foreseeable abuse.

[41 FR 2751, Jan. 19, 1976, as amended at 43 FR 58813, Dec. 18, 1978]

§ 1207.5 Design.

(a) *Strength*. The strength of the assembled and installed swimming pool slide shall be such that no structural failures of any component part shall cause failures of any other component part of the slide as described in the performance tests in paragraphs (d)(4) and (f)(9) of this section.

(b) *Edges*. Edges of swimming pool slide runways, ladders, handrails, and deck anchor flanges shall be designed, finished (deburred, polished, etc.), or protected in such a manner as to prevent cutting human tissue on casual contact and intended use. If edge guards are used, they shall be permanently affixed to the structure in a tamper-proof fashion.

(c) *Ladders, steps, stairs, or ramps*—(1) *General*. Swimming pool slide ladders, steps, stairs, or ramps shall have treads, not rungs, if the angle of the incline is 15° or greater from a plumbline.

(2) *Angle*. Swimming pool slide ladders not using rungs shall be designed and installed in such a manner that the user's center of gravity will be approximately positioned directly over each step during the use of the ladder. When tread design ladders are used, the minimum installed angle shall be not less than 15° from a plumbline dropped from a ladder step as shown in figure A. If stairs or ramps are used to ascent to the top of the slide, they shall be designed in accordance with reference (c) of § 1207.11, pages 457–463.

(NOTE: To convert the English system values given in the figures to metric values, the following conversion factors should be used: 1 inch=2.54 cm., 1 foot=30.48 cm., 1 square inch=6.452 sq. cm., 1 lb. (mass)=0.4536 kg., 1 lb. (force)=4.448 newtons, and 1 ft.-lb.=1.356 newton-meters.)

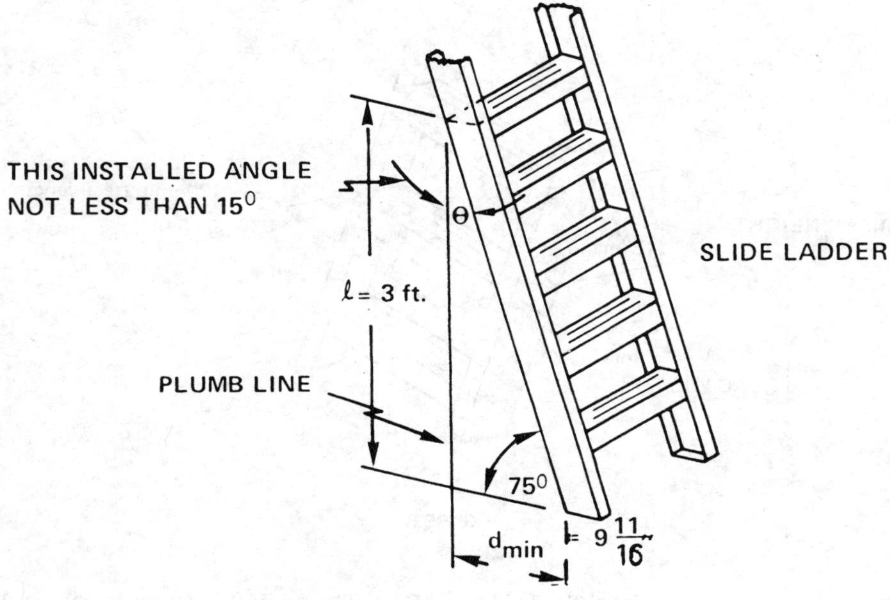

FIGURE A

(3) *Steps*—(i) *Dimensions.* Slide ladder treads may have flat or curved tread surfaces and shall be designed so that they have a minimum tread width of 2 inches (5.08 cm) and a minimum length of 12 inches (30.48 cm) (reference (c) of § 1207.11). The riser height of slide ladder treads shall be no more than 12 inches (30.5 cm) nor less than 7 inches (17.8 cm) and shall be constant over the entire height of the ladder (reference (c) of § 1207.11).

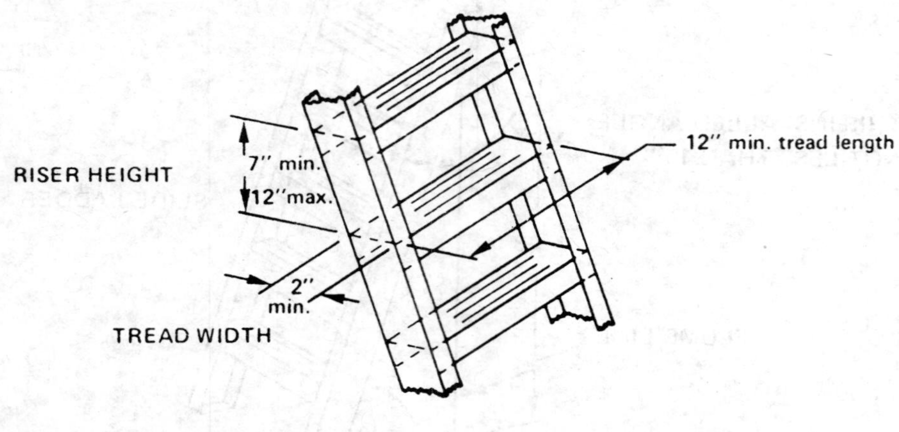

FIGURE B

(ii) *Tread curvature.* If slide ladder tread surfaces are curved, they shall not have a radius of curvature less than seven times the tread width.

(iii) *Slip resistant surfaces*—(A) *General.* The tread surface of all swimming pool slide ladders shall have a slip-resistant surface that is either an integral part of or permanently attached to the ladder steps. The performance test is designed to insure that all tread slip-resistant surfaces shall have the ability to maintain a barefooted 50-percentile adult male (reference (d) of § 1207.11) at an angle of repose of 33° ±1° without movement with a safety factor of 2.0. The angle of repose is the angle formed by the intersection of the ladder rails and the line connecting the user's feet and center of gravity. The tread and the foot shall be wet for this test.

(B) *Performance test.* A wooden block shall be prepared in accordance with figure C. The contact surface area of the block shall be 8 square inches (51.61 square cm) to simulate the ball of the foot (reference (d) of § 1207.11). It shall be covered with ¼±⅛ inch (.64±.32 cm) of natural or silicone rubber sponge capped with porous soft leather as shown in figure C.

TEST BLOCK FOR SLIP-RESISTANCE MEASUREMENTS OF SLIDE LADDER TREADS

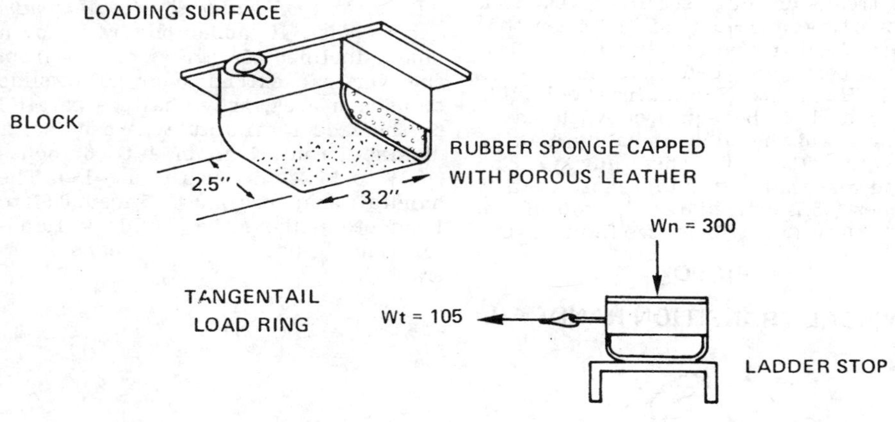

FIGURE C

The tests shall be carried out on a slide assembled and installed according to the manufacturer's instructions. The block shall be soaked in pool water for at least 3 minutes and placed at the midpoint of the wet step with the centroid of load of the block on the longitudinal axis of the step. The block shall be loaded symmetrically on its upper bearing surface with a weight of 300±2 pounds (136.1±.9 kg). A controlled and measured force shall be applied at the tangential load ring of the block tangent to the horizontal and increased at a rate of no more than 20 pounds (88.96 newtons) per second. If the block does not move at the point that the tangential load is equal to 105 pounds (467.1 newtons), the tread surface passes this performance test. Other force-creating means that produce equal forces on the block (300±2lbs, 1,334 newtons) may be substituted for weights if they result in substantially identical slip-resistance measurements.

(iv) *Fastener requirements.* Ladder treads shall be attached to the ladder rails in such a manner that continued intended use or reasonably foreseeable abuse shall not cause any fastener to loosen, crack, or break. All attachment methods that are used to hold the ladder tread to the ladder rails shall be permanent and tamperproof. If fasteners are used for the tread-rail attachment, the number and placement of such fasteners shall not cause a failure of the tread under the ladder loading conditions specified in this paragraph (c)(3).

(v) *Aboveground pool ladders.* Aboveground pool slides equipped with swing-up ladders shall be designed so that the ladders may be fixed in the up position by a tamperproof lock.

(vi) *Ladder platforms.* Swimming pool slides whose height above the surface upon which the slide is mounted is greater than 7.5 feet (2.29 meters) shall have a platform built into the ladder. This platform shall be located at least 6 feet (1.83 meters) above the deck and shall have minimum dimensions of 12 by 12 inches (30.48×30.48 cm.). The floor of the platform shall have a slip-resistant surface whose performance exceeds the requirements of the tests specified in paragraph (c)(3)(iii)(B) of this section. A minimum dimension of two times the riser height shall be maintained from the platform to the top of the slide runway. Transitional handrails shall be provided when a platform is used.

(vii) *Static load performance test.* Ladder treads or rungs shall be capable of supporting a 300-pound (1,334–newton) static load in the center without failure or permanent deformation.

(d) *Handrails.* Swimming pool slide ladders shall be equipped with handrails to aid the slider in safely making the transition to the runway. The handrails shall extend no more than 18 inches (45.72 cm) above the top of the slide runway platform (see figure D_1).

FIG. D_1

TYPICAL TRANSITION HANDRAIL

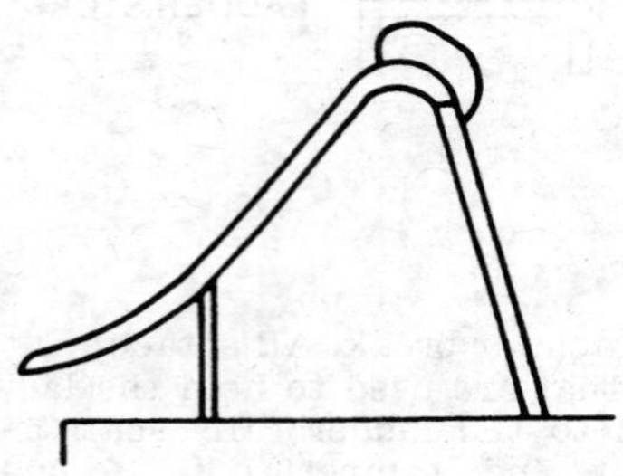

(1) *Size.* The outside diameter of handrails shall be between 1.00 and 1.90 inches (2.54 and 4.83 cm) (references (c) and (d) of § 1207.11).

(2) *Extent of handrails*—(i) *Maximum angle ladder.* If ladder handrails for a ladder inclined 15 degrees or less from the vertical extend below the slide transition area, they shall be parallel to the ladder rails at a perpendicular distance from them of 4 to 6 inches (10.16 to 15.24 cm) (see figure D_2). The handrail shall begin 3 to 5 feet (0.91 to 1.52 meters) above the pool deck. Handrails should not provide a means of entrapment.

FIG. D_2

MAXIMUM/MINIMUM DIMENSIONS FOR SLIDE LADDER HANDRAILS

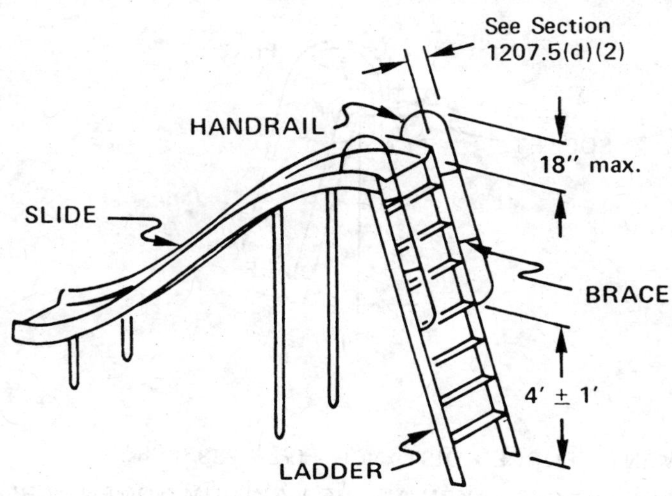

(ii) *Extent of handrails for ladders, steps, stairs, or ramps.* For slides not using the minimum angle ladder (15 degrees or less from the vertical), the perpendicular distance between the ladder handrails and the ladder rails below the slide transition area shall be the distance "*l*" as shown in table 1.

TABLE 1—VARIATIONS OF *l*

Ladders:	$15° < \theta < 40°$	$L = (34.09\theta_{rad} - 3.86) \pm 1''$ $= (86.59\theta_{rad} - 9.80) \pm 2.54$ cm
Stairs:	$40° < \theta < 70°$ ...	$l = 34'' \pm 1''$ $= 86.36 \pm 2.54$ cm
Ramps:	$\theta < 70°$	$l = 42'' \pm 1''$ $= 106.68 \pm 2.54$ cm

(3) *Bracing of handrails.* If handrail braces are used, they shall withstand intended use and reasonably foreseeable abuse.

(4) *Attachment and strength of handrails.* Handrails and their fasteners shall withstand allowable shear, bending, and cyclical loading in intended use and reasonably foreseeable abuse. All fasteners for handrail connections shall be vibrationproof, selflocking, and tamperproof. Threaded fasteners shall be capable of withstanding a 1-foot-pound (1,356-newton meter) back-off torque.

(i) *Sockets performance test.* If handrail sockets are used, the handrail end shall be permanently fixed in the socket so that it cannot be pulled out or bent at the socket by a moment of 233 foot-pounds (316 newton-meters) applied clockwise around point A in figure E. The socket shall not permanently deform under the maximum applied loads.

FIG. E
APPLICATION OF HANDRAIL MOMENTS

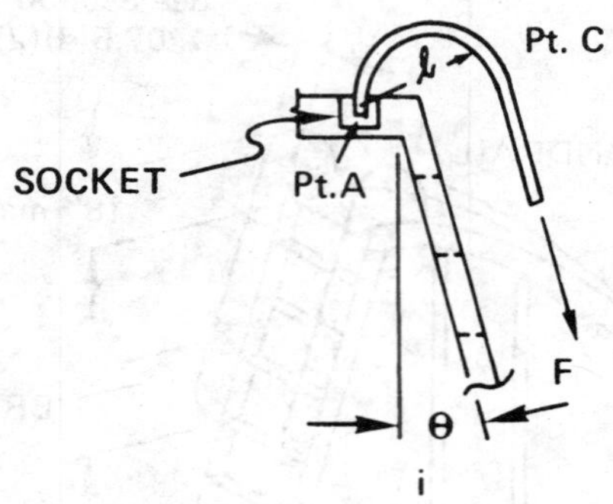

MOMENT = FORCE x DISTANCE = f×ℓ = 233 ft. lbs.

WHERE : Pt. C IS TAKEN AT THE MAXIMUM MOMENT ARM "ℓ FROM Pt. A.

(ii) *Side forces.* If the handrail is in a socket or attached to the side of the slide runway rail, the attachment methods must be capable of withstanding all shear and bending forces induced by a 172-foot-pound (233-newton-meter) moment counterclockwise around point A in figure F.

FIG. F
APPLICATION OF HANDRAILS MO.

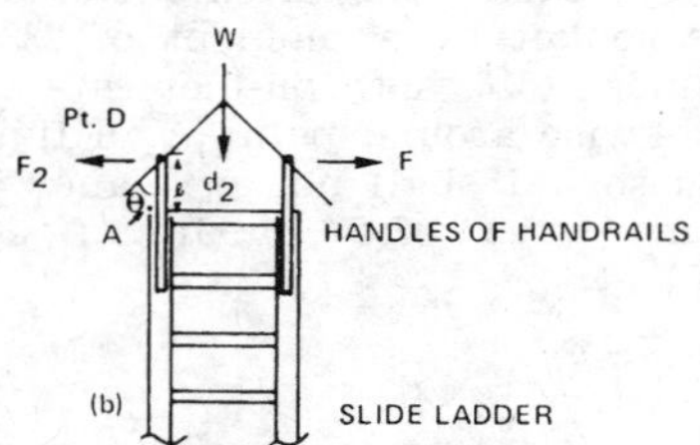

MOMEMT = $F_2 \times d_2$ = FORCE x DISTANCE = 172 ft. lbs.

(iii) *Performance tests*—(A) *Strength for climbing and falls.* (*1*) Attach a pull loop to point C of the upper handrail (figure E). Point C is the point where a perpendicular to the axis of the handrail passes through point A, the socket, or other attachment point. Attach a stranded steel cable or wire rope to point C. All cables and ropes shall have at least a 1,000-pound (4,448-newton) tensile capacity. Attach a 162-pound (73.5-kg) weight to this cable at least 4 feet (1.22 meters) below point C. Observe any permanent deformation or bending on the hand-rail at point A. If none exists, the handrail passes this performance test.

(*2*) Lift the weight one foot (30.48 cm) from its maximum static position and drop it. Observe any permanent deformation of the handrail or its attachments at point A. If each handrail will still support the 162-pound (73.5-kg) weight for a period of 15 minutes and has not been bent more than 45° from its original direction, it passes this performance test.

(B) *Transition handrail strength.* Rotate the assembled slide into the horizontal position on its side on a loading dock or other platform. Move the slide into such a position that the entire handrail assembly overhangs the platform and level the slide. Fasten the slide firmly in this position and attach a 115-pound (52.2-kg) weight to point D, as shown in figure F, and check for any visible permanent deformation of the handrail at point A. If none exists, the handrails pass this performance test.

(e) *Lubrication.* Swimming pool slides shall either be equipped with a method of lubrication (for example, water) or have a similar coefficient of friction so that the slider has a smooth, continuous slide. If water is used, the nozzles, piping, or hoses that deliver water to the runway shall be recessed or designed in such a fashion as not to interfere with a slider's progress down the slide or create tripping hazards on the slide.

(f) *Runways*—(1) *Curvature.* Slide runway curvature between the front and rear support legs of the slide shall be consistent with maintaining the slider safely on the slide during intended use and reasonably foreseeable abuse.

(2) *Dynamic equilibrium.* (i) Swimming pool slide runways, whether straight or curved, shall be designed as "balanced curves." On a balanced curve, the test fixture discussed in paragraph (f)(2)(ii) of this section shall stay on a trajectory that keeps it within a distance of ±41 percent of the runway width to the runway centerline at all points along the runway without contacting the runway rails.

(ii) *Performance test*—(A) *Direct measurement.* Build a wooden pallet no larger than 5 by 5 inches (12.7×12.7 cm), as shown in figure G. Securely attach a lead rod or bar on the pallet. Size the bar so that the weight-to-area ratio of the assembly is 1.30±0.05 lbs./sq. in. (8,960±340 newtons/sq. meter) and the pallet does not tip over when in motion. Attach a felt pen or other suitable marking device to the pallet assembly as shown in figure G to mark the slide during descent.

(B) *Test.* Lubricate the slide in accordance with the manufacturer's instructions. Center the pallet at the top of the slide runway and release. Observe the pallet's descent and note if it touches the slide's side rails. If it touches, check alignment and installation again. With water off and the slide dry, center the pallet at the top of the runway and release. Measure the distance from the felt pen marked line to the centerline of the runway. If within ±41 percent of the width measured from the centerline along the entire path and if the pallet does not contact the runway rails, the slide is dynamically balanced and passes this performance test.

(3) *Runway side rails.* Swimming pool slide runways shall have permanent runway side rails of at least 2 inches (5.08 cm) and height to prevent lateral discharge of the slider off the slide under intended use and reasonably foreseeable abuse.

(4) *Runway side-rail heights.* Runway side-rail heights shall be designed as a function of the maximum slide-slope angle (as shown in figure H). Table 2 that follows shows side-rail height versus maximum slide-slope angle. If the maximum slide-slope angle is not shown in table 2, the next higher side-rail height must be used. Maximum slide-slope angles shall not exceed 75°. (See figure H.)

FIG. G
ASSEMBLY FOR MEASUREMENT OF RUNWAY EQUILIBRIUM

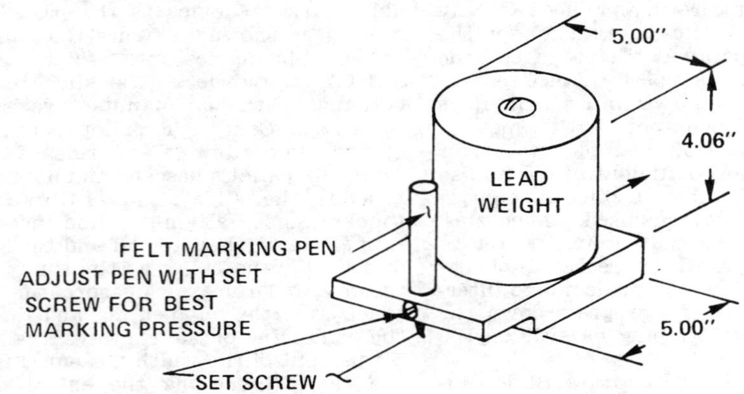

TABLE 2

ψ=Maximum slide-slope angle	Runway side-rail height inches (centimeters)
<60°	2 (5.08)
60–70°	3 (7.62)
70–75°	3½ (8.89)

FIG. H
MAXIMUM SLIDE SLOPE ANGLE "ψ

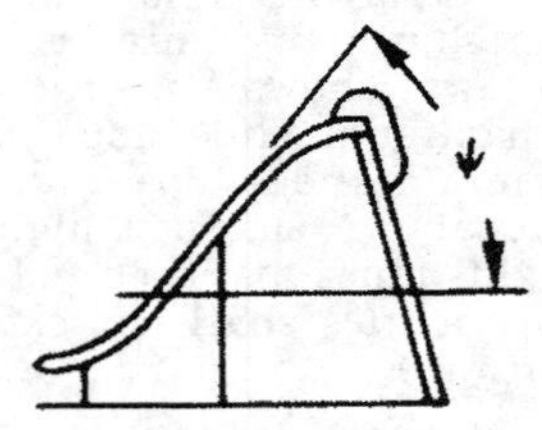

(5) *Slide geometry*. Swimming pool slide runways shall have a smooth transition section and have geometry such that the path of the center of gravity of the slider is not more than ±10° from the horizontal at the center of gravity's exit off the slide and such that the slider's angle of attack (α), shown in figure I and defined below, shall be at least +15° when the slider's feet leave the slide. (See figure I.)

(i) *Performance tests*. Measurement of the 50th-percentile adult male (71±2 inches and 162±5 pounds, 180.34±5.08 cm and 73.5±2.3 kg)[1] slider's angle of attack shall be made using any of the following methods or their equivalent:

(A) Motion picture cameras (36 frames per second or more).

(B) Still cameras with strobe lights and reflectors on the head and hip of the slider.

(C) Still cameras with rotating shutters and lights on the head and hip of the slider.

(D) Video tape recorder.

(ii) Measurements shall be made from the still water level as the horizontal. The path angle shall be determined by measuring the angle between a tangent to the path of the center of gravity (line X) and the horizontal taken through the center of gravity (line Y). At least five consecutive runs with the same subject shall be made in order that an average may be computed.[2] Angle of attack shall be taken as the angle between the slider's longitudinal axis (*Z*) and the tangent to the path of his center of gravity (*X*). The slider's longitudinal axis shall be located by the vertical line that passes through his center of gravity when he stands erect. The slider shall wear usual swimming attire. The angle-of-attack measurement shall be made after the

[1] See reference (f) of § 1207.11 for full discussion.

[2] Maximum measurement variation of ±15 percent.

slider's feet have cleared the slide, the distance between the end of the slide and his feet being less than 8 inches (20.3 cm). The slider's descent must be headfirst, prone, belly-down, and with arms extended in front. Except when starting, the slider shall not augment the slide trip by forcibly reacting with the slide through the use of his hands, arms, feet and/or legs. The slider's starting reactions with the slide shall be only as strong as necessary to start him moving. If the average angle of attack measured and computed in the above manner is equal to or greater than +15°, the slide passes this performance test.

FIG. I

MEASUREMENT OF ANGLE OF ATTACK

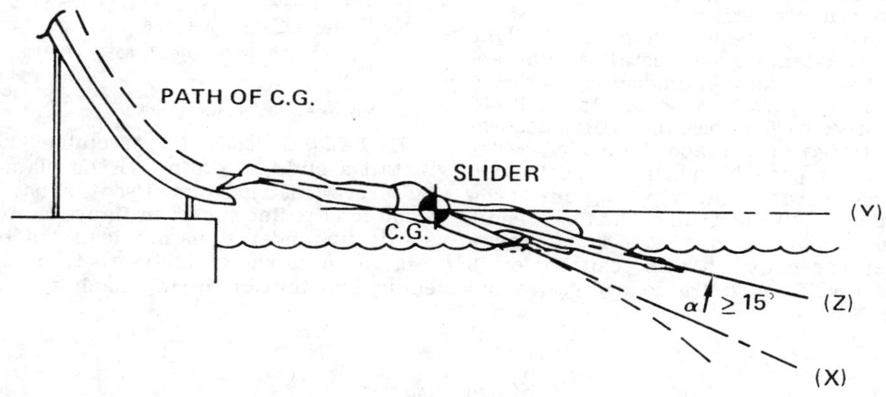

(6) *Runway exit lips.* All runway exit lips of swimming pool slides shall be smoothly faired into the runway surface with a radius of curvature at the exit lip of the slide of at least 2¼ inches (5.72 cm) (see figure J).

FIG. J

RUNWAY EXIT ANGLE θ

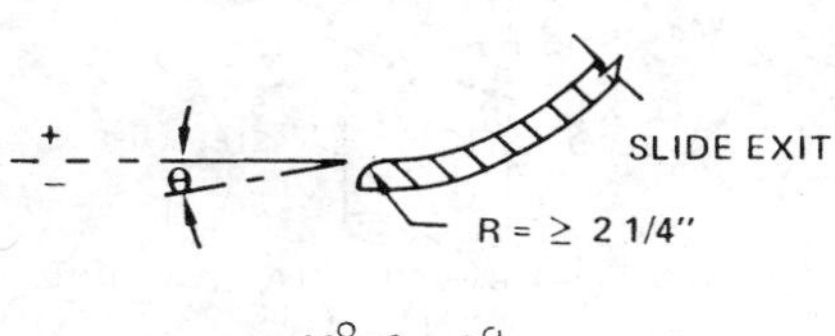

(7) *Runway exit vertical angle.* The angle of the runway at exit of the slide () shall be −3 to −11 degrees from the horizontal as shown in figure J.

(8)(i) *Runway exit ramp lateral curvature and exit lip horizontal angle.* No net lateral forces on the slider shall exist in that portion of the runway exit ramp beyond the forward support points of the slide. All slides shall be designed and constructed so that the exit lip of the slide is level at all points along the width of the runway at the runway exit lip line drawn at the point where the lip curvature shown in figure J is tangent to the runway. The slide shall be designed so that any side forces on the user induced by prior lateral curvature will be reduced to zero upon exit from the slide runway.

(ii) *Performance tests.* Those tests described in paragraph (f)(2)(ii) of this section are also applicable to paragraph (f)(8) of this section, and the path of the test fixture must be parallel to the centerline of the slide at the exit lip (within 5°) and not touching the side rails of the runway.

(9) *Strength of slide runways and supports*—(i) *Static loads.* A properly assembled and installed slide runway shall be

capable of supporting a static load of at least 350 pounds (1,557 newtons) applied normal to the runway over an area of no more than 20 square inches (129.03 square cm) at any point along its length or width.

(ii) *Dynamic loading.* Properly assembled and installed slide runways shall be capable of supporting, without structural failure except as defined in paragraph (f)(9)(iii)(B)(*3*) of this section, a dynamic load of at least 450 foot-pounds (610.2 newton-meters) dropped on an area of 20 square inches (129.03 square cm) at the midpoints of the upper runway platform and the lower runway exit ramp.

(iii) *Performance tests*—(A) *Static loads.* Assemble and install a slide according to the manufacturer's instructions. Prepare a 20-square-inch (129.03 square cm) load-bearing pallet according to figure K. Place the loaded pallet on the upper slide platform, positioned between the runway rails, until the scale on the hoist line reads between 0 and 10 pounds (0 and 44.48 newtons). Keep the pallet in this position for 10 minutes. Remove the loaded pallet and observe the runway for any significant structural failure such as permanent deformations or cracks. If there are none, the slide passes the test. Repeat the same test on the lower runway exit ramp.

FIG. K
STATIC LOAD TEST FOR
SLIDE BED

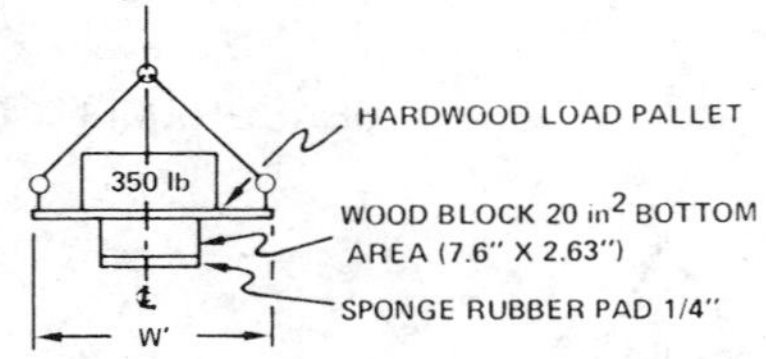

(B) *Dynamic loads.* (*1*) Assemble and install a slide according to the manufacturer's instructions. Use the hardwood load pallet shown in figure K and set it up under dynamic load guides fabricated as shown in figure L, or an equivalent impact-testing machine.

FIG. L
DYNAMIC LOAD TEST

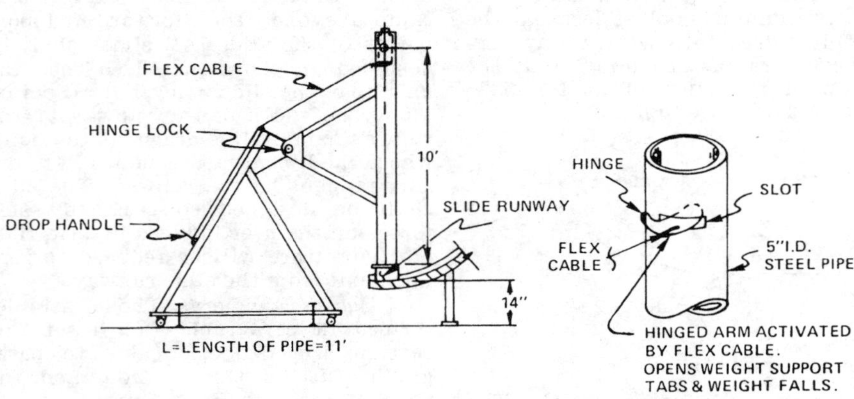

(*2*) Fabricate a 45-pound (20.4–kg) billet of 4.900±0.005-inch (12.45±.01 cm) steel rod as shown in figure M, or equivalent, and load into the pipe above the trigger slot. The length of the pipe from the trigger slot to the impact pallet shall be 10.0±0.1 feet (3.05 meters±3.05 cm).

FIG. M

TYPICAL BILLET FOR IMPACT TESTING

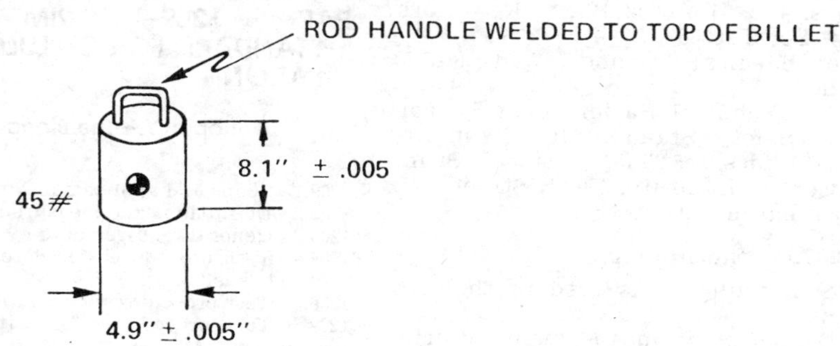

(*3*) Drop the billet onto the pallet and observe the slide for any permanent deformations or cracks. If the slide runway can still support a static load of 350 pounds (1,557 newtons) on the pallet without further crack propagation, it passes this test.

(*4*) Perform the test on the entrance and exit platforms of the slide runway.

[41 FR 2751, Jan. 19, 1976; 41 FR 9307, Mar. 4, 1976; 41 FR 10062, Mar. 9, 1976, as amended at 41 FR 12638, Mar. 26, 1976; 41 FR 13911, Apr. 1, 1976]

§§ 1207.6–1207.8 [Reserved]

§ 1207.9 Product certification.

(a) Certification shall be in accordance with section 14(a)(1) of the Consumer Product Safety Act (15 U.S.C. 2063(a)(1)).

(b) A certificate shall accompany the swimming pool slide (in the form of a permanent label on the shipping container(s) or in the form of a separate certificate) to all distributors and retailers to whom the material is delivered certifying that the slide conforms to this part 1207. The certificate or permanent label issued under this section shall be based upon either a test of each product or a reasonable testing program, shall state the name of the manufacturer or private labeler issuing the certificate, and shall include the date and place of manufacture.

(c) Any certificate shall be based upon the test procedures and requirements specified in this part 1207.

§ 1207.10 Handling, storage, and marking.

(a) *Marking.* The manufacturer's or private labeler's identification shall appear on the slide and shipping container. Such identification shall include the identity and address of the manufacturer or private labeler. If a private labeler's name is used, the marking shall include a code mark that will permit an identification of the manufacturer.

(b) *Shipping, handling, and storage.* The slide shall be designed, constructed, or packaged so that reasonably foreseeable shipping, handling, and storage will not cause defects in the slide that will prevent the slide from complying with the requirements of this part 1207.

§ 1207.11 References.

(a) "Statistical Abstract of the United States 1973," U.S. Dept. of Commerce, pp. 181–185, 192.

(b) "Human Engineering Guide for Equipment Designers," Woodson and Conover, pp. 2–166 through 2–169 published by the University of California Press, 2223 Fulton St., Berkeley, California 94720.

(c) "Human Engineering Guide to Equipment Design," Van Cott and KinKade, published by U.S. Dept. of

Defense, 1972, Library of Congress Card No. 72–600054, pp. 457–465.

(d) "The Measure of Man—Human Factors in Design," by Henry Dreyfuss, published by Watson-Guptill Publications, Inc., 1 Astor Plaza, New York, New York, 10036.

(e) "Medical Tribune", Wed., 8/15/73, p. 21.

(f) "Technical Rationale in Support of A Safety Standard for Swimming Pool Slides," 5/30/75. National Swimming Pool Institute, 2000 K Street NW., Washington, D.C. 20006.

§ 1207.12 Stockpiling.

(a) *Definitions.* As used in this section:

(1) *Stockpiling* means manufacturing or importing swimming pool slides between the date of promulgation of part 1207 in the FEDERAL REGISTER and its effective date at a rate greater than five percent more than the rate at which the slides were manufactured or imported during the base period.

(2) *Base period* means, at the option of the manufacturer or importer concerned, any period of 180 consecutive days beginning on or after January 2, 1974, and ending on or before December 31, 1974.

(3) *Rate of production (or importation)* means the total number of swimming pool slides manufactured (or imported) during a stated time period. In determining whether a slide was manufactured (or imported) during a stated time period, the later of the date on which the slide runway was manufactured (or imported) or the date on which the accompanying ladder and other support parts were manufactured (or imported) shall be used.

(b) *Prohibited acts.* Manufacturers and importers of swimming pool slides, as these products are defined in § 1207.3(a)(28) shall not manufacture or import slides that do not comply with the requirements of this part 1207 between January 19, 1976, and July 17, 1976, at a rate which is greater than the rate of production or importation during the base period plus five percent of that rate.

(c) Manufacturers and importers shall maintain appropriate documentation to be able to substantiate to the Commission that they are in compliance with the provisions of this section.

[41 FR 2751, Jan. 19, 1976, as amended at 41 FR 15003, Apr. 9, 1976]

PART 1209—INTERIM SAFETY STANDARD FOR CELLULOSE INSULATION

Subpart A—The Standard

Subpart B—Certification

SOURCE: 44 FR 39966, July 6, 1979, unless otherwise noted.

Subpart A—The Standard

AUTHORITY: Sec. 35(c)(2), Pub. L. 95–319, 92 Stat. 388–389 (15 U.S.C. 2082).

§ 1209.1 Scope and application.

(a) *Scope.* This part 1209, an interim consumer product safety standard, prescribes flame resistance and corrosiveness requirements for cellulose insulation that is a consumer product. These requirements are intended to reduce or eliminate an unreasonable risk of injury to consumers from flammable and corrosive cellulose insulation. The requirements are based upon the flame resistance and corrosiveness requirements of General Services Administration Specification HH-I-515D.

(b) *Application.* This part 1209 shall apply to cellulose insulation that is a consumer product, that is, cellulose insulation produced or distributed for sale to, or for the personal use, consumption, or enjoyment of consumers in or around a permanent or temporary household or residence, a school, in recreation, or otherwise. The interim standard applies to cellulose insulation that is produced or distributed for sale to consumers for their direct installation or use, as well as cellulose insulation that is produced or distributed for installation by professionals. This part 1209 applies only to cellulose insulation manufactured after October 15, 1979.

§ 1209.2 Definitions and measurements.

(a) As used in this part 1209, *Cellulose insulation* means cellulosic fiber, loose fill, thermal insulation that is suitable for blowing or pouring applications.

(b) The definitions given in section 3 of the Consumer Product Safety Act are applicable to this part 1209.

(c) For the purposes of conformance with the technical requirements of this standard, the figures are given in the metric system of measurement. The inch-pound system approximations of these figures are provided in parentheses for convenience and information only. For numerical quantities for which no specific tolerances are given, the tolerance shall be one half of the unit value of the last significant digit given in the dimension. Where numerical quantities are given without tolerances in both the metric and inch-pound system of measurements, the tolerance shall be one half of the last significant digit of the metric equivalent of the numerical quantity.

(d) The specifications and dimensions in the test methods below are given in metric units, with the English equivalents in parentheses. For enforcement purposes the Commission will use metric units.

§ 1209.3 General requirements.

(a) All cellulose insulation to which this interim standard applies, as described in § 1209.1, shall be noncorrosive when tested in accordance with the test procedures at § 1209.5 and evaluated using the criteria at § 1209.5(c). This means that after the product is tested, the six metal coupons used in the test shall not have any perforations (excluding notches extending into the coupon 3 mm or less from any edge) when the coupons are observed over a 40–W appliance light bulb.

(b) All cellulose insulation to which this interim standard applies, as described in § 1209.1, shall have a critical radiant flux equal to or greater than 0.12 W/cm^2 for each of the three specimens when tested in accordance with the test procedures at § 1209.6.

(c) All cellulose insulation to which this interim standard applies, as described in § 1209.1, shall have no evidence of flaming combustion and shall also have weight loss of 15 percent or less of the initial weight, for each of the three specimens, when tested in accordance with the test procedures at § 1209.7.

(d) All containers of cellulose insulation to which this interim standard applies, as described in § 1209.1, shall have a labeling statement in accordance with the labeling requirements at § 1209.9.

§ 1209.4 Test procedures for determining settled density.

The settled density of lose fill insulation must be determined before the corrosiveness test (§ 1209.5) and the smoldering combustion test (§ 1209.7) can be performed. This section describes the procedure for determining the settled density of loose fill insulation.

(a) *Apparatus and materials.* (1) An insulation specimen container with a flat bottom and an inside diameter of 15.0±1 cm, straight sides [without a flared lip or spout, (Apparatus #1)]. The height of the beaker shall be such that the distance between the bottom of the cyclone and the top edge of the beaker is 8.5 cm±1.0 cm. (3.39 in±.39 in).

(2) A flat-rigid disc with a total weight of 75±5 g (2.65±0.18 oz) and of a suitable diameter to fit loosely into the specimen container. Weight may be added to the center of the disc to bring the total weight to the required 75±5 g (Apparatus #2).

(3) A balance of 2 kg (4.4 lbs) capacity accurate at least to 0.2 g (0.007 oz) (Apparatus #3).

(4) Blower apparatus, two units (supply and overflow) meeting the following specifications: (The Commission staff has found that a Breuer Electric Manufacturing Co., Model 98805 blower is suitable for this purpose, although other blowers may be suitable.) (Apparatus #4).

(i) Each blower apparatus shall be capable of blowing an average of 272.2 kg (600 lbs.) of insulation per hour.

(ii) Each blower apparatus shall have a nominal air flow of 2.1 cm^3/min. (75 ft^3/min.)

(iii) Each blower apparatus shall have a nominal motor speed of 16,450 revolutions per minute at 115 VAC.

(5) A shaker unit capable of shaking 4.5 kg (10 lb) of weight with a vertical motion of 0.5 g Root Mean Square (RMS) acceleration at an approximate frequency of 9 Hertz (Hz) and displacement of approximately 1.17 cm ($^{15}\!/_{32}$±$^{1}\!/_{32}$ in.) ±.08 cm peak to peak. (The Commission staff has found that a Tyler Industries, Portable Sieve Shaker Model Rx–24 is suitable for this purpose, although other shakers may be suitable.) (Apparatus #5).

(6) Fill chamber with inside dimensions of 45.7 cm (18 in) high × 38.1 cm (15 in) wide × 38.1 cm (15 in) deep, with covered openings that will allow a radiant panel tray to be slid through the chamber, (see Figure 1 for details) (Apparatus #6).

(7) A cyclone receiver (see Figure 2 for complete details). (Apparatus #7).

(8) Various lengths of nominally 2-inch diameter hose (see Figure 1 for details), as follows:

(i) A supply source hose, 274.3±5.1 cm (9 ft±2 in) (Apparatus #8(i)).

(ii) A cyclone receiver hose, 182.9±5.1 cm (6 ft±2 in) (Apparatus #8(ii)).

(iii) A fill chamber exit hose, 91,.4±5.1 cm (3 ft±2 in) (Apparatus #8(iii)).

(iv) An overflow exhaust hose, length as needed (Apparatus #8(iv)).

(9) Blower Control(s) capable of operating the two blowers at 40 volts RMS. As an example, a variac for each of the two blowers with sufficient rating to operate at 40 volts and 12 amperes RMS would be acceptable (Apparatus #9).

(10) An insulation holding container to hold a sufficient quantity of insulation to fill the specimen container four times.

(11) A garden rake, 50.8 cm (20 in) wide (Apparatus #11).

(12) A shovel (Apparatus #12).

(b) *Conditioning.* Specimens shall be conditioned to equilibrium at 21±5 °C (69.8±9 °F) and 50±5 % relative humidity. A less than 1% change in net weight of the specimen in two consecutive weighings with two hours between each weighing constitutes equilibrium.

(c) *Test specimen preparation*—(1) *Insulation intended for pneumatic applications.* If the insulation is intended for pneumatic applications, the test specimens shall be prepared in the following manner:

(i) If ambient laboratory conditions are different from the conditioning requirements specified in (b) above, begin testing the specimen for settled density within 10 minutes after it has been removed from the conditioned area.

(ii) Pour the conditioned insulation into the holding box (Apparatus #10) in sufficient quantity to fill the specimen container (Apparatus #1 shown in Figure 1) four times. Manually break up any large clumps of material that might cause feeding problems.

(2) *Insulation intended for pouring applications.* If the insulation is intended for pouring applications, the test specimens shall be prepared in the following manner:

(i) If ambient laboratory conditions are different from the conditioning requirements specified in (b) above, begin testing 10 minutes after it has been removed from the conditioned area.

(ii) Pour loose fill insulation into a simulated attic space until full. The attic space shall be formed by two nominal 2 × 6 (243 cm) (8 ft) long joists placed 40.6 cm (16 in) on center with 1.27 cm (½ in) plywood nailed to the ends and bottom. Fluff the material with a garden rake (Apparatus #11), applying a series of small amplitude strokes while moving the rake slowly along the joist. Repeat the fluffing process six times.

(d) *Procedures*—(1) *Procedures for insulation intended for pneumatic applications.* If the insulation is intended for pneumatic applications, conduct the following procedures:

(i) The test shall be conducted in an area conditioned to the requirements of § 1209.4(b).

(ii) The apparatus shall be set up as shown in Figure 1. (Apparatus #9 and #10 are not shown in Figure 1, but are described at § 1209.4(a)). Connect one end of the supply source hose (Apparatus #8.i) to the intake of the supply blower (Apparatus #4). The other end will be used to pick up insulation from the holding container (Apparatus #10). Connect one end of the cyclone receiver hose (Apparatus #8.ii) to the outlet of the supply blower and the other end to the cyclone receiver (Apparatus #7). Connect one end of the fill chamber exit hose (Apparatus #8.iii) to the intake of the overflow blower (Apparatus #4) and the other end to the fill chamber (Apparatus #6). The fill chamber shall be placed on a flat and level surface. Connect one end of the variable length overflow exhaust hose (Apparatus #8.iv) to the outlet of the overflow blower. The other end should be conveniently placed to reduce insulation dust in the test area.

(iii) Weigh the empty insulation specimen container and record its weight.

(iv) Place the empty insulation specimen container in the fill chamber (Apparatus #6) centered under the cyclone receiver (Apparatus #7), and close the front cover.

(v) Adjust the blower control(s) (Apparatus #9) such that the supply and overflow blowers will operate at a no load voltage of 40 volts RMS.

(vi) Turn on the blowers simultaneously and proceed to fill the insulation specimen container by picking up material from the holding container using the supply source hose.

(vii) The container may fill unevenly, i.e. a void may tend to form off center in the container. If this occurs, stop the blowing process and rotate the container 180 degrees and continue the blowing process until the container just begins to overflow. If, for any reason, the filling process is interrupted for more than one minute or for more than the one time allowed to rotate the container, begin the process again.

(viii) Gently screed the excess material using a straight edge so as to leave a uniform surface of the insulation flush with the top of the container.

(ix) Weigh the filled and leveled container and record the weight. Take care not to bump or jar the container so as not to introduce any extraneous settling of the insulation.

(x) Cover the container to prevent spilling and secure the container to the shaker. Operate the shaker for a period of 5 minutes±15 seconds.

(xi) Remove the container from the shaker and uncover, taking care not to bump or jar it. Lower the disc (Apparatus #2) very slowly into the container until it starts to contact the insulation. At this point, release the disc and allow it to settle onto the insulation under its own weight.

(xii) Measure the volume of the space occupied by the settled insulation using the bottom edge of the disc as the upper datum point. If the disc is not level, measure the high and low points of the bottom of the disc and average the readings and use this as the height measurement in calculating the volume (V_s). This settled insulation volume and insulation weight (w) shall be used to calculate the settled density.

(xiii) Repeat this procedure [steps (i through xi)] using another specimen of the insulation until four settled densities are obtained for a given material. Then average these figures to arrive at a final settled density.

(2) *Procedures for insulation intended for pouring applications.* If the insulation is intended for pouring applications, conduct the following procedures:

(i) Weigh the empty insulation specimen container and record its weight.

(ii) Using a shovel (Apparatus #12) remove insulation from the simulated attic space and place it into the specimen container until the container just begins to overflow.

(iii) Follow steps (vi) through (xii) as specified under *Procedures for insulation intended for pneumatic applications.*

(iv) Repeat this procedure (steps (i) through (iii)) using another specimen of the insulation until four settled densities are obtained for a given material. Then average these figures to arrive at a final settled density.

(e) *Insulation intended for pouring and pneumatic applications.* If the insulation is intended for both pouring and pneumatic applications, or if it is uncertain whether the insulation will be poured or installed pneumatically, the insulation shall be tested for settled density using the test specimen preparation and test procedures at § 1209.4 (c) and (d) for each of the applications. The larger of the two settled density values shall be used in performing the corrosiveness test at § 1209.5 and the smoldering combustion test at § 1209.7.

(f) *Calculations.* Calculate the settled density of each specimen using the following formula:

Settled Density in kg/m^3=W/V_s, where

W=combined weight of the container and insulation in grams, minus the weight of the container in grams.

V_s=volume of insulation in liters after shaking.

§ 1209.5 Test procedures for corrosiveness.

This section prescribes the procedures for determining the corrosiveness of cellulose insulation. Cellulose insulation shall be tested for corrosiveness using the measured settled density, obtained by following the test procedure at § 1209.4, to calculate the amount of distilled or deionized water to add to the test specimens. Determination of corrosiveness shall be in accordance with the following test procedure:

(a) *Apparatus and materials*—(1) *Humidity chamber.* A forced-air humidity chamber capable of maintaining 48.9±1.7 °C (120±3 °F) and 97 ±1.5 percent relative humidity.

(2) *Crystallizing dishes.* Six glass crystallizing dishes, 90 mm (3.54 in) diameter by 50 mm (1.9 in) height.

(3) *Test coupons.* (i) Two aluminum coupons. 3003 bare aluminum, zero temper.

(ii) Two copper coupons. ASTM B 152, type ETP, Cabra No. 110 soft copper.

(iii) Two steel coupons. Low carbon, commercial quality, cold rolled, less than 30 carbon content, shim steel.

Each coupon shall be 50.8 by 50.8 mm (2 by 2 in) by 0.076 mm (0.003 in) thick metal free of tears, punctures, or crimps.

(4) Test specimens: Six test specimens of insulation shall be used for one test. Each specimen shall weigh 20g (0.7 oz).

(b) *Procedure*—(1) *General procedures for cleaning all metal coupons.* The metal coupons shall be cleaned by the following method:

(i) At no time during the fabrication, cleaning or testing shall the metal coupons be touched by ungloved hands.

(ii) Gloves shall be clean and in good condition.

(iii) All chemicals used shall be of American Chemical Society reagent grade or better, free from oily residues and other contaminants.

(iv) Water shall be distilled or deionized water.

(v) Handle cleaned coupons only with clean forceps.

(vi) In order to avoid exposing laboratory personnel to toxic fumes, the commission recommends that all cleaning procedures be performed in a fume hood.

(vii) Clean the coupons by vapor degreasing with 1,1,1-trichloroethane for ten minutes. Following vapor degreasing, subject the coupons to caustic and/or detergent washing as appropriate. Following caustic or detergent washing, rinse the coupons in flowing water to remove residues. Inspect each coupon for a water-break free surface. (A water-break is a break, separation, beading or retraction of the water film as the coupon is held vertically after wetting. As the coupons are cleaned, the water film should become gradually thinner at the top and heavier at the bottom.) Hot air dry the coupons at 105 °C (221 °F).

(2) Specimens of cellulose insulation submitted for testing shall be blown, combed, or otherwise mixed to reasonably assure homogeneity in the cellulose insulation test specimens.

(3) Before presaturating each 20g (0.7 oz) test specimen, subdivide it into two 10g (0.35 oz) portions. The quantity of distilled or deionized water to be used for each 10g (0.35 oz) portion shall be determined using the following formula:

ml distilled water = 46 / (settled density, Kg/m^3) × 75

or

ml distilled water = 2.9 / (settled density, lb/ft^3) × 75

(4) Presaturate each 10g (0.35 oz) portion with the determined amount of water. Place one presaturated 10g (0.35 oz) portion into a crystallizing dish, tamp level using the bottom of a clean suitably sized glass beaker. Place a metal coupon onto the presaturated insulation portion and center it in a horizontal plane. Place the other presaturated 10g (0.35 oz) portion into the crystallizing dish on the metal coupon and tamp the composite specimen (metal coupon plus saturated insulation in the crystallizing dish) to assure an even distribution of this material and to assure good contact of the insulation with the metal. Exercise care in preparing the composite specimens to eliminate air pockets from forming next to the metal coupons.

(5) Do not cover the crystallizing dish. (Care should be taken to avoid evaporation from the composite specimen while it is being prepared until it is placed in the humidity chamber.) If dripping occurs in the chamber, position a drip guard in the chamber to divert condensation to the chamber floor. Repeat the above for the other metal coupons. Place all six composite specimens into the humidity chamber. The chamber shall be preconditioned to 48.9 ±1.7 °C (120 ±3 °F) and 97 ±1.5 percent relative humidity. The specimens shall remain in the chamber for 336 ±4 hours. (Keep the chamber door open a minimum of time while placing composite specimens in and removing them from the chamber.)

(6) Upon completion of the test disassemble the composite specimens. Thoroughly wash the metal coupons under running water and lightly brush them using a soft nylon bristle brush or equivalent to remove loose corrosion products. Remove the remaining corrosion products from the metal coupons by cleaning them in accordance with the following practices:[1]

(i) Technique #1—Electrolytic Cleaning. This technique can be used for post-cleaning the tested copper, steel and aluminum coupons.

Description: Electrolyze the coupons as follows: Make a solution containing 28 ml of sulfuric acid (specific gravity 1.84), 2 ml of organic inhibitor, e.g. aobut 0.5 g/liter of such inhibitors as diorthotolyl thiourea, quinoline ethiodide, or betanaphthol quinoline may be used, and 970 ml of water. The solution shall be at 75 °C (167 °F). The anode shall be carbon or lead, and the cathode shall be one metal coupon. The electrolyzing shall run for 3 minutes at a current density of 20 A/dm^2. *Caution:* If lead anodes are used, lead may deposit on the coupon. If the coupon is resistant to nitric acid, the lead may be removed by a flash dip in 1 + 1 nitric acid (plus water). To avoid injury in this and subsequent techniques when mixing acid and water, gradually pour the acid into the water with continuous stirring, provide cooling if necessary.

(ii) Technique #2—Copper. This technique or Technique #1 can be used for post-cleaning the tested copper coupons only.

Description: Make a solution containing 500 ml of hydrochloric acid (specific gravity 1.19), 100 ml of sulfuric acid (specific gravity 1.84), and 400 ml of water. To avoid injury, prepare the solution by slowly adding the sulfuric acid to the water with continuous stirring. Cool, then add the hydrochloric

[1] These practices are the recommended practices in "ASTM G1—Standard Recommended Practice for Preparing, Cleaning, and Evaluating Corrosion Test Specimens," published by American Society for Testing and Materials, 1916 Race Street, Philadelphia, Pa. 19103.

acid slowly with continuous stirring. The solution shall be at room temperature. Dip the coupons in the solution for 1 to 3 minutes.

(iii) Technique #3—Steel. This technique or technique #1 can be used for post-cleaning the tested steel coupons only.

Description: Use one of the following two solutions:

Solution #1. Add 100 ml of sulfuric acid (specific gravity 1.84), 1.5 ml organic inhibitor, and water to make a 1 liter solution. The solution shall be 50 °C (120 °F). Dip the coupons in this solution.

Solution #2 (also referred to as Clarke's solution). Add 20 g of antimony trioxide and 50 g of stannous chloride to 1 liter of hydrochloric acid (specific gravity 1.19). The solution shall be stirred and be used at room temperature. Dip the coupons in this solution stirring the solution at a rate such that deformation of the coupons does not occur. This dipping shall last for up to 25 minutes.

(iv) Technique #4—Aluminum. This technique or technique #1 can be used for post-cleaning the tested aluminum coupons only.

Description: Make a 1 liter solution by adding 20g of chromic acid, and 50 ml of phosphoric acid (specific gravity 1.69), to water. The solution shall be 80 °C (176 °F). Dip the coupons in this solution for 5–10 minutes. If a film remains, dip the coupons in nitric acid (specific gravity 1.42) for 1 minute. Repeat the chromic acid dip. Nitric acid alone may be used if there are no deposits.

(7) After cleaning, examine the metal coupons over a 40–W appliance light bulb for perforation.

(c) *Noncorrosiveness*. Noncorrosiveness shall be determined by the absence of any perforations (excluding notches which extend into the coupon 3 mm or less from any edge) on each of the six test coupons when the coupons are observed over a 40–W appliance light bulb.

§ 1209.6 Test procedures for critical radiant flux.

This section provides the test procedure for determining the critical radiant flux of exposed attic floor insulation using a radiant heat energy source.

(a) *Apparatus and description of test procedure*. Test chamber (Figures 3 and 4 paragraph (b) of this section). An air-gas fueled radiant heat energy panel or equivalent panel inclined at 30° above and directed at a horizontally-mounted attic floor insulation specimen. The radiant panel generates a radiant energy flux distribution ranging along the approximately 100-cm length of the test specimen from a nominal maximum of 1.0 W/cm.^{2} to a minimum of 0.1 W/cm^2. The test is initiated by open flame ignition from a pilot burner. The distance burned to flame-out is converted to W/cm^2 from the flux profile graph (Figure 8) and reported as critical radiant flux, W/cm^2. Section 1209.8 provides a procedure for calibrating the radiation pyrometer used to standardize the thermal output of the panel.

(b) *Construction and instrumentation of the radiant panel test chamber*. The radiant panel test chamber shall be constructed and instrumented as follows:

(1) The radiant panel test chamber employed for this test shall be located in a draft protected area maintained at 21±3 °C (69.8±9 °F) and relative humidity of 50±20%. The radiant panel test chamber, (Figures 3 and 4) shall consist of an enclosure 140 cm (55 in) long by 50 cm (19½ in) deep by 71 cm (28 in) above the test specimen. The sides, ends, and top shall be of 1.3 cm nominal (½ in) calcium silicate board, such as Marinite I, 0.74 g/cm^3 (46 lb/ft^3) nominal density, with a thermal conductivity at 177 °C (350 °F) of 1.11 cal (g)/hr cm^2 °C/cm [0.89 Btu/(hr) (ft^2) (°F/in)]. One side shall be provided with an approximately 10 cm × 110 cm (4 × 44 inches) draft tight fire resistant glass window so that the entire length of the test specimen may be observed from ourside the fire test chamber. On the same side and below the observation window is a door which, when open, allows the specimen platform to be moved out for mounting or removal of test specimens. A draft tight, fire resistant observation window may be installed at the low flux end of the chamber.

(2) The bottom of the test chamber shall consist of a sliding steel platform which has provisions for rigidly securing the test specimen holder in a fixed and level position. The free, or air access, area around the platform shall be

in the range of 1935–3225 cm² (300–500 square in). The top of the chamber shall have an exhaust stack with interior dimensions of 10.2 cm (4 in) wide by 38 cm (15 in) deep by 31.8 cm (12.5 in) high at the opposite end of the chamber from the radiant energy source. The radiant heat energy source shall be a panel of porous refractory material mounted in a cast iron frame, with a radiation surface of 30.5×45.7 cm nominal (12 by 18 in). The panel fuel system shall consist of a venturi-type aspirator or equivalent system for mixing gas and air at approximately atmospheric pressure, a clean dry air supply capable of providing 28.3 NTP (Normal Temperature and Pressure m³ per hr (1000 standard cubic feet per hour) at 7.6 cm (3.0 in) of water, and suitable instrumentation for monitoring and controlling the flow of fuel to the panel.

(3) The radiant heat energy panel shall be mounted in the chamber 30±0.5° to the horizontal specimen plane. The horizontal distance from the 0 mark on the specimen fixture to the bottom edge (projected) of the radiating surface of the panel is 8.9 cm±0.1 (3½±1⁄32 in). The panel to specimen vertical distance is 14.0 cm±0.1 (5½±1⁄32 in) (see Figure 5). The angle and dimensions given above are critical in order to obtain the required radiant flux. The radiation pyrometer for standardizing the thermal output of the panel shall be suitable for viewing a circular area 25.0 cm (10 in) in diameter at a range of about 1.37 m (54 in). It shall be calibrated over the black body temperature range of 490–510 °C (914–950 °F) in accordance with the procedure described in § 1209.8. A high impedance voltmeter with a suitable millivolt range shall be used to monitor the output of the radiation pyrometer described. The dummy holder (see Figure 6), shall be constructed from 14 gauge heat-resistant stainless steel (AISI Type 300 (UNA-N08330)) or equivalent thickness 0.198 cm (0.078 in), having overall dimension of 114 cm (45 in) by 32 cm (12¾ in) with a specimen opening of 20 cm (7.9 inches) by 100 cm (39.4 in). Six slots are cut in the flange on either side of the holder to reduce warping. The holder is fastened to the platform with two stud bolts at each end.

(4) The specimen tray (see Figure 7) shall be constructed from 14 gauge heat-resistant stainless steel (AISI Type 300 (UNA-N08330)) or equivalent, thickness 0.198 cm (0.078 in). The depth of the tray is 5.0±0.2 cm (2±5⁄64 in). The flanges of the specimen tray are drilled to accommodate two stud bolts at each end; the bottom surface of the flange is 2.1±0.1 cm (0.83±0.04 in) below the top edge of the specimen tray. The overall dimensions of the tray and the width of the flanges are not critical and should be chosen so that the tray essentially fills the open space in the sliding platform. Tray must be adequate to contain a specimen at least 100 cm long and 25 cm wide. It is important to note that the zero reference point on the dummy specimen coincides with the pilot burner flame impingement point (see Figure 5).

(5) The pilot burner used to ignite the specimen shall be a propane venturi torch with an axially sysmmetric burner tip having a propane supply tube with an orifice diameter of 0.0076±0.0013 cm (0.003±0.0005 in). In operation, the propane flow is adjusted to give a pencil flame blue inner cone length of 1.3 cm (½ in). The pilot burner is positioned so that the flame generated will impinge on the centerline of the specimen at the zero reference point and at right angles to the specimen length (see Figures 3 and 4). The burner shall be capable of being swung out of the ignition position so that the flame is horizontal and at least 5 cm (2 in) above the specimen plane.

(6) Two 3.2 mm nominal (⅛ in) diameter stainless steel sheathed, grounded junction chromel alumel thermocouples are located in the flooring radiant panel test chamber (see Figures 3 and 4). Thermocouples shall be kept clean to ensure accuracy of readout. The chamber thermocouple is located in the longitudinal central vertical plane of the chamber 2.5 cm±0.1 (1±1⁄32 in) down from the top and 10.2 cm±0.1 (4 in±1⁄32) back from the inside of the exhaust stack. The exhaust stack thermocouple is centrally located 15.2±0.1 cm (6±1⁄32 in) from the top. A temperature indicating device with a range of 100–500 °C (212–932 °F) may be used to determine the chamber temperatures prior to a test.

(7) An exhaust duct with a capacity of 28.3–85 NTP m^3 per minute (1000–3000 standard cubic feet per minute) decoupled from the chamber stack by at least 7.6 cm (3 in) on all sides and with an effective area of the canopy slightly larger than the plane area of the chamber with the specimen platform in the out position shall be used to remove combustion products from the chamber. With the panel turned on and dummy specimen in place, there shall be no measurable difference in air flow through the chamber stack with the exhaust on or off.

(8) The dummy specimen which is used in the flux profile determination shall be made of 1.9±0.1 cm (¾±1⁄32 in) 0.74 g/cm^3 (46 lb/ft^3) nominal density calcium silicate board, such as Marinite I (see Figure 6). It is 25 cm (10 in) wide by 107 cm (42 in) long with 2.7±0.1 cm (1¹⁄16±1⁄32 in) diameter holes centered on and along the centerline at the 10, 20, 30, 40, 50, 60, 70, 80, 90 cm locations (within ±0.1 cm), measured from the zero reference point at the maximum flux end of the specimen. The total heat flux transducer used to determine the flux profile of the chamber in conjunction with the dummy specimen should be of the Schmidt-Boelter type, having a range of 0–1.5 W/cm^2 (0–1.32 Btu/ft^2 s), and shall be calibrated over the operating flux level range of .10 to 1.5 W/cm^2 in accordance with the procedure outlined in § 1209.8. The incoming cooling water flowing through the instrument shall be 15–25 °C (59–77 °F). A high impedance voltmeter with a resolution of at least 0.01 mV shall be used to measure the output of the total heat flux transducer during the flux profile determination. A timer shall be used for measuring preheat and pilot contact time.

(c) *Safety procedures*. The possibility of a gas-air fuel explosion in the test chamber should be recognized. Suitable safeguards consistent with sound engineering practice should be installed in the panel fuel supply system. These may include one or more of the following:

(1) A gas feed cut-off activated when the air supply fails,

(2) A fire sensor directed at the panel surface that stops fuel flow when the panel flame goes out,

(3) A commercial gas water heater or gas-fired furnace pilot burner control thermostatic shut-off, which is activated when the gas supply fails, or other suitable and approved device.

Manual reset is considered a desirable feature of any safeguard system used. In view of the potential hazard from products of combustion, the exhaust system must be so designed and operated that the laboratory environment is protected from smoke and gas. The operator should be instructed to minimize exposure to combustion products by following sound safety practices, such as ensuring that the exhaust system is working properly and wearing appropriate clothing, including gloves.

(d) *Test specimens*—(1) *Specimens of insulation intended for pneumatic applications*. (i) Insulation shall be installed into the specimen tray using the blower/cyclone apparatus described in § 1209.4(a).

(ii) Insulation shall be conditioned as described in § 1209.4(b).

(iii) Apparatus #4, 6, 7, 8, 9 and 10 shall be used as described in § 1209.4(d)(1)(i) with the following additional requirements.

(iv) The fill chamber (apparatus #6) shall be equipped with openings in the front and back so that a radiant panel specimen tray can be slid through the fill chamber.

(v) Adjust the blower control(s) (apparatus #9) such that the supply and overflow blowers will operate at a no load voltage of 40 volts RMS.

(vi) Turn on the blowers simultaneously and proceed to fill the fill chamber by picking up material from the box using the supply source hose. Large clumps of insulation shall be broken by hand before feeding them into the hose. Continue filling the chamber until large amounts of insulation are being drawn into the overflow hose.

(vii) Slowly slide the specimen tray through the fill chamber so that the low flux end of the tray is parallel with the back of the fill chamber filling the tray by sliding the tray forward to allow an excess of insulation to build up in the tray.

(viii) Shut off the blowers and remove the specimen tray and gently screed the insulation so that the insulation is level across the top of the tray. Take care not to compact the insulation or to leave large voids in the material. The tray may now be inserted into the radiant panel.

(2) *Specimens of insulation intended for pouring applications.* Insulation intended for pouring applications shall be poured into the tray until the tray is overfilled and then carefully screeded to the top of the tray taking care not to compact the insulation or leave large voids in the surface of the material.

(3) *Specimens of insulation intended for pouring and pneumatic applications.* If the insulation is intended for both pouring and pneumatic applications, or if it is uncertain whether the insulation will be poured or blown, the insulation shall be tested using the test procedures at paragraphs (d) (1) and (2) of this section for each of the applications. Three specimens shall be tested under the test procedure for each application. All of the specimens shall meet the criteria at §1209.3(b) for passing the attic floor radiant panel test.

(e) *Radiant heat energy flux profile standardization.* In a continuing program of tests, determine the flux profile at least once a week. Where the time interval between tests is greater than one week, determine the flux profile at the start of the test series.

(1) Mount the dummy specimen in the mounting frame and attach the assembly to the sliding platform. With the sliding platform out of the chamber, ignite the radiant panel. Allow the unit to heat for 1 hour. The pilot burner is off during this determination. Adjust the fuel mixture to give an air-rich flame. Make fuel flow settings to bring the panel to an apparent black body temperature as measured by the radiation pyrometer, of approximately 500 °C (932 °F), and bring the chamber to a temperature of approximately 180 °C (356 °F). When equilibrium has been established, move the specimen platform into the chamber. Allow 0.5 hour for the closed chamber to reach equilibrium.

(2) Measure the radiant heat energy flux level at the 40 cm point with the total flux meter instrumentation. This is done by inserting the flux meter in the opening so that its detecting plane is 0.16–0.32 cm (1⁄16-1⁄8 inch) above and parallel to the plane of the dummy specimen and reading its output after 30±10 seconds. If the level is within the limits specified, the flux profile determination is started. If it is not, make the necessary adjustments in the panel fuel flow. A suggested flux profile data log format is shown in Figure 9.

(3) The test shall be run under chamber operating conditions which give a flux profile as shown in Figure 8. The radiant heat energy incident on the dummy specimen shall be between 0.87 and .95 W/cm^2 (0.77 and .83 Btu/ft^2 sec) at the 20 cm point, between 0.48 and 0.52 W/cm^2 (0.42 and 0.46 Btu/ft^2 sec) at the 40 cm point, and between 0.22 and 0.26 W/cm^2 (0.19 and 0.23 Btu/ft^2 sec) at the 60 cm point. Insert the flux meter in the 10 cm opening, following the procedure given above. Read the millivolt output at 30±10 seconds and proceed to the 20 cm point. Repeat the 10 cm procedure. The 30 to 90 cm flux levels are determined in the same manner. Following the 90 cm measurement, make a check reading at 40 cm. If this is within the limits set forth, the test chamber is in calibration, and the profile determination is completed. If not, carefully adjust fuel flow, allow 0.5 hour for equilibrium and repeat the procedure. Plot the radiant heat energy flux data as a function of distance along the specimen plane on rectangular coordinate graph paper. Carefully draw the best smooth curve through the data points. This curve will hereafter be referred to as the flux profile curve.

(4) Determine the open chamber apparent black body and chamber temperatures that are identified with the standard flux profile by opening the door and moving the specimen platform out. Allow 0.5 hour for the chamber to reach equilibrium. Read the radiation pyrometer output and record the apparent black body temperature. This is the temperature setting that can be used in subsequent test work in lieu of measuring the radiant flux at 20 cm, 40 cm, and 60 cm using the dummy specimen. The chamber temperature also shall be determined again after 0.5

hour and is an added check on operating conditions.

(f) *Conditioning.* Test specimens shall be conditioned to equilibrium at 21±3 °C (69.8±5.4 °F) and a relative humidity of 50±5 percent immediately prior to testing. A less than 1% change in net weight of the specimen in two consecutive weighings with two hours between each weighing constitutes equilibrium. The maximum cumulative time a conditioned sample may be exposed to conditions different from 21±3 °C (69.8±5.4 °F) and relative humidity of 50±5% before insertion in to the radiant panel chamber for testing is 10 minutes.

(g) *Test Procedure.* (1) With the sliding platform out of the chamber, ignite the radiant panel. Allow the unit to heat for 1 hour. It is recommended that a sheet of inorganic millboard be used to cover the opening when the hinged portion of the front panel is open and the specimen platform is moved out of the chamber. The millboard is used to prevent heating of the specimen and to protect the operator. Read the panel apparent black body temperature and the chamber temperature. When these temperatures are in agreement to within ±5 °C (±9 °F) with those determined previously, during the flux profile standardization procedure, the chamber is ready for use.

(2) Mount the specimen tray with insulation on the sliding platform and position with stud bolts (see Figure 9). Ignite the pilot burner, move the specimen into the chamber, and close the door. Start the timer. After 2 minutes ±5 seconds preheat, with the pilot burner on and set so that the flame is horizontal and about 5 cm above the specimen, bring the pilot burner flame into contact with the center of the specimen at the 0 mark. Leave the pilot burner flame in contact with the specimen for 2 minutes ±5 seconds, or until all flaming other than in the area of the pilot burner has ceased, then remove to a position of at least 5 cm above the specimen and leave burning until the test is terminated.

(3) If the specimen does not ignite within 2 minutes following pilot burner flame application, the test is terminated by extinguishing the pilot burner flame. For specimens that do ignite, the test is continued until the flame goes out. When the test is completed, the door is opened, and the specimen platform is pulled out.

(4) Measure the distance burned, (the point of farthest advance of the flame front) to the nearest 0.1 cm (.03 in). From the flux profile curve, convert the distance to W/cm^2 (Btu/ft2sec) critical radiant heat flux at flame out. Read to two significant figures. A suggested data log format is shown in Figure 10.

(5) Remove the specimen tray from the moveable platform. The succeeding test can begin as soon as the panel apparent black body temperature and chamber temperature are verified. The specimen tray should be at room temperature before the next specimen is inserted.

§ 1209.7 Test procedures for smoldering combustion.

This section provides the test method for determining smoldering combustion characteristics of materials used for thermal insulation. This test shall be conducted on materials at the measured settled density as provided in § 1209.4.

(a) *Apparatus.* (1) The specimen holder shall be an open-top 20±0.2 cm (7.87±.08 in) square box, 10±0.2 cm (3.94±.08 in) in height, fabricated from a single piece of 0.61±0.08 mm thick (24 U.S. Standard gauge) stainless steel sheet with the vertical edges of the box overlapped, not to exeed 7 mm (.28 in) in seam width, and soldered so as to be watertight. A removable extension top extending 8±.5 cm. above the top of the smolder box shall also be provided. The specimen holder during test use shall rest upon a pad of unfaced glass fiberboard or equivalent having dimensions equal to or greater than those of the bottom of the specimen holder. The unfaced glass fiberboard shall be approximately 2.5 cm (1 in) thick with a thermal conductivity of 0.30±0.05 cal(g)/hr cm^2 °C/cm (0.24±0.04 Btu/hr ft^2 °F/in) at 23.9 °C (75 °F).

(2) Ignition source. The ignition source shall be a cigarette without filter tip made from natural tobacco, 85±2 mm (3.35±.08 in) long with a tobacco packing density of 0.270±0.020 g/cm^3 (16.9±1.25 lb/ft^3) and a total weight of 1.1±0.1 gm (0.039±0.004 oz).

(3) Balance. A balance of 1 kg (2.2 lb) capacity, accurate at least to 0.1 g (0.004 oz), is required.

(4) Test area. The test area shall be draft-protected and equipped with a suitable system for exhausting smoke and/or noxious gases produced by testing. Air velocities as measured by a hot wire anemometer in the vicinity of the surface of the specimen shall not exceed 0.5 m/sec (1.64 ft/sec). The test area shall be at 21±3 °C (69.8±5.4 °F) and 50±5 percent relative humidity at the time the test begins.

(b) *Test procedure.* (1) Specimens and cigarettes shall be conditioned in air at a temperature of 21±3 °C (69.8±5.4 °F) and a relative humidity of 50±5 percent to equilibrium prior to test. A change of less than 1% in net weight of the specimen in two consecutive weighings with two hours between each weighing constitutes equilibrium. Cigarettes shall be removed from any packaging and exposed in a suitable manner to permit free movement of air around them during conditioning. Calculate the weight of material necessary to fill the holder (volume 4,000 cm^3or 0.14 ft^3) at the settled density as determined in § 1209.4(e). The material shall be blown, combed, or otherwise mixed to remove lumps and shall be loaded uniformly into each specimen holder, level and flush to the top of the holder. The weight of each specimen shall be measured to the nearest 0.2 g (0.007 oz) or less by weighing the holder before and after filling. If the weight of the specimen is less than that calculated, a removable extension top shall be placed on top of the holder, the necessary amount of insulation is placed inside the extension and the loaded holder shall be dropped from a height no greater than 7.6 cm. (3 in) onto a hard flat surface. This process shall be repeated until the calculated weight of material completely fills the holder. The extension top is then removed. With the specimen in the holder and placed on the insulated pad, a rod of 8 mm (.31 in) diameter with a pointed end shall be inserted vertically into the approximate center of the material being tested and withdrawn to form an appropriate cavity for the ignition source, such that the cigarette fits snugly and maintains uniform contact with the specimen. A well lit cigarette, burned not more than 8 mm (0.31 in), shall be inserted in the formed cavity, with the lit end upward and flush with the specimen surface. Burning of the cigarette and specimen shall be allowed to proceed undisturbed in the test area for at least 2 hours or until the smoldering is no longer progressing, whichever period is longer.

(2) After completion of burning and after the holder has cooled down to approximately room temperature, the specimen holder with its material residue shall be weighed, at least to the nearest 0.1 g (0.003 oz), and the percent weight loss of the original specimen calculated. The weight of the cigarette residue is ignored in this calculation. (That is, the weight of the cigarette residue is not subtracted from the net weight of the specimen holder's contends at the conclusion of the test.)

(3) Three specimens per sample shall be tested.

§ 1209.8 Procedure for calibration of radiation instrumentation.

This procedure is used to calibrate the radiation instruments used in the test procedures for measuring critical radiant flux.

(a) *Radition pyrometer.* Calibrate the radiation pyrometer by means of a conventional black body enclosure placed within a furnace and maintained at uniform temperatures of 490, 500, and 510 °C (914, 932, and 950 °F). The black body enclosure may consist of a closed chromel metal cylinder with a small sight hole in one end. Sight the radiation pyrometer upon the opposite end of the cylinder where a thermocouple indicates the black body temperature. Place the thermocouple within a drilled hole and in good thermal contact with the black body. When the black body enclosure has reached the appropriate temperature equilibrium, read the output of the radiation pyrometer. Repeat for each temperature.

(b) *Total heat flux meter.* The total flux meter shall be calibrated by the National Bureau of Standards, (direct request for such calibration services to the: Radiometric Physics Division, 534, National Bureau of Standards (NBS),

Washington, DC 20234.), or, alternatively, its calibration shall be developed by transfer calibration methods with an NBS calibrated flux meter. This latter calibration shall make use of the radiant panel tester as the heat source. Measurements shall be made at each of the nine dummy specimen positions and the mean value of these results shall constitute the final calibration.

(c) *Recommendation.* It is recommended that each laboratory maintain a dedicated calibrated reference flux meter against which one or more working flux meters can be compared as needed. The working flux meters should be calibrated according to this procedure at least once per year.

§ 1209.9 Labeling requirement.

(a) Manufacturers, importers, and private labelers of cellulose insulation shall place on all containers of cellulose insulation the following statement:

This product meets the amended CPSC standard for flame resistance and corrosiveness of cellulose insulation.

To meet this requirement manufacturers, importers, and private labelers may use any type of label, including one which is pressure sensitive or glued on, provided the label is made in such a manner that it will remain attached to the container for the expected time interval between the manufacture of the product and its installation.

(b) This label shall appear prominently and conspicuously on the container in letters which are at least one-fourth inch in height. The labeling statement shall be printed with legible type in a color which contrasts with the background on which the statement is printed.

§ 1209.10 Certification and enforcement.

(a) While this part 1209 prescribes test methods to determine whether cellulose insulation subject to this interim standard meets its requirements, the interim standard itself does not require that a manufacturer or private labeler test any cellulose insulation. However, section 14 of the Consumer Product Safety Act (15 U.S.C. 2063) requires manufacturers and private labelers of products subject to safety standards to certify that the product conforms to the standard based on either a test of each product or a reasonable testing program. (Elsewhere in this issue of the FEDERAL REGISTER, 44 FR 39983, the Commission has issued a certification rule that prescribes requirements that manufacturers and private labelers shall follow to certify that their cellulose insulation complies with the requirements of the amended standard.)

(b) The Commission intends to use the test procedures set forth in this part 1209 to determine whether insulation subject to the interim standard meets the requirements of the interim standard.

§ 1209.11 Effective date.

All cellulose insulation that is a consumer product and that is manufactured after October 15, 1979 shall meet the requirements of this standard, including the labeling requirement of § 1209.9.

FIGURE 1 TO SUBPART A OF PART 1209—PARTIAL INSULATION PREPARATION APPARATUS

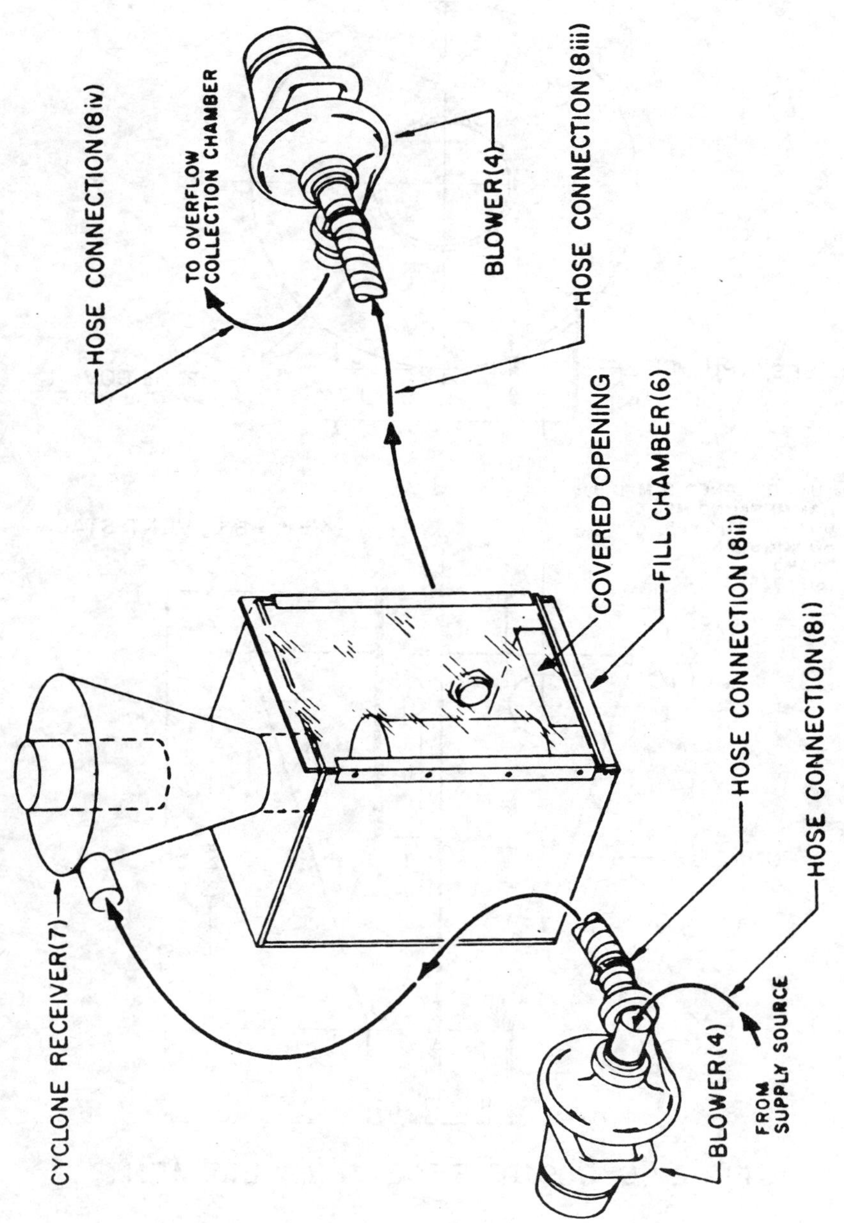

FIG 1—PARTIAL INSULATION PREPARATION APPARATUS

FIGURE 2 TO SUBPART A OF PART 1209—CYCLONE RECEIVER WELDMENT

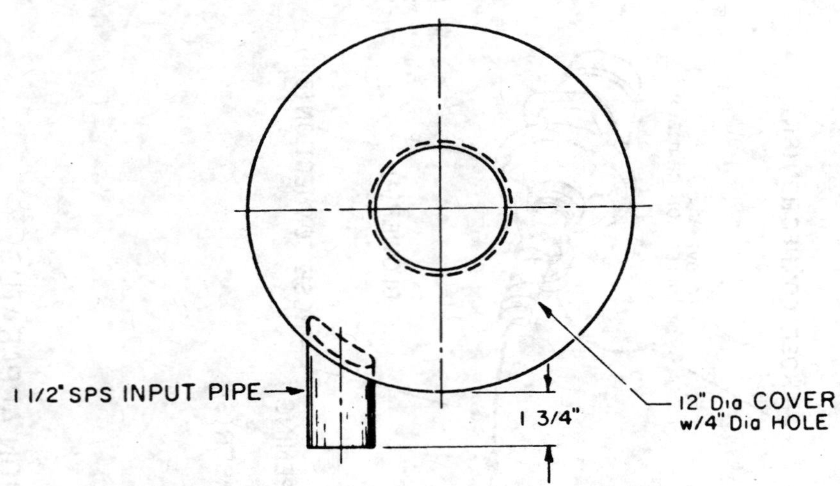

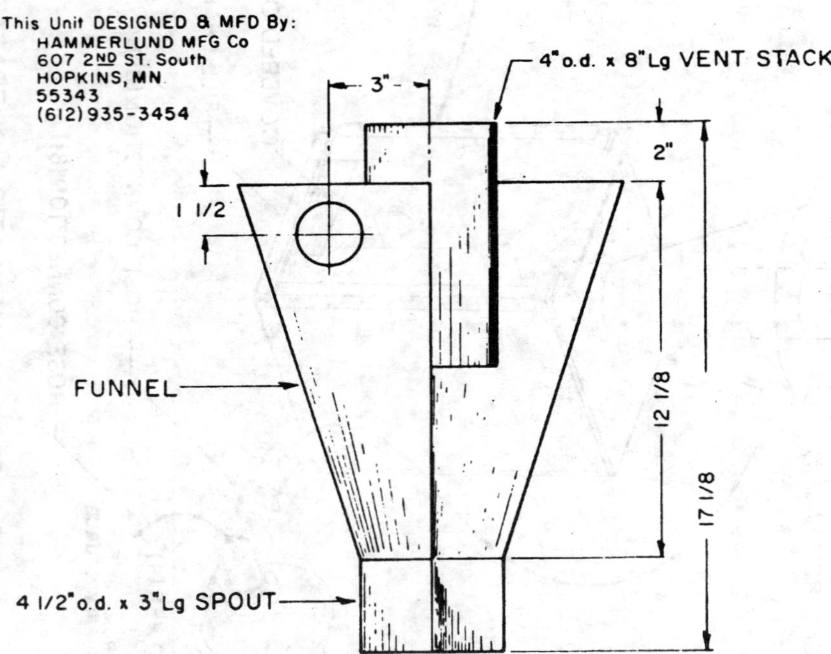

FIG 2—CYCLONE RECEIVER WELDMENT

FIGURE 3 TO SUBPART A OF PART 1209—FLOORING RADIANT TESTER SCHEMATIC SIDE ELEVATION

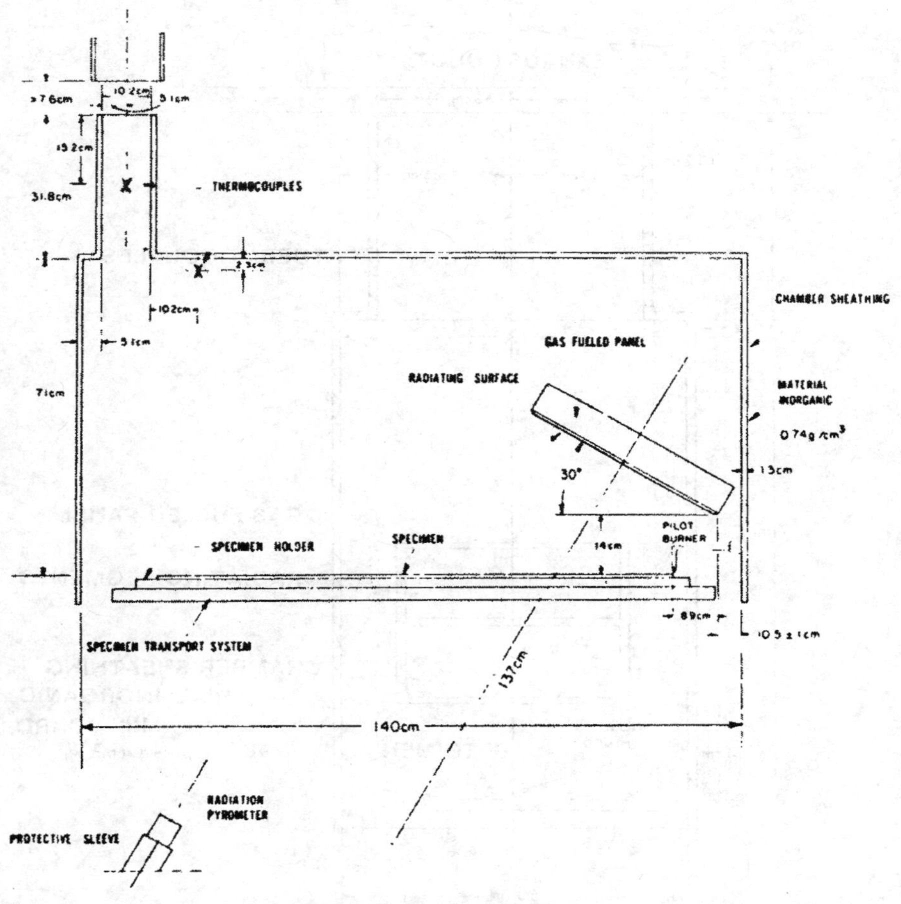

FIG 3 — FLOORING RADIANT TESTER SCHEMATIC

SIDE ELEVATION

FIGURE 4 TO SUBPART A OF PART 1209—FLOORING RADIANT PANEL TESTER SCHEMATIC LOW FLUX END, ELEVATION

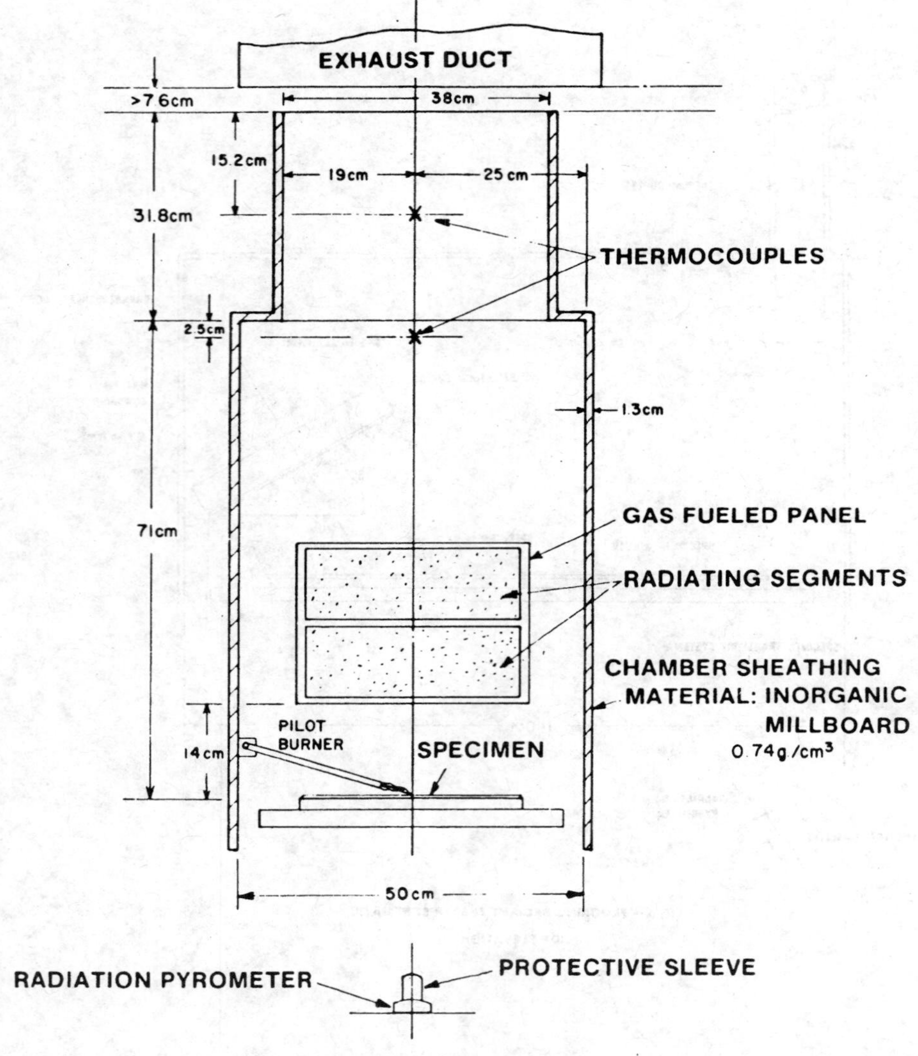

FIG 4 — **FLOORING RADIANT PANEL TESTER SCHEMATIC LOW FLUX END, ELEVATION**

FIGURE 5 TO SUBPART A OF PART 1209—ZERO REFERENCE POINT RELATED TO DETECTING PLANE

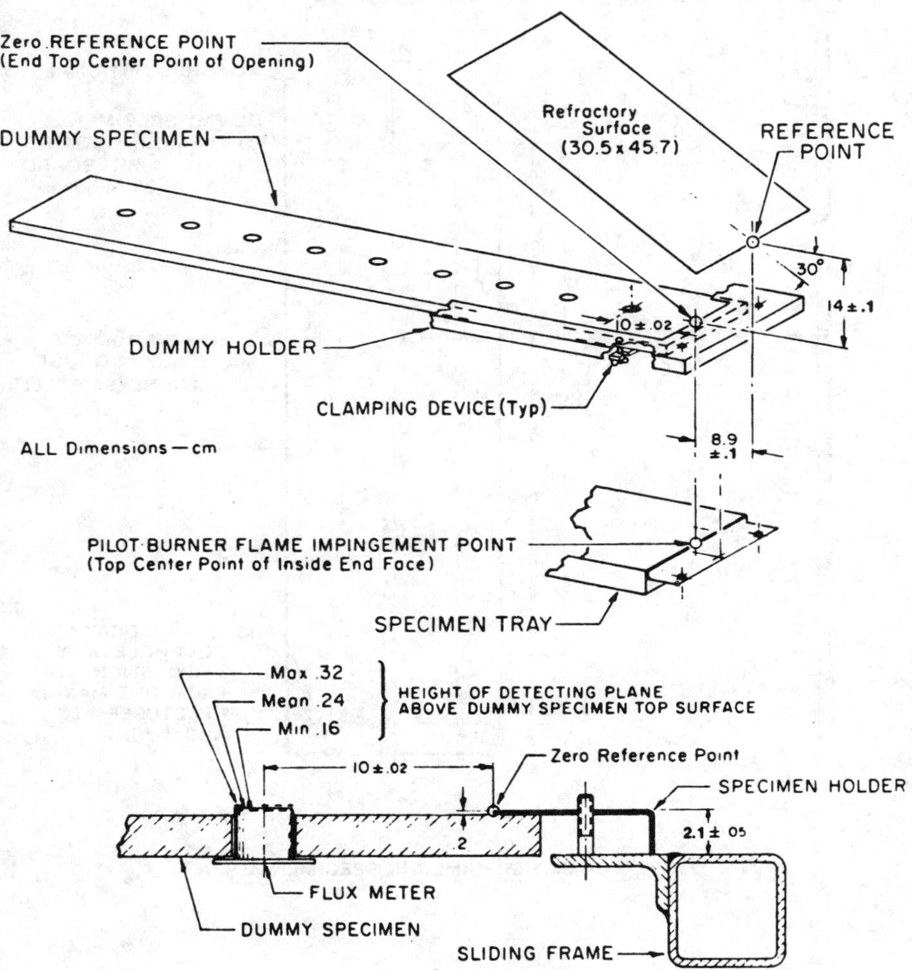

FIG 5 — ZERO REFERENCE POINT RELATED TO DETECTING PLANE

FIGURE 6 TO SUBPART A OF PART 1209—DUMMY SPECIMEN IN SPECIMEN HOLDER

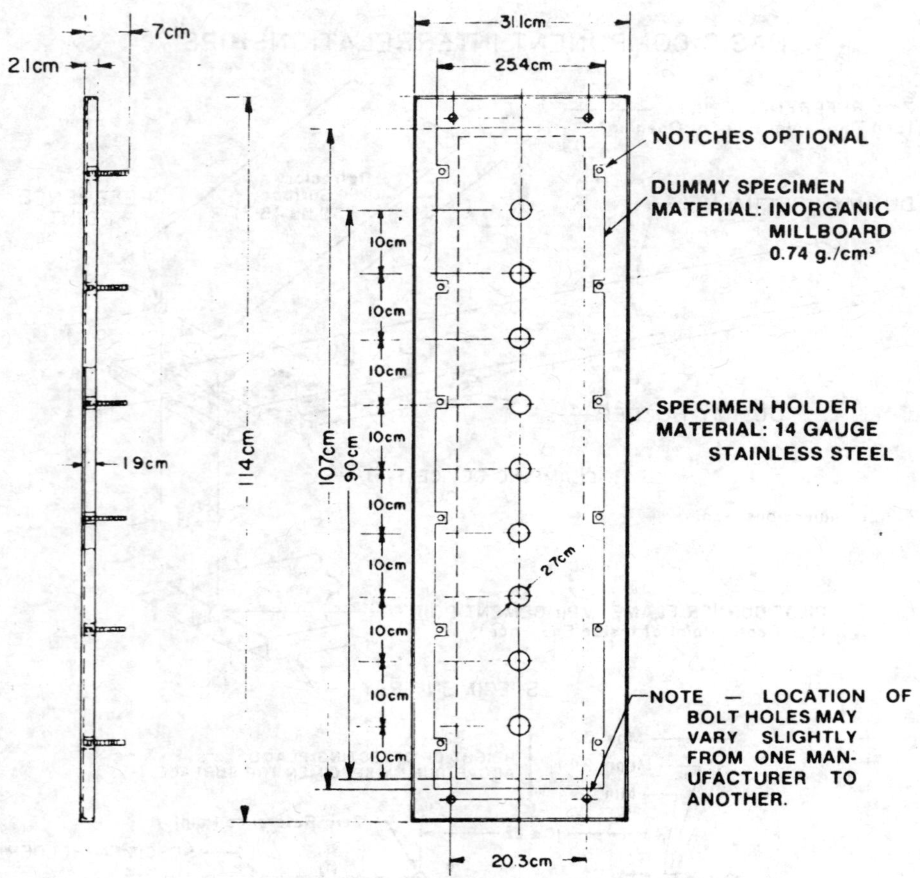

FIG 6 — **DUMMY SPECIMEN IN SPECIMEN HOLDER**

FIGURE 7 TO SUBPART A OF PART 1209—SPECIMEN TRAY

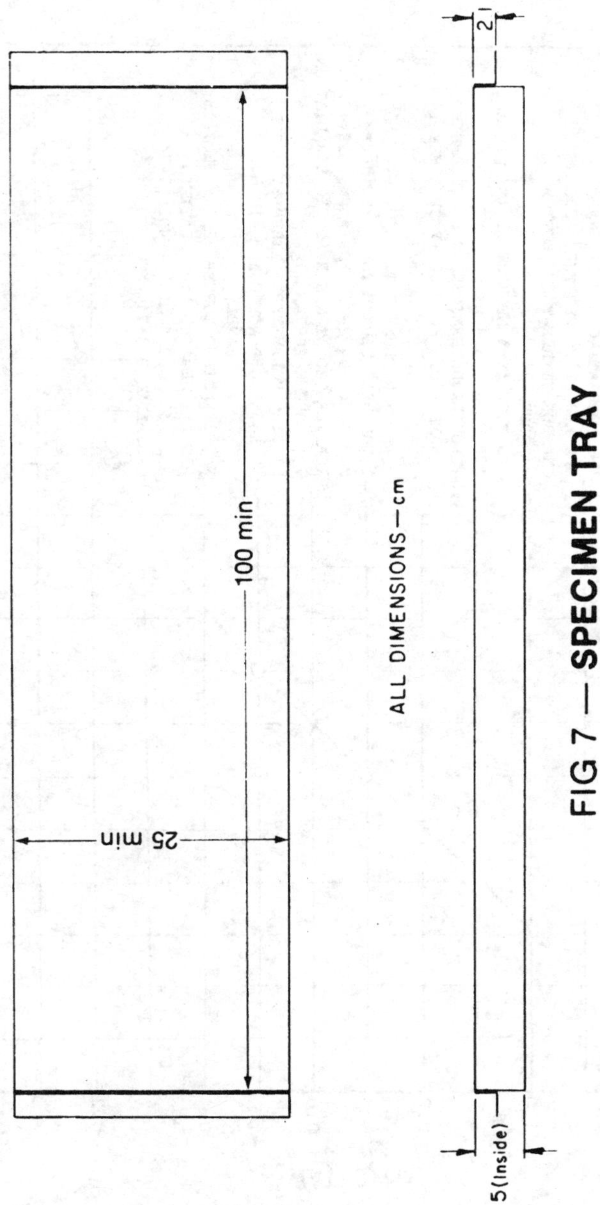

FIG 7 — SPECIMEN TRAY

FIGURE 8 TO SUBPART A OF PART 1209—STANDARD RADIANT HEAT ENERGY FLUX PROFILE

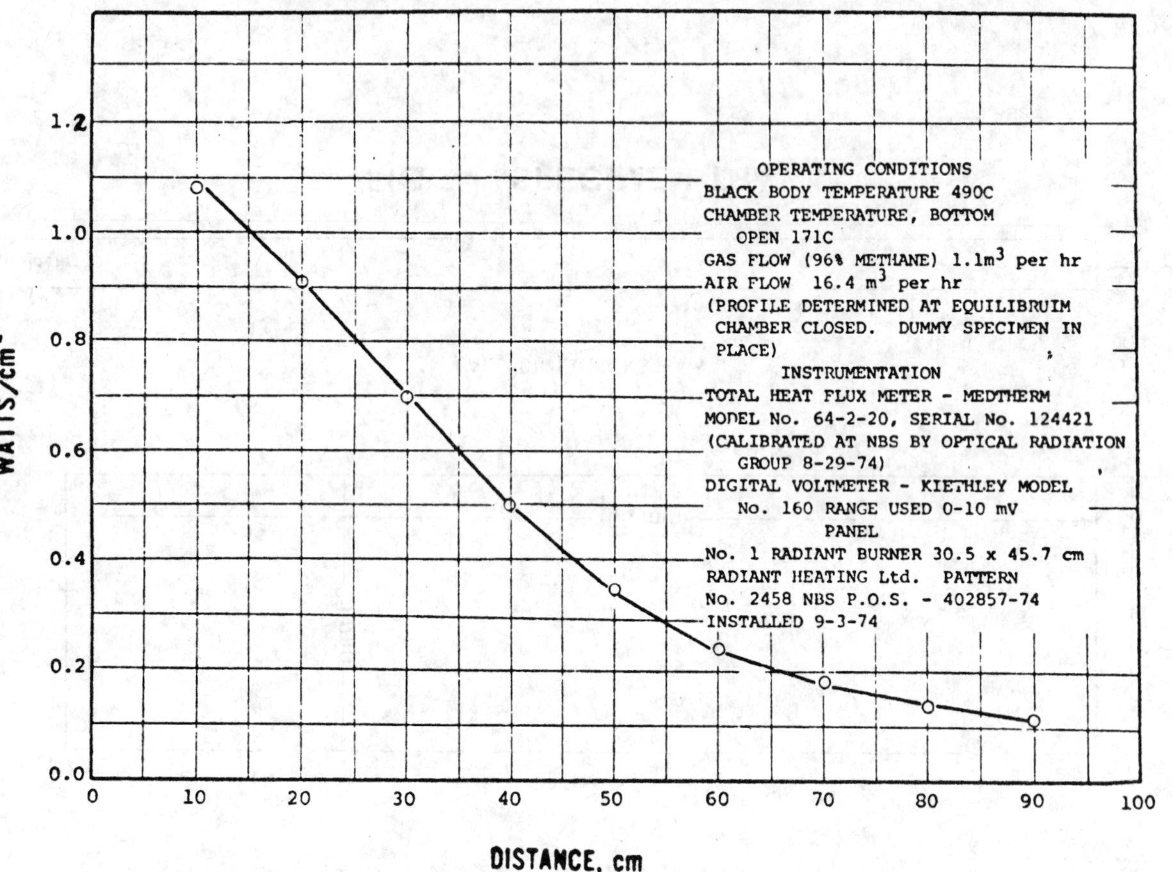

FIG 8 — STANDARD RADIANT HEAT ENERGY FLUX PROFILE

FIGURE 9 TO SUBPART A OF PART 1209—FLUX PROFILE DATA LOG FORMAT

RADIANT FLUX PROFILE

Date __________

Black Body Temperature ______m.v. ______°C (°F)

Gas Flow ______NTPm^{3}H (SCFH) Air Flow ______NTPm^{3}H (SCFH)

Room Temperature ______°C(°F)

Air Pressure __________ Gas _______ cm (in) of H_2O

Flux Meter ____________ Conversion Factor ____________

Radiometer No. ________ From Calibration on __________

Distance (cm)	MV	Watts/cm^2
10	_____	________
20	_____	________
30	_____	________
40	_____	________
50	_____	________
60	_____	________
70	_____	________
80	_____	________
90	_____	________

Signed _____________

FIG. 9 Flux Profile Data Log Format

FIGURE 10 TO SUBPART A OF PART 1209—INSULATION RADIANT PANEL TEST DATA LOG FORMAT

Test Number __________ Date __________ Time __________

Laboratory ___________________________

Specimen Identification/Code No. _____________________

Test Assembly: _______________________________________

Panel: Temperature _____°C (°F)

Flow: Gas ______NTPm^{3}H (SCFH) Air ________ NTPm^{3}H

Pressure, cm (in) H_2O: Initial, Air _____ Gas _______

Chamber Temperature (Initial) ___________°C (°F)

Room: Temperature _____°C (°F) Hood Draft ____cm (in) water

Total Burn Length _____________________________cm (in)

Critical Radiant Flux watts/cm^2 ____________________

Flux Profile Reference _____________________________

Observations:

Signed _______________________

FIG. 10 - Insulation Radiant Panel Test Data Log Format

Subpart B—Certification

AUTHORITY: Secs. 14, 16; 86 Stat. 1220, 1222; (15 U.S.C. 2063, 2065).

§ 1209.31 Purpose and applicability.

(a) *Purpose.* The purpose of this subpart B of part 1209 is to establish requirements that manufacturers, importers, and private labelers must follow to certify that their products comply with the Amended Interim Standard for Cellulose Insulation (16 CFR part 1209, subpart A). This subpart B includes requirements for conducting a reasonable testing program, certifying with labels and separate certificates, and recordkeeping.

(b) *Applicability.* (1) Cellulose insulation which is subject to the standard includes all cellulose insulation, manufactured after the effective date (as described in § 1209.41), produced or distributed for sale to, or for the personal use, consumption, or enjoyment of, consumers in or around a permanent or temporary household or residence, a school, in recreation or otherwise. The standard applies to cellulose insulation that is produced or distributed for sale to consumers, for their direct installation or use, as well as cellulose insulation that is produced or distributed for installation by professionals.

(2) The term *cellulose insulation* is defined in § 1209.2(a) of the standard to mean cellulosic fiber, loose fill, thermal insulation that is suitable for blowing or pouring applications.

§ 1209.32 Definitions.

In addition to the definitions set forth in section 3 of the act and in § 1209.2 of the standard, the following definitions shall apply to this subpart:

Private labeler means an owner of a brand or trademark which is used on the label of cellulose insulation subject to the standard which bears a private label as defined in section 3(a)(7) of the act (15 U.S.C. 2052(a)(7)).

Production interval means a time span determined by the manufacturer, private labeler, or importer to be appropriate for conducting a test or series of tests on samples of the cellulose insulation being produced to demonstrate that the product meets the requirements of the standard. An appropriate production interval may vary from test to test. The time period for a production interval shall be short enough to ensure that if the samples selected for testing comply with the standard or a portion of the standard, the insulation produced during the period will meet the standard or the appropriate portion of the standard.

§ 1209.33 Reasonable testing program.

(a) *General.* Section 14(a) of the Consumer Product Safety Act (15 U.S.C. 2063(a)) requires each manufacturer, importer, or private labeler of a product which is subject to a consumer product safety standard to issue a certificate of compliance with the applicable standard and to base that certificate upon a test of each item or upon a reasonable testing program. Because it is not practical to test each item subject to the standard, a reasonable testing program shall be used to support certificates of compliance for cellulose insulation.

(b) *Requirements of testing program.* A reasonable testing program for cellulose insulation is one which demonstrates with reasonable certainty that insulation certified to comply with the standard will meet all requirements of the standard. Manufacturers, private labelers, and importers shall determine the types and frequency of testing for their own reasonable testing programs. A reasonable testing program may include either the tests prescribed by the standard, or any other reasonable test procedures. However, a reasonable testing program cannot consist of tests which the party issuing the certificate of compliance knows (or through the exercise of reasonable diligence should know) will pass or accept insulation which will yield failing results when subjected to any of the tests in the standard. All reasonable testing programs shall consist of four elements:

(1) Qualification tests which must be performed on samples of the manufacturer's cellulose insulation to demonstrate that the product is capable of passing the tests prescribed by the standard.

(2) A description of the cellulose insulation which passed the qualification testing. This description is known as the "product specification."

(3) Production tests, which must be performed at appropriate production intervals as long as the cellulose insulation is being manufactured.

(4) Corrective action, which must be taken whenever samples of the cellulose insulation yield unacceptable or failing test results.

(c) *Commission testing.* The Commission will test for compliance with the standard by using the test procedures contained in the standard, and will base enforcement actions for violation of the standard on the results of such testing.

(d) *Testing by third parties.* At the option of the manufacturer, importer, or private labeler, some or all of the testing for the reasonable testing program may be performed by a commercial testing laboratory. However, the manufacturer, importer, or private labeler is responsible for ensuring that all testing used to support the certificate of compliance has been properly performed with passing or acceptable results and for maintaining all records of such tests in accordance with § 1209.38 below.

§ 1209.34 Qualification testing.

(a) *Requirement.* Before any manufacturer, importer, or private labeler begins distribution in commerce of cellulose insulation which is subject to the standard, samples of the insulation shall be tested for compliance with the standard. Manufacturers, importers, and private labelers shall determine the types of tests for qualification testing.

(b) *Timing, Sampling.* Any or all of the qualification testing required by this § 1209.34 may be performed before the effective date of the standard. Manufacturers, private labelers, or importers may select samples for qualification testing of a product in any manner they desire.

§ 1209.35 Product specification.

(a) *Requirement.* Before any manufacturer, importer, or private labeler distributes in commerce cellulose insulation which is subject to the standard, it shall ensure that the insulation is described in a written product specification.

(b) *Contents of Specification.* The product specification shall include the following information:

(1) A description of the equipment used to manufacture the insulation, including the model number and names of the equipment manufacturers, and details of any modification made to any item of equipment.

(2) A description of the cellulosic stock material used to manufacture the insulation, identifying the extent of impurities allowed.

(3) The formulation of the fire-retardant chemicals added, including their chemical constituents and their form (for example, granulated, powdered, or liquid); the amount of fire-retardant chemicals present in the finished insulation, expressed as a percentage of the total weight of chemicals and cellulosic stock; the average weight of chemicals per bag; and the name and address of each chemical supplier. Where the chemical composition or formula of a commercially premixed fire retardant is not known to the insulation manufacturer, the premixed fire retardant may be described simply by the name and address of the supplier and its brand or trade name.

(4) A description of the tests which were used to qualify the product as well as the dates of performance and results and actual values, where applicable, of the tests.

(5) Any other information necessary to describe the insulation.

(c) *Distribution in Commerce.* After the qualification testing required by § 1209.34 has been completed with acceptable results and the product specification required by this § 1209.35 has been recorded, the cellulose insulation may be manufactured and distributed in commerce, subject to the provisions of § 1209.36.

(d) *New Product.* Whenever a manufacturer, private labeler, or importer makes any change to any item of equipment, cellulosic stock material, or formulation of a fire-retardant chemical, or any other factor which is likely to affect the ability of the cellulose insulation to meet the standard, that change will result in a new cellulose insulation product, requiring the preparation of a new product specification. The new product must be subjected to qualification tests and must yield passing or acceptable results.

§ 1209.36 Production testing.

(a) *General.* Manufacturers, private labelers, and importers shall test the cellulose insulation periodically as it is manufactured to demonstrate that the product being manufactured is substantially similar to the product which passed the qualification testing and to demonstrate that the product being manufactured meets the requirements of the standard.

(b) *Types and frequency of testing.* Manufacturers, private labelers, and importers shall determine the types of tests for production testing. Each production test shall be conducted at a production interval short enough to ensure that if the samples selected for testing meet the standard or a portion of the standard, the insulation produced during the interval will also meet the standard or the appropriate portion of the standard.

(c) *Test failure.* If any test yields failing results, production must cease and the faulty manufacturing process must be corrected (see § 1209.37). In addition, the material from which the samples were taken may not be distributed in commerce unless the material can be corrected (see § 1209.37) so as to yield passing results and meet the standard. Cellulose insulation that does not comply with the standard cannot be sold or offered for sale.

§ 1209.37 Corrective actions.

(a) *Test failure.* When any test required by § 1209.36 yields failing or unacceptable results, corrective action must be taken. Corrective action includes changes to the manufacturing process as well as reworking the insulation product itself. Corrective action may consist of equipment adjustment, equipment repair, equipment replacement, change in chemical formulation, change in chemical quantity, change in cellulosic stock, or other action deemed appropriate by the manufacturer, private labeler or importer to achieve passing or acceptable test results.

(b) *New product.* If any corrective action required by this § 1209.37 results in a change in the product specification and a new cellulose insulation product (see § 1209.34(b)), the product specification for the new product must be recorded in accordance with § 1209.35, and qualification tests must be performed with passing or acceptable results in accordance with § 1209.34, before the new product is distributed in commerce.

§ 1209.38 Records.

(a) *Establishment and maintenance.* Each manufacturer, importer, and private labeler of cellulose insulation subject to the standard shall establish and maintain the following records which shall be available to any designated officer or employee of the Commission upon request in accordance with section 16(b) of the act (15 U.S.C. 2965(b)):

(1) A record of each product specification containing all information required by § 1209.35. (This includes information concerning the types of qualification tests as well as the results from these tests.)

(2) Records to demonstrate compliance with the requirements for production testing in § 1209.36, including a description of the types of production tests conducted and the production interval selected for performance of each production test.

(3) Records of all corrective actions taken in accordance with § 1209.37, including the specific action taken, the date the action was taken, and the test failure which necessitated the action. Records of corrective action must relate the corrective action taken to the product specification of the insulation product which was the subject of that corrective action, and the product specification of any new product which results from any corrective action.

(4) Records indicating exactly which insulation material is covered by each certificate of compliance issued.

(b) *Retention*—(1) *Product specification.* The records of each product specification shall be retained for as long as the cellulose insulation covered by that specification is manufactured and for a period of two (2) years thereafter.

(2) *Other records.* Records of production testing, corrective actions taken, and certificates issued shall be maintained for a period of two (2) years.

(c) *Confidentiality.* Requests for confidentiality of records provided to the Commission will be handled in accordance with section 6(a)(2) of the CPSA (15 U.S.C. 2055(a)(2)), the Freedom of Information Act as amended (5 U.S.C. 552), and the Commission's regulations under that act (16 CFR part 1015, February 22, 1977).

§ 1209.39 Certification of compliance.

(a)(1) *Responsibilities of manufacturer for insulation sold in bags.* Manufacturers of cellulose insulation subject to the standard which is sold in bags or other containers shall certify compliance with the standard by marking each bag or container with the following information:

(i) The statement "This product meets the amended CPSC standard for flame resistance and corrosiveness of cellulose insulation." (This statement is the same statement provided in § 1209.9 of the standard; it need not appear twice on the bag or container.)

(ii) The name of the manufacturer, private labeler, or importer issuing the certificate of compliance. See paragraphs (b) and (c), below.

(iii) The date of manufacture by day, month, and year.

(iv) The place of manufacture, by city, state, and zip code, or in the case of products manufactured outside the United States, by city and country.

The information required by this § 1209.39(a) may appear anywhere on the bag or container. The information required need not appear at the same place on the bag or container. The information shall be permanent until the bag or container is opened and used. The information shall be conspicuous and must appear in letters and figures at least ¼ inch in height. The date and place of manufacture may be in code, provided the person or firm issuing the certificate maintains a written record of the meaning of the code that can be made available to consumers, persons in the chain of distribution, and the Commission upon request.

(2) *Insulation not sold in bags or containers.* The manufacturer of cellulose insulation subject to the standard which is not sold in bags or other containers shall certify compliance with the standard by accompanying each shipment or delivery of the product, with a document such as an invoice, bill, statement, or separate document, which states the following: "This product meets the amended CPSC standard for flame resistance and corrosiveness of cellulose insulation. This material was manufactured on (insert day, month, and year of manufacture) at (insert city, state, and zip code, or in the case of insulation manufactured outside the United States, city and country)." The certificate of compliance must also contain the name of the manufacturer, private labeler, or importer issuing the certificate. See paragraphs (b) and (c), below. The certificate of compliance must appear in letters and figures which are conspicuous and legible. The date and place of manufacture may be in code, provided the person or firm issuing the certificate maintains a written record of the meaning of the code that can be made available to consumers, persons in the chain of distribution, and the Commission upon request.

(b) *Responsibilities of private labelers.* A private labeler who distributes a product subject to the standard which is manufactured by another person or firm but which is sold under the private labeler's name, brand, or trademark must issue the certificate of compliance required by section 14 of the Consumer Product Safety Act and this section. If the testing required by this subpart has been performed by or for the manufacturer of the product, the private labeler may rely on any such tests to support the certificate of compliance if the records of such tests are maintained in accordance with § 1209.38, above. The private labeler is responsible for ensuring that all testing used to support the certificate of compliance has been performed properly with passing or acceptable results, and that all records of such tests are accurate and complete.

(c) *Responsibilities of importers.* The importer of any product subject to the standard must issue the certificate of compliance required by section 14(a) of the act and this § 1209.39. If the testing required by this subpart B of part 1209 has been performed by or for the foreign manufacturer of the product, the importer may rely on any such tests to support the certificate of compliance if the importer is a resident of the U.S. or has a resident agent in the U.S. and the records are maintained in the U.S. in accordance with § 1209.38 above. The importer is responsible for ensuring that all testing used to support the certificate of compliance has been performed properly with passing or acceptable results, and that all records of such tests are accurate and complete.

§ 1209.40 Certification responsibility, multiple parties.

If there is more than one party (i.e., manufacturer, private labeler, or importer) otherwise subject to the requirements of this subpart B of part 1209 for certain cellulose insulation, only the party closest to the consumer in the distribution chain is required to issue a certificate.

§ 1209.41 Effective date.

The requirements of this subpart B of part 1209 shall become effective on October 16, 1979. Any cellulose insulation manufactured after October 15, 1979 must be certified as complying with the standard. Cellulose insulation which is sold in bags or other containers is "manufactured" when the insulation is packaged in the bag or other container in which it will be sold. Insulation which is not sold in bags or containers is "manufactured" when the insulation leaves the manufacturing site to be sold.

PART 1210—SAFETY STANDARD FOR CIGARETTE LIGHTERS

Subpart A—Requirements for Child Resistance

Subpart B—Certification Requirements

Subpart C—Stockpiling

SOURCE: 58 FR 37584, July 12, 1993, unless otherwise noted.

Subpart A—Requirements for Child Resistance

AUTHORITY: 15 U.S.C. 2056, 2058, 2079(d).

§ 1210.1 Scope, application, and effective date.

This part 1210, a consumer product safety standard, prescribes requirements for disposable and novelty lighters. These requirements are intended to make the lighters subject to the standard's provisions resistant to successful operation by children younger than 5 years of age. This standard applies to all disposable and novelty lighters, as defined in § 1210.2, that are manufactured or imported after July 12, 1994.

§ 1210.2 Definitions.

As used in this part 1210:

(a) *Cigarette lighter*. See *lighter*.

(b) *Disposable lighter*—means a lighter that either is:

(1) Not refillable with fuel or

(2)(i) Its fuel is butane, isobutane, propane, or other liquified hydrocarbon, or a mixture containing any of these, whose vapor pressure at 75 °F (24 °C) exceeds a gage pressure of 15 psi (103 kPa), and

(ii) It has a Customs Valuation or ex-factory price under $2.00, as adjusted every 5 years, to the nearest $0.25, in accordance with the percentage changes in the appropriate monthly Producer Price Index (Producer Price Index for Miscellaneous Fabricated Products) from June 1993. The adjusted figure, based on the change in that Index since June 1993 as finalized in November 2003, is $2.25.

(c) *Lighter*, also referred to as *cigarette lighter*, means a flame-producing product commonly used by consumers to ignite cigarettes, cigars, and pipes, although they may be used to ignite other materials. This term does not include matches or any other lighting device intended primarily for igniting materials other than smoking materials, such as fuel for fireplaces or for charcoal or gas-fired grills. When used in this part 1210, the term *lighter* includes only the disposable and novelty lighters to which this regulation applies.

(d) *Novelty lighter* means a lighter that has entertaining audio or visual effects, or that depicts (logos, decals, art work, etc.) or resembles in physical form or function articles commonly recognized as appealing to or intended for use by children under 5 years of age. This includes, but is not limited to, lighters that depict or resemble cartoon characters, toys, guns, watches, musical instruments, vehicles, toy animals, food or beverages, or that play musical notes or have flashing lights or other entertaining features. A novelty lighter may operate on any fuel, including butane or liquid fuel.

(e) *Successful operation* means one signal of any duration from a surrogate lighter within either of the two 5-minute test periods specified in § 1210.4(f).

(f) *Surrogate lighter* means a device that: approximates the appearance, size, shape, and weight of, and is identical in all other factors that affect child resistance (including operation and the force(s) required for operation), within reasonable manufacturing tolerances, to, a lighter intended for use by consumers; has no fuel; does not produce a flame; and produces an audible or visual signal that will be clearly discernible when the surrogate lighter is activated in each manner that would normally produce a flame in a production lighter. (This definition does not require a lighter to be modified with electronics or the like to produce a signal. Manufacturers may use a lighter without fuel as a surrogate lighter if a distinct signal such as a ''click'' can be heard clearly when the mechanism is operated in each manner that would produce a flame in a production lighter and if a flame cannot be produced in a production lighter without the signal. *But see* § 1210.4(f)(1).)

(g) *Model* means one or more cigarette lighters from the same manufacturer or importer that do not differ in design or other characteristics in any manner that may affect child-resistance. Lighter characteristics that may affect child-resistance include, but are not limited to, size, shape, case material, and ignition mechanism (including child-resistant features).

[58 FR 37584, July 12, 1993, as amended at 69 FR 19763, Apr. 14, 2004]

§ 1210.3 Requirements for cigarette lighters.

(a) A lighter subject to this part 1210 shall be resistant to successful operation by at least 85 percent of the child-test panel when tested in the manner prescribed by § 1210.4.

(b) The mechanism or system of a lighter subject to this part 1210 that makes the product resist successful operation by children must:

(1) Reset itself automatically after each operation of the ignition mechanism of the lighter,

(2) Not impair safe operation of the lighter when used in a normal and convenient manner,

(3) Be effective for the reasonably expected life of the lighter, and

(4) Not be easily overriden or deactivated.

§ 1210.4 Test protocol.

(a) *Child test panel.* (1) The test to determine if a lighter is resistant to successful operation by children uses a panel of children to test a surrogate lighter representing the production lighter intended for use. Written informed consent shall be obtained from a parent or legal guardian of a child before the child participates in the test.

(2) The test shall be conducted using at least one, but no more than two, 100-child test panels in accordance with the provisions of § 1210.4(f).

(3) The children for the test panel shall live within the United States.

(4) The age and sex distribution of each 100-child panel shall be:

(i) 30 +or- 2 children (20 +or- 1 males; 10 +or- 1 females) 42 through 44 months old;

(ii) 40 +or- 2 children (26 +or- 1 males; 14 +or- 1 females) 45 through 48 months old;

(iii) 30 +or- 2 children (20 +or- 1 males; 10 +or- 1 females) 49 through 51 months old.

NOTE: To calculate a child's age in months:

1. Subtract the child's birth date from the test date.

	Month	Day	Year
Test Date	8	3	94
Birth Date	6	23	90
Difference	2	-20	4

2. Multiply the difference in years by 12 months.

4 years × 12 months = 48 months.

3. Add the difference in months.

48 months + 2 months = 50 months.

4. If the difference in days is greater than 15 (e.g. 16, 17), add 1 month.

If the difference in days is less than -15 (e.g., -16, -17) subtract 1 month.

50 months - 1 month = 49 months.

If the difference in days is between -15 and 15 (e.g., -15, -14, ... 14, 15), do *not* add or subtract 1 month.

(5) No child with a permanent or temporary illness, injury, or handicap that would interfere with the child's ability to operate the surrogate lighter shall be selected for participation.

(6) Two children at a time shall participate in testing of surrogate lighters. Extra children whose results will

not be counted in the test may be used if necessary to provide the required partner for test subjects, if the extra children are within the required age range and a parent or guardian of each such child has signed a consent form.

(7) No child shall participate in more than one test panel or test more than one surrogate lighter. No child shall participate in both child-resistant package testing and surrogate lighter testing on the same day.

(b) *Test sites, environment, and adult testers.* (1) Surrogate lighters shall be tested within the United States at 5 or more test sites throughout the geographical area for each 100-child panel if the sites are the customary nursery schools or day care centers of the participating children. No more than 20 children shall be tested at each site. In the alternative, surrogate lighters may be tested within the United States at one or more central locations, provided the participating children are drawn from a variety of locations within the geographical area.

(2) Testing of surrogate lighters shall be conducted in a room that is familiar to the children on the test panel (for example, a room the children frequent at their customary nursery school or day care center). If the testing is conducted in a room that initially is unfamiliar to the children (for example, a room at a central location), the tester shall allow at least 5 minutes for the children to become accustomed to the new environment before starting the test. The area in which the testing is conducted shall be well-lighted and isolated from distractions. The children shall be allowed freedom of movement to work with their surrogate lighters, as long as the tester can watch both children at the same time. Two children at a time shall participate in testing of surrogate lighters. The children shall be seated side by side in chairs approximately 6 inches apart, across a table from the tester. The table shall be normal table height for the children, so that they can sit up at the table with their legs underneath and so that their arms will be at a comfortable height when on top of the table. The children's chairs shall be "child-size."

(3) Each tester shall be at least 18 years old. Five or 6 adult testers shall be used for each 100-child test panel. Each tester shall test an approximately equal number of children from a 100-child test panel (20 +or- 2 children each for 5 testers and 17 +or- 2 children each for 6 testers).

NOTE: When a test is initiated with five testers and one tester drops out, a sixth tester may be added to complete the testing. When a test is initiated with six testers and one tester drops out, the test shall be completed using the five remaining testers. When a tester drops out, the requirement for each tester to test an approximately equal number of children does not apply to that tester. When testing is initiated with five testers, no tester shall test more than 19 children until it is certain that the test can be completed with five testers.

(c) *Surrogate lighters.* (1) Six surrogate lighters shall be used for each 100-child panel. The six lighters shall represent the range of forces required for operation of lighters intended for use. All surrogate lighters shall be the same color. The surrogate lighters shall be labeled with sequential numbers beginning with the number one. The same six surrogate lighters shall be used for the entire 100-child panel. The surrogate lighters may be used in more than one 100-child panel test. The surrogate lighters shall not be damaged or jarred during storage or transportation. The surrogate lighters shall not be exposed to extreme heat or cold. The surrogate lighters shall be tested at room temperature. No surrogate lighter shall be left unattended.

(2) Each surrogate lighter shall be tested by an approximately equal number of children in a 100-child test panel (17 +or- 2 children).

NOTE: If a surrogate lighter is permanently damaged, testing shall continue with the remaining lighters. When a lighter is dropped out, the requirement that each lighter be tested by an approximately equal number of children does not apply to that lighter.

(3) Before each 100-child panel is tested, each surrogate lighter shall be examined to verify that it approximates the appearance, size, shape, and weight of a production lighter intended for use.

(4) Before and after each 100-child panel is tested, force measurements shall be taken on all operating components that could affect child resistance

to verify that they are within reasonable operating tolerances for a production lighter intended for use.

(5) Before and after testing surrogate lighters with each child, each surrogate lighter shall be operated outside the presence of any child participating in the test to verify that the lighters produce a signal. If the surrogate lighter will not produce a signal before the test, it shall be repaired before it is used in testing. If the surrogate lighter does not produce a signal when it is operated after the test, the results for the preceding test with that lighter shall be eliminated. The lighter shall be repaired and tested with another eligible child (as one of a pair of children) to complete the test panel.

(d) *Encouragement.* (1) Prior to the test, the tester shall talk to the children in a normal and friendly tone to make them feel at ease and to gain their confidence.

(2) The tester shall tell the children that he or she needs their help for a special job. The children shall not be promised a reward of any kind for participating, and shall not be told that the test is a game or contest or that it is fun.

(3) The tester shall not discourage a child from attempting to operate the surrogate lighter at any time unless a child is in danger of hurting himself or another child. The tester shall not discuss the dangers of lighters or matches with the children to be tested prior to the end of the 10-minute test.

(4) Whenever a child has stopped attempting to operate the surrogate lighter for a period of approximately one minute, the tester shall encourage the child to try by saying "keep trying for just a little longer."

(5) Whenever a child says that his or her parent, grandparent, guardian, etc., said never to touch lighters, say "that's right — never touch a real lighter — but your [parent, etc.] said it was OK for you to try to make a noise with this special lighter because it can't hurt you."

(6) The children in a pair being tested may encourage each other to operate the surrogate lighter and may tell or show each other how to operate it. (This interaction is *not* considered to be disruption as described in paragraph (e)(2) below.) However, neither child shall be allowed to operate the other child's lighter. If one child takes the other child's surrogate lighter, that surrogate lighter shall be immediately returned to the proper child. If this occurs, the tester shall say "No. He(she) has to try to do it himself(herself)."

(e) *Children who refuse to participate.* (1) If a child becomes upset or afraid, and cannot be reassured before the test starts, select another eligible child for participation in that pair.

(2) If a child disrupts the participation of another child for more than one minute during the test, the test shall be stopped and both children eliminated from the results. An explanation shall be recorded on the data collection record. These two children should be replaced with other eligible children to complete the test panel.

(3) If a child is not disruptive but refuses to attempt to operate the surrogate lighter throughout the entire test period, that child shall be eliminated from the test results and an explanation shall be recorded on the data collection record. The child shall be replaced with another eligible child (as one of a pair of children) to complete the test panel.

(f) *Test procedure.* (1) To begin the test, the tester shall say "I have a special lighter that will not make a flame. It makes a noise like this." Except where doing so would block the child's view of a visual signal, the adult tester shall place a 8½ by 11 inch sheet of cardboard or other rigid opaque material upright on the table in front of the surrogate lighter, so that the surrogate lighter cannot be seen by the child, and shall operate the surrogate lighter once to produce its signal. The tester shall say "Your parents [or other guardian, if applicable] said it is OK for you to try to make that noise with your lighter." The tester shall place a surrogate lighter in each child's hand and say "now *you* try to make a noise with your lighter. Keep trying until I tell you to stop."

(2) The adult tester shall observe the children for 5 minutes to determine if either or both of the children can successfully operate the surrogate lighter

by producing one signal of any duration. If a child achieves a spark without defeating the child-resistant feature, say "that's a spark — it won't hurt you — try to make the noise with your lighter." If any child successfully operates the surrogate lighter during this period, the surrogate lighter shall be taken from that child and the child shall not be asked to try to operate the lighter again. The tester shall ask the successful child to remain until the other child is finished.

(3) If either or both of the children are unable to successfully operate the surrogate lighter during the 5-minute period specified in §1210.4(f)(2), the adult tester shall demonstrate the operation of the surrogate lighter. To conduct the demonstration, secure the children's full attention by saying "Okay, give me your lighters now." Take the lighters and place them on the table in front of you out of the children's reach. Then say, "I'll show you how to make the noise with your lighters. First I'll show you with (child's name)'s lighter and then I'll show you with (child's name)'s lighter." Pick up the first child's lighter. Hold the lighter approximately two feet in front of the children at their eye level. Hold the lighter in a vertical position in one hand with the child-resistant feature exposed (not covered by fingers, thumb, etc.) Orient the child-resistant mechanism on the lighter toward the children. (This may require a change in your orientation to the children such as sitting sideways in the chair to allow a normal hand position for holding the lighter while assuring that both children have a clear view of the mechanism. You may also need to reposition your chair so your hand is centered between the children.) Say "now watch the lighter." Look at each child to verify that they are looking at the lighter. Operate the lighter one time in a normal manner according to the manufacturer's instructions. Do not exaggerate operating movements. Do not verbally describe the lighter's operation. Place the first child's lighter back on the table in front of you and pick up the second child's lighter. Say, "Okay, now watch this lighter." Repeat the demonstration as described above using the second child's lighter.

NOTE: Testers shall be trained to conduct the demonstration in a uniform manner, including the words spoken to the children, the way the lighter is held and operated, and how the tester's hand and body is oriented to the children. All testers must be able to operate the surrogate lighters using only appropriate operating movements in accordance with the manufacturer's instructions. If any of these requirements are not met during the demonstration for any pair of children, the results for that pair of children shall be eliminated from the test. Another pair of eligible children shall be used to complete the test panel.

(4) Each child who fails to successfully operate the surrogate lighter in the first 5 minutes is then given another 5 minutes in which to attempt the successful operation of the surrogate lighter. After the demonstrations give their original lighters back to the children by placing a lighter in each child's hand. Say "Okay, now you try to make the noise with your lighters - keep trying until I tell you to stop." If any child successfully operates the surrogate lighter during this period, the surrogate lighter shall be taken from that child and the child shall not be asked to try to operate the lighter again. The tester shall ask the successful child to remain until the other child is finished.

(5) At the end of the second 5-minute test period, take the surrogate lighter from any child who has not successfully operated it.

(6) After the test is over, ask the children to stand next to you. Look at the children's faces and say: "These are special lighters that don't make fire. Real lighters can burn you. Will you both promise me that you'll never try to work a real lighter?" Wait for an affirmative response from each child; then thank the children for helping.

(7) Escort the children out of the room used for testing.

(8) After a child has participated in the testing of a surrogate lighter, and on the same day, provide written notice of that fact to the child's parent or guardian. This notification may be in the form of a letter provided to the school to be given to the parents or guardian of each child. The notification shall state that the child participated, shall ask the parent or guardian to warn the child not to play with

lighters, and shall remind the parent or guardian to keep all lighters and matches, whether child resistant or not, out of the reach of children. For children who operated the surrogate lighter, the notification shall state that the child was able to operate the child-resistant lighter. For children who do not defeat the child-resistant feature, the notification shall state that, although the child did not defeat the child-resistant feature, the child may be able to do so in the future.

(g) *Data collection and recording.* Except for recording the times required for the children to activate the signal, recording of data should be avoided while the children are trying to operate the lighters, so that the tester's full attention is on the children during the test period. If actual testing is videotaped, the camera shall be stationary and shall be operated remotely in order to avoid distracting the children. Any photographs shall be taken *after* actual testing and shall simulate actual test procedure(s) (for example, the demonstration). The following data shall be collected and recorded for each child in the 100-child test panel:

(1) Sex (male or female).

(2) Date of birth (month, day, year).

(3) Age (in months, to the nearest month, as specified in § 1210.4(a)(4)).

(4) The number of the lighter tested by that child.

(5) Date of participation in the test (month, day, year).

(6) Location where the test was given (city, state, country, and the name of the site or an unique number or letter code that identifies the test site).

(7) The name of the tester who conducted the test.

(8) The elapsed time (to the nearest second) at which the child achieved any operation of the surrogate signal in the first 5-minute test period.

(9) The elapsed time (to the nearest second) at which the child achieved any operation of the surrogate signal in the second 5-minute test period.

(10) For a single pair of children from each 100-child test panel, photograph(s) or video tape to show how the lighter was held in the tester's hand, and the orientation of the tester's body and hand to the children, during the demonstration.

(h) *Evaluation of test results and acceptance criterion.* To determine whether a surrogate lighter resists operation by at least 85 percent of the children, sequential panels of 100 children each, up to a maximum of 2 panels, shall be tested as prescribed below.

(1) If no more than 10 children in the first 100-child test panel successfully operated the surrogate lighter, the lighter represented by the surrogate lighter shall be considered to be resistant to successful operation by at least 85 percent of the child test panel, and no further testing is conducted. If 11 through 18 children in the first 100-child test panel successfully operate the surrogate lighter, the test results are inconclusive, and the surrogate lighter shall be tested with a second 100-child test panel in accordance with this § 1210.4. If 19 or more of the children in the first 100-child test panel successfully operated the surrogate lighter, the lighter represented by the surrogate shall be considered not resistant to successful operation by at least 85 percent of the child test panel, and no further testing is conducted.

(2) If additional testing of the surrogate lighter is required by § 1210.4(h)(1), conduct the test specified by this § 1210.4 using a second 100-child test panel and record the results. If a total of no more than 30 of the children in the combined first and second 100-child test panels successfully operated the surrogate lighter, the lighter represented by the surrogate lighter shall be considered resistant to successful operation by at least 85 percent of the child test panel, and no further testing is performed. If a total of 31 or more children in the combined first and second 100-child test panels successfully operate the surrogate lighter, the lighter represented by the surrogate lighter shall be considered not resistant to successful operation by 85 percent of the child test panel, and no further testing is conducted.

TABLE 1—EVALUATION OF TEST RESULTS—§ 1210.4(E)

Test panel	Cumulative Number of Children	Successful Lighter Operations		
		Pass	Continue	Fail
1	100	0-10	11-18	19 or more
1	200	11-30	—	31 or more

§ 1210.5 Findings.

Section 9(f) of the Consumer Product Safety Act, 15 U.S.C. 2058(f), requires the Commission to make findings concerning the following topics and to include the findings in the rule.

(a) *The degree and nature of the risk of injury the rule is designed to eliminate or reduce.* The standard is designed to reduce the risk of death and injury from accidental fires started by children playing with lighters. From 1988 to 1990, an estimated 160 deaths per year resulted from such fires. About 150 of these deaths, plus nearly 1,100 injuries and nearly $70 million in property damage, resulted from fires started by children under the age of 5. Fire-related injuries include thermal burns — many of high severity — as well as anoxia and other, less serious injuries. The annual cost of such fires to the public is estimated at about $385 million (in 1990 dollars). Fires started by young children (under age 5) are those which the standard would be most effective at reducing.

(b) *The approximate number of consumer products, or types or classes thereof, subject to the rule.* The standard covers certain flame-producing devices, commonly known as lighters, which are primarily intended for use in lighting cigarettes and other smoking materials. Lighters may be gas- or liquid-fueled, mechanical or electric, and of various physical configurations. Over 600 million lighters are sold annually to consumers in the U.S.; over 100 million are estimated to be in use at any given time. Over 95 percent of all lighters sold are pocket-sized disposable butane models; of the remaining 5 percent, most are pocket refillable butane models. A small proportion of refillables is comprised of pocket liquid-fuel models; still smaller proportions are represented by table lighters and by "novelty" lighters, that is, those having the physical appearance of other specific objects. Approximately 600 million pocket butane disposables (nonrefillable), 15-20 million pocket butane refillables, 5-10 million pocket liquid-fuel refillables, and 1-3 million novelty and other lighters were sold to consumers in 1991. The standard covers disposable lighters, including inexpensive butane refillables, and novelty lighters. Roughly 30 million households have at least one lighter; ownership of more than one lighter is typical, especially among smoking households.

(c) *The need of the public for the consumer products subject to the rule, and the probable effect of the rule on the utility, cost, or availability of such products to meet such need.* Consumers use lighters primarily to light smoking materials. Most other lighting needs that could be filled by matches may also be filled by lighters. Disposable butane lighters are, chiefly by virtue of their low price and convenience, the closest available substitutes for matches. Although matches are found in far more households, lighters have steadily replaced matches since the 1960's as the primary light source among American consumers. The standard generally requires that lighters not be operable by most children under 52 months of age. This would likely be achieved by modifying products to incorporate additional-action switches, levers, or buttons, thereby increasing the difficulty of product activation. Depending on the method of compliance chosen by manufacturers, there could be some adverse effect on the utility of lighters. This may occur to the extent that operation of the products by adult users is made more difficult by the incorporation of child-resistant features. This may lead some consumers to switch to matches, at least temporarily, which could reduce the expected level of safety provided by the standard. In addition, some "novelty" lighters will probably be discontinued, due to the technical difficulty of incorporating child-resistant features or designs. Some loss of utility derived from those products by collectors or other users may result, though many novelty models will probably remain on the market. The cost of producing lighters subject to the standard is expected to increase due to manufacturers' and importers' expenditures in the areas of research and development, product redesign, tooling and assembly process changes, certification and testing, and other administrative activities. Total per-unit production costs for the various lighter types may increase by 10-40 percent, with an average of less than 20 percent. Cost increases will likely be passed on to consumers in the form of higher retail prices. Disposable lighters may increase in price by 10-40 cents per unit; prices of other lighters may increase by as much as $1-3. The estimated average per-unit price increase for all lighters subject to the standard is about 20 cents. The total annual cost of the standard to consumers is estimated at about $90 million. The estimated cost of the standard per life saved is well under $1 million after considering the benefits of reduced injuries and property damage; this is well below the consensus of estimates of the statistical value of life. A wide range of lighter types and models will continue to be available to consumers. As noted above, some models of novelty lighters — all of which account for less than 1 percent of lighters sold — will likely be discontinued; this should not have a significant impact on the overall availability of lighters to consumers.

(d) *Any means of achieving the objective of the order while minimizing adverse effects on competition or disruption or dislocation of manufacturing and other commercial practices consistent with the public health and safety.* The Commission considered the potential effects on competition and business practices of various aspects of the standard, and, as noted below, incorporated some burden-reducing elements into the proposal. The Commission also encouraged and participated in the development of a draft voluntary standard addressing the risk of child-play fires. A draft voluntary safety standard was developed by members of an ASTM task group (now a subcommittee) to address much of the risk addressed by the proposed CPSC rule. This draft voluntary standard contained performance requirements similar, but not identical, to those in the CPSC proposal. Development work on the voluntary standard ceased in 1991; industry representatives requested that the Commission issue the draft ASTM provisions in a mandatory rule. One possible alternative to this mandatory standard would be for the Commission to rely on voluntary conformance to this draft standard to provide safety to consumers. The expected level of conformance to a voluntary standard is uncertain, however; although some of the largest firms may market some child-resistant lighters that conform to these requirements, most firms (possibly including some of the largest) probably would not. Even under generous assumptions about the level of voluntary conformance, net benefits to consumers would be substantially lower under this alternative than under the standard. Thus, the Commission finds that reliance on voluntary conformance to the draft ASTM standard would not adequately reduce the unreasonable risk associated with lighters.

(e) *The rule (including its effective date) is reasonably necessary to eliminate or reduce an unreasonable risk.* The Commission's hazard data and regulatory analysis demonstrate that lighters covered by the standard pose an unreasonable risk of death and injury to consumers. The Commission considered a number of alternatives to address this risk, and believes that the standard strikes the most reasonable balance between risk reduction benefits and potential costs. Further, the amount of time before the standard becomes effective will provide manufacturers and importers of most products adequate time to design, produce, and market safer lighters. Thus, the Commission finds that the standard and its effective date are reasonably necessary to reduce the risk of fire-related death and injury associated with young children playing with lighters.

(f) *The benefits expected from the rule bear a reasonable relationship to its costs.* The standard will substantially reduce the number of fire-related deaths, injuries, and property damage associated with young children playing with lighters. The cost of these accidents, which is estimated to be about $385 million annually, will also be greatly reduced. Estimated annual benefits of the standard are $205-$270 million; estimated annual costs to the public are about $90 million. Expected annual net benefits would therefore be $115-$180 million. Thus, the Commission finds that a reasonable relationship exists between potential benefits and potential costs of the standard.

(g) *The rule imposes the least burdensome requirement which prevents or adequately reduces the risk of injury for which the rule is being promulgated.* (1) In the final rule, the Commission incorporated a number of changes from the proposed rule in order to minimize the potential burden of the rule on industry and consumers. The Commission also considered and rejected several alternatives during the development of the standard to reduce the potential burden on industry (especially small importers) and on consumers. These alternatives involve different performance and test requirements and different definitions determining the scope of coverage among products. Other alternatives generally would be more burdensome to industry and would have higher costs to consumers. Some less burdensome alternatives would have lower risk-reduction benefits to consumers; none has been identified that would have higher expected net benefits than the standard.

(2) The scope of this mandatory standard is limited to disposable lighters and novelty lighters; it does not apply to "luxury" lighters (including most higher priced refillable butane and liquid-fuel models). This is similar but not identical to the scope of a draft voluntary industry standard developed in response to the Commission's advance notice of proposed rulemaking of March 3, 1988 (53 FR 6833). This exclusion significantly reduces the potential cost of the standard without significantly affecting potential benefits.

(3) The Commission narrowed the scope of the final rule with respect to novelty lighters, and considered limiting the scope further to exclude all nondisposable novelty lighters. Though further limiting the scope would ease the potential burden of the standard on manufacturers and importers slightly, inherently less safe non-child-resistant lighters that are considered to be especially appealing to children would remain on the market, thereby reducing the potential safety benefits to the public. The Commission finds that it would not be in the public interest to exclude novelty lighters.

(4) The Commission considered the potential effect of alternate performance requirements during the development of the standard. A less stringent acceptance criterion of 80 percent (rather than the standard's 85 percent) might slightly reduce costs to industry and consumers. The safety benefits of this alternative, however, would likely be reduced disproportionately to the potential reduction in costs. A higher (90 percent) acceptance criterion was also considered. This higher performance level is not commercially or technically feasible for many firms, however; the Commission believes that this more stringent alternative would have substantial adverse effects on manufacturing and competition, and would increase costs disproportionate to benefits. The Commission believes that the requirement that complying lighters not be operable by at least 85 percent of children in prescribed tests strikes a reasonable balance between improved safety for a substantial majority of young children and other potential fire victims and the potential for adverse competitive effects and manufacturing disruption.

(5) The Commission believes that the standard should become effective as soon as reasonably possible. The standard will become effective 12 months from its date of publication in the FEDERAL REGISTER. The Commission also considered an effective date of 6 months after the date of issuance of the final rule. While most lighters sold in the U.S. could probably be made child resistant within 6 months, some disruptive effects on the supply of some imported lighters would result; this could have a temporary adverse impact on the competitive positions of some U.S. importers. The 12-month period in the standard would tend to minimize this potential effect, and would allow more time for firms to design, produce, and import complying lighters. The Commission estimates that there would be no significant adverse impact

on the overall supply of lighters for the U.S. market.

(h) *The promulgation of the rule is in the public interest.* As required by the CPSA and the Regulatory Flexibility Act, the Commission considered the potential benefits and costs of the standard and various alternatives. While certain alternatives to the final rule are estimated to have net benefits to consumers, the adopted rule maximizes these net benefits. Thus, the Commission finds that the standard, if promulgated on a final basis, would be in the public interest.

Subpart B—Certification Requirements

AUTHORITY: 15 U.S.C. 2063, 2065(b), 2066(g), 2076(e), 2079(d).

§ 1210.11 General.

Section 14(a) of the Consumer Product Safety Act (CPSA), 15 U.S.C. 1263(a), requires every manufacturer, private labeler, or importer of a product that is subject to a consumer product safety standard and that is distributed in commerce to issue a certificate that such product conforms to the applicable standard and to base that certificate upon a test of each item or upon a reasonable testing program. The purpose of this subpart B of part 1210 is to establish requirements that manufacturers, importers, and private labelers must follow to certify that their products comply with the Safety Standard for Cigarette Lighters. This subpart B describes the minimum features of a reasonable testing program and includes requirements for labeling, recordkeeping, and reporting pursuant to sections 14, 16(b), 17(g), and 27(e) of the CPSA, 15 U.S.C. 2063, 2065(b), 2066(g), and 2076(e).

§ 1210.12 Certificate of compliance.

(a) *General requirements*—(1) *Manufacturers (including importers).* Manufacturers of any lighter subject to the standard must issue the certificate of compliance required by section 14(a) of the CPSA and this subpart B, based on a reasonable testing program or a test of each product, as required by §§ 1210.13-1210.14 and 1210.16. Manufacturers must also label each lighter subject to the standard as required by paragraph (c) of this section and keep the records and make the reports required by §§ 1210.15 and 1210.17. For purposes of this requirement, an importer of lighters shall be considered the "manufacturer."

(2) *Private labelers.* Because private labelers necessarily obtain their products from a manufacturer or importer that is already required to issue the certificate, private labelers are not required to issue a certificate. However, private labelers must ensure that the lighters are labeled in accordance with paragraph (c) of this section and that any certificate of compliance that is supplied with each shipping unit of lighters in accordance with paragraph (b) of this section is supplied to any distributor or retailer who receives the product from the private labeler.

(3) *Testing on behalf of importers.* If the required testing has been performed by or for a foreign manufacturer of a product, an importer may rely on such tests to support the certificate of compliance, provided that the importer is a resident of the United States or has a resident agent in the United States, the records are in English, and the records and the surrogate lighters tested are kept in the United States and can be provided to the Commission within 48 hours (§ 1210.17(a)) or, in the case of production records, can be provided to the Commission within 7 calendar days in accordance with § 1210.17(a)(3). The importer is responsible for ensuring that the foreign manufacturer's records show that all testing used to support the certificate of compliance has been performed properly (§§ 1210.14-1210.16), the records provide a reasonable assurance that all lighters imported comply with the standard (§ 1210.13(b)(1)), the records exist in English (§ 1210.17(a)), (4) the importer knows where the required records and lighters are located and that records required to be located in the United States are located there, arrangements have been made so that any records required to be kept in the United States will be provided to the Commission within 48 hours of a request and any records not kept in the United States will be provided to the Commission within 7 calendar days

(§ 1210.17(a)), and the information required by § 1210.17(b) to be provided to the Commission's Division of Regulatory Management has been provided.

(b) *Certificate of compliance*. A certificate of compliance must accompany each shipping unit of the product (for example, a case), or otherwise be furnished to any distributor or retailer to whom the product is sold or delivered by the manufacturer, private labeler, or importer. The certificate shall state:

(1) That the product "complies with the Consumer Product Safety Standard for Cigarette Lighters (16 CFR 1210),"

(2) The name and address of the manufacturer or importer issuing the certificate or of the private labeler, and

(3) The date(s) of manufacture and, if different from the address in paragraph (b)(2) of this section, the address of the place of manufacture.

(c) *Labeling*. The manufacturer or importer must label each lighter with the following information, which may be in code.

(1) An identification of the period of time, not to exceed 31 days, during which the lighter was manufactured.

(2) An identification of the manufacturer of the lighter, unless the lighter bears a private label. If the lighter bears a private label, it shall bear a code mark or other label which will permit the seller of the lighter to identify the manufacturer to the purchaser upon request.

[58 FR 37584, July 12, 1993, as amended at 59 FR 67621, Dec. 30, 1994]

§ 1210.13 Certification tests.

(a) *General*. As explained in § 1210.11 of this subpart, certificates of compliance required by section 14(a) of the CPSA must be based on a reasonable testing program.

(b) *Reasonable testing programs*—(1) *Requirements*. (i) A reasonable testing program for lighters is one that demonstrates with a high degree of assurance that all lighters manufactured for sale or distributed in commerce will meet the requirements of the standard, including the requirements of § 1210.3. Manufacturers and importers shall determine the types and frequency of testing for their own reasonable testing programs. A reasonable testing program should be sufficiently stringent that it will detect any variations in production or performance during the production interval that would cause any lighters to fail to meet the requirements of the standard.

(ii) All reasonable testing programs shall include qualification tests, which must be performed on surrogates of each model of lighter produced, or to be produced, to demonstrate that the product is capable of passing the tests prescribed by the standard (see § 1210.14), and production tests, which must be performed during appropriate production intervals as long as the product is being manufactured (see § 1210.16).

(iii) Corrective action and/or additional testing must be performed whenever certification tests of samples of the product give results that do not provide a high degree of assurance that all lighters manufactured during the applicable production interval will pass the tests of the standard.

(2) *Testing by third parties*. At the option of the manufacturer or importer, some or all of the testing of each lighter or lighter surrogate may be performed by a commercial testing laboratory or other third party. However, the manufacturer or importer must ensure that all certification testing has been properly performed with passing results and that all records of such tests are maintained in accordance with § 1210.17 of this subpart.

§ 1210.14 Qualification testing.

(a) *Testing*. Before any manufacturer or importer of lighters distributes lighters in commerce in the United States, surrogate lighters of each model shall be tested in accordance with § 1210.4, above, to ensure that all such lighters comply with the standard. However, if a manufacturer has tested one model of lighter, and then wishes to distribute another model of lighter that differs from the first model only by differences that would not have an *adverse* effect on child resistance, the second model need not be tested in accordance with § 1210.4.

(b) *Product modifications*. If any changes are made to a product after initial qualification testing that could adversely affect the ability of the product to meet the requirements of the standard, additional qualification tests must be made on surrogates for the changed product before the changed lighters are distributed in commerce.

(c) *Requalification.* If a manufacturer or importer chooses to requalify a lighter design after it has been in production, this may be done by following the testing procedures at § 1210.4.

§ 1210.15 Specifications.

(a) *Requirement.* Before any lighters that are subject to the standard are distributed in commerce, the manufacturer or importer shall ensure that the surrogate lighters used for qualification testing under § 1210.14 are described in a written product specification. (Section 1210.4(c) requires that six surrogate lighters be used for testing each 100-child panel.)

(b) *Contents of specification.* The product specification shall include the following information:

(1) A complete description of the lighter, including size, shape, weight, fuel, fuel capacity, ignition mechanism, and child-resistant features.

(2) A detailed description of all dimensions, force requirements, or other features that could affect the child-resistance of the lighter, including the manufacturer's tolerances for each such dimension or force requirement.

(3) Any further information, including, but not limited to, model names or numbers, necessary to adequately describe the lighters and any child-resistant features.

§ 1210.16 Production testing.

(a) *General.* Manufacturers and importers shall test samples of lighters subject to the standard as they are manufactured, to demonstrate that the lighters meet the specifications, required under § 1210.15, of the surrogate that has been shown by qualification testing to meet the requirements of the standard.

(b) *Types and frequency of testing.* Manufacturers, private labelers, and importers shall determine the types of tests for production testing. Each production test shall be conducted at a production interval short enough to provide a high degree of assurance that, if the samples selected for testing pass the production tests, all other lighters produced during the interval will meet the standard.

(c) *Test failure*—(1) *Sale of lighters.* If any test yields results which indicate that any lighters manufactured during the production interval may not meet the standard, production and distribution in commerce of lighters that may not comply with the standard must cease until it is determined that the lighters meet the standard or until corrective action is taken. (It may be necessary to modify the lighters or perform additional tests to ensure that only complying lighters are distributed in commerce. Lighters from other production intervals having test results showing that lighters from that interval comply with the standard could be produced and distributed unless there was some reason to believe that they might not comply with the standard.)

(2) *Corrective actions.* When any production test fails to provide a high degree of assurance that all lighters comply with the standard, corrective action must be taken. Corrective action may include changes in the manufacturing process, the assembly process, the equipment used to manufacture the product, or the product's materials or design. The corrective action must provide a high degree of assurance that all lighters produced after the corrective action will comply with the standard. If the corrective action changes the product from the surrogate used for qualification testing in a manner that could adversely affect its child resistance, the lighter must undergo new qualification tests in accordance with § 1210.14, above.

§ 1210.17 Recordkeeping and reporting.

(a) *Records.* Every manufacturer and importer of lighters subject to the standard shall maintain the following records in English on paper, microfiche, or similar media and make such records available to any designated officer or employee of the Commission in accordance with section 16(b) of the Consumer Product Safety Act, 15 U.S.C. 2065(b). Such records must also be kept in the United States and provided to the Commission within 48 hours of receipt of a request from any employee of the Commission, except as provided in paragraph (b)(3) of this section. Legible copies of original records may be used to comply with these requirements.

(1) Records of qualification testing, including a description of the tests, photograph(s) or a video tape for a single pair of children from each 100-child test panel to show how the lighter was held in the tester's hand, and the orientation of the tester's body and hand to the children, during the demonstration, the dates of the tests, the data required by § 1210.4(d), the actual surrogate lighters tested, and the results of the tests, including video tape records, if any. These records shall be kept until 3 years after the production of the particular model to which such tests relate has ceased. If requalification tests are undertaken in accordance with § 1210.14(c), the original qualification test results may be discarded 3 years after the requalification testing, and the requalification test results and surrogates, and the other information required in this subsection for qualifications tests, shall be kept in lieu thereof.

(2) Records of procedures used for production testing required by this subpart B, including a description of the types of tests conducted (in sufficient detail that they may be replicated), the production interval selected, the sampling scheme, and the pass/reject criterion. These records shall be kept until 3 years after production of the lighter has ceased.

(3) Records of production testing, including the test results, the date and location of testing, and records of corrective actions taken, which in turn includes the specific actions taken to improve the design or manufacture or to correct any noncomplying lighter, the date the actions were taken, the test result or failure that triggered the actions, and the additional actions taken to ensure that the corrective action had the intended effect. These records shall be kept for 3 years following the date of testing. Records of production testing results may be kept on paper, microfiche, computer tape, or other retrievable media. Where records are kept on computer tape or other retrievable media, however, the records shall be made available to the Commission on paper copies upon request. A manufacturer or importer of a lighter that is not manufactured in the United States may maintain the production records required by paragraph (a)(3) of this section outside the United States, but shall make such records available to the Commission in the United States within 1 week of a request from a Commission employee for access to those records under section 16(b) of the CPSA, 15 U.S.C. 2065(b).

(4) Records of specifications required under § 1210.15 shall be kept until 3 years after production of each lighter model has ceased.

(b) *Reporting.* At least 30 days before it first imports or distributes in commerce any model of lighter subject to the standard, every manufacturer and importer must provide a written report to the Division of Regulatory Management, Consumer Product Safety Commission, Washington, D.C. 20207. Such report shall include:

(1) The name, address, and principal place of business of the manufacturer or importer,

(2) A detailed description of the lighter model and the child-resistant feature(s) used in that model,

(3) A description of the qualification testing, including a description of the surrogate lighters tested, the specification of the surrogate lighter required by § 1210.15, a summary of the results of all such tests, the dates the tests were performed, the location(s) of such tests, and the identity of the organization that conducted the tests,

(4) An identification of the place or places that the lighters were or will be manufactured,

(5) The location(s) where the records required to be maintained by paragraph (a) of this section are kept, and

(6) A prototype or production unit of that lighter model.

(c) *Confidentiality.* Persons who believe that any information required to be submitted or made available to the Commission is trade secret or otherwise confidential shall request that the information be considered exempt from disclosure by the Commission, in accordance with 16 CFR 1015.18. Requests for confidentiality of records provided to the Commission will be handled in accordance with section 6(a)(2) of the

CPSA, 15 U.S.C. 2055(a)(2), the Freedom of Information Act as amended, 5 U.S.C. 552, and the Commission's regulations under that act, 16 CFR part 1015.

§ 1210.18 Refusal of importation.

(a) *For noncompliance with reporting and recordkeeping requirements.* The Commission has determined that compliance with the recordkeeping and reporting requirements of this subpart is necessary to ensure that lighters comply with this part 1210. Therefore, pursuant to section 17(g) of the CPSA, 15 U.S.C. 2066(g), the Commission may refuse to permit importation of any lighters with respect to which the manufacturer or importer has not complied with the recordkeeping and reporting requirements of this subpart. Since the records are required to demonstrate that production lighters comply with the specifications for the surrogate, the Commission may refuse importation of lighters if production lighters do not comply with the specifications required by this subpart or if any other recordkeeping or reporting requirement in this part is violated.

(b) *For noncompliance with this standard and for lack of a certification certificate.* As provided in section 17(a) of the CPSA, 15 U.S.C. 2066(a), products subject to this standard shall be refused admission into the customs territory of the United States if, among other reasons, the product fails to comply with this standard or is not accompanied by the certificate required by this standard.

Subpart C—Stockpiling

AUTHORITY: 15 U.S.C. 2058(g)(2), 2079(d).

§ 1210.20 Stockpiling.

(a) *Definition. Stockpiling* means to manufacture or import a product that is subject to a consumer product safety rule between the date of issuance of the rule and its effective date at a rate which is significantly greater than the rate at which such product was produced or imported during a base period.

(b) *Base Period.* For purposes of this rule, *base period* means, at the option of the manufacturer or importer, any 1-year period during the 5-year period prior to July 12, 1993.

(c) *Prohibited act.* Manufacturers and importers of disposable and novelty cigarette lighters shall not manufacture or import lighters that do not comply with the requirements of this part between July 12, 1993 and July 12, 1994, at a rate that is greater than the rate of production or importation during the base period plus 20 per cent of that rate.

PART 1211—SAFETY STANDARD FOR AUTOMATIC RESIDENTIAL GARAGE DOOR OPERATORS

Subpart A—The Standard

Subpart B—Certification

Subpart C—Recordkeeping

AUTHORITY: Sec. 203 of Pub. L. 101–608, 104 Stat. 3110; 15 U.S.C. 2063 and 2065.

Subpart A—The Standard

SOURCE: 57 FR 60455, Dec. 21, 1992, unless otherwise noted.

§1211.1 Effective date.

This standard applies to all residential garage door operators manufactured on or after January 1, 1993 for sale in the United States.

§1211.2 Definition.

As used in this part 1211: *Residential garage door operator* means a vehicular door operator which:

(a) Serves a residential building of one to four single family units;

(b) Is rated 600 volts or less; and

(c) Is intended to be employed in ordinary locations in accordance with the National Electrical Code, NFPA 70, 1999 edition. This incorporation by reference was approved by the Director of the Federal Register in accordance with 5 U.S.C. 552(a) and 1 CFR part 51. Copies may be obtained from the National Fire Protection Association, 1 Batterymarch Park, Quincy, Mass. 02269–9101, tel. 1–800–344–3555. Copies may be inspected at the Consumer Product Safety Commission, Office of the Secretary, 4330 East West Highway, Bethesda, Maryland or at the National Archives and Records Administration (NARA). For information on the availability of this material at NARA, call 202–741–6030, or go to: *http://www.archives.gov/federal_register/code_of_federal_regulations/ibr_locations.html.*

[57 FR 60455, Dec. 21, 1992, as amended at 62 FR 46667, Sept. 4, 1997; 65 FR 70657, Nov. 27, 2000]

§1211.3 Units of measurement.

If a value for measurement is followed by a value in other units, in parentheses, the second value may be only approximate. The first stated value is the requirement.

[57 FR 60455, Dec. 21, 1992, as amended at 65 FR 70657, Nov. 27, 2000]

§1211.4 General requirements for protection against risk of injury.

(a) If an automatically reset protective device is employed, automatic restarting of a motor shall not result in a risk of injury to persons.

(b) A residential garage door operator is considered to comply with the requirement in paragraph (a) of this section if some means is provided to prevent the motor from restarting when the protector closes.

(c) An electronic or solid-state circuit that performs a back-up, limiting, or other function intended to reduce the risk of fire, electric shock, or injury to persons, including entrapment protection circuits, shall comply with the requirements in the Standard for Safety for Tests for Safety-Related Controls Employing Solid-State Devices, UL 991, second edition, dated June 23, 1995, including environmental and stress tests appropriate to the intended usage of the end-product. This incorporation by reference was approved by the Director of the Federal Register in accordance with 5 U.S.C. 552(a) and 1 CFR part 51. Copies may be obtained from Global Engineering Documents, 15 Inverness Way East, Englewood, CO 80112, Telephone (800) 854–7179 or Global Engineering Documents, 7730 Carondelet Ave., Suite 470, Clayton, MO 63105, Telephone (800) 854–7179. Copies may be inspected at the Consumer Product Safety Commission, Office of the Secretary, 4330 East West Highway, Bethesda, Maryland or at the National Archives and Records Administration (NARA). For information on the availability of this material at NARA, call 202–741–6030, or go to: *http://www.archives.gov/federal_register/code_of_federal_regulations/ibr_locations.html.*

[57 FR 60455, Dec. 21, 1992, as amended at 62 FR 46667, Sept. 4, 1997; 65 FR 70657, Nov. 27, 2000]

§1211.5 General testing parameters.

(a) The following test parameters are to be used in the investigation of the circuit covered by §1211.4(c) for compliance with the Standard for Safety for Tests for Safety-Related Controls Employing Solid-State Devices, UL 991, second edition, dated June 23, 1995, as incorporated by reference in paragraph (b)(3) of this section:

(1) With regard to electrical supervision of critical components, an operator being inoperative with respect to

downward movement of the door meets the criteria for trouble indication.

(2) A field strength of 3 volts per meter is to be used for the Radiated EMI Test.

(3) The Composite Operational and Cycling Test is to be used for 14 days at temperature extremes of minus 35 °Celsius (minus 31 °F) and 70 °C (158 °F).

(4) Exposure Class H5 is to be used for the Humidity Test.

(5) A vibration level of 5g is to be used for the Vibration Test.

(6) When a Computational Investigation is conducted, λ_p shall not be greater than 6 failures/10^6 hours for the entire system. For external secondary entrapment protection devices that are sold separately, λ_p shall not be greater than 0 failures/10^6 hours. For internal secondary entrapment protection devices whether or not they are sold separately, λ_p shall not be greater than 0 failures/10^6 hours. The operational test is conducted for 14 days. An external secondary entrapment protection device that is sold separately, and that has a λ_p greater than 0 failures/10^6 hours meets the intent of the requirement when for the combination of the operator and the specified external secondary entrapment protection device λ_p does not exceed 6 failures/10^6 hours. See § 1211.15(i) and (k).

(7) When the Demonstrated Method Test is conducted, the multiplier is to be based on the continuous usage level, and a minimum of 24 units for a minimum of 24 hours per unit are to be tested.

(8) The Endurance test is to be conducted concurrently with the Operational test. The control shall perform its intended function while being conditioned for fourteen days in an ambient air temperature of 60 °C (140 °F), or 10 °C (18 °F) greater than the operating temperature of the control, whichever is higher. During the test, the control is to be operated in a manner representing the opening and closing of the door at a rate of one open-close operation per minute.

(9) For the Electrical Fast Transient Burst Test, test level 3 is to be used for residential garage door operators.

(b) In the evaluation of entrapment protection circuits used in residential garage door operators, the critical condition flow chart shown in figure 1 shall be used:

(1) To conduct a failure-mode and effect analysis (FMEA);

(2) In investigating the performance during the Environmental Stress Tests; and

(3) During the Power Cycling Safety for Tests in accordance with the Standard for Safety for Tests for Safety-Related Controls Employing Solid-State Devices, UL 991, second edition, dated June 23, 1995. This incorporation by reference was approved by the Director of the Federal Register in accordance with 5 U.S.C. 552(a) and 1 CFR part 51. Copies may be obtained from Global Engineering Documents, 15 Inverness Way East, Englewood, CO 80112, Telephone (800) 854–7179 or Global Engineering Documents, 7730 Carondelet Ave., Suite 470, Clayton, MO 63105, Telephone (800) 854–7179. Copies may be inspected at the Consumer Product Safety Commission, Office of the Secretary, 4330 East West Highway, Bethesda, Maryland or at the National Archives and Records Administration (NARA). For information on the availability of this material at NARA, call 202–741–6030, or go to: *http://www.archives.gov/federal_register/code_of_federal_regulations/ibr_locations.html.*

[57 FR 60455, Dec. 21, 1992, as amended at 62 FR 46667, Sept. 4, 1997; 65 FR 70657, Nov. 27, 2000]

§ 1211.6 General entrapment protection requirements.

(a) A residential garage door operator system shall be provided with primary inherent entrapment protection that complies with the requirements as specified in § 1211.7.

(b) In addition to the primary inherent entrapment protection as required by paragraph (a) of this section, a residential garage door operator shall comply with one of the following:

(1) Shall be constructed to:

(i) Require constant pressure on a control to lower the door,

(ii) Reverse direction and open the door to the upmost position when constant pressure on a control is removed prior to operator reaching its lower limit, and

(iii) Limit a portable transmitter, when supplied, to function only to cause the operator to open the door;

(2) Shall be provided with a means for connection of an external secondary entrapment protection device as described in §§ 1211.8, 1211.10, and 1211.11; or

(3) Shall be provided with an inherent secondary entrapment protection device as described in §§ 1211.8, 1211.10, and 1211.12.

(c) A mechanical switch or a relay used in an entrapment protection circuit of an operator shall withstand 100,000 cycles of operation controlling a load no less severe (voltage, current, power factor, inrush and similar ratings) than it controls in the operator, and shall function normally upon completion of the test.

(d) In the event malfunction of a switch or relay (open or short) described in paragraph (c) of this section results in loss of any entrapment protection required by §§ 1211.7(a), 1211.7(f), or 1211.8(a), the door operator shall become inoperative at the end of the opening or closing operation, the door operator shall move the door to, and stay within, 1 foot (305 mm) of the uppermost position.

[57 FR 60455, Dec. 21, 1992, as amended at 65 FR 70657, Nov. 27, 2000]

§ 1211.7 Inherent entrapment protection requirements.

(a)(1) Other than for the first 1 foot (305mm) of door travel from the full upmost position both with and without any external entrapment protection device functional, the operator of a downward moving residential garage door shall initiate reversal of the door within 2 seconds of contact with the obstruction as specified in paragraph (b) of this section. After reversing the door, the operator shall return the door to, and stop at, the full upmost position. Compliance shall be determined in accordance with paragraphs (b) through (i) of this section.

(2) The door operator is not required to return the door to, and stop the door at, the full upmost position when the operator senses a second obstruction during the upward travel.

(3) The door operator is not required to return the door to, and stop the door at, the full upmost position when a control is actuated to stop the door during the upward travel—but the door can not be moved downward until the operator reverses the door a minimum of 2 inches (50.8 mm).

(b)(1) A solid object is to be placed on the floor of the test installation and at various heights under the edge of the door and located in line with the driving point of the operator. When tested on the floor, the object shall be 1 inch (25.4 mm) high. In the test installation, the bottom edge of the door under the driving force of the operator is to be against the floor when the door is fully closed.

(2) For operators other than those attached to the door, a solid object is not required to be located in line with the driving point of the operator. The solid object is to be located at points at the center, and within 1 foot of each end of the door.

(3) To test operators for compliance with requirements in paragraphs (a)(3), (f)(3), and (g)(3) of this section, § 1211.10(a)(6)(iii), and § 1211.13(c), a solid rectangular object measuring 4 inches (102 mm) high by 6 inches (152 mm) wide by a minimum of 6 inches (152 mm)long is to be placed on the floor of the test installation to provide a 4-inch (102 mm) high obstruction when operated from a partially open position.

(c) An operator is to be tested for compliance with paragraph (a) of this section for 50 open-and-close cycles of operation while the operator is connected to the type of residential garage door with which it is intended to be used or with the doors specified in paragragh (e) of this section. For an operator having a force adjustment on the operator, the force is to be adjusted to the maximum setting or at the setting that represents the most severe operating condition. Any accessories having an effect on the intended operation of entrapment protection functions that are intended for use with the operator, are to be attached and the test is to be repeated for one additional cycle.

(d) For an operator that is to be adjusted (limit and force) according to instructions supplied with the operator, the operator is to be tested for 10 additional obstruction cycles using the solid object described in paragraph (b) of this section at the maximum setting or at the setting that represents the most severe operating condition.

(e) For an operator that is intended to be used with more than one type of door, one sample of the operator is to be tested on a sectional door with a curved track and one sample is to be tested on a one-piece door with jamb hardware and no track. For an operator that is not intended for use on either or both types of doors, a one-piece door with track hardware or a one-piece door with pivot hardware shall be used for the tests. For an operator that is intended for use with a specifically dedicated door or doors, a representative door or doors shall be used for the tests. See the marking requirements at §1211.16.

(f)(1) An operator, using an inherent entrapment protection system that monitors the actual position of the door, shall initiate reversal of the door and shall return the door to, and stop the door at, the full upmost position in the event the inherent door operating "profile" of the door differs from the originally set parameters. The entrapment protection system shall monitor the position of the door at increments not greater than 1 inch (25.4 mm).

(2) The door operator is not required to return the door to, and stop the door at, the full upmost position when an inherent entrapment circuit senses an obstruction during the upward travel.

(3) The door operator is not required to return the door to, and stop the door at, the full upmost position when a control is actuated to stop the door during the upward travel—but the door can not be moved downward until the operator reverses the door a minimum of 2 inches (50.8 mm).

(g)(1) An operator, using an inherent entrapment protection system that does not monitor the actual position of the door, shall initiate reversal of the door and shall return the door to and stop the door at the full upmost position, when the lower limiting device is not actuated in 30 seconds or less following the initiation of the close cycle.

(2) The door operator is not required to return the door to, and stop the door at, the full upmost position when an inherent entrapment circuit senses an obstruction during the upward travel. When the door is stopped manually during its descent, the 30 seconds shall be measured from the resumption of the close cycle.

(3) The door operator is not required to return the door to, and stop the door at, the full upmost position when a control is actuated to stop the door during the upward travel—but the door can not be moved downward until the operator reverses the door a minimum of 2 inches (50.8 mm). When the door is stopped manually during its descent, the 30 seconds shall be measured from the resumption of the close cycle.

(h) To determine compliance with paragraph (f) or (g) of this section, an operator is to be subjected to 10 open-and-close cycles of operation while connected to the door or doors specified in paragraphs (c) and (e) of this section. The cycles are not required to be consecutive. Motor cooling-off periods during the test meet the intent of the requirement. The means supplied to comply with the requirement in paragraph (a) of this section and §1211.8(a) are to be defeated during the test. An obstructing object is to be used so that the door is not capable of activating a lower limiting device.

(i) During the closing cycle, the system providing compliance with §§1211.7(a) and 1211.7(f) or 1211.7(a) and 1211.7(g) shall function regardless of a short- or open-circuit anywhere in any low-voltage external wiring, any external entrapment devices, or any other external component.

[65 FR 70657, Nov. 27, 2000, as amended at 72 FR 54817, Sept. 27, 2007]

§ 1211.8 Secondary entrapment protection requirements.

(a) A secondary entrapment protection device supplied with, or as an accessory to, an operator shall consist of:

(1) An external photoelectric sensor that when activated results in an operator that is closing a door to reverse direction of the door and the sensor prevents an operator from closing an open door,

(2) An external edge sensor installed on the edge of the door that, when activated results in an operator that is closing a door to reverse direction of

the door and the sensor prevents an operator from closing an open door,

(3) An inherent door sensor independent of the system used to comply with § 1211.7 that, when activated, results in an operator that is closing a door to reverse direction of the door and the sensor prevents an operator from closing an open door, or

(4) Any other external or internal device that provides entrapment protection equivalent to paragraphs (a)(1), (a)(2), or (a)(3) of this section.

(b) With respect to paragraph (a) of this section, the operator shall monitor for the presence and correct operation of the device, including the wiring to it, at least once during each close cycle. In the event the device is not present or a fault condition occurs which precludes the sensing of an obstruction, including an open or short circuit in the wiring that connects an external entrapment protection device to the operator and device's supply source, the operator shall be constructed such that:

(1) A closing door shall open and an open door shall not close more than 1 foot (305 mm) below the upmost position, or

(2) The operator shall function as required by § 1211.6(b)(1).

(c) An external entrapment protection device shall comply with the applicable requirements in §§ 1211.10, 1211.11 and 1211.12.

(d) An inherent secondary entrapment protection device shall comply with the applicable requirements in § 1211.13. Software used in an inherent entrapment protection device shall comply with the Standard for Safety for Software in Programmable Components, UL 1998, Second Edition, May 29, 1998. This incorporation by reference was approved by the Director of the Federal Register in accordance with 5 U.S.C. 552(a) and 1 CFR part 51. Copies may be obtained from Global Engineering Documents, 15 Inverness Way East, Englewood, CO 80112, Telephone (800) 854–7179 or Global Engineering Documents, 7730 Carondelet Ave., Suite 470, Clayton, MO 63105, Telephone (800) 854–7179. Copies may be inspected at the Consumer Product Safety Commission, Office of the Secretary, 4330 East West Highway, Bethesda, Maryland or at the National Archives and Records Administration (NARA). For information on the availability of this material at NARA, call 202–741–6030, or go to: *http://www.archives.gov/federal_register/code_of_federal_regulations/ibr_locations.html.*

[65 FR 70658, Nov. 27, 2000]

§ 1211.9 Additional entrapment protection requirements.

(a) A means to manually detach the door operator from the door shall be supplied. The gripping surface (handle) shall be colored red and shall be easily distinguishable from the rest of the operator. It shall be capable of being adjusted to a height of 6 feet (1.8 m) above the garage floor when the operator is installed according to the instructions specified in § 1211.14(a)(2). The means shall be constructed so that a hand firmly gripping it and applying a maximum of 50 pounds (223 N) of force shall detach the operator with the door obstructed in the down position. The obstructing object, as described in § 1211.7(b), is to be located in several different positions. A marking with instructions for detaching the operator shall be provided as required by § 1211.15(i).

(b) A means to manually detach the door operator from the door is not required for a door operator that is not directly attached to the door and that controls movement of the door so that:

(1) The door is capable of being moved open from any position other than the last (closing) 2 inches (50.8 mm) of travel, and

(2) The door is capable of being moved to the 2-inch point from any position between closed and the 2-inch point.

(c) Actuation of a control that initiates movement of a door shall stop and may reverse the door on the down cycle. On the up cycle, actuation of a control shall stop the door but not reverse it.

(d) An operator shall be constructed so that adjustment of limit, force or other user controls and connection of external entrapment protection devices can be accomplished without exposing normally enclosed live parts or wiring.

[57 FR 60455, Dec. 21, 1992, as amended at 65 FR 70658, Nov. 27, 2000]

§ 1211.10 Requirements for all entrapment protection devices.

(a) General requirements. (1) An external entrapment protection device shall perform its intended function when tested in accordance with paragraphs (a)(2) through (4) and (6) of this section.

(2) The device is to be installed in the intended manner and its terminals connected to circuits of the door operator as indicated by the installation instructions.

(3) The device is to be installed and tested at minimum and maximum heights and widths representative of recommended ranges specified in the installation instructions. For doors, if not specified, devices are to be tested on a minimum 7 foot (2.1 m) wide door and maximum 20 foot (6.1 m) wide door.

(4) If powered by a separate source of power, the power-input supply terminals are to be connected to supply circuits of rated voltage and frequency.

(5) An external entrapment protection device requiring alignment, such as a photoelectric sensor, shall be provided with a means, such as a visual indicator, to show proper alignment and operation of the device.

(6)(i) An operator using an external entrapment protection device, upon detecting a fault or an obstruction in the path of a downward moving door, shall initiate reversal and shall return the door to, and stop the door at, the full upmost position.

(ii) The door operator is not required to return the door to, and stop the door at, the full upmost position when an inherent entrapment circuit senses an obstruction during the upward travel.

(iii) The door operator is not required to return the door to, and stop the door at, the full upmost position when a control is actuated to stop the door during the upward travel—but the door can not be moved downward until the operator has reversed the door a minimum of 2 inches (50.8 mm).

(b) *Current protection test.* (1) There shall be no damage to the entrapment protection circuitry if low voltage field-wiring terminals or leads are shortened or miswired to adjacent terminals.

(2) To determine compliance with paragraph (b)(1) of this section, an external entrapment protection device is to be connected to a door operator or other source of power in the intended manner, after which all connections to low voltage terminals or leads are to be reversed as pairs, reversed individually, or connected to any low voltage lead or adjacent terminal.

(c) *Splash test.* (1) An external entrapment protection device intended to be installed inside a garage 3 feet or less above the floor shall withstand a water exposure as described in paragraph (c)(2) of this section without resulting in a risk of electric shock and shall function as intended. After exposure, the external surface of the device may be dried before determining its functionality.

(2) External entrapment protection devices are to be indirectly sprayed using a hose having the free end fitted with a nozzle as illustrated in figure 2 and connected to a water supply capable of maintaining a flow rate of 5 gallons (19 liters) per minute as measured at the outlet orifice of the nozzle. The water from the hose is to be played, from all sides and at any angle against the floor under the device in such a manner most likely to cause water to splash the enclosure of electric components. However, the nozzle is not to be brought closer than 10 feet (3.05 m) horizontally to the device. The water is to be sprayed for 1 minute.

Figure 2

NOZZLE

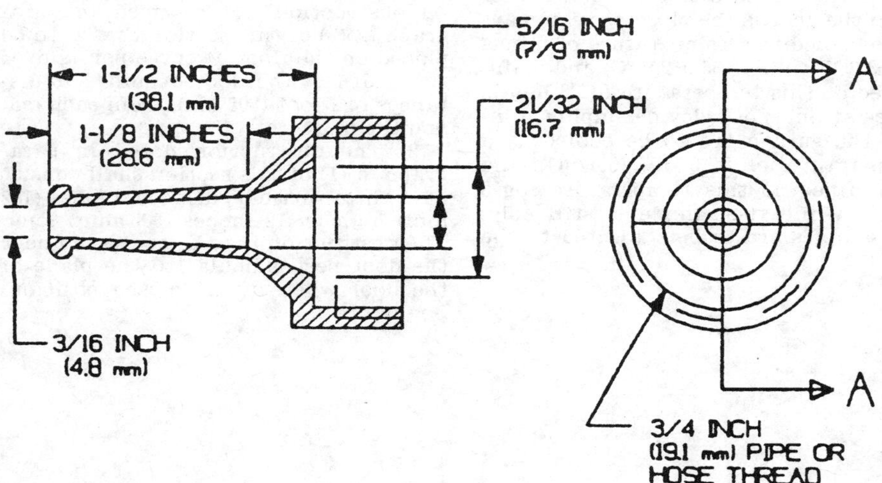

(d) *Ultraviolet light exposure test.* A polymeric material used as a functional part of a device that is exposed to outdoor weather conditions shall comply with the Ultraviolet Light Exposure Test described in the Standard for Safety for Polymeric Materials—Use in Electrical Equipment Evaluations, UL 746C, 4th ed., dated December 27, 1995. This incorporation by reference was approved by the Director of the Federal Register in accordance with 5 U.S.C. 552(a) and 1 CFR part 51. Copies may be obtained from Global Engineering Documents, 15 Inverness Way East, Englewood, CO 80112, Telephone (800) 854–7179 or Global Engineering Documents, 7730 Carondelet Ave., Suite 470, Clayton, MO 63105, Telephone (800) 854–7179. Copies may be inspected at the Consumer Product Safety Commission, Office of the Secretary, 4330 East West Highway, Bethesda, Maryland or at the National Archives and Records Administration (NARA). For information on the availability of this material at NARA, call 202–741–6030, or go to: *http://www.archives.gov/federal_register/code_of_federal_regulations/ibr_locations.html.*

(e) *Resistance to impact test.* (1) An external entrapment protection device employing a polymeric or elastomeric material as a functional part shall be subjected to the impact test specified in paragraph (e)(2) of this section. As a result of the test:

(i) There shall be no cracking or breaking of the part, and

(ii) The part shall operate as intended or, if dislodged after the test, is capable of being restored to its original condition.

(2) Samples of the external entrapment protection device are to be subjected to the Impact Test described in the Standard for Polymeric Materials—

Use in Electrical Equipment Evaluations, UL 746C, 4th ed., dated December 27, 1995, as incorporated by reference in paragraph (d) of this section. The external entrapment protection device is to be subjected to 5 foot-pound (6.8 J) impacts. Three samples are to be tested, each sample being subjected to three impacts at different points.

(3) Each of three additional samples of a device exposed to outdoor weather when the door is the closed position are to be cooled to a temperature of minus 31.0±3.6 °F (minus 35.0±2.0 °C) and maintained at this temperature for 3 hours. Three samples of a device employed inside the garage are to be cooled to a temperature of 32.0 °F (0.0 °C) and maintained at this temperature for 3 hours. While the sample is still cold, the samples are to be subjected to the impact test described in paragraph (e)(1) of this section.

[57 FR 60455, Dec. 21, 1992, as amended at 62 FR 46667, Sept. 4, 1997; 65 FR 70659, Nov. 27, 2000; 72 FR 54817, Sept. 27, 2007]

§ 1211.11 Requirements for photoelectric sensors.

(a) *Normal operation test.* (1) When installed as described in § 1211.10(a) (1)–(4), a photoelectric sensor shall sense an obstruction as described in paragraph (a)(2) of this section that is to be placed on the floor at three points over the width of the door opening, at distances of 1 foot (305 mm) from each end and the midpoint.

(2) The obstruction noted in paragraph (a)(1) of this section shall consist of a white vertical surface 6 inches (152 mm) high by 12 inches (305 mm) long. The obstruction is to be centered under the door perpendicular to the plane of the door when in the closed position. See figure 3.

Figure 3

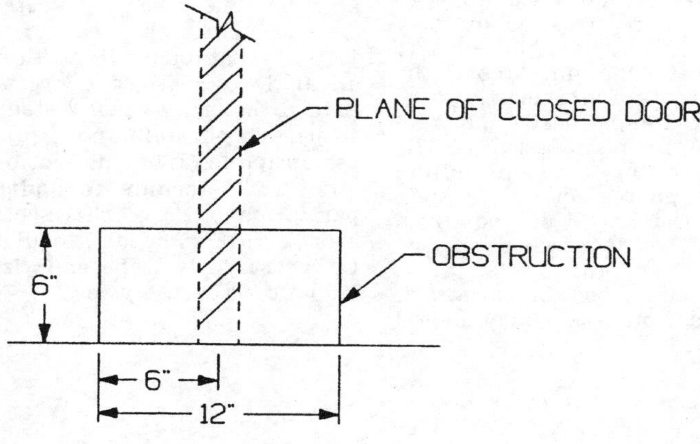

Figure 4

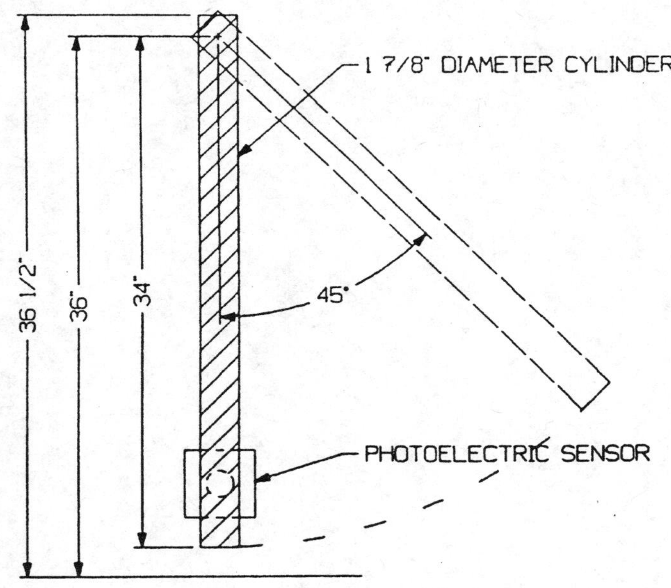

(b) *Sensitivity test.* (1) When installed as described in § 1211.10(a)(1)–(4), a photoelectric sensor shall sense the presence of a moving object when tested according to paragraph (b)(2) of this section.

(2) The moving object is to consist of a 1⅞ inch (47.6 mm) diameter cylindrical rod, 34½ inches (876 mm) long, with the axis point being 34 inches (864 mm) from the end. The axis point is to be fixed at a point centered directly above the beam of the photoelectric sensor 36 inches (914 mm) above the floor. The photoelectric sensor is to be mounted at the highest position as recommended by the manufacturer. The rod is to be swung as a pendulum through the photoelectric sensor's beam from a position 45 degrees from the plane of the door when in the closed position. See figure 4.

(3) The test described in paragraph (b)(2) of this section is to be conducted at three points over the width of the door opening, at distances of 1 foot (305 mm) from each end and the midpoint.

(c) *Ambient light test.* (1) A photoelectric sensor shall operate as specified in § 1211.8 (a) and (b) when subjected to ambient light impinging at an angle of 15 to 20 degrees from the axis of the beam when tested according to paragraph (c)(2) and, if appropriate, paragraph (c)(3) of this section.

(2) To determine compliance with paragraph (c)(1) of this section, a 500 watt, 3600K Photo Floodlamp, type DXC RFL–2, is to be energized from a 120-volt, 60-hertz source.

Figure 5

AMBIENT LIGHT TEST

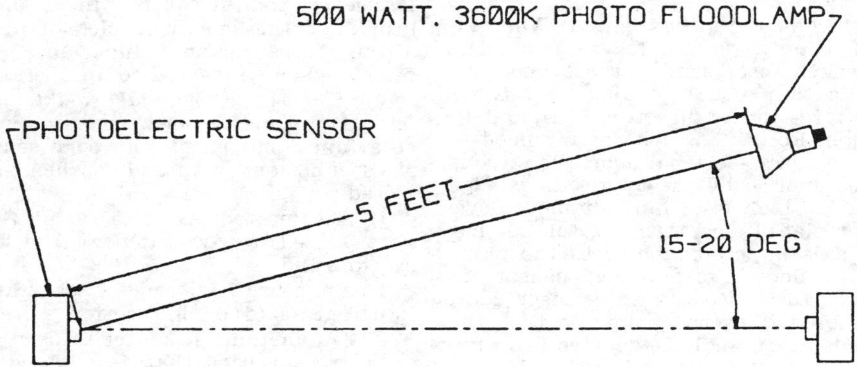

Figure 6

EDGE SENSOR NORMAL OPERATION TEST

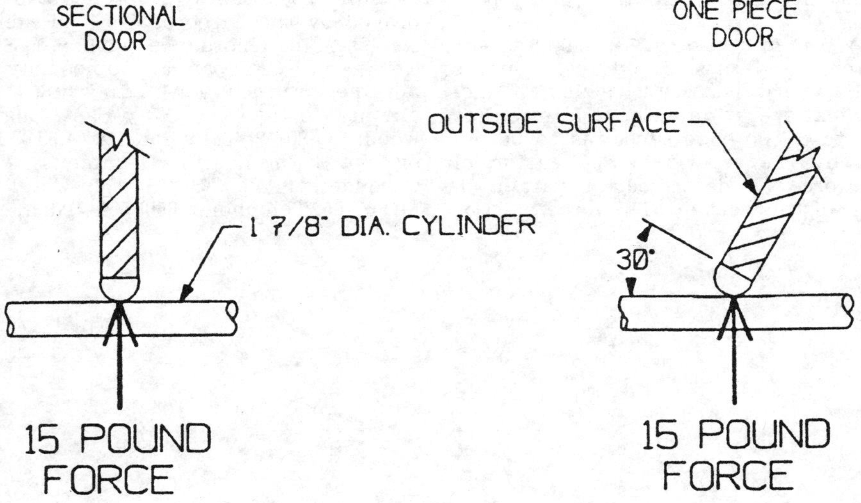

The lamp is to be positioned 5 feet from the front of the receiver and aimed directly at the sensor at an angle of 15 to 20 degrees from the axis of the beam. See figure 5.

(3) If the photoelectric sensor uses a reflector, this test is to be repeated with the lamp aimed at the reflector.

§ 1211.12 Requirements for edge sensors.

(a) *Normal operation test.* (1) When installed on a representative door edge, an edge sensor shall actuate upon the application of a 15 pounds (66.7 N) or less force in the direction of the application. For an edge sensor intended to be used on a sectional door, the force is to be applied by the longitudinal edge of a 1⅞ inch (47.6 mm) diameter cylinder placed across the switch so that the axis is perpendicular to the plane of the door. For an edge sensor intended to be used on a one piece door, the force is to be applied so that the axis is at an angle 30 degrees from the direction perpendicular to the plane of the door. See figure 6.

(2) With respect to the test of paragraph (a)(1) of this section, the test is to be repeated at various representative points of the edge sensor across the width of the door.

(3) Exception: The edge sensor need not be sensitive to actuation two inches (50.4 mm) or less from each end of the intended width of the door opening.

(b) *Endurance test.* An edge sensor system and associated components shall withstand 30,000 cycles of mechanical operation without failure. For this test, the edge sensor is to be cycled by the repetitive application of the force as described in paragraph (a)(1) of this section. The force is to be applied to the same location for the entire test. For an edge sensor system employing integral electric contact strips, this test shall be conducted with the contacts connected to a load no less severe than it controls in the operator. For the last 50 cycles of operation, the sensor shall function as intended when connected to an operator.

(c) *Elastomeric material conditioning test.* (1) An elastomeric material used as a functional part of an edge sensor shall function as intended when subjected to:

(i) Accelerated Aging Test of Gaskets, stated in paragraph (c)(3) of this section, and

(ii) Puncture Resistance Test, stated in paragraph (d) of this section.

(2) An elastomeric material used for a functional part that is exposed to outdoor weather conditions when the door is in the closed position shall have physical properties as specified in table 1 after being conditioned in accordance with the Ultraviolet Light Exposure Test described in the Standard for Safety for Polymeric Materials—Use in Electrical Equipment Evaluations, UL 746C, 4th ed., dated December 27, 1995. This incorporation by reference was approved by the Director of the Federal Register in accordance with 5 U.S.C. 552(a) and 1 CFR part 51. Copies may be obtained from Global Engineering Documents, 15 Inverness Way East, Englewood, CO 80112, Telephone (800) 854–7179 or Global Engineering Documents, 7730 Carondelet Ave., Suite 470, Clayton, MO 63105, Telephone (800) 854–7179.

Table 1

PHYSICAL PROPERTIES OF GASKET-ACCELERATED AGING TEST

	Before Accelerated Aging	After Accelerated Aging
Recovery -- Maximum set when 2-inch (50.8-mm) gauge marks are stretched to 5 inches (127 mm), held for 2 minutes, and measured 2 minutes after release	1/2 inch (12.7 mm)	--
Elongation -- Minimum increase in distance between 2-inch gauge marks at break	250 percent [2 to 7 inches (50.8 – 178.8 mm)]	65 percent of original
Tensile Strength -- Minimum force at breaking point	850 pounds per square inch (59 mPa)	75 percent of original

Copies may be inspected at the Consumer Product Safety Commission, Office of the Secretary, 4330 East West Highway, Bethesda, Maryland or at the National Archives and Records Administration (NARA). For information on the availability of this material at NARA, call 202–741–6030, or go to: *http://www.archives.gov/federal_register/code_of_federal_regulations/ibr_locations.html.*

(3) Rubber compounds forming gaskets that are depended upon for protection from rain shall have physical properties as specified in table 1, before and after conditioning for 168 hours in an air-circulating oven at 70 °C (158 °F).

(d) *Puncture resistance test.* (1) After being subjected to the test described in paragraph (d)(2) of this section, an elastomeric material that is a functional part of an edge sensor shall:

(i) Not be damaged in a manner that would adversely affect the intended operation of the edge sensor, and

(ii) Maintain enclosure integrity if it serves to reduce the likelihood of contamination of electrical contacts.

(2) A sample of the edge sensor is to be installed in the intended manner on a representative door edge. The probe described in figure 7 is to be applied with a 20 pound-force (89N) to any point on the sensor that is 3 inches or less above the floor is to be applied in the direction specified in the Edge Sensor Normal Operation Test, figure 6. The test is to be repeated on three locations on each surface of the sensor being tested.

Figure 7

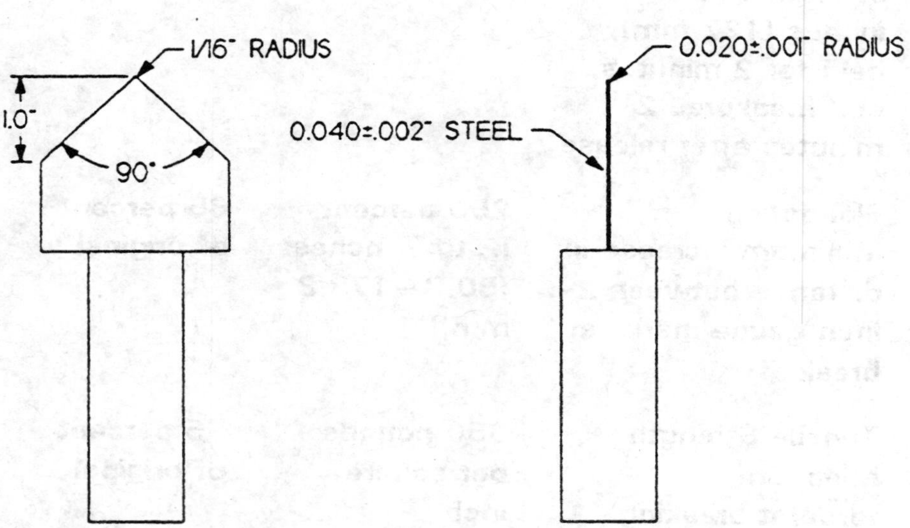

[57 FR 60455, Dec. 21, 1992, as amended at 62 FR 46667, Sept. 4, 1997; 65 FR 70659, Nov. 27, 2000]

§ 1211.13 Inherent force activated secondary door sensors.

(a) *Normal operation test.* (1) A force activated door sensor of a door system installed according to the installation instructions shall actuate when the door applies a 15 pound (66.7 N) or less force in the down or closing direction and when the door applies a 25 pound (111.2 N) or less force in the up or opening direction. For a force activated door sensor intended to be used in an operator intended for use only on a sectional door, the force is to be applied by the door against the longitudinal edge of a 1⅞ (47.6 mm) diameter cylinder placed across the door so that the axis is perpendicular to the plane of the door. See Figure 6 of this part. The weight of the door is to be equal to the maximum weight rating of the operator.

(2) The test described in paragraph (a)(1) of this section is to be repeated and measurements made at various representative points across the width and height of the door. For this test, a door sensor system and associated components shall withstand a total of 9 cycles of mechanical operation without failure with the force applied as follows:

(i) At the center at points one, three, and five feet from the floor,

(ii) Within 1 foot of the end of the door, at points one, three, and five feet from the floor,

(iii) Within 1 foot of the other end of the door at points one, three, and five feet from the floor.

(3) The cycles are not required to be consecutive. Continuous operation of the motor without cooling is not required.

(b) *Adjustment of door weight.* (1) With the door at the point and at the weight determined by the tests of paragraphs (a)(2) and (b)(2) of this section to be the most severe, the door sensor and associated components shall withstand 50 cycles of operation without failure.

(2) At the point determined by the test in paragraphs (a)(1) and (a)(2) of this section to be the most severe, weight is to be added to the door in 5.0 pound (2.26 Kg) increments and the test repeated until a total of 15.0 pounds (66.72 N) has been added to the door. Before performing each test cycle, the door is to be cycled 2 times to update the profile. Similarly, starting from normal weight plus 15.0 pounds, the test is to be repeated by subtracting weight in 5.0 pound increments until a total of 15.0 pounds has been subtracted from the door.

(c) Obstruction test. For a door traveling in the downward direction, when an inherent secondary entrapment protection device senses an obstruction and initiates a reversal, a control activation shall not move the door downward until the operator reverses the door a minimum of 2 inches (50.8 mm). The test is to be performed as described in § 1211.7(b)(3).

[65 FR 70659, Nov. 27, 2000, as amended at 72 FR 54817, Sept. 27, 2007]

§ 1211.14 Instruction manual.

(a) *General.* (1) A residential garage door operator shall be provided with an instruction manual. The instruction manual shall give complete instructions for the installation, operation, and user maintenance of the operator.

(2) Instructions that clearly detail installation and adjustment procedures required to effect proper operation of the safety means provided shall be provided with each door operator.

(3) A residential garage door or door operator shall be provided with complete and specific instructions for the correct adjustment of the control mechanism and the need for periodic checking and, if needed, adjustment of the control mechanism so as to maintain satisfactory operation of the door.

(4) The instruction manual shall include the important instructions specified in paragraphs (b)(1) and (2) of this section. All required text shall be legible and contrast with the background. Upper case letters of required text shall be no less than 5⁄64 inch (2.0 mm) high and lower case letters shall be no less than 1⁄16 inch (1.6 mm) high. Heading such as "Important Installation Instructions," "Important Safety Instructions," "Save These Instructions" and the words "Warning—To reduce the risk of severe injury or death to persons:" shall be in letters no less than 3⁄16 inch (4.8 mm) high.

(5) The instructions listed in paragraphs 1211.13(b)(1) and (2) shall be in the exact words specified or shall be in equally definitive terminology to those specified. No substitutes shall be used for the word "Warning." The items may be numbered. The first and last items specified in paragraph (b)(2) of this section shall be first and last respectively. Other important and precautionary items considered appropriate by the manufacturer may be inserted.

(6) The instructions listed in paragraph (b)(1) of this section shall be located immediately prior to the installation instructions. The instructions listed in paragraph (b)(2) of this section shall be located immediately prior to user operation and maintenance instructions. In each case, the instructions shall be separate in format from other detailed instructions related to

installation, operation and maintenance of the operator. All instructions, except installation instructions, shall be a permanent part of the manual(s).

(b) *Specific required instructions.* (1) The Installation Instructions shall include the following instructions:

Important Installation Instructions

Warning—To reduce the risk of severe injury or death:

1. Read and follow all Installation Instructions.

2. Install only a properly balanced garage door. An improperly balanced door could cause severe injury. Have a qualified service person make repairs to cables, spring assemblies and other hardware before installing opener.

3. Remove all ropes and remove or make inoperative all locks connected to the garage door before installing opener.

4. Where possible, install door opener 7 feet or more above the floor. For products requiring an emergency release, mount the emergency release 6 feet above the floor.

5. Do not connect opener to source of power until instructed to do so.

6. Locate control button: (a) within sight of door, (b) at a minimum height of 5 feet so small children cannot reach it, and (c) away from all moving parts of the door.

7. Install Entrapment Warning Label next to the control button in a prominent location. Install the Emergency Release Marking. Attach the marking on or next to the emergency release.

8. After installing opener, the door must reverse when it contacts a 1½ inch high object (or a 2 by 4 board laid flat) on the floor.

(2) The User Instructions shall include the following instructions:

Important Safety Instructions

Warning—To reduce the risk of severe injury or death:

1. Read and follow all instructions.

2. Never let children operate, or play with door controls. Keep the remote control away from children.

3. Always keep the moving door in sight and away from people and objects until it is completely closed. No one should cross the path of the moving door.

4. NEVER GO UNDER A STOPPED PARTIALLY OPEN DOOR.

5. Test door opener monthly. The garage door MUST reverse on contact with a 1½ inch object (or a 2 by 4 board laid flat) on the floor. After adjusting either the force or the limit of travel, retest the door opener. Failure to adjust the opener properly may cause severe injury or death.

6. For products requiring an emergency release, if possible, use the emergency release only when the door is closed. Use caution when using this release with the door open. Weak or broken springs may allow the door to fall rapidly, causing injury or death.

7. Keep garage door properly balanced. See owner's manual. An improperly balanced door could cause severe injury or death. Have a qualified service person make repairs to cables, spring assemblies and other hardware.

8. Save these Instructions.

[57 FR 60455, Dec. 21, 1992. Redesignated and amended at 65 FR 70659, Nov. 27, 2000; 72 FR 54818, Sept. 27, 2007]

§ 1211.15 Field-installed labels.

(a) A residential garage door operator shall be provided with labels for field installation and constructed as specified in paragraphs (c) through (i) of this section. The labels shall be acceptable for permanent installation. The instruction manual shall specify where the labels are to be located.

(b) If labels secured by adhesive are used, the instruction shall specify that an additional mechanical means shall be used to secure the labels to surfaces to which the adhesive will not adhere.

(c) A residential garage door operator shall be provided with a cautionary label intended for permanent installation to identify the possible risk of entrapment. The instruction manual shall direct that the label be affixed near the wall-mounted control button.

(d) The label required in accordance with paragraph (c) of this section shall be in a vertical layout with three panels:

(1) A signal word panel,

(2) A pictorial panel, and

(3) A message panel, with adjacent panels delineated from each other by a horizontal black line. The entire label shall be surrounded by a black border and shall measure at least 5 inches (127 mm) wide by 6¼ inches (159 mm) long overall.

(e) The signal word panel as specified in paragraph (d) of this section shall contain the word "WARNING," in uppercase letters, preceded by a safety alert symbol consisting of an orange exclamation mark on a black solid equilateral triangle background with the point of the triangle oriented upward. The word "WARNING" and the safety alert symbol shall be centered on one line and shall be in black letters at least 7⁄16 inch (11.1 mm) high on an orange background.

(f) The pictorial panel as specified in paragraph (d) of this section shall be positioned between the signal word panel and the message panel. The pictorial shall be black on a white background and shall clearly depict a child running toward or under a garage door. A red prohibition symbol (slash, oriented from the upper left to the lower right, through a circle) shall be superimposed over, and totally surround, the pictorial. The pictorial shall have an overall diameter of 1-7⅛ inch (47.6 mm) minimum.

(g) The message panel as specified in paragraph (d) of this section shall include the following text or an equivalent wording:

(1) Possible Risk and Consequence Statement—"There is a risk of a child becoming trapped under an automatic garage door resulting in severe injury or death."

(2) Avoidance Statements—

(i) "Do not allow children to walk or run under a closing door."

(ii) "Do not allow children to operate door operator controls."

(iii) "Always keep a closing door within sight."

(iv) "In the event a person is trapped under the door, push the control button or use the emergency release." For products not having an emergency release use instead "In the event a person is trapped under the door, push the control button."

(3) Instructions—

(i) "Test Door Operator Monthly: Use a 1½ inch thick object placed on the floor under the closing door. In the event the door does not reverse upon contact, adjust, repair, or replace the operator."

(ii) Additional instructions on not removing or painting over the label, mounting the label adjacent to the wall control, and mounting the wall control out of children's reach shall be provided. These additional instruction shall be in less prominent lettering than those in paragraph (g)(3)(i) of this section.

(h) The lettering of the message panel described in paragraph (g) of this section shall be black on a white background and shall be sans serif letters in combinations of upper case and lower case letters. The upper case letters of the Possible Risk and Consequence Statements and Avoidance Statements shall be ⅛ inch (3.18 mm) high minimum. The lettering of the Possible Risk and Consequence Statement shall be in italics, underlined, bold, or the like, and shall be double spaced from the Avoidance Statements. All other instructions shall be in letters less prominent than the Possible Risk and Consequence Statements and shall be separated with at least a single space between individual instructions.

(i) Except for door operators complying with § 1211.9(b), a residential garage door operator shall be provided with a cautionary marking attached to or adjacent at all times to the means provided to detach the operator from the garage door. The marking shall include the following statement or the equivalent: "If the door becomes obstructed, detach door from operator as follows: (The method to detach the operator shall be shown on the marking.)"

[57 FR 60455, Dec. 21, 1992. Redesignated and amended at 65 FR 70659, Nov. 27, 2000]

§ 1211.16 UL marking requirements.

(a) Unless specifically excepted, marking required in this standard shall be permanent. Ink-printed and stenciled markings, decalcomania labels, and pressure sensitive labels are among the types of marking that are considered acceptable if they are acceptably applied and are of good quality.

(b) Except as provided below, a garage door operator shall be plainly marked, at a location where the marking will be readily visible—after installation, in the case of a permanently connected appliance—with:

(1) The manufacturer's name, trademark, or other descriptive marking by which the organization responsible for the product may be identified—hereinafter referred to as the manufacturer's name;

(2) The catalog number or the equivalent;

(3) The voltage, frequency, and input in amperes or watts; and

(4) The date or other dating period of manufacture not exceeding any three consecutive months.

(c) The ampere rating shall be included unless the full-load power factor is 80 percent or more, or, for a cord-connected operator, unless the rating is 50 watts or less. The number of phases shall be indicated if an operator is for use on a polyphase circuit. The date code repetition cycle shall not be less than 20 years.

(d) Exception No. 1: The manufacturer's identification may be in a traceable code if the operator is identified by the brand or trademark owned by a private labeler.

(e) Exception No. 2: The date of manufacture may be abbreviated or in an established or otherwise accepted code.

(f) If a manufacturer produces or assembles operators at more than one factory, each finished operator shall have a distinctive marking, which may be in code, to identify it as the product of a particular factory.

(g) The carton and the instruction manual for an operator shall be marked with the word "WARNING" and the following or the equivalent: "To reduce the risk of injury to persons—Use this operator only with (a) _____ door(s)."

(h) A residential garage door operator shall be marked with the word "WARNING" and the following or equivalent, "Risk of entrapment. After adjusting either the force or limits of travel adjustments, insure that the door reverses on a 1½ inch (or a 2 by 4 board laid flat) high obstruction on the floor."

(i) A separately supplied accessory, including external entrapment protection device, intended for installation with an appliance or appliances shall be marked with the manufacturer's name and catalog or model number and the type of appliance or appliances with which it is intended to be used—such as a residential garage door operator. Additionally, installation instructions, accompanying specifications sheet, or packaging of the accessory shall identify the appliance or appliances with which it is intended to be used by specifying the manufacturer's name and catalog or model number or by any other positive means to serve the identification purpose.

(j) An appliance provided with terminals or connectors for connection of a separately supplied accessory, such as an external entrapment protection device, shall be marked to identify the accessory intended to be connected to the terminals or connectors. The accessory identification shall be by manufacturer's name and catalog or model number or other means to allow for the identification of accessories intended for use with the appliance.

(k) With reference to paragraph (k) of this section, instructions for installing a separately supplied accessory shall be provided. A statement shall be included in the instructions warning the user that the appliance must be disconnected from the source of supply before attempting the installation of the accessory.

[57 FR 60455, Dec. 21, 1992. Redesignated at 65 FR 70659, Nov. 27, 2000]

§ 1211.17 Statutory labeling requirement.

(a) A manufacturer selling or offering for sale in the United States an automatic residential garage door operator manufactured on or after January 1, 1991, shall clearly identify on any container of the system and on the system the month or week and year the system was manufactured and its conformance with the requirements of this part.

(b) The display of the UL logo or listing mark, and compliance with the date marking requirements of UL–325 now stated in § 1211.5 of this subpart, on both the container and the system, shall satisfy the requirements of this subpart.

[57 FR 60455, Dec. 21, 1992. Redesignated at 65 FR 70659, Nov. 27, 2000]

Subpart B—Certification

SOURCE: 57 FR 60468, Dec. 21, 1992, unless otherwise noted.

§ 1211.20 Purpose, scope, and application.

(a) *Purpose.* Section 14(a) of the Consumer Product Safety Act, 15 U.S.C. 2063(a), requires every manufacturer (including importers) and private labeler of a product which is subject to a consumer product safety standard to issue a certificate that the product conforms to the applicable standard, and to base that certificate either on a test of each product or on a "reasonable testing program." The purpose of this subpart is to establish requirements that manufacturers and importers of automatic residential garage door operators subject to the Safety Standard for Automatic Residential Garage Door Operators (16 CFR part 1211, subpart A), shall issue certificates of compliance in the form specified.

(b) *Scope and application.* The provisions of this subpart apply to all residential garage door operators which are subject to the requirements of the Safety Standard for Automatic Residential Garage Door Operators that take effect on January 1, 1993 or later.

§ 1211.21 Effective date.

Under the Consumer Product Safety Act, automatic residential garage door operators must certify that they comply with requirements of subpart A of this part. This certification requirement is currently in effect. The specific labeling requirement of the certification rule in this subpart will become effective for any automatic residential garage door operator manufactured on or after January 21, 1993.

§ 1211.22 Definitions.

The following definitions shall apply to this subpart:

(a) *Private labeler* means an owner of a brand or trademark which is used on an operator subject to the standard and which is not the brand or trademark of the manufacturer of the operator, provided the owner of the brand or trademark caused or authorized the operator to be so labeled and the brand or trademark of the manufacturer of such operator does not appear on the label.

(b) *Production lot* means a quantity of garage door operators from which certain operators are selected for testing prior to certifying the lot. All garage door operators in a lot must be essentially identical in those design, construction, and material features which relate to the ability of an operator to comply with the standard.

(c) *Reasonable testing program* means any test or series of tests which are identical or equivalent to, or more stringent than, the tests defined in the standard and which are performed on one or more garage door operators of the production lot for the purpose of determining whether there is reasonable assurance that the operators in that lot comply with the requirements of the standard.

§ 1211.23 Certification testing.

(a) *General.* Manufacturers and importers shall either test each individual garage door operator (or have it tested) or shall rely upon a reasonable testing program to demonstrate compliance with the requirements of the standard.

(b) *Reasonable testing program.* This paragraph provides guidance for establishing a reasonable testing program.

(1) A reasonable testing program for automatic residential garage door operators is one that provides reasonable assurance that the operators comply with the standard. Manufacturers and importers may define their own testing programs. Such reasonable testing programs may, at the option of manufacturers and importers, be conducted by an independent third party qualified to perform such testing programs.

(2) To conduct a reasonable testing program, the garage door operators should be divided into production lots. Sample operators from each production lot should be tested in accordance with the reasonable testing program so that there is a reasonable assurance that if the operators selected for testing meet the standard, all operators in the lot will meet the standard. Where there is a change in parts, suppliers of parts, or production methods that could affect the ability of the operator to comply with the requirements of the standard, the manufacturer should establish a new production lot for testing.

(3) The Commission will test for compliance with the standard by using the test procedures contained in the standard. However, a manufacturer's reasonable testing program may include either tests prescribed in the standard or any other reasonable test procedures.

(4) If the reasonable testing program shows that an operator does not comply with one or more requirements of

the standard, no operator in the production lot can be certified as complying until all non-complying operators in the lot have been identified and destroyed or altered by repair, redesign, or use of a different material or components to the extent necessary to make them conform to the standard. The sale or offering for sale of garage door operators that do not comply with the standard is a prohibited act and a violation of section 19(a) of the CPSA (15 U.S.C. 2068(a)), regardless of whether the operator has been validly certified.

§ 1211.24 Product certification and labeling by manufacturers.

(a) *Form of permanent label of certification.* Manufacturers (including importers) shall issue certificates of compliance for automatic residential garage door operators manufactured after the effective date of the standard in the form of a permanent label which can reasonable be expected to remain on the operator during the entire period the operator is capable of being used. Such labeling shall be deemed to be a "certificate" of compliance as that term is used in section 14 of the CPSA, 15 U.S.C. 2063.

(b) *Exception for UL listed operators.* The certification labeling requirement of paragraph (a) of this section shall be satisfied by display of the Underwriters Laboratories, Inc. (UL) logo or listing mark, and compliance with the date marking requirements of UL Standard for Safety 325, on both the operator system and its container. Operators displaying the UL logo or listing mark and complying with the UL standard are exempt from the requirements of paragraphs (c) and (d) of this section.

(c) *Contents of certification label.* The certification labels required by this section shall clearly and legibly contain the following information:

(1) The statement "Meets CPSC ______ (insert 1993 or later date of applicable standard) garage door operator entrapment protection requirements."

(2) An identification of the production lot.

(d) *Placement of the label.* The label required by this section must be affixed to the operator. If the label is not immediately visible to the ultimate purchaser of the garage door operator prior to purchase because of packaging or other marketing practices, a second label that states: "Meets CPSC ______ (insert 1993 or later date of applicable standard) garage door operator entrapment protection requirements," along with the month or week and year of manufacture must appear on the container or, if the container is not visible, on the promotional material used with the sale of the operator.

§ 1211.25 Product certification and labeling by importers.

(a) *General.* The importer of any automatic residential garage door operator subject to the standard in subpart A of this part must issue the certificate of compliance required by section 14(a) of the CPSA and § 1211.24 of this subpart. If testing of each operator, or a reasonable testing program, meeting the requirements of this subpart has been performed by or for the foreign manufacturer of the product, the importer may rely in good faith on such tests to support the certificate of compliance provided the importer is a resident of the United States or has a resident agent in the United States and the records of such tests required by § 1211.31 of subpart C of this part are maintained in the United States.

(b) *Responsibility of importer.* If the importer relies on tests by the foreign manufacturer to support the certificate of compliance, the importer bears the responsibility for examining the records supplied by the manufacturer to determine that the records of such tests appear to comply with § 1211.31 of subpart C of this part.

Subpart C—Recordkeeping

SOURCE: 57 FR 60468, Dec. 21, 1992, unless otherwise noted.

§ 1211.30 Effective date.

The recordkeeping requirements in this subpart shall become effective on January 21, 1993, and shall apply to automatic residential garage door operators manufactured on or after that date.

§1211.31 Recordkeeping requirements.

(a) *General.* Every person issuing certificates of compliance for automatic residential garage door operators subject to the standard set forth in subpart A of this part shall maintain written records which show that the certificates are based on a test of each operator or on a reasonable testing program. The records shall be maintained for a period of at least three years from the date of certification of each operator or the last operator in each production lot. These records shall be available to any designated officer or employee of the Commission upon request in accordance with section 16(b) of the CPSA, 15 U.S.C. 2065(b).

(b) *Content of records.* Records shall identify the operators tested and the production lot and describe the tests the operators were subjected to in sufficient detail so the tests may be replicated. Records shall also provide the results of the tests including the precise nature of any failures, and specific actions taken to address any failures.

(c) *Format for records.* The records required to be maintained by this section may be in any appropriate form or format that clearly provides the required information.

PART 1212—SAFETY STANDARD FOR MULTI-PURPOSE LIGHTERS

Subpart A—Requirements for Child-Resistance

Sec.

Subpart B—Certification Requirements

Subpart C—Stockpiling

APPENDIX A TO PART 1212—FINDINGS UNDER THE CONSUMER PRODUCT SAFETY ACT

SOURCE: 64 FR 71872, Dec. 22, 1999, unless otherwise noted.

Subpart A—Requirements for Child-Resistance

AUTHORITY: 15 U.S.C. 2056, 2058, 2079(d).

§1212.1 Scope, application, and effective date.

This part 1212, a consumer product safety standard, prescribes requirements for multi-purpose lighters. These requirements are intended to make the multi-purpose lighters subject to the standard's provisions resistant to successful operation by children younger than 5 years of age. This standard applies to all multi-purpose lighters, as defined in §1212.2, that are manufactured in the United States, or imported, on or after December 22, 2000.

§1212.2 Definitions.

As used in this part 1212:

(a)(1) Multi-purpose lighter, (also known as grill lighter, fireplace lighter, utility lighter, micro-torch, or gas match, etc.) means: A hand-held, flame-producing product that operates on fuel, incorporates an ignition mechanism, and is used by consumers to ignite items such as candles, fuel for fireplaces, charcoal or gas-fired grills, camp fires, camp stoves, lanterns, fuel-fired appliances or devices, or pilot lights, or for uses such as soldering or brazing. Some multi-purpose lighters have a feature that allows for hands-free operation.

(2) The following products are not multi-purpose lighters:

(i) Devices intended primarily for igniting cigarettes, cigars, and pipes, whether or not such devices are subject to the requirements of the Safety Standard for Cigarette Lighters (16 CFR part 1210).

(ii) Devices containing more than 10 oz. of fuel.

(iii) Matches.

(b) *Successful operation* means one signal of any duration from a surrogate multi-purpose lighter within either of the two 5-minute test periods specified in §1212.4(f).

(c)(1) *Surrogate multi-purpose lighter* means a device that

(i) Approximates the appearance, size, shape, and weight of, and is identical in all other factors that affect child resistance (including operation and the force(s) required for operation), within reasonable manufacturing tolerances, to, a multi-purpose lighter intended for use by consumers,

(ii) Has no fuel,

(iii) Does not produce a flame, and

(iv) produces an audible, or audible and visual, signal that will be clearly discernible when the surrogate multi-purpose lighter is activated in each manner that would produce a flame in a fueled production multi-purpose lighter.

(2) This definition does not require a multi-purpose lighter to be modified with electronics or the like to produce a signal. Manufacturers may use a multi-purpose lighter without fuel as a surrogate multi-purpose lighter if a distinct audible signal, such as a "click," can be heard clearly when the mechanism is operated in each manner that would produce a flame in a production lighter and if a flame cannot be produced in a production multi-purpose lighter without the signal. But see §1212.4(f)(1).

(d) *Child-resistant mechanism* means the mechanism of a multi-purpose lighter that makes the lighter resist successful operation by young children, as specified in §1212.3.

(e) *Model* means one or more multi-purpose lighters from the same manufacturer or importer that do not differ in design or other characteristics in any manner that may affect child resistance. Lighter characteristics that may affect child resistance include, but are not limited to, size, shape, case material, and ignition mechanism (including child-resistant features).

§ 1212.3 Requirements for multi-purpose lighters.

(a) A multi-purpose lighter subject to this part 1212 shall be resistant to successful operation by at least 85% of the child-test panel when tested in the manner prescribed by §1212.4.

(b) The child-resistant mechanism of a multi-purpose lighter subject to this part 1212 must:

(1) Operate safely when used in a normal and convenient manner,

(2) Comply with this §1212.3 for the reasonably expected life of the lighter,

(3) Not be easy to deactivate or prevent from complying with this §1212.3.

(4) Except as provided in paragraph (b)(5) of this section, automatically reset when or before the user lets go of the lighter.

(5) The child-resistant mechanism of a multi-purpose lighter subject to this part 1212 that allows hands-free operation must:

(i) Require operation of an additional feature (e.g., lock, switch, etc.) after a flame is achieved before hands-free operation can occur;

(ii) Have a manual mechanism for turning off the flame when the hands-free function is used; and either

(iii) Automatically reset when or before the user lets go of the lighter when the hands-free function is not used; or

(iv) Automatically reset when or before the user lets go of the lighter after turning off the flame when the hands-free feature is used.

§ 1212.4 Test protocol.

(a) *Child test panel.* (1) The test to determine if a multi-purpose lighter is resistant to successful operation by children uses a panel of children to test a surrogate multi-purpose lighter representing the production multi-purpose lighter. Written informed consent shall be obtained from a parent or legal guardian of a child before the child participates in the test.

(2) The test shall be conducted using at least one, but no more than two, 100-child test panels in accordance with the provisions of §1212.4(f).

(3) The children for the test panel shall live within the United States.

(4) The age and sex distribution of each 100-child panel shall be:

(i) 30±2 children (20 ±1 males; 10±1 females) 42 through 44 months old;

(ii) 40±2 children (26±1 males; 14±1 females) 45 through 48 months old;

(iii) 30±2 children (20±1 males; 10±1 females) 49 through 51 months old.

NOTE TO PARAGRAPH (a)(4): To calculate a child's age in months: Subtract the child's birth date from the test date. The following calculation shows how to determine the age of the child at the time of the test. Both dates are expressed numerically as Month-Day-Year.

Example: Test Date (*e.g.*, 8/3/94) minus Birth Date—(*e.g.*, 6/23/90). Subtract the number for the year of birth from the number for the year of the test (*i.e.*, 94 minus 90 = 4). Multiply the difference in years by 12 months (*i.e.*, 4 years × 12 months = 48 months). Subtract the number for the month of the birth date from the number of the month of the test date (*i.e.*, 8 minus 6 = 2 months). Add the difference in months obtained above to the number of months represented by the difference in years described above (48 months + 2 months = 50 months). If the difference in days is greater than 15 (*e.g.*, 16, 17 . . .), add 1 month. If the difference in days is less than −15 (*e.g.*, −16, −17), subtract 1 month (*e.g.*, 50 months − 1 month = 49 months). If the difference in days is between −15 and 15 (*e.g.*, −15, −14, . . . 14, 15), do not add or subtract a month.

(5) No child with a permanent or temporary illness, injury, or handicap that would interfere with the child's ability to operate the surrogate multi-purpose lighter shall participate.

(6) Two children at a time shall participate in testing of surrogate multi-purpose lighters. Extra children whose results will not be counted in the test may be used if necessary to provide the required partner for test subjects, if the extra children are within the required age range and a parent or guardian of each such child has signed a consent form.

(7) No child shall participate in more than one test panel or test more than one surrogate multi-purpose lighter. No child shall participate in both surrogate multi-purpose lighter testing and either surrogate cigarette lighter testing or child-resistant package testing on the same day.

(b) *Test sites, environment, and adult testers.* (1) Surrogate multi-purpose lighters shall be tested within the United States at 5 or more test sites throughout the geographical area for each 100-child panel if the sites are the customary nursery schools or day care centers of the participating children. No more than 20 children shall be tested at each site. In the alternative, surrogate multi-purpose lighters may be tested within the United States at one or more central locations, provided the participating children are drawn from a variety of geographical locations.

(2) Testing of surrogate multi-purpose lighters shall be conducted in a room that is familiar to the children on the test panel (for example, a room the children frequent at their customary nursery school or day care center). If the testing is conducted in a room that initially is unfamiliar to the children (for example, a room at a central location), the tester shall allow at least 5 minutes for the children to become accustomed to the new environment before starting the test. The area in which the testing is conducted shall be well-lighted and isolated from distractions. The children shall be allowed freedom of movement to work with their surrogate multi-purpose lighters, as long as the tester can watch both children at the same time. Two children at a time shall participate in testing of surrogate multi-purpose lighters. The children shall be seated side by side in chairs approximately 6 inches apart, across a table from the tester. The table shall be normal table height for the children, so that they can sit up at the table with their legs underneath and so that their arms will be at a comfortable height when on top of the table. The children's chairs shall be "child size."

(3) Each tester shall be at least 18 years old. Five or 6 adult testers shall be used for each 100-child test panel. Each tester shall test an approximately equal number of children from the 100-child test panel (20±2 children each for 5 testers and 17±2 children each for 6 testers).

NOTE: When a test is initiated with five testers and one tester drops out, a sixth tester may be added to complete the testing. When a test is initiated with six testers and one tester drops out, the test shall be completed using the five remaining testers. When a tester drops out, the requirement for each tester to test an approximately equal number of children does not apply to that tester. When testing is initiated with five testers, no tester shall test more than 19 children until it is certain that the test can be completed with five testers.

(c) *Surrogate multi-purpose lighters.* (1) Six surrogate multi-purpose lighters shall be used for each 100-child panel. The six multi-purpose lighters shall represent the range of forces required for operation of multi-purpose lighters intended for use. All of these surrogate multi-purpose lighters shall have the same visual appearance, including color. The surrogate multi-purpose lighters shall be labeled with sequential numbers beginning with the number one. The same six surrogate multi-purpose lighters shall be used for the entire 100-child panel. The surrogate multi-purpose lighters may be used in more than one 100-child panel test. The surrogate multi-purpose lighters shall not be damaged or jarred during storage or transportation. The surrogate multi-purpose lighters shall not be exposed to extreme heat or cold. The surrogate multi-purpose lighters shall be tested at room temperature. No surrogate multi-purpose lighter shall be left unattended.

(2) Each surrogate multi-purpose lighter shall be tested by an approximately equal number of children in a 100-child test panel (17±2 children).

NOTE: If a surrogate multi-purpose lighter is permanently damaged, testing shall continue with the remaining multi-purpose lighters. When a multi-purpose lighter is dropped out, the requirement that each multi-purpose lighter be tested by an approximately equal number of children does not apply to that lighter.

(3) Before each 100-child panel is tested, each surrogate multi-purpose lighter shall be examined to verify that it approximates the appearance, size, shape, and weight of a production multi-purpose lighter intended for use.

(4) Before and after each 100-child panel is tested, force measurements shall be taken on all operating components that could affect child resistance to verify that they are within reasonable operating tolerances for the corresponding production multi-purpose lighter.

(5) Before and after testing surrogate multi-purpose lighters with each child, each surrogate multi-purpose lighter shall be operated outside the presence of any child participating in the test to verify that it produces a signal. If the surrogate multi-purpose lighter will not produce a signal before the test, it shall be repaired before it is used in testing. If the surrogate multi-purpose lighter does not produce a signal when it is operated after the test, the results for the preceding test with that multi-purpose lighter shall be eliminated. An explanation shall be recorded on the data collection record. The multi-purpose lighter shall be repaired and tested with another eligible child (as one of a pair of children) to complete the test panel.

(d) *Encouragement.* (1) Prior to the test, the tester shall talk to the children in a normal and friendly tone to make them feel at ease and to gain their confidence.

(2) The tester shall tell the children that he or she needs their help for a special job. The children shall not be promised a reward of any kind for participating, and shall not be told that the test is a game or contest or that it is fun.

(3) The tester shall not discourage a child from attempting to operate the surrogate multi-purpose lighter at any time (either verbally or with body language such as facial expressions), unless a child is in danger of hurting himself or another child. The tester shall not discuss the dangers of multi-purpose lighters or matches with the children to be tested prior to the end of the 10-minute test.

(4) Whenever a child has stopped attempting to operate the surrogate multi-purpose lighter for a period of approximately one minute, the tester shall encourage the child to try by saying "keep trying for just a little longer."

(5) Whenever a child says that his or her parent, grandparent, guardian, etc., said never to touch lighters, say "that's right—never touch a real lighter—but your [parent, etc.] said it was OK for you to try to make a noise with this special lighter because it can't hurt you."

(6) The children in a pair being tested may encourage each other to operate the surrogate multi-purpose lighter and may tell or show each other how to operate it. (This interaction is not considered to be disruption as described in paragraph (e)(2) of this section.) However, neither child shall be allowed to touch or operate the other child's multi-purpose lighter. If one child takes the other child's surrogate multi-purpose lighter, that surrogate lighter shall be immediately returned to the proper child. If this occurs, the

tester shall say "No. He (she) has to try to do it himself (herself)."

(e) *Children who refuse to participate.* (1) If a child becomes upset or afraid, and cannot be reassured before the test starts, select another eligible child for participation in that pair.

(2) If a child disrupts the participation of another child for more than 1 minute during the test, the test shall be stopped and both children eliminated from the results. An explanation shall be recorded on the data collection record. These two children should be replaced with other eligible children to complete the test panel.

(3) If a child is not disruptive but refuses to attempt to operate the surrogate multi-purpose lighter throughout the entire test period, that child shall be eliminated from the test results and an explanation shall be recorded on the data collection record. The child shall be replaced with another eligible child (as one of a pair of children) to complete the test panel.

(f) *Test procedure.* (1) To begin the test, the tester shall say "I have a special lighter that will not make a flame. It makes a noise like this." Except where doing so would block the child's view of a visual signal, the adult tester shall place a 8½ by 11 inch sheet of cardboard or other rigid opaque material upright on the table in front of the surrogate multi-purpose lighter, so that the surrogate multi-purpose lighter cannot be seen by the child, and shall operate the surrogate multi-purpose lighter once to produce its signal. The tester shall say "Your parents said it is OK for you to try to make that noise with your lighter." The tester shall place a surrogate multi-purpose lighter in each child's hand and say "now you try to make a noise with your lighter. Keep trying until I tell you to stop."

NOTE: For multi-purpose lighters with an "off/on" switch, the surrogate lighter shall be given to the child with the switch in the "on," or unlocked, position.

(2) The adult tester shall observe the children for 5 minutes to determine if either or both of the children can successfully operate the surrogate multi-purpose lighter by producing one signal of any duration. If a child achieves a spark without defeating the child-resistant feature, say "that's a spark—it won't hurt you—try to make a noise with your lighter." If any child successfully operates the surrogate multi-purpose lighter during this first 5-minute period, the lighter shall be taken from that child and the child shall not be asked to try to operate the lighter again. The tester shall ask the successful child to remain until the other child is finished.

(3) If either or both of the children are unable to successfully operate the surrogate multi-purpose lighter during the 5-minute period specified in §1212.4(f) (3), the adult tester shall demonstrate the operation of the surrogate multi-purpose lighter. To conduct the demonstration, secure the children's full attention by saying "Okay, give me your lighter(s) now." Take the surrogate multi-purpose lighters and place them on the table in front of you out of the children's reach. Then say, "I'll show you how to make the noise with your lighters. First I'll show you with (child's name) lighter and then I'll show you with (child's name) lighter." Pick up the first child's surrogate multi-purpose lighter. Hold the lighter approximately 2 feet in front of the children at their eye level. Hold the surrogate multi-purpose lighter in a comfortable operating position in one hand so both children can see the operation of the child-resistant mechanism and the ignition mechanism during each demonstration. Say "now watch the lighter." Look at each child to verify that they are both looking at the lighter. Operate the multi-purpose lighter one time in a normal manner according to the manufacturer's instructions. Do not exaggerate operating movements. Do not verbally describe the lighter's operation. Place the first child's lighter back on the table in front of you and pick up the second child's lighter. Say, "Okay, now watch this lighter." Repeat the demonstration as described above using the second child's multi-purpose lighter.

NOTE TO PARAGRAPH (f)(3): The demonstration is conducted with each child's lighter, even if one child has successfully operated the lighter. Testers shall conduct the demonstration in a uniform manner, including the words spoken to the children, the way the multi-purpose lighter is held and operated, and how the tester's hand and body is oriented to the children. All testers must be able to operate the surrogate multi-purpose lighters using only appropriate operating movements in accordance with the manufacturer's instructions. If any of these requirements are not met during the demonstration for any pair of children, the results for that pair of children shall be eliminated from the test. Another pair of eligible children shall be used to complete the test panel.

(4) Each child who fails to successfully operate the surrogate multi-purpose lighter in the first 5 minutes is then given another 5 minutes in which to attempt to complete the successful operation of the surrogate multi-purpose lighter. After the demonstrations, give the same surrogate multi-purpose lighter back to each child who did not successfully operate the surrogate multi-purpose lighter in the first 5 minutes by placing the multi-purpose lighter in the child's hand. Say "Okay, now you try to make the noise with your lighter(s)—keep trying until I tell you to stop." If any child successfully operates the surrogate multi-purpose lighter during this period, the surrogate multi-purpose lighter shall be taken from that child and the child shall not be asked to try to operate the lighter again. If the other child has not yet successfully operated the surrogate multi-purpose lighter, the tester shall ask the successful child to remain until the other child is finished.

NOTE: Multi-purpose lighters with an on/off switch shall have the switch returned to the position the child left it at the end of the first 5-minute test period before returning the lighter to the child.

(5) At the end of the second 5-minute test period, take the surrogate multi-purpose lighter from any child who has not successfully operated it.

(6) After the test is over, ask the children to stand next to you. Look at the children's faces and say: "These are special lighters that don't make fire. Real lighters can burn you. Will you both promise me that if you find a real lighter you won't touch it and that you'll tell a grownup right away?" Wait for an affirmative response from each child; then thank the children for helping.

(7) Escort the children out of the room used for testing.

(8) After a child has participated in the testing of a surrogate multi-purpose lighter, and on the same day, provide written notice of that fact to the child's parent or guardian. This notification may be in the form of a letter provided to the school to be given to a parent or guardian of each child. The notification shall state that the child participated, shall ask the parent or guardian to warn the child not to play with lighters or matches, and shall remind the parent or guardian to keep all lighters and matches, whether child-resistant or not, out of the reach of children. For children who operated the surrogate multi-purpose lighter, the notification shall state that the child was able to operate the child-resistant multi-purpose lighter. For children who do not defeat the child-resistant feature, the notification shall state that, although the child did not defeat the child-resistant feature, the child may be able to do so in the future.

(g) *Data collection and recording.* Except for recording the times required for the children to activate the signal, recording of data should be avoided while the children are trying to operate the multi-purpose lighters, so that the tester's full attention is on the children during the test period. If actual testing is videotaped, the camera shall be stationary and shall be operated remotely in order to avoid distracting the children. Any photographs shall be taken after actual testing and shall simulate actual test procedure(s) (for example, the demonstration). The following data shall be collected and recorded for each child in the 100-child test panel:

(1) Sex (male or female).

(2) Date of birth (month, day, year).

(3) Age (in months, to the nearest month).

(4) The number of the multi-purpose lighter tested by that child.

(5) Date of participation in the test (month, day, year).

(6) Location where the test was given (city, state, and the name of the site).

(7) The name of the tester who conducted the test.

(8) The elapsed time at which the child achieved any operation of the surrogate signal in the first 5-minute test period.

(9) The elapsed time at which the child achieved any operation of the surrogate signal in the second 5-minute test period.

(10) For a single pair of children from each 100-child test panel, photograph(s) or video tape to show how the multi-purpose lighter was held in the tester's hand, and the orientation of the tester's body and hand to the children, during the demonstration.

(h) *Evaluation of test results and acceptance criterion.* To determine whether a surrogate multi-purpose lighter resists operation by at least 85% of the children, sequential panels of 100 children each, up to a maximum of 2 panels, shall be tested as prescribed below.

(1) If no more than 10 children in the first 100-child test panel successfully operated the surrogate multi-purpose lighter, the multi-purpose lighter represented by the surrogate multi-purpose lighter shall be considered to be resistant to successful operation by at least 85% of the child test panel, and no further testing is conducted. If 11 through 18 children in the first 100-child test panel successfully operate the surrogate multi-purpose lighter, the test results are inconclusive, and the surrogate multi-purpose lighter shall be tested with a second 100-child test panel in accordance with this §1212.4. If 19 or more of the children in the first 100-child test panel successfully operated the surrogate multi-purpose lighter, the lighter represented by the surrogate shall be considered not resistant to successful operation by at least 85% of the child test panel, and no further testing is conducted. (2)(i) If additional testing of the surrogate multi-purpose lighter is required by paragraph (h)(1) of this section, conduct the test specified by this §1212.4 using a second 100-child test panel and record the results. If a total of no more than 30 of the children in the combined first and second 100-child test panels successfully operated the surrogate multi-purpose lighter, the multi-purpose lighter represented by the surrogate multi-purpose lighter shall be considered resistant to successful operation by at least 85% of the child test panel, and no further testing is performed. If a total of 31 or more children in the combined first and second 100-child test panels successfully operate the surrogate multi-purpose lighter, the multi-purpose lighter represented by the surrogate shall be considered not resistant to successful operation by 85% of the child test panel, and no further testing is conducted.

(ii) Thus, for the first panel of 100 children, the surrogate passes if there are 0–10 successful operations by the children; the surrogate fails if there are 19 or greater successful operations; and testing is continued if there are 11–18 successes. If testing is continued with a second panel of children, the surrogate passes if the combined total of the successful operations of the two panels is 30 or less, and it fails if there are 31 or more.

§1212.5 Findings.

(a) Before issuing a final rule, the Consumer Product Safety Act (CPSA), 15 U.S.C. 2058(f)(1), requires the Commission to consider and make appropriate findings for inclusion in the rule with respect to:

(1) The degree and nature of the risk of injury the rule is designed to eliminate or reduce;

(2) The approximate number of consumer products, or types or classes thereof, subject to such rule;

(3) The need of the public for the consumer products subject to such rule, and the probable effect of such rule, upon the utility, cost, or availability of such products to meet such need; and

(4) Any means of achieving the objective of the order while minimizing adverse effects on competition or disruption or dislocation of manufacturing and other commercial practices consistent with the public health and safety

(b) The CPSA, 15 U.S.C. 2058(f)(3), also requires the Commission to make the following findings before it promulgates a rule, and to include such findings in the rule:

(1) That the rule (including its effective date) is reasonably necessary to eliminate or reduce an unreasonable risk of injury associated with such product;

(2) That the promulgation of the rule is in the public interest;

(3) That the benefits expected from the rule bear a reasonable relationship to its costs; and

(4) That the rule imposes the least burdensome requirement that prevents or adequately reduces the risk of injury for which the rule is being promulgated.

(c) The required findings are included as appendix A to this part 1212.

Subpart B—Certification Requirements

AUTHORITY: 15 U.S.C. 2063, 2065(b), 2066(g), 2076(e), 2079(d).

§ 1212.11 General.

Section 14(a) of the Consumer Product Safety Act (CPSA), 15 U.S.C. 2063(a), requires every manufacturer, private labeler, or importer of a product that is subject to a consumer product safety standard and that is distributed in commerce to issue a certificate that such product conforms to the applicable standard and to base that certificate upon a test of each item or upon a reasonable testing program. The purpose of this subpart B of part 1212 is to establish requirements that manufacturers, importers, and private labelers must follow to certify that their products comply with the Safety Standard for Multi-purpose lighters. This Subpart B describes the minimum features of a reasonable testing program and includes requirements for labeling, recordkeeping, and reporting pursuant to sections 14, 16(b), 17(g), and 27(e) of the CPSA, 15 U.S.C. 2063, 2065(b), 2066(g), and 2076(e).

§ 1212.12 Certificate of compliance.

(a) *General requirements*—(1) *Manufacturers (including importers).* Manufacturers of any multi-purpose lighter subject to the standard must issue the certificate of compliance required by section 14(a) of the CPSA, 15 U.S.C. 2063(a), and this subpart B, based on a reasonable testing program or a test of each product, as required by §§ 1212.13, 1212.14, and 1212.16. Manufacturers must also label each multi-purpose lighter subject to the standard as required by paragraph (c) of this section and keep the records and make the reports required by §§ 1212.15 and 1212.17. For purposes of this requirement, an importer of multi-purpose lighters shall be considered the "manufacturer."

(2) *Private labelers.* Because private labelers necessarily obtain their products from a manufacturer or importer that is already required to issue the certificate, private labelers are not required to issue a certificate. However, private labelers must ensure that the multi-purpose lighters are labeled in accordance with paragraph (c) of this section and that any certificate of compliance that is supplied with each shipping unit of multi-purpose lighters in accordance with paragraph (b) of this section is supplied to any distributor or retailer who receives the product from the private labeler.

(3) *Testing on behalf of importers.* (i) If the required testing has been performed by or for a foreign manufacturer of a product, an importer may rely on such tests to support the certificate of compliance, provided that:

(A) The importer is a resident of the United States or has a resident agent in the United States and

(B) The records are in English and the records and the surrogate multi-purpose lighters tested are kept in the United States and can be provided to the Commission within 48 hours (§ 1212.17(a)) or, in the case of production records, can be provided to the Commission within 7 calendar days in accordance with § 1212.17(a)(3).

(ii) The importer is responsible for ensuring that:

(A) The foreign manufacturer's records show that all testing used to support the certificate of compliance has been performed properly (§§ 1212.14–1212.16),

(B) The records provide a reasonable assurance that all multi-purpose lighters imported comply with the standard (§ 1212.13(b)(1)),

(C) The records exist in English (§ 1212.17(a)),

(D) The importer knows where the required records and multi-purpose lighters are located and that records required to be located in the United States are located there,

(E) Arrangements have been made so that any records required to be kept in the United States will be provided to the Commission within 48 hours of a request and any records not kept in the United States will be provided to the Commission within 7 calendar days (§ 1212.17(a)), and

(F) The information required by § 1212.17(b) to be provided to the Commission's Office of Compliance has been provided.

(b) *Certificate of compliance.* A certificate of compliance must accompany each shipping unit of the product (for example, a case), or otherwise be furnished to any distributor or retailer to whom the product is sold or delivered by the manufacturer, private labeler, or importer. The certificate shall state:

(1) That the product "complies with the Consumer Product Safety Standard for Multi-purpose lighters (16 CFR part 1212)",

(2) The name and address of the manufacturer or importer issuing the certificate or of the private labeler, and

(3) The date(s) of manufacture and, if different from the address in paragraph (b)(2) of this section, the address of the place of manufacture.

(c) *Labeling.* The manufacturer or importer must label each multi-purpose lighter with the following information, which may be in code.

(1) An identification of the period of time, not to exceed 31 days, during which the multi-purpose lighter was manufactured.

(2) An identification of the manufacturer of the multi-purpose lighter, unless the multi-purpose lighter bears a private label. If the multi-purpose lighter bears a private label, it shall bear a code mark or other label that will permit the seller of the multi-purpose lighter to identify the manufacturer to the purchaser upon request.

§ 1212.13 Certification tests.

(a) *General.* As explained in § 1212.11 of this subpart, certificates of compliance required by section 14(a) of the CPSA, 15 U.S.C. 2063(a), must be based on a reasonable testing program.

(b) *Reasonable testing programs*—(1) *Requirements.* (i) A reasonable testing program for multi-purpose lighters is one that demonstrates with a high degree of assurance that all multi-purpose lighters manufactured for sale or distributed in commerce will meet the requirements of the standard, including the requirements of § 1212.3. Manufacturers and importers shall determine the types and frequency of testing for their own reasonable testing programs. A reasonable testing program should be sufficiently stringent that it will detect any variations in production or performance during the production interval that would cause any multi-purpose lighters to fail to meet the requirements of the standard.

(ii) All reasonable testing programs shall include:

(A) Qualification tests, which must be performed on surrogates of each model of multi-purpose lighter produced, or to be produced, to demonstrate that the product is capable of passing the tests prescribed by the standard (see § 1212.14) and

(B) Production tests, which must be performed during appropriate production intervals as long as the product is being manufactured (see § 1212.16).

(iii) Corrective action and/or additional testing must be performed whenever certification tests of samples of the product give results that do not provide a high degree of assurance that all multi-purpose lighters manufactured during the applicable production interval will pass the tests of the standard.

(2) *Testing by third parties.* At the option of the manufacturer or importer, some or all of the testing of each multi-purpose lighter or multi-purpose lighter surrogate may be performed by a commercial testing laboratory or other third party. However, the manufacturer or importer must ensure that all certification testing has been properly performed with passing results and that all records of such tests are maintained in accordance with § 1212.17 of this subpart.

§ 1212.14 Qualification testing.

(a) *Testing.* Before any manufacturer or importer of multi-purpose lighters distributes multi-purpose lighters in commerce in the United States, surrogate multi-purpose lighters of each model shall be tested in accordance with § 1212.4 to ensure that all such multi-purpose lighters comply with the standard. However, if a manufacturer has tested one model of multi-purpose lighter, and then wishes to distribute another model of multi-purpose lighter that differs from the first model only by differences that would not have an adverse effect on child resistance, the second model need not be tested in accordance with § 1212.4.

(b) *Product modifications.* If any changes are made to a product after initial qualification testing that could adversely affect the ability of the product to meet the requirements of the standard, additional qualification tests must be made on surrogates for the changed product before the changed multi-purpose lighters are distributed in commerce.

(c) *Requalification.* If a manufacturer or importer chooses to requalify a multi-purpose lighter design after it has been in production, this may be done by following the testing procedures at § 1212.4.

§ 1212.15 Specifications.

(a) *Requirement.* Before any multi-purpose lighters that are subject to the standard are distributed in commerce, the manufacturer or importer shall ensure that the surrogate multi-purpose lighters used for qualification testing under § 1212.14 are described in a written product specification. (Section 1212.4(c) requires that six surrogate multi-purpose lighters be used for testing each 100-child panel.)

(b) *Contents of specification.* The product specification shall include the following information:

(1) A complete description of the multi-purpose lighter, including size, shape, weight, fuel, fuel capacity, ignition mechanism, and child-resistant features.

(2) A detailed description of all dimensions, force requirements, or other features that could affect the child-resistance of the multi-purpose lighter, including the manufacturer's tolerances for each such dimension or force requirement.

(3) Any further information, including, but not limited to, model names or numbers, necessary to adequately describe the multi-purpose lighters and any child-resistant features.

§ 1212.16 Production testing.

(a) *General.* Manufacturers and importers shall test samples of multi-purpose lighters subject to the standard as they are manufactured, to demonstrate that the multi-purpose lighters meet the specifications, required under § 1212.15, of the surrogate that has been shown by qualification testing to meet the requirements of the standard.

(b) *Types and frequency of testing.* Manufacturers, private labelers, and importers shall determine the types of tests for production testing. Each production test shall be conducted at a production interval short enough to provide a high degree of assurance that, if the samples selected for testing pass the production tests, all other multi-purpose lighters produced during the interval will meet the standard.

(c) *Test failure*—(1) *Sale of multi-purpose lighters.* If any test yields results which indicate that any multi-purpose lighters manufactured during the production interval may not meet the standard, production and distribution in commerce of multi-purpose lighters that may not comply with the standard must cease until it is determined that the lighters meet the standard or until corrective action is taken. (It may be necessary to modify the multi-purpose lighters or perform additional tests to ensure that only complying multi-purpose lighters are distributed in commerce. Multi-purpose lighters from other production intervals having test results showing that multi-purpose lighters from that interval comply with the standard could be produced and distributed unless there was some reason to believe that they might not comply with the standard.)

(2) *Corrective actions.* When any production test fails to provide a high degree of assurance that all multi-purpose lighters comply with the standard, corrective action must be taken. Corrective action may include changes in the manufacturing process, the assembly process, the equipment used to manufacture the product, or the product's materials or design. The corrective action must provide a high degree of assurance that all multi-purpose lighters produced after the corrective action will comply with the standard. If the corrective action changes the

product from the surrogate used for qualification testing in a manner that could adversely affect its child-resistance, the multi-purpose lighter must undergo new qualification tests in accordance with § 1212.14.

§ 1212.17 Recordkeeping and reporting.

(a) Every manufacturer and importer of lighters subject to the standard shall maintain the following records in English on paper, microfiche, or similar media and make such records available to any designated officer or employee of the Commission in accordance with section 16(b) of the Consumer Product Safety Act, 15 U.S.C. 2065(b). Such records must also be kept in the United States and provided to the Commission within 48 hours of receipt of a request from any employee of the Commission, except as provided in paragraph (a)(3) of this section. Legible copies of original records may be used to comply with these requirements.

(1) Records of qualification testing, including a description of the tests, photograph(s) or a video tape for a single pair of children from each 100-child test panel to show how the lighter was held in the tester's hand, and the orientation of the tester's body and hand to the children, during the demonstration, the dates of the tests, the data required by § 1212.4(d), the actual surrogate lighters tested, and the results of the tests, including video tape records, if any. These records shall be kept for a period of 3 years after the production of the particular model to which such tests relate has ceased. If requalification tests are undertaken in accordance with § 1212.14(c), the original qualification test results may be discarded 3 years after the requalification testing, and the requalification test results and surrogates, and the other information required in this subsection for qualifications tests, shall be kept in lieu thereof.

(2) Records of procedures used for production testing required by this subpart B, including a description of the types of tests conducted (in sufficient detail that they may be replicated), the production interval selected, the sampling scheme, and the pass/reject criterion. These records shall be kept for a period of 3 years after production of the lighter has ceased.

(3) Records of production testing, including the test results, the date and location of testing, and records of corrective actions taken, which in turn includes the specific actions taken to improve the design or manufacture or to correct any noncomplying lighter, the date the actions were taken, the test result or failure that triggered the actions, and the additional actions taken to ensure that the corrective action had the intended effect. These records shall be kept for a period of 3 years following the date of testing. Records of production testing results may be kept on paper, microfiche, computer tape, or other retrievable media. Where records are kept on computer tape or other retrievable media, however, the records shall be made available to the Commission on paper copies upon request. A manufacturer or importer of a lighter that is not manufactured in the United States may maintain the production records required by this paragraph (a)(3) outside the United States, but shall make such records available to the Commission in the United States within 1 week of a request from a Commission employee for access to those records under section 16(b) of the CPSA, 15 U.S.C. 2065(b).

(4) Records of specifications required under § 1212.15 shall be kept for 3 years after production of each lighter model has ceased.

(b) *Reporting.* At least 30 days before it first imports or distributes in commerce any model of lighter subject to the standard, every manufacturer and importer must provide a written report to the Office of Compliance, Consumer Product Safety Commission, 4330 East-West Highway, Room 610, Bethesda, Maryland 20814–4408. Such report shall include:

(1) The name, address, and principal place of business of the manufacturer or importer,

(2) A detailed description of the lighter model and the child-resistant feature(s) used in that model,

(3) A description of the qualification testing, including a description of the surrogate lighters tested (including a

description of the point in the operation at which the surrogate will signal operation—e.g., the distance by which a trigger must be moved), the specification of the surrogate lighter required by § 1212.15, a summary of the results of all such tests, the dates the tests were performed, the location(s) of such tests, and the identity of the organization that conducted the tests,

(4) An identification of the place or places that the lighters were or will be manufactured,

(5) The location(s) where the records required to be maintained by paragraph (a) of this section are kept, and

(6) A prototype or production unit of that lighter model.

(c) *Confidentiality.* Persons who believe that any information required to be submitted or made available to the Commission is trade secret or otherwise confidential shall request that the information be considered exempt from disclosure by the Commission, in accordance with 16 CFR 1015.18. Requests for confidentiality of records provided to the Commission will be handled in accordance with section 6(a)(2) of the CPSA, 15 U.S.C. 2055(a)(2), the Freedom of Information Act as amended, 5 U.S.C. 552, and the Commission's regulations under that act, 16 CFR part 1015.

§ 1212.18 Refusal of importation.

(a) *For noncompliance with reporting and recordkeeping requirements.* The Commission has determined that compliance with the recordkeeping and reporting requirements of this subpart is necessary to ensure that lighters comply with this part 1212. Therefore, pursuant to section 17(g) of the CPSA, 15 U.S.C. 2066(g), the Commission may refuse to permit importation of any lighters with respect to which the manufacturer or importer has not complied with the recordkeeping and reporting requirements of this subpart. Since the records are required to demonstrate that production lighters comply with the specifications for the surrogate, the Commission may refuse importation of lighters if production lighters do not comply with the specifications required by this subpart, or if any other recordkeeping or reporting requirement in this part is violated.

(b) *For noncompliance with this standard or for lack of a certification certificate.* As provided in section 17(a) of the CPSA, 15 U.S.C. 2066(a), products subject to this standard shall be refused admission into the customs territory of the United States if, among other reasons, the product either fails to comply with this standard or is not accompanied by the certificate required by this standard.

Subpart C—Stockpiling

AUTHORITY: 15 U.S.C. 2058(g)(2), 2065(b), 2079(d)

§ 1212.20 Stockpiling.

(a) *Definition.* "Stockpiling" means to manufacture or import a product that is subject to a consumer product safety rule between the date of issuance of the rule and its effective date at a rate which is significantly greater than the rate at which such product was produced or imported during a base period.

(b) *Base period.* For purposes of this rule, "base period" means the 1-year period ending December 21, 1999.

(c) *Prohibited act.* Manufacturers and importers of multi-purpose lighters shall not manufacture or import such lighters that do not comply with the requirements of this part between December 22, 1999 and December 22, 2000, at a rate that is greater than the rate of production or importation during the base period plus 20 per cent of that rate.

(d) *Reporting and recordkeeping requirements.* All firms and persons who make or import multi-purpose lighters, after the date of publication of this rule, that do not meet the requirements of this standard, shall supply the Commission's Office of Compliance with:

(1) Supporting information to establish the number of multi-purpose lighters made or imported during the base period. This information shall be submitted by January 21, 2000.

(2) Supporting information to establish the number of lighters made or imported during the year following publication of the final rule. This information shall be submitted within 10 days

of the end of each calendar month, for lighters shipped within that month.

(3) Supporting information shall be sufficient to identify the manufacturer or importer, the party to which the lighters were sold, the destination of the lighters, and shall include copies of relevant invoices and importation documents.

Appendix A to Part 1212—Findings Under the Consumer Product Safety Act

Section 9(f) of the Consumer Product Safety Act (15 U.S.C. 2058(f)) requires the Commission to make findings concerning the following topics and to include the findings in the rule. Because the findings are required to be published in the rule, they reflect the information that was available to the Consumer Product Safety Commission ("CPSC" or "Commission") when the standard was issued on December 22, 1999.

A. *The degree and nature of the risk of injury the rule is designed to eliminate or reduce.* The standard is designed to reduce the risk of death and injury from accidental fires started by children playing with multi-purpose lighters. The Commission has identified 196 fires that occurred from 1995 through 1998 that were started by children under age 5 playing with multi-purpose lighters. These fires resulted in a total of 35 deaths and 81 injuries. Fire-related injuries include thermal burns—many of high severity—as well as anoxia and other, less serious injuries. The societal costs of these fires is estimated to include $175 million in deaths, $13.7 million in injuries, and over $5 million in property damage. Because these data are from known fires rather than national estimates, the extent of the total problem may be greater. Fires started by children under age 5 are those which the standard would most effectively reduce.

B. *The approximate number of consumer products, or types or classes thereof, subject to the rule.* The standard covers certain flame-producing devices, commonly known as multi-purpose lighters, that are defined in §1212.2(a) of 16 CFR part 1212. This definition includes products that are referred to as micro-torches. Multi-purpose lighters may use any fuel and may be refillable or nonrefillable. Approximately 21 million multi-purpose lighters are expected to be sold to consumers in the U.S. during 1999. Multi-purpose lighters manufactured in the United States, or imported, on or after December 22, 2000 will be required to meet child-resistance requirements. The following products are not multi-purpose lighters: devices intended primarily for igniting cigarettes, cigars, and pipes, whether or not such devices are subject to the requirements of the Safety Standard for Cigarette Lighters (16 CFR part 1210); devices that contain more than 10 oz. of fuel; and matches.

C. *The need of the public for the consumer products subject to the rule, and the probable effect of the rule on the utility, cost, or availability of such products to meet such need.* Consumers use multi-purpose lighters primarily to ignite items such as candles, fuel for fireplaces, charcoal or gas-fired grills, camp fires, camp stoves, lanterns, or fuel-fired appliances or devices or their pilot lights.

1. There will be several types of costs associated with the rule. Manufacturers would have to devote some resources to the development or modification of technology to produce child-resistant multi-purpose lighters. Before being marketed, the lighters must be tested and certified to the new standard. It is also possible that manufacturing child-resistant lighters may require more labor or material than non-child-resistant lighters.

2. Manufacturers will have to modify their existing multi-purpose lighters to comply with the rule. In general, costs that manufacturers would incur in developing, producing, and selling new complying lighters include the following:

- Research and development toward finding the most promising approaches to improving child resistance, including building prototypes and surrogate lighters for preliminary child panel testing;
- Retooling and other production equipment changes required to produce more child-resistant multi-purpose lighters, beyond normal periodic changes made to the plant and equipment;
- Labor and material costs of the additional assembly steps, or modification of assembly steps, in the manufacturing process;
- The additional labeling, recordkeeping, certification, testing, and reporting that will be required for each new model;
- Various administrative costs of compliance, such as legal support and executive time spent at related meetings and activities; and
- Lost revenue if sales are adversely affected.

3. Industry sources have not been able to provide firm estimates of these costs. One major manufacturer has introduced a child-resistant multi-purpose lighter. However, because that company did not previously manufacture a non-child-resistant lighter, it was unable to estimate the incremental cost of developing and manufacturing child-resistant multi-purpose lighters.

4. Assuming that there are 20 manufacturers and that each invests an average of $2 million to develop and market complying lighters, the total industry cost for research development, retooling, and compliance testing would be approximately $40 million. If

amortized over a period of 10 years, and assuming a modest 1% sales growth each year, the average of these costs would be about $0.23 per unit. For a manufacturer with a large market share (i.e., selling several million units or more a year) the cost per unit of the development costs could be lower than the estimated $0.23 per unit, even at the high end of the estimates. On the other hand, for manufacturers with a small market share, the per-unit development costs would be greater. Some manufacturers with small market shares may even drop out of the market (at least temporarily) or delay entering the market.

5. In addition to the research, development, retooling, and testing costs, material and labor costs are likely to increase. For example, additional labor will be required to add the child-resistant mechanism to the lighter during assembly. Additional materials may also be needed to produce the child-resistant mechanism. While CPSC was unable to obtain reliable estimates, some industry sources indicated that they believed that these costs would be relatively low, probably less than $0.25 per unit.

6. Multi-purpose lighters will also be required to have a label that identifies the manufacturer and the approximate date of manufacture. However, virtually all products are already labeled in some way. Since the requirement in the rule allows substantial flexibility to the manufacturer in terms of things such as color, size, and location, this requirement is not expected to increase the costs significantly.

7. Certification and testing costs include costs of producing surrogate lighters; conducting child panel tests; and issuing and maintaining records for each model. The largest component of these costs is believed to be building surrogates and conducting child panel tests, which, based on CPSC experience, may cost about $25,000 per lighter model. Administrative expenses associated with the compliance and related activities are difficult to quantify, since many such activities associated with the rule would probably be carried out anyway and the marginal impact of the recommended rule is probably slight.

8. Multi-purpose lighters are sold in countries other than the United States. Some manufacturers may develop lighters that meet the requirements of the rule for distribution in the United States, but continue to distribute the current, non-child-resistant models in other countries. Thus, some manufacturers may incur the incremental costs associated with producing multiple lines of similar products. These costs could include extra administrative costs required to maintain different lines and the incremental costs of producing different lines of similar products, such as using different molds or different assembly steps. These costs would, however, be mitigated if similar or identical standards were adopted by other countries. In total, the rule will likely increase the cost of manufacturing multi-purpose lighters by about $0.48 per unit.

9. At the present time, one manufacturer has about 80–90% of the market for multi-purpose lighters. The other manufacturers, importers, and private labelers divide up the remaining 10–20% of the market. Thus, there is already a very high degree of concentration in the market. Even so, at least two manufacturers have already entered the market with models that are believed to meet the requirements of the rule and at least one other firm is believed to be actively developing a child-resistant lighter. Therefore, the rule is not expected to have any significant impact on competition. Moreover, other firms are expected to enter the market for multi-purpose lighters, and thereby increase competition, as the market expands. Firms that market child-resistant multi-purpose lighters before the standard's effective date may gain an initial competitive advantage. However, any differential impact is likely to be slight and short-lived. Other manufacturers can be expected to have child-resistant multi-purpose lighters developed and ready to market before or soon after the rule goes into effect.

D. *Impact on consumers*. Aside from increased safety, the rule is likely to affect consumers in two ways. First, the increased cost for producing the child-resistant models will likely result in higher retail prices for multi-purpose lighters. Second, the utility derived from child-resistant lighters may be decreased if complying lighters are less easy to operate.

1. Assuming a 100% markup over the incremental cost to manufacturers (estimated at $0.48/unit), the rule may be expected to increase the retail price of multi-purpose lighters by $0.96 per unit. The per-unit price increase for micro-torches and other high-end multi-purpose lighters may be higher due to the smaller numbers of such lighters produced.

2. The utility that consumers receive from multi-purpose lighters may be reduced if the rule makes the lighters more difficult to operate. This could result in some consumers switching to substitute products, such as matches. However, as with child-resistant cigarette lighters, the increased difficulty of operating child-resistant multi-purpose lighters is expected to be slight. Moreover, even if some consumers do switch to other products, the risk of fire is not expected to increase significantly. Most cigarette lighters (one possible substitute) must already meet the same child-resistant standard as those applicable to multi-purpose lighters. Although consumers that switch to matches may increase the risk of child-play fires somewhat, matches seem to be inherently

more child resistant than are non-child-resistant multi-purpose lighters. Previously, the CPSC determined that non-child-resistant cigarette lighters were 1.4 times as likely as matches to be involved in child-play fires and 3.9 times as likely to be involved in a child-play death. Thus, even if some consumers did switch to using matches, the risk of child-play fires would still likely be less than if they continued to use non-child-resistant multi-purpose lighters.

3. The total societal costs of fires known to have been started during 1995 through 1998 by children under age 5 playing with multi-purpose lighters was approximately $194.2 million, or $48.6 million per year. This is probably an underestimate, since it only includes the cases of which CPSC is aware. During the same period, an estimated 20 million multi-purpose lighters were available for use each year. The societal costs of the fires started by young children attempting to operate multi-purpose lighters is, therefore, about $2.43 per lighter ($48.6 million ÷ 20 million lighters) per year. The rule is expected to reduce this cost by 75 to 84%. Therefore, the expected societal benefit of the rule in terms of reduced fires, deaths, injuries, and property damage is expected to be at least $1.82 per complying lighter sold.

4. As discussed above, the rule may increase the cost of manufacturing multi-purpose lighters by $0.48 and may increase the retail prices by as much as $0.96. Therefore, assuming that sales of multi-purpose lighters remain the same, the net benefit (benefits minus costs) of the rule to consumers is expected to be at least $0.86 per unit ($1.82—$0.96). Based on annual sales of approximately 20 million units per year, the rule would result in an annual net benefit to consumers at least $17.2 million (20 million × $0.86) annually.

5. The actual level of benefits observed could be higher if some multi-purpose lighters are stored with the on/off switch in the "on" position. If a significant number of consumers commonly store multi-purpose lighters with the switch on, the effective level of child resistance of multi-purpose lighters currently in use may be lower than indicated by CPSC's baseline testing. This would increase the effectiveness of the rule and the value of the net benefits.

E. *Any means of achieving the objective of the order while minimizing adverse effects on competition or disruption or dislocation of manufacturing and other commercial practices consistent with the public health and safety.* 1. The performance requirements of this part 1212 are based on the Commission's Safety Standard for Cigarette Lighters, 16 CFR part 1210. In developing that standard, the Commission considered the potential effects on competition and business practices of various aspects of the standard, and incorporated some burden-reducing elements into the standard.

2. One possible alternative to this mandatory standard would be for the Commission to rely on voluntary conformance to the requirements of the standard to provide safety to consumers. The expected level of conformance to a voluntary standard is uncertain, however. Although some of the largest firms may market some child-resistant multi-purpose lighters that conform to these requirements, most firms (possibly including some of the largest) probably would not. Even under generous assumptions about the level of voluntary conformance, net benefits to consumers would be substantially lower under this alternative than under the standard. Thus, the Commission finds that reliance on voluntary conformance to the provisions of this part 1212 would not adequately reduce the unreasonable risk associated with multi-purpose lighters.

F. *The rule (including its effective date) is reasonably necessary to eliminate or reduce an unreasonable risk of injury.* The Commission's hazard data and regulatory analysis demonstrate that multi-purpose lighters covered by the standard pose an unreasonable risk of death and injury to consumers. The Commission considered a number of alternatives to address this risk, and believes that the standard strikes the most reasonable balance between risk reduction benefits and potential costs. Further, the amount of time before the standard becomes effective (one year after publication of the final rule) will provide manufacturers and importers of most products adequate time to design, produce, and market safer multi-purpose lighters. Thus, the Commission finds that the standard and its effective date are reasonably necessary to reduce the risk of fire-related death and injury associated with young children playing with multi-purpose lighters.

G. *The benefits expected from the rule bear a reasonable relationship to its costs.* The standard will substantially reduce the number of fire-related deaths, injuries, and property damage associated with young children playing with multi-purpose lighters. The cost of these accidents, which is estimated to be greater than $48.6 million annually, will also be greatly reduced. The rule is expected to reduce this societal cost by 75–84%, or by greater than $36.5 million. The estimated annual costs to the public are expected to be less than $20 million. Therefore, substantial net benefits will accrue to consumers. Thus, the Commission finds that a reasonable relationship exists between the expected benefits and the expected costs of the standard.

H. *The rule imposes the least burdensome requirement which prevents or adequately reduces the risk of injury for which the rule is being promulgated.* 1. The Commission incorporated a number of features from the cigarette lighter standard, 16 CFR part 1210, in order to minimize the potential burden of the rule on industry and consumers. The Commission also considered alternatives involving different performance and test requirements and different definitions determining the scope of coverage among products. Alternatives that would be more burdensome to industry would have higher costs to consumers. Less burdensome alternatives would have lowered the risk-reduction benefits to consumers. No alternative has been identified that would result in a higher level of net benefits to consumers.

2. A less stringent acceptance criterion of 80% (rather than the standard's 85%) might slightly reduce costs to industry and consumers. The safety benefits of this alternative, however, would likely be reduced disproportionately to the potential reduction in costs. A higher (90%) acceptance criterion was also considered. This higher performance level may not be commercially or technically feasible for many firms, however. The Commission believes that this more stringent alternative would have substantial adverse effects on manufacturing and competition, and would increase costs disproportionate to benefits. The Commission believes that the requirement that complying multi-purpose lighters not be operable by at least 85% of children in prescribed tests strikes a reasonable balance between improved safety for a substantial majority of young children and other potential fire victims and the potential for adverse competitive effects and manufacturing disruption.

3. The standard becomes effective 12 months after it is issued December 22, 2000. The Commission also considered an effective date of 6 months after the date of issuance of the final rule. Although most multi-purpose lighters sold in the U.S. could probably be made child-resistant within 6 months, the supply of some imported multi-purpose lighters would be disrupted. The 12-month period in the standard would minimize this potential effect, and would allow more time for firms to design, produce, and import complying multi-purpose lighters. The Commission estimates that there would be no significant adverse impact on the overall supply of multi-purpose lighters for the U.S. market. A longer effective date was deemed unsuitable because it would unduly delay the lifesaving benefits of the standard and would penalize firms that have already begun to develop child-resistant multi-purpose lighters.

I. *The promulgation of the rule is in the public interest.* As required by the CPSA and the Regulatory Flexibility Act, the Commission considered the potential benefits and costs of the standard and various alternatives. The standard provides substantial net benefits to society. Although certain alternatives to the final rule were estimated to also have net benefits to consumers, they would decrease the level of safety. Therefore, the Commission finds that the standard is in the public interest.

PART 1213—SAFETY STANDARD FOR ENTRAPMENT HAZARDS IN BUNK BEDS

AUTHORITY: 15 U.S.C. 2056, 2058.

SOURCE: 64 FR 71899, Dec. 22, 1999, unless otherwise noted.

§ 1213.1 Scope, application, and effective date.

(a) *Scope, basis, and purpose.* This part 1213, a consumer product safety standard, prescribes requirements for bunk beds to reduce or eliminate the risk that children will die or be injured from being trapped between the upper bunk and the wall, in openings below guardrails, or in other structures in the bed.

(b) *Application and effective date.* The standard in this part applies to all bunk beds, except those manufactured only for institutional use, that are manufactured in the United States, or imported, on or after June 19, 2000. (Facilities intended for use by children under age 6 are not considered to be institutions.) Bunk beds intended for use by children are subject to the requirements in 16 CFR 1500.18(a)(18) and 16 CFR part 1513, and not to this part 1213. However, those regulations are substantively identical to the requirements in this part 1213.

§ 1213.2 Definitions.

As used in this part 1213:

Bed. See *Bunk bed.*

Bed end structure means an upright unit at the head and foot of the bed to which the side rails attach.

Bunk bed means a bed in which the underside of any foundation is over 30 inches (760 mm) from the floor.

Foundation means the base or support on which a mattress rests.

Guardrail means a rail or guard on a side of the upper bunk to prevent a sleeping occupant from falling or rolling out.

§ 1213.3 Requirements.

(a) *Guardrails.* (1) Any bunk bed shall provide at least two guardrails, at least one on each side of the bed, for each bed having the underside of its foundation more than 30 inches (760 mm) from the floor.

(2) One guardrail shall be continuous between each of the bed's end structures. "Continuous" means that any gap between the guardrail and end structure shall not exceed 0.22 inches (5.6 mm) (so as to not cause a finger entrapment hazard for a child).

(3) The other guardrail may terminate before reaching the bed's end structures, providing there is no more than 15 inches (380 mm) between either end of the guardrail and the nearest bed end structures.

(4) For bunk beds designed to have a ladder attached to one side of the bed, the continuous guardrail shall be on the other side of the bed.

(5) Guardrails shall be attached so that they cannot be removed without either intentionally releasing a fastening device or applying forces sequentially in different directions.

(6) The upper edge of the guardrails shall be no less than 5 inches (130 mm) above the top surface of the mattress when a mattress of the maximum thickness specified by the bed manufacturer's instructions is on the bed. This requirement does not prohibit a wall-side guardrail that terminates in a quarter-circle bend and attaches to the side rail of the upper bunk foundation.

(7) With no mattress on the bed, there shall be no openings in the structure between the lower edge of the uppermost member of the guardrail and the underside of the upper bunk's foundation that would permit passage of the wedge block shown in Figure 1 of this part when tested in accordance with the procedure at § 1213.4(a).

(b) *Bed end structures.* (1) The upper edge of the upper bunk end structures shall be at least 5 inches (130 mm) above the top surface of the mattress for at least 50 percent of the distance between the two posts at the head and foot of the upper bunk when a mattress and foundation of the maximum thickness specified by the manufacturer's instructions is on the bed.

(2) With no mattress on the bed, there shall be no openings in the end structures above the foundation of the upper bunk that will permit the free passage of the wedge block shown in Figure 1 when tested in accordance with the procedure at § 1213.4(b).

(3) When tested in accordance with § 1213.4(c), there shall be no openings in the end structures between the underside of the foundation of the upper bunk and upper side of the foundation of the lower bunk that will permit the free passage of the wedge block shown in Figure 1, unless the openings are also large enough to permit the free passage of a 9-inch (230-mm) diameter rigid sphere.

(4) All portions of the boundary of any opening required by §§ 1213.4(c)(1) and (2) to be probed by the wedge block of Figure 1, and that permits free passage of a 9-inch diameter sphere, must conform to the neck entrapment requirements of § 1213.4(c)(3).

§ 1213.4 Test methods.

(a) *Guardrails* (see § 1213.3(a)(6)). With no mattress on the bed, place the wedge block shown in Figure 1, tapered side first, into each opening in the bed structure below the lower edge of the uppermost member of the guardrail and above the underside of the upper bunk's foundation. Orient the block so that it is most likely to pass through the opening (*e.g.*, the major axis of the block parallel to the major axis of the opening) ("most adverse orientation"). Then gradually apply a 33-lbf (147–N) force in a direction perpendicular to the plane of the large end of the block. Sustain the force for 1 minute.

(b) *Upper bunk end structure* (see § 1213.3(b)(2)). Without a mattress or foundation on the upper bunk, place the wedge block shown in Figure 1 into each opening, tapered side first, and in the most adverse orientation. Determine if the wedge block can pass freely through the opening.

(c) *Lower bunk end structure* (see § 1213.3(b)(3)). (1) Without a mattress or foundation on the lower bunk, place the wedge block shown in Figure 1, tapered side first, into each opening in the lower bunk end structure in the most adverse orientation. Determine whether the wedge block can pass freely through the opening. If the wedge block passes freely through the opening, determine whether a 9-inch (230-mm) diameter rigid sphere can pass freely through the opening.

(2) With the manufacturer's recommended maximum thickness mattress and foundation in place, repeat the test in paragraph (c)(1) of this section.

(3) All portions of the boundary of any opening that is required to be probed by the wedge block of Figure 1 by paragraphs (c)(1) and (c)(2) of this section, and that permits free passage of a 9-inch diameter sphere, must satisfy the requirements of paragraphs (c)(3)(i) and (c)(3)(ii) of this section addressing neck entrapment.

(i) Insert the "A" section of the test template shown in Figure 2 of this part into the portion of the boundary of the opening to be tested, with the plane of the template in the plane of the opening and with the centerline of the top of the template (as shown in Figure 2) aligned parallel to the centerline of the opening, until motion is stopped by contact between the test template and the boundaries of the opening (see Figure 3 of this part). By visual inspection, determine if there is simultaneous contact between the boundary of the opening and both sides of the "A" section of the template. If simultaneous contact occurs, mark the contact points on the boundary of the opening and conduct the additional test described in paragraph (c)(3)(ii) of this section.

(ii) To check the potential for neck entrapment, place the neck portion of the "B" section of the template into the opening, with its plane perpendicular to both the plane of the opening and the centerline of the opening (see Figure 4 of this part). If the neck portion of the "B" section of the template completely enters the opening (passes 0.75 inch or more beyond the points previously contacted by the "A" section of the template), the opening is considered to present a neck entrapment hazard and fails the test, unless its lower boundary slopes downward at 45° or more for the whole distance from the narrowest part of the opening the neck can reach to the part of the opening that will freely pass a 9-inch diameter sphere.

§ 1213.5 Marking and labeling.

(a) There shall be a permanent label or marking on each bed stating the name and address (city, state, and zip code) of the manufacturer, distributor, or retailer; the model number; and the month and year of manufacture.

(b) The following warning label shall be permanently attached to the inside of an upper bunk bed end structure in a location that cannot be covered by the bedding but that may be covered by the placement of a pillow.

⚠ **WARNING**

To help prevent serious or fatal injuries from entrapment or falls:

- Never allow a child under 6 years on upper bunk
- Use only a mattress that is __ inches long and __ inches wide on upper bunk
- Ensure thickness of mattress and foundation combined does not exceed __ inches and that mattress surface is at least 5 inches below upper edge of guardrails

DO NOT REMOVE THIS LABEL

§ 1213.6 Instructions.

Instructions shall accompany each bunk bed set, and shall include the following information.

(a) *Size of mattress and foundation.* The length and width of the intended mattress and foundation shall be clearly stated, either numerically or in conventional terms such as twin size, twin extra-long, etc. In addition, the maximum thickness of the mattress and foundation required for compliance with § 1213.3(a)(5) and (b)(1) shall be stated.

(b) *Safety warnings.* The instructions shall provide the following safety warnings:

(1) Do not allow children under 6 years of age to use the upper bunk.

(2) Use guardrails on both sides of the upper bunk.

(3) Prohibit horseplay on or under beds.

(4) Prohibit more than one person on upper bunk.

(5) Use ladder for entering or leaving upper bunk.

(6) If the bunk bed will be placed next to a wall, the guardrail that runs the full length of the bed should be placed against the wall to prevent entrapment between the bed and the wall. (This applies only to bunk beds without two full-length guardrails.)

§ 1213.7 Findings.

The Consumer Product Safety Act requires that the Commission, in order to issue a standard, make the following findings and include them in the rule. 15 U.S.C. 2058(f)(3). These findings are contained in the appendix to this part 1213.

(a) The rule in this part (including its effective date of June 19, 2000 is reasonably necessary to eliminate or reduce an unreasonable risk of injury associated with the product.

[These findings are contained in the appendix to this part 1213.]

(b) Promulgation of the rule is in the public interest.

(c) Where a voluntary standard has been adopted and implemented by the affected industry, that compliance with such voluntary standard is not likely to result in the elimination or adequate reduction of the risk of injury; or it is unlikely that there will be substantial compliance with such voluntary standard.

(d) The benefits expected from the rule bear a reasonable relationship to its costs.

(e) The rule imposes the least burdensome requirement that prevents or adequately reduces the risk of injury for which the rule is being promulgated.

FIGURE 1 TO PART 1213—WEDGE BLOCK FOR TESTS IN §1213.4(a), (b) AND (c)

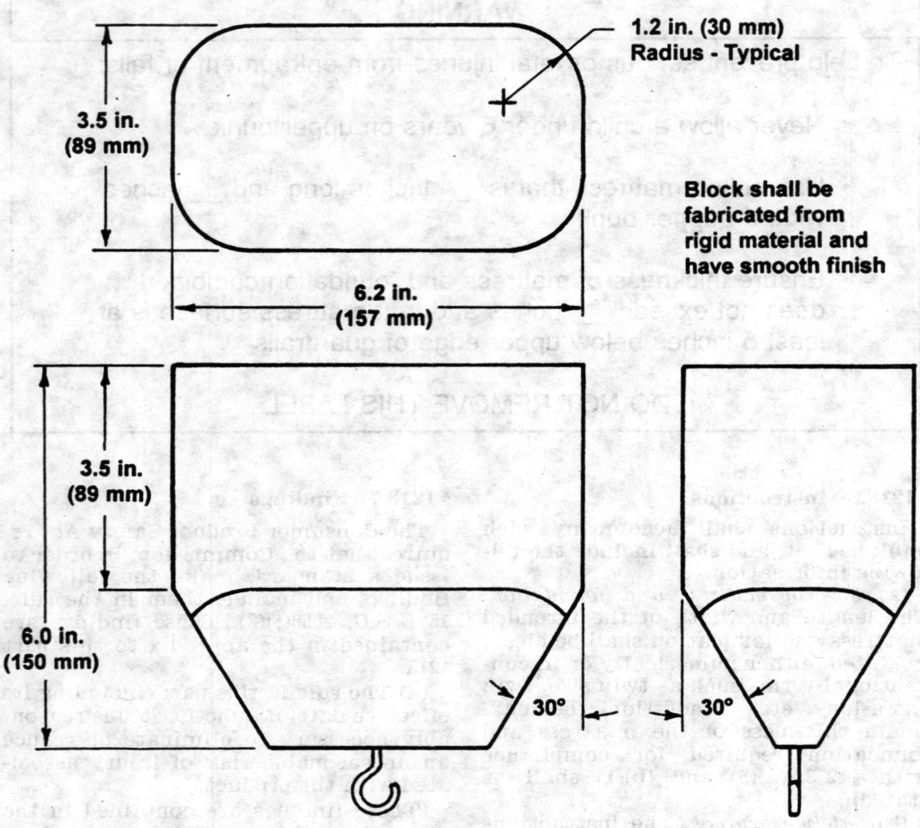

Figure 1 to Part 1213 - Wedge Block for Tests in § 1213.4(a), (b) and (c)

FIGURE 2 TO PART 1213—TEST TEMPLATE FOR NECK ENTRAPMENT

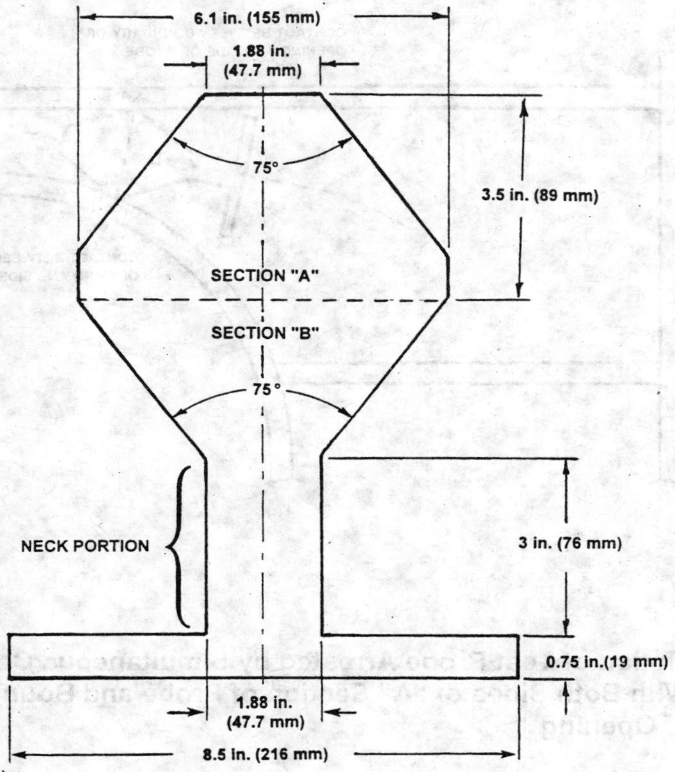

NOTE – Probe to be constructed from any rigid material 0.75 in. (19 mm) thick

Fig. 2 – Test Probe for Neck Entrapment

FIGURE 3 TO PART 1213—MOTION OF TEST TEMPLATE ARRESTED BY SIMULTANEOUS CONTACT WITH BOTH SIDES OF "A" SECTION AND BOUNDARIES OF OPENING

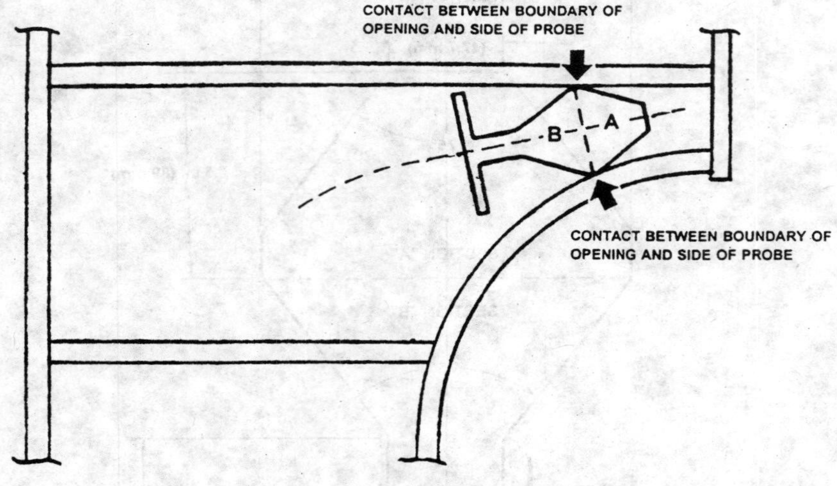

Fig. 3 – Motion of Test Probe Arrested by Simultaneous Contact With Both Sides of "A" Section of Probe and Boundaries of Opening

FIGURE 4 TO PART 1213—NECK PORTION OF "B" SECTION OF TEMPLATE ENTERS COMPLETELY INTO OPENING

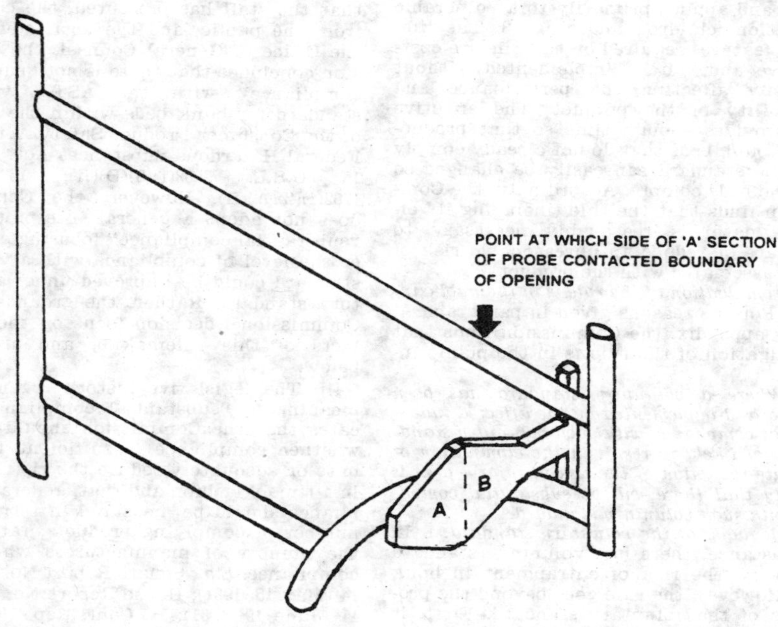

Fig 4 – Neck Portion of "B" Section of Probe Enters Completely into Opening

APPENDIX TO PART 1213—FINDINGS UNDER THE CONSUMER PRODUCT SAFETY ACT

The Consumer Product Safety Act requires that the Commission, in order to issue a standard, make the following findings and include them in the rule. 15 U.S.C. 2058(f)(3). Because of this, the facts and determinations in these findings apply as of the date the rule was issued, December 22, 1999.

A. *The rule in this part* (including its effective date of June 19, 2000) *is reasonably necessary to eliminate or reduce an unreasonable risk of injury associated with the product.*

1. For a recent 9.6-year period, the CPSC received reports of 57 deaths of children under age 15 who died when they were trapped between the upper bunk of a bunk bed and the wall or when they were trapped in openings in the bed's structure. Over 96% of those who died in entrapment incidents were age 3 or younger. On average, averting these deaths is expected to produce a benefit to society with a present value of about $175 to $350 for each bed that otherwise would not have complied with one or more of the rule's requirements.

2. This increased safety will be achieved in two ways. First, all bunk beds will be required to have a guardrail on both sides of the bed. If the bed is placed against a wall, the guardrail on that side is expected to prevent a child from being entrapped between the bed and the wall. The guardrail on the wall side of the bed must extend continuously from one end to the other. Second, the end structures of the bed must be constructed so that, if an opening in the end structure is large enough so a child can slip his or her body through it, it must be large enough that the child's head also can pass through.

3. For the reasons discussed in paragraph D. of this appendix, the benefits of the

changes to bunk beds caused by this rule will have a reasonable relationship to the changes' costs. The rule addresses a risk of death, and applies primarily to a vulnerable population, children under age 3. The lifesaving features required by the rule are cost-effective and can be implemented without adversely affecting the performance and availability of the product. The effective date provides enough time so that production of bunk beds that do not already comply with the standard can easily be changed so that the beds comply. Accordingly, the Commission finds that the rule (including its effective date) is reasonably necessary to eliminate or reduce an unreasonable risk of injury associated with the product.

B. *Promulgation of the rule is in the public interest.* For the reasons given in paragraph A. of this appendix, the Commission finds that promulgation of the rule is in the public interest.

C. *Where a voluntary standard has been adopted and implemented by the affected industry, that compliance with such voluntary standard is not likely to result in the elimination or adequate reduction of the risk of injury; or it is unlikely that there will be substantial compliance with such voluntary standard.*

1. *Adequacy of the voluntary standard.* i. In this instance, there is a voluntary standard addressing the risk of entrapment in bunk beds. However, the rule goes beyond the provisions of the voluntary standard. First, it eliminates the voluntary standard's option to have an opening of up to 15 inches at each end of the wall-side guardrail. Second, it requires more of the lower bunk end structures to have entrapment protection. The voluntary standard protects against entrapment only within the 9-inch space immediately above the upper surface of the lower bunk's mattress. The mandatory standard extends this area of protection upward to the level of the underside of the upper bunk foundation. Both of these provisions, which are in the rule but not in the voluntary standard, address fatalities and, as noted in paragraph D of this appendix, have benefits that bear a reasonable relationship to their costs.

ii. Therefore, the Commission finds that compliance with the voluntary standard is not likely to result in the elimination or adequate reduction of the risk of entrapment injury or death.

2. *Substantial compliance.* i. Neither the CPSA nor the FHSA define "substantial compliance." The March 3, 1999 Notice of Proposed Rulemaking summarized an interpretation of "substantial compliance" that the Office of General Counsel provided to the Commission. 64 Fed. Reg. 10245, 10248–49 (March 3, 1999). The Commission specifically invited public comment on that interpretation from "all persons who would be affected by such an interpretation." *Id.* at 10249. The Commission received more than 20 comments on the interpretation.

ii. Having now considered all the evidence that the staff has presented, the comments from the public, and the legal advice from the Office of General Counsel, the Commission concludes that there is not "substantial compliance" with the ASTM voluntary standard for bunk beds within the meaning of the Consumer Product Safety Act and the Federal Hazardous Substances Act. See, *e.g.*, 15 U.S.C. 2058(f)(3)(D)(ii); 15 U.S.C. 1262(i)(2)(A)(ii). However, the Commission does not adopt a general interpretation of "substantial compliance" focusing on whether the level of compliance with a voluntary standard could be improved under a mandatory standard. Rather, the grounds for the Commission's decision focus on the specific facts of this rulemaking and are stated below.

iii. The legislative history regarding the meaning of "substantial compliance" indicates that the Commission should consider whether compliance is sufficient to eliminate or adequately reduce the risk of injury in a timely fashion and that, generally, compliance should be measured in terms of the number of complying products, rather than the number of manufacturers who are in compliance. *E.g.*, Senate Report No. 97–102, p. 14 (May 15, 1981); House Report No. 97–158, p. 11 (June 19, 1981); H. Conf. Rep. No. 97–208, 97th Cong., 1st Sess. 871, reprinted in 1981 U.S. Code Cong. & Admin. News 1010, 1233.

iv. Given this Congressional guidance, the Commission believes it appropriate to examine the number of conforming products as the starting point for analysis. However, the Commission does not believe that there is any single percentage of conforming products that can be used in all cases to define "substantial compliance." Instead, the percentage must be viewed in the context of the hazard the product presents. Thus, the Commission must examine what constitutes substantial compliance with a voluntary standard in light of its obligation to safeguard the American consumer.

v. There are certain factors the agency considers before it initiates regulatory action, such as the severity of the potential injury, whether there is a vulnerable population at risk, and the risk of injury. See 16 CFR 1009.8. These and other factors also appropriately inform the Commission's decision regarding whether a certain level of conformance with a voluntary standard is substantial. In the light of these factors, industry's compliance rate with the voluntary standard for bunk beds is not substantial.

vi. In this case, the Commission deals with the most severe risk—death—to one of the most vulnerable segments of our population—infants and young children. While the risk of death is not high, it exists whenever a young child is in a residence with a nonconforming bunk bed.

vii. Additionally, some products, such as hairdryers without shock protection devices, require some intervening action (dropping the hair dryer into water) to create the hazard. By contrast, deaths in bunk beds occur during the intended use of the product—a child rolling over in bed or climbing in or out of it—without any intervening action.

viii. The Commission must also consider that bunk beds have a very long product life, frequently being passed on to several families before being discarded. Thus, a number of children may be exposed to a bed during its useful life. Every noncomplying bed that poses an entrapment hazard presents the potential risk of death to any young child in the house. It is a risk that is hard for a parent to protect against, as children find their way onto these beds even if they are not put to sleep in them.

ix. Bunk beds are products that can be made relatively easily by very small companies, or even by a single individual. The Office of Compliance believes smaller entities will always present a compliance problem, because new manufacturers can enter the marketplace relatively easily and need little expertise to make a wooden bunk bed. The evidence seems to support the view that there will always be an irreducible number of new, smaller bunk bed manufacturers who will not follow the voluntary standard.

x. What constitutes substantial compliance is also a function of what point in time the issue is examined. In 1989, the Commission denied a petition for a mandatory bunk bed rule. At that time, industry was predicting that by April of 1989, 90% of all beds being manufactured would comply with the voluntary guidelines. But that was in the context of years of steadily increasing conformance and the hope that conformance would continue to grow and that deaths and near-misses would begin to decline. But the conformance level never grew beyond the projection for 1989 and deaths and near-misses have not dropped.

xi. Even with the existing compliance rate, the Commission is contemplating the prospect of perhaps 50,000 nonconforming beds a year (or more) entering the marketplace, with many beds remaining in use for perhaps 20 years or longer. Under these circumstances, a 10% rate of noncompliance is too high.

xii. It is now clear that the bunk bed voluntary standard has not achieved an adequate reduction of the unreasonable risk of death to infants and children in a timely fashion, and it is unlikely to do so. Accordingly, the Commission finds that substantial compliance with the voluntary standard for bunk beds is unlikely.

xiii. Products that present some or all of the following factors might not be held to as strict a substantial compliance analysis. Those which:

—Rarely or never cause death;
—Cause only less severe injuries;
—Do not cause deaths or injuries principally to a vulnerable segment of the population;
—Are not intended for children and which have no special attraction for children;
—Have a relatively short life span;
—Are made by a few stable manufacturers or which can only be made by specialized manufacturers needing a significant manufacturing investment to produce the product;
—Are covered by a voluntary standard which continues to capture an increasing amount of noncomplying products; or
—Require some additional intervening action to be hazardous.

xiv. And, in analyzing some other product, there could be other factors that would have to be taken into consideration in determining what level of compliance is adequate to protect the public. The tolerance for nonconformance levels has to bear some relationship to the magnitude and manageability of the hazard addressed.

xv. The Commission emphasizes that its decision is not based on the argument that a mandatory rule provides more powerful enforcement tools. If this were sufficient rationale, mandatory rules could always displace voluntary standards, and this clearly was not Congress's intent. But, with a mandatory standard, the necessity of complying with a mandatory federal regulation will be understandable to small manufacturers. State and local governments will have no doubt about their ability to help us in our efforts to locate these manufacturers.

D. *The benefits expected from the rule bear a reasonable relationship to its costs.*

1. *Bunk beds that do not comply with ASTM's requirements for guardrails.* The cost of providing a second guardrail for bunk beds that do not have one is expected to be from $15–40 per otherwise noncomplying bed. If, as expected, the standard prevents virtually all of the deaths it addresses, the present value of the benefits of this modification are estimated to be from $175–350 per otherwise noncomplying bed. Thus, the benefit of this provision is about 4–23 times its cost.

2. *Bunk beds that comply with ASTM's requirements for guardrails.* The voluntary standard allows up to a 15-inch gap in the coverage of the guardrail on the wall side of the upper bunk. Additional entrapment deaths are addressed by requiring that the wall-side guardrail be continuous from one end of the bed to the other. The estimated present value of the benefits of this requirement is $2.40 to $3.50 per otherwise noncomplying bed. The Commission estimates that

the materials cost to extend one guardrail an additional 30 inches (760 mm) will be less than the present value of the benefits of making the change. Further, the costs of any design changes can be amortized over the number the bunk beds manufactured after the design change is made. Thus, the costs of any design change will be nominal.

3. *Lower bunk end structures.* The Commission is aware of a death, involving entrapment in the end structures of the lower bunk, occurring in a scenario not currently addressed by the voluntary standard. This death would be addressed by extending the voluntary standard's lower bunk end structures entrapment provisions from 9 inches above the lower bunk's sleeping surface to the bottom of the upper bunk and by also including a test for neck entrapment in this area. The Commission expects the costs of this requirement to be design-related only, and small. Indeed, for some bunk beds, materials costs may decrease since less material may be required to comply with these requirements than is currently being used. Again, the design costs for these modifications to the end structures can be amortized over the subsequent production run of the bed.

4. *Effect on market.* The small additional costs from any wall-side guardrails and end-structure modifications are not expected to affect the market for bunk beds, either alone or added to the costs of compliance to ASTM's provisions.

5. *Conclusion.* The Commission has no reason to conclude that any of the standard's requirements will have costs that exceed the requirement's expected benefits. Further, the total effect of the rule is that the benefits of the rule will exceed its costs by about 4–23 times. Accordingly, the Commission concludes that the benefits expected from the rule bear a reasonable relationship to its costs.

E. *The rule imposes the least burdensome requirement that prevents or adequately reduces the risk of injury for which the rule is being promulgated.* 1. The Commission considered relying on the voluntary standard, either alone or combined with a third-party certification program. However, the Commission concluded that a mandatory program will be more effective in reducing these deaths, each of which is caused by an unreasonable risk of entrapment. Accordingly, these alternatives would not prevent or adequately reduce the risk of injury for which the rule is being promulgated.

2. The Commission also considered a suggestion that bunk beds that conformed to the voluntary standard be so labeled. Consumers could then compare conforming and nonconforming beds at the point of purchase and make their purchase decisions with this safety information in mind. This, however, would not necessarily reduce injuries, because consumers likely would not know there is a voluntary standard and thus would not see any risk in purchasing a bed that was not labeled as conforming to the standard.

3. For the reasons stated in this appendix, no alternatives to a mandatory rule have been suggested that would adequately reduce the deaths caused by entrapment of children in bunk beds. Accordingly, the Commission finds that this rule imposes the least burdensome requirement that prevents or adequately reduces the risk of injury for which the rule is being promulgated.

PART 1215—SAFETY STANDARD FOR INFANT BATH SEATS

AUTHORITY: Sections 3 and 104 of Pub. L. 110–314, 122 Stat. 3016 (August 14, 2008); section 3 of Pub. L. 112–28, 125 Stat. 273 (August 12, 2011).

SOURCE: 75 FR 31698, June 4, 2010, unless otherwise noted.

§ 1215.1 Scope.

This part 1215 establishes a consumer product safety standard for infant bath seats manufactured or imported on or after December 6, 2010.

§ 1215.2 Requirements for infant bath seats.

Each infant bath seat shall comply with all applicable provisions of ASTM F1967–11a, Standard Consumer Safety Specification for Infant Bath Seats, approved September 1, 2011. The Director of the Federal Register approves the incorporation by reference listed in this section in accordance with 5 U.S.C. 552(a) and 1 CFR part 51. You may obtain a copy of these ASTM standards from ASTM International, 100 Barr Harbor Drive, P.O. Box C700, West Conshohocken, PA 19428–2959 USA, phone: 610–832–9585; *http://www.astm.org/* . You may inspect copies at the Office of the Secretary, U.S. Consumer Product Safety Commission, Room 820, 4330 East West Highway, Bethesda, MD 20814, telephone 301–504–7923, or at the National Archives and Records Administration (NARA). For information on the availability of this material at NARA, call 202–741–6030, or go to: *http://www.archives.gov/federal_register/*

code__of__federal regulations/ ibr__locations.html.

[77 FR 45245, July 31, 2012]

PART 1216—SAFETY STANDARD FOR INFANT WALKERS

AUTHORITY: The Consumer Product Safety Improvement Act of 2008, Pub. L. 110–314, §104, 122 Stat. 3016 (August 14, 2008).

SOURCE: 75 FR 35273, June 21, 2010, unless otherwise noted.

§ 1216.1 Scope.

This part 1216 establishes a consumer product safety standard for infant walkers manufactured or imported on or after December 21, 2010.

§ 1216.2 Requirements for infant walkers.

(a) Except as provided in paragraph (b) of this section, each infant walker shall comply with all applicable provisions of ASTM F 977–07, Standard Consumer Safety Specification for Infant Walkers, approved April 1, 2007. The Director of the Federal Register approves this incorporation by reference in accordance with 5 U.S.C. 552(a) and 1 CFR part 51. You may obtain a copy from ASTM International, 100 Bar Harbor Drive, P.O. Box 0700, West Conshohocken, PA 19428; telephone 610–832–9585; *http://www.astm.org*. You may inspect a copy at the Office of the Secretary, U.S. Consumer Product Safety Commission, Room 820, 4330 East West Highway, Bethesda, MD 20814, telephone 301–504–7923, or at the National Archives and Records Administration (NARA). For information on the availability of this material at NARA, call 202–741–6030, or go to: *http://www.archives.gov/federal__register/ code__of__federal__regulations/ ibr__locations.html.*

(b) Comply with the ASTM F 977–07 standard with the following additions or exclusions:

(1) Instead of Figure 1 of ASTM F 977–07, comply with the following:

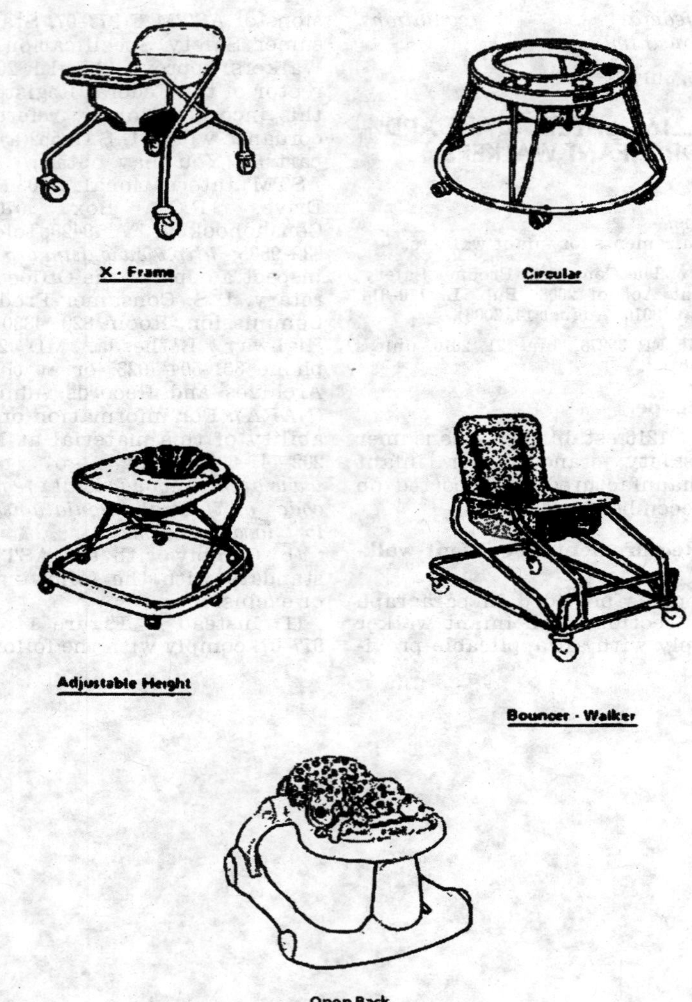

Figure 1 Illustration of Types of Infant Walkers

(2) Instead of complying with section 4.6 through 4.6.8 of ASTM F 977–07, comply with the following:

(i) 4.6 The following guidelines shall apply to force gauges used for testing:

(ii) 4.6.1 *Equipment*—Force gauge with a range of 0 to 25 lbf (110 N), tolerance of ±0.25 lbf (1.1 N). A calibration interval shall be maintained for the force guage which will ensure that the accuracy does not drift beyond the stated tolerance.

(iii) 4.6.2 *Equipment*—Force gauge with a range 0 to 100 lbf (500 N) tolerance of ±1 lbf (4.44 N). A calibration shall be maintained for the force gauge which will ensure that the accuracy does not drift beyond the stated tolerance.

(3) In addition to complying with section 6.3 of ASTM F 977–07, comply with the following:

(i) 6.4 *Parking Device (applicable to walkers equipped with parking brakes)*—The walker shall have a maximum displacement of 1.97 inches (50 mm) for each test in each direction (forward, rearward, and sideward) when tested in accordance with 7.7.

(ii) [Reserved]

(4) In addition to complying with section 7.6.1.2 of ASTM F 977–07, comply with the following:

(i) 7.6.1.2 The dummy's head shall remain unrestrained for all the step tests.

(ii) [Reserved]

(5) Following section 7.6.2 of ASTM F 977–07, use the following table instead of Table 1 Summary of Step(s) Tests:

(i) *Table 1 Summary of Step(s) Tests*

Section No.	Facing direction of walker	Weight of CAMI dummy, lb.	Simulated speed, ft/s	Apply tipover test
7.6.3	Forward	17	4	Yes.
7.6.3.6	Forward	28 (vest)	4	Yes.
7.6.4	Sideward	17	2	Yes.
7.6.4.6	Sideward	28 (vest)	2	Yes.
7.6.5	Rearward	17	4	No.
7.6.5.5	Rearward	28 (vest)	4	No.

(ii) [Reserved]

(6) Instead of complying with section 7.6.3.1 of ASTM F 977–07, comply with the following:

(i) 7.6.3.1 Center the walker on the test platform facing forward so that Plane A is perpendicular to the front edge of the platform and the walker is distance *d* from the center of the most forward wheel(s) to the edge of the test platform,

$$d_{CAMI} - \frac{\left(V_f^2 - V_o^2\right) * \left(W_{CAMI} + W_{walker} + W_{drop\ weight}\right)}{2g\left(W_{drop\ weight} - \mu_k N_{CAMI}\right)}$$

Where

V_f = Maximum velocity of walker at edge of platform = 4 ft/sec

V_o = Initial velocity = 0

W_{CAMI} = Measured weight of CAMI dummy

W_{walker} = Weight of the walker

$W_{drop\ weight}$ = Drop weight = 8 lb

μ_k = Dynamic coefficient of friction = 0.05

N_{CAMI} = Normal force (for CAMI dummy scenario) = weight of CAMI dummy and walker

g = acceleration of gravity = 32.2 ft/sec^2

Position the swivel wheels in such a way that the walker moves forward in a straight line parallel to Plane A.

(ii) [Reserved]

(7) Instead of complying with section 7.6.3.2 of ASTM F 977–07, comply with the following:

(i) 7.6.3.2 Place a CAMI infant dummy Mark II in the walker and position it as shown in Fig. 11 with the torso contacting the front of the occupant seating area and arms placed on the walker tray.

(ii) [Reserved]

(8) Instead of complying with section 7.6.3.3 of ASTM F 977–07, comply with the following:

(i) 7.6.3.3 While holding the walker stationary, attach an 8 lb (3.6 kg) weight to the front of the walker base at Plane A by means of a 7-strand military rope with 550 lb tensile strength (*e.g.*, paracord 550) and a stainless steel ball bearing pulley with an outside diameter of 1.25 in (32mm) and adjust the pulley so that the force is applied horizontally (0 ±0.5° with respect to the table surface).

(ii) [Reserved]

(9) Instead of complying with section 7.6.3.6 of ASTM F 977–07, comply with the following:

(i) 7.6.3.6 Repeat 7.6.3.1–7.6.3.5 using the CAMI dummy with the weighted vest and with distance d, computed using the following equation:

$$d_{CAMI\ w/vest} \frac{\left(V_f^2 - V_o^2\right) * \left(W_{CAMI\ w/vest} + W_{walker} + W_{drop\ weight}\right)}{2g\left(W_{drop\ weight} - \mu_k N_{CAMI\ w/vest}\right)}$$

Where

V_f = Maximum velocity of walker at edge of platform = 4 ft/sec

V_o = Initial velocity = 0

$W_{CAMI\ w/vest}$ = Measured weight of CAMI dummy and weighted vest

W_{walker} = Weight of the walker

$W_{drop\ weight}$ = Drop weight = 8 lb

μ_k = Dynamic coefficient of friction = 0.05

$N_{CAMI\ w/vest}$ = Normal force (for CAMI dummy fitted with 11 lb vest scenario) = weight of CAMI dummy + vest weight + walker weight

g = acceleration of gravity = 32.2 ft/sec²

(ii) [Reserved]

(10) In addition to complying with section 7.6.3.6 of ASTM F 977–07, comply with the following:

(i) 7.6.3.7 Repeat tests in the following sequence: Section 7.6.3.4, section 7.6.3.5, and section 7.6.3.6 two additional times.

(ii) [Reserved]

(11) Instead of complying with 7.6.4.1 of ASTM F 977–07, comply with the following:

(i) 7.6.4.1 Center the walker on the test platform facing sideways so that Plane B is perpendicular to the front edge of the platform and the walker is distance *d* from the center of the most sideward wheel(s) to the edge of the test platform,

$$d_{CAMI} = \frac{\left(V_f^2 - V_o^2\right) * \left(W_{CAMI} + W_{walker} + W_{drop\ weight}\right)}{2g\left(W_{drop\ weight} - \mu_k N_{CAMI}\right)}$$

Where

V_f = Maximum velocity of walker at edge of platform = 2 ft/sec

V_o = Initial velocity = 0

W_{CAMI} = Measured weight of CAMI dummy

W_{walker} = Weight of the walker

$W_{drop\ weight}$ = Drop weight = 8 lb

μ_k = Dynamic coefficient of friction = 0.05

N_{CAMI} = Normal force (for CAMI dummy scenario) = weight of CAMI dummy and walker

g = acceleration of gravity = 32.2 ft/sec²

Position the swivel wheels in such a way that the walker moves sideward in a straight line parallel to Plane B.

(ii) [Reserved]

(12) Instead of complying with section 7.6.4.3 of ASTM F 977–07, comply with the following:

(i) 7.6.4.3 While holding the walker stationary, attach an 8 lb (3.6 kg) weight to the side of the walker base at Plane B by means of a rope (as specified in 7.6.3.3) and a pulley (as specified in 7.6.3.3) and adjust the pulley so that the force is applied horizontally (0 ±0.5° with respect to the table surface).

(ii) [Reserved]

(13) Instead of complying with section 7.6.4.6 of ASTM F 977–07, comply with the following:

(i) 7.6.4.6 Repeat 7.6.4.1 through 7.6.4.5 using the CAMI dummy with the weighted vest (see Fig. 12) and with distance d, computed using the following equation:

$$d_{CAMI\ w/vest} = \frac{\left(V_f^2 - V_o^2\right) * \left(W_{CAMI\ w/vest} + W_{walker} + W_{drop\ weight}\right)}{2g\left(W_{drop\ weight} - \mu_k N_{CAMI\ w/vest}\right)}$$

Where

V_f = Maximum velocity of walker at edge of platform = 2 ft/sec
V_o = Initial velocity = 0
$W_{CAMI\ w/vest}$ = Measured weight of CAMI dummy and weighted vest
W_{walker} = Weight of the walker
$W_{drop\ weight}$ = Drop weight = 8 lb
μ_k = Dynamic coefficient of friction = 0.05
$N_{CAMI\ w/vest}$ = Normal force (for CAMI dummy fitted with 11 lb vest scenario) = weight of CAMI dummy + vest weight + walker weight
g = acceleration of gravity = 32.2 ft/sec^{2}"

(ii) [Reserved]

(14) In addition to complying with section 7.6.4.6 of ASTM F 977–07, comply with the following:

(i) 7.6.4.7 Repeat tests in the following sequence: section 7.6.4.4, section 7.6.4.5, and section 7.6.4.6 two additional times.

(ii) [Reserved]

(15) Instead of complying with Figure 10, use the following:

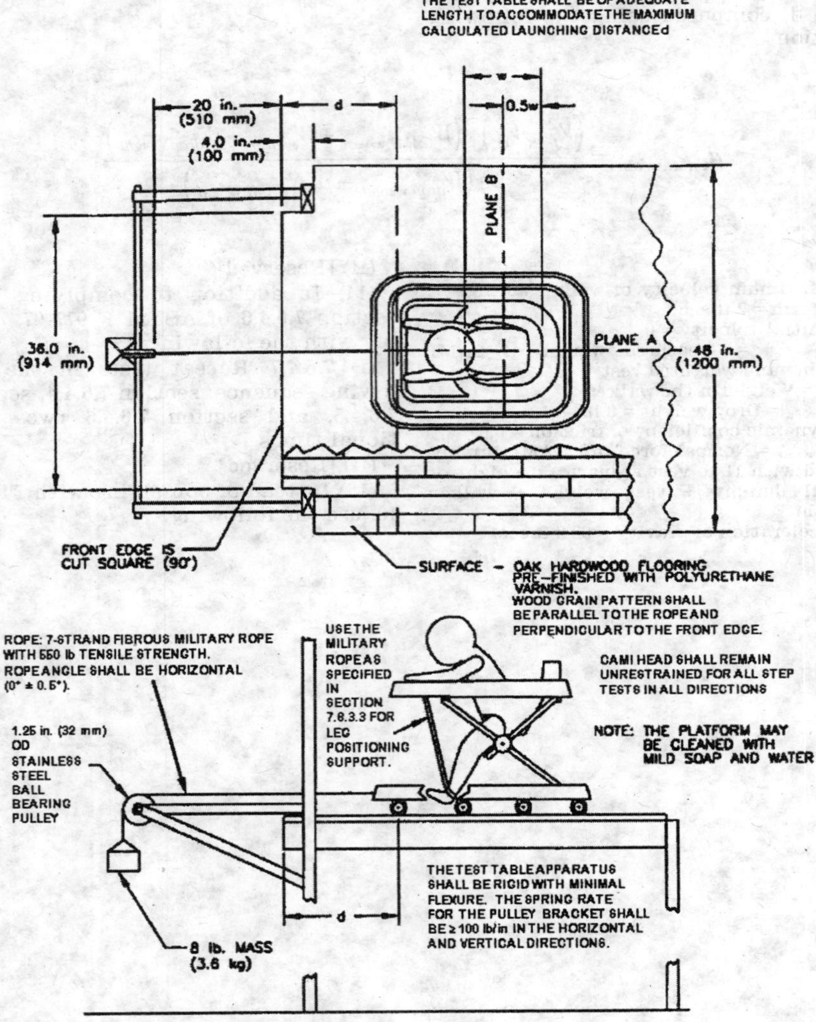
THE TEST TABLE SHALL BE OF ADEQUATE LENGTH TO ACCOMMODATE THE MAXIMUM CALCULATED LAUNCHING DISTANCE d
20 in. (510 mm)
d
4.0 in. (100 mm)
w
0.5w
PLANE B
PLANE A
36.0 in. (914 mm)
48 in. (1200 mm)
FRONT EDGE IS CUT SQUARE (90°)
SURFACE - OAK HARDWOOD FLOORING PRE-FINISHED WITH POLYURETHANE VARNISH.
WOOD GRAIN PATTERN SHALL BE PARALLEL TO THE ROPE AND PERPENDICULAR TO THE FRONT EDGE.
ROPE: 7-STRAND FIBROUS MILITARY ROPE WITH 550 lb TENSILE STRENGTH. ROPE ANGLE SHALL BE HORIZONTAL (0° ± 0.5°).
USE THE MILITARY ROPE AS SPECIFIED IN SECTION 7.8.3.3 FOR LEG POSITIONING SUPPORT.
CAMI HEAD SHALL REMAIN UNRESTRAINED FOR ALL STEP TESTS IN ALL DIRECTIONS
NOTE: THE PLATFORM MAY BE CLEANED WITH MILD SOAP AND WATER
1.25 in. (32 mm) OD STAINLESS STEEL BALL BEARING PULLEY
THE TEST TABLE APPARATUS SHALL BE RIGID WITH MINIMAL FLEXURE. THE SPRING RATE FOR THE PULLEY BRACKET SHALL BE ≥ 100 lb/in IN THE HORIZONTAL AND VERTICAL DIRECTIONS.
d
8 lb. MASS (3.6 kg)

Figure 10 Test Platform Specifications

(16) Instead of complying with section 7.6.5.1 of ASTM F 977–07, comply with the following:

(i) 7.6.5.1 Center the walker on the test platform facing rearward so that Plane A is perpendicular to the front edge of the platform and the walker is distance d from the center of the most rearward wheel(s) to the edge of the test platform,

$$d_{CAMI} = \frac{\left(V_f^2 - V_o^2\right) * \left(W_{CAMI} + W_{walker} + W_{drop\ weight}\right)}{2g\left(W_{drop\ weight} - \mu_k N_{CAMI}\right)}$$

Where

V_f = Maximum velocity of walker at edge of platform = 4 ft/sec

V_o = Initial velocity = 0

W_{CAMI} = Measured weight of CAMI dummy

W_{walker} = Weight of the walker

$W_{drop\ weight}$ = Drop weight = 8 lb

μ_k = Dynamic coefficient of friction = 0.05

N_{CAMI} = Normal force (for CAMI dummy scenario) = weight of CAMI dummy and walker

g = acceleration of gravity = 32.2 ft/sec^2

Position the swivel wheels in such a way that the walker moves rearward in a straight line parallel to Plane A. If the walker has an open back design, attach the 1 in aluminum angle used in 7.3.4 to span the back frame.

(ii) [Reserved]

(17) Instead of complying with section 7.6.5.3 of ASTM F 977–07, comply with the following:

(i) 7.6.5.3 While holding the walker stationary, attach an 8 lb (3.6 kg) weight to the rear of the walker base at Plane A by means of a rope (as specified in 7.6.3.3) and a pulley (as specified in 7.6.3.3) and adjust the pulley so that the force is applied horizontally (0 ±0.5° with respect to the table surface).

(ii) [Reserved]

(18) Instead of complying with section 7.6.5.5 of ASTM F 977–07, comply with the following:

(i) 7.6.5.5 Repeat 7.6.5.1 through 7.6.5.4 using the CAMI dummy with the weighted vest (see Fig. 12) and with distance d, computed using the following equation:

$$d_{CAMI\ w/vest} = \frac{\left(V_f^2 - V_o^2\right) * \left(W_{CAMI\ w/vest} + W_{walker} + W_{drop\ weight}\right)}{2g\left(W_{drop\ weight} - \mu_k N_{CAMI\ w/vest}\right)}$$

Where

V_f = Maximum velocity of walker at edge of platform = 4 ft/sec

V_o = Initial velocity = 0

$W_{CAMI\ w/vest}$ = Measured weight of CAMI dummy and weighted vest

W_{walker} = Weight of the walker

$W_{drop\ weight}$ = Drop weight = 8 lb

μ_k = Dynamic coefficient of friction = 0.05

$N_{CAMI\ w/vest}$ = Normal force (for CAMI dummy fitted with weighted vest scenario) = Measured weight of CAMI dummy + measured weight of vest + walker weight

g = acceleration of gravity = 32.2 ft/sec^2″

(19) In addition to complying with section 7.6.5.5 of ASTM F 977–07, comply with the following:

(i) 7.6.5.6 Repeat tests in the following sequence: section 7.6.5.3, and section 7.6.5.5 two additional times.

(ii) [Reserved]

(20) In addition to complying with section 7.6 of ASTM F 977–07, comply with the following:

(i) 7.7 *Parking Device Test* (see 6.4):

(A) 7.7.1 Perform the parking device test using a Test Mass that is A rigid cylinder 6.30 in ±0.04 in (160mm ±1 mm) in diameter, 11.02 in ±0.04 in (280 mm ±1 mm) in height with a mass of 16.9 lb (7.65 kg), with its center of gravity in the center of the cylinder.

(B) 7.7.2 Adjust the walker seat to the highest position (if applicable). Place the Test Mass vertically in the walker seat. Set any manual speed control to the fastest position (if applicable). Establish a vertical plane A that passes through the center of the seating area and is parallel to the direction the child faces. Establish a vertical plane B that is perpendicular to plane A and passes through the center of the seating area.

(C) 7.7.3 Perform the parking device test in the forward, sideward, and rearward directions.

(D) 7.7.4 *Forward facing test of parking devices.*

(E) 7.7.4.1 Position the walker including the Test Mass facing forward so that plane A is perpendicular to the front edge of the platform (see fig. 10) and passes through the center of the pulley. Engage all parking devices in accordance with the manufacturer's instructions.

(F) 7.7.4.2 Within one minute of placing the walker with the Test Mass on the platform, attach an 8 lb weight gradually within 5 seconds to the walker frame base at plane A by means of a rope and a pulley per the test apparatus specifications in the step test procedure, adjusted so that the force is applied horizontally (rope angle shall be 0 ±0.5°). Remove the 8 lb weight after 1 minute. Measure the displacement.

(G) 7.7.5 *Sideward facing test of parking devices.*

(H) 7.7.5.1 Position the walker including the Test Mass facing sideward so that plane B is perpendicular to the front edge of the platform and passes through the center of the pulley. Engage all parking devices in accordance with the manufacturer's instructions.

(I) 7.7.5.2 Within one minute of placing the walker with the Test Mass on the platform, attach an 8 lb weight gradually within 5 seconds to the walker frame base at plane B by means of a rope and a pulley per the test apparatus specifications in the step test procedure, adjusted so that the force is applied horizontally (rope angle shall be 0 ±0.5°). Remove the 8 lb weight after 1 minute. Measure the displacement.

(J) 7.7.5.3 If the walker is equipped with fixed direction rear wheels and the walker is displaced in a curved path, establish the location of the rope attachment as the reference point and measure the linear displacement of that reference point after performing the procedure as described in 7.7.5.1 and 7.7.5.2.

(K) 7.7.6 *Rearward facing test of parking devices.*

(L) 7.7.6.1 Position the walker including the Test Mass facing rearward so that plane A is perpendicular to the front edge of the platform and passes through the center of the pulley. Engage all parking devices in accordance with the manufacturers' instructions.

(M) 7.7.6.2 Within one minute of placing the walker with the Test Mass on the platform, attach an 8 lb weight gradually within 5 seconds to the walker frame base at plane A by means of a rope and a pulley per the test apparatus specifications in the step test procedure, adjusted so that the force is applied horizontally (rope angle shall be 0 ±0.5°). Remove the 8 lb weight after 1 minute. Measure the displacement.

(ii) [Reserved]

(21) In addition to complying with section 8.2.3.2 of ASTM F 977–07, comply with the following:

(i) 8.2.3.3 If the walker is equipped with a parking brake, a warning statement shall address the following:

WARNING: Parking brake use does not totally prevent walker movement. Always keep child in view when in the walker, even when using the parking brakes.

(ii) [Reserved]

(22) Instead of complying with section 8.2.4.2 of ASTM F 977–07, comply with the following:

(i) 8.2.4.2 The stairs warning shall be stated exactly as follows:

⚠ WARNING – STAIR HAZARD
Avoid serious injury or death
Block stairs/steps securely before using walker, even when using parking brake.

(ii) [Reserved]

[75 FR 35273, June 21, 2010, as amended at 75 FR 51178, Aug. 19, 2010]

PART 1217—SAFETY STANDARD FOR TODDLER BEDS

AUTHORITY: Sections 3 and 104 of Pub. L. 110–314, 122 Stat. 3016 (August 14, 2008).

SOURCE: 76 FR 22028, Apr. 20, 2011, unless otherwise noted.

§ 1217.1 Scope, application, and effective date.

This part 1217 establishes a consumer product safety standard for toddler beds manufactured or imported on or after October 20, 2011.

§ 1217.2 Requirements for toddler beds.

(a) The Director of the Federal Register approves the incorporations by reference listed in this section in accordance with 5 U.S.C. 552(a) and 1 CFR part 51. You may obtain a copy of these ASTM standards from ASTM International, 100 Barr Harbor Drive, P.O. Box C700, West Conshohocken, PA 19428–2959 USA, phone: 610–832–9585; *http://www.astm.org/*. You may inspect copies at the Office of the Secretary, U.S. Consumer Product Safety Commission, Room 820, 4330 East West Highway, Bethesda, MD 20814, telephone 301–504–7923, or at the National Archives and Records Administration (NARA). For information on the availability of this material at NARA, call 202–741–6030, or go to: *http://www.archives.gov/federal_register/code_of_federal regulations/ibr_locations.html.*

(b) Except as provided in paragraph (c) of this section, each toddler bed as defined in ASTM F 1821–09, *Standard Consumer Safety Specification for Toddler Beds*, approved April 1, 2009, shall comply with all applicable provisions of ASTM F 1821–09.

(c) Comply with ASTM F 1821–09 with the following additions or exclusions.

(1) Do not comply with sections 6.1 through 6.1.2 of ASTM F 1821–09.

(2) Instead of complying with section 6.5 of ASTM F 1821–09, comply with the following:

(i) 6.5 *Guardrails:*

(ii) 6.5.1 For products with guardrails, there shall be no opening in the guardrail structure below the lowest surface of the uppermost member of the guardrail and above the mattress support structure that will permit complete passage of the wedge block shown in Figure 2 when tested in accordance with 7.4.

(iii) 6.5.2 The upper edge of the guardrails shall be at least 5 in. (130 mm) above the sleeping surface when a mattress of a thickness that is the maximum specified by the manufacturer's instructions is used. If no maximum mattress thickness is specified, the guardrail height shall be based on a mattress thickness of 6 in. (152 mm).

(iv) 6.5.3 When tested in accordance with 7.9, the guardrail shall not break, detach, or create a condition that would present any of the hazards described in Section 5. Guardrails that do not have any free ends, that is, they are attached to both the headboard and the footboard, are exempt from this test. For guardrails with two free ends, perform this test at each free end.

(3) In addition to complying with section 6.7 of ASTM F 1821–09 comply with the following:

(i) 6.8 *Spindle/Slat Static Load Strength:*

(A) 6.8.1 Toddler beds that contain wooden or metal spindles/slats shall meet the performance requirements outlined in section 6.8.2 or 6.8.3.

(B) 6.8.2 Except as provided in section 6.8.3, after testing in accordance with the procedure in 7.10, there shall be no complete breakage of a spindle/slat or complete separation of a spindle/slat from the guardrails, side rails, or end structures.

(C) 6.8.3 Toddler beds that convert from a full-size crib, also known as convertible cribs, shall meet the requirements specified in section 6.7 of ASTM F 1169–10 *Safety Standard for Full-Size Baby Cribs*, approved June 1, 2010, instead of the requirements of 6.8.2. See 16 CFR Part 1219 for complete requirements for full-size cribs.

(ii) [Reserved]

(4) Do not comply with sections 7.1.2 through 7.1.6 of ASTM F 1821–09,

(5) In addition to complying with section 7.8.5 of ASTM F 1821–09, comply with the following:

(i) 7.9 *Test Method for Guardrail Structural Integrity:*

(A) 7.9.1 Firmly secure the toddler bed on a stationary flat surface using clamps. Gradually over a period of 5 s apply a 50 lbf (222.4 N) to the guardrail from the inside of the toddler bed, outward and perpendicular to the place of the rail, and hold for 10 s. The force is to be applied to the geometric center of a 3 × 6 × ½ in. (7.62 × 15.24 × 1.27 cm) piece of plywood with the long end parallel to the floor (see Fig. 11).

(B) 7.9.2 For guardrails with a rectangular shape, the plywood shall be placed with the upper long edge of the plywood even with a line drawn parallel to the rail, which is 11 inches (27.94 cm) from the mattress support and the short edge even with the free short edge of the rail.

(C) 7.9.3 For contoured guardrails that are not rectangular, the plywood shall be placed with the upper long edge of the plywood even with a line drawn parallel to the rail which is 11 inches (27.94 cm) from the mattress support and the short edge placed so that the downward slope of the free rail edge intersects the corner of the plywood.

(ii) 7.10 *Spindle/Slat Testing for Guardrails, Side Rails, and End Structures:*

(A) 7.10.1 The spindle/slat static force test shall be performed with the spindle/slat assemblies removed from the bed and supported only on the rail corners through a contact area not more than 3 square inches (7.6 cm²) when measured from the end of the rail in a direction parallel to the longitudinal axis of the rail. Besides the corners, the upper and lower horizontal rails of both linear and contoured rails shall be free to deflect under the applied force. For toddler beds incorporating folding or moveable sides for purposes of easier access to the occupant, storage and/or transport, each side segment (portion of side separated by hinges for folding) shall be tested separately as described above.

(B) 7.10.2 Gradually, over a period of not less than 2 s nor greater than 5 s, apply an 80 lbf (355.8 N) perpendicular to the plane of the side at the midpoint, between the top and bottom of the spindle/slat being tested. This force shall be applied through a force measuring device and contact area 1 ±1⁄16 in. (25.4 ±1.6 mm) wide by a length at least equal to the width of the spindle/slat being tested at the point of application. This force shall be maintained for 10 s. The force measuring device must be capable of recording the force at breakage, if breakage occurs during this test. This force measuring device must be capable of a maximum measurement resolution of 0.25 lbf (1.11 N).

(C) 7.10.3 Test, according to 7.10.2, 25% (rounding up to the nearest percentage, if necessary) of all spindles/slats. Spindles/slats that offer the least resistance to bending based upon their geometry shall be selected to be tested within this grouping of 25% except that adjacent spindles/slats shall not be tested.

(D) 7.10.4 Upon completion of testing as defined in 7.10.2 and 7.10.3, no spindle/slat shall have failed at an applied force less than or equal to 60 lbf. If no more than one spindle/slat fails and that failure occurs only as the result of an applied force greater than 60 lbf, then an additional 25% of spindles/slats shall be tested per 7.10.2 and 7.10.3. During testing of this second 25%, any spindle/slat failure (at or below 80 lbf) shall constitute failure of the test.

(E) 7.10.5 End vertical rails that are joined between the slat assembly top and bottom rails are not considered slats and do not require testing under 7.10.

(6) Instead of complying with sections 8.4.2 through 8.4.4.5 of ASTM F 1821–09, comply with the following:

(i) 8.4.2 The safety alert symbol '⚠'

and the word "WARNING" or "CAUTION" must be at least 0.2 in. (5 mm) high, and the remainder of the text shall be characters whose upper case shall be at least 0.1 in. (2.5 mm) high, sans serif.

(ii) 8.4.3 Except as provided in 8.4.4 and 8.4.5, the following warnings must appear on all toddler beds, exactly as depicted.

⚠ WARNING

INFANTS HAVE DIED IN TODDLER BEDS FROM ENTRAPMENT.

Openings in and between bed parts can entrap head and neck of a small child.

NEVER use bed with children younger than 15 months.

ALWAYS follow assembly instructions.

⚠ WARNING

STRANGULATION HAZARD

NEVER place bed near windows where cords from blinds or drapes may strangle a child.

NEVER suspend strings over bed.

NEVER place items with a string, cord, or ribbon, such as hood strings or pacifier cords, around a child's neck. These items may catch on bed parts.

⚠ CAUTION

ENTRAPMENT HAZARD

To avoid dangerous gaps, any mattress used in this bed shall be a full-size crib mattress at least 51 ⅝ in. (1310 mm) in length, 27 ¼ in. (690 mm) in width, and 4 in. (100 mm) in thickness.

(iii) 8.4.4 Toddler beds that convert from a full-size crib, also known as convertible cribs, must meet the warning requirements specified in section 8 of ASTM F 1169–10, instead of the requirements of 8.4.3. See 16 CFR Part 1219 for complete requirements for full-size cribs.

(iv) 8.4.5 Any toddler bed that can convert from a full-size crib, and has the warning specified in section 8.1.3 of ASTM F 1169–10, must include additional text at the end of that warning that specifies the minimum mattress thickness of 4 inches (100 mm). See 16 CFR Part 1219 for complete requirements for full-size cribs.

(7) In addition to figure 10 of ASTM F 1821–09, use the following:

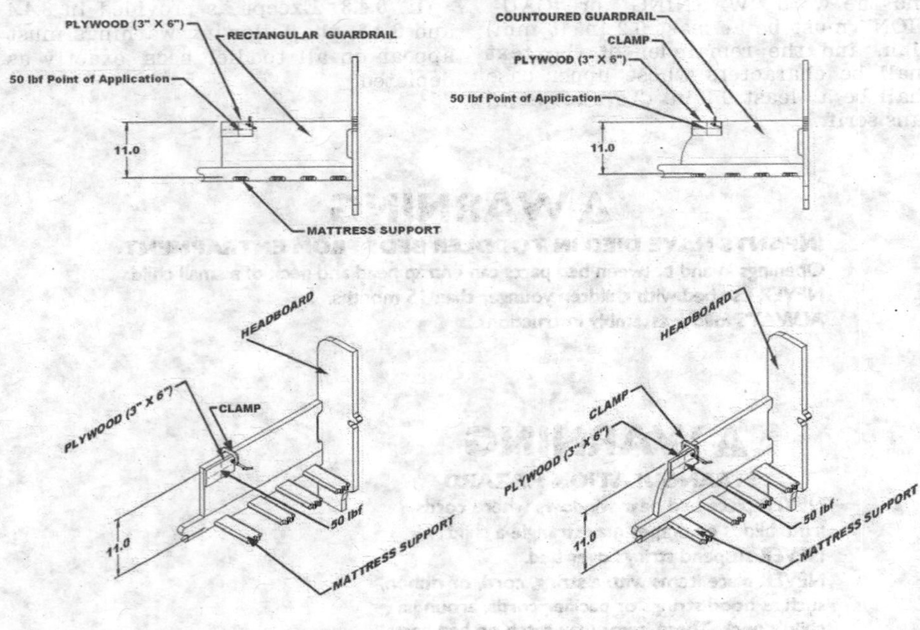

FIGURE 11 -- Guardrail Structural Integrity Test

[76 FR 22028, Apr. 20, 2011, as amended at 76 FR 27882, May 13, 2011]

PART 1219—SAFETY STANDARD FOR FULL-SIZE BABY CRIBS (Eff. June 28, 2011)

AUTHORITY: The Consumer Product Safety Improvement Act of 2008, Pub. L. 110–314, Sec. 104, 122 Stat. 3016 (August 14, 2008); section 3 of Pub. L. 112–28, 125 Stat. 273 (August 12, 2011).

SOURCE: 75 FR 81786, Dec. 28, 2010, unless otherwise noted.

§ 1219.1 Scope, compliance dates, and definitions.

(a) *Scope*. This part establishes a consumer product safety standard for new and used full-size baby cribs.

(b) *Compliance dates*. (1) Except as provided in paragraph (b)(2) of this section, compliance with this part 1219 shall be required on June 28, 2011, and applies to the manufacture, sale, contract for sale or resale, lease, sublet, offer, provision for use, or other placement in the stream of commerce of a new or used full-size baby crib on or after that date.

(2) Child care facilities, family child care homes, and places of public accommodation affecting commerce shall be required to comply with this part on December 28, 2012, but this provision applies only to the offer or provision for use of cribs by child care facilities, family child care homes, and places of public accommodation affecting commerce and not the sale, resale, or other placement in the stream of commerce of cribs by these entities.

(c) *Definitions*. (1) *Full-size baby crib* means a bed that is:

(i) Designed to provide sleeping accommodations for an infant;

(ii) Intended for use in the home, in a child care facility, a family child care home, or place of public accommodation affecting commerce; and

(iii) Within a range of ±5.1 cm (±2 in.) of the following interior dimensions: The interior dimensions shall be 71 ±1.6 cm (28 ±5⁄8 in.) wide as measured between the innermost surfaces of the crib sides and 133 ±1.6 cm (52 3⁄8 ±5⁄8 in.) long as measured between the innermost surfaces of the crib end panels, slats, rods, or spindles. Both measurements are to be made at the level of the mattress support spring in each of its adjustable positions and no more than 5 cm (2 in.) from the crib corner posts or from the first spindle to the corresponding point of the first spindle at the other end of the crib. If a crib has contoured or decorative spindles, in either or both of the sides or ends, the measurement shall be determined from the largest diameter of the first turned spindle within a range of 10 cm (4 in.) above the mattress support spring in each of its adjustable positions, to a corresponding point on the first spindle or innermost surface of the opposite side of the crib.

(2) *Place of public accommodation affecting commerce* means any inn, hotel, or other establishment that provides lodging to transient guests, except that such term does not include an establishment treated as an apartment building for purposes of any State or local law or regulation or an establishment located within a building that contains not more than five rooms for rent or hire and that is actually occupied as a residence by the proprietor of such establishment.

§ 1219.2 Requirements for full-size baby cribs.

Each full-size baby crib shall comply with all applicable provisions of ASTM F1169–11, Standard Consumer Safety Specification for Full-Size Baby Cribs, approved August 15, 2011. The Director of the Federal Register approves this incorporation by reference in accordance with 5 U.S.C. 552(a) and 1 CFR part 51. You may obtain a copy from ASTM International, 100 Barr Harbor Drive, P.O. Box 0700, West Conshohocken, PA 19428; telephone 610–832–9585; *www.astm.org.* You may inspect a copy at the Office of the Secretary, U.S. Consumer Product Safety Commission, Room 820, 4330 East West Highway, Bethesda, MD 20814, telephone 301–504–7923, or at the National Archives and Records Administration (NARA). For information on the availability of this material at NARA, call 202–741–6030, or go to: *http://www.archives.gov/federal_register/code_of_federal_regulations/ibr_locations.html.*

[77 FR 45245, July 31, 2012]

PART 1220—SAFETY STANDARD FOR NON-FULL-SIZE BABY CRIBS (Eff. June 28, 2011)

AUTHORITY: The Consumer Product Safety Improvement Act of 2008, Pub. L. 110–314, § 104, 122 Stat. 3016 (August 14, 2008).

SOURCE: 75 FR 81787, Dec. 28, 2010, unless otherwise noted.

§ 1220.1 Scope, compliance dates, and definitions.

(a) *Scope.* This part establishes a consumer product safety standard for new and used non-full-size baby cribs.

(b) *Compliance dates.* (1) Except as provided in paragraph (b)(2) of this section, compliance with this part 1220 shall be required on June 28, 2011, and applies to the manufacture, sale, contract for sale or resale, lease, sublet, offer, provision for use, or other placement in the stream of commerce of a new or used non-full-size baby crib on or after that date.

(2) Child care facilities, family child care homes, and places of public accommodation affecting commerce shall be required to comply with this part on December 28, 2012, but this provision applies only to the offer or provision for use of cribs by child care facilities, family child care homes, and places of public accommodation affecting commerce and not the sale, resale, or other placement in the stream of commerce of cribs by these entities.

(c) *Definitions.* (1) *Non-full-size baby crib* means a bed that is:

(i) Designed to provide sleeping accommodations for an infant;

(ii) Intended for use in or around the home, for travel, in a child care facility, in a family child care home, in a place of public accommodation affecting commerce and other purposes;

(iii) Has an interior length dimension either greater than 139.7 cm (55 in.) or smaller than 126.3 cm (49 ¾ in.), or, an interior width dimension either greater than 77.7 cm (30⅝ in.) or smaller than 64.3 cm (25⅜ in.), or both;

(iv) Includes, but is not limited to, the following:

(A) *Portable crib*—a non-full-size baby crib designed so that it may be folded or collapsed, without disassembly, to occupy a volume substantially less than the volume it occupies when it is used.

(B) *Crib pen*—a non-full-size baby crib with rigid sides the legs of which may be removed or adjusted to provide a play pen or play yard for a child.

(C) *Specialty crib*—an unconventionally shaped (circular, hexagonal, etc.) non-full-size baby crib incorporating a special mattress or other unconventional components.

(D) *Undersize crib*—a non-full-size baby crib with an interior length dimension smaller than 126.3 cm (49¾ in.), or an interior width dimension smaller than 64.3 cm (25⅜ in.), or both.

(E) *Oversize crib*—a non-full-size baby crib with an interior length dimension greater than 139.7 cm (55 in.), or an interior width dimension greater than 77.7 cm (30⅝ in.), or both.

(v) Does not include mesh/net/screen cribs, nonrigidly constructed baby cribs, cradles (both rocker and pendulum types), car beds, baby baskets, and bassinets (also known as junior cribs).

(2) *Play yard* means a framed enclosure that includes a floor and has mesh or fabric sided panels primarily intended to provide a play or sleeping environment for children. It may fold for storage or travel.

(3) *Place of public accommodation affecting commerce* means any inn, hotel, or other establishment that provides lodging to transient guests, except that such term does not include an establishment treated as an apartment building for purposes of any State or local law or regulation or an establishment located within a building that contains not more than five rooms for rent or hire and that is actually occupied as a residence by the proprietor of such establishment.

§ 1220.2 Requirements for non-full-size baby cribs.

(a) Except as provided in paragraph (b) of this section, each non-full-size baby crib shall comply with all applicable provisions of ASTM F 406–10a, Standard Consumer Safety Specification for Non-Full-Size Baby Cribs/Play Yards, approved October 15, 2010. The Director of the Federal Register approves this incorporation by reference in accordance with 5 U.S.C. 552(a) and 1 CFR part 51. You may obtain a copy from ASTM International, 100 Bar Harbor Drive, PO Box 0700, West Conshohocken, PA 19428; telephone 610–832–9585; *http://www.astm.org.* You may inspect a copy at the Office of the Secretary, U.S. Consumer Product Safety Commission, Room 820, 4330 East West Highway, Bethesda, MD 20814, telephone 301–504–7923, or at the National Archives and Records Administration (NARA). For information on the availability of this material at NARA, call 202–741–6030, or go to: *http://www.archives.gov/federal_register/code_of_federal_regulations/ibr_locations.html.*

(b) Comply with the ASTM F 406–10a standard with the following additions or exclusions:

(1) Do not comply with sections 5.6.2 through 5.6.2.4 of ASTM F 406–10a.

(2) Do not comply with section 5.16.2 of ASTM F 406–10a.

(3) Do not comply with section 6.10 of ASTM F 406–10a.

(4) Do not comply with section 7, *Performance Requirements for Mesh/Fabric Products*, of ASTM F 406–10a.

(5) Instead of complying with section 8.10.1 of ASTM F 406–10a, comply with the following:

(i) The spindle/slat static force test shall be performed with the spindle/slat assemblies removed from the crib and rigidly supported within 3 in. of each end of the upper and lower horizontal rails in a manner that shall not interfere with a spindle/slat deflecting under the applied force. For cribs incorporating foldable or moveable sides for purposes of easier access to the occupant, storage and/or transport, each side segment (portion of side separated by hinges for folding) shall be tested separately.

(ii) [Reserved]

(6) Do not comply with sections 8.11 through 8.11.2.4 of ASTM F 406–10a.

(7) Do not comply with sections 8.12 through 8.12.2.2 of ASTM F 406–10a.

(8) Do not comply with section 8.14 through 8.14.2 of ASTM F 406–10a.

(9) Do not comply with sections 8.15 through 8.15.3.3 of ASTM F 406–10a.

(10) Do not comply with sections 8.16 through 8.16.3 of ASTM F 406–10a.

(11) Do not comply with section 9.3.2 through 9.3.2.4 of ASTM F 406–10a.

(12) Instead of complying with section 9.4.2.6 of ASTM F 406–10a, comply with the following warning requirement:

(i) Child can become entrapped and die when improvised netting or covers are placed on top of product. Never add such items to confine child in product.

(ii) [Reserved]

PART 1221—SAFETY STANDARD FOR PLAY YARDS

AUTHORITY: The Consumer Product Safety Improvement Act of 2008, Pub. L. 110–314, section 104, 122 Stat. 3016 (August 14, 2008).

SOURCE: 77 FR 52228, Aug, 29, 2012, unless otherwise noted.

EFFECTIVE DATE NOTE: At 77 FR 52228, Aug, 29, 2012, part 1221 was added, effective Feb. 28, 2013.

§ 1221.1 Scope.

This part establishes a consumer product safety standard for play yards manufactured or imported on or after February 28, 2013.

§ 1221.2 Requirements for play yards.

(a) Except as provided in paragraph (b) of this section, each play yard must comply with all applicable provisions of ASTM F406–12a, Standard Consumer Safety Specification for Non-Full-Size Baby Cribs/Play Yards, approved on May 1, 2012. The Director of the Federal Register approves this incorporation by reference in accordance with 5 U.S.C. 552(a) and 1 CFR part 51. You may obtain a copy from ASTM International, 100 Bar Harbor Drive, P.O. Box 0700, West Conshohocken, PA 19428; *http://www.astm.org*. You may inspect a copy at the Office of the Secretary, U.S. Consumer Product Safety Commission, Room 820, 4330 East-West Highway, Bethesda, MD 20814, telephone 301–504–7923, or at the National Archives and Records Administration (NARA). For information on the availability of this material at NARA, call 202–741–6030, or go to: *http://www.archives.gov/federal_register/code_of_federal_regulations/ibr_locations.html*.

(b) Comply with the ASTM F406–12a standard with the following exclusions:

(1) Do not comply with section 5.17 of ASTM F406–12a.

(2) Do not comply with section 5.19 of ASTM F406–12a.

(3) Do not comply with section 5.20 of ASTM F406–12a.

(4) Do not comply with section 6, Performance Requirements for Rigid-Sided Products, of ASTM F406–12a, in its entirety.

(5) Do not comply with sections 8.1 through 8.10.5 of ASTM F406–12a.

(6) Instead of complying with section 9.4.2.10 of ASTM F406–12a, comply with only the following:

(i) 9.4.2.10 For products that have a separate mattress that is not permanently fixed in place: Use ONLY mattress/pad provided by manufacturer.

(ii) [Reserved]

(7) Do not comply with section 10.1.1.1 of ASTM F406–12a.

PART 1223—SAFETY STANDARD FOR INFANT SWINGS

AUTHORITY: The Consumer Product Safety Improvement Act of 2008, Pub. L. 110–314, Sec. 104, 122 Stat. 3016 (August 14, 2008).

EFFECTIVE DATE NOTE: At 77 FR 66713, Nov. 7, 2012, part 1223 was added, effective May 7, 2013.

§ 1223.1 Scope.

This part establishes a consumer product safety standard for infant swings.

§ 1223.2 Requirements for infant swings.

(a) Except as provided in paragraph (b) of this section, each infant swing must comply with all applicable provisions of ASTM F2088—12a, Standard Consumer Safety Specification for Infant Swings, approved on September 1, 2012. The Director of the Federal Register approves this incorporation by reference in accordance with 5 U.S.C. 552(a) and 1 CFR part 51. You may obtain a copy from ASTM International, 100 Bar Harbor Drive, P.O. Box 0700, West Conshohocken, PA 19428; *http://www.astm.org*. You may inspect a copy at the Office of the Secretary, U.S. Consumer Product Safety Commission, Room 820, 4330 East West Highway, Bethesda, MD 20814, telephone 301–504–7923, or at the National Archives and Records Administration (NARA). For information on the availability of this material at NARA, call 202–741–6030, or go to: *http://www.archives.gov/federal_register/code_of_federal_regulations/ibr_locations.html*.

(b)(1) Instead of complying with section 8.3.1 of ASTM F2088–12a, comply with the following:

(i) 8.3.1 The warning statements shall address the following at a minimum:

(ii) 8.3.1.1 Products having an adjustable seat recline with a maximum seatback angle greater than 50 degrees from horizontal measured in accordance with 7.13 shall address the following:

Keep swing seat fully reclined until child is at least 4 months old AND can hold up head without help. Young infants have limited head and neck control. If seat is too upright, infant's head can drop forward, compress the airway, and result in DEATH.

(iii) 8.3.1.2 To prevent serious injury or death from infants falling or being strangled in straps:

(A) Always secure infant in the restraint system provided.

(B) Never leave infant unattended in swing.

(C) Discontinue use of swing when infant attempts to climb out.

(D) Travel swings (see 3.1.11) shall address the following:

Always place swing on floor. Never use on any elevated surface.

(2) Instead of complying with section 7.12.2 of ASTM F2088–12a, comply with the following:

(i) 7.12.2 Place the back of the swing in the most upright position. Remove positioning accessories, including pillows. Position the segments of the restraint system to limit interaction with the Hinged Weight Gage—Infant (see Fig. 10) when placed in the seat. Place the Hinged Weight Gage—Infant with the hinge located at the junction of the swing back and seat bottom (see Fig. 8). Determine if the lowest point of the toy positioned over the occupant is within 25.25 in. (641.5 mm) of the top surface of the Lower Plate (see Fig. 10)—throughout the swing seat's range of motion. Proceed to 7.12.3 if the distance is 25.25 in. (641.5 mm) or less. The toy is considered out of reach and not tested to 7.12.3 if the distance is greater than 25.25 in. (641.5 mm).

(ii) [Reserved]

PART 1224—SAFETY STANDARD FOR PORTABLE BED RAILS

Sec.

AUTHORITY: Sections 3 and 104 of Pub. L. 110–314, 122 Stat. 3016 (August 14, 2008).

SOURCE: 77 FR 12197, Feb. 29, 2012, unless otherwise noted.

§ 1224.1 Scope, application, and effective date.

This part establishes a consumer product safety standard for portable bed rails manufactured or imported on or after August 29, 2012.

§ 1224.2 Requirements for portable bed rails.

(a) Each portable bed rail as defined in ASTM F2085–12, *Standard Consumer Safety Specification for Portable Bed Rails*, approved January 1, 2012, must comply with all applicable provisions of ASTM F2085–12. The Director of the Federal Register approves this incorporation by reference in accordance with

5 U.S.C. 552(a) and 1 CFR part 51. You may obtain a copy of this ASTM standard from ASTM International, 100 Barr Harbor Drive, P.O. Box C700, West Conshohocken, PA 19428–2959 USA, phone: 610–832–9585; *http://www.astm.org/*. You may inspect copies at the Office of the Secretary, U.S. Consumer Product Safety Commission, Room 820, 4330 East West Highway, Bethesda, MD 20814, telephone 301–504–7923, or at the National Archives and Records Administration (NARA). For information on the availability of this material at NARA, call 202–741–6030, or go to: *http://www.archives.gov/federal_register/code_of_federal regulations/ibr_locations.html.*

(b) [Reserved]

PART 1301—BAN OF UNSTABLE REFUSE BINS

AUTHORITY: Secs. 8, 9, 86 Stat. 1215–1217, as amended, 90 Stat. 506; 15 U.S.C. 2057, 2058.

SOURCE: 42 FR 30300, June 13, 1977, unless otherwise noted.

§ 1301.1 Scope and application.

(a) In this part 1301 the Consumer Product Safety Commission (Commission) declares that certain unstable refuse bins are banned hazardous products under sections 8 and 9 of the Consumer Product Safety Act (CPSA) (15 U.S.C. 2057 and 2058).

(b) This ban applies to those refuse bins of metal construction that are being distributed in commerce on or after the effective date of this rule, which do not meet the criteria of § 1301.5 and which are produced or distributed for sale to, or for the personal use, consumption or enjoyment of consumers, in or around a permanent or temporary household or residence, a school, in recreation or otherwise. The Commission has found that (1) these refuse bins are being, or will be distributed in commerce; (2) they present an unreasonable risk of injury; and (3) no feasible consumer product safety standard under the CPSA would adequately protect the public from the unreasonable risk of injury associated with these products. The ban is applicable to those refuse bins having an internal volume one cubic yard or greater by actual measurement, which will tip over when subjected to either of the forces described in § 1301.7 and which are in commerce or being distributed in commerce on or after the effective date of the ban.

(c) When such refuse bins are the subject of rental or lease transactions between owners of refuse bins or between refuse collection agencies and persons who make such refuse bins available for use by the public, such transactions are considered to be distributions in commerce and therefore come within the scope of this ban. Refuse collection agencies or owners of refuse bins who rent or lease refuse bins to persons who make them available for use by consumers are considered to be distributors; the persons to whom refuse bins are rented or leased are not considered to be distributors.

(d) On or after the effective date of this rule it shall be unlawful to manufacture for sale, offer for sale, or distribute in commerce, the unstable refuse bins described in this rule.

(e) This rule, effective November 13, 1981, is partially revoked and therefore does not apply to front-loading, straight-sided refuse bins without trunnion bars having an internal volume capacity of 1, 1½, or 2 cubic yards, of the following external dimensions:

Internal volume	Length (inches)	Width (inches)	Height[1]		Weight (lbs)
			High side (inches)	Low side (inches)	
1 cubic yard ...	70–72	21–23	29–31	29–31	313–347
1½ cubic yards	70–72	29–31	33–36	29–32	346–382
2 cubic yards	70–72	32–35	39–43	31–36	409–453

[1] Does not include height of wheels.

(Sec. 9(h), Pub. L. 97–35, Pub. L. 92–573, 86 Stat. 1215, 15 U.S.C. 2058(h))

[42 FR 30300, June 13, 1977, as amended at 46 FR 55925, Nov. 13, 1981]

§ 1301.2 Purpose.

The purpose of this rule is to ban those refuse bins which come under the scope of this ban because they present an unreasonable risk of injury due to tip-over that can result in serious injury or death from crushing.

§ 1301.3 Findings.

(a) *Risk of injury*. The Commission has studied 19 in-depth investigation reports of accidents associated with tip-over of unstable refuse bins. The 19 accidents, which involved 21 victims, resulted in 13 deaths. Of the 21 victims, 20 were children 10 years of age and under. Additionally, Commission records show three death certificates for victims, under 5 years of age, who were killed by refuse bins tipping over. Therefore, the Commission finds that unreasonable risks of injury or death from crushing due to tip-over are associated with certain unstable refuse bins having an internal volume one cubic yard or greater, which unreasonable risk this banning rule is designed to eliminate or reduce.

(b) *Products subject to this ban*. (1) The Commission finds that the types of products subject to this ban are those manufactured metal receptacles known in the solid waste collection trade as containers, refuse bins, buckets, boxes or hoppers, with actual internal volumes of one cubic yard or greater, used for the storage and transportation of solid waste. They are fabricated in numerous sizes and configurations for use with rear, side, front, hoist and roll-off loaded trash collection trucks and are used by private firms and public agencies.

(2) Although unstable refuse bins subject to this ban may be in various forms and shapes, the Commission's in-depth investigations into accidents associated with metal refuse containers indicate that most accidents have occurred with slant-sided metal refuse bins which are used by rear and side-loaded trucks. Therefore, the Commission bases its economic analysis of the potential impact of the ban upon the population of these bins. Certain refuse bins such as front loaded, roll-off, box and other types of large or broad based bins, because of their configuration, bulk and weight are likely to be inherently stable and are therefore not included in the population of potentially unstable bins studied in this economic analysis.

(3) The Commission estimates that there may be approximately 638,000–716,000 slant-sided, metal refuse bins with an internal volume one cubic yard or greater, which may be unstable. The population of potentially unstable bins owned by some 10,000–15,000 private solid waste collection firms in all parts of the United States and its territories is estimated to be 359,000–371,000. These figures are discussed in the Commission's *Economic Impact Statement* of April 22, 1977, which is available for review from the Commission's Office of the Secretary, Washington, D.C. 20207.

(c) *Need of the public for the product and effects on utility, cost, and availability*. (1) The public need for refuse bins is substantial since these products are used for the containment of solid waste and thus contribute to public hygiene. The U.S. Environmental Protection Agency estimates that 135,000,000 tons of solid waste were collected in 1976 from residential, commercial and industrial sources. Approximately 101,250,000 tons (75%) were collected by private firms and the remainder by public agencies.

(2) The Commission finds that the ban will not affect the utility that consumers derive from the general use of refuse bins. The interest of the public is in continuity, availability and price of solid waste collection. The ban could result in a shift from bins which are subject to the ban to other types of storage containers. Such a shift would not affect solid waste collection and would entail a small price increase for individual consumers. To the extent that injuries and deaths associated with the use of unstable bins are reduced or eliminated as a result of the ban, the public utility derived from the use of the product will be increased.

(3)(i) The Commission finds that, based on its analysis of industrial estimates, newly produced complying refuse bins will cost approximately 1–10% more than currently produced noncomplying bins and that existing inventories of unstable bins can be modified (depending upon size) for about

$45–$75 each. This modification cost estimate includes the cost of material, shop labor, retrieval and return to service, and the substitution of one bin for another for on-site service.

(ii) The Commission estimates that the ban will not result in any significant price increases for the delivery of solid waste collection service to the general public because of the competitive structure of the solid waste collection industry.

(4) The Commission finds that the ban will have no effect on the availability of solid waste collection service to the general public. Solid waste collection haulers who use products subject to this ban can modify these refuse bins so that these products can continue to be used for solid waste collection.

(d) *Alternatives.* (1) The Commission has considered other means of achieving the objective of this ban, but has found none that it believes would have fewer adverse effects on competition or that would cause less disruption or dislocation of manufacturing, servicing or other commercial practices consistent with public health and safety. The Commission estimates that this ban may, because of capital and testing costs and maintenance capacity limitations, have an adverse effect on individual firms within some markets.

(2) The Commission estimates that the ban will not have an adverse effect on the competitive structure of the solid waste collection industry. The competitive nature of solid waste collection firms is fostered because of low starting costs, particularly if a firm is owner-operated. The rate of entry and exit into and out of the industry for small operators tends to be high relative to larger firms in the industry. The ban will most likely not increase the degree of market concentration among the larger firms nor affect the rate of entry into or exit out of the industry by relatively smaller firms.

(3) Table 3 of the Economic Impact Statement indicates that about 85 percent of the private sector trash haulers are those with a fleet size of about 10 trucks and have annual revenues under $1 million. These might be classified as small business firms. All firms in the trash hauling business would have two possible problems associated with the ban: cost and time to retrofit, and access to capital for retrofitting. The problem of raising capital to retrofit should not be a burden to small firms unless they are denied credit for factors not associated with this ban. The revised effective date from 9 to 12 months will extend both the time to retrofit and the time to search for capital sources, if necessary. We conclude that the small firms in the trash hauling industry will not experience undue hardship relative to their larger competitors.

(e) *Conclusion.* (1) The Commission finds that this rule is reasonably necessary to eliminate or reduce the unreasonable risks of injury associated with refuse bins, as they are defined in § 1301.4, and which fail to meet the criteria specified in § 1301.5

(2) Based on all of the above findings, the Commission finds that the issuance of this rule is in the public interest.

(3) The Commission is aware of the fact that refuse bins are used for many years before being discarded. Estimates of their useful life range from 10 to 15 years. Although other products which may be hazardous may also have a long life in the hands of individual consumers, a substantial number of unstable refuse bins remain in commerce because they are rented or leased and are constantly available for use by large numbers of consumers. The combination of the long life of refuse bins plus the fact that unstable refuse bins could remain in commerce and be available for use by many people, persuaded the Commission to make this finding that no feasible consumer product safety standard under the CPSA could adequately protect the public from the unreasonable risk of injury associated with those unstable refuse bins coming under the coverage of this ban.

§ 1301.4 Definitions.

(a) The definitions in section 3 of the Consumer Product Safety Act (15 U.S.C. 2052) apply to this part 1301.

(b) *Refuse bin* means a metal receptacle having an internal volume one cubic yard or greater, by actual measurement, which temporarily receives and holds refuse for ultimate disposal either by unloading into the body or loading hopper of a refuse collection vehicle or by other means.

(c) *Internal volume* means the actual volumetric capacity of the container. This may not necessarily correspond to the nominal size rating used by industry.

(d) *Tip over* means that during the application of either test force described in § 1301.7(a), the refuse bin begins to rotate forward about its forwardmost ground supports.

§ 1301.5 Banning criteria.

(a) Any refuse bin of metal construction produced or distributed, for sale to, or for the personal use, consumption or enjoyment of consumers, in or around a permanent or temporary household or residence, a school, in recreation or otherwise, which is in commerce or being distributed in commerce on or after the effective date of this ban and which has an actual internal volume one cubic yard or greater and tips over when tested under the conditions of § 1301.6 and using the procedures described in § 1301.7, is a banned hazardous product.

(b) The Commission considers a refuse bin to tip over when it begins to rotate forward about its forwardmost ground supports.

§ 1301.6 Test conditions.

(a) The refuse bin shall be empty and have its lids or covers in a position which would most adversely affect the stability of the bin when tested.

(b) The refuse bin shall be tested on a hard, flat surface. During testing, the bin shall not be tilted from level in such a way as to increase its stability.

(c) Those refuse bins equipped with casters or wheels shall have the casters or wheels positioned in a position which would most adversely affect the stability of the bin and shall be chocked to prevent movement.

(d) The stability of the refuse bin shall be tested without dependence upon non-permanent attachments or restraints such as chains or guys.

(e) For purposes of enforcement, bins will be tested by the Commission in that position which most adversely affects their stability.

§ 1301.7 Test procedures.

(a) The refuse bin shall be tested by applying forces as described in paragraphs (a) (1) and (2) of this section one after the other.

(1) A horizontal force of 70 pounds (311 N) shall be applied at a point and in a direction most likely to cause tipping, and

(2) A vertically downward force of 191 pounds (850 N) shall be applied to a point most likely to cause tipping. (See Figure 1.)

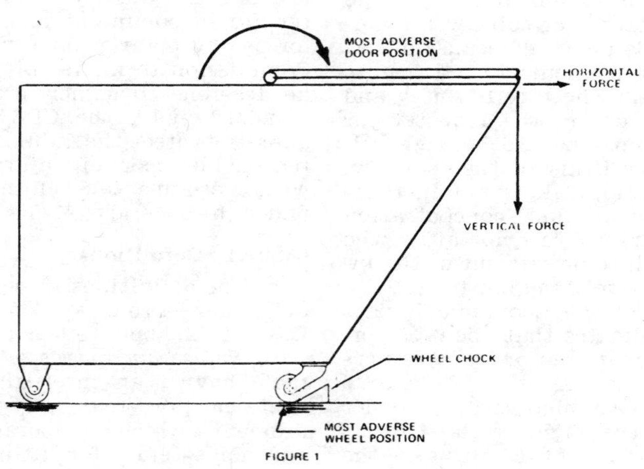

FIGURE 1

(b) These forces shall be applied separately and the bin shall not tip over under the application of either action cited above in paragraph (a)(1) or (a)(2).

§ 1301.8 Effective date.

The effective date of this ban shall be June 13, 1978.

PART 1302—BAN OF EXTREMELY FLAMMABLE CONTACT ADHESIVES

AUTHORITY: Secs. 8, 9; 86 Stat. 1215–1217 as amended; 90 Stat. 506; (15 U.S.C. 2057, 2058).

SOURCE: 42 FR 63731, Dec. 19, 1977, unless otherwise noted.

§ 1302.1 Scope and application.

(a) In this part 1302 the Consumer Product Safety Commission (Commission) declares extremely flammable contact adhesives and similar liquid or semiliquid consumer products to be banned hazardous products under sections 8 and 9 of the Consumer Product Safety Act (CPSA) (15 U.S.C. 2057 and 2058). This ban applies to those extremely flammable contact adhesives and similar liquid or semiliquid consumer products, as defined in § 1302.3(b), which are in commerce or are being distributed in commerce on or after the effective date of this regulation, and which are consumer products (as defined in section 3(a) of the Act (15 U.S.C. 2052) customarily produced or distributed for sale to, or for the personal use, consumption or enjoyment of consumers in or around a permanent or temporary household or residence, a school, in recreation or otherwise.

(b) An extremely flammable contact adhesive as defined in § 1302.3(b) is a banned hazardous product if the manufacturer, distributor, or retailer customarily produces or distributes the product for sale to, or use by consumers, or if the manufacturer, distributor, or retailer fosters or facilitates the product's sale to, or use by, consumers. For example, contact adhesives available in retail stores, such as lumber yards or hardware stores, for sale to consumers would be included in the scope of the ban even though such outlets may sell such products primarily to industrial or professional users. The manufacturer who markets an extremely flammable contact adhesive which would be subject to the ban if sold to consumers has the responsibility for determining the distribution and use patterns of its product and for taking all reasonable steps to ensure that the product is not made available for sale to consumers. The test of whether a contact adhesive is banned shall be whether the product, under any customary or reasonably foreseeable condition of distribution, or sale, is made available for purchase by consumers.

(c) Contact adhesives that are labeled as, marketed, and sold solely for industrial or professional use are not within the scope of this ban. However, merely labeling a contact adhesive for industrial or professional use only would not exclude such products from this ban. In addition, packaging a contact adhesive in a large size container would not in itself exclude the product from this ban.

(d) The Commission has found that the contact adhesives covered by this ban are being, or will be distributed in commerce; and present an unreasonable risk of injury; and that no feasible consumer product safety standard under the CPSA would adequately protect the public from the unreasonable risk of injury associated with these products.

§ 1302.2 Purpose.

The purpose of this rule is to ban extremely flammable contact adhesives which have been found to present an unreasonable risk of injury to consumers of burns resulting from explosive and flashback fire.

§ 1302.3 Definitions.

(a) The definitions in section 3 of the Consumer Product Safety Act (15 U.S.C. 2052) apply to this part 1302.

(b) The term *extremely flammable contact adhesive and similar liquid or semiliquid consumer products* means consumer products that have each of the following product characteristics:

(1) Show a flash point at or below 20 degrees Farenheit as determined by the Tagliabue open-cup test method prescribed by 16 CFR 1500.43; and

(2) Are intended to be applied to two surfaces to be bonded together and allowed to dry partially until there is little residual tack, and adhere to themselves instantaneously when the coated surfaces are joined under low or moderate pressure; and

(3) Are composed of a high percentage (70–90 percent by weight) of solvents and a low percentage of solids (10–30 percent by weight); and

(4) Are substances that are non-aerosols and are free-flowing, having a wet viscosity within the range of 300–6,000 centipoise at 70 degrees Fahrenheit when measured by an RVF Brookfield viscometer; and

(5) Are packaged in containers of more than one-half pint.

(c) The term *flash point* means the lowest temperature corrected to a pressure of 101.3 RPa (1013 millibars) of a substance at which application of an ignition source causes the vapor above the substance to ignite under specified conditions of test. A blue light (blue halo) or other colored light which sometimes surrounds the test flame should not be confused with the true ignition of the vapors (flash point).

(d) *Initial introduction into commerce* occurs when the manufacturer ships a product covered by this regulation from a facility of the manufacturer to a distributor, retailer, or consumer.

§ 1302.4 Banned hazardous products.

Any extremely flammable contact adhesive and similar liquid or semiliquid consumer product as defined in § 1302.3 (b), which has been manufactured or initially introduced into commerce after January 17, 1978, is a banned hazardous product. In addition, any other extremely flammable contact adhesive and similar liquid or semiliquid consumer product, as defined in § 1302.3(b), no matter when manufactured or initially introduced into commerce, is a banned hazardous product after June 13, 1978.

§ 1302.5 Findings.

(a) *The degree and nature of the risk of injury.* The Commission finds that the risk of injury which this regulation is designed to eliminate or reduce is the risk of injury of burns from explosive vapor ignition and flashback fire associated with extremely flammable contact adhesives as defined in this rule.

(1) *Degree of the risk of injury presented by extremely flammable contact adhesives.* (i) In October 1976, the Commission's staff prepared a report entitled Hazard Analysis on Contact Adhesive Fires. According to the Hazard Analysis, three factors that measure burn severity are percent of body burned, days hospitalized, and whether clothing ignition occurs. Injury data sources summarized in the Hazard Analysis reveal that contact adhesive fires often result in a high percent of body burned, result in many days hospitalized, and usually involve clothing ignition burns.

(ii) The American Burn Association (ABA) participated in a special survey with the Commission to obtain an estimate of the incidence and severity of burns associated with the use of contact adhesive cements. In January 1976, the President of the ABA sent a letter to the 1,300 ABA members asking the members to record any thermal injuries or deaths that have occurred between January 1975 and March 1976 associated with contact adhesives. In November 1976, the Chairman of the ABA Committee on Burn Prevention submitted a statement to the Commission estimating that between 45 and 125 contact adhesive related injuries are treated annually in hospital emergency rooms. Although ABA members reported an annual rate of 20 severe burn injuries for the January 1975 to March 1976 period, the actual rate of severe burn injuries may be higher, since only approximately 400 hospitals, less than 10 percent of the country's short-term hospitals, are represented in ABA membership. The results of the ABA survey, as reported by the ABA Chairman, showed that the injuries treated by members resulted in an average hospitalization of 42 days, almost double the length of stay for all burn victims in special facilities for burns. According to the ABA Chairman, when a burn victim experiences such a lengthy stay, it is an indication of very severe injury and predicts a lengthy period of recuperation and potentially permanent physical and psychological consequences.

(iii) The Hazard Analysis prepared by the Commission's staff also contains a summary of the results of the ABA survey. According to the Commission's staff, the ABA survey revealed 33 incidents with sufficient details for analysis. Nine of the victims died from their burns and 21 were hospitalized. The average body area burned was 40 percent. In addition, the victims' clothing ignited on all except three of the 33 victims.

(iv) The Hazard Analysis also contains a summary of contact adhesive related fires in the National Fire Protection Association's (NFPA) Fire Incident Data Organization (FIDO), a computerized file of fire experience that includes data collected from 1971 to 1975. The NFPA files contained reports of 38 fires from 1971 to 1975, seven of which occurred in residences. These seven fires resulted in injuries to fifteen persons and deaths to three persons.

(v) In addition to the above injury information, the Hazard Analysis also indicates that the Commission has received three death certificates specifying the involvement of an adhesive.

(vi) According to the hazard analysis, after cases from the various data sources were verified as being mutually exclusive, at least 130 persons have been injured in contact adhesive fires since 1970. Fifteen of these persons subsequently died from the injuries they sustained in these accidents.

(vii) Technical analysis of extremely flammable contact adhesives by the Commission's staff indicates that the degree of the hazard associated with these products is such that as little as one pint of extremely flammable contact adhesive may produce a substantial explosion hazard.

(2) *Nature of the risk of injury presented by flammable contact adhesives.* (i) Technical analysis of these substances by the Commission's staff indicates that extremely flammable contact adhesives have a low flash point (20 °F or below), a rapid evaporation rate (as a result of a high percentage of solvents, 70–90 percent by weight), a low percentage of solids, 10–30 percent by weight, and a low wet-viscosity (300–6,000 centipoise when measured by an RVF Brookfield viscometer).

(ii) Flash point, viscosity, low solid to high solvent ratio, evaporation rate, size of the application area, and rate of application are factors which determine the potential for creating an ignitable vapor situation. The rapid rate of evaporation of extremely volatile, low flash point solvents from extremely flammable contact adhesives is capable of creating a highly explosive atmosphere. The flammable nature of these contact adhesives is such that the vaporized solvents from these products can be ignited by a sparking electric motor or an overlooked pilot light in an area remote from the site of use. Analysis of actual injury reports by the Commission's staff reveals that extremely flammable contact adhesives have, in fact, been ignited by many ignition sources including oven and stove pilot lights, water heater and furnace pilot lights, electric space heaters (without any visible flame), sparks from a refrigerator motor and a wall receptacle, and friction. Analysis of available injury reports has shown that these ignition sources are frequently located in areas of the house remote from the room in which the contact adhesive is being used.

(iii) The possibility of ignition from a source in another room or another part of the house may well be overlooked by the public, in spite of warnings on the label of the product. Ignition of the vapors may result in a sudden, flash back fire from the source of vapor ignition to the container of adhesive with little or no warning to the consumer and with the potential for serious or fatal injury to the user or bystanders. The injury information available to the Commission shows that the vast majority of accidents occur while the product is being used for its intended purpose. The potential for serious injury, therefore, appears to be present during normal use of the product.

(iv) Although the Commission has in the past required the extremely flammable contact adhesives now subject to this ban to bear minimum cautionary labeling for the hazard caused by the extreme flammability of the mixture, the Commission finds that this cautionary labeling is inadequate to protect the public. An analysis prepared by the Commission staff of the available injury data indicates that in spite of the cautionary labeling, accidents have continued to occur, inflicting serious injuries in much the same manner as those accidents that occurred prior to the issuance of the 1970 labeling regulation. The cautionary labeling presently required could be revised to include more explicit and graphic warnings. However, as a result of the degree and nature of the risk of injury presented by the product, this labeling would also provide inadequate protection to the public. The degree and nature of the risk of injury is such that a bystander or visitor could present an ignition source resulting in an accident. Since the bystander or visitor would not normally have an opportunity to read the warning label on the product, additional labeling would not benefit these potential victims. The possibility of ignition from a source in another room or another part of the house may well be overlooked by the public, in spite of warnings on the label of the product.

(b) *Products subject to this ban.* (1) The products banned by this rule are listed in § 1302.1.

(2) The Commission finds that the types of products subject to this ban are those contact adhesives that are extremely flammable and are packaged in containers of more than one-half pint. The average annual consumption of all types of contact adhesives in the United States is estimated at approximately 25 million gallons. Of this, it is estimated that 4–5 million gallons are sold in containers of 1 gallon or less, the sizes consumers generally buy. Professional users are estimated to purchase about half of the contact adhesives in this size range with most purchases probably of gallon containers. Therefore, consumers probably purchase 2–2.5 million gallon of all contact adhesives, most of which is estimated to be in quart containers, and a smaller amount in containers of one pint or less.

(3) In early 1976, contact adhesive sales were estimated as 80 percent extremely flammable, 10 percent chlorinated-solvent based, and 10 percent water-based. Since that time, a flammable petroleum solvent based contact adhesive has been developed and there has been a trend away from extremely flammable to flammable and nonflammable for consumer use. Although this trend is evident, reliable estimates of current market shares are not available. A rough estimate would be that perhaps 50 percent of contact adhesives in container sizes of more than one-half pint to 1 gallon are extremely flammable.

(c) Need of the public for the products and effects of the rule on their utility, cost, and availability.

(1) *The need for contact adhesives.* Contact adhesives are used primarily for bonding plastic laminates to counter and table tops, for applying tile board to walls, and for applying some types of flooring. Other uses include bonding metals, wood, leather, linoleum, tiles, rubber and plastics. Contact adhesives may also be used in furniture construction and repairs. There are contact adhesives available other than the extremely flammable type and other alternatives to contact adhesives that consumers can use.

(2) *Probable effects of the ban on the utility of contact adhesives.* Of the three general types of contact adhesive other than extremely flammable contact adhesives, flammable and non-flammable (chlorinated) contact adhesives have about the same general performance characteristics as extremely flammable contact adhesives. Therefore, because these two products are available to the public, the Commission believes the ban will have little impact on the utility of contact adhesives. In terms of performance characteristics, there is little difference between flammable and extremely flammable contact adhesives. Although the extremely flammable product requires approximately 10 minutes of drying time before the item can be bonded, the flammable product requires about 20 minutes. This difference in time is not likely to be significant for most consumers who do ordinary home improvement or repair work. The performance characteristics of non-flammable chlorinated based contact adhesives are similar to those of the extremely flammable type

for most applications. Non-flammable chlorinated based contact adhesives may be unacceptable for applications involving leather. Water based contact adhesives may not be as satisfactory, in terms of performance characteristics, as the other contact adhesives. The drying time for water-based contact adhesives varies with humidity. Although manufacturers of water-based neoprene contact adhesives claim that their products will dry in 30 minutes, for most of the country a drying time from one to four hours is probably more realistic. It is possible that the adhesive will never dry in some areas of the country with very high humidity. The time needed for the adhesive to adhere after joining (open time) will also vary with the humidity. Water-based acrylic contact adhesives are similar to neoprene type adhesives in terms of the effect of humidity on drying time. The neoprene and acrylic based adhesives are not completely satisfactory for binding some substances with non-porous surfaces, such as metals. In addition, the water in these adhesives might have an adverse effect on leather. Neoprene water-based adhesives may become unstable if frozen and thawed several times. This may occur during shipping or storage in some areas of the country during deaths associated with the extreme winter. To the extent that injuries and flammable contact adhesives are reduced or eliminated as a result of the ban, the utility of contact adhesives will be increased.

(3) *Probable effects of the ban upon the cost of contact adhesives.* For gallon containers, the Commission estimates that the contact adhesives available as substitutes for the extremely flammable type may cost in the range of $1–$6 more than the extremely flammable type. Although a gallon of extremely flammable contact adhesive may cost $7.50–$10.50, a gallon of flammable contact adhesive may cost from $8–$11, a gallon of nonflammable chlorinated base contact adhesive may cost from $12–$15, a gallon of water-based neoprene contact adhesive may cost from $11–$16, and a gallon of water-based acrylic contact adhesive may cost from $10–$15.

(4) *Probable effect of the ban on the availability of contact adhesives to meet the need of the public.* The Commission estimates that the ban will not have any effect on the availability or use of contact adhesives. Manufacturers are most likely to switch production to flammable petroleum-based and to 1,1,1,-trichloroethane (1,1,1,-TCE) based or water-based contact adhesives.

(d) *Alternatives.* (1) The Commission has considered other means of achieving the objective of this rule, such as labeling, but has found none that would achieve the objective of this ban, consistent with the public health and safety.

(2) The Commission believes that any adverse effects of the ban should be minimal and would be expected to be confined to some shift in distribution patterns to accommodate professional users, including methods of distinguishing between professional users and consumers.

(3) The Commission finds that competition should not be significantly affected by this rule.

(e) *Conclusion.* The Commission finds that this rule, including its effective date, is reasonably necessary to eliminate or reduce the unreasonable risk of injury of burns from explosive vapor ignition and flashback fire that is associated with the banned products described in §1302.3(b). The Commission also finds that issuance of the rule is in the public interest. The Commission also finds that no feasible consumer product safety standard under the act would adequately protect the public from the unreasonable risk of injury associated with the product.

§1302.6 Effective date.

This rule becomes effective January 18, 1978.

PART 1303—BAN OF LEAD-CONTAINING PAINT AND CERTAIN CONSUMER PRODUCTS BEARING LEAD-CONTAINING PAINT

Sec.

AUTHORITY: Secs. 8, 9, 86 Stat. 1215–1217, as amended 90 Stat. 506, 122 Stat. 3016, (15 U.S.C. 2057, 2058), Sec. 101, 122 Stat. 3016.

SOURCE: 42 FR 44199, Sept. 1, 1977, unless otherwise noted.

§ 1303.1 Scope and application.

(a) In this part 1303, the Consumer Product Safety Commission declares that paint and similar surface-coating materials for consumer use that contain lead or lead compounds and in which the lead content (calculated as lead metal) is in excess of 0.06 percent (0.06 percent is reduced to 0.009 percent effective August 14, 2009 as mandated by Congress in section 101(f) of the Consumer Product Safety Improvement Act of 2008, Pub. L. 110–314) of the weight of the total nonvolatile content of the paint or the weight of the dried paint film (which paint and similar surface-coating materials are referred to hereafter as "lead-containing paint") are banned hazardous products under sections 8 and 9 of the Consumer Product Safety Act (CPSA), 15 U.S.C. 2057, 2058. The following consumer products are also declared to be banned hazardous products:

(1) Toys and other articles intended for use by children that bear "lead-containing paint".

(2) Furniture articles for consumer use that bear "lead-containing paint".

(b) This ban applies to the products in the categories described in paragraph (a) of this section that are manufactured after February 27, 1978, and which are "consumer products" as that term is defined in section 3(a)(1) of the Consumer Product Safety Act. Accordingly, those of the products described above that are customarily produced or distributed for sale to or for use, consumption, or enjoyment of consumers in or around a household, in schools, in recreation, or otherwise are covered by the regulation. Paints and coatings for motor vehicles and boats are not included within the scope of the ban because they are outside the statutory definition of "consumer product". In addition to those products which are sold directly to consumers, the ban applies to products which are used or enjoyed by consumers after sale, such as paints used in residences, schools, hospitals, parks, playgrounds, and public buildings or other areas where consumers will have direct access to the painted surface.

(c) The Commission has issued the ban because it has found that there is an unreasonable risk of lead poisoning in children associated with lead content of over 0.06 percent in paints and coatings to which children have access and that no feasible consumer product safety standard under the CPSA would adequately protect the public from this risk. The 0.06 percent is reduced to 0.009 percent effective August 14, 2009 as mandated by Congress in section 101(f) of the Consumer Product Safety Improvement Act of 2008, Public Law 110–314.

(d) Any ban or rule promulgated under 16 CFR 1303.1 shall be considered a regulation of the Commission promulgated under or for the enforcement of section 2(q) of the Federal Hazardous Substances Act (15 U.S.C. 1261(q)).

[42 FR 44199, Sept. 1, 1977, as amended at 73 FR 77493, Dec. 19, 2008]

§ 1303.2 Definitions.

(a) The definitions in section 3 of the Consumer Product Safety Act (15 U.S.C. 2052) shall apply to this part 1303.

(b) For purposes of this part:

(1) *Paint and other similar surface-coating materials* means a fluid, semi-fluid, or other material, with or without a suspension of finely divided coloring matter, which changes to a solid film when a thin layer is applied to a metal, wood, stone, paper, leather, cloth, plastic, or other surface. This term does not include printing inks or those materials which actually become a part of the substrate, such as the pigment in a plastic article, or those materials which are actually bonded to the substrate, such as by electroplating or ceramic glazing.

(2) *Lead-containing paint* means paint or other similar surface coating materials containing lead or lead compounds and in which the lead content (calculated as lead metal) is in excess of 0.06 percent (0.06 percent is reduced to 0.009 percent effective August 14, 2009) by weight of the total nonvolatile content of the paint or the weight of the dried paint film.

(3) *Toys and other articles intended for use by children* means those toys and other articles which are intended to be entrusted to or for use by children. This would not include all articles to which children might have access simply because they are present in a household.

(4) *Furniture article* means those movable articles: (i) Used to support people or things; (ii) other functional or decorative furniture articles, including, but not limited to, products such as beds, bookcases, chairs, chests, tables, dressers, desks, pianos, console televisions, and sofas. The term "furniture article" does not include appliances, such as ranges, refrigerators, dishwashers, clothes washers and dryers, air conditioners, humidifiers, and dehumidifiers; fixtures such as bathroom fixtures, built-in cabinets, chandeliers, windows, and doors; or household items such as window shades, venetian blinds, or wall hangings and draperies.

[42 FR 44199, Sept. 1, 1977, as amended at 73 FR 77493, Dec. 19, 2008]

§ 1303.3 Exemptions.

(a) The categories of products listed in paragraph (b) of this section are exempted from the scope of the ban established by this part 1303, provided:

(1) That these products bear on the main panel of their label, in addition to any labeling that may be otherwise required, the signal word "Warning" (unless some other signal word is required) and the following statement: "Contains Lead. Dried Film of This Paint May Be Harmful If Eaten or Chewed."

(2)(i) That these products also bear on their label the following additional statement or its practical equivalent:

Do not apply on toys and other children's articles, furniture, or interior surfaces of any dwelling or facility which may be occupied or used by children.

Do not apply on exterior surfaces of dwelling units, such as window sills, porches, stairs, or railings, to which children may be commonly exposed.

Keep out of reach of children.

(ii) If the statement required by the preceding paragraph (a)(2)(i) is placed on a label panel other than the main panel, the label statement required to be on the main panel by paragraph (a)(1) of this section shall contain the following additional statement: "See other cautions on __ (insert 'side' or 'back', as appropriate) panel."

(3) That the placement, conspicuousness, and contrast of the label statements required by this section (a) comply with the requirements of the Federal Hazardous Substances Act at 16 CFR 1500.121.

(b) The following products are exempt from the scope of the ban established by this part 1303, provided they comply with the requirements of paragraph (a) of this section:

(1) Agricultural and industrial equipment refinish coatings.

(2) Industrial (and commercial) building and equipment maintenance coatings, including traffic and safety marking coatings.

(3) Graphic art coatings (i.e., products marketed solely for application on billboards, road signs, and similar uses and for identification marking in industrial buildings).

(4) Touchup coatings for agricultural equipment, lawn and garden equipment, and appliances.

(5) Catalyzed coatings marketed solely for use on radio-controlled model powered aircraft.

(c) The following products are exempt from the scope of the ban established by part 1303 (no cautionary labeling is required):

(1) Mirrors which are part of furniture articles to the extent that they bear lead-containing backing paint.

(2) Artists' paints and related materials.

(3) Metal furniture articles (but not metal children's furniture) bearing factory-applied (lead) coatings.

[42 FR 44199, Sept. 1, 1977, as amended at 43 FR 8515, Mar. 2, 1978]

§ 1303.4 Banned hazardous products.

The following consumer products, manufactured after February 27, 1978, unless exempted by § 1303.3, are banned hazardous products (see definitions in § 1303.2):

(a) Paint and other similar surface-coating materials which are "lead-containing paint."

(b) Toys and other articles intended for use by children that bear "lead-containing paint."

(c) Furniture articles that bear "lead-containing paint."

§ 1303.5 Findings.

(a) *The degree and nature of the risk of injury.* (1) The Commission finds that the risk of injury which this regulation is designed to eliminate or reduce is lead poisoning in children. The adverse effects of this poisoning in children can cause a range of disorders such as hyperactivity, slowed learning ability, withdrawal, blindness, and even death. The final Environmental Impact Statement on Lead in Paint which is on file with the President's Council on Environmental Quality (and available for inspection in the Office of the Secretary) contains in appendix A a detailed discussion of the health effects of lead in paint. These effects will only be summarized here.

(2) Lead is a cumulative toxic heavy metal which, in humans, exerts its effects on the renal, hematopoietic, and nervous systems. Newer concepts indicate that there are three stages to childhood lead poisoning. The adverse health effects in the first stage are not clinically present but metabolic changes can be observed. During the second stage or symptomatic stage such symptoms as loss of appetite, vomiting, apathy, drowsiness, and inability to coordinate voluntary muscle movements occur. The after effects of this stage include seizure disorders as well as various behavioral and functional disorders which are often included under the heading of minimal brain dysfunction. Studies suggest that this syndrome may include hyperactivity, impulsive behavior, prolonged reaction time, perceptual disorders and slowed learning ability. The adverse health effects of the third stage may be permanent and can include blindness, mental retardation, behavior disorders, and death.

(3) The Commission notes that children with pica are of special concern with regard to lead poisoning. Pica, the repetitive ingestion of nonfood substances, occurs in 50 percent of children between the ages of one and three, and studies indicate that at this age lead is absorbed more rapidly than lead is absorbed in adults. Pica for paint is believed to be episodic and can occur 2 to 3 times a week.

(4) The Commission also notes that there are no reports of injuries caused by lead paint poisoning in the Commission's National Electronic Injury Surveillance System (NEISS) data, which reflect hospital emergency room treatment. Lead paint poisonings result from a chronic hazard rather than from an acute hazard of the type generally treated in emergency rooms; and NEISS reporting, therefore, does not reflect this type of chronic hazard or injuries.

(5) Former U.S. Surgeon-General Jesse L. Steinfeld, however, estimated in 1971 that 400,000 pre-school American children have elevated body lead burdens. The National Bureau of Standards in 1972 estimated that 600,000 young children have unduly high lead blood content.

(b) *Products subject to this ban.* (1) The products banned by this rule are listed in § 1303.4.

(2) The term *paint* comprises a variety of coating materials such as interior and exterior household paints, varnishes, lacquers, stains, enamels, primers, and similar coatings formulated for use on various surfaces. Based on 1976 data, the Commission estimates that over 400 million gallons of paint a year valued at approximately $2.5 billion could potentially be subject to this rule.

(3) All products commonly known as toys and other articles intended for the use of children are subject to this rule. The categories of products within this classification are numerous and include items and equipment for play, amusement, education, physical fitness, and care of children. Retail sales in 1976 of products considered to be toys or other articles intended for use of children are estimated at around $4 billion.

(4) For the purposes of this rule, furniture articles are certain movable articles used to support people or things or other functional or decorative furniture articles such as couches, beds, tables, chairs, chests, and the like. Appliances and similar equipment, household fixtures, and certain other household items such as window shades, blinds, wall hangings, and the like are not included within the definition of furniture. The regulation applies to furniture for use in households, schools, in recreation, or otherwise. In

1972, the value of shipments of items of furniture such as those named above was as follows: wood household furniture $2,716 million; metal household furniture $859 million; wood television and radio cabinets $293 million; and $190 million for other household furniture made of plastic, reed and rattan. (Not included in the above are some $2 billion worth of upholstered furniture and $300 million in convertible sofas, chair beds and studio couches.)

(c) *Need of the public for the products and effects of the rule on their utility, cost, and availability.* (1) The public need for paints of various types and for furniture and other articles is substantial and well established. The Commission finds that the need of the public for paint containing more than 0.06 percent lead or for the affected products that are coated with materials containing more than 0.06 percent lead is limited. The Commission has determined that there are products containing more than the 0.06 percent level of lead which meet a public need and for which substitutes are either not available or are not sufficiently effective and to which access by children to the coatings or the surfaces to which they are applied is unlikely. Accordingly, these products have been specifically exempted from the scope of the regulation in §1303.3.

(2) The Commission finds that the effects of this rule on the cost, utility, and availability of paints and painted articles will be small. The Commission notes that over 95 percent of latex-based and nearly 70 percent of oil-based paints have lead levels at or below the level set by part 1303.

(i) *Costs.* The Commission estimates that the added costs to the consumer for paints affected by this rule will not exceed 5 to 10 cents per gallon. Costs to consumers for furniture and for toys and other articles intended for the use of children are not expected to increase as the result of compliance with the regulation.

(ii) *Utility.* The Commission finds that for water-based or latex paints and coatings subject to this rule, reducing the amount of allowable lead to 0.06 percent will not have adverse effects on their utility. For certain solvent-thinned coatings, however, lead driers will have to be replaced by nonlead driers such as zirconium to comply with the 0.06 percent level (Driers are not used in latex paints). An impact on the paint industry may result because current nonlead driers may not dry satisfactorily in low temperatures or high humidity conditions, and so the painting industry in some areas at certain times of the year may suffer a reduction of effective painting time.

(iii) *Availability.* Substitutes at comparable prices are available for paints and for products banned by this rule. The Commission believes that the reduction of lead to a level of 0.06 percent will not affect the availabilty of water-based or latex paints. Sales of such coatings currently exceed sales of solvent-based coatings, and because of the drying problem mentioned above, the trend toward increased use of water-based paints may be accelerated somewhat by the effects of the ban.

(d) *Alternatives.* (1) The Commission has considered other means of achieving the objective of this rule, but has found none that would cause less disruption or dislocation of manufacturing and other commercial practices, consistent with public health and safety.

(2) The Commission estimates that this ban may, because of testing costs and the necessity for improved housekeeping practices in the manufacture of paint and similar surface-coating materials to prevent lead containimation, have some relatively minor adverse effect on individual firms within some markets.

(3) The Commission, however, finds that competition will not be adversely affected by this rule. Although costs of reformulation and testing may be relatively higher for small manufacturers than large manufacturers, these costs are not so onerous as to lead to greater concentration in the industry. The period of time before the effective date is sufficient to minimize problems of compliance with the rule.

(4) The reduction of the permissible level of lead in paint will affect paint manufacturers, raw materials suppliers, professional and non-professional painters, and manufacturers of furniture and children's articles. For

those producers of paint which are already subject to the regulations under the Federal Hazardous Substances Act (FHSA), the impact of this CPSA ban will involve only a change to non-lead driers since lead pigments are precluded from practical use under the 0.5 percent lead restriction now in effect under the FHSA (16 CFR 1500.17(a)(6)). The manufacturers of some painted furniture who were not affected by the 0.5 percent limit under the FHSA may now be, if they use lead pigments or driers. Producers of children's articles who were subject to the 0.5 percent FHSA limit will have to ensure that the paint they use conforms to the 0.06 percent level.

(e) *Conclusion.* The Commission finds that this rule, including its effective date, is reasonably necessary to eliminate or reduce the unreasonable risk of lead poisoning of young children that is associated with the banned products which are described in §1303.4 and that promulgation of the rule is in the public interest.

PART 1304—BAN OF CONSUMER PATCHING COMPOUNDS CONTAINING RESPIRABLE FREE-FORM ASBESTOS

AUTHORITY: Secs. 8, 9, 86 Stat. 1215–1217, as amended 90 Stat. 506, 15 U.S.C. 2057, 2058.

SOURCE: 42 FR 63362, Dec. 15, 1977, unless otherwise noted.

§1304.1 Scope and application.

(a) In this part 1304 the Consumer Product Safety Commission declares that consumer patching compounds containing intentionally-added respirable freeform asbestos in such a manner that the asbestos fibers can become airborne under reasonably foreseeable conditions of use, are banned hazardous products under sections 8 and 9 of the Consumer Product Safety Act (CPSA) (15 U.S.C. 2057 and 2058). This ban applies to patching compounds which are (1) used to cover, seal or mask cracks, joints, holes and similar openings in the trim, walls, ceiling, etc. of building interiors, which after drying are sanded to a smooth finish and (2) are produced and distributed for sale to or for the personal use, consumption or enjoyment of a consumer in or around a permanent or temporary household or residence, a school, in recreation or otherwise.

(b) The Commission has found that (1) these patching compounds are being or will be distributed in commerce; (2) that they present an unreasonable risk of injury; and (3) that no feasible consumer product safety standard under the CPSA would adequately protect the public from the unreasonable risk of injury associated with these products. This rule applies to the banned hazardous products defined in §1304.3 and described further in §1304.4.

(c) Only consumer products are subject to this regulation. Patching compounds which are consumer products include those which a consumer can purchase. Merely labeling a patching compound for industrial use would not exclude such articles from the ban. If the sale or use of the product by consumers is facilitated, it is subject to the ban. Patching compounds which are labeled as, marketed, and sold solely for industrial use in non-consumer environments are not subject to the ban. In addition to those products which can be sold directly to consumers, the ban applies to patching compounds containing respirable free-form asbestos which are used in residences, schools, hospitals, public buildings or other areas where consumers have customary access.

§1304.2 Purpose.

The purpose of this rule is to ban consumer patching compounds containing intentionally added respirable, free-form asbestos. These products present an unreasonable risk of injury due to inhalation of fibers which increase the risk of developing cancer, including lung cancer and mesothelioma, diseases which have been demonstrated to be caused by exposure to asbestos fibers.

§ 1304.3 Definitions.

(a) The definitions in section 3 of the Consumer Product Safety Act (15 U.S.C. 2052) apply to this part 1304.

(b) *Asbestos* means a group of mineral fibers composed of hydrated silicates, oxygen, hydrogen, and other elements such as sodium, iron, magnesium, and calcium in diverse combinations and are: Amosite, chrysotile, crocidolite, anthophyllite asbestos, actinolite asbestos, and tremolite asbestos.

(c) *Free-form asbestos* is that which is not bound, or otherwise "locked-in" to a product by resins or other bonding agents, or which can readily become airborne with any reasonably foreseeable use.

(d) *Patching compounds* are mixtures of talc, pigments, clays, casein, ground marble, mica or other similar materials and a binding material such as asbestos which are sold in a dry form ready to be mixed with water, or such combinations in ready-mix paste form.

(e) *Consumer patching compounds* are those that are customarily produced or distributed for sale to or for the personal use, consumption or enjoyment of consumers in or around a permanent or temporary household or residence, a school, in recreation or otherwise. The Commission considers that patching compounds for application in these consumer environments are either distributed for sale to or are for the personal use or enjoyment of consumers.

(f) *Intentionally-added asbestos* is asbestos which is (1) added deliberately as an ingredient intended to impart specific characteristics; or, (2) contained in the final product as the result of knowingly using a raw material containing asbestos. Whenever a manufacturer finds out that the finished product contains asbestos, the manufacturer will be considered as knowingly using a raw material containing asbestos, unless the manufacturer takes steps to reduce the asbestos to the maximum extent feasible.

(g) *Initial introduction into commerce* occurs when the manufacturer ships a product covered by this regulation from a facility of the manufacturer to a distributor, retailer, or user.

§ 1304.4 Consumer patching compounds as banned hazardous products.

On the basis that airborne asbestos fibers present the hazards of cancer, including lung cancer and mesothelioma to the public, consumer patching compounds containing intentionally-added, respirable free-form asbestos, which have been manufactured or initially introduced into commerce after January 16, 1978, are banned hazardous products. In addition, all other consumer patching compounds containing intentionally-added, respirable free-form asbestos, no matter when manufactured or initially introduced into commerce, are banned hazardous products after June 11, 1978.

§ 1304.5 Findings.

(a) *The degree and nature of the risk of injury.* The Commission finds that the risk of injury which this regulation is designed to eliminate or reduce is from cancer, including lung cancer and mesothelioma. In assessing the degree and nature of the risk of injury to consumers, the Commission has reviewed experimental data and human experience information. The Commission noted that in the scientific literature, there is general agreement that there is no known threshold level below which exposure to respirable free-form asbestos would be considered safe. Further, on the basis of such scientific opinion, it appears to the Commission that children are particularly vulnerable to carcinogens because of their longer potential lifetime and their rapid rate of growth. In areas of the country where asbestos may not be prevalent in the environment, the major risk of exposure for children and others may occur in the household. In areas of the country where more asbestos fibers are present in the environment, the public is exposed to additional risks from the presence of asbestos fibers in households and other consumer environments. The Commission concluded on the basis of these factors that consumer patching compounds containing respirable free-form asbestos present an unreasonable risk of injury to the public. In addition, a risk assessment was made. For purposes of this assessment, the Commission considered the use of patching compounds by the consumer, for six hours a day four times a year, to be a high yet reasonably foreseeable exposure. The increased risk of death from respiratory cancer induced by this exposure is estimated at between 10 and 2,000 per million. For five years of exposure at these levels, the risk increases geometrically and is estimated at between 1,000 and 12,000 per million. The lower estimate of 10 per million is closer to the actual risk for a one-year exposure. Nevertheless, in view of the seriousness of the injury and the cumulative effects of asbestos exposure, even this minimum figure represents an unacceptable risk. The Commission believes that reducing exposure to respirable free-form asbestos in the home represents a substantial decrease in risk to consumers, since, for many people, the major exposure to inhalable asbestos is in the home.

(b) *Products subject to the ban.* Consumer patching compounds as defined in §1034.3 (d), (e), (f) includes such products as drywall spackling compounds and tape joint compounds (commonly known as "joint cement" or "tape joint mud"). The Commission estimates annual shipments of patching compounds subject to the ban at approximately 30–50 million "units," or individual packages, of various sizes from 0.5 to 25 pounds (dry) or 0.5 to 5 gallons (wet). The Commission believes that about half the patching compounds sold in 1977, and intended for sale to or use or enjoyment by consumers, were formulated with asbestos. Many others containing significant levels of asbestos contamination will also be affected by the ban.

(c) *Need of the public for the products and effects of the rule on their utility, cost and availability.* Patching compounds, though used primarily by commercial construction workers, are also used by consumers, and are used for the patching and sealing of cracks and joints in and around the household and in other consumer environments either by consumers or professional applicators. The compounds are used to cover areas on gypsum drywall which might otherwise be aesthetically undesirable or which might lead to structural damage, energy loss or lower property value. The asbestos in these compounds acts as a structural reinforcing agent which helps to reduce cracking and shrinkage of the compound over time, and which renders the compound more pliable or "workable" upon application.

(1) *Utility.* The elimination of asbestos from these products may result in the increased use or new development of substitutes which have similar properties to those of asbestos, or which impart similar qualities to the product. In current reformulations, asbestos is replaced by a combination of substances, of which the most common is attapulgite, a fibrous clay. Some nonasbestos formulations are reportedly not as effective as those containing asbestos in controlling shrinkage and cracking over time. The workability of some compounds may be diminished as well. This may adversely affect the utility derived from the product by consumers, and by professional contractors until such time as improved formulations are developed and available to end-users.

(2) *Cost.* Asbestos-free patching compound formulations may require more time to use. This would tend to increase the direct labor costs of residential and other construction and renovation. The expected increase is between 10 and 25 percent. The Commission estimates that the annual labor cost of drywall finishing in these consumer environments is on the order of $1 billion. The use of nonasbestos patching compound formulations in all applications may increase this cost by $50–$125 million, assuming that roughly half the current labor costs (i.e., that portion now associated with the use of asbestos formulations) are affected by the 10–25 percent increase. The burden of this cost is expected to fall directly on owners of existing homes who may engage in some renovation, and on purchasers of newly-renovated or newly-constructed homes. These increased costs are expected to diminish over time as formulations improve and as applicators become more accustomed to using nonasbestos formulations. The use of asbestos substitutes may also lead to cost increases in the manufacture of patching compounds. The Commission

estimates this cost, which may vary widely from firm to firm, at an average of 5–15 percent. This is made up primarily of increased costs of raw materials and of formulation research and development. It is expected that the price of many patching compounds may rise as a result. Producers, distributors, and retailers of patching compounds may also have to incur costs associated with the disposal of products in inventory. The Commission estimates that the wholesale value of manufacturers' and distributors' inventories at the time the ban becomes effective will be approximately $15 million. These costs may be reflected in the prices charged for asbestos-free patching compound formulations, and in the prices of other drywall and paint products. It appears that, because of competitive pressure from asbestos-containing compounds, producers of asbestos-free formulations have not yet passed on to purchasers their increased costs. If the increased production costs of asbestos-free formulations can be passed on completely as a result of the ban, the total annual price effect for the year following the issuance of the ban may be $10–$60 million. The magnitude of this effect may be reduced significantly in successive years following the issuance of the ban as producers' development costs are amortized, as raw materials become more widely available, and as price competition is strengthened because of market pressure and economies of sale associated with production.

(3) *Availability*. The supply of asbestos substitutes, particularly attapulgite clay and relatively uncontaminated talc, for use in the manufacture of patching compounds may be insufficient to meet the short-run demand which is expected to be stimulated by the promulgation of the ban. Further, many small producers probably lack the technical capability to reformulate their products, and may be forced to cease production, at least until formulations of satisfactory cost and performance are developed. This may affect some professional contractors. In the short run, consumers may be indirectly affected by delays in drywall finishing and building completion.

(d) *Any means of achieving the objective of the ban while minimizing adverse effects on competition or disruption or dislocation of manufacturing and other commercial practices consistent with the public health and safety*. The adverse effects of the ban on patching compounds containing asbestos is reduced by limiting the ban to intentionally added asbestos. Other alternatives such as limiting the scope of the ban only to products purchased and used by consumers or to issuing a ban with a later effective date, were considered by the Commission. However, none was found that would cause less disruption or dislocation of manufacturing and other commercial practices, consistent with public health and safety.

PART 1305—BAN OF ARTIFICIAL EMBERIZING MATERIALS (ASH AND EMBERS) CONTAINING RESPIRABLE FREE-FORM ASBESTOS

AUTHORITY: Secs. 8, 9, 30(d), Pub. L. 92–573, as amended, Pub. L. 94–284; 86 Stat. 1215–17, as amended, 90 Stat. 506 (15 U.S.C. 2057, 2058).

SOURCE: 42 FR 63364, Dec. 15, 1977, unless otherwise noted.

§ 1305.1 Scope and application.

In this part 1305 the Consumer Product Safety Commission declares that artificial emberizing materials (ash and embers) containing respirable free-form asbestos generally packaged in an emberizing kit for use in fireplaces, and designed for use in such a manner that the asbestos fibers can become airborne under reasonably foreseeable conditions of use are banned hazardous products under sections 8 and 9 of the Consumer Product Safety Act (CPSA) (15 U.S.C. 2057 and 2058). This ban applies to artificial emberizing materials available in separate kits or with artificial fireplace logs for use in fireplaces and sprinkled or coated by consumers on the artificial logs to simulate live embers and ashes and give a glowing appearance when subjected to high temperatures. Bags of material containing asbestos that are sold separately to be sprinkled on and under artificial logs to simulate burning and glowing ashes also come within the scope of this ban.

§ 1305.2 Purpose.

The purpose of this rule is to ban artificial emberizing materials containing respirable free-form asbestos. These products present an unreasonable risk of injury due to inhalation of fibers which increase the risk of developing cancers such as lung cancer and mesothelioma, diseases which have been demonstrated to be caused by exposure to asbestos fibers.

§ 1305.3 Definitions.

(a) The definitions in section 3 of the Consumer Product Safety Act (15 U.S.C. 2052) apply to this part 1305.

(b) *Asbestos* means a group of mineral fibers composed of hydrated silicates, oxygen, hydrogen and other elements such as sodium, iron, magnesium and calcium in diverse combinations and are: Amosite, chrysotile, crocidolite, anthophyllite asbestos, actinolite asbestos, and tremolite asbestos.

(c) *Free-form asbestos* is that which is not bound, woven, or otherwise ''locked-in'' to a product by resins or other bonding agents, or those from which fibers can readily become airborne with any reasonably foreseeable use.

(d) *Emberizing materials* means an asbestos-containing material generally packed in an ''emberizing'' kit to be placed under artificial logs in gas-burning fireplace systems or in artificial fireplaces for decorative purposes. The product is also glued to artificial logs, either at a factory or by a consumer using an emberizing kit. (Synthetic logs manufactured of cellulostic products which are consumed by flames are not included in this definition. Electric artificial logs and artificial ash beds used in electric fireplaces, which do not contain respirable free-form asbestos are not included in this definition.)

§ 1305.4 Artificial fireplace ash and embers as banned hazardous products.

On the basis that airborne asbestos fibers present the hazards of cancer such as lung cancer and mesothelioma to the public, artificial fireplace ash and embers containings respirable free-form asbestos are banned hazardous products.

§ 1305.5 Findings.

(a) *The degree and nature of the risk of injury.* The Commission finds that the risk of injury which this regulation is designed to eliminate or reduce is from cancer, including lung cancer and mesothelioma. Measurements are not available of the amounts of asbestos in the air from asbestos-containing emberizing materials in homes. However, it appears that the amount of airborne asbestos in such homes would increase when air currents in the home are created by downdrafts from a fireplace chimney or other activities that stir air in any room. Since emberizing materials may contain up to 50 percent asbestos, which if not permanently bound into artificial fireplace logs would be in respirable form, the risk associated with emberizing materials is considerable, especially since it continues to exist 24 hours a day.

(b) *Products subject to the ban.* Artificial emberizing materials are decorative simulated ashes or embers, used in certain gas-buring fireplace systems, which glow to give the appearance of real burning embers. The material is sprinkled on or glued to gas logs, or sprinkled on fireplace floors.

(c) *Need of the public for the products and effects of the rule on their utility, cost, and availability.* Artificial fireplace emberizing material serves a strictly decorative purpose and does not materially affect the actual performance of the fireplace gas system in terms of its ability to provide heat. A certain degree of aesthetic desirability exists, however, since the product ''system'' itself (the gas log, ashes, and embers) is intended to simulate burning wooden logs. Gas logs may be sold with artificial emberizing material attached at the factory (the log commonly referred to as being ''frosted''), or with the ''embers'' in a separate kit, often mixed with simulated "ashes." Virtually all gas logs are either frosted or packaged with an emberizing kit; however, the majority of gas logs produced in 1977 were packaged with non-asbestos-containing emberizing kits. The Commission estimates annual sales of artificial gas logs at approximately 100,000 units. Some 25,000–30,000 of these would be subject to the ban. Approximately 100,000 gas logs frosted or treated by consumers with asbestos are estimated to be in existence. The Commission believes that the majority of gas logs are sold with emberizing kits; this gives the consumer a choice as to whether or not to use the artificial embers and ashes.

(1) *Utility*. Manufacturers of artificial gas log emberizing material are currently using four substitutes for asbestos in their products: vermiculite, rock wool, mica, and a synthetic fiber. None of the four is claimed to be as aesthetically effective as asbestos. Thus, the utility derived by consumers from some gas-burning fireplace systems may be adversely affected.

(2) *Cost*. No effect on the overall price level of gas logs is anticipated as a result of the ban. The average price of emberizing kits may rise somewhat; the Commission estimates the total price effect of the ban on consumers at under $25,000.

(3) *Availability*. The Commission believes that all producers of artificial emberizing material will have eliminated asbestos from their products by the time the ban becomes effective. No significant impact on the availability of asbestos substitutes to producers nor on the availability of gas logs or emberizing kits to retail dealers and consumers is expected as a result of the ban.

(d) *Any means of achieving the objective of the ban while minimizing adverse effects on competition or disruption or dislocation of manufacturing and other commercial practices consistent with the public health and safety*. The Commission believes that there will be minimal disruption to the market for artificial emberizing materials as a consequence of the ban and that no further reduction in adverse effects is feasible.

PART 1306—BAN OF HAZARDOUS LAWN DARTS

AUTHORITY: 15 U.S.C. 2058–2060.

SOURCE: 53 FR 46839, Nov. 18, 1988, unless otherwise noted.

§ 1306.1 Scope and application.

(a) In this part 1306, the Commission declares lawn darts, described in § 1306.3, to be banned hazardous products.

(b) Lawn darts and similar products that are articles intended for use by children are not covered by this ban, but are banned under the Federal Hazardous Substances Act at 16 CFR 1500.18(a)(4).

§ 1306.2 Purpose.

The purpose of this rule is to prohibit the sale of lawn darts, which have been found to present an unreasonable risk of skull puncture injuries to children.

§ 1306.3 Banned hazardous products.

Any lawn dart is a banned hazardous product.

§ 1306.4 Findings.

(a) The Commission has found that lawn darts are being distributed in commerce and present an unreasonable risk of injury.

(b) *The degree and nature of the risk of injury*. (1) The risk that the Commission intends to address in this proceeding is that of puncture of the skulls of children caused by lawn darts being used by children. The potential for these devices to cause these types of injuries is not necessarily obvious to parents or other adults who might buy these items or allow their children to play with them, much less to the children themselves. This is because the tips do not appear sharp enough to present an obvious danger of puncture. The combined factors of weight, the narrow elongated shaft, the speed that the dart is traveling at the time of impact, and the thickness of the child's skull at the point of impact present the risk. The Commission has concluded that all lawn darts have the potential for skull puncture during reasonably foreseeable use or misuse.

(2) Because all lawn darts are being banned, the elimination of lawn darts that can cause skull puncture injuries will also eliminate the punctures of other parts of the body, as well as the lacerations, fractures, and other injuries that have been associated with lawn darts in the past. The Commission's staff estimates that about 670 injuries from lawn darts are treated in U.S. hospital emergency rooms per year. About 40 percent of these are puncture wounds. Approximately 57 percent of the injuries involved the head, face, eye, or ear. Approximately 4 percent of the injured victims were hospitalized (on the average, approximately 25 per year), including all of the injuries reported as fractures. Over 75 percent of the victims were under age 15; about 50 percent of the victims were under age 10. In addition, Commission records dating back to 1970 show that at least three children have been killed by injuries associated with lawn darts. These children were 4, 7, and 13 years old. In the 25 lawn dart injury reports for which information about the user of the lawn darts was available, the reports indicated that children were playing with the lawn darts, despite the ban and exemption which were developed to keep the product out of the hands of children.

(c) *Products subject to this ban.* (1) Lawn darts are devices with elongated tips that are intended to be used outdoors and that are designed so that when they are thrown into the air they will contact the ground tip first. Often, lawn darts are used in a game where the darts are thrown at a target or other feature on the ground. The types of lawn darts that have generally been available in the past and that have demonstrated their ability to cause skull puncture injuries typically have a metal or weighted plastic body, on the front of which is an elongated metal shaft about ¼ inch in diameter. These darts have a shaft on the rear of the body containing plastic fins. These darts are about a foot in length and weigh about one quarter to one half pound. These darts are intended to stick in the ground when thrown. Prior to this rule, annual sales of these lawn darts were estimated at 1–1.5 million units.

(2) The definition for lawn darts in this rule is not intended to include arrows or horseshoes, nor is it intended to apply to indoor dart games that use a vertically-placed target, such as "English darts" or "American darts."

(d) *The need of the public for lawn darts, and the effects of the rule on their utility, cost, and availability.* The need of the public for lawn darts is for recreational enjoyment. Substitute recreational enjoyment can be obtained from other products. Lawn darts will not be available through commercial channels after the effective date of the ban.

(e) *Alternatives.* (1) The Commission considered various labeling requirements and limitations on the marketing of lawn darts that would be intended to discourage the marketing of the product to children and the use of the product by children. The Commission concluded, however, that these types of requirements would not preclude substantial use of the product by children and would not reduce adequately the risk of injury addressed by this rule.

(2) The Commission also considered the possibility of performance requirements for lawn darts to determine which lawn darts present an unreasonable risk of injury of skull penetration to children, but such requirements were determined not to be feasible.

(f) *Conclusion.* The Commission finds:

(1) That this rule, including its effective date, is reasonably necessary to eliminate or adequately reduce the unreasonable risk of skull puncture wounds to children associated with lawn darts and will also eliminate or reduce the other injuries, including puncture wounds, that have been associated with this product.

(2) That issuance of the rule is in the public interest.

(3) That no feasible consumer product safety standard would adequately protect the public from the unreasonable risk associated with lawn darts.

(4) That the benefits expected from this rule bear a reasonable relationship to its costs.

(5) That the rule imposes the least burdensome requirement which prevents or adequately reduces the risk of injury for which the rule is being promulgated.

§ 1306.5 Effective date.

This rule is effective December 19, 1988 and applies to all lawn darts in the chain of distribution on or after that date.

PART 1401—SELF PRESSURIZED CONSUMER PRODUCTS CONTAINING CHLOROFLUOROCARBONS: REQUIREMENTS TO PROVIDE THE COMMISSION WITH PERFORMANCE AND TECHNICAL DATA; REQUIREMENTS TO NOTIFY CONSUMERS AT POINT OF PURCHASE OF PERFORMANCE AND TECHNICAL DATA

AUTHORITY: Secs. 2(b), 27(e), Pub. L. 92–573, 86 Stat. 1208, 1228 (15 U.S.C. 2051(b), 2076(e)).

SOURCE: 42 FR 42783, Aug. 24, 1977, unless otherwise noted.

§ 1401.1 Scope.

This part 1401 establishes requirements under section 27(e) of the Consumer Product Safety Act (15 U.S.C. 2076(e)) for marketers and importers of self-pressurized consumer products that contain chlorofluorocarbons as propellants to provide notification of certain performance and technical data to prospective purchasers of such products at the time of original purchase and to the first purchaser of such products for purposes other than resale. The notification shall consist of a label on the product stating that it contains a chlorofluorocarbon that may harm the public health and environment by reducing the ozone in the upper atmosphere. Also, manufacturers and importers must provide the commission with reports identifying which of the self-pressurized consumer products sold by them contain chlorofluorocarbon propellants.

§ 1401.2 Purpose.

Chlorofluorocarbons are used as propellants in self-pressurized containers of a variety of products subject to the Commission's jurisdiction. Scientific research has indicated that chlorofluorocarbons may pose a risk of depletion of ozone in the stratosphere. The stratospheric ozone shield is of great importance in protecting life on earth from shortwave ultra-violet rays of the sun. Ozone depletion allows more of these rays to reach the earth, and the consequences include a possibility of a significant increase in human skin cancer and other effects of unknown magnitude on man, animals, and plants. Chlorofluorocarbon release may also cause climatic change, both by reducing stratospheric ozone and by increasing infrared absorption in the atmosphere. The Commission believes that the requirements of this part 1401 will enable consumers to make a conscious choice of whether to use products that contain chlorofluorocarbon propellants. The Commission also believes that these requirements are necessary in order to carry out the purposes of the Consumer Product Safety Act of (a) helping to protect the public against unreasonable risks of injury associated with consumer products and (b) assisting consumers in evaluating the comparative safety of consumer products.

§ 1401.3 Definitions.

For the purposes of this part 1401:

(a) *Chlorofluorocarbon* means any fully halogenated chlorofluoroalkane.

(b) *Finished product* means a product which has been completely manufactured, packaged, and labeled.

(c) *Initially introduced into interstate commerce* means the first shipment of the product into interstate commerce by the firm marketing the product. There must be both physical movement in interstate commerce and passage of title to the product. Thus, mere shipment of a product across state lines from a contract filler to the marketer of the product would not constitute initial introduction into interstate commerce. All products initially introduced into interstate commerce before the effective date may continue to be distributed and sold even though they do not bear the warning statement.

(d) *Manufacturer* means any person who manufactures or imports a consumer product. The term includes both a person who manufactures the product at the direction of another (such as a contract filler of aerosol products) and the person at whose direction the product is manufactured (such as the marketer of the brand).

(e) *Propellent* means a liquefied or compressed gas in a container, where a purpose of the liquefied or compressed gas is to expel material from the container. The material to be expelled may be the propellant itself and/or a material different from the propellent.

(f) The definitions given in section 3 of the Consumer Product Safety Act (15 U.S.C. 2052) shall, where applicable, apply to this part 1401.

§ 1401.4 [Reserved]

§ 1401.5 Providing performance and technical data to purchasers by labeling.

(a) Manufacturers of self-pressurized consumer products containing a chlorofluorocarbon propellant shall provide performance and technical data concerning such products that they import or initially introduce into interstate commerce after February 19, 1978, to prospective purchasers at the time of original purchase and to the first purchaser for purposes other than resale. The data shall consist of the following identification and warning statement: "WARNING—Contains a chlorofluorocarbon that may harm the public health and environment by reducing ozone in the upper atmosphere."

(b) The identification and warning statement required by paragraph (a) of this section shall be in addition to any other required labeling and shall be sufficiently prominent and conspicuous as to be likely to be read and understood by ordinary individuals under normal conditions of purchase. This identification and warning statement shall appear on the immediate container of the product and also on any outside container or wrapper in which the product is normally offered for sale at retail. The identification and warning statement may appear on a firmly affixed tag, tape, card, or sticker or similar overlabeling attached to the package.

[42 FR 42783, Aug. 24, 1977; 42 FR 46285, Sept. 15, 1977]

§ 1401.6 Effective date.

This part becomes effective February 20, 1978.

PART 1402—CB BASE STATION ANTENNAS, TV ANTENNAS, AND SUPPORTING STRUCTURES

Sec.

AUTHORITY: 15 U.S.C. 2051, 2076.

SOURCE: 43 FR 28392, June 29, 1978, unless otherwise noted.

§ 1402.1 Scope.

(a) This part 1402 requires manufacturers (including importers) of Citizens Band (CB) base station antennas, outdoor television (TV) antennas, and their supporting structures to provide notification of ways to avoid the hazard of electrocution which exists when these products are allowed to come near powerlines while the antennas are being put up or taken down. The notification must be provided to (1) prospective purchasers of such products at the time of original purchase and (2) the first purchaser of such products for purposes other than resale. The notification consists of instructions to accompany the products, warning labels on the products, and warning statements on the packaging or parts container. Samples of the instructions, labels, and warning statements must also be provided to the Consumer Product Safety Commission.

(b) This part 1402 applies to any of the following that are "consumer products" as defined in section 3 of the Consumer Product Safety Act (15 U.S.C. 2052) and that are manufactured or imported, or packaged or sold by the manufacturer or importer, after September 26, 1978.

(1) Antennas designed or intended to be used as outdoor CB base station antennas (referred to in this rule as "CB base station antennas").

(2) Antennas designed or intended to be used as outdoor TV receiving antennas (referred to in this rule as "TV antennas").

(3) Antenna supporting structures, which are elements over 5 feet in length that are intended to support these types of antennas at a higher elevation. These structures include towers, tripods, and masts. Devices which merely secure the antenna in place are not included.

[43 FR 28392, June 29, 1978, as amended at 43 FR 47722, Oct. 17, 1978]

§ 1402.2 Background.

As a result of numerous electrocutions which have occurred when consumers contacted powerlines with CB base station and outside TV antennas while putting these antennas up or taking them down, the Consumer Product Safety Commission has determined that it is necessary to require that warnings and instructions be furnished with these antennas and their supporting structures so that consumers can be made aware of the hazards involved and of safe ways to put up and take down these antennas. The Commission anticipates that this regulation will help protect the public against the unreasonable risk of injury associated with CB base station antennas, outside TV antennas, and supporting structures due to contact with overhead powerlines.

§ 1402.3 Definitions.

(a) The definitions in section 3 of the Consumer Product Safety Act (15 U.S.C. 2052) apply to this part 1402.

(b) *Antenna supporting structures, CB base station antennas*, and *TV antennas* are defined in § 1402.1(b)(1) through (3).

§ 1402.4 Requirements to provide performance and technical data by labeling and instructions.

(a) *Notice to purchasers.* Manufacturers of CB base station antennas, TV antennas, and antenna supporting structures shall give notification of performance and technical data related to performance and safety to prospective purchasers of such products at the time of original purchase and to the first purchaser of such product for purposes other than resale, in the manner set forth below.

(1) *Antennas.* CB base station antennas and TV antennas shall be provided with the following:

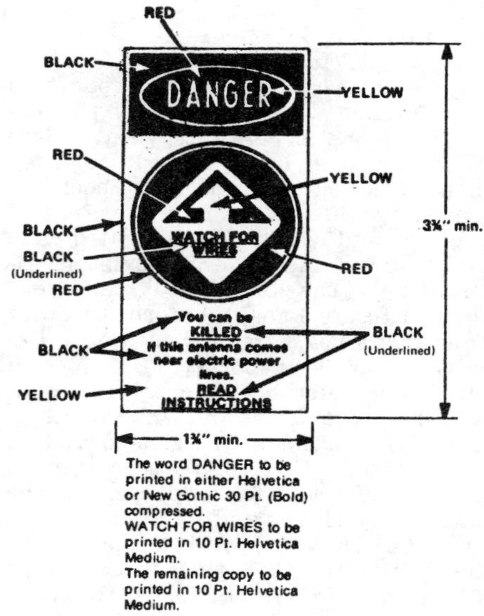

FIGURE 1

(i) *Label.* (A) The antenna shall bear the label shown in fig. 1 so that the label will be conspicuous to the installer during installation.

(B) If pipe or tubular nontelescoping masts are a suitable supporting structure for the antenna, a separate label as shown in fig. 1 shall accompany the antenna. The label shall be suitable for mounting by the consumer on such a mast.

(C) The label in figure 1 shall be made and attached in such a manner that it will be legible for an average expected life of at least 3 years.

(D) The word "product" may be substituted for "antenna" in the label of fig. 1.

(E)(*1*) The colors in figure 1 shall conform to ANSI Standard Z53.1–1971, "Safety Color Code for Marking Physical Hazards," published in 1971 by the American National Standards Institute, which is incorporated by reference. Copies of this document are available from the American National Standards Institute, 1430 Broadway, New York, New York 10018. This standard is also available for inspection at the National Archives and Records Administration (NARA). For information on the availability of this material at NARA, call 202–741–6030, or go to: *http://www.archives.gov/federal_register/code_of_federal_regulations/ibr_locations.html.* This incorporation by reference was approved by the Director of the Federal Register. These materials are incorporated as they exist in the edition which has been approved by the Director of the Federal Register and which has been filed with the Office of the Federal Register. Alternatively, the colors "red" and "yellow" in figure 1 may conform to Color Tolerance Charts, published by the Department of Transportation. Copies of the Color Tolerance Charts are available from the Office of Hazardous Materials, Department of Transportation, Washington, DC 20590. These materials are also available for inspection at the National Archives and Records Administration (NARA). For information on the availability of this material at NARA, call 202–741–6030, or go to: *http://www.archives.gov/federal_register/code_of_federal_regulations/ibr_locations.html.*

(*2*) Color limit values shall be determined by ASTM D 1535–68, "Specifying Color by the Munsell System," published in 1968 by the American Society for Testing and Materials. Copies of ASTM D 1535–68 are available from the American Society for Testing and Materials, 1916 Race Street, Philadelphia, Pennsylvania 19103. These materials are also available for inspection at the National Archives and Records Administration (NARA). For information on the availability of this material at NARA, call 202–741–6030, or go to: *http://www.archives.gov/federal_register/code_of_federal_regulations/ibr_locations.html.* This incorporation by reference was approved by the Director of the Federal Register. These materials are incorporated as they exist in the edition which has been approved by the Director of the Federal Register and which has been filed with the Office of the Federal Register. Alternatively, color limit values for red or yellow may be determined by the Department of Transportation Color Tolerance Charts, which display the desired color within the tolerance limits.

(ii) *Instructions.* CB base station antennas and TV antennas shall be accompanied by instructions that include the following:

(A) The following warning statement, placed on the first page of the document(s) containing the instructions and at the beginning of the body of the instructions: "WARNING: INSTALLATION OF THIS PRODUCT NEAR POWERLINES IS DANGEROUS. FOR YOUR SAFETY, FOLLOW THE INSTALLATION DIRECTIONS". This statement shall be legible and conspicuous and shall be in type that is at least as large as the largest type used on the remainder of the page, with the exception of the logo and any identification of the manufacturer, brand, model, or similar designations, and that is preferably no smaller than 10 point type.

(B) The information set forth below, which shall be in a part of the instructions that is conspicuously identified as containing information concerning the risk of electrocution caused by contact with powerlines. No particular wording is required for this information, but it shall be in legible English and readily understandable to a user with a sixth grade reading ability (other languages may be included as appropriate).

(*1*) An explanation of the risk of electrocution caused by contacting powerlines while putting up or taking down the antenna.

(*2*) An identification of the generally available types and sizes of antenna supporting structures that are suitable for use with the antenna. If a generally available type or size of supporting structure is not identified as suitable, an explanation of why it is not suitable shall be included.

(*3*) If pipe or tubular non-telescoping masts are a suitable supporting structure for the antenna, the instructions shall contain the following in relation to installation of the antenna on such masts:

(*i*) How to select and measure the installation site.

(*ii*) An explanation (pictorial where appropriate) of methods that can be used to reduce the possibility of contact with powerlines when putting up and taking down the antenna mast.

(*iii*) Instructions for properly attaching the separate label that is required to accompany the antenna by paragraph (a)(1)(i)(B) of this section.

(*iv*) A statement that if the supporting structure to be used with the antenna does not have a label of the type provided by the manufacturer, the provided label should be attached to the base of the supporting structure by the installer.

(2) *Antenna supporting structures.* Antenna supporting structures, except pipe or tubular nontelescoping mast sections less than 11 ft. (335 cm.) in length that are not individually packaged or otherwise contained in a package intended for distribution to the consumer, shall comply with the following requirements:

(i) *Label.* (A) Antenna supporting structures shall bear the label shown in fig. 1, which shall be legible for an average expected life of at least 3 years. The label shall be attached so that it is conspicuous during installation and is 3 to 5 ft. (91 to 152 cm.) from the base of the supporting structure.

(B) The word "product" may be substituted for "antenna" in the label, as may "tower", "tripod", or other term, if it accurately describes the supporting structure.

(ii) *Instructions.* Antenna supporting structures shall be accompanied by instructions that include the following:

(A) The following warning statement, placed on the first page of the document(s) containing the instructions and at the beginning of the body of the instructions: "WARNING: INSTALLATION OF THIS PRODUCT NEAR POWERLINES IS DANGEROUS. FOR YOUR SAFETY, FOLLOW THE INSTALLATION DIRECTIONS." This statement shall be legible and conspicuous and shall be in type that is at least as large as the largest type used on the remainder of the page, with the exception of the logo and any identification of the manufacturer, brand, model, and similar designations, and that is preferably no smaller than 10 point type.

(B) The information set forth below, which shall be in a part of the instructions that is conspicuously identified as containing information concerning the risk of electrocution caused by contact with powerlines. No particular wording is required for this information, but it shall be in legible English and understandable to a user with a sixth grade reading ability (other languages may be included as appropriate).

(*1*) An explanation of the risk of electrocution caused by contacting powerlines while putting up or taking down the supporting structure.

(*2*) How to select and measure the installation site.

(*3*) An explanation (pictorial where appropriate) of methods that can be used to reduce the possibility of contact with powerlines when putting up and taking down the supporting structure.

(3) *Packaging.* (i) The following warning statement shall legibly and conspicuously appear on either the packaging or the parts container of any CB base station antenna, TV antenna, or antenna supporting structure: "Warning: Installation of this product near powerlines is dangerous. For your safety, follow the enclosed installation directions."

(b) *Data provided to the Commission.* (1) Manufacturers of CB base station antennas, TV antennas, and antenna supporting structures shall provide to the Commission samples of all the labels, warning statements, and instructions which will be used to satisfy the requirements of paragraph (a) of this section. These samples shall be provided to the Assistant Executive Director for Compliance, Consumer Product Safety Commission, 4330 East West Highway, Bethesda, Md. 20207, by October 27, 1978, or, in the event of a subsequent change in the warning statements or instructions or if a new product is introduced, within 30 days after the change or introduction.

(2) Manufacturers need not submit a separate sample for each model of antenna or supporting structure where different models use the same label and warning statement and where the portion of the instructions required by this part is the same for the different models (even though the remainder of the instructions may be different for each model). Changes in instructions which do not affect the portions of the instructions required by this part do not require the submission of additional samples.

(3) The reporting requirement contained in this section has been approved by the U.S. General Accounting Office under No. B–180232 (R0555).

[43 FR 28392, June 29, 1978, as amended at 43 FR 47722, Oct. 17, 1978; 46 FR 63250, Dec. 31, 1981; 62 FR 46667, Sept. 4, 1997]

APPENDIX I TO PART 1402—RECOMMENDED OUTLINE FOR INSTRUCTION BOOKLET ON "HOW TO SAFELY INSTALL YOUR CB BASE STATION ANTENNA"

I. Required Warning Label Statement.
II. Statement of Hazard.
III. General Safety Instructions:
A. Seek professional assistance.
B. Select your site with safety in mind.
C. Call your electric power company.
D. Plan your procedure.
E. What to do if the assembly starts to drop.
F. What to do if the assembly contacts powerlines.
G. What to do in case of electric shock.
IV. Site Selection (How to select and measure the installation site):
A. Distance from powerlines.
B. FCC height limitations.
C. Alternate locations:
1. Roof.
2. Chimney.
3. Side of house.
4. Free standing.
V. Types and Sizes of Support Structures and Mountings:
A. Tripod:
1. Where it can be used.
2. Limitations.
3. Suitable mounting methods.
B. Tubular Mast:
1. Non-telescopic:
a. Where it can be used.
b. Limitations.
c. Suitable mounting methods.
2. Telescopic: *
a. Where it can be used.
b. Limitations.
c. Suitable mounting methods.
C. Tower:*
1. Where it can be used.
2. Limitations.
3. Suitable mounting methods.
VI. Installation Instructions:
A. General Instructions:
1. Materials.
2. Assembly.
3. How to walk-up a tubular mast:
a. Height limitations.
b. Tying off.
c. Raising the mast with an X-frame.
d. Raising the mast without an X-frame.
4. Guy Wires.
B. How to Install a Tripod:
1. Preparation.
2. Erecting the assembly.
3. Securing the assembly.
C. How to Install a Non-telescopic Tubular Mast:
1. Roof Mount:
a. Preparation.
b. Erecting the assembly.
c. Securing the assembly.
2. Chimney Mount:
a. Preparation.
b. Erecting the assembly.
c. Securing the assembly.
3. Side of House Mount:
a. Preparation.
b. Erecting the assembly.
c. Securing the assembly.
4. Free Standing Mount:
a. Preparation.
b. Erecting the assembly.
c. Securing the assembly.
VII. Grounding Your Antenna:
D. How to Install a Telescopic Mast:*
1. Preparation.
2. Erecting the assembly.
3. Securing the assembly.
E. How to Install a Tower:*
1. Preparation.
2. Erecting the assembly.
3. Securing the assembly.
VIII. Instructions for Attaching Label to Antenna and Supporting Structure.

PART 1404—CELLULOSE INSULATION

Sec.

---

*Detailed instructions for installing these supports would come with the product.

AUTHORITY: Secs. 2, 27, 35, Pub. L. 92–573, Pub. L. 95–319; 86 Stat. 1207, 1228; 92 Stat. 386 (15 U.S.C. 2051, 2076, 2082).

SOURCE: 44 FR 40001, July 6, 1979, unless otherwise noted.

§ 1404.1 Scope, application, and effective date.

(a) *Scope*. This part 1404 establishes a requirement for manufacturers, including importers, of cellulose insulation to notify (1) prospective purchasers of such products at the time of original purchase and (2) the first purchasers of such products for purposes other than resale (installers and consumers) of ways to avoid the fire hazard that exists where cellulose insulation is installed too close to the sides or over the top of a recessed electrical light fixture or where cellulose insulation is installed too close to the exhaust flues from heat-producing devices or apparatus such as furnaces, water heaters, and space heaters. The notification consists of a warning label on the containers of cellulose insulation.

(b) *Application and effective date*. This rule applies to cellulose insulation that is for sale to consumers for installation in households or residences, as well as insulation that is produced or distributed for installation by professionals in households or residences. Cellulose insulation that is labeled as, marketed, and sold solely for nonresidential installation is not included within the scope of this proceeding. The rule applies to all products manufactured after October 15, 1979.

§ 1404.2 Background.

Based on available fire incident information, engineering analysis of the probable fire scenarios, and laboratory tests, the Consumer Product Safety Commission has determined that fires can occur where cellulose insulation is improperly installed too close to the sides or over the top of recessed electrical light fixtures, or installed too close to the exhaust flues from heat producing devices or apparatus such as furnaces, water heaters, and space heaters. These fires may result in serious injuries or deaths. Presently available information indicates that fires may occur where cellulose insulation is improperly installed even though the cellulose insulation complies with the Commission's amended interim standard for cellulose insulation (16 CFR part 1209) based on GSA Specification HH-I-515D. The Commission has determined that it is necessary to require labeling to inform persons installing cellulose insulation and consumers in whose homes the insulation is installed of the fire hazard associated with improperly installed cellulose insulation and the method of properly installing the insulation to prevent this hazard. The Commission anticipates that this regulation will accomplish the purpose of helping protect the public against the unreasonable risk of injury associated with improperly installed cellulose insulation.

§ 1404.3 Definitions.

The definitions in section 3 of the Consumer Product Safety Act (15 U.S.C. 2052) apply to this part 1404.

Cellulose insulation is cellulosic fiber, loose fill, thermal insulation that is suitable for blowing or pouring applications.

Manufacturer means any person who manufactures or imports a consumer product. The term includes both a person who manufactures the product at the direction of another (such as a packager) and the person at whose direction the product is manufactured (such as the marketer of the brand).

§ 1404.4 Requirements to provide performance and technical data by labeling—Notice to purchasers.

(a) Manufacturers of cellulose insulation shall give notification of performance and technical data related to performance and safety (1) to prospective purchasers at the time of original purchase and (2) to the first purchaser of such products for purposes other than resale in the following manner. Manufacturers of cellulose insulation shall label all containers of cellulose insulation with the following statement, using capital letters as indicated:

CAUTION

Potential Fire Hazard: Keep cellulose insulation at least three inches away from the sides of recessed light fixtures. Do not place insulation over such fixtures so as to entrap heat.

Also keep this insulation away from exhaust flues of furnaces, water heaters, space heaters, or other heat-producing devices.

To be sure that insulation is kept away from light fixtures and flues, use a barrier to permanently maintain clearance around these areas. Check with local building or fire officials for guidance on installation and barrier requirements.

Request to Installer: Remove this label and give it to the consumer at completion of job.

Manufacturers of cellulose insulation may substitute the phrase "TO HELP AVOID FIRE" for the phrase "POTENTIAL FIRE HAZARD" in the label described above. Manufacturers may also delete the word "cellulose from the first sentence of the label and may delete the word "this" from the third sentence of the label. The remainder of the label statement shall appear exactly as described above.

(b) The labeling statement required by §1404.4(a) shall appear prominently and conspicuously on the container. The word "CAUTION" shall appear in capital letters at least one-fourth inch in height. The words "POTENTIAL FIRE HAZARD" and "REQUEST TO INSTALLER" shall appear in capital letters at least three-sixteenths inch in height. The remainder of the statement shall appear in capital letters at least three-sixteenths inch in height, with lower case letters in corresponding proportion but at least one-eighth inch in height. The labeling statement shall be enclosed within a rectangle formed with lines at least one-sixteenth inch in width. The labeling statement shall be printed with legible type in a color which contrasts with the background on which the statement is printed.

(c) To meet this requirement, manufacturers may use any type of label, including one which is pressure sensitive or glued-on, provided the label is made in such a manner that it will remain attached to the container for the expected time interval between the manufacture of the product and its installation.

[44 FR 40001, July 6, 1979, as amended at 49 FR 21701, May 23, 1984]

PART 1406—COAL AND WOOD BURNING APPLIANCES—NOTIFICATION OF PERFORMANCE AND TECHNICAL DATA

AUTHORITY: 15 U.S.C. 2051, 2076.

§1406.1 Scope, purpose, and effective date.

(a) *Scope.* This part 1406 requires manufacturers, including importers, of coal and wood burning appliances, as defined in §1406.3(a), to provide consumers with a specified notification concerning the installation, operation, and maintenance of the appliances. The notification is intended to provide consumers with technical and performance information related to the safety of the appliances. This part 1406 also requires these manufacturers to provide to the Commission a copy of the notification to consumers and a statement of the reasons supporting the manufacturer's conclusion that certain clearance distances contained in the notification are appropriate for preventing fires.

(b) *Purpose.* This regulation is intended to reduce the unreasonable risk of injury from fire associated with inadequate information provided with coal and wood burning appliances. This rule does not replace any voluntary standards applicable to these appliances or any state or local requirements applicable to the installation, use, or maintenance of such appliances that are not inconsistent with this rule. Thus, for example, a local code could require the actual installation of appliances at different distances from combustibles than those specified on the label required by this rule, and voluntary standards or local codes could require labeling or instructions in addition to those required by this rule. The fact that a product complies with this regulation is not intended to be a substitute for the performance tests and other criteria established by listing organizations whose approval is required to meet some state or local requirements applicable to these appliances.

(c) *Effective date.* (1) Except as provided in paragraphs (c)(2) and (c)(3) of this section, manufacturers, including importers, of coal and wood burning appliances as defined in §1406.3(a) must comply with this regulation with respect to stoves that are manufactured or imported after October 17, 1983, or that are first introduced into United States commerce after May 16, 1984, regardless of the date of manufacture. For the purposes of this rule, an appliance is manufactured when no further assembly of the appliance is required (i) before shipment by the manufacturer or (ii), if the product is not so shipped, before delivery to the first purchaser. A product manufactured in the United States (U.S.) is first introduced into U.S. commerce when it is shipped by the manufacturer or delivered to the next purchaser, whichever comes first. A product manufactured outside the U.S. is first introduced into U.S. commerce when it is first brought within a U.S. port of entry.

(2) The requirements of §1406.4(c) apply to sales catalogs and point of sale literature provided by manufacturers after May 16, 1984.

(3) Section 1406.5 is effective December 6, 1983.

(Information collection requirements contained in paragraph (a) were approved by the Office of Management and Budget under control number 3041–0040)

[48 FR 21914, May 16, 1983; 48 FR 26761, June 10, 1983, as amended at 48 FR 50706, Nov. 3, 1983; 48 FR 52889, Nov. 23, 1983]

§ 1406.2 Background.

(a) Fire data analyzed by the Consumer Product Safety Commission disclose a number of incidents involving coal and wood burning appliances. Many of these cases involve improper installation of the appliances, especially where they are installed with insufficient clearances to adjacent combustibles such as walls, ceilings, floors, draperies, carpets, or furnishings. Another common installation problem involves the use of improper types of chimneys or chimney connectors and insufficient clearances between these devices and combustibles. Other incidents involve improper operation of the appliance, such as by overfiring it or using flammable liquids to start the fire. Still other incidents occur when appliances are improperly maintained and develop mechanical defects or excessive deposits of flammable creosote.

(b) After considering the available data on the causes of fires in these appliances, the Commission concludes that there is an unreasonable risk of injury associated with appliances that are sold without notifying consumers of the information they need to prevent many of these occurrences. Accordingly, the Commission has determined that disclosure of the information required by §1406.4 is necessary to help the Commission in carrying out the purposes of the Consumer Product Safety Act of (1) helping to protect the public against unreasonable risks of injury associated with consumer products and (2) assisting consumers in evaluating the comparative safety of consumer products.

(c) The Commission has also determined that in carrying out these purposes of the act, it is necessary for manufacturers to provide to the Commission a copy of the information provided to consumers and a statement of the reasons why some of the information was selected, in accordance with §1406.5.

[48 FR 21914, May 16, 1983, as amended at 48 FR 50706, Nov. 3, 1983]

§ 1406.3 Definitions.

For the purposes of this rule:

(a) *Coal and wood burning appliances* means fireplace stoves, room heater/fireplace stove combinations, cookstoves and ranges, and radiant and circulating heaters. It does not include central heating units, masonry fireplaces and chimneys, fireplace inserts, or factory built fireplaces (zero clearance fireplaces).

(b) *Central heating units* include boilers, furnaces, and furnace add-ons. These appliances are designed to be connected to hot water distribution or ductwork systems for heating several rooms. The furnace add-on converts an existing gas, oil, or electric heating system to one capable of using solid fuel as well as its original fuel.

(c) A *chimney* is a vertical or nearly vertical enclosure containing one or more passageways called flue passages for conveying combustion wastes to the outside atmosphere.

(d) A *chimney connector* is the stovepipe which connects the appliance flue with the chimney flue.

(e) *Cookstoves and ranges* are chimney connected solid fuel burning appliances that are used primarily for cooking. In addition to the firechamber, there may be one or more ovens or warmer compartments and several removable cooking space pothole lids. The intensity of the fire is controlled by damper and draft regulators.

(f) A *factory built fireplace* is a firechamber and chimney assembly consisting entirely of factory made parts. It is designed for component assembly without requiring field construction. These "zero clearance" units are fabricated for safe installation against combustible surfaces and for burning fireplace fuel.

(g) *Fireplace inserts* are heating units that fit into a fireplace and connect to the fireplace flue. These units function like radiant and circulating heaters.

(h) A *fireplace stove* is a freestanding, chimney-connected firechamber which is constantly open to view. It is designed to burn regular fireplace fuel and function as a decorative fireplace.

(i) A *masonry chimney* is a chimney field-constucted of solid masonry units, brick, stones, or reinforced concrete.

(j) A *masonry fireplace* is an open firechamber built into a structure along with a chimney and hearth. It is constructed of solid masonry units such as bricks, stones, or reinforced concrete.

(k) *Radiant and circulating heaters* have firechambers which may be airtight[1] or non-airtight and are available in a number of sizes, shapes, and designs. The firechamber is closed in use, but there may be a window of specially formulated glass for viewing the fire. Drafts and dampers are used to control the burning process. There may be a secondary combustion chamber, baffles, a thermostat, a blower, or other components which function to improve combustion efficiency or to control heat output. The primary function of these appliances is as space heaters. However, some have lift-off cooking pothole lids, and the top surface of most can be used for cooking. The fuel may be wood, coal, or both. Radiant heaters transmit heat primarily by direct radiation. Circulating heaters have an outer jacket surrounding the fire chamber. Air enters from the bottom, is warmed by passing over the fire chamber, and exits at the top. Movement is by natural convection or forced air circulation.

(l) A "room heater/fireplace stove combination" is a freestanding, chimney-connected fire chamber with doors. It is designed to be used to burn fireplace fuels with the firechamber either open or closed to view. This appliance functions as a decorative fireplace when the doors are open and as a non-airtight heater when the doors are closed.

[48 FR 21914, May 16, 1983]

§ 1406.4 Requirements to provide performance and technical notice to prospective purchasers and purchasers.

Manufacturers, including importers, of coal and wood burning appliances as defined in § 1406.3 shall give notification of performance and technical data related to performance and safety to prospective purchasers at the time of original purchase and to the first purchaser of such products for purposes other than resale, in the manner set forth below:

(a) *Written notice on appliance.* (1) The appliance shall bear a legible notice containing the following performance and technical data.

(i) Appropriate minimum clearances from unprotected combustibles to avoid the occurrence of fire.[2] The clearances shall include:

[1] An airtight stove is defined as "A stove in which a large fire can be suffocated by shutting the air inlets, resulting ultimately in a large mass of unburned fuel remaining in the stove." Jay W. Shelton, *Wood Heat Safety*, Garden Way Publishing, Charlotte, Vermont (1979), p. 160.

[2] Appropriate distances are to be determined by the manufacturer. The Commission expects that test procedures utilized by a nationally recognized testing organization

(A) Distance from the back and sides of the appliance, and the chimney connector, to walls, stated in diagrammatic form.

(B) Distance to be maintained between the chimney connector and ceilings, in either diagrammatic or written form.

(ii) Type and dimensions of floor protection, if necessary to protect combustible floors.

(iii) Proper type(s) of chimney and chimney connector to be used with the appliance. This information should include the proper designations so that the chimney and chimney connector are of suitable design and construction to withstand the temperature of the flue gases and other probable environmental stresses and so that the inside dimensions are suitable to adequately vent the products of combustion. See Figs. 1 and 2 for examples of an acceptable designation for a chimney and chimney connector.

(iv) Identification of parts or precautions required for passing a chimney through combustible walls or ceilings or for passing a chimney connector through combustible walls. The following statement is an example of one that complies with this requirement:

Special methods are required when passing through a wall or ceiling. See instructions or building codes.

(v) A statement not to overfire the appliance, and a description of at least 1 condition which signals overfiring.

(vi) A statement of how often the chimney and chimney connector should be inspected and that it should be cleaned when necessary.

(vii) Information explaining that the appliance should be installed and used only in accordance with the manufacturer's directions and local building codes.

(viii) A direction to contact local building or fire officials about restrictions and installation inspection requirements.

(ix) A statement that furnishings and combustible materials should be kept a considerable distance from the appliance or a statement to keep furnishings and other combustibles far away.

(x) The types of fuel suitable for use in the appliance.

(xi) The name and address of the manufacturer, importer or private labeler to which the owner can write for a copy of the manufacturer's directions or for additional information, and a sufficient identification of the appliance model so that the appropriate information can be supplied.

(2) No specific wording is required on the written notice, but the information shall be printed in legible English in clear and readily understandable language. Examples of acceptable labels are given in Figs. 1 and 2, appendix I.

(3) The written notice shall be placed in a location that is conspicuous before the appliance is installed. In addition, the written information required by paragraphs (a)(1)(v), (a)(1)(vi), (a)(1)(ix), and (a)(1)(x) of this section shall be readily visible during normal use of the appliance. A label on the back of the stove would not be considered "readily visible" during normal use if the stove is suitable for installation with its back within a few feet of the wall. Locations within compartments or behind doors or panels may be readily visible during normal use if the location is readily visible when the door or panel is opened or removed and the door or panel must be opened or removed, or the compartments used, as part of the normal operating procedures for the appliance. An example of a notice format where the information required to be readily visible during normal use is separated from the remainder of the notice is given in Fig. 1, appendix I. The Commission recommends the use of this 2 label format in order to provide more consumer awareness of the operation and maintenance information after the appliance is installed, since this information would be on a simpler label that would not have installation information competing for the consumer's attention.

(4) The written notice shall be provided so that it will remain legible for the maximum expected useful life of the appliance in normal operation.

(b) *Directions.* All appliances covered by this rule shall be accompanied by directions that include the following

---

would be suitable for determining appropriate distances.

technical and performance information:

(1) The following notice shall be placed on the first page of the document(s) containing the directions and at the beginning of the directions:

SAFETY NOTICE: IF THIS _____ IS NOT PROPERLY INSTALLED, A HOUSE FIRE MAY RESULT. FOR YOUR SAFETY, FOLLOW THE INSTALLATION DIRECTIONS. CONTACT LOCAL BUILDING OR FIRE OFFICIALS ABOUT RESTRICTIONS AND INSTALLATION INSPECTION REQUIREMENTS IN YOUR AREA.

This statement shall be conspicuous and in type that is at least as large as the largest type used on the remainder of the page, with the exception of the logo and any identification of the manufacturer, brand, model, and similar designations. At the manufacturer's option, other information may be added to this notice.

(2) Step by step installation directions shall be provided, including all necessary information regarding parts and materials. This information shall include an explanation of the consequences which could result from failure to install the appliance properly. These directions shall include a direction to refer to the chimney and chimney connector manufacturers' instructions and local building codes for installation through combustible walls or ceilings.

(3) These directions shall also include a clearly identified section containing complete use directions, including what types of fuel(s) can be used and how to fire the unit to avoid fire hazards, and a clearly identified section containing complete maintenance directions, including how and when to clean the chimney and chimney connector. A statement that flammable liquids should not be used with the appliance shall also be included where applicable. These sections shall contain a description of the consequences that could result from failure to use or maintain the appliance properly.

(4) The directions required by paragraphs (b)(2) and (b)(3) of this section shall include all the information required by paragraph (a)(1) of this section and shall be in legible English in readily understandable language. A recommended outline for the directions is given in appendix II.

(c) *Catalogs and point of sale literature.* Literature for the appliance that is intended to induce an immediate order or sale (such as catalogs and point of sale literature) and that is provided by the manufacturer, shall legibly and conspicuously include the information required by paragraph (a)(1)(viii) of this section and shall state the appropriate minimum clearances, to avoid the occurrence of fire, from the back and sides of the appliance to walls.

NOTE: General advertising would not be subject to this requirement.

APPENDIX I TO § 1406.4—RECOMMENDED FORMAT AND WORDING FOR WRITTEN NOTICE

The following are examples of formats and suggested wording for the written notice required by § 1406.4(a). Information to be supplied by the manufacturer is indicated by underlined blank spaces or by asterisks. The Commission recommends the "two label" format shown in Fig. 1.

Fig.1 - Example of how written notice requirements are satisfied with two labels. Label (A) is located so that it is conspicuous before installation. Label (B) is located so that it is readily visible during normal use. Insert appropriate information or numbers at "_*_". Words or diagrams should be changed to suit particular appliance.

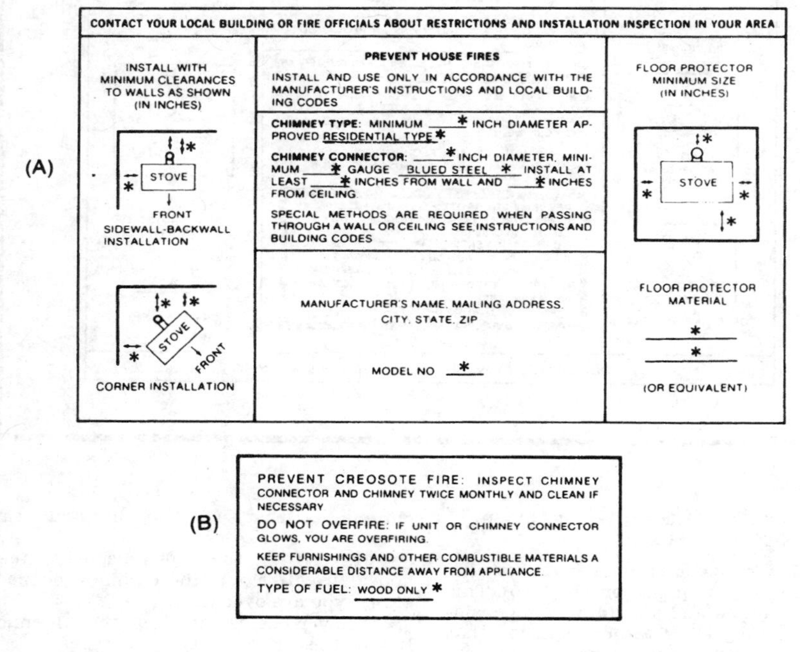

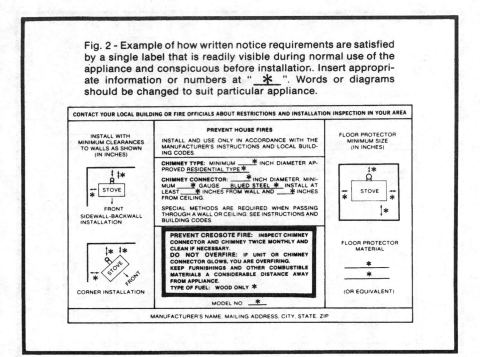

Fig. 2 - Example of how written notice requirements are satisfied by a single label that is readily visible during normal use of the appliance and conspicuous before installation. Insert appropriate information or numbers at "___*___". Words or diagrams should be changed to suit particular appliance.

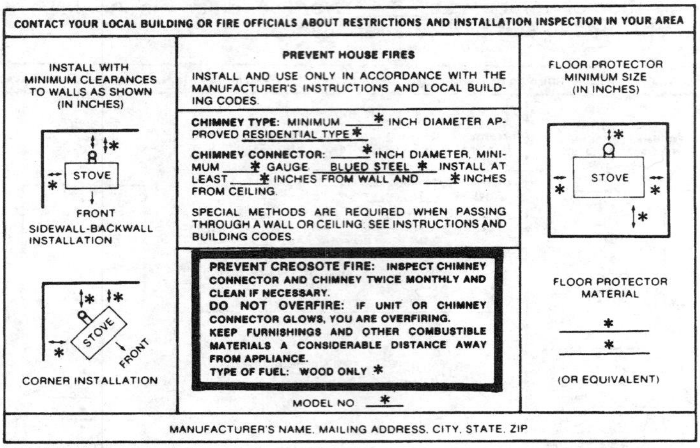

CONTACT YOUR LOCAL BUILDING OR FIRE OFFICIALS ABOUT RESTRICTIONS AND INSTALLATION INSPECTION IN YOUR AREA

INSTALL WITH MINIMUM CLEARANCES TO WALLS AS SHOWN (IN INCHES)

STOVE

FRONT

SIDEWALL-BACKWALL INSTALLATION

STOVE

FRONT

CORNER INSTALLATION

PREVENT HOUSE FIRES

INSTALL AND USE ONLY IN ACCORDANCE WITH THE MANUFACTURER'S INSTRUCTIONS AND LOCAL BUILDING CODES.

CHIMNEY TYPE: MINIMUM ___*___ INCH DIAMETER APPROVED RESIDENTIAL TYPE *

CHIMNEY CONNECTOR: ___*___ INCH DIAMETER, MINIMUM ___*___ GAUGE ___BLUED STEEL *___ INSTALL AT LEAST ___*___ INCHES FROM WALL AND ___*___ INCHES FROM CEILING.

SPECIAL METHODS ARE REQUIRED WHEN PASSING THROUGH A WALL OR CEILING. SEE INSTRUCTIONS AND BUILDING CODES.

PREVENT CREOSOTE FIRE: INSPECT CHIMNEY CONNECTOR AND CHIMNEY TWICE MONTHLY AND CLEAN IF NECESSARY.
DO NOT OVERFIRE: IF UNIT OR CHIMNEY CONNECTOR GLOWS, YOU ARE OVERFIRING.
KEEP FURNISHINGS AND OTHER COMBUSTIBLE MATERIALS A CONSIDERABLE DISTANCE AWAY FROM APPLIANCE.
TYPE OF FUEL: WOOD ONLY *

MODEL NO. ___*___

FLOOR PROTECTOR MINIMUM SIZE (IN INCHES)

STOVE

FLOOR PROTECTOR MATERIAL

___*___

___*___

(OR EQUIVALENT)

MANUFACTURER'S NAME, MAILING ADDRESS, CITY, STATE, ZIP

APPENDIX II TO §1406.4—RECOMMENDED OUTLINE FOR DIRECTIONS

The following is a recommended outline for the directions required by §1406.4(b). This outline is a guide and should not be considered as including all of the information that may be necessary for the proper installation, use, and maintenance of the appliance since the necessary information may vary from product to product.

"HOW TO INSTALL, USE, AND MAINTAIN YOUR ______"

I. SAFETY PRECAUTIONS

A. The Safety Notice required by this rule.

- "SAFETY NOTICE: IF THIS ______ IS NOT PROPERLY INSTALLED, A HOUSE FIRE MAY RESULT. FOR YOUR SAFETY, FOLLOW THE INSTALLATION DIRECTIONS. CONTACT LOCAL BUILDING OFFICIALS ABOUT RESTRICTIONS AND INSTALLATION INSPECTION REQUIREMENTS IN YOUR AREA."

B. Statements of other important safety messages, including:

- "Creosote may build up in the chimney connector and chimney and cause a house fire. Inspect the chimney connector and chimney at least twice monthly and clean if necessary."
- "Overfiring the appliance may cause a house fire. If a unit or chimney connector glows, you are overfiring."
- "Never use gasoline or other flammable liquids to start or 'freshen up' a fire."
- "Dispose of ashes in a metal container."

II. INSTALLATION INSTRUCTIONS

A. The parts and materials required, including:

- The size and type of chimney to which the appliance is to be connected.
- The size and thickness or gage of metal of the chimney connector.
- The thimble or type of connection through a combustible wall or ceiling.

B. The step-by-step directions for installing the appliance and its accessories, chimney connector, and chimney. The directions would include:

- Clearances from the appliance and chimney connector to combustibles,
- Methods to safely join the chimney connector to the chimney and how to pass these parts through a combustible wall or to pass the chimney through a ceiling.

• The joining of two or more parts to constitute a safe assembly such as attaching and securing the chimney connector to the appliance and to each adjoining section, and,

• Where required, the parts or materials to be used for the floor protector (hearth). The minimum areas to be covered and their relation to the appliance should be stated.

III. USE INSTRUCTIONS

A. Recommendations about building and maintaining a fire, warnings against overfiring, and condition(s) that signal(s) overfiring.

B. Caution against the use and storage of flammable liquids, as follows: "Do not use gasoline, gasoline-type lantern fuel, kerosene, charcoal lighter fluid, or similar liquids to start or 'freshen up' a fire in this appliance. Keep these flammable liquids well away from this appliance while it is in use."

C. Explanation about the use or nonuse of grates, irons and or other methods of supporting the fuel.

D. How to use manual or thermostatic controls.

E. Explanation about the use of any electrical assemblies including care and routing of power supply cord.

F. Caution about disposing of ashes, as follows:

Disposal of Ashes

Ashes should be placed in a metal container with a tight fitting lid. The closed container of ashes should be placed on a noncombustible floor or on the ground, away from all combustible materials, pending final disposal. The ashes should be retained in the closed container until all cinders have thoroughly cooled.

G. Keep furnishings and other combustible materials away from appliance.

IV. MAINTENANCE INSTRUCTIONS

A. How to inspect and maintain the appliance, chimney, and chimney connector.

B. Explanation about the formation and removal of creosote buildup in the chimney connector and chimney as follows:

Creosote Formation and Need for Removal

When wood is burned slowly, it produces tar and other vapors, which combine with moisture to form creosote. Creosote vapors condense in the relatively cool chimney flue, and creosote residue accumulates on the flue lining. When ignited, this creosote make an extremely hot fire.

The chimney connector and chimney should be inspected at least twice monthly during the heating season to determine if creosote buildup has occurred.

If creosote has accumulated, it should be removed to reduce the chance of a chimney fire.

C. Explain how to remove creosote.

V. REFERENCES

A. The name and address of the manufacturer or private labeler from which the owner can obtain additional information if needed. Include other sources of information as appropriate.

B. The manufacturer's or private labeler's catalog designations, model numbers or the equivalent for the appliance and related parts.

[48 FR 21914, May 16, 1983, as amended at 48 FR 28230, June 21, 1983]

§ 1406.5 Performance and technical data to be furnished to the Commission.

Manufacturers, including importers, of coal and wood burning appliances as defined in § 1406.3(a) shall provide to the Commission the following performance and technical data related to performance and safety.

(a) *Written notice.* Manufacturers shall provide to the Commission copies of the written notice required by § 1406.4(a). If the written notice is provided to purchasers in a way, such as by casting or stamping the notice into the stove, that makes it impractical to furnish a sample of the actual notice to the Commission, the manufacturer will provide an actual-size copy of the notice and a description of the forming process.

(b) *Directions.* Manufacturers shall provide to the Commission a copy of the directions required by § 1406.4(b).

(c) *Rationale.* Manufacturers shall provide to the Commission a statement of how the distances to combustibles required to be stated by § 1406.4(a)(1) were determined. In addition, the maufacturer will state the type of appliance, its fuel, size, and weight, and the material of which it is constructed, unless this information is included in the directions submitted under paragraph (b) of this section.

(d) *General.* (1) The information required to be submitted under paragraphs (a) through (c) of this section shall be submitted for each distinct design or model of appliance manufactured. An appliance will be considered to be a distinct design or model if it differs from other appliances of the same manufacturer by functional differences such as performance, weight, size, or capacity. Differences in cosmetic or other nonfunctional features do not require the submission of additional information.

(2) The written notice, directions, and rationale shall be provided to the Assistant Executive Director for Compliance, Consumer Product Safety Commission, Washington, DC 20207, by December 6, 1983. If there is a subsequent change in the component materials or design features of a model for which this information was previously submitted that could cause the model to require different clearances from combustibles or a different type of chimney, or if a new product is introduced into United States commerce, the required information shall be submitted within 30 days after the change or introduction.

(Approved by Office of Management and Budget under control number 3041–0040)

[48 FR 50706, Nov. 3, 1983, as amended at 62 FR 46667, Sept. 4, 1997]

PART 1407—PORTABLE GENERATORS: REQUIREMENTS TO PROVIDE PERFORMANCE AND TECHNICAL DATA BY LABELING

AUTHORITY: 15 U.S.C. 2076(e).

SOURCE: 72 FR 1450, Jan. 12, 2007, unless otherwise noted.

§ 1407.1 Purpose, scope, and effective date.

This part 1407 establishes requirements under section 27(e) of the Consumer Product Safety Act (15 U.S.C. 2076(e)) for manufacturers to provide consumers with a specified notification concerning the carbon monoxide poisoning hazard associated with the use of portable generators. The notification is intended to provide consumers with technical and performance information related to the safety of portable generators. This part applies to any generator manufactured or imported on or after May 14, 2007.

§ 1407.2 Definitions.

(a) The definitions in section 3 of the Consumer Product Safety Act (15 U.S.C. 2052) apply to this part 1407.

(b) A portable generator is an internal combustion engine-driven electric generator rated no higher than 15 kilowatts and 250 volts that is intended to be moved for temporary use at a location where utility-supplied electric power is not available. It has receptacle outlets for the alternating-current (AC) output circuits, and may have alternating- or direct-current (DC) sections for supplying energy to battery charging circuits.

§ 1407.3 Providing performance and technical data to purchasers by labeling.

(a) *Notice to purchasers.* Manufacturers of portable generators shall give notification of performance and technical data related to performance and safety to prospective purchasers of such products at the time of original purchase and to the first purchaser of such product for purposes other than resale, in the manner set forth below.

(1) *On-product label.* The CO poisoning hazard label shown in fig. 1 shall be used on the product. A different representation of the generator may be substituted for accuracy if consumers are more likely to recognize the substituted representation as the generator to which this label is affixed. Alternate-language versions of this label may appear on the product in addition to the label specified in figure 1. If the product label is also provided by the manufacturer in additional language(s), it shall appear adjacent to or below the English-language version of the product label, and shall be no larger than the English-language version of the label. Versions of the product label that are in a language other than English may appear without the pictograms that appear in the English-language versions.

(i) The signal word "DANGER" shall be in letters not less than 0.15 inch (3.8 mm) high. The remaining text shall be in type whose uppercase letters are not less than 0.1 inch (2.5 mm) high.

(ii) The signal word "DANGER" shall appear in white letters on a safety red background. The safety alert symbol shown in fig. 2 shall appear immediately before and next to the signal word and be no smaller than the height of the signal word with the base of the triangle on the same horizontal line as the base of the signal word. The solid portion of the triangle (within the lines of the triangle, around the exclamation mark) shall be white and the exclamation mark shall be safety red. The prohibition circle-slash symbols shall be opaque.

(iii) The on-product hazard label shown in fig. 1 shall be located:

(A) On a part of the portable generator that cannot be removed without the use of tools, and

(B) On a location that is prominent and conspicuous to an operator while performing at least two of the following actions: Filling the fuel tank, accessing the receptacle panel, and starting the engine.

(iv) The on-product hazard label shown in fig. 1 shall be designed to remain permanently affixed, intact, legible, and largely unfaded in the environment in which the product is expected to be operated and stored over the life of the product.

(2) *Carbon monoxide poisoning hazard label for package.* The CO poisoning hazard label shown in fig. 3 shall be affixed to the principal display panel(s) of the package, as well as the surface containing the top flaps of the package. The principal display panel(s) of the package is the portion(s) of the outer packaging that is designed to be most prominently displayed, shown, presented, or examined under conditions of retail sale. Any panel of the package that includes text in a language other than English shall also include a CO poisoning hazard label in that language. Alternate-language versions of the label, in addition to the label specified in figure 3, may also appear on the top flaps of the package as long as they are physically separate from one another. A different representation of the generator may be substituted for accuracy if consumers are more likely to recognize the substituted representation as the generator contained within the packaging.

(i) The signal word "DANGER" shall be in letters not less than 0.15 inch (3.8 mm) high. The remaining text shall be in type whose uppercase letters are not less than 0.1 inch (2.5 mm) high.

(ii) The signal word "DANGER" shall appear in white letters on a safety red background. The safety alert symbol shown in fig. 2 shall appear immediately before and next to the signal word and be no smaller than the height of the signal word with the base of the triangle on the same horizontal line as the base of the signal word. The solid portion of the triangle (within the lines of the triangle, around the exclamation mark) shall be white and the exclamation mark shall be safety red. The prohibition circle-slash symbols shall be opaque.

(b) [Reserved]

⚠ DANGER

Using a generator indoors CAN KILL YOU IN MINUTES.

Generator exhaust contains carbon monoxide. This is a poison you cannot see or smell.

NEVER use inside a home or garage, EVEN IF doors and windows are open.	**Only use OUTSIDE and far away from windows, doors, and vents.**

⚠ DANGER

Using a generator indoors CAN KILL YOU IN MINUTES.

Generator exhaust contains carbon monoxide. This is a poison you cannot see or smell.

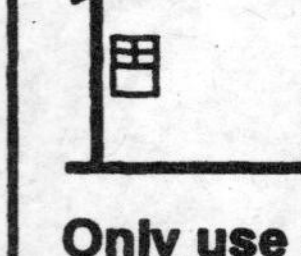

NEVER use inside a home or garage, EVEN IF doors and windows are open.	**Only use OUTSIDE and far away from windows, doors, and vents.**

Avoid other generator hazards.
READ MANUAL BEFORE USE.

[72 FR 1450, Jan. 12, 2007, as amended at 72 FR 2184, Jan. 18, 2007]

PART 1420—REQUIREMENTS FOR ALL TERRAIN VEHICLES

AUTHORITY: The Consumer Product Safety Improvement Act of 2008, Pub. Law 110–314, §232, 122 Stat. 3016 (August 14, 2008).

SOURCE: 73 FR 67386, Nov. 14, 2008, unless otherwise noted.

§ 1420.1 Scope, application and effective date.

This part 1420, a consumer product safety standard, prescribes requirements for all terrain vehicles. The requirements for four-wheel ATVs in §1420.3 take effect on April 30, 2012, and apply to new assembled or unassembled ATVs manufactured or imported on or after that date. The restrictions on three-wheel ATVs stated in §1420.4 take effect September 13, 2008.

[73 FR 67386, Nov. 14, 2008, as amended at 77 FR 12200, Feb. 29, 2012]

§ 1420.2 Definitions.

In addition to the definitions in section 3 of the Consumer Product Safety Act (15 U.S.C. 2052), the following definitions apply for purposes of this Part 1420.

(a) *All terrain vehicle or ATV* means:

(1) Any motorized, off-highway vehicle designed to travel on 3 or 4 wheels, having a seat designed to be straddled by the operator and handlebars for steering control; but

(2) Does not include a prototype of a motorized, off-highway, all-terrain vehicle that is intended exclusively for research and development purposes unless the vehicle is offered for sale.

(b) *ATV action plan* means a written plan or letter of undertaking that describes actions the manufacturer or distributor agrees to take to promote ATV safety, including rider training, dissemination of safety information, age recommendations, other policies governing marketing and sale of the ATVs, the monitoring of such sales, and other safety related measures, and that is substantially similar to the plans described under the heading "The Undertakings of the Companies" in the Commission Notice published in the FEDERAL REGISTER on September 9, 1998 (63 FR 48199–48204).

§ 1420.3 Requirements for four-wheel ATVs.

(a) Each ATV shall comply with all applicable provisions of the American National Standard for Four-Wheel All-Terrain Vehicles (American National Standards Institute, Inc. ANSI/SVIA 1-2010), approved December 23, 2010. The Director of the Federal Register approves this incorporation by reference in accordance with 5 U.S.C. 552(a) and 1 CFR part 51. You may obtain a copy from the Specialty Vehicle Institute of America, 2 Jenner, Suite 150, Irvine, CA 92618–3806; telephone 949–727–3727 ext.3023; *www.svia.org*. You may inspect a copy at the Office of the Secretary, U.S. Consumer Product Safety Commission, Room 820, 4330 East West Highway, Bethesda, MD 20814, telephone 301–504–7923, or at the National Archives and Records Administration (NARA). For information on the availability of this material at NARA, call 202–741–6030, or go to: *http://www.archives.gov/federal_register/code_of_federal_regulations/ibr_locations.html*.

(b) Each ATV must be subject to an ATV action plan filed with the Commission before August 14, 2008 or subsequently filed with and approved by the Commission, and shall bear a label certifying such compliance and identifying the manufacturer, importer or private labeler and the ATV action plan to which it is subject.

(c) The ATV manufacturer or distributor shall be in compliance with all provisions of the applicable ATV action plan.

[73 FR 67386, Nov. 14, 2008, as amended at 77 FR 12200, Feb. 29, 2012]

§ 1420.4 Restrictions on three-wheel ATVs.

Until a mandatory consumer product safety standard applicable to three-wheel ATVs promulgated pursuant to the Consumer Product Safety Act is in effect, new three wheel ATVs may not be imported into or distributed in commerce in the United States.

PART 1450—VIRGINIA GRAEME BAKER POOL AND SPA SAFETY ACT REGULATIONS

AUTHORITY: 15 U.S.C. 2051–2089, 86 Stat. 1207; 15 U.S.C. 8001–8008, 121 Stat. 1794.

SOURCE: 75 FR 21987, Apr. 27, 2010, unless otherwise noted.

§§ 1450.1–1450.2 [Reserved]

§ 1450.3 Incorporation by reference.

(a) Each swimming pool or spa drain cover manufactured, distributed, or entered into commerce in the United States shall conform to the entrapment protection standards of ANSI/APSP–16 2011, *Suction Fittings for Use in Swimming Pools, Wading Pools, Spas, and Hot Tubs*, approved on February 17, 2011. The Director of the Federal Register approves this incorporation by reference in accordance with 5 U.S.C. 552(a) and 1 CFR part 51. You may obtain a copy from the Association of Pool & Spa Professionals, 2111 Eisenhower Avenue, Alexandria, Virginia 22314; *http://www.apsp.org*, telephone 703–838–0083. You may inspect a copy at the Office of the Secretary, U.S. Consumer Product Safety Commission, Room 820, 4330 East West Highway, Bethesda, MD 20814, telephone 301–504–7923, or at the National Archives and Records Administration (NARA). For information on the availability of this material at NARA, call 202–741–6030 or go to: *http://www.archives.gov/federal_register/code_of_federal_regulations/ibr_locations.html*.

(b) [Reserved]

[76 FR 47438, July 5, 2011]

SUBCHAPTER C—FEDERAL HAZARDOUS SUBSTANCES ACT REGULATIONS

PART 1500—HAZARDOUS SUBSTANCES AND ARTICLES; ADMINISTRATION AND ENFORCEMENT REGULATIONS

AUTHORITY: 15 U.S.C. 1261–1278, 122 Stat. 3016; the Consumer Product Safety Improvement Act of 2008, Pub. L. 110–314, § 104, 122 Stat. 3016 (August 14, 2008).

SOURCE: 38 FR 27012, Sept. 27, 1973, unless otherwise noted.

§ 1500.1 Scope of subchapter.

Set forth in this subchapter C are the regulations of the Consumer Product Safety Commission issued pursuant to and for the implementation of the Federal Hazardous Substances Act as amended (see § 1500.3(a)(1)).

§ 1500.2 Authority.

Authority under the Federal Hazardous Substances Act is vested in the Consumer Product Safety Commission by section 30(a) of the Consumer Product Safety Act (15 U.S.C. 2079(a)).

§ 1500.3 Definitions.

(a) *Certain terms used in this part.* As used in this part:

(1) *Act* means the Federal Hazardous Substances Act (Pub. L. 86–613, 74 Stat. 372–81 (15 U.S.C. 1261–74)) as amended by:

(i) The Child Protection Act of 1966 (Pub. L. 89–756, 80 Stat. 1303–05).

(ii) The Child Protection and Toy Safety Act of 1969 (Pub. L. 91–113, 83 Stat. 187–90).

(iii) The Poison Prevention Packaging Act of 1970 (Pub. L. 91–601, 84 Stat. 1670–74).

(2) *Commission* means the Consumer Product Safety Commission established May 14, 1973, pursuant to provisions of the Consumer Product Safety Act (Pub. L. 92–573, 86 Stat. 1207–33 (15 U.S.C. 2051–81)).

(b) *Statutory definitions.* Except for the definitions given in section 2 (c) and (d) of the act, which are obsolete, the definitions set forth in section 2 of the act are applicable to this part and are repeated for convenience as follows (some of these statutory definitions are interpreted, supplemented, or provided with alternatives in paragraph (c) of this section):

(1) *Territory* means any territory or possession of the United States, including the District of Columbia and the Commonwealth of Puerto Rico but excluding the Canal Zone.

(2) *Interstate commerce* means (i) commerce between any State or territory and any place outside thereof and (ii) commerce within the District of Columbia or within any territory not organized with a legislative body.

(3) *Person* includes an individual, partnership, corporation, and association.

(4)(i) *Hazardous substance* means:

(A) Any substance or mixture of substances which is toxic, corrosive, an irritant, a strong sensitizer, flammable or combustible, or generates pressure through decomposition, heat, or other means, if such substance or mixture of substances may cause substantial personal injury or substantial illness during or as a proximate result of any customary or reasonably foreseeable handling or use, including reasonably foreseeable ingestion by children.

(B) Any substance which the Commission by regulation finds, pursuant to the provisions of section 3(a) of the act, meet the requirements of section 2(f)(1)(A) of the act (restated in (A) above).

(C) Any radioactive substance if, with respect to such substance as used in a particular class of article or as packaged, the Commission determines by regulation that the substance is sufficiently hazardous to require labeling in accordance with the act in order to protect the public health.

(D) Any toy or other article intended for use by children which the Commission by regulation determines, in accordance with section 3(e) of the act, presents an electrical, mechanical, or thermal hazard.

(ii) *Hazardous substance* shall not apply to pesticides subject to the Federal Insecticide, Fungicide, and Rodenticide Act, to foods, drugs, and cosmetics subject to the Federal Food, Drug, and Cosmetic Act, nor to substances intended for use as fuels when stored in containers and used in the heating, cooking, or refrigeration system of a house. "Hazardous substance" shall apply, however, to any article which is not itself a pesticide within the meaning of the Federal Insecticide, Fungicide, and Rodenticide Act but which is a hazardous substance within the meaning of section 2(f)(1) of the Federal Hazardous Substances Act (restated in paragraph (b)(4)(i) of this section) by reason of bearing or containing such a pesticide.

(iii) *Hazardous substance* shall not include any source material, special nuclear material, or byproduct material as defined in the Atomic Energy Act of 1954, as amended, and regulations issued pursuant thereto by the Atomic Energy Commission.

(5) *Toxic* shall apply to any substance (other than a radioactive substance) which has the capacity to produce personal injury or illness to man through ingestion, inhalation, or absorption through any body surface.

(6)(i) *Highly toxic* means any substance which falls within any of the following categories:

(A) Produces death within 14 days in half or more than half of a group of 10 or more laboratory white rats each weighing between 200 and 300 grams, at a single dose of 50 milligrams or less per kilogram of body weight, when orally administered; or

(B) Produces death within 14 days in half or more than half of a group of 10 or more laboratory white rats each weighing between 200 and 300 grams, when inhaled continuously for a period of 1 hour or less at an atmospheric concentration of 200 parts per million by volume or less of gas or vapor or 2 milligrams per liter by volume or less of mist or dust, provided such concentration is likely to be encountered by man when the substance is used in any reasonably foreseeable manner; or

(C) Produces death within 14 days in half or more than half of a group of 10 or more rabbits tested in a dosage of 200 milligrams or less per kilogram of body weight, when administered by continuous contact with the bare skin for 24 hours or less.

(ii) If the Commission finds that available data on human experience with any substance indicate results different from those obtained on animals in the dosages and concentrations specified in paragraph (b)(6)(i) of this section, the human data shall take precedence.

(7) *Corrosive* means any substance which in contact with living tissue will cause destruction of tissue by chemical action, but shall not refer to action on inanimate surfaces.

(8) *Irritant* means any substance not corrosive within the meaning of section 2(i) of the act (restated in paragraph (b)(7) of this section) which on immediate, prolonged, or repeated contact with normal living tissue will induce a local inflammatory reaction.

(9) *Strong sensitizer* means a substance which will cause on normal living tissue through an allergic or photodynamic process a hypersensitivity which becomes evident on reapplication of the same substance and which is designated as such by the Commission. Before designating any substance as a strong sensitizer, the Commission, upon consideration of the frequency of occurrence and severity of the reaction, shall find that the substance has a significant potential for causing hypersensitivity.

(10) The terms *extremely flammable, flammable,* and *combustible* as they apply to any substances, liquid, solid, or the contents of any self-pressurized container, are defined by regulations issued by the Commission and published at § 1500.3(c)(6).

(11) *Radioactive substance* means a substance which emits ionizing radiation.

(12) *Label* means a display of written, printed, or graphic matter upon the immediate container of any substance or, in the cases of an article which is unpackaged or is not packaged in an

immediate container intended or suitable for delivery to the ultimate consumer, a display of such matter directly upon the article involved or upon a tag or other suitable material affixed thereto. A requirement made by or under authority of the act that any word, statement, or other information appear on the label shall not be considered to be complied with unless such word, statement, or other information also appears (i) on the outside container or wrapper, if any there be, unless it is easily legible through the outside container or wrapper and (ii) on all accompanying literature where there are directions for use, written or otherwise.

(13) *Immediate container* does not include package liners.

(14) *Misbranded hazardous substance* means a hazardous substance (including a toy, or other article intended for use by children, which is a hazardous substance, or which bears or contains a hazardous substance in such manner as to be susceptible of access by a child to whom such toy or other article is entrusted) intended, or packaged in a form suitable, for use in the household or by children, if the packaging or labeling of such substance is in violation of an applicable regulation issued pursuant to section 3 or 4 of the Poison Prevention Packaging Act of 1970 or if such substance, except as otherwise provided by or pursuant to section 3 of the act (Federal Hazardous Substances Act), fails to bear a label:

(i) Which states conspicuously:

(A) The name and place of business of the manufacturer, packer, distributor, or seller;

(B) The common or usual name or the chemical name (if there be no common or usual name) of the hazardous substance or of each component which contributes substantially to its hazard, unless the Commission by regulation permits or requires the use of a recognized generic name;

(C) The signal word "DANGER" on substances which are extremely flammable, corrosive, or highly toxic;

(D) The signal word "WARNING" or "CAUTION" on all other hazardous substances;

(E) An affirmative statement of the principal hazard or hazards, such as "Flammable," "Combustible," "Vapor Harmful," "Causes Burns," "Absorbed Through Skin," or similar wording descriptive of the hazard;

(F) Precautionary measures describing the action to be followed or avoided, except when modified by regulation of the Commission pursuant to section 3 of the act;

(G) Instruction, when necessary or appropriate, for first-aid treatment;

(H) The word *Poison* for any hazardous substance which is defined as "highly toxic" by section 2(h) of the act (restated in paragraph (b)(6) of this section);

(I) Instructions for handling and storage of packages which require special care in handling or storage; and

(J) The statement (*1*) "Keep out of the reach of children" or its practical equivalent, or, (*2*) if the article is intended for use by children and is not a banned hazardous substance, adequate directions for the protection of children from the hazard; and

(ii) On which any statements required under section 2(p)(1) of the act (restated in paragraph (b)(14)(i) of this section) are located prominently and are in the English language in conspicuous and legible type in contrast by typography, layout, or color with other printed matter on the label.

Misbranded hazardous substance also means a household substance as defined in section 2(2)(D) of the Poison Prevention Packaging Act of 1970 if it is a substance described in section 2(f)(1) of the Federal Hazardous Substances Act (restated in paragraph (b)(4)(i)(A) of this section) and its packaging or labeling is in violation of an applicable regulation issued pursuant to section 3 or 4 of the Poison Prevention Packaging Act of 1970.

(15)(i) *Banned hazardous substance* means:

(A) Any toy, or other article intended for use by children, which is a hazardous substance, or which bears or contains a hazardous substance in such manner as to be susceptible of access by a child to whom such toy or other article is entrusted; or

(B) Any hazardous substance intended, or packaged in a form suitable, for use in the household, which the Commission by regulation classifies as a "banned hazardous substance" on the basis of a finding that, notwithstanding such cautionary labeling as is or may be required under the act for that substance, the degree or nature of the hazard involved in the presence or use of such substance in households is such that the objective of the protection of the public health and safety can be adequately served only by keeping such substance, when so intended or packaged, out of the channels of interstate commerce; *Provided,* That the Commission by regulation (*1*) shall exempt from section 2(q)(1)(A) of the act (restated in paragraph (b)(15)(i)(A) of this section) articles, such as chemistry sets, which by reason of their functional purpose require the inclusion of the hazardous substance involved, or necessarily present an electrical, mechanical, or thermal hazard, and which bear labeling giving adequate directions and warnings for safe use and are intended for use by children who have attained sufficient maturity, and may reasonably be expected, to read and heed such directions and warnings, and (*2*) shall exempt from section 2(q)(1)(A) of the act (restated in paragraph (b)(15)(i)(A) of this section), and provide for the labeling of, common fireworks (including toy paper caps, cone fountains, cylinder fountains, whistles without report, and sparklers) to the extent that the Commission determines that such articles can be adequately labeled to protect the purchasers and users thereof.

(ii) Proceedings for the issuance, amendment, or repeal of regulations pursuant to section 2(q)(1)(B) of the act (restated in paragraph (b)(15)(i)(B) of this section) shall be governed by the provisions of section 701 (e), (f), and (g) of the Federal Food, Drug, and Cosmetic Act: *Provided,* That if the Commission finds that the distribution for household use of the hazardous substance involved presents an imminent hazard to the public health, the Commission may by order published in the FEDERAL REGISTER give notice of such finding, and thereupon such substance when intended or offered for household use, or when so packaged as to be suitable for such use, shall be deemed to be a "banned hazardous substance" pending the completion of proceedings relating to the issuance of such regulations.

(16) "Electrical hazard"—an article may be determined to present an electrical hazard if, in normal use or when subjected to reasonably foreseeable damage or abuse, its design or manufacture may cause personal injury or illness by electric shock.

(17) "Mechanical hazard"—an article may be determined to present a mechanical hazard if, in normal use or when subjected to reasonably foreseeable damage or abuse, its design or manufacture presents an unreasonable risk of personal injury or illness:

(i) From fracture, fragmentation, or disassembly of the article;

(ii) From propulsion of the article (or any part or accessory thereof);

(iii) From points or other protrusions, surfaces, edges, openings, or closures;

(iv) From moving parts;

(v) From lack or insufficiency of controls to reduce or stop motion;

(vi) As a result of self-adhering characteristics of the article;

(vii) Because the article (or any part or accessory thereof) may be aspirated or ingested;

(viii) Because of instability; or

(ix) Because of any other aspect of the article's design or manufacture.

(18) "Thermal hazard"—an article may be determined to present a thermal hazard if, in normal use or when subjected to reasonably foreseeable damage or abuse, its design or manufacture presents an unreasonable risk of personal injury or illness because of heat as from heated parts, substances, or surfaces.

(c) *Certain statutory definitions interpreted, supplemented, or provided with alternatives.* The following items interpret, supplement, or provide alternatives to definitions set forth in section 2 of the act (and restated in paragraph (b) of this section):

(1) To provide flexibility as to the number of animals tested, the following is an alternative to the definition of "highly toxic" in section 2(h) of the act (and paragraph (b)(6) of this section); *Highly toxic* means:

(i) A substance determined by the Commission to be highly toxic on the basis of human experience; and/or

(ii) A substance that produces death within 14 days in half or more than half of a group of:

(A) White rats (each weighing between 200 and 300 grams) when a single dose of 50 milligrams or less per kilogram of body weight is administered orally;

(B) White rats (each weighing between 200 and 300 grams) when a concentration of 200 parts per million by volume or less of gas or vapor, or 2 milligrams per liter by volume or less of mist or dust, is inhaled continuously for 1 hour or less, if such concentration is likely to be encountered by man when the substance is used in any reasonably foreseeable manner; and/or

(C) Rabbits (each weighing between 2.3 and 3.0 kilograms) when a dosage of 200 milligrams or less per kilogram of body weight is administered by continuous contact with the bare skin for 24 hours or less by the method described in §1500.40.

The number of animals tested shall be sufficient to give a statistically significant result and shall be in conformity with good pharmacological practices.

(2) To give specificity to the definition of "toxic" in section 2(g) of the act (and restated in paragraph (b)(5) of this section), the following supplements that definition. The following categories are not intended to be inclusive.

(i) *Acute toxicity. Toxic* means any substance that produces death within 14 days in half or more than half of a group of:

(A) White rats (each weighing between 200 and 300 grams) when a single dose of from 50 milligrams to 5 grams per kilogram of body weight is administered orally. Substances falling in the toxicity range between 500 milligrams and 5 grams per kilogram of body weight will be considered for exemption from some or all of the labeling requirements of the act, under §1500.82, upon a showing that such labeling is not needed because of the physical form of the substances (solid, a thick plastic, emulsion, etc.), the size or closure of the container, human experience with the article, or any other relevant factors;

(B) White rats (each weighing between 200 and 300 grams) when an atmospheric concentration of more than 200 parts per million but not more than 20,000 parts per million by volume of gas or vapor, or more than 2 but not more than 200 milligrams per liter by volume of mist or dust, is inhaled continuously for 1 hour or less, if such concentration is likely to be encountered by man when the substance is used in any reasonably foreseeable manner: and/or

(C) Rabbits (each weighing between 2.3 and 3.0 kilograms) when a dosage of more than 200 milligrams but not more than 2 grams per kilogram of body weight is administered by continuous contact with the bare skin for 24 hours by the method described in §1500.40.

The number of animals tested shall be sufficient to give a statistically significant result and shall be in conformity with good pharmacological practices. "Toxic" also applies to any substance that is "toxic" (but not "highly toxic") on the basis of human experience.

(ii) *Chronic toxicity.* A substance is toxic because it presents a chronic hazard if it falls into one of the following categories. (For additional information see the chronic toxicity guidelines at 16 CFR 1500.135.)

(A) *For Carcinogens.* A substance is toxic if it is or contains a known or probable human carcinogen.

(B) *For Neurotoxicological Toxicants.* A substance is toxic if it is or contains a known or probable human neurotoxin.

(C) *For Developmental or Reproductive Toxicants.* A substance is toxic if it is or contains a known or probable human developmental or reproductive toxicant.

(3) The definition of *corrosive* in section 2(i) of the act (restated in paragraph (b)(7) of this section) is interpreted to also mean the following: *Corrosive* means a substance that causes visible destruction or irreversible alterations in the tissue at the site of contact. A test for a corrosive substance is whether, by human experience, such tissue destruction occurs at the site of application. A substance would be considered corrosive to the skin if, when tested on the intact skin

of the albino rabbit by the technique described in § 1500.41, the structure of the tissue at the site of contact is destroyed or changed irreversibly in 24 hours or less. Other appropriate tests should be applied when contact of the substance with other than skin tissue is being considered.

(4) The definition of *irritant* in section 2(j) of the act (restated in paragraph (b)(8) of this section) is supplemented by the following: *Irritant* includes "primary irritant to the skin" as well as substances irritant to the eye or to mucous membranes. *Primary irritant* means a substance that is not corrosive and that human experience data indicate is a primary irritant and/or means a substance that results in an empirical score of five or more when tested by the method described in § 1500.41. *Eye irritant* means a substance that human experience data indicate is an irritant to the eye and/or means a substance for which a positive test is obtained when tested by the method described in § 1500.42.

(5) The definition of *strong sensitizer* in section 2(k) of the Federal Hazardous Substances Act (restated in 16 CFR 1500.3(b)(9)) is supplemented by the following definitions:

(i) *Sensitizer*. A *sensitizer* is a substance that will induce an immunologically-mediated (allergic) response, including allergic photosensitivity. This allergic reaction will become evident upon reexposure to the same substance. Occasionally, a sensitizer will induce and elicit an allergic response on first exposure by virtue of active sensitization.

(ii) *Strong*. In determining that a substance is a "strong" sensitizer, the Commission shall consider the available data for a number of factors. These factors should include any or all of the following (if available): Quantitative or qualitative risk assessment, frequency of occurrence and range of severity of reactions in healthy or susceptible populations, the result of experimental assays in animals or humans (considering dose-response factors), with human data taking precedence over animal data, other data on potency or bioavailability of sensitizers, data on reactions to a cross-reacting substance or to a chemical that metabolizes or degrades to form the same or a cross-reacting substance, the threshold of human sensitivity, epidemiological studies, case histories, occupational studies, and other appropriate *in vivo* and *in vitro* test studies.

(iii) *Severity of reaction*. The minimal severity of reaction for the purpose of designating a material as a "strong sensitizer" is a clinically important allergic reaction. For example, strong sensitizers may produce substantial illness, including any or all of the following: physical discomfort, distress, hardship, and functional or structural impairment. These may, but not necessarily, require medical treatment or produce loss of functional activities.

(iv) *Significant potential for causing hypersensitivity*. "Significant potential for causing hypersensitivity" is a relative determination that must be made separately for each substance. It may be based upon the chemical or functional properties of the substance, documented medical evidence of allergic reactions obtained from epidemiological surveys or individual case reports, controlled in *vitro* or *in vivo* experimental assays, or susceptibility profiles in normal or allergic subjects.

(v) *Normal living tissue*. The allergic hypersensitivity reaction occurs in normal living tissues, including the skin and other organ systems, such as the respiratory or gastrointestinal tract, either singularly or in combination, following sensitization by contact, ingestion, or inhalation.

(6) The Consumer Product Safety Commission, by the regulations published in this section, defines the terms *extremely flammable*, *flammable*, and *combustible*, appearing in section 2(1) of the Federal Hazardous Substances Act, as follows:

(i) The term *extremely flammable* shall apply to any substance which has a flashpoint at or below 20 °F (−6.7 °C) as determined by the test method described at § 1500.43a, except that, any mixture having one component or more with a flashpoint higher than 20 °F (−6.7 °C) which comprises at least 99 percent of the total volume of the mixture is not considered to be an extremely flammable substance.

(ii) The term *flammable* shall apply to any substance having a flashpoint above 20 °F (−6.7 °C) and below 100 °F (37.8 °C), as determined by the method described at § 1500.43a, except that:

(A) Any mixture having one component or more with a flashpoint at or above 100 °F (37.8 °C) which comprises at least 99 percent of the total volume of the mixture is not considered to be a flammable substance; and

(B) Any mixture containing 24 percent or less of water miscible alcohols, by volume, in aqueous solution is not considered to be flammable if the mixture does not present a significant flammability hazard when used by consumers.

(iii) The term *combustible* shall apply to any substance having a flashpoint at or above 100 °F (37.8 °C) to and including 150 °F (65.6 °C) as determined by the test method described at § 1500.43a, except that:

(A) Any mixture having one component or more with a flashpoint higher than 150 °F (65.6 °C) which comprises at least 99 percent of the total volume of the mixture is not considered to be a combustible hazardous substance; and

(B) Any mixture containing 24 percent or less of water miscible alcohols, by volume, in aqueous solution is not considered to be combustible if the mixture does not present a significant flammability hazard when used by consumers.

(iv) To determine flashpoint temperatures for purposes of enforcing and administering requirements of the Federal Hazardous Substances Act applicable to "extremely flammable," "flammable," and "combustible" hazardous substances, the Commission will follow the procedures set forth in § 1500.43a. However, the Commission will allow manufacturers and labelers of substances and products subject to those requirements to rely on properly conducted tests using the Tagliabue opencup method which was in effect prior to the issuance of § 1500.43a (as published at 38 FR 27012, September 27, 1973, and set forth below), and the defintions of the terms "extremely flammable," "flammable," and "combustible" in this section before its amendment (as published at 38 FR 27012, September 27, 1983, and amended 38 FR 30105, November 1, 1973, set forth in the note following this section) if all of the following conditions are met:

(A) The substance or product was subject to and complied with the requirements of the Federal Hazardous Substances Act for "extremely flammable," "flammable," or "combustible" hazardous substances before the effective date of § 1500.43a; and

(B) No change has been made to the formulation or labeling of such substance or product after the effective date of § 1500.43a, prescribing a closed-cup test apparatus and procedure.

(v) *Extremely flammable solid* means a solid substance that ignites and burns at an ambient temperature of 80 °F or less when subjected to friction, percussion, or electrical spark.

(vi) *Flammable solid* means a solid substance that, when tested by the method described in § 1500.44, ignites and burns with a self-sustained flame at a rate greater than one-tenth of an inch per second along its major axis.

(vii) *Extremely flammable contents of self-pressurized container* means contents of a self-pressurized container that, when tested by the method described in § 1500.45, a flashback (a flame extending back to the dispenser) is obtained at any degree of valve opening and the flashpoint, when tested by the method described in § 1500.43a is less than 20 °F (−6.7 °C).

(viii) *Flammable contents of self-pressurized container* means contents of a self-pressurized container that, when tested by the method described in § 1500.45, a flame projection exceeding 18 inches is obtained at full valve opening, or flashback (a flame extending back to the dispenser) is obtained at any degree of valve opening.

(7) The definition of *hazardous substance* in section 2(f)(1)(A) of the act (restated in paragraph (b)(4)(i)(A) of this section) is supplemented by the following definitions or interpretations or terms used therein:

(i) A substance or mixture of substances that "generates pressure through decomposition, heat, or other means" is a hazardous substance:

(A) If it explodes when subjected to an electrical spark, percussion, or the flame of a burning paraffin candle for 5 seconds or less.

(B) If it expels the closure of its container, or bursts its container, when held at or below 130 °F. for 2 days or less.

(C) If it erupts from its opened container at a temperature of 130 °F. or less after having been held in the closed container at 130 °F. for 2 days.

(D) If it comprises the contents of a self-pressurized container.

(ii) *Substantial personal injury or illness* means any injury or illness of a significant nature. It need not be severe or serious. What is excluded by the word "substantial" is a wholly insignificant or negligible injury or illness.

(iii) *Proximate result* means a result that follows in the course of events without an unforeseeable, intervening, independent cause.

(iv) *Reasonably foreseeable handling or use* includes the reasonably foreseeable accidental handling or use, not only by the purchaser or intended user of the product, but by all others in a household, especially children.

(8) The definition of "radioactive substance" in section 2(m) of the act (restated in paragraph (b)(11) of this section) is supplemented by the following: *Radioactive substance* means a substance which, because of nuclear instability, emits electromagnetic and/or particulate radiation capable of producing ions in its passage through matter. Source materials, special nuclear material, and byproduct materials described in section 2(f)(3) of the act are exempt.

(9) In the definition of "label" in section 2(n) of the act (restated in paragraph (b)(12) of this section), a provision stipulates that words, statements, or other information required to be on the label must also appear on all accompanying literature where there are directions for use, written or otherwise. To make this provision more specific, "accompanying literature" is interpreted to mean any placard, pamphlet, booklet, book, sign, or other written, printed, or graphic matter or visual device that provides directions for use, written or otherwise, and that is used in connection with the display, sale, demonstration, or merchandising of a hazardous substance intended for or packaged in a form suitable for use in the household or by children.

(10) The definition of "misbranded hazardous substance" in section 2(p) of this act (restated in paragraph (b)(14) of this section) is supplemented by the following definitions or interpretations of terms used therein:

(i) *Hazardous substances intended, or packaged in a form suitable, for use in the household* means any hazardous substance, whether or not packaged, that under any customary or reasonably foreseeable condition of purchase, storage, or use may be brought into or around a house, apartment, or other place where people dwell, or in or around any related building or shed including, but not limited to, a garage, carport, barn, or storage shed. The term includes articles, such as polishes or cleaners, designed primarily for professional use but which are available in retail stores, such as hobby shops, for nonprofessional use. Also included are items, such as antifreeze and radiator cleaners, that although principally for car use may be stored in or around dwelling places. The term does not include industrial supplies that might be taken into a home by a serviceman. An article labeled as, and marketed solely for, industrial use does not become subject to this act because of the possibility that an industrial worker may take a supply for his own use. Size of unit or container is not the only index of whether the article is suitable for use in or around the household; the test shall be whether under any reasonably foreseeable condition of purchase, storage, or use the article may be found in or around a dwelling.

(ii) *Conspicuously* in section 2(p)(1) of the act and *prominently* and *conspicuous* in section 2(p)(2) of the act mean that, under customary conditions of purchase, storage, and use, the required information shall be visible, noticeable, and in clear and legible English. Some factors affecting a warning's prominence and conspicuousness are: Location, size of type, and contrast of printing against background. Also bearing on the effectiveness of a warning might be the effect of the package contents if spilled on the label.

NOTE: The definitions of *extremely flammable*, *flammable*, and *combustible* hazardous substances set forth above in paragraphs (b)(10) and (c)(6) are effective August 10, 1987. The definitions remaining in effect until August 10, 1987, as published at 38 FR 27012, Sept. 27, 1973, and amended at 38 FR 30105, Nov. 1, 1973, are set forth below. Manufacturers and labelers of products subject to the Federal Hazardous Substances Act may continue to use these definitions for labeling of those products under the conditions set forth in § 1500.3(c)(6)(iv), as amended.

(b)(10) *Extremely flammable* shall apply to any substance which has a flashpoint at or below 20 °F. as determined by the Tagliabue Open Cup Tester; *flammable* shall apply to any substance which has a flashpoint of above 20 °F., to and including 80 °F., as determined by the Tagliabue Open Cup Tester; and *combustible* shall apply to any substance which has a flashpoint above 80 °F. to and including 150 °F., as determined by the Tagliabue Open Cup Tester; except that the flammability or combustibility of solids and of the contents of self-pressurized containers shall be determined by methods found by the Commission to be generally applicable to such materials or containers, respectively, and established by regulations issued by the Commission, which regulations shall also define the terms *flammable, combustible,* and *extremely flammable* in accord with such methods.

* * * * *

(c)(6)(i) *Extremely flammable* means any substance that has a flashpoint at or below 20 °F. as determined by the method described in § 1500.43.

(ii) *Flammable* means any substance that has a flashpoint of above 20 °F., to and including 80 °F., as determined by the method described in § 1500.43.

[38 FR 27012, Sept. 27, 1973, as amended at 38 FR 30105, Nov. 1, 1973; 49 FR 22465, May 30, 1984; 51 FR 28536, Aug. 8, 1986; 51 FR 29096, Aug. 14, 1986; 51 FR 30209, Aug. 25, 1986; 57 FR 46669, Oct. 9, 1992]

EFFECTIVE DATE NOTE: At 77 FR 73293, Dec. 10, 2012, § 1500.3 was amended by revising paragraph (c)(1) introductory text; adding paragraph (c)(1)(iii); revising paragraph (c)(2) introductory text; revising paragraph (c)(2)(i) and revising paragraphs (c)(3) and (4), effective Jan. 9, 2013. For the convenience of the user, the added and revised text is set forth as follows:

§ 1500.3 Definitions

* * * * *

(c) * * *

(1) To provide flexibility as to the number of animals tested, and to emphasize *in vitro* testing methods, the following is an alternative to the definition of "highly toxic" in section 2(h) of the act (and paragraph (b)(6) of this section); *Highly toxic* means:

* * * * *

(iii) A substance that produces a result of 'highly toxic' in any of the approved test methods described in the CPSC's animal testing policy set forth in 16 CFR 1500.232, including data from *in vitro* or *in silico* test methods that the Commission has approved; or a validated weight-of-evidence analysis comprising all of the following that are available: existing human and animal data, structure activity relationships, physicochemical properties, and chemical reactivity data.

(2) To give specificity to the definition of "toxic" in section 2(g) of the act (and restated in paragraph (b)(5) of this section), the following supplements that definition. "Toxic" applies to any substance that is "toxic" (but not "highly toxic") on the basis of human experience. The following categories are not intended to be inclusive. * * *

(i) The number of animals tested shall be sufficient to give a statistically significant result and shall be in conformity with good pharmacological practices. *Toxic* also applies to any substance that can be labeled as such, based on the outcome of any of the approved test methods described in the CPSC's animal testing policy set forth in 16 CFR 1500.232, including data from, including data from *in vitro* or *in silico* test methods that the Commission has approved; or a validated weight-of-evidence analysis comprising all of the following that are available: existing human and animal data, structure activity relationships, physicochemical properties, and chemical reactivity data.

* * * * *

(3) Corrosive means a substance that causes visible destruction or irreversible alterations in the tissue at the site of contact. A test for a corrosive substance is whether, by human experience, such tissue destruction occurs at the site of application. A substance would be considered corrosive to the skin if a weight-of-evidence analysis suggests that it is corrosive, or validated *in vitro* test method suggests that it is corrosive, or if, when tested by the *in vivo* technique described in § 1500.41, the structure of the tissue at the site of contact is destroyed or changed irreversibly in 24 hours or less. Other appropriate tests should be applied when contact of the substance with other than skin tissue is being considered. A substance could also be labeled corrosive based on the outcome of any of the approved test methods described in the CPSC's animal testing policy set forth in 16 CFR 1500.232, including data from *in*

vitro or *in silico* test methods that the Commission has approved; or a validated weight-of-evidence analysis comprising all of the following that are available: Existing human and animal data, structure activity relationships, physicochemical properties, and chemical reactivity data.

(4) The definition of irritant in section 2(j) of the act (restated in paragraph (b)(8) of this section) is supplemented by the following: *Irritant* includes primary irritant to the skin, as well as substances irritant to the eye or to mucous membranes. *Primary irritant* means a substance that is not corrosive and that human experience data indicate is a primary irritant; and/or means a substance that results in an empirical score of five or more when tested by the method described in 1500.41; and/or a substance that can be considered a primary irritant based on the outcome of any of the approved test methods described in the CPSC's animal testing policy set forth in 16 CFR 1500.232, including data from *in vitro* or *in silico* test methods that the Commission has approved; or a validated weight-of-evidence analysis comprising all of the following that are available: existing human and animal data, structure activity relationships, physicochemical properties, and chemical reactivity data. *Eye irritant* means a substance that human experience data indicate is an irritant to the eye; and/or means a substance for which a positive test is obtained when tested by the method described in 1500.42; and/or means a substance that can be considered an eye irritant based on the outcome of any of the approved test methods described in the CPSC's animal testing policy set forth in 16 CFR 1500.232, including data from *in vitro* or *in silico* test methods that the Commission has approved; or a validated weight-of-evidence analysis comprising all of the following that are available: existing human and animal data, structure activity relationships, physicochemical properties, and chemical reactivity data.

* * * * *

§ 1500.4 Human experience with hazardous substances.

(a) Reliable data on human experience with any substance should be taken into account in determining whether an article is a "hazardous substance" within the meaning of the act. When such data give reliable results different from results with animal data, the human experience takes precedence.

(b) Experience may show that an article is more or less toxic, irritant, or corrosive to man than to test animals. It may show other factors that are important in determining the degree of hazard to humans represented by the substance. For example, experience shows that radiator antifreeze is likely to be stored in the household or garage and likely to be ingested in significant quantities by some persons. It also shows that a particular substance in liquid form is more likely to be ingested than the same substance in a paste or a solid and that an aerosol is more likely to get into the eyes and the nasal passages than a liquid.

§ 1500.5 Hazardous mixtures.

For a mixture of substances, the determination of whether the mixture is a "hazardous substance" as defined by section 2(f) of the act (repeated in § 1500.3(b)(4)) should be based on the physical, chemical, and pharmacological characteristics of the mixture. A mixture of substances may therefore be less hazardous or more hazardous than its components because of synergistic or antagonistic reactions. It may not be possible to reach a fully satisfactory decision concerning the toxic, irritant, corrosive, flammable, sensitizing, or pressure-generating properties of a substance from what is known about its components or ingredients. The mixture itself should be tested.

§ 1500.12 Products declared to be hazardous substances under section 3(a) of the act.

(a) The Commission finds that the following articles are hazardous substances within the meaning of the act because they are capable of causing substantial personal injury or substantial illness during or as a proximate result of any customary or reasonably foreseeable handling or use:

(1) Charcoal briquettes and other forms of charcoal in containers for retail sale and intended for cooking or heating.

(2) Metal-cored candlewicks that have a lead content of more than 0.06 percent of the total weight of the metal core, and candles made with such wicks.

(b) [Reserved]

[38 FR 27012, Sept. 27, 1973, as amended at 68 FR 19147, Apr. 18, 2003]

§ 1500.13 Listing of "strong sensitizer" substances.

On the basis of frequency of occurrence and severity of reaction information, the Commission finds that the following substances have a significant potential for causing hypersensitivity and therefore meet the definition for "strong sensitizer" in section 2(k) of the act (repeated in § 1500.3(b)(9)):

(a) Paraphenylenediamine and products containing it.

(b) Powdered orris root and products containing it.

(c) Epoxy resins systems containing in any concentration ethylenediamine, diethylenetriamine, and diglycidyl ethers of molecular weight of less than 200.

(d) Formaldehyde and products containing 1 percent or more of formaldehyde.

(e) Oil of bergamot and products containing 2 percent or more of oil of bergamot.

§ 1500.14 Products requiring special labeling under section 3(b) of the act.

(a) Human experience, as reported in the scientific literature and to the Poison Control Centers and the National Clearing House for Poison Control Centers, and opinions of informed medical experts establish that the following substances are hazardous:

(1) Diethylene glycol and mixtures containing 10 percent or more by weight of diethylene glycol.

(2) Ethylene glycol and mixtures containing 10 percent or more by weight of ethylene glycol.

(3) Products containing 5 percent or more by weight of benzene (also known as benzol) and products containing 10 percent or more by weight of toluene (also known as toluol), xylene (also known as xylol), or petroleum distillates such as kerosine, mineral seal oil, naphtha, gasoline, mineral spirits, stoddard solvent, and related petroleum distillates.

(4) Methyl alcohol (methanol) and mixtures containing 4 percent or more by weight of methyl alcohol (methanol).

(5) Turpentine (including gum turpentine, gum spirits of turpentine, steam-distilled wood turpentine, sulfate wood turpentine, and destructively distilled wood turpentine) and mixtures containing 10 percent or more by weight of such turpentine.

(b) The Commission finds that the following substances present special hazards and that, for these substances, the labeling required by section 2(p)(1) of the act is not adequate for the protection of the public health. Under section 3(b) of the act, the following specific label statements are deemed necessary to supplement the labeling required by section 2(p)(1) of the act:

(1) *Diethylene glycol.* Because diethylene glycol and mixtures containing 10 percent or more by weight of diethylene glycol are commonly marketed, stored, and used in a manner increasing the possibility of accidental ingestion, such products shall be labeled with the signal word "warning" and the statement "Harmful if swallowed."

(2) *Ethylene glycol.* Because ethylene glycol and mixtures containing 10 percent or more by weight of ethylene glycol are commonly marketed, stored, and used in a manner increasing the possibility of accidental ingestion, such products shall be labeled with the signal word "warning" and the statement "Harmful or fatal if swallowed."

(3) *Benzene, toluene, xylene, petroleum distillates.* (i) Because inhalation of the vapors of products containing 5 percent or more by weight of benzene may cause blood dyscrasias, such products shall be labeled with the signal word "danger," the statement of hazard "Vapor harmful," the word "poison," and the skull and crossbones symbol. If the product contains 10 percent or more by weight of benzene, it shall bear the additional statement of hazard "Harmful or fatal if swallowed" and the additional statement "Call physician immediately."

(ii) Because products containing 10 percent or more by weight of toluene, xylene, or any of the other substances listed in paragraph (a)(3) of this section may be aspirated into the lungs, with resulting chemical pneumonitis, pneumonia, and pulmonary edema, such products shall be labeled with the signal word "danger," the statement or hazard "Harmful or fatal if swallowed," and the statement "Call physician immediately."

(iii) Because inhalation of the vapor of products containing 10 percent or more by weight of toluene or xylene may cause systemic injury, such products shall bear the statement of hazard "Vapor harmful" in addition to the statements prescribed in paragraph (b)(3)(ii) of this section.

(4) *Methyl alcohol* (*methanol*). Because death and blindness can result from the ingestion of methyl alcohol, the label for this substance and for mixtures containing 4 percent or more by weight of this substance shall include the signal word "danger," the additional word "poison," and the skull and crossbones symbol. The statement of hazard shall include "Vapor harmful" and "May be fatal or cause blindness if swallowed." The label shall also bear the statement "Cannot be made nonpoisonous."

(5) *Turpentine*. Because turpentine (including gum turpentine, gum spirits of turpentine, steam-distilled wood turpentine, sulfate wood turpentine, and destructively distilled wood turpentine) and products containing 10 percent or more by weight of such turpentine, in addition to oral toxicity resulting in systemic poisoning, may be aspirated into the lungs with resulting chemical pneumonitis, pneumonia, and pulmonary edema, such products shall be labeled with the signal word "danger" and the statement of hazard "Harmful or fatal if swallowed."

(6) *Charcoal*. Charcoal briquettes and other forms of charcoal in containers for retail sale and intended for cooking or heating.

(i)(A) Because inhalation of the carbon monoxide produced by burning charcoal indoors or in confined areas may cause serious injury or death, containers of such products packaged before November 3, 1997, shall bear the following borderlined statement:

WARNING: Do Not Use for Indoor Heating or Cooking Unless Ventilation Is Provided for Exhausting Fumes to Outside. Toxic Fumes May Accumulate and Cause Death

(B) For bags of charcoal packaged before November 3, 1997, the statement specified in paragraph (b)(6)(i) of this section shall appear within a heavy borderline in a color sharply contrasting to that of the background, on both front and back panels in the upper 25 percent of the panels of the bag at least 2 inches below the seam, and at least 1 inch above any reading material or design elements in type size as follows: The signal word "WARNING" shall appear in capital letters at least three-eighths inch in height; the remaining text of the warning statement shall be printed in letters at least three-sixteenths inch in height.

(ii)(A) Because inhalation of the carbon monoxide produced by burning charcoal indoors or in confined areas can cause serious injury or death, containers of such products packaged on or after November 3, 1997, shall bear the following borderlined label.

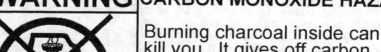

⚠WARNING

CARBON MONOXIDE HAZARD

Burning charcoal inside can kill you. It gives off carbon monoxide, which has no odor.

NEVER burn charcoal inside homes, vehicles or tents.

(B) Except as provided in paragraph (b)(6)(ii)(C) of this section, the following requirements apply to bags of charcoal subject to paragraph (b)(6)(ii)(A) of this section. The label specified in paragraph (b)(6)(ii)(A) of this section shall appear within a heavy borderline, in a color sharply contrasting to that of the background, on both the front and back panels in the upper 25 percent of the panels of the bag, and with the outer edge of the borderline at least 2.54 cm (1 inch) below the seam and at least 2.54 cm (1 inch) above any other reading material or design elements. The signal word "WARNING" shall be in bold capital letters in at least 7.14 mm (9⁄32 inch) type. The remaining text of the warning statement shall be in at least 4.763 mm (3⁄16 inch) type. The phrase "CARBON MONOXIDE HAZARD" shall be in bold. This phrase and the word "NEVER" shall be in all capital letters. The lettering shall have a strokewidth-to-height ratio of 1:6 to 1:8. The label shall be at least 50.8 mm (2 inches) high and 147.5 mm (5 13⁄16 inches) wide. The label's lettering, spacing between the bottom of the letters of one line and the top of the letter of the next line, and pictogram shall have the size relation to each other and to the remainder of the label shown in paragraph (b)(6)(ii)(A) of this section.

(C) For bags of charcoal subject to paragraph (b)(6)(ii)(A) of this section that are 6 inches or less wide, the minimum label height may be reduced to 38 mm (1.5 inches) and the minimum width may be reduced to 139.7 mm (5.5 inches). The signal word "WARNING" shall be in capital letters in at least 6.32 mm (0.249 inch) type. The remaining text of the warning shall be in at least 4.23 mm (0.166 inch) type. All other requirements of paragraphs 6(b)(ii) (A) and (B) of this section shall apply to these bags.

(7) *Fireworks devices.* Because of the special hazards presented by fireworks devices if not used in a certain manner, the following listed fireworks devices shall be labeled as indicated:

(i) *Fountains.*

WARNING (OR CAUTION)

FLAMMABLE (or EMITS SHOWERS OF SPARKS, if more descriptive).
Use only under [close] adult supervision. (Use of the word close is optional.)
For outdoor use only.
Place on level surface.
Light fuse and get away.

(ii) *California candles.*

WARNING (OR CAUTION) EMITS SHOWERS OF SPARKS

Use only under [close] adult supervision. (Use of the word close is optional.)
For outdoor use only.
Hold in hand at bottom of tube.
Point away from body so that neither end points toward body.

(iii) *Spike and handle cylindrical fountains.*

(A) *Spike fountains.*

WARNING (OR CAUTION) EMITS SHOWERS OF SPARKS

Use only under [close] adult supervision. (Use of the word close is optional.)
For outdoor use only.
Stick firmly in ground in an upright position.
Do not hold in hand.
Light fuse and get away.

(B) *Handle fountains.*

WARNING (OR CAUTION) EMITS SHOWERS OF SPARKS

Use only under [close] adult supervision. (Use of the word close is optional.)
For outdoor use only.
Hold in hand—point away from body.
Light fuse.

(iv) *Roman Candles.*

WARNING (OR CAUTION) SHOOTS FLAMING BALLS

Use only under [close] adult supervision. (Use of the word close is optional.)
For outdoor use only.
Stick butt end in ground.
Do not hold in hand.
Light fuse and get away.

(v) *Rockets with sticks.*

WARNING (OR CAUTION) FLAMMABLE

Use only under [close] adult supervision. (Use of the word close is optional.)
For outdoor use only.
Place in wooden trough or iron pipe at 75° angle, pointing away from people or flammable material.
Do not hold in hand.
Light fuse and get away.

(vi) *Wheels.*

WARNING (OR CAUTION) FLAMMABLE (OR EMITS SHOWERS OF SPARKS, IF MORE DESCRIPTIVE)

Use only under [close] adult supervision. (Use of the word close is optional.)
For outdoor use only.
Attach securely by means of a nail through the hole (or place on hard flat surface, for ground spinners).
Light fuse and get away.

(vii) *Illuminating torches.*

WARNING (OR CAUTION) FLAMMABLE (OR EMITS SHOWERS OF SPARKS, IF MORE DESCRIPTIVE)

Use only under [close] adult supervision. (Use of the word close is optional.)
For outdoor use only.
Hold in hand—point away from body, clothing, or other flammable material (or place upright on level ground. Do not hold in hand, if more descriptive).
Light fuse (or light fuse and get away, if more descriptive).

(viii) *Sparklers.*

On the front and back panels:

WARNING (OR CAUTION) FLAMMABLE

On the side, front, back, top, or bottom panel.

CAUTION

Use only under [close] adult supervision. (Use of the word close is optional.)
For outdoor use only.
Do not touch glowing wire (or do not touch hot plastic, wood, etc., if more descriptive).
Hold in hand with arm extended away from body.
Keep burning end or sparks away from wearing apparel or other flammable material.

(ix) *Mines and shells.*

WARNING (OR CAUTION) EMITS SHOWERS OF SPARKS (OR SHOOTS FLAMING BALLS, IF MORE DESCRIPTIVE)

Use only under [close] adult supervision. (Use of the word close is optional.)
For outdoor use only.
Place on hard smooth surface (or place upright on level ground, if more descriptive).
Do not hold in hand.
Light fuse and get away.

(x) *Whistles without report.*

WARNING (OR CAUTION) FLAMMABLE

SHOOTS WHISTLE IN AIR (if applicable)
Use only under [close] adult supervision. (Use of the word close is optional.)
For outdoor use only.
Do not hold in hand.
Light fuse and get away.

(xi) *Toy smoke devices and flitter devices.*

WARNING (OR CAUTION) FLAMMABLE (OR EMITS SHOWERS OF SPARKS, IF MORE DESCRIPTIVE)

Use only under [close] adult supervision. (Use of the word close is optional.)
For outdoor use only.
Do not hold in hand.
Light fuse and get away.

(xii) *Helicopter-type rockets.*

WARNING (OR CAUTION) FLAMMABLE (OR EMITS SHOWERS OF SPARKS, IF MORE DESCRIPTIVE)

Use only under [close] adult supervision. (Use of the word close is optional.)
For outdoor use only.
Place on hard, open surface.
Light fuse and get away.

(xiii) *Party poppers.*

WARNING (OR CAUTION) FLAMMABLE

Use only under [close] adult supervision. (Use of the word close is optional.)
Do not point either end toward face or other person.
Hold in hand—jerk string.

(xiv) *Missile-type rockets.*

WARNING (OR CAUTION) FLAMMABLE (OR EMITS SHOWERS OF SPARKS, IF MORE DESCRIPTIVE)

Use only under [close] adult supervision. (Use of the word close is optional.)
For outdoor use only.
Place on hard, open surface.
Light fuse and get away.

(xv) *Labeling—General.* Any fireworks device not required to have a specific label as indicated above shall carry a warning label indicating to the user where and how the item is to be used and necessary safety precautions to be observed. All labels required under this section shall comply with the requirements of §1500.121 of these regulations. (See also §1500.17(a) (3), (8) and (9); §1500.83(a)(27); §1500.85(a)(2); and part 1507).

(8) *Art materials.*

NOTE: The Labeling of Hazardous Art Materials Act ("LHAMA"), 15 U.S.C. 1277 (Pub. L. 100–695, enacted November 18, 1988) provides that, as of November 18, 1990, "the requirements for the labeling of art materials set forth in the version of the standard of the American Society for Testing and Materials ["ASTM"] designated D–4236 that is in effect on [November 18, 1988] * * * shall be deemed to be a regulation issued by the Commission under section 3(b)" of the Federal Hazardous Substances Act, 15 U.S.C. 1262(b). For the convenience of interested persons, the Commission is including the requirements of ASTM D–4236 in paragraph (b)(8)(i) of this section, along with other requirements (stated in paragraph (b)(8)(ii) of this section) made applicable to art materials by the LHAMA. The substance of the requirements specified in LHAMA became effective on November 18, 1990, as mandated by Congress.

(i) *ASTM D–4236*—(A) *Scope*—(*1*) This section describes a procedure for developing precautionary labels for art materials and provides hazard and precautionary statements based upon knowledge that exists in the scientific and medical communities. This section concerns those chronic health hazards known to be associated with a product or product component(s), when the component(s) is present in a physical form, volume, or concentration that in the opinion of a toxicologist (see paragraph (b)(8)(i)(B)(*11*) of this section) has the potential to produce a chronic adverse health effect(s).

(*2*) This section applies exclusively to art materials packaged in sizes intended for individual users of any age or those participating in a small group.

(*3*) Labeling determinations shall consider reasonably foreseeable use or misuse.

(*4*) Manufacturers or repackagers may wish to have compliance certified by a certifying organization. Guidelines for a certifying organization are given in paragraph (b)(8)(i)(H) of this section.

(B) Descriptions of Terms Specific to This Standard. (*1*) Art material or art material product—any raw or processed material, or manufactured product, marketed or represented by the producer or repackager as intended for and suitable for users as defined herein.

(*2*) Users—artists or crafts people of any age who create, or recreate in a limited number, largely by hand, works which may or may not have a practical use, but in which aesthetic considerations are paramount.

(*3*) Chronic adverse health effect(s)—a persistent toxic effect(s) that develops over time from a single, prolonged, or repeated exposure to a substance. This effect may result from exposure(s) to a substance that can, in humans, cause sterility, birth defects, harm to a developing fetus or to a nursing infant, cancer, allergenic sensitization, damage to the nervous system, or a persistent adverse effect to any other organ system.

(*4*) chronic health hazard(s) (hereafter referred to as ''chronic hazard'')—a health risk to humans, resultant from exposure to a substance that may cause a chronic adverse health effect.

(*5*) Analytical laboratory—a laboratory having personnel and apparatus capable of performing quantitative or qualitative analyses of art materials, which may yield information that is used by a toxicologist for evaluation of potentially hazardous materials.

(*6*) Label—a display of written, printed, or graphic matter upon the immediate container of any art material product. When the product is unpackaged, or is not packaged in an immediate container intended or suitable for delivery to users, the label can be a display of such matter directly upon the article involved or upon a tag or other suitable labeling device attached to the art material.

(*7*) Producer—the person or entity who manufactures, processes, or imports an art material.

(*8*) Repackager—the person or entity who obtains materials from producers and without making changes in such materials puts them in containers intended for sale as art materials to users.

(*9*) Sensitizer—a substance known to cause, through an allergic process, a chronic adverse health effect which becomes evident in a significant number of people on re-exposure to the same substance.

(*10*) Toxic—applies to any substance that is likely to produce personal injury or illness to humans through ingestion, inhalation, or skin contact.

(*11*) Toxicologist—an individual who through education, training, and experience has expertise in the field of toxicology, as it relates to human exposure, and is either a toxicologist or physician certified by a nationally recognized certification board.

(*12*) Bioavailability—the extent that a substance can be absorbed in a biologically active form.

(C) Requirements. (*1*) The producer or repackager of art materials shall submit art material product formulation(s) or reformulation(s) to a toxicologist for review, such review to be in accordance with paragraph (b)(8)(l)(D) of this section. The toxicologist shall be required to keep product formulation(s) confidential.

(*2*) Unless otherwise agreed in writing by the producer or repackager, no one other than the toxicologists shall have access to the formulation(s); except that the toxicologists shall furnish a patient's physician, on a confidential basis, the information necessary to diagnose or treat cases of exposure or accidental ingestion.

(*3*) The producer or repackager, upon advice given by a toxicologist in accordance with paragraph (b)(8)(i)(D) of this section and based upon generally accepted, well-established evidence that a component substance(s) is known to cause chronic adverse health effects adopt precautionary labeling in accordance with paragraph (b)(8)(i)(E) of this section.

(*4*) Labeling shall conform to any labeling practices prescribed by federal and state statutes or regulations and shall not diminish the effect of required acute toxicity warnings.

(*5*) The producer or repackager shall supply a poison exposure management information source the generic formulation information required for dissemination to poison control centers or shall provide a 24-hour cost-free telephone number to poison control centers.

(*6*) The producer or repackager shall have a toxicologist review as necessary, but at least every 5 years, art material product formulation(s) and associated label(s) based upon the then-current, generally accepted, well-established scientific knowledge.

(*7*) Statement of Conformance—"Conforms to ASTM Practice D–4236," or "Conforms to ASTM D–4236," or "Conforms to the health requirements of ASTM D–4236." This statement may be combined with other conformance statements. The conformance statement should appear whenever practical on the product; however, it shall also be acceptable to place the statement on one or more of the following:

(*i*) The individual product package,

(*ii*) a display or sign at the point of purchase,

(*iii*) separate explanatory literature available on requirements at the point of purchase,

(*iv*) a response to a formal request for bid or proposal.

(D) Determination of Labeling. (*1*) An art material is considered to have the potential for producing chronic adverse health effects if any customary or reasonably foreseeable use can result in a chronic hazard.

(*2*) In making the determination, a toxicologist(s) shall take into account the following:

(*i*) Current chemical composition of the art material, supplied by an analytical laboratory or by an industrial chemist on behalf of a manufacturer or repackager.

(*ii*) Current generally accepted, well-established scientific knowledge of the chronic toxic potential of each component and the total formulation.

(*iii*) Specific physical and chemical form of the art material product, bioavailability, concentration, and the amount of each potentially chronic toxic component found in the formulation.

(*iv*) Reasonably foreseeable uses of the art material product as determined by consultation with users and other individuals who are experienced in use of the material(s), such as teachers, or by market studies, unless such use information has previously been determined with respect to the specific art material(s) under review.

(*v*) Potential for known synergism and antagonism of the various components of the formulation.

(*vi*) Potentially chronic adverse health effects of decomposition or combustion products, if known, from any reasonably foreseeable use of the hazardous art material product.

(*vii*) Opinions of various regulatory agencies and scientific bodies, including the International Agency for Research on Cancer and the National Cancer Institute, on the potential for chronic adverse health effects of the various components of the formulation.

(*3*) Based upon the conclusion reached in conformance with review determinations set forth herein, the toxicologist(s) shall recommend precautionary labeling consistent with paragraph (b)(8)(i)(E) of this section.

(E) Labeling Practices—(*1*) Signal Word. (*i*) When a signal word for an acute hazard(s) is mandated and a chronic hazard(s) exists, the signal word shall be that for the acute hazard.

(*ii*) When only a chronic hazard(s) exists, the signal word WARNING shall be used.

(*iii*) The signal word shall be prominently visible and set in bold capitals in a size equal to or greater than the statement of potential chronic hazards.

(*2*) List of Potentially Chronic Hazards—Potentially chronic hazards, as determined under the procedures of paragraph (b)(8)(i)(D) of this section, shall be stated substantially in accordance with the statements listed in paragraph (b)(8)(i)(F) of this section. Potentially chronic hazards noted shall be those that are clinically significant and that might be expected with any reasonably foreseeable use of the art material. The hazards should be grouped in the order of relative descending severity.

(*3*) Name of Chronically Hazardous Component(s)—All components and known decomposition products of the formulation with a potential for chronic hazards, as determined under the procedures of paragraph (b)(8)(i)(D) of this section, shall be listed prominently. Generically equivalent names may be used.

(*4*) Safe Handling Instructions—Appropriate precautionary statements as to work practices, personal protection, and ventilation requirements shall be used substantially conforming with those listed in paragraph (b)(8)(i)(G) of this section.

(*5*) List of Sensitizing Components—To protect users from known sensitizers found within art materials, each label shall contain a list of those sensitizers present in sufficient amounts to contribute significantly to a known skin or respiratory sensitization.

(*6*) Combined Statement—If an art material contains more than one component capable of causing a chronic adverse health effect, or if a single chemical can cause several different chronic adverse health effects, the potential effects may be combined into one statement.

(*7*) Information Sources—The precautionary label shall contain a statement identifying a source for additional health information substantially in conformance with one of the phrases listed below:

(*i*) For more health information—(24 hour cost-free U.S. telephone number),

(*ii*) Contact a physician for more health information, or

(*iii*) Call your local poison control center for more health information.

(*8*) Labeling Content, Product Size—Any art material product in a container larger in size than one fluid ounce (30 ml) (if the product is sold by volume) or one ounce net weight (28 g) (if the product is sold by weight) shall have full precautionary labeling, as described in paragraph (b)(8)(i) (E) of this section. Any art material product in a container equal to or smaller than one fluid ounce or one ounce net weight shall have a label that includes a signal word in conformance with paragraph (b)(8)(i)(E)(*1*) of this section and a list of potentially harmful or sensitizing components in conformance with paragraphs (b)(8)(i)(E) (*3*) and (*5*) of this section.

(*9*) The information described in paragraph (b)(8)(i)(E) of this section must appear on:

(*i*) The outside container or wrapper, if any, unless it is easily legible through the outside container or wrapper and

(*ii*) All accompanying literature where there are directions for use, written or otherwise. Where a product that requires warning labels under paragraphs (b)(8)(i) (D) and (E) of this section is packed within a point-of-sale package that obscures the warning statement(s), the point-of-sale package shall carry the signal word conforming to paragraph (b)(8)(i)(E)(*1*) and the following wording: "Contains: (list hazardous product(s)) that may be harmful if misused. Read cautions on individual containers carefully. Keep out of the reach of children."

(*10*) Statements required under paragraphs (b)(8)(i) (D) and (E) of this section must be in the English language and located prominently in conspicuous and legible type in contrast by topography, layout, or color with other printed matter on the label.

(*11*) Supplemental Information—Where appropriate, more detailed information that relates to chronic hazard(s), such as physical properties, decomposition products, detailed safety instructions, or disposal recommendations, shall be included in supplemental documents, such as Material Safety Data Sheets, technical brochures, technical data sheets etc.

(F) chronic Hazard Statements

MAY CAUSE STERILITY.

CONTACT MAY CAUSE PERMANENT EYE DAMAGE.

MAY BE HARMFUL BY BREATHING VAPORS/DUSTS.

MAY BE HARMFUL IF SWALLOWED.

MAY BE HARMFUL BY SKIN CONTACT.

MAY PRODUCE BIRTH DEFECTS IN THE DEVELOPING FETUS.

MAY BE EXCRETED IN HUMAN MILK.

MAY CAUSE HARM TO THE NURSING INFANT.

CANCER AGENT! EXPOSURE MAY PRODUCE CANCER.

CANCER AGENT BASED ON TESTS WITH LABORATORY ANIMALS.

POSSIBLE CANCER AGENT BASED ON TESTS WITH LABORATORY ANIMALS.

MAY PRODUCE ALLERGIC REACTION BY INGESTION/INHALATION/SKIN CONTACT.

MAY PRODUCE NUMBNESS OR WEAKNESS IN THE EXTREMITIES.

EXPOSURE MAY CAUSE (SPECIFY THE ORGAN(S)) DAMAGE.

HEATING/COMBUSTION MAY CAUSE HAZARDOUS DECOMPOSITION PRODUCTS.

(G) Precautionary Statements

Keep out of reach of children.

When using do not eat, drink, or smoke.

Wash hands immediately after use.

Avoid inhalation/ingestion/skin contact.

Avoid fumes from combustion.

Keep container tightly closed when not in use.

Store in well-ventilated area.

Wear protective clothing (specify type).

Wear protective goggles/face shield.

Wear NIOSH-certified mask for dusts/mists/fumes.

Wear NIOSH-certified respirator with an appropriate cartridge for (specify).

Wear NIOSH-certified supplied-air respirator.

Use window exhaust fan to remove vapors and ensure adequate cross ventilation. (Specify explosion-proof if necessary.)

Do not heat above (specify temperature) without adequate ventilation.

Use (specify type) local exhausting hood.

Do not use/mix with (specify material).

(ii) The following shall apply with respect to the standard for art materials set forth in § 1500.14(b)(8)(i).

(A) The term *art material or art material product* shall mean any substance marketed or represented by the producer or repackager as suitable for use in any phase of the creation of any work of visual or graphic art of any medium. The term does not include economic poisons subject to the Federal Insecticide, Fungicide, and Rodenticide Act or drugs, devices, or cosmetics subject to the Federal Food, Drug, and Cosmetics Act.

(B) The standard referred to in paragraph (b)(8)(i) of this section applies to art materials intended for users of any age.

(C) Each producer or repackager of art materials shall describe in writing the criteria used to determine whether an art material has the potential for producing chronic adverse health effects. Each producer or repackager shall submit, to the Commission's Division of Regulatory Management, Consumer Product Safety Commission, Washington, DC 20207, the written description of the criteria described above and a list of art materials that require hazard warning labels under this section. Upon request of the Commission, a producer or repackager shall submit to the Commission product formulations.

(D) All art materials that require chronic hazard labeling pursuant to this section must include on the label the name and United States address of the producer or repackager of the art materials, an appropriate United States telephone number that can be contacted for more information on the hazards requiring warning labels under this section, and a statement that such art materials are inappropriate for use by children.

(E) If an art material producer or repackager becomes newly aware of any significant information regarding the hazards of an art material or ways to protect against the hazard, this new information must be incorporated into the labels of such art materials that are manufactured after 12 months from the date of discovery. If a producer or repackager reformulates an art material, the new formulation must be evaluated and labeled in accordance with the standard set forth §1500.14(b)(8)(i).

(F) In determining whether an art material has the potential for producing chronic adverse health effects, including carcinogenicity and potential carcinogenicity, the toxicologist to whom the substance is referred under the standard described above shall take into account opinions of various regulatory agencies and scientific bodies, including the U.S. Consumer Product Safety Commission (CPSC), the U.S. Environmental Protection Agency (EPA), and the International Agency for Research on Cancer (IARC).

(iii) Pursuant to the LHAMA, the Commission has issued guidelines which, where possible, specify criteria for determining when any customary or reasonably foreseeable use of an art material can result in a chronic hazard. These guidelines include criteria for determining when art materials may produce chronic adverse effects in children and adults, criteria for determining which substances contained in art materials have the potential for producing chronic adverse effects and what those effects are, criteria for determining the bioavailability of chronically hazardous substances contained in art materials when the products are used in a customary or reasonably foreseeable manner, and criteria for determining acceptable daily intake levels for chronically hazardous substances contained in art materials. Because these guidelines apply to hazardous substances in general as well as to hazardous substances in art materials, the guidelines are set forth in §1500.135 and a definition of "chronic toxicity" is provided in §1500.3(c)(2)(ii) as part of supplementation of the term "toxic" in section 2(q) of the FHSA.

(iv) *Policies and interpretations.*

(A) For purposes of enforcement policy, the Commission will not consider as sufficient grounds for bringing an enforcement action under the Labeling of Hazardous Art Materials Act ("LHAMA") the failure of the following types of products to meet the requirements of §1500.14(b)(8) (i) through (iii).

(*1*) Products whose intended general use is not to create art (e.g., common wood pencils, and single colored pens, markers, and chalk), unless the particular product is specifically packaged, promoted, or marketed in a manner that would lead a reasonable person to conclude that it is intended for use as an art material. Factors the Commission would consider in making this determination are how an item is packaged (e.g., packages of multiple colored pencils, chalks, or markers unless promoted for non-art materials uses are likely to be art materials), how it is marketed and promoted (e.g., pencils and pens intended specifically for sketching and drawing are likely to be art materials), and where it is sold (e.g., products sold in an art supply store are likely to be art materials). The products described in this paragraph do not meet the statutory definition of "art material."

(*2*) Tools, implements, and furniture used in the creation of a work of art such as brushes, chisels, easels, picture frames, drafting tables and chairs, canvas stretchers, potter's wheels, hammers, air pumps for air brushes, kilns, and molds.

(*3*) Surface materials upon which an art material is applied, such as coloring books and canvas, unless, as a result of processing or handling, the consumer is likely to be exposed to a chemical in or on the surface material in a manner which makes that chemical susceptible to being ingested, absorbed, or inhaled.

(*4*) The following materials whether used as a surface or applied to one, unless, as a result of processing or handling, the consumer is likely to be exposed to a chemical in or on the surface material in a manner which makes that chemical susceptible to being ingested, absorbed, or inhaled: paper, cloth, plastics, films, yarn, threads, rubber, sand, wood, stone, tile, masonry, and metal.

(B) For purposes of LHAMA enforcement policy, the Commission will enforce against materials including, but not limited to, paints, crayons, colored pencils, glues, adhesives, and putties, if such materials are sold as part of an art, craft, model, or hobby kit. The Commission will enforce the LHAMA requirements against paints or other materials sold separately which are intended to decorate art, craft, model, and hobby items. Adhesives, glues, and putties intended for general repair or construction uses are not subject to LHAMA. However, the Commission will enforce the LHAMA requirements against adhesives, glues, and putties sold separately (not part of a kit) if they are intended for art and craft and model construction uses. This paragraph (b)(8)(iv)(B) applies to products introduced into interstate commerce on or after August 14, 1995.

(C) Commission regulations at §1500.14(b)(8)(i)(C)(7) require that a statement of conformance appear with art materials that have been reviewed in accordance with the Commission standard. The Commission interprets this provision to require a conformance statement regardless of the presence of any chronic hazard warnings.

(D) Nothing in this enforcement statement should be deemed to alter any of the requirements of the Federal Hazardous Substances Act ("FHSA"), such as, but not limited to, the requirement that any hazardous substance intended or packaged in a form suitable for household use must be labeled in accordance with section 2(p) of the FHSA.

APPENDIX A TO §1500.14(B)(8)—GUIDELINES FOR A CERTIFYING ORGANIZATION (NOT MANDATORY)

(a) The term "certifying organization," as used in this paragraph, refers to an organization or an institute that, after assuring that all provisions are met, certifies that an art material does conform to the labeling requirements of this practice.

(b) The certifying body may be funded by member manufacturers, but should include users or their representatives, as well as manufacturers' chemists, on its technical and certifying committees.

(c) Representative samples of art materials, labeled as conforming to this section and bought at retail, should be analyzed at random and from time to time by an analytical laboratory to ensure they are the same as the formulation used by the toxicologist(s) for determining labeling requirements.

(d) The methods used by the toxicologist(s) in review and determination of the need and content of precautionary labeling for potentially chronic adverse health effects should be periodically reviewed by an advisory board composed of not less than three or more than five toxicologists, at least one of whom is certified in toxicology by a nationally recognized certification board.

(e) In cases where there is disagreement by participating producers or participating users, with the determination of the toxicologist(s), there should be a method whereby the toxicologist's decision can be presented to the advisory board of toxicologists for arbitration.

[38 FR 27012, Sept. 27, 1973, as amended at 41 FR 22934, June 8, 1976; 48 FR 16, Jan. 3, 1983; 53 FR 3018, Feb. 3, 1988; 57 FR 46669, Oct. 9, 1992; 60 FR 8193, Feb. 27, 1995; 61 FR 19829, May 3, 1996; 61 FR 33175, June 26, 1996]

§ 1500.15 Labeling of fire extinguishers.

When a substance or mixture of substances labeled for use in or as a fire extinguisher produces substances that are toxic within the meaning of §1500.3(c) (1) and (2) when used according to label directions to extinguish a fire, the containers for such substances shall bear the following labeling:

(a) When substances are produced that meet the definition of highly toxic in §1500.3(c)(1), the signal word "Danger" and the statement of hazard "Poisonous gases formed when used to extinguish flame or on contact with heat" are required labeling.

(b) When substances are produced that meet the definition of toxic in §1500.3(c)(2), the signal word "Caution" or "Warning" and the statement of hazard "Dangerous gas formed when used to extinguish flame or on contact with heat" are required labeling.

(c) Regardless of whether paragraph (a) or (b) of this section applies, any substance or mixture of substances labeled for use as a fire extinguisher that, if applied to an electrical fire, would subject the user to the likelihood of electrical shock shall be conspicuously labeled "Caution: Do not use on electrical wires."

(d) The statements specified in paragraphs (a), (b), and (c) of this section shall be in addition to any other that may be required under the act. All such substances or mixtures of substances shall also bear the additional statements "Use in an enclosed place may be fatal" and "Do not enter area until well ventilated and all odor of chemical has disappeared."

§ 1500.17 Banned hazardous substances.

(a) Under the authority of section 2(q)(1)(B) of the act, the Commission declares as banned hazardous substances the following articles because they possess such a degree or nature of hazard that adequate cautionary labeling cannot be written and the public health and safety can be served only by keeping such articles out of interstate commerce:

(1) Mixtures that are intended primarily for application to interior masonry walls, floors, etc., as a water repellant treatment and that are "extremely flammable" within the meaning of section 2(1) of the act (repeated in § 1500.3(b)(10)).

(2) Carbon tetrachloride and mixtures containing it (including carbon tetrachloride and mixtures containing it used in fire extinguishers), excluding unavoidable manufacturing residues of carbon tetrachloride in other chemicals that under reasonably foreseeable conditions of use do not result in an atmospheric concentration of carbon tetrachloride greater than 10 parts per million.

(3) Fireworks devices intended to produce audible effects (including but not limited to cherry bombs, M–80 salutes, silver salutes, and other large firecrackers, aerial bombs, and other fireworks designed to produce audible effects, and including kits and components intended to produce such fireworks) if the audible effect is produced by a charge of more than 2 grains of pyrotechnic composition; except that this provision shall not apply to such fireworks devices if all of the following conditions are met:

(i) Such fireworks devices are distributed to farmers, ranchers, or growers through a wildlife management program administered by the U.S. Department of the Interior (or by equivalent State or local government agencies); and

(ii) Such distribution is in response to a written application describing the wildlife management problem that requires use of such devices, is of a quantity no greater than required to control the problem described, and is where other means of control are unavailable or inadequate. (See also § 1500.14(b)(7); § 1500.17(a) (8) and (9); § 1500.83(a)(27); § 1500.85(a)(2); and part 1507).

(4) Liquid drain cleaners containing 10 percent or more by weight of sodium and/or potassium hydroxide; except that this subparagraph shall not apply to such liquid drain cleaners if packaged in accordance with a standard for special packaging of such articles promulgated under the Poison Prevention Packaging Act of 1970 (Pub. L. 91–601, 84 Stat. 1670–74 (15 U.S.C. 1471–76)).

(5) Products containing soluble cyanide salts, excluding unavoidable manufacturing residues of cyanide salts in other chemicals that under reasonable and foreseeable conditions of use will not result in a concentration of cyanide greater than 25 parts per million.

(6)(i) Any paint or other similar surface-coating material intended, or packaged in a form suitable, for use in or around the household that:

(A) Is shipped in interstate commerce after December 31, 1973, and contains lead compounds of which the lead content (calculated as the metal) is in excess of 0.06 percent of the total weight of the contained solids or dried paint film; or

(B) Is shipped in interstate commerce after December 31, 1972, and contains lead compounds of which the lead content (calculated as the metal) is in excess of 0.5 percent of the total weight of the contained solids or dried paint film.

(C) [Reserved]

(D) The provisions of paragraph (a)(6)(i) of this section do not apply to artists' paints and related materials.

(ii) Any toy or other article intended for use by children that:

(A) Is shipped in interstate commerce after December 31, 1973, and bears any paint or other similar surface-coating material containing lead compounds of which the lead content (calculated as the metal) is in excess of 0.06 percent of the total weight of the contained solids or dried paint film; or

(B) Is shipped in interstate commerce after December 31, 1972, and bears any paint or other similar surface-coating material containing lead compounds of which the lead content (calculated as the metal) is in excess of 0.5 percent of the total weight of the contained solids or dried paint film.

(iii) Since the Commission has issued comprehensive regulations for lead-containing paint and certain consumer products bearing such paint at the 0.06 percent level under the Consumer Product Safety Act (see 16 CFR part 1303), paragraphs (i) and (ii) of §1500.17(a)(6) are revoked as to the subject products manufactured after February 27, 1978.

NOTE: The effective date of paragraphs (a)(6)(i)(A) and (a)(6)(ii)(A) was stayed by an order published in the FEDERAL REGISTER of August 10, 1972 (37 FR 16078).

(7) General-use garments containing asbestos (other than garments having a bona fide application for personal protection against thermal injury and so constructed that the asbestos fibers will not become airborne under reasonably foreseeable conditions of use).

(8) Firecrackers designed to produce audible effects, if the audible effect is produced by a charge of more than 50 milligrams (.772 grains) of pyrotechnic composition (not including firecrackers included as components of a rocket), aerial bombs, and devices that may be confused with candy or other foods, such as "dragon eggs," and "cracker balls" (also known as "ball-type caps"), and including kits and components intended to produce such fireworks except such devices which meet all of the following conditions:

(i) The fireworks devices are distributed to farmers, ranchers, or growers through a wildlife management program administered by the U.S. Department of Interior (or by equivalent State or local governmental agencies); and

(ii) Such distribution is in response to a written application describing the wildlife management problem that requires use of such devices, is of a quantity no greater than required to control the problem described, and is where other means of control is unavailable or inadequate. (See also §1500.17(a) (3) and (9)).

(9) All fireworks devices, other than firecrackers, including kits and components intended to produce such fireworks, not otherwise banned under the act, that do not comply with the applicable requirements of part 1507 of this chapter, except fireworks devices which meet all the following conditions:

(i) The fireworks devices are distributed to farmers, ranchers, or growers through a wildlife management program administered by the U.S. Department of the Interior (or by equivalent State or local government agencies); and

(ii) Such distribution is in response to a written application describing the wildlife management problem that requires use of such devices, is of a quantity no greater than required to control the problem described, and is where other means of control is unavailable or inadequate. (See also §1500.17(a) (3) and (8)).

(10) Self-pressurized products intended or suitable for household use that contain vinyl chloride monomer as an ingredient or in the propellant manufactured or imported on or after October 7, 1974. (See also §1500.17(a) (3) and (8)).

(11)(i) Reloadable tube aerial shell fireworks devices that use shells larger than 1.75 inches in outer diameter and that are imported on or after October 8, 1991.

(ii) *Findings*. (A) *General*. In order to issue a rule under section 2(q)(1) of the Federal Hazardous Substances Act ("FHSA"), 15 U.S.C. 1261(q)(1), classifying a substance or article as a banned hazardous substance, the FHSA requires the Commission to make certain findings and to include these findings in the regulation. These findings are discussed below.

(B) *Voluntary standard*. Although a voluntary standard relating to the risk of injury associated with reloadable tube aerial shells has been adopted, it has not been implemented. Thus, the Commission is not required to make findings covering the likelihood that the voluntary standard would result in elimination or adequate reduction of the risk of injury or that there would be substantial compliance with the voluntary standard.

(C) *Relationship of benefits to costs.* The Commission estimates that the removal of large reloadable shells from the market is likely to virtually eliminate the number of associated injuries, with only a slight offsetting increase in the number of injuries due to the use of substitute Class C fireworks products available to consumers. The estimated net benefits range from essentially zero to close to $1 million annually. The annual costs of a ban are estimated to be very low. Included are potential costs to foreign manufacturers and U.S. importers from sales losses, production changes, and inventory retrofitting, and slightly reduced market choices for consumers who purchase aerial display fireworks. Costs to each of these sectors are estimated to be slight, and are reduced to the extent that alternative products are perceived as adequate substitutes for large reloadable shells. Thus, the Commission finds that the benefits expected from the regulation bear a reasonable relationship to its costs.

(D) *Least burdensome requirement.* The Commission considered several alternatives to the ban. These included: Design or performance criteria; additional or alternative labeling; inclusion of some reloadable shells 1.75 inches or smaller in the ban; and no action in reliance on the voluntary standard. The Commission determined that a ban of reloadable shells larger than 1.75 inches in outer diameter is the least burdensome alternative that would prevent or adequately reduce the risk of injury.

(*1*) Regarding design or performance criteria, the Commission considered requirements similar to those stated in the voluntary standard of the American Fireworks Standards Laboratory (''AFSL''). However, such criteria may increase the cost of the product and would not address all factors involved in the incidents. Further, concerns exist about the feasibility of criteria and quality control.

(*2*) Regarding additional or alternative labeling, the users' perception and experience concerning the amount of time available to get away may lead them to disregard an inconsistent warning. There are no data to suggest that a significant number, if any, incidents would be avoided if large reloadable shells carried more detailed labels or instructions than they currently do. It cannot be concluded that potential benefits would be greater than zero.

(*3*) The Commission considered including reloadable shells that are 1.75 inches or less in outer diameter and have the ''equivalent explosive power'' of larger shells. A kinetic energy level of 70 joules was considered to evaluate explosive power. However, any potential benefits are uncertain since the Commission concluded that a clear relation between kinetic energy and injury potential could not be established. Also, costs could be slightly higher.

(*4*) The Commission also considered imposing no mandatory requirements on large reloadable shells and relying instead on the AFSL voluntary standard. However, it is uncertain whether any net benefits to consumers would result from this alternative, since the level of injury reduction could be near zero if, as is probable, some firms chose not to conform with some or all of the AFSL standard.

(12)(i) *Large multiple-tube devices.* Multiple-tube mine and shell fireworks devices that first enter commerce or are imported on or after March 26, 1997, that have any tube measuring 1.5 inches (3.8 cm) or more in inner diameter, and that have a minimum tip angle less than 60 degrees when tested in accordance with the procedure of §1507.12 of this part.

(ii) *Findings*—(A) *General.* In order to issue a rule under the section 2(q)(1) of the FHSA, 15 U.S.C. 1261(q)(1), classifying a substance or article as a banned hazardous substance, the FHSA requires the Commission to make certain findings and to include these in the regulation. These findings are discussed in paragraphs (a)(12)(ii) (B) through (D) of this section.

(B) *Voluntary standard.* (*1*) One alternative to the tip-angle requirement that the Commission considered is to take no mandatory action, and to depend on a voluntary standard. The

American Fireworks Safety Laboratory (AFSL) has a standard for mines and shells intended to address the potential tip-over hazard associated with multiple-tube fireworks devices. AFSL's Voluntary Standard for Mines and Shells—Single or Multiple Shot requires that large multiple-tube devices not tip over (except as the result of the last shot) when shot on a 2-inch thick medium-density foam pad. The Commission cannot conclude that AFSL's existing voluntary standard adequately reduces the risk of injury from large devices that tip over while functioning. The Commission's tests using polyurethane foam did not find sufficient agreement between performance on foam and on grass. No other data are available to show that this dynamic test is reliable.

(*2*) In addition, even if the AFSL standard is effective, the Commission does not believe that compliance with the standard will be adequate. AFSL reports that it has been testing in accordance with its standard since January 1994. However, the results of CPSC's compliance testing indicate that multiple-tube devices still tip over while functioning. In fiscal year 1994, all 24 imported devices the Commission tested, and 1 of 8 domestic devices, tipped over while functioning. In fiscal year 1995, 22 of 27 imported devices and 1 of 5 domestic devices tipped over during Commission testing. The Commission finds that there is unlikely to be substantial compliance with the voluntary standard applicable to multiple-tube devices.

(C) *Relationship of benefits to costs.* The Commission estimates that the 60-degree tip-angle standard will eliminate the unreasonable tip-over risk posed by these devices. This will provide benefits of saving one life about every 3 years, and preventing an unknown number of nonfatal injuries. The annual cost of modifying affected devices is estimated to be between $1.5 million and $2.7 million. The Commission finds that the benefits from the regulation bear a reasonable relationship to its costs.

(D) *Least burdensome requirement.* The Commission considered the following alternatives: a ban of all multiple-tube devices with inner tube diameters 1.5 inches or greater; a dynamic performance standard; additional labeling requirements; and relying on the voluntary standard. Although a ban of all large multiple-tube devices would address the risk of injury, it would be more burdensome than the tip-angle standard. The Commission was unable to develop a satisfactory dynamic standard that would reduce the risk of injury. Neither additional labeling requirements nor reliance on the voluntary standard would adequately reduce the risk of injury. Thus, the Commission finds that a standard requiring large multiple-tube devices to have a minimum tip angle greater than 60 degrees is the least burdensome requirement that would prevent or adequately reduce the risk of injury.

(13)(i) *Candles made with metal-cored wicks.* Candles manufactured or imported on or after October 15, 2003, made with metal-cored candlewicks, unless:

(A) The metal core of each candlewick has a lead content (calculated as the metal) of not more than 0.06 percent of the total weight of the metal core; and

(B) Each outer container or wrapper in which candles subject to paragraph (a)(13)(i)(A) of this section are shipped, including each outer container or wrapper in which such candles are distributed to a retail outlet, is labeled "Conforms to 16 CFR 1500.17(a)(13)." For purposes of this paragraph (B), the term "outer container or wrapper" does not include the immediate container in which candle(s) is/are intended to be displayed at retail or during use in the home, unless that container or wrapper is also the only container or wrapper in which the candle(s) is/are shipped to a retailer.

(ii) *Metal-cored candlewicks.* Metal-cored candlewicks manufactured or imported on or after October 15, 2003, unless:

(A) The metal core of each candlewick has a lead content (calculated as the metal) of not more than 0.06 percent of the total weight of the metal core; and

(B) Each outer container or wrapper in which candlewicks subject to paragraph (a)(13)(ii)(A) of this section is shipped, including each outer container or wrapper of a shipment distributed to a retail outlet, is labeled "Conforms to 16 CFR 1500.17(a)(13)." For purposes of this paragraph (B), the term "outer container or wrapper" does not include the immediate container in which candlewick(s) is/are intended to be displayed or sold at retail, unless that container or wrapper is also the only container or wrapper in which the candlewick(s) is/are shipped to a retailer.

(iii) *Findings*—(A) *General.* To issue a rule under section 2(q)(1) of the FHSA, 15 U.S.C. 1261(q)(1), classifying a substance or article as a banned hazardous substance, the Commission must make certain findings and include them in the regulation. These findings are discussed in paragraphs (a)(13)(iii)(B) through (D) of this section.

(B) *Voluntary Standard.* One alternative to the ban that the Commission considered is to take no mandatory action, and to depend on a voluntary standard. One organization has a standard for candlewicks intended to address the potential for substantial illness posed by such wicks and candles with such wicks. The Commission has found that the standard is technically unsound and that substantial compliance with it is unlikely. Furthermore, there is no evidence that the standard has been adopted and implemented by candlewick or candle manufacturers.

(C) *Relationship of Benefits to Costs.* The Commission estimates that the ban will reduce the potential for exposure to lead and resulting lead poisoning because there is no "safe" level of lead in the blood. The annual cost to the candle/wick industry of the ban is estimated by the Commission to be in the range of $100,000 to $300,000. On a percentage basis these costs represent only 0.005 to 0.015 percent of the overall value of candle shipments in 2000, which was approximately $2 billion. Accordingly, the Commission finds that the benefits from the regulation bear a reasonable relationship to its costs.

(D) *Least burdensome requirement.* The Commission considered the following alternatives: no action; labeling all metal-cored candles with wicks containing more than 0.06 percent lead by weight of the metal; recordkeeping for shipments of wicks containing 0.06 percent or less lead by weight of the metal and of candles with such wicks; and relying on the voluntary standard. Neither no action, nor labeling, nor reliance on the voluntary standard would adequately reduce the risk of illness. Recordkeeping for shipments of wicks and of candles was not the least burdensome requirement that would prevent or adequately reduce the risk of illness. Therefore the Commission finds that a ban on candlewicks containing more than 0.06 percent lead by weight of the metal and candles with such wicks is the least burdensome requirement that would prevent or adequately reduce the risk of illness.

(b) [Reserved]

(Secs. 2(f)(1), (A), (B), (g), (q)(1)(B), 3(a), 74 Stat. 372, 374, as amended 80 Stat. 1304–05, 83 Stat. 187–189, 90 Stat. 503 (15 U.S.C. 1261, 1262); sec. 701 (e), (f), (g), 52 Stat. 1055–56, as amended 70 Stat. 919, 72 Stat. 948 (21 U.S.C. 371 (e), (f), (g)), sec. 30(a), 86 Stat. 1231 (15 U.S.C. 2079(a)))

[38 FR 27012, Sept. 27, 1973, as amended at 38 FR 27514, Oct. 4, 1973; 38 FR 31520, Nov. 15, 1973; 39 FR 30114, Aug. 21, 1974; 39 FR 42903, Dec. 9, 1974; 41 FR 22935, June 8, 1976; 42 FR 44202, Sept. 1, 1977; 43 FR 12310, Mar. 24, 1978; 48 FR 16, Jan. 3, 1983; 56 FR 37837, Aug. 9, 1991; 61 FR 13095, Mar. 26, 1996; 61 FR 18245, Apr. 25, 1996; 68 FR 19147, Apr. 18, 2003]

§ 1500.18 Banned toys and other banned articles intended for use by children.

(a) *Toys and other articles presenting mechanical hazards.* Under the authority of sections 2(f)(1)(D) and 24 of the act and pursuant to the provisions of section 3(e) of the act, the Commission has determined that the following types of toys or other articles intended for use by children present a mechanical hazard within the meaning of section 2(s) of the act because in normal use, or when subjected to reasonably foreseeable damage or abuse, the design or manufacture presents an unreasonable risk of personal injury or illness:

(1) Any toy rattle containing, either internally or externally, rigid wires, sharp protrusions, or loose small objects that have the potential for causing lacerations, puncture wound injury, aspiration, ingestion, or other injury. (But see § 1500.86(a)(1)).

(2) Any toy having noisemaking components or attachments capable of being dislodged by the operating features of the toy or capable of being deliberately removed by a child, which toy has the potential for causing laceration, puncture wound injury, aspiration, ingestion, or other injury.

(3) Any doll, stuffed animal, or other similar toy having internal or external components that have the potential for causing laceration, puncture wound injury, or other similar injury. (But see § 1500.86(a)(2)); (See also §§ 1500.48 and 1500.49).

(4) Lawn darts and other similar sharp-pointed toys usually intended for outdoor use and having the potential for causing puncture wound injury.

(5) Caps (paper or plastic) intended for use with toy guns and toy guns not intended for use with caps if such caps when so used or such toy guns produce impulse-type sound at a peak pressure level at or above 138 decibels, referred to 0.0002 dyne per square centimeter, when measured in an anechoic chamber at a distance of 25 centimeters (or the distance at which the sound source ordinarily would be from the ear of the child using it if such distance is less than 25 centimeters) in any direction from the source of the sound. This paragraph is an interim regulation pending further investigation to determine whether prevention of damage to the hearing of children requires revision hereof.

(6) Any article known as a "baby-bouncer" or "walker-jumper" and any other similar article (referred to in this paragraph as "article(s)"), except an infant walker subject to part 1216, which is intended to support very young children while sitting, bouncing, jumping, and/or reclining, and which because of its design has any exposed parts capable of causing amputation, crushing, lacerations, fractures, hematomas, bruises, or other injuries to fingers, toes, or other parts of the anatomy of young children. Included among, but not limited to, the design features of such articles which classify the articles as banned hazardous substances are:

(i) The areas about the point on each side of the article where the frame components are joined together to form an "X" shape capable of producing a scissoring, shearing, or pinching effect.

(ii) Other areas where two or more parts are joined in such a manner as to permit a rotational movement capable of exerting a scissoring, shearing, or pinching effect.

(iii) Exposed coil springs which may expand sufficiently to allow an infant's finger, toe, or any other part of the anatomy to be inserted, in whole or in part, and injured by being caught between the coils of the spring or between the spring and another part of the article.

(iv) Holes in plates or tubes which provide the possibility of insertion, in whole or in part, of a finger, toe, or any part of the anatomy that could then be injured by the movement of another part of the article.

(v) Design and construction that permits accidental collapse while in use. (But see § 1500.86(a)(4)).

(7) Toys usually known as clacker balls and consisting of two balls of plastic or another material connected by a length of line or cord or similar connector (referred to as "cord" in § 1500.86(a)(5)), intended to be operated in a rhythmic manner by an upward and downward motion of the hand so that the two balls will meet forcefully at the top and bottom of two semicircles thus causing a "clacking" sound, which toys present a mechanical hazard because their design or manufacture presents an unreasonable risk of personal injury from fracture, fragmentations, or disassembly of the toy and from propulsion of the toy or its part(s). (But see § 1500.86(a)(5).) This does not include products that are constructed so that the connecting members consist of plastic rods integrally molded to the balls and are mounted on a pivot so that movement of the balls is essentially limited to a single plane.

(8) Any pacifier that does not meet the requirements of 16 CFR part 1511 and that is introduced into interstate commerce after February 26, 1978.

(9) Any toy or other article intended for use by children under 3 years of age which presents a choking, aspiration, or ingestion hazard because of small parts as determined by part 1501 of this chapter and which is introduced into

interstate commerce after January 1, 1980. For purposes of this regulation, introduction into interstate commerce is defined as follows: A toy or children's article manufactured outside the United States is introduced into interstate commerce when it is first brought within a U.S. port of entry. A toy or children's article manufactured in the United States is introduced into interstate commerce (1) at the time of its first interstate sale, or (2) at the time of its first intrastate sale if one or more of its components and/or raw materials were received interstate, whichever occurs earlier. Part 1501 defines the term "toy or other article intended for use by children under 3," as used in this regulation, and exempts certain products from banning under this regulation.

(10)–(11) [Reserved]

(12) Any bicycle as defined in §1512.2(a) of this chapter (except a bicycle that is a "track bicycle" or a "one-of-a-kind bicycle" as defined in §1512.2 (d) and (e) of this chapter) that is introduced into interstate commerce on or after May 11, 1976, and that does not comply with the requirements of part 1512 of this chapter, except for §§1512.5(c)(3), 1512.9(a), 1512.18(e) and 1512.18(f) which become effective November 13, 1976.

(15) Any rattle (as defined in §1510.2 of this chapter) that is introduced into interstate commerce on or after August 21, 1978, and that does not comply with the requirements of part 1510 of this chapter. For purposes of the regulation, introduction into interstate commerce is defined as follows: A rattle manufactured outside the United States is introduced into interstate commerce when it is first brought within a U.S. port of entry. A rattle manufactured in the United States is introduced into interstate commerce (a) at the time of its first interstate sale, or (b) at the time of its first intrastate sale if one or more of its components and/or raw materials were received interstate.

(16) (i) Any article known as an "infant cushion" or "infant pillow," and any other similar article, which has all of the following characteristics (But see §1500.86(a)(9)):

(A) Has a flexible fabric covering. The term *fabric* includes those materials covered by the definition of "fabric" in section 2(f) of the Flammable Fabrics Act, 15 U.S.C. 1191(f).

(B) Is loosely filled with a granular material, including but not limited to, polystyrene beads or pellets.

(C) Is easily flattened.

(D) Is capable of conforming to the body or face of an infant.

(E) Is intended or promoted for use by children under one year of age.

(ii) *Findings*—(A) *General*. In order to issue a rule under section 2(q)(1) of the Federal Hazardous Substance Act (FHSA), 15 U.S.C. 1261(q)(1), classifying a substance or article as a banned hazardous substance, the FHSA requires the Commission to make certain findings and to include these findings in the regulation. These findings are discussed in paragraphs (a)(16)(ii) (B) through (D) of this section.

(B) *Voluntary standard*. No findings concerning compliance with or adequacy of a voluntary standard are necessary since no voluntary standard addressing infant cushions has been adopted or implemented.

(C) *Relationship of benefits to costs*. The Commission estimates that the removal of infant cushions from the market will result in total annual benefits of approximately five million dollars. The potential costs to businesses are expected to be offset by production of other products, and the potential costs to consumers are likely to be offset by the availability of substitutes for a comparable price.

(D) *Least burdensome requirement*. The Commission considered labeling and a design or performance standard as alternatives to the ban. The Commission does not believe that any form of labeling would have a significant effect in preventing the hazard associated with infant cushions. The Commission also concluded that no feasible standard exists that would address the hazard. Thus, the Commission determined that a ban of infant cushions is the least burdensome alternative that would prevent or adequately reduce the risk of injury.

(17) Any ball intended for children under three years of age that, under the influence of its own weight, passes,

in any orientation, entirely through a circular hole with a diameter of 1.75 inches (44.4 mm.) in a rigid template ¼ inches (6 mm.) thick. In testing to evaluate compliance with this paragraph, the diameter of opening in the Commission's test template shall be no greater than 1.75 inches (44.4 mm.).

(i) For the purposes of this paragraph, the term "ball" includes any spherical, ovoid, or ellipsoidal object that is designed or intended to be thrown, hit, kicked, rolled, dropped, or bounced. The term "ball" includes any spherical, ovoid, or ellipsoidal object that is attached to a toy or article by means of a string, elastic cord, or similar tether. The term "ball" also includes any multi-sided object formed by connecting planes into a generally spherical, ovoid, or ellipsoidal shape that is designated or intended to be used as a ball, and any novelty item of a generally spherical, ovoid, or ellipsoidal shape that is designated or intended to be used as a ball.

(ii) The term "ball" does not include dice, or balls permanently enclosed inside pinball machines, mazes, or similar outer containers. A ball is permanently enclosed if, when tested in accordance with 16 CFR 1500.52, the ball is not removed from the outer container.

(iii) In determining whether such a ball is intended for use by children under three years of age, the criteria specified in 16 CFR 1501.2(b) and the enforcement procedure established by 16 CFR 1501.5 shall apply.

(18)(i) Any bunk bed (as defined in § 1513.2(c) of this chapter) that does not comply with the requirements of part 1513 of this chapter.

(ii) *Findings.* In order to issue a rule under Section 3(e) of the Federal Hazardous Substances Act (FHSA), 15 U.S.C. 1262(e), classifying a toy or other article intended for use by children as a hazardous substance on the basis that it presents a mechanical hazard (as defined in Section 2(s) of the FHSA), the FHSA requires the Commission to make the following findings and to include these findings in the regulation: Bunk beds present a mechanical hazard; Where a voluntary standard has been adopted and implemented by the affected industry, that compliance with such voluntary standard is not likely to result in the elimination or adequate reduction of the risk of injury, or it is unlikely that there will be substantial compliance with such voluntary standard; The benefits expected from the rule bear a reasonable relationship to its costs; and The rule imposes the least burdensome requirement that prevents or adequately reduces the risk of injury for which the rule is being promulgated. These findings are made in the appendix to Part 1513.

(19)(i) Dive sticks, and other similar articles, that are used in swimming pools or other water environments for such activities as underwater retrieval games or swimming instruction, and which, when placed in the water, submerge and rest at the bottom of the pool. This includes products that are pre-weighted to sink to the bottom and products that are designed to allow the user to adjust the weight. Dive sticks and similar articles that come to rest underwater at an angle greater than 45 degrees from vertical when measured under the test at § 1500.86(a)(7) and dive sticks and similar articles that maintain a compressive force of less than 5-lbf under the test at § 1500.86(a)(8) are exempt from this banning rule. Articles that have a continuous circular shape, such as dive rings and dive disks are also exempt.

(ii)(A) *Findings.* In order for the Commission to issue a rule under section 2(q)(1) of the FHSA classifying a substance or article as a banned hazardous substance, the Commission must make certain findings and include these findings in the regulation. 15 U.S.C. 1262(i)(2). These findings are discussed in paragraphs (a)(18)(ii)(B) through (D) of this section.

(B) *Voluntary standard.* No findings concerning compliance with and adequacy of a voluntary standard are necessary because no relevant voluntary standard addressing the risk of injury posed by dive sticks has been adopted and implemented.

(C) *Relationship of benefits to costs.* The Commission estimates the potential benefits of removing hazardous dive sticks from the market to be 2 to 4 cents per dive stick. With the availability of substitutes and the expected low cost of modifying dive sticks to conform to the rule, the Commission anticipates that necessary changes will be minimal. The Commission estimates that the costs of the rule will be no more than 2 to 4 cents per dive stick. Thus, the Commission finds that there is a reasonable relationship between the expected benefits of the rule and its costs.

(D) *Least burdensome requirement.* The Commission considered pursuing voluntary recalls, following a voluntary standard, requiring labeling or changing the scope of the rule. A banning rule would be more effective than case-by-case recalls because the impalement hazard affects all dive sticks, not a specific brand or model. Awaiting recalls would allow these hazardous items on the market until the Commission obtained recalls. No applicable voluntary standard exists, and compliance may be low if one did. Although labeling could help reduce the risk of injuries from dive sticks, it would be less effective than a banning rule. It may be difficult for a label to convey the necessary information at the time of use. Modifying the scope so that the rule would only apply to pre-weighted dive sticks would continue to permit hazardous items because the unweighted dive sticks can easily be weighted to stand vertically at the bottom of the water. Thus, the Commission finds that a ban of dive sticks with the hazardous characteristics it has identified is the least burdensome alternative that would adequately reduce the risk of injury.

(b) *Electrically operated toys and other electrical operated children's articles presenting electrical, thermal, and/or certain mechanical hazards.* Under the authority of section 2(f)(1)(D) of the act and pursuant to provisions of section 3(e) of the act, the Commission has determined that the following types of electrically operated toys or other electrically operated articles intended for use by children present electrical, thermal, and/or certain mechanical hazards within the meaning of section 2 (r), (s), and/or (t) of the act because in normal use or when subjected to reasonably foreseeable damage or abuse, the design or manufacture may cause personal injury or illness by electric shock and/or presents an unreasonable risk of personal injury or illness because of heat as from heated parts, substances, or surfaces, or because of certain mechanical hazards.

(1) Any electrically operated toy or other electrically operated article intended for use by children (as defined in § 1505.1(a)(1)) that is introduced into interstate commerce and which does not comply with the requirements of part 1505 of this chapter.

NOTE: Paragraph (b)(1) was originally promulgated as 21 CFR 191.9a(b)(1) with an effective date of September 3, 1973 (38 FR 6138).

(2) [Reserved]

(c) *Toys and other articles (not electrically operated) presenting electric hazards.* Under the authority of section 2(f)(1)(D) of the act and pursuant to provisions of section 3(e) of the act, the Commission has determined that the following types of toys or other articles intended for use by children (not electrically operated) present an electrical hazard within the meaning of section 2(r) of the act.

(1) Any kite 10 inches or greater in any dimension constructed of aluminized polyester film or any kite having a tail or other component consisting of a piece of aluminized polyester film 10 inches or greater in any dimension presents an electrical hazard and is a banned hazardous substance because its design (specifically its size and electrical conductivity) presents a risk of personal injury from electric shock due to its ability to conduct electricity and to become entangled in or otherwise contact high voltage electric power lines.

(2) [Reserved]

(15 U.S.C. 1261 (f)(1)(D), (g)(1)(A), (r); 15 U.S.C. 1262(e)(1); 15 U.S.C. 2079(a))

[38 FR 27012, Sept. 27, 1973]

EDITORIAL NOTE: For FEDERAL REGISTER citations affecting § 1500.18, see the List of CFR Sections Affected, which appears in the Finding Aids section of the printed volume and at *www.fdsys.gov*.

§ 1500.19 Misbranded toys and other articles intended for use by children.

(a) *Definitions.* For the purposes of this section, the following definitions shall apply.

(1) *Ball* means a spherical, ovoid, or ellipsoidal object that is designed or intended to be thrown, hit, kicked, rolled, dropped, or bounced. The term "ball" includes any spherical, ovoid, or ellipsoidal object that is attached to a toy or article by means of a string, elastic cord, or similar tether. The term "ball" also includes any multi-sided object formed by connecting planes into a generally, spherical, ovoid, or ellipsoidal shape that is designated or intended to be used as a ball, and any novelty item of a generally spherical, ovoid, or ellipsoidal shape that is designated or intended to be used as a ball. The term "ball" does not include dice, or balls permanently enclosed inside pinball machines, mazes, or similar outer containers. A ball is permanently enclosed if, when tested in accordance with 16 CFR 1500.53, it is not removed from the outer container.

(2) *Small ball* means a ball that, under the influence of its own weight, passes, in any orientation, entirely through a circular hole with a diameter of 1.75 inches (44.4 mm.) in a rigid template ¼ inches (6 mm.) thick. In testing to evaluate compliance with this regulation, the diameter of opening in the Commission's test template shall be no greater than 1.75 inches (44.4 mm.).

(3) *Latex balloon* means a toy or decorative item consisting of a latex bag that is designed to be inflated by air or gas. The term does not include inflatable children's toys that are used in aquatic activities such as rafts, water wings, swim rings, or other similar items.

(4) *Marble* means a ball made of a hard material, such as glass, agate, marble or plastic, that is used in various children's games, generally as a playing piece or marker. The term "marble" does not include a marble permanently enclosed in a toy or game. A marble is permanently enclosed if, when tested in accordance with 16 CFR 1500.53, it is not removed from the toy or game.

(5) *Small part* means any object which, when tested in accordance with the procedures contained in 16 CFR 1501.4(a) and 1501.4(b)(1), fits entirely within the cylinder shown in Figure 1 appended to 16 CFR part 1501. The use and abuse testing provisions of 16 CFR 1500.51 through 1500.53 and 1501.4(b)(2) do not apply to this definition.

(6) *Package* or packaging refers to the immediate package in which a product subject to labeling under section 24 of the act is sold, as well as to any outer container or wrapping for that package.

(7) *Descriptive material* means any discrete piece of written material separate from the label of the package that contains an instruction (whether written or otherwise) for the use of a product subject to these labeling requirements, any depiction of the product, and any written material that specifically describes any function, use, warnings, user population, design or material specification, or other characteristic of the product. A catalog or other marketing material or advertisement that depicts other products in addition to the product it accompanies is not "descriptive material" unless it contains additional information, such as instructions for use of the product it accompanies or lists of accessories exclusively for use with that product, that are designed to focus the purchaser's attention on the product. Descriptive material "accompanies" a product subject to the labeling requirements when it is packaged with the product or when it is intended to be distributed with the product at the time of sale or delivery to the purchaser. "Descriptive material" does not include statements that appear on the package of a product subject to the labeling requirements. "Descriptive material" does not include material intended solely for use by children if the package it accompanies contains a separate package insert prominently identified as a warning for parents that contains the required precautionary statements.

(8) *Bin* and *container for retail display* mean containers in which multiple unpackaged and unlabeled items are held for direct selection by and sale to consumers.

(b) *Misbranded toys and children's articles.* Pursuant to sections 2(p) and 24 of the FHSA, the following articles are misbranded hazardous substances if their packaging, any descriptive material that accompanies them, and, if unpackaged and unlabeled, any bin in which they are held for sale, any container in which they are held for retail display, or any vending machine from which they are dispensed, fails to bear the labeling statements required in paragraphs (b) (1) through (4) and paragraph (f)(3) of this section, or if such labeling statements fail to comply with the prominence and conspicuousness requirements of paragraph (d) of this section.

(1) With the exception of books and other articles made of paper, writing materials such as crayons, chalk, pencils, and pens, modeling clay and similar products, fingerpaints, watercolors, and other paint sets, and any other article identified in 16 CFR 1501.3 (other than balloons), any article that is a toy or game intended for use by children who are at least three years old but less than six years of age shall bear or contain the following cautionary statement if the toy or game includes a small part:

WARNING:

CHOKING HAZARD--Small parts
Not for children under 3 yrs.

(2) Any latex balloon, or toy or game that contains a latex balloon, shall bear the following cautionary statement:

WARNING:

CHOKING HAZARD--Children under 8 yrs. can
choke or suffocate on uninflated or broken balloons.
Adult supervision required.

Keep uninflated balloons from children.
Discard broken balloons at once.

(3)(i) Any small ball intended for children three years of age or older shall bear the following cautionary statement:

WARNING:

CHOKING HAZARD--This toy is a small ball.
Not for children under 3 yrs.

(ii) Any toy or game intended for children who are at least three years old but less than eight years of age that contains a small ball shall bear the following cautionary statement:

WARNING:

**CHOKING HAZARD--Toy contains a small ball.
Not for children under 3 yrs.**

(4)(i) Any marble intended for children three years of age or older shall bear the following cautionary statement:

WARNING:

**CHOKING HAZARD--This toy is a marble.
Not for children under 3 yrs.**

(ii) Any toy or game intended for children who are at least three years old but less than eight years of age that contains a marble shall bear the following cautionary statement:

WARNING:

**CHOKING HAZARD--Toy contains a marble.
Not for children under 3 yrs.**

(c) *Age of intended user.* In determining the ages of the children for which any toy or article subject to this section is intended, the following factors are relevant: the manufacturer's stated intent (such as the age stated on a label) if it is reasonable; the advertising, marketing, and promotion of the article; and whether the article is commonly recognized as being intended for children in this age group. In enforcing this provision, the Commission will follow the procedures set forth in 16 CFR 1501.5.

(d) *Prominence and conspicuousness of labeling statements.* The requirements of 16 CFR 1500.121 relating to the prominence and conspicuousness of precautionary labeling statements for hazardous substances shall apply to any labeling statement required under § 1500.19(b) and (f), with the following clarifications and modifications.

(1) All labeling statements required by § 1500.19(b) and (f) shall be in the

English language. The statements required by paragraph (b) need not appear in the format and layout depicted in paragraph (b). The statements required by 16 CFR 1500.19(b) and (f) shall be blocked together within a square or rectangular area, with or without a border. This means that the statements must appear on at least two lines. The statements shall be separated from all other graphic material by a space no smaller than the minimum allowable height of the type size for other cautionary material (e.g., the phrase "Not for children under 3 yrs."). If not separated by that distance, the labeling statements must be surrounded by a border line. Label design, the use of vignettes, or the proximity of other labeling or lettering shall not obscure or render inconspicuous any labeling statement required under § 1500.19(b) and (f). This means that such statements shall appear on a solid background, which need not differ from the background color or any other color on the package label.

(2) The words "WARNING" or "SAFETY WARNING" required by section 24 of the FHSA shall be regarded as signal words.

(3) The statement "CHOKING HAZARD" shall be regarded as a statement of the principal hazard associated with the products subject to this section.

(4) All other remaining statements required by this section shall be regarded as "other cautionary material" as that term is defined in 16 CFR 1500.121(a)(2)(viii).

(5) The principal display panel for a bin, container for retail display, or vending machine shall be the side or surface designed to be most prominently displayed, shown, or presented to, or examined by, prospective purchasers. In the case of bins or containers for retail display, the cautionary material may be placed on a display card of a reasonable size in relationship to the surface area of the bin or container. The area of the display card shall constitute the area of the principal display panel. In the case of vending machines that contain a display card, the cautionary label may be placed either on the display card, on the coinage indicator decal, or on the glass or clear plastic of the machine. If there is no display card inside a vending machine, the size of the principal display panel will be calculated in accordance with 16 CFR 1500.121(c) based on the size of the front of the container from which items are dispensed, exclusive of the area of metal attachments, coin inserts, bases, etc. Any other side or surface of such a bin, container for retail sale, or vending machine that bears information, such as price or product description, for examination by purchasers shall be deemed to be a principal display panel, excluding any side or surface with information that only identifies the company that owns or operates a vending machine.

(6) All of the labeling statements required by this section, including those classified as "other cautionary material," must appear on the principal display panel of the product, except as provided for by § 1500.19(f). Any signal word shall appear on the same line and in close proximity to the triangle required by section 24 of the act. Multiple messages should be provided with sufficient space between them, when feasible, to prevent them from visually blending together.

(7) All labeling statements required by this section shall comply with the following type size requirements. 16 CFR 1500.121(c)(1) explains how to compute the area of the principal display panel and letter height.

Area sq. in	0–2	+2–5	+5–10	+10–15	+15–30	+30–100	+100–400	+400
Type Size								
Sig. Wd	3/64″	1/16″	3/32″	7/64″	1/8″	5/32″	1/4″	1/2″
St. Haz	3/64″	3/64″	1/16″	3/32″	3/32″	7/64″	5/32″	1/4″
Oth. Mat	1/32″	3/64″	1/16″	1/16″	5/64″	3/32″	7/64″	5/32″

(8) Labeling required by this section that appears on a bin, container for retail display, or vending machine shall be in reasonable proximity to any pricing or product information contained on the principal display panel, or, if such information is not present, in

close proximity to the article that is subject to the labeling requirements.

(9) Descriptive material that accompanies a product subject to the labeling requirements, including accompanying material subject to the alternative allowed by §1500.19(f), shall comply with the requirements of 16 CFR 1500.121(c)(6) relating to literature containing instructions for use which accompanies a hazardous substance. If the descriptive material contains instructions for use, the required precautionary labeling shall be in reasonable proximity to such instructions or directions and shall be placed together within the same general area (see 16 CFR 1500.121(c)(6)).

(10) In the case of any alternative labeling statement permitted under §1500.19(e), the requirements of 16 CFR 1500.121(b)(3) and 1500.121(c)(2)(iii) shall apply to statements or indicators on the principal display panel directing attention to the complete cautionary labeling that appears on another display panel.

(11) Any triangle required by this section shall be an equilateral triangle. The height of such a triangle shall be equal to or exceed the height of the letters of the signal word "WARNING". The height of the exclamation point inside the triangle shall be at least half the height of the triangle, and the exclamation point shall be centered vertically in the triangle. The triangle shall be separated from the signal word by a distance at least equal to the space occupied by the first letter of the signal word. In all other respects, triangles with exclamation points shall conform generally to the provisions of 16 CFR 1500.121 relating to signal words.

(e) *Combination of labeling statements.* The labels of products that contain more than one item subject to the requirements of this section may combine information relating to each of the respective hazards, if the resulting condensed statement contains all of the information necessary to describe the hazard presented by each article. However, in the case of a product that contains a balloon and another item subject to the labeling requirements, only the signal word and statement of hazard may be combined.

(f) *Alternative labeling statements for small packages.* Any cautionary statement required by section 1500.19(b) may be displayed on a display panel of the package of a product subject to the labeling requirement other than the principal display panel only if:

(1) The package has a principal display panel of 15 square inches or less,

(2) The full labeling statement required by paragraph (b) of this section is displayed in three or more languages on another display panel of the package of the product, and

(3)(i) In the case of a toy or game subject to §1500.19(b)(1), a small ball subject to §1500.19(b)(3), a marble subject to §1500.19(b)(4), or a toy or game containing such a ball or marble, the principal display panel of the package bears the statement:

 **SAFETY WARNING**

and bears an arrow or other indicator pointing toward or directing the purchaser's attention to the display panel on the package where the full labeling statement appears, or

(ii) In the case of a balloon subject to §1500.19(b)(2) or a toy or game containing such a balloon, the principal display panel bears the statement:

WARNING--CHOKING HAZARD

and bears an arrow or other indicator pointing toward or directing the purchaser's attention to the display panel on the package where the full labeling statement appears.

(g) *Alternative for products manufactured outside the United States.* In the case of a product subject to the labeling requirements of § 1500.19(b) which is manufactured outside the United States and is shipped directly from the manufacturer to the consumer by United States mail or other delivery service in an immediate package that contains descriptive material, the descriptive material inside the immediate package of the product need not bear the required labeling statement only if the shipping container of the product contains other accompanying material that bears the required statements displayed in a prominent and conspicuous manner. Products shipped from abroad to a U.S. affiliate for shipment to consumers are included within the scope of this exception.

(h) *Preemption.* Section 101(e) of the Child Safety Protection Act of 1994 prohibits any state or political subdivision of a state from enacting or enforcing any requirement relating to cautionary labeling addressing small parts hazards or choking hazards associated with any toy, game, marble, small ball, or balloon intended or suitable for use by children unless the state or local requirement is identical to a requirement established by section 24 of the FHSA or by 16 CFR 1500.19. Section 101(e) allows a state or political subdivision of a state to enforce a non-identical requirement relating to cautionary labeling warning of small parts hazards or choking hazards associated with any toy subject to the provisions of section 24 of FHSA until January 1, 1995, if the non-identical requirement was in effect on October 2, 1993.

[60 FR 10752, Feb. 27, 1995, as amended at 60 FR 41802, Aug. 14, 1995]

§ 1500.20 Labeling requirement for advertising toys and games.

(a) *Scope.* This section applies to catalogue and other printed material advertisements which provide a direct means of purchase or order of products requiring cautionary labeling under sections 24(a) and (b) of the FHSA.

(b) *Effective Date.* Under the Consumer Product Safety Improvement Act of 2008, Public Law 110–314, 122 Stat. 3016 (August 14, 2008), ("CPSIA"), the effective date of the CPSIA's amendment to Section 24 of the FHSA to require cautionary statements in catalogues and other printed materials is February 10, 2009. By this rule, the Commission is providing a grace period of 180 days, or until August 9, 2009, during which catalogues and other printed materials printed prior to February 10, 2009, may be distributed without such cautionary statements. Catalogues and other printed materials that are printed on or after February 10, 2009, must have the required cautionary statements. All catalogues and other printed materials distributed on or after August 9, 2009, must comply with this rule. This rule addresses only catalogues and other printed materials; however, the CPSIA extends the requirements for cautionary statements to Internet advertisements as well. Internet advertisements must comply with Section 24 of the FHSA as amended by the CPSIA no later than December 12, 2008.

(c) *Definitions.* For the purposes of this section, the following definitions shall apply.

(1) *Ball* means a spherical, ovoid, or ellipsoidal object that is designed or intended to be thrown, hit, kicked, rolled, dropped, or bounced. The term "ball" includes any spherical, ovoid, or ellipsoidal object that is attached to a toy or article by means of a string, elastic cord, or similar tether. The term "ball" also includes a multi-sided object formed by connecting planes

into a generally spherical, ovoid, or ellipsoidal shape that is designated or intended to be used as a ball, and any novelty item of a generally spherical, ovoid, or ellipsoidal shape that is designated or intended to be used as a ball. The term "ball" does not include dice, or balls permanently enclosed inside pinball machines, mazes, or similar other containers. A ball is permanently enclosed if, when tested in accordance with 16 CFR 1500.53, it is not removed from the outer container.

(2) *Small ball* means a ball that, under the influence of its own weight, passes in any orientation, entirely through a circular hole with a diameter of 1.75 inches (44.4 mm) in a rigid template ¼ inches (6 mm) thick. In testing to evaluate compliance with this regulation, the diameter of opening in the Commission's test template shall be no greater than 1.75 inches (44.4 mm).

(3) *Latex balloon* means a toy or decorative item consisting of a latex bag that is designed to be inflated by air or gas. The term does not include inflatable children's toys that are used in aquatic activities such as rafts, water wings, swim rings, or other similar items.

(4) *Marble* means a ball made of hard material, such as glass, agate, marble, or plastic, that is used in various children's games, generally as a playing piece or marker. The term "marble" does not include a marble permanently enclosed in a toy or game. A marble is permanently enclosed if, when tested in accordance with 16 CFR 1500.53, it is not removed from the toy or game.

(5) *Small part* means any object which, when tested in accordance with the procedures contained in 16 CFR 1501.4(a) and 1501.4(b)(1), fits entirely within the cylinder shown in Figure 1 appended to 16 CFR part 1501. The use and abuse testing provisions of 16 CFR 1500.51 through 1500.53 and 1501.4(b)(2) do not apply to this definition.

(6) *Direct means of purchase or order* means any method of purchase that allows the purchaser to order the product without being in the physical presence of the product. Advertising that provides a direct means of purchase or order of a product would include catalogues or other printed advertising material that contain order blanks, telephone numbers or fax numbers for placing orders, and Internet Web sites that enable consumers to purchase a product online or through the use of a telephone number or fax number provided on the Internet Web site.

(d) *Advertising requirements*. Any toy or game that requires a cautionary statement about the choking hazard associated with small parts, balloons, small balls, or marbles must bear that cautionary statement in the product's advertising if the advertising provides a direct means to purchase or order the product.

(1) The advertising for any article that is a toy or game intended for use by children who are at least three years old but less than six years of age shall bear or contain the following cautionary statement if the toy or game includes a small part:

FIGURE 1

WARNING:

CHOKING HAZARD--Small parts
Not for children under 3 yrs.

(2) The advertising for any latex balloon, or toy or game that contains a latex balloon, shall bear the following cautionary statement:

FIGURE 2

WARNING:

CHOKING HAZARD--Children under 8 yrs. can choke or suffocate on uninflated or broken balloons. Adult supervision required.

Keep uninflated balloons from children. Discard broken balloons at once.

(3)(i) The advertising for any small ball intended for children three years of age or older shall bear the following cautionary statement:

FIGURE 3

WARNING:

CHOKING HAZARD--This toy is a small ball. Not for children under 3 yrs.

(ii) The advertising for any toy or game intended for children who are at least three years old but less than eight years of age that contains a small ball shall bear the following cautionary statement:

FIGURE 4

WARNING:

CHOKING HAZARD--Toy contains a small ball. Not for children under 3 yrs.

(4)(i) The advertising for any marble intended for children three years of age or older shall bear the following cautionary statement:

FIGURE 5

WARNING:

CHOKING HAZARD--This toy is a marble. Not for children under 3 yrs.

(ii) The advertising for any toy or game intended for children who are at least three years old but less than eight years of age that contains a marble shall bear the following cautionary statement:

FIGURE 6

WARNING:

CHOKING HAZARD--Toy contains a marble. Not for children under 3 yrs.

(e) *Abbreviated warnings for catalogues and other printed materials.* Abbreviated versions of the required cautionary statements are permitted in each individual product advertisement, provided that the corresponding full cautionary statements appear in the catalogue and a statement referring to the precise location of the full cautionary statements—such as the page number on which the cautionary statements can be found—is located at the bottom of each catalogue page that contains one or more abbreviated cautionary statements. If abbreviated cautionary statements are used:

(1) The full cautionary statements associated with the abbreviated cautionary statements shall appear:

(i) Near the beginning of the catalogue, before any catalogue pages that contain advertisements of products available for purchase, or

(ii) Adjacent to the ordering information or order form in the catalogue.

(2) The full cautionary statements shall be in conspicuous and legible type in contrast by typography, layout or color.

(3) The full cautionary statements shall be clearly numbered according to the following scheme:

Required cautionary statement	Number
16 CFR 1500.19(b)(1) [1]	1
16 CFR 1500.19(b)(2) [2]	2
16 CFR 1500.19(b)(3)(i) [3]	3
16 CFR 1500.19(b)(3)(ii) [4]	4
16 CFR 1500.19(b)(4)(i) [5]	5
16 CFR 1500.19(b)(4)(ii) [6]	6

[1] See figure 1.
[2] See Figure 2.
[3] See Figure 3.
[4] See Figure 4.
[5] See Figure 5.
[6] See Figure 6.

(4) The abbreviated cautionary statements shall consist of items 1500.20(e)(3)(i) through 1500.20(e)(3)(iv):

(i) A safety alert symbol substantially similar to that shown in figure 7.

FIGURE 7

(ii) The phrase, "CHOKING HAZARD," written in capital letters.

(iii) Numbers, separated by commas and enclosed within a single set of parentheses, that identify the applicable cautionary statements for the product being advertised, followed by a period. These numbers shall match the numbers used to identify each full cautionary statement, as specified in 1500.20(e)(2).

(iv) A single prohibited age range written as either "Not for under 3 yrs" or "Not for under 8 yrs," based on the most restrictive age range for all required cautionary statements for that product. Thus, if an advertised product requires the cautionary statement specified in 16 CFR 1500.19(b)(2), the prohibited age range in the abbreviated cautionary statement shall be "Not for under 8 yrs."

(v) For example, see Figure 8 for the abbreviated cautionary statement for an advertisement of a product that requires the cautionary statements specified in 16 CFR 1500.19(b)(1) and 16 CFR 1500.19(b)(2).

FIGURE 8

⚠ CHOKING HAZARD (1,2). Not for under 8 yrs.

(f) *Alternatives to cautionary statements for individual product advertisements in catalogues and other printed materials.* Multiple identical full or abbreviated cautionary statements may be replaced with a single full cautionary statement under the following circumstances:

(1) If all products available for purchase within a catalogue require the same cautionary statement, that cautionary statement, in full, may appear on the front cover, or equally conspicuous location, of the catalogue in lieu of repeating the cautionary statement within the catalogue, provided that it is communicated to consumers that the cautionary statement applies to all products in the catalogue.

(2) If all products on one catalogue page or on two facing catalogue pages require the same cautionary statement, that cautionary statement, in full, may appear at the top of the page or pages in lieu of repeating the cautionary statement in each product advertisement, provided that it is communicated to consumers that the cautionary statement applies to all products on the catalogue page or pages.

(g) *Prominence and conspicuousness of labeling statements.* The type size of abbreviated cautionary statements shall be reasonably related to the type size of any other printed matter in the product advertisement, and must be in conspicuous and legible type by typography, layout, or color with other printed matter in the advertisement and separated from other graphic matter.

(h) *Business to Business Catalogue Exception.* The requirements of section 24(c)of the Federal Hazardous Substances Act, as amended by section 105 of the CPSIA, do not apply to catalogues and other printed materials distributed solely between businesses unless the recipient business is one that could be expected to be purchasing the product for the use of children (instead of for resale, e.g.). Examples of businesses that can be expected to be purchasing products for the use of children include day care centers, schools, and churches.

[73 FR 67736, Nov. 17, 2008, as amended at 73 FR 71545, Nov. 25, 2008]

§ 1500.40 Method of testing toxic substances.

The method of testing the toxic substances referred to in § 1500.3(c)(1)(ii)(C) and (2)(iii) is as follows:

(a) *Acute dermal toxicity (single exposure).* In the acute exposures, the agent is held in contact with the skin by means of a sleeve for periods varying up to 24 hours. The sleeve, made of rubber dam or other impervious material, is so constructed that the ends are reinforced with additional strips and should fit snugly around the trunk of the animal. The ends of the sleeve are tucked, permitting the central portion to "balloon" and furnish a reservoir for the dose. The reservoir must have sufficient capacity to contain the dose without pressure. In the following table are given the dimensions of sleeves and the approximate body surface exposed to the test substance. The sleeves may vary in size to accommodate smaller or larger subjects. In the testing of unctuous materials that adhere readily to the skin, mesh wire screen may be employed instead of the sleeve. The screen is padded and raised approximately 2 centimeters from the exposed skin. In the case of dry powder preparations, the skin and substance are moistened with physiological saline prior to exposure. The sleeve or screen is then slipped over the gauze that holds the dose applied to the skin. In the case of finely divided powders, the measured dose is evenly distributed on cotton gauze which is then secured to the area of exposure.

DIMENSIONS OF SLEEVES FOR ACUTE DERMAL TOXICITY TEST

[Test animal—Rabbits]

Measurements in centimeters		Range of weight of animals (grams)	Average area of exposure (square centimeters)	Average percentage of total body surface
Diameter at ends	Overall length			
7.0	12.5	2,500–3,500	240	10.7

(b) *Preparation of test animal.* The animals are prepared by clipping the skin of the trunk free of hair. Approximately one-half of the animals are further prepared by making epidermal abrasions every 2 or 3 centimeters longitudinally over the area of exposure. The abrasions are sufficiently deep to penetrate the stratum corneum (horny layer of the epidermis) but not to distrub the derma; that is, not to obtain bleeding.

(c) *Procedures for testing.* The sleeve is slipped onto the animal which is then placed in a comfortable but immobilized position in a multiple animal holder. Selected doses of liquids and solutions are introduced under the sleeve. If there is slight leakage from the sleeve, which may occur during the first few hours of exposure, it is collected and reapplied. Dosage levels are adjusted in subsequent exposures (if necessary) to enable a calculation of a dose that would be fatal to 50 percent of the animals. This can be determined from mortality ratios obtained at various doses employed. At the end of 24 hours the sleeves or screens are removed, the volume of unabsorbed material (if any) is measured, and the skin reactions are noted. The subjects are cleaned by thorough wiping, observed for gross symptoms of poisoning, and then observed for 2 weeks.

EFFECTIVE DATE NOTE: At 77 FR 73294, Dec. 10, 2012, § 1500.40 was amended by revising the introductory text, effective Jan. 9, 2013. For the convenience of the user, the revised text is set forth as follows:

§ 1500.40 Method of testing toxic substances.

Guidelines for testing the toxicity of substances, including testing that does not require animals, are presented in the CPSC's animal testing policy set forth in 16 CFR 1500.232. A weight-of-evidence analysis, including any of the following: existing human and animal data, structure activity relationships, physicochemical properties; and chemical reactivity, or validated *in vitro* or *in silico* testing are recommended to evaluate existing information before *in vivo* tests are considered. If *in vivo* testing is conducted, a sequential testing strategy is recommended to reduce the number of test animals. The method of testing the toxic substances referred to in § 1500.3(c)(1)(ii)(C) and (c)(2)(iii) is as follows:

* * * * *

§ 1500.41 Method of testing primary irritant substances.

Primary irritation to the skin is measured by a patch-test technique on the abraded and intact skin of the albino rabbit, clipped free of hair. A minimum of six subjects are used in abraded and intact skin tests. Introduce under a square patch, such as surgical gauze measuring 1 inch by 1 inch and two single layers thick, 0.5 milliliter (in the case of liquids) or 0.5 gram (in the case of solids and semisolids) of the test substance. Dissolve solids in an appropriate solvent and apply the solution as for liquids. The animals are immobilized with patches secured in place by adhesive tape. The entire trunk of the animal is then wrapped with an impervious material, such as rubberized cloth, for the 24-hour period of exposure. This material aids in maintaining the test patches in position and retards the evaporation of volatile substances. After 24 hours of exposure, the patches are removed and the resulting reactions are evaluated on the basis of the designated values in the following table:

Skin reaction	Value [1]
Erythema and eschar formation:	
No erythema	0
Very slight erythema (barely perceptible)	1
Well-defined erythema	2
Moderate to severe erythema	3
Severe erythema (beet redness) to slight eschar formations (injuries in depth)	4
Edema formation:	
No edema	0
Very slight edema (barely perceptible)	1
Slight edema (edges of area well defined by definite raising)	2
Moderate edema (raised approximately 1 millimeter)	3
Severe edema (raised more than 1 millimeter and extending beyond the area of exposure)	4

[1] The "value" recorded for each reading is the average value of the six or more animals subject to the test.

Readings are again made at the end of a total of 72 hours (48 hours after the first reading). An equal number of exposures are made on areas of skin that have been previously abraded. The abrasions are minor incisions through the stratum corneum, but not sufficiently deep to disturb the derma or to produce bleeding. Evaluate the reactions of the abraded skin at 24 hours and 72 hours, as described in this paragraph. Add the values for erythema and eschar formation at 24 hours and at 72 hours for intact skin to the values on abraded skin at 24 hours and at 72 hours (four values). Similarly, add the values for edema formation at 24 hours and at 72 hours for intact and abraded skin (four values). The total of the eight values is divided by four to give the primary irritation score; for example:

Skin reaction	Exposure time (hours)	Evaluation value
Erythema and eschar formation:		
Intact skin	24	2
Do	72	1
Abraded skin	24	3
Do	72	2
Subtotal		8
Edema formation:		
Intact skin	24	0
Do	72	1
Abraded skin	24	1
Do	72	2
Subtotal		4
Total		12

Thus, the primary irritation score is 12÷4=3.

EFFECTIVE DATE NOTE: At 77 FR 73294, Dec. 10, 2012, § 1500.41 was amended by adding five sentences at the beginning of the introductory text, effective Jan. 9, 2013. For the convenience of the user, the added text is set forth as follows:

§ 1500.41 Method of testing primary irritant substances.

Guidelines for testing the dermal irritation and corrosivity properties of substances, including testing that does not require animals, are presented in the CPSC's animal testing policy set forth in 16 CFR 1500.232. A weight-of-evidence analysis or a validated *in vitro* test method is recommended to evaluate existing information before *in vivo* tests are considered. This analysis should include all of the following that are available: human and animal data, structure activity relationships, physicochemical properties, and dermal toxicity. If *in vivo* testing is conducted, a sequential testing strategy is recommended to reduce the number of test animals. The method of testing the dermal corrosivity and primary irritation of substances referred to in § 1500.3(c)(3) and (4), respectively, is a patch-test technique on the abraded and intact skin of the albino rabbit, clipped free of hair. * * *

* * * * *

§ 1500.42 Test for eye irritants.

(a)(1) Six albino rabbits are used for each test substance. Animal facilities for such procedures shall be so designed and maintained as to exclude sawdust, wood chips, or other extraneous materials that might produce eye irritation. Both eyes of each animal in the test group shall be examined before testing, and only those animals without eye defects or irritation shall be used. The animal is held firmly but gently until quiet. The test material is placed in one eye of each animal by gently pulling the lower lid away from the eyeball to form a cup into which the test substance is dropped. The lids are then gently held together for one second and the animal is released. The other eye, remaining untreated, serves as a control. For testing liquids, 0.1 milliliter is used. For solids or pastes, 100 milligrams of the test substance is used, except that for substances in flake, granule, powder, or other particulate form the amount that has a volume of 0.1 milliliter (after compacting as much as possible without crushing or altering the individual particles, such as by tapping the measuring container) shall be used whenever this volume weighs less than 100 milligrams. In such a case, the weight of the 0.1 milliliter test dose should be recorded. The eyes are not washed following instillation of test material except as noted below.

(2) The eyes are examined and the grade of ocular reaction is recorded at 24, 48, and 72 hours. Reading of reactions is facilitated by use of a binocular loupe, hand slit-lamp, or other expert means. After the recording of observations at 24 hours, any or all eyes may be further examined after applying fluorescein. For this optional test, one drop of fluorescein sodium ophthalmic solution U.S.P. or equivalent is dropped directly on the cornea. After flushing out the excess fluorescein with sodium chloride solution U.S.P. or equivalent, injured areas of the cornea appear yellow; this is best visualized in a darkened room under ultraviolet illumination. Any or all eyes may be washed with sodium chloride solution U.S.P. or equivalent after the 24-hour reading.

(b)(1) An animal shall be considered as exhibiting a positive reaction if the test substance produces at any of the readings ulceration of the cornea (other than a fine stippling), or opacity of the cornea (other than a slight dulling of the normal luster), or inflammation of the iris (other than a slight deepening of the folds (or rugae) or a slight circumcorneal injection of the blood vessels), or if such substance produces in the conjunctivae (excluding the cornea and iris) an obvious swelling with partial eversion of the lids or a diffuse crimson-red with individual vessels not easily discernible.

(2) The test shall be considered positive if four or more of the animals in the test group exhibit a positive reaction. If only one animal exhibits a positive reaction, the test shall be regarded as negative. If two or three animals a positive reaction, the test is repeated using a different group of six animals. The second test shall be considered positive if three or more of the animals exhibit a positive reaction. If only one or two animals in the second test exhibit a positive reaction, the test shall be repeated with a different group of six animals. Should a third test be needed, the substance will be regarded as an irritant if any animal exhibits a positive response.

(c) To assist testing laboratories and other interested persons in interpreting the results obtained when a substance is tested in accordance with the method described in paragraph (a) of this section, an ''Illustrated Guide for Grading Eye Irritation by Hazardous Substances'' will be sold by the Superintendent of Documents, U.S. Government Printing Office, Washington, D.C. 20402.[1] The guide will contain color plates depicting responses of varying intensity to specific test solutions. The grade of response and the substance used to produce the response will be indicated.

[38 FR 27012, Sept. 27, 1973; 38 FR 30105, Nov. 1, 1973; 62 FR 46667, Sept. 4, 1997]

EFFECTIVE DATE NOTE: At 77 FR 73294, Dec. 10, 2012, § 1500.42 was amended by adding introductory text, revising the first sentence of paragraph (a)(1), and revising paragraph (c), effective Jan. 9, 2013. For the convenience of the user, the added and revised text is set forth as follows:

§ 1500.42 Test for eye irritants.

Guidelines for *in vivo* and *in vitro* testing of ocular irritation of substances, including

[1] The Illustrated Guide is out of print and, as of January 1, 1981, no longer available. However, information about the test method, and black and white photocopies may be obtained by writing to the Directorate for Epidemiology and Health Sciences, CPSC, Washington, D.C. 20207, (301) 504–0957.

testing that does not require animals, are presented in the CPSC's animal testing policy set forth in 16 CFR 1500.232. A weight-of-evidence analysis or a validated *in vitro* test method is recommended to evaluate existing information before *in vivo* tests are considered. This analysis should include any of the following: Existing human and animal data on ocular or dermal irritation, structure activity relationships, physicochemical properties, and chemical reactivity. If *in vivo* testing is conducted, a sequential testing strategy is recommended to reduce the number of test animals. Additionally, the routine use of topical anesthetics, systemic analgesics, and humane endpoints to avoid or minimize pain and distress in ocular safety testing is recommended.

(a)(1) In the method of testing the ocular irritation of a substance referred to in § 1500.3(c)(4), six albino rabbits are used for each test substance * * *

* * * * *

(c) To assist testing laboratories and others interested in interpreting ocular irritation test results, the CPSC animal testing policy Web page at *http://www.cpsc.gov/library/animaltesting.html* will contain the scoring system defined in the U.S. EPA's Test Guideline, OPPTS 870.2400: Acute Eye Irritation[1] or the OECD Test Guideline 405: Acute Eye Irritation/Corrosion.[2]

§ 1500.43 Method of test for flashpoint of volatile flammable materials by Tagliabue open-cup apparatus.

SCOPE

1. (a) This method describes a test procedure for the determination of open-cup flashpoints of volatile flammable materials having flashpoints below 175 °F.

(b) This method, when applied to paints and resin solutions which tend to skin over or which are very viscous, gives less reproducible results than when applied to solvents.

OUTLINE OF METHOD

2. The sample is placed in the cup of a Tag Open Tester, and heated at a slow but constant rate. A small test flame is passed at a uniform rate across the cup at specified intervals. The flashpoint is taken as the lowest temperature at which application of the test flame causes the vapor at the surface of the liquid to flash, that is, ignite but not continue to burn.

APPARATUS

3. The Tag open-cup tester is illustrated in Fig. 1. It consists of the following parts, which must conform to the dimensions shown, and have the additional characteristics as noted:

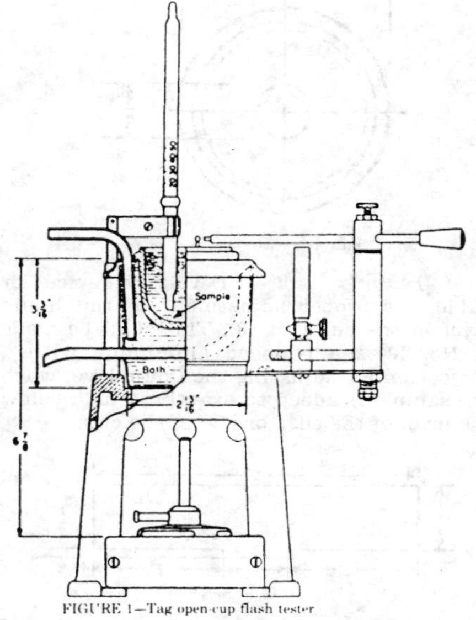

FIGURE 1—Tag open-cup flash tester

(a) *Copper bath*, preferably equipped with a constant level overflow so placed as to maintain the bath liquid level ⅛-inch below the rim of the glass cup.

(b) *Thermometer holder*. Support firmly with ringstand and clamp.

(c) *Thermometer*. For flashpoints above 40 °F., use the ASTM Tag Closed Tester Thermometer, range of +20 to +230 °F., in 1 °F. divisions, and conforming to thermometer 9F. of ASTM Standard E 1. For flashpoints from 20 °F. to 40 °F., use ASTM Tag Closed Tester, Low Range, Thermometer 57F. For flashpoints below 20 °F., use ASTM Thermometer 33F. The original Tag Open-Cup (Paper Scale) Thermometer will be a permissible alternate until January 1, 1962. It is calibrated to −20 °F.

(d) *Glass test cup*. Glass test cup (Fig. 2), of molded clear glass, annealed, heat-resistant, and free from surface defects.

[1] EPA. 1998. Health Effects Test Guidelines, OPPTS 870.2400 Acute Eye Irritation. EPA 712–C–98–195. Washington, DC: U.S. Environmental Protection Agency. (Available: *http://iccvam.niehs.nih.gov/SuppDocs/FedDocs/EPA/EPA_870_2400.pdf*)

[2] OECD. 2002. OECD Guideline for the Testing of Chemicals 405: Acute Eye Irritation/Corrosion. Paris: Organisation for Economic Co-operation and Development. (Available: *http://iccvam.niehs.nih.gov/SuppDocs/FedDocs/OECD/OECDtg405.pdf*)

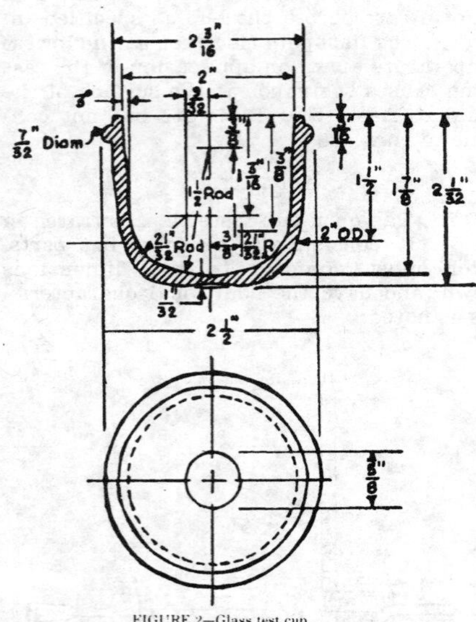

FIGURE 2—Glass test cup

(e) *Leveling device.* Leveling device or guide, for proper adjustment of the liquid level in the cup (Fig. 3). This shall be made of No. 18-gage polished aluminum, with a projection for adjusting the liquid level when the sample is added to exactly ⅛-inch below the level of the edge or rim of the cup.

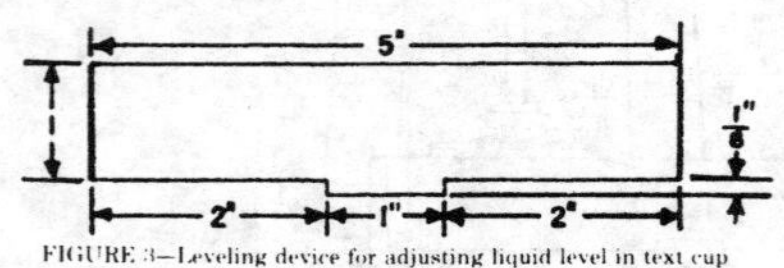

FIGURE 3—Leveling device for adjusting liquid level in text cup

(f) "Micro," or small gas burner of suitable dimensions for heating the bath. A screw clamp may be used to help regulate the gas. A small electric heater may be used.

(g) Ignition taper, which is a small straight, blow-pipe type gas burner. The test flame torch prescribed in the method of test for flash and fire points by Cleveland Open Cup (ASTM designation: D 92) is satisfactory.

(h) Alternative methods for maintaining the ignition taper in a fixed horizontal plane above the liquid may be used, as follows:

(1) Guide wire, 3⁄32-inch in diameter and 3½ inches in length, with a right-angle bend ½-inch from each end. This wire is placed snugly in holes drilled in the rim of the bath, so that the guide wire is ⅝-inch from the center of the cup and resting on the rim of the cup.

(2) Swivel-type taper holder, such as is used in ASTM METHOD D 92. The height and position of the taper are fixed by adjusting the holder on a suitable ringstand support adjacent to the flash cup.

(i) Draft shield, consisting of two rectangular sheets of noncombustible material, 24 inches × 28 inches, are fastened together along the 28-inch side, preferably by hinges. A triangular sheet, 24 inches × 24 inches × 34 inches is fastened by hinges to one of the lateral sheets (to form a top when shield is open). The interior of the draft shield shall be painted a flat black.

PROCEDURE

4. (a) Place the tester on a solid table free of vibration, in a location free of perceptible draft, and in a dim light.

(b) Run water, brine, or water-glycol solution into the bath to a predetermined level, which will fill the bath to ⅛-inch below the top when the cup is in place. An overflow is permissible for water-level control.

(c) Firmly support the thermometer vertically halfway between the center and edge of the cup on a diameter at right angles to the guide wire, or on a diameter passing through the center of the cup and the pivot of the taper. Place so that the bottom of the bulb is ¼-inch from the inner bottom surface of the cup. If the old Tagliabue thermometer is used, immerse to well cover the mercury bulb, but not the wide body of the thermometer.

(d) Fill the glass cup with the sample liquid to a depth just ⅛-inch below the edge, as determined by the leveling device.

(e) Place the guide wire or swivel device in position, and set the draft shield around the tester so that the sides from right angles with each other and the tester is well toward the back of the shield.

(f) If a guide wire is used, the taper, when passed, should rest lightly on the wire, with the end of the jet burner just clear of the edge of the guide wire. If the swivel-type holder is used, the horizontal and vertical positions to the jet are so adjusted that the jet passes on the circumference of a circle, having a radius of at least 6 inches, across the center of the cup at right angles to the diameter passing through the thermometer, and in a plane ⅛-inch above the upper edge of the cup. The taper should be kept in the "off" position, at one end or the other of the swing, except when the flame is applied.

(g) Light the ignition flame and adjust it to form a flame of spherical form matching in size the 5⁄32-inch sphere on the apparatus.

(h) Adjust heater source under bath so that the temperature of the sample increases at a rate of 2±0.5 °F. per minute. With viscous materials this rate of heating cannot always be obtained.

INITIAL TEST

5. Determine an approximate flashpoint by passing the taper flame across the sample at

intervals of 2 °F. Each pass must be in one direction only. The time required to pass the ignition flame across the surface of the sample should be 1 second. Remove bubbles from the surface of the sample liquid before starting a determination. Meticulous attention to all details relating to the taper, size of taper flame, and rate of passing the taper is necessary for good results. When determining the flashpoint of viscous liquids and those liquids that tend to form a film of polymer, etc., on the surface, the surface film should be disturbed mechanically each time before the taper flame is passed.

RECORDED TESTS

6. Repeat the procedure by cooling a fresh portion of the sample, the glass cup, the bath solution, and the thermometer at least 20 °F. below the approximate flashpoint. Resume heating, and pass the taper flame across the sample at two intervals of 2 °F. until the flashpoint occurs.

REPORTING DATA

7. The average of not less than three recorded tests, other than the initial test, shall be used in determining the flashpoint and flammability of the substance.

STANDARDIZATION

8. (a) Make determinations in triplicate on the flashpoint of standard paraxylene and of standard isopropyl alcohol which meet the following specifications:

(i) *Specifications for p-xylene, flashpoint check grade. p-xylene shall conform to the following requirements;*

Specific gravity: 15.56 °C./15.56 °C., 0.860 minimum, 0.866 maximum

Boiling range: 2 °C. maximum from start to dry point when tested in accordance with the method of test for distillation of industrial aromatic hydrocarbons (ASTM designation: D 850), or the method of test for distillation range of lacquer solvents and diluents (ASTM) designation D 1078). The range shall include the boiling point of pure *P*-xylene, which is 138.35 °C. (281.03 °F.).

Purity: 95 percent minimum, calculated in accordance with the method of test for determination of purity from freezing points of high-purity compounds (ASTM designation: D 1016), from the experimentally determined freezing point, measured by the method of test for measurement of freezing points of high-purity compounds for evaluation of purity (ASTM designation: D 1015).

(ii) *Specifications for ispropanol, flash point check grade.* Isopropanol shall conform to the following requirements:

Specific gravity: 0.8175 to 0.8185 at 20 °C./20 °C. as determined by means of a calibrated pycnometer.

Distillation range: Shall entirely distill within a 1.0 °C. range which shall include the temperature 80.4 °C. as determined by ASTM method D 1078.

Average these values for each compound. If the difference between the values for these two compounds is less than 15 °F. (8.5 °C.) or more than 27 °F. (16 °C.), repeat the determinations or obtain fresh standards.

(b) Calculate a correction factor as follows:

$X = 92 - \mathrm{A}$
$Y = 71 - \mathrm{B}$

Correction = $(X + Y) / 2$.

Where:

A=Observed flash of *p*- xylene, and
B=Observed flash of isopropyl alcohol.

Apply this correction of all determinations. Half units in correction shall be discarded.

PRECISION

9. (a) For hydrocarbon solvents having flashpoints between 60 °F. and 110 °F., repeatability is ±2 °F. and the reproducibility is ±5 °F.

(b) If results from two tests differ by more than 10 °F., they shall be considered uncertain and should be checked. This calibration procedure provided in this method will cancel out the effect of barometric pressure if calibration and tests are run at the same pressure. Data supporting the precision are given appendix III of the 1956 Report of Committee D–1 on Paint, Varnish, Lacquers and Related Products, Proceedings, Am. Soc. Testing Mats., Vol. 56 (1956).

NOTE: The test apparatus and procedure described in § 1500.43 may be used by manufacturers and labelers of products subject to the Federal Hazardous Substances Act to determine flashpoint temperatures of those products under the conditions set forth in § 1500.3(c)(6)(iv), as amended.

[51 FR 28537, Aug. 8, 1986]

§ 1500.43a Method of test for flashpoint of volatile flammable materials.

(a) *Scope.* (1) This method describes the test procedure which the Commission will use for the determination of the flashpoint of volatile flammable materials, using a Setaflash[1] low-range closed tester, or an apparatus producing equivalent results. The method described in this section is essentially a Setaflash equilibrium procedure

[1] Setaflash is a registered trademark of Stanhope-Seta Limited, Surrey, England.

which closely parallels the test method designated ASTM D 3828-81, "Standard Test Methods for Flash Point by Setaflash Closed Tester," published by the American Society for Testing and Materials (ASTM), 1916 Race Street, Philadelphia, Pennsylvania 19103. Manufacturers and labelers of products subject to labeling and other requirements under the Federal Hazardous Substances Act may use other apparatus and/or test methods which produce equivalent results.

(2) At the option of the user, the procedures described in this section may be used to determine the actual flashpoint temperature of a sample or to determine whether a product will or will not flash at a specified temperature (flash/no flash).

(3) If the substance to be tested has a viscosity greater than 150 Stokes at 77 °F (25 °C), see paragraph (n) of this section for modifications to the testing procedure.

(4) If the Commission has reason to believe on the basis of reliable experience or other relevant information or data that the flammability hazard of a substance is greater or less than its flammability classification based on flashpoint temperature determined in accordance with this § 1500.43a and that the substance should be reclassified, the Commission will initiate a rulemaking proceeding for reclassification of the substance. Product manufacturers and labelers may use reliable experience or other relevant information or data in addition to the flashpoint temperature of a substance as a basis for compliance with any applicable requirements of the Federal Hazardous Substances Act in the absence of a rule issued by the Commission to reclassify the substance.

(b) *Summary of test methods.* (1) Method A—Flash/No Flash Test. A specified volume of sample is introduced by a syringe into the cup of the apparatus that is set and maintained at the specified temperature. After a specific time a test flame is applied and an observation made as to whether or not a flash occurred. Test procedures are set forth in detail in § 1500.43a(i).

(2) Method B—Finite (or Actual) Flashpoint. (i) A specified voume of sample is introduced into the cup of the apparatus that is maintained at the expected flashpoint. After a specified time a test flame is applied and the observation made whether or not a flash occurred.

(ii) The specimen is removed from the cup, the cup cleaned, and the cup temperature adjusted 5 °C (9 °F), lower or higher depending on whether or not a flash occurred previously. A fresh specimen is introduced and tested. This procedure is repeated until the flashpoint is established within 5 °C (9 °F).

(iii) The procedure is then repeated at 1 °C (2 °F) intervals until the flashpoint is determined to the nearest 1 °C (2 °F).

(iv) If improved accuracy is desired the procedure is repeated at 0.5 °C (1 °F). Test procedures are set forth in detail at § 1500.43a(j).

(3) The test procedures will be modified, where necessary, to ensure that the results obtained reflect the hazard of the substance under reasonably foreseeable conditions of use. Thus, for example, the material, if a mixture, will normally be tested as it comes from the container, and/or after a period of evaporation. The period of evaporation for a material which is a mixture will normally be the time required for the mixture to evaporate in an open beaker under ambient conditions to 90 percent of its original volume, or a period of four hours, whichever occurs first. However, this period of evaporation will be changed if the results obtained do not represent the hazard of the substance under reasonably foreseeable conditions of use.

(c) *Definition of flashpoint.* The lowest temperature of the sample, corrected to a barometric pressure of 101.3 kPa (760 mm Hg), at which application of a test flame causes the vapor of the sample to ignite under specified conditions of test. The sample is deemed to have flashed when a large flame appears and instantaneously propagates itself over the surface of the sample. Occasionally, particularly near actual flashpoint, the application of the test flame will cause a halo or an enlarged flame; this is not a flash and should be ignored.

(d) *Test apparatus.* The test apparatus is an equilibrium closed-cup tester with a range up to 100 °C (212 °F). The essential dimensions and requirements are shown in figure 1 and table 3, and are described in § 1500.43a(m). Closed-cup flashpoint testers and accessories meeting these requirements are available from commercial suppliers and distributors of laboratory equipment.

(e) *Safety precautions.* The operator must exercise and take appropriate safety precautions during the initial application of the test flame to the sample. Samples containing low-flash material may give an abnormally strong flash when the test flame is first applied.

(f) *Preparation of samples.* (1) Erroneously high flashpoints may be obtained if precautions are not taken to avoid the loss of volatile material. In preliminary tests of materials taken directly from the container, do not open containers unnecessarily and make a transfer unless the sample temperature is at least 10 °C (18 °F) below the expected flashpoint. Do not use samples in leaky containers for this test.

(2) Do not store samples in plastic (polyethylene, polypropylene, etc.) bottles since volatile material may diffuse through the walls of the bottle.

(3) A 2-ml specimen is required for each test. If possible, obtain at least a 50-ml sample from the bulk test site and store in a clean, tightly closed container.

(g) *Preparation of apparatus.* (1) Place the tester on a level, stable surface. Unless tests are made in a draft-free area, surround the tester on three sides with a shield for protection. Do not rely on tests made in a laboratory draft hood or near ventilators.

(2) Read the manufacturer's instructions on the care and servicing of the instrument and for correct operation of its controls.

(h) *Calibration and standardization.* (1) Before initial use determine and plot the relationship between the temperature control dial and the thermometer readings at each major (numbered) dial division as follows:

Turn the temperature control knob[2] fully counterclockwise ("O" reading). Advance the temperature control knob clockwise until the indicator light is illuminated.[3] Advance the knob clockwise to the next numbered line. After the thermometer mercury column ceases to advance, record the dial reading and the temperature. Advance the knob clockwise to the next numbered line. After the thermometer mercury column ceases to advance, read the dial reading and the temperature. Repeat this procedure through the full range of the instrument. Plot the dial readings versus the respective temperatures.

(2) Standardize the instrument using a sample of material meeting the specifications in table 1. If the average of two determinations falls within the acceptable limits the instrument is assumed to be operating properly. If the average of the two determinations does not fall within this range, check the manufacturer's operating and maintenance instructions and determine that they are being followed. In particular, be sure that the cup lid assembly makes a vapor-tight seal with the cup, the shutter provides a light-tight seal, and that adequate heat transfer paste surrounds the thermometer bulb and the immersed portion of the barrel.

(i) *Test Method A—for determining Flash/No Flash.* (1) Determine the target flashpoint as follows:

(i) Target flashpoint, °C=S_c—0.25 (101.3—A)

(ii) Target flashpoint, °C=S_c—0.03 (760–B)

(iii) Target flashpoint, °F=S_f—0.06 (760–B)

where:

S_c=specification, or uncorrected target, flashpoint, °C,

S_f=specification, or uncorrected target, flashpoint, °F,

[2] If the instrument has two temperature control knobs, set the fine control (center, small knob) at its mid-position and allow it to remain there throughout the calibration. The calibration is determined by adjusting the coarse control (large, outer knob) only.

[3] When using the tester, it will be found that the indicator light may not illuminate and the temperature may not rise until a temperature control dial setting between one and two is reached.

B=ambient barometric pressure, mm Hg,[4] and
A=ambient barometer pressure, kPa.[4]

(2) Inspect the inside of the sample cup, lid, and shutter mechanism for cleaniness and freedom from contamination. Use an absorbent paper tissue to wipe clean, if necessary. Put cover in place and lock securely. The filing orifice may be convenienty cleaned with a pipe cleaner.

(3) Set the instrument at the target temperature.

(i) For target temperature below ambient. The instrument power switch is to be in the off position. Fill the refigerant-charged cooling block with a suitable material.[5] Raise the lid and shutter assembly, and position the base of the block in the sample cup, being careful not to injure or mar the cup. When the thermometer reads approximately 6 to 10 °C (10 to 20 °F) below the target temperature, remove the cooling block and quickly dry the cup with a paper tissue to remove any moisture. Immediately close the lid and shutter assembly and secure. Prepare to introduce the sample using the syringe, both of which have been precooled to a temperature 5 to 10 °C (10 to 20 °F) below the target temperature.

(A) Caution: Do not cool the sample block below −38 °C, the freezing point of mercury.

(B) Caution: Acetone is extremely flammable. Keep away from heat, sparks, and flames and keep container closed when not actually pouring acetone. Use only in a well-ventilated area. Avoid inhalation and contact with the eyes or skin. Use cloth or leather gloves, goggles or safety shield, and keep dry ice in a canvas bag, especially when cracking.

(ii) For target temperature above ambient. Switch the instrument on and turn the coarse temperature control knob fully clockwise (full on) causing the indicator light to illuminate.[6] When the thermometer indicates a temperature about 3 °C (5 °F) below the target (or specification) temperature, reduce the heat input to the sample cup by turning the coarse temperature control knob counter-clockwise to the desired control point (see §1500.43a(i)(1)). When the indicator light slowly cycles on and off read the temperature on the thermometer. If necessary, adjust the fine (center) temperature control knob to obtain the desired test (target) temperature. When the test temperature is reached and the indicator lamp slowly cycles on and off, prepare to introduce the sample.

(4) Charge the syringe with a 2-ml specimen of the sample[7] to be tested; transfer the syringe to the filling orifice, taking care not to lose any sample; discharge the test specimen into the cup by fully depressing the syringe plunger, remove the syringe.

(5)(i) Set the timer[8] by rotating its knob clockwise to its stop. Open the gas control valve and light the pilot and test flames. Adjust the test flame with the pinch valve to conform to the size of the 4-mm (5/32-in.) gage.

(ii) After the time signal indicates the specimen is at test temperature[8], apply the test flame by slowly and uniformly opening the shutter and closing

[4] The barometric pressure used in this calculation must be the ambient pressure for the laboratory at the time of test. Many aneroid barometers, such as those used at weather stations and airports, are precorrected to give sea-level readings; these must not be used.

[5] If the target or specification temperature is not less than 5 °C (40 °F) crushed ice and water may be used as charging (cooling) fluid. If below 5 °C (40 °F), a suitable charging (cooling) fluid is solid carbon dioxide (dry ice) and acetone. If the refrigerant charged cooling module is unavailable, refer to the manufacturer's instruction manual for alternative methods of cooling.

[6] The target temperature may be attained by originally turning the coarse temperature control knob to the proper setting (see §1500.43a(h)(1) for the temperature desired rather than the maximum setting (full on). The elapsed time to reach the temperature will be greater, except for maximum temperature. However, less attention will be required during the intervening period.

[7] For target or expected temperatures below ambient, both syringe and sample must be precooled to cup temperature (see §1500.43a(i)(3)(i)) before the specimen is taken.

[8] For target temperatures below ambient, do not set the timer. Adjust the test flame and allow the temperature to rise under ambient conditions until the target temperature is reached. Immediately apply the test flame as detailed.

it completely over a period of approximately 2½ s.[9] Watch closely for a flash at the cup openings.

(iii) The sample is deemed to have flashed when a large flame appears and instantaneously propagates itself over the surface of the sample (see §1500.43a(c)).

(6) Record the test results as "flash" or "no flash" and the test temperature.

(7) Turn off the pilot and test flames using the gas control valve. Remove the sample and clean the instrument. It may be necessary to allow the cup temperature to decline to a safe level before cleaning.

(j) *Test Method B—for determining Finite or Actual Flashpoint.* (1) Inspect the inside of the sample cup, lid, and shutter mechanism for cleanliness and freedom from contamination. Use an absorbent paper tissue to wipe clean, if necessary. Put cover in place and lock securely. The filling orifice may be conveniently cleaned with a pipe cleaner.

(2) For expected flashpoints below ambient. (i) The instrument power switch is to be in off position. Fill the refrigerant-charged cooling block with a suitable material.[5] Raise the lid and shutter assembly, and position the base of the block in the sample cup, being careful not to injure or mar the cup. When the thermometer reaches a temperature 5 to 10 °C (10 to 20 °F) below the expected flashpoint, remove the cooling block and quickly dry the cup with a paper tissue to remove any moisture. Immediately close the lid and shutter assembly and secure. Prepare to introduce the sample using the syringe, both of which have been precooled to a temperature 5 to 10 °C (10 to 20 °F) below the expected temperature (See §1500.43a(j)(5)).

(ii) Caution: Do not cool the sample block below −38 °C, the freezing point of mercury.

(3) For tests where the expected flashpoint is above ambient. Turn the coarse temperature control knob fully clockwise (full on) causing the indicator light to illuminate. When the thermometer reaches a temperature 3 °C (5 °F) below the estimated flashpoint, turn the coarse temperature knob counter-clockwise to the dial reading representing the estimated flashpoint temperature as shown on the calibration curve (See §1500.43a(h)(1)). When the indicator light slowly cycles on and off, read the temperature on the thermometer. If necessary, adjust the fine temperature control knob to obtain the exact desired temperature.

(4)(i) Charge the syringe[7] with a 2 ml specimen of the sample[7] to be tested; transfer the syringe to the filling orifice, taking care not to lose any sample; discharge the test specimen into the cup by fully depressing the syringe plunger; remove the syringe.

(ii) Set the timer[10] by rotating its knob clockwise to its stop. Open the gas control valve and ignite the pilot and test flames. Adjust the test flame with the pinch valve to conform to the size of the 4-mm (5⁄32-in.) gage.

(iii) After the audible time signal indicates the specimen is at test temperature,[10] apply the test flame by slowly and uniformly opening the shutter and then closing it completely over a period of approximately 2½ s. Watch closely for a flash at the cup opening.

(iv) The sample is deemed to have flashed only if a large flame appears and instantaneously propagates itself over the surface of the sample. (See §1500.43a(c).)

(v) Turn off the pilot and test flames using the gas control valve. When the cup temperature declines to a safe level, remove the sample and clean the instrument.

(5)(i) If a flash was observed in §1500.43a(j)(4)(iii) repeat the procedure given in §1500.43a(j)(2) or (3), and in §1500.43a(j)(4), testing a new specimen at a temperature 5 °C (9 °F) below that at which the flash was observed.

(ii) If necessary, repeat the procedure in §1500.43a(j)(5)(i), lowering the temperature 5 °C (9 °F) each time, until no flash is observed.[9]

---

[9] Never apply the test flame to the specimen more than once. Fresh portions of the sample must be used for each test.

[10] For expected flashpoint below ambient, do not set the timing device. Adjust the test flame. Allow the temperature to rise under ambient conditions until the temperature reaches 5 °C (9 °F) below the expected flashpoint. Immediately apply the test flame.

(iii) Proceed to § 1500.43a(j)(7).

(6)(i) If no flash was observed in § 1500.43a(j)(4)(iii) repeat the procedure given in § 1500.43a(j)(2) or (3), and in § 1500.43a(j)(4), testing a fresh specimen at a temperature 5 °C (9 °F) above that at which the specimen was tested in § 1500.43a(j)(4)(iii).

(ii) If necessary repeat the procedure in § 1500.43a(j)(6)(i), above, raising the temperature 5 °C (9 °F) each time until a flash is observed.[9]

(7) Having established a flash within two temperatures 5 °C (9 °F) apart, repeat the procedure at 1 °C (2 °F) intervals from the lower of the two temperatures until a flash is observed.[9] Record the temperature of the test when this flash occurs as the flashpoint, allowing for any known thermometer correction. Record the barometric pressure.[4]

(8) The flashpoint determined in § 1500.43a(j)(7) will be to the nearest 1 °C (2 °F). If improved accuracy is desired (that is, to the nearest 0.5 °C (1 °F)), test a fresh specimen at a temperature 0.5 °C (1 °F) below that at which the flash was observed in § 1500.43a(j)(7). If no flash is observed, the temperature recorded in § 1500.43a(j)(7), is the flashpoint to the nearest 0.5 °C (1 °F). If a flash is observed at the lower temperature, record this latter temperature as the flashpoint.

(9) Turn off the pilot and test flames using the gas control valve. When the cup temperature declines to a safe level, remove the sample and clean the instrument.

(k) *Calculations*. If it is desired to correct the observed finite flashpoint for the effect of barometric pressure, proceed as follows: Observe and record the ambient barometric pressure[4] at the time of the test. If the pressure differs from 101.3 kPa (760 mm Hg), correct the flashpoint as follows:

(1) Corrected flashpoint (°C)=C+0.25 (101.3–A)

(2) Corrected flashpoint (°F)=F+0.06 (760–B)

(3) Corrected flashpoint (°C)=C+0.03 (760–B)

Where: F=Observed flashpoint, °F,
C=observed flashpoint, °C,
B=ambient barometric pressure, mm Hg; and
A=ambient barometric pressure, kPa.

(l) *Precision*. The precision of the method as determined by statistical examination of interlaboratory results is as follows:

(1) Repeatability. The difference between two test results obtained by the same operator with the same apparatus under constant operating conditions on identical test material, would, in the long run, in the normal and correct operation of the test method, exceed the values shown in table 2 only in 1 case in 20.

(2) Reproducibility. The difference between two single and independent results obtained by different operators working in different laboratories on identical test material, would, in the long run, in the normal and correct operation of the test method, exceed the values shown in table 2 only in 1 case in 20.

(m) *Flash Test Apparatus*. (1)(i) Unit consisting of an aluminum alloy or nonrusting metal block of suitable conductivity with a cylindrical depression, or sample cup, over which is fitted a cover. A thermometer is embedded in the block.

(ii) The cover is fitted with an opening slide and a device capable of inserting an ignition flame (diameter 4±0.5 mm) into the well when the slide device shall intersect the plane of the underside of the cover. The cover is also provided with an orifice extending into the sample well for insertion of the test sample and also a suitable clamping device for securing the cover tightly to the metal block. The three openings in the cover shall be within the diameter of the sample well. When the slide is in the open position, the two openings in the slide shall coincide exactly with the two corresponding openings in the cover.

(iii) Electrical heaters are attached to the bottom of the cup in a manner that provides efficient transfer of heat. An electronic heat control is required to hold the equilibrium temperature, in a draft-free area, within 0.1 °C (0.2 °F) for the low-temperature tester. A visual indicator lamp shows when energy is or is not being applied. Energy may be supplied from 120 or 240 V, 50 or 60 Hz main service.

(2)(i) Test flame and pilot flame-regulatable test flame, for dipping into the sample cup to try for flash, and a pilot flame, to maintain the test flame, are required. These flames may be fueled by piped gas service. A gage ring 4mm (5/32 in.) in diameter, engraved on the lid near the test flame, is required to ensure uniformity in the size of the test flame.

(ii) Caution: Never recharge the self-contained gas tank at elevated temperature, or with the pilot or test flames lighted, nor in the vicinity of other flames.

(iii) Audible Signal is required. The audiable signal is given after 1 min in the case of the low-temperature tester.

(iv) Syringe. 2ml capacity, equipped with a needle suitable for use with the apparatus, adjusted to deliver 2.00±0.05 ml.

(3) Essential dimensions of the test apparatus are set forth in table 3.

(n) *Testing high-viscosity liquids.* (1) High-viscosity materials may be added to the cup by the following procedure:

(i) Back load a 5 or 10-ml syringe with the sample to be tested and extrude 2 ml into the cup. Spread the specimen as evenly as possible over the bottom of the cup.

(ii) If the sample cannot be loaded into a syringe and extruded, other means of adding the sample to the cup may be used such as a spoon. Add approximately 2 ml of material to the spoon and then push the material from the spoon into the cup.

(iii) If the test specimen does not close the sampling port in the cup, seal the cup externally by suitable means.

(2) Using the appropriate procedure, either Method A in § 1500.43a(i) or Method B in § 1500.43a(j), determine the flashpoint of the specimen which has been added to the tester in accordance with § 1500.43a(n)(i), except that the time specified is increased from 1 to 5 minutes for samples at or above ambient temperature.

TABLE 1—CALIBRATION OF TESTER

Material	*p*-xylene[A] (Caution).[B]
Specific gravity. 15.6/15.6 °C (60/60 °F).	0.850 to 0.866.
Boiling range	2 °C maximum including 138.35 °C (281.03 °F).
Freezing point	11.23 °C (52.2 °F) minimum.
Flashpoint °C (acceptable range).	25.6±0.5 (78±1 Φ).

[A] Available as Flash Point Check Fluid (p-xylene) from Special Products Div., Phillips Petroleum Co., Drawer 'O,' Borger, Texas 79007.

[B] Caution: Handle xylene with care. Avoid inhalation; use only in a well-ventilated area. Avoid prolonged or repeated contact with skin. Keep away from flames and heat, except as necessary for the actual flash point determination.

TABLE 2—REPEATABILITY AND REPRODUCIBILITY

Temperature, °C (°F)	Repeatability, °C (°F)	Reproducibility, °C (°F)
20(68)	0.5(0.9)	1.4(2.6)
70(158)	0.5(0.9)	2.9(5.3)
93(200)	1.3(2.3)	4.9(8.8)
150(300)	2.0(3.6)	7.5(13.5)
200(400)	2.6(4.7)	9.9(17.9)
260(500)	3.3(5.9)	12.4(22.3)

TABLE 3—ESSENTIAL DIMENSIONS OF FLASH TEST APPARATUS[A,B]

Sample Block	
Block diameter	61.5–62.5
Sample well diameter	49.40–49.70
Sample well depth	9.70–10.00
Top of block to center of thermometer hole	16.00–17.00
Diameter of thermometer hole (approx.)	7.0004
Cover	
Large opening length	12.42–12.47
Large opening width	10.13–10.18
Small opening length	5.05–5.10
Small opening width	7.60–7.65
Distance between extreme edges of small openings	48.37–48.32
Filling orifice diameter	4.00–4.50
Bore or filler tube	1.80–1.85
Maximum distance of filler tube from base of well with cover closed (max.)	0.75
Slide	
Large opening length	12.42–12.47
Large opening width	10.13–10.18
Small opening length	5.05–5.10
Small opening width	7.60–7.65
Near edge of large opening to end of slide	12.80–12.85
Extremes of large and small openings	30.40–30.45
Jet	
Length of jet	18.30–18.40
External diameter at end of jet	2.20–2.60
Bore of jet	1.60–1.65
Height of jet center above top surface of cover	11.00–11.20
Jet pivot to center of block with cover closed	12.68–12.72

[A] The O-seal or gasket which provides a seal when the cover is shut, should be made of a heat-resistant material capable of withstanding temperatures up to 150 °C for the low-range apparatus.

[B] When in position, the thermometer bulb should be surrounded with heat-conducting thermoplastic compound, such as a paste comprised of zinc oxide and mineral oil.

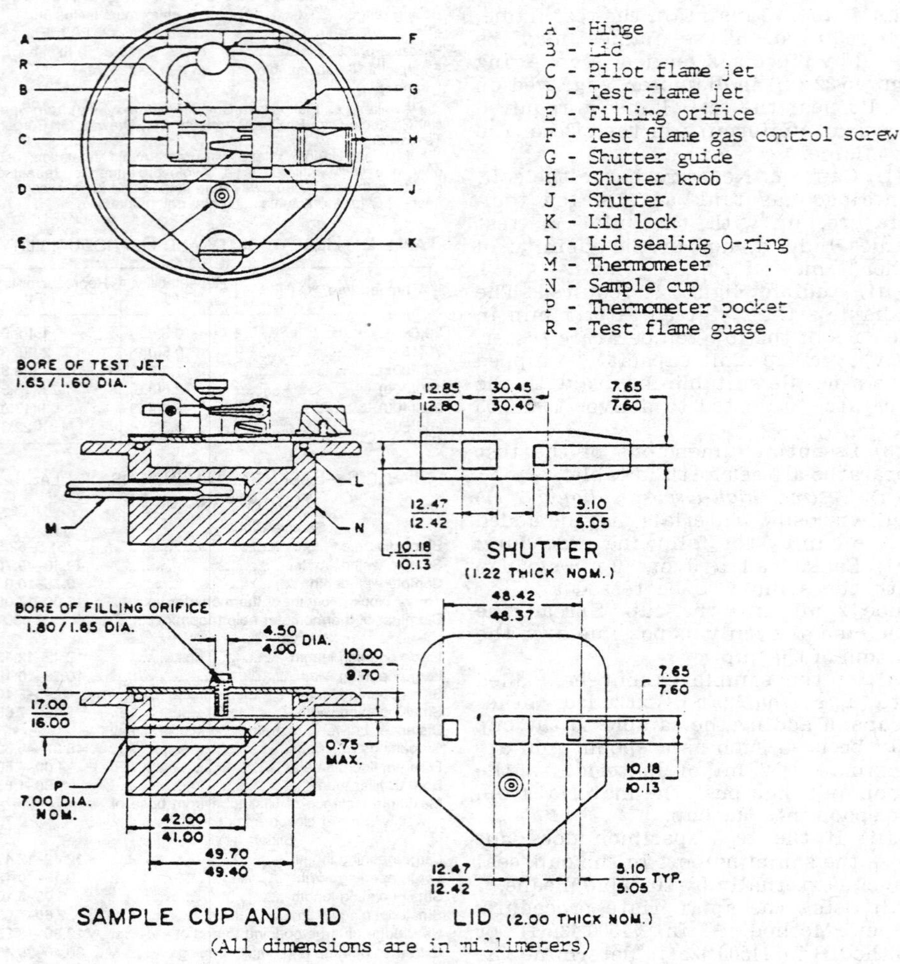

FIGURE 1 - Closed-cup tester

[51 FR 28539, Aug. 8, 1986]

§ 1500.44 Method for determining extremely flammable and flammable solids.

(a) *Preparation of samples*—(1) *Granules, powders, and pastes.* Pack the sample into a flat, rectangular metal boat with inner dimensions 6 inches long × 1 inch wide × one-fourth inch deep.

(2) *Rigid and pliable solids.* Measure the dimensions of the sample and support it by means of metal ringstands, clamps, rings, or other suitable devices as needed, so that the major axis is oriented horizontally and the maximum surface is freely exposed to the atmosphere.

(b) *Procedure.* Place the prepared sample in a draft-free area that can be ventilated and cleared after each test. The temperature of the sample at the time of testing shall be between 68 °F. and 86 °F. Hold a burning paraffin candle whose diameter is at least 1 inch, so that the flame is in contact with the surface of the sample at the end of the major axis for 5 seconds or until the sample ignites, whichever is less. Remove the candle. By means of a stopwatch, determine the time of combustion with self-sustained flame. Do not exceed 60 seconds. Extinguish flame with a CO_2 or similar nondestructive type extinguisher. Measure the dimensions of the burnt area and calculate the rate of burning along the major axis of the sample.

§ 1500.45 Method for determining extremely flammable and flammable contents of self-pressurized containers.

(a) *Equipment required.* The test equipment consists of a base 8 inches wide, 2 feet long, marked in 6-inch intervals. A rule 2 feet long and marked in inches is supported horizontally on the side of the base and about 6 inches above it. A paraffin candle 1 inch or more in diameter, and of such height that the top third of the flame is at the height of the horizontal rule, is placed at the zero point in the base.

(b) *Procedure.* The test is conducted in a draft-free area that can be ventilated and cleared after each test. Place the self-pressurized container at a distance of 6 inches from the flame source. Spray for periods of 15 seconds to 20 seconds (one observer noting the extension of the flame and the other operating the container) through the top third of the flame and at a right angle to the flame. The height of the flame should be approximately 2 inches. Take three readings for each test, and average. As a precaution do not spray large quantities in a small, confined space. Free space of previously discharged material.

§ 1500.46 Method for determining flashpoint of extremely flammable contents of self-pressurized containers.

Use the apparatus described in § 1500.43a. Use some means such as dry ice in an open container to chill the pressurized container. Chill the container, the flash cup, and the bath solution of the apparatus (brine or glycol may be used) to a temperature of about 25 °F below zero. Puncture the chilled container to exhaust the propellant. Transfer the chilled formulation to the test apparatus and test in accordance with the method described in § 1500.43a.

[51 FR 28544, Aug. 8, 1986]

§ 1500.47 Method for determining the sound pressure level produced by toy caps.

(a) *Equipment required.* The equipment for the test includes a microphone, a preamplifier (if required), and an oscilloscope.

(1) The microphone-preamplifier system shall have a free-field response uniform to within ±2 decibels from 50 hertz to 70 kilohertz or beyond and a dynamic range covering the interval 70 to 160 decibels relative to 20 micronewtons per square meters. Depending on the model, the microphone shall be used at normal or at grazing incidence, whichever gives the most uniform free-field response. The microphone shall be calibrated both before and after the test of a model of cap. The calibration shall be accurate to within ±1 decibel. If the calibration is of the pressure type or of the piston-phone plus electrostatic actuator type, it shall be corrected to free-field conditions in accordance with the manufacturer's instructions.

(2) The oscilloscope shall be the storage type or one equipped with a camera. It shall have a response uniform to within ±1 decibel from 50 hertz to 250 kilohertz or higher. It shall be calibrated to within ±1 decibel against an external voltage source periodically during the tests.

(b) *Procedure.* (1) Use the type pistol that would ordinarily be used with the caps being tested. Place the pistol and testing equipment so that neither the pistol nor the microphone is closer than 1 meter from any wall, floor, ceiling, or other large obstruction. Locate the pistol and the microphone in the same horizontal plane with a distance of 25 centimeters between the diaphragm of the microphone and the position of the explosive. Measure the peak sound pressure level at each of the six designated orientations of the pistol with respect to the measuring microphone. The 0° orientation corresponds to the muzzle of the pistol pointing at the microphone. The 90°, 180°, and 270° orientations are measured in a clockwise direction when looking down on the pistol with its barrel horizontal, as illustrated by the following figure:

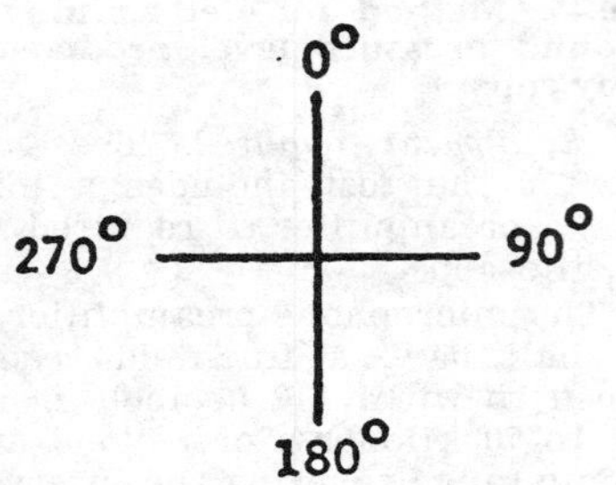

(2) The hammer and trigger orientations are obtained by rotating the pistol about the axis of the barrel, when the pistol is in the 90° or 270° orientation, so that the hammer and the trigger are each respectively closest to and in the same horizontal plane with the microphone.

(3) Fire 10 shots at each of the six orientations, obtaining readings on the oscilloscope of the maximum peak voltage for each shot. Average the results of the 10 firings for each of the six orientations.

(4) Using the orientation that yields the highest average value, convert the value to sound pressure levels in decibels relative to 20 micronewtons per square meter using the response to the calibrated measuring microphone.

§ 1500.48 Technical requirements for determining a sharp point in toys and other articles intended for use by children under 8 years of age.

(a) *Objective.* The sharp point test prescribed by paragraph (d) of this section will be used by the Commission in making a preliminary determination that points on toys and other articles intended for use by children under 8 years of age, and such points exposed in normal use or as a result of reasonably foreseeable damage or abuse of such toys and articles, present a potential risk of injury by puncture or laceration under section 2(s) of the Federal Hazardous Substances Act (15 U.S.C. 1261(s)). The Commission will further evaluate points that are identified as presenting a potential risk of puncture or laceration injury to determine the need for individual product regulatory action.

(b) *Scope*—(1) *General.* The sharp point test of paragraph (d) of this section is applicable to toys or other articles that are introduced into interstate commerce on or after December 22, 1978. The sharp point test shall be applied to any accessible portion of the test sample before and after subjecting the test sample to the use and abuse tests of §§ 1500.51, 1500.52, and 1500.53 (excluding the bite test-paragraph (c) of each section).

(2) *Exemptions.* (i) Toys and other children's articles that are the subject of any of the following regulations are exempt from this § 1500.48: The regulations for bicycles, non-full-size baby cribs, and full-size baby cribs (parts 1508, 1509, and 1512, of this chapter).

(ii) Toys that by reason of their functional purpose necessarily present the hazard of sharp points and that do not have any nonfunctional sharp points are exempt from this § 1500.48: *Provided,* Each toy is identified by a conspicuous, legible, and visible label at the time of any sale, as having functional sharp points. An example of such toys is a toy sewing machine with a needle.

(iii) Articles, besides toys, intended for use by children that by reason of their functional purpose necessarily present the hazard of sharp points and that do not have any nonfunctional sharp points are exempt from this § 1500.48. An example of such articles is a ball-point pen.

(c) *Accessibility*—(1) *General.* Any point that is accessible either before or after these tests of §§ 1500.51, 1500.52, and 1500.53 (excluding the bite test—paragraph (c) of each section) are performed shall be subject to the sharp point test of paragraph (d) of this section.

(2) *Accessible points.* (i) An accessible point for a toy or article intended for children 3 years of age or less is one that can be contacted by any portion forward of the collar of the accessibility probe designated as probe A in figure 2 of this section.

(ii) An accessible point for a toy or article intended for children over 3 years up to 8 years of age is one that can be contacted by any portion forward of the collar of the accessibility probe designated as probe B in figure 2 of this section.

(iii) An accessible point for a toy or article intended for children of ages spanning both age groups is one that can be contacted by any portion forward of the collar of either probe A or B, as shown in figure 2 of this section.

(3) *Insertion depth for accessibility.* (i) For any hole, recess, or opening having a minor dimension (The minor dimension of an opening is the diameter of the largest sphere that will pass through the opening.) smaller than the collar diameter of the appropriate probe, the total insertion depth for accessibility shall be up to the collar on the appropriate probe. Each probe joint may be rotated up to 90 degrees to simulate knuckle movement.

(ii) For any hole, recess, or opening having a minor dimension larger than the collar diameter of probe A but less than 7.36 inches (186.9 millimeters), when probe A is used, or a minor dimension larger than the collar diameter of probe B but less than 9.00 inches (228.6 millimeters), when probe B is used, the total insertion depth for accessibility shall be determined by inserting the appropriate probe with the extension shown in figure 2 in any direction up to two and one-quarter times the minor dimension of the probe, recess, or opening, measured from any point in the plane of the opening. Each probe joint may be rotated up to 90 degrees to simulate knuckle movement.

(iii) For any hole, recess, or opening having a minor dimension of 7.36 inches (186.9 millimeters) or larger when probe A is used, or a minor di-mension of 9.00 inches (228.6 millimeters), or larger when probe B is used, the total insertion depth for accessibility is unrestricted unless other holes, recesses, or openings within the original hole, recess, or opening are encountered with dimensions specified in paragraph (c)(3) (i) or (ii) of this section. In such instances, the appropriate paragraphs (c)(3) (i) or (ii) of this section shall be followed. If both probes are to be used, a minor dimen-sion that is 7.36 inches (186.9 millimeters or larger shall determine unrestricted access.

(4) *Inaccessible points.* Points shall be considered inaccessible without testing with a probe if they lie adjacent to a surface of the test sample and any gap between the point and the adjacent surface does not exceed 0.020 inch (0.50 millimeter) either before or after the tests of §§ 1500.51, 1500.52, and 1500.53 (excluding the bite test—paragraph (c) of each section) are performed.

(d) *Sharp point test method*—(1) *Principle of operation.* The principle of operation of the sharp point tester shown in figure 1 of this section is as follows (Detailed engineering drawings for a suggested sharp point tester are available from the Commission's Office of the Secretary.): A rectangular opening measuring 0.040 inch (1.02 millimeters) wide by 0.045 inch (1.15 millimeters) long in the end of the slotted cap establishes two reference dimensions. Depth of penetration of the point being tested determines sharpness. If the point being tested can contact a sensing head that is recessed a distance of 0.015 inch (0.38 millimeter) below the end cap and can move the sensing head a further 0.005 inch (0.12 millimeter) against a 0.5-pound (2.2-newton) force of a return spring, the point shall be identified as sharp. A sharp point tester of the general configuration shown in figure 1 of this section or one yielding equivalent results shall identify a sharp point. In conducting tests to determine the presence of sharp points, the Commission will use the sharp point tester shown in figure 1 of this section and the accessibility probes designated as A or B in figure 2 of this section.

(2) *Procedure.* (i) The sample to be tested shall be held in such a manner that it does not move during the test.

(ii) Part of the test sample may need to be removed to allow the sharp point testing device to test a point that is accessible by the criteria of paragraph (c) of this section. Such dismantling of the test sample could affect the rigidity of the point in question. The sharp point test shall be performed with the point supported so that its stiffness approximates but is not greater than the point stiffness in the assembled sample.

(iii) Using the general configuration shown in figure 1 of this section, the adjustment and operation of the sharp point tester is as follows: Hold the sharp point tester and loosen the lock ring by rotating it so that it moves towards the indicator lamp assembly a sufficient distance to expose the calibration reference marks on the barrel. Rotate the gaging can clockwise until the indicator lamp lights. Rotate the cap counterclockwise until an equivalent of five divisions (the distance between the short lines on the cap) have passed the calibration reference mark. Lock the gaging cap in this position by rotating the lock ring until it fits firmly against the cap. Insert the point into the gaging slot in all directions in which it was accessible by the criteria of paragraph (c) of this section, and apply a force of 1.00 pound (4.45 newtons). A glowing light identifies the point as sharp.

(iv) The test instruments used by the Commission in its tests for compliance with this regulation shall have gaging slot opening dimensions no greater than 0.040 inch by 0.045 inch and shall have the sensing head recessed a depth of no less than 0.015 inch. The force applied by the Commission when inserting a point into the gaging slot shall be no more than 1.00 pound.

(e) For the purpose of conformance with the technical requirements prescribed by this § 1500.48, the English figures shall be used. The metric approximations are provided in parentheses for convenience and information only.

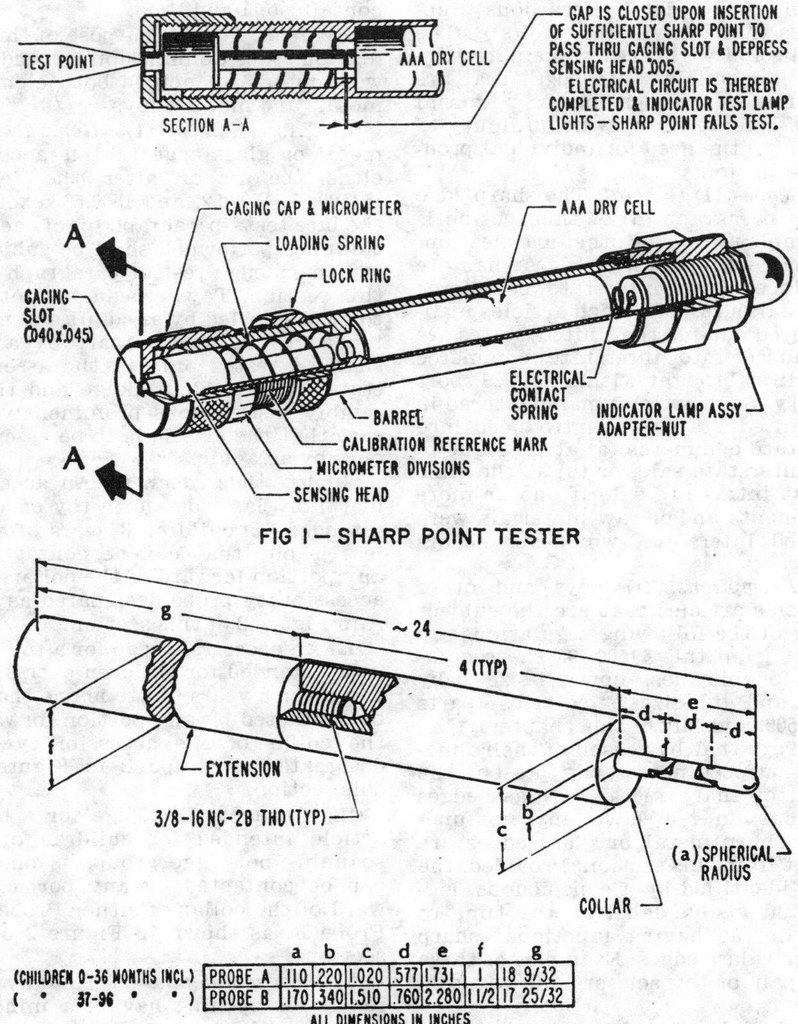

FIG 1—SHARP POINT TESTER

		a	b	c	d	e	f	g
(CHILDREN 0-36 MONTHS INCL)	PROBE A	.110	.220	1.020	.577	1.731	1	18 9/32
(" 37-96 " ")	PROBE B	.170	.340	1.510	.760	2.280	1 1/2	17 25/32

ALL DIMENSIONS IN INCHES

FIG 2—ACCESSIBILITY PROBES

§1500.49 Technical requirements for determining a sharp metal or glass edge in toys and other articles intended for use by children under 8 years of age.

(a) *Objective.* The sharp edge test method prescribed by paragraph (d) of this section will be used by the Commission in making a preliminary determination that metal or glass edges on toys and other articles intended for use by children under 8 years of age, and such edges exposed in normal use or as a result of reasonably forseeable damage or abuse of such toys and articles, present a potential risk of injury by laceration or avulsion under section 2(s) of the Federal Hazardous Substances Act (15 U.S.C. 1261(s)). The Commission will further evaluate toys and other articles with edges that are identified as presenting a potential risk of laceration or avulsion injury to determine the need for individual product regulation.

(b) *Scope*—(1) *General.* The sharp edge test of paragraph (d) of this section is applicable to toys or other articles containing metal or glass edges that are introduced into interstate commerce after March 26, 1979. Such articles manufactured outside the United States are introduced into interstate commerce when first brought within as U.S. port of entry. Such articles manufactured in the United States are introduced into interstate commerce (a) at the time of first interstate sale, or (b) at the time of first intrastate sale if one or more components and/or raw materials were received interstate, whichever occurs earlier.

(2) *Exemptions.* (i) Toys and other children's articles that are the subject of any of the following regulations are exempt from this § 1500.49: The regulations for bicycles, non-full-size baby cribs, and full-size baby cribs (parts 1508, 1509, and 1512 of this chapter).

(ii) Toys that by reason of their functional purpose necessarily present the hazard of sharp metal or glass edges and that do not have any nonfunctional sharp metal or glass edges are exempt from this section: Provided, the toy is identified by a conspicuous, legible, and visible label at the time of any sale, as having functional sharp metal or glass edges. Examples of these are a pair of toy scissors and toy tool kits.

(iii) Articles, besides toys, intended for use by children that by reason of their functional purpose necessarily present the hazard of sharp metal or glass edges and that do not have any non-functional sharp metal or glass edges are exempt from this section. Examples of these are children's ice skates and children's cutlery.

(3) *Definitions*—(i) *Glass.* For the purpose of this regulation the Commission defines glass as a hard, brittle, amorphous substance produced by fusion, usually consisting of mutually dissolved silica and silicates that also contain soda and lime.

(ii) *Metal.* For the purpose of this regulation the Commission intends the word metal to include both elemental metals and metal alloys.

(c) *Accessibility*—(1) *General.* Any metal or glass edge that is accessible either before or after the test of §§ 1500.51, 1500.52, and 1500.53 (excluding the bite test—paragraph (c) of each section) are performed shall be subject to the sharp edge test of paragraph (d) of this section. Toys reasonably intended to be assembled by an adult and not intended to be taken apart by a child shall be tested only in the assembled state if the shelf package and the assembly instructions prominently indicate that the article is to be assembled only by an adult.

(2) *Accessible edges.* (i) An accessible metal or glass edge for a toy or article intended for children 3 years of age or less is one that can be contacted by any portion forward of the collar of the accessibility probe designated as probe A in Figure 2 of this section.

(ii) An accessible edge for a toy or article intended for children over 3 years and up to 8 years of age is one that can be contacted by any portion forward of the collar of the accessibility probe designated as Probe B in Figure 2 of this section.

(iii) An accessible edge for a toy or article intended for children of ages spanning both age groups is one that can be contacted by any portion forward of the collar of either Probe A or Probe B, as shown in Figure 2 of this section.

(3) *Insertion depth.* (i) For any hole, recess, or opening having a minor dimension (the minor dimension of an opening is the diameter of the largest sphere that will pass through the opening), smaller than the collar diameter of the appropriate probe, the total insertion depth for accessibility shall be up to the collar on the appropriate probe. Each probe joint may be rotated up to 90 degrees to simulate knuckle movement.

(ii) For any hole, recess, or opening having a minor dimension larger than the collar diameter of Probe A, but less than 7.36 inches (186.9 millimeters), when Probe A is used, or a minor dimension larger than the collar diameter of Probe B, but less than 9.00 inches (228.6 millimeters), when Probe B is used, the total insertion depth for accessibility shall be determined by inserting the appropriate probe with the extension, shown in Figure 2, in any direction up to 2¼ times the minor dimension of the hole, recess, or opening, measured from any point in the plane of the opening. Each probe joint may be rotated up to 90 degrees to simulate knuckle movement.

(iii) For any hole, recess, or opening having a minor dimension of 7.36 inches (186.9 millimeters) or larger when Probe A is used, or a minor dimension of 9.00 inches (228.6 millimeters) or larger when Probe B is used, the total insertion depth for accessibility is unrestricted unless other holes, recesses, or openings within the original hole, recess, or opening are encountered with dimensions specified in paragraph (c)(3) (i) or (ii) of this section. In such instances, the appropriate paragraphs (c)(3) (i) or (ii) of this section shall be followed. If both probes are to be used, a minor dimension that is 7.36 inches (186.9 millimeters or larger shall determine unrestricted access.

(4) *Inaccessible edges.* Metal or glass edges shall be considered inaccessible without testing with a probe if they lie adjacent to a surface of the test sample, and any gap between the edge and the adjacent surface does not exceed 0.020 inch (0.50 millimeter) both before and after the tests of §§ 1500.51, 1500.52, and 1500.53 (excluding the bite test—paragraph (c) of each section) are performed. For example, in a lap joint in which a metal edge is overlapped by a parallel surface, any burr or feather-edge on the side closest to the protecting parallel surface is considered inaccessible if the gap between the edge and the parallel surface is no greater than 0.020 inch (0.50 millimeter). As an additional example, when sheet metal has a hemmed edge a portion of the sheet adjacent to the edge is folded back upon itself, approximately 180 degrees, so that it is roughly parallel to the main sheet. Any burrs or feathering on the inside edge, the side closest to the protecting parallel surface of the main sheet, will be considered inaccessible if the gap between the inside edge and the parallel surface does not exceed 0.020 inch (0.50 millimeter).

(d) *Sharp edge test method*—(1) *Principle of operation.* The test shall be performed with a sharp edge tester which contains a cylindrical mandrel capable of rotation at a constant velocity. (Engineering drawings for a suitable portable sharp edge test instrument are available from the Commission's Office of the Secretary.) The full circumference of the mandrel shall be wrapped with a single layer of polytetrafluoroethylene (TFE) tape as specified in paragraph (e)(3) of this section. The mandrel shall be applied to the edge to be tested with a normal force of 1.35 pounds (6.00 Newtons) such that the edge contacts the approximate center of the width of the tape as shown in Figure 1 of this section. The mandrel shall be rotated through one complete revolution while maintaining the force against the edge constant. Linear motion of the mandrel along the line of the edge shall be prevented. The edge shall be identified as sharp if it completely cuts through the tape for a length of not less than ½ inch (13 millimeters) at any force up to 1.35 pounds (6.00 Newtons).

(2) *Procedure.* (i) The edge of the sample to be tested shall be held in such a manner that it does not move during the test. If the full mandrel force of 1.35 pounds (6.00 Newtons) causes the edge to bend, a reduced mandrel force may be used.

(ii) Part of the test sample may need to be removed to allow the sharp edge testing device to test an edge that is accessible by the criteria of paragraph (c) of this section. Such dismantling of the test sample could affect the rigidity of the edge in question. The sharp edge test shall be performed with the edge supported so that its stiffness approximates but is not greater than the edge stiffness in the assembled sample.

(iii) Conduct of a sharp edge test is as follows: Wrap one layer of polytetrafluoroethylene (TFE) tape, described in paragraph (e)(3) of this section, around the full circumference of the mandrel in an unstretched state. The ends of the tape shall be either butted or overlapped not more than 0.10 inch (2.5 millimeters). Apply the mandrel, at the approximate center of the tape, to the edge of the test sample with a force of 1.35 pounds (6.00 Newtons) measured in a direction at right angles to the mandrel axis. The mandrel shall be placed so that its axis is at 90 degrees ±5 degrees to the line of a straight test edge or 90 degrees ±5 degrees to a tangent at the point of contact with a curved test edge. The point of contact between the test edge and the mandrel shall be in the approximate center of the width of the tape. The axis of the mandrel may be positioned anywhere in a plane which is at right angles to either the line of a straight test edge or to a tangent at the point of contact with a curved test edge. The operator should seek the orientation most likely to cause the edge to cut the tape. Maintain the force against the edge and rotate the mandrel through one complete revolution while preventing any linear motion of the mandrel along the edge. Release the mandrel from the edge and remove the tape without enlarging any cut or causing any score to become a cut. A cut in the tape with a length of not less than ½ inch (13 millimeters) identifies an edge as sharp. (The test instruments used by the Commission in its test for compliance with the regulation will be calibrated to insure that the force with which the mandrel is applied to a test edge does not exceed 1.35 pounds.)

(e) *Specifications for sharp edge test equipment.* The following specifications shall apply to the equipment to be used in the sharp edge test described in paragraph (d) of this section:

(1) The rotation of the mandrel shall produce a constant tangential velocity of 1.00±0.08 inch per second (25.4±2.0 millimeters per second) during the center 75 percent of its rotation and shall have a smooth start and stop.

(2) The mandrel shall be made of steel. The test surface of the mandrel shall be free of scratches, nicks, or burrs and shall have a surface roughness no greater than 16 microinches (0.40 micron). The test surface shall have a hardness no less than 40 as measured on the Rockwell "C" scale, as determined pursuant to ASTM E 18–74 entitled "Standard Test Methods for Rockwell Hardness and Rockwell Superficial Hardness of Metallic Materials," published July 1974 and which is incorporated by reference in this regulation. (Copies are available from American Society for Testing and Materials, 1916 Race Street, Philadelphia, Pa. 19103.) The diameter of the mandrel shall be 0.375±0.005 inch (9.35±0.12 millimeters). The mandrel shall be of suitable length to carry out the test.

(3) The tape shall be pressure-sensitive polytetrafluoroethylene (TFE) high temperature electrical insulation tape as described in Military Specification MIL-I-23594B (1971) which is incorporated by reference in this regulation. (Copies are available from Naval Publications and Forms Center, 5801 Tabor Ave., Philadelphia, Pa. 19120.) The thickness of the polytetrafluoroethylene backing shall be between 0.0026 inch (0.066 millimeter) and 0.0035 inch (0.089 millimeter).[1] The adhesive shall be pressure-sensitive silicone polymer with a nominal thickness of 0.003 inch (.08 millimeter). The width of the tape shall not be less than ¼ inch (6 millimeters). While conducting sharp edge tests the temperature of the tape shall be maintained between 70 °F (21.1 °C) and 80 °F (26.6 °C).

(f) For the purpose of conformance with the technical requirements prescribed by this § 1500.49, the English figures shall be used. The metric approximations are provided in parentheses for convenience and information only.

[1] The tape that the Commission will use for the sharp edge test is CHR type "T" manufactured by The Connecticut Hard Rubber Co., New and East Streets, New Haven, Conn. 06509.

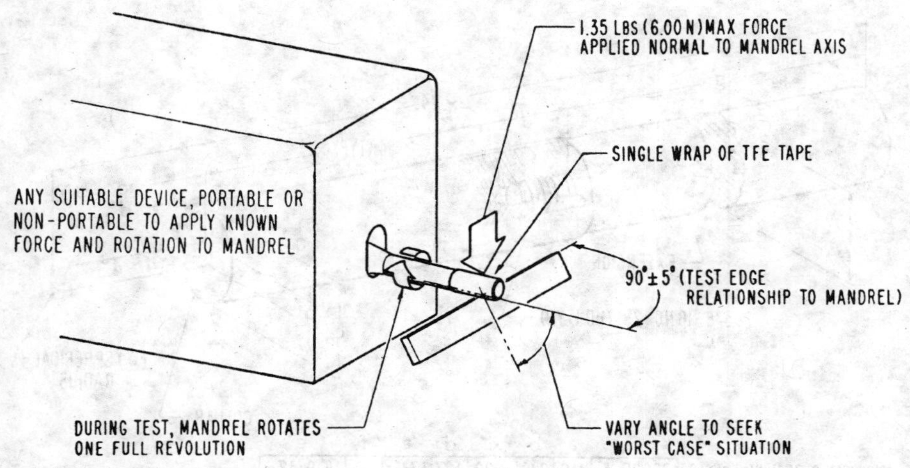

FIG I–PRINCIPLE OF SHARP EDGE TEST

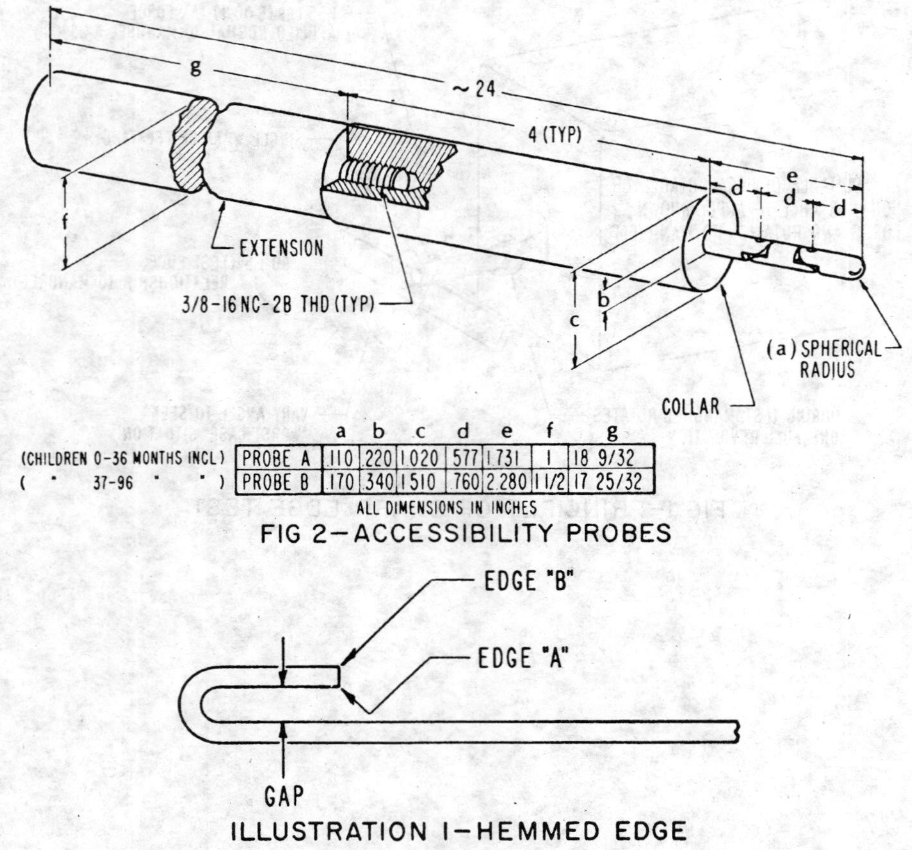

		a	b	c	d	e	f	g
(CHILDREN 0-36 MONTHS INCL)	PROBE A	.110	.220	1.020	.577	1.731	1	18 9/32
(" 37-96 " ")	PROBE B	.170	.340	1.510	.760	2.280	1 1/2	17 25/32

ALL DIMENSIONS IN INCHES

FIG 2—ACCESSIBILITY PROBES

ILLUSTRATION I—HEMMED EDGE

(Secs. 2(s), 10(a), 74 Stat. 378 (15 U.S.C. 1261, 1269))

[43 FR 12645, Mar. 24, 1978, as amended at 43 FR 21324, May 17, 1978]

§ 1500.50 Test methods for simulating use and abuse of toys and other articles intended for use by children.

(a) *Objective.* The objective of §§ 1500.51, 1500.52, and 1500.53 is to describe specific test methods for simulating normal use of toys and other articles intended for use by children as well as the reasonably foreseeable damage or abuse to which the articles may be subjected. The test methods are for use in exposing potential hazards that would result from the normal use or the reasonably foreseeable damage or abuse of such articles intended for children.

(b) *Application—general.* (1)(i) The test methods described in §§ 1500.51, 1500.52 and 1500.53 are to be used in determining what is normal use and reasonably foreseeable damage or abuse when specifically referenced under § 1500.18. Other banning regulations may also reference these use and abuse toy test procedures.

(ii) The test methods described in §§ 1500.51, 1500.52, and 1500.53 have been established for articles intended for the specified age groups of children: 18 months of age or less, over 18 months but not over 36 months of age, and over 36 months but not over 96 months of age. If an article is marked, labeled, advertised, or otherwise intended for children of ages spanning more than one of these age groups, the article will be subjected to the tests providing the most stringent requirements. If an article is not age-labeled in a clear and conspicuous manner or, based on such factors as marketing practices and the customary patterns of usage of a product by children, is inappropriately age-labeled, and is intended or appropriate for children 96 months of age or less, it will also be subjected to the most stringent test requirements.

(2) For purposes of compliance with the test methods prescribed in §§ 1500.51, 1500.52, and 1500.53, the English system shall be used. The metric approximations are provided in parentheses for convenience and information only.

(3) Each of the test methods described in §§ 1500.51, 1500.52, and 1500.53 shall be applied to a previously untested sample except the tension test which shall be conducted with the test sample used in the torque test.

(4) Prior to testing, each sample shall be subjected to a temperature of 73°±3 °F. (23°±2 °C.) as a relative humidity of 20 − 70 percent for a period of at least 4 hours. The toy testing shall commence within five minutes after the toy has been removed from the preconditioning atmosphere.

(5) Toys reasonably intended to be assembled by an adult and not intended to be taken apart by a child shall be tested only in the assembled state if the shelf package and the assembly instructions prominently indicate that the article is to be assembled only by an adult.

(6) Toys intended to be repeatedly assembled and taken apart shall have the individual pieces as well as the completed article subjected to these test procedures.

(7) In situations where a test procedure may be applied in more than one way to a toy test component, the point (or direction) of force (or torque) application which results in the most severe conditions shall be used.

(c) *Definitions.* As used in this section and in §§ 1500.51, 1500.52, and 1500.53:

(1) *Toy* means any toy, game, or other article designed, labeled, advertised, or otherwise intended for use by children.

(2) *Mouth toy* means any toy reasonably intended to be placed into or in contact with a child's mouth.

[40 FR 1483, Jan. 7, 1975; 40 FR 16191, Apr. 10, 1975]

§ 1500.51 Test methods for simulating use and abuse of toys and other articles intended for use by children 18 months of age or less.

(a) *Application.* The test methods described in this section shall be used to simulate the normal and reasonably foreseeable use, damage, or abuse of toys and other articles intended for use by children 18 months of age or less in conjunction with § 1500.18.

(b) *Impact test*—(1) *Application.* Except as provided in paragraph (b)(4) of this section, toys having a weight of less than 3.0 pounds ±0.01 pound (1.4 kilograms) shall be subject to this test.

(2) *Impact medium.* The impact medium shall consist of a ⅛-inch (0.3-centimeter) nominal thickness of type IV vinyl-composition tile, composition 1—asbestos free, as specified by paragraphs 1.2 and 3.1.4 of Interim Amendment-1(YD), dated November 14, 1979, to the Federal Specification entitled Tile, Floor: Asphalt, Rubber, Vinyl, Vinyl-Asbestos, SS-T-312B, dated October 10, 1974,[1] over at least a 2.5-inch (6.4-centimeter) thickness of concrete. The impact area shall be at least 3 square feet (0.3 square meter). The Commission recognizes that this specified impact medium is the equivalent of, and will yield the same impact test results as, a surface covered with vinyl-asbestos tile meeting the requirements of Federal Specification SS-T-312A.

(3) *Testing procedure.* Except as provided in paragraphs (b)(4) (i) and (ii) of this section, the toy shall be dropped 10 times from a height of 4.5 feet ±0.5 inch (1.37 meters) onto the impact medium described in paragraph (b)(2) of this section. The toy shall be dropped in random orientation. After each drop,

[1] These documents may be ordered from the General Services Administration, Specifications Unit, Room 6654, 7th and D Streets, S.W., Washington, DC 20407. The price of the specification and amendment is $1.00.

the test sample shall be allowed to come to rest and shall be examined and evaluated before continuing.

(4) *Large and bulky toys.* (i) A toy that has a projected base area of 400 or more square inches (2,560 or more square centimeters), shall be tested for impact in accordance with paragraph (b)(4)(iii) of this section. The base area for toys with permanently attached legs shall be measured by calculating the area enclosed by straight lines connecting the outermost edge of each leg of the perimeter.

(ii) A toy that has a volume of more than 3 cubic feet (0.085 cubic meter), calculated by the major dimensions without regard to minor appendages, shall be tested for impact in accordance with paragraph (b)(4)(iii) of this section.

(iii) The toys described in paragraph (b)(4)(i) and (ii) of this section shall be tested for impact by tipping them over three times by pushing the samples slowly past their centers of balance onto the impact medium described in paragraph (b)(2) of this section.

(c) *Bite test*—(1) *Application.* A toy (or component or any accessible portion thereof) that has an external dimension of 1.25 inches ±0.05 inch (3.18 centimeters) or less and a design configuration that would permit a child to insert a portion into the mouth in any orientation up to a biting thickness of 1.25 inches ±0.05 inch (3.18 centimeters), for a penetration of at least 0.25 inch (0.635 centimeter), shall be subject to this test.

(2) *Test equipment*—(i) *Contact mechanism.* The contact mechanism shall be two metal strips or plates each measuring 0.25 inch ±0.002 inch (0.635 centimeter) high and each having a contact edge radius of 0.020 inch ±0.002 inch (0.05 centimeter), for at least a 150-degree cross-sectional arc. A suggested contact mechanism appears in figure 1 of this section.

(ii) *Loading device.* The loading device shall be a scale or force gauge having an accuracy of ±0.5 pound (±225 grams).

(3) *Testing procedure.* The test article shall be placed in the contact mechanism in any reasonable position for a penetration of 0.25 to 0.5 inch (0.64 to 1.27 centimeters), which position utilizes less than 180 degrees of the arc of the contact mechanism, and a test load increasing to 25 pounds ±0.5 pound (11.35 kilograms) shall be evenly applied within 5 seconds. This load shall be maintained for an additional 10 seconds.

(d) *Flexure test*—(1) *Application.* This test shall be applied to each component of a toy containing metal wire(s), or other metal material(s), for stiffening or for retention of form if the component can be bent through a 60-degree arc by a maximum force of 10 pounds ±0.5 pound (4.55 kilograms), applied perpendicularly to the major axis of the component at a point 2 inches (5 centimeters) from the intersection of the component with the main body of the toy or at the end of the component if the component is less than 2 inches ±0.05 inch (5 centimeters) long.

(2) *Testing procedure.* The toy shall be secured in a vise equipped with vise shields that are fabricated from 13-gauge cold-rolled steel or other similar material and that have a 0.375-inch (0.95-centimeter) inside radius. The component shall then be bent through a 60-degree arc by a force applied at a point on the component 2 inches ±0.05 inch (5 centimeters) from the intersection of the component with the main body of the toy or applied at the end of the component if the component is less than 2 inches (5 centimeters) long. The component shall then be bent in the reverse direction through a 120-degree arc. This process shall be repeated for 30 cycles at a rate of one cycle per two seconds with a 60-second rest period occurring after each 10 cycles. Two 120-degree arc bends shall constitute one cycle.

(e) *Torque test*—(1) *Application*—(i) *General.* A toy with a projection, part, or assembly that a child can grasp with at least the thumb and forefinger or the teeth shall be subject to this test.

(ii) *Toys with rotating components.* Projections, parts, or assemblies that are rigidly mounted on an accessible rod or shaft designed to rotate along with the projections, parts, or assemblies shall be tested with the rod or shaft clamped to prevent rotation.

(2) *Test equipment*—(i) *Loading device.* The loading device shall be a torque gauge, torque wrench, or other appropriate device having an accuracy of ±0.2

inch-pound (±0.23 kilogram-centimeter).

(ii) *Clamp*. The clamp shall be capable of holding the test component firmly and transmitting a torsional force.

(3) *Testing procedure*. With the toy rigidly fastened in any reasonable test position, the clamp is fastened to the test object or component. A torque of 2 inch-pounds ±0.2 inch-pound (2.30 kilogram-centimeters) shall be applied evenly within a period of 5 seconds in a clockwise direction until a rotation of 180 degrees from the original position has been attained or 2 inch-pounds (2.30 kilogram-centimeters) exceeded. The torque or maximum rotation shall be maintained for an additional 10 seconds. The torque shall then be removed and the test component permitted to return to a relaxed condition. This procedure shall then be repeated in a counterclockwise direction.

(f) *Tension test*—(1) *Application*—(i) *General*. Any projection of a toy that the child can grasp with at least the thumb and forefinger or the teeth shall be subject to this test. This test is to be conducted on the same toy that has been subjected to the torque test described in paragraph (e) of this section.

(ii) *Stuffed toys and beanbags*. A stuffed toy or beanbag constructed of pliable materials having seams (such as fabrics) shall have the seams subjected to 10 pounds ±0.5 pound (4.55 kilograms) of force applied in any direction.

(2) *Test equipment*—(i) *Clamps*. One clamp capable of applying a tension load to the test component is required. A second clamp suitable for applying a tension load perpendicularly to the major axis of the test component is also required.

(ii) *Loading device*. The loading device is to be a self-indicating gauge or other appropriate means having an accuracy of ±0.5 pound (±225 grams).

(3) *Testing procedure*. With the test sample fastened in a convenient position, an appropriate clamp shall be attached to the test object or component. A 10-pound ±0.5 pound (4.55–kilogram) direct force shall be evenly applied, within a period of 5 seconds, parallel to the major axis of the test component and maintained for an additional 10 seconds. The tension clamp shall then be removed and a second clamp appropriate for pulling at 90 degrees shall be attached to the test object or component. A 10-pound ±0.5 pound (4.55-kilogram) tensile force shall be evenly applied, within a period of 5 seconds, perpendicularly to the major axis of the test component and maintained for an additional 10 seconds.

(g) *Compression test*—(1) *Application*. Any area on the surface of a toy that is accessible to a child and inaccessible to flat-surface contact during the impact test shall be subject to this test.

(2) *Test apparatus*. The loading device shall be a rigid metal disc 1.125 inches ±0.015 inch (2.86 centimeters) in diameter and 0.375 inch (0.95 centimeter) in thickness. The perimeter of the disc shall be rounded to a radius of 1/32 inch (0.08 centimeter) to eliminate irregular edges. The disc shall be attached to an appropriate compression scale having an accuracy of ±0.5 pound (±225 grams).

(3) *Testing procedure*. The disc shall be positioned so that the contact surface is parallel to the surface under test. A direct force of 20 pounds ±0.5 pound (9.1 kilograms) shall be evenly applied within 5 seconds through the disc. This load shall be maintained for an additional 10 seconds. During the test the toy is to rest on a flat, hard surface in any convenient position.

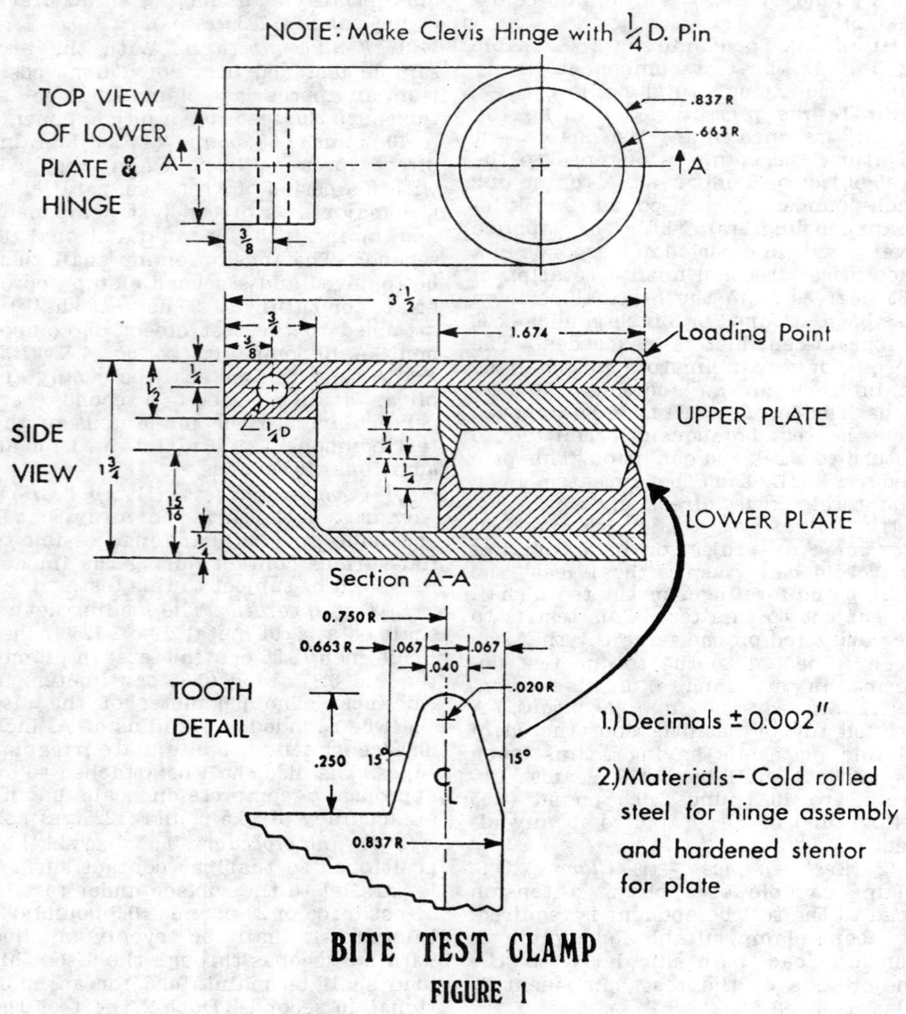

BITE TEST CLAMP

FIGURE 1

[40 FR 1484, Jan. 7, 1975; 40 FR 6210, Feb. 10, 1975; 40 FR 16192, Apr. 10, 1975; 40 FR 17746, Apr. 22, 1975; as amended at 55 FR 52040, Dec. 19, 1990; 56 FR 9, Jan. 2, 1991; 56 FR 558, Jan. 7, 1991]

§ 1500.52 Test methods for simulating use and abuse of toys and other articles intended for use by children over 18 but not over 36 months of age.

(a) *Application*. The test methods described in this section, shall be used to simulate the normal and reasonably foreseeable use, damage, or abuse of toys and other articles intended for use by children over 18 but not over 36 months of age in conjunction with § 1500.18.

(b) *Impact test*—(1) *Application*. Except as provided in paragraph (b)(4) of this section, toys having a weight of less than 4.0 pounds ±0.01 pound (1.8 kilograms) shall be subject to this test.

(2) *Impact medium.* The impact medium shall consist of a ⅛-inch (0.3-centimeter) nominal thickness of type IV vinyl-composition tile, composition 1—asbestos free, as specified by paragraphs 1.2 and 3.1.4 of Interim Amendment-1(YD), dated November 14, 1979, to the Federal Specification entitled Tile, Floor: Asphalt, Rubber, Vinyl, Vinyl-Asbestos, SS-T-312B, dated October 10, 1974,[1] over at least a 2.5-inch (6.4-centimeter) thickness of concrete. The impact area shall be at least 3 square feet (0.3 square meter). The Commission recognizes that this specified impact medium is the equivalent of, and will yield the same impact test results as, a surface covered with vinyl-asbestos tile meeting the requirements of Federal Specification SS-T-312A.

(3) *Testing procedure.* Except as provided in paragraph (b)(4) (i) and (ii) of this section, the toy shall be dropped four times from a height of 3 feet ±0.5 inch (0.92 meter) onto the impact medium described in paragraph (b)(2) of this section. The toy shall be dropped in random orientation. After each drop, the test sample shall be allowed to come to rest and shall be examined and evaluated before continuing.

(4) *Large and bulky toys.* (i) A toy that has a projected base area of 400 or more square inches (2,560 or more square centimeters) shall be tested for impact in accordance with paragraph (b)(4)(iii) of this section. The base area for toys with permanently attached legs shall be measured by calculating the area enclosed by straight lines connecting the outermost edge of each leg of the perimeter.

(ii) A toy that has a volume of more than 3 cubic feet (0.085 cubic meter), calculated by the major dimensions without regard to minor appendages, shall be tested for impact in accordance with paragraph (b)(4)(iii) of this section.

(iii) The toys described in paragraph (b)(4) (i) and (ii) of this section shall be tested for impact by tipping them over three times by pushing the samples slowly past their centers of balance onto the impact medium described in paragraph (b)(2) of this section.

(c) *Bite test*—(1) *Application.* A toy (or component or any accessible portion thereof) that has an external dimension of 1.25 inches ±0.05 inch (3.18 centimeters) or less and a design configuration that would permit a child to insert a portion into the mouth in any orientation up to a biting thickness of 1.25 inches ±0.05 inches (3.18 centimeters), for a penetration of at least 0.25 inch (0.635 centimeter), shall be subject to this test.

(2) *Test equipment*—(i) *Contact mechanism.* The contact mechanism shall be two metal strips or plates each measuring 0.25 inch ±0.002 inch (0.635 centimeter) high and each having a contact edge radius of 0.020 inch ±0.002 inch (0.05 centimeter) for at least a 150-degree cross-sectional arc. A suggested contact mechanism appears in figure 1 of §1500.51.

(ii) *Loading device.* The loading device shall be a scale or force gauge having an accuracy of ±0.5 pound (±225 grams).

(3) *Testing procedure.* The test article shall be placed in the contact mechanism in any reasonable position for a penetration of 0.25 to 0.5 inch (0.64 to 1.27 centimeters), which position utilizes less than 180 degrees of the arc of the contact mechanism, and a test load increasing to 50 pounds ±0.5 pound (22.74 kilograms) shall be evenly applied within 5 seconds. This load shall be maintained for an additional 10 seconds.

(d) *Flexure test*—(1) *Application.* This test shall be applied to each component of a toy containing metal wire(s), or other metal material(s), for stiffening or for retention of form if the component can be bent through a 60-degree arc by a maximum force of 15 pounds ±0.5 pound (6.80 kilograms) applied perpendicularly to the major axis of the component at a point 2 inches ±0.05 inch (5 centimeters) from the intersection of the component with the main body of the toy or at the end of the component if the component is less than 2 inches ±0.05 inch (5 centimeters) long.

(2) *Testing procedure.* The toy shall be secured in a vise equipped with vise shields that are fabricated from 13-gauge cold-rolled steel or other similar material and that have a 0.375-inch (0.95-centimeter) inside radius. The

[1] See footnote 1 to §1500.51.

component shall then be bent through a 60-degree arc by a force applied at a point on the component 2 inches ±0.05 inch (5 centimeters) from the intersection of the component with the main body of the toy or applied at the end of the component if the component is less than 2 inches (5 centimeters) long. The component shall then be bent in the reverse direction through a 120-degree arc. This process shall be repeated for 30 cycles at a rate of one cycle per two seconds with a 60-second rest period occurring after each 10 cycles. Two 120-degree arc bends shall constitute one cycle.

(e) *Torque test*—(1) *Application*—(i) *General.* A toy with a projection, part, or assembly that a child can grasp with at least the thumb and forefinger or the teeth shall be subject to this test.

(ii) *Toys with rotating components.* Projections, parts, or assemblies that are rigidly mounted on an accessible rod or shaft designed to rotate along with the projections, parts, or assemblies shall be tested with the rod or shaft clamped to prevent rotation.

(2) *Test equipment*—(i) *Loading device.* The loading device shall be a torque gauge, torque wrench, or other appropriate device having an accuracy of ±0.2 inch-pound (±0.23 kilogram-centimeter).

(ii) *Clamp.* The clamp shall be capable of holding the test component firmly and transmitting a torsional force.

(3) *Testing procedure.* With the toy rigidly fastened in any reasonable test position, the clamp is fastened to the test object or component. A torque of 3 inch-pounds ±0.2 inch-pound (3.46 kilogram-centimeters) shall be applied evenly within a period of 5 seconds in a clockwise direction until a rotation of 180 degrees from the original position has been attained or 3 inch-pounds ±0.2 inch-pound (3.46 kilogram-centimeters) exceeded. The torque or maximum rotation shall be maintained for an additional 10 seconds. The torque shall then be removed and the test component permitted to return to a relaxed condition. This procedure shall then be repeated in a counterclockwise direction.

(f) *Tension test*—(1) *Application*—(i) *General.* Any projection of a toy that the child can grasp with at least the thumb and forefinger or the teeth shall be subject to this test. This test is to be conducted on the same toy that has been subjected to the torque test described in paragraph (e) of this section.

(ii) *Stuffed toys and beanbags.* A stuffed toy or beanbag constructed of pliable materials having seams (such as fabrics) shall have the seams subjected to 15 pounds ±0.5 pound (6.80 kilograms) of force applied in any direction.

(2) *Test equipment*—(i) *Clamps.* One clamp capable of applying a tension load to the test component is required. A second clamp suitable for applying a tension load perpendicularly to the major axis of the test component is also required.

(ii) *Loading device.* The loading device is to be a self-indicating gauge or other appropriate means having an accuracy of ±0.5 pound (±255 grams).

(3) *Testing procedure.* With the test sample fastened in a convenient position, an appropriate clamp shall be attached to the test object or component. A 15-pound ±0.5 pound (6.80-kilogram) direct force shall be evenly applied, within a period of 5 seconds, parallel to the major axis of the test component and maintained for an additional 10 seconds. The tension clamp shall then be removed and a second clamp appropriate for pulling at 90 degrees shall be attached to the test object or component. A 15-pound ±0.5 pound (6.80-kilogram) tensile force shall be evenly applied, within a period of 5 seconds, perpendicularly to the major axis of the test component and maintained for an additional 10 seconds.

(g) *Compression test*—(1) *Application.* Any area on the surface of a toy that is accessible to a child and inaccessible to flat-surface contact during the impact test shall be subject to this test.

(2) *Test apparatus.* The loading device shall be a rigid metal disc 1.125 inches ±0.015 inch (2.86 centimeters) in diameter and 0.375 inch (0.95 centimeter) in thickness. The perimeter of the disc shall be rounded to a radius of 1/32 inch (0.08 centimeter) to eliminate irregular edges. The disc shall be attached to an appropriate compression scale having an accurancy of ±0.5 pound (±225 grams).

(3) *Testing procedure.* The disc shall be positioned so that the contact surface

is parallel to the surface under test. A direct force of 25 pounds ±0.5 pound (11.4 kilograms) shall be evenly applied within 5 seconds through the disc. This load shall be maintained for an additional 10 seconds. During the test the toy is to rest on a flat, hard surface in any convenient position.

[40 FR 1485, Jan. 7, 1975; 40 FR 6210, Feb. 10, 1975; 40 FR 16192, Apr. 10, 1975; as amended at 56 FR 10, Jan. 2, 1991]

§ 1500.53 Test methods for simulating use and abuse of toys and other articles intended for use by children over 36 but not over 96 months of age.

(a) *Application.* The test methods described in this section shall be used to simulate the normal and reasonably foreseeable use, damage, or abuse of toys and other articles intended for use by children over 36 but not over 96 months of age in conjunction with § 1500.18.

(b) *Impact test*—(1) *Application.* Except as provided in paragraph (b)(4) of this section, toys having a weight of less than 10.0 pounds ±0.01 pound (4.6 kilograms) shall be subject to this test.

(2) *Impact medium.* The impact medium shall consist of a ⅛-inch (0.3-centimeter) nominal thickness of type IV vinyl-composition tile, composition 1—asbestos free, as specified by paragraphs 1.2 and 3.1.4 of Interim Amendment-1(YD), dated November 14, 1979, to the Federal Specification entitled Tile, Floor: Asphalt, Rubber, Vinyl, Vinyl-Asbestos, SS-T-312B, dated October 10, 1974,[1] over at least a 2.5-inch (6.4-centimeter) thickness of concrete. The impact area shall be at least 3 square feet (0.3 square meter). The Commission recognizes that this specified impact medium is the equivalent of, and will yield the same impact test results as, a surface covered with vinyl-asbestos tile meeting the requirements of Federal Specification SS-T-312A.

(3) *Testing procedure.* except as provided in paragraph (b)(4) (i) and (ii) of this section, the toy shall be dropped four times from a height of 3 feet ±0.5 inch (0.92 meter) onto the impact medium described in paragraph (b)(2) of this section. The toy shall be dropped in random orientation. After each drop, the test sample shall be allowed to come to rest and shall be examined and evaluated before continuing.

(4) *Large and bulky toys.* (i) A toy that has a projected base area of 400 or more square inches (2,560 or more square centimeters) shall be tested for impact in accordance with paragraph (b)(4)(iii) of this subsection. The base area for toys having permanently attached legs shall be measured by calculating the area enclosed by straight lines connecting the outermost edge of each leg of the perimeter.

(ii) A toy that has a volume of more than 3 cubic feet (0.085 cubic meter), calculated by the major dimensions without regard to minor appendages, shall be tested for impact in accordance with paragraph (b)(4)(iii) of this section.

(iii) The toys described in paragraph (b)(4) (i) and (ii) of this section shall be tested for impact by tipping them over three times by pushing the samples slowly past their centers of balance onto the impact medium described in paragraph (b)(2) of this section.

(c) *Bite test*—(1) *Application.* A toy (or component) that is a mouth toy shall be subject to this test.

(2) *Test equipment*—(i) *Contact mechanism.* The contact mechanism shall be two metal strips or plates each measuring 0.25 inch ±0.002 inch (0.635 centimeter) high and each having a contact edge radius of 0.020 inch ±0.002 inch (0.5 centimeter) for at least a 150-degree cross-sectional arc. A suggested contact mechanism appears in figure 1 of § 1500.51.

(ii) *Loading device.* The loading device shall be a scale or force gauge having an accuracy of ±0.5 pound (±225 grams).

(3) *Testing procedure.* The test article shall be placed in the contact mechanism in any reasonable position for a penetration of 0.25 to 0.5 inch (0.64 to 1.27 centimeters), which position utilizes less than 180 degrees of the arc of the contract mechanism, and a test load increasing to 100 pounds ±0.5 pound (45.50 kilograms) shall be evenly applied within 5 seconds. This load shall be maintained for an additional 10 seconds.

(d) *Flexure test*—(1) *Application.* This test shall be applied to each component of a toy containing metal wire(s), or other metal material(s), for stiffening or for retention of form if the component can be bent through a 60-degree arc by a maximum force of 15 pounds ±0.5 pound (6.80 kilograms) applied perpendicularly to the major axis of the component at a point 2 inches ±0.05 inch (5 centimeters) from the intersection of the component with the main body of the toy or at the end of the component if the component is less than 2 inches ±0.05 inch (5 centimeters) long.

(2) *Testing procedure.* The toy shall be secured in a vise equipped with vise shields that are fabricated from 13-gauge cold-rolled steel or other similar material and that have a 0.375-inch (0.95-centimeter) inside radius. The component shall then be bent through a 60-degree arc by a force applied at a point on the component 2 inches (5 centimeters) from the intersection of the component with the main body of the toy or applied at the end of the component if the component is less than 2 inches (5 centimeters) long. The component shall then be bent in the reverse direction through a 120-degree arc. This process shall be repeated for 30 cycles at a rate of one cycle per two seconds with a 60-second rest period occurring after each 10 cycles. Two 120-degree arc bends shall constitute one cycle.

(e) *Torque test*—(1) *Application*—(i) *General.* A toy with a projection, part, or assembly that a child can grasp with at least the thumb and forefinger or the teeth shall be subject to this test.

(ii) *Toys with rotating components.* Projections, parts, or assemblies that are rigidly mounted on an accessible rod or shaft designed to rotate along with the projections, parts, or assemblies shall be tested with the rod or shaft clamped to prevent rotation.

(2) *Test equipment*—(i) *Loading device.* The loading device shall be a torque gauge, torque wrench, or other appropriate device having an accuracy of ±0.2 inch-pound (±0.23 kilogram-centimeter).

(ii) *Clamp.* The clamp shall be capable of holding the test component firmly and transmitting a torsional force.

(3) *Testing procedure.* With the toy rigidly fastened in any reasonable test position, the clamp is fastened to the test object or component. A torque of 4 inch-pounds ±0.2 inch-pound (4.60 kilogram-centimeters) shall be applied evenly within a period of 5 seconds in a clockwise direction until a rotation of 180 degrees from the original position has been attained or 4 inch-pounds ±0.2 inch-pound (4.60 kilogram-centimeters) exceeded. The torque or maximum rotation shall be maintained for an additional 10 seconds. The torque shall then be removed and the test component permitted to return to a relaxed condition. This procedure shall then be repeated in a counterclockwise direction.

(f) *Tension test*—(1) *Application*—(i) *General.* Any projection of a toy that the child can grasp with at least the thumb and forefinger or the teeth shall be subject to this test. This test is to be conducted on the same toy that has been subjected to the torque test described in paragraph (e) of this section.

(ii) *Stuffed toys and beanbags.* A stuffed toy or beanbag constructed of pliable materials having seams (such as fabrics) shall have the seams subjected to 15 pounds ±0.5 pound (6.80 kilograms) of force applied in any direction.

(2) *Test equipment*—(i) *Clamps.* One clamp capable of applying a tension load to the test component is required. A second clamp suitable for applying a tension load perpendicularly to the major axis of the test component is also required.

(ii) *Loading device.* The loading device is to be a self-indicating gauge or other appropriate means having an accuracy of ±0.5 pound (±225 grams).

(3) *Testing procedure.* With the test sample fastened in a convenient position, and appropriate clamp shall be attached to the test object or component. A 15-pound ±0.5 pound (6.80-kilogram) direct force shall be evenly applied, within a period of 5 seconds, parallel to the major axis of the test component and maintained for an additional 10 seconds. The tension clamp shall then be removed and a second clamp appropriate for pulling at 90 degrees shall be attached to the test object or component. A 15-pound ±0.5 pound (6.80-kilogram) tensile force shall be evenly applied, within a period of 5 seconds, perpendicularly to the major axis of the

test component and maintained for an additional 10 seconds.

(g) *Compression test*—(1) *Application*. Any area on the surface of a toy that is accessible to a child and inaccessible to flat-surface contact during the impact test shall be subject to this test.

(2) *Test apparatus*. The loading device shall be a rigid metal disc 1.125 inches ±0.015 inch (2.86 centimeters) in diameter and 0.375 inch (0.95 centimeter) in thickness. The perimeter of the disc shall be rounded to a radius of 1⁄32 inch (0.08 centimeter) to eliminate irregular edges. The disc shall be attached to an appropriate compression scale having an accuracy of ±0.5 pound (±225 grams).

(3) *Testing procedure*. The disc shall be positioned so that the contact surface is parallel to the surface under test. A direct force of 30 pounds ±0.5 pound (13.6 kilograms) shall be evenly applied within 5 seconds through the disc. This load shall be maintained for an additional 10 seconds. During the test the toy is to rest on a flat, hard surface in any convenient position.

[40 FR 1486, Jan. 7, 1975; 40 FR 16192, Apr. 10, 1975, as amended at 56 FR 10, Jan. 2, 1991]

§ 1500.81 Exemptions for food, drugs, cosmetics, and fuels.

(a) *Food, drugs, and cosmetics*. Substances subject to the Federal Food, Drug, and Cosmetic Act are exempted by section 2(f)(2) of the act; but where a food, drug, or cosmetic offers a substantial risk of injury or illness from any handling or use that is customary or usual it may be regarded as misbranded under the Federal Food, Drug, and Cosmetic Act because its label fails to reveal material facts with respect to consequences that may result from use of the article (21 U.S.C. 321(n)) when its label fails to bear information to alert the householder to this hazard.

(b) *Fuels*. A substance intended to be used as a fuel is exempt from the requirements of the act when in containers that are intended to be or are installed as part of the heating, cooling, or refrigeration system of a house. A portable container used for delivery or temporary or additional storage, and containing a substance that is a hazardous substance as defined in section 2(f) of the act, is not exempt from the labeling prescribed in section 2(p) of the act, even though it contains a fuel to be used in the heating, cooking, or refrigeration system of a house.

§ 1500.82 Exemption from full labeling and other requirements.

(a) Any person who believes a particular hazardous substance intended or packaged in a form suitable for use in the household or by children should be exempted from full label compliance otherwise applicable under the act, because of the size of the package or because of the minor hazard presented by the substance, or for other good and sufficient reason, may submit to the Commission a request for exemption under section 3(c) of the act, presenting facts in support of the view that full compliance is impracticable or is not necessary for the protection of the public health. The Commission shall determine on the basis of the facts submitted and all other available information whether the requested exemption is consistent with adequate protection of the public health and safety. If the Commission so finds, it shall detail the exemption granted and the reasons therefor by an appropriate order published in the FEDERAL REGISTER.

(b) The Commission may on its own initiative determine on the basis of facts available to it that a particular hazardous substance intended or packaged in a form suitable for use in the household or by children should be exempted from full labeling compliance otherwise applicable under the act because of the size of the package or because of the minor hazard presented by the substance or for other good and sufficient reason. If the Commission so finds, it shall detail the exemption granted and the reasons therefor by an appropriate order in the FEDERAL REGISTER.

(c) Any person who believes a particular article should be exempted from being classified as a "banned hazardous substance" as defined by section 2(q)(1)(A) of the act (repeated in §1500.3(b)(15)(i)(A)), because its functional purpose requires inclusion of a hazardous substance, it bears labeling giving adequate directions and warnings for safe use, and it is intended for use by children who have attained sufficient maturity, and may reasonably be expected, to read and heed such directions and warnings, may submit to the Commission a request for exemption under section 2(q)(1)(B)(i) of the act (repeated in proviso (*1*) under § 1500.3(b)(15(i)), presenting facts in support of his contention. The commission shall determine on the basis of the facts submitted, and all other available information, whether the requested exemption is consistent with the purposes of the act. If the Commission so finds, it shall detail the exemption granted and the reasons therefor by an appropriate order in the FEDERAL REGISTER.

(d) On its own initiative, the Commission may determine on the basis of available facts that a particular banned hazardous substance should be exempted from section 2(q)(1)(A) of the act (repeated in § 1500.3(b)(15)(i)(A)), because its functional purpose requires inclusion of a hazardous substance, it bears labeling giving adequate directions and warnings for safe use, and it is intended for use by children who have obtained sufficient maturity, and may reasonably be expected, to read and heed such directions and warnings. If the Commission so finds, it shall detail the exemption granted and the reasons therefor by an appropriate order in the FEDERAL REGISTER.

§ 1500.83 Exemptions for small packages, minor hazards, and special circumstances.

(a) The following exemptions are granted for the labeling of hazardous substances under the provisions of § 1500.82:

(1) When the sole hazard from a substance in a self-pressurized container is that it generates pressure or when the sole hazard from a substance is that it is flammable or extremely flammable, the name of the component which contributes the hazards need not be stated.

(2) Common matches, including book matches, wooden matches, and so-called "safety" matches are exempt from the labeling requirements of section 2(p)(1) of the act (repeated in § 1500.3(b)(14)(i)) insofar as they apply to the product being considered hazardous because of being an "extremely flammable solid" or "flammable solid" as defined in § 1500.3(c)(6)(v) and (vi).

(3) Paper items such as newspapers, wrapping papers, toilet and cleansing tissues, and paper writing supplies are exempt from the labeling requirements of section 2(p)(1) of the act (repeated in § 1500.3(b)(14)(i)) insofar as they apply to the products being considered hazardous because of being an "extremely flammable solid" or "flammable solid" as defined in § 1500.3(c)(6)(v) and (vi).

(4) Thread, string, twine, rope, cord, and similar materials are exempt from the labeling requirements of section 2(p)(1) of the act (repeated in § 1500.3(b)(14)(i)) insofar as they apply to the products being considered hazardous because of being an "extremely flammable solid" or "flammable solid" as defined in Sec. 1500.3(c)(6)(v) and (vi).

(5) Laboratory chemicals intended only for research or investigational and other laboratory uses (except those in home chemistry sets) are exempt from the requirements of placement provided in § 1500.121 if all information required by that section and the act appears with the required prominence on the label panel adjacent to the main panel.

(6) [Reserved]

(7) Rigid or semirigid ballpoint ink cartridges are exempt from the labeling requirements of section 2(p)(1) of the act (repeated in § 1500.3(b)(14)(i)), insofar as such requirements would be necessary because the ink contained therein is a "toxic" substance as defined in § 1500.3(c)(2)(i), if:

(i) The ballpoint ink cartridge is of such construction that the ink will, under any reasonably foreseeable conditions of manipulation or use, emerge only from the ballpoint end;

(ii) When tested by the method described in § 1500.3(c)(2)(i), the ink does not have an LD–50 single oral dose of less than 500 milligrams per kilogram of body weight of the test animal; and

(iii) The cartridge does not have a capacity of more than 2 grams of ink.

(8) Containers of paste shoe waxes, paste auto waxes, and paste furniture and floor waxes containing toluene (also known as toluol), xylene (also known as xylol), petroleum distillates, and/or turpentine in the concentrations described in § 1500.14(a)(3) and (5) are exempt from the labeling requirements

of § 1500.14(b)(3)(ii) and (5) if the visicosity of such products is sufficiently high so that they will not flow from their opened containers when inverted for 5 minutes at a temperature of 80 °F., and are exempt from bearing a flammability warning statement if the flammability of such waxes is due solely to the presence of solvents that have flashpoints above 80 °F. when tested by the method described in § 1500.43.

(9) Porous-tip ink-marking devices are exempt from the labeling requirements of section 2(p)(1) of the act (repeated in § 1500.3(b)(14)(i)) and from the labeling requirements of § 1500.14(b)(1), (2), and (3)(ii) and (iii) insofar as such requirements would be necessary because the ink contained therein is a toxic substance as defined in § 1500.3(c)(2)(i), and/or because the ink contains 10 percent or more by weight of toluene (also known as toluol), xylene (also known as xylol), or petroleum distillates as defined in § 1500.14(a)(3), and/or because the ink contains 10 percent or more by weight of ethylene glycol; provided that:

(i) The porous-tip ink-marking devices are of such construction that:

(A) The ink is held within the device by an absorbent material so that no free liquid is within the device; and

(B) Under any reasonably foreseeable conditions of manipulation and use, including reasonably foreseeable abuse by children, the ink will emerge only through the porous writing nib of the device; and

(ii)(A) The device has a capacity of not more than 10 grams of ink and the ink, when tested by methods described in § 1500.3(c)(2)(i), has an LD–50 single oral dose of not less than 2.5 grams per kilogram of body weight of the test animal; or

(B) The device has a capacity of not more than 12 grams of ink and the ink, when tested by methods described in § 1500.3(c)(2)(i), has an LD–50 single oral dose of not less than 3.0 grams per kilogram of body weight of the test animal.

(10) Viscous nitrocellulose-base adhesives containing more than 4 percent methyl alcohol by weight are exempt from the label statement "Cannot be be made nonpoisonous" required by § 1500.14(b)(4) if:

(i) The total amount of methyl alcohol by weight in the product does not exceed 15 percent; and

(ii) The contents of any container does not exceed 2 fluid ounces.

(11) Packages containing polishing or cleaning products which consist of a carrier of solid particulate or fibrous composition and which contain toluene (also known as toluol), xylene (also known as xylol), or petroleum distillates in the concentrations described in § 1500.14(a) (1) and (2) are exempt from the labeling requirements of § 1500.14(b)(3)(ii) if such toluene, xylene, or petroleum distillate is fully absorbed by the solid, semisolid, or fibrous carrier and cannot be expressed therefrom with any reasonably foreseeable conditions of manipulation.

(12) Containers of dry ink intended to be used as a liquid ink after the addition of water are exempt from the labeling requirements of section 2(p)(1) of the act (repeated in § 1500.3(b)(14)(i)) and from the labeling requirements of § 1500.14(b) (1) and (2) insofar as such requirements would be necessary because the dried ink contained therein is a toxic substance as defined in § 1500.3(c)(2)(i) and/or because the ink contains 10 percent or more of ethylene glycol as defined in § 1500.14(a)(2); provided that:

(i) When tested by the method described in § 1500.3(c)(2)(i), the dry ink concentrate does not have an LD–50 (lethal dose, median; lethal for 50 percent or more of test group) single oral dose of less than 1 gram per kilogram of body weight of the test animal.

(ii) The dry ink concentrate enclosed in a single container does not weigh more than 75 milligrams.

(iii) The dry ink concentrate does not contain over 15 percent by weight of ethylene glycol.

(13) Containers of liquid and semisolid substances such as viscous-type paints, varnishes, lacquers, roof coatings, rubber vulcanizing preparations, floor covering adhesives, glazing compounds, and other viscous products containing toluene (also known as toluol), xylene (also known as xylol), or petroleum distillates in concentrations described in § 1500.14(a)(3) are exempt from the labeling requirements of

§ 1500.14(b)(3)(ii) insofar as that subdivision applies to such toluene, xylene, or petroleum distillates, provided that the viscosity of the substance or of any liquid that may separate or be present in the container is not less than 100 Saybolt universal seconds at 100 °F.

(14) Customer-owned portable containers that are filled by retail vendors with gasoline, kerosene (kerosine), or other petroleum distillates are exempt from the provision of section 2(p)(1)(A) of the act (which requires that the name and place of business of the manufacturer, distributor, packer, or seller appear on the label of such containers) provided that all the other label statements required by section 2(p)(1) of the act and § 1500.14(b)(3) appear on the labels of containers of the substances named in this subparagraph.

(15) Cellulose sponges are exempt from the labeling requirements of section 2(p)(1) of the act and § 1500.14(b)(1) insofar as such requirements would be necessary because they contain 10 percent or more of diethylene glycol as defined in § 1500.14(a)(1), provided that:

(i) The cellulose sponge does not contain over 15 percent by weight of diethylene glycol; and

(ii) The diethylene glycol content is completely held by the absorbent cellulose material so that no free liquid is within the sponge as marketed.

(16) Containers of substances which include salt (sodium chloride) as a component are exempt from the labeling requirements of section 2(p)(1) of the act (repeated in § 1500.3(b)(14)(i)) insofar as such requirements would be necessary because the salt contained therein is present in a quantity sufficient to render the article "toxic" as defined in § 1500.3(3)(2)(i), provided that the labels of such containers bear a conspicuous statement that the product contains salt.

(17) The labeling of substances containing 10 percent or more of ferrous oxalate is exempt from the requirement of § 1500.129(f) that it bear the word "poison" which would be required for such concentration of a salt of oxalic acid.

(18) Packages containing articles intended as single-use spot removers, and which consist of a cotton pad or other absorbent material saturated with a mixture of drycleaning solvents, are exempt from the labeling requirements of section 2(p)(1) of the act (repeated in § 1500.3(b)(14)(i)) insofar as they apply to the "flammable solid" hazard as defined in § 1500.3(c)(6)(vi), provided that:

(i) The article is packaged in a sealed foil envelope;

(ii) The total amount of solvent in each package does not exceed 4.5 milliliters; and

(iii) The article will ignite only when in contact with an open flame, and when so ignited, the article burns with a sooty flame.

(19) Packages containing articles intended as single-use spot removers, and which consist of a cotton pad or other absorbent material containing methyl alcohol, are exempt from the labeling requirements of § 1500.14(b)(4), if:

(i) The total amount of cleaning solvent in each package does not exceed 4.5 milliliters of which not more than 25 percent is methyl alcohol; and

(ii) The liquid is completely held by the absorbent materials so that no free liquid is within the packages marketed.

(20) Cigarette lighters containing petroleum distillate fuel are exempt from the labeling requirements of section 2(p)(1) of the act (repeated in § 1500.3(b)(14)(i)) and § 1500.14(b)(3) insofar as such requirements would be necessary because the petroleum distillate contained therein is flammable and because the substance is named in § 1500.14(a)(3) as requiring special labeling, provided that:

(i) Such lighters contain not more than 10 cubic centimeters of fuel at the time of sale; and

(ii) Such fuel is contained in a sealed compartment that cannot be opened without the deliberate removal of the flush-set, screw-type refill plug of the lighter.

(21) Containers of dry granular fertilizers and dry granular plant foods are exempt from the labeling requirements of section 2(p)(1) of the act (repeated in § 1500.3(b)(14)(i)) insofar as such requirements would be necessary because the fertilizer or plant food contained therein is a toxic substance as defined in § 1500.3(c)(2)(i), provided that:

(i) When tested by the method described in § 1500.3(c)(2)(i), the product has a single dose LD–50 of not less than 3.0 grams per kilogram of body weight of the test animal;

(ii) The label of any such exempt dry granular fertilizers discloses the identity of each of the hazardous ingredients;

(iii) The label bears the name and address of the manufacturer, packer, distributor, or seller; and

(iv) The label bears the statement "Keep out of the reach of children" or its practical equivalent.

(22) Small plastic capsules containing a paste composed of powdered metal solder mixed with a liquid flux are exempt from the requirements of section 2(p)(1) of the act (repeated in §1500.3(b)(14)(i)), if:

(i) The capsule holds not more than one-half milliliter of the solder mixture;

(ii) The capsule is sold only as a component of a kit; and

(iii) Adequate caution statements appear on the carton of the kit and on any accompanying labeling which bears directions for use.

(23) Chemistry sets and other science education sets intended primarily for use by juveniles, and replacement containers of chemicals for such sets, are exempt from the requirements of section 2(p)(1) of the act (repeated in §1500.3(b)(14)(i)), if:

(i) The immediate container of each chemical that is hazardous as defined in the act and regulations thereunder bears on its main panel the name of such chemical, the appropriate signal word for that chemical, and the additional statement "Read back panel before using" (or "Read side panel before using," if appropriate) and bears on the back (or side) panel of the immediate container the remainder of the appropriate cautionary statement for the specific chemical in the container;

(ii) The experiment manual or other instruction book or booklet accompanying such set bears on the front page thereof, as a preface to any written matter in it (or on the cover, if any there be), the following caution statement within the borders of a rectangle and in the type size specified in §1500.121:

WARNING—This set contains chemicals that may be harmful if misused. Read cautions on individual containers carefully. Not to be used by children except under adult supervision

; and

(iii) The outer carton of such set bears on the main display panel within the borders of a rectangle, and in the type size specified in §1500.121, the caution statement specified in paragraph (a)(23)(ii) of this section.

(24) Fire extinguishers containing fire extinguishing agents which are stored under pressure or which develop pressure under normal conditions of use are exempt from the labeling requirements of section 2(p)(1) of the act (repeated in §1500.3(b)(14)(i)) insofar as such requirements apply to the pressure hazard as defined in §1500.3(c)(7)(i), provided that:

(i) If the container is under pressure both during storage and under conditions of use, it shall be designed to withstand a pressure of at least 6 times the charging pressure at 70 °F., except that carbon dioxide extinguishers shall be constructed and tested in accordance with applicable Interstate Commerce Commission specifications; or

(ii) If the container is under pressure only during conditions of use, it shall be designed to withstand a pressure of not less than 5 times the maximum pressure developed under closed nozzle conditions at 70 °F. or 1½ times the maximum pressure developed under closed nozzle conditions at 120 °F., whichever is greater.

(25) Cleaning and spot removing kits intended for use in cleaning carpets, furniture, and other household objects; kits intended for use in coating, painting, antiquing, and similarly processing furniture, furnishings, equipment, sidings, and various other surfaces; and kits intended for use in photographic color processing are exempt from the requirements of section 2(p)(1) of the act (repeated in §1500.3(b)(14)(i)) and from the requirements of §1500.14, provided that:

(i) The immediate container of each hazardous substance in the kit is fully labeled and in conformance with the requirements of the act and regulations thereunder; and

(ii) The carton of the kit bears on the main display panel (or panels) within a borderline, and in the type size specified in § 1500.121, the caution statement "(Insert proper signal word as specified in paragraph (a)(25)(iii) of this section). This kit contains the following chemicals that may be harmful if misused: (List hazardous chemical components by name.) Read cautions on individual containers carefully. Keep out of the reach of children."

(iii) If either the word "POISON" or "DANGER" is required on the container of any component of the kit, the same word shall be required to appear as part of the caution statement on the kit carton. If both "POISON" and "DANGER" are required in the labeling of any component or components in the kit, the word "POISON" shall be used. In all other cases the word "WARNING" or "CAUTION" shall be used.

(26) Packages containing articles intended as single-use spot removers and containing methyl alcohol are exempt from the labeling specified in § 1500.14(b)(4), if:

(i) The total amount of cleaning solvent in each unit does not exceed 1 milliliter, of which not more than 40 percent is methyl alcohol;

(ii) The liquid is contained in a sealed glass ampoule enclosed in a plastic container with a firmly attached absorbent wick at one end through which the liquid from the crushed ampoule must pass, under the contemplated conditions of use; and

(iii) The labeling of each package of the cleaner bears the statement "WARNING—Keep out of the reach of children," or its practical equivalent, and the name and place of business of the manufacturer, packer, distributor, or seller.

(27) Packaged fireworks assortments intended for retail distribution are exempt from section 2(p)(1) of the act (repeated in § 1500.3(b)(14)(i)), if:

(i) The package contains only fireworks devices suitable for use by the public and designed primarily to produce visible effects by combustion, except that small devices designed to produce audible effects may also be included if the audible effect is produced by a charge of not more than 2 grains of pyrotechnic composition;

(ii) Each individual article in the assortment is fully labeled and in conformance with the requirements of the act and regulations thereunder; and

(iii) The outer package bears on the main display panel (or panels), within the borders of a rectangle and in the type size specified in § 1500.121, the caution statement "WARNING—This assortment contains items that may be hazardous if misused and should be used only under adult supervision. IMPORTANT—Read cautions on individual items carefully." (See also § 1500.14(b)(7); § 1500.17(a) (3), (8) and (9); § 1500.85(a)(2); and part 1507).

(28) Packages containing felt pads impregnated with ethylene glycol are exempt from the labeling requirements of § 1500.14(b)(1), if:

(i) The total amount of ethylene glycol in each pad does not exceed 1 gram; and

(ii) The liquid is held by the felt pad so that no free ethylene glycol is within the package.

(29) Cigarette lighters containing butane and/or isobutane fuel are exempt from the labeling requirements of section 2(p)(1) of the act (repeated in § 1500.3(b)(14)(i)) insofar as such requirements would otherwise be necessary because the fuel therein is extremely flammable and under pressure, provided that:

(i) The lighters contain not more than 12 grams of fuel at the time of sale; and

(ii) The fuel reservoir is designed to withstand a pressure of at least 1½ times the maximum pressure which will be developed in the container at 120 °F.

(30) The outer retail containers of solder kits each consisting of a small tube of flux partially surrounded by a winding of wire-type cadmium-free silver solder are exempt from the labeling requirements of section 2(p)(1) of the act (repeated in § 1500.3(b)(14)(i)), if:

(i) The metal solder contains no cadmium and is not otherwise hazardous under the provisions of the act;

(ii) The tube of flux in the kit is fully labeled and in conformance with the act and regulations thereunder, and any accompanying literature that bears directions for use also bears all the information required by section 2(p) of the act; and

(iii) The main panel of the outer container bears in type size specified in §1500.121 the following: (A) The signal word; (B) a statement of principal hazard or hazards; (C) the statement "Keep out of the reach of children," or its practical equivalent; and (D) instructions to read other cautionary instructions on the tube of flux within.

(31) Visual novelty devices consisting of sealed units, each of which unit is a steel and glass cell containing perchloroethylene (among other things), are exempt from the requirements of §1500.121(a) that would otherwise require a portion of the warning statement to appear on the glass face of the device, provided that:

(i) The device contains not more than 105 milliliters of perchloroethylene and contains no other component that contributes substantially to the hazard; and

(ii) The following cautionary statement appears on the device (other than on the bottom) in the type size specified in §1500.121 (c) and (d):

CAUTION—IF BROKEN, RESULTANT VAPORS MAY BE HARMFUL

Contains perchloroethylene. Do not expose to extreme heat. If broken indoors, open windows and doors until all odor of chemical is gone.

Keep out of the reach of children.

A practical equivalent may be substituted for the statement "Keep out of the reach of children."

(32) Hollow plastic toys containing mineral oil are exempt from the labeling specified in §1500.14(b)(3)(ii), if:

(i) The article contains no other ingredient that would cause it to possess the aspiration hazard specified in §1500.14(b)(3)(ii);

(ii) The article contains not more than 6 fluid ounces of mineral oil;

(iii) The mineral oil has a viscosity of at least 70 Saybolt universal seconds at 100 °F.;

(iv) The mineral oil meets the specifications in the N.F. for light liquid petrolatum; and

(v) The container bears the statement "CAUTION—Contains light liquid petrolatum N.F. Discard if broken or leak develops."

(33) Containers of mineral oil having a capacity of not more than 1 fluid ounce and intended for use in producing a smoke effect for toy trains are exempt from the labeling specified in §1500.14(b)(3), if:

(i) The mineral oil meets the specifications in the N.F. for light liquid petrolatum;

(ii) The mineral oil has a viscosity of at least 130 Saybolt universal seconds at 100 °F.;

(iii) The article contains no other ingredient that contributes to the hazard; and

(iv) The label declares the presence light liquid petrolatum and the name and place of business of the manufacturer, packer, distributor, or seller.

(34) Viscous products containing more than 4 percent by weight of methyl alcohol, such as adhesives, asphalt-base roof and tank coatings, and similar products, are exempt from bearing the special labeling required by §1500.14(b)(4), if:

(i) The product contains not more than 15 percent by weight of methyl alcohol;

(ii) The methyl alcohol does not separate from the other ingredients upon standing or through any foreseeable use or manipulation;

(iii) The viscosity of the product is not less than 7,000 centipoises at 77 °F., unless the product is packaged in a pressurized container and is dispensed as a liquid unsuitable for drinking; and

(iv) The labeling bears the statement "Contains methyl alcohol. Use only in well-ventilated area. Keep out of the reach of children."

(35) Individual detonators or blasting caps are exempt from bearing the statement, "Keep out of the reach of children," or its practical equivalent, if:

(i) Each detonator or cap bears conspicuously in the largest type size practicable the statement, "DANGEROUS—BLASTING CAPS—EXPLOSIVE" or "DANGEROUS—DETONATOR—EXPLOSIVE"; and

(ii) The outer carton and any accompanying printed matter bear appropriate, complete cautionary labeling.

(36) Individual toy rocket propellant devices and separate delay train and/or

recovery system activation devices intended for use with premanufactured model rocket engines are exempt from bearing the full labeling required by section 2(p)(1) of the act (repeated in § 1500.3(b)(14)(i)) insofar as such requirements would be necessary because the articles are flammable or generate pressure, provided that:

(i) The devices are designed and constructed in accordance with the specifications in § 1500.85(a)(8), (9) or (14);

(ii) Each individual device or retail package of devices bears the following:

(A) The statement "WARNING—FLAMMABLE: Read instructions before use";

(B) The common or usual name of the article;

(C) A statement of the type of engine and use classification;

(D) Instructions for safe disposal; and

(E) Name and place of business of manufacturer or distributor; and

(iii) Each individual rocket engine or retail package of rocket engines distributed to users is accompanied by an instruction sheet bearing complete cautionary labeling and instructions for safe use and handling of the individual rocket engines.

(37) Glues with a cyanoacrylate base in packages containing 3 grams or less are exempt from the requirement of § 1500.121(d) that labeling which is permitted to appear elsewhere than on the main label panel must be in type size no smaller than 6 point type, provided that:

(i) The main panel of the immediate container bears both the proper signal word and a statement of the principal hazard or hazards associated with this product, as provided by § 1500.121 (a) and (c);

(ii) The main panel of the immediate container also bears an instruction to read carefully additional warnings elsewhere on the label and on any outer package, accompanying leaflet, and display card. The instruction to read additional warnings must comply with the size, placement, conspicuousness, and contrast requirements of § 1500.121; and

(iii) The remainder of the cautionary labeling required by the act that is not on the main label panel must appear elsewhere on the label in legible type and must appear on any outer package, accompanying leaflet, and display card. If there is no outer package, accompanying leaflet, or display card, then the remainder of the required cautionary labeling must be displayed on a tag or other suitable material that is securely affixed to the article so that the labeling will remain attached throughout the conditions of merchandising and distribution to the ultimate consumer. That labeling which must appear on any outer package, accompanying leaflet, tag, or other suitable material must comply with the size, placement, contrast, and conspicuousness requirements of § 1500.121(d).

(38) Rigid or semi-rigid writing instruments and ink cartridges having a writing point and an ink reservoir are exempt from the labeling requirements of section 2(p)(1) of the act (repeated in § 1500.3(b)(14)(i) of the regulations) and of regulations issued under section 3(b) of the act (§ 1500.14(b)(1, 2)) insofar as such requirements would be necessary because the ink contained therein is a "toxic" substance as defined in § 1500.3(c)(2)(i) and/or because the ink contains 10 percent or more by weight ethylene glycol or diethylene glycol, if all the following conditions are met:

(i) The writing instrument or cartridge is of such construction that the ink will, under any reasonably foreseeable condition of manipulation and use, emerge only from the writing tip.

(ii) When tested by the method described in § 1500.3(c)(2)(i), the ink does not have an LD–50 single oral dose of less than 2.5 grams per kilogram of body weight of the test animal.

(iii) If the ink contains ethylene glycol or diethylene glycol, the amount of such substance, either singly or in combination, does not exceed 1 gram per writing instrument or cartridge.

(iv) The amount of ink in the writing instrument or cartridge does not exceed 3 grams.

[38 FR 27012, Sept. 27, 1973; 42 FR 33026, June 29, 1977, as amended at 43 FR 32745, July 28, 1978; 43 FR 47176, Oct. 13, 1978; 44 FR 42678, July 20, 1979; 46 FR 11513, Feb. 9, 1981; 48 FR 16, Jan. 3, 1983; 68 FR 4699, Jan. 30, 2003; 74 FR 27249, June 9, 2009; 75 FR 49380, Aug. 13, 2010]

§ 1500.85 Exemptions from classification as banned hazardous substances.

(a) The term *banned hazardous substances* as used in section 2(q)(1)(A) of the act shall not apply to the following articles provided that these articles bear labeling giving adequate directions and warnings for safe use:

(1) Chemistry sets and other science education sets intended primarily for juveniles, and replacement components for such sets, when labeled in accordance with § 1500.83(a)(23).

(2) Firecrackers designed to produce audible effects, if the audible effect is produced by a charge of not more than 50 milligrams (.772 grains) of pyrotechnic composition. (See also § 1500.14(b)(7); § 1500.17(a) (3), (8) and (9); and part 1507).

(3) [Reserved]

(4) Educational materials such as art materials, preserved biological specimens, laboratory chemicals, and other articles intended and used for educational purposes.

(5) Liquid fuels containing more than 4 percent by weight of methyl alcohol that are intended and used for operation of miniature engines for model airplanes, boats, cars, etc.

(6) Novelties consisting of a mixture of polyvinyl acetate, U.S. Certified Colors, and not more than 25 percent by weight of acetone, and intended for blowing plastic balloons.

(7) Games containing, as the sole hazardous component, a self-pressurized container of soap solution or similar foam-generating mixture provided that the foam-generating component has no hazards other than being in a self-pressurized container.

(8) Model rocket propellant devices designed for use in light-weight, recoverable, and reflyable model rockets, provided such devices:

(i) Are designed to be ignited by electrical means.

(ii) Contain no more than 62.5 grams (2.2 ounces) of propellant material and produce less than 80 newton-seconds (17.92 pound seconds) of total impulse with thrust duration not less than 0.050 second.

(iii) Are constructed such that all the chemical ingredients are preloaded into a cylindrical paper or similarly constructed nonmetallic tube that will not fragment into sharp, hard pieces.

(iv) Are designed so that they will not burst under normal conditions of use, are incapable of spontaneous ignition, and do not contain any type of explosive or pyrotechnic warhead other than a small parachute or recovery-system activation charge.

(9) Separate delay train and/or recovery system activation devices intended for use with premanufactured model rocket engines wherein all of the chemical ingredients are preloaded so the user does not handle any chemical ingredient and are so designed that the main casing or container does not rupture during operation.

(10) Solid fuel pellets intended for use in miniature jet engines for propelling model jet airplanes, speed boats, racing cars, and similar models, provided such solid fuel pellets:

(i) Weigh not more than 11.5 grams each.

(ii) Are coated with a protective resinous film.

(iii) Contain not more than 35 percent potassium dichromate.

(iv) Produce a maximum thrust of not more than 7½ ounces when used as directed.

(v) Burn not longer than 12 seconds each when used as directed.

(11) Fuses intended for igniting fuel pellets exempt under subparagraph (10) of this paragraph.

(12) Kits intended for construction of model rockets and jet propelled model airplanes requiring the use of difluorodichloromethane as a propellant, provided the outer carton bears on the main panel in conspicuous type size the statement "WARNING—Carefully read instructions and cautions before use."

(13) Flammable wire materials intended for electro-mechanical actuation and release devices for model kits described in paragraph (12) of this section, provided each wire does not exceed 15 milligrams in weight.

(14) Model rocket propellant devices (model rocket motors) designed to propel rocket-powered model cars, provided—

(i) Such devices:

(A) Are designed to be ignited electrically and are intended to be operated from a minimum distance of 15 feet (4.6 m) away;

(B) Contain no more than 4 g. of propellant material and produce no more than 2.5 Newton-seconds of total impulse with a thrust duration not less than 0.050 seconds;

(C) Are constructed such that all the chemical ingredients are pre-loaded into a cylindrical paper or similarly constructed non-metallic tube that will not fragment into sharp, hard pieces;

(D) Are designed so that they will not burst under normal conditions of use, are incapable of spontaneous ignition, and do not contain any type of explosive or pyrotechnic warhead other than a small recovery system activation charge;

(E) Bear labeling, including labeling that the devices are intended for use by persons age 12 and older, and include instructions providing adequate warnings and instructions for safe use; and

(F) Comply with the requirements of 16 CFR 1500.83(a)(36)(ii and iii); and

(ii) The surface vehicles intended for use with such devices:

(A) Are lightweight, weighing no more than 3.0 oz. (85 grams), and constructed mainly of materials such as balsa wood or plastics that will not fragment into sharp, hard pieces;

(B) Are designed to utilize a braking system such as a parachute or shock absorbing stopping mechanism;

(C) Are designed so that they cannot accept propellant devices measuring larger than 0.5″ (13 mm) in diameter and 1.75″ (44 mm) in length;

(D) Are designed so that the engine mount is permanently attached by the manufacturer to a track or track line that controls the vehicle's direction for the duration of its movement;

(E) Are not designed to carry any type of explosive or pyrotechnic material other than the model rocket motor used for primary propulsion;

(F) Bear labeling and include instructions providing adequate warnings and instructions for safe use; and

(G) Are designed to operate on a track or line that controls the vehicles' direction for the duration of their movement and either cannot operate off the track or line or, if operated off the track or line, are unstable and fail to operate in a guided fashion so that they will not strike the operator or bystanders.

(b) [Reserved]

[38 FR 27012, Sept. 27, 1973, as amended at 41 FR 22935, June 8, 1976; 42 FR 43391, Aug. 29, 1977; 48 FR 16, Jan. 3, 1983; 68 FR 4699, Jan. 30, 2003]

§ 1500.86 Exemptions from classification as a banned toy or other banned article for use by children.

(a) The term *banned hazardous substance* as used in section 2(q)(1)(A) of the act (repeated in §1500.3(b)(15)(i)(A)) of the act shall not apply to the following articles:

(1) Toy rattles described in §1500.18(a)(1) in which the rigid wires, sharp protrusions, or loose small objects are internal and provided that such rattles are constructed so that they will not break or deform to expose or release the contents either in normal use or when subjected to reasonably foreseeable damage or abuse.

(2) Dolls and stuffed animals and other similar toys described in §1500.18(a)(3) in which the components that have the potential for causing laceration, puncture wound injury, or other similar injury are internal, provided such dolls, stuffed animals, and other similar toys are constructed so that they will not break or deform to expose such components either in normal use or when subjected to reasonably foreseeable damage or abuse.

(3) [Reserved]

(4) Any article known as a "baby-bouncer" or "walker-jumper" and any other similar article (referred to in this paragraph as "article(s)"), except an infant walker subject to part 1216 of this chapter, described in §1500.18(a)(6) provided:

(i) The frames are designed and constructed in a manner to prevent injury from any scissoring, shearing, or pinching when the members of the frame or other components rotate about a common axis or fastening point or otherwise move relative to one another; and

(ii) Any coil springs which expand when the article is subjected to a force that will extend the spring to its maximum distance so that a space between successive coils is greater than one-eighth inch (0.125 inch) are covered or otherwise designed to prevent injuries; and

(iii) All holes larger than one-eighth inch (0.125 inch) in diameter and slots, cracks, or hinged components in any portion of the article through which a child could insert, in whole or in part a finger, toe, or any other part of the anatomy are guarded or otherwise designed to prevent injuries; and

(iv) The articles are designed and constructed to prevent accidental collapse while in use; and

(v) The articles are designed and constructed in a manner that eliminates from any portion of the article the possibility of presenting a mechanical hazard through pinching, bruising, lacerating, crushing, breaking, amputating, or otherwise injuring portions of the human body when in normal use or when subjected to reasonably foreseeable damage or abuse; and

(vi) Any article which is introduced into interstate commerce after the effective date of this subparagraph is labeled:

(A) With a conspicuous statement of the name and address of the manufacturer, packer, distributor, or seller; and

(B) With a code mark on the article itself and on the package containing the article or on the shipping container, in addition to the invoice(s) or shipping document(s), which code mark will permit future identification by the manufacturer of any given model (the manufacturer shall change the model number whenever the article undergoes a significant structural or design modification); and

(vii) The manufacturer or importer of the article shall make, keep, and maintain for 3 years records of sale, distribution, and results of inspections and tests conducted in accordance with this subparagraph and shall make such records available at all reasonable hours upon request by any officer or employee of the Consumer Product Safety Commission and shall permit such officer or employee to inspect and copy such records, to make such stock inventories as he deems necessary, and to otherwise check the correctness of such records.

(5) Clacker balls described in §1500.18(a)(7) that have been designed, manufactured, assembled, labeled, and tested in accordance with the following requirements, and when tested at the point of production or while in interstate commerce or while held for sale after shipment in interstate commerce do not exceed the failure rate requirements of the table in paragraph (a)(5)(vi) of this section:

(i) The toy shall be so designed and fabricated that:

(A) Each ball: Weighs less than 50 grams; will not shatter, crack, or chip; is free of cracks, flash (ridges due to imperfect molding), and crazing (tiny surface cracks); and is free of rough or sharp edges around any hole where the cord enters or over any surface with which the cord may make contact. Each ball is free of internal voids (holes, cavities, or air bubbles) if the balls are made of materials other than those materials (such as ABS (acrylonitrile butadiene styrene), nylon, and high-impact polystyrene) that are injection-molded and possess high-impact characteristics.

(B) The cord: Is of high tensile strength, synthetic fibers that are braided or woven, having a breaking strength in excess of 445 Newtons (100 pounds); is free of fraying or any other defect that might tend to reduce its strength in use; is not molded in balls made of casting resins which tend to wick up or run up on the outside of the cord; and is affixed to a ball at the center of the horizontal plane of the ball when it is suspended by the cord. Clacker balls where the mass of each ball is less than 12 grams (0.42 oz.) and the distance between the center of the pivot and the center of the ball cannot exceed 180 mm (7.1 inches) may have a minimum cord breaking strength of less than 445 Newtons (100 pounds), as computed by the following formula:

Adjusted Cord Breaking Strength in Newtons=0.1382(m_b) (R_p), where m_b=mass of a single ball in grams and

R_p=pivot length in mm.

(C) When the cord is attached to the ball by means of a knot, the end beneath the knot is chemically fused or otherwise treated to prevent the knot from slipping out or untying in use.

(ii) The toy shall be tested at the time of production:

(A) By using the sampling procedure described in the table in subdivision (vi) of this subparagraph to determine the number of units to be tested.

(B) By subjecting each ball tested to 10 drops of a 2.25 kg (5-pound) steel impact rod or weight (57-mm (2¼-inch) diameter with a flat head) dropped 1220 mm (48 inches) in a vented steel or aluminum tube (60-mm (2⅜-inch) inside diameter) when the ball is placed on a steel or cast iron mount. Clacker balls where the mass of each ball is less than 12 grams (0.42 oz.) and the distance between the center of the pivot and the center of the ball cannot exceed 180 mm (7.1 inches) may be tested by dropping the impact weight from a height of less than 1220 mm (48 in.), where the height is computed as follows:

Adjusted drop height in mm=$179\times10^{-5}(m_b)(R_p2)$, where m_b=mass of a single ball in grams and

R_p=pivot length in mm.

Any ball showing any chipping, cracking, or shattering shall be counted as a failure within the meaning of the third column of the table in paragraph (a)(5)(vi) of this section.

(C) By inspecting each ball tested for smoothness of finish on any surface of the ball which may come in contact with the cord during use. A cotton swab shall be rubbed vigorously over each such surface or area of the ball; if any cotton fibers are removed, the ball shall be counted as a failure within the meaning of the fourth column of the table in subdivision (vi) of this paragraph. The toy shall also be checked to ascertain that there is no visibly perceptible "wicking up" or "running up" of the casting resins on the outside of the cord in the vicinity where the ball is attached.

(D) By fully assembling the toy and testing the cord in such a manner as to test both the strength of the cord and the adequacy with which the cord is attached to the ball and any holding device such as a tab or ring included in the assembly. The fully assembled article shall be vertically suspended by one ball and a 445-Newton (100-pound) test applied to the bottom ball. Clacker balls where the mass of each ball is less than 12 grams (0.42 oz.) and the distance between the center of the pivot and the center of the ball cannot exceed 180 mm (7.1 inches) may be tested with a force of under 445 Newtons (100 pounds). The test force for these clacker balls shall be the same as the cord breaking strength calculated in §1500.86(a)(5)(i)(B). Any breaking, fraying, or unraveling of the cord or any sign of slipping, loosening, or unfastening shall be counted as a failure within the meaning of the fourth column of the table in paragraph (a)(5)(vi) of this section.

(E) By additionally subjecting any ring or other holding device to a 222-Newton (50-pound) test load applied to both cords; the holding device is to be securely fixed horizontally in a suitable clamp in such a manner as to support 50 percent of the area of such holding device and the balls are suspended freely. Clacker balls where the mass of each ball is less than 12 grams (0.42 oz.) and the distance between the center of the pivot and the center of the ball cannot exceed 180 mm (7.1 inches) may have their holding device tested with a force of less than 222 Newtons (50 pounds). The holding device test force for these clacker balls shall be half of the cord breaking strength calculated in §1500.86(a)(5)(i)(B). Any breaking, cracking, or crazing of the ring or other holding device shall be counted as a failure within the meaning of the fourth column of the table in paragraph (a)(5)(vi) of this section.

(F) By cutting each ball tested in half and then cutting each half perpendicularly to the first cut into three or more pieces of approximately equal thickness. Each portion is to be inspected before and after cutting, and any ball showing any flash, crack, crazing, or internal voids on such inspection is to be counted as a failure within the meaning of the fourth column of the table in paragraph (a)(5)(vi) of this section. Balls that are injection-molded and possess high-impact characteristics (such as injection-molded balls made of ABS, nylon, or high-impact polystyrene) though exempt from the requirements that there be no internal voids, must be tested to determine the presence of any flash, crack or grazing. A transparent ball shall be subjected to the same requirements except that it may be visually inspected without cutting.

(iii) The toy shall be fully assembled for use at time of sale, including the proper attachments of balls, cords, knots, loops, or other holding devices.

(iv) The toy shall be labeled:

(A) With a conspicuous statement of the name and address of the manufacturer, packer, distributor, or seller.

(B) To bear on the toy itself and/or the package containing the toy and/or the shipping container, in addition to the invoice(s) and shipping document(s), a code or mark in a form and manner that will permit future identification of any given batch, lot, or shipment by the manufacturer.

(C) To bear a conspicuous warning statement on the main panel of the retail container and display carton and on any accompanying literature: That if cracks develop in a ball or if the cord becomes frayed or loose or unfastened, use of the toy should be discontinued; and if a ring or loop or other holding device is present, the statement "In use, the ring or loop must be placed around the middle finger and the two cords positioned over the forefinger and held securely between the thumb and forefinger," or words to that effect which will provide adequate instructions and warnings to prevent the holding device from accidentally slipping out of the hand. Such statements shall be printed in sharply contrasting color within a borderline and in letters at least 6 mm (1/4 inch) high on the main panel of the container and at least 3 mm (1/8) high on all accompanying literature.

(v) The manufacturer of the toy shall make, keep, and maintain for 3 years records of sale, distribution, and results of inspections and tests conducted in accordance with this subparagraph and shall make such records available upon request at all reasonable hours by any officer or employee of the Consumer Product Safety Commission, and shall permit such officer or employee to inspect and copy such records and to make such inventories of stock as he deems necessary and otherwise to check the correctness of such records.

(vi) The lot size, sample size, and failure rate for testing clacker balls are as follows:

Number of units in batch, shipment, delivery, lot, or retail stock	Number of units in random sample	Failure rate constituting rejection when testing per § 1500.86(a)(5)(ii)(B)	Failure rate constituting rejection when testing per § 1500.86(a)(5)(ii) (C), (D), (E), and (F)
50 or less	8	1	1
51 to 90	13	1	1
91 to 150	20	1	1
151 to 280	32	1	2
281 to 500	50	1	2
501 to 1,200	80	2	4
1,201 to 3,200	125	2	6
3,201 to 10,000	200	3	10
10,001 to 35,000	315	4	16
35,001 to 150,000	500	6	25
150,001 to 500,000	800	8	40
500,001 and over	1,250	11	62

(vii) Applicability of the exemption provided by this paragraph shall be determined through use of the table in paragraph (a)(5)(vi) of this section. A random sample of the number of articles as specified in the second column of the table shall be selected according to the number of articles in a particular batch, shipment, delivery, lot, or retail stock per the first column. A failure rate as shown in either the third or fourth column shall indicate that the entire batch, shipment, delivery, lot, or retail stock has failed and thus is not exempted under this paragraph from classification as a banned hazardous substance.

(6) Caps (paper or plastic) described in § 1500.18(a)(5), provided:

(i) Such articles do not produce peak sound pressure levels greater than 158 decibels when tested in accordance with § 1500.47, and provided any such articles producing peak sound pressure levels greater than 138 decibels but not greater than 158 decibels when tested in accordance with § 1500.47 shall bear the following statement on the carton and in the accompanying literature in accordance with § 1500.121: "WARNING—Do not fire closer than 1 foot to the ear. Do not use indoors."

(ii) Any person who elects to distribute toy caps in accordance with paragraph (a)(6)(i) of this section shall promptly notify the Consumer Product Safety Commission, Bureau of Compliance, Washington, D.C. 20207, of their intention and shall conduct or participate in a program to develop caps that produce a sound pressure level of not more than 138 decibels when tested in accordance with § 1500.47.

(iii) Any person who elects to distribute caps in accordance with paragraph (a)(6)(i) of this section shall, after notification of his intentions to the Commission in accordance with paragraph (a)(6)(ii) of this section, submit to the Consumer Product Safety Commission, Bureau of Compliance, Washington, DC 20207, a progress report not less frequently than once every 3 months concerning the status of his program to develop caps that produce a sound level of not more than 138 decibels when tested in accordance with § 1500.47.

(7) Dive sticks and similar articles described in § 1500.18(a)(19) that come to rest at the bottom of a container of water in a position in which the long axis of the article is greater than 45 degrees from vertical when measured in accordance with the following test method:

(i) Test equipment.

(A) A container that is filled with tap water to a depth at least 3 inches [76 mm] greater than the longest dimension of the dive stick. The container shall:

(*1*) Be sufficiently wide to allow the dive stick to lie along the bottom with its long axis in a horizontal position,

(*2*) Have clear side walls to permit observation of the dive stick under water, and

(*3*) Be placed on a level surface and have a flat bottom.

(B) A protractor or other suitable angle measurement device that has an indicator for 45 degrees from vertical.

(ii) Testing procedure

(A) If the dive stick is sold such that the consumer is required to attach an additional component(s) to the dive stick, then the product shall be tested both with and without the attachment(s).

(B) From just above the water surface, drop the dive stick into the container.

(C) Let the dive stick sink and come to rest at the bottom of the container. If the dive stick is designed so that the weight can be adjusted by adding water or other substance, adjust the weight so that the dive stick sinks and comes to rest with its long axis positioned as close to vertical as possible.

(D) Align the angle measurement device alongside the dive stick underwater and wait for the dive stick to come to rest if there is any water disturbance. Determine whether the long axis of the dive stick is greater than or less than 45 degrees from vertical.

(8) Dive sticks and similar articles described in § 1500.18(a)(19) in which the maximum force measured in the following test method is less than 5–lbf [22N]. The test shall be conducted in the ambient environment of the laboratory and not under water.

(i) Test equipment.

(A) A compression rig that has a force gauge or equivalent device that is calibrated for force measurements within a minimum range of 0 to 5 lbf [0–22 N] and with an accuracy of ±0.1 lbf [±0.44 N] or better. The test rig shall have a system to guide this force application in the vertical direction and shall have a means to adjust the rate of load application.

(B) Compression disk—the loading device that is attached to the force gauge shall be a rigid metal disk with a minimum diameter of 1.125 inches [29 mm].

(C) Vise or other clamping device.

(ii) Testing procedure

(A) Position the bottom of the dive stick in the clamping device so that the longest axis of the dive stick is vertical. The bottom end of the dive stick is the end that sinks to the bottom of a pool of water. Secure the bottom of the dive stick in the clamp such that the clamping mechanism covers no more than the bottom ½ inch [13 mm] of the dive stick.

(B) Apply a downward force at a rate of 0.05 in/sec (±0.01 in/sec) [1.3 mm.sec ±0.3 mm/sec] at the top of the dive stick with the compression disk positioned so that the plane of the disk contact surface is perpendicular to the long axis of the dive stick.

(C) Apply the load for a period of 40 seconds or until the maximum recorded force exceeds 5-lbf [22 N].

(D) Record the maximum force that was measured during the test.

(b) [Reserved]

(9) Boston Billow Nursing Pillow and substantially similar nursing pillows that are designed to be used only as a nursing aide for breastfeeding mothers. For example, are tubular in form, C- or crescent-shaped to fit around a nursing mother's waist, round in circumference and filled with granular material.

[38 FR 27012, Sept. 27, 1973, as amended at 53 FR 46839, Nov. 18, 1988; 59 FR 9076, 9077, Feb. 25, 1994; 66 FR 13651, Mar. 7, 2001; 68 FR 70140, Dec. 17, 2003; 73 FR 77495, Dec. 19, 2008; 75 FR 35282, June 21, 2010]

§ 1500.87 Children's products containing lead: inaccessible component parts.

(a) The Consumer Product Safety Improvement Act (CPSIA) provides for specific lead limits in children's products. Section 101(a) of the CPSIA provides that by February 10, 2009, products designed or intended primarily for children 12 and younger may not contain more than 600 ppm of lead. After August 14, 2009, products designed or intended primarily for children 12 and younger cannot contain more than 300 ppm of lead. On August 14, 2011, the limit may be further reduced to 100 ppm after three years, unless the Commission determines that it is not technologically feasible to have this lower limit.

(b) Section 101 (b)(2) of the CPSIA provides that the lead limits do not apply to component parts of a product that are not accessible to a child. This section specifies that a component part is not accessible if it is not physically exposed by reason of a sealed covering or casing and does not become physically exposed through reasonably foreseeable use and abuse of the product including swallowing, mouthing, breaking, or other children's activities, and the aging of the product, as determined by the Commission. Paint, coatings, or electroplating may not be considered to be a barrier that would render lead in the substrate to be inaccessible to a child.

(c) Section 101(b)(2)(B) of the CPSIA directs the Commission to promulgate by August 14, 2009, this interpretative rule to provide guidance with respect to what product components or classes of components will be considered to be inaccessible.

(d) The accessibility probes specified for sharp points or edges under the Commissions' regulations at 16 CFR 1500.48–1500.49 will be used to assess the accessibility of lead-component parts of a children's product. A lead-containing component part would be considered accessible if it can be contacted by any portion of the specified segment of the accessibility probe. A lead-containing component part would be considered inaccessible if it cannot be contacted by any portion of the specified segment of the accessibility probe.

(e) For products intended for children that are 18 months of age or less, the use and abuse tests set forth under the Commission's regulations at 16 CFR 1500.50 and 16 CFR 1500.51 (excluding the bite test of § 1500.51(c)), will be used to evaluate accessibility of lead-containing component parts of a children's product as a result of normal and reasonably foreseeable use and abuse of the product.

(f) For products intended for children that are over 18 months but not over 36 months of age, the use and abuse tests set forth under the Commission's regulations at 16 CFR 1500.50 and 16 CFR 1500.52 (excluding the bite test of § 1500.52(c)), will be used to evaluate accessibility of lead-containing component parts of a children's product as a result of normal and reasonably foreseeable use and abuse of the product.

(g) For products intended for children that are over 36 months but not over 96 months of age, the use and abuse tests set forth under the Commission's regulations at 16 CFR 1500.50 and 16 CFR 1500.53 (excluding the bite test of § 1500.53(c)), will be used to evaluate accessibility of lead-containing component parts of a children's product as a result of normal and reasonably foreseeable use and abuse of the product.

(h) For products intended for children over 96 months through 12 years of age, the use and abuse tests set forth under the Commission's regulations at 16 CFR 1500.50 and 16 CFR 1500.53 (excluding the bite test of §1500.53(c)) intended for children aged 37–96 months will be used to evaluate accessibility of lead-containing component parts of a children's product as a result of normal and reasonably foreseeable use and abuse of the product.

(i) A children's product that is or contains a lead-containing part which is enclosed, encased, or covered by fabric and passes the appropriate use and abuse tests on such covers, is inaccessible to a child unless the product or part of the product in one dimension is smaller than 5 centimeters.

(j) The intentional disassembly or destruction of products by children older than age 8 years by means or knowledge not generally available to younger children, including use of tools, will not be considered in evaluating products for accessibility of lead-containing components.

[74 FR 39540, Aug. 7, 2009]

§ 1500.88 Exemptions from lead limits under section 101 of the Consumer Product Safety Improvement Act for certain electronic devices.

(a) The Consumer Product Safety Improvement Act (CPSIA) provides for specific lead limits in children's products. Section 101(a) of the CPSIA provides that by February 10, 2009, products designed or intended primarily for children 12 and younger may not contain more than 600 ppm of lead. After August 14, 2009, products designed or intended primarily for children 12 and younger cannot contain more than 300 ppm of lead. On August 14, 2011, the limit will be further reduced to 100 ppm, unless the Commission determines that it is not technologically feasible to meet this lower limit. Section 101(b)(2) of the CPSIA further provides that the lead limits do not apply to component parts of a product that are not accessible to a child. This section specifies that a component part is not accessible if it is not physically exposed by reason of a sealed covering or casing and does not become physically exposed through reasonably foreseeable use and abuse of the product including swallowing, mouthing, breaking, or other children's activities, and the aging of the product, as determined by the Commission. Paint, coatings, or electroplating may not be considered to be a barrier that would render lead in the substrate to be inaccessible to a child.

(b) Section 101(b)(4) of the CPSIA provides that if the Commission determines that it is not technologically feasible for certain electronic devices to comply with the lead limits, the Commission must issue requirements by regulation to eliminate or minimize the potential for exposure to and accessibility of lead in such electronic devices and establish a compliance schedule unless the Commission determines that full compliance is not technologically feasible within a schedule set by the Commission.

(c) Certain accessible lead-containing component parts in children's electronic devices unable to meet the lead limits set forth in paragraph (a) of this section due to technological infeasibility are granted the exemptions that follow in paragraph (d) of this section below, provided that use of lead is necessary for the proper electronic functioning of the component part and it is not technologically feasible for the component part to meet the lead content limits set forth in paragraph (a) of this section.

(d) Exemptions for lead as used in certain electronic components parts in children's electronic devices include:

(1) Lead blended into the glass of cathode ray tubes, electronic components, and fluorescent tubes.

(2) Lead used as an alloying element in steel. The maximum amount of lead shall be less than 0.35% by weight (3,500 ppm).

(3) Lead used in the manufacture of aluminum. The maximum amount of lead shall be less than 0.4% by weight (4,000 ppm).

(4) Lead used in copper-based alloys. The maximum amount of lead shall be less than 4% by weight (40,000 ppm).

(5) Lead used in lead-bronze bearing shells and bushings.

(6) Lead used in compliant pin connector systems.

(7) Lead used in optical and filter glass.

(8) Lead oxide in plasma display panels (PDP) and surface conduction electron emitter displays (SED) used in structural elements; notably in the front and rear glass dielectric layer, the bus electrode, the black stripe, the address electrode, the barrier ribs, the seal frit and frit ring, as well as in print pastes.

(9) Lead oxide in the glass envelope of Black Light Blue (BLB) lamps.

(e) Components of electronic devices that are removable or replaceable, such as battery packs and light bulbs that are inaccessible when the product is assembled in functional form or are otherwise granted an exemption, are not subject to the lead limits in paragraph (a) of this section.

(f) Commission staff is directed to reevaluate and report to the Commission on the technological feasibility of compliance with the lead limits in paragraph (a) of this section for children's electronic devices, including the technological feasibility of making accessible component parts inaccessible, and the status of the exemptions, no less than every five years after publication of a final rule in the FEDERAL REGISTER on children's electronic devices.

[75 FR 3158, Jan. 20, 2010]

§ 1500.89 Procedures and requirements for determinations regarding lead content of materials or products under section 101(a) of the Consumer Product Safety Improvement Act.

(a) The Consumer Product Safety Improvement Act provides for specific lead limits in children's products. Section 101(a) of the CPSIA provides that by February 10, 2009, products designed or intended primarily for children 12 years of age or younger may not contain more than 600 ppm of lead. After August 14, 2009, products designed or intended primarily for children 12 years of age or younger cannot contain more than 300 ppm of lead. On August 14, 2011, the limit will be further reduced to 100 ppm, unless the Commission determines that this lower limit is not technologically feasible. Paint, coatings or electroplating may not be considered a barrier that would make the lead content of a product inaccessible to a child or prevent the absorption of any lead in the human body through normal and reasonably foreseeable use and abuse of the product.

(b) The Commission may, either on its own initiative or upon the request of any interested person, make a determination that a material or product does not contain leads levels that exceed 600 ppm, 300 ppm, or 100 ppm, as applicable.

(c) A determination by the Commission under paragraph (b) of this section that a material or product does not contain lead levels that exceed 600 ppm, 300 ppm, or 100 ppm, as applicable does not relieve the material or product from complying with the applicable lead limit as provided under paragraph (a) of this section.

(d) To request a determination under paragraph (b) of this section, the request must:

(1) Be e-mailed to *cpsc-os@cpsc.gov.* and titled "Section 101 Request for Lead Content Determination." Requests may also be mailed, preferably in five copies, to the Office of the Secretary, Consumer Product Safety Commission, Room 502, 4330 East West Highway, Bethesda, Maryland 20814, or delivered to the same address.

(2) Be written in the English language.

(3) Contain the name and address, and e-mail address or telephone number, of the requestor.

(4) Provide documentation including:

(i) A detailed description of the product or material and how it is used by a child;

(ii) Representative data on the lead content of parts of the product or materials used in the production of a product;

(iii) All relevant data or information on manufacturing processes through which lead may be introduced into the material or product;

(iv) An assessment of the likelihood or lack thereof that the manufacturing processes will result in lead contamination of a material or product that ordinarily does not contain lead;

(v) All relevant data or information on the facilities used to manufacture the material or product, and any other materials used in the product;

(vi) An assessment of the likelihood or lack thereof that the use of leaded materials in a facility will result in lead contamination of a material or product that ordinarily does not contain lead;

(vii) Any other information relevant to the potential for lead content of the product or material to exceed the statutory lead limit specified in the request, that is 600 ppm, 300 ppm, or 100 ppm, as applicable;

(viii) Detailed information on the relied upon test methods for measuring lead content of products or materials including the type of equipment used or any other techniques employed and a statement as to why the data is representative of the lead content of such products or materials generally; and

(ix) Any data or information that is unfavorable to the request that is reasonably available to the requestor.

(e) Where a submission fails to meet all of the requirements of paragraph (d) of this section, the Office of the Secretary shall notify the person submitting it, describe the deficiency, and explain that the request may be resubmitted when the deficiency is corrected.

(f) Upon receipt of a complete request for a determination, the Office of Hazard Identification and Reduction (EXHR) will assess the request to determine whether the product or material is one that does not contain lead in excess of the limits as provided under paragraph (a) of this section. EXHR will make an initial recommendation within thirty (30) calendar days, to the extent practicable. EXHR may request an extension from the Executive Director of the CPSC, if necessary, to make its initial determination. A complete request is one that does not require additional information from the requestor for EXHR to make an initial recommendation to the Commission.

(g) Where the Office of Hazard Identification and Reduction's (EXHR) initial recommendation is to deny the request for a lead content determination, it will provide, in a staff memorandum to the Commission, submitted to the Commission for ballot vote, the basis for the denial with sufficient detail for the Commission to make an informed decision that reasonable grounds for a determination are not presented. The Commission, by ballot vote, will render a decision on the staff's recommendation. The ballot vote and the staff memorandum will be posted on the CPSC Web site. Any determination by the Commission to grant a request will be published in the FEDERAL REGISTER for comment. If the Commission concludes that the request shall be denied, the requestor shall be notified in writing of the denial from the Office of the Secretary along with the official ballot results and the EXHR staff's memorandum of recommendation.

(h) Where the Office of Hazard Identification and Reduction's (EXHR) initial recommendation is to grant the request for a lead content determination, it will submit the basis for that recommendation to the Commission in a memorandum to be voted on by ballot, with sufficient detail for the Commission to make an informed decision that reasonable grounds for a determination are presented. If the notice of proposed rulemaking (NPR) is published, it will invite public comment in the FEDERAL REGISTER. EXHR will review and evaluate any comments and supporting documentation before making its final recommendation to the Commission for final agency action, by staff memorandum submitted to the Commission. If the Commission, after review of the staff's final recommendation, determines that a material or product does not and would not exceed the lead content limits, it will decide by ballot vote, on whether to publish a final rule in the FEDERAL REGISTER.

(i) The filing of a request for a determination does not have the effect of staying the effect of any provision or limit under the statutes and regulations enforced by the Commission. Even though a request for a determination has been filed, unless a Commission determination is issued in final form after notice and comment, materials or products subject to the lead limits under section 101 of the CPSIA must be tested in accordance with section 102 of the CPSIA, unless the testing requirement is otherwise stayed by the Commission.

[74 FR 10480, Mar. 11, 2009]

§ 1500.90 Procedures and requirements for exclusions from lead limits under section 101(b) of the Consumer Product Safety Improvement Act.

(a) The Consumer Product Safety Improvement Act provides for specific lead limits in children's products. Section 101(a) of the CPSIA provides that by February 10, 2009, products designed or intended primarily for children 12 years of age or younger may not contain more than 600 ppm of lead. After August 14, 2009, products designed or intended primarily for children 12 years of age or younger cannot contain more than 300 ppm of lead. On August 14, 2011, the limit will be further reduced to 100 ppm, unless the Commission determines that this lower limit is not technologically feasible. Paint, coatings or electroplating may not be considered a barrier that would make the lead content of a product inaccessible to a child or prevent the absorption of any lead in the human body through normal and reasonably foreseeable use and abuse of the product.

(b) Section 101(b)(1) of the CPSIA provides that the Commission may exclude a specific product or material from the lead limits established for children's products under the CPSIA if the Commission, after notice and a hearing, determines on the basis of the best-available, objective, peer-reviewed, scientific evidence that lead in such product or material will neither:

(1) Result in the absorption of any lead into the human body, taking into account normal and reasonably foreseeable use and abuse of such product by a child, including swallowing, mouthing, breaking, or other children's activities, and the aging of the product; nor

(2) Have any other adverse impact on public health or safety.

(c) To request an exclusion from the lead limits as provided under paragraph (a) of this section, the request must:

(1) Be e-mailed to *cpsc-os@cpsc.gov.* and titled "Section 101 Request for Exclusion of a Material or Product." Requests may also be mailed, preferably in five copies, to the Office of the Secretary, Consumer Product Safety Commission, Room 502, 4330 East West Highway, Bethesda, Maryland 20814, or delivered to the same address.

(2) Be written in the English language.

(3) Contain the name and address, and e-mail address or telephone number, of the requestor.

(4) Provide documentation including:

(i) A detailed description of the product or material and how it is used by a child;

(ii) Representative data on the lead content of parts of the product or materials used in the production of a product;

(iii) All relevant data or information on manufacturing processes through which lead may be introduced into the product or material;

(iv) Any other information relevant to the potential for lead content of the product or material to exceed the CPSIA lead limits that is reasonably available to the requestor;

(v) Detailed information on the relied upon test methods for measuring lead content of products or materials including the type of equipment used or any other techniques employed and a statement as to why the data is representative of the lead content of such products or materials generally; and

(vi) An assessment of the manufacturing processes which strongly supports a conclusion that they would not be a source of lead contamination of the product or material, if relevant.

(5) Provide best-available, objective, peer-reviewed, scientific evidence to support a request for an exclusion demonstrating that the normal and reasonably foreseeable use and abuse activity by a child (including swallowing, mouthing, breaking, or other children's activities) and the aging of the material or product for which exclusion is sought, will not result in the absorption of any lead into the human body, nor have any other adverse impact on public health or safety. This literature should support a request for exclusion that addresses how much lead is present in the product, how much lead comes out of the product, and the conditions under which that may happen and information relating to a child's interaction, if any, with the product.

(6) Provide best-available, objective, peer-reviewed, scientific evidence that is unfavorable to the request that is reasonably available to the requestor.

(d) Where a submission fails to meet all of the requirements of paragraph (c) of this section, the Office of the Secretary shall notify the person submitting it, describe the deficiency, and explain that the request may be resubmitted when the deficiency is corrected.

(e) Upon receipt of a complete request for an exclusion, the Office of Hazard Identification and Reduction (EXHR) will assess the request to determine whether, on the basis of its review of the submitted materials, that the normal and reasonably foreseeable use and abuse activity by a child (including swallowing, mouthing, breaking, or other children's activities) and the aging of the material or product for which exclusion is sought, will not result in the absorption of any lead into the human body nor have any other adverse impact on health or safety.

EXHR will make an initial recommendation within thirty (30) calendar days to the extent practicable. EXHR may request an extension from the Executive Director of the CPSC, if necessary, to make its initial recommendation. A complete request is one that does not require additional information from the requestor for EXHR to make an initial recommendation to the Commission.

(f) Where the Office of Hazard Identification and Reduction's (EXHR) initial recommendation is to deny the request for an exclusion, it will provide in a staff memorandum to the Commission, submitted to the Commission for ballot vote, the basis for denial with sufficient detail for the Commission to make an informed decision that reasonable grounds for an exclusion are not presented. The Commission, by ballot vote, will render a decision on the staff's recommendation. The ballot vote and the staff memorandum will be posted on the CPSC Web site. Any determination by the Commission to grant a request will be published in the FEDERAL REGISTER for comment. If the Commission concludes that the request shall be denied, the requestor shall be notified in writing of the denial from the Office of the Secretary along with the official ballot results and the EXHR's staff's memorandum of recommendation.

(g) Where the Office of Hazard Identification and Reduction's (EXHR) initial recommendation is to grant the exclusion, it will submit the basis for that recommendation to the Commission in a memorandum to be voted on by ballot, with sufficient detail for the Commission to make an informed decision that reasonable grounds for a determination are presented. If the notice of proposed rulemaking (NPR) is published, it will invite public comment in the FEDERAL REGISTER. EXHR will review and evaluate the comments and supporting documentation before making its final recommendation to the Commission, by staff memorandum submitted to the Commission, for final agency action. If the Commission, after review of the staff's final recommendation, determines that an exclusion is supported by the evidence, it will decide by ballot vote, on whether to publish a final rule in the FEDERAL REGISTER.

(h) The filing of a request for exclusion does not have the effect of staying the effect of any provision or limit under the statutes and regulations enforced by the Commission. Even though a request for an exclusion has been filed, unless an exclusion is issued in final form by the Commission after notice and comment, materials or products subject to the lead limits under section 101 of the CPSIA are considered to be banned hazardous substances if they do not meet the lead limits as provided under paragraph (a) of this section.

[74 FR 10480, Mar. 11, 2009]

§ 1500.91 Determinations regarding lead content for certain materials or products under section 101 of the Consumer Product Safety Improvement Act.

(a) The Consumer Product Safety Improvement Act provides for specific lead limits in children's products. Section 101(a) of the CPSIA provides that by February 10, 2009, products designed or intended primarily for children 12 and younger may not contain more than 600 ppm of lead. After August 14, 2009, products designed or intended primarily for children 12 and younger cannot contain more than 300 ppm of lead. On August 14, 2011, the limit may be further reduced to 100 ppm, unless the Commission determines that it is not technologically feasible to have this lower limit. Paint, coatings or electroplating may not be considered a barrier that would make the lead content of a product inaccessible to a child. Materials used in products intended primarily for children 12 and younger that are treated or coated with paint or similar surface-coating materials that are subject to 16 CFR part 1303, must comply with the requirements for lead paint under section 14(a) of the Consumer Product Safety Act (CPSA), as amended by section 102(a) of the CPSIA.

(b) Section 3 of the CPSIA grants the Commission general rulemaking authority to issue regulations, as necessary, either on its own initiative or upon the request of any interested person, to make a determination that a material or product does not exceed the lead limits as provided under paragraph (a) of this section.

(c) A determination by the Commission under paragraph (b) of this section that a material or product does not contain lead levels that exceed 600 ppm, 300 ppm, or 100 ppm, as applicable, does not relieve the material or product from complying with the applicable lead limit as provided under paragraph (a) of this section if the product or material is changed or altered so that it exceeds the lead content limits.

(d) The following materials do not exceed the lead content limits under section 101(a) of the CPSIA provided that these materials have neither been treated or adulterated with the addition of materials that could result in the addition of lead into the product or material:

(1) Precious gemstones: diamond, ruby, sapphire, emerald.

(2) Semiprecious gemstones and other minerals, provided that the mineral or material is not based on lead or lead compounds and is not associated in nature with any mineral based on lead or lead compounds (excluding any mineral that is based on lead or lead compounds including, but not limited to, the following: aragonite, bayldonite, boleite, cerussite, crocoite, galena, linarite, mimetite, phosgenite, vanadinite, and wulfenite).

(3) Natural or cultured pearls.

(4) Wood.

(5) Paper and similar materials made from wood or other cellulosic fiber, including, but not limited to, paperboard, linerboard and medium, and coatings on such paper which become part of the substrate.

(6) CMYK process printing inks (excluding spot colors, other inks that are not used in CMYK process, inks that do not become part of the substrate under 16 CFR part 1303, and inks used in after-treatment applications, including screen prints, transfers, decals, or other prints).

(7) Textiles (excluding after-treatment applications, including screen prints, transfers, decals, or other prints) consisting of:

(i) Natural fibers (dyed or undyed) including, but not limited to, cotton, kapok, flax, linen, jute, ramie, hemp, kenaf, bamboo, coir, sisal, silk, wool (sheep), alpaca, llama, goat (mohair, cashmere), rabbit (angora), camel, horse, yak, vicuna, qiviut, guanaco;

(ii) Manufactured fibers (dyed or undyed) including, but not limited to, rayon, azlon, lyocell, acetate, triacetate, rubber, polyester, olefin, nylon, acrylic, modacrylic, aramid, spandex.

(8) Other plant-derived and animal-derived materials including, but not limited to, animal glue, bee's wax, seeds, nut shells, flowers, bone, sea shell, coral, amber, feathers, fur, leather.

(e) The following metals and alloys do not exceed the lead content limits under section 101(a) of the CPSIA, provided that no lead or lead-containing metal is intentionally added but does not include the non-steel or non-precious metal components of a product, such as solder or base metals in electroplate, clad, or fill applications:

(1) Surgical steel and other stainless steel within the designations of Unified Numbering System, UNS S13800–S66286, not including the stainless steel designated as 303Pb (UNS S30360).

(2) Precious metals: Gold (at least 10 karat); sterling silver (at least 925/1000); platinum; palladium; rhodium; osmium; iridium; ruthenium, titanium.

[74 FR 43041, Aug. 26, 2009]

§ 1500.121 Labeling requirements; prominence, placement, and conspicuousness.

(a)(1) *Background and scope.* Section 2(p)(1) of the Federal Hazardous Substances Act (FHSA) or ''the Act''), 15 U.S.C. 1261(p)(1), requires that hazardous substances bear certain cautionary statements on their labels. These statements include: signal words; affirmative statements of the principal hazard(s) associated with a hazardous substance; the common or usual name, or chemical name, of the hazardous substance; the name and place of business of the manufacturer, packer, distributor, or seller; statements of precautionary measures to follow; instructions, when appropriate, for special handling and storage; the statement ''Keep Out of the Reach of Children'' or its practical equivalent;

and, when appropriate, first-aid instructions. Section 2(p)(2) of the Act specifies that all such statements shall be located prominently on the label of such a substance and shall appear in conspicuous and legible type in contrast by typography, layout, or color with other printed matter on the label. This regulation contains the Commission's interpretations and policies for the type size and placement of cautionary material on the labels of hazardous substances and contains other criteria for such cautionary statements that are acceptable to the Commission as satisfying section 2(p)(2) of the Act. Labels that do not comply with this regulation may be considered misbranded.

(2) *Definitions*. For the purposes of this section:

(i) *Container* means the immediate package from which a hazardous substance may be dispensed and also any article, package or wrapping, such as a tube or cone used for a firework or a wet cell battery casing containing sulfuric acid, which is necessary for the substance to function during actual use.

(ii) *Cautionary material, cautionary labeling,* and *cautionary labeling required by the Act* mean all items of labeling information required by sections 2(p)(1) of the FHSA (repeated in 16 CFR 1500.3(b)(14)(i) or by the regulations which require additional labeling under section 3(b) of the Act.

(iii) *Display panel* means any surface of the immediate container, and of any outer container or wrapping, which bears labeling.

(iv) *Principal display panel* means the portion(s) of the surface of the immediate container, and of any outer container or wrapping, which bear(s) the labeling designed to be most prominently displayed, shown, presented, or examined under conditions of retail sale. (See paragraph (c)(1) of this section.)

(v) *Type size* means the actual height of the printed image of each upper case or capital letter as it appears on the label of a hazardous substance. (See paragraph (c)(2) of this section.)

(vi) *Signal word* means the appropriate word "DANGER," "WARNING," or "CAUTION," as required by sections 2(p)(1) (C) or (D) of the Act.

(vii) *Statement of principal hazard(s)* means that wording descriptive of the principal or primary hazard(s) associated with a hazardous substance required by section 2(p)(1)(E) of the Act. Some examples of such statements are "HARMFUL OR FATAL IF SWALLOWED," "VAPOR HARMFUL," "FLAMMABLE," and "SKIN AND EYE IRRITANT."

(viii) *Other cautionary material* means all labeling statements, other than "signal words" or "statement(s) of principal hazard(s)," required by the Act or by regulations issued under the Act.

(b) *Prominent label placement*. To satisfy the requirement of the Act that cautionary labeling statements shall appear "prominently" on the label of a hazardous substance, all such statements shall be placed on the label as follows:

(1) *Horizontal placement of labeling statements*. Except for the name and place of business of the manufacturer, packer, distributor, or seller, all cautionary material required by the Act shall appear in lines that are generally parallel to any base on which the package rests as it is designed to be displayed for sale or, on display panels other than the principal display panel, in lines generally parallel to all other labeling on that panel. This requirement does not apply to labeling on collapsible tubes, cylindrical containers with a narrow diameter, or F-type containers where both the "front" and "back" of the container are principal display panels. (See paragraph (e) of this section.)

(2) *Principal display panel labeling*. (i) All items of cautionary labeling required by the Act may appear on the principal display panel on the immediate container and, if appropriate, on any other container or wrapper. See paragraph (b)(4) of this section for requirements and exceptions for labeling outer containers and wrappings.

(ii) The signal word, the statement of principal hazard(s), and, if appropriate, instructions to read carefully any cautionary material that may be placed elsewhere on the label shall be blocked together within a square or rectangular area, with or without a border, on the principal display panel on the immediate container and, where required by paragraph (b)(4) of this section, on any outer container or wrapping. All cautionary statements placed on the principal display panel shall be separated on all sides from other printed or graphic matter, with the exception of the declaration of net contents required under the Fair Packaging and Labeling Act, 15 U.S.C. 1453(a) (2) and (3), by a border line or by a space no smaller than the minimum allowable height of the type size for cautionary material required by the Act (exclusive of signal words and statements of hazard) on the principal display panel.

(iii) Depending on the design of the package or the configuration of the label, or both, a package may have more than one principal display panel. If so, each principal display panel must bear, at a minimum, the signal word, statement of principal hazard or hazards, and, if appropriate, instructions to read carefully any cautionary material that may be placed elsewhere on the label.

(A) Where the principal display panel of the immediate container consists of a lid, cap, or other item which may be separated from the immediate container and discarded, the container shall be deemed to have a second principal display panel elsewhere on the immediate container which must bear, at a minimum, the signal word, statement of principal hazard(s), and instructions, if appropriate, to read any cautionary material which may be placed elsewhere on the label.

(3) *Prominent label placement—other display panel labeling.* All items of cautionary labeling required by the Act which do not appear on the principal display panel shall be placed together on a display panel elsewhere on the container. The name and place of business of the manufacturer, packer, distributor, or seller may appear separately on any display panel. Where cautionary material appears on a display panel other than the principal display panel, the principal display panel shall bear the statement "Read carefully other cautions on the ______ panel," or its practical equivalent. [A description of the location of the other panel is to be inserted in the blank space.]

(4) *Outer container or wrappings.* All cautionary labeling appearing on the immediate container of a hazardous substance shall also appear on any outer container or wrapping used in the retail display of the substance, in the same manner as required for the immediate container. Those cautionary labeling statements appearing on the immediate container which are clearly legible through any outer container or wrapper used in retail display need not appear on the outer container or wrapping itself. (See section 2(n)(1) of the Act.)

(5) *Placement of the word "Poison" and the skull and crossbones symbol.* The word "poison" and, when appropriate, the skull and crossbones symbol shall appear on the label of a hazardous substance as follows:

(i) If a hazardous substance is "highly toxic," as defined in §1500.3(c)(i) and section 2(h)(1) of the FHSA, the label must bear the word "poison" in accordance with section 2(p)(1)(H) of the Act, in addition to the signal word "DANGER," and must also bear the skull and crossbones symbol. Some products, under §1500.14(b) of the regulations, may, in addition to any required signal word, be required to bear the word "poison" and the skull and crossbones symbol because of the special hazard associated with their ingredients. In both instances, the word "poison" and the skull and crossbones symbol need not appear on the principal display panel on the container, unless all other cautionary labeling required by the Act appears on the principal display panel. The word "poison" and the skull and crossbones symbol, when required, must appear either together with other cautionary labeling on a display panel other than the principal display panel or together with the signal word and statement(s) of principal hazard on the principal display panel.

(ii) Where, pursuant to a regulation issued under section 3(b) of the Act, the label of a hazardous substance requires the word "poison" instead of a signal word, the word, "POISON" shall appear in capital letters on the principal display panel, together with the statement(s) of the principal hazard. Certain substances for which the word "poison" is required instead of any signal word are listed in § 1500.129.

(c) *Conspicuousness—type size and style.* To satisfy the requirement that cautionary labeling statements under the Act be conspicuous and legible, such statements shall conform to the following requirements:

(1) *Area of principal display panel.* The area of the principal display panel is the area of the side or surface of the immediate container, or of the side or surface of any outer container or wrapping, that bears the labeling designed to be most prominently displayed, shown, presented, or examined under conditions of retail sale. This area is not limited to the portion of the surface covered with labeling; rather, it includes the entire surface. Flanges at the tops and bottoms of cans, conical shoulders of cans, handles, and shoulders and necks of bottles and jars are excluded in measuring the area. For the purposes of determining the proper type size for cautionary labeling, the area of the principal display panel (or other panel bearing cautionary labeling, under paragraph (c)(2)(ii) of this section) is to be computed as follows:

(i) In the case of a rectangular package, where one entire side is the principal display panel, the product of the height times the width of that side shall be the area of the principal display panel.

(ii) In the case of a cylindrical or nearly cylindrical container or tube on which the principal display panel appears on the side, the area of the principal display panel shall be 40 percent of the product of the height of the container times its circumference.

(iii) In the case of any other shape of container, the area of the principal display panel shall be 40 percent of the total surface of the container, excluding those areas, such as flanges at tops and bottoms, specified in paragraph (c)(1) above. However, if such a container presents an obvious principal display panel (such as an oval or hourglass shaped area on the side of a container for dishwashing detergent), the area to be measured shall be the entire area of the obvious principal display panel.

(2) *Type-size requirements.* (i) The term *type size* refers to the height of the actual printed image of each upper case or capital letter as it appears on the label. The size of cautionary labeling shall be reasonably related to the type size of any other printing appearing on the same panel, but in any case must meet the minimum size requirements in table 1.

(ii) When an item of labeling is required to be in a specified type size, all upper case, or capital, letters must be at least equal in height to the required type size, and all other letters must be the same style as the upper case or capital letters. Unless otherwise specified in the regulations (examples appear at §§ 1500.14(b)(6), 1512.19, 1508.9, and part 1505), the type size of all cautionary statements appearing on any display panel shall comply with the specifications in table 1 when the area of the display panel is measured by the method in paragraph (c)(1) above:

TABLE I

Area of principal display panel in square inches	0–2	>2–5	>5–10	>10–15	>15–30	>30
Type size in inches *						
Signal word **	3/64	1/16	3/32	7/64	1/8	5/32
Statement of hazard	3/64	3/64	1/16	3/32	3/32	7/64
Other cautionary material ***	1/32	3/64	1/16	1/16	5/64	3/32

> means "greater than."

* minimum height of printed image of capital or upper case letters.

** including the word "poison" when required instead of a signal word by Section 3(b) of the Act (§ 1500.129).

*** size of lettering for other cautionary material is based on the area of the display panel on which such cautionary material appears.

(iii) If all of the required cautionary labeling does not appear on the principal display panel, the statement to "Read carefully other cautions on the _____ panel," or its practical equivalent, must appear in, as a minimum, the same type size as that required in table 1 for the other cautionary material which appears elsewhere on the label of a hazardous substance. The size of the cautionary labeling that does not appear on the principal display panel is determined by the area of the panel on which it does appear.

(3) *Type style—proportion.* The ratio of the height of a capital or uppercase letter to its width shall be such that the height of the letter is no more than 3 times its width.

(4) *Signal word and statements of hazard—capital letters.* The signal word, the word "poison" if required instead of a signal word (see § 1500.129), and the statement of principal hazard or hazards shall be in capital letters.

(5) *Multiple statement of hazard—type size and style.* All statements of principal hazard or hazards on a label shall appear in the same size and style of type, and shall appear in the same color or have the same degree of boldness.

(6) *Accompanying literature containing directions for use.* Where literature accompanying the package of a hazardous substance has directions for use, written or otherwise, section 2(n) of the Act requires the literature to bear cautionary labeling.

(i) All such cautionary labeling shall be in reasonable proximity to any direction for use and shall be placed together within the same general area.

(ii) The type size of such cautionary labeling shall be reasonably related to the type size of any other printed matter in the accompanying literature and must be in conspicuous and legible type by typography, layout, or color with other printed matter on the label. The signal word and statement of principal hazard or hazards shall appear in capital letters.

(d) *Conspicuousness—contrast.* To satisfy the requirement that cautionary labeling statements appear in conspicuous and legible type which is in contrast by typography, layout, or color with the other printed matter on the label, such statements shall conform to the following requirements:

(1) *Color.* Where color is the primary method used to achieve appropriate contrast, the color of any cautionary labeling statement shall be in sharp contrast with the color of the background upon which such a statement appears. Examples of combinations of colors which may not satisfy the requirement for sharp contrast are: black letters on a dark blue or dark green background, dark red letters on a light red background, light red letters on a reflective silver background, and white letters on a light gray or tan background.

(2) *Interference with conspicuousness—labeling design, vignettes, or other printed material.* For cautionary information appearing on panels other than the principal display panel, the label design, the use of vignettes, or the proximity of other labeling or lettering shall not be such that any cautionary labeling statement is obscured or rendered inconspicuous.

(e) *Collapsible metal tubes.* Collapsible metal tubes containing hazardous substances shall be labeled so that all cautionary labeling required by the Act appears as close to the dispensing end of the container as possible. The placement and conspicuousness of these statements shall conform to the provisions of paragraphs (b), (c), and (d) of this section.

(f) *Unpackaged hazardous substances.* Where practicable, unpackaged hazardous substances intended, or distributed in a form suitable, for use in or around a household or by children shall be labeled so that all items of information required by the Act appear upon the article itself. In instances where this is impracticable (for example, because of the size or nature of the article), the required cautionary labeling must be displayed by means of a tag or other suitable material that is no less than five square inches in area and is securely affixed to the article so that the labeling will remain attached throughout conditions of merchandising and distribution to the ultimate consumer. The placement and conspicuousness of all cautionary labeling appearing on such a tag or material, or on an unpackaged article, shall conform to the provisions of paragraphs (b), (c), and (d) of this section. For the purposes of determining the proper type size to use on a tag or other material, the area of one side of the tag or other material shall be the area of the principal display panel.

(g) *Exemptions.* All requirements of the Act are satisfied by compliance with this § 1500.121. However, exemptions can be granted under section 3(c) of the Act and § 1500.83, or under the provisions of another statute should this section be incorporated in regulations under another statute. Section 1500.82 contains the requirements for exemption requests under the Federal Hazardous Substances Act.

(h) *Effective date.* The provisions of this rule apply to hazardous substances bearing labels printed after December 30, 1985. Labels printed prior to the effective date of this rule may be applied until not later than December 28, 1987. This rule applies to all hazardous substances to which labels are applied after December 28, 1987.

[49 FR 50383, Dec. 28, 1984]

§ 1500.122 Deceptive use of disclaimers.

A hazardous substance shall not be deemed to have met the requirements of section 2(p) (1) and (2) of the act (repeated in § 1500.3(b)(14) (i) and (ii)) if there appears in or on the label (or in any accompanying literature; words, statements, designs, or other graphic material that in any manner negates or disclaims any of the label statements required by the act; for example, the statement "Harmless" or "Safe around pets" on a toxic or irritant substance.

§ 1500.123 Condensation of label information.

Whenever the statement of the principal hazard or hazards itself provides the precautionary measures to be followed or avoided, a clear statement of the principal hazard will satisfy the requirements of section 2(p)(1) (E) and (F) of the act (repeated in § 1500.3(b)(14)(i) (E) and (F)). When the statement of precautionary measures in effect provides instruction for first-aid treatment, the statement of the precautionary measures will satisfy the requirements of section 2(p)(1) (F) and (G) of the act (repeated in § 1500.3(b)(14)(i) (F) and (G)).

§ 1500.125 Labeling requirements for accompanying literature.

When any accompanying literature includes or bears any directions for use (by printed word, picture, design, or combination thereof), such placard, pamphlet, booklet, book, sign, or other graphic or visual device shall bear all the information required by section 2(p) of the act (repeated in § 1500.3(b)(14)).

§ 1500.126 Substances determined to be "special hazards."

Whenever the Commission determines that for a particular hazardous substance intended or packaged in a form suitable for use in the household or by children, the requirements of section 2(p) of the act (repeated in § 1500.3(b)(14)) are not adequate for the protection of the public health and safety because of some special hazard, the Commission, by an appropriate order in the FEDERAL REGISTER, shall specify such reasonable variations or additional label requirements that it finds are necessary for the protection of the public health and safety. Such order shall specify a date that is not less than 90 days after the order is published (unless emergency conditions stated in the order specify an earlier date) after which any such hazardous substance intended, or packaged in a form suitable, for use in the household or by children that fails to bear a label in accordance with such order shall be deemed to be a misbranded hazardous substance.

§ 1500.127 Substances with multiple hazards.

(a) Any article that presents more than one type of hazard (for example, if the article is both toxic and flammable) must be labeled with: An affirmative statement of each such hazard; the precautionary measures describing the action to be followed or avoided for each such hazard; instructions, when necessary or appropriate, for first-aid treatment of persons suffering from the ill effects that may result from each such hazard; instructions for handling and storage of articles that require special care in handling and storage because of more than one type of hazard presented by the article; and the common or usual name (or the chemical name if there is no common or usual name) for each hazardous component present in the article.

(b) Label information referring to the possibility of one hazard may be combined with parallel information concerning any additional hazards presented by the article if the resulting condensed statement contains all of the information needed for dealing with each type of hazard presented by the article.

[38 FR 27012, Sept. 27, 1973; 38 FR 30105, Nov. 1, 1973]

§ 1500.128 Label comment.

The Commission will offer informal comment on any proposed label and accompanying literature involving a hazardous substance if furnished with:

(a) Complete labeling or proposed labeling, which may be in draft form.

(b) Complete quantitative formula.

(c) Adequate clinical pharmacological, toxicological, physical, and chemical data applicable to the possible hazard of the substance.

(d) Any other information available that would facilitate preparation of a suitable label, such as complaints of injuries resulting from the product's use or other evidence that would furnish human-experience data.

§ 1500.129 Substances named in the Federal Caustic Poison Act.

The Commission finds that for those substances covered by the Federal Caustic Poison Act (44 Stat. 1406), the requirements of section 2(p)(1) of the Federal Hazardous Substances Act (repeated in § 1500.3(b)(14)(i)) are not adequate for the protection of the public health. Labeling for those substances, in the concentrations listed in the Federal Caustic Poison Act, were required to bear the signal word "poison." The Commission concludes that the lack of the designation "poison" would indicate to the consumer a lesser hazard and that such would not be in the interest of the public health. Under the authority granted in section 3(b) of the act, the Commission therefore finds that for the following substances, and at the following concentrations, the word "poison" is necessary instead of any signal word:

(a) Hydrochloric acid and any preparation containing free or chemically unneutralized hydrochloric acid (HCl) in a concentration of 10 percent or more.

(b) Sulfuric acid and any preparation containing free or chemically unneutralized sulfuric acid ($H_2 SO_4$) in a concentration of 10 percent or more.

(c) Nitric acid or any preparation containing free or chemically unneutralized nitric acid (HNO_3) in a concentration of 5 percent or more.

(d) Carbolic acid ($C_6 H_5 OH$), also known as phenol, and any preparation containing carbolic acid in a concentration of 5 percent or more.

(e) Oxalic acid and any preparation containing free or chemically unneutralized oxalic acid ($H_2 C_2 O_4$) in a concentration of 10 percent or more.

(f) Any salt of oxalic acid and any preparation containing any such salt in a concentration of 10 percent or more.

(g) Acetic acid or any preparation containing free or chemically unneutralized acetic acid ($HC_2 H_2 O_2$) in a concentration of 20 percent or more.

(h) Hypochlorous acid, either free or combined, and any preparation containing the same in a concentration that will yield 10 percent or more by weight of available chlorine.

(i) Potassium hydroxide and any preparation containing free or chemically unneutralized potassium hydroxide (KOH), including caustic potash and vienna paste (vienna caustic), in a concentration of 10 percent or more.

(j) Sodium hydroxide and any preparation containing free or chemically unneutralized sodium hydroxide ($NaOH$), including caustic soda and lye in a concentration of 10 percent or more.

(k) Silver nitrate, sometimes known as lunar caustic, and any preparation containing silver nitrate ($AgNO_3$) in a concentration of 5 percent or more.

(l) Ammonia water and any preparation containing free or chemically uncombined ammonia (NH_3), including ammonium hydroxide and "hartshorn," in a concentration of 5 percent or more.

§ 1500.130 Self-pressurized containers: labeling.

(a) Self-pressurized containers that fail to bear a warning statement adequate for the protection of the public health and safety may be misbranded under the act, except as otherwise provided pursuant to section 3 of the act.

(b) The following warning statement will be considered as meeting the requirements of section 2(p)(1) of the act (repeated in § 1500.3(b)(14)(i)) if the only hazard associated with an article is that the contents are under pressure:

WARNING—CONTENTS UNDER PRESSURE

Do not puncture or incinerate container. Do not expose to heat or store at temperatures above 120 °F. Keep out of the reach of children.

The word "CAUTION" may be substituted for the word "WARNING". A practical equivalent may be substituted for the statement "Keep out of the reach of children."

(c) That portion of the warning statement set forth in paragraph (b) of this section in capital letters should be printed on the main (front) panel of the container in capital letters of the type size specified in § 1500.121(c). The balance of the cautionary statements may appear together on another panel if the front panel also bears a statement such as "Read carefully other cautions on ______ panel."

(d) If an article has additional hazards, such as skin or eye irritancy, toxicity, or flammability, appropriate additional front and rear panel precautionary labeling is required.

§ 1500.133 Extremely flammable contact adhesives; labeling.

(a) Extremely flammable contact adhesives, also known as contact bonding cements, when distributed in containers intended or suitable for household use may be misbranded under the act if the containers fail to bear a warning statement adequate for the protection of the public health and safety.

(b) The following warning statement is considered as the minimum cautionary labeling adequate to meet the requirements of section 2(p)(1) of the act (repeated in § 1500.3(b)(14)(i)) with respect to containers of more than one-half pint of contact adhesive and similar liquid or semiliquid articles having a flashpoint at or below 20 °F. as determined by the method in § 1500.43, when the only hazard foreseeable is that caused by the extreme flammability of the mixture:

DANGER

EXTREMELY FLAMMABLE

VAPORS MAY CAUSE FLASH FIRE

Vapors may ignite explosively.

Prevent buildup of vapors—open all windows and doors—use only with cross-ventilation.

Keep away from heat, sparks, and open flame.

Do not smoke, extinguish all flames and pilot lights, and turn off stoves, heaters, electric motors, and other sources of ignition during use and until all vapors are gone.

Close container after use.

Keep out of the reach of children.

(c) The words that are in capital letters in the warning statement set forth in paragraph (b) of this section should be printed on the main (front) panel or panels of the container in capital letters of the type size specified in § 1500.121(c). The balance of the cautionary information may appear together on another panel provided the front panel bears a statement such as "Read carefully other cautions on ______ panel," the blank being filled in with the identification of the specific label panel bearing the balance of the cautionary labeling. It is recommended that a borderline be used in conjunction with the cautionary labeling.

(d) If an article has additional hazards, or contains ingredients listed in § 1500.14 as requiring special labeling, appropriate additional front and rear panel precautionary labeling is required.

(e) Since the Commission has issued a regulation banning under the Consumer Product Safety Act extremely flammable contact adhesives covered by this labeling regulation (sec. 16 CFR part 1302), paragraphs (a), (b), (c) and (d) of this section are revoked as to the subject products after June 13, 1978.

[38 FR 27012, Sept. 27, 1973, as amended at 42 FR 63742, Dec. 19, 1977]

§ 1500.134 Policy on first aid labeling for saline emesis.

(a) This section states the Consumer Product Safety Commission's policy concerning first aid instructions for the use of a salt solution to induce vomiting (saline emesis) in the event of ingestion of hazardous substances.

(b) In many cases where hazardous substances are ingested, the recommended first aid instructions for inducing vomiting have contained a statement that this should be accomplished by drinking a solution of salt (sodium chloride) in warm water. At one time, this direction was considered medically acceptable. However, the Commission has obtained information showing that the instruction to perform saline emesis is no longer appropriate. This is because the use of salt to induce vomiting can cause severe hypernatremia (salt poisoning) with potentially toxic effects, particularly in children 5 years old or younger, the age group most often involved in accidental poisonings. In view of the availability of safer and more effective emetics such as ipecac syrup, the Commission no longer recommends a direction to perform saline emesis as a first aid direction for inducing vomiting.

(c) The Commission believes that, for products for which directions for saline emesis have been given in the past, ipecac syrup, U.S.P., is the most appropriate emetic, unless a particular contraindication exists in connection with any particular hazardous substance.

(d) The Commission wishes to emphasize that this policy does not require that any specific first aid instruction or wording be used. Where appropriate, the label may include directions (1) that the victim immediately contact a doctor or poison control center and/or (2) that vomiting be induced using methods other than salt. It is, of course, the manufacturer's responsibility to insure that the label provides enough information in addition to first aid instructions to fulfill all other labeling required by statute or regulation.

(Sec. 30(a), 86 Stat. 1231 (15 U.S.C. 2079(a)))

[43 FR 33704, Aug. 1, 1978]

§ 1500.135 Summary of guidelines for determining chronic toxicity.

A substance may be toxic due to a risk of a chronic hazard. (A regulatory definition of "toxic" that pertains to chronic toxicity may be found at 16 CFR 1500.3(c)(2).) The following discussions are intended to help clarify the complex issues involved in assessing risk from substances that may potentially cause chronic hazards and, where possible, to describe conditions under which substances should be considered toxic due to a risk of the specified chronic hazards. The guidelines are not intended to be a static classification system, but should be considered along with available data and with expert judgment. They are not mandatory. Rather, the guidelines are intended as an aid to manufacturers in determining whether a product subject to the FHSA presents a chronic hazard. All default assumptions contained in the guidelines on hazard and risk determination are subject to replacement when alternatives which are supported by appropriate data become available. The following are brief summaries of more extensive discussions contained in the guidelines. Thus, the guidelines should be consulted in conjunction with these summaries. Copies of the guidelines may be obtained from the Office of Compliance and Enforcement, Consumer Product Safety Commission, Washington, DC 20207. (In addition to the chronic hazards discussed below, issues relating to the chronic hazard of sensitization are discussed in 16 CFR 1500.3(c)(5).)

(a) *Carcinogenicity.* Substances are toxic by reason of their potential carcinogenicity in humans when they are known or probable human carcinogenic substances as defined below. Substances that are possible human carcinogenic substances or for which there is no evidence of carcinogenic effect under the following categories lack sufficient evidence to be considered toxic by virtue of their potential carcinogenicity.

(1) *Known Human carcinogenic Substances ("sufficient evidence" in humans).* Substances are toxic by reason of their carcinogenicity when they meet the "sufficient evidence" criteria of carcinogenicity from studies in humans, which require that a causal relationship between exposure to an agent and cancer be established. This category is similar to the Environmental Protection Agency's (EPA) Group A, the International Agency for Research on Cancer's (IARC) Group 1, or the

American National Standards Institute's (ANSI) Category 1. A causal relationship is established if one or more epidemiological investigations that meet the following criteria show an association between cancer and exposure to the agent.

(i) No identified bias that can account for the observed association has been found on evaluation of the evidence.

(ii) All possible confounding factors which could account for the observed association can be ruled out with reasonable confidence.

(iii) Based on statistical analysis, the association has been shown unlikely to be due to chance.

(2) *Probable Human Carcinogenic Substances.* Substances are also toxic by reason of their probable carcinogenicity when they meet the "limited evidence" criteria of carcinogenicity in humans or the "sufficient evidence" criteria of carcinogenicity in animals described below. This category is similar to EPA's Group B, IARC's Group 2, or ANSI's Categories 2 and 3. Evidence derived from animal studies that has been shown not to be relevant to humans is not included. For example, such evidence would result when there was an identified mechanism of action for a chemical that causes cancer in animals that has been shown not to apply to the human situation. It is reasonable, for practical purposes, to regard an agent for which there is "sufficient" evidence of carcinogenicity in animals as if it presented a carcinogenic risk to humans.

(i) *"Limited evidence" of carcinogenicity in humans.* The evidence is considered limited for establishing a causal relationship between exposure to the agent and cancer when a causal interpretation is credible, but chance, bias, or other confounding factors could not be ruled out with reasonable confidence.

(ii) *"Sufficient evidence" of carcinogenicity in animals.* Sufficient evidence of carcinogenicity requires that the substance has been tested in well-designed and -conducted studies (e.g., as conducted by National Toxicology Program (NTP), or consistent with the Office of Science Technology Assessment and Policy (OSTP) guidelines) and has been found to elicit a statistically significant ($p < 0.05$) exposure-related increase in the incidence of malignant tumors, combined malignant and benign tumors, or benign tumors if there is an indication of the ability of such benign tumors to progress to malignancy:

(A) In one or both sexes of multiple species, strains, or sites of independent origin; or experiments using different routes of administration or dose levels; or

(B) To an unusual degree in a single experiment (one species/strain/sex) with regard to unusual tumor type, unusual tumor site, or early age at onset of the tumor.

The presence of positive effects in short-term tests, dose-response effects data, or structure-activity relationship are considered additional evidence.

(3) *Possible Human Carcinogenic Substance ("limited evidence" animal carcinogen).* In the absence of "sufficient" or "limited" human data, agents with "limited" evidence of carcinogenicity from animal studies fall into this category. Such substances, and those that do not fall into any other group, are not considered "toxic." This does not imply that the substances are or are not carcinogens, only that the evidence is too uncertain to provide for a determination. This category is similar to EPA's Group C, IARC's Group 3, or ANSI's category 4.

(b) *Neurotoxicity.* Substances are toxic by reason of their potential neurotoxicity in humans when they meet the "sufficient evidence" or "limited evidence" criteria of neurotoxicity in humans, or when they meet the "sufficient evidence" criteria of neurotoxicity in animals.

(1) *Known Neurotoxic Substances ("sufficient evidence in humans").* Substances are toxic by reason of their neurotoxicity and are considered "known neurotoxic substances" when they meet the "sufficient evidence" criteria of neurotoxicity derived from studies in humans which require that a causal association between exposure to an agent and neurotoxicity be established with a reasonable degree of certainty. Substances in this category meet the definition of "neurotoxic" as stated above. "Sufficient evidence,"

derived from human studies, for a causal association between exposure to a chemical and neurotoxicity is considered to exist if the studies meet the following criteria.

(i) A consistent pattern of neurological dysfunction is observed.

(ii) The adverse effects/lesions account for the neurobehavioral dysfunction with reasonable certainty.

(iii) All identifiable bias and confounding factors are reasonably discounted after consideration.

(iv) The association has been shown unlikely to be due to chance, based on statistical analysis.

(2) *Probable Neurotoxic Substances.* Substances are also toxic by reason of their probable neurotoxicity when they meet the "limited evidence" criteria of neurotoxicity in humans, or the "sufficient evidence" criteria derived from animal studies. Evidence derived from animal studies that has been shown not to be relevant to humans is not included. Such evidence would result, for example, when there was an identified mechanism of action for a chemical that causes neurotoxicity in animals that has been shown not to apply to the human situation.

(i) *"Limited evidence" of neurotoxicity in humans.* The evidence derived from human studies is considered limited for neurotoxicity when the evidence is less than convincing, i.e., one of the criteria of "sufficient evidence" of neurotoxicity for establishing a causal association between exposure to the agent and neurotoxicity is not met, leaving some uncertainties in establishing a causal association.

(ii) *"Sufficient evidence" of neurotoxicity in animals.* Sufficient evidence of neurotoxicity derived from animal studies for a causal association between exposure to a chemical and neurotoxicity requires that:

(A) The substance has been tested in well-designed and -conducted studies (e.g., NTP's neurobehavioral battery, or conforming to EPA's neurotoxicity test guidelines); and

(B) The substance has been found to elicit a statistically significant ($p < 0.05$) increase in any neurotoxic effect in one or both sexes of multiple species, strains, or experiments using different routes of administration and dose-levels.

(3) *Possible Neurotoxic Substances.* "Possible neurotoxic substances" are the substances which meet the "limited evidence" criteria of neurotoxicity evidence derived from animal studies in the absence of human data, or in the presence of inadequate human data, or data which do not fall into any other group. Substances in this category are not considered "toxic."

(c) *Developmental and Reproductive Toxicity*—(1) *Definitions of "Sufficient" and "Limited" Evidence.* The following definitions apply to all categories stated below.

(i) "Sufficient evidence" from human studies for a causal association between human exposure and the subsequent occurrence of developmental or reproductive toxicity is considered to exist if the studies meet the following criteria:

(A) No identified bias that can account for the observed association has been found on evaluation of the evidence.

(B) All possible confounding factors which could account for the observed association can be ruled out with reasonable confidence.

(C) Based on statistical analysis, the association has been shown unlikely to be due to chance.

(ii) "Limited evidence" from human studies exists when the human epidemiology meets all but one of the criteria for "sufficient evidence"; i.e., the statistical evidence is borderline as opposed to clear-cut, there is a source of bias, or there are confounding factors that have not been and cannot be accounted for.

(iii) "Sufficient evidence" from animal studies exists when

(A) Obtained from a good quality animal study; and

(B) The substance has been found to elicit a statistically significant ($p<0.05$) treatment-related increase in multiple endpoints in a single species/strain, or in the incidence of a single endpoint at multiple dose levels or with multiple routes of administration in a single species/strain, or increase in the incidence of a single endpoint in multiple species/strains/ experiments.

(iv) "Limited evidence" from animal studies exists when:

(A) Obtained from a good quality study and there is a statistically significant ($p<0.05$) treatment-related increase in the incidence of a single endpoint in a single species/strain/experiment at a single dose level administered through only one route and such evidence otherwise does not meet the criteria for "sufficient evidence"; or

(B) The evidence is derived from studies which can be interpreted to show positive effects but have some qualitative or quantitative limitations with respect to experimental procedures (e.g., doses, exposure, follow-up, number of animals/group, reporting of the data, etc.) which would prevent classification of the evidence in the group of "sufficient evidence."

(2) *Developmental Toxicants.* Substances are toxic by reason of their potential developmental or reproductive toxicity when they meet the "sufficient evidence" or "limited evidence" criteria of developmental or reproductive toxicity in humans, or when they meet the "sufficient evidence" criteria of developmental or reproductive toxicity in animals. The Food and Drug Administration (FDA) and the European Economic Community (EEC) have developed categories for teratogens but not other developmental toxicants. The teratogen guidelines limit the information only to structural birth defects and do not include other hazards of developmental toxicity such as embryonal death, fetal death, or functional deficiencies which are also important in assessing the overall toxicity of a substance when administered during pregnancy. Recently, EPA has proposed a system for classifying developmental toxicity. The Occupational Safety and Health Administration (OSHA) has not yet developed any classification for developmental toxicity. The commission has established the following categories for determination of developmental toxicity according to the available evidence.

(i) *Known Human Developmental Toxicant ("sufficient evidence in humans").* A substance is considered a "known human developmental toxicant" if there is "sufficient" human evidence to establish a causal association between human exposure and the subsequent occurrence of developmental toxicity manifested by death of the conceptus (embryo or fetus), or structural or functional birth defects. This category (Human Developmental Toxicant) is comparable to category 1 of the EEC and categories D and X of FDA, except that these guidelines are limited to teratogens. This category is also comparable to the category "definitive evidence for human developmental toxicity" proposed by EPA.

(ii) *Probable Human Developmental Toxicant.* A substance is considered a "probable human developmental toxicant" if there is "limited" human evidence or "sufficient" animal evidence to establish a causal association between human exposure and subsequent occurrence of developmental toxicity. This group (Probable Human Developmental Toxicant) is comparable to the category "adequate evidence for human developmental toxicity" proposed by EPA. This category is also comparable to category 2 of the EEC and category A1 of FDA, except that these guidelines are limited to teratogens.

(iii) *Possible Human Developmental Toxicant.* A substance is considered a "possible human developmental toxicant" if there is "limited" animal evidence, in the absence of human data, or in the presence of inadequate human data, or which does not fall into any other group, to establish a causal association between human exposure and subsequent occurrence of developmental toxicity. EEC, FDA, and EPA have not developed a category comparable to this group. The Commission believes that data from well planned animal studies are important to consider even though they may provide only limited evidence of developmental toxicity.

(3) *Male Reproductive Toxicants.* Male reproductive toxicants can be grouped into the following different categories based on evidence obtained from human or animal studies.

(i) *Known Human Male Reproductive Toxicant.* A substance is considered a "known human male reproductive toxicant" if there is "sufficient" human evidence to establish a causal association between human exposure and the adverse effects on male reproductive main endpoints which are mating ability, fertility, and prenatal and postnatal development of the conceptus. This category is comparable to the one termed "Known Positive" in the EPA guidelines on male reproductive risk assessment.

(ii) *Probable Human Male Reproductive Toxicant.* A substance is considered a "probable human male reproductive toxicant" if there is "limited" human evidence or "sufficient" animal evidence to establish a causal association between human exposure and the adverse effects on male reproductive main endpoints. This category is comparable to the one termed "Probable Positive" in the EPA guidelines on male reproductive risk assessment. However, the EPA category is based only on sufficient animal evidence. CPSC believes that limited human evidence is also sufficient for a chemical to be placed in this category.

(iii) *Possible Human Male Reproductive Toxicant.* A substance is considered a "possible human male reproductive toxicant" if there is limited animal evidence, in the absence of human data, or in the presence of inadequate human data, or which does not fall into any other group, to establish a causal association between human exposure and adverse effects on male reproductive main endpoints. This category is comparable to the one termed "Possible Positive A" in the EPA guidelines on male reproductive risk assessment. EPA proposes to use either limited human or limited animal evidence data to classify a toxicant as a "Possible Positive A" toxicant. As described above, CPSC would elevate limited human evidence to the category "Probable Human Male Reproductive Toxicant."

(4) *Female Reproductive Toxicants.* Female reproductive toxicants can be grouped into the following different categories based on evidence obtained from human or animal studies. EPA has proposed guidelines for assessing female reproductive risk but has not yet proposed a specific system for categorization of female reproductive toxicants.

(i) *Known Human Female Reproductive Toxicant.* A substance is considered a "known human female reproductive toxicant" if there is "sufficient" human evidence to establish a causal association between human exposure and adverse effects on female reproductive function such as mating ability, fertility, and prenatal and postnatal development of the conceptus.

(ii) *Probable Human Female Reproductive Toxicant.* A substance is considered a "probable human female reproductive toxicant" if there is "limited" human evidence or "sufficient" animal evidence to establish a causal association between human exposure and adverse effects on female reproductive function.

(iii) *Possible Human Female Reproductive Toxicant.* A substance is considered a "possible human female reproductive toxicant" if there is "limited" animal evidence, in the absence of human data, or in the presence of inadequate human data, or which does not fall into any other group, to establish a causal association between human exposure and adverse effects on female reproductive function.

(d) *Other Subjects Related to the Determination that a Substance is Toxic.* Under the FHSA, for a toxic substance to be considered hazardous, it must not only have the potential to be hazardous but there must also be the potential that persons are exposed to the substance, that the substance can enter the body, and that there is a significant risk of an adverse health effect associated with the customary handling and use of the substance. Under these guidelines, existence of an adverse health effect means that such exposure is above the "acceptable daily intake" ("ADI"). The ADI is based on the risks posed by the substance, and whether they are acceptable under the FHSA. This section addresses those issues by providing guidelines concerning assessment of exposure, assessment of bioavailability, determination of acceptable risks and the ADI to children and adults, and assessment of risk.

(1) *Assessment of Exposure.* An exposure assessment may comprise a single exposure scenario or a distribution of exposures. Reasonably foreseeable use, as well as accidental exposure, should be taken into consideration when designing exposure studies. The following

guidelines should be used in the assessment of exposure.

(i) *Inhalation*. Inhalation studies to assess exposure should be reliable studies using direct monitoring of populations, predictions of exposure through modeling, or surrogate data.

(A) *Direct Monitoring*. Populations to be monitored should be selected randomly to be representative of the general population, unless the exposure of a particular subset population is the desired goal of the assessment. The monitoring technique should be appropriate for the health effect of interest.

(B) *Modeling*. Predictions of exposure to a chemical using mathematical models can be based on physical and chemical principles, such as mass balance principles. Mass balance models should consider the source strength of the product of interest, housing characteristics, and ambient conditions likely to be encountered by the studied population.

(C) *Surrogate Data*. Surrogate data should only be used when data concerning the chemical of interest are sparse or unavailable and when there is a reasonable assurance that the surrogate data will accurately represent the chemical of interest.

(ii) *Oral Ingestion*. Oral ingestion studies may involve direct monitoring of sources of chemicals as well as laboratory simulations. The estimation of exposure from ingestion of chemicals present in consumer products is predicted based upon estimates of use of the product and absorption of the chemical from the gastrointestinal tract. The following criteria should be established for laboratory simulations to estimate exposure:

(A) A simulant or range of simulants should be carefully selected to mimic the possible range of conditions which occur in humans, such as full and empty stomachs, or various saliva compositions at different times of the day.

(B) The mechanical action to which a product is submitted must be chosen to represent some range of realistic conditions to which a human may subject the product.

(iii) *Dermal Exposure*. (A) Dermal exposure involves estimating the amount of substance contacting the skin. This may involve experiments measuring the amount of material leached from a product contacting a liquid layer which interfaces with the skin, or the amount of substance which migrates from a product (in solid or liquid form) which is in contact with the skin.

(B) Parameters to be considered include: Surface area of the skin contacted, duration of contact, frequency of contact, and thickness of a liquid interfacial layer.

(2) *Assessment of Bioavailability*. (i) The need to consider bioavailability in estimating the risk from use of a product containing a toxic substance only arises when it is anticipated that the absorption characteristics of a substance to which there is human exposure will differ from those characteristics for the substance tested in the studies used to define the dose-response relationship.

(ii) In determining the need to assess bioavailability, the factors to be examined include:

(A) The physical or chemical form of the substance,

(B) The route of exposure (inhalation, ingestion, or through the skin),

(C) The presence of other constituents in the product which interfere with or alter absorption of the toxic substance, and

(D) Dose.

(3) *Assessment of Risk*. This section on quantitative risk assessment applies to estimates of risk for substances that are toxic by reason of their carcinogenicity.

(i) Generally, the study leading to the highest risk should be used in the risk assessment; however, other factors may influence the choice of study.

(ii) Risk should be based on the maximum likelihood estimate from a multistage model (such as Global83 or later version) unless the maximum likelihood estimate is not linear at low dose, in which case the 95% upper confidence limit on risk should be used.

(iii) For systemic carcinogens, if estimates of human risk are made based on animal data, a factor derived from dividing the assumed human weight (70 kg) by the average animal weight during the study and taking that to the ⅓ power should be used. There is the possibility that this factor may be changed, using the 1/4 power instead of the 1/3 power, as part of a unified Federal regulatory approach. If such an approach is adopted, it will apply here.

(iv) When dose is expressed as parts per million, and the carcinogen acts at the site of contact, humans and animals exposed to the same amount for the same proportion of lifetime should be assumed to be equally sensitive.

(v) If no experimental study having the same route of exposure as that anticipated for human use of a substance is available, a study by another route of exposure may be used. Pharmacokinetic methods may be used if sufficient data are available.

(vi) When exposure scenarios are different from those used in the underlying study upon which estimates of risk are based, proportionality should be applied. If pharmacokinetic methods are used to adjust for risks at high versus low exposure levels, level-time measures should not be combined without taking the non-linearity into account.

(4) *Acceptable Risks*—(i) *ADI for Carcinogens.* The maximum acceptable daily intake ("ADI") is that exposure of a toxic (by virtue of its carcinogenicity) substance that is estimated to lead to a lifetime excess risk of one in a million. Exposure refers to the anticipated exposure from normal lifetime use of the product, including use as a child as well as use as an adult.

(ii) *ADI for Neurotoxicological and Developmental/Reproductive Agents.* Due to the difficulties in using a numerical risk assessment method to determine risk for neurotoxicological or developmental/reproductive toxicants, the Commission is using a safety factor approach, as explained below.

(A) *Human Data.* If the hazard is ascertained from human data, a safety factor of ten will be applied to the lowest No Observed Effect Level ("NOEL") seen among the relevant studies. If no NOEL can be determined, a safety factor of 100 will be applied to the Lowest Observed Effect Level ("LOEL"). Both the NOEL and LOEL are defined in terms of daily dose level.

(B) *Animal Data.* If the hazard is ascertained from animal data, a safety factor of one hundred will be applied to the lowest NOEL. If no NOEL can be determined, a safety factor of one thousand will be applied to the lowest LOEL. Both the NOEL and LOEL are defined in terms of daily dose level.

[57 FR 46665, Oct. 9, 1992]

§ 1500.210 Responsibility.

The provisions of these regulations (16 CFR subchapter C of chapter II) with respect to the doing of any act shall be applicable also to the causing of such act to be done.

§ 1500.211 Guaranty.

In the case of the giving of a guaranty or undertaking referred to in section 5(b)(2) of the act, each person signing such guaranty or undertaking, or causing it to be signed, shall be considered to have given it. Each person causing a guaranty or undertaking to be false is chargeable with violations of section 4(d) of the act.

§ 1500.212 Definition of guaranty; suggested forms.

(a) A guaranty or undertaking referred to in section 5(b)(2) of the act may be:

(1) Limited to a specific shipment or other delivery of an article, in which case it may be a part of or attached to the invoice or bill of sale covering such shipment of delivery; or

(2) General and continuing, in which case, in its application to any shipment or other delivery of an article, it shall be considered to have been given at the date such article was shipped or delivered, or caused to be shipped or delivered, by the person who gives the guaranty of undertaking.

(b) The following are suggested forms of guaranty or undertaking referred to in section 5(b)(2) of the act. (1) *Limited form for use on invoice or bill of sale.*

(Name of person giving the guaranty or undertaking)

hereby guarantees that no article listed herein is misbranded within the meaning of the Federal Hazardous Substances Act.

(Signature and post-office address of person giving the guaranty or undertaking)

(2) *General and continuing forms.*

The article comprising each shipment or other delivery hereafter made by ________

(Name of person giving the guaranty or undertaking)

to, or on the order of ______________

(Name and post-office address of person to whom the guaranty or undertaking is given)

is hereby guaranteed, as of the date of such shipment or delivery, to be, on such date, not misbranded within the meaning of the Federal Hazardous Substances Act.

(Signature and post-office address of person giving the guaranty or undertaking)

(c) The application of a guaranty or undertaking referred to in section 5(b)(2) of the act to any shipment or other delivery of an article shall expire when such article, after shipment or delivery by the person who gave such guaranty or undertaking, becomes misbranded within the meaning of the act.

§ 1500.213 Presentation of views under section 7 of the act.

(a) Presentation of views under section 7 of the act shall be private and informal. The views presented shall be confined to matters relevant to the contemplated proceeding. Such views may be presented by letter or in person by the person to whom the notice was given, or by his representative. In case such person holds a guaranty or undertaking referred to in section 5(b)(2) of the act applicable to the article on which such notice was based, such guaranty or undertaking, or a verified copy thereof, shall be made a part of such presentation of views.

(b) Upon request, reasonably made, by the person to whom a notice appointing a time and place for the presentation of views under section 7 of the act has been given, or by his representative, such time or place, or both such time and place, may be changed if the request states reasonable grounds therefor. Such request shall be addressed to the office of the Consumer Product Safety Commission that issued the notice.

§ 1500.214 Examinations and investigations; samples.

When any officer or employee of the Commission collects a sample of a hazardous substance for analysis under the act, the sample shall be designated as an official sample if records or other evidence is obtained by him or any other officer or employee of the Commission indicating that the shipment or other lot of the article from which such sample was collected was introduced or delivered for introduction into interstate commerce, or was in or was received in interstate commerce, or was manufactured within a Territory not organized with a legislative body. Only samples so designated by an officer or employee of the Commission shall be considered to be official samples:

(a) For the purpose of determining whether or not a sample is collected for analysis, the term "analysis" includes examinations and tests.

(b) The owner of a hazardous substance of which an official sample is collected is the person who owns the shipment or other lot of the article from which the sample is collected.

§ 1500.230 Guidance for lead (Pb) in consumer products.

(a) *Summary*. (1) The U.S. Consumer Product Safety Commission issues this guidance to manufacturers, importers, distributors, and retailers to protect children from hazardous exposure to lead in consumer products.[1] The Commission identifies the major factors that it considers when evaluating products that contain lead, and informs the public of its experience with products that have exposed children to potentially hazardous amounts of lead.

(2) To reduce the risk of hazardous exposure to lead, the Commission requests manufacturers to eliminate the use of lead that may be accessible to children from products used in or around households, schools, or in recreation. The Commission also recommends that, before purchasing products for resale, importers, distributors, and retailers obtain assurances from manufacturers that those products do not contain lead that may be accessible to children.

(b) *Hazard*. Young children are most commonly exposed to lead in consumer products from the direct mouthing of objects, or from handling such objects and subsequent hand-to-mouth activity. The specific type and frequency of

[1] This guidance is not a rule. It is intended to highlight certain obligations under the Federal Hazardous Substances Act. Companies should read that Act and the accompanying regulations in this part for more detailed information.

behavior that a child exposed to a product will exhibit depends on the age of the child and the characteristics and pattern of use of the product. The adverse health effects of lead poisoning in children are well-documented and may have long-lasting or permanent consequences. These effects include neurological damage, delayed mental and physical development, attention and learning deficiencies, and hearing problems. Because lead accumulates in the body, even exposures to small amounts of lead can contribute to the overall level of lead in the blood and to the subsequent risk of adverse health effects. Therefore, any unnecessary exposure of children to lead should be avoided. The scientific community generally recognizes a level of 10 micrograms of lead per deciliter of blood as a threshold level of concern with respect to lead poisoning. To avoid exceeding that level, young children should not chronically ingest more than 15 micrograms of lead per day from consumer products.

(c) *Guidance.* (1) Under the Federal Hazardous Substances Act (FHSA), 15 U.S.C. 1261(f)(1), household products that expose children to hazardous quantities of lead under reasonably foreseeable conditions of handling or use are "hazardous substances." A household product that is not intended for children but which creates such a risk of injury because it contains lead requires precautionary labeling under the Act. 15 U.S.C. 1261(p). A toy or other article intended for use by children which contains a hazardous amount of lead that is accessible for children to ingest is a banned hazardous substance. 15 U.S.C. 1261(q)(1)(B). In evaluating the potential hazard associated with products that contain lead, the Commission staff considers these major factors on a case-by-case basis: the total amount of lead contained in a product, the bioavailability of the lead, the accessibility of the lead to children, the age and foreseeable behavior of the children exposed to the product, the foreseeable duration of the exposure, and the marketing, patterns of use, and life cycle of the product.

(2) Paint and similar surface coatings containing lead have historically been the most commonly-recognized sources of lead poisoning among the products within the Commission's jurisdiction. The Commission has, by regulation, banned paint and other similar surface coatings that contain more than 0.06% lead ("lead-containing paint"), toys and other articles intended for use by children that bear lead-containing paint, and furniture articles for consumer use that bear lead-containing paint. 16 CFR Part 1303. In recent years, however, the Commission staff has identified a number of disparate products—some intended for use by children and others simply used in or around the household or in recreation—that presented a risk of lead poisoning from sources other than paint. These products included vinyl miniblinds, crayons, figurines used as game pieces, and children's jewelry.

(3) In several of these cases, the staff's determination that the products presented a risk of lead poisoning resulted in recalls or in the replacement of those products with substitutes, in addition to an agreement to discontinue the use of lead in future production. The Commission believes that, had the manufacturers of these lead-containing products acted with prudence and foresight before introducing the products into commerce, they would not have used lead at all. This in turn would have eliminated both the risk to young children and the costs and other consequences associated with the corrective actions.

(4) The Commission urges manufacturers to eliminate lead in consumer products to avoid similar occurrences in the future. However, to avoid the possibility of a Commission enforcement action, a manufacturer who believes it necessary to use lead in a consumer product should perform the requisite analysis before distribution to determine whether the exposure to lead causes the product to be a "hazardous substance." If the product is a hazardous substance and is also a children's product, it is banned. If it is a hazardous household substance but is not intended for use by children, it requires precautionary labeling. This same type of analysis also should be performed on materials substituted for lead.

(5) The Commission also notes that, under the FHSA, any firm that purchases a product for resale is responsible for determining whether that product contains lead and, if so, whether it is a "hazardous substance." The Commission, therefore, recommends that, prior to the acquisition or distribution of such products, importers, distributors, and retailers obtain information and data, such as analyses of chemical composition or accessibility, relevant to this determination from manufacturers, or have such evaluations conducted themselves.

[63 FR 70649, Dec. 22, 1998]

§ 1500.231 Guidance for hazardous liquid chemicals in children's products.

(a) *Summary.* The U.S. Consumer Product Safety Commission issues this guidance to manufacturers, importers, distributors, and retailers to protect children from exposure to hazardous chemicals found in liquid-filled children's products, such as rolling balls, bubble watches, necklaces, pens, paperweights, keychains, liquid timers, and mazes.[1] The Commission identifies the major factors that it considers when evaluating liquid-filled children's products that contain hazardous chemicals, and informs the public of its experience with exposure to these hazardous chemicals to children. To reduce the risk of exposure to hazardous chemicals, such as mercury, ethylene glycol, diethylene glycol, methanol, methylene chloride, petroleum distillates, toluene, xylene, and related chemicals, the Commission requests manufacturers to eliminate the use of such chemicals in children's products. The Commission also recommends that, before purchasing products for resale, importers, distributors, and retailers obtain assurances from manufacturers that liquid-filled children's products do not contain hazardous liquid chemicals.

(b) *Hazard.* During reasonably foreseeable handling or use of liquid-filled children's products, hazardous chemicals may become accessible to young children in a manner that places children at risk. Young children are exposed to the chemicals from directly mouthing them or from handling such objects and subsequent hand-to-mouth or hand-to-eye activity. The specific type and frequency of behavior that a child exposed to a product will exhibit depends on the age of the child and the characteristics and pattern of use of the product. The adverse health effects of these chemicals to children include chemical poisoning from ingestion of the chemicals, pneumonia from aspiration of the chemicals into the lungs, and skin and eye irritation from exposure to the chemicals. The chemicals may also be combustible.

(c) *Guidance.* (1) Under the Federal Hazardous Substances Act (FHSA), products that are toxic or irritants and that may cause substantial injury or illness under reasonably foreseeable conditions of handling or use, including reasonably foreseeable ingestion by children, are "hazardous substances." 15 U.S.C. 1261(f)(1). A product that is not intended for children, but that creates a risk of substantial injury or illness because it contains hazardous chemicals, requires precautionary labeling under the Act. 15 U.S.C. 1261(p). A toy or other article intended for use by children that contains an accessible and harmful amount of a hazardous chemical is banned. 15 U.S.C. 1261(q)(1)(A). In evaluating the potential hazard associated with children's products that contain hazardous chemicals, the Commission's staff considers certain factors on a case-by-case basis, including: the total amount of the hazardous chemical in a product, the accessibility of the hazardous chemicals to children, the risk presented by that accessibility, the age and foreseeable behavior of the children exposed to the product, and the marketing, patterns of use, and life cycle of the product.

(2) The Commission's staff has identified a number of liquid-filled children's products, such as rolling balls, bubble watches, necklaces, pens, paperweights, maze toys, liquid timers, and keychains, that contain hazardous chemicals. In several of these cases,

[1] This guidance is not a rule. It is intended to highlight certain obligations under the Federal Hazardous Substances Act. Companies should read that Act and the accompanying regulations in this part for more detailed information.

the staff determined that these products violated the FHSA because they presented a risk of chemical poisoning and/or chemical pneumonia from aspiration. This determination resulted in recalls or in the replacement of those products with substitutes, as well as in agreements with the manufacturers to discontinue the use of hazardous chemicals in liquid-filled children's products in future production. The Commission believes that these hazardous substances pose a risk to young children and, consequently, manufacturers should not have included them in the product design or manufacturing process.

(3) Therefore, the Commission considers the use of hazardous chemicals in children's products such as those described above to be ill-advised and encourages manufacturers to avoid using them in such products. Further, the Commission recommends that, before purchasing such products for resale, importers, distributors, and retailers obtain assurances from the manufacturers that liquid-filled children's products do not contain hazardous liquid chemicals.

[63 FR 70648, Dec. 22, 1998]

§ 1500.232 Statement on animal testing policy.

(a) *Summary.* (1) The U.S. Consumer Product Safety Commission issues this statement of policy on animal testing and alternatives to animal testing of hazardous substances regulated under the Federal Hazardous Substances Act (FHSA). The FHSA requires appropriate cautionary labeling on certain hazardous household products to alert consumers to the potential hazard(s) that the products may present. Among the hazards addressed by the FHSA are toxicity, corrosivity, sensitization, and irritation.

(2) In order to determine the appropriate cautionary labeling, it is necessary to have objective criteria by which the existence of each hazard can be determined. Hazards such as toxicity, tissue corrosiveness, eye irritancy, and skin irritancy result from the biological response of living tissue and organs to the presence of the hazardous substance. One means of characterizing these hazards is to use animal testing as a proxy for the human reaction. In fact, the FHSA defines the hazard category of "highly toxic" in terms of animal toxicity when groups of 10 or more rats are exposed to specified amounts of the substance. The Commission's regulations under the FHSA concerning toxicity and irritancy allow the use of animal tests to determine the presence of the hazard when human data or existing animal data are not available.

(3) Neither the FHSA nor the Commission's regulations requires animal testing. The FHSA and its implementing regulations only require that a product be labeled to reflect the hazards associated with that product. If animal testing is conducted, Commission policy supports limiting such tests to a minimum number of animals and advocates measures that eliminate or reduce the pain or discomfort to animals that can be associated with such tests. The Commission has prepared this statement of policy with respect to animal testing to encourage the manufacturers subject to the FHSA to follow a similar policy.

(4) In making the appropriate hazard determinations, manufacturers of products subject to the FHSA should use existing alternatives to animal testing whenever possible. These include: prior human experience (*e.g.*, published case studies), *in vitro* or *in silico* test methods that have been approved by the Commission, literature sources containing the results of prior animal testing or limited human tests (*e.g.*, clinical trials, dermal patch testing), and expert opinion (*e.g.*, hazard assessment, structure-activity analysis). If a manufacturer or other entity performs a hazard test for FHSA labeling purposes that has not been previously approved by the Commission, CPSC staff will consider the data on a case-by-case basis and, upon review, determine whether to post the test method on the animal testing Web site. The Commission recommends resorting to animal testing only when the other information sources have been exhausted. At this time, the Commission recommends use of the most humane procedures with the fewest animals possible to achieve reliable results. Recommended

procedures are summarized in the following statement and can be accessed on the Commission's Web page at: *http://www.cpsc.gov/library/animaltesting.html*. If a manufacturer or other entity performs a hazard test for FHSA labeling purposes that has not been previously approved by the Commission (*e.g.*, an ICCVAM-recommended test method or one of the tests described in the current version of the FHSA), CPSC staff will consider the data on a case-by-case basis and, upon review, determine whether to post the test method on the animal testing Web site.

(b) *Statement of policy on animal testing*. (1) Neither the FHSA nor the Commission's regulations requires animal testing. Reliable human experience always takes precedence over results from animal data. In the cases where animal tests are conducted, the Commission prefers test methods that reduce stress and suffering in test animals and that use fewer animals while maintaining scientific integrity. To this end, the Commission reviews recommendations on alternative test methods developed by the scientific and regulatory communities. Current descriptions of test method recommendations approved by or known to the Commission can be accessed via the Internet at: *http://www.cpsc.gov/library/animaltesting.html*. The Commission strongly supports the use of scientifically sound alternatives to animal testing. The following parts of this section outline some of these alternatives. Testing laboratories and other interested persons requiring assistance interpreting the results obtained when a substance is tested in accordance with the methods described here, or in following the testing strategies outlined in the section, should refer to the Commission's animal testing Web page at: *http://www.cpsc.gov/library/animaltesting.html*.

(i) *Acute toxicity*. The traditional FHSA animal test for acute toxicity determines the median lethal dose (LD50) or lethal concentration (LC50), the dose or concentration that is expected to kill half the test animals. Procedures for determining the median LD50/LC50 are described in section 2(h)(1) of the Act and supplemented in §1500.3(c)(1) and (2) and the test method outlined in §1500.40. The Commission recommends *in vitro* alternatives over *in vivo* LD50/LC50 tests, or using modifications of the traditional LD50/LC50 test during toxicity testing that reduce the number of animals tested whenever possible. Data from *in vitro* or *in silico* test methods that have not been approved by the Commission may be submitted to the Commission for consideration of their acceptability. Commission-approved testing alternatives are identified on the Web site at: *http://www.cpsc.gov/library/animaltesting.html* and include:

(A) *In vitro* and *in vivo* test methods that have been scientifically validated and approved for use in toxicity testing by the Commission;

(B) Valid *in vitro* methods to estimate a starting dose for an acute *in vivo* test;

(C) A sequential version of the traditional LD50/LC50 tests described in §1500.3(c)(1) and (2) and the test method described in §1500.40, in which dose groups are run successively rather than simultaneously;

(D) A limit-dose test where the LD50/LC50 is determined as a point estimate, which can still be used to categorize a hazard, although it gives no information on hazard dose-response. In the limit test, animals (10 rats) each receive a single dose of product at 5g per kilogram of body weight. If not more than one animal dies in 14 days, the product is considered to have an LD50 of greater than 5g/kg, and thus, deemed to be nontoxic. Only if two or more animals die is a second group of 10 rats tested (at a lower dose). This procedure reduces the number of animals tested from the 80 to 100 animals involved in a full LD50 test to, typically, 10 to 20 rats per product. This reduction in the number of animals tested is justified because an exact LD50 is not required by either the FHSA or the regulations. The FHSA requires only a categorical determination that the toxicity is greater than 5g/kg, between 50 mg/kg and 5g/kg, or less than 50 mg/kg.

(ii) *Dermal irritation/corrosivity*. An acceptable *in vitro* test method or weight-of-evidence analysis is recommended before *in vivo* dermal irritation testing is considered to determine appropriate cautionary labeling. The weight-of-evidence analysis should incorporate any existing data on humans and animals, validated *in vitro* or *in silico* test results (valid tests are identified on the Commission's animal testing Web site at: *http://www.cpsc.gov/library/animaltesting.html*), the substance's dermal toxicity, evidence of corrosivity/irritation of one or more structurally related substances or mixtures of such substances, data demonstrating low or high pH (≤2 or ≥11.5) of the substance, and any other relevant physicochemical properties that indicate the substance might be a dermal corrosive or irritant. If there is any indication from this analysis that the substance is either corrosive or irritating to the skin, the substance should be labeled appropriately. If the substance is not corrosive *in vitro*, but no data exist regarding its irritation potential, human patch testing should be considered. If *in vitro* data are unavailable, human patch testing is not an option, and there are insufficient data to determine the weight-of-evidence, a tiered *in vivo* animal test is recommended.

(A) In a tiered *in vivo* dermal study, a single rabbit is tested initially. If the outcome is positive for corrosivity, testing is stopped, and the substance is labeled appropriately. If the substance is not corrosive, two more rabbits should be patch-tested to complete the assessment of skin irritation potential.

(B) If a tiered test is not feasible, the Commission recommends the test method described in §1500.41. Note that in any *in vivo* dermal irritation test method, the Commission recommends using a semiocclusive patch to cover the animal's test site and eliminating the use of stocks for restraint during the exposure period, thereby allowing the animal free mobility and access to food and water.

(iii) *Ocular irritation*. A weight-of-evidence analysis is recommended to evaluate existing information before any *in vivo* ocular irritation testing is considered. This analysis should incorporate any existing data on humans and animals, validated *in vitro* or *in silico* test data (identified on the Commission's animal testing Web site at: *http://www.cpsc.gov/library/animaltesting.html*), the substance's dermal corrosivity/irritation (primary skin irritants and corrosives are also usually eye irritants and therefore do not need to be tested in the eye), evidence of ocular irritation of one or more structurally related substances or mixtures of such substances, data demonstrating high acidity or alkalinity of the substance, and any other relevant physicochemical properties that indicate the substance might be a dermal corrosive or irritant or ocular irritant.

(A) When the weight-of-evidence is insufficient to determine a substance's ocular irritation, a Commission-approved *in vitro* or *in silico* assay for ocular irritancy should be run to assess eye irritation potential and determine labeling. Examples of Commission-validated *in vitro* assays are identified on the Commission's animal testing Web site at: *http://www.cpsc.gov/library/animaltesting.html*). If no valid *in vitro* test exists, the test strategy for determining dermal corrosion/irritation outlined in paragraph (b)(1)(ii)(B) of this section can be followed to determine ocular irritation.

(B) If the dermal test strategy outlined in section paragraph (b)(1)(ii)(B) of this section leads to a conclusion of not corrosive, a tiered *in vivo* ocular irritation test should be performed, in which a single rabbit is exposed to the substance initially. If the outcome of this initial test is positive, testing is stopped, and the substance is labeled an eye irritant. If the outcome of this initial test is negative, one to two more rabbits are tested for ocular irritation, and the outcome of this test will determine the label. If a tiered test is not feasible, the Commission recommends the test method described in §1500.42.

(C) When any ocular irritancy testing on animals is conducted, including the method described in §1500.42, the Commission recommends a threefold plan to reduce animal suffering: The use of preemptive pain management, including topical anesthetics and systemic analgesics that eliminate or reduce suffering that may occur as a result of the application process or from the test substance itself (an example of a typical preemptive pain treatment is two applications of tetracaine ophthalmic anesthetic, 10–15 minutes apart, prior to instilling the test material to the eye); post-treatment with systemic analgesics for pain relief; and implementation of humane endpoints, including scheduled observations, monitoring, and recording of clinical signs of distress and pain, and recording the nature, severity, and progression of eye injuries. The specific techniques that have been approved by the Commission can be found at: *http://www.cpsc.gov/library/animaltesting.html*.

(iv) *Dermal sensitization*. An acceptable *in vitro* test method (examples of valid *in vitro* tests are identified on the Commission's animal testing Web site at: *http://www.cpsc.gov/library/animaltesting.html*), or weight-of-evidence analysis is recommended before *in vivo* animal sensitization testing is considered to determine appropriate cautionary labeling. The weight-of-evidence analysis should incorporate any existing data on humans and animals, validated *in vitro* or *in silico* test results, and any relevant physicochemical properties that indicate the substance might be a dermal sensitizer. If there is any indication from this analysis that the substance is sensitizing to the skin, the substance should be labeled appropriately.

(2) [Reserved]

[77 FR 73288, Dec. 10, 2012]

EFFECTIVE DATE NOTE: At77 FR 73288, Dec. 10, 2012, §1500.232 was added, effective Jan. 9, 2013.

IMPORTS

§ 1500.265 Imports; definitions.

For the purposes of the regulations prescribed under section 14 of the act:

(a) The term *owner or consignee* means the person who has the rights of a consignee under the provisions of the Tariff Act of 1930 (secs. 483, 484, 485, 46 Stat. 721 as amended; 19 U.S.C. 1483, 1484, 1485).

(b) The term *area office director* means the director of the area office of the Consumer Product Safety Commission having jurisdiction over the port of entry through which a hazardous substance is imported or offered for import, or such officer of the area office as he may designate to act in his behalf in administering and enforcing the provisions of section 14 of the act.

§ 1500.266 Notice of sampling.

When a sample of a hazardous substance offered for import has been requested by the director of the area office, the collector of customs having jurisdiction over the hazardous substance shall give to the owner or consignee prompt notice of delivery of, or intention to deliver, such sample. Upon receipt of the notice, the owner or consignee shall hold such hazardous substance and not distribute it until further notice from the area office director or the collector of customs of the results of examination of the sample.

§ 1500.267 Payment for samples.

The Consumer Product Safety Commission will pay for all import samples that are found to be in compliance with the requirements of the act. Billing for reimbursement should be made by the owner or consignee to the Commission area office headquarters in the territory of which the shipment was offered for import. Payment for samples will not be made if the hazardous substance is found to be in violation of the act, even though subsequently brought into compliance under the terms of an authorization to bring the article into compliance.

§ 1500.268 Hearing.

(a) If it appears that the hazardous substance may be subject to refusal of admission, the area office director shall give the owner or consignee a written notice to that effect, stating the reasons therefor. The notice shall specify a place and a period of time during which the owner or consignee shall have an opportunity to introduce testimony. Upon timely request, giving reasonable grounds therefor, such time and place may be changed. Such testimony shall be confined to matters relevant to the admissibility of the hazardous substance, and may be introduced orally or in writing.

(b) If such owner or consignee submits or indicates his intention to submit an application for authorization to relabel or perform other action to bring the hazardous substance into compliance with the act, such testimony shall include evidence in support of such application. If such application is not submitted at or prior to the hearing, the area office director shall specify a time limit, reasonable in the light of the circumstances, for filing such application.

§ 1500.269 Application for authorization.

Application for authorization to relabel or perform other action to bring the hazardous substance into compliance with the act may be filed only by the owner or consignee and shall:

(a) Contain detailed proposals for bringing the article into compliance with the act.

(b) Specify the time and place where such operations will be carried out and the approximate time for their completion.

§ 1500.270 Granting of authorization.

(a) When authorization contemplated by § 1500.269 is granted, the area office director shall notify the applicant in writing, specifying:

(1) The procedure to be followed:

(2) That the operations are to be carried out under the supervision of an officer of the Consumer Product Safety Commission or the Bureau of Customs, as the case may be;

(3) A time limit, reasonable in the light of the circumstances, for completion of the operations; and

(4) Such other conditions as are necessary to maintain adequate supervision and control over the article.

(b) Upon receipt of a written request for extension of time to complete such operations, containing reasonable grounds therefor, the area office director may grant such additional time as he deems necessary.

(c) An authorization may be amended upon a showing of reasonable grounds therefor and the filing of an amended application for authorization with the area office director.

(d) If ownership of a hazardous substance covered by an authorization changes before the operations specified in the authorization have been completed, the original owner will be held responsible, unless the new owner has executed a bond and obtained a new authorization. Any authorization granted under this section shall supersede and nullify any previously granted authorization with respect to the article.

§ 1500.271 Bonds.

(a) The bonds required under section 14(b) of the act may be executed by the owner or consignee on the appropriate form of a customs single-entry or term bond, containing a condition for the redelivery of the merchandise or any part thereof upon demand of the collector of customs and containing a provision for the performance of conditions as may legally be imposed for the relabeling or other action necessary to bring the hazardous substance into compliance with the act in such manner as is prescribed for such bond in the customs regulations in force on the date of request for authorization. The bond shall be filed with the collector of customs.

(b) The collector of customs may cancel the liability for liquidated damages incurred under the above-mentioned provisions of such a bond, if he receives an application for relief therefrom, upon the payment of a lesser amount or upon such other terms and conditions as shall be deemed appropriate under the law and in view of the circumstances, but the collector shall not act under this regulation in any case unless the area office director is in full agreement with the action.

§ 1500.272 Costs chargeable in connection with relabeling and reconditioning inadmissible imports.

The cost of supervising the relabeling or other action necessary in connection with an import of a hazardous substance that fails to comply with the act shall be paid by the owner or consignee who files an application requesting such action and executes a bond, pursuant to section 14(b) of the act. The cost of such supervision shall include, but not be restricted to, the following:

(a) Travel expenses of the supervising officer.

(b) Per diem in lieu of subsistence of the supervising officer when away from his home station as provided by law.

(c) Services of the supervising officer, to be calculated at the rate of a GS 11, step 1 employee, except that such services performed by a customs officer and subject to the provisions of the Act of February 13, 1911, as amended (sec. 5, 36 Stat. 901 as amended; 19 U.S.C. 267), shall be calculated as provided in that Act.

(d) Services of the analyst, to be calculated at the rate of a GS 12, step 1 employee (which shall include the use of the chemical laboratories and equipment of the Consumer Product Safety Commission).

(e) The minimum charge for services of supervising officers and of analysts shall be not less than the charge for 1 hour, and time after the first hour shall be computed in multiples of 1 hour, disregarding fractional parts less than one-half hour.

[38 FR 27012, Sept. 27, 1973, as amended at 57 FR 28605, June 26, 1992]

PART 1501—METHOD FOR IDENTIFYING TOYS AND OTHER ARTICLES INTENDED FOR USE BY CHILDREN UNDER 3 YEARS OF AGE WHICH PRESENT CHOKING, ASPIRATION, OR INGESTION HAZARDS BECAUSE OF SMALL PARTS

Sec.

AUTHORITY: Secs. 2(f)(1)(D), (q)(1)(A), (s), 3(e)(1), and 10; 74 Stat. 372, 374, 375 as amended; 80 Stat. 1304–05, 83 Stat. 187–89 (15 U.S.C. 1261, 1262, 1269).

SOURCE: 44 FR 34903, June 15, 1979, unless otherwise noted.

§ 1501.1 Purpose.

Section 1500.18(a)(9) of this chapter classifies as a banned hazardous substance any toy or other article intended for use by children under 3 years of age that presents a choking, aspiration, or ingestion hazard because of small parts. This part 1501 describes certain articles that are subject to § 1500.18(a)(9); lists certain articles that are specifically exempted; and provides a test method for determining whether an article is hazardous to children under 3 because it, or one of its components that can be detached or broken off during normal or reasonable foreseeable use, is too small.

§ 1501.2 Scope.

(a) This regulation (§ 1500.18(a)(9) and the criteria described in § 1501.4 below) applies to all toys and other articles intended for use by children under 3 years (36 months) of age that are introduced into interstate commerce after the effective date. Such articles include, but are not to limited to: squeeze toys; teethers; crib exercisers; crib gyms; crib mobiles; other toys or articles intended to be affixed to a crib, stroller, playpen, or baby carriage; pull and push toys; pounding toys; blocks and stacking sets; bathtub, wading pool and sand toys; rocking, spring, and stick horses and other figures; chime and musical balls and carousels; jacks-in-the-box; stuffed, plush, and flocked animals and other figures; preschool toys, games and puzzles intended for use by children under 3; riding toys intended for use by children under 3; infant and juvenile furniture articles which are intended for use by children under 3 such as cribs, playpens, baby bouncers and walkers, strollers and carriages; dolls which are intended for use by children under 3 such as baby dolls, rag dolls, and bean bag dolls; toy cars, trucks, and other vehicles intended for use by children under 3. In addition, such articles include any other toys or articles which are intended, marketed or labeled to be entrusted to or used by children under 3 years of age.

(b) In determining which toys and other articles are intended for use by children under 3 years (36 months) of age, for purposes of this regulation, the following factors are relevant: the manufacturer's stated intent (such as on a label) if it is a reasonable one; the advertising, promotion, and marketing of the article; and whether the article is commonly recognized as being intended for children under 3.

(c) This regulation does not apply to toys or articles which are solely intended for use by children 3 years of age or older. In addition, it does not apply to all articles to which children under 3 years of age might have access simply because of presence in a household. Certain articles which are specifically exempted from this regulation are listed in § 1501.3 below.

§ 1501.3 Exemptions.

The following articles are exempt from this regulation (§§ 1500.18(a)(9) and 1501.4 below):

(a) Balloons;

(b) Books and other articles made of paper;

(c) Writing materials such as crayons, chalk, pencils, and pens;

(d) Children's clothing and accessories, such as shoe lace holders and buttons;

(e) Grooming, feeding, and hygiene products, such as diaper pins and clips, barrettes, toothbrushes, drinking glasses, dishes and eating utensils;

(f) Phonograph records;

(g) Modeling clay and similar products;

(h) Fingerpaints, watercolors, and other paint sets;

(i) Rattles (as defined at 16 CFR 1510.2); and

(j) Pacifiers (as defined at 16 CFR 1511.2(a)).

§ 1501.4 Size requirements and test procedure.

(a) No toy or other children's article subject to § 1500.18(a)(9) and to this part 1501 shall be small enough to fit entirely within a cylinder with the dimensions shown in Figure 1, when tested in accordance with the procedure in paragraph (b) of this section. In testing to ensure compliance with this regulation, the dimensions of the Commission's test cylinder will be no greater than those shown in Figure 1. (In addition, for compliance purposes, the English dimensions shall be used. The metric approximations are included only for convenience.)

(b)(1) Place the article, without compressing it, into the cylinder. If the article fits entirely within the cylinder, in any orientation, it fails to comply with the test procedure. (Test any detached components of the article the same way.)

(2) If the article does not fit entirely within the cylinder, subject it to the appropriate "use and abuse" tests of 16 CFR 1500.51 and 1500.52 (excluding the bite tests of §§ 1500.51(c) and 1500.52(c)). Any components or pieces (excluding paper, fabric, yarn, fuzz, elastic, and string) which have become detached from the article as a result of the use and abuse testing shall be placed into the cylinder, one at a time. If any such components or pieces fit entirely within the cylinder, in any orientation and without being compressed, the article fails to comply with the test procedure.

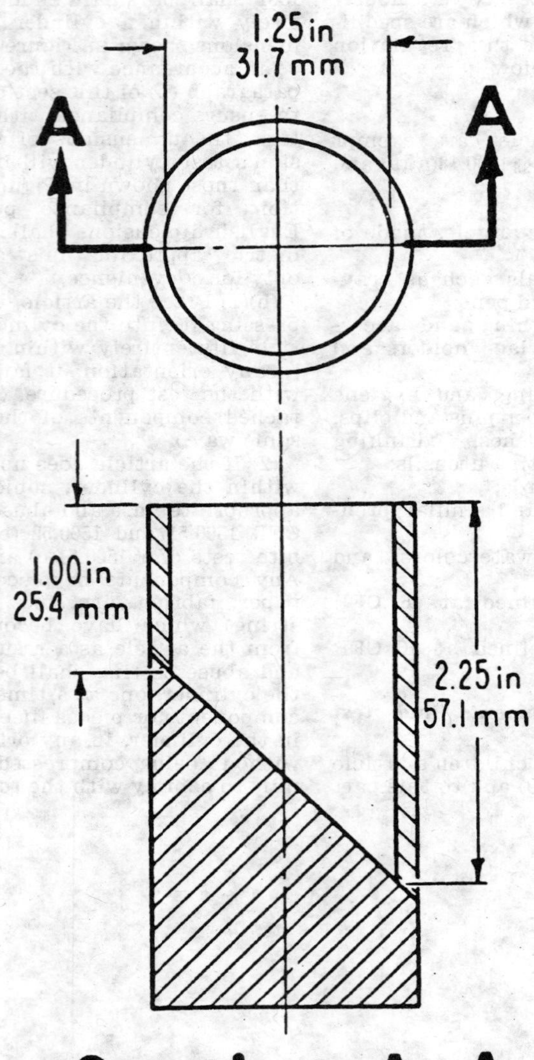

Section A-A

FIG 1—SMALL PARTS CYLINDER

§ 1501.5 Enforcement procedure.

The Commission will enforce this regulation, unless it determines that an emergency situation exists, only in accordance with Chapter 2, Guide 2.05—Letter of Advice/Notices of Noncompliance of the CPSC Enforcement Policy and Procedural Guides, issued in January 1990 and available from the Office of the Secretary, Consumer Product Safety Commission, Washington, DC 20207. Under the procedure described in this chapter, firms must be informed by letter that they or their products may be the subject of enforcement action and must be provided ten days within which to submit evidence and arguments that the products are not violative or are not covered by the regulation, prior to the initiation of enforcement action by the Commission or by its delegated staff member. The function of approving such enforcement actions is currently delegated by the Commission to the Assistant Executive Director for Compliance and Enforcement (copies of the existing delegation documents are also available from the CPSC's Office of the Secretary).

[56 FR 46986, Sept. 17, 1991]

PART 1502—PROCEDURES FOR FORMAL EVIDENTIARY PUBLIC HEARING

AUTHORITY: 15 U.S.C. 1261(q)(1)(B), 1262(a), 1262(e), 1269(a); 15 U.S.C. 1474(a); 21 U.S.C. 371(e)–(g).

SOURCE: 56 FR 9278, Mar. 6, 1991, unless otherwise noted.

Subpart A—General Provisions

§1502.1 Scope.

The procedures in this part apply when—

(a) A person has a right to an opportunity for a hearing under sections 2(q)(1)(B) or 3(a) of the Federal Hazardous Substances Act ("FHSA") and 701(e) of the Federal Food, Drug, and Cosmetic Act ("FDCA") (15 U.S.C. 1261(q)(1)(B) and 1262(a), and 21 U.S.C. 371(e));

(b) The Commission elects to hold a hearing under section 3(e)(1) of the FHSA or section 5 of the Poison Prevention Packaging Act ("PPPA") and section 701(e) of the FDCA (15 U.S.C. 1262(e)(1) and 1474(a), and 21 U.S.C. 371(e)); or

(c) The Commission concludes that it is in the public interest to hold a formal evidentiary public hearing on any matter before it in such a proceeding.

§ 1502.2 Computation of time periods.

Whenever a time period for taking action is specified by these procedures, by the presiding officer, or by the Commission, Saturdays, Sundays, and Federal holidays are included in computing time. However, if the last day for taking such action falls on a Saturday, Sunday, or Federal holiday, the action shall be timely if taken on or before the next Federal Government business day.

§ 1502.3 Confidential information.

Whenever any participant desires or is required to submit information in any proceeding under this part 1502, and the participant believes that such information consists of trade secret or other confidential business or financial information that should not be disclosed publicly, the participant may, instead of submitting such information, file a motion for a protective order containing a general description of the information desired to be withheld, together with a detailed argument supporting the claim that the information should be held in confidence.

§ 1502.4 Office of the Secretary.

(a) The mailing address of the Commission's Office of the Secretary is:

Office of the Secretary, Consumer Product Safety Commission, Washington, DC 20207.

(b) The address for delivery to the Office of the Secretary is:

Office of the Secretary, Room 502, 4330 East West Highway, Bethesda, Maryland 20816.

(c) The telephone number of the Office of the Secretary is (301)504-0800.

[56 FR 9278, Mar. 6, 1991, as amended at 62 FR 46667, Sept. 4, 1997]

Subpart B—Initiation of Proceedings

§ 1502.5 Initiation of a hearing involving the issuance, amendment, or revocation of a regulation.

(a) The FEDERAL REGISTER notice promulgating the final regulation will describe how to submit objections and requests for hearing.

(b) On or before the 30th day after the date of publication of a final regulation in the FEDERAL REGISTER, a person may file written objections, with or without a request for a hearing, with the Commission. The 30-day period may not be extended, except that additional information supporting an objection may be received after 30 days upon a showing of inadvertent omission or for other good cause shown, if consideration of the additional information will not delay review of the objection and request for hearing.

§ 1502.6 Filing objections and requests for a hearing on a regulation.

(a) Objections and requests for a hearing under § 1502.5(a) must be filed with the Office of the Secretary and will be accepted for filing if they meet the following conditions:

(1) They are submitted within the time specified in § 1502.5(b).

(2) Each objection is separately numbered.

(3) Each objection specifies with particularity the provision(s) of the regulation to which that objection is directed.

(4) Each objection on which a hearing is requested specifically requests a hearing. Failure to request a hearing on an objection constitutes a waiver of the right to a hearing on that objection.

(5) Each objection for which a hearing is requested includes a detailed description of the basis for the objection and the factual information or analysis in support thereof. Failure to include a description and analysis for an objection constitutes a waiver of the right

to a hearing on that objection. The description and analysis may be used only for the purpose of determining whether a hearing has been justified under § 1502.8, and do not limit the evidence that may be presented if a hearing is granted.

(i) A copy of any report, article, survey, or other written document relied upon must be submitted, unless the document is—

(A) A CPSC document that is routinely publicly available; or

(B) A recognized medical or scientific textbook or journal in the public domain.

(ii) A summary of the non-documentary testimony to be presented by any witnesses relied upon must be submitted.

(b) If an objection or request for a public hearing fails to meet the requirements of this section the Office of the General Counsel shall notify the Office of the Secretary of the deficiency. The Office of the Secretary shall return it with a copy of the applicable regulations, indicating those provisions not complied with. A deficient objection or request for a hearing may be supplemented and subsequently filed if submitted within the 30-day time period specified in § 1502.5(b).

(c) If another person objects to a regulation issued in response to a petition, the petitioner may submit a written reply to the Office of the Secretary on or before the 15th day after the last day for filing objections.

§ 1502.7 Notice of filing of objections.

As soon as practicable after the expiration of the time for filing objections to and requests for hearing on agency action involving the issuance, amendment, or revocation of a regulation under the FHSA or the PPPA and section 701(e) of the Federal Food, Drug, and Cosmetic Act, the Commission shall publish a notice in the FEDERAL REGISTER specifying those parts of the regulation that have been stayed by the filing of proper objections and, if no objections have been filed, stating that fact. The notice does not constitute a determination that a hearing is justified on any objections or requests for hearing that have been filed. When to do so will cause no undue delay, the notice required by this section may be combined with the notices described in §§ 1502.10 and 1502.13.

§ 1502.8 Ruling on objections and requests for hearing.

(a) As soon as practicable, the Commission will review all objections and requests for hearing filed under § 1502.6 and determine—

(1) Whether the regulation should be modified or revoked under § 1502.9; and

(2) Whether a hearing has been justified.

(b) A request for a hearing will be granted if the material submitted shows the following:

(1) There is a genuine and substantial issue of fact for resolution at a hearing. A hearing will not be granted on issues of policy or law.

(2) The factual issue can be resolved by available and specifically identified reliable evidence. A hearing will not be granted on the basis of mere allegations or denials or general descriptions of positions and contentions.

(3) The data and information submitted, if established at a hearing, would be adequate to justify resolution of the factual issue in the way sought by the person. A hearing will be denied if the Commission concludes that the data and information submitted, even though accurate, are insufficient to justify the factual determination urged.

(4) Resolution of the factual issue in the way sought by the person is adequate to justify the action requested. A hearing will not be granted on factual issues that are not determinative with respect to the action requested, e.g., if the Commission concludes that the Commission's action would be the same even if the factual issue were resolved in the way sought, or if a request is made that a final regulation include a provision not reasonably encompassed by the proposal.

(5) The action requested is not inconsistent with any provision in the FHSA or any regulation in 16 CFR subchapter C explaining or particularizing the requirements of the FHSA.

(6) The requirements in other applicable regulations, and in the notice promulgating the final regulation or

the notice of opportunity for hearing are met.

(c) In making the determinations specified in paragraph (a) of this section, the Commission may issue an appropriate order on the determinations without further notice or opportunity for comment from interested parties. However, the Commission, at its option, may use the procedure specified in 16 CFR part 1052 or any other applicable public procedure available to it.

(d) If it is uncertain whether a hearing has been justified under the principles in paragraph (b) of this section, and the Commission concludes that summary decision against the person requesting a hearing should be considered, the Commission may serve upon the person by registered mail a proposed order denying a hearing. The person has 30 days after receipt of the proposed order to demonstrate that the submission justifies a hearing.

§ 1502.9 Modification or revocation of regulation or order.

If, upon review of an objection or request for hearing, the Commission determines that the regulation should be modified or revoked, the Commission will promptly take such action by notice in the FEDERAL REGISTER. Further objections to or requests for hearing on the modification or revocation may be submitted under §§ 1502.5 and 1502.6, but no further issue may be taken with other provisions in the regulation. Objections and requests for hearing that are not affected by the modification or revocation will remain on file and be acted upon in due course.

§ 1502.10 Denial of hearing in whole or in part.

(a) If the Commission determines upon review of the objections or requests for hearing that a hearing is not justified, in whole or in part, a notice of the determination will be published in the FEDERAL REGISTER.

(b) The notice will state whether the hearing is denied in whole or in part. If the hearing is denied in part, the notice will be combined with the notice of hearing required by § 1502.13, and will specify the objections and requests for hearing that have been granted and denied.

(c) Any denial will be explained. A denial based on an analysis of the information submitted to justify a hearing will explain the inadequacy of the information.

(d) The notice will confirm, modify, or stay the effective date of the regulation involved.

(e) The record of the administrative proceeding relating to denial in whole or in part of a public hearing on an objection or request for hearing consists of the following:

(1) The entire rulemaking record;

(2) The objections and requests for hearing filed by the Office of the Secretary; and

(3) The notice denying a formal evidentiary public hearing.

(f) The record specified in paragraph (e) of this section is the exclusive record for the Commission's decision on the complete or partial denial of a hearing. The record of the proceeding will be closed as of the date of the Commission's decision denying a hearing, unless another date is specified. A person who requested and was denied a hearing may submit a petition for reconsideration or a petition for stay of the Commission's action. A person who wishes to rely upon information or views not included in the administrative record shall submit them to the Commission with a petition to modify the final regulation.

(g) Denial of a request for a hearing in whole or in part is final agency action reviewable in the courts, under the statutory provisions governing the matter involved, as of the date of publication of the denial in the FEDERAL REGISTER.

(1) Before requesting a court for a stay of the Commission's action pending judicial review, a person shall first submit a petition to the Commission for a stay of action.

(2) The time for filing a petition for judicial review of a denial of a hearing on an objection or issue begins on the date the denial is published in the FEDERAL REGISTER. The failure to file a petition for judicial review within the period established in the statutory provision governing the matter involved constitutes a waiver of the right to judicial review of the objection or issue,

regardless whether a hearing has been granted on other objections and issues.

§ 1502.11 Judicial review after waiver of hearing on a regulation.

(a) A person with a right to submit objections and a request for hearing under § 1502.5(a) may submit objections and waive the right to a hearing. The waiver may be either an explicit statement, or a failure to request a hearing, as provided in § 1502.6(a)(4).

(b) If a person waives the right to a hearing, the Commission will rule upon the person's objections under §§ 1502.8 through 1502.10. As a matter of discretion, the Commission may also order a hearing on the matter.

(c) If the Commission rules adversely on a person's objection, the person may petition for judicial review in a U.S. court of appeals under the appropriate statute.

(1) The record for judicial review is the record designated in § 1502.10(e).

(2) The time for filing a petition for judicial review begins on the date of publication of the Commission's ruling on the objections in the FEDERAL REGISTER.

§ 1502.12 Request for alternative form of hearing.

(a) A person with a right to request a formal hearing may waive that right and request a hearing before the Commission under 16 CFR part 1052.

(b) The request—

(1) May be on the person's own initiative or at the suggestion of the Commission;

(2) Must be submitted by the person in the form of a petition before publication of a notice of hearing under § 1502.13 or a denial of hearing under § 1502.10; and

(3) Must be—

(i) In lieu of a request for a formal hearing under § 1502.5; or,

(ii) If submitted with or after a request for formal hearing, accompanied by a waiver of the right to a formal hearing, conditioned on the request for the alternative form of hearing. Upon acceptance by the Commission, the waiver becomes binding and may be withdrawn only by waiving any right to any form of hearing, unless the Commission determines otherwise.

(c) When more than one person requests and justifies a formal hearing under these procedures, an alternative form of hearing may be used only if all the persons concur and waive their right to request a formal hearing.

(d) The Commission will determine whether an alternative form of hearing should be used after considering the requests submitted and the appropriateness of the alternative hearing for the issues raised in the objections. The Commission's determination is binding unless, for good cause, the Commission subsequently determines otherwise.

(e) If the Commission determines that an alternative form of hearing will be used, the Commission will publish a notice in the FEDERAL REGISTER setting forth the following information:

(1) A description of the regulation that is the subject of the hearing.

(2) A statement specifying any part of the regulation that has been stayed by operation of law or in the Commission's discretion.

(3) The time, date, and place of the hearing, or a statement that such information will be contained in a later notice.

(4) The parties to the hearing.

(5) The issues at the hearing. The statement of issues determines the scope of the hearing.

§ 1502.13 Notice of hearing; stay of action.

(a) If the Commission determines upon review of the objections and requests for hearing that a hearing is justified on any issue, the Commission will publish a notice setting forth the following:

(1) A description of the regulation that is the subject of the hearing.

(2) A statement specifying any part of the regulation or order that has been stayed by operation of law or in the Commission's discretion.

(3) The parties to the hearing.

(4) The issues of fact on which a hearing has been justified.

(5) A statement of any objections or requests for hearing for which a hearing has not been justified, which are subject to § 1502.10.

(6) The presiding officer, or a statement that the presiding officer will be designated in a later notice.

(7) The time within which notices of participation should be filed under § 1502.16.

(8) The date, time, and place of the prehearing conference, or a statement that the date, time, and place will be announced in a later notice. The prehearing conference may not commence until after the time expires for filing the notice of participation required by § 1502.16(a).

(9) The time within which participants should submit written information and views under § 1502.25(b). Additional copies of material already submitted under § 1502.25 need not be included with any later submissions.

(10) The contents of the portions of the administrative record relevant to the issues at the hearing. Except for trade secrets or other confidential information, the disclosure of which is prohibited by statute, the portions listed will be placed on public display in the Office of the Secretary before the notice is published.

(b) The statement of the issues determines the scope of the hearing and the matters on which evidence may be introduced. The issues may be revised by the presiding officer. A participant may obtain interlocutory review by the Commission of a decision by the presiding officer to revise the issues to include an issue on which the Commission has not granted a hearing or to eliminate an issue on which a hearing has been granted.

(c) A hearing is deemed to begin on the date of publication of the notice of hearing.

§ 1502.14 Effective date of a regulation when no objections are filed.

(a) If no objections are filed and no hearing is requested on a regulation under § 1502.5, the regulation is effective on the date specified in the regulation as promulgated.

(b) The Commission shall publish a confirmation of the effective date of the regulation. The FEDERAL REGISTER document confirming the effective date of the regulation may extend the time for compliance with the regulation.

Subpart C—Appearance and Participation

§ 1502.15 Appearance.

(a) A person who has filed a notice of participation under § 1502.16 may appear in person or by counsel or other representative in any hearing and, subject to § 1502.27, may be heard concerning all relevant issues.

(b) The presiding officer may strike a person's appearance for violation of the requirements regarding conduct in § 1502.28.

§ 1502.16 Notice of participation.

(a) Within 30 days after publication of the notice of hearing under § 1502.13, a person desiring to participate in a hearing is to file with the Office of the Secretary a notice of participation in the following form:

(Date)

Office of the Secretary, Consumer Product Safety Commission, Room 502, 4330 East West Highway, Bethesda, MD. Mailing address: Office of the Secretary, Consumer Product Safety Commission, Washington, DC 20207.

Notice of Participation

(Title of Regulation)
Docket No. ________________
Please enter the participation of:
(Name) ________________
(Street address) ________________
(City, State, and Zip Code) ________________
____
(Telephone number) ________________
Service on the above will be accepted by:
(Name) ________________
(City, State, and Zip Code) ________________
____
(Telephone number) ________________

The following statements are made as part of this notice of participation:

A. *Specific interests.* (A statement of the specific interest of the person in the proceeding, including the specific issues of fact concerning which the person desires to be heard. This part need not be completed by a party to the proceeding.)

B. *Commitment to participate.* (A statement that the person will present documentary evidence or testimony at the hearing and will comply with the requirements of § 1502.25 of these procedures.)

(Signed) ________________

(b) Any amendment to a notice of participation should be filed with the Office of the Secretary and served on all participants.

(c) No person may participate in a hearing who has not filed a written notice of participation or whose participation has been stricken under paragraph (e) of this section.

(d) The presiding officer may permit the late filing of a notice of participation upon a showing of good cause.

(e) The presiding officer may strike the participation of a person for nonparticipation in the hearing or for failure to comply with any requirement of this subpart, e.g., disclosure of information as required by § 1502.25 or the prehearing order issued under § 1502.30. Any person whose participation is stricken may petition the Commission for interlocutory review of that decision.

[56 FR 9278, Mar. 6, 1991, as amended at 62 FR 46667, Sept. 4, 1997]

§ 1502.17 Advice on public participation in hearings.

(a) All inquiries from the public about scheduling, location, and general procedures should be addressed to the Office of the Secretary, Consumer Product Safety Commission, Washington, DC 20207, or telephone (301) 504–0800.

(b) Requests by hearing participants for changes in the schedule of a hearing or for filing documents, briefs, or other pleadings should be made in writing directly to the presiding officer.

(c) Under no circumstances will the Office of the General Counsel of CPSC directly provide advice about a hearing to any person who is participating or may participate in the hearing. In every hearing, certain attorneys in the office are designated to represent the staff. Other members of the office, ordinarily including the General Counsel, are designated to advise the Commission on a final decision in the matter. It is not compatible with these functions, nor would it be professionally responsible, for the attorneys in the Office of the General Counsel also to advise other participants in a hearing, or for any attorney who may be called on to advise the Commission to respond to inquiries from other participants in the hearing; such participants may be urging views contrary to those of the staff involved or to what may ultimately be the final conclusions of the Commission. Accordingly, members of the Office of the General Counsel, other than the attorneys responsible for representing the staff, will not answer questions about the hearing from any participant or potential participant.

(d) Participants in a hearing may communicate with the attorneys responsible for representing the staff, in the same way that they may communicate with counsel for any other party in interest about the presentation of matters at the hearing. It would be inappropriate to bar discussion of such matters as stipulations of fact, joint presentation of witnesses, or possible settlement of hearing issues. Members of the public, including participants at hearings, are advised, however, that all such communications, including those by telephone, will be recorded in memoranda that can be filed with the Office of the Secretary.

(e) Separation of functions and *ex parte* communications will be handled as follows.

(1) An interested person may meet or correspond with any CPSC representative concerning a matter prior to publication of a notice announcing a formal evidentiary public hearing on the matter. The provisions of 16 CFR part 1012 apply to such meetings.

(2) Upon publication of a notice announcing a formal evidentiary public hearing, the following rules concerning separation of functions apply:

(i) The CPSC staff members responsible for preparing evidence and participating in the hearing in the matter are, as a party to the hearing, responsible for all investigative functions and for presentation of the position of the staff at the hearing and in any pleading or oral argument before the Commission. These representatives of the staff may not participate or advise in any decision except as witnesses or counsel in public proceedings. Except as provided herein, there shall be no other communication between representatives of the staff and representatives of the various Commissioners' offices concerning the matter prior to the decision of the Commission. The Commission may, however, designate other representatives of the staff to advise the Commission. The designation will be in writing and filed with the Office of the Secretary no later than the time specified in paragraph (f)(2) of this section for the application of separation of functions. All employees of the CPSC other than representatives of the involved staff (except for those specifically designated otherwise) may be called upon to advise and participate with the offices of the Commissioners in their functions relating to the hearing and the final decision.

(ii) The General Counsel of CPSC shall designate members of the Office of the General Counsel to advise and participate with the staff in its functions in the hearing and shall designate other members of the Office of the General Counsel to advise the offices of the Commissioners in their functions related to the hearing and the final decision. The members of the Office of the General Counsel designated to advise the staff may not participate or advise in any decision of the Commission except as counsel in public proceedings. The designation shall be in the form of a memorandum filed with the Office of the Secretary and made a part of the administrative record in the proceeding. There may be no other communication between those members of the Office of the General Counsel designated to advise the offices of the Commissioners and any other person in the Office of the General Counsel or in the involved staff with respect to the matter prior to the decision of the Commission. The General Counsel may assign different attorneys to advise either the staff or the offices of the Commissioners at any stage of the proceedings. The General Counsel will ordinarily advise and participate with the offices of the Commissioners in their functions relating to the hearing and the final decision.

(iii) The Commissioners are responsible for the agency review and final decision of the matter, with the advice and participation of anyone in CPSC other than representatives of the responsible staff and those members of the Office of the General Counsel designated to assist in the staff functions in the hearing.

(iv) Between the date that separation of functions applies and the date of the Commission's decision on the matter, communication concerning the matter involved in the hearing will be restricted as follows:

(A) No person outside CPSC may have an *ex parte* communication with the presiding officer or any person representing the offices of the Commissioners concerning the matter in the hearing. Neither the presiding officer nor any person representing the offices of the Commissioners may have any *ex parte* communications with a person outside CPSC concerning the matter in the hearing. All communications are to be public communications, as witness or counsel under the applicable procedures.

(B) A participant in the hearing may submit a written communication concerning a proposal for settlement to the presiding officer with a request that it be transmitted to the Commission. These communications are to be in the form of pleadings, served on all other participants, and filed with the Office of the Secretary like any other pleading.

(C) A written communication contrary to this section must be immediately served on all other participants and filed with the Office of the Secretary by the presiding officer at the hearing, or by the Commissioner, depending on who received the communication. An oral communication contrary to this section must be immediately recorded in a written memorandum and similarly served on all other participants and filed with the Office of the Secretary. A person, including a representative of a participant in the hearing, who is involved in an oral communication contrary to this section, must, if possible, be made available for cross-examination during the hearing with respect to the substance of that conversation. Rebuttal testimony pertinent to a written or oral communication contrary to this section will be permitted. Cross-examination and rebuttal testimony will be transcribed and filed with the Office of the Secretary.

(D) The making of a communication contrary to this section may, consistent with the interests of justice and the policy of the underlying statute, result in a decision adverse to the person knowingly making or causing the making of such a communication.

[56 FR 9278, Mar. 6, 1991, as amended at 62 FR 46667, Sept. 4, 1997]

Subpart D—Presiding Officer

§ 1502.18 Presiding officer.

The presiding officer in a hearing will be an administrative law judge qualified under 5 U.S.C. 3105.

§ 1502.19 Commencement of functions.

The functions of the presiding officer begin upon designation and end upon the filing of the initial decision.

§ 1502.20 Authority of presiding officer.

The presiding officer has all powers necessary to conduct a fair, expeditious, and orderly hearing, including the power to—

(a) Specify and change the date, time, and place of oral hearings and conferences;

(b) Establish the procedures for use in developing evidentiary facts, including the procedures in § 1502.30(b) and to rule on the need for oral testimony and cross-examination under § 1502.26(b);

(c) Prepare statements of the areas of factual disagreement among the participants;

(d) Hold conferences to settle, simplify, or determine the issues in a hearing or to consider other matters that may expedite the hearing;

(e) Administer oaths and affirmations;

(f) Control the course of the hearing and the conduct of the participants;

(g) Examine witnesses and strike or limit their testimony if they fail to respond fully to proper questions;

(h) Admit, exclude, or limit evidence;

(i) Set the time for filing pleadings;

(j) Rule on motions and other procedural matters;

(k) Rule on motions for summary decision under § 1502.31;

(l) Conduct the hearing in stages if the number of parties is large or the issues are numerous and complex;

(m) Waive, suspend, or modify any procedure in this subpart if the presiding officer determines that no party will be prejudiced, the ends of justice will be served, and the action is in accordance with law;

(n) Strike the participation of any person under § 1502.16(e) or exclude any person from the hearing under § 1502.28, or take other reasonable disciplinary action; and

(o) Take any other action required for the fair, expeditious, and orderly conduct of the hearing.

§ 1502.21 Disqualification of presiding officer.

(a) A participant may request the presiding officer to disqualify himself/herself and withdraw from the proceeding. The ruling on any such request may be appealed in accordance with § 1502.35(b).

(b) A presiding officer who is aware of grounds for disqualification, whether or not raised by a participant, shall withdraw from the proceeding.

§ 1502.22 Unavailability of presiding officer.

(a) If the presiding officer is unable to act for any reason, the Commission will assign the powers and duties to another presiding officer. The substitution will not affect the hearing, except as the new presiding officer may order.

(b) Any motion based on the substitution must be made within 10 days.

Subpart E—Hearing Procedures

§ 1502.23 Filing and service of submissions.

(a) Submissions, including pleadings in a hearing, are to be filed with the Office of the Secretary. Two copies shall be filed. To determine compliance with filing deadlines in a hearing, a submission is considered filed on the day of filing with or mailing to the Office of the Secretary. When this part allows a response to a submission and prescribes a period of time for the filing of the response, an additional 3 days are allowed for the filing of the response if the submission is served by mail.

(b) The person making a submission shall serve copies of it on the other participants.

(c) Service is accomplished by mailing a submission to the address shown in the notice of participation or by personal delivery.

(d) All submissions are to be accompanied by a certificate of service or by a statement that service is not required, stating the reason therefor.

(e) No written submission or other portion of the administrative record may be held in confidence, except as provided in § 1502.3.

§ 1502.24 Petition to participate *in forma pauperis*.

(a) A participant who believes that compliance with the filing and service requirements of this section constitutes an unreasonable financial burden may submit to the Commission a petition to participate *in forma pauperis*.

(b) The petition will be captioned: "Request to Participate *In Forma Pauperis*, Docket No. ______." Filing and service requirements for the petition are described in paragraph (c) of this section, whether or not the petition is granted; The petition must demonstrate that either:

(1) The participant is indigent and a strong public interest justifies participation, or

(2) The participant's participation is in the public interest because it can be considered of primary benefit to the general public.

(c) The Commission may grant or deny the petition. If the petition is granted, the participant need file only one copy of each submission with the Office of the Secretary. The Office of the Secretary will make sufficient additional copies for the administrative record, and serve a copy on each other participant.

§ 1502.25 Disclosure of data and information to be relied on by the participants.

(a) Before the notice of hearing is published under § 1502.13, the Assistant General Counsel for Regulatory Affairs shall submit the following to the Office of the Secretary:

(1) The relevant portions of the administrative record of the proceeding. Portions of the administrative record not relevant to the issues in the hearing are not required to be submitted.

(2) All other documentary data and information relied upon.

(3) A narrative position statement on the factual issues in the notice of hearing and the type of supporting evidence the Assistant General Counsel intends to introduce.

(b) Within 60 days of the publication of the notice of hearing or, if no participant will be prejudiced, within another period of time set by the presiding officer, each participant shall submit to the Office of the Secretary all data and information specified in paragraph (a) (2) and (3) of this section and any objections that the administrative record filed under paragraph (a)(1) of this section is incomplete, and any documents in the participants' files containing factual information, whether favorable or unfavorable to the regulation issued by the Commission, which relates to the issues involved in the hearing.

(c) Submissions required by paragraphs (a) and (b) of this section may be supplemented later in the proceeding, with the approval of the presiding officer, upon a showing that the material in the supplement was not reasonably known or available when the submission was made, that the relevance of the material contained in the supplement could not reasonably have been foreseen, or that admission of the material in the supplement is necessary for a fair determination of the issues involved in the hearing.

(d) A participant's failure to comply substantially and in good faith with this section constitutes a waiver of the right to participate further in the hearing; failure of a party to comply constitutes a waiver of the right to a hearing.

(e) Participants may reference each other's submissions. To reduce duplicative submissions, participants are encouraged to exchange and consolidate lists of documentary evidence. If a particular document is bulky or in limited supply and cannot reasonably be reproduced, and it constitutes relevant evidence, the presiding officer may authorize submission of a reduced number of copies.

(f) The presiding officer will rule on questions relating to this section.

§ 1502.26 Purpose; oral and written testimony; burden of proof.

(a) The objective of a formal evidentiary hearing is the fair determination of relevant facts consistent with the right of all interested persons to participate and the public interest in promptly settling controversial matters affecting the public health and welfare.

(b) Accordingly, the evidence at a hearing is to be developed to the maximum extent through written submissions, including written direct testimony, which may be in narrative or in question-and-answer form.

(1) Direct testimony will be submitted in writing, except on a showing that written direct testimony is insufficient for a full and true disclosure of relevant facts and that the participant will be prejudiced if unable to present oral direct testimony. If the proceeding involves particular issues, each party may determine whether, and the extent to which, each wishes to present direct testimony orally or in writing.

(2) Oral cross-examination of witnesses will be permitted if it appears that alternative means of developing the evidence are insufficient for a full and true disclosure of the facts and that the party requesting oral cross-examination will be prejudiced by denial of the request or that oral cross-examination is the most effective and efficient means to clarify the matters at issue.

(3) Witnesses shall give testimony under oath.

(c) A participant who proposes to substitute a new provision for a provision objected to has the burden of proof in relation to the new provision.

§ 1502.27 Participation of nonparties.

(a) A nonparty participant may—

(1) Attend all conferences (including the prehearing conference), oral proceedings, and arguments;

(2) Submit written testimony and documentary evidence for inclusion in the record;

(3) File written objections, briefs, and other pleadings; and

(4) Present oral argument.

(b) A nonparty participant may not—

(1) Submit written interrogatories; or

(2) Conduct cross-examination.

(c) A person whose petition is the subject of the hearing has the same right as a party.

(d) A nonparty participant will be permitted additional rights if the presiding officer concludes that the participant's interests would not be adequately protected otherwise or that broader participation is required for a full and true disclosure of the facts, but the rights of a nonparty participant may not exceed the rights of a party.

§ 1502.28 Conduct at oral hearings or conferences.

All participants in a hearing will conduct themselves with dignity and observe judicial standards of practice and ethics. They may not indulge in personal attacks, unseemly wrangling, or intemperate accusations or characterizations. Representatives of parties shall, to the extent possible, restrain clients from improprieties in connection with any proceeding. Disrespectful, disorderly, or contumacious language or conduct, refusal to comply with directions, use of dilatory tactics, or refusal to adhere to reasonable standards of orderly and ethical conduct during any hearing shall constitute grounds for immediate exclusion from the proceeding by the presiding officer.

§ 1502.29 Time and place of prehearing conference.

A prehearing conference will commence at the date, time, and place announced in the notice of hearing, or in a later notice, or as specified by the presiding officer in a notice modifying a prior notice. At the prehearing conference, insofar as practicable at that time, the presiding officer will establish the methods and procedures to be used in developing the evidence, determine reasonable time periods for the conduct of the hearing, and designate the times and places for the production of witnesses for direct and cross-examination, if leave to conduct oral examination is granted on any issue.

§ 1502.30 Prehearing conference procedure.

(a) Participants in a hearing are to appear at the prehearing conference prepared to discuss and resolve all matters specified in paragraph (b) of this section.

(1) To expedite the hearing, participants are encouraged to prepare in advance for the prehearing conference. Participants should cooperate with each other, and should request information and begin preparation of testimony at the earliest possible time. Failure of a participant to appear at the prehearing conference or to raise matters that reasonably could be anticipated and resolved at that time will not delay the progress of the hearing and constitutes a waiver of the rights of the participant regarding such matters as objections to the agreements reached, actions taken, or rulings issued by the presiding officer at or as a result of the prehearing conference and may be grounds for striking the participation under §1502.16.

(2) Participants shall bring to the prehearing conference the following specific information, which will be filed with the Office of the Secretary under §1502.23:

(i) Any additional information desired to supplement the submission filed under §1502.25; the supplement may be filed if approved under §1502.25.

(ii) A list of all witnesses whose testimony will be offered, orally or in writing, at the hearing, with a full curriculum vitae for each. Additional witnesses may be identified later, with the approval of the presiding officer, on a showing that the witness was not reasonably available at the time of the prehearing conference, that the relevance of the witness's views could not reasonably have been foreseen at that time, or for other good cause shown, as where a previously identified witness is unforeseeably unable to testify.

(iii) All prior written statements, including articles and any written statement signed or adopted, or a recording or transcription of an oral statement made, by persons identified as witnesses if—

(A) The statement is available without making a request to the witness;

(B) The statement relates to the subject matter of the witness's testimony; and

(C) The statement either was made before the time the person agreed to become a witness or has been made publicly available by the person.

(b) The presiding officer will conduct a prehearing conference for the following purposes:

(1) To determine the areas of factual disagreement to be considered at the hearing. The presiding officer may hold conferences off the record in an effort to reach agreement on disputed factual questions, subject to the *ex parte* limitations in §1502.17(f).

(2) To identify the most appropriate techniques for developing evidence on issues in controversy and the manner and sequence in which they will be used, including, where oral examination is to be conducted, the sequence in which witnesses will be produced for, and the time and place of, oral examination. The presiding officer may consider, but is not limited to, the following techniques.

(i) Submission of narrative statements of position on factual issues in controversy.

(ii) Submission of evidence or identification of previously submitted evidence to support such statements, such as affidavits, verified statements of fact, data, studies, and reports.

(iii) Exchange of written interrogatories directed to particular witnesses.

(iv) Written requests for the production of additional documentation, data, or other relevant information.

(v) Submission of written questions to be asked by the presiding officer of a specific witness.

(vi) Identification of facts for which oral examination and/or cross-examination is appropriate.

(3) To group participants with substantially like interests for presenting evidence, making motions and objections, including motions for summary decision, filing briefs, and presenting oral argument.

(4) To hear and rule on objections to admitting information submitted under §1502.25 into evidence.

(5) To obtain stipulations and admissions of facts.

(6) To take other action that may expedite the hearing.

(c) The presiding officer shall issue, orally or in writing, a prehearing order reciting the actions taken at the prehearing conference and setting forth the schedule for the hearing. The order will control the subsequent course of the hearing unless modified by the presiding officer for good cause.

§ 1502.31 Summary decisions.

(a) After the hearing commences, a participant may move, with or without supporting affidavits, for a summary decision on any issue in the hearing. Any other participant may, within 10 days after service of the motion, which time may be extended for an additional 10 days for good cause, serve opposing affidavits or countermove for summary decision. The presiding officer may set the matter for argument and call for the submission of briefs.

(b) The presiding officer will grant the motion if the objections, requests for hearing, other pleadings, affidavits, and other material filed in connection with the hearing, or matters officially noticed, show that there is no genuine issue as to any material fact and that a participant is entitled to summary decision.

(c) Affidavits should set forth facts that would be admissible in evidence and show affirmatively that the affiant is competent to testify to the matters stated. When a properly supported motion for summary decision is made, a participant opposing the motion may not rest upon mere allegations or denials or general descriptions of positions and contentions; affidavits or other responses must set forth specific facts showing that there is a genuine issue of fact for the hearing.

(d) Should it appear from the affidavits of a participant opposing the motion that for sound reasons stated, facts essential to justify the opposition cannot be presented by affidavit, the presiding officer may deny the motion for summary decision, allow additional time to permit affidavits or additional evidence to be obtained, or issue other just order.

(e) If on motion under this section a summary decision is not rendered upon the whole case or for all the relief asked, and evidentiary facts need to be developed, the presiding officer will issue an order specifying the facts that appear without substantial controversy and directing further evidentiary proceedings. The facts so specified will be deemed established.

(f) A participant submitting or opposing a motion for summary decision may obtain interlocutory review by the Commission of a summary decision of the presiding officer.

§ 1502.32 Receipt of evidence.

(a) A hearing consists of the development of evidence and the resolution of factual issues as set forth in this subpart and in the prehearing order.

(b) All orders, transcripts, written statements of position, written direct testimony, written interrogatories and responses, and any other written material submitted in the proceeding comprise the administrative record of the hearing, and will be promptly placed on public display in the Office of the Secretary, except as ordered by the presiding officer.

(c) Written evidence, identified as such, is admissible unless a participant objects and the presiding officer excludes it on objection of a participant or on the presiding officer's own initiative.

(1) The presiding officer may exclude written evidence as inadmissible only if—

(i) The evidence is irrelevant, immaterial, unreliable, or repetitive;

(ii) Exclusion of part or all of the written evidence of a participant is necessary to enforce the requirements of this subpart; or

(iii) The evidence was not submitted as required by § 1502.25.

(2) Items of written evidence are to be submitted as separate documents, sequentially numbered, except that a voluminous document may be submitted in the form of a cross-reference to the documents filed under § 1502.25.

(3) Written evidence excluded by the presiding officer as inadmissible remains a part of the administrative record, as an offer of proof, for judicial review.

(d) Testimony, whether on direct or on cross-examination, is admissible as evidence unless a participant objects and the presiding officer excludes it.

(1) The presiding officer may exclude oral evidence as inadmissible only if—

(i) The evidence is irrelevant, immaterial, unreliable, or repetitive; or

(ii) Exclusion of part or all of the evidence is necessary to enforce the requirements of these procedures.

(2) If oral evidence is excluded as inadmissible, the participant may take written exception to the ruling in a brief to the Commission, without taking oral exception at the hearing. Upon review, the Commission may reopen the hearing to permit the evidence to be admitted if the Commission determines that its exclusion was erroneous and prejudicial.

(e) The presiding officer may schedule conferences as needed to monitor the progress of the hearing, narrow and simplify the issues, and consider and rule on motions, requests, and other matters concerning the development of the evidence.

(f) The presiding officer will conduct such proceedings as are necessary for the taking of oral testimony, for the oral examination of witnesses by the presiding officer on the basis of written questions previously submitted by the parties, and for the conduct of cross-examination of witnesses by the parties. The presiding officer shall exclude irrelevant or repetitious written questions and limit oral cross-examination to prevent irrelevant or repetitious examination.

(g) The presiding officer shall order the proceedings closed for the taking of oral testimony relating only to trade secrets and privileged or confidential commercial or financial information. Participation in closed proceedings will be limited to the witness, the witness's counsel, and Federal Government employees.

§ 1502.33 Official notice.

(a) Official notice may be taken of such matters as might be judicially noticed by the courts of the United States or of any other matter peculiarly within the general knowledge of CPSC as an expert agency.

(b) If official notice is taken of a material fact not appearing in the evidence of record, a participant, on timely request, will be afforded an opportunity to show the contrary.

§ 1502.34 Briefs and arguments.

(a) Promptly after the taking of evidence is completed, the presiding officer will announce a schedule for the filing of briefs. Briefs are to be filed ordinarily within 45 days of the close of the hearing. Briefs must include a statement of position on each issue, with specific and complete citations to the evidence and points of law relied on. Briefs must contain proposed findings of fact and conclusions of law.

(b) The presiding officer may, as a matter of discretion, permit oral argument after the briefs are filed.

(c) Briefs and oral argument shall refrain from disclosing specific details of written and oral testimony and documents relating to trade secrets and privileged or confidential commercial or financial information, except as specifically authorized in a protective order issued by the presiding officer.

§ 1502.35 Interlocutory appeal from ruling of presiding officer.

(a) Except as provided in paragraph (b) of this section and in §§ 1502.13(b), 1502.16(e), 1502.31(f), and 1502.37(d) authorizing interlocutory appeals, rulings of the presiding officer may not be appealed to the Commission before the Commission's consideration of the entire record of the hearing.

(b) A ruling of the presiding officer is subject to interlocutory appeal to the Commission if the presiding officer certifies on the record or in writing that immediate review is necessary to prevent exceptional delay, expense, or prejudice to any participant or substantial harm to the public interest.

(c) When an interlocutory appeal is made to the Commission, a participant may file a brief with the Commission only if such is specifically authorized by the presiding officer or the Commission, and, if such authorization is granted, within the period the Commission directs. If a participant is authorized to file a brief, any other participant may file a brief in opposition, within the period the Commission directs. If no briefs are authorized, the appeal will be presented as an oral argument to the Commission. The oral argument will be transcribed. If briefs are authorized, oral argument will be heard only at the discretion of the Commission.

§ 1502.36 Official transcript.

(a) The presiding officer will arrange for a verbatim stenographic transcript of oral testimony and for necessary copies of the transcript.

(b) One copy of the transcript will be placed on public display in the Office of the Secretary upon receipt.

(c) Copies of the transcript may be obtained by application to the official reporter and payment of costs thereof.

(d) Witnesses, participants, and counsel have 30 days from the time the transcript becomes available to propose corrections in the transcript of oral testimony. Corrections are permitted only for transcription errors. The presiding officer shall promptly order justified corrections.

§ 1502.37 Motions.

(a) Except for a motion made in the course of an oral hearing before the presiding officer, a motion on any matter relating to the proceeding shall be filed under § 1502.23 and must include a draft order.

(b) A response may be filed within 10 days of service of a motion. The time may be shortened or extended by the presiding officer for good cause shown.

(c) The moving party has no right to reply, except as permitted by the presiding officer.

(d) The presiding officer shall rule upon the motion and may certify that ruling to the Commission for interlocutory review.

Subpart F—Administrative Record

§ 1502.38 Administrative record of a hearing.

(a) The record of a hearing consists of—

(1) The regulation or notice of opportunity for hearing that gave rise to the hearing;

(2) All objections and requests for hearing filed with the Office of the Secretary under §§ 1502.5 and 1502.6;

(3) The notice of hearing published under § 1502.13;

(4) All notices of participation filed under § 1502.16;

(5) All FEDERAL REGISTER notices pertinent to the proceeding;

(6) All submissions filed under § 1502.24, e.g., the submissions required by § 1502.25, all other documentary evidence and written testimony, pleadings, statements of position, briefs, and other similar documents;

(7) The transcript, written order, and all other documents relating to the prehearing conference, prepared under § 1502.30;

(8) All documents relating to any motion for summary decision under § 1502.31;

(9) All documents of which official notice is taken under § 1502.33;

(10) All pleadings filed under § 1502.34;

(11) All documents relating to any interlocutory appeal under § 1502.35;

(12) All transcripts prepared under § 1502.36; and

(13) Any other document relating to the hearing and filed with the Office of the Secretary by the presiding officer or any participant.

(b) The record of the administrative proceeding is closed—

(1) With respect to the taking of evidence, when specified by the presiding officer; and

(2) With respect to pleadings, at the time specified in § 1502.34(a) for the filing of briefs.

(c) The presiding officer may reopen the record to receive further evidence at any time before the filing of the initial decision.

§ 1502.39 Examination of record.

Except as provided in § 1502.3, documents in the record will be publicly available. Documents available for examination or copying will be placed on public display in the Office of the Secretary promptly upon receipt in that office.

Subpart G—Initial and Final Decision

§ 1502.40 Initial decision.

(a) The presiding officer shall prepare and file an initial decision as soon as practicable after the filing of briefs and oral argument.

(b) The initial decision shall contain—

(1) Findings of fact based upon relevant, material, and reliable evidence of record;

(2) Conclusions of law;

(3) A discussion of the reasons for the findings and conclusions, including a discussion of the significant contentions made by any participant;

(4) Citations to the record supporting the findings and conclusions;

(5) An appropriate regulation supported by substantial evidence of record and based upon the findings of fact and conclusions of law (unless the initial decision is to not issue a regulation);

(6) An effective date for the regulation (if any), together with an explanation of why the effective date is appropriate; and

(7) The periods of time for filing exceptions to the initial decision with the Office of the Secretary and for filing replies to such exceptions, in accordance with §1502.41(a)–(c).

(c) The initial decision must refrain from disclosing specific details of trade secrets and privileged or confidential commercial or financial information, except as specifically authorized in a protective order issued by the presiding officer.

(d) The initial decision is to be filed with the Office of the Secretary and served upon all participants. Once the initial decision is filed with the Office of the Secretary, the presiding officer has no further jurisdiction over the matter, and any motions or requests filed with the Office of the Secretary will be decided by the Commission.

(e) The initial decision becomes the final decision of the Commission by operation of law unless a participant files exceptions with the Office of the Secretary under §1502.41(a) or the Commission files a notice of review under §1502.41(f).

(f) Notice that an initial decision has become the decision of the Commission without appeal to or review by the Commission will be published in the FEDERAL REGISTER. The Commission also may publish the decision when it is of widespread interest.

§ 1502.41 Appeal from or review of initial decision.

(a) A participant may appeal an initial decision to the Commission by filing exceptions with the Office of the Secretary, and serving them on the other participants within the period specified in the initial decision. The period for appeal to the Commission may not exceed 30 days, unless extended by the Commission under paragraph (d) of this section.

(b) Exceptions must specifically identify alleged errors in the findings of fact or conclusions of law in the initial decision, and provide supporting citations to the record. Oral argument before the Commission may be requested in the exceptions.

(c) Any reply to the exceptions shall be filed and served within the period specified in the initial decision. The period may not exceed 30 days after the end of the period (including any extensions) for filing exceptions, unless extended by the Commission under paragraph (d) of this section.

(d) The Commission may extend the time for filing exceptions or replies to exceptions for good cause shown.

(e) If the Commission decides to hear oral argument, the participants will be informed of the date, time, and place of the argument, the amount of time allotted to each participant, and the issues to be addressed.

(f) Within 10 days following the expiration of the time for filing exceptions (including any extensions), the Commission may file with the Office of the Secretary, and serve on the participants, a notice of the Commission's determination to review the initial decision. The Commission may invite the participants to file briefs or present oral argument on the matter. The time for filing briefs or presenting oral argument will be specified in that or a later notice.

§ 1502.42 Decision by Commission on appeal or review of initial decision.

(a) On appeal from or review of the initial decision, the Commission has all the powers given to the presiding officer with respect to the initial decision. On the Commission's own initiative or on motion, the Commission may remand the matter to the presiding officer for any further action necessary for a proper decision.

(b) The scope of the issues at the public hearing is the same as the scope of the issues on appeal at the public hearing unless the Commission specifies otherwise.

(c) As soon as possible after the filing of briefs and the presentation of any oral argument, the Commission will issue a final decision in the proceeding, which meets the requirements established in § 1502.40 (b) and (c).

(d) The Commission may adopt the initial decision as the final decision.

(e) Notice of the Commission's decision will be published in the FEDERAL REGISTER. The Commission may also publish the decision when it is of widespread interest.

§ 1502.43 Reconsideration and stay of Commission's action.

Following notice or publication of the final decision, a participant may petition the Commission for reconsideration of any part or all of the decision or may petition for a stay of the decision.

Subpart H—Judicial Review

§ 1502.44 Review by the courts.

(a) The Commission's final decision constitutes final agency action from which a participant may petition for judicial review under the statutes governing the matter involved. Before requesting an order from a court for a stay of the Commission's action pending judicial review, a participant shall first submit a petition for a stay of action under § 1502.43.

(b) Under 28 U.S.C. 2112(a), CPSC will request consolidation of all petitions related to a particular matter.

§ 1502.45 Copies of petitions for judicial review.

The General Counsel of CPSC has been designated by the Commission as the officer on whom copies of petitions for judicial review are to be served. This officer is responsible for filing the record on which the final decision is based. The record of the proceeding is certified by the Secretary of the Commission.

PART 1505—REQUIREMENTS FOR ELECTRICALLY OPERATED TOYS OR OTHER ELECTRICALLY OPERATED ARTICLES INTENDED FOR USE BY CHILDREN

Subpart A—Regulations

Subpart B—Policies and Interpretations

AUTHORITY: 15 U.S.C. 1261–1262, 2079.

SOURCE: 38 FR 27032, Sept. 27, 1973, unless otherwise noted.

Subpart A—Regulations

§ 1505.1 Definitions.

(a) The following definitions apply to this part 1505:

(1) The term "electrically operated toy or other electrically operated article intended for use by children" means any toy, game, or other article designed, labeled, advertised, or otherwise intended for use by children which is intended to be powered by electrical current from nominal 120 volt (110–125 v.) branch circuits. Such articles are referred to in this part in various contexts as "toy" or "electrically operated toy." If the package (including packing materials) of the toy or other article is intended to be used with the product, it is considered to be part of the toy or other article. This definition does not include components which are powered by circuits of 30 volts r.m.s. (42.4 volts peak) or less, articles designed primarily for use by adults which may be used incidentally by children, or video games.

(2) The term *video games* means video game hardware systems, which are games that both produce a dynamic video image, either on a viewing screen that is part of the video game or,

through connecting cables, on a television set, and have some way to control the movement of at least some portion of the video image.

[38 FR 27032, Sept. 27, 1973, as amended at 58 FR 40335, July 28, 1993]

§ 1505.2 Scope of part.

This part sets forth the requirements whereby electrically operated toys and other electrically operated articles intended for use by children (as defined in § 1505.1(a)(1)) are not banned toys or banned articles under § 1500.18(b)(1) of this chapter.

§ 1505.3 Labeling.

(a) *General.* Electrically operated toys, and the instruction sheets and outer packaging thereof, shall be labeled in accordance with the requirements of this section and any other applicable requirements of the Federal Hazardous Substances Act and regulations promulgated thereunder. All labeling shall be prominently and conspicuously displayed under customary conditions of purchase, storage, and use. All required information shall be readily visible, noticeable, clear, and, except where coding is permitted, shall be in legible English (other languages may also be included as appropriate). Such factors governing labeling as location, type size, and contrast against background may be based on necessary condensations to provide a reasonable display.

(b) *Specific items.* (1) The toy shall be marked in accordance with the provisions of paragraph (d) of this section to indicate:

(i) The electrical ratings required by paragraph (c) of this section.

(ii) Any precautionary statements required by paragraph (e) of this section.

(iii) The date (month and year) of manufacture (or appropriate codes). As an alternative to putting this information on the toy itself, it may be included in the instructions provided with the toy (see paragraph (b)(3) of this section).

(2) The shelf pack or package of the toy shall be labeled in accordance with the provisions of paragraph (d) of this section to indicate:

(i) The date (month and year) of manufacture (or appropriate codes).

(ii) The electrical ratings required by paragraph (c) of this section.

(iii) Any precautionary statements required by paragraph (e) of this section.

(3) Each toy shall be provided with adequate instructions that are easily understood by children of those ages for which the toy is intended. The instructions shall describe the applicable installation, assembly, use, cleaning, maintenance (including lubrication), and other functions as appropriate. Applicable precautions shall be included as well as the information required by paragraphs (b) (1) and (2) of this section, except that the date of manufacture information described in paragraph (b)(1)(iii) of this section need not be included in the instructions provided with the toy if it is placed on the toy itself. The instructions shall also contain a statement addressed to parents recommending that the toy be periodically examined for potential hazards and that any potentially hazardous parts be repaired or replaced.

(4) If a toy is produced or assembled at more than one establishment, the toy and its shelf pack or package shall have a distinctive mark (which may be in code) identifying the toy as the product of a particular establishment.

(c) *Rating.* (1) A toy shall be marked to indicate its rating in volts and also in amperes and/or watts.

(2) If a toy utilizes a single motor as its only electric energy consuming component, the electrical rating may be marked on a motor nameplate and need not be marked elsewhere on the toy if the nameplate is readily visible after the motor has been installed in the toy.

(3) A toy shall be rated for alternating current only, direct current only, or both alternating and direct current.

(4) The alternating current rating shall include the frequency or frequency range requirement, if necessary because of a special component.

(d) *Markings.* (1) The markings required on the toy by paragraph (b) of this section shall be of a permanent nature, such as paint-stenciled, die-stamped, molded, or indelibly stamped. The markings shall not be permanently obliterable by spillage of any material intended for use with the toy and shall not be readily removable by cleaning with ordinary household cleaning substances. All markings on the toy and labeling of the shelf pack or package required by paragraph (b) of this section shall contrast sharply with the background (whether by color, projection, or indentation) and shall be readily visible and legible. Such markings and labeling shall appear in lettering of a height not less than that specified in paragraph (d)(2) of this section, except that those words shown in capital letters in paragraph (e) of this section shall appear in capital lettering of a height not less than twice that specified in paragraph (d)(2) of this section.

(2) Minimum lettering heights shall be as follows:

SURFACE AREA DISPLAY MARKING, MINIMUM HEIGHT OF LETTERING

Square inches	Inches
Under 5	1/16
5 or more and under 25	1/8
25 or more and under 100	3/16
100 or more and under 400	1/4
400 or more	1/2

(e) *Precautionary statements*—(1) *General*. Electrically operated toys shall bear the statement: "CAUTION—ELECTRIC TOY." The instruction booklet or sheet accompanying such toys shall bear on the front page thereof (in the type size specified in § 1500.121), as a preface to any written matter contained therein, and the shelf pack or package of such toys shall bear in the upper right hand quarter of the principal display panel, the statement: "CAUTION—ELECTRIC TOY: Not recommended for children under ___ years of age. As with all electric products, precautions should be observed during handling and use to prevent electric shock." The blank in the preceding statement shall be filled in by the manufacturer, but in no instance shall the manufacturer indicate that the article is recommended for children under 8 years of age if it contains a heating element. In the case of other electrically operated products which may not be considered to be "toys" but are intended for use by children, the term "ELECTRICALLY OPERATED PRODUCT" may be substituted for the term "ELECTRIC TOY."

(2) *Thermal hazards*. (i) Toys having Type C or Type D surfaces (described in § 1505.6(g)(2)) which reach temperatures greater than those shown in paragraph (e)(2)(ii) of this section shall be defined as hot and shall be marked where readily noticeable when the hot surface is in view with the statement: "HOT—Do Not Touch." When the marking is on other than the hot surface, the word "HOT" shall be followed by appropriate descriptive words such as "Molten Material," "Sole Plate," or "Heating Element," and the statement "Do Not Touch." An alternative statement for a surface intended to be handheld as a functional part of the toy shall be "HOT ______ Handle Carefully," the blank being filled in by the manufacturer with a description of the potential hazard such as "Curler" or "Cooking Surface."

(ii) Surfaces requiring precautionary statements of thermal hazards are those exceeding the following temperatures when measured by the test described in § 1505.6(g)(4):

Surface type (see § 1505.6 (g)(2))	Thermal inertia type [1]	Temperature	
		Degrees C.	Degrees F.
C	1	65	149
C	2	75	167
C	3	85	185
C	4	95	203
D	1	55	131
D	2	70	158
D	3	80	176
D	4	90	194

[1] Thermal inertia types are defined in terms of lambda as follows:

Type 1: Greater than 0.0045 (e.g., most metals).

Type 2: More than 0.0005 but not more than 0.0045 (e.g., glass).

Type 3: More than 0.0001 but not more than 0.0005 (e.g., most plastics).

Type 4: 0.0001 or less (e.g., future polymeric materials).

The thermal inertia of a material can be obtained by multiplying the thermal conductivity (cal./em./sec./degrees C.) by the density (gm./cm.^{3}) by the specific heat (cal./gm./degrees C.)

(3) *Lamp hazards*—(i) *Replaceable incandescent lamps*. A toy with one or more replaceable incandescent lamps, having a potential difference of more than 30 volts r.m.s. (42.4 volts peak) between any of its electrodes or lampholder contacts and any other part or ground, shall be marked inside the lamp compartment where readily noticeable during lamp replacement with the statement: "WARNING—Do

not use light bulbs larger than ___ watts", the blank being filled in by the manufacturer with a number specifying the wattage rating of the lamp. Such toys shall bear the statement: "WARNING—Shock Hazard. Pull plug before changing light bulb" on the outside of the lamp compartment where it will be readily noticed before gaining access to the lamp compartment.

(ii) *Nonreplacement incandescent lamps.* A toy which utilizes one or more nonreplaceable incandescent lamps (other than pilot or indicator lamps) shall be marked where clearly visible with the statement: "SEALED UNIT—Do not attempt to change light bulb" or equivalent.

(4) *Water.* If not suitable for immersion in water, a toy cooking appliance (such as a corn popper, skillet, or candy-maker) or other article which may conceivably be immersed in water shall be marked with the statement: "DANGER—To prevent electric shock, do not immerse in water; wipe clean with damp cloth" or equivalent.

[38 FR 27032, Sept. 27, 1973, as amended at 42 FR 34280, July 5, 1977; 42 FR 43392, Aug. 29, 1977]

§ 1505.4 Manufacturing requirements.

(a) *General.* (1) Only materials safe and suitable for the particular use for which the electrically operated toy is intended shall be employed.

(2) Toys shall be produced in accordance with detailed material specifications, production specifications, and quality assurance programs. Quality assurance programs shall be established and maintained by each manufacturer to assure compliance with all requirements of this part.

(3) The manufacturer or importer shall keep and maintain for 3 years after production or importation of each lot of toys (i) the material and production specifications and the description of the quality assurance program required by paragraph (a)(2) of this section, (ii) the results of all inspections and tests conducted, and (iii) records of sale and distribution. These records shall be made available upon request at reasonable times to any officer or employee of the Consumer Product Safety Commission. The manufacturer or importer shall permit such officer or employee to inspect and copy such records, to make such inventories of stock as he deems necessary, and to otherwise verify the accuracy of such records.

(4) Toys shall be constructed and finished with a high degree of uniformity and as fine a grade of workmanship as is practicable in a well-equipped manufacturing establishment. Each component of a toy shall comply with the requirements set forth in this part.

(b) [Reserved]

(c) *Protective coatings.* Iron and steel parts shall be suitably protected against corrosion if the lack of a protective coating would likely produce a hazardous condition in normal use or when the toy is subjected to reasonably foreseeable damage or abuse.

(d) *Mechanical assembly*—(1) *General.* A toy shall be designed and constructed to have the strength and rigidity necessary to withstand reasonably foreseeable damage and abuse without producing or increasing a shock, fire, or other accident hazard. An increase in hazards may be due to total or partial structural collapse of the toy resulting in a reduction of critical spacings, loosening or displacement of one or more components, or other serious defects.

(2) *Mounting.* Each switch, lampholder, motor, automatic control, transformer, and similar component shall be securely mounted and shall be prevented from turning, unless the turning of such component is part of the design of the toy and produces no additional hazard such as reduced spacings below acceptable levels or stress on the connection. Friction between tight-fitting surfaces shall not be considered sufficient for preventing the turning of components. The proper use of a suitable lockwasher or a keyed and notched insert plus a suitable lockwasher for single-hole mountings shall be acceptable. Each toy shall be designed and constructed so that vibrations occurring during normal operation and after reasonably foreseeable damage or abuse will not affect it adversely. Brush caps shall be tightly threaded or otherwise designed to prevent loosening.

(3) *Structural integrity.* Heating elements shall be supported in a substantial and reliable manner and shall be structurally prevented from making contacts inside or outside of the toy which may produce shock hazards. The current-carrying component(s) of the heating element shall be enclosed, and the enclosure shall be designed or insulated to prevent the development of a shock or fire hazard that may result from element failure. A toy operating with a gas or liquid under pressure, such as an electrically operated steam engine, shall be tested with respect to its explosion hazard and shall be provided with a pressure relief device that will discharge in the safest possible direction; that is, avoiding direct human contact and avoiding the wetting of electrical contacts.

(e) *Insulating material.* (1) Material to be used for mounting uninsulated live electrical elements shall be generally accepted as suitable for the specific application, particularly with regard to electrical insulation (voltage breakdown) and good aging characteristics (no significant change in insulating characteristics over the expected lifetime of the toy).

(2) Material used to insulate a heating element from neighboring parts shall be suitable for the purpose. If plain asbestos in a glass braid is used to so insulate the heating element, it shall be tightly packed and totally enclosed by the braid, and the overall thickness, including the braid, shall not be less than one-sixteenth inch. Hard fiber may be used for electrically insulating bushings, washers, separators, and barriers, but is not sufficient as the sole support of uninsulated live metal parts.

(f) *Enclosures*—(1) *General.* Each toy shall have an enclosure constructed of protective material suitable for the particular application, for the express purpose of housing all electrical parts that may present a fire, shock, or other accident hazard under any conditions of normal use or reasonably foreseeable damage or abuse. Enclosures shall meet the performance requirements prescribed by § 1505.6(b).

(2) *Accessibility.* An enclosure containing a wire, splice, brush cap, connection. electrical component, or uninsulated live part or parts at a potential of more than 30 volts r.m.s. (42.4 volts peak) to any other part or to ground:

(i) Shall be sealed by welding, riveting, adhesive bonding, and/or by special screws or other fasteners not removable with a common household tool (screwdriver, pliers, or other similar household tool) used as intended; and

(ii) Shall have no opening permitting entry of a 0.010-inch-diameter music wire that could contact a live part. Cross-notch-head screws, spring clips, bent tabs, and similar fasteners shall not be considered suitable sealing devices for enclosures since they are easy to remove with common household tools. Bent tabs shall be acceptable if, due to metal thickness or other factors, they successfully resist forceful attempts to dislodge them with ordinary tools.

(3) *Nonapplication.* The requirements of this paragraph are not applicable to an insulating husk enclosure or equivalent that covers the electrodes of a replaceable incandescent lamp and its lampholder contacts. The primary function of an enclosure containing a lamp shall be to protect it from breakage during normal use or reasonably foreseeable damage or abuse.

(g) *Spacings.* The distance, through air or across the surface of an insulator, between uninsulated live metal parts and a metallic enclosure and between uninsulated live metal parts and all other metal parts shall be suitable for the specific application as determined by the dielectric strength requirements prescribed by § 1505.6(e)(2). Electrical insulating linings on barriers shall be held securely in place.

(h) *Special safety features*—(1) *Moving parts.* If the normal use of a toy involves accident hazards, suitable protection shall be provided for the reduction of such hazards to an acceptable minimum. For example, rotors, pulleys, belting, gearing, and other moving parts shall be enclosed or guarded to prevent accidental contact during normal use or when subjected to reasonably foreseeable damage or abuse. Such enclosure or guard shall not contain openings that permit entrance of a ¼-inch-diameter rod and present a hazardous condition.

(2) *Switch marking.* Any toy having one or more moving parts which perform an inherent function of the toy and which may cause personal injury shall have a switch that can deenergize the toy by a simple movement to a plainly marked "OFF" position. Momentary contact switches which are normally in the "OFF" position need not be so marked.

(3) *Electrically operated sewing machines.* Electrically operated toy sewing machines shall be designed and constructed to eliminate the possibility of a child's finger(s) being pierced by a needle. For the purpose of this paragraph, a clearance of not more than five thirty-seconds of an inch below the point of the needle when in its uppermost position or below the presser foot, if provided, shall be considered satisfactory.

(4) *Pressure relief valves.* A pressurized enclosure shall have an automatic pressure relief device and shall be capable of withstanding hydrostatic pressure equal to at least five times the relief pressure.

(5) *Containers for heated materials.* Containers intended for holding molten compounds and hot liquids shall be designed and constructed to minimize accidental spillage. A pot or pan having a lip and one or more properly located pouring spouts and an adequately thermally insulated handle may provide satisfactory protection. Containers intended solely for baking need not be designed and constructed to minimize accidental spillage. Containers shall be of such material and construction t+at they will not deform or melt when subjected to the maximum operating temperature occurring during normal use or after reasonably foreseeable damage or abuse.

(6) *Water.* Electrically operated toys (such as toy irons) shall not be designed or manufactured to be used with water except for toy steam engines or other devices in which the electrical components are separate from the water reservoir and are completely contained in a sealed chamber. Toys requiring occasional or repeated cleaning with a wet cloth shall be constructed to prevent seepage of water into any electrically active area that may produce a hazardous condition.

§ 1505.5 Electrical design and construction.

(a) *Switches.* (1) Switches and other control devices of electrically operated toys shall be suitable for the application and shall have a rating not less than that of the load they control (see § 1505.6(e)(5)(ii) regarding electrical switch overload). A switch that controls a replaceable incandescent lamp, electrode, or lampholder contact which is at a potential of more than 30 volts r.m.s. (42.4 volts peak) to any other part or to ground shall open both sides of the circuit and shall have a marked "OFF" position. A switch that may reasonably be expected to be subjected to temperatures higher than 50 °C. (122 °F.) shall be constructed of materials which are suitable for use at such temperatures.

(2) Switches shall be located and protected so that they are not subject to mechanical damage that would produce a hazard in normal use or from reasonably foreseeable damage or abuse (see § 1505.6(b)).

(b) *Lamps.* (1) A replaceable incandescent lamp having a voltage of more than 30 volts r.m.s. (42.4 volts peak) between any of its electrodes or lampholder contacts and any other part or ground shall be in an enclosure that has at least one door or cover permitting access to the lamp. Such door(s) or cover(s) of the enclosure shall be so designed and constructed that they cannot be opened manually or with a flat bladed screwdriver or pliers.

(2) With all access doors and covers closed, the lamp enclosure shall have no opening that will permit entry of a straight rod 6 inches long and one-fourth inch in diameter if such entry would present an electrical hazard. The lamp shall be located no less than one-half inch from any ¼-inch-diameter opening in the enclosure.

(3) A toy having one or more lampholders shall be designed and constructed so that no live parts other than the contacts of the lampholders are exposed to contact by persons removing or replacing lamps. The shells of all lampholders for incandescent lamps shall be at the same potential.

(4) If the potential between the contacts of a lampholder for a replaceable

incandescent lamp and any other part or ground is greater than 30 volts r.m.s. (42.4 volts peak), the contacts shall be located in an insulating husk or equivalent.

(c) *Transformers.* Transformers that are integral parts of toys shall be of the 2-coil insulated type.

(d) *Automatic controls.* Automatic controls for temperature regulations shall have the necessary capacity and reliability for their particular application.

(e) *Power supply connections (cords and plugs).* (1) A toy shall be provided with a suitable means for attachement to the power supply circuit.

(2) A toy requiring a power cord shall have a flexible cord that is permanently attached to the toy.

(3) The perimeter of the face of the attachment-plug cap shall be not less than five-sixteenths of an inch from any point on either blade of the plug.

(4) The body of the attachment-plug cap shall decrease in cross section from the face but shall have an expansion of the body, after a suitable distance from the face, sufficient to provide an effective finger grip.

(5) A flexible electrical power cord provided on a toy shall be type SP–2 (as defined in the "National Electrical Code," Chapter 4, article 400, pages 230–241 (1978)[1], or its equivalent, or a heavier general-use type, and shall be not less than 5 feet nor more than 10 feet in length when measured as the overall length of the attached cord outside the enclosure of the toy, including fittings, up to the face of the attachment-plug cap. However, hand-held educational or hobby-type products intended for heating such as woodburning tools, shall use one of the type cords designated below, in accordance with the weight of the product without the cord:

WEIGHT OF APPLIANCE (WITHOUT CORD) AND CORD TYPE

½ lb. (0.227 kg) and lighter: SP–1, SPT–1, HPD. Heavier than ½ lb. (0.227 kg): SP–2, SPT–2, SV, SVO, SVT, SVTO, HPD, HPN, SJ, SJO, SJT, SJTO.

(6) A flexible cord and plug shall have a current-carrying capacity of not less than the ampere rating of the toy, and the conductor of the cord shall have a cross sectional area no less than No. 18 AWG (American wire gauge).

(7) Cords on toys which are intended to come in direct contact with water or other liquids during use shall be of a jacketed type. Cords on toys with which water or other liquids are to be indirectly used (such as for cooling a mold) shall be plastic covered.

(8) Transformers in which the primary coil connects directly to the branch circuit outlet shall not be subject to the requirements of paragraphs (e) (2), (4), and (5) of this section.

(f) *Bushings.* (1) At the point where a power supply cord passes through an opening in a wall, barrier, or the overall enclosure of a toy, a suitable and substantial bushing, insulating bushing, or equivalent shall be reliably secured in place and shall have smooth surfaces and well-rounded edges against which the cord may bear.

(2) If a cord hole is in wood, porcelain, phenolic composition, or other suitable insulating material, the surface of the hole is acceptable without a bushing if the edges of the hole are smooth and well-rounded. Where a separate insulating bushing is required, a bushing made of ceramic material or a suitable molded composition is acceptable if its edges are smooth and well-rounded.

(3) In no instance shall a separate bushing of wood, rubber, or any of the hot-molded shellac-and-tar compositions be considered acceptable.

(g) *Wiring.* (1) The internal wiring of a toy shall consist of suitable insulated conductors having adequate mechanical strength, dielectric properties, and

[1] NFPA No. 70–1978, 1978 edition of National Electrical Code, Article 400, "Flexible Cords and Cables," pages 70–230 through 70–240, published by the National Fire Protection Association, which is incorporated by reference. Copies of this document are available from the National Fire Protection Administration, 60 Batterymarch Park, Quincy, Massachusetts 02269. This document is also available for inspection at the National Archives and Records Administration (NARA). For information on the availability of this material at NARA, call 202–741–6030, or go to: *http://www.archives.gov/federal_register/code_of_federal_regulations/ibr_locations.html.* This incorporation by reference was approved by the Director of the Federal Register. These materials are incorporated as they exist in the edition which has been approved by the Director of the Federal Register and which has been filed with the Office of the Federal Register.

electrical capacity for the particular application.

(2) Wireways shall be smooth and entirely free of sharp edges, burrs, fins, and moving parts that may abrade conductor insulation. Each splice and connection shall be mechanically secure, shall provide adequate and reliable electrical contact, and shall be provided with insulation at least equivalent to that of the wire involved unless adequate spacing between the splice and all other metal parts is permanently assured.

(3) A wire connector for making a splice in a toy shall be a type that is applied by a tool and for which the application force of the tool is independent of the force applied by the operator.

(4) Soldered connections shall be made mechanically secure before soldering.

(5) Current-carrying parts shall be made of silver, copper, a copper alloy, or other electrically conductive material suitable for the particular application.

(h) *Strain relief.* (1) A means of strain relief shall be provided to prevent mechanical stress on a flexible cord from being transmitted to terminals, splices, or interior wiring.

(2) If suitable auxiliary insulation is provided under a clamp for mechanical protection, clamps of any material are acceptable for use on Type SP–2 (as defined in the "National Electrical Code," chapter 4, article 400, pages 184–194 (1971)[2]) or equivalent rubber-insulated cord. For heavier types of thermoplastic-insulated cord, clamps may be without auxiliary insulation unless the clamp may damage the cord insulation.

(3) A flexible cord shall be prevented from being pushed into the toy through the cord-entry hole if such displacement would result in a hazardous condition.

(4) A knot in the cord shall not be considered an acceptable means of strain relief, but a knot associated with a loop around a smooth, fixed structural component shall be considered acceptable.

(i) *Additional requirements.* Except for the electrodes of a replaceable incandescent lamp and its lampholder contacts, a potential of more than 30 volts r.m.s. (42.4 volts peak) shall not exist between any exposed live part in a toy and any other part or ground.

(Sec. 30(a), 86 Stat. 1231 (15 U.S.C. 2079(a)))

[38 FR 27032, Sept. 27, 1973, as amended at 43 FR 45552, Oct. 3, 1978; 46 FR 63251, Dec. 31, 1981]

§ 1505.6 Performance.

(a) *General.* Electrically operated toys and components thereof shall be tested by the appropriate methods described in this section and shall pass the tests in such a manner as to provide the necessary assurance that normal use and reasonably foreseeable damage or abuse will not produce a hazard or a potentially hazardous condition. The toy shall be capable of passing all applicable tests with any door, cover, handle, operable part, or accessory placed in any normal position. A toy shall not present a fire, casualty, or shock hazard when operated continuously for 6 hours under conditions of normal use and reasonably foreseeable damage or abuse, including the most hazardous position in which the toy can be left.

(b) *Enclosures.* For the purposes of this section, the term *enclosure* means any surface or surrounding structure which prevents access to a real or potential hazard. An enclosure shall withstand impact, compression, and pressure tests (see paragraphs (b)(1),

[2] NFPA No. 70–1971, 1971 edition of National Electrical Code, Article 400, "Flexible Cords and Cables," pages 70–184 through 70–194, published by the National Fire Protection Association, which is incorporated by reference. Copies of this document are available from the National Fire Protection Association, 60 Batterymarch Park, Quincy, Massachusetts 02269. This document is also available for inspection at the National Archives and Records Administration (NARA). For information on the availability of this material at NARA, call 202–741–6030, or go to: *http://www.archives.gov/federal_register/code_of_federal_regulations/ibr_locations.html.* This incorporation by reference was approved by the Director of the Federal Register. These materials are incorporated as they exist in the edition which has been approved by the Director of the Federal Register and which has been filed with the Office of the Federal Register.

(2), and (3) of this section) without developing any openings above those specified, reduction of electrical spacings below those specified, or other fire, casualty, or shock hazards, including the loosening or displacement of components but excluding breakage of a lamp. After completion of each test, the toy shall comply with the requirements of the dielectric strength test described in paragraph (e)(2) of this section and, upon visual examination, shall not evidence the development of any hazards. Rupture of a fuse shall be considered a test failure.

(1) *Impact test.* A toy weighing 10 pounds or less shall be dropped four times from a height of 3 feet onto a 2½ inch thick concrete slab covered with 0.125 inch nominal thickness vinyl title. The impact area shall be at least 3 square feet. The test shall be conducted while the toy is energized and operating and with all dead metal of the toy that may be energized connected together electrically and grounded through a 3-ampere plug fuse. The toy shall be dropped in random orientation. After each drop the test sample shall be allowed to come to rest and examined and evaluated before continuing.

(2) *Compression test.* Any area on the surface of the enclosure that is accessible to a child and inaccessible to flat-surface contact during the impact test shall be subjected to a direct force of 20 pounds for 1 minute. The force shall be applied over a period of 5 seconds through the axis of a ½-inch-diameter metal rod having a flat end with the edge rounded to a radius of one thirty-seconds of an inch to eliminate sharp edges. The axis of the rod shall be perpendicular to the surface being tested. During the test the toy shall rest on a flat, hard surface in any test-convenient position.

(3) *Pressure test.* If any portion of the top of a toy has a flat surface measuring 24 square inches or more and a minor dimension of at least 3 inches, that surface shall be subjected to a direct vertical pressure increasing to 50 pounds over a period of 5 seconds and maintained for 1 minute. The force shall be applied through a steel ball 2 inches in diameter. During the test the toy shall be in an upright position on a flat, horizontal solid surface.

(c) *Handles and knobs*—(1) *General.* For the purposes of tests in this paragraph, the parts of a lifting handle on a toy that are within seven-sixteenths of an inch of the surface to which the handle is attached, or the parts of a lifting knob that are within one-fourth inch of the surface to which the knob is attached, are considered to be for support purposes, and the remainder of the handle or knob is considered to be generally functional in nature. A handle or knob shall withstand crushing and lifting tests (see paragraphs (c)(2) and (3) of this section) without fracture of the handle or knob, development of an opening that may pinch the hand, or breakage of the means used to fasten the handle or knob in place.

(2) *Crushing test.* The functional portion of a handle or knob shall be subjected to a crushign force increasing to 20 pounds over a period of 5 seconds and maintained for 1 minute. The force shall be applied through two flat and parallel hardwood blocks, each at least 2½ inches thick and each having dimensions slightly exceeding those of the handle or knob being tested. The crushing force between the blocks shall be exerted in any direction perpendicular to the major axis of the handle or knob.

(3) *Lifting test.* The support portion of a handle or knob shall be subjected to a force equal to four times the weight of the object it is intended to support. The direction of the lifting force shall be as intended by the design of the toy and shall be applied through a ½-inch-wide strap through or around a handle or by fingers or the equivalent on a knob. The force shall be applied over a period of 5 seconds through the center of gravity of the toy and maintained for 1 minute.

(d) *Stability.* A toy shall not overturn while resting in an upright position on a flat surface inclined 15° from horizontal. No spillage of molten material or hot liquids from containers shall occur while the toy is operating in this position under normal conditions of use. During this test, casters, if any, shall be in the position most likely to result in tipping, but shall not be artificially held in one position to prevent a natural rotation to another position.

(e) *Electrical*—(1) *Power input.* The actual current flow in a toy without a heating element shall not exceed 110 percent of the rated value, and shall not exceed 5.5 amperes, at rated voltage. The power input to a toy with a heating element shall not exceed 105 percent of the rated value at rated voltage. The power input rating of a toy employing one or more incandescent lamps as the only power-consuming components shall be considered to be the total rated wattage of such lamps. The rated voltage shall be considered to be the mean value of a marked voltage range.

(2) *Dielectric strength.* (i) A toy shall be capable of withstanding without breakdown for 1 minute a 60-cycle-per-second (60 Hertz) essentially sinusoidal potential of 1,000 volts applied between live parts and any dead metal parts.

(ii) If a toy employs a low-voltage secondary winding (either in the form of a conventional transformer or as an insulated coil of a motor), the toy shall also be capable of withstanding without breakdown for 1 minute a sinusoidal test potential applied between the high-voltage and low-voltage windings. The test potential shall be applied at the rated frequency of the toy and shall have a value of 1,000 volts plus twice the rated voltage of the high-voltage winding. The test potential shall be supplied from a suitable capacity-testing transformer, the output voltage of which can be regulated. The waveform of the test voltage shall approximate a sine wave as closely as possible.

(iii) The applied test potential shall be increased rapidly and uniformly from zero until the required test value is reached and shall be held at that value for 1 minute. Unless otherwise specified, the toy shall be at the maximum operating temperature reached in normal use prior to conducting the tests.

(iv) The dielectric strength requirements of this subparagraph may also be determined by subjecting the toy to a 60-cycle-per-second (60 Hertz) essentially sinusoidal potential of 1,200 volts for 1 second. If the dielectric strength is determined by this method, the toy need not be in a heated condition.

(3) *Leakage current and repeated dielectric withstand tests.* (i) Both before and after being conditioned, a toy intended to operate from a source exceeding 42.4 volts peak shall:

(A) Not have a leakage current exceeding 0.5 milliampere, except that during the interval beginning 5 seconds and terminating 10 minutes after the toy is first energized, the leakage current of toys with heating elements other than lamps shall not exceed 2.5 milliamperes; and

(B) Comply with the requirements of a repeated dielectric withstand test both with and without preheating.

(ii) All accessible parts of a toy shall be tested for leakage current. If an insulating material is used for the enclosure or part of the enclosure, the leakage current shall be measured using a metal foil with an area not exceeding 10 by 20 centimeters in contact with accessible surfaces of such insulating material. Where the accessible surface of insulating material is less than 10 by 20 centimeters, the metal foil shall be the same size as the surface. The metal foil shall be so applied that it will not affect the temperature of the toy. The accessible parts shall be tested individually, collectively, and from one part to another.

(iii) Following the initial leakage current test, the toy shall be cooled down or heated up to 32 °C. (90 °F.). The toy shall then be conditioned for 48 hours in air at a temperature of 32° ±2 °C. (89.6° ±3.6 °F.) and with a relative humidity of 90–95 percent. The specified relative humidity shall be maintained inside a closed compartment in which a saturated solution of potassium sulphate is kept in a suitable container. Leakage current measurements shall be made, as specified in paragraph (e)(3)(ii) of this section and before the toy is energized, while the toy is in the humidity compartment.

(iv) With the connections intended for the source of supply connected thereto and then connected to the ungrounded side of a power supply circuit having a voltage equal to 110 percent of the rated voltage of the toy, the leakage current through a noninductive 1,500-ohm resistor connected between the gounded side of the supply circuit and each dead metal part (accessible and inaccessible) shall, when stable, be measured in accordance with the test provisions established in ANSI Standard C 101.1–1971, "American National Standard for Leakage Current for Appliances," approved November 17, 1970, which is incorporated by reference. Copies of this document are available from American National Standards Institute, 1430 Broadway, New York, New York 10018. This document is also available for inspection at the National Archives and Records Administration (NARA). For information on the availability of this material at NARA, call 202–741–6030, or go to: *http://www.archives.gov/federal_register/code_of_federal_regulations/ibr_locations.html.* This incorporation by reference was approved by the Director of the Federal Register. These materials are incorporated as they exist in the edition which has been approved by the Director of the Federal Register and which has been filed with the Office of the Federal Register.

(v) For a toy whose outer enclosure consists wholly or partly of insulating material, the term *dead metal part* means metal foil tightly wrapped around the exterior of the enclosure in a manner that covers, but does not enter into, any enclosure openings.

(4) *Motor operation.* (i) A motor provided as part of a toy shall be capable of driving its maximum normal load in the toy without introducing any potentially hazardous condition. The performance of the toy shall be considered unacceptable if, during the test, temperatures in excess of those specified in § 1505.7 for Type D surfaces are attained on any accessible surface. The performance of the toy shall also be considered unacceptable if the rise in temperature during the test causes melting, scorching, embrittlement, or other evidence of thermal damage to the insulating material used to prevent exposure of live metal parts.

(ii) A motor-operated toy shall be tested with the motor stalled if the construction of the toy is such that any person can touch moving parts associated with the motor from outside the toy. The performance of the toy shall be considered unacceptable if, during the test, temperatures higher than those specified in § 1505.8 are attained or if temperatures higher than those specified for Type C surfaces in § 1505.7 are attained on any accessible surface of the motor. (See also § 1505.50.)

(5) *Overload*—(i) *Motor.* A motor-control switch that is a part of a toy shall be horsepower-rated to cover the load or shall be capable of performing acceptably when subjected to an overload test consisting of 50 cycles of operation by making and breaking the stalled-rotor current of the toy at maximum rated voltage. There shall be no electrical or mechanical failure nor any visible burning or pitting of the switch contacts as a result of this test.

(ii) *Switch.* To determine if a motor-control switch is capable of performing acceptably when subjected to overload conditions, the toy shall be connected to a grounded supply circuit of rated frequency and maximum rated voltage with the rotor of the motor locked into position. During the test, exposed dead metal parts of the toy shall be connected to ground through a 3-ampere plug fuse such that any single pole, current-rupturing device will be located in the ungrounded conductor of the supply circuit. If the toy is intended for use on direct current, or on direct current as well as alternating current, the exposed dead metal parts of the toy shall be so connected as to be positive with respect to a single pole, current-rupturing device. The switch shall be operated at a rate of not more than 10 cycles per minute. The performance of the toy shall be considered unacceptable if the fuse in the grounding connection is blown during the test.

(f) *Hydrokinetic*—(1) *General.* Electrically operated toy steam engines shall be capable of performing acceptably when subjected to the tests described in this paragraph.

(2) *Preliminary test.* The ultimate strength of the boiler assembly shall first be determined by applying a hydrostatic pressure to the boiler with all openings blocked (the pressure-relief valve, steam exhausts, and any whistle or other accessory shall be removed

and the resulting openings sealed); however, a water or other type of gage shall be left in place. The hydrostatic pressure shall be applied slowly and the ultimate value which is attained shall be recorded.

(3) *Pressure-relief test.* A pressure gage shall be connected to the boiler assembly which shall then be operated normally. The pressure at which the pressure-relief valve functions shall be noted while the engine is shut off (if a shutoff valve is provided) and with the whistle, if any, turned off. The test shall be discontinued and shall be considered a failure if the observed pressure exceeds one-fifth the value attained in the preliminary test described in paragraph (f)(2) of this section.

(4) *Operating pressure test.* If the boiler is still intact and no failure has occurred, the pressure-relief valve shall then be rendered inoperable and all other valves (such as a whistle and exhaust from the assembly) shall be tightly closed. Operations shall be continued until the pressure becomes constant. This test shall be discontinued and shall be considered a failure if the observed pressure exceeds one-third the value attained in the preliminary test described in paragraph (f)(2) of this section. During this test, all valves, gaskets, joints, and similar components shall be sufficiently tightened to prevent leakage. Rupture of the boiler or of any other fittings supplied with the engine shall be considered a failure.

(5) *Hydrostatic test.* If there has been no failure, two previous untested toys shall withstand for 1 minute a hydrostatic pressure of 5 times the pressure at which the safety valve operated or 3 times the constant pressure observed with the pressure-relief valve inoperable, whichever is greater. During this test, all openings shall be blocked (the pressure-relief valve, steam exhaust from the assembly, and any whistle or other outlet); however, a water or other type of gage shall remain in place. Rupture of the boiler or of a gage shall be considered a failure.

(g) *Thermal*—(1) *General.* The normal operation of a toy includes performance in normal use and after being subjected to reasonably foreseeable damage or abuse likely to produce the highest temperatures or, in the case of motor-operated toys, the load that most closely approximates the severest conditions of normal use or reasonably foreseeable damage or abuse.

(2) *Classification.* Parts or surfaces of a toy are classified according to their use or function as follows (for the purposes of paragraph (g)(2) (v), (vi), and (vii) of this section, accessibility shall be defined as the ability to reach a heated surface with a ¼-inch-diameter rod 3 inches long as described in § 1505.51(a)):

(i) *Type A.* A part or surface of a toy (such as a handle) likely to be grasped by the hand or fingers for the purpose of carrying the toy or lifting a separable lid.

(ii) *Type B.* A part or surface of a toy that is (*a*) part of a handle, knob, or similar component, as in Type A (described in paragraph (g)(2)(i) of this section), but which is not normally grasped or contacted by the hand or fingers for carrying (including parts of a handle within 7⁄16 inch of the surface to which the handle is attached and parts of a finger knob within ¼ inch of the surface to which the knob is attached, if the remainder of the knob is large enough to be grasped), or (*b*) a handle, knob, or part that may be touched but which need not be grasped for carrying the toy or lifting a lid, door, or cover (e.g., support part of a handle or knob).

(iii) *Type C.* A part or surface of a toy that can be touched by casual contact or that can be touched without employing the aid of a common household tool (screwdriver, pliers, or other similar household tool) and that is either (*a*) a surface that performs an intended heating function (e.g., the soleplate of a flat-iron, a cooking surface, or a heating element surface), or (*b*) a material heated by the element and intended to be used as the product of the toy, excluding pans, dishes, or other containers used to hold the material to be cooked or baked if a common utensil or other device is supplied with the toy and specific instructions are established for using such a device to remove the container from the heated area. (See also § 1505.51(b))

(iv) *Type C marked.* A Type C surface which has been marked with a precautionary statement of thermal hazards in accordance with § 1505.3(e)(2). (See also § 1505.51(b))

(v) *Type D.* An accessible part or surface of a toy other than Types A, B, C or E (see paragraph (g)(2) (i), (ii), (iii) and (vii) of this paragraph).

(vi) *Type D marked.* A Type D surface which has been marked with a precautionary statement of thermal hazards in accordance with § 1505.3(e)(2).

(vii) *Type E.* A heated surface in an oven or other article that is inaccessible or protected by an electrical-thermal safety interlock. Such interlocks shall prohibit the operation of a heating device whenever such surfaces are accessible and shall not allow accessibility to such surfaces until the temperatures of those surfaces have been reduced to levels below those established for Type D surfaces (paragraph (g)(2)(v) of this section).

(3) *Requirements.* When tested under the conditions described in paragraph (g)(4) of this section, a toy shall not attain a temperature at any point sufficiently high to constitute a fire hazard or to adversely affect any materials employed and shall not show a maximum temperature higher than those established by §§ 1505.7 and 1505.8. These maximum surface temperature requirements are not applicable to educational-or hobby-type products such as lead-casting sets and wood-burning tools which are appropriately labeled on the shelf pack or package as being intended only for children over 12 years of age provided that the maximum surface temperature of any such toy does not exceed that reasonably required to accomplish the intended technical effect. Such toys shall be provided with specific instructions and the warning statements required by and in accordance with § 1505.3 (d) and (e), and shall be appropriately identified as educational or hobby-type products.

(4) *Test conditions*—(i) *General.* Tests shall be conducted while the toy is connected to a circuit of 60-cycle-per-second (60 Hertz) current using the materials supplied with the toy or using materials otherwise intended to be used with the toy. Following such tests, the toy shall be energized for a 6-hour period to determine that no hazardous conditions would result from unattended use of the toy.

(ii) *Temperature.* Normally, tests shall be performed at an ambient (room) temperature of 25 °C. (77 °F.); however, a test may be conducted at any ambient temperature within the range of 21° to 30 °C. (69.8° to 86 °F.).

(iii) *Voltage.* The toy shall be tested at the voltage indicated in the manufacturer's rating or at 120 volts, whichever is greater.

(5) *Temperature measurements*—(i) *General.* Temperatures shall be measured by means of instruments utilizing thermocouples of No. 30 AWG (American Wire Gage) wire (either copper and constantan or iron and constantan) and potentiometer-type instruments that are accurate and are calibrated in accordance with current good laboratory practices. The thermocouple wire shall conform with the requirements for "special" thermocouples as listed in the table of limits of error of thermocouples (Table VIII) in ANSI Standard C 96.1–1964, "American Standard for Temperature Measurement Thermocouples," approved June 9, 1964, which is incorporated by reference. Copies of this document are available from American National Standards Institute, 1430 Broadway, New York, New York 10018. This standard is also available for inspection at the National Archives and Records Administration (NARA). For information on the availability of this material at NARA, call 202–741–6030, or go to: *http://www.archives.gov/federal_register/code_of_federal_regulations/ibr_locations.html.* This incorporation by reference was approved by the Director of the Office of the Federal Register. These materials are incorporated as they exist in the edition which has been approved by the Director of the Federal Register and which has been filed with the Office of the Federal Register.

(ii) *Test procedures.* The thermocouple junction and adjacent thermocouple lead wire shall be securely held in good thermal contact with the surface of the material whose temperature is being measured. In most cases, good thermal contact will result from securely taping or cementing the thermocouple in place. If a metal surface is involved, brazing or soldering the thermocouple to the metal may be necessary. The surface temperatures of a toy shall be measured with the toy operating in any unattended condition (e.g., with and without opening and closing doors or covers) for a sufficient period of time to allow temperatures to become constant, or, in the case of a toy with a thermostatically controlled heating element, for a sufficient period of time to determine the maximum surface temperature attained. A temperature shall be considered to be constant when three successive readings taken at 15-minute intervals indicate no change.

(iii) *Heating devices.* Toy ovens, casting toys, popcorn and candy makers, and other toys requiring the insertion of any materials or substances shall be additionally tested by feeding crumpled strips of newspaper and tissue paper into or onto the toy in place of the intended materials or substances. The test strips shall be conditioned for at least 48 hours in air at a temperature of 25° ±4 °C. (77° ±7 °F.) and a relative humidity of 50 percent ±5 percent. The test strips shall be 2 inches wide by 8 inches long before crumpling. The crumpled paper shall occupy not more than 25 percent of the accessible volume. The performance of the toy shall be considered unacceptable if flaming occurs within a 60-minute period following the attainment of normal operating temperatures. If a light bulb is used for heating purposes, the test shall be conducted using the largest wattage bulb that can be easily inserted into the socket.

(h) *Strain-relief test.* (1) The strain-relief means provided on the flexible power cord of a toy shall be capable of withstanding a direct pull of 35 pounds applied to the cord for 2 minutes without displacement of the strain-relief unit or a deformation of the anchoring surface that would produce a stress which would result in a potentially hazardous condition. A 35-pound weight shall be attached to the cord and supported by the toy in such a manner that the strain-relief means is stressed from any angle that the construction of the toy permits. The test shall be conducted with the electrical connection within the toy disconnected.

(2) The initial 2-minute test shall be conducted with the force vector parallel to the longitudinal axis of the cord and perpendicular to the anchoring surface of the strain-relief unit. Each test at other angles of stress shall be conducted for periods of 1 minute. The strain-relief means is not acceptable if, at the point of disconnection of the cord, there is any movement of the cord to indicate that stress would have resulted on the conections.

(3) Except for toys weighing more than 10 pounds, the strain-relief unit and its support base shall be designed and constructed in such a manner that no indication of stress would result which would produce a hazard when the cord is held firmly in place 3 feet from the strain-relief unit and the toy is dropped the 3 feet at any angle.

[38 FR 27032, Sept. 27, 1973; 38 FR 30105, Nov. 1, 1973, as amended at 43 FR 26428 June 20, 1978; 46 FR 63251, Dec. 31, 1981; 51 FR 34199, Sept. 26, 1986]

§ 1505.7 Maximum acceptable surface temperatures.

The maximum acceptable surface temperatures for electrically operated toys shall be as follows:

Surface type (as described—in § 1505.6 (g)(2))	Thermal inertia type [1]	Temperatures	
		°C.	°F.
A	1	50	122
A	2	55	131
A	3	60	140
B	1	55	131
B	2	65	149
B	3	75	167
C (unmarked)	1	65	149
C (unmarked)	2	75	167
C (unmarked)	3	85	185
C (unmarked)	4	95	203
C marked	1	70	158
C marked	2	90	194
C marked	3	110	230
C marked	4	130	266
D (unmarked)	1	55	131
D (unmarked)	2	70	158
D (unmarked)	3	80	176
D (unmarked)	4	90	194
D marked	1	60	140
D marked	2	75	167
D marked	3	100	212
D marked	4	125	257
E	(2)	(3)	(3)

[1] Thermal inertia types are defined in terms of lambda as follows:

Type 1: Greater than 0.0045 (e.g., most metals).

Type 2: More than 0.0005 but not more than 0.0045 (e.g., glass).

Type 3: More than 0.0001 but not more than 0.0005 (e.g., most plastics).

Type 4: 0.0001 or less (e.g., future polymeric materials).

The thermal inertia of a material can be obtained by multiplying the thermal conductivity (cal./cm./sec./degrees C.) by the density (gm./cm.³) by the specific heat (cal./gm./degrees C.).

[2] All types.
[3] No limit.

§ 1505.8 Maximum acceptable material temperatures.

The maximum acceptable material temperatures for electrically operated toys shall be as follows (Classes 105, 130, A, and B are from "Motors and Generators," Standard MG–1–1967[1] published by the National Electrical Manufacturers Association):

Material	Degrees C.	Degrees F.
Capacitors	(1)	(1)
Class 105 insulation on windings or relays, solenoids, etc.:		
Thermocouple method[2]	90	194
Resistance method	110	230
Class 130 insulation system	110	230
Insulation:		
Varnished-cloth insulation	85	185
Fiber used as electrical insulation	90	194

	Class A	Class B	Class A	Class B
Insulation on coil windings of a.c. motors (not including universal motors) and on vibrator coils:				
In open motors and on vibrator coils—thermocouple or resistance method[2]	100	120	212	248
In totally enclosed motors—thermocouple or resistance method[2]	105	125	221	257
Insulation on coil windings of d.c. motors and of universal motors:				
In open motors:				
Thermocouple method[2]	90	110	194	230
Resistance method	100	120	212	248
In totally enclosed motors:				
Thermocouple method[2]	95	115	203	239
Resistance method	105	125	221	257
Phenolic composition[3]	....	150	302	....
Rubber- or thermoplastic-insulated wires and cords[3]	....	60	140	....
Sealing compound	....	(4)	(5)	....
Supporting surface while the toy is operating normally	....	90	194	....
Wood and other similar combustible material	....	90	194	....

[1] If the capacitor has no marked temperature limit, the maximum acceptable temperature will be assumed to be 65 °C. (149 °F.) for an electrolytic type and 90 °C. (194 °F.) for other than an electrolytic type.
[2] The temperature indicated refers to the hottest spot on the outside surface of the coil measured by the thermocouple method.
[3] The limitations on rubber- and thermoplastic-insulated wires and cords and on phenolic composition do not apply if the insulation or the phenolic has been investigated and found to have special heat-resistant properties, or if the insulation meets the thermal requirements.
[4] 40 less than melting point.
[5] 104 less than melting point.

Subpart B—Policies and Interpretations

§ 1505.50 Stalled motor testing.

(a) § 1505.6(e)(4)(ii) requires that a motor-operated toy be tested with the motor stalled if the construction of the toy is such that any person can touch moving parts associated with the motor from outside the toy. The performance of the toy shall be considered unacceptable if, during the test, temperatures higher than those specified in § 1505.8 are attained or if temperatures higher than those specified for Type C surfaces in § 1505.7 are attained on any accessible surface of the motor.

(b) To determine if a moving part associated with the motor can be touched from outside the toy, the Commission staff will use a ¼-inch diameter rod, as referenced in § 1505.4(h)(1). If the rod, when inserted into openings in the toy, can touch any moving part associated with the motor, the toy will be tested with the motor stalled.

[1] Copies may be obtained from: National Electrical Manufacturers Association, 155 East 44th Street, New York, NY 10017.

(c) The requirement that temperatures higher than those specified in § 1505.8 not be attained applies to those internal components which are described in § 1505.8. Additionally, temperatures of accessible surfaces shall not exceed those specified for Type C surfaces in § 1505.7.

(Secs. 2(q)(1)(A), 2(r), 3(e), 10(a), 74 Stat. 372, 378, 80 Stat. 1303–1304, 83 Stat. 187–189 (15 U.S.C. 1261, 1262, 1269); sec. 30(a), 86 Stat. 1231 (15 U.S.C. 2079(a)))

[43 FR 26428, June 20, 1978]

§ 1505.51 Hot surfaces.

(a) *Test probe.* Section 1505.6(g)(2) defines accessibility, for certain paragraphs, as the ability to reach a heated surface with a ¼-inch-diameter rod 3 inches long. To test for accessibility using this test probe, it shall be inserted no more than 3 inches into any opening in the toy. Unless the probe contacts a surface within 3 inches of the plane of the toy's opening, that surface is not accessible.

(b) *Accessibility of Type C and C-marked surfaces.* Under § 1505.6(g)(2) (iii) and (iv), touching by casual contact or without employing the aid of a common household tool shall be determined by use of the accessibility test probe described in §§ 1505.6(g)(2) and 1505.51(a).

[51 FR 34199, Sept. 26, 1986]

PART 1507—FIREWORKS DEVICES

Sec.

AUTHORITY: 15 U.S.C. 1261–1262, 2079(d); 21 U.S.C. 371(e).

SOURCE: 41 FR 22935, June 8, 1976, unless otherwise noted.

CROSS REFERENCE: See also 1500.14(b)(7); 1500.17(a) (3), (8) and (9); 1500.83(a)(27) and 1500.85(a)(2).

§ 1507.1 Scope.

This part 1507 prescribes requirements for those fireworks devices (other than firecrackers) not otherwise banned under the act. Any fireworks device (other than firecrackers) which fails to conform to applicable requirements is a banned hazardous substance and is prohibited from the channels of interstate commerce. Any fireworks device not otherwise banned under the act shall not be a banned hazardous substance by virtue of the fact that there are no applicable requirements prescribed herein.

§ 1507.2 Prohibited chemicals.

Fireworks devices shall not contain any of the following chemicals:

(a) Arsenic sulfide, arsenates, or arsenites.

(b) Boron.

(c) Chlorates, except:

(1) In colored smoke mixtures in which an equal or greater amount of sodium bicarbonate is included.

(2) In caps and party poppers.

(3) In those small items (such as ground spinners) wherein the total powder content does not exceed 4 grams of which not greater than 15 percent (or 600 milligrams) is potassium, sodium, or barium chlorate.

(d) Gallates or gallic acid.

(e) Magnesium (magnesium/aluminum alloys, called magnalium, are permitted).

(f) Mercury salts.

(g) Phosphorus (red or white). Except that red phosphorus is permissible in caps and party poppers.

(h) Picrates or picric acid.

(i) Thiocyanates.

(j) Titanium, except in particle size greater than 100-mesh.

(k) Zirconium.

§ 1507.3 Fuses.

(a) Fireworks devices that require a fuse shall:

(1) Utilize only a fuse that has been treated or coated in such manner as to reduce the possibility of side ignition. Devices such as ground spinners that require a restricted orifice for proper thrust and contain less than 6 grams of pyrotechnic composition are exempted from § 1507.3(a)(1).

(2) Utilize only a fuse which will burn at least 3 seconds but not more than 9 seconds before ignition of the device.

(b) The fuse shall be securely attached so that it will support either the weight of the fireworks device plus 8 ounces of dead weight or double the weight of the device, whether is less, without separation from the fireworks device.

[41 FR 22935, June 8, 1976, as amended at 61 FR 67200, Dec. 20, 1996; 61 FR 67200, Dec. 20, 1996]

§ 1507.4 Bases.

The base or bottom of fireworks devices that are operated in a standing upright position shall have the minimum horizontal dimensions or the diameter of the base equal to at least one-third of the height of the device including any base or cap affixed thereto.

§ 1507.5 Pyrotechnic leakage.

The pyrotechnic chamber in fireworks devices shall be sealed in a manner that prevents leakage of the pyrotechnic composition during shipping, handling, and normal operation.

§ 1507.6 Burnout and blowout.

The pyrotechnic chamber in fireworks devices shall be constructed in a manner to allow functioning in a normal manner without burnout or blowout.

§ 1507.7 Handles and spikes.

(a) Fireworks devices which are intended to be hand-held and are so labeled shall incorporate a handle at least 4 inches in length (see § 1500.14(b)(7)). Handles shall remain firmly attached during transportation, handling and full operation of the device, or shall consist of an integral section of the device at least four inches below the pyrotechnic chamber.

(b) Spikes provided with fireworks devices shall protrude at least 2 inches from the base of the device and shall have a blunt tip not less than ⅛-inch in diameter of ⅛-inch square.

§ 1507.8 Wheel devices.

Drivers in fireworks devices commonly known as "wheels" shall be securely attached to the device so that they will not come loose in transportation, handling, and normal operation. Wheel devices intended to operate in a fixed location shall be designed in such a manner that the axle remains attached to the device during normal operation.

§ 1507.9 Toy smoke devices and flitter devices.

(a) Toy smoke devices shall be so constructed that they will neither burst nor produce external flame (excluding the fuse and firstfire upon ignition) during normal operation.

(b) Toy smoke devices and flitter devices shall not be of such color and configuration so as to be confused with banned fireworks such as M–80 salutes, silver salutes, or cherry bombs.

(c) Toy smoke devices shall not incorporate plastic as an exterior material if the pyrotechnic composition comes in direct contact with the plastic.

§ 1507.10 Rockets with sticks.

Rockets with sticks (including skyrockets and bottle rockets) shall utilize a straight and rigid stick to provide a direct and stable flight. Such sticks shall remain straight and rigid and attached to the driver so as to prevent the stick from being damaged or detached during transportation, handling, and normal operation.

§ 1507.11 Party poppers.

Party poppers (also known by other names such as "Champagne Party Poppers," and "Party Surprise Poppers,") shall not contain more than 0.25 grains of pyrotechnic composition. Such devices may contain soft paper or cloth inserts provided any such inserts do not ignite during normal operation.

§ 1507.12 Multiple-tube fireworks devices.

(a) *Application.* Multiple-tube mine and shell fireworks devices with any tube measuring 1.5 inches (3.8 cm) or more in inside diameter and subject to § 1500.17(a)(12) of this part shall not tip over when subjected to the tip-angle test described in this section.

(b) *Testing procedure.* The device shall be placed on a smooth surface that can be inclined at 60 degrees from the horizontal, as shown in Figure 1 of this section. The height and width of the inclined plane (not including the portion of the plane below the mechanical stop) shall be at least 1 inch (2.54 cm) greater than the largest dimension of the base of the device to be tested. The test shall be conducted on a smooth, hard surface that is horizontal as measured by a spirit level or equivalent instrument. The mechanical stop on the inclined plane shall be 1/16 inches (1.6 mm) in height and perpendicular to the inclined plane. The stop shall be positioned parallel to the bottom edge of the inclined plane and so that no portion of the device to be tested or its base touches the horizontal surface. The device shall not tip over when the plane is inclined at 60-degrees from the horizontal. The procedure shall be repeated for each edge of the device.

FIGURE 1 TO § 1507.12

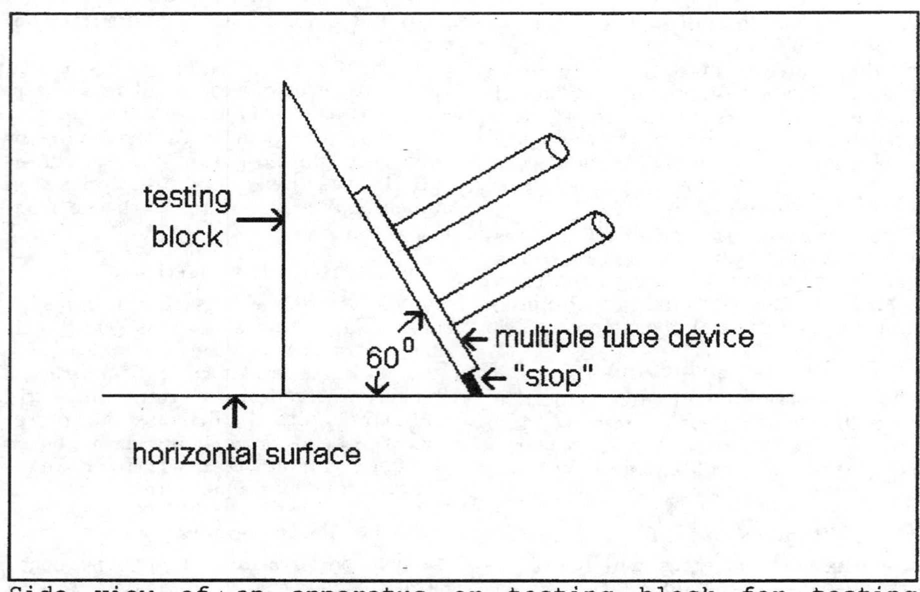

Side view of an apparatus or testing block for testing compliance with the proposed 60-degree tilt angle standard.

[61 FR 13096, Mar. 26, 1996]

FIGURE 2 TO PART 1508—HEADFORM PROBE

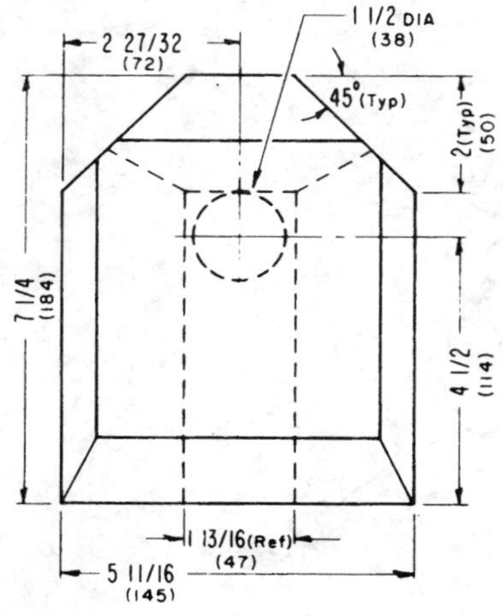

FIG 2—HEADFORM PROBE

DIMENSIONS ARE SHOWN IN INCHES AND WILL BE USED FOR COMPLIANCE PURPOSES. MILLIMETERS, SHOWN IN PARENTHESIS, ARE FOR CONVENIENCE ONLY.

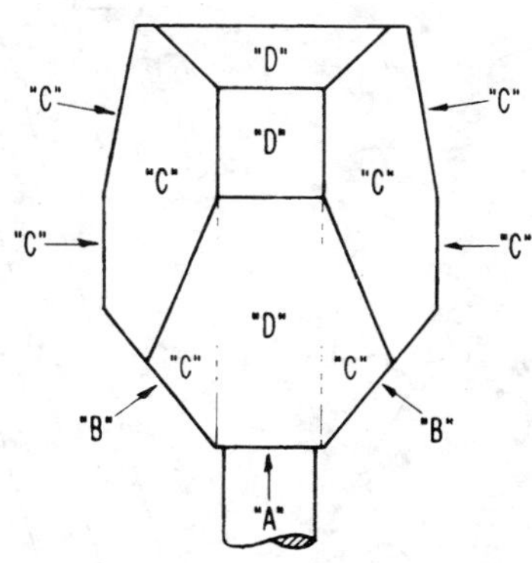

REAR VIEW—
IDENTIFYING SURFACES

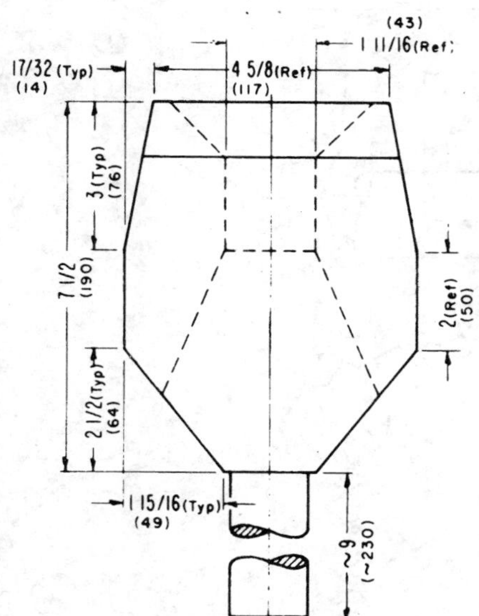

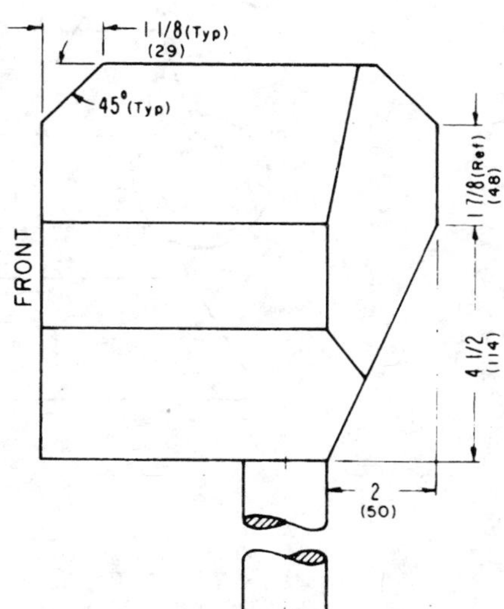

[47 FR 47544, Oct. 27, 1982]

FIGURE 3 TO PART 1508

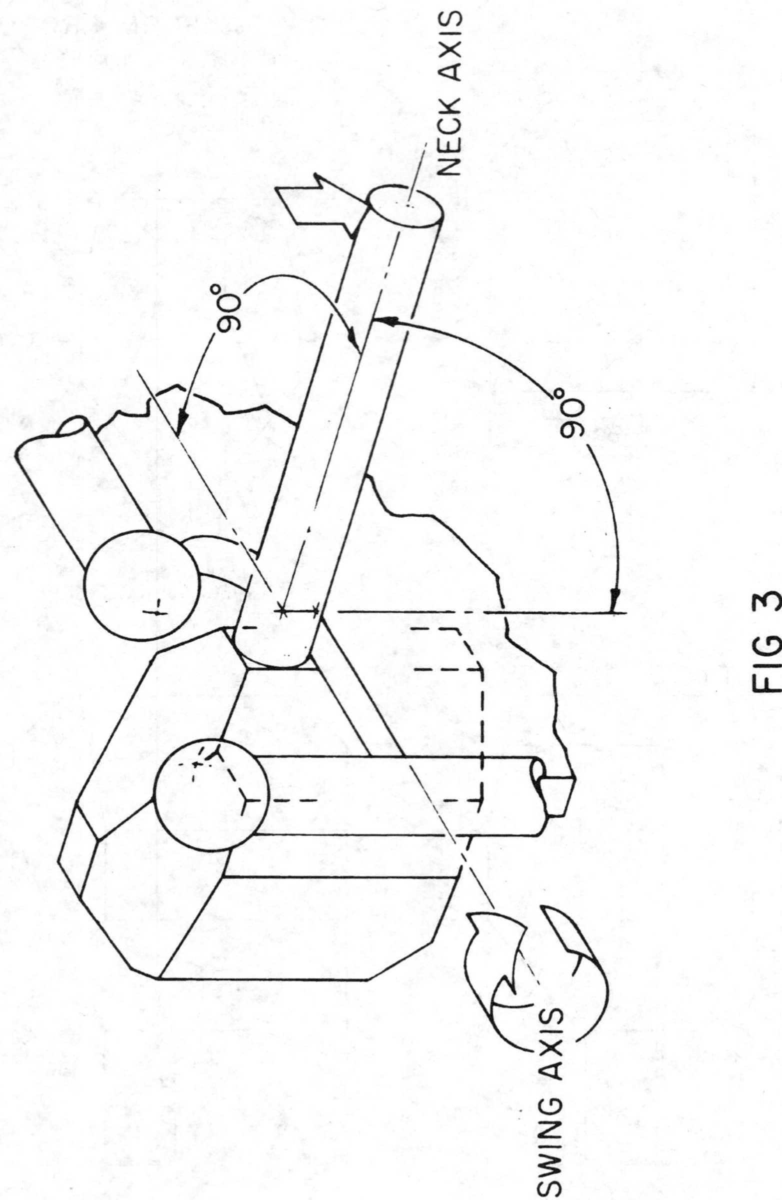

[47 FR 47544, Oct. 27, 1982]

PART 1510—REQUIREMENTS FOR RATTLES

AUTHORITY: Secs. 2(f)(1)(D), (q)(1)(A), (s), 3(e)(1), 64 Stat. 372, 374, 375, as amended 80 Stat. 1304–05, 83 Stat. 187–89 (15 U.S.C. 1261, 1262); sec. 30(a), 86 Stat. 1231 (15 U.S.C. 2079(a)).

SOURCE: 43 FR 22002, May 23, 1978, unless otherwise noted.

§ 1510.1 Scope and purpose of part 1510.

This part 1510 sets forth the requirement whereby rattles (as defined in § 1510.2) are not banned articles under § 1500.18(a)(15) of this chapter. The purpose of these requirements is to ensure that certain infant rattles which may cause choking and/or suffocation because their design or construction permits them to enter into an infant's mouth and become lodged in the throat are eliminated from interstate commerce.

§ 1510.2 Definition.

For the purposes of this part 1510, a rattle is an infant's toy, intended to be hand held, usually containing pellets or other small objects and which produces sounds when shaken. Examples of products which may have similar noisemaking characteristics but which are excluded from the scope of this definition are: dolls, stuffed animals, crib exercisers, crib mobiles, pull toys, shoe lace holders, bells which are not part of the noisemaking component of a rattle, plastic keys or other figures on loops or chains which produce sound by striking together, games, puzzles and musical instruments such as tambourines, castanets, and maracas.

§ 1510.3 Requirements.

No portion of a rattle, when tested in accordance with the procedure of § 1510.4 below, shall be capable of entering and penetrating to the full depth of a cavity in a test fixture with dimensions shown in figure 1. (In determining these dimensions for compliance purposes, the English measurements shall be used. Metric equivalents are included for convenience.) Rattles shall meet this requirement both before and after performing the use and abuse tests of § 1500.51 of this chapter (excluding the bite and flexure tests of paragraphs (c) and (d)).

§ 1510.4 Test procedure.

Place the test fixture shown in Figure 1 on a horizontal plane surface. Under its own weight and in a non-compressed state apply any portion of the test sample in the most adverse orientation to the opening in the test fixture. Repeat this procedure after performing the use and abuse tests of § 1500.51 (excluding the bite and flexure tests of paragraphs (c) and (d) of this section). In testing to ensure compliance with this regulation, the measurements of the opening of the Commission's test fixture will be no greater than those shown in Figure 1 and the depth of the fixture used will be no less than that shown in Figure 1.

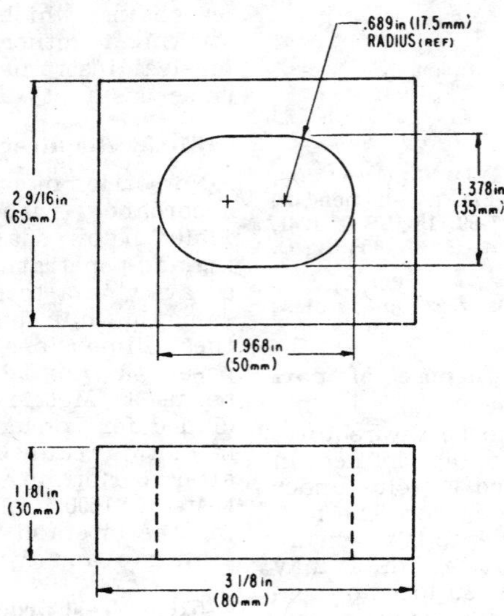

FIG 1—RATTLE TEST FIXTURE

PART 1511—REQUIREMENTS FOR PACIFIERS

AUTHORITY: Secs. 2(f)(1)(D), (q)(1)(A), (s), 3(e)(1), 74 Stat. 372, 374, 375, as amended 80 Stat. 1304–05, 83 Stat. 187–89; 15 U.S.C. 1261, 1262.

SOURCE: 42 FR 33279, June 30, 1977, unless otherwise noted.

§ 1511.1 Scope of part 1511.

This part 1511 sets forth the requirements whereby pacifiers (as defined in § 1511.2(a)) are not banned articles under § 1500.18(a)(8) of this chapter.

§ 1511.2 Definitions.

(a) A *pacifier* is an article consisting of a nipple that is intended for a young child to suck upon, but is not designed to facilitate a baby's obtaining fluid, and usually includes a guard or shield and a handle or ring.

(b) *Guard or shield* means the structure located at the base of the nipple used to prevent the pacifier from being completely drawn into the child's mouth.

(c) *Handle or ring* means the structure usually located adjacent to the guard or shield used for holding or grasping the pacifier. A hinged handle or ring is one that is free to pivot about an axis parallel to the plane of the guard or shield.

§ 1511.3 Guard or shield requirements.

(a) *Performance requirements*. Place the pacifier in the opening of the fixture illustrated in Figure 1(a) of this part so that the nipple of the pacifier is centered in the opening and protrudes through the back of the fixture as shown in Figure 1(b). For pacifiers with non-circular guards or shields, align the major axis of the guard or shield with the major axis of the opening in the fixture. Apply a tensile force to the pacifier nipple in the direction shown. The force shall be applied gradually attaining but not exceeding 2.0 pounds (8.9 newtons) within a period of 5 seconds and maintained at 2.0 pounds for an additional 10 seconds. Any pacifier which can be completely drawn through an opening with dimensions no greater than those of Figure 1(a) by such a force shall fail the test in this part.

(b) *Ventilation holes.* The pacifier guard or shield shall contain at least two holes symmetrically located and each being at least 0.20 inches (5 millimeters) in minor dimension. The edge of any hole shall be no closer than 0.20 inches (5 millimeters) to the perimeter of the pacifier guard or shield.

§ 1511.4 Protrusions.

(a) *Protrusions limitation.* No protrusion from the face of the guard or shield opposite from the nipple shall exceed 0.63 inches (16mm) when measured in accordance with the procedure specified in paragraph (b) of this section.

(b) *Protrusion test.* Secure the pacifier by clamping the nipple with its axis horizontal. For pacifiers with hinged handles or rings the orientation of the hinge axis shall be horizontal. A plane surface shall be applied to any protrusion from the guard or shield with a force gradually attaining but not exceeding 2.0 pounds (8.9 newtons) applied in a direction along the axis of the nipple. The normal of the plane surface shall be maintained parallel to the axis of the nipple. Any protrusion shall be allowed to flex or rotate about its hinge as the plane surfact is applied to it. Measure the distance from the plane surface to the guard or shield at the base of the nipple.

§ 1511.5 Structural integrity tests.

(a) *Nipple.* Hold the pacifier by the shield or guard, grasp the nipple end of the pacifier and gradually apply a tensile force to the pacifier nipple in any possible direction. The force shall be applied gradually, attaining but not exceeding 10.0 pounds (44.5 newtons) within a period of 5 seconds and maintained at 10.0 pounds for an additional 10 seconds.

(b) *Handle or ring.* Hold the pacifier by the shield or guard or base of the nipple, and push or pull on the handle or ring in any possible direction. The force shall be applied gradually attaining but not exceeding 10.0 pounds (44.5 newtons) within a period of 5 seconds and maintained at 10.0 pounds for an additional 10 seconds.

(c) *Heat cycle deterioration.* After the testing prescribed in paragraphs (a) and (b) of this section, all pacifiers shall be subject to the following: submerge the pacifier in boiling water for 5 minutes and then remove the pacifier and allow it to cool for 5 minutes in room temperature air, 60° to 80 °F. (16° to 27 °C). After the cooling period, resubmerge the pacifier in the boiling water for 5 minutes. The process shall be repeated for a total of 6 boiling/cooling cycles. After the sixth cycle, the pacifier shall again be subjected to the structural tests in paragraphs (a) and (b) of this section and section 1511.3.

(d) *Small parts.* Any components or fragments which are released as a result of the tests specified in paragraphs (a), (b) and (c) of this section shall be placed in the truncated cylinder shown in Figure 2, such that the component or fragment is in the lowest position in the cylinder. If the uppermost edge of the component or fragment is below the plane of the top of the cylinder, the pacifier shall fail the test in this section.

§ 1511.6 Ribbons, strings, cords, or other attachments.

A pacifier shall not be sold or distributed with any ribbon, string, cord, chain, twine, leather, yarn or similar attachments.

§ 1511.7 Labeling.

(a) As required by paragraphs (b) and (c) of this section, pacifiers shall be labeled with the statement: "Warning—Do Not Tie Pacifier Around Child's Neck as it Presents a Strangulation Danger."

(b) The labeling statement required by paragraph (a) of this section shall appear legibly and conspicuously on any retail display carton containing two or more pacifiers.

(c) Each individually packaged pacifier shall bear the labeling statement required in paragraph (a) of this section on the package legibly and conspicuously.

§ 1511.8 Metric references.

For purposes of compliance with the test procedure prescribed by this § 500.46, the English figures shall be used. The metric approximations are provided in parentheses for convenience and information only.

FIGURE 1 TO PART 1511—PACIFIER TEST FIXTURE

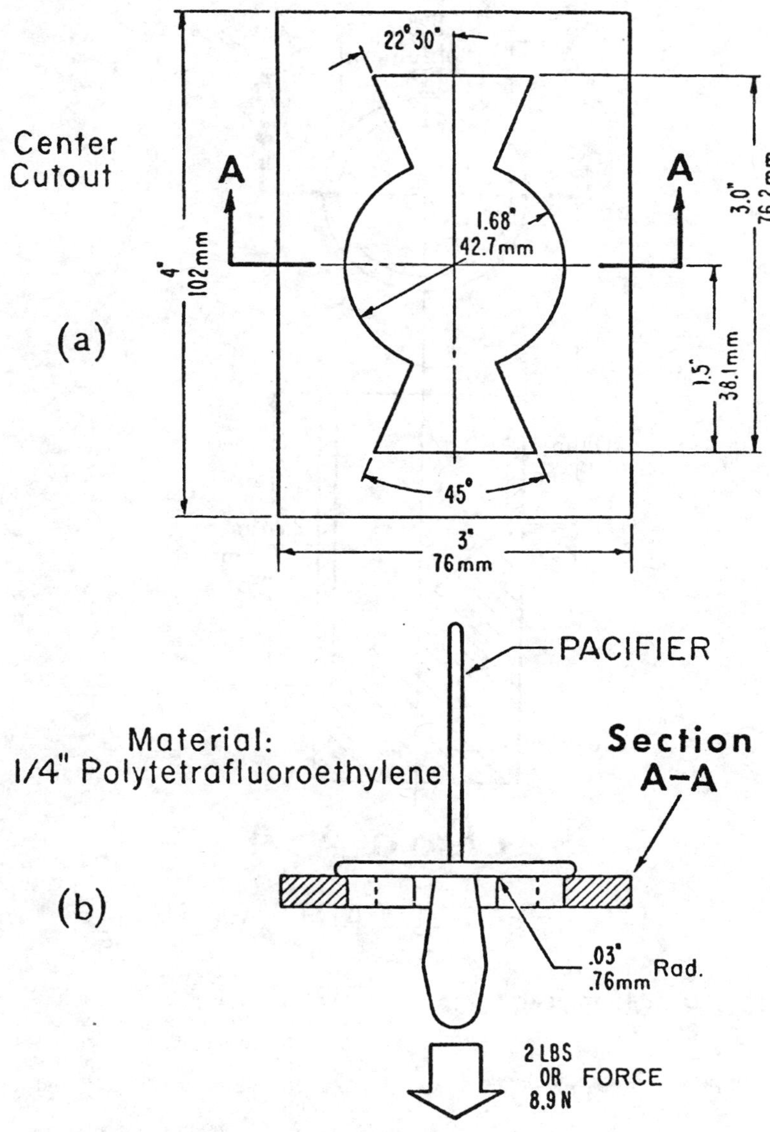

FIG 1 – PACIFIER TEST FIXTURE

FIGURE 2 TO PART 1511—SMALL PARTS GAGE

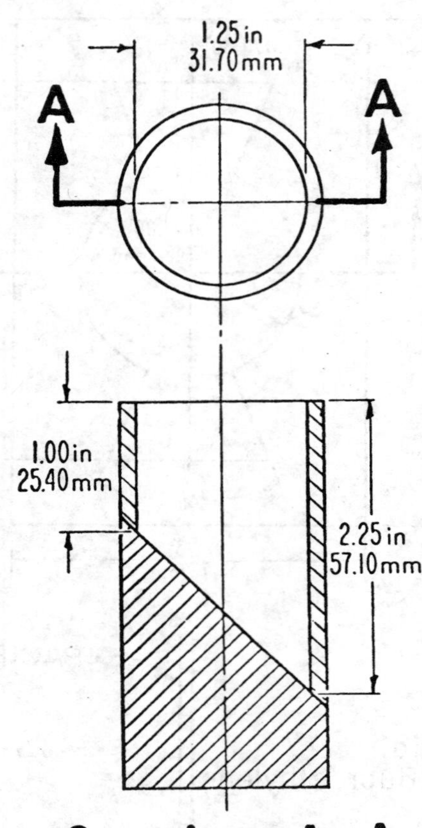

FIG 2-SMALL PARTS GAGE

PART 1512—REQUIREMENTS FOR BICYCLES

Subpart A—Regulations

Subpart B—Policies and Interpretations [Reserved]

AUTHORITY: Secs. 2(f)(1)(D), (q)(1)(A), (s), 3(e)(1), 74 Stat. 372, 374, 375, as amended, 80 Stat. 1304–05, 83 Stat. 187–89 (15 U.S.C. 1261, 1262); Pub. L. 107–319, 116 Stat. 2776.

SOURCE: 43 FR 60034, Dec. 22, 1978, unless otherwise noted.

Subpart A—Regulations

§ 1512.1 Scope.

This part sets forth the requirements for a bicycle as defined in § 1512.2(a) (except a bicycle that is a "track bicycle" or a "one-of-a-kind bicycle" as defined in § 1512.2 (d) and (e)) which is not a banned article under § 1500.18(a)(12) of this chapter.

§ 1512.2 Definitions.

For the purposes of this part:

(a) Bicycle means:

(1) A two-wheeled vehicle having a rear drive wheel that is solely human-powered;

(2) A two- or three-wheeled vehicle with fully operable pedals and an electric motor of less than 750 watts (1 h.p.), whose maximum speed on a paved level surface, when powered solely by such a motor while ridden by an operator who weighs 170 pounds, is less than 20 mph.

(b) *Sidewalk bicycle* means a bicycle with a seat height of no more than 635 mm (25.0 in); the seat height is measured with the seat adjusted to its highest position. Recumbent bicycles are not included in this definition.

(c) *Seat height* means the dimension from the point on the seat surface intersected by the seat post center line (or the center of the seating area if no seat post exists) and the ground plane, as measured with the wheels aligned and in a plane normal to the ground plane.

(d) *Track bicycle* means a bicycle designed and intended for sale as a competitive velodrome machine having no brake levers or calipers, single crank-to-wheel ratio, and no free-wheeling feature between the rear wheel and the crank.

(e) *One-of-a-kind bicycle* means a bicycle that is uniquely constructed to the order of an individual consumer other than by assembly of stock or production parts.

(f) *Normal riding position* means that the rider is seated on the bicycle with both feet on the pedals and both hands on the handlegrips (and in a position that allows operation of handbrake levers if so equipped); the seat and handlebars may be adjusted to positions judged by the rider to be comfortable.

(g) *Recumbent bicycle* means a bicycle in which the rider sits in a reclined position with the feet extended forward to the pedals.

[43 FR 60034, Dec. 22, 1978, as amended at 68 FR 7073, Feb. 12, 2003; 76 FR 27888, May 13, 2011]

§ 1512.3 Requirements in general.

Any bicycle subject to the regulations in this part shall meet the requirements of this part in the condition to which it is offered for sale to consumers; any bicycle offered for sale to consumers in disassembled or partially assembled condition shall meet these requirements after assembly according to the manufacturer's instructions. For the purpose of compliance with this part, where the metric and English units are not equal due to the conversion process the less stringent requirement will prevail.

§ 1512.4 Mechanical requirements.

(a) *Assembly*. Bicycles shall be manufactured such that mechanical skills required of the consumer for assembly shall not exceed those possessed by an adult of normal intelligence and ability.

(b) *Sharp edges.* There shall be no unfinished sheared metal edges or other sharp parts on assembled bicycles that are, or may be, exposed to hands or legs; sheared metal edges that are not rolled shall be finished so as to remove any feathering of edges, or any burrs or spurs caused during the shearing process.

(c) *Integrity.* There shall be no visible fracture of the frame or of any steering, wheel, pedal, crank, or brake system component resulting from testing in accordance with: The handbrake loading and performance test, § 1512.18(d); the foot brake force and performance test, § 1512.18(e); and the road test, § 1512.18(p) (or the sidewalk bicycle proof test, § 1512.18(q)).

(d) *Attachment hardware.* All screws, bolts, or nuts used to attach or secure components shall not fracture, loosen, or otherwise fail their intended function during the tests required in this part. All threaded hardware shall be of sufficient quality to allow adjustments and maintenance. Recommended quality thread form is specified in Handbook H28, "Screw Thread Standards for Federal Service,"[1] issued by the National Bureau of Standards, Department of Commerce; recommended mechanical properties are specified in ISO Recommendation R898, "Mechanical Properties of Fasteners," and in ISO Recommendations 68, 262, and 263, "General Purpose Screw Threads."[2]

(e)–(f) [Reserved]

(g) *Excluded area.* There shall be no protrusions located within the area bounded by (1) a line 89 mm (3½ in) to the rear of and parallel to the handlebar stem; (2) a line tangent to the front tip of the seat and intersecting the seat mast at the top rear stay; (3) the top surface of the top tube; and (4) a line connecting the front of the seat (when adjusted to its highest position) to the junction where the handlebar is attached to the handlebar stem. The top tube on a female bicycle model shall be the seat mast and the down tube or tubes that are nearest the rider in the normal riding position. Control cables no greater than 6.4 mm (¼ in) in diameter and cable clamps made from material not thicker than 4.8 mm (3⁄16 in) may be attached to the top tube.

(h) [Reserved]

(i) *Control cable ends.* Ends of all accessible control cables shall be provided with protective caps or otherwise treated to prevent unraveling. Protective caps shall be tested in accordance with the protective cap and end-mounted devices test, § 1512.18(c), and shall withstand a pull of 8.9 N (2.0 lbf).

(j) *Control cable abrasion.* Control cables shall not abrade over fixed parts and shall enter and exit cable sheaths in a direction in line with the sheath entrance and exit so as to prevent abrading.

[43 FR 60034, Dec. 22, 1978, as amended at 76 FR 27888, May 13, 2011]

§ 1512.5 Requirements for braking system.

(a) *Braking system.* Bicycles shall be equipped with front- and rear-wheel brakes or rear-wheel brakes only.

(b) *Handbrakes.* Handbrakes shall be tested at least ten times by applying a force sufficient to cause the handlever to contact the handlebar, or a maximum of 445 N (100 lbf), in accordance with the loading test, § 1512.18(d)(2), and shall be rocked back and forth with the weight of a 68.1 kg (150 lb) rider on the seat with the same handbrake force applied in accordance with the rocking test, § 1512.18(d)(2)(iii); there shall be no visible fractures, failures, movement of clamps, or misalignment of brake components.

(1) *Stopping distance.* A bicycle equipped with only handbrakes shall be tested for stopping distance by a rider of at least 68.1 kg (150 lb) weight in accordance with the performance test, § 1512.18(d)(2) (v) and (vi), and shall have a stopping distance of no greater than 4.57 m (15 ft) from the actual test speed as determined by the equivalent ground speed specified in § 1512.18(d)(2)(vi).

(2) *Hand lever access.* Hand lever mechanisms shall be located on the handlebars in a position that is readily accessible to the rider when in a normal riding position.

[1] Copies may be obtained from: Superintendent of Documents, U.S. Government Printing Office, Washington, D.C. 20402.

[2] Copies may be obtained from: American National Standards Institute, 1430 Broadway, New York, New York 10018.

(3) *Grip dimension*. The grip dimension (maximum outside dimension between the brake hand lever and the handlebars in the plane containing the centerlines of the handgrip and the hand brake lever) shall not exceed 89 mm (3½ in) at any point between the pivot point of the lever and lever midpoint; the grip dimension for sidewalk bicycles shall not exceed 76 mm (3 in). The grip dimension may increase toward the open end of the lever but shall not increase by more than 12.7 mm (½ in) except for the last 12.7 mm (½ in) of the lever. (See figure 5 of this part 1512.)

(4) *Attachment*. Brake assemblies shall be securely attached to the frame by means of fasteners with locking devices such as a lock washer, locknut, or equivalent and shall not loosen during the rocking test, §1512.18(d)- (2)(iii). The cable anchor bolt shall not cut any of the cable strands.

(5) *Operating force*. A force of less than 44.5 N (10 lbf) shall cause the brake pads to contact the braking surface of the wheel when applied to the handlever at a point 25 mm (1.0 in) from the open end of the handlever.

(6) *Pad and pad holders*. Caliper brake pad shall be replaceable and adjustable to engage the braking surface without contacting the tire or spokes and the pad holders shall be securely attached to the caliper assembly. The brake pad material shall be retained in its holder without movement when the bicycle is loaded with a rider of at least 68.1 kg (150 lb) weight and is rocked forward and backward as specified in the rocking test, §1512.18(d)(2)(iii).

(7) [Reserved]

(8) *Hand lever location*. The rear brake shall be actuated by a control located on the right handlebar and the front brake shall be actuated by a control located on the left handlebar. The left-hand/right-hand locations may be reversed in accordance with an individual customer order. If a single hand lever is used to actuate both front and rear brakes, it shall meet all applicable requirements for hand levers and shall be located on either the right or left handlebar in accordance with the customer's preference.

(9) *Hand lever extensions*. Bicycles equipped with hand lever extensions shall be tested with the extension levers in place and the hand lever extensions shall also be considered to be hand levers.

(c) *Footbrakes*. All footbrakes shall be tested in accordance with the force test, §1512.18(e)(2), and the measured braking force shall not be less than 178 N (40 lbf) for an applied pedal force of 310 N (70 lbf).

(1) *Stopping distance*. Bicycles equipped with footbrakes (except sidewalk bicycles) shall be tested in accordance with the performance test, §1512.18(e)(3), by a rider of at least 68.1 kg (150 lb) weight and shall have a stopping distance of no greater than 4.57 m (15 ft) from an actual test speed of at least 16 km/h (10 mph). If the bicycle has a footbrake only and the equivalent groundspeed of the bicycle is in excess of 24 km/h (15 mph) (in its highest gear ratio at a pedal crank rate of 60 revolutions per minute),[3] the stopping distance shall be 4.57 m (15 ft) from an actual test speed of 24 km/h (15 mph) or greater.

(2) *Operating force*. Footbrakes shall be actuated by a force applied to the pedal in a direction opposite to that of the drive force, except where brakes are separate from the drive pedals and the applied force is in the same direction as the drive force.

(3) *Crank differential*. The differential between the drive and brake positions of the crank shall be not more than 60° with the crank held against each position under a torque of no less than 13.6 N-m (10 ft-lb).

(4) *Independent operation*. The brake mechanism shall function independently of any drive-gear positions or adjustments.

(d) *Footbrakes and handbrakes in combination*. Bicycles equipped with footbrakes and handbrakes shall meet all the requirements for footbrakes in §1512.5(c), including the tests specified. In addition, if the equivalent ground speed of the bicycle is 24 km/h (15 mph) or greater (in its highest gear ratio at a pedal crank rate of 60 revolutions per

[3] This is proportional to a gear development greater than 6.67 m (21.9 ft) in the bicycle's highest gear ratio. Gear development is the distance the bicycle travels in meters, in one crank revolution.

minute),[3] the actual test speed specified in § 1512.18(e)(3) shall be increased to 24 km/h (15 mph) and both braking systems may be actuated to achieve the required stopping distance of 4.57 m (15 ft).

(e) *Sidewalk bicycles.* (1) Sidewalk bicycles shall not have handbrakes only.

(2) Sidewalk bicycles with a seat height of 560 mm (22 in) or greater (with seat height adjusted to its lowest position) shall be equipped with a footbrake meeting all the footbrake requirements of § 1512.5(c), including the specified tests except that the braking force transmitted to the rear wheel shall be in accordance with the sidewalk bicycle footbrake force tests, § 1512.18(f).

(3) Sidewalk bicycles with a seat height less than 560 mm (22 in) (with seat height adjusted to its lowest position) and not equipped with a brake shall not have a freewheel feature. Such sidewalk bicycles equipped with a footbrake shall be tested for brake force in accordance with the sidewalk bicycle footbrake force test, § 1512.18(f). Such sidewalk bicycles not equipped with brakes shall be identified with a permanent label clearly visible from a distance of 3.1 m (10 ft) in daylight conditions and promotional display material and shipping cartons shall prominently display the words "No Brakes."

§ 1512.6 Requirements for steering system.

(a) *Handlebar stem insertion mark.* Quill-type handlebar stems shall contain a permanent ring or mark which clearly indicates the minimum insertion depth of the handlebar stem into the fork assembly. The insertion mark shall not affect the structural integrity of the stem and shall not be less than 2½ times the stem diameter from the lowest point of the stem. The stem strength shall be maintained for at least a length of one shaft diameter below the mark.

(b) *Handlebar stem strength.* The handlebar stem shall be tested for strength in accordance with the handlebar stem test, § 1512.18(g), and shall withstand a force of 2000 N (450 lbf) for bicycles and 1000 N (225 lbf) for sidewalk bicycles.

(c) *Handlebar.* Handlebars shall allow comfortable and safe control of the bicycle. Handlebar ends shall be symmetrically located with respect to the longitudinal axis of the bicycle and no more than 406 mm (16 in) above the seat surface when the seat is in its lowest position and the handlebar ends are in their highest position. This requirement does not apply to recumbent bicycles.

(d) *Handlebar ends.* The ends of the handlebars shall be capped or otherwise covered. Handgrips, end plugs, control shifters, or other end-mounted devices shall be secure against a removal force of no less than 66.8 N (15 lbf) in accordance with the protective cap and end-mounted devices test, § 1512.18(c).

(e) *Handlebar and clamps.* The handlebar and clamps shall be tested in accordance with the handlebar test, § 1512.18(h). Directions for assembly of the bicycle required in the instruction manual by § 1512.19(a)(2) shall include an explicit warning about the danger of damaging the stem-to-fork assembly and the risk of injury to the rider that can result from overtightening the stem bolt or other clamping device. The directions for assembly shall also contain a simple, clear, and precise statement of the procedure to be followed to avoid damaging the stem-to-fork assembly when tightening the stem bolt or other clamping device.

[43 FR 60034, Dec. 22, 1978, as amended at 76 FR 27888, May 13, 2011]

§ 1512.7 Requirements for pedals.

(a) *Construction.* Pedals shall have right-hand/left-hand symmetry. The tread surface shall be present on both top and bottom surfaces of the pedal except that if the pedal has a definite preferred position, the tread surface need only be on the surface presented to the rider's foot.

(b) *Toe clips.* Pedals intended to be used only with toe clips shall have toe clips securely attached to them and need not have tread surfaces. Pedals designed for optional use of toe clips shall have tread surfaces.

(c) *Pedal reflectors.* Pedals for bicycles other than sidewalk bicycles shall have reflectors in accordance with § 1512.16(e). Pedals for sidewalk bicycles are not required to have reflectors.

§ 1512.8 Requirements for drive chain.

The drive chain shall operate over the sprockets without catching or binding. The tensile stength of the drive chain shall be no less than 8010 N (1,800 lbf) or 6230 N (1,400 lbf) for sidewalk bicycles.

§ 1512.9 Requirements for protective guards.

(a) *Chain guard.* Bicycles having a single front sprocket and a single rear sprocket shall have a chain guard that shall cover the top strand of the chain and at least 90° of the perimeter where the drive chain contacts the drive sprocket as shown in figure 7. The chain guard shall extend rearward to a point at least 8 cm (3.2 in.) forward of the centerline of the rear axle. The minimum width of the top area of the chain guard shall be twice the width of the chain in that portion forward of the rear wheel rim. The rear part of the top area may be tapered. The minimum width at the rear of the guard shall be one-half the chain width. Such chain guard shall prevent a rod of 9.4 mm (3⁄8 in.) diameter and 76 mm (3.0 in.) length from entrapment between the upper junction of the chain and the sprocket when introduced from the chain side of the bicycle in any direction within 45° from a line normal to the sprocket.

(b) *Derailleur guard.* Derailleurs shall be guarded to prevent the drive chain from interfering with or stopping the rotation of the wheel through improper adjustments or damage.

§ 1512.10 Requirements for tires.

The manufacturer's recommended inflation pressure shall be molded into or onto the sidewall of the tire in lettering no less than 3.2 mm (1⁄8 in.) in height. The statement of recommended inflation pressure shall be in the English language utilizing Arabic numerals. (The following language is suggested to indicate recommended inflation pressure: "Inflate to ___ PSI.") After inflation to 110 percent of the recommended inflation pressure, the tire shall remain intact on the rim, including while being tested under a load of 2,000 N (450 lbf) in accordance with the rim test, § 1512.18(j). Tubular sew-up tires, nonpneumatic tires, and non-molded wired-on tires are exempt from this section.

§ 1512.11 Requirements for wheels.

(a) *Spokes.* There shall be no missing spokes.

(b) *Alignment.* The wheel assembly shall be aligned such that no less than 1.6 mm (1⁄16 in.) clearance exists between the tire and fork or any frame member when the wheel is rotated to any position.

(c) *Rims.* Rims shall retain the spokes and tire when side-loaded with 2000 N (450 lbf) and tested in accordance with the rim test, § 1512.18(j). Sidewalk bicycles need not meet this requirement.

§ 1512.12 Requirements for wheel hubs.

All bicycles (other than sidewalk bicycles) shall meet the following requirements:

(a) *Locking devices.* Wheels shall be secured to the bicycle frame with a positive lock device. Locking devices on threaded axles shall be tightened to the manufacturer's specifications.

(1) *Rear wheels.* There shall be no relative motion between the axle and the frame when a force of 1,780 N (400 lbf) is applied symmetrically to the axle for a period of 30 seconds in the direction of wheel removal.

(2) *Front wheels.* Locking devices, except quick-release devices, shall withstand application of a torque in the direction of removal of 17 N-m (12.5 ft-lb).

(b) *Quick-release devices.* Lever-operated, quick-release devices shall be adjustable to allow setting the lever position for tightness. Quick-release levers shall be clearly visible to the rider and shall indicate whether the levers are in a locked or unlocked position. Quick-release clamp action shall emboss the frame or fork when locked, except on fiber reinforced plastics.

(c) *Front hubs.* Front hubs not equipped with lever-operated quick-release devices shall have a positive retention feature that shall be tested in accordance with the front hub retention test, § 1512.18(j)(3), to assure that when the locking devices are released the wheel will not separate from the fork.

[43 FR 60034, Dec. 22, 1978, as amended at 76 FR 27888, May 13, 2011]

§ 1512.13 Requirements for front fork.

The front fork shall be tested for strength by application of at least 39.5 J (350 in-lb) of energy in accordance with the fork test, § 1512.18(k)(1), without visible evidence of fracture. Sidewalk bicycles need not meet this requirement.

§ 1512.14 Requirements for fork and frame assembly.

The fork and frame assembly shall be tested for strength by application of a load of 890 N (200 lbf) or at least 39.5 J (350 in-lb) of energy, whichever results in the greater force, in accordance with the frame test, § 1512.18(k)(2), without visible evidence of fracture or frame deformation that significantly limits the steering angle over which the wheel can be turned. Sidewalk bicycles are exempt from this section.

§ 1512.15 Requirements for seat.

(a) *Seat limitations.* No part of the seat, seat supports, or accessories attached to the seat shall be more than 125 mm (5.0 in) above the top of the seat surface at the point where the seat surface is intersected by the seat post axis. This requirement does not apply to recumbent bicycles.

(b) *Seat post.* The seat post shall contain a permanent mark or ring that clearly indicates the minimum insertion depth (maximum seat-height adjustment); the mark shall not affect the structural integrity of the seat post. This mark shall be located no less than two seat-post diameters from the lowest point on the post shaft, and the post strength shall be maintained for at least a length of one shaft diameter below the mark. This requirement does not apply to bicycles with integrated seat masts, however, a permanent mark or other means to clearly indicate that the seat or seat posts is safely installed shall be provided.

(c) *Adjustment clamps.* The seat adjustment clamps shall be capable of securing the seat in any position to which it can be adjusted and preventing movement of the seat in any direction under normal conditions of use. Following the road test, § 1512.18(p) (or the sidewalk bicycle proof test, § 1512.18(q), as applicable), the seat clamps shall be tested in accordance with the seat adjustment clamps and load test, § 1512.18(l).

[43 FR 60034, Dec. 22, 1978, as amended at 76 FR 27888, May 13, 2011]

§ 1512.16 Requirements for reflectors.

Bicycles shall be equipped with reflective devices to permit recognition and identification under illumination from motor vehicle headlamps. The use of reflector combinations off the center plane of the bicycle (defined in § 1512.18(m)(2)) is acceptable if each reflector meets the requirements of this section and of § 1512.18 (m) and (n) and the combination of reflectors has a clear field of view of ±10° vertically and ±50° horizontally. Sidewalk bicycles are not required to have reflectors.

(a) *Front, rear, and pedal reflectors.* There shall be an essentially colorless front-facing reflector, essentially colorless or amber pedal reflectors, and a red rear-facing reflector.

(b) *Side reflectors.* There shall be retroreflective tire sidewalls or, alternatively, reflectors mounted on the spokes of each wheel, or, for non-caliper rim brake bicycles, retroreflective wheel rims. The center of spoke-mounted reflectors shall be within 76 mm (3.0 in.) of the inside of the rim. Side reflective devices shall be visible on each side of the wheel.

(c) *Front reflector.* The reflector or mount shall not contact the ground plane when the bicycle is resting on that plane in any orientation. The optical axis of the reflector shall be directed forward within 5° of the horizontal-vertical alignment of the bicycle when the wheels are tracking in a straight line, as defined in § 1512.18(m)(2). The reflectors and/or mounts shall incorporate a distinct, preferred assembly method that shall insure that the reflector meets the optical requirements of this paragraph (c) when the reflector is attached to the bicycle. The front reflector shall be tested in accordance with the reflector mount and alignment test, § 1512.18(m).

(d) *Rear reflector.* The reflector or mount shall not contact the ground plane when the bicycle is resting on that plane in any orientation. The reflector shall be mounted such that it is to the rear of the seat mast with the top of the reflector at least 76 mm (3.0

in) below the point on the seat surface that is intersected by the line of the seat post. The optical axis of the reflector shall be directed rearward within 5° of the horizontal-vertical alignment of the bicycle when the wheels are traveling in a straight line, as defined in § 1512.18(m)(2). The reflectors and/or mounts shall incorporate a distinct, preferred assembly method that shall insure that the reflector meets the optical requirements of this paragraph (d) when the reflector is attached to the bicycle. The rear reflector shall be tested in accordance with the reflector mount and alignment test, § 1512.18(m).

(e) *Pedal reflectors.* Each pedal shall have reflectors located on the front and rear surfaces of the pedal. The reflector elements may be either integral with the construction of the pedal or mechanically attached, but shall be sufficiently recessed from the edge of the pedal, or of the reflector housing, to prevent contact of the reflector element with a flat surface placed in contact with the edge of the pedal.

(f) *Side reflectors.* Reflectors affixed to the wheel spokes shall be mounted either flat on the spokes or within the spoke cage such that the angle between the optical axis and the normal to the plane of the wheel shall not exceed the angle of the spokes with the plane of the wheel. The reflectors shall not interfere with any wheel adjustments. The side-mounted reflector devices shall be essentially colorless or amber on the front wheel and essentially colorless or red on the rear wheel.

(g) *Reflector tests.* The pedal, front-mount, rear-mount, and side-mount reflectors shall be tested in accordance with the reflector test, § 1512.18(n), to assure the reflectance values over the angles given in tables 1 and 2.

(h) *Retroreflective tire sidewalls.* When retroreflective tire sidewalls are used in lieu of spoke-mounted reflectors, the reflecting material shall meet the following requirements:

(1) The retroreflective material shall form a continuous circle on the sidewall.

(2) The retroreflective material shall adhere to the tire such that after the tire has been subjected to a temperature of 50° ±3 °C (122° ±5.4 °F) for 30 minutes, the retroreflective material cannot be peeled or scraped away without removal of tire material.

(3) The retroreflective material shall be as resistant to abrasion as is the adjacent sidewall material so that when retroreflective material is removed from the inflated tire by abrasion with a wet, steel bristle brush, tire material will be removed along with the retroreflective material.

(4) The retroreflective material shall be tested for performance in accordance with the retroreflective tire test, § 1512.18(o), to assure the reflectance properties over the angles given in table 3. When a portion of the retroreflective material is selected (and the remainder is masked as specified in § 1512.18(o)(2)(i)), the selected portion shall not contact the ground plane when the assembled bicycle is resting on that plane in any orientation.

(i) *Retroreflective rims.* When retroreflective rims are used in lieu of spoke-mounted reflectors or retroreflective tire sidewalls, the reflecting material shall meet the following requirements:

(1) The retroreflective material shall form a continuous circle on the rim.

(2) If the retroreflective material is applied to the rim in the form of a self-adhesive tape, the following requirement must be met: Use a sharp knife, razor blade, or similar instrument to carefully release an end of the tape material sufficient to be grasped between the thumb and finger. Grasp the freed tape end and gradually pull in a direction 90° to the plane of the rim. The tape material must break before additional separation (peeling) from the rim is observed.

(3) After the retroreflective material is abraded in accordance with the abrasion test for retroreflective rims at § 1512.18(r), the rim must then be tested for performance in accordance with the retroreflective tire and rim test at § 1512.18(o), to assure the reflectance properties over the angles given in table 3.

[43 FR 60034, Dec. 22, 1978, as amended at 45 FR 82627, 82628, Dec. 16, 1980]

§ 1512.17 Other requirements.

(a) *Road test.* Bicycles, other than sidewalk bicycles, shall be ridden at least 6.4 km (4.0 mi.) by a rider weighing at least 68.1kg (150 lb.) and travel five times over a 30.5 m (100 ft.) cleated course in accordance with the road test, § 1512.18(p), and shall exhibit stable handling, turning, and steering characteristics without difficulty of operation. There shall be no system or component failure of the structure, brakes, or tires, and there shall be no loosening or misalignment of the seat, handlebars, controls, or reflectors during or resulting from this test.

(b) *Sidewalk bicycle proof test.* Sidewalk bicycles shall be dropped a distance of at least 300 mm (1.0 ft.) three times onto a paved surface with weights attached in accordance with the sidewalk bicycle proof test, § 1512.18(q). There shall be no fracture of wheels, frame, seat, handlebars, or fork during or resulting from this test.

(c) *Ground clearance.* With the pedal horizontal and the pedal crank in its lowest position and any training wheels removed, it shall be possible to tilt the bicycle at least 25° from the vertical without the pedal or any other part (other than tires) contacting the ground plane.

(d) *Toe clearance.* Bicycles not equipped with positive foot-retaining devices (such as toe clips) shall have at least 89 mm (3½ in) clearance between the pedal and the front tire or fender (when turned to any position). The clearance shall be measured forward and parallel to the longitudinal axis of the bicycle from the center of either pedal to the arc swept by the tire or fender, whichever results in the least clearance. (See figure 6 of this part 1512.)

§ 1512.18 Tests and test procedures.

(a) *Sharp edge test.* [Reserved]

(b) [Reserved]

(c) *Protective cap and end-mounted devices test.* (Ref. § 1512.4(i), § 1512.6(d).) Any device suitable for exerting a removal force of at least 67 N (15 lbf) for protective caps and 8.9 N (2.0 lbf) for end caps at any point and in any direction may be used. All protective caps and end-mounted handlebar devices shall be tested to determine that they cannot be removed by application of the specified forces.

(d) *Handbrake loading and performance test:* (Ref. § 1512.5(b)).

(1) *Apparatus.* A spring scale or other suitable device for measuring the specified forces on the handbrake levers and a dry, clean, level, paved surface of adequate length.

(2) *Procedure.* The loading test, § 1512.18(d)(2)(i), and the rocking test, § 1512.18(d)(2)(iii), shall be performed before the performance test, § 1512.18(d)(2)(v), is performed and no adjustments shall be made between these tests.

(i) *Loading test procedure.* The hand levers shall be actuated with a force applied at a point no more than 25 mm (1.0 in) from the open end of the lever. If the hand lever contacts the handlebar (bottoms) before a force of 445 N (100 lbf) is reached, the loading may be stopped at that point, otherwise the loading shall be increased to at least 445 N (100 lbf).[4] Application of the loading force shall be repeated for a total of 10 times and all brake components shall be inspected.

(ii) *Loading test criteria.* There shall be no visible fractures, failures, misalignments, and clearances not in compliance with applicable parts of § 1512.5.

(iii) *Rocking test procedure.* A weight of at least 68.1 kg (150 lb) shall be placed on the seat; the force required for the hand levers to contact the handlebars or 445 N (100 lbf), as determined in § 1512.18(d)(2), shall be applied to the hand levers;[4] and the bicycle shall be rocked forward and backward over a dry, clean, level, paved surface at least six times and for a distance of at least 76 mm (3 in) in each direction.

(iv) *Rocking test criteria.* There shall be no loosening of the brake pads, pad holders, or cable and hand-lever securing devices or any other functional brake component.

(v) *Performance test procedure.* The following test conditions, unless otherwise specified in this part 1512, shall be followed:

(A) The bicycle shall be ridden over a dry, clean, smooth paved test course

[4] For hand lever extensions, the loading shall be continued until a force of 445 N (100 lbf) is reached or the hand lever extension is in the same plane as the upper surface of the handlebars or the extension lever contacts the handlebars.

free from protruding aggregate. The test course shall provide a coefficient of friction of less then 1.0 and shall have a slope of less than 1 percent.

(B) The wind velocity shall be less than 11 km/h (7 mph).

(C) Only the brake system under test shall be actuated.

(D) The bicycle shall attain the specified ground speed while the rider is in the normal riding position.

(E) The rider shall remain in the normal riding position throughout the test.

(F) The bicycle must be moving in a straight line at the start of brake application.

(G) Corrections for velocity at the initiation of braking may be made. The corrected braking distance shall be computed as follow:

$S_c = (V_s / V_m)^2 S_m$

where:

S_c = Corrected braking distance,
V_s = Specified test velocity.
V_m = Measured test velocity,
S_m = Measured braking distance.

The test run is invalid if at the commencement of the test, the measured test speed of the bicycle is not less than nor greater than the test speed required by this part 1512 by 1.5 km/h (0.9 mph).

(H) Four test runs are required. The stopping distance shall be determined by averaging the results of the four test runs.

(I) The stopping distances specified are based on a rider weight of at least 68.1 kg (150 lb) and a maximum rider and weight combination of 91 kg (200 lb). Greater stopping distances are allowable for heavier riders and test equipment weights at the rate of 0.30 m per 4.5 kg (1.0 ft per 10 lb).

(J) A test run is invalid if front-wheel lockup occurs.

(vi) *Performance test criteria.* The stopping force applied to the hand lever at a point no closer than 25 mm (1.0 in) from the open end shall not exceed 178 N (40 lbf). Bicycles with an equivalent ground speed in excess of 24 km/h (15 mph) (in its highest gear ratio at a pedal crank rate of 60 revolutions per minute)[3] shall stop from an actual test speed of 24 km/h (15 mph) or greater within a distance of 4.57 m (15 ft); when the equivalent ground speed is less than 24 km/h (15 mph) under the same conditions, the bicycle shall stop from an actual test speed of 16 km/h (10 mph) or greater within a distance of 4.57 m (15 ft).

(e) *Footbrake force and performance test.* (Ref. § 1512.5(c) (1) and (2)):

(1) *Apparatus.* Suitable devices for exerting and measuring the required forces and a dry, clean, level, paved surface of adequate length.

(2) *Force test.* The braking force shall be measured as the wheel is rotated in a direction of forward motion, and the braking force is measured in a direction tangential to the tire during a steady pull after the wheel completes one-half revolution but before the wheel completes one revolution. The brake shall be capable of producing a linearly proportional brake force for a gradually applied pedal force from 89 N to 310 N (20 to 70 lbf) and shall not be less than 178 N (40 lbf) for an applied pedal force of 310 N (70 lbf). All data points must fall within plus or minus 20 percent of the brake force, based on the measured brake load using the least square method of obtaining the best straight line curve.

(3) *Performance test.* The procedure of § 1512.18(d)(2)(v) shall be followed to test the footbrake performance. The stopping distance shall be less than 4.57 m (15 ft) from an actual test speed of 16 km/h (10 mph). In addition, if the equivalent ground speed of the bicycle is in excess of 24 km/h (15 mph) (in its highest gear ratio at a pedal crank rate of 60 revolutions per minute),[3] the stopping distance shall be 4.57 m (15 ft) from an actual test speed of 24 km/h (15 mph) or greater.

NOTE: No allowance shall be made for rider weight. See § 1512.5(d) for additional requirements for bicycles with both handbrakes and footbrakes.

(f) *Sidewalk bicycle footbrake force test.* For sidewalk bicycles, the footbrake force test is the same as for bicycles except; the brake force transmitted to the rear wheel shall continually increase as the pedal force is increased from 44.5 N to 225 N (10 to 50 lbf). The ratio of applied pedal force to braking

[3] See footnote 3 to § 1512.5.

force shall not be greater than two-to-one.

(g) *Handlebar stem test.* (Ref. § 1512.6(b)):

(1) *Procedure.* The handlebar stem shall be tested for strength by applying a force of 2000 N (450 lbf), in a forward direction, for bicycles, or 1000 N (225 lbf) for sidewalk bicycles, at a point in line with the handlbar attachment point and at an angle of 45° from the stem centerline (See fig. 2).

(2) *Criteria.* No visible fractures shall result from this test.

(h) *Handlebar test.* (Ref. § 1512.6(e)):

(1) *Stem-to-fork clamp test*—(i) *Procedure.* The handlebar and handlebar stem shall be assembled to the bicycle in accordance with the manufacturer's instructions. The handlebar-fork assembly shall be subjected to a torque applied about the axis of the stem, and shall then be disassembled and examined for signs of structural damage including cracking, splitting, stripping of threads, bearing damage, and bulging of the stem and fork structures. The handlebar and handlebar stem components shall be inspected for visible signs of galling, gouging, and scoring not due to normal assembly and disassembly operations.

(ii) *Criteria.* There shall be no visible movement between the stem and fork when a torque of 47+3, −0 N-m (35+2, −0 ft=lb) for bicycles and 20+3, −0 N-m (15+2, −0 ft=lb) for sidewalk bicycles is applied to the handlebar about the stem-to-fork axis. There shall be no visible signs of damage to the stem-to-fork assembly or any component part thereof.

(2) *Handlebar strength and clamp test*—(i) *Procedure.* The stem shall be in place on the bicycle or in an equivalent test fixture and secured according to manufacturer's instructions. A load shall be applied equally to each handlebar end in a direction to cause the greatest torque about the handlebar-to-stem clamp; deflection shall be measured along the line of applied force.

(ii) *Criteria.* The handlebars shall support a force of no less than 445 N (100 lbf) or absorb no less than 22.6 J (200 in-lb) of energy through a maximum deflection of no more than 76 mm (3.0 in.); the handlebar clamp shall prevent rotational movement of the handlebars relative to the clamp, and there shall be no visible fractures.

(i) *Pedal slip test.* [Reserved]

(j) *Rim test.* (Ref. §§ 1512.10 and 1512.11(c)):

(1) *Procedure.* Only one wheel need be tested if the front and rear wheel are of identical construction. The wheel to be tested shall be removed from the bicycle and be supported circumferentially around the tire sidewall. A load of 2000 N (450 lbf) shall be applied to the axle and normal to the plane of the wheel for at least 30 seconds. If the wheel hub is offset, the load shall be applied in the direction of the offset.

(2) *Criteria.* The wheel and tire assembly shall be inspected for compliance with the requirements of § 1512.11(a) and shall be remounted on the bicycle according to the manufacturer's instructions and shall turn freely without roughness and shall comply with the requirement of § 1512.11(b).

(3) *Front hub retention test.* (Ref. § 1512.12(c)).

(i) *Procedures.* Front hub locking devices shall be released. When threaded nuts and axles are used, the nuts shall be open at least 360° from a finger tight condition. A separation force of at least 111 N (25 lb) shall be applied to the hub on a line along the slots in the fork ends.

(ii) *Criteria.* The front hub shall not separate from the fork; fenders, mudguards, struts, and brakes shall not be allowed to restrain the separation.

(k) *Fork and frame test.* (Ref. §§ 1512.13 and 1512.14):

(1) *Fork test*—(i) *Procedure.* With the fork stem supported in a 76 mm (3.0 in) vee block and secured by the method illustrated in figure 1 of this part 1512, a load shall be applied at the axle attachment in a direction perpendicular to the centerline of the stem and against the direction of the rake. Load and deflection readings shall be recorded and plotted at the point of loading.

(ii) *Criteria.* Energy of at least 39.5 J (350 in-lb) shall be absorbed with a deflection in the direction of the force of no more than 64 mm (2½ in.).

(2) *Fork and frame assembly test*—(i) *Procedure.* The fork, or one identical to that tested in accordance with the fork test, § 1512.18(k)(1), shall be replaced on

the bicycle in accordance with the manufacturer's instructions; and a load of 890 N (200 lbf), or an energy of at least 39.5 J (350 in-lb), whichever results in the greater force, shall be applied to the fork at the axle attachment point against the direction of the rake in line with the rear wheel axle. The test load shall be counteracted by a force applied at the location of the rear axle during this test.

(ii) *Criteria.* There shall be no visible evidence of fracture and no deformation of frame that significantly limits the steering angle over which the front wheel can be turned.

(l) *Seat adjustment clamps and load test.* (Ref. §1512.15(c)).

(1) *Procedure.* A force of at least 668 N (150 lbf) shall be applied vertically downward (334 N (75 lbf) for sidewalk bicycles) to a point within 25 mm (1.0 in.) from either the front or rear of the seat, whichever produces the greatest torque on the seat clamp. After removal of this force, a force of 222 N (50 lbf) shall then be applied horizontally (111 N (25 lbf) for sidewalk bicycles) to a point within 25 mm (1.0 in.) from either the front or rear of the seat, whichever produces the greatest torque on the clamp.

(2) *Criteria.* No movement of the seat with respect to the seat post, or of the seat post with respect to the bicycle frame, shall have resulted from application of the forces specified.

(m) *Reflector mount and alignment test.* (Ref. §1512.16 (c) and (d)):

(1) *Procedure.* A force of 89 N (20 lbf) shall be applied to the reflector mount in at least three directions selected as most likely to affect its alignment. At least one of those directions shall be selected to represent a force that would be expected in lifting the bicycle by grasping the reflector.

(2) *Criteria.* (i) *During test:* The optical axis of the reflector shall remain parallel within 15° to the line or intersection of the ground plane and the center plane of the bicycle defined as a plane containing both wheels and the centerlines of the down tube and seat mast.

(ii) *Post test:* The optical axis of the reflector shall remain parallel within 5° to the line or intersection of the ground plane and the center plane of the bicycle defined as a plane containing both wheels and the centerlines of the down tube and seat mast.

(n) *Reflector test.* (Ref. §1512.16(g)):

(1) *Conditioning.* The following conditioning in the order given shall be performed prior to testing for performance.

(i) *Warpage conditioning.* The reflector shall be held in a preheated oven for at least one hour at 50° ±5 °C (122±5.4 °F). A pedal reflector may be conditioned integrally with its pedal.

(ii) *Mechanical impact conditioning.* The reflector shall be mounted faceup in a manner similar to the way in which it is mounted on the bicycle. A 13 mm (½ in.) diameter polished steel ball shall be dropped normal to the center of the face of the reflector from a height of 0.76 m (30 in.). The ball may be guided by a tube with holes, but not restricted in free fall. Pedal reflectors are exempt from this impact conditioning.

(iii) *Moisture conditioning.* The reflector shall be submerged in tap water in a suitable container. The container shall be pressurized in 17.2 kN/m^2 (2.5 psi) (equivalent to 1.7 m (5¾ ft.)) of water for 15 minutes and then released.

(2) *Reflector performance test.* (i) Arrangements for the reflector performance test shall be as shown in figure 3 and the distance *D* between the light source and the reflector shall be 30.5 m (100 ft.). The source of illumination shall be a lamp with a 51 mm (2.0 in.) effective diameter and a filament operating at 2,856±10 percent color temperature. The observation point shall be colocated (as close as practicable) with the source of illumination. The reflector shall be mounted with the center of the reflector at the center of rotation and at the same horizontal level as the source of illumination. Photometric measurements shall be made at the observation angles and entrance angles given in tables 1 and 2.

(ii) The observation angle is the angle formed by a line from the point of observation to the center of the reflector with a second line from the center of the reflector to the source of illumination. The entrance angle is the angle between the optical axis of the reflector and a line from the center of the reflector to the source of illumination. The entrance angle shall be designated left, right, up, and down in accordance with the position of the source of illumination with respect to the axis of the reflector as viewed from behind the reflector when the plane of the observation angle is vertical and the receiver is above the source.

(iii) Photometric measurements shall be made either visually or photoelectrically. With either method, the light reflected to the observation point shall be determined. Also, the illumination on the reflector from the source shall be measured.

(iv) For visual measurements a comparison lamp, emitting light similar in spectral quality to the reflector, shall be located adjacent to the reflector (at an angle not to exceed ½°) and arranged so that the candlepower can be varied from 0.01 to 0.25 to make the intensity duplicate that of the reflector under test. The candlepower of the source of the illumination of the reflector under test shall be known or determined for this test. Means shall be provided to change the intensity of the source of illumination without changing the filament color temperature. The comparison lamp shall be designed to avoid reflection from the source of illumination back in the direction of the observer. It shall be of such size and so diffused that when viewed by the observer (through a 2½× reducing monocular), the candlepower can be readily compared and adjusted to that of the reflector. The observer shall have at least 10 minutes of dark adaption before making observations. For photoelectric measurements, the opening to the photocell shall not be more than ½ inch vertical by 1 inch horizontal.

(v) Reflectors that mount on the bicycle in a fixed rotational position with respect to the bicycle, or the bicycle component on which they are mounted (such as pedals or spokes), shall be tested with a single orientation. Reflectors that do not mount on the bicycle in a fixed rotational position with respect to the bicycle shall be rotated about their axis through 360° to find the minimum candlepower per footcandle for each test point. If the measurement falls below the minimum requirement at any test point, the reflector shall be rotated ±5° about its axis from the angle where the minimum occurs, and the maximum candlepower per footcandle within this angle shall be the measured value.

(vi) Should uncolored reflections from the front surface interfere with photometric readings at any test point the lowest reading and location within 1° above, below, right, and left of the test point shall meet the minimum requirement for the test point.

(vii) A recommended coordinate system for definition of color is the "Internationale de l'Eclairage (CIE 1931)" system. In the coordinate system and when illuminated by the source defined in table 4 of this part 1512, a reflector will be considered to be red if its color falls within the region bounded by the red spectrum locus and the lines $y = 0.980 - x$ and $y = 0.335$; a reflector will be considered to be amber if its color falls within the region bounded by the yellow spectrum locus and the lines $y = 0.382$, $y = 0.790 - 0.667x$, and $y = x - 0.120$.

(o) Reflective tire and rim test (Ref. § 1512.16(h) and (i)):

(1) *Apparatus.* Arrangements for the reflective intensity measurement shall be as shown in figure 3 of this part 1512. A light projector (having a maximum effective lens diameter of *D*/500, where *D* is the distance from the source to the retroreflective surface being measured) capable of projecting light of uniform intensity shall be used to illuminate the sample. The light falling on the sample shall have a color temperature of 2856°K+*10*% (equivalent to a tungsten filament lamp operated at a color temperature of 2856°K+*10*% having approximately the relative energy distribution given in table 4 of this part 1512). The light reflected from the test surface shall be measured with a photoelectric receiver, the response of which has been corrected for the spectral sensitivity of the average photopic human eye. The dimensions of the active area of the receiver shall be such that no point on the perimeter of the receiver is more than *D*/100 from its center (where *d* is the distance from the receiver to the retroreflective surface). Wheels used for the measurement of retroreflective tires or rims shall

have all exposed metallic surfaces, including spokes, masked in flat black so that when measured these surfaces indicate no appreciable reflectance. The tire shall be mounted and fully inflated. Distances shall be measured from the plane of the wheel and the center of the hub. For the tests, the distance *D* between the projector and the center of the wheel and distance *d* between the center of the wheel and the receiver shall each be at least 15 m (50 ft.).

(2) *Procedure*—(i) *Masking.* The reflecting strip to be tested shall be within two concentric circles, the larger of which is no more than 0.02 m (0.79 in.) greater in radius than the smaller. While additional reflecting material is permitted outside such boundaries, such additional material shall not be counted in determining the average width of the reflecting strip and shall be masked off with opaque, matte black tape in testing the reflecting material.

(ii) *Orientation.* Every position of the reflecting strip on the rim or the mounted and fully inflated tire to be tested shall be oriented so that the normal to this portion is within 40° of parallel to the axis of rotation of the wheel.

(iii) *Measurement.* Measure the distance *d* from the receiver to the center of the wheel and the minimum distance *r* from the axis of rotation of the wheel to the unmasked portion of the reflective strip. Measure the illumination incident on the reflective strip at uniform intervals of no more than 45° around the wheel, with the receiver oriented in the direction of the incident radiation. The average of such readings will be the mean illumination of the sample *E*. If any one of such readings differs by more than 10 percent from the mean illumination, then a more uniform source must be obtained. Measure the illumination of the receiver due to reflection from the retroreflective surface for each entrance angle and each observation angle given in table 3 of this part 1512. The entrance angle and the observation angle shall be in the same plane. A negative entrance angle (figure 3 of this part 1512) is specified when the entrance angle is small because the location of the receiver with respect to the direction of illumination becomes important for distinguishing between ordinary mirror-like reflection and retroreflection. The illumination incident on the test surface and the receiver shall be measured in the same units on a linear scale. Compute the ratio *A* for each combination of entrance angle and observation angle listed in table 3 as follows:

$$A = [(E_r / E_s)(d^2 / r)]$$

Where:

A = Ratio in meters,
E_r = Illumination incident upon the receiver,
E_s = Illumination incident upon a plane perpendicular to the incident ray at the specimen position (see instructions above in this paragraph (o)(2)(iii) for averaging), measured in the same units as E_r,
d = The distance in meters from the receiver to the center of the wheel,
r = The minimum radius in meters of the boundary circles of the retroreflective strip.

The minimum value of *A* shall be that listed in table 3 of this part 1512 for each combination of entrance angle and observation angle. The plane containing the entrance angle and the plane containing the observation angle shall coincide. In table 3, a positive entrance angle corresponds to the case in which the line of sight to the receiver lies between the line of incidence and the optic axis of the reflector, and a negative entrance angle corresponds to the case in which the line of incidence lies between the line of sight of the receiver and optic axis of the reflector.

(iv) *Criteria.* The ratio A as defined in § 1512.18(o)(2)(iii) shall not be less than:

$$A = 4\mathrm{Cos}^2\theta/[1+(\Phi/0.225)^{3/2}]$$

where A is ratio in meters, θ is the entrance angle in degrees, and Φ is the observation angle in degrees. The criterion applies only for entrance angles from 0° to 40° and observation angles from 0.2° to 1.5°, and performance is not specified beyond this range. The values of *A* in table 3 are obtained from the above formula by rounding up to two significant figures. Except in cases in which the performance of the reflector is seriously questionable, a reflector with *A* at least the value given in table

3 at each of the six combinations of entrance and observation angles will be considered to satisfy this criteria.

(p) *Road test.* (Ref. §§ 1512.15(c) and 1512.17(a)):

(1) *Procedure.* The bicycle shall be ridden at least 6.4 km (4.0 mi.) by a rider weighing at least 68.1 kg (150 lb.) with the tires inflated to maximum recommended pressure. Travel shall include riding the bicycle five times over a 30 m (100 ft.) course of wooden cleats fastened to a paved surface. The cleats shall be a full 25 mm (1.0 in.) high by 51 mm (2.0 in.) wide lumber with a 12 mm by 12 mm (½ in. by ½ in.) chamfer of 45° on the corners contacting the tires. The cleats shall be spaced every 1.8 m (6.0 ft.) over the 30 m (100 ft.) course. The bicycle shall be ridden over the cleated course at a speed of at least 24 km/hr (15 mph) with the rider firmly seated.

(2) *Criteria.* The bicycle shall exhibit stable handling, turning, and steering characteristics without difficulty of operation. There shall be no system or component failure of the structure, brakes, or tires and there shall be no loosening or misalignment of the seat, handlebars, controls, or reflectors.

(q) *Sidewalk bicycle proof test.* (Ref. §§ 1512.15(c) and 1512.17(b)):

(1) *Procedure.* The bicycle shall be loaded with weights of 13.6 kg (30 lb.) on the seat surface and 4.5 kg (10 lb.) attached to the end of each handle grip for a total load of 22.7 kg (50 lb.). The bicycle shall be lifted a distance of 0.3 m (1.0 ft.) and dropped (while maintaining an upright position) three times onto a paved surface. Following this and with weight removed, it shall be allowed to fall in any configuration and attitude from an upright position to the paved surface three times on each side.

(r) *Abrasion test for retroreflective rims.* (Ref. § 1512.16(i)):

(1) This test consists of a steel wire cup brush rotating at a constant velocity of 60 rpm that is applied at a force of 2 N (0.45 lbf) to the retroreflective material on one side of a bicycle wheel rim. The rim is rotated about the axle at a linear velocity of 0.23 m/sec (9 in./sec). The test is complete when the wheel has completed 1000 revolutions.

(2) *Apparatus.* Figure 8 of this part 1512 illustrates the following test fixture arrangement that is suitable to perform this abrasion test:

(i) *Test fixture.* The test fixture contains a clamp to hold the axle of a bicycle wheel so that the wheel can rotate freely about the axle. The axis of rotation is capable of being inclined from the vertical to bring that portion of the side of the wheel rim containing the retroreflective material into a horizontal plane as it passes beneath the abrading brush. A drive mechanism to rotate the bicycle wheel contains a means to adjust the rotational velocity to obtain the specified linear velocity measured at a point on the wheel rim on the axis of the abrading brush.

(ii) *Abrader.* The abrader is a cup brush meeting the specification in paragraph (r)(3)(v) of this section. It is mounted in a chuck attached to a motor that rotates about a vertical axis at the specified rotational velocity. A means is provided to apply the rotating cup brush at the specified force against the retroreflective material on the bicycle wheel rim. The axis of the abrading brush is positioned on the mid point in the width of the retroreflective material. The force is produced by deadweights applied to a pan on the axis of the counterbalanced motor/brush assembly.

(3) *Specifications.* (i) The linear velocity of the reflective band on wheel rim shall be 0.23 m/sec (9 in./sec) measured at a point on the axis of the abrading brush.

(ii) The rotational velocity of the abrading brush shall be 60 rpm.

(iii) The force normal to the plane of the retroreflective material at which the abrading brush is to be applied shall be 2 N (0.45 lbf).

(iv) The bicycle wheel shall make 1000 complete revolutions per test.

(v) The abrader shall be a cup brush having bristles that are 0.005 in. (approx. 0.13mm) diameter low carbon steel wire; an outside diameter of 0.5 inch (aprox. .13mm); a wire bristle length of 0.25 inch (approx. 6.4mm); and a cup diameter of 0.405 inch (approx. 10.29mm).[6]

(vi) The abrasion test shall be conducted at an ambient temperature of between 16 °C (60 °F) and 27 °C (80 °F).

(4) *Procedure.* (i) The retroreflective bicycle rim to be tested shall be an unused sample free from grit, grime and grease. Prior to beginning the test, remove, according to instructions supplied with the bicycle, any protective coating or material used to prevent damage in shipping.

(ii) Test the wheel in a suitable test fixture, according to the specifications in paragraph (r)(3) of this section.

(iii) Clamp the wheel by its axle in the test fixture and align the axis of rotation so that the portion of the reflective material below the axis of the abrading brush is horizontal.

(iv) Shape the cup brush by hand to the specified 0.5 (approx. 13mm) diameter. Any stray wire bristles projecting more than 1⁄32 in. (approx. 1 mm) beyond the tip of the bulk of the bristles should be clipped off. Adjust the position of the brush so that its axis is centered over the mid-point in the width of the retroreflective material.

(v) Adjust the rotational velocity of the bicycle wheel to obtain a linear velocity of 0.23 m/sec (9 in./sec) measured at the mid-point in the width of the retroreflective material. Adjust the force to obtain a force normal to the surface under the brush of 2 N (0.45 lbf).

(vi) Apply the abrading brush to the retroreflective material on the wheel rim, and continue the test for 1000 complete revolutions of the bicycle wheel.

[43 FR 60034, Dec. 22, 1978, as amended at 45 FR 82628, Dec. 16, 1980; 46 FR 3204, Jan. 14, 1981; 68 FR 52691, Sept. 5, 2003; 76 FR 27888, May 13, 2011]

§ 1512.19 Instructions and labeling.

A bicycle shall have an instruction manual attached to its frame or included with the packaged unit.

(a) The instruction manual shall include at least the following:

(1) Operations and safety instructions describing operation of the brakes and gears, cautions concerning wet weather and night-time operation, and a guide for safe on-and-off road operation.

(2) Assembly instructions for accomplishing complete and proper assembly.

(3) Maintenance instructions for proper maintenance of brakes, control cables, bearing adjustments, wheel adjustments, lubrication, reflectors, tires and handlebar and seat adjustments; should the manufacturer determine that such maintenance is beyond the capability of the consumer, specifics regarding locations where such maintenance service can be obtained shall be included.

(b) A bicycle less than fully assembled and fully adjusted shall have clearly displayed on any promotional display material and on the outside surface of the shipping carton the following: (1) A list of tools necessary to properly accomplish assembly and adjustment, (2) a drawing illustrating the minimum leg-length dimension of a rider and a method of measurement of this dimension.

(c) The minimum leg-length dimension shall be readily understandable and shall be based on allowing no less than one inch of clearance between (1) the top tube of the bicycle and the ground plane and (2) the crotch measurement of the rider. A girl's style frame shall be specified in the same way using a corresponding boys' model as a basis.

(d) [Reserved]

(e) Every bicycle subject to the requirements of this part 1512 shall bear a marking or label that is securely affixed on or to the frame of the bicycle in such a manner that the marking or label cannot be removed without being defaced or destroyed. The marking or label shall identify the name of the manufacturer or private labeler and shall also bear some form of marking from which the manufacturer can identify the month and year of manufacture or from which the private labeler can identify the manufacturer and the month and year of manufacture. For purposes of this paragraph, the term *manufacture* means the completion by the manufacturer of a bicycle of those construction or assembly operations

[6] For compliance testing the Commission will use a brush meeting this description distributed by Dremel Manufacturing Company, Racine, Wisconsin as Dremel Part No. 442. This brush is manufactured by Weiler Brush Company as No. 26074, MC–10 Wire.

that are performed by the manufacturer before the bicycle is shipped from the manufacturer's place of production for sale to distributors, retailers, or consumers.

[43 FR 60034, Dec. 22, 1978, as amended at 60 FR 62990, Dec. 8, 1995]

§ 1512.20 Separability.

If any section or portion thereof of this part 1512 or its application to any person or circumstance is held invalid, the remainder of the section(s) and its (their) application to other persons or circumstances is not thereby affected.

Subpart B—Policies and Interpretations [Reserved]

FIGURE 1 TO PART 1512—BICYCLE FRONT FORK CANTILEVER BENDING TEST RIG

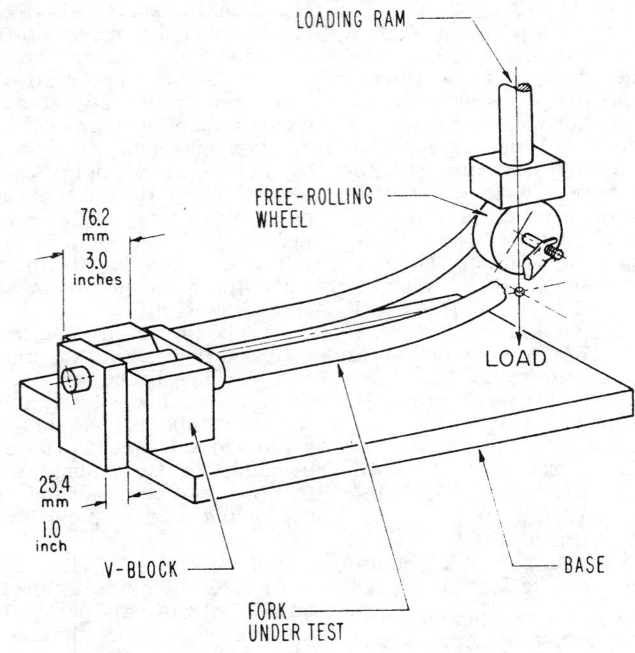

FIG I-BICYCLE FRONT FORK CANTILEVER BENDING TEST RIG

FIGURES 2 AND 3 TO PART 1512—HANDLEBAR STEM LOADING AND ENTRANCE 8 OBSERVATION ANGLES

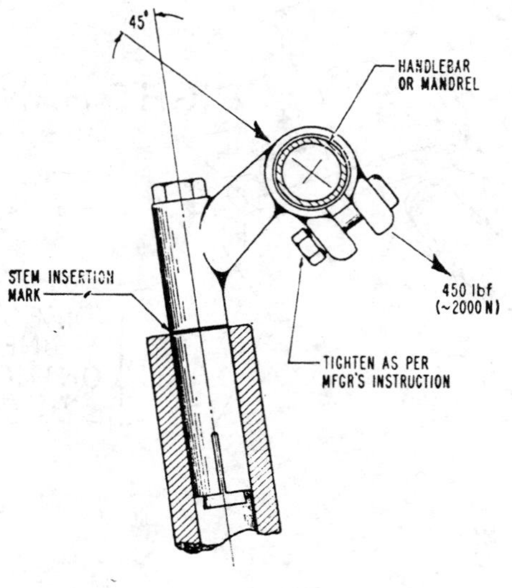

FIG 2—HANDLEBAR STEM LOADING

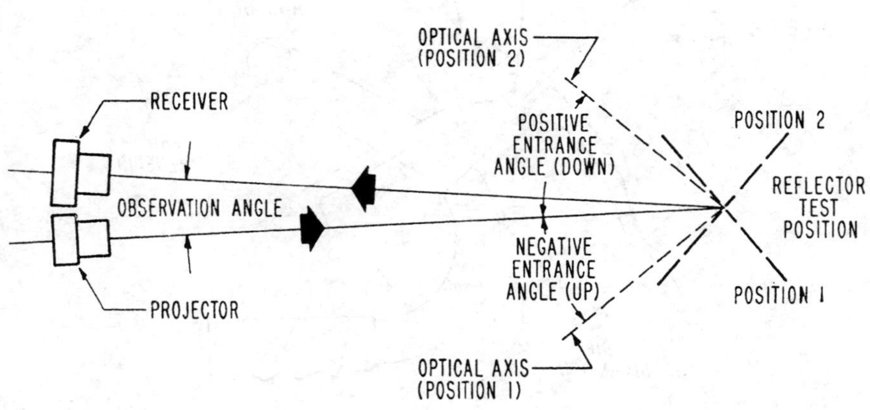

Side View

FIG. 3—ENTRANCE & OBSERVATION ANGLES

[FIG 4-REVOKED]

FIGURE 5 TO PART 1512—TYPICAL HANDBRAKE ACTUATOR SHOWING GRIP DIMENSION

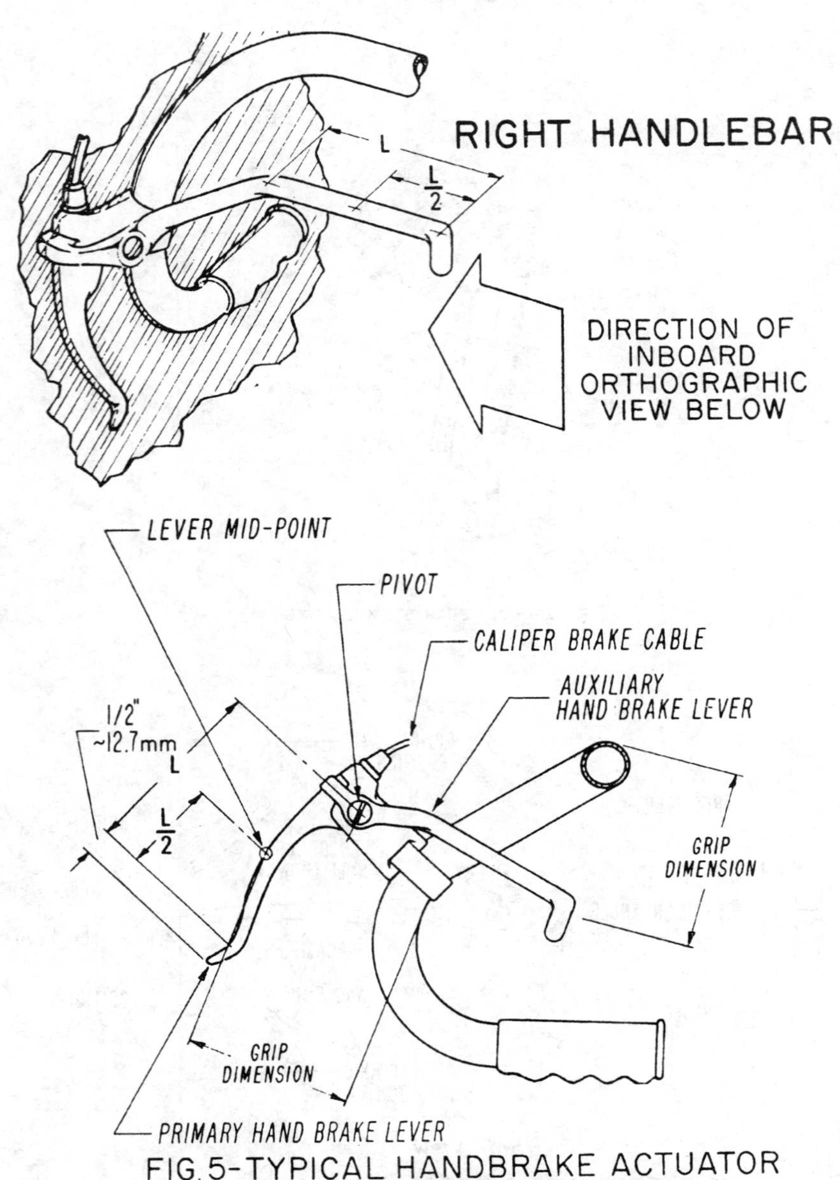

FIG. 5-TYPICAL HANDBRAKE ACTUATOR SHOWING GRIP DIMENSION

FIGURES 6 AND 7 TO PART 1512—TOE CLEARANCE AND CHAIN GUARD REQUIREMENTS

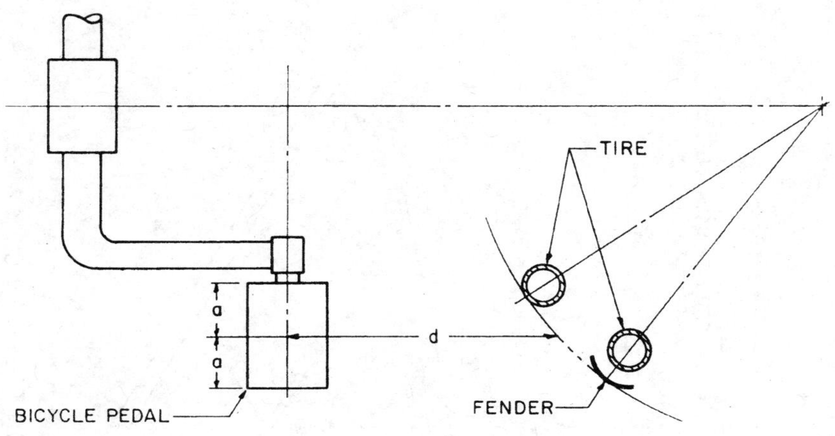

FIG 6–TOE CLEARANCE

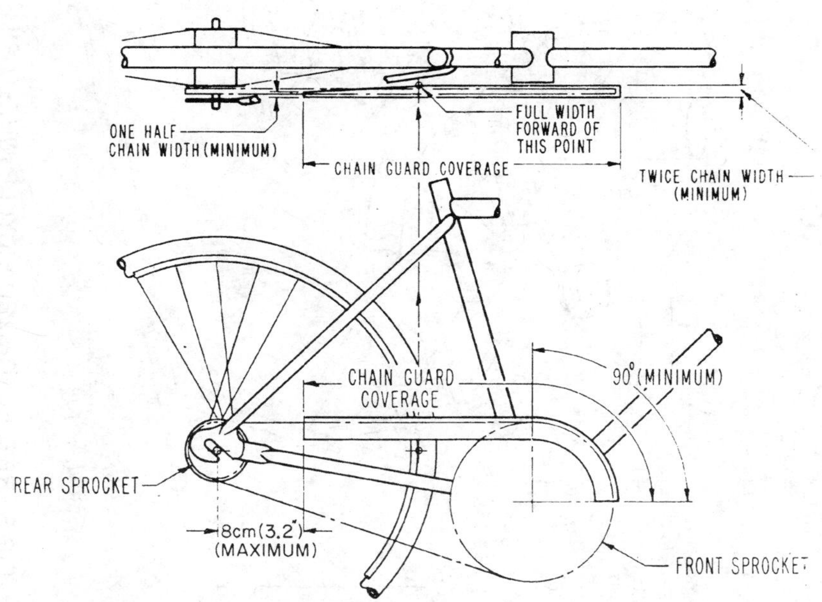

FIG 7–CHAIN GUARD REQUIREMENTS

FIGURE 8 TO PART 1512—REFLECTORIZED BICYCLE WHEEL RIM ABRASION TEST DEVICE

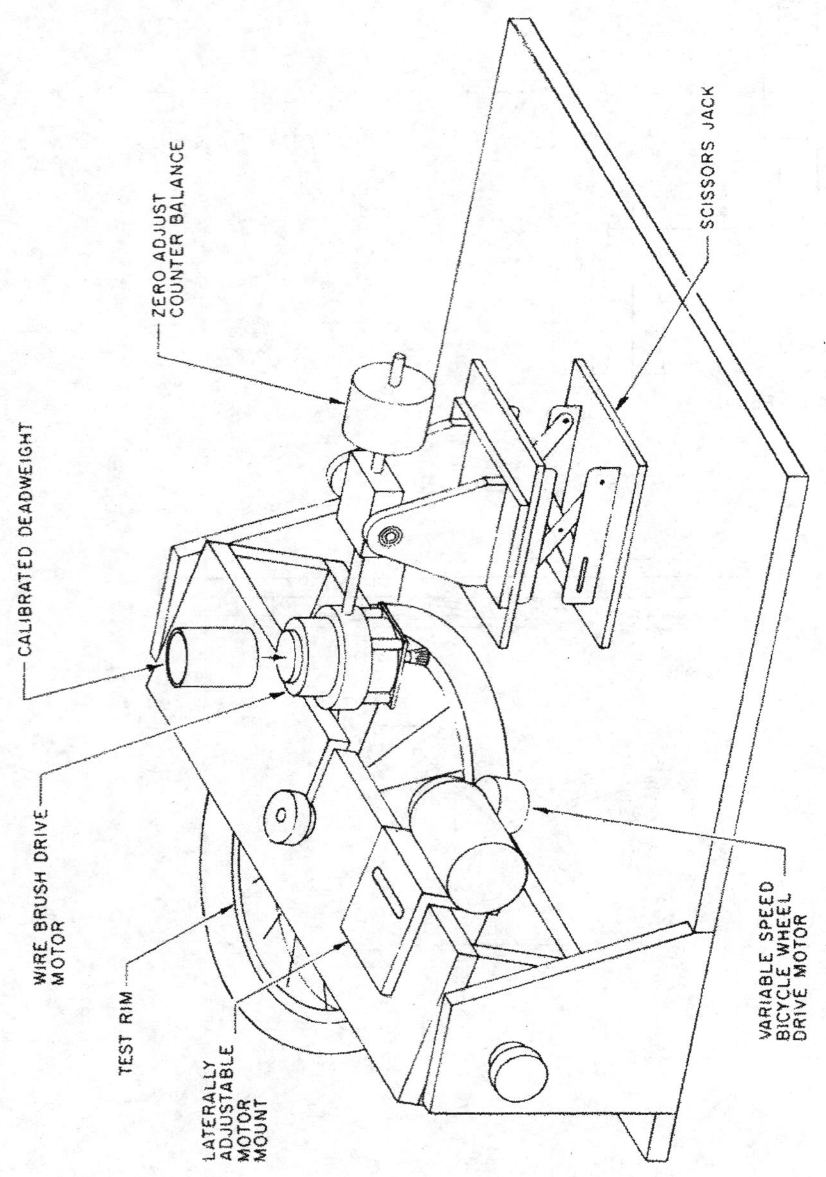

FIG 8—REFLECTORIZED BICYCLE WHEEL RIM ABRASION TEST DEVICE

TABLE 1 TO PART 1512—MINIMUM CANDLEPOWER PER INCIDENT FOOT-CANDLE FOR CLEAR REFLECTOR[1]

Observation angle	Front, rear, and side reflectors; entrance angle in degrees			Pedal reflectors; entrance angle in degrees		
	0	10 up/down	20 left/right	0	10 up/down	20 left/right
0.2	27.0	18.0	9.0	7.5	6.0	3.0
0.3	....	....	....	6.0	4.8	2.4
1.5	.28	.20	.12	.28	.20	.12

[1] Amber values shall be 5/8 × clear values. Red values shall be 1/4 clear values.

TABLE 2 TO PART 1512—MINIMUM CANDLEPOWER PER INCIDENT FOOT-CANDLE FOR CLEAR REFLECTOR[1]

Observation angle	Front, rear, and side reflectors; entrance angle in degrees		
	30 left/right	40 left/right	50 left/right
0.2	8.0	7.0	6.0
1.5	.12	.12	.12

[1] Amber values shall be 5/8 × clear values. Red values shall be 1/4 × clear values.

TABLE 3 TO PART 1512—MINIMUM ACCEPTABLE VALUES FOR THE QUANTITY A DEFINED IN THE RETROREFLECTIVE TIRE AND RIM TEST PROCEDURE

Observation angle (degrees)	Entrance angle (degrees)	Minimum acceptable value of A	
		Meters	Feet
0.2	−4	2.2	7.25
.2	20	1.9	6.27
.2	40	1.3	4.29
1.5	−4	.22	.73
1.5	20	.19	.63
1.5	40	.13	.43

[43 FR 60034, Dec. 22, 1978, as amended at 45 FR 82631, Dec. 16, 1980; 46 FR 3204, Jan. 14, 1981]

TABLE 4 TO PART 1512—RELATIVE ENERGY DISTRIBUTION OF SOURCES

Wave length (nanometers)	Relative energy
380	9.79
390	12.09
400	14.71
410	17.68
420	21.00
430	24.67
440	28.70
450	33.09
460	37.82
470	42.87
480	48.25
490	53.91
500	59.86
510	66.06
520	72.50
530	79.13
540	85.95
550	92.91
560	100.00
570	107.18
580	114.44
590	121.73
600	129.04
610	136.34
620	143.62
630	150.83
640	157.98
650	165.03
660	171.96
670	178.77
680	185.43
690	191.93
700	198.26
710	204.41
720	210.36
730	216.12
740	221.66
750	227.00
760	232.11

PART 1513—REQUIREMENTS FOR BUNK BEDS

AUTHORITY: 15 U.S.C. 1261(f)(1)(D), 1261(s), 1262(e)(1), 1262(f)–(i).

SOURCE: 64 FR 71907, Dec. 22, 1999, unless otherwise noted.

§ 1513.1 Scope, application, and effective date.

(a) *Scope, basis, and purpose.* This part 1513 prescribes requirements for bunk beds to reduce or eliminate the risk that children will die or be injured from being trapped between the upper bunk and the wall or in openings below guardrails or in other structures in the bed. Bunk beds meeting these requirements are exempted from 16 CFR 1500.18(a)(18).

(b) *Application and effective date.* This part applies to all bunk beds, except those manufactured only for institutional use, that are manufactured in the United States, or imported, on or after June 19, 2000. (Facilities intended for use by children under age 6 are not considered to be institutions.) Bunk beds, as described in this section, that are not intended for use by children are subject to the requirements in 16 CFR part 1213, and not to 16 CFR 1500.18(a)(18). However, the provisions of 16 CFR 1213 are substantively identical to the requirements in this part 1513.

§ 1513.2 Definitions.

As used in this part 1513:

Bed. See Bunk bed.

Bed end structure means an upright unit at the head and foot of the bed to which the side rails attach.

Bunk bed means a bed in which the underside of any foundation is over 30 inches (760 mm) from the floor.

Foundation means the base or support on which a mattress rests.

Guardrail means a rail or guard on a side of the upper bunk to prevent a sleeping occupant from falling or rolling out.

§ 1513.3 Requirements.

(a) *Guardrails.* (1) Any bunk bed shall provide at least two guardrails, at least one on each side of the bed, for each bed having the underside of its foundation more than 30 inches (760 mm) from the floor.

(2) One guardrail shall be continuous between each of the bed's end structures. "Continuous" means that any gap between the guardrail and end structure shall not exceed 0.22 inches (5.6 mm) (so as to not cause a finger entrapment hazard for a child).

(3) The other guardrail may terminate before reaching the bed's end structures, providing there is no more than 15 inches (380 mm) between either end of the guardrail and the nearest bed end structure.

(4) For bunk beds designed to have a ladder attached to one side of the bed, the continuous guardrail shall be on the other side of the bed.

(5) Guardrails shall be attached so that they cannot be removed without either intentionally releasing a fastening device or applying forces sequentially in different directions.

(6) The upper edge of the guardrails shall be no less than 5 inches (130 mm) above the top surface of the mattress when a mattress of the maximum thickness specified by the manufacturer's instructions is on the bed. This requirement does not prohibit a wall-side guardrail that terminates in a quarter-circle bend and attaches to the side rail of the upper bunk foundation.

(7) With no mattress on the bed, there shall be no openings in the structure between the lower edge of the uppermost member of the guardrail and the underside of the upper bunk's foundation that would permit passage of the wedge block shown in Figure 1 of this part when tested in accordance with the procedure at § 1513.4(a).

(b) *Bed end structures.* (1) The upper edge of the upper bunk end structures shall be at least 5 inches (130 mm) above the top surface of the mattress for at least 50 percent of the distance between the two posts at the head and foot of the upper bunk when a mattress and foundation of the maximum thickness specified by the manufacturer's instructions is on the bed.

(2) With no mattress on the bed, there shall be no openings in the rigid end structures above the foundation of the upper bunk that will permit the free passage of the wedge block shown in Figure 1 when tested in accordance with the procedure at § 1513.4(b).

(3) When tested in accordance with § 1513.4(c), there shall be no openings in the end structures between the underside of the foundation of the upper bunk and upper side of the foundation of the lower bunk that will permit the free passage of the wedge block shown in Figure 1, unless the openings are also large enough to permit the free passage of a 9-inch (230-mm) diameter rigid sphere.

(4) All portions of the boundary of any opening required by §§ 1513.4(c)(1) and (2) to be probed by the wedge block

of Figure 1, and that permits free passage of a 9-inch diameter sphere, must conform to the neck entrapment requirements of § 1513.4(c)(3).

§ 1513.4 Test methods.

(a) *Guardrails* (see § 1513.3(a)(6)). With no mattress on the bed, place the wedge block shown in Figure 1, tapered side first, into each opening in the rigid bed structure below the lower edge of the uppermost member of the guardrail and above the underside of the upper bunk's foundation. Orient the block so that it is most likely to pass through the opening (*e.g.*, the major axis of the block parallel to the major axis of the opening) ("most adverse orientation"). Then, gradually apply a 33-lbf (147–N) force in a direction perpendicular to the plane of the large end of the block. Sustain the force for 1 minute.

(b) *Upper bunk end structure* (see § 1513.3(b)(2)). Without a mattress or foundation on the upper bunk, place the wedge block shown in Figure 1 into any opening, tapered side first, and in the most adverse orientation. Determine if the wedge block can pass freely through the opening.

(c) *Lower bunk end structure* (see § 1513.3(b)(3)). (1) Without a mattress or foundation on the lower bunk, place the wedge block shown in Figure 1, tapered side first, into each opening in the lower bunk end structure in the most adverse orientation. Determine whether the wedge block can pass freely through the opening. If the wedge block passes freely through the opening, determine whether a 9-inch (230-mm) diameter rigid sphere can pass freely through the opening.

(2) With the manufacturer's recommended maximum thickness mattress and foundation in place, repeat the test in paragraph (c)(1) of this section.

(3) All portions of the boundary of any opening that is required to be probed by the wedge block of Figure 1 by paragraphs (c)(1) and (c)(2) of this section, and that permits free passage of a 9-inch diameter sphere, must satisfy the requirements of paragraphs (c)(3)(i) and (c)(3)(ii) of this section addressing neck entrapment:

(i) Insert the "A" section of the test template shown in Figure 2 of this part into the portion of the boundary to be tested, with the plane of the template in the plane of the opening and with the centerline of the top of the template (as shown in Figure 2) aligned parallel to the centerline of the opening, until motion is stopped by contact between the test template and the boundaries of the opening (see Figure 3 of this part). By visual inspection, determine if there is simultaneous contact between the boundary of the opening and both sides of the "A" section of the template. If simultaneous contact occurs, mark the contact points on the boundary of the opening and conduct the additional test described in paragraph (c)(3)(ii) of this section.

(ii) To check the potential for neck entrapment, place the neck portion of the "B" section of the template into the opening, with its plane perpendicular to both the plane of the opening and the centerline of the opening (see Figure 4 of this part). If the neck portion of the "B" section of the template can completely enter the opening (passes 0.75 inch or more beyond the points previously contacted by the "A" section of the template), the opening is considered to present a neck entrapment hazard and fails the test, unless its lower boundary slopes downward at 45" or more for the whole distance from the narrowest part of the opening the neck can reach to the part of the opening that will freely pass a 9-inch diameter sphere.

§ 1513.5 Marking and labeling.

(a) There shall be a permanent label or marking on each bed stating the name and address (city, state, and zip code) of the manufacturer, distributor, or retailer; the model number; and the month and year of manufacture.

(b) The following warning label shall be permanently attached to the inside of an upper bunk bed end structure in a location that cannot be covered by the bedding but that may be covered by the placement of a pillow.

⚠ WARNING
To help prevent serious or fatal injuries from entrapment or falls: • Never allow a child under 6 years on upper bunk • Use only a mattress that is __ inches long and __ inches wide on upper bunk • Ensure thickness of mattress and foundation combined does not exceed __ inches and that mattress surface is at least 5 inches below upper edge of guardrails DO NOT REMOVE THIS LABEL

§ 1513.6 Instructions.

Instructions shall accompany each bunk bed set, and shall include the following information.

(a) *Size of mattress and foundation.* The length and width of the intended mattress and foundation shall be clearly stated, either numerically or in conventional terms such as twin size, twin extra-long, etc. In addition, the maximum thickness of the mattress and foundation required for compliance with § 1513.3 (a)(5) and (b)(1) of this part shall be stated.

(b) *Safety warnings.* The instructions shall provide the following safety warnings:

(1) Do not allow children under 6 years of age to use the upper bunk.

(2) Use guardrails on both sides of the upper bunk.

(3) Prohibit horseplay on or under beds.

(4) Prohibit more than one person on upper bunk.

(5) Use ladder for entering or leaving upper bunk.

(6) If the bunk bed will be placed next to a wall, the guardrail that runs the full length of the bed should be placed against the wall to prevent entrapment between the bed and the wall. (This applies only to bunk beds without two full-length guardrails.)

FIGURE 1 TO PART 1513—WEDGE BLOCK FOR TESTS IN § 1513.4 (a), (b), AND (c)

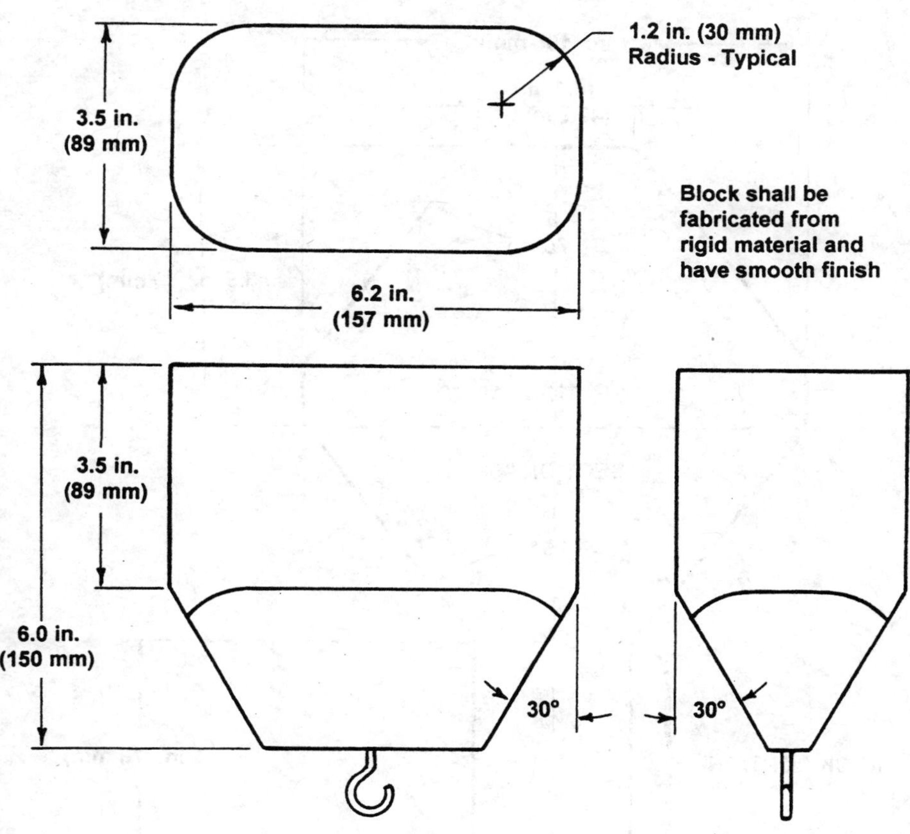

Figure 1 to Part 1513 - Wedge Block for Tests in § 1513.4(a), (b) and (c)

FIGURE 2 TO PART 1513—TEST PROBE FOR NECK ENTRAPMENT

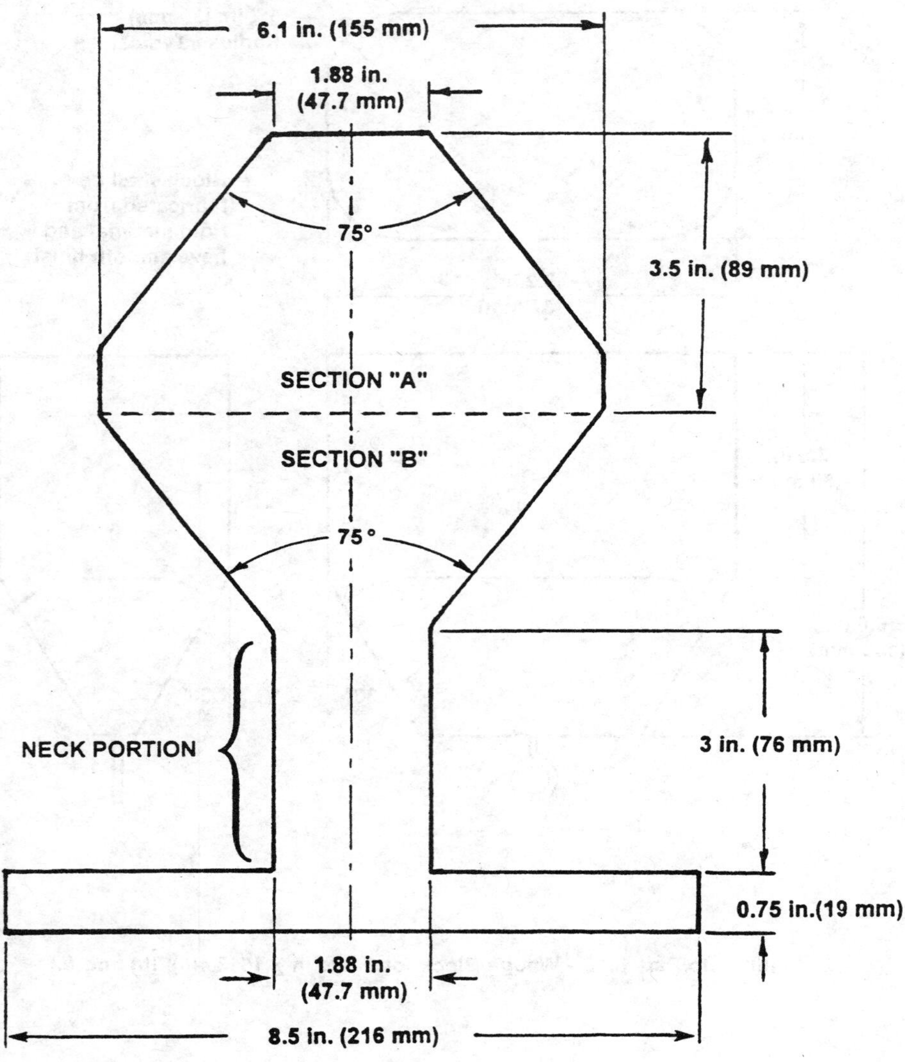

NOTE – Probe to be constructed from any rigid material 0.75 in. (19 mm) thick

Fig. 2 – Test Probe for Neck Entrapment

FIGURE 3 TO PART 1513—MOTION OF TEST PROBE ARRESTED BY SIMULTANEOUS CONTACT WITH BOTH SIDES OF "A" SECTION OF PROBE AND BOUNDARIES OF OPENING

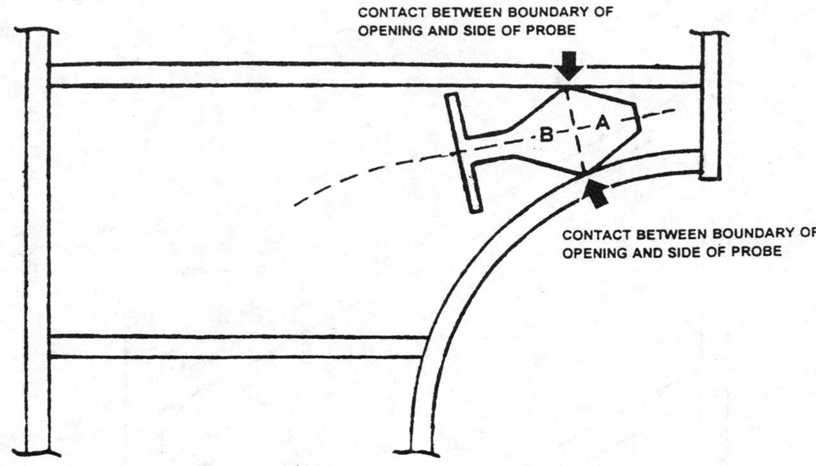

Fig. 3 – Motion of Test Probe Arrested by Simultaneous Contact With Both Sides of "A" Section of Probe and Boundaries of Opening

FIGURE 4 TO PART 1513—NECK PORTION OF "B" SECTION OF PROBE ENTERS COMPLETELY INTO OPENING

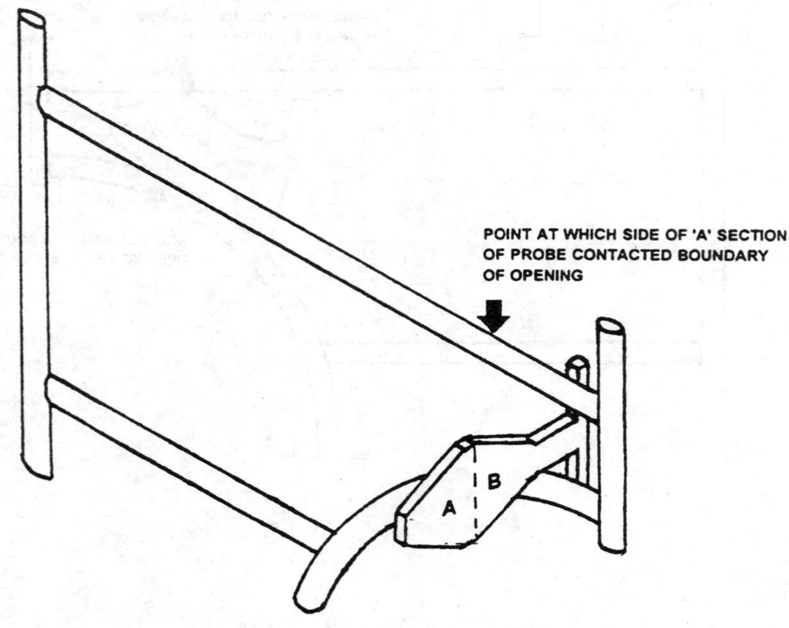

Fig 4 – Neck Portion of "B" Section of Probe Enters Completely into Opening

APPENDIX TO PART 1513—FINDINGS UNDER THE FEDERAL HAZARDOUS SUBSTANCES ACT

The Federal Hazardous Substances Act (FHSA) requires that the Commission, in order to issue part 1513, make the following findings and include them in the rule. 15 U.S.C. 1261(s), 1262(i). Because of this, the facts and determinations in these findings apply as of the date the rule was issued, December 22, 1999.

A. *Bunk beds present a mechanical hazard.* Section 2(s) of the FHSA states that an "article may be determined to present a mechanical hazard if, in normal use or when subjected to reasonably foreseeable damage or abuse, its design or manufacture presents an unreasonable risk of personal injury or illness * * * (3 from * * * surfaces, edges, openings, or closures * * * , or (9) because of any other aspect of the articles design or manufacture." 15 U.S.C. 1261(s).

2. For a recent 9.6-year period, the CPSC received reports of 57 deaths of children under age 15 who died when they were trapped between the upper bunk of a bunk bed and the wall or when they were trapped in openings in the bed's structure. Over 96% of those who died in entrapment incidents were age 3 or younger. On average, averting these deaths is expected to produce a benefit to society with a present value of about $175 to $350 for each bed that otherwise would not have complied with one or more of the rule's requirements.

3. This increased safety will be achieved in three main ways. First, all bunk beds will be required to have a guardrail on both sides of the bed. If the bed is placed against a wall, the guardrail on that side is expected to prevent a child from being entrapped between the bed and the wall. The guardrail on the

wall side of the bed must extend continuously from one end to the other. Second, the end structures of the bed must be constructed so that, if an opening in the end structure is large enough so a child can slip his or her body through it, it must be large enough that the child's head also can pass through. Third, this area must also be constructed so that a child cannot insert his or her head into an opening and move to another part of the opening where the head cannot be pulled out and the neck can become entrapped.

4. For the reasons discussed in paragraph C of this appendix, the benefits of the changes to bunk beds caused by this rule will have a reasonable relationship to the changes' costs. The rule addresses a risk of death, and applies primarily to a vulnerable population, children under age 3. The life-saving features required by the rule are cost-effective and can be implemented without adversely affecting the performance and availability of the product. The effective date provides enough time so that production of bunk beds that do not already comply with the standard can easily be changed so that the beds comply. Accordingly, the Commission finds that there is an unreasonable risk of entrapment injury associated with bunk beds that do not comply with part 1513.

B. *Where a voluntary standard has been adopted and implemented by the affected industry, that compliance with such voluntary standard is not likely to result in the elimination or adequate reduction of the risk of injury, or it is unlikely that there will be substantial compliance with such voluntary standard.*

1. *Adequacy of the voluntary standard.* In this instance, there is a voluntary standard addressing the risk of entrapment in bunk beds. However, the rule goes beyond the provisions of the voluntary standard. First, it eliminates the voluntary standard's option to have an opening of up to 15 inches at each end of the wall-side guardrail. Second, it requires more of the lower bunk end structures to have entrapment protection. The voluntary standard protects against entrapment only within the 9-inch space immediately above the upper surface of the lower bunk's mattress. The mandatory standard extends this area of protection upward to the level of the underside of the upper bunk foundation. Both of these provisions, which are in the rule but not in the voluntary standard, address fatalities and, as noted in this paragraph (a)(18), have benefits that bear a reasonable relationship to their costs.

Therefore, the Commission finds that compliance with the voluntary standard is not likely to result in the elimination or adequate reduction of the risk of entrapment injury or death.

2. *Substantial compliance.* i. The FHSA does not define "substantial compliance." The March 3, 1999 Notice of Proposed Rulemaking summarized an interpretation of "substantial compliance" that the Office of General Counsel provided to the Commission. 64 FR 10245, 10248–49 (March 3, 1999). The Commission specifically invited public comment on that interpretation from "all persons who would be affected by such an interpretation." Id. at 10249. The Commission received more than 20 comments on the interpretation.

ii. Having now considered all the evidence that the staff has presented, the comments from the public, and the legal advice from the Office of General Counsel, the Commission concludes that there is not "substantial compliance" with the ASTM voluntary standard for bunk beds within the meaning of the Consumer Product Safety Act and the Federal Hazardous Substances Act. See, e.g., 15 U.S.C. 2058(f)(3)(D)(ii); 15 U.S.C. 1262(i)(2)(A)(ii). However, the Commission does not adopt a general interpretation of "substantial compliance" focusing on whether the level of compliance with a voluntary standard could be improved under a mandatory standard. Rather, the grounds for the Commission's decision focus on the specific facts of this rulemaking and are stated below.

iii. The legislative history regarding the meaning of "substantial compliance" indicates that the Commission should consider whether compliance is sufficient to eliminate or adequately reduce the risk of injury in a timely fashion and that, generally, compliance should be measured in terms of the number of complying products, rather than the number of manufacturers who are in compliance. E.g., Senate Report No. 97-102, p. 14 (May 15, 1981); House Report No. 97-158, p. 11 (June 19, 1981); H. Conf. Rep. No. 97-208, 97th Cong., 1st Sess. 871, reprinted in 1981 U.S. Code Cong. & Admin. News 1010, 1233.

iv. Given this Congressional guidance, the Commission believes it appropriate to examine the number of conforming products as the starting point for analysis. However, the Commission does not believe that there is any single percentage of conforming products that can be used in all cases to define "substantial compliance." Instead, the percentage must be viewed in the context of the hazard the product presents. Thus, the Commission must examine what constitutes substantial compliance with a voluntary standard in light of its obligation to safeguard the American consumer.

v. There are certain factors the agency considers before it initiates regulatory action, such as the severity of the potential injury, whether there is a vulnerable population at risk, and the risk of injury. See 16 CFR 1009.8. These and other factors also appropriately inform the Commission's decision regarding whether a certain level of conformance with a voluntary standard is substantial. In the light of these factors, industry's compliance rate with the voluntary standard for bunk beds is not substantial.

vi. In this case, the Commission deals with the most severe risk—death—to one of the most vulnerable segments of our population—infants and young children. While the risk of death is not high, it exists whenever a young child is in a residence with a nonconforming bunk bed.

vii. Additionally, some products, such as hairdryers without shock protection devices, require some intervening action (dropping the hair dryer into water) to create the hazard. By contrast, deaths in bunk beds occur during the intended use of the product—a child rolling over in bed or climbing in or out of it—without any intervening action.

viii. The Commission must also consider that bunk beds have a very long product life, frequently being passed on to several families before being discarded. Thus, a number of children may be exposed to a bed during its useful life. Every noncomplying bed that poses an entrapment hazard presents the potential risk of death to any young child in the house. It is a risk that is hard for a parent to protect against, as children find their way onto these beds even if they are not put to sleep in them.

ix. Bunk beds are products that can be made relatively easily by very small companies, or even by a single individual. The Office of Compliance believes smaller entities will always present a compliance problem, because new manufacturers can enter the marketplace relatively easily and need little expertise to make a wooden bunk bed. The evidence seems to support the view that there will always be an irreducible number of new, smaller bunk bed manufacturers who will not follow the voluntary standard.

x. What constitutes substantial compliance is also a function of what point in time the issue is examined. In 1989, the Commission denied a petition for a mandatory bunk bed rule. At that time, industry was predicting that by April of 1989, 90% of all beds being manufactured would comply with the voluntary guidelines. But that was in the context of years of steadily increasing conformance and the hope that conformance would continue to grow and that deaths and near-misses would begin to decline. But the conformance level never grew beyond the projection for 1989 and deaths and near-misses have not dropped.

xi. Even with the existing compliance rate, the Commission is contemplating the prospect of perhaps 50,000 nonconforming beds a year (or more) entering the marketplace, with many beds remaining in use for perhaps 20 years or longer. Under these circumstances, a 10% rate of noncompliance is too high.

xii. It is now clear that the bunk bed voluntary standard has not achieved an adequate reduction of the unreasonable risk of death to infants and children in a timely fashion, and it is unlikely to do so. Accordingly, the Commission finds that substantial compliance with the voluntary standard for bunk beds is unlikely.

xiii. Products that present some or all of the following factors might not be held to as strict a substantial compliance analysis. Those which:

—Rarely or never cause death;
—Cause only less severe injuries;
—Do not cause deaths or injuries principally to a vulnerable segment of the population;
—Are not intended for children and which have no special attraction for children;
—Have a relatively short life span;
—Are made by a few stable manufacturers or which can only be made by specialized manufacturers needing a significant manufacturing investment to produce the product;
—Are covered by a voluntary standard which continues to capture an increasing amount of noncomplying products; or
—Require some additional intervening action to be hazardous.

xiv. And, in analyzing some other product, there could be other factors that would have to be taken into consideration in determining what level of compliance is adequate to protect the public. The tolerance for nonconformance levels has to bear some relationship to the magnitude and manageability of the hazard addressed.

xv. The Commission emphasizes that its decision is not based on the argument that a mandatory rule provides more powerful enforcement tools. If this were sufficient rationale, mandatory rules could always displace voluntary standards, and this clearly was not Congress's intent. But, with a mandatory standard, the necessity of complying with a mandatory federal regulation will be understandable to small manufacturers. State and local governments will have no doubt about their ability to help us in our efforts to locate these manufacturers.

C. *The benefits expected from the rule bear a reasonable relationship to its costs.*

1. *Bunk beds that do not comply with ASTM's requirements for guardrails.* The cost of providing a second guardrail for bunk beds that do not have one is expected to be from $15–40 per otherwise noncomplying bed. If, as expected, the standard prevents virtually all of the deaths it addresses, the present value of the benefits of this modification are estimated to be from $175–350 per otherwise noncomplying bed. Thus, the benefit of this provision is about 4–23 times its cost.

2. *Bunk beds that comply with ASTM's requirements for guardrails.* The voluntary standard allows up to a 15-inch gap in the coverage of the guardrail on the wall side of the upper bunk. Additional entrapment deaths are addressed by requiring that the

wall-side guardrail be continuous from one end of the bed to the other. The estimated present value of the benefits of this requirement will be $2.40 to $3.50 per otherwise noncomplying bed. The Commission estimates that the materials cost to extend one guardrail an additional 30 inches (760 mm) will be less than the present value of the benefits of making the change. Further, the costs of any design changes can be amortized over the number of bunk beds produced after the design change is made. Thus, any design costs are nominal.

3. *Lower bunk end structures*. The Commission is aware of a death, involving entrapment in the end structures of the lower bunk, occurring in a scenario not currently addressed by the voluntary standard. This death is addressed by extending the upper limit of the voluntary standard's lower bunk end structures entrapment provisions from 9 inches above the lower bunk's sleeping surface to the bottom of the upper bunk and by also including a test for neck entrapment in this area. The Commission expects the costs of this requirement to be design-related only, and small. Indeed, for some bunk beds, material costs may decrease since less material may be required to comply with these requirements than are currently being used. Again, the design costs for these modifications to the end structures can be amortized over the subsequent production run of the bed.

4. *Effect on market*. The small additional costs from any wall-side guardrail and end-structure modifications are not expected to affect the market for bunk beds, either alone or added to the costs of compliance to ASTM's provisions.

5. *Conclusion*. The Commission has no reason to conclude that any of the standard's requirements have costs that exceed the requirement's expected benefits. Further, the total effect of the rule is that the benefits of the rule will exceed its costs by about 4–23 times. Accordingly, the Commission concludes that the benefits expected from the rule will bear a reasonable relationship to its costs.

D. *The rule imposes the least burdensome requirement that prevents or adequately reduces the risk of injury for which the rule is being promulgated*. 1. The Commission considered relying on the voluntary standard, either alone or combined with a third-party certification program. However, the Commission concludes that a mandatory program will be more effective in reducing these deaths, each of which is caused by an unreasonable risk of entrapment. Accordingly, these alternatives would not prevent or adequately reduce the risk of injury for which the rule is being promulgated.

2. The Commission also considered a suggestion that bunk beds that conformed to the voluntary standard be so labeled. Consumers could then compare conforming and nonconforming beds at the point of purchase and make their purchase decisions with this safety information in mind. This, however, would not necessarily reduce injuries, because consumers likely would not know there is a voluntary standard and thus would not see any risk in purchasing a bed that was not labeled as conforming to the standard.

SUBCHAPTER D—FLAMMABLE FABRICS ACT REGULATIONS

PART 1602—STATEMENTS OF POLICY OR INTERPRETATION

§ 1602.1 Enforcement policy.

(a) On May 14, 1973, the responsibilities of the Federal Trade Commission for enforcement of the Flammable Fabrics Act, as amended (15 U.S.C. 1191–1204), were transferred to the Consumer Product Safety Commission pursuant to section 30(b) of the Consumer Product Safety Act (Pub. L. 92–573), 86 Stat. 1231 (15 U.S.C. 2079(b)).

(b) The Consumer Product Safety Commission intends to discharge its responsibilities under the Flammable Fabrics Act vigorously, expeditiously, and without compromise in order to protect the public from the hazards to life, health, and property caused by dangerously flammable products.

(c) The Consumer Product Safety Commission has determined that its enforcement policy for the Flammable Fabrics Act, will be to have available for use in each case the full range of enforcement procedures under that act without qualification or modification. Accordingly, notice is given that the Consumer Product Safety Commission hereby institutes an enforcement policy of using in each case arising under the Flammable Fabrics Act any and all appropriate enforcement procedures available under that act.

(d) In order to effectuate this policy, the above stated policy has been adopted and substituted for any conflicting determinations and policies of the Federal Trade Commission. The following determinations and policies of the Federal Trade Commission insofar as they apply to this Commission are terminated and set aside pursuant to section 30(e)(2) of the Consumer Product Safety Act (86 Stat. 1232 (15 U.S.C. 2079(e)(2))):

(1) The Federal Trade Commission's "Flammable Fabrics Enforcement Policy" published as a notice in the FEDERAL REGISTER of November 10, 1971 (36 FR 21544), as amended by a notice published April 25, 1973 (38 FR 10184), which was corrected May 8, 1973 (38 FR 11492).

(2) Any Federal Trade Commission policy or directive modifying or interpreting said Enforcement Policy, as amended.

(e) All other rules, regulations, orders, and determinations of the Federal Trade Commission under the Flammable Fabrics Act will continue in effect until modified, terminated, superseded, set aside, or repealed by the Consumer Product Safety Commission, by any court of competent jurisdiction, or by operation of law.

(Sec. 1, et seq., 81 Stat. 568–74 (15 U.S.C. 1191–1204, note under 1191))

[40 FR 59884, Dec. 30, 1975]

PART 1605—INVESTIGATIONS, INSPECTIONS AND INQUIRIES PURSUANT TO THE FLAMMABLE FABRICS ACT

Subpart A—Procedures for Investigations, Inspections and Inquiries

Subpart B—Consent Order Agreements

AUTHORITY: Sec. 5, 67 Stat. 112, as amended (15 U.S.C. 1194); sec. 6, 38 Stat. 721, as amended (15 U.S.C. 46); sec. 9, 38 Stat. 722, as amended (15 U.S.C. 49); sec. 10, 38 Stat.723, as amended (15 U.S.C. 50); sec. 16, Pub. L. 92–573, 86 Stat. 1222 (15 U.S.C. 2065); sec. 27, Pub. L. 92–573, 86 Stat. 1227 (15 U.S.C. 2076); sec. 30(b), Pub. L. 92–573, 86 Stat. 1231 (15 U.S.C. 2079(b)); sec. 30(d), as amended, Pub. L. 94–284, 90 Stat. 510, (15 U.S.C. 2079(d)).

SOURCE: 42 FR 61023, Nov. 30, 1977, unless otherwise noted.

Subpart A—Procedures for Investigations, Inspections and Inquiries

§ 1605.1 Purposes, delegation, finding and how initiated.

(a) An investigation under these rules is an undertaking by the Commission to obtain information for the purposes of enforcing or determining compliance with the Flammable Fabrics Act (15 U.S.C. 1191 et seq.) ("FFA"); the regulations, rules, standards, and orders promulgated thereunder; and those sections of the Federal Trade Commission Act (15 U.S.C. 41 et seq.) ("FTCA") which are relevant to the enforcement and administration of the Flammable Fabrics Act. The term investigation includes, but is not limited to inspections (§ 1605.2); investigational hearings (§ 1605.6); and inquiries, employing orders of access (§ 1605.4), subpoenas (§ 1605.5), depositions (§ 1605.7), written interrogatories (§ 1605.9), and general or special orders (§ 1605.10).

(b) An inspection as described in § 1605.2 is initiated when the Commission or its delegee authorizes the issuance of a written notice of inspection (hereinafter notice), described in § 1605.2(c). Investigations and inquiries will be initiated by the Commission in such manner as it deems proper.

(c) The Commission hereby delegates to the Associate Executive Director for Compliance and Enforcement, the Director of the Enforcement Division, the Solicitor, and the Directors of Area Offices, the power to initiate inspections in the same manner as the Commission.

(d) Finding. The Commission found on November 3, 1977 pursuant to section 30(d) of the Consumer Product Safety Act, as amended ("CPSA") (15 U.S.C. 2079(d)) that the risk of injury associated with products regulated under the Flammable Fabrics Act cannot be eliminated or reduced to a sufficient extent by the issuance of procedures for investigations, inspections and inquiries under the Flammable Fabrics Act and the Federal Trade Commission Act (15 U.S.C. 41 et seq.). This finding is made to eliminate any confusion and uncertainty that may exist concerning the scope of the Commission's statutory authority under the Flammable Fabrics Act and Federal Trade Commission Act to conduct inspections and collect samples. The Commission is supplementing the authority granted to it under the FFA and FTCA with its powers under the CPSA while retaining the procedural safeguards and requirements of all of these acts. Accordingly, the Commission issues these rules pursuant to sections 16 and 27 of the CPSA (15 U.S.C. 2065 and 2076) and makes them applicable to products regulating under the FFA.

§ 1605.2 Conduct and scope of inspections.

(a) After an inspection is initiated as set forth in § 1605.1, an officer or employee duly designated by the Commission shall issue the notice. Upon presenting such notice, along with appropriate credentials, to the person, or agent-in-charge of the sole proprietorship, partnership, or corporation to be inspected, the Commission officer or employee may seek, for the purposes set forth in § 1605.1 (a):

(1) To enter, at reasonable times, any factory, warehouse, or establishment in which a product, fabric, or related material is manufactured, processed, packaged, tested or to which it is delivered or in which it is held in connection with its importation, introduction, distribution, transportation, receipt, and/or sale in commerce;

(2) To enter any conveyance being used to transport, deliver, or hold any such product, fabric, or related material in connection with its importation, introduction, distribution, transportation, receipt, and/or sale in commerce;

(3) To inspect at all reasonable times, in a reasonable manner, and within reasonable limits, any factory, warehouse, establishment, or conveyance described in paragraph (a) (1) and (2) of this section and all appropriate records, reports, books, documents and papers including, but not limited to, those relating to production, inventory, testing, distribution, sale, transportation, importation, or receipt of any product, fabric, or related material and all pertinent equipment, materials, substances, products, fabrics, related materials, containers, packages and

packaging, and labels, and labeling therein:

(4) To have access to and copy at all reasonable times: (i) All records, reports, books, documents, papers, or labeling required by the Commission to be established, made, or maintained; (ii) all documents showing or relating to the production inventory, testing, distribution, sale, transportation, importation, or receipt of any product, fabric, or related material; and (iii) all other appropriate records, reports, books, documents, papers, packages and packaging, and labels and labeling;

(5) To obtain: (i) Information, both oral and written, concerning the production, inventory, testing, distribution, sale, transportation, importation or receipt of any product, fabric or related material and the organization, business, conduct, practices, and management of any person, sole proprietorship, partnership, or corporation being inspected and its relation to any other person, sole proprietorship, partnership, or corporation; (ii) samples of items, materials, substances, products, fabrics, related materials, containers, packages and packaging, labels and labeling, and have the same analyzed, tested, or examined; and (iii) information, both oral and written, concerning any matter referred to in these rules.

(b) A separate notice shall be given for each inspection, but a notice shall not be required for each entry made during the course of the same inspection. Each such inspection shall be commenced at a reasonable time and be completed within a reasonable time.

(c) The notice of inspection shall include: the name and address of the person, sole proprietorship, partnership, or corporation being inspected; the name and title of the inspector; the date and time of the anticipated entry; pertinent extracts from the statutory provisions upon which the right to access is based; pertinent extracts from the statutory provisions upon which the penalties for refusal of access are based; pertinent extracts from §1605.2 of these rules setting forth the authority of inspectors and the types of information and items they are authorized to obtain; a statement which sets forth the purposes of the inspection and the nature of the information and items to be obtained and/or copied; and a statement that those from whom information is requested should state whether any of the information submitted is believed to contain or relate to a trade secret or other matter which should be considered by the Commission to be confidential in accordance with section 4(c) of the Flammable Fabrics Act (15 U.S.C. 1193(c)) and whether any of the information is believed to be entitled to exemption from disclosure by the Commission under the provisions of the Freedom of Information Act (5 U.S.C. 552) or section 6(f) of the Federal Trade Commission Act (15 U.S.C. 46(f)). Any statement asserting this claim of confidentiality must be in writing, and any request for exemption of the information from disclosure must be made in accordance with the Commission's Freedom of Information Act regulations, 16 CFR part 1015, 42 FR 10490, February 22, 1977 or as amended.

(d) If upon being presented with a notice, the person, or agent-in-charge of the sole proprietorship, partnership, or corporation being inspected fails to allow access to documentary evidence for the purpose of inspecting and making copies of such evidence, the inspector shall notify that individual that he or she may be in violation of the law and subject to the penalties therein and immediately thereafter refer such individual to the appropriate provisions of the notice which set forth such penalties. If the individual still refuses to comply, in whole or in part, with the authorized request for access, the inspector shall leave the premises; and the Commission shall take such action as it deems appropriate. If the person in charge refuses to accept the notice upon its presentation, the inspector shall affix the notice to a public entrance way on the premises.

§ 1605.3 Compulsory processes and the service thereof.

(a) In addition to or in lieu of authorizing the issuance of a notice, the Commission may elect to use any of the following means to initiate investigations, inspections, or inquiries to obtain information for the purposes set forth in §1605.1(a):

(1) Orders for Access;

(2) Subpoenas;

(3) Investigational Hearings;

(4) Depositions;

(5) Written Interrogatories; and

(6) General or special Orders.

(b) Service of notice in connection with any of the compulsory processes enumerated in §1605.3(a) shall be effected as follows:

(1) By personal service upon the person, or agent-in-charge of the sole proprietorship, partnership, or corporation being investigated, inspected, or inquired of; or

(2) By mail (registered or certified) or delivery to the last known residence or business address of anyone being investigated, inspected, or inquired of.

(c) The date of service of any form of compulsory process shall be the date on which the document is mailed, or delivered in person, whichever is applicable. Whenever a party is required or permitted to do an act within a prescribed period after service of a document and the document is served by mail, three (3) days shall be added to the prescribed period.

(d) These rules shall be referred to in any form of compulsory process served upon a person, sole proprietorship, partnership, or corporation.

(e) Anyone submitting information in response to any of the compulsory processes referred to in §1605.4(a) hereof should state whether any of the information submitted is believed to contain or relate to a trade secret or other matter which should be considered by the Commission to be confidential in accordance with section 4(c) of the Flammable Fabrics Act (15 U.S.C. 1193(c)) and whether any of the information is believed to be entitled to exemption from disclosure by the Commission under the provisions of the Freedom of Information Act (15 U.S.C. 552) or section 6(f) of the Federal Trade Commission Act (15 U.S.C. 46(f)). Any statement asserting this claim of confidentiality must be in writing, and any request for exemption of the information from disclosure must be made in accordance with the Commission's Freedom of Information Act regulations, 16 CFR part 1015, 42 FR 10490, February 22, 1977 or as amended.

§ 1605.4 Orders for access.

(a) In the event an inspection pursuant to §1605.2 herein is refused, in whole or in part, or prior to any such inspection, the Commission may issue an order requiring any person, sole proprietorship, partnership, or corporation to allow access to a duly-designated officer or employee of the Commission for the purpose of conducting an inspection. Such order will be issued by the Commission upon the demonstration by the staff of a justifiable need to gain access. Inspections conducted after service of an order for access shall be conducted in accordance with the procedures provided in §1605.2.

(b) After issuance of an order for access, the staff may, upon request of the recipient of the order, agree to modify the order to limit its scope, impose conditions or extend the time for compliance. If an agreement cannot be voluntarily reached, the recipient of the order may file a motion to limit or quash the order. Any such motion shall set forth the reasons why the order should be limited or quashed; and may be accompanied by memoranda, affidavits, or other documents submitted in support of the motion. Unless a different period of time for filing a motion is specified in the order, the motion must be received in the Office of the Secretary of the Commission within ten calendar days after the order is mailed or delivered in person to such person, sole proprietorship, partnership, or corporation unless the Commission, upon a showing of good cause, grants an extension of time within which to file a motion to limit or quash an order of access.

(c) Upon receipt of a motion to limit or quash the order for access, the Office of the Secretary shall immediately notify and trasmit a copy of the motion to Associate Executive Director for Compliance and Enforcement or the General Counsel, as appropriate. Unless a different period of time is specified in the order, the Associate Executive Director for Compliance and Enforcement or General Counsel shall file an answer with the Office of the Secretary within ten calendar days after receipt of a copy of the motion. A copy of the answer shall be served upon the moving party or the counsel of the moving party. No reply to the answer will be permitted.

(d) All motions to limit or quash shall be ruled upon by the Commission. The Office of the Secretary shall serve the decision on the motion to limit or quash the order of access upon the moving party or the counsel of the moving party and shall furnish a copy of the decision to the Associate Executive Director for Compliance and Enforcement or the General Counsel, as appropriate. The decision on the motion to limit or quash shall be the final decision on the matter. Motions for reconsideration will not be received.

§ 1605.5 Subpoenas.

(a) The Commission may issue to any person, sole proprietorship, partnership, or corporation a subpoena requiring the production of documentary evidence (subpoena duces tecum) and/or the attendance and testimony of witnesses (subpoena ad testificandum) relating to any matter under investigation. The Commission hereby delegates to the Associate Executive Director for Compliance and Enforcement, the Director of the Enforcement Division, the Solicitor, or the General Counsel, depending upon which officer is involved with the subpoena, the power to negotiate and approve the terms of satisfactory compliance with such subpoena.

(b) The person, sole proprietorship, partnership, or corporation upon whom a subpoena is served may file a motion to limit or quash the subpoena. Any such motion shall set forth the reasons why the subpoena should be quashed or limited and may be accompanied by memoranda, affidavits, or other documents submitted in support of the motion. Unless a different period of time for filing a motion is specified in the subpoena, the motion must be received in the Office of the Secretary of the Commission within ten calendar days after the subpoena is mailed or delivered to such person, sole proprietorship, partnership, or corporation unless the Commission, upon a showing of good cause, grants an extension of time within which to file a motion to limit or quash a subpoena.

(c) Upon receipt of any such motion, the Office of the Secretary shall immediately notify and transmit a copy of the motion to the Associate Executive Director for Compliance and Enforcement or the General Counsel, as appropriate. Unless a different period of time is specified in the subpoena, the Associate Executive Director for Compliance and Enforcement or the General Counsel shall file an answer with the Office of the Secretary within ten calendar days after receipt of a copy of the motion. A copy of the answer shall be served upon the moving party or the counsel of the moving party. No reply to the answer will be permitted.

(d) All motions to limit or quash a subpoena shall be ruled upon by the Commission. The Office of the Secretary shall serve the decision on the motion to limit or quash the subpoena upon the moving party or the counsel of the moving party and shall furnish a copy of the decision to the Associate Executive Director for Compliance and Enforcement or the General Counsel, as appropriate. The decision on the motion to limit or quash shall be the final decision on the matter. Motions for reconsideration will not be received.

§ 1605.6 Investigational hearings.

(a) The Commission may order, and by subpoena, may compel any person, sole proprietorship, partnership, or corporation to provide information at an investigational hearing. Such hearings shall be for the purpose of taking the testimony, under oath, of witnesses and receiving documents and other data relating to any subject under investigation. Such hearings shall be presided over by the commission, by one or more of its members, an Administrative Law Judge, hearing examiner, attorney-examiner or by a duly designated officer or employee. The hearings shall be stenographically reported, and a transcript thereof shall be made a part of the record.

(b) A Commissioner who participates in such a hearing or other investigation, inspection, or inquiry shall not be disqualified by reason of such participation from subsequently sharing in a Commission decision in the matter.

(c) All investigational hearings shall be closed to the public, unless otherwise ordered by the Commission.

(d) The release of the record of such hearing shall be governed by the Commission's regulations under the Freedom of Information Act, 5 U.S.C. 552, and/or other applicable laws or regulations.

§ 1605.7 Depositions.

(a) The Commission may order and, by subpoena, may compel testimony to be taken by deposition at any stage of any investigation. Such depositions may be taken before any person designated by the Commission who has the power to administer oaths. The testimony given shall be reduced to writing by the person taking the deposition or under such person's direction and shall then be submitted to the deponent for signature unless the deponent waives the right to sign the deposition. All depositions shall be closed to the public, unless otherwise ordered by the Commission. The release of the record of such depositions shall be governed by the Commission's regulations under the Freedom of Information Act, 5 U.S.C. 552, and/or other applicable laws or regulations.

(b) Any changes in form or substance which the deponent desires to make shall state the reasons for such changes. The deposition shall then be signed by the deponent, unless the deponent waives the right to sign, cannot be found, or is unable or refuses to sign. If the deposition is not signed by the deponent within 30 days of its submission to the deponent, or such shorter time as the Commission may designate, the Commission designee shall sign it and state on the record the fact of the waiver of the right to sign or of the illness or absence of the deponent, or the fact of the deponent's inability or refusal to sign together with the reason, if any, given therefor. The deposition referred to herein may be used in any investigation or any administrative or judical adjudicative proceeding.

§ 1605.8 Rights of witnesses at investigational hearings and of deponents at depositions.

(a) Any person, or agent or officer of a sole proprietorship, partnership, or corporation who is required to produce documentary evidence or give testimony as a witness at an investigational hearing conducted under provisions of § 1605.6 or as a deponent at a deposition taken in accordance with provisions of § 1605.7 may be accompanied by an attorney or an official or employee of the person, sole proprietorship, parnership, or corporation, who may act as counsel for the witness or the deponent. However, a person who is subpoenaed to produce documentary evidence or give testimony at an investigational hearing or deposition cannot act as counsel for another witness or deponent at the same proceeding. The term attorney refers to members of the bar of a Federal Court or the courts of any State or Territory of the United States, the Commonwealth of Puerto Rico, or the District of Columbia. The witness or deponent and his or her counsel may act as follows during the course of an investigational hearing or deposition:

(1) A witness or deponent may confer, in confidence, with his or her counsel concerning any questions asked of the witness or deponent. If the witness or deponent or counsel objects to a question, the objection and basis thereof shall be stated on the record. In the case of an objection based upon the privilege against self incrimination, the privilege must be asserted by the witness or deponent. If a witness at an investigationl hearing refuses to answer a question or provide other information, the presiding officer shall have the authority to immediately order the witness or deponent to answer the question or provide the information requested, except in circumstances where an immediate ruling would be unwarranted and except where such refusal is based upon the privilege against self incrimination, which shall be handled in accordance with the procedure set forth in 18 U.S.C. 6002 and 6004. Otherwise, all objections shall be ruled upon by the presiding officer at the time the objection is made.

(2) Objections timely made under the provisions of § 1605.8(a) shall be noted on the record, shall be treated as continuing, and shall be preserved throughout the course of the proceeding without the necessity of repetition during similar lines of inquiry.

(3) Except as provided by this § 1605.8(a), counsel for a witness or a deponent may not interrupt the examination of the witness or the deponent by making objections or statements on the record.

(4) Upon completion of the examination of a witness or a deponent, the witness or deponent may clarify on the record any of his or her answers.

(b) Any such person, agent, or officer who is required to appear in person at an investigational hearing or at a deposition shall testify as to matters and information known and/or reasonably available to the person, sole proprietorship, parnership, or corporation involved.

(c) Any such person, agent, or officer who is compelled by subpoena to appear in person at an investigational hearing or at a deposition shall receive the same fees and mileage allowances as are paid witnesses in the courts of the United States.

(d) Any such person, agent, or officer who is required to appear in person at an investigational hearing or at a deposition shall be entitled to retain a copy of any document submitted by him or her and, upon payment of lawfully prescribed costs, shall be entitled to procure a copy of his or her own testimony as recorded.

(e) The Commission designee who presides at an investigational hearing or before whom a deposition is taken shall take all necessary action to regulate the course of the hearing or the deposition, to avoid delay and to assure that reasonable standards of orderly and ethical conduct are maintained. Such designee shall, for reasons stated on the record, immediately report to the Commission any instance in which counsel for a witness or a deponent has refused to comply with the designee's directions, or to adhere to reasonable standards of orderly and ethical conduct in the course of the hearing or the deposition. The Commission shall thereupon take such action as the circumstances warrant.

§ 1605.9 Written interrogatories.

(a) The Commission may order any person, sole proprietorship, partnership, or corporation being investigated to answer written interrogatories. Such interrogatories shall be answered by the individual or by any agent or officer of the sole proprietorship, partnership, or corporation who shall furnish information on behalf of the sole proprietorship, partnership, or corporation. The information provided shall be that which is known or reasonably available to the person or organization involved and shall be submitted after reasonable inquiry to obtain the information requested.

(b) Each interrogatory shall be answered separately and fully in writing, under oath, unless it is objected to, in which event the reason for the objection shall be stated in lieu of an answer. The answers shall be signed by the individual or the officer or agent making them. The person, sole proprietorship, parnership, or corporation upon whom the interrogatories have been served shall furnish the Commission a copy of the answers and objections, if any, within 30 days after service of the interrogatories or within such shorter time as the commission may designate. Interrogatories submitted hereunder are continuing in character so as to require the person, sole proprietorship, partnership, or corporation answering to file supplementary answers upon obtaining further or different information.

§ 1605.10 General or special orders seeking information.

The Commission may require by the issuance of general or special orders, any person, sole proprietorship, partnership, or corporation to file with the Commission in such form as the Commission may prescribe annual and/or special reports or answers in writing to specific questions which furnish to the Commission such information as it may require as to its organization, business, conduct, practices, management, and relation to any person, sole proprietorship, partnership, or corporation. Such reports and answers shall be made under oath, or otherwise, as the Commission may prescribe and shall be filed with the Commission within such time as the Commission may prescribe, unless additional time may be granted in any case by the Commission.

§ 1605.11 Remedies for failure to permit authorized investigations.

In the event of failure to comply with any investigative process authorized by these rules, the Commission may seek appropriate action pursuant to the authority conferred by the Federal Trade Commission Act, including actions for enforcement, forfeitures, penalities, or criminal sanctions.

§ 1605.12 Nonexclusive delegation of power.

No provision contained herein delegating any of the Commission's powers shall be construed as limiting the actual authority of the Commission to exercise the same powers.

Subpart B—Consent Order Agreements

§ 1605.13 Procedures for Consent Order Agreements.

(a) The Consent Order Agreement is a document executed by a person, sole proprietorship, partnership, or corporation (Consenting Party) and a Commission staff representative which incorporates both a proposed complaint setting forth the staff's charges and a proposed order by which such charges are resolved. A consent order agreement shall contain the following provisions, as appropriate:

(1) An admission of all jurisdictional facts by the consenting parties;

(2) A waiver of any rights to an administrative or judicial hearing and of any other procedural steps including any rights to seek judicial review or otherwise challenge or contest the validity of the Commission's order;

(3) A statement that the agreement is in settlement of the staff's charges and does not constitute an admission by the Consenting Party that the law has been violated;

(4) A statement that the Commission's order is issued under the provisions of the Federal Trade Commission Act (15 U.S.C. 41 et seq.), the Flammable Fabrics Act (15 U.S.C. 1191 et seq.), and the Consumer Product Safety Act (15 U.S.C. 2051 et seq.) and that a violation of such an order subjects the Consenting Party to civil penalties under the provisions of the Federal Trade Commission Act;

(5) An acknowledgement that the consent order agreement only becomes effective upon its final acceptance by the Commission and its service upon the Consenting Party;

(6) An acknowledgement that the Commission may disclose terms of the consent order agreement to the public;

(7) A statement that the Consulting Party shall cease and desist from certain acts and practices;

(8) A statement that the Consenting Party shall perform certain acts and practices pursuant to the consent order agreement;

(9) An acknowledgement that the requirements of the order are in addition to, and not to the exclusion of, other remedies such as criminal penalties which may be pursued under section 7 of the Flammable Fabrics Act.

(b) At any time in the course of an investigation, the staff, with the approval of the Commission may propose to the person, sole proprietorship, partnership, or corporation being investigated, that any alleged violation be resolved by an agreement containing a consent order. Additionally, such a proposal may be made to the Commission staff by such person, sole proprietorship, partnership, or corporation.

(c) Upon receiving an executed agreement, the Commission may: (1) Provisionally accept it; (2) reject it and issue its complaint (in which case the matter will be scheduled for hearing in accordance with the Commission's Rules of Practice for Adjudicative Proceedings (16 CFR part 1025, June 21, 1977, or as later revised)); or (3) take such other action as it may deem appropriate.

(d) If the agreement is provisionally accepted, the Commission shall place the agreement on the public record and shall announce provisional acceptance of the agreement in the FEDERAL REGISTER. Any interested person may ask the Commission not to accept the agreement by filing a request in the office of the Secretary. Such request must be received in the Office of the Secretary no later than the close of business of the fifteenth calendar day following the date the announcement is published in the FEDERAL REGISTER.

(e) Unless the Commission orders otherwise, the agreement shall be deemed finally accepted by the Commission on the 20th calendar day after the date of announcement in the FEDERAL REGISTER. The Commission shall then issue its complaint and order in such form as the circumstances, may require. The order is a final order in disposition of the proceeding and is effective immediately upon its service upon the Consenting Party pursuant to these rules. The Consenting Party shall thereafter be bound by and take immediate action in accordance with such final order.

(f) If the Commission does not accept the agreement on a final basis, it shall so notify the Consenting Party. Such notification constitutes withdrawal of the Commission's provisional acceptance unless the Commission orders otherwise. The Commission may then issue its complaint, may order further investigation, or may take such other action it considers appropriate.

PART 1608—GENERAL RULES AND REGULATIONS UNDER THE FLAMMABLE FABRICS ACT

AUTHORITY: Sec. 5, 67 Stat. 112, as amended, 81 Stat. 570, 15 U.S.C. 1194.

SOURCE: 40 FR 59887, Dec. 30, 1975, unless otherwise noted.

§ 1608.0 Scope.

The rules and regulations in this part are applicable to all standards issued under the Flammable Fabrics Act.

§ 1608.1 Terms defined.

As used in the rules and regulations in this subchapter D, unless the context otherwise specifically requires:

(a) The term *act* means the Flammable Fabrics Act, sec. 1 et seq., 67 Stat. 111–115, as amended, 68 Stat. 770, 81 Stat. 568–74 (15 U.S.C. 1191–1204, note under 1191).

(b) The terms *rule, rules, regulations,* and *rules and regulations,* mean the rules and regulations prescribed by the Commission pursuant to section 5(c) of the act.

(c) The term *United States* means, the several States, the District of Columbia, the Commonwealth of Puerto Rico and the Territories and Possessions of the United States.

(d) The terms *marketing or handling* means the transactions referred to in section 3 of the act.

(e) The definition of terms contained in section 2 of the act shall be applicable also to such terms when used in rules promulgated under the act.

§ 1608.2 Form of separate guaranty.

The forms which follow are suggested forms of separate guaranties under section 8 of the act for use by guarantors residing in the United States. Representations contained in these suggested forms of separate guaranties with respect to reasonable and representative tests may be based upon a guaranty received and relied upon in good faith by the guarantor, tests performed by or for a guarantor, or class tests, where permitted under these rules. Where the forms are used as part of an invoice or other paper relating to the marketing or handling of products, fabrics, or related materials subject to the act, wording may be varied to limit the guaranty to specific items in such invoice or other paper. The name, address of the guarantor, and date on the invoice or other paper will suffice to meet the signature, address, and date requirements indicated on the forms.

(a) *General form.*

The undersigned hereby guarantees that reasonable and representative tests, made in accordance with procedures prescribed and applicable standards or regulations issued, amended, or continued in effect under the Flammable Fabrics Act, as amended, show that the product, fabric, or related material covered and identified by, and in the form delivered under this document conforms to the applicable standard or regulation issued, amended, or continued in effect.

Date: ____________________
Name ____________________
Address ____________________

(b) *Form for guaranty based on guaranty.*

Based upon a guaranty received, the undersigned hereby guarantees that reasonable and representative tests, made in accordance with procedures prescribed pursuant to the Flammable Fabrics Act, as amended, show that the product, fabric, or related material covered and identified by, and in the form delivered under this document conforms to the applicable standard or regulation issued, amended, or continued in effect.

Date: ______

Name ______

Address ______

(Sec. 5 of the Act, 67 Stat. 112, as amended by 81 Stat. 570, 15 U.S.C. sec. 1194; sec. 8 of the Act, 67 Stat. 114, as amended by 81 Stat. 572, 15 U.S.C. sec. 1197)

§ 1608.3 Continuing guaranties.

(a) Any person residing in the United States may file with the Office of the Secretary of the Consumer Product Safety Commission a continuing guaranty under section 8 of the act applicable to any product, fabric, or related material marketed or handled by such person. When filed with the Commission, a continuing guaranty shall be fully executed in duplicate and execution of each copy shall be acknowledged before a notary public. Forms for use in preparing continuing guaranties to be filed with the Commission will be supplied by the Office of the Secretary of the Commission upon request. To remain in effect, such guaranties must be renewed every 3 years and at such other times as any change occurs in the legal business status of the person filing the guaranty. It is therefore required that any person who has filed a continuing guaranty with the Commission shall promptly advise the Commission in writing of any change in the legal status of the guarantor or in the address of the guarantor's principal office and place of business. Representations contained in the prescribed form of continuing guaranty with respect to reasonable and representative tests may be based upon (1) a guaranty received and relied upon in good faith by the guarantor, (2) tests performed by or for a guarantor, or (3) class tests, where permitted under these rules.

(b) The following is the prescribed form of continuing guaranty for filing with the Commission:

CONTINUING GUARANTY UNDER THE FLAMMABLE FABRICS ACT FOR FILING WITH CONSUMER PRODUCTS SAFETY COMMISSION

The undersigned, ______, a ______ (Corporation, partnership, proprietorship) residing in the United States and having principal office and place of business at ______ (Street and number) ______, (City) ______, (State or territory, ZIP code) and being engaged in the marketing or handling of products, fabrics, or related materials subject to the Flammable Fabrics Act, as amended, and regulations thereunder,

Hereby guarantee(s) that with regard to all the products, fabrics, or related materials [described as follows: ______

______]

(If guaranty is limited to certain products, fabrics, or related materials, list the general categories here. If guaranty is not so limited, leave these lines blank.)

hereafter marketed or handled by the undersigned, and for which flammability standards have been issued, amended, or continued in effect under the Flammable Fabrics Act, as amended, reasonable and representative tests as prescribed by the Consumer Product Safety Commission have been performed, which shows that the products, fabrics, or related materials conform to such of the above-mentioned flammability standards as are applicable thereto.

Dated, signed, and executed this ______ day of ______, 19___, at ______ (City), ______ (State or Territory)

(Impression of corporate seal, if corporation.) (Name under which business is conducted.)

______

(If firm is a partnership list partners below.) (Signature of proprietor, partner, or authorized official of corporation.)

______

State of ______, *ss:*

County of ______

On this ______ day of ______, 19___, before me personally appeared the said ______, (Signer of guaranty) proprietor, partner (strike nonapplicable words) ______ (If corporation, give title of signing official) of ______, (Firm name) to me personally known, and acknowledged the execution of the foregoing instrument on behalf of the firm, for the uses and purposes therein stated.

(Impression of notary seal required here.) Notary Public in and for County of __________ State of __________. My commission expires __________

(c) Any person who has a continuing guaranty on file with the Commission may, during the effective period of the guaranty, give notice of such fact by setting forth on the invoice or other paper covering the marketing or handling of the product, fabric, or related material guaranteed the following:

Continuing guaranty under the Flammable Fabrics Act filed with the Consumer Product Safety Commission.

Provided, however, That such statement may not be used where the guaranty is limited and the invoice or other paper covers any product, fabric, or related material, subject to a flammability standard under the act, which is not covered by the guaranty because of its limited nature.

(d) Any person who falsely represents that he has a continuing guaranty on file with the Commission when such is not a fact, or who falsely represents that a limited continuing guaranty he does have on file with the Commission covers any product, fabric, or related material when such is not the case, shall be deemed to have furnished a false guaranty under section 8(b) of the act.

(e) Any seller residing in the United States may give a continuing guaranty under section 8 of the act to a buyer applicable to any product, fabric, or related material sold or to be sold to said buyer by seller. All such continuing guaranties shall be fully executed in duplicate and execution of each copy shall be acknowledged before a notary public. To remain in effect, such guaranties must be renewed every 3 years and at such other times as any change occurs in the legal business status of the person giving the guaranty. Representations contained in the prescribed form of continuing guaranty from seller to buyer with respect to reasonable and representative tests may be based upon: (1) A guaranty received and relied upon in good faith by the guarantor, (2) tests performed by or for a guarantor, or (3) class tests, where permitted under these rules.

(f) The following is the prescribed form of continuing guaranty from seller to buyer:

CONTINUING GUARANTY FROM SELLER TO BUYER UNDER THE FLAMMABLE FABRICS ACT

The undersigned, __________ a __________ (Corporation, partnership, proprietorship) residing in the United States and having its principal office and place of business at __________, __________, (Street and number) __________ (City), __________ (State or Territory and ZIP code), and being engaged in the marketing or handling of products, fabrics, or related materials subject to the Flammable Fabrics Act, as amended, and Regulations thereunder,

Hereby guarantee(s) to __________ (Name and address), buyer, that with regard to all the products, fabrics, or related materials [described as follows: __________ (If guaranty is limited to certain products, fabrics, or related materials, list the general categories here. If guaranty is not so limited, leave these lines blank.) hereafter sold or to be sold to buyer by the undersigned, and for which flammability standards have been issued, amended, or continued in effect under the Flammable Fabrics Act, as amended, reasonable and representative tests as prescribed by the Consumer Product Safety Commission have been performed show that the products, fabrics, or related materials, at the time of their shipment or delivery by the undersigned, conform to such of the abovementioned flammability standards as are applicable thereto.

Dated, signed, and executed this __________ day of __________ 19___, at __________, (City) __________ (State or Territory).

(Impression of corporate seal, if corporation.) (Name under which business is conducted.)

____

(If firm is a partnership list partners below.) (Signature of proprietor, partner, or authorized official of corporation.)

____

STATE OF __________, *ss:*
County of __________,

On this _____ day of __________, 19___, before me personally appeared the said __________ (Signer of guaranty), proprietor, partner (Strike non-applicable words) __________ (If corporation, give title of signing official) of __________ (Firm name), to me personally known, and acknowledged the execution of the foregoing instrument on behalf of the firm, for the uses and purposes therein stated.

(Impression of notary seal required here.) Notary Public in and for County of __________, State of __________. My commission expires __________

(Sec. 5 of the Act, 67 Stat. 112, as amended by 81 Stat. 570, 15 U.S.C. 1194: section 8 of the Act 67 Stat. 114, as amended by 81 Stat. 572, 15 U.S.C. 1197)

[40 FR 59887, Dec. 30, 1975, as amended at 52 FR 48810, Dec. 28, 1987]

§ 1608.4 Guaranties furnished by nonresidents of the U.S. no bar to prosecution.

A guaranty furnished under section 8 of the act by a person who is not a resident of the United States may not be relied upon as a bar to prosecution under section 7 of the act for a violation of section 3 of the act.

§ 1608.5 Salvage operations of common carriers and others.

For the purposes of this act the ordinary course of business of common carriers, contract carriers or freight forwarders, as referred to in section 11 of the act, shall not include the marketing or handling of products, fabrics, or related materials subject to the act in the course of performance of salvage or lien realizing operations.

§ 1608.6 Reference to guaranty by Government prohibited.

No representation nor suggestion shall be made in advertising or otherwise marketing or handling products, fabrics or related materials subject to the act that the act, the Government, or any branch thereof, guarantees, in any manner that such product, fabric, or related material conforms to a flammability standard in effect under the act.

PART 1609—TEXT OF THE FLAMMABLE FABRICS ACT OF 1953, AS AMENDED IN 1954, PRIOR TO 1967 AMENDMENT AND REVISION

§ 1609.1 Text of the Flammable Fabrics Act of 1953, as amended in 1954.

The following is the text of the Flammable Fabrics Act of 1953, ch. 164, 67 Stat. 111, as amended, ch. 833, 68 Stat. 770 (1954):

AN ACT

To prohibit the introduction or movement in interstate commerce of articles of wearing apparel and fabrics which are so highly flammable as to be dangerous when worn by individuals, and for other purposes.

Be it enacted by the Senate and House of Representatives of the United States of America in Congress assembled,

SHORT TITLE

SECTION 1. This Act may be cited as the "Flammable Fabrics Act."

DEFINITIONS

Sec. 2. As used in this Act—

(a) The term *person* means an individual, partnership, corporation, association, or any other form of business enterprise.

(b) The term *commerce* means commerce among the several States or with foreign nations, or in any Territory of the United States or in the District of Columbia, or between any such Territory and another, or between any such Territory and any State or foreign nation, or between the District of Columbia and any State or Territory or foreign nation.

(c) The term *Territory* includes the insular possessions of the United States and also any Territory of the United States.

(d) The term *article of wearing apparel* means any costume or article of clothing worn or intended to be worn by individuals except hats, gloves, and footwear: Provided, however, That such hats do not constitute or form part of a covering for the neck, face, or shoulders when worn by individuals: Provided further, That such gloves are not more than fourteen inches in length and are not affixed to or do not form an integral part of another garment: And provided further, That such footwear does not consist of hosiery in whole or in part and is not affixed to or does not form an integral part of another garment.

(e) The term *fabric* means any material (other than fiber, filament, or yarn) woven, knitted, felted, or otherwise produced from or in combination with any natural or synthetic fiber, film, or substitute therefor which is intended or sold for use in wearing apparel except that interlining fabrics when intended or sold for use in wearing apparel shall not be subject to this Act.

(f) The term *interlining* means any fabric which is intended for incorporation into an article of wearing apparel as a layer between an outer shell and an inner lining.

(g) The term *Commission* means the Federal Trade Commission.

(h) The term *Federal Trade Commission Act* means the Act of Congress entitled "An Act to create a Federal Trade Commission, to define its powers and duties, and for other purposes," approved September 26, 1914, as amended.

PROHIBITED TRANSACTIONS

SEC. 3. (a) The manufacture for sale, the sale, or the offering for sale, in commerce, or the importation into the United States, or the introduction, delivery for introduction, transportation or causing to be transported in commerce or for the purpose of sale or delivery after sale in commerce, of any article of wearing apparel which under the provisions of section 4 of this Act is so highly flammable as to be dangerous when worn by individuals, shall be unlawful and shall be an unfair method of competition and an unfair and deceptive act or practice in commerce under the Federal Trade Commission Act.

(b) The sale or the offering for sale, in commerce, or the importation into the United States, or the introduction, delivery for introduction, transportation or causing to be transported in commerce or for the purpose of sale or delivery after sale in commerce, of any fabric which under the provisions of section 4 of this Act is so highly flammable as to be dangerous when worn by individuals, shall be unlawful and shall be an unfair method of competition and an unfair and deceptive act or practice in commerce under the Federal Trade Commission Act.

(c) The manufacture for sale, the sale, or the offering for sale, of any article of wearing apparel made of fabric which under section 4 is so highly flammable as to be dangerous when worn by individuals and which has been shipped or received in commerce shall be unlawful and shall be an unfair method of competition and an unfair and deceptive act or practice in commerce under the Federal Trade Commission Act.

STANDARD OF FLAMMABILITY

SEC. 4. (a) Any fabric or article of wearing apparel shall be deemed so highly flammable within the meaning of section 3 of this Act as to be dangerous when worn by individuals if such fabrics or any uncovered or exposed part of such article of wearing apparel exhibits rapid and intense burning when tested under the conditions and in the manner prescribed in the Commercial Standard promulgated by the Secretary of Commerce effective January 30, 1953, and identified as "Flammability of Clothing Textiles, Commercial Standard 191–53," or exhibits a rate of burning in excess of that specified in paragraph 3.11 of the Commercial Standard promulgated by the Secretary of Commerce effective May 22, 1953, and identified as "General Purpose Vinyl Plastic Film, Commercial Standard 192–53." For the purposes of this Act, such Commercial Standard 191–53 shall apply with respect to the hats, gloves, and footwear covered by section 2(d) of this Act, notwithstanding any exception contained in such Commercial Standard with respect to hats, gloves, and footwear.

(b) If at any time the Secretary of Commerce finds that the Commercial Standards referred to in subsection (a) of this section are inadequate for the protection of the public interest, he shall submit to the Congress a report setting forth his findings together with such proposals for legislation as he deems appropriate.

(c) Notwithstanding the provisions of paragraph 3.1 Commercial Standard 191–53, textiles free from nap, pile, tufting, flock or other type of raised fiber surface when tested as described in said standard shall be classified as class 1, normal flammability, when the time of flame spread is three and one-half seconds or more, and as class 3, rapid and intense burning when the time of flame spread is less than three and one-half seconds. [Approved August 23, 1954.]

ADMINISTRATION AND ENFORCEMENT

SEC. 5. (a) Except as otherwise specifically provided herein, sections 3, 5, 6, and 8(b) of this Act shall be enforced by the Commission under rules, regulations and procedures provided for in the Federal Trade Commission Act.

(b) The Commission is authorized and directed to prevent any person from violating the provisions of section 3 of this Act in the same manner, by the same means and with the same jurisdiction, powers and duties as though all applicable terms and provisions of the Federal Trade Commission Act were incorporated into and made a part of this Act; and any such person violating any provision of section 3 of this Act shall be subject to the penalties and entitled to the privileges and immunities provided in said Federal Trade Commission Act as though the applicable terms and provisions of the said Federal Trade Commission Act were incorporated into and made a part of this Act.

(c) The Commission is authorized and directed to prescribe such rules and regulations as may be necessary and proper for purposes of administration and enforcement of this Act.

(d) The Commission is authorized to—

(1) cause inspections, analyses, tests, and examinations to be made of any article of

wearing apparel or fabric which it has reason to believe falls within the prohibitions of this Act; and

(2) cooperate on matters related to the purposes of this Act with any department or agency of the Government; with any State, Territory, or possession or with the District of Columbia; or with any department, agency, or political subdivision thereof; or with any person.

INJUNCTION AND CONDEMNATION PROCEEDINGS

SEC. 6. (a) Whenever the Commission has reason to believe that any person is violating or is about to violate section 3 of this Act, and that it would be in the public interest to enjoin such violation until complaint under the Federal Trade Commission Act is issued and dismissed by the Commission or until order to cease and desist made thereon by the Commission has become final within the meaning of the Federal Trade Commission Act or is set aside by the court on review, the Commission may bring suit in the district court of the United States or in the United States court of any Territory for the district or Territory in which such person resides or transacts business, to enjoin such violation and upon proper showing a temporary injunction or restraining order shall be granted without bond.

(b) Whenever the Commission has reason to believe that any article of wearing apparel has been manufactured or introduced into commerce or any fabric has been introduced in commerce in violation of section 3 of this Act, it may institute proceedings by process of libel for the seizure and confiscation of such article of wearing apparel or fabric in any district court of the United States within the jurisdiction of which such article of wearing apparel or fabric is found. Proceedings in cases instituted under the authority of this section shall conform as nearly as may be to proceedings in rem in admiralty, except that on demand of either party and in the discretion of the court, any issue of fact shall be tried by jury. Whenever such proceedings involving identical articles of wearing apparel or fabrics are pending in two or more jurisdictions, they may be consolidated for trial by order of any such court upon application seasonably made by any party in interest upon notice to all other parties in interest. Any court granting an order of consolidation shall cause prompt notification thereof to be given to other courts having jurisdiction in the cases covered thereby and the clerks of such other courts shall transmit all pertinent records and papers to the court designated for the trial of such consolidated proceedings.

(c) In any such action the court upon application seasonably made before trial shall by order allow any party in interest, his attorney or agent, to obtain a representative sample of the article of wearing apparel or fabric seized.

(d) If such articles of wearing apparel or fabrics are condemned by the court they shall be disposed of by destruction, by delivery to the owner or claimant thereof upon payment of court costs and fees and storage and other proper expenses and upon execution of good and sufficient bond to the effect that such articles of wearing apparel or fabrics will not be disposed of for wearing apparel purposes until properly and adequately treated or processed so as to render them lawful for introduction into commerce, or by sale upon execution of good and sufficient bond to the effect that such articles of wearing apparel or fabrics will not be disposed of for wearing apparel purposes until properly and adequately treated or processed so as to render them lawful for introduction into commerce. If such products are disposed of by sale the proceeds, less costs and charges, shall be paid into the Treasury of the United States.

PENALTIES

SEC. 7. Any person who willfully violates section 3 or 8(b) of this Act shall be guilty of a misdemeanor, and upon conviction thereof shall be fined not more than $5,000 or be imprisoned not more than one year or both in the discretion of the court: Provided, That nothing herein shall limit other provisions of this Act.

GUARANTY

SEC. 8. (a) No person shall be subject to prosecution under section 7 of this Act for a violation of section 3 of this Act if such person (1) establishes a guaranty received in good faith signed by and containing the name and address of the person by whom the wearing apparel or fabric guaranteed was manufactured or from whom it was received, to the effect that reasonable and representative tests made under the procedures provided in section 4 of this Act show that the fabric covered by the guaranty, or used in the wearing apparel covered by the guaranty, is not, under the provisions of section 4 of this Act, so highly flammable as to be dangerous when worn by individuals, and (2) has not, by further processing, affected the flammability of the fabric or wearing apparel covered by the guaranty which he received. Such guaranty shall be either (1) a separate guaranty specifically designating the wearing apparel or fabric guaranteed, in which case it may be on the invoice or other paper relating to such wearing apparel or fabric; or (2) a continuing guaranty filed with the Commission applicable to any wearing apparel or fabric handled by a guarantor, in such form as the Commission by rules or regulations may prescribe.

(b) It shall be unlawful for any person to furnish, with respect to any wearing apparel or fabric, a false guaranty (except a person relying upon a guaranty to the same effect received in good faith signed by and containing the name and address of the person by whom the wearing apparel or fabric guaranteed was manufactured or from whom it was received) with reason to believe the wearing apparel or fabric falsely guaranteed may be introduced, sold, or transported in commerce, and any person who violates the provisions of this subsection is guilty of an unfair method of competition, and an unfair or deceptive act or practice, in commerce within the meaning of the Federal Trade Commission Act.

SHIPMENTS FROM FOREIGN COUNTRIES

SEC. 9. Any person who has exported or who has attempted to export from any foreign country into the United States any wearing apparel or fabric which, under the provisions of section 4, is so highly flammable as to be dangerous when worn by individuals may thenceforth be prohibited by the Commission from participating in the exportation from any foreign country into the United States of any wearing apparel or fabric except upon filing bond with the Secretary of the Treasury in a sum double the value of said products and any duty thereon, conditioned upon compliance with the provisions of this Act.

INTERPRETATION AND SEPARABILITY

SEC. 10. The provisions of this Act shall be held to be in addition to, and not in substitution for or limitation of, the provisions of any other law. If any provision of this Act or the application thereof to any person or circumstances is held invalid the remainder of the Act and the application of such provisions to any other person or circumstances shall not be affected thereby.

EXCLUSIONS

SEC. 11. The provisions of this Act shall not apply (a) to any common carrier, contract carrier, or freight forwarder with respect to an article of wearing apparel or fabric shipped or delivered for shipment into commerce in the ordinary course of its business; or (b) to any converter, processor, or finisher in performing a contract or commission service for the account of a person subject to the provisions of this Act: Provided, That said converter, processor, or finisher does not cause any article of wearing apparel or fabric to become subject to this Act contrary to the terms of the contract or commission service; or (c) to any article of wearing apparel or fabric shipped or delivered for shipment into commerce for the purpose of finishing or processing to render such article or fabric not so highly flammable, under the provisions of section 4 of this Act, as to be dangerous when worn by individuals.

EFFECTIVE DATE

SEC. 12. This Act shall take effect one year after the date of its passage.

AUTHORIZATION OF NECESSARY APPROPRIATIONS

SEC. 13. There is hereby authorized to be appropriated such sums as may be necessary to carry out the provisions of this Act.

[40 FR 59889, Dec. 30, 1975]

PART 1610—STANDARD FOR THE FLAMMABILITY OF CLOTHING TEXTILES

Subpart A—The Standard

Subpart B—Rules and Regulations

Subpart C—Interpretations and Policies

SOURCE: 73 FR 15640, Mar. 25, 2008, unless otherwise noted.

AUTHORITY: 15 U.S.C. 1191–1204.

Subpart A—The Standard

§ 1610.1 Purpose, scope and applicability.

(a) *Purpose.* The purpose of this standard is to reduce danger of injury and loss of life by providing, on a national basis, standard methods of testing and rating the flammability of textiles and textile products for clothing use, thereby prohibiting the use of any dangerously flammable clothing textiles.

(b) *Scope.* The Standard provides methods of testing the flammability of clothing and textiles intended to be used for clothing, establishes three classes of flammability, sets forth the requirements which textiles shall meet to be classified, and warns against the use of those textiles which have burning characteristics unsuitable for clothing. Hereafter, "clothing and textiles intended to be used for clothing" shall be referred to as "textiles."

(c) *Specific exceptions.* This standard shall not apply to: (1) Hats, provided they do not constitute or form part of a covering for the neck, face, or shoulders when worn by individuals;

(2) Gloves, provided they are not more than 14 inches in length and are not affixed to or do not form an integral part of another garment;

(3) Footwear, provided it does not consist of hosiery in whole or part and is not affixed to or does not form an integral part of another garment;

(4) Interlining fabrics, when intended or sold for use as a layer between an outer shell and an inner lining in wearing apparel.

(d) *Specific exemptions.* Experience gained from years of testing in accordance with the Standard demonstrates that certain fabrics consistently yield acceptable results when tested in accordance with the Standard. Therefore, persons and firms issuing an initial guaranty of any of the following types of fabrics, or of products made entirely from one or more of these fabrics, are exempt from any requirement for testing to support guaranties of those fabrics:

(1) Plain surface fabrics, regardless of fiber content, weighing 2.6 ounces per square yard or more; and

(2) All fabrics, both plain surface and raised-fiber surface textiles, regardless of weight, made entirely from any of the following fibers or entirely from combination of the following fibers: acrylic, modacrylic, nylon, olefin, polyester, wool.

(e) *Applicability.* The requirements of this part 1610 shall apply to textile fabric or related material in a form or state ready for use in an article of wearing apparel, including garments and costumes finished for consumer use.

§ 1610.2 Definitions.

In addition to the definitions given in Section 2 of the Flammable Fabrics Act as amended (15 U.S.C. 1191), the following definitions apply for this part 1610.

(a) *Base burn* (also known as base fabric ignition or fusing) means the point at which the flame burns the ground (base) fabric of a raised surface textile fabric and provides a self-sustaining flame. Base burns, used to establish a Class 3 fabric, are those burns resulting from surface flash that occur on specimens in places other than the point of impingement when the warp and fill yarns of a raised surface textile fabric undergo combustion. Base burns can be identified by an opacity change, scorching on the reverse side of the fabric, or when a physical hole is evident.

(b) *Burn time* means the time elapsed from ignition until the stop thread is severed as measured by the timing mechanism of the test apparatus.

(c) *Dry cleaning* means the cleaning of samples in a commercial dry cleaning machine under the conditions described in § 1610.6.

(d) *Film* means any non-rigid, unsupported plastic, rubber or other synthetic or natural film or sheeting, subject to the Act, or any combination thereof, including transparent, translucent, and opaque material, whether plain, embossed, molded, or otherwise surface treated, which is in a form or state ready for use in wearing apparel, and shall include film or sheeting of any thickness.

(e) *Flammability* means those characteristics of a material that pertain to its relative ease of ignition and relative ability to sustain combustion.

(f) *Flame application* time means the 1 second during which the ignition flame is applied to the test specimen.

(g) *Ignition* means that there is a self-sustaining flame on the specimen after the test flame is removed.

(h) *Interlining* means any textile which is intended for incorporation into an article of wearing apparel as a layer between an outer shell and an inner lining.

(i) *Laundering* means washing with an aqueous detergent solution and includes rinsing, extraction and tumble drying as described in § 1610.6.

(j) *Long dimension* means the 150 mm (6 in) length of test specimen.

(k) *Plain surface textile* fabric means any textile fabric which does not have an intentionally raised fiber or yarn surface such as a pile, nap, or tuft, but shall include those fabrics that have fancy woven, knitted or flock-printed surfaces.

(l) *Raised surface textile fabric* means any textile fabric with an intentionally raised fiber or yarn surface, such as a pile, including flocked pile, nap, or tufting.

(m) *Refurbishing* means dry cleaning and laundering in accordance with § 1610.6.

(n) *Sample* means a portion of a lot of material which is taken for testing or for record keeping purposes.

(o) *Specimen* means a 50 mm by 150 mm (2 in by 6 in) section of sample.

(p) *Stop thread supply* means No. 50, white, mercerized, 100% cotton sewing thread.

(q) *Surface flash* means a rapid burning of the pile fibers and yarns on a raised fiber surface textile that may or may not result in base burning.

(r) *Textile fabric* means any coated or uncoated material subject to the Act, except film and fabrics having a nitrocellulose fiber, finish, or coating, which is woven, knitted, felted or otherwise produced from any natural or manmade fiber, or substitute therefore, or combination thereof, of 50 mm (2 in) or more in width, and which is in a form or state ready for use in wearing apparel, including fabrics which have undergone further processing, such as dyeing and finishing, in garment form, for consumer use.

§ 1610.3 Summary of test method.

The Standard provides methods of testing the flammability of textiles from or intended to be used for apparel; establishes three classes of flammability; sets forth the requirements for classifying textiles; and prohibits the use of single or multi-layer textile fabrics that have burning characteristics that make them unsuitable for apparel. All textiles shall be tested before and after refurbishing according to § 1610.6. Each specimen cut from the textile shall be inserted in a frame, brushed if it has a raised-fiber surface, and held in a special apparatus at an angle of 45°. A standardized flame shall be applied to the surface near the lower end of the specimen for 1 second, and the time required for the flame to proceed up the fabric a distance of 127 mm (5 in) shall be recorded. A notation shall be made as to whether the base of a raised-surface textile fabric ignites or fuses.

§ 1610.4 Requirements for classifying textiles.

(a) *Class 1, Normal Flammability.* Class 1 textiles exhibit normal flammability and are acceptable for use in clothing. This class shall include textiles which meet the minimum requirements set forth in paragraph (a)(1) or paragraph (a)(2) of this section.

(1) *Plain surface textile fabric.* Such textiles in their original state and/or after being refurbished as described in § 1610.6(a) and § 1610.6(b), when tested as described in § 1610.6 shall be classified as Class 1, Normal flammability, when the burn time is 3.5 seconds or more.

(2) *Raised surface textile fabric.* Such textiles in their original state and/or after being refurbished as described in

§ 1610.6(a) and § 1610.6(b), when tested as described in § 1610.6, shall be classified as Class 1, Normal flammability, when the burn time is more than 7 seconds, or when they burn with a rapid surface flash (0 to 7 seconds), provided the intensity of the flame is so low as not to ignite or fuse the base fabric.

(b) *Class 2, Intermediate flammability.* Class 2 fabrics, applicable only to raised-fiber surface textiles, are considered to be of intermediate flammability, but may be used for clothing. This class shall include textiles which meet the minimum requirements set forth in paragraph (b)(2) of this section.

(1) *Plain surface textile fabric.* Class 2 is not applicable to plain surface textile fabrics.

(2) *Raised surface textile fabric.* Such textiles in their original state and/or after being refurbished as described in § 1610.6(a) and § 1610.6(b), when tested as described in § 1610.6, shall be classified as Class 2, Intermediate flammability, when the burn time is from 4 through 7 seconds, both inclusive, and the base fabric ignites or fuses.

(c) *Class 3, Rapid and intense burning.* Class 3 textiles exhibit rapid and intense burning, are dangerously flammable and shall not be used for clothing. This class shall include textiles which have burning characteristics as described in paragraphs (c)(1) and (c)(2) of this section. Such textiles are considered dangerously flammable because of their rapid and intense burning.

(1) *Plain surface textile fabric.* Such textiles in their original state and/or after refurbishing as described in § 1610.6(a) and § 1610.6(b), when tested as described in § 1610.6, shall be classified as Class 3 Rapid and Intense Burning when the time of flame spread is less than 3.5 seconds.

(2) *Raised surface textile fabric.* Such textiles in their original state and/or after refurbishing as described in § 1610.6(a) and § 1610.6(b), when tested as described in § 1610.6, shall be classified as Class 3 Rapid and Intense Burning when the time of flame spread is less than 4 seconds, and the base fabric starts burning at places other than the point of impingement as a result of the surface flash (test result code SFBB).

TABLE 1 TO § 1610.4—SUMMARY OF TEST CRITERIA FOR SPECIMEN CLASSIFICATION
[SEE § 1610.7]

Class	Plain surface textile fabric	Raised surface textile fabric
1	Burn time is 3.5 seconds or more ACCEPTABLE (3.5 sec is a pass).	(1) Burn time is greater than 7.0 seconds; or (2) Burn time is 0–7 seconds with no base burns (SFBB). Exhibits rapid surface flash only. ACCEPTABLE.
2	Class 2 is not applicable to plain surface textile fabrics	Burn time is 4–7 seconds (inclusive) with base burn (SFBB). ACCEPTABLE.
3	Burn time is less than 3.5 seconds. NOT ACCEPTABLE.	Burn time is less than 4.0 seconds with base burn (SFBB). NOT ACCEPTABLE.

§ 1610.5 Test apparatus and materials.

(a) *Flammability apparatus.* The flammability test apparatus consists of a draft-proof ventilated chamber enclosing a standardized ignition mechanism, sample rack, and automatic timing mechanism. The flammability apparatus shall meet the minimum requirements for testing as follows.

(1) *Test chamber—(i) Test chamber structure.* The test chamber shall be a metal, draft-proof ventilated chamber. The test chamber shall have inside dimensions of 35.3 cm high by 36.8 cm wide by 21.6 cm deep (14 in by 14.5 in by 8.5 in). There shall be eleven or twelve 12.7 mm diameter (0.5 in) holes equidistant along the rear of the top closure. The front of the chamber shall be a close fitting door with an insert made of clear material (i.e., glass, plexiglass) to permit observation of the entire test. A ventilating strip is provided at the base of the door in the front of the apparatus. The test chamber to be used in this test method is illustrated in Figures 1 and 2 of this part.

(ii) *Specimen rack.* The specimen rack provides support for the specimen holder (described in paragraph (a)(1)(iii) of this section) in which the specimen is mounted for testing. The angle of inclination shall be 45°. Two guide pins projecting downward from the center of the base of the rack travel in slots provided in the floor of the chamber so that adjustment can be made for the thickness of the specimen in relation to the test flame. A stop shall be provided in the base of the chamber to assist in adjusting the position of the rack. The specimen rack shall be constructed so that: It supports the specimen holder in a way that does not obstruct air flow around the bottom edge of the fabric specimen; and the fabric specimen is properly aligned with the igniter tip during flame impingement. The specimen rack to be used in this test method is illustrated in Figures 1 through 3 of this part. Movable rack: Refer to the manufacturers' instruction in relation to the adjustment procedure to move the rack into the appropriate position for the indicator finger alignment.

(iii) *Specimen holder.* The specimen holder supports and holds the fabric specimen. The specimen holder shall consist of two 2 mm (0.06 in) thick U-shaped matched metal plates. The plates are slotted and loosely pinned for alignment. The specimen shall be firmly sandwiched in between the metal plates with clamps mounted along the sides. The two plates of the holder shall cover all but 3.8 cm (1.5 in) of the width of the specimen for its full length. See Figures 1 and 3 of this part. The specimen holder shall be supported in the draft-proof chamber on the rack at an angle of 45°.

(iv) *Indicator finger.* The position of the specimen rack (described in paragraph (a)(1)(ii) of this section) shall be adjusted, so the tip of the indicator finger just touches the surface of the specimen. An indicator finger is necessary to ensure that the tip of the test flame will impinge on the specimen during testing. The indicator finger to be used in this test method is illustrated in Figures 1, 2 and 4 of this part.

(v) *Ignition mechanism.* The ignition mechanism shall consist of a motor driven butane gas jet formed around a 26-gauge hypodermic needle and creates the test flame. The test flame shall be protected by a shield. See Figure 5. The test flame is adjusted to 16 mm (0.625 in) and applied to the specimen for 1 second. A trigger device is located in the front of the apparatus, the pulling or pushing of which activates the test flame impingement and timing device. Electro-mechanical devices (*i.e.*, servo-motors, solenoids, micro-switches, and electronic circuits, in addition to miscellaneous custom made cams and rods, shock absorbing linkages, and various other mechanical components) can be used to control and apply the flame impingement. See Figure 6 of this part.

(vi) *Draft ventilator strip.* A draft ventilator strip shall be placed across the front opening, sealing the space between the sliding door when in lowered position and the base on which the grid rack is attached. (See Figure 1 of this part.)

(vii) *Stop weight.* The weight, attached by means of a clip to the stop thread, in dropping actuates the stop motion for the timing mechanism. The weight shall be 30g ±5g (1.16 oz. ±0.18 oz).

(viii) *Door.* The door shall be a clear (*i.e.* glass or plexiglass) door, close fitting and allows for viewing of the entire test.

(ix) *Hood.* The hood or other suitable enclosure shall provide a draft-proof environment surrounding the test chamber. The hood or other suitable enclosure shall have a fan or other means for exhausting smoke and/or fumes produced by testing.

(2) *Stop thread and thread guides—(i) Stop thread.* The stop thread shall be stretched from the spool through suitable thread guides provided on the specimen holder and chamber walls.

(ii) *Stop thread supply.* This supply, consisting of a spool of No. 50, white, mercerized, 100% cotton sewing thread, shall be fastened to the side of the chamber and can be withdrawn by releasing the thumbscrew holding it in position.

(iii) *Thread Guides.* The thread guides permit the lacing of the stop thread in the proper position exactly 127 mm (5 in) from the point where the center of the ignition flame impinges on the test specimen. The stop thread shall be 9.5 mm (0.37 in) above and parallel to the lower surface of the top plate of the specimen holder. This condition can be achieved easily and reproducibly with the use of a thread guide popularly referred to as a "sky hook" suspended down from the top panel along with two L-shaped thread guides attached to the upper end of the top plate of the specimen holder. Two other thread guides can be installed on the rear panel to draw the thread away from directly over the test flame. The essential condition, however, is the uniform height of 9.5 mm (0.37 in) for the stop thread and not the number, placement or design of the thread guides.

(iv) *Stop weight thread guide.* This thread guide shall be used to guide the stop thread when attaching the stop weight.

(3) *Supply for test flame.* (i) The fuel supply shall be a cylinder of chemically pure (c. p.) butane.

(ii) The fuel-tank control valve shall consist of a sensitive control device for regulating the fuel supply at the tank.

(iii) The flow control device, such as a manometer or flow meter, shall be sufficient to maintain a consistent flame length of 16 mm (5⁄8 in).

(4) *Timing Device.* The timing device consists of a timer, driving mechanism and weight. The timer, by means of special attachments, is actuated to start by connection with the gas jet. A trigger device (described in paragraph (a)(1)(v) of this section) activates the flame impingement, causing the driving mechanism to move the gas jet to its most forward position and automatically starts the timer at the moment of flame impact with the specimen. The falling weight, when caused to move by severance of the stop thread, stops the timer. Time shall be read directly and recorded as a burn time. Read burn time to 0.1 second. An electronic or mechanical timer can be used to record the burn time, and electro-mechanical devices (*i.e.*, servomotors, solenoids, micro-switches, and electronic circuits, in addition to miscellaneous custom made cams and rods, shock absorbing linkages, and various other mechanical components) can be used to control and apply the flame impingement.

(b) *Specimen preparation equipment and materials*—(1) *Laboratory drying oven.* This shall be a forced circulation drying oven capable of maintaining 105° ±3 °C (221° ±5 °F) for 30 ±2 minutes to dry the specimens while mounted in the specimen holders.

(2) *Desiccator.* This shall be an airtight and moisture tight chamber capable of holding the specimens horizontally without contacting each other during the cooling period following drying, and shall contain silica gel desiccant.

(3) *Desiccant.* Anhydrous silica gel shall be used as the desiccant.

(4) *Automatic washing machine.* The automatic washing machine shall be as described in § 1610.6(b)(1)(ii).

(5) *Automatic tumble dryer.* The automatic tumble dryer shall be as described in § 1610.6(b)(1)(ii).

(6) *Commercial dry cleaning machine.* The commercial dry cleaning machine shall be capable of providing a complete automatic dry-to-dry cycle using perchloroethylene solvent and a cationic drycleaning detergent as specified in § 1610.6(b)(1)(i).

(7) *Dry cleaning solvent.* The solvent shall be perchloroethylene, commercial grade.

(8) *Dry cleaning detergent.* The dry cleaning detergent shall be cationic class.

(9) *Laundering detergent.* The laundering detergent shall be as specified in § 1610.6(b)(1)(ii).

(10) *Brushing device.* The brushing device shall consist of a base board over which a small carriage is drawn. See Figure 7 of this part. This carriage runs on parallel tracks attached to the edges of the upper surface of the base board. The brush is hinged with pin hinges at the rear edge of the base board and rests on the carriage vertically with a pressure of 150 gf (0.33 lbf). The brush shall consist of two rows of stiff nylon bristles mounted with the tufts in a staggered position. The bristles are 0.41 mm (0.016 in) in diameter and 19 mm (0.75 in) in length. There are 20 bristles per tuft and 4 tufts per inch. See Figure 8 of this part. A clamp is attached to the forward edge of the movable carriage to permit holding the specimen on the carriage during the brushing operation.

The purpose of the metal plate or "template" on the carriage of the brushing device is to support the specimen during the brushing operation. The template shall be 3.2 mm (0.13 in) thick. See Figure 9 of this part.

[73 FR 15640, Mar. 25, 2008, as amended at 73 FR 62187, Oct. 20, 2008]

§ 1610.6 Test procedure.

The test procedure is divided into two steps. Step 1 is testing in the original state; Step 2 is testing after the fabric has been refurbished according to paragraph (b)(1) of this section.

(a) *Step 1—Testing in the original state.* (1) Tests shall be conducted on the fabric in a form or state ready for use in wearing apparel. Determine whether the fabric to be tested is a plain surface textile fabric or a raised surface textile fabric as defined in § 1610.2 (k) and (l). There are some fabrics that require extra attention when preparing test specimens because of their particular construction characteristics. Examples of these fabrics are provided in paragraphs (a)(1)(i) through (vi) of this section along with guidelines for preparing specimens from these fabrics. This information is not intended to be all-inclusive.

(i) *Flocked fabrics.* Fabrics that are flocked overall are treated as raised surface textile fabrics as defined in § 1610.2(l). Flock printed fabrics (usually in a pattern and not covering the entire surface) shall be treated as plain surface textile fabrics as defined in § 1610.2(k).

(ii) *Cut velvet fabrics.* Cut velvet fabrics with a patterned construction shall be considered a raised surface textile fabric as defined in § 1610.2(l).

(iii) *Metallic thread fabrics.* Metallic thread fabrics shall be considered plain surface textile fabrics provided the base fabric is smooth. The specimens shall be cut so that the metallic thread is parallel to the long dimension of the specimen and arranged so the test flame impinges on a metallic thread.

(iv) *Embroidery.* Embroidery on netting material shall be tested with two sets of preliminary specimens to determine the most flammable area (which offers the greatest amount of netting or embroidery in the 150 mm (6 in.) direction). One set of netting only shall be tested and the other set shall consist mainly of embroidery with the specimens cut so that the test flame impinges on the embroidered area. Test the most flammable area according to the plain surface textile fabric requirements. The full test shall be completed on a sample cut from the area that has the fastest burn rate.

(v) *Burn-out patterns.* Flat woven constructions with burn-out patterns shall be considered plain surface textile fabrics as defined in § 1610.2(k).

(vi) *Narrow fabrics and loose fibrous materials.* Narrow fabrics and loose fibrous materials manufactured less than 50 mm (2 in) in width in either direction shall not be tested. If a 50 mm by 150 mm (2 in by 6 in) specimen cannot be cut due to the nature of the item, *i.e.* hula skirts, leis, fringe, loose feathers, wigs, hairpieces, etc., do not conduct a test.

(2) *Plain surface textile fabrics:*

(i) *Preliminary trials.* Conduct preliminary trials to determine the quickest burning direction. The specimen size shall be 50 mm by 150 mm (2 in by 6 in). Cut one specimen from each direction of the fabric. Identify the fabric direction being careful not to make any identifying marks in the exposed area to be tested. Preliminary specimens shall be mounted and conditioned as described in paragraphs (a)(2)(ii) through (iv) of this section and then tested following the procedure in paragraph (c) of this section to determine if there is a difference in the burning characteristics with respect to the direction of the fabric.

(ii) *Identify and cut test specimens.* Cut the required number of test specimens to be tested (refer to § 1610.7(b)(1)). Each specimen shall be 50 mm by 150 mm (2 in by 6 in), with the long dimension in the direction in which burning is most rapid as established in the preliminary trials. Be careful not to make any identifying marks in the exposed area to be tested.

(iii) *Mount specimens.* Specimens shall be placed in the holders, with the side to be burned face up. Even though plain surface textile fabrics are not brushed, all specimens shall be mounted in a specimen holder placed on the carriage that rides on the brushing device to ensure proper position in the holder. A specimen shall be placed between the two metal plates of a specimen holder and clamped. Each specimen shall be mounted and clamped prior to conditioning and testing.

(iv) *Condition specimens.* All specimens mounted in the holders shall then be placed in a horizontal position on an open metal shelf in the oven to permit free circulation of air around them. The specimens shall be dried in the oven for 30 ±2 minutes at 105° ±3 °C (221° ±5 °F), removed from the oven and placed over a bed of anhydrous silica gel desiccant in a desiccator until cool, but not less than 15 minutes.

(v) *Flammability test.* Follow the test procedure in paragraph (c) of this section and also follow the test sequence in §1610.7(b)(1).

(3) *Raised surface textile fabrics*—(i) Preliminary trials. The most flammable surface of the fabric shall be tested. Conduct preliminary trials and/or visual examination to determine the quickest burning area. The specimen size shall be 50 mm by 150 mm (2 in by 6 in). For raised surface textile fabrics, the direction of the lay of the surface fibers shall be parallel with the long dimension of the specimen. Specimens shall be taken from that part of the raised-fiber surface that appears to have the fastest burn time. For those fabrics where it may be difficult to visually determine the correct direction of the lay of the raised surface fibers, preliminary tests can be done to determine the direction of the fastest burn time. For textiles with varying depths of pile, tufting, etc., the preliminary test specimens are taken from each depth of pile area to determine which exhibits the quickest rate of burning. A sufficient number of preliminary specimens shall be tested to provide adequate assurance that the raised surface textile fabric will be tested in the quickest burning area. Preliminary specimens shall be mounted and conditioned as described below and tested following the procedure in paragraph (c) of this section.

(ii) *Identify and cut test specimens.* Cut the required number of specimens (refer to §1610.7(b)(3)) to be tested. Each specimen shall be 50 mm by 150 mm (2 in by 6 in), with the specimen taken from the direction in which burning is most rapid as established in the preliminary trials and/or visual examination. Be careful not to make any identifying marks in the exposed area to be tested.

(iii) *Mount specimens.* Prior to mounting the specimen, run a fingernail along the 150 mm (6 in) edge of the fabric not more than 6.4 mm (0.25 in) in from the side to determine the lay of the surface fibers. All specimens shall be mounted in a specimen holder placed on the carriage that rides on the brushing device. The specimens shall be mounted with the side to be burned face up and positioned so the lay of the surface fibers is going away from the closed end of the specimen holder. The specimen must be positioned in this manner so that the brushing procedure described in paragraph (a)(3)(iv) of this section will raise the surface fibers, *i.e.*, the specimen is brushed against the direction of the lay of the surface fibers. The specimen shall be placed between the two metal plates of the specimen holder and clamped.

(iv) *Brush specimens.* After mounting in the specimen holder (and with the holder still on the carriage that rides on the brushing device) each specimen shall be brushed one time. The carriage is pushed to the rear of the brushing device, see Figure 7, and the brush, see Figure 8, lowered to the face of the specimen. The carriage shall be drawn forward by hand once against the lay of the surface fibers at a uniform rate. Brushing of a specimen shall be performed with the specimen mounted in a specimen holder. The purpose of the metal plate or "template" on the carriage of the brushing device is to support the specimen during the brushing operation. See Figure 9.

(v) *Condition specimens.* All specimens (mounted and brushed) in the holders shall be then placed in a horizontal position on an open metal shelf in the oven to permit free circulation of air around them. The specimens shall be dried in the oven for 30 ±2 minutes at 105° ±3 °C (221 ° ±5 °F) removed from the oven and placed over a bed of anhydrous silica gel desiccant in a desiccator until cool, but not less than 15 minutes.

(vi) *Conduct flammability test.* Follow the procedure in paragraph (c) of this section and follow the test sequence in §1610.7(b)(3).

(b) *Step 2—Refurbishing and testing after refurbishing.*

(1) The refurbishing procedures are the same for both plain surface textile fabrics and raised fiber surface textile fabrics. Those samples that result in a Class 3, Rapid and Intense Burning after Step 1 testing in the original state shall not be refurbished and shall not undergo Step 2.

(i) *Dry cleaning procedure.* (A) All samples shall be dry cleaned before they undergo the laundering procedure. Samples shall be dry cleaned in a commercial dry cleaning machine, using the following prescribed conditions:

Solvent: Perchloroethylene, commercial grade

Detergent class: Cationic.

Cleaning time: 10–15 minutes.

Extraction time: 3 minutes.

Drying Temperature: 60–66 °C (140–150 °F).

Drying Time: 18–20 minutes.

Cool Down/Deodorization time: 5 minutes.

Samples shall be dry cleaned in a load that is 80% of the machine's capacity.

(B) If necessary, ballast consisting of clean textile pieces or garments, white or light in color and consisting of approximately 80% wool fabric pieces and 20% cotton fabric pieces, shall be used.

(ii) *Laundering procedure.* The sample, after being subjected to the dry cleaning procedure, shall be washed and dried one time in accordance with sections 8.2.2, 8.2.3 and 8.3.1(A) of AATCC Test Method 124–2006 "Appearance of Fabrics after Repeated Home Laundering" (incorporated by reference at §1610.6(b)(1)(B)(iii)). Washing shall be performed in accordance with sections 8.2.2 and 8.2.3 of AATCC Test Method 124–2006 using AATCC 1993 Standard Reference Detergent, powder and wash water temperature (IV) (120° ±5 °F; 49° ±3 °C) specified in Table II of that method, and the water level, agitator speed, washing time, spin speed and final spin cycle specified for "Normal/Cotton Sturdy" in Table III of that method. A maximum wash load shall be 8 pounds (3.63 kg) and may consist of any combination of test samples and dummy pieces. Drying shall be performed in accordance with section 8.3.1(A) of that test method, Tumble Dry, using the exhaust temperature (150° ±10 °F; 66° ±5 °C) and cool down time of 10 minutes specified in the "Durable Press" conditions of Table IV.

(iii) AATCC Test Method 124–2006 "Appearance of Fabrics after Repeated Home Laundering," is incorporated by reference. The Director of the Federal Register approves this incorporation by reference in accordance with 5 U.S.C. 552(a) and 1 CFR part 51. You may obtain a copy from the American Association of Textile Chemists and Colorists, P.O. Box 12215, Research Triangle Park, North Carolina 27709. You may inspect a copy at the Office of the Secretary, Consumer Product Safety Commission, Room 502, 4330 East West Highway, Bethesda, Maryland 20814 or at the National Archives and Records Administration (NARA). For information on the availability of this material at NARA, call 202–741–6030, or go to *http://www.archives.gov/federal_register/code_of_federal_regulations/ibr_locations.html.*

(2) *Testing plain surface textile fabrics after refurbishing.* The test procedure is the same as for Step 1—Testing in the original state described in paragraph (a)(1) of this section; also follow the test sequence §1610.7(b)(2).

(3) *Testing raised fiber surface textile fabrics after refurbishing.* The test procedure is the same as for Step 1—Testing in the original state as described in paragraph (a)(3) of this section; also follow the test sequence in §1610.7(b)(4).

(c) *Procedure for testing flammability.* (1) The test chamber shall be located under the hood (or other suitable enclosure) with the fan turned off. Open the control valve in the fuel supply. Allow approximately 5 minutes for the air to be drawn from the fuel line, ignite the gas and adjust the test flame to a length of 16 mm (⅝ in), measured from its tip to the opening in the gas nozzle.

(2) Remove one mounted specimen from the desiccator at a time and place it in position on the specimen rack in the chamber of the apparatus. Thick fabrics may require adjustment of the specimen rack so that the tip of the indicator finger just touches the surface of the specimen.

(3) Adjust the position of the specimen rack of the flammability test chamber so that the tip of the indicator finger just touches the face of the mounted specimen.

(4) String the stop thread through the guides in the upper plate of the specimen holder across the top of the specimen, and through any other thread guide(s) of the chamber. Hook the stop weight in place close to and just below the stop weight thread guide. Set the timing mechanism to zero. Close the door of the flammability test chamber.

(5) Begin the test within 45 seconds of the time the specimen was removed from the desiccator. Activate the trigger device to impinge the test flame. The trigger device controls the impingement of the test flame onto the specimen and starts the timing device. The timing is automatic and stops when the weight is released by the severing of the stop thread.

(6) At the end of each test, turn on the hood fan to exhaust any fumes or smoke produced during the test.

(7) Record the burn time (reading of the timer) for each specimen, along with visual observation using the test result codes given in §1610.8. If there is no burn time, record the visual observation using the test result codes. Please note for raised-fiber surface textile fabrics, specimens should be allowed to continue burning, even though a burn rate is measured, to determine if the base fabric will fuse.

(8) After exhausting all fumes and smoke produced during the test, turn off the fan before testing the next specimen.

[73 FR 15640, Mar. 25, 2008, as amended at 73 FR 62187, Oct. 20, 2008]

§ 1610.7 Test sequence and classification criteria.

(a) *Preliminary and final classifications.* Preliminary classifications are assigned based on the test results both before and after refurbishing. The final classification shall be the preliminary classification before or after refurbishing, whichever is the more severe flammability classification.

(b) *Test sequence and classification criteria.* (1) Step 1, Plain Surface Textile Fabrics in the original state.

(i) Conduct preliminary tests in accordance with §1610.6(a)(2)(i) to determine the fastest burning direction of the fabric.

(ii) Prepare and test five specimens from the fastest burning direction. The burn times determine whether to assign the preliminary classification and proceed to §1610.6(b) or to test five additional specimens.

(iii) Assign the preliminary classification of Class 1, Normal Flammability and proceed to §1610.6(b) when:

(A) There are no burn times; or

(B) There is only one burn time and it is equal to or greater than 3.5 seconds; or

(C) The average burn time of two or more specimens is equal to or greater than 3.5 seconds.

(iv) Test five additional specimens when there is either only one burn time, and it is less than 3.5 seconds; or there is an average burn time of less than 3.5 seconds. Test these five additional specimens from the fastest burning direction as previously determined by the preliminary specimens. The burn times for the 10 specimens determine whether to:

(A) Stop testing and assign the final classification as Class 3, Rapid and Intense Burning only when there are two or more burn times with an average burn time of less than 3.5 seconds; or

(B) Assign the preliminary classification of Class 1, Normal Flammability and proceed to §1610.6(b) when there are two or more burn times with an average burn time of 3.5 seconds or greater.

(v) If there is only one burn time out of the 10 test specimens, the test is inconclusive. The fabric cannot be classified.

(2) Step 2, Plain Surface Textile Fabrics after refurbishing in accordance with §1610.6(b)(1).

(i) Conduct preliminary tests in accordance with §1610.6(a)(2)(i) to determine the fastest burning direction of the fabric.

(ii) Prepare and test five specimens from the fastest burning direction. The burn times determine whether to stop testing and assign the preliminary classification or to test five additional specimens.

(iii) Stop testing and assign the preliminary classification of Class 1, Normal Flammability, when:

(A) There are no burn times; or

(B) There is only one burn time, and it is equal to or greater than 3.5 seconds; or

(C) The average burn time of two or more specimens is equal to or greater than 3.5 seconds.

(iv) Test five additional specimens when there is only one burn time, and it is less than 3.5 seconds; or there is an average burn time less than 3.5 seconds. Test five additional specimens from the fastest burning direction as previously determined by the preliminary specimens. The burn times for the 10 specimens determine the preliminary classification when:

(A) There are two or more burn times with an average burn time of 3.5 seconds or greater. The preliminary classification is Class 1, Normal Flammability; or

(B) There are two or more burn times with an average burn time of less than 3.5 seconds. The preliminary and final classification is Class 3, Rapid and Intense Burning; or

(v) If there is only one burn time out of the 10 specimens, the test results are inconclusive. The fabric cannot be classified.

(3) Step 1, Raised Surface Textile Fabric in the original state.

(i) Determine the area to be most flammable per § 1610.6(a)(3)(i).

(ii) Prepare and test five specimens from the most flammable area. The burn times and visual observations determine whether to assign a preliminary classification and proceed to § 1610.6(b) or to test five additional specimens.

(iii) Assign the preliminary classification and proceed to § 1610.6(b) when:

(A) There are no burn times. The preliminary classification is Class 1, Normal Flammability; or

(B) There is only one burn time and it is less than 4 seconds without a base burn, or it is 4 seconds or greater with or without a base burn. The preliminary classification is Class 1, Normal Flammability; or

(C) There are no base burns regardless of the burn time(s). The preliminary classification is Class 1, Normal Flammability; or

(D) There are two or more burn times with an average burn time of 0–7 seconds with a surface flash only. The preliminary classification is Class 1, Normal Flammability; or

(E) There are two or more burn times with an average burn time greater than 7 seconds with any number of base burns. The preliminary classification is Class 1, Normal Flammability; or

(F) There are two or more burn times with an average burn time of 4 through 7 seconds (both inclusive) with no more than one base burn. The preliminary classification is Class 1, Normal Flammability; or

(G) There are two or more burn times with an average burn time less than 4 seconds with no more than one base burn. The preliminary classification is Class 1, Normal Flammability; or

(H) There are two or more burn times with an average burn time of 4 through 7 seconds (both inclusive) with two or more base burns. The preliminary classification is Class 2, Intermediate Flammability.

(iv) Test five additional specimens when the tests of the initial five specimens result in either of the following: There is only one burn time and it is less than 4 seconds with a base burn; or the average of two or more burn times is less than 4 seconds with two or more base burns. Test these five additional specimens from the most flammable area. The burn times and visual observations for the 10 specimens will determine whether to:

(A) Stop testing and assign the final classification only if the average burn time for the 10 specimens is less than 4 seconds with three or more base burns. The final classification is Class 3, Rapid and Intense Burning; or

(B) Assign the preliminary classification and continue on to § 1610.6(b) when:

(*1*) The average burn time is less than 4 seconds with no more than two base burns. The preliminary classification is Class 1, Normal Flammability; or

(*2*) The average burn time is 4–7 seconds (both inclusive) with no more than 2 base burns. The preliminary classification is Class 1, Normal Flammability, or

(*3*) The average burn time is greater than 7 seconds. The preliminary classification is Class 1, Normal Flammability; or

(*4*) The average burn time is 4 through 7 seconds (both inclusive) with three or more base burns. The preliminary classification is Class 2, Intermediate Flammability, or

(v) If there is only one burn time out of the 10 specimens, the test is inconclusive. The fabric cannot be classified.

(4) Step 2, Raised Surface Textile Fabric After Refurbishing in accordance with § 1610.6(b).

(i) Determine the area to be most flammable in accordance with § 1610.6(a)(3)(i).

(ii) Prepare and test five specimens from the most flammable area. Burn times and visual observations determine whether to stop testing and determine the preliminary classification or to test five additional specimens.

(iii) Stop testing and assign the preliminary classification when:

(A) There are no burn times. The preliminary classification is Class 1, Normal Flammability; or

(B) There is only one burn time, and it is less than 4 seconds without a base burn; or it is 4 seconds or greater with or without a base burn. The preliminary classification is Class 1, Normal Flammability; or

(C) There are no base burns regardless of the burn time(s). The preliminary classification is Class 1, Normal Flammability; or

(D) There are two or more burn times with an average burn time of 0 to 7 seconds with a surface flash only. The preliminary classification is Class 1, Normal Flammability; or

(E) There are two or more burn times with an average burn time greater than 7 seconds with any number of base burns. The preliminary classification is Class 1, Normal Flammability; or

(F) There are two or more burn times with an average burn time of 4 through 7 seconds (both inclusive) with no more than one base burn. The preliminary classification is Class 1, Normal Flammability; or

(G) There are two or more burn times with an average burn time less than 4 seconds with no more than one base burn. The preliminary classification is Class 1, Normal Flammability; or

(H) There are two or more burn times with an average burn time of 4 through 7 seconds (both inclusive) with two or more base burns. The preliminary classification is Class 2, Intermediate Flammability.

(iv) Test five additional specimens when the tests of the initial five specimens result in either of the following: There is only one burn time, and it is less than 4 seconds with a base burn; or the average of two or more burn times is less than 4 seconds with two or more base burns.

(v) If required, test five additional specimens from the most flammable area. The burn times and visual observations for the 10 specimens determine the preliminary classification when:

(A) The average burn time is less than 4 seconds with no more than two base burns. The preliminary classification is Class 1, Normal Flammability; or

(B) The average burn time is less than 4 seconds with three or more base burns. The preliminary and final classification is Class 3, Rapid and Intense Burning; or

(C) The average burn time is greater than 7 seconds. The preliminary classification is Class 1, Normal Flammability; or

(D) The average burn time is 4–7 seconds (both inclusive), with no more than two base burns. The preliminary classification is Class 1, Normal Flammability; or

(E) The average burn time is 4–7 seconds (both inclusive), with three or more base burns. The preliminary classification is Class 2, Intermediate Flammability; or

(vi) If there is only one burn time out of the 10 specimens, the test is inconclusive. The fabric cannot be classified.

§ 1610.8 Reporting results.

(a) The reported result shall be the classification before or after refurbishing, whichever is the more severe; and based on this result, the textile shall be placed in the proper final classification as described in § 1610.4.

(b) *Test result codes.* The following are the definitions for the test result codes, which shall be used for recording flammability results for each specimen that is burned.

(1) For Plain Surface Textile Fabrics:

DNI Did not ignite.

IBE Ignited, but extinguished.

__.__ sec. Actual burn time measured and recorded by the timing device.

(2) For Raised Surface Textile Fabrics:

SF uc Surface flash, under the stop thread, but does not break the stop thread.

SF pw Surface flash, part way. No time shown because the surface flash did not reach the stop thread.

SF poi Surface flash, at the point of impingement only (equivalent to "did not ignite" for plain surfaces).

__.__ sec. Actual burn time measured by the timing device in 0.0 seconds.

__.__ SF only Time in seconds, surface flash only. No damage to the base fabric.

__.__ SFBB Time in seconds, surface flash base burn starting at places other than the point of impingement as a result of surface flash.

__.__ SFBB poi Time in seconds, surface flash base burn starting at the point of impingement.

__.__ SFBB poi* Time in seconds, surface flash base burn possibly starting at the point of impingement. The asterisk is accompanied by the following statement: "Unable to make absolute determination as to source of base burns." This statement is added to the result of any specimen if there is a question as to origin of the base burn.

Subpart B—Rules and Regulations

§ 1610.31 Definitions.

In addition to the definitions provided in section 2 of the Flammable Fabrics Act as amended (15 U.S.C. 1191), and in § 1610.2 of the Standard, the following definitions apply for this subpart.

(a) *Act* means the "Flammable Fabrics Act" (approved June 30, 1953, Pub. Law 88, 83d Congress, 1st sess., 15 U.S.C. 1191; 67 Stat. 111) as amended, 68 Stat. 770, August 23, 1954.

(b) *Rule, rules, regulations, and rules and regulations,* mean the rules and regulations prescribed by the Commission pursuant to section 5(c) of the act.

(c) *United States* means, the several States, the District of Columbia, the Commonwealth of Puerto Rico and the Territories, and Possessions of the United States.

(d) *Marketing or handling* means the transactions referred to in section 3 of the Flammable Fabrics Act, as amended in 1967.

(e) *Test* means the application of the relevant test method prescribed in the procedures provided under section 4(a) of the Act (16 CFR Part 1609).

(f) *Finish type* means a particular finish, but does not include such variables as changes in color, pattern, print, or design, or minor variations in the amount or type of ingredients in the finish formulation. Examples of finish types would be starch finishes, resin finishes or parchmentized finishes.

(g) *Uncovered or exposed part* means that part of an article of wearing apparel that might during normal wear be open to flame or other means of ignition. The outer surface of an undergarment is considered to be an uncovered or exposed part of an article of wearing apparel, and thus subject to the Act. Other examples of exposed parts of an article of wearing apparel subject to the Act include, but are not limited to:

(1) Linings, with exposed areas, such as full front zippered jackets;

(2) Sweatshirts with exposed raised fiber surface inside and capable of being worn napped side out;

(3) Unlined hoods;

(4) Rolled cuffs.

(h) *Coated fabrics* means a flexible material composed of a fabric and any adherent polymeric material applied to one or both surfaces.

§ 1610.32 General requirements.

No article of wearing apparel or fabric subject to the Act and regulations shall be marketed or handled if such article or fabric, when tested according to the procedures prescribed in section 4(a) of the Act (16 CFR 1609), is so highly flammable as to be dangerous when worn by individuals.

§ 1610.33 Test procedures for textile fabrics and film.

(a)(1) All textile fabrics (except those with a nitro-cellulose fiber, finish or coating) intended or sold for use in wearing apparel, and all such fabrics contained in articles of wearing apparel, shall be subject to the requirements of the Act, and shall be deemed to be so highly flammable as to be dangerous when worn by individuals if such fabrics or any uncovered or exposed part of such articles of wearing apparel exhibits rapid and intense burning when tested under the conditions and in the manner prescribed in subpart A of this part 1610.

(2) Notwithstanding the provisions of paragraph (a)(1) of this section, coated fabrics, except those with a nitro-cellulose coating, may be tested under the procedures outlined in part 1611, Standard for the Flammability of Vinyl Plastic Film, and if such coated fabrics do not exhibit a rate of burning in excess of that specified in § 1611.3 they shall not be deemed to be so highly flammable as to be dangerous when worn by individuals.

(b) All film, and textile fabrics with a nitro-cellulose fiber, finish or coating intended or sold for use in wearing apparel, and all film and such textile fabrics referred to in this rule which are contained in articles of wearing apparel, shall be subject to the requirements of the Act, and shall be deemed to be so highly flammable as to be dangerous when worn by individuals if such film or such textile fabrics or any uncovered or exposed part of such articles of wearing apparel exhibit a rate of burning in excess of that specified in part 1611, Standard for the Flammability of Vinyl Plastic Film.

§ 1610.34 Only uncovered or exposed parts of wearing apparel to be tested.

(a) In determining whether an article of wearing apparel is so highly flammable as to be dangerous when worn by individuals, only the uncovered or exposed part of such article of wearing apparel shall be tested according to the applicable procedures set forth in § 1610.6.

(b) If the outer layer of plastic film or plastic-coated fabric of a multilayer fabric separates readily from the other layers, the outer layer shall be tested under part 1611—Standard for the Flammability of Vinyl Plastic Film. If the outer layer adheres to all or a portion of one or more layers of the underlaying fabric, the multi-layered fabric may be tested under either part 1610—Standard for the Flammability of Clothing Textiles or part 1611. However, if the conditioning procedures required by § 1610.6(a)(2)(iv) and § 1610.6(a)(3)(v) would damage or alter the physical characteristics of the film or coating, the uncovered or exposed layer shall be tested in accordance with part 1611.

(c) Plastic film or plastic-coated fabric used, or intended for use as the outer layer of disposable diapers is exempt from the requirements of the Standard, provided that a sample taken from a full thickness of the assembled article passes the test in the Standard (part 1610 or part 1611) otherwise applicable to the outer fabric or film when the flame is applied to the exposed or uncovered surface. See § 1610.36(f) and § 1611.36(f).

§ 1610.35 Procedures for testing special types of textile fabrics under the standard.

(a) *Fabric not customarily washed or dry cleaned.* (1) Except as provided in paragraph (a)(2) of this section, any textile fabric or article of wearing apparel which, in its normal and customary use as wearing apparel would not be dry cleaned or washed, need not be dry cleaned or washed as prescribed in § 1610.6(b) when tested under the Standard if such fabric or article of wearing apparel, when marketed or handled, is marked in a clear and legible manner with the statement: "Fabric may be dangerously flammable if dry cleaned or washed." An example of the type of fabric referred to in this paragraph is bridal illusion.

(2) Section 1610.3, which requires that all textiles shall be refurbished before testing, shall not apply to disposable fabrics and garments. Additionally, such disposable fabrics and garments shall not be subject to the labeling requirements set forth in paragraph (a)(1) of this section.

(b) A coated fabric need not, upon test under the procedures outlined in subpart A of part 1610, be dry cleaned as set forth in § 1610.6(b)(1)(i).

(c) In determining whether a textile fabric having a raised-fiber surface, which surface is to be used in the covered or unexposed parts of articles of wearing apparel, is so highly flammable as to be dangerous when worn by individuals, only the opposite surface or surface intended to be exposed need be tested under the applicable procedures set forth in § 1610.6, providing an invoice or other paper covering the marketing or handling of such fabric is given which clearly designates that the raised-fiber surface is to be used only in the covered or unexposed parts of articles of wearing apparel.

§ 1610.36 Application of Act to particular types of products.

(a) *Interlinings.* Fabrics intended or sold for processing into interlinings or other covered or unexposed parts of articles of wearing apparel shall not be subject to the provisions of section 3 of the Act: *Provided*, that an invoice or other paper covering the marketing or handling of such fabrics is given which specifically designates their intended end use: *And provided further*, that with respect to fabrics which under the provisions of section 4 of the Act, as amended, are so highly flammable as to be dangerous when worn by individuals, any person marketing or handling such fabrics maintains records which show the acquisition, disposition and intended end use of such fabrics, and any person manufacturing articles of wearing apparel containing such fabrics maintains records which show the acquisition, and use and disposition of such fabrics. Any person who fails to maintain such records or to furnish such invoice or other paper shall be deemed to have engaged in the marketing or handling of such products for purposes subject to the requirements of the Act and such person and the products shall be subject to the provisions of sections 3, 6, 7, and 9 of the Act.

(b) *Hats, gloves, and footwear.* Fabrics intended or sold for use in those hats, gloves, and footwear which are excluded under the definition of articles of wearing apparel in section 2(d) of the Act shall not be subject to the provisions of section 3 of the Act: *Provided*, that an invoice or other paper covering the marketing or handling of such fabrics is given which specifically designates their intended use in such products: *And provided further*, that with respect to fabrics which under the provisions of section 4 of the Act, as amended, are so highly flammable as to be dangerous when worn by individuals, any person marketing or handling such fabrics maintains records which show the acquisition, disposition, and intended end use of such fabrics, and any person manufacturing hats, gloves, or footwear containing such fabrics maintains records which show the acquisition, end use and disposition of such fabrics. Any person who fails to maintain such records or to furnish such invoice or other paper shall be deemed to have engaged in the marketing or handling of such products for purposes subject to the requirements of the Act and such person and the products shall be subject to the provisions of sections 3, 6, 7, and 9 of the Act.

(c) *Veils and hats.* (1) Ornamental millinery veils or veilings when used as a part of, in conjunction with, or as a hat, are not to be considered such a "covering for the neck, face, or shoulders" as would, under the first proviso of section 2(d) of the Act, cause the hat to be included within the definition of the term "article of wearing apparel" where such ornamental millinery veils or veilings do not extend more than nine (9) inches from the tip of the crown of the hat to which they are attached and do not extend more than two (2) inches beyond the edge of the brim of the hat.

(2) Where hats are composed entirely of ornamental millinery veils or veilings such hats will not be considered as subject to the Act if the veils or veilings from which they are manufactured were not more than nine (9) inches in width and do not extend more than nine (9) inches from the tip of the crown of the completed hat.

(d) *Handkerchiefs.* (1) Except as provided in paragraph (d)(2) of this section, handkerchiefs not exceeding a finished size of twenty-four (24) inches on any side or not exceeding five hundred seventy-six (576) square inches in area are not deemed "articles of wearing apparel" as that term is used in the Act.

(2) Handkerchiefs or other articles affixed to, incorporated in, or sold as a part of articles of wearing apparel as decoration, trimming, or for any other purpose, are considered an integral part of such articles of wearing apparel, and the articles of wearing apparel and all parts thereof are subject to the provisions of the Act. Handkerchiefs or other articles intended or sold to be affixed to, incorporated in or sold as a part of articles of wearing apparel as aforesaid constitute "fabric" as that term is defined in section 2(e) of the Act and are subject to the provisions of the Act, such handkerchiefs or other articles constitute textile fabrics as the term "textile fabric" is defined in § 1610.2(r).

(3) If, because of construction, design, color, type of fabric, or any other factor, a piece of cloth of a finished type or any other product of a finished type appears to be likely to be used as a covering for the head, neck, face, shoulders, or any part thereof, or otherwise appears likely to be used as an article of clothing, garment, such product is not a handkerchief and constitutes an article of wearing apparel as defined in and subject to the provisions of the Act, irrespective of its size, or its description or designation as a handkerchief or any other term.

(e) *Raised-fiber surface wearing apparel.* Where an article of wearing apparel has a raised-fiber surface which is intended for use as a covered or unexposed part of the article of wearing apparel but the article of wearing apparel is, because of its design and construction, capable of being worn with the raised-fiber surface exposed, such raised-fiber surface shall be considered to be an uncovered or exposed part of the article of wearing apparel. Examples of the type of products referred to in this paragraph are athletic shirts or so-called "sweat shirts" with a raised-fiber inner side.

(f) *Multilayer fabric and wearing apparel with a film or coating on the uncovered or exposed surface.* Plastic film or plastic-coated fabric used, or intended for use, as the outer layer of disposable diapers is exempt from the requirements of the standard, provided that a full thickness of the assembled article passes the test in the Standard otherwise applicable to the outer fabric or film when the flame is applied to the exposed or uncovered surface.

§ 1610.37 Reasonable and representative tests to support guaranties.

(a) *Purpose.* The purpose of this § 1610.37 is to establish requirements for reasonable and representative tests to support initial guaranties of products, fabrics, and related materials which are subject to the Standard for the Flammability of Clothing Textiles (the Standard, 16 CFR part 1610).

(b) *Statutory provisions.* (1) Section 8(a) of the Act (15 U.S.C. 1197(a)) provides that no person shall be subject to criminal prosecution under section 7 of the Act (15 U.S.C. 1196) for a violation of section 3 of the Act (15 U.S.C. 1192) if such person establishes a guaranty received in good faith to the effect that the product, fabric, or related material complies with the applicable flammability standard. A guaranty does not provide the holder any defense to an administrative action for an order to cease and desist from violation of the applicable standard, the Act, and the Federal Trade Commission Act (15 U.S.C. 45), nor to any civil action for injunction or seizure brought under section 6 of the Act (15 U.S.C. 1195).

(2) Section 8 of the Act provides for two types of guaranties:

(i) An initial guaranty based on "reasonable and representative tests" made in accordance with the applicable standard issued under the Act; and

(ii) A guaranty based on a previous guaranty, received in good faith, to the effect that reasonable and representative tests show conformance with the applicable standard.

(c) *Requirements.* (1) Each person or firm issuing an initial guaranty of a product, fabric, or related material subject to the Standard shall devise and implement a program of reasonable and representative tests to support such a guaranty.

(2) The term program of reasonable and representative tests as used in this § 1610.37 means at least one test with results demonstrating conformance

with the Standard for the product, fabric or related material which is the subject of an initial guaranty. The program of reasonable and representative tests required by this § 1610.37 may include tests performed before the effective date of this section, and may include tests performed by persons or firms outside of the territories of the United States or other than the one issuing the initial guaranty. The number of tests and the frequency of testing shall be left to the discretion of the person or firm issuing the initial guaranty.

(3) In the case of an initial guaranty of a fabric or related material, a program of reasonable and representative tests may consist of one or more tests of the particular fabric or related material which is the subject of the guaranty, or of a fabric or related material of the same "class" of fabrics or related materials as the one which is the subject of the guaranty. For purposes of this § 1610.37, the term class means a category of fabrics or related materials having general constructional or finished characteristics, sometimes in association with a particular fiber, and covered by a class or type description generally recognized in the trade.

§ 1610.38 Maintenance of records by those furnishing guaranties.

(a) Any person or firm issuing an initial guaranty of a product, fabric, or related material which is subject to the Standard for the Flammability of Clothing Textiles (the Standard, 16 CFR part 1610) shall keep and maintain a record of the test or tests relied upon to support that guaranty. The records to be maintained shall show:

(1) The style or range number, fiber composition, construction and finish type of each textile fabric or related material covered by an initial guaranty; or the identification, fiber composition, construction and finish type of each textile fabric (including those with a nitrocellulose fiber, finish or coating), and of each related material, used or contained in a product of wearing apparel covered by an initial guaranty.

(2) The results of the actual test or tests made of the textile fabric or related material covered by an initial guaranty; or of any fabric or related material used in the product of wearing apparel covered by an initial guaranty.

(3) When the person or firm issuing an initial guaranty has conducted the test or tests relied upon to support that guaranty, that person or firm shall also include with the information required by paragraphs (a) (1) and (2) of this section, a sample of each fabric or related material which has been tested.

(b) Persons furnishing guaranties based upon class tests shall maintain records showing:

(1) Identification of the class test.

(2) Fiber composition, construction and finish type of the fabrics, or the fabrics used or contained in articles of wearing apparel so guaranteed.

(3) A swatch of each class of fabrics guaranteed.

(c) Persons furnishing guaranties based upon guaranties received by them shall maintain records showing the guaranty received and identification of the fabrics or fabrics contained in articles of wearing apparel guaranteed in turn by them.

(d) The records referred to in this section shall be preserved for a period of 3 years from the date the tests were performed, or in the case of paragraph (c) of this section from the date the guaranties were furnished.

(e) Any person furnishing a guaranty under section 8(a) of the Act who neglects or refuses to maintain and preserve the records prescribed in this section shall be deemed to have furnished a false guaranty under the provisions of section 8(b) of the Act.

§ 1610.39 Shipments under section 11(c) of the Act.

(a) The invoice or other paper relating to the shipment or delivery for shipment in commerce of articles of wearing apparel or textile fabrics for the purpose of finishing or processing to render them not so highly flammable as to be dangerous when worn by individuals, shall contain a statement disclosing such purpose.

(b) An article of wearing apparel or textile fabric shall not be deemed to fall within the provisions of section 11(c) of the Act as being shipped or delivered for shipment in commerce for the purpose of finishing or processing to render such article of wearing apparel or textile fabric not so highly flammable under section 4 of the Act, as to be dangerous when worn by individuals, unless the shipment or delivery for shipment in commerce of such article of wearing apparel or textile fabric is made directly to the person engaged in the business of processing or finishing textile products for the prearranged purpose of having such article of apparel or textile fabric processed or finished to render it not so highly flammable under section 4 of the Act, as to be dangerous when worn by individuals, and any person shipping or delivering for shipment the article of wearing apparel or fabric in commerce for such purpose maintains records which establish that the textile fabric or article of wearing apparel has been shipped for appropriate flammability treatment, and that such treatment has been completed, as well as records to show the disposition of such textile fabric or article of wearing apparel subsequent to the completion of such treatment.

(c) The importation of textile fabrics or articles of wearing apparel may be considered as incidental to a transaction involving shipment or delivery for shipment for the purpose of rendering such textile fabrics or articles of wearing apparel not so highly flammable under the provisions of section 4 of the Act, as to be dangerous when worn by individuals, if:

(1) The importer maintains records which establish that: (i) The imported textile fabrics or articles of wearing apparel have been shipped for appropriate flammability treatment, and

(ii) Such treatment has been completed, as well as records to show the disposition of such textile fabrics or articles of wearing apparel subsequent to the completion of such treatment.

(2) The importer, at the time of importation, executes and furnishes to the U.S. Customs and Border Protection an affidavit stating: These fabrics (or articles of wearing apparel) are dangerously flammable under the provisions of section 4 of the Act, and will not be sold or used in their present condition but will be processed or finished by the undersigned or by a duly authorized agent so as to render them not so highly flammable under the provisions of section 4 of the Flammable Fabrics Act, as to be dangerously flammable when worn by individuals. The importer agrees to maintain the records required by 16 CFR 1610.39(c)(1).

(3) The importer, if requested to do so by the U.S. Customs and Border Protection, furnishes an adequate specific-performance bond conditioned upon the complete discharge of the obligations assumed in paragraphs (c)(1) and (2) of this section.

(d) The purpose of section 11(c) of the Act is only to permit articles of wearing apparel or textile fabrics which are dangerously flammable to be shipped or delivered for shipment in commerce for the purpose of treatment or processing to render them not dangerously flammable. Section 11(c)of the Act does not in any other respect limit the force and effect of sections 3, 6, 7, and 9 of the Act. In particular, section 11(c) of the Act does not authorize the sale or offering for sale of any article of wearing apparel or textile fabric which is in fact dangerously flammable at the time of sale or offering for sale, even though the seller intends to ship the article for treatment prior to delivery to the purchaser or has already done so. Moreover, under section 3 of the Act a person is liable for a subsequent sale or offering for sale if, despite the purported completion of treatment to render it not dangerously flammable, the article in fact remains dangerously flammable.

§ 1610.40 Use of alternate apparatus, procedures, or criteria for tests for guaranty purposes.

(a) Section 8(a) of the Act provides that no person shall be subject to criminal prosecution under section 7 of the Act (15 U.S.C. 1196) for a violation of section 3 of the Act (15 U.S.C. 1192) if that person establishes a guaranty received in good faith which meets all requirements set forth in section 8 the Act. One of those requirements is that the guaranty must be based upon "reasonable and representative tests" in accordance with the applicable standard.

(b) Subpart A of this part 1610 prescribes apparatus and procedures for testing fabrics and garments subject to its provisions. See §§ 1610.5 & 1610.6. Subpart A prescribes criteria for classifying the flammability of fabrics and garments subject to its provisions as "Normal flammability, Class 1," "Intermediate flammability, Class 2," and "Rapid and Intense Burning, Class 3." See § 1610.4. Sections 3 and 4 of the Act prohibit the manufacture for sale, importation into the United States, or introduction in commerce of any fabric or article of wearing apparel subject to the Standard which exhibits "rapid and intense burning" when tested in accordance with the Standard. See 16 CFR part 1609.

(c) The Commission recognizes that for purposes of supporting guaranties, "reasonable and representative tests" could be either the test in Subpart A of this part, or alternate tests which utilize apparatus or procedures other than those in Subpart A of this part. This § 1610.40 sets forth conditions under which the Commission will allow use of alternate tests with apparatus or procedures other than those in Subpart A of this part to serve as the basis for guaranties.

(d)(1) Persons and firms issuing guaranties that fabrics or garments subject to the Standard meet its requirements may base those guaranties on any alternate test utilizing apparatus or procedures other than those in Subpart A of this part, if such alternate test is as stringent as, or more stringent than, the test in Subpart A of this part. The Commission considers an alternate test to be "as stringent as, or more stringent than" the test in Subpart A of this part if, when testing identical specimens, the alternate test yields failing results as often as, or more often than, the test in Subpart A of this part. Any person using such an alternate test must have data or information to demonstrate that the alternate test is as stringent as, or more stringent than, the test in Subpart A of this part.

(2) The data or information required by this paragraph (d) of this section to demonstrate equivalent or greater stringency of any alternate test using apparatus or procedures other than those in Subpart A of this part must be in the possession of the person or firm desiring to use such alternate test before the alternate test may be used to support guaranties of items subject to the Standard.

(3) The data or information required by paragraph (d) of this section to demonstrate equivalent or greater stringency of any alternate test using apparatus or procedures other than those in Subpart A of this part must be retained for as long as that alternate test is used to support guaranties of items subject to the Standard, and for one year thereafter.

(e) Specific approval from the Commission in advance of the use of any alternate test using apparatus or procedures other than those in Subpart A is not required. The Commission will not approve or disapprove any specific alternate test utilizing apparatus or procedures other than those in Subpart A of this part.

(f) Use of any alternate test to support guaranties of items subject to the Standard without the information required by this section may result in violation of section 8(b), of the Act (15 U.S.C. 1197(b)), which prohibits the furnishing of a false guaranty.

(g) The Commission will test fabrics and garments subject to the Standard for compliance with the Standard using the apparatus and procedures set forth in Subpart A of this part. The Commission will consider any failing results from compliance testing as evidence that:

(1) The manufacture for sale, importation into the United States, or introduction in commerce of the fabric or garment which yielded failing results was in violation of the Standard and of section 3 of the Act; and

(2) The person or firm using the alternate test as the basis for a guaranty has furnished a false guaranty, in violation of section 8(b) of the Act. (Reporting requirements contained in paragraph (d) were approved by Office of Management and Budget under control number 3041–0024.)

Subpart C—Interpretations and Policies

§ 1610.61 Reasonable and representative testing to assure compliance with the standard for the clothing textiles.

(a) *Background.* (1) The CPSC administers the Flammable Fabrics Act ("the Act"), 15 U.S.C. 1191–1204. Under the Act, among other things, the Commission enforces the Standard for the Flammability of Clothing Textiles ("the Standard"), 16 CFR part 1610. That Standard establishes requirements for the flammability of clothing and textiles intended to be used for clothing (hereinafter "textiles").

(2) The Standard applies both to fabrics and finished garments. The Standard provides methods of testing the flammability of textiles, and sets forth the requirements that textiles must meet to be classified into one of three classes of flammability (classes 1, 2 and 3). § 1610.4. Class 1 textiles, those that exhibit normal flammability, are acceptable for use in clothing. § 1610.4(a)(1) & (2). Class 2 textiles, applicable only to raised-fiber surfaces, are considered to be of intermediate flammability, but may be used in clothing. § 1610.4(b)(1) & (2). Finally, Class 3 textiles, those that exhibit rapid and intense burning, are dangerously flammable and may not be used in clothing. § 1610.4(c)(1) & (2). The manufacture for sale, offering for sale, importation into the U.S., and introduction or delivery for introduction of Class 3 articles of wearing apparel are among the acts prohibited by section 3(a) of the Act, 15 U.S.C. 1192(a).

(3) CPSC currently uses retail surveillance, attends appropriate trade shows, follows up on reports of noncompliance and previous violations, and works with U.S. Customs and Border Protection in an effort to find textiles that violate CPSC's standards. The Commission has a number of enforcement options to address prohibited acts. These include bringing seizure actions in federal district court against violative textiles, seeking an order through an administrative proceeding that a firm cease and desist from selling violative garments, pursuing criminal penalties, or seeking the imposition of civil penalties for "knowing" violations of the Act. Of particular relevance to the latter two remedies is whether reasonable and representative tests were performed demonstrating that a textile or garment meets the flammability standards for general wearing apparel. Persons who willfully violate flammability standards are subject to criminal penalties.

(4) Section 8(a) of the Act, 15 U.S.C. 1197(a), exempts a firm from the imposition of criminal penalties if the firm establishes that a guaranty was received in good faith signed by and containing the name and address of the person who manufactured the guarantied wearing apparel or textiles or from whom the apparel or textiles were received. A guaranty issued by a person who is not a resident of the United States may not be relied upon as a bar to prosecution. 16 CFR 1608.4. The guaranty must be based on the exempted types of fabrics or on reasonable and representative tests showing that the fabric covered by the guaranty or used in the wearing apparel covered by the guaranty is not so highly flammable as to be dangerous when worn by individuals, i.e., is not a Class 3 material. (The person proffering a guaranty to the Commission must also not, by further processing, have affected the flammability of the fabric, related material or product covered by the guaranty that was received.) Under § 1610.37, a person, to issue a guaranty, should first evaluate the type of fabric to determine if it meets testing exemptions in accordance with § 1610.1(d). (Some textiles never exhibit unusual burning characteristics and need not be tested.) § 1610.1(d). Such textiles include plain surface fabrics, regardless of fiber content, weighing 2.6 oz. or more per sq. yd., and plain and raised surface fabrics made of acrylic, modacrylic, nylon, olefin, polyester, wool, or any combination of these fibers, regardless of weight.) If no exemptions apply, the person issuing the guaranty must devise and implement a program of reasonable and representative tests to support the guaranty. The number of tests and frequency of testing is left to the discretion of that person, but at least one test is required.

(5) In determining whether a firm has committed a "knowing" violation of a flammability standard that warrants imposition of a civil penalty, the CPSC considers whether the firm had actual knowledge that its products violated the flammability requirements. The CPSC also considers whether the firm should be presumed to have the knowledge that would be possessed by a reasonable person acting in the circumstances, including knowledge that would have been obtainable upon the exercise of due care to ascertain the truth of representations. 15 U.S.C. 1194(e). The existence of results of flammability testing based on a reasonable and representative program and, in the case of tests performed by another entity (such as a guarantor), the steps, if any, that the firm took to verify the existence and reliability of such tests, bear directly on whether the firm acted reasonably in the circumstances.

(b) *Applicability.* (1) When tested for flammability, a small number of textile products exhibit variability in the test results; that is, even though they may exhibit Class 1 or Class 2 burning characteristics in one test, a third test may result in a Class 3 failure. Violative products that the Commission has discovered between 1994 and 1998 include sheer 100% rayon skirts and scarves; sheer 100% silk scarves; 100% rayon chenille sweaters; rayon/nylon chenille and long hair sweaters; polyester/cotton and 100% cotton fleece/sherpa garments, and 100% cotton terry cloth robes. Between August 1994 and August 1998, there have been 21 recalls of such dangerously flammable clothing, and six retailers have paid civil penalties to settle Commission staff allegations that they knowingly sold garments that violated the general wearing apparel standard.

(2) The violations and resulting recalls and civil penalties demonstrate the critical necessity for manufacturers, distributors, importers, and retailers to evaluate, prior to sale, the flammability of garments made from the materials described above, or to seek appropriate guaranties that assure that the garments comply. Because of the likelihood of variable flammability in the small group of textiles identified above, one test is insufficient to assure reasonably that these products comply with the flammability standards. Rather, a person seeking to evaluate garments made of such materials should assure that the program tests a sufficient number of samples to provide adequate assurance that such textile products comply with the general wearing apparel standard. The number of samples to be tested, and the corresponding degree of confidence that products tested will comply, are to be specified by the individual designing the test program. However, in assessing the reasonableness of a test program, the Commission staff will specifically consider the degree of confidence that the program provides.

(c) *Suggestions.* The following are some suggestions to assist in complying with the Standard:

(1) Purchase fabrics or garments that meet testing exemptions listed in §1610.1(d). (If buyers or other personnel do not have skills to determine if the fabric is exempted, hire a textile consultant or a test lab for an evaluation.)

(2) For fabrics that are not exempt, conduct reasonable and representative testing before cutting and sewing, using standard operating characteristic curves for acceptance sampling to determine a sufficient number of tests.

(3) Purchase fabrics or garments that have been guarantied and/or tested by the supplier using a reasonable and representative test program that uses standard operating characteristic curves for acceptance sampling to determine a sufficient number of tests. Firms should also receive and maintain a copy of the guaranty.

(4) Periodically verify that your suppliers are actually conducting appropriate testing.

FIGURE 1 TO PART 1610—SKETCH OF FLAMMABILITY APPARATUS

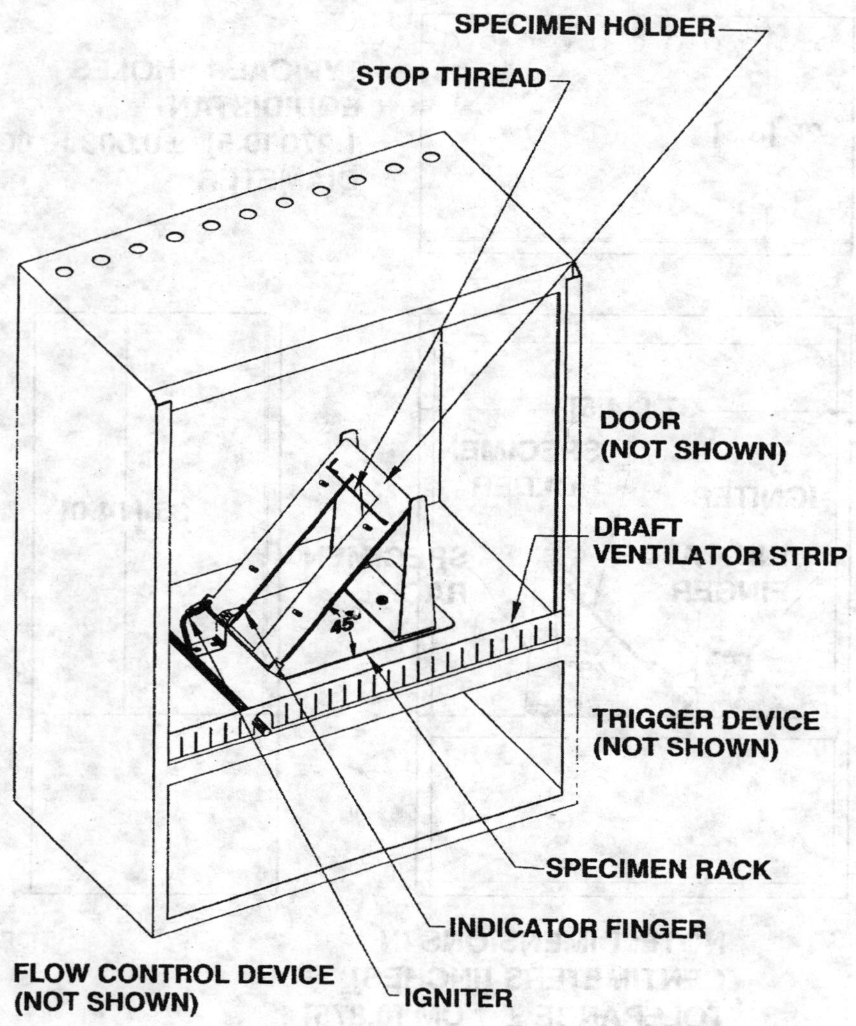

SKETCH OF FLAMMABILITY APPARATUS
FIGURE 1

FIGURE 2 TO PART 1610—FLAMMABILITY APPARATUS VIEWS

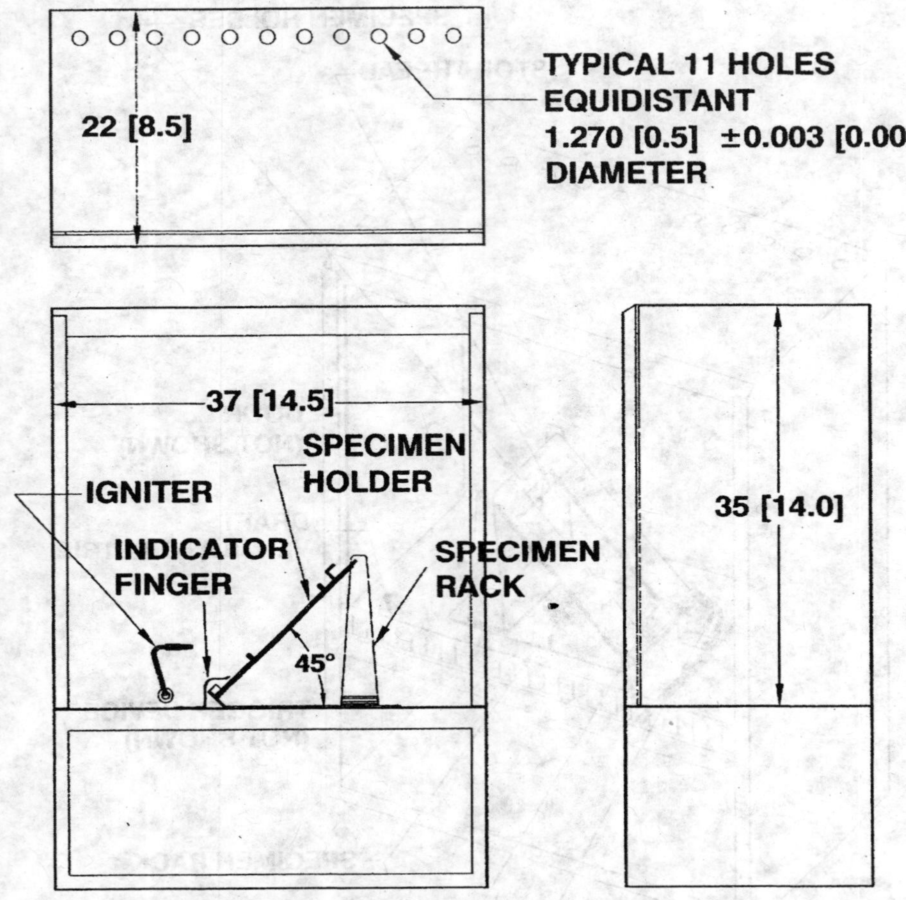

NOTE: DIMENSIONS IN CENTIMETERS [INCHES] TOLERANCE ± 1 CM [0.375] UNLESS OTHERWISE NOTED

FLAMMABILITY APPARATUS VIEWS
FIGURE 2

FIGURE 3 TO PART 1610—SPECIMEN HOLDER SUPPORTED IN SPECIMEN RACK

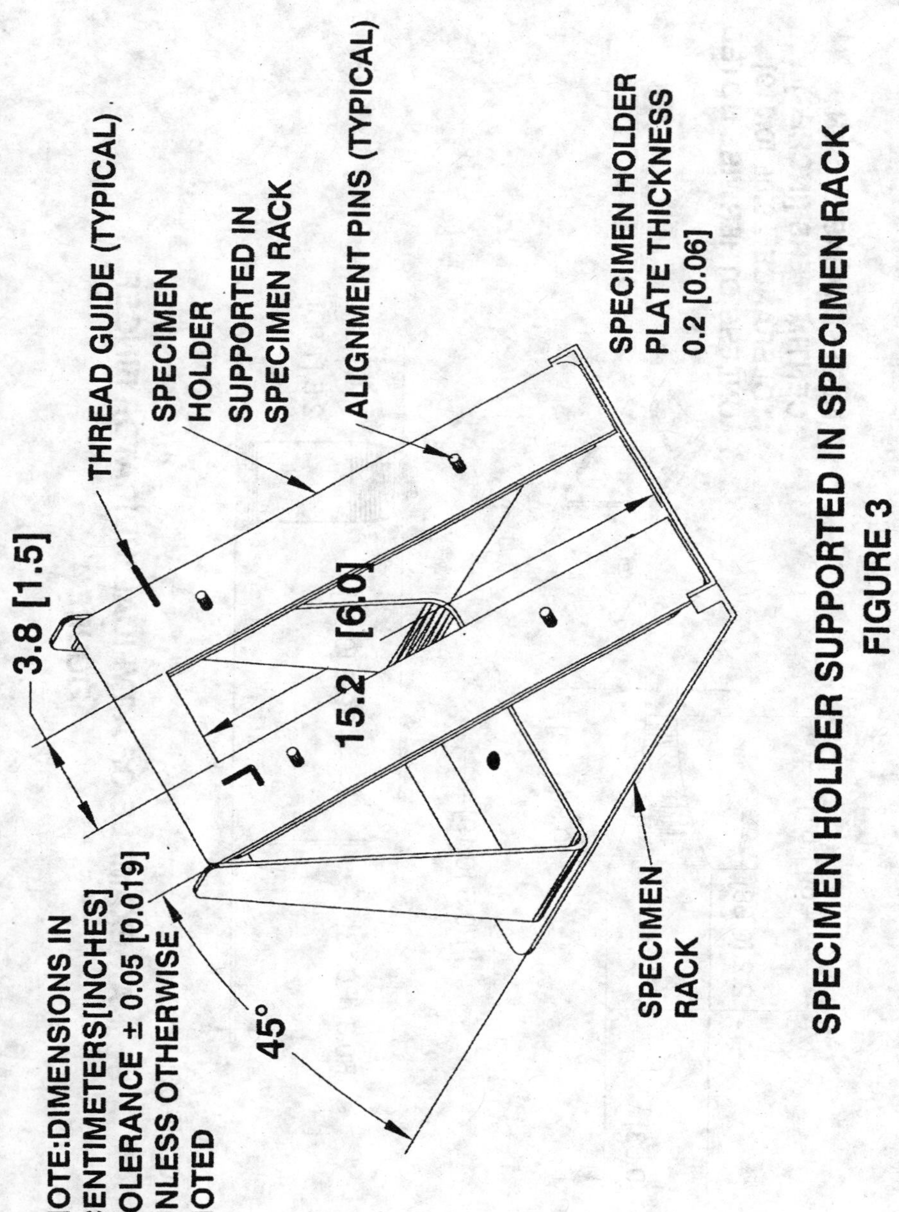

FIGURE 4 TO PART 1610—AN EXAMPLE OF A TYPICAL INDICATOR FINGER

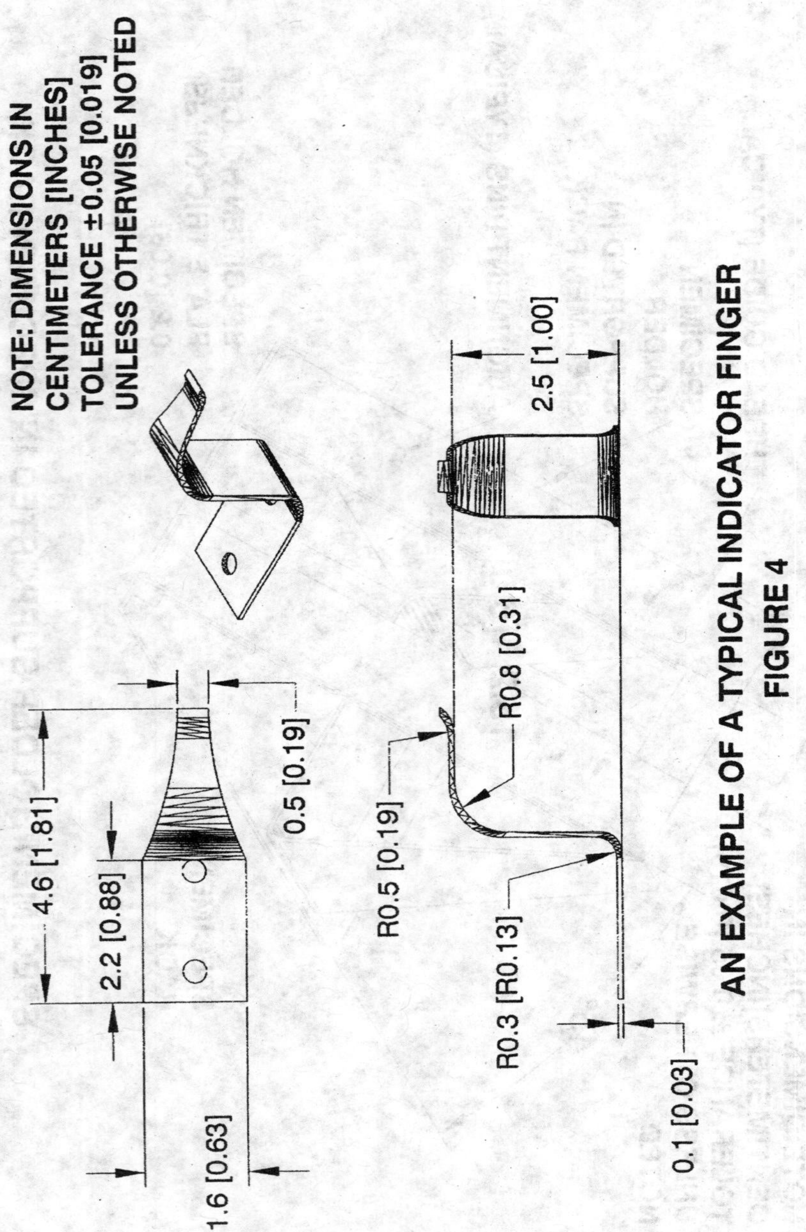

FIGURE 5 TO PART 1610—AN EXAMPLE OF A TYPICAL GAS SHIELD

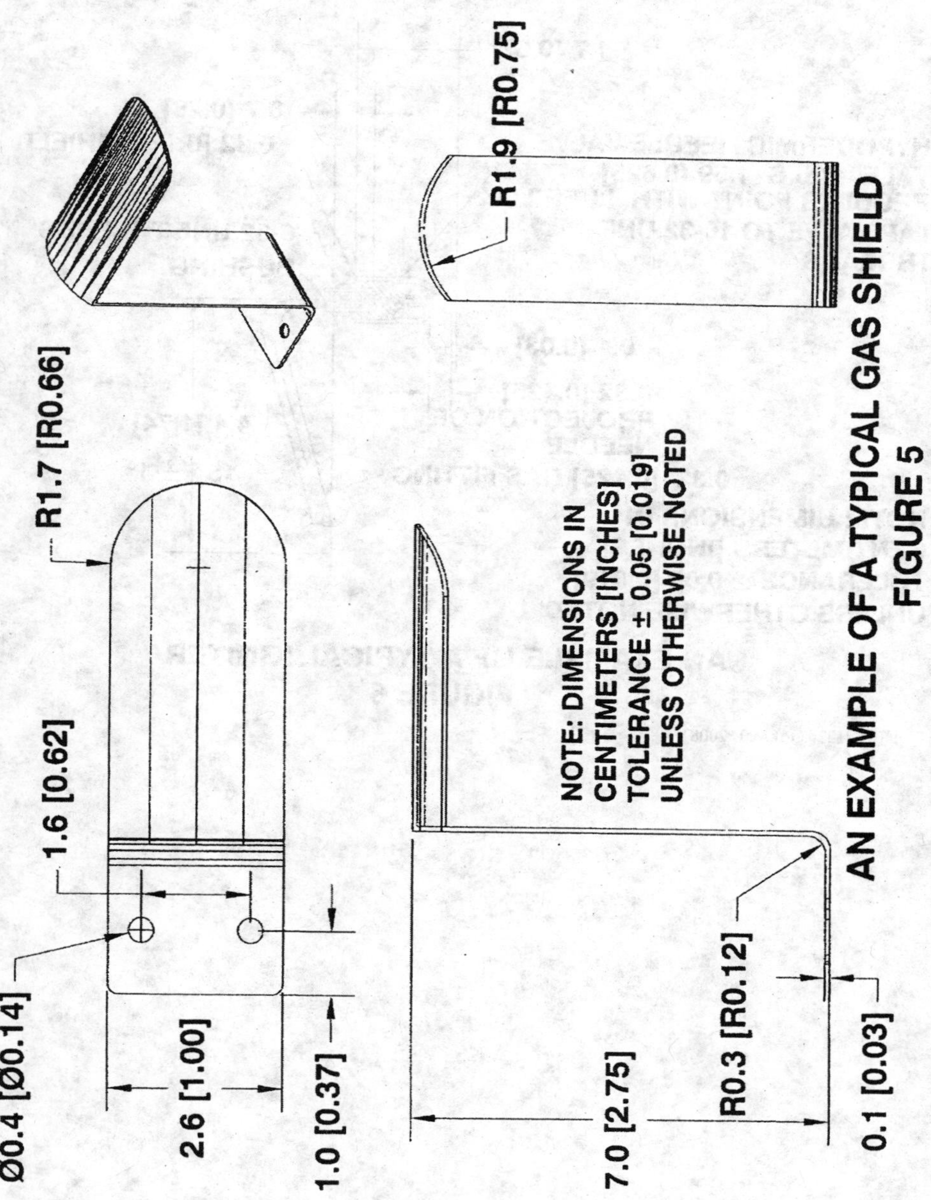

FIGURE 6 TO PART 1610—IGNITER

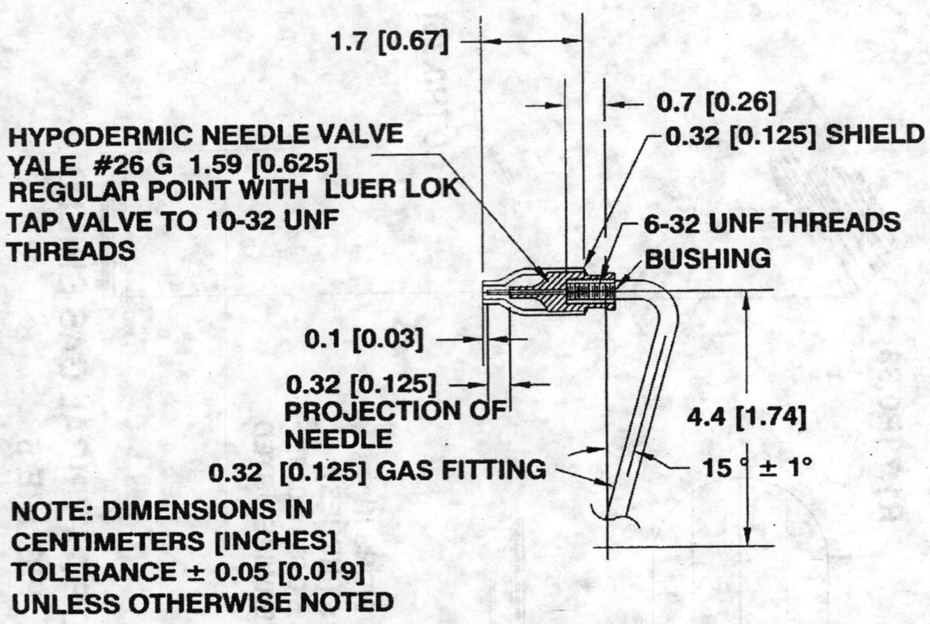

AN EXAMPLE OF A TYPICAL IGNITER
FIGURE 6

[73 FR 62187, Oct. 20, 2008]

FIGURE 7 TO PART 1610—BRUSHING DEVICE

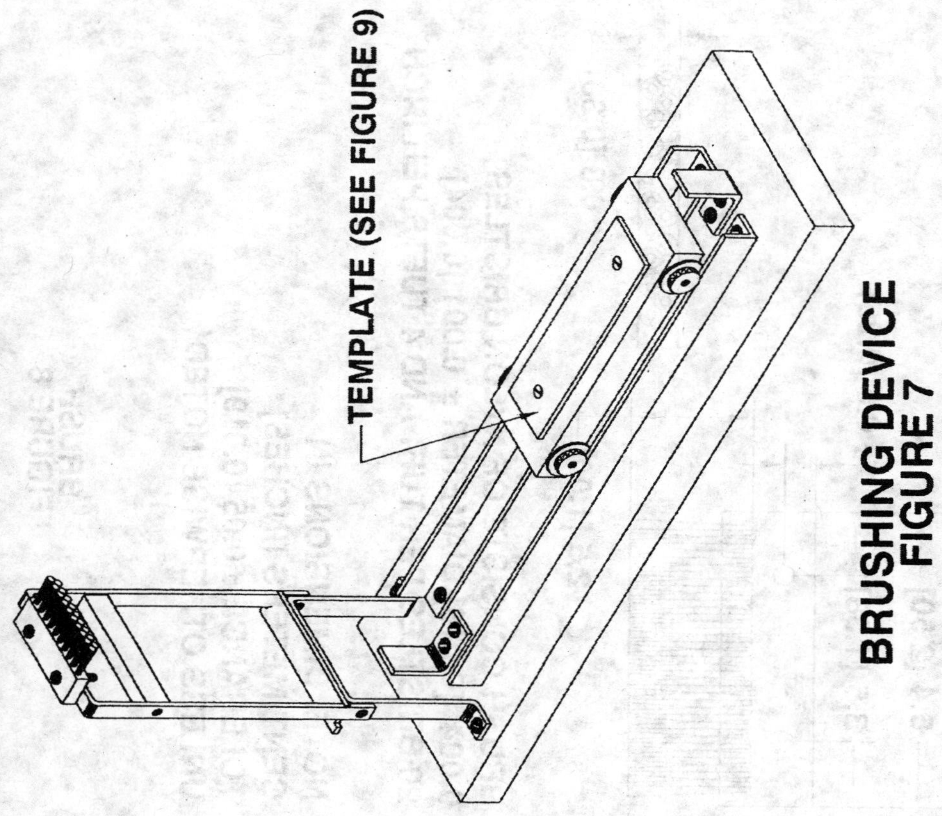

FIGURE 8 TO PART 1610—BRUSH

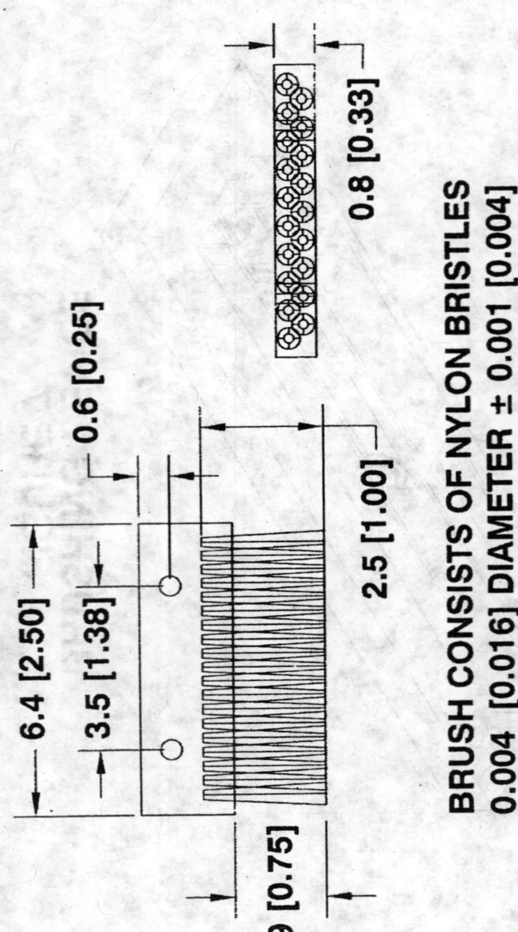

BRUSH CONSISTS OF NYLON BRISTLES
0.004 [0.016] DIAMETER ± 0.001 [0.004]
20 BRISTLES PER TUFT AND 4 TUFTS PER INCH

NOTE: DIMENSIONS IN
CENTIMETERS [INCHES]
TOLERANCE ±0.05 [0.019]
UNLESS OTHERWISE NOTED

BRUSH
FIGURE 8

FIGURE 9 TO PART 1610—BRUSHING DEVICE TEMPLATE

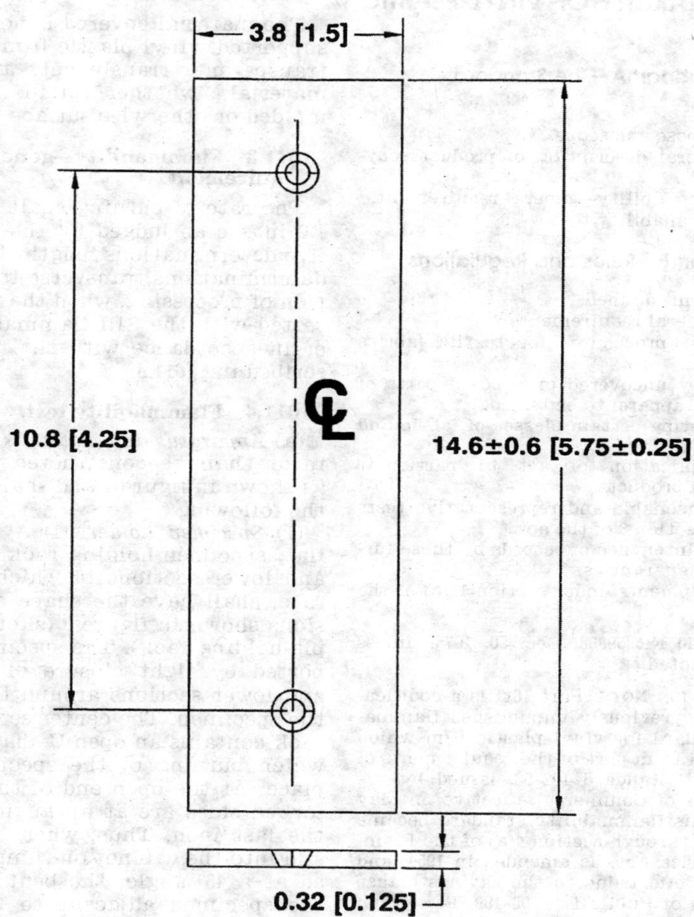

NOTES:

1. TWO HOLES Ø 0.16 [0.0625] COUNTERSINK FOR FLAT HEAD SCREW
2. DIMENSIONS IN CENTIMETERS [INCHES]
3. TOLERANCE ± 0.05 [0.019] UNLESS OTHERWISE NOTED

AN EXAMPLE OF A TYPICAL BRUSHING DEVICE TEMPLATE FIGURE 9

[73 FR 62187, Oct. 20, 2008]

PART 1611—STANDARD FOR THE FLAMMABILITY OF VINYL PLASTIC FILM

Subpart A—The Standard

Subpart B—Rules and Regulations

SOURCE: 40 FR 59898, Dec. 30, 1975, unless otherwise noted.

CODIFICATION NOTE: Part 1611 is a codification of the previously unpublished flammability standard for vinyl plastic film which was derived from part of the requirements of Commercial Standard 192–53, issued by the Department of Commerce, effective on May 22, 1953. This flammability standard became mandatory through section 4(a) of the Flammable Fabrics Act, as amended in 1954, and remains in effect due to the savings clause (section 11) of Public Law 90–189. Paragraph 3.11 of the Commercial Standard, referred to in the 1954 act, has been codified as §1611.3 16 CFR part 1609 containes the text of the Flammable Fabrics Act of 1953, as amended in 1954.

Subpart A—The Standard

AUTHORITY: Sec. 4, Pub. L. 83–88, 67 Stat. 112, as amended, 68 Stat. 770 (15 U.S.C. 1193); sec. 11, Pub. L. 90–189, 81 Stat. 568.

§1611.1 Purpose and scope.

The purpose of this standard is to promulgate a minimum standard for flammability of vinyl plastic film which are subject to the requirements of the Flammable Fabrics Act.

§1611.2 General description of products covered.

The material covered is nonrigid, unsupported, vinyl plastic film, including transparent, translucent, and opaque material, whether plain, embossed, molded or otherwise surface treated.[a]

§1611.3 Flammability—general requirement.

The rate of burning shall not exceed 1.2 in./sec as judged by the average of five determinations lengthwise and five determinations transverse to the direction of processing, when the material is tested with the SPI flammability tester in accordance with the method described in §1611.4.

§1611.4 Flammability test.

(a) *Apparatus and materials.* The apparatus shall be constructed essentially as shown in figure 1 and shall consist of the following:

(1) *Specimen holder.* (i) A removable, flat, specimen-holding rack, the upper and lower sections of which are separate, shall have the shape and dimensions shown in figure 2 (sketch of sample-holding rack). The specimen is supported by tight closure of the upper and lower sections around the sides of the specimen. The center section of the rack contains an open U-shaped area in which burning of the specimen takes place. At the open end of the rack the forked sides are at an angle of 45° for the last inch. Thus, when the rack is slid into the cabinet on runners mounted at a 45° angle, the bent portion of the specimen adjacent to the igniter flame is vertical and the remainder is at 45°.

(ii) The switch actuators consist of suitable springs mounted on the side of

[a] Refer to sections 2 and 4 of the Flammable Fabrics Act of 1953, as amended in 1954, set out at 16 CFR part 1609 for the scope of this standard. The vinyl plastic film covered by Commercial Standard 192–53, as promulgated by the Secretary of Commerce was vinyl plastic film 10 mils and less in thickness (see §1.3 of the voluntary standard). After CS 191–53 and CS 192–53 were made mandatory by section 4 of the act, the Federal Trade Commission clarified the scope of the standards in rules and regulations now found at §§1611.31(i) and 1611.33(b) (formerly 16 CFR 302.1(a)(9) and 302.3(b)).

the rack, one just beyond the curved portion at the open end, and the other at the closed end of the U-shaped holder. The springs are depressed and held in position prior to ignition by means of cotton thread suitably wound across the specimen and securely attached to the rack. As flame reaches these threads, the springs are released, thus activating the microswitches of the stop clocks.

(2) *Igniter flame.* The igniter flame shall be produced at the tip of a No. 22 hypodermic needle jet. The igniter shall be so located in the cabinet that the tip of the needle is 9⁄16 in. from the surface of the specimen when the specimen rack is in place.

(3) *Cabinet.* The cabinet shall protect the igniter flame and specimen from air currents during tests, yet contain a suitable door or window for visual operation, provision for inserting the specimen holder, and adjustable vents to supply sufficient air for combustion of the specimen. It should also be capable of rapid ventilation following a test so that all combustion products can be removed between tests. A hood may be used if its exhaust fan is turned off during the test.

(4) *Timing mechanism.* The burning rate shall be determined by a stop clock through microswitches mounted on the specimenholder rack. The clock is started when the specimen flame burns the first thread, and is stopped when the thread at the upper end of the holder, 6 in. from the first thread, burns apart. The timing mechanism shall be capable of indicating time interval to 0.1 second.

(5) *Butane.* Unless otherwise specified, butane gas shall be used for the igniter flame.

(6) *Thread.* J. & P. Coats heavy-duty white cotton thread.

(7) *Microburner.*

(b) *Test specimens.* (1) Test specimens shall be 3 in. in width and 9 in. in length. They shall be free from folds or wrinkles. Five specimens from each direction (machine and transverse) of a given material shall be tested.

(2) *Conditioning.* The conditioning procedure shall conform to the requirements of procedure B of ASTM D618, Tentative Methods of Conditioning Plastics and Electrical Insulating Materials for Testing.

(c) *Procedure.* (1) After preparing the specimens, the holder shall be threaded so as to depress the switch actuators (springs) at least ¼ in. from the edge of the holder. Each actuator shall be separately threaded, the thread passing down through the J-slots and under the upper jaws so that the thread is adjacent to the specimen when the holder is closed.

(2) The specimen shall be inserted into the holder so that it extends down into the lock springs and is held firmly between the two wires at the open end of the burning channel. These wires insure that the end of the specimen is always the correct distance from the igniter flame. The sample shall be free from wrinkles or distortion when the holder is closed. The specimen should not extend beyond the outer edge of the lower plate, otherwise the rack may not slide freely on the slide channel on introducing it into the cabinet.

(3) Prior to introducing the specimen and holder into the cabinet, both electrical switches shall be set for automatic timing. The needle valve regulating the butane flow shall be adjusted to provide a ½-in. flame. (When the specimen is in place its surface is 9⁄16 in. from the tip of the needle and the flame is just barely flattened against the specimen. This can be checked by using a specimen made of asbestos in place of a plastic specimen.)

(4) With the hood fan off, clocks zeroed, and the flame adjusted as mentioned, the door is closed and the specimen holder is then inserted at a constant rate. The holder should be allowed to slide down the rails by gravity, taking about one-half second to travel the length of the slide. Any hesitation in bringing the specimen holder fully into burning position may cause erroneous ignition results.

(5) The burning time shall be read from the stop clock and the rate of burning calculated. Results that deviate from the mean value of all tests should be rejected if the deviation of the doubtful value is more than five times the average deviation from the mean obtained by excluding the doubtful value. Such doubtful values shall be discarded and retests made.

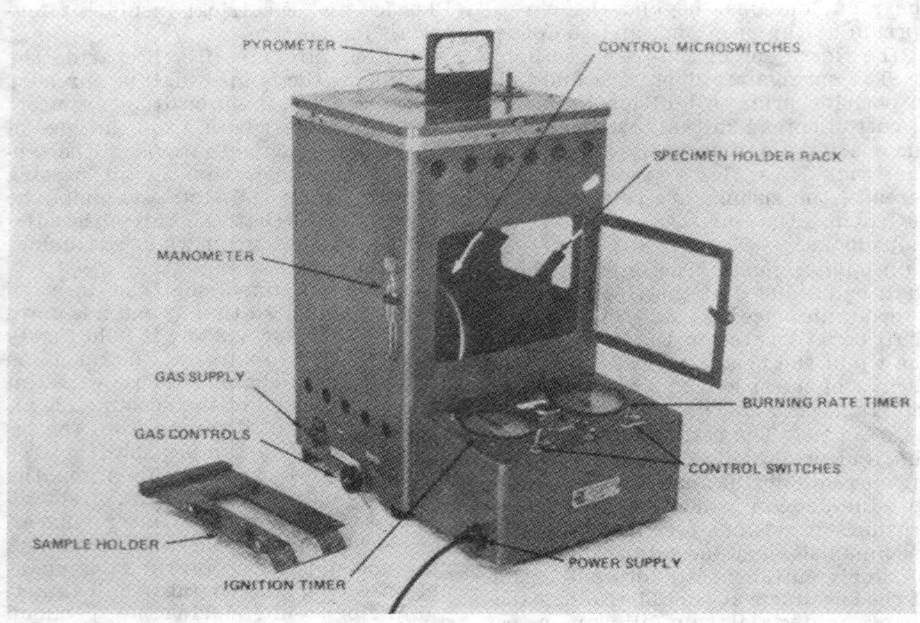

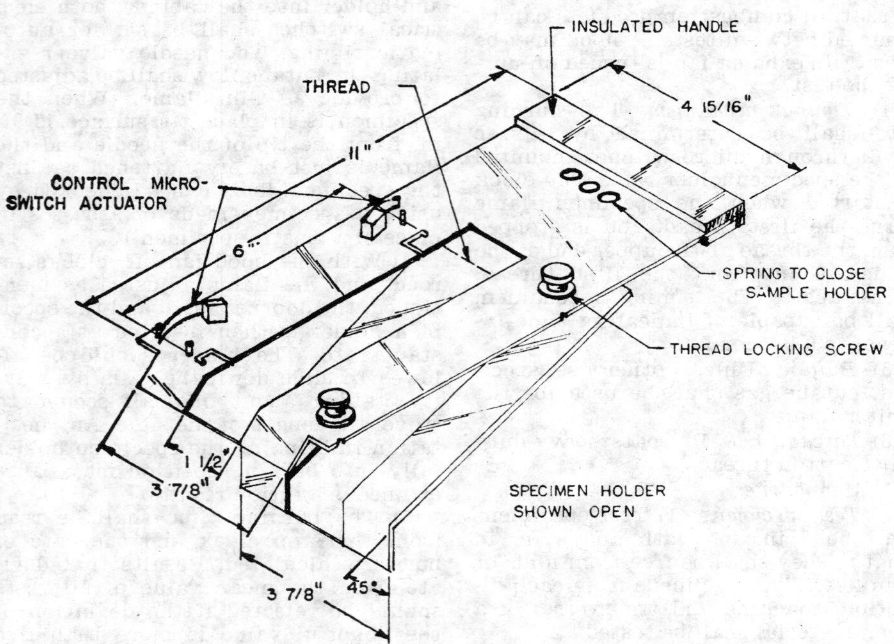

FIGURE 2 —Specimen holder

Subpart B—Rules and Regulations

AUTHORITY: Sec. 5, 15 U.S.C. 1194.

NOTE: An interpretation, with respect to Ornamental Veils or Veilings, issued by the Federal Trade Commission at 32 FR 11850, Aug. 17, 1967, provides as follows:

Ornamental millinery veils or veilings when used as a part of, in conjunction with, or as a hat, are not to be considered such a "covering for the neck, face, or shoulders" as would, under the first proviso of section 2(d) of the Flammable Fabrics Act, cause the hat to be included within the definition of the term "article of wearing apparel" where such ornamental millinery veils or veilings do not extend more than nine (9) inches from the tip of the crown of the hat to which they are attached and do not extend more than two (2) inches beyond the edge of the brim of the hat.

Where hats are composed entirely of ornamental millinery veils or veilings such hats will not be considered as subject to the Flammable Fabrics Act if the veils or veilings from which they are manufactured were not more than nine (9) inches in width and do not extend more than nine (9) inches from the tip of the crown of the completed hat.

§ 1611.31 Terms defined.

As used in this part, unless the context otherwise specifically requires:

(a) The term *act* means the "Flammable Fabrics Act" (approved June 30, 1953, Pub. Law 88, 83d Congress, 1st sess., 15 U.S.C. 1191; 67 Stat. 111), as amended, 68 Stat. 770, August 23, 1954.

(b) The terms *rule, rules, regulations*, and *rules and regulations*, mean the rules and regulations prescribed by the Commission pursuant to section 5(c) of the act.

(c) The term *United States* means the several States, the District of Columbia, the Commonwealth of Puerto Rico and the Territories and Possessions of the United States.

(d) The terms *marketing or handling* means the transactions referred to in section 3 of the Flammable Fabrics Act, as amended in 1967.

(e) The terms *uncovered or exposed part* of an article of wearing apparel as used in section 4(a) of the act, means that part of such article of apparel which might during normal wear be open to flame or other means of ignition.

NOTE: The outer surface of an undergarment is considered to be an uncovered or exposed part of an article of wearing apparel, and thus subject to the act.

(f) The term *textile fabric* means any coated or uncoated material subject to the act, except film and fabrics having a nitro-cellulose fiber, finish, or coating, which is woven, knitted, felted or otherwise produced from any natural or man-made fiber, or substitute therefore, or combination thereof, of two inches or more in width, and which is in a form or condition ready for use in wearing apparel.

(g) The term *plain surface textile fabric* means any textile fabric which does not have an intentionally raised fiber or yarn surface such as a pile, nap, or tuft, but shall include those fabrics having fancy woven, knitted or flock printed surfaces.

(h) The term *raised surface textile fabric* means any textile fabric which has an intentionally raised fiber or yarn surface such as a pile, nap, or tufting.

(i) The term *film* means any nonrigid, unsupported plastic, rubber or other synthetic or natural film or sheeting, subject to the act, or any combination thereof, including transparent, translucent, and opaque material, whether plain, embossed, molded, or otherwise surface treated, which is in a form or condition ready for use in wearing apparel, and shall include film or sheeting exceeding 10 mils in thickness.

(j) The term *test* means the application of the relevant test method prescribed in the procedures provided under section 4(a) of the act.

(k) The term *initial test* means tests made under the procedures prescribed in section 4(a) of the act of specimens taken from two separate pieces of a textile fabric, or textile fabric with a nitro-cellulose fiber, finish or coating, having the same weight, construction and finish type, or from two separate runs of film having the same formula, finish, color, and thickness.

(l) The term *finish type* means a particular finish, but does not include such variables as changes in color, pattern, print, or design, or minor variations in the amount or type of ingredients in the finish formulation. Examples of finish types would be starch finishes, resin finishes or parchmentized finishes.

(m) The definition of terms contained in section 2 of the act shall be applicable also to such terms when used in rules promulgated under the act.

§ 1611.32 General requirements.

(a) No article of wearing apparel or fabric subject to the act and regulations shall be marketed or handled if such article or fabric, when tested according to the procedures prescribed in section 4(a) of the act, is so highly flammable to be dangerous when worn by individuals.

(b)(1) In the application of the requirements of § 1611.3 of the Standard to any item of film, coated fabric, or wearing apparel, compute the average burn rate from five specimens burned transverse to the direction of processing and the average burn rate from an additional five specimens burned lengthwise to the direction of processing. If either the average burn rate from the five specimens burned transverse or the average burn rate from the five specimen burned lengthwise exceeds 1.2 inches per second, the test results shall be interpreted as a failure.

(2) To compute the average burn rate for each set of five specimens, at least two of the specimens must ignite and burn the stop cord for the specimen. However, if fewer than two specimens of any given set of five specimens ignite and burn the stop cord for the specimen, the test results shall be interpreted according to provisions of paragraphs (b)(2)(i) through (iii) of this section:

(i) If no specimen ignites and burns the stop cord, the test results of that set of specimens shall be regarded as passing.

(ii) If only one specimen of the set of five specimens ignites and burns the stop cord with passing results, the results of that set of specimens will be regarded as passing.

(iii) If only one specimen of the set of five specimens ignites and burns the stop cord with failing results, test another set of five specimens from the same direction of processing. Compute the average burn rate for all ten specimens in the same direction of processing. If two or more of the 10 specimens ignite and burn the stop cord, average the results from all 10 specimens which ignited and burned the stop cord. If only one of the 10 specimens ignites and burns the stop cord, the test is inconclusive. The Commission will take no enforcement action on the basis of that test. The Commission may conduct additional testing of the article of film, coated fabric, or wearing apparel, but the results of any inconclusive test shall not be averaged with results obtained from any other test.

[50 FR 7762, Feb. 26, 1985; 50 FR 11848, Mar. 26, 1985]

§ 1611.33 Test procedures for textile fabrics and film.

(a)(1) All textile fabrics (except those with a nitro-cellulose fiber, finish or coating) intended or sold for use in wearing apparel, and all such fabrics contained in articles of wearing apparel, shall be subject to the requirements of the act, and shall be deemed to be so highly flammable as to be dangerous when worn by individuals if such fabrics or any uncovered or exposed part of such articles of wearing apparel exhibits rapid and intense burning when tested under the conditions and in the manner prescribed in subpart A of this part, and identified as "Flammability of Clothing Textiles, Commercial Standard 191–53".

(2) Notwithstanding the provisions of paragraph (a)(1) of this section, coated fabrics, except those with a nitro-cellulose coating, may be tested under the procedures outlined in part 1611, the flammability standard incorporated in the Commercial Standard promulgated by the Secretary of Commerce effective May 22, 1953, and identified as "General Purpose Vinyl Plastic Film, Commercial Standard 192–53", and if such coated fabrics do not exhibit a rate of burning in excess of that specified in § 1611.3 they shall not be deemed to be so highly flammable as to be dangerous when worn by individuals.

(b) All film, and textile fabrics with a nitro-cellulose fiber, finish or coating intended or sold for use in wearing apparel, and all film and such textile fabrics referred to in this rule which are contained in articles of wearing apparel, shall be subject to the requirements of the act, and shall be deemed to be so highly flammable as to be dangerous when worn by individuals if such film or such textile fabrics or any uncovered or exposed part of such articles of wearing apparel exhibit a rate of burning in excess of that specified in part 1611, the flammability standard incorporated in the Commercial Standard promulgated by the Secretary of Commerce effective May 22, 1953, and identified as "General Purpose Vinyl Plastic Film, Commercial Standard 192–53."

§ 1611.34 Only uncovered or exposed parts of wearing apparel to be tested.

In determining whether an article of wearing apparel is so highly flammable as to be dangerous when worn by individuals, only the uncovered or exposed part of such article of wearing apparel shall be tested according to the applicable procedures set forth in section 4(a) of the act.

NOTE: If the outer layer of plastic film or plastic-coated fabric of a multilayer fabric separates readily from the other layers, the outer layer shall be tested under part 1611—Standard for the Flammability of Vinyl Plastic Film. If the outer layer adheres to all or a portion of one or more layers of the underlying fabric, the multilayered fabric may be tested under either part 1611 or Part 1610—Standard for the Flammability of Clothing Textiles. However, if the conditioning procedures required by § 1610.4(f) of the Standard for the Flammability of Cloth Textiles would damage or alter the physical characteristics of the film or coating, the uncovered or exposed layer shall be tested in accordance with part 1611.

Plastic film or plastic-coated fabric used, or intended for use, as the outer layer of disposable diapers is exempt from the requirements of the standard, provided that a sample taken from a full thickness of the assembled article passes the test in the standard (part 1610 or part 1611) otherwise applicable to the outer fabric or film when the flame is applied to the exposed or uncovered surface. See §§ 1610.36(f) and 1611.36(f).

[50 FR 7762, Feb. 26, 1985]

§ 1611.35 Testing certain classes of fabric and film.

(a) *Fabric not customarily washed or dry cleaned.* (1) Except as provided in paragraph (a)(2) of this section, any textile fabric or article of wearing apparel, which, in its normal and customary use as wearing apparel would not be dry cleaned or washed, need not be dry cleaned or washed as prescribed in §§ 1610.4 (d) and (e) when tested under the Standard for the Flammability of Clothing Textiles if such fabric or article of wearing apparel, when marketed or handled, is marked in a clear and legible manner with the statement: "Fabric may be dangerously flammable if dry cleaned or washed." An example of the type of fabric referred to in this paragraph is bridal illusion.

(2) Section 1610.4(a)(4) of the Standard for the Flammability of Clothing Textiles, which requires that certain samples shall be dry cleaned or washed before testing, shall not apply to disposable fabrics and garments. Additionally, such disposable fabrics and garments shall not be subject to the labeling requirements set forth in paragraph (a)(1) of this section.

(b) A coated fabric need not, upon test under the procedures outlined in subpart A of part 1610, be dry cleaned as set forth in § 1610.4(d).

(c) In determining whether a textile fabric having a raised-fiber surface, which surface is to be used in the covered or unexposed parts of articles of wearing apparel, is so highly flammable as to be dangerous when worn by individuals, only the opposite surface or surface intended to be exposed need be tested under the applicable procedures set forth in section 4(a) of the act, providing an invoice or other paper covering the marketing or handling of such fabric is given which clearly designates that the raised-fiber surface is to be used only in the covered or unexposed parts of articles of wearing apparel.

(d)(1) Items which are subject to the Standard for the Flammability of Vinyl Plastic Film from which a test specimen 3 inches by 9 inches cannot be taken lengthwise to the direction of processing shall not be tested in the lengthwise direction.

(2) Items which are subject to the Standard for the Flammability of Vinyl Plastic Film from which a test specimen 3 inches by 9 inches cannot be taken transverse to the direction of processing shall not be tested in the transverse direction.

[40 FR 59898, Dec. 30, 1975, as amended at 50 FR 51671, Dec. 19, 1985]

§ 1611.36 Application of act to particular types of products.

(a) Fabrics intended or sold for processing into interlinings or other covered or unexposed parts of articles of wearing apparel shall not be subject to the provisions of section 3 of the act: *Provided,* That an invoice or other paper covering the marketing or handling of such fabrics is given which specifically designates their intended end use: *And provided further,* That with respect to fabrics which under the provisions of section 4 of the act, as amended, are so highly flammable as to be dangerous when worn by individuals, any person marketing or handling such fabrics maintains records which show the acquisition, disposition and intended end use of such fabrics, and any person manufacturing articles of wearing apparel containing such fabrics maintains records which show the acquisition, and use and disposition of such fabrics. Any person who fails to maintain such records or to furnish such invoice or other paper shall be deemed to have engaged in the marketing or handling of such products for purposes subject to the requirements of the act and such person and the products shall be subject to the provisions of sections 3, 6, 7, and 9 of the act.

(b) Fabrics intended or sold for use in those hats, gloves, and footwear which are excluded under the definition of articles of wearing apparel in section 2(d) of the act shall not be subject to the provisions of section 3 of the act: *Provided,* That an invoice or other paper covering the marketing or handling of such fabrics is given which specifically designates their intended use in such products: *And provided further,* That with respect to fabrics which under the provisions of section 4 of the act, as amended, are so highly flammable as to be dangerous when worn by individuals, any person marketing or handling such fabrics maintains records which show the acquisition, disposition, and intended end use of such fabrics, and any person manufacturing hats, gloves, or footwear containing such fabrics maintains records which show the acquisition, end use and disposition of such fabrics. Any person who fails to maintain such records or to furnish such invoice or other paper shall be deemed to have engaged in the marketing or handling of such products for purposes subject to the requirements of the act and such person and the products shall be subject to the provisions of sections 3, 6, 7, and 9 of the act.

(c) Except as provided in paragraph (d) of this section, handkerchiefs not exceeding a finished size of twenty-four (24) inches on any side or not exceeding five hundred seventy-six (576) square inches in area are not deemed "articles of wearing apparel" as that term is used in the act.

(d) Handkerchiefs or other articles affixed to, incorporated in, or sold as a part of articles of wearing apparel as decoration, trimming, or for any other purpose, are considered an integral part of such articles of wearing apparel, and the articles of wearing apparel and all parts thereof are subject to the provisions of the act. Handkerchiefs or other articles intended or sold to be affixed to, incorporated in or sold as a part of articles of wearing apparel as aforesaid constitute "fabric" as that term is defined in section 2(e) of the act and are subject to the provisions of the act which such handkerchiefs or other articles constitute textile fabrics as the term "textile fabric" is defined in § 1611.31(f).

(e) Where an article of wearing apparel has a raised-fiber surface which is intended for use as a covered or unexposed part of the article of wearing apparel but the article of wearing apparel is, because of its design and construction, capable of being worn with the raised-fiber surface exposed, such raised-fiber surface shall be considered to be an uncovered or exposed part of the article of wearing apparel. Examples of the type of products referred to in this paragraph are athletic shirts or so-called "sweat shirts" with a raised fiber inner side.

(f) *Multilayer fabric and wearing apparel with a film or coating on the uncovered or exposed surface.* Plastic film or plastic-coated fabric used, or intended for use, as the outer layer of disposable diapers is exempt from the requirements of the standard, provided that a full thickness of the assembled article passes the test in the standard otherwise applicable to the outer fabric or film when the flame is applied to the exposed or uncovered surface. (15 U.S.C. 1193, 1194; 15 U.S.C. 2079(b))

NOTE: An interpretation to §302.6(c) issued by the Federal Trade Commission, 30 FR 16106, Dec. 28, 1965, provides as follows:

"§1611.36(c) does not exclude products from the act on the sole basis of the size, description or designation of such product.

"If, because of construction, design, color, type of fabric, or any other factor, a piece of cloth of a finished type or any other product of a finished type appears to be likely to be used as a covering for the head, neck, face, shoulders, or any part thereof, or otherwise appears likely to be used as an article of clothing, garment, or costume, such product is not a handkerchief and constitutes an article of wearing apparel as defined in and subject to the provisions of the Flammable Fabrics Act, irrespective of its size, or its description or designation as a handkerchief or any other term."

(Secs. 4, 5, 67 Stat. 112, 113, as amended, 68 Stat. 770, 81 Stat. 571, 90 Stat. 515 (15 U.S.C. 1193, 1194); sec. 30(b), 86 Stat. 1207 (15 U.S.C. 2079(b))

[40 FR 59898, Dec. 30, 1975, as amended at 50 FR 7763, Feb. 26, 1985]

§ 1611.37 Reasonable and representative tests under section 8 of the Act.

EXPLANATION: Section 8 of the Act, among other things, provides that no person shall be subject to prosecution under section 7 of the Act for a violation of section 3 of the Act if such person establishes a guaranty received in good faith signed by and containing the name and address of the person by whom the wearing apparel or fabric guaranteed was manufactured or from whom it was received, to the effect that reasonable and representative tests made under the procedures provided in section 4(a) of the Act show that the fabric covered by the guaranty, or used, or contained in the wearing apparel, is not, under the provisions of section 4(a) of the Act, so highly flammable as to be dangerous when worn by individuals.

While one establishing a guaranty received in good faith would not be subject to criminal prosecution under section 7 of the Act, he, or the merchandise involved, would nevertheless, remain subject to the administrative processes of the Consumer Product Safety Commission under section 5 of the Act, as well as the injunction and condemnation procedures under section 6 of the Act.

The furnishing of guaranties is not mandatory under the Act. The purpose of this rule is to establish minimum requirements for the reasonable and representative tests on which guaranties may be based.

(a) The following shall constitute reasonable and representative tests, as that term is used in section 8 of the Act, for those textile fabrics which by reason of their composition, construction, finish type or weight may be tested upon a class basis. The word "class" as used in this section means a category of textile fabrics having certain general constructional or finished characteristics, sometimes in association with a particular fiber, and covered by a class or type description generally recognized by the trade. In certain instances the use of class tests is restricted by this section to a particular textile fabric of the same fiber composition, construction and finish type. The results of such class tests may be used by any person as a basis for furnishing guaranties under section 8 of the Act on all textile fabrics of the same class.

(1) *Plain surface textile fabrics weighing two ounces or more per square yard.* (i) One test of any plain surface textile fabric weighing two ounces or more per square yard, exclusive of metallic ornamentation, or one test of any fabric in a particular class of such fabrics, shall suffice for any such fabric or class of fabrics.

(2) *Plain surface textile fabrics weighing less than two ounces per square yard.* (i) When, on the initial test of any plain surface textile fabric weighing less than two ounces per square yard, such fabric exhibits a burning time of 3.5 seconds or more, such test may suffice for any fabric of the same fiber composition, construction and finish type. This class of fabric shall be tested at least once at intervals of not more than three months thereafter while in production. If, after four consecutive interval production tests have been made, none of such test results show the flame spread to have been less than 4.5 seconds, no further tests of such class of fabric need be made.

(ii) When, on the initial test of any plain surface textile fabric weighing less than two ounces per square yard, none of the specimens ignite, such initial test may suffice for any fabric of the same fiber composition, construction and finish type.

(iii) When, on the initial test of any plain surface textile fabric weighing less than two ounces per square yard, such fabric ignites but the flame is extinguished before the stop cord is burned, such test may suffice for any fabric of the same fiber composition, construction and finish type. This class of fabric shall be tested at least once at intervals of not more than one year thereafter while in production.

(3) *Certain raised fiber surface textile fabrics.* (i) When a test of any raised fiber surface textile fabric which has a dense cut pile of uniform short length or looped yarns, does not exhibit a surface flash and does not ignite, such test shall suffice for any such fabric having a dense cut pile of the same length or the same looped yarns and of the same fiber composition, construction and finish type. Examples of the types of fabrics referred to are velvet, velveteens, velours, and corduroys.

(ii) One test of any raised fiber surface textile fabric, the raised fiber surface of which consists of not less than ninety percentum (90%) protein fiber, or one test of any fabric in a particular class of such fabrics, shall suffice for any such fabric or class of fabrics.

(iii) When, on the initial test of any raised surface textile fabric which has a surface composed of looped yarns, such fabric exhibits a burning time in excess of 12 seconds, such test may suffice for any such fabric having the same looped yarns and of the same fiber composition, construction and finish type. An example of the type of fabric referred to is "terry cloth".

(b) Raised fiber surface textile fabrics: When, on the initial test of a raised fiber surface textile fabric, such fabric:

(1)(i) Falls within Class 2 as provided in §1610.3(a)(2)(i), the fabric shall be tested at least once at intervals of not more than one month while in production, or if the production exceeds 50,000 yards per month, the fabric shall be tested thereafter every 50,000 yards or fraction thereof.

(ii) If, after two such intervals, production tests have been made, the test results do not show the flame spread to have been less than 4 seconds, with the base fabric ignited or fused, the fabric shall be tested at least once at intervals of not more than three months while in production, or if the production exceeds 100,000 yards per three months, the fabric shall be tested thereafter every 100,000 yards or fraction thereof.

(2) Has a flame spread in excess of 7 seconds with the base fabric ignited or fused, the fabric shall be tested at least once at intervals of not more than six months thereafter while in production.

(3) Has a surface flash, but the base fabric does not ignite nor fuse, the fabric shall be tested at least once at intervals of not more than six months thereafter while in production.

(4) Does not have a surface flash and does not ignite, the initial test shall suffice.

(c) When, on initial test a film or a textile fabric with a nitro-cellulose fiber, finish or coating, does not exhibit a burning rate in excess of 1.2 inches per second, one test each year thereafter while in production shall be deemed reasonable and representative tests for such film or textile fabric.

(d) Reasonable and representative tests of fabrics and fabrics contained in articles of wearing apparel, subject to the act, produced prior to the effective date of the act, and which have not been tested under the applicable requirements of paragraphs (a), (b), or (c) of this section, shall be an initial test for each class of such fabrics, and such tests shall be applicable to all fabrics having the same fiber composition, construction and finish type.

(e) In the case of articles of wearing apparel which are not made from fabrics but directly from yarns, the fabrics contained in such articles of wearing apparel shall be tested by the testing requirements provided in paragraphs (a) and (b) of this section.

(f) Where fabrics or fabrics contained in articles of wearing apparel have not been tested when in production by the applicable testing requirements provided in paragraphs (a), (b) or (c) of this section, one test of each such fabrics shall be made every 10,000 yards or fraction thereof, or of the fabric contained in one of every 5,000 of such articles of wearing apparel or fraction thereof, and these shall be deemed reasonable and representative tests of such fabrics.

(g) In the case of textile fabrics or textile fabrics contained in articles of wearing apparel having an appliqued, overstitched, or embroidered type of design of a loop, pile, nap, or tufted construction, tests shall be conducted according to paragraph (b) of this section on each type of applique, overstitch, or embroidery.

(h) If tests of any textile fabric made subsequent to the initial test show a burning time of another category, then such fabric shall be tested thereafter under the testing requirements of such changed time.

(i) The application of this section, insofar as it relates to the testing of plain surface textile fabrics or such fabrics contained in articles of wearing apparel weighing two ounces or more per square yard, shall be limited to fabrics made of fibers in use or capable of being used as of May 31, 1954. Such fabrics weighing two ounces or more per square yard made in whole or in part of fibers developed and used subsequent to May 31, 1954, shall be tested in accordance with the testing requirements set out in paragraph (a)(2) of this section.

§ 1611.38 Maintenance of records by those furnishing guaranties.

(a) In order to properly administer and enforce section 8 of the act relating to guaranties, it is required that any person furnishing either a separate or continuing guaranty who has made the tests prescribed by the act and regulations shall keep and maintain records of such tests. The records to be maintained shall show:

(1) The style or range number, fiber composition, construction and finish type of each textile fabric and each textile fabric (including those with a nitro-cellulose fiber, finish or coating) used or contained in an article of wearing apparel covered by the guaranty, including a swatch of the fabric tested.

(2) The stock or formula number, color, thickness and general description of each film or film used in an article of wearing apparel covered by the guaranty, including a sample of the film tested.

(3) The results of the actual tests made on the textile fabric and film or the fabric and film used or contained in an article of wearing apparel.

(b) Persons furnishing guaranties based upon class tests shall maintain records showing:

(1) Identification of the class test.

(2) Fiber composition, construction and finish type of the fabrics, or the fabrics used or contained in articles of wearing apparel so guaranteed.

(3) A swatch of each class of fabrics guaranteed.

(c) Persons furnishing guaranties based upon guaranties received by them shall maintain records showing:

(1) The guaranty received and identification of the fabrics or fabrics contained in articles of wearing apparel guaranteed in turn by them.

(2) [Reserved]

(d) The records referred to in this section shall be preserved for a period of three years from the date the tests were performed, or in the case of paragraph (c) of this section the guaranties were furnished.

(e) Any person furnishing a guaranty under section 8(a) of the act who neglects or refuses to maintain and preserve the records prescribed in this section shall be deemed to have furnished a false guaranty under the provisions of section 8(b) of the act.

§ 1611.39 Shipments under section 11(c) of the act.

(a) The invoice or other paper relating to the shipment or delivery for shipment in commerce of articles of wearing apparel or textile fabrics for the purpose of finishing or processing to render them not so highly flammable as to be dangerous when worn by individuals, shall contain a statement disclosing such purpose.

(b) An article of wearing apparel or textile fabric shall not be deemed to fall within the provisions of section 11(c) of the act as being shipped or delivered for shipment in commerce for the purpose of finishing or processing to render such article of wearing apparel or textile fabric not so highly flammable under section 4 of the act, as to be dangerous when worn by individuals, unless the shipment or delivery for shipment in commerce of such article of wearing apparel or textile fabric is made direct to person engaged in the business of processing or finishing textile products for the prearranged purpose of having such article of apparel or textile fabric processed or finished to render it not so highly flammable under section 4 of the act, as to be dangerous when worn by individuals, and any person shipping or delivering for shipment the article of wearing apparel or fabric in commerce for such purpose maintains records which establish (1) that the textile fabric or article of wearing apparel has been shipped for appropriate flammability treatment, and (2) that such treatment has been completed, as well as records to show the disposition of such textile fabric or article of wearing apparel subsequent to the completion of such treatment.

(c) The importation of textile fabrics or articles of wearing apparel may be considered as incidental to a transaction involving shipment or delivery for shipment for the purpose of rendering such textile fabrics or articles of wearing apparel not so highly flammable under the provisions of section 4 of the act, as to be dangerous when worn by individuals, if:

(1) The importer maintains records which establish (i) that the imported textile fabrics or articles of wearing apparel have been shipped for appropriate flammability treatment, and (ii) that such treatment has been completed, as well as records to show the disposition of such textile fabrics or articles of wearing apparel subsequent to the completion of such treatment.

(2) The importer, at the time of importation, execute and furnishes to the Bureau of Customs an affidavit stating

These fabrics (or articles of wearing apparel) are dangerously flammable under the provisions of section 4 of the Flammable Fabrics Act, and will not be sold or used in their present condition but will be processed or finished by the undersigned or by a duly authorized agent so as to render them not so highly flammable under the provisions of section 4 of the Flammable Fabrics Act, as to be dangerously flammable when worn by individuals. The importer agrees to maintain the records required by 16 CFR 1610.39(c)(1).

(3) The importer, if requested to do so by the Bureau of Customs, furnishes an adequate specific-performance bond conditioned upon the complete discharge of the obligations assumed in paragraphs (c) (1) and (2) of this section.

NOTE: The purpose of section 11(c) is only to permit articles of wearing apparel or textile fabrics which are dangerously flammable to be shipped or delivered for shipment in commerce for the purpose of treatment or processing to render them not dangerously flammable. Section 11(c) does not in any other respect limit the force and effect of sections 3, 6, 7, and 9 of the act. In particular, section 11(c) does not authorize the sale or offering for sale of any article of wearing apparel or textile fabric which is in fact dangerously flammable at the time of sale or offering for sale, even though the seller intends to ship the article for treatment prior to delivery to the purchaser or has already done so. Moreover, under section 3 of the act a person is liable for a subsequent sale or offering for sale if, despite the purported completion of treatment to render it not dangerously flammable, the article in fact remains dangerously flammable.

PART 1615—STANDARD FOR THE FLAMMABILITY OF CHILDREN'S SLEEPWEAR: SIZES 0 THROUGH 6X (FF 3–71)

Subpart A—The Standard

Sec.

Subpart B—Rules and Regulations

Subpart C—Interpretations and Policies

SOURCE: 40 FR 59903, Dec. 30, 1975, unless otherwise noted.

Subpart A—The Standard

AUTHORITY: Sec. 429, Pub. L. 105–276; Sec. 4, 67 Stat. 112, as amended, 81 Stat. 569–570; 15 U.S.C. 1193.

§ 1615.1 Definitions.

In addition to the definitions given in section 2 of the Flammable Fabrics Act, as amended (15 U.S.C. 1191), the following definitions apply for purposes of this Standard:

(a) *Children's Sleepwear* means any product of wearing apparel up to and including size 6X, such as nightgowns, pajamas, or similar or related items, such as robes, intended to be worn primarily for sleeping or activities related to sleeping, except:

(1) Diapers and underwear;

(2) "Infant garments," as defined by section 1615.1(c), below; and

(3) "Tight-fitting garments," as defined by section 1615.1(o), below.

(b) *Size 6X* means the size defined as 6X in Department of Commerce Voluntary Product Standard, previously identified as Commercial Standard, CS 151–50 "Body Measurements for the Sizing of Apparel for Infants, Babies, Toddlers, and Children."[1]

(c) *Infant garment* means a garment which:

(1) Is sized nine months or smaller;

(2) If a one-piece garment, does not exceed 64.8 centimeters (25.75 inches) in length; if a two-piece garment, has no piece exceeding 40 centimeters (15.75 inches) in length;

(3) Complies with all applicable requirements of the Standard for the Flammability of Clothing Textiles (16 CFR part 1610) and the Standard for the Flammability of Vinyl Plastic Film (16 CFR part 1611); and

(4) Bears a label stating the size of the garment, expressed in terms of months of age. For example, "0 to 3 mos." or "9 mos." If the label is not visible to the consumer when the garment is offered for sale at retail, the same information must appear legibly on the package of the garment.

(d) *Item* means any product of children's sleepwear, or any fabric or related material intended or promoted for use in children's sleepwear.

(e) *Trim* means decorative materials, such as ribbons, laces, embroidery, or ornaments. This definition does not include (1) individual pieces less than 2 inches in their longest dimension, provided that such pieces do not constitute or cover in aggregate a total of more than 20 square inches of the item, or (2) functional materials (findings), such as zippers, buttons, or elastic bands, used in the construction of garments.

(f) *Test Criteria* means the maximum char length which a sample or specimen may exhibit in order to pass an individual test.

(g) *Char Length* means the distance from the original lower edge of the specimen exposed to the flame in accordance with the procedure specified in § 1615.4 *Test procedure* to the end of the tear or void in the charred, burned, or damaged area, the tear being made in accordance with the procedure specified in § 1615.4(g)(2).

(h) [Reserved]

(i) *Afterglow* means the continuation of glowing of parts of a specimen after flaming has ceased.

(j) *Fabric Piece* (Piece) means a continuous, unseamed length of fabric, one or more of which make up a unit.

(k) *Fabric Production Unit* (Unit) means any quantity of finished fabric up to 5,000 linear yards for normal sampling or 10,000 linear yards for reduced sampling which has a specific identity that remains unchanged throughout the Unit except for color or print pattern as specified in § 1615.4(b). For purposes of this definition, finished fabric means fabric in its final form after completing its last processing steps as a fabric except for slitting.

(l) *Garment Production Unit* (Unit) means any quantity of finished garments up to 500 dozen which have a specific identity that remains unchanged throughout the Unit except

[1] Copies available from the National Technical Information Service, 5285 Port Royal Street, Springfield, VA 22151, and should be ordered as CS 15150.

for size, trim, findings, color, and print patterns as specified in § 1615.4(b).

(m) *Sample* means five test specimens.

(n) *Specimen* means an 8.9 × 25.4 cm. (3.5 × 10 in.) section of fabric. For garment testing the specimen will include a seam or trim.

(o) Tight-fitting garment means a garment which:

(1)(i) In each of the sizes listed below does not exceed the maximum dimension specified below for the chest, waist, seat, upper arm, thigh, wrist, or ankle:

	Chest	Waist	Seat	Upper arm	Thigh	Wrist	Ankle
Size 9–12 mos							
Maximum dimension:							
Centimeters	48.3	48.3	48.3	14.3	26.7	10.5	13
(inches)	(19)	(19)	(19)	(5⅝)	(10½)	(4⅛)	(5⅛)
Size 12–18 mos							
Maximum dimension:							
Centimeters	49.5	49.5	50.8	14.9	28.3	10.5	13.1
(inches)	(19½)	(19½)	(20)	(5⅞)	(11⅛)	(4⅛)	(5⅛)
Size 18–24 mos							
Maximum dimension:							
Centimeters	52.1	50.8	53.3	15.6	29.5	11	13.6
(inches)	(20½)	(20)	(21)	(6⅛)	(11⅝)	(4¼)	(5⅜)
Size 2							
Maximum dimension:							
Centimeters	52.1	50.8	53.3	15.6	29.8	11.4	14
(inches)	(20½)	(20)	(21)	(6⅛)	(11¾)	(4½)	(5½)
Size 3							
Maximum dimension:							
Centimeters	53.3	52.1	56	16.2	31.4	11.7	14.9
(inches)	(21)	(20½)	(22)	(6⅜)	(12⅜)	(4⅝)	(5⅞)
Size 4							
Maximum dimension:							
Centimeters	56	53.3	58.4	16.8	33.0	12.1	15.9
(inches)	(22)	(21)	(23)	(6⅝)	(13)	(4¾)	(6¼)
Size 5							
Maximum dimension:							
Centimeters	58.4	54.6	61.0	17.5	34.6	12.4	16.8
(inches)	(23)	(21½)	(24)	(6⅞)	(13⅝)	(4⅞)	(6⅝)
Size 6							
Maximum dimension:							
Centimeters	61.0	55.9	63.5	18.1	36.2	12.7	17.8
(inches)	(24)	(22)	(25)	(7⅛)	(14¼)	(5)	(7)
Size 6X							
Maximum dimension:							
Centimeters	62.9	57.2	65.4	18.7	37.8	13.0	18.7
(inches)	(24¾)	(22½)	(25¾)	(7⅜)	(14⅞)	(5⅛)	(7⅜)

(ii) Note: Measure the dimensions on the front of the garment. Lay garment, right side out, on a flat, horizontal surface. Smooth out wrinkles. Measure distances as specified below and multiply them by two. Measurements should be equal to or less than the maximum dimensions given in the standards.

(A) Chest—measure distance from arm pit to arm pit (A to B) as in Diagram 1.

(B) Waist—See Diagram 1. *One-piece garment*, measure at the narrowest location between arm pits and crotch (C to D). *Two-piece garment*, measure width at both the bottom/ sweep of the upper piece (C to D) and, as in Diagram 3, the top of the lower piece (C to D).

(C) Wrist—measure the width of the end of the sleeve (E to F), if intended to extend to the wrist, as in Diagram 1.

(D) Upper arm—draw a straight line from waist/sweep D through arm pit B to G. Measure down the sleeve fold from G to H. Refer to table below for G to H distances for each size. Measure the upper arm of the garment (perpendicular to the fold) from H to I as shown in Diagram 1.

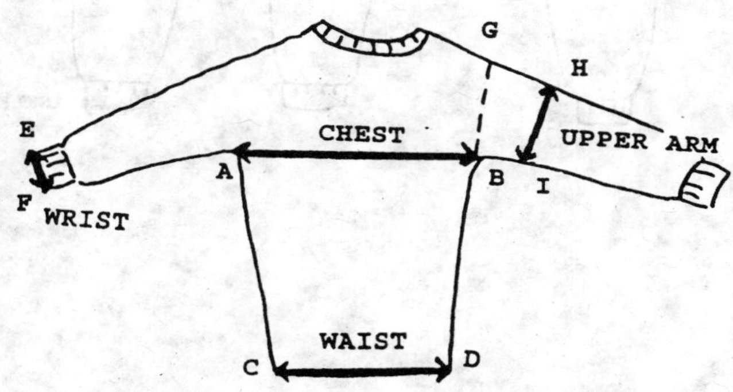

Diagram 1

DISTANCE FROM SHOULDER (G) TO (H) FOR UPPER ARM MEASUREMENT FOR SIZES 9 MONTHS THROUGH 6X

9–12 mo	12–18 mo	18–24 mo	2	3	4	5	6	6x
5.8 cm 2⅛″	6.6 cm 2⅝″	7.4 cm 2⅞″	7.4 cm 2⅞″	8.1 cm 3¼″	8.8 cm 3½″	9.5 cm 3¾″	10.3cm 4″	11 cm 4⅜″

(E) Seat—Fold the front of the pant in half to find the bottom of thecrotch at J as in Diagram 2. The crotch seam and inseam intersect at J. Mark point K on the crotch seam at 4 inches above and perpendicular to the bottom of the crotch. Unfold the garment as in Diagram 3. Measure the seat from L to M through K as shown.

(F) Thigh—measure from the bottom of the crotch (J) 1 inch down the inseam to N as in Diagram 2. Unfold the garment and measure the thigh from the inseam at N to O as shown in Diagram 3.

(G) Ankle—measure the width of the end of the leg (P to Q), if intended to extend to the ankle, as in Diagram 3.

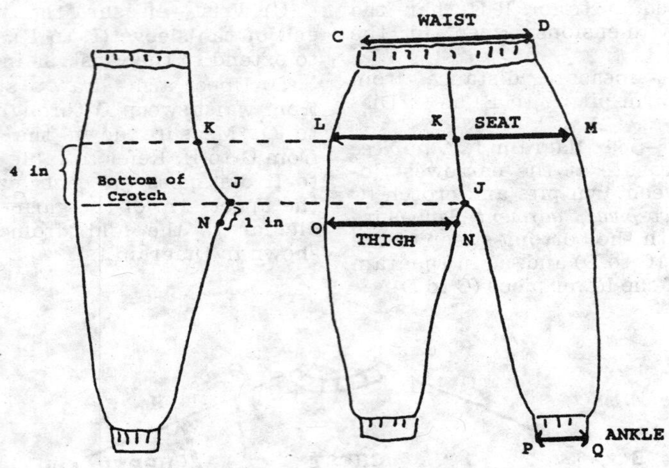

Diagram 2 Diagram 3

(2) Has no item of fabric, ornamentation or trim, such as lace, appliques, or ribbon, which extends more than 6 millimeters (¼ inch) from the point of attachment to the outer surface of the garment;

(3) Has sleeves which do not exceed the maximum dimension for the upper arm at any point between the upper arm and the wrist, and which diminish in width gradually from the top of the shoulder (point G in Diagram 1) to the wrist;

(4) Has legs which do not exceed the maximum dimension for the thigh at any point between the thigh and the ankle, and which diminish in width gradually from the thigh to the ankle;

(5) In the case of a one-piece garment, has a width which does not exceed the maximum dimension for the chest at any point between the chest and the waist and which diminishes gradually from the chest to the waist; and has a width which does not exceed the maximum dimension for the seat at any point between the seat and the waist and which diminishes gradually from the seat to the waist;

(6) In the case of a two-piece garment has an upper piece with a width which does not exceed the maximum dimension for the chest at any point between the chest and the bottom of that piece and which diminishes gradually from the chest to the bottom of that piece; in the case of an upper piece with fastenings, has the lowest fastening within 15 centimeters (6 inches) of the bottom of that piece;

(7) In the case of a two-piece garment, has a lower piece with a width which does not exceed the maximum dimension for the seat at any point between the seat and the top of the lower piece and which diminishes gradually from the seat to the top of that piece;

(8) Complies with all applicable requirements of the Standard for the Flammability of Clothing Textiles (16 CFR part 1610) and the Standard for the

Flammability of Vinyl Plastic Film (16 CFR part 1611); and

(9) Bears a label stating the size of the garment in terms of age in months, or by child's size; for example: "Size 9 to 12 mos." or "Size 2." If the label is not visible to the consumer when the garment is offered for sale at retail, the same information must appear legibly on the package of the garment.

(10)(i) *Hangtags.* Bears a hangtag as shown following this paragraph stating "For child's safety, garment should fit snugly. This garment is not flame resistant. Loose-fitting garment is more likely to catch fire." The hangtag must measure 1½″×6¼″. The text must be enclosed in a text box that measures 1″×5¾″ and must be in 18 point Arial/Helvetica font. The hangtag must have a yellow background and black lettering. The color yellow must meet the specifications for Standard Safety Yellow (Hue 5.OY; Value/Chroma 8.0/12) as described in American National Standard ANSI Z535.1–1998, Safety Color Code, p.6, under Munsell Notation.[2] One side of the hangtag must display only this message. The reverse side of the hangtag may display sizing information, but otherwise must be blank. The text must not be obscured by the hole provided for attaching the hangtag to the garment. The hangtag must be prominently displayed on the garment.

For child's safety, garment should fit snugly.
This garment is not flame resistant.
Loose-fitting garment is more likely to catch fire.

(ii) *Packages.* If the garments are sold in packages, the package must have a label as shown following this paragraph with the same language that would appear on the hangtag. The label must have a text box that measures ¾″×3¾″. The text must be 11 point Arial/Helvetica in black lettering against a yellow background. The packages must be prominently, conspicuously, and legibly labeled with the required message. The package label may be adhesive.

For child's safety, garment should fit snugly.
This garment is not flame resistant.
Loose-fitting garment is more likely to catch fire.

[2] ANSI Z535.1–1998, Standard for Safety Color Code, p.6, published by National Electrical Manufacturers Association is incorporated by reference. Copies of this document are available from the National Electrical Manufacturers Association, 1300 N. 17th Street, Suite 1847, Rossylyn, Virginia 22209. This document is also available for inspection at the National Archives and Records Administration (NARA). For information on the availability of this material at NARA, call 202–741–6030, or go to: *http://www.archives.gov/federal_register/code_of_federal_regulations/ibr_locations.html.* The incorporation by reference was approved by the Director of the Federal Register in accordance with 5 U.S.C. 552(a) and 1 CFR part 51.

(11) Bears a label as shown following this paragraph stating "Wear Snug-fitting, Not Flame Resistant." The text must be printed on the front of the sizing label located on the center back of the garment and must be immediately below the size designation. The text must be a minimum of 5 point sans serif font in all capital letters and must be set apart from other label text by a line border. The text must contrast with the background color of the label. The label must not be covered by any other label or tag.

WEAR SNUG-FITTING NOT FLAME RESISTANT

Example in 10 pt Arial font

[40 FR 59903, Dec. 30, 1975, as amended at 43 FR 4853, Feb. 6, 1978; 50 FR 53307, Dec. 31, 1985; 61 FR 47644, Sept. 9, 1996; 64 FR 2838, Jan. 19, 1999; 64 FR 34533, 34535, June 28, 1999; 65 FR 1435, Jan. 10, 2000; 72 FR 13689, Mar. 23, 2007]

§ 1615.2 Scope and application.

(a) This Standard provides a test method to determine the flammability of items as defined in § 1615.1(d).

(b) All items as defined in § 1615.1(d) are subject to requirements of this standard.

(c) The flammability standards for clothing textiles and vinyl plastic film, parts 1610 and 1611 of this chapter, are superseded by this part insofar as they apply to items defined in § 1615.1(d).

[40 FR 59903, Dec. 30, 1975, as amended at 64 FR 34533, June 28, 1999]

§ 1615.3 General requirements.

(a) *Summary of test method.* Five conditioned specimens, 8.9 × 25.4 cm. (3.5 × 10 in.), are suspended one at a time vertically in holders in a prescribed cabinet and subjected to a standard flame along their bottom edge for a specified time under controlled conditions. The char length is measured.

(b) *Test criteria.* The test criteria when the testing is done in accordance with § 1615.4 *Test procedure* are:

(1) *Average char length.* The average char length of five specimens shall not exceed 17.8 cm. (7.0 in.).

(2) *Full specimen burn.* No individual specimen shall have a char length of 25.4 cm. (10 in.).

[40 FR 59903, Dec. 30, 1975, as amended at 43 FR 4853, Feb. 6, 1978]

§ 1615.4 Test procedure.

(a) *Apparatus*—(1) *Test chamber.* The test chamber shall be a steel cabinet with inside dimensions of 32.9 cm. (12 15/16 in.) wide, 32.9 cm. (12 15/16 in.) deep, and 76.2 cm. (30 in.) high. It shall have a frame which permits the suspension of the specimen holder over the center of the base of the cabinet at such a height that the bottom of the specimen holder is 1.7 cm. (3/4 in.) above the highest point of the barrel of the gas burner specified in paragraph (c) of this section and perpendicular to the front of the cabinet. The front of the cabinet shall be a close fitting door with a glass insert to permit observation of the entire test. The cabinet floor may be covered with a piece of asbestos paper, whose length and width are approximately 2.5 cm. (1 in.) less than the cabinet floor dimensions. The cabinet to be used in this test method is illustrated in Figure 1 and detailed in Engineering Drawings, Nos. 1 to 7.

(2) *Specimen holder.* The specimen holder is designed to permit suspension of the specimen in a fixed vertical position and to prevent curling of the specimen when the flame is applied. It shall consist of two U-shaped 0.20 cm. (14 ga. USS) thick steel plates, 42.2 cm. (16 5/8 in.) long, and 8.9 cm. (3.5 in.) wide, with

aligning pins. The openings in the plates shall be 35.6 cm. (14 in.) long and 5.1 cm. (2 in.) wide. The specimen shall be fixed between the plates, which shall be held together with side clamps. The holder to be used in this test method is illustrated in Figure 2 and detailed in Engineering Drawing No. 7.

(3) *Burner.* The burner shall be substantially the same as that illustrated in Figure 1 and detailed in Engineering Drawing No. 6. It shall have a tube of 1.1 cm. (0.43 in.) inside diameter. The input line to the burner shall be equipped with a needle valve. It shall have a variable orifice to adjust the height of the flame. The barrel of the burner shall be at an angle of 25° from the vertical. The burner shall be equipped with an adjustable stop collar so that it may be positioned quickly under the test specimen. The burner shall be connected to the gas source by rubber or other flexible tubing.

(4) *Gas supply system.* There shall be a pressure regulator to furnish gas to the burner under a pressure of 129±13mm. Hg (2½±¼ lbs. per sq. in.) at the burner inlet.

(5) *Gas.* The gas shall be at least 97 percent pure methane.

(6) *Hooks and weights.* Metal hooks and weights shall be used to produce a series of loads for char length determinations. Suitable metal hooks consist of No. 19 gauge steel wire, or equivalent, made from 7.6 cm. (3 in.) lengths of the wire, bent 1.3 cm. (0.5 in.) from one end to a 45° angle hook. The longer end of the wire is fastened around the neck of the weight to be used and the other in the lower end of each burned specimen to one side of the burned area. The requisite loads are given in table 1.

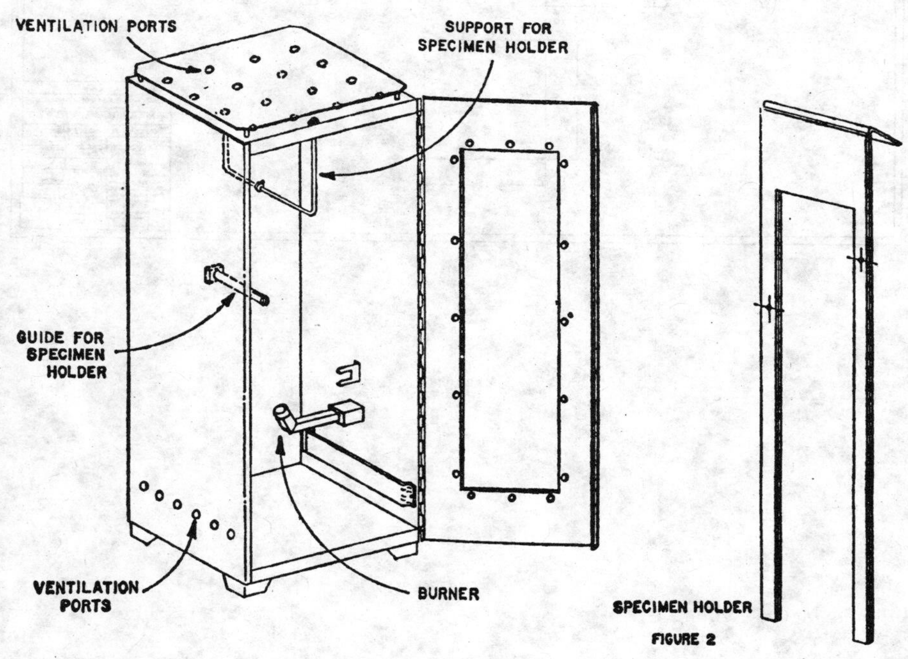

FIGURE 2

VERTICAL TEST CABINET

FIGURE 1

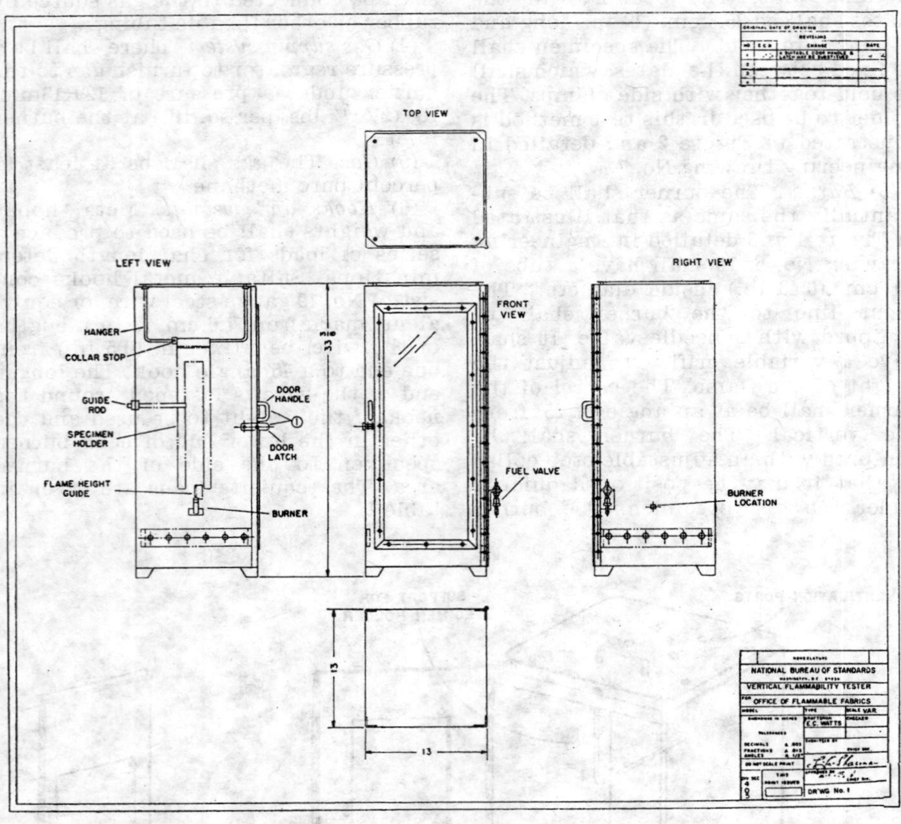
TOP VIEW
LEFT VIEW
RIGHT VIEW
FRONT VIEW
HANGER
COLLAR STOP
GUIDE ROD
SPECIMEN HOLDER
FLAME HEIGHT GUIDE
BURNER
DOOR HANDLE
DOOR LATCH
FUEL VALVE
BURNER LOCATION
33
13
13
NATIONAL BUREAU OF STANDARDS
VERTICAL FLAMMABILITY TESTER
OFFICE OF FLAMMABLE FABRICS
E.C. WATTS
DR'WG No. 1

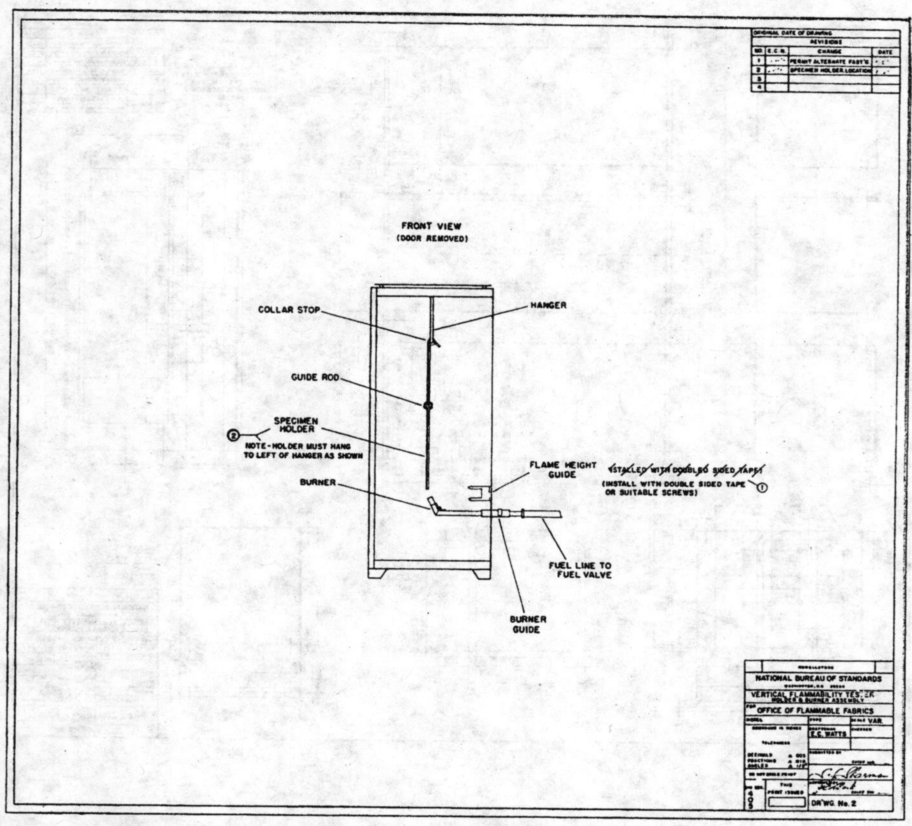
ORIGINAL DATE OF DRAWING
REVISIONS
NO. E.C.N. CHANGE DATE
1 PERMIT ALTERNATE FAST'G
2 SPECIMEN HOLDER LOCATION
3
4
FRONT VIEW
(DOOR REMOVED)
COLLAR STOP
HANGER
GUIDE ROD
SPECIMEN HOLDER
2 NOTE-HOLDER MUST HANG TO LEFT OF HANGER AS SHOWN
FLAME HEIGHT GUIDE
INSTALLED WITH DOUBLED SIDED TAPE
(INSTALL WITH DOUBLE SIDED TAPE OR SUITABLE SCREWS) 1
BURNER
FUEL LINE TO FUEL VALVE
BURNER GUIDE
NATIONAL BUREAU OF STANDARDS
VERTICAL FLAMMABILITY TESTER
HOLDER & BURNER ASSEMBLY
FOR OFFICE OF FLAMMABLE FABRICS
SCALE VAR.
E.C. WATTS
THIS PRINT ISSUED
405
DR'WG. No. 2

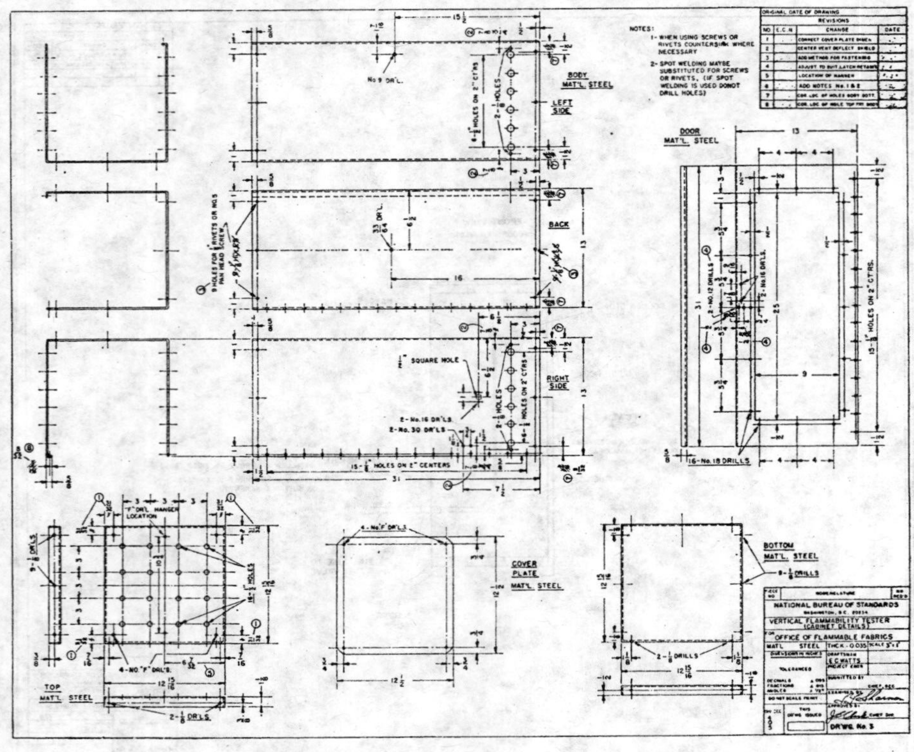
NOTES:
1- WHEN USING SCREWS OR RIVETS COUNTERSINK WHERE NECESSARY
2- SPOT WELDING MAYBE SUBSTITUTED FOR SCREWS OR RIVETS, (IF SPOT WELDING IS USED DONOT DRILL HOLES)
ORIGINAL DATE OF DRAWING
REVISIONS
NO. E.C.N. CHANGE DATE
6 ADD NOTES No. 1 & 2
BODY MAT'L. STEEL
LEFT SIDE
BACK
RIGHT SIDE
SQUARE HOLE
2-No.16 DR'LS.
2-No.30 DR'LS.
HOLES ON 2" CENTERS
DOOR MAT'L. STEEL
16-No.18 DRILLS
"F" DR'L HANGER LOCATION
4-NO."F" DR'LS.
TOP MAT'L. STEEL
COVER PLATE MAT'L. STEEL
BOTTOM MAT'L. STEEL
NATIONAL BUREAU OF STANDARDS
VERTICAL FLAMMABILITY TESTER (CABINET DETAILS)
OFFICE OF FLAMMABLE FABRICS
MAT'L STEEL THCK - 0.035
E.C. WATTS
DR'WG. No. 3

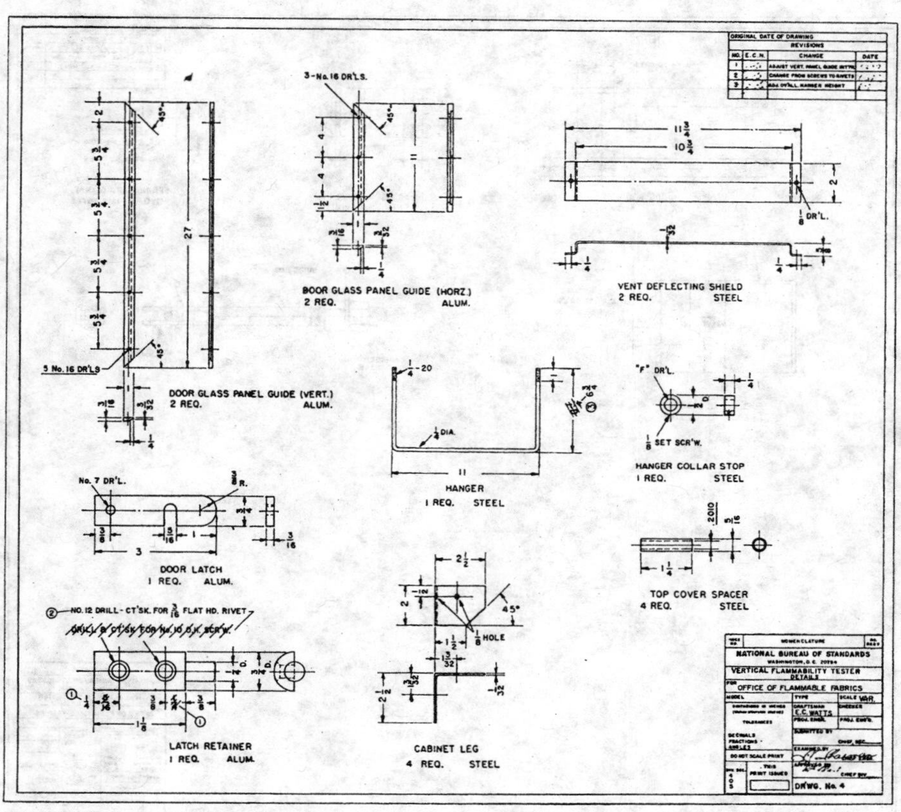
3-No.16 DR'LS.
5 No.16 DR'LS
DOOR GLASS PANEL GUIDE (VERT.)
2 REQ. ALUM.
DOOR GLASS PANEL GUIDE (HORZ.)
2 REQ. ALUM.
VENT DEFLECTING SHIELD
2 REQ. STEEL
HANGER
1 REQ. STEEL
"F" DR'L.
SET SCR'W.
HANGER COLLAR STOP
1 REQ. STEEL
No. 7 DR'L.
DOOR LATCH
1 REQ. ALUM.
TOP COVER SPACER
4 REQ. STEEL
NO. 12 DRILL - CT'SK. FOR 3/16 FLAT HD. RIVET
LATCH RETAINER
1 REQ. ALUM.
HOLE
CABINET LEG
4 REQ. STEEL
NATIONAL BUREAU OF STANDARDS
VERTICAL FLAMMABILITY TESTER
DETAILS
OFFICE OF FLAMMABLE FABRICS
E.C. WATTS
DRWG. No. 4

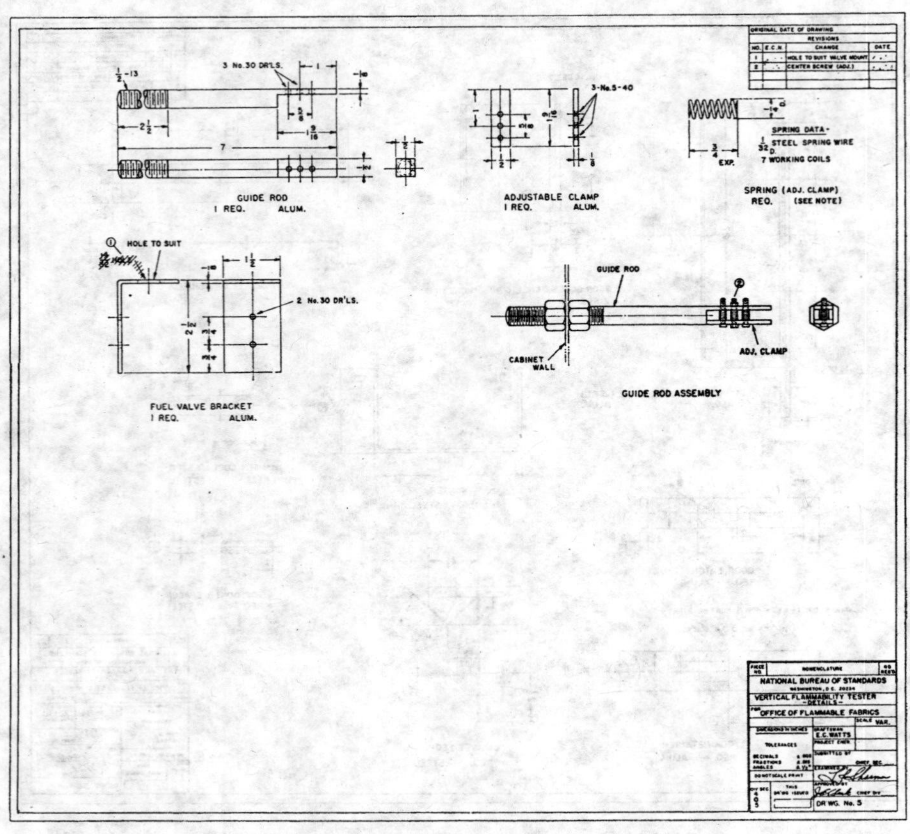
GUIDE ROD
1 REQ. ALUM.
ADJUSTABLE CLAMP
1 REQ. ALUM.
SPRING DATA-
STEEL SPRING WIRE
7 WORKING COILS
SPRING (ADJ. CLAMP)
REQ. (SEE NOTE)
HOLE TO SUIT
2 No. 30 DR'LS.
FUEL VALVE BRACKET
1 REQ. ALUM.
GUIDE ROD
CABINET WALL
ADJ. CLAMP
GUIDE ROD ASSEMBLY
NATIONAL BUREAU OF STANDARDS
VERTICAL FLAMMABILITY TESTER
OFFICE OF FLAMMABLE FABRICS
E.C. WATTS
DR WG. No. 5

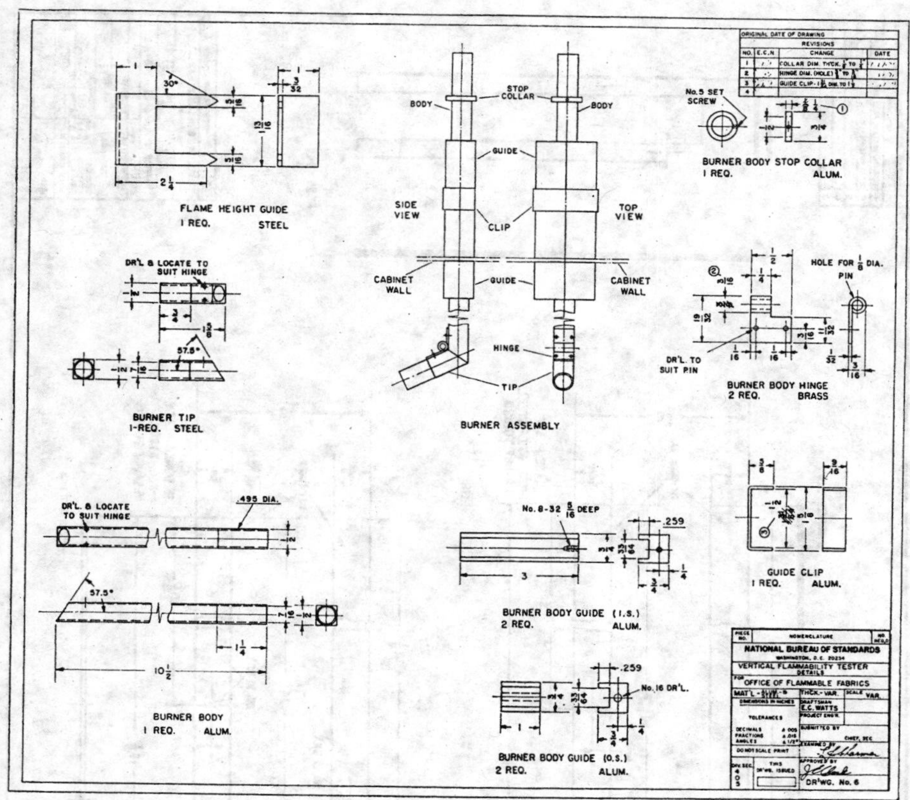
FLAME HEIGHT GUIDE
1 REQ. STEEL
BURNER TIP
1-REQ. STEEL
BURNER ASSEMBLY
SIDE VIEW
TOP VIEW
STOP COLLAR
BODY
GUIDE
CLIP
CABINET WALL
HINGE
TIP
No.5 SET SCREW
BURNER BODY STOP COLLAR
1 REQ. ALUM.
HOLE FOR 1/8 DIA. PIN
DR'L. TO SUIT PIN
BURNER BODY HINGE
2 REQ. BRASS
DR'L. & LOCATE TO SUIT HINGE
.495 DIA.
BURNER BODY
1 REQ. ALUM.
No. 8-32 5/16 DEEP
BURNER BODY GUIDE (I.S.)
2 REQ. ALUM.
No.16 DR'L.
BURNER BODY GUIDE (O.S.)
2 REQ. ALUM.
GUIDE CLIP
1 REQ. ALUM.
ORIGINAL DATE OF DRAWING
REVISIONS
NATIONAL BUREAU OF STANDARDS
VERTICAL FLAMMABILITY TESTER
DETAILS
OFFICE OF FLAMMABLE FABRICS
E.C. WATTS
DR'WG. No. 6

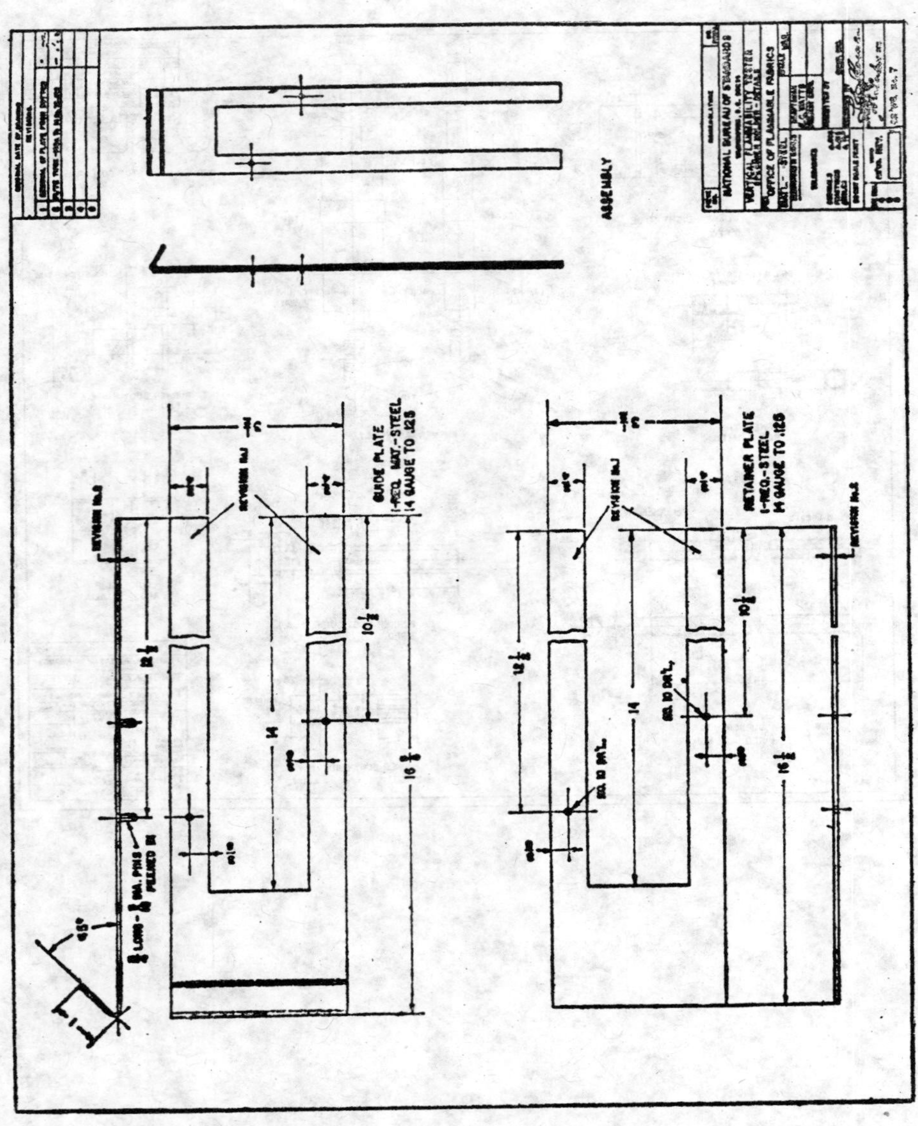
ASSEMBLY
GUIDE PLATE
1-REQ. MAT.-STEEL
14 GAUGE TO .125
RETAINER PLATE
1-REQ.-STEEL
14 GAUGE TO .125
NATIONAL BUREAU OF STANDARDS
OFFICE OF FLAMMABLE FABRICS

TABLE 1—ORIGINAL FABRIC WEIGHT[1]

Grams per square meter	Ounces per square yard	Loads	
		Grams	Pounds
Less than 101	Less than 3	54.4	0.12
101 to 207	3 to 6	113.4	.25
207 to 338	6 to 10	226.8	.50
Greater than 338	Greater than 10	340.2	.75

[1] Weight of the original fabric, containing no seams or trim, is calculated from the weight of a specimen which has been conditioned for at least 8 h at 21±1.1 °C (70±2 °F) and 65±2 pct relative humidity. Shorter conditioning times may be used if the change in weight of a specimen in successive weighings made at intervals of not less than 2 h does not exceed 0.2 pct of the weight of the specimen.

(7) *Stopwatch.* A stopwatch or similar timing device shall be used to measure time to 0.1 second.

(8) *Scale.* A linear scale graduated in millimeters or 0.1 inch divisions shall be used to measure char length.

(9) *Circulating Air Oven.* A forced circulation drying oven capable of maintaining the specimens at 105±2.8 °C. (221±5 °F.), shall be used to dry the specimen while mounted in the specimen holders.[3]

(10) *Desiccator.* An air-tight and moisture-tight desiccating chamber shall be used for cooling mounted specimens after drying. Anhydrous silica gel shall be used as the desiccant in the desicating chamber.

(11) *Hood.* A hood or other suitable enclosure shall be used to provide a draft-free environment surrounding the test chamber. This enclosure shall have a fan or other suitable means for exhausting smoke and/or toxic gases produced by testing.

(b) *Specimens and sampling—General.* (1) The test criteria of § 1615.3(b) shall be used in conjunction with the following fabric and garment sampling plan, or any other approved by the Consumer Product Safety Commission that provides at least the equivalent level of fire safety to the consumer. Alternate sampling plans submitted for approval shall have operating characteristics such that the probability of Unit acceptance at any percentage defective does not exceed the corresponding probability of Unit acceptance of the following sampling plan in the region of the latter's operating characteristic curves that lies between 5 and 95 percent acceptance probability.

(2) Different colors or different print patterns of the same fabric may be included in a single Fabric or Garment Production Unit, provided such colors or print patterns demonstrate char lengths that are not significantly different from each other as determined by previous testing of at least three samples from each color or print pattern to be included in the Unit.

(3) Garments with different trim and findings may be included in a single Garment Production Unit providing the other garment characteristics are identical except for size, color, and print pattern.

(4) For fabrics whose flammability characteristics are not dependent on chemical additives or chemical reactants to fiber, yarns, or fabrics, the laundering requirement of paragraph (g)(4) of this section is met on subsequent Fabric Production Units if results of testing an initial Fabric Production Unit demonstrate acceptability according to the requirements of paragraph (c) of this section, Normal Sampling, both before and after the appropriate laundering.

(5) If the fabric has been shown to meet the laundering requirement, paragraph (g)(4) of this section, the garments produced from that fabric are not required to be laundered.

(6) Each Sample (five specimens) for all Fabric Sampling shall be selected so that two specimens are in one fabric direction (machine or cross-machine) and three specimens are in the other fabric direction except for the additional Sample selected after a failure, in which case, all five specimens shall be selected in the same fabric direction in which the specimen failure occurred.

(7) Fabric Samples may be selected from fabric as outlined in paragraph (c) of this section entitled Fabric Sampling, or, for verification purposes, from randomly selected garments.

(8) Multilayer fabrics shall be tested with a hem of approximately 2.5 cm. (1 in.) sewn at the bottom edge of the specimen with a suitable thread and

[3] Option 1 of ASTM, D2654–67T, "Method of Test for Amount of Moisture in Textile Materials," describes a satisfactory oven (1970 Book of ASTM Standards, part 24, published by the American Society for Testing and Materials, 1916 Race Street, Philadelphia, Pa. 19103).

stitch. The specimen shall include each of the components over its entire length. Garments manufactured from multilayer fabrics shall be tested with the edge finish at the bottom edge of the specimen which is used in the garment.

(c) *Specimens and Sampling—Fabric Sampling.* A Fabric Production Unit (Unit) is either accepted or rejected in accordance with the following plan:

(1) *Normal Sampling.* Select one Sample from the beginning of the first Fabric Piece (Piece) in the Unit and one Sample from the end of the last Piece in the Unit, or select a sample from each end of the Piece if the Unit is made up of only one Piece. Test the two selected Samples. If both Samples meet all the Test Criteria of §1615.3(b), accept the unit. If either or both of the Samples fail the 17.8 cm. (7.0 in.) average char length criterion, §1615.3(b)(1), reject the Unit. If two or more of the individual specimens, from the 10 selected specimens fail, the 25.4 cm. (10 in.) char length, .3(b)(2), reject the Unit. If only one individual specimen, from the 10 selected specimens, fails the 25.4 cm. (10 in.) char length, §1615.3(b)(2), select five additional specimens from the same end of the Piece in which the failure occurred, all five to be taken in the fabric direction in which the specimen failure occurred. If this additional Sample passes all the test criteria, accept the Unit. If this additional Sample fails any part of the test criteria, reject the Unit.

(2) *Reduced Sampling.* (i) The level of sampling required for fabric acceptance may be reduced provided the preceding 15 Units of the fabric have all been accepted using the Normal Sampling plan.

(ii) The Reduced Sampling plan shall be the same as for Normal Sampling except that the quantity of fabric in the Unit may be increased to 10,000 linear yards.

(iii) Select and test two Samples in the same manner as in Normal Sampling. Accept or reject the Unit on the same basis as with Normal Sampling.

(iv) Reduced Sampling shall be discontinued and Normal Sampling resumed if a Unit is rejected.

(3) *Tightened Sampling.* The level of sampling required for acceptance shall be increased when a Unit is rejected under the Normal Sampling plan. The Tightened Sampling shall be the same as Normal Sampling except that one additional Sample shall be selected and cut from a middle Piece in the Unit. If the Unit is made up of less than two pieces, the Unit shall be divided into at least two Pieces. The division shall be such that the Pieces produced by the division shall not be smaller than 100 linear yards or greater than 2,500 linear yards. If the unit is made up of two Pieces, the additional Sample shall be selected from the interior end of one of the Pieces. Test the three selected Samples. If all three selected Samples meet all the test criteria of §1615.3(b), accept the unit. If one or more of the three selected Samples fail the 17.8 cm. (7.0 in.) average char length criterion, §1615.3(b)(1), reject the Unit. If two or more of the individual specimens from the 15 selected specimens fail the 25.4 cm. (10 in.) char length, §1615.3(b)(2), reject the unit. If only one individual specimen, of the 15 selected Specimens fails the 25.4 cm. (10 in.) char length, §1615.3(b)(2), select five additional specimens from the same end of the same piece in which the failure occurred, all five to be taken in the fabric direction in which the Specimen failure occurred. If this additional Sample passes all the test criteria, accept the Unit. If this additional Sample fails any part of the test criteria, reject the Unit. Tightened Sampling may be discontinued and Normal Sampling resumed after five consecutive Units have all been accepted using Tightened Sampling. If Tightened Sampling remains in effect for 15 consecutive units, production of the specific fabric in Tightened Sampling must be discontinued until that part of the process or component which is causing failure has been identified and the quality of the end product has been improved.

(4) *Disposition of Rejected Units.* (i) The Piece or Pieces which have failed and resulted in the initial rejection of the Unit may not be retested, used, or promoted for use in children's sleepwear as defined in §1615.1(a) except after reworking to improve the flammability characteristics and subsequent retesting in accordance with the procedures in Tightened Sampling.

(ii) The remainder of a rejected Unit, after removing the Piece or Pieces the failure of which resulted in Unit rejection, may be accepted if the following test plan is successfully concluded at all required locations. The required locations are those adjacent to each such failed Piece. (Required locations exist on both sides of the "Middle Piece" tested in Tightened Sampling if failure of that Piece resulted in Unit rejection.) Failure of a Piece shall be deemed to have resulted in Unit rejection if Unit rejection occurred and a Sample or specimen from the Piece failed any test criterion of § 1615.3(b).

(iii) The Unit should contain at least 15 Pieces for disposition testing after removing the failing Pieces. If necessary for this purpose, the Unit shall be demarcated into at least 15 approximately equal length Pieces unless such division results in Pieces shorter than 100 linear yards. In this latter case, the Unit shall be demarcated into roughly equal length Pieces of approximately 100 linear yards each. If such a division results in five Pieces or less in the Unit for each failing Piece after removing the failing Pieces, only the individual Piece retest procedure (described subsequently) may be used.

(iv) Select and cut a Sample from each end of each adjoining Piece beginning adjacent to the Piece which failed. Test the two Samples from the Piece. If both Samples meet all the test criteria of § 1615.3(b), the Piece is acceptable. If one or both of the two selected Samples fail the 17.8 cm. (7.0 in.) average char length criterion, § 1615.3(b)(1), the Piece is unacceptable. If two or more of the individual Specimens, from the 10 selected specimens, fail the 25.4 cm. (10 in.) char length § 1615.3(b)(2), the Piece is unacceptable. If only one individual specimen, from the 10 selected specimens, fails the 25.4 cm. (10 in.) char length, § 1615.3(b)(2), select five additional specimens from the same end of the Piece in which the failure occurred, all five to be taken in the fabric direction in which the specimen failure occurred. If this additional Sample passes all the test criteria, the Piece is acceptable. If this additional Sample fails any part of the test criteria, the Piece is unacceptable.

(v) Continue testing adjoining Pieces until a Piece has been found acceptable. Then continue testing adjoining Pieces until three successive adjoining Pieces, not including the first acceptable Piece, have been found acceptable or until five such Pieces not including the first acceptable Piece, have been tested, whichever occurs sooner. Unless three successive adjoining Pieces have been found acceptable among five such Pieces, testing shall be stopped and the entire Unit rejected without further testing. If three successive Pieces have been found acceptable among five such Pieces, accept the three successive acceptable Pieces and the remaining Pieces in the Unit.

(vi) Alternatively, individual Pieces from a rejected Unit containing three or more Pieces may be tested and accepted or rejected on a Piece-by-Piece basis according to the following plan, after removing the Piece or Pieces, the failure of which resulted in Unit rejection. Select four Samples (two from each end) from the Piece. Test the four selected Samples. If all four Samples meet all the Test Criteria of § 1615.3(b), accept the Piece. If one or more of the Samples fail the 17.8 cm. (7 in.) average char length criterion, § 1615.3(b)(1), reject the Piece. If two or more of the individual Specimens from the 20 selected specimens, fail the 25.4 cm. (10 in.) char length, § 1615.3(b)(1), reject the Piece. If only one individual specimen, from the 20 selected specimens, fails the 25.4 cm. (10 in.) char length, § 1615.3(b)(2), select two additional Samples from the same end of the Piece in which the failure occurred. If these additional two Samples meet all the Test Criteria of § 1615.3(b), accept the Piece. If one or both of the two additional Samples fail any part of the Test Criteria, reject the Piece.

(vii) The Pieces of a Unit rejected after retesting may not be retested, used, or promoted for use in children's sleepwear as defined in § 1615.1(a) except after reworking to improve the flammability characteristics, and subsequent retesting in accordance with the procedures set forth in Tightened Sampling.

(5) *Records*. Records of all Unit sizes, test results, and the disposition of rejected Pieces and Units must be maintained by the manufacturer upon the effective date of this Standard. Rules and regulations may be established by the Consumer Product Safety Commission.

(d) *Specimens and Sampling—Garment Sampling*. (1)(i) The garment sampling plan is made up of two parts: (A) Prototype Testing and (B) Production Testing. Prior to production, prototypes must be tested to assure that the design characteristics of the garments are acceptable. Garment Production Units (Units) are then accepted or rejected on an individual Unit basis.

(ii) Edge finishes such as hems and binding are excluded from testing except that when trim is used on an edge the trim must be subjected to prototype testing. Seams attaching findings are excluded from testing.

(2) *Prototype Testing*. Preproduction prototypes of a garment style or type shall be tested to assure that satisfactory garment specifications in terms of flammability are set up prior to production.

(i) *Seams*. Make three Samples (15 specimens) using the longest seam type and three Samples using each other seam type 10 inches or longer that is to be included in the garment. Prior to testing, assign each specimen to one of the three Samples. Test each set of three Samples and accept or reject each seam design in accordance with the following plan:

(A) If all three Samples meet all the test criteria of §1615.3(b), accept the seam design. If one or more of the three Samples fail the 17.8 cm. (7 in.) average char length criterion, §1615.3(b)(1), reject the seam design. If three or more of the individual Specimens from the 15 selected specimens fail the 25.4 cm. (10 in.) char length, §1615.3(b)(2), reject the seam design. If only one of the individual specimens from the 15 selected specimens fails the 25.4 cm. (10 in.) char length, §1615.3(b)(2), accept the seam design.

(B) If two of the individual specimens from the 15 selected specimens, fail the 25.4 cm. (10 in.) char length, §1615.3(b)(2), select three more Samples (15 specimens) and retest. If all three additional Samples meet all the test criteria of §1615.3(b) accept the seam design. If one or more of the three additional Samples fail the 17.8 cm. (7 in.) average char length criterion, §1615.3(b)(1), reject the seam design. If two or more of the individual specimens from the 15 selected specimens, fail the 25.4 cm. (10 in.) char length, §1615.3(b)(2) reject the seam design. If only one of the individual specimens from the 15 selected specimens, fails the 25.4 cm. (10 in.) char length §1615.3(b)(2) accept the seam design.

(ii) *Trim*. (A)(*1*) Make three samples (15 specimens) from each type of trim to be included in the garment. For trim used only in a horizontal configuration on the garment, specimens shall be prepared by sewing or attaching the trim horizontally to the bottom edge of an appropriate section of untrimmed fabric. Sleeve and neckline trim may not be tested in this manner. Where more than one row of trim is used on the garment, specimens shall be prepared with the same configuration (same number of rows and spacing between rows up to the limit of the specimen size) as the garment.

(*2*) For trim used in other than a horizontal configuration, specimens shall be prepared by sewing or attaching the trim to the center of the vertical axis of an appropriate section of untrimmed fabric, beginning the sewing or attachment at the lower edge of each specimen.

(*3*) For either configuration, the sewing or attachment shall be made in the manner in which the trim is attached in the garment.

(B)(*1*) Sewing or otherwise attaching the trim shall be done with thread or fastening material of the same composition and size to be used for this purpose in the garment and using the same stitching or seamtype. Trim used in the horizontal configuration shall be sewn or fastened the entire width (smaller dimension) of the specimen. Trim used in other than the horizontal configuration shall be sewn or fastened the entire length (longer dimension) of the specimen.

(*2*) Prior to testing, assign each specimen to one of the three samples. Test the sets of three samples and accept or reject the type of trim and design on the same basis as seam design. A type of trim and design accepted when tested in a vertical configuration may be used in a horizontal configuration without further testing.

(3) *Production Testing.* A Unit is either accepted or rejected according to the following plan:

(i)(A) From each Unit select at random sufficient garments and cut three Samples (15 specimens) from the longest seam type. No more than five specimens may be cut from a single garment. Prior to testing, assign each specimen to one of the three Samples. All specimens cut from a single garment must be included in the same Sample. Test the three selected Samples. If all three Samples meet all the test criteria of § 1615.3(b), accept the Unit. If one or more of the three Samples fail the 17.8 cm. (7 in.) average char length criterion, § 1615.3(b)(1), reject the Unit. If four or more of the individual specimens, from the 15 selected specimens, fail the 25.4 cm (10 in.) char length, § 1615.3(b)(2), reject the Unit. If three or less of the individual specimens, from the 15 selected specimens, fail the 25.4 cm. (10 in.) char length, § 1615.3(b)(2), accept the Unit.

(B)(*1*) If the garment under test does not have a 10-inch seam in the largest size in which it is produced, the following selection and testing procedure shall be followed.

(*2*) Select and cut specimens 8.9 cm. (3.5 in.) wide by the maximum available seam length, with the seam in the center of the specimen and extending the entire specimen length. Cut three Samples (15 specimens). These specimens shall be placed in specimen holders so that the bottom edge is even with the bottom of the specimen holder and the seam begins in the center of the bottom edge. Prior to testing, assign each specimen to one of the three Samples. All specimens cut from a single garment must be included in the same Sample.

(*3*) Test the three Samples. If all three Samples pass the 17.8 cm. (7 in.) average char length criterion, § 1615.3(b)(1), and if three or less individual specimens fail by charring the entire specimen length, accept the Unit. If the Unit is not accepted in the above test, three Samples (15 specimens) of the longest seam type shall be made using fabric and thread from production inventory and sewn on production machines by production operators. The individual fabric sections prior to sewing must be no larger than 20.3 × 63.3 cm. (8 in. × 25 in.) and must be selected from more than one area of the base fabric. Test the three prepared Samples. Accept or reject the Unit as described previously in this subsection.

(*4*) *Disposition of Rejected Units.* Rejected Units shall not be retested, used, or promoted for use in children's sleepwear as defined in § 1615.1(a), except after reworking to improve the flammability characteristics and subsequent retesting in accordance with the procedures set forth in garment production testing.

(*5*) *Records.* Records of all Unit sizes, test results, and the disposition of rejected Units must be maintained by the manufacturer upon the effective date of this standard. Rules and regulations may be established by the Consumer Product Safety Commission.

(e) *Specimens and Sampling—Compliance Market Sampling Plan.* Sampling plans for use in market testing of items covered by this Standard may be issued by the Consumer Product Safety Commission. Such plans shall define noncompliance of a production Unit to exist only when it is shown, with a high level of statistical confidence, those production Units represented by tested items which fail such plans will, in fact, fail this standard. Production units found to be non-complying under the provisions of paragraph (e) of this section shall be deemed not to conform to this Standard. The Consumer Product Safety Commission may publish such plans in the FEDERAL REGISTER.

(f) *Mounting and conditioning of specimens.* (1) The specimens shall be placed in specimen holders so that the bottom edge of each specimen is even with the bottom of the specimen holder. Mount the specimen in as close to a flat configuration as possible. The sides of the specimen holder shall cover 1.9 cm. (¾ in.) of the specimen width along each long edge of the specimen, and thus shall expose 5.1 cm. (2 in.) of the specimen width. The sides of the specimen holder shall be clamped with a sufficient number of clamps or shall be taped to prevent the specimen from being displaced during handling and testing. The specimens may be taped in the holders if the clamps fail to hold them. Place the mounted specimens in the drying oven in a manner that will permit free circulation of air at 105 °C. (221 °F.) around them for 30 minutes.[4]

(2) Remove the mounted specimens from the oven and place them in the desiccator for 30 minutes to cool. No more than five specimens shall be placed in a desiccator at one time. Specimens shall remain in the desiccator no more than 60 minutes.

(g) *Testing*—(1) *Burner adjustment.* With the hood fan turned off, use the needle valve to adjust the flame height of the burner to 3.8 cm. (1½ in.) above the highest point of the barrel of the burner. A suitable height indicator is shown in Engineering Drawing No. 6 and Figure 1.

(2) Specimen Burning and Evaluation. (i) One at a time, the mounted specimens shall be removed from the desiccator and suspended in the cabinet for testing. The cabinet door shall be closed and the burner flame impinged on the bottom edge of the specimen for 3.0±0.2 seconds. Flame impingement is accomplished by moving the burner under the specimen for this length of time, and then removing it.

(ii) When afterglow has ceased, remove the specimen from the cabinet and holder, and place it on a clean flat surface. Fold the specimen lengthwise along a line through the highest peak of the charred or melted area; crease the specimen firmly by hand. Unfold the specimen and insert the hook with the correct weight as shown in table 1 in the specimen on one side of the charred area 6.4 mm. (¼ in.) from the lower edge.

(iii) Tear the specimen by grasping the other lower corner of the fabric and gently raising the specimen and weight clear of the supporting surface.[5] Measure the char length as the distance from the end of the tear to the edge of the specimen exposed to the flame. After testing each specimen, vent the hood and cabinet to remove the smoke and/or toxic gases.

(3) *Report.* Report the value of char length, in centimeters (inches), for each specimen, as well as the average char length for each set of five specimens.

(4) *Laundering.* (i) The procedures described in sections 1615.4(b) through (g) shall be carried out on finished items (as produced or after one washing and drying) and after they have been washed and dried 50 times in accordance with sections 8.2.2, 8.2.3, and 8.3.1(A) of AATCC Test Method 124–1996 "Appearance of Fabrics after Repeated Home Laundering," Technical Manual of the American Association of Textile Chemists and Colorists, vol. 73, 1997, which is incorporated by reference. Copies of this document are available from the American Association of Textile Chemists and Colorists, P.O. Box 12215, Research Triangle Park, North Carolina 27709. This document is also available for inspection at the National Archives and Records Administration (NARA). For information on the availability of this material at NARA, call 202–741–6030, or go to: *http://www.archives.gov/federal_register/code_of_federal_regulations/ibr_locations.html.* This incorporation by reference was approved by the Director of the Federal Register in accordance with 5 U.S.C. 552(a) and 1 CFR part 51. Items which do not withstand 50 launderings shall be tested at the end of their useful service life.

(ii) Washing shall be performed in accordance with sections 8.2.2 and 8.2.3 of AATCC Test Method 124–1996, using wash temperature V (60° ±3 °C, 140° ±5 °F) specified in Table II of that method, and the water level, agitator speed, washing time, spin speed and final spin cycle specified for "Normal/Cotton Sturdy" in Table III. A maximum

[4] If the specimens are moist when received, permit them to air dry at laboratory conditions prior to placement in the oven. A satisfactory preconditioning procedure may be found in ASTM D 1776–67, "Conditioning Textiles and Textile Products for Testing." ("1970 Book of ASTM Standards," part 24, published by the American Society for Testing and Materials, 1916 Race Street, Philadelphia, PA 19103.)

[5] A figure showing how this is done is given in AATCC 34–1969, Technical Manual of the American Association of Textile Chemists and Colorists, vol. 46, 1970, published by AATCC, Post Office Box 12215, Research Triangle Park, N.C. 27709.

washer load shall be 3.64 Kg (8 pounds) and may consist of any combination of test samples and dummy pieces. Drying shall be performed in accordance with section 8.3.1(A) of that test method, Tumble Dry, using the exhaust temperature (66° ±5 °C, 150° ±10 °F) and cool down time of 10 minutes specified in the "Durable Press" conditions of Table IV. Alternatively, a different number of times under another washing and drying procedure may be specified and used, if that procedure has previously been found to be equivalent by the Consumer Product Safety Commission. Such laundering is not required of items which are not intended to be laundered, as determined by the Consumer Product Safety Commission.

(iii) Items which are not susceptible to being laundered and are labeled "dry-clean only" shall be drycleaned by a procedure which has previously been found to be acceptable by the Consumer Product Safety Commission.

(iv) For the purpose of the issuance of a guarantee under section 8 of the act, finished sleepwear garments to be tested according to paragraphs (b) through (e) of this section need not be laundered or drycleaned provided all fabrics used in making the garments (except trim) have been guaranteed by the fabric producer to be acceptable when tested according to paragraphs (b) through (e) of this section.

[40 FR 59903, Dec. 30, 1975; 41 FR 1061, Jan. 6, 1976; 41 FR 8032, Feb. 24, 1976, as amended at 43 FR 4853, Feb. 6, 1978; 46 FR 63251, Dec. 31, 1981; 64 FR 24526, June 28, 1999; 65 FR 12927, Mar. 10, 2000; 72 FR 13689, Mar. 23, 2007]

§1615.5 Labeling requirements.

(a) *Care labels.* All items of children's sleepwear shall be labeled with precautionary instructions to protect the items from agents or treatments which are known to cause deterioration of their flame resistance. If the item has been initially tested under §1615.4(g)(4) after one washing and drying, it shall be labeled with instructions to wash before wearing. Such labels shall be permanent and otherwise in accordance with rules and regulations established by the Consumer Product Safety Commission.

(b) [Reserved]

[40 FR 59903, Dec. 30, 1975, as amended at 61 FR 1116, Jan. 16, 1996]

Subpart B—Rules and Regulations

AUTHORITY: Sec. 5, 67 Stat. 112–113, as amended, 81 Stat. 570, 15 U.S.C. 1194.

§1615.31 Labeling, recordkeeping, advertising, retail display and guaranties.

(a) *Definitions.* For the purposes of this section, the following definitions apply:

(1) *Standard* means the Standard for the Flammability of Children's Sleepwear: Sizes 0 through 6X (FF 3–71) (subpart A of this part) promulgated by the Secretary of Commerce in the FEDERAL REGISTER of July 29, 1971 (36 FR 14062), and amended by him in the FEDERAL REGISTER of July 21, 1972 (37 FR 14624).

(2) *Children's sleepwear* means "children's sleepwear" as defined in §1615.1(a) of the Standard; that is, "any product of wearing apparel up to and including size 6X, such as nightgowns, pajamas, or similar or related items, such as robes, intended to be worn primarily for sleeping or activities related to sleeping. Diapers and underwear are excluded from this definition."

(3) *Item* means "item" as defined in §1615.1(c) of the Standard; that is, "any product of children's sleepwear, or any fabric or related material intended or promoted for use in children's sleepwear."

(4) *Marketing or handling* or *marketed or handled* means any one or more of the transactions set forth in section 3 of the Flammable Fabrics Act (15 U.S.C. 1192).

(5) The definitions of terms set forth in §1615.1 of the Standard shall also apply to this section.

(b) *Labeling.* (1) Where any agent or treatment is known to cause deterioration of flame resistance or otherwise enhances the flammability characteristics of an item, such item shall be prominently, permanently, conspicuously, and legibly labeled with precautionary care and treatment instructions to protect the item from such agent or treatment: Provided:

(i) Where items required to be labeled in accordance with this paragraph are marketed at retail in packages, and the required label is not readily visible to the prospective purchaser, the packages must also be prominently, conspicuously, and legibly labeled with the required information, and

(ii) Where items are required to be labeled in accordance with this paragraph, the precautionary care and treatment instructions may appear on the reverse side of the permanent label if

(A) The precautionary care and treatment instructions are legible, prominent and conspicuous, and

(B) The phrase "CARE INSTRUCTIONS ON REVERSE" or the equivalent appears permanently, prominently, conspicuously, and legibly on the side of the permanent label that is visible to the prospective purchaser when the item is marketed at retail, and

(C) The item which is so labeled is marketed at retail in such a manner that the prospective purchaser is able to manipulate the label so the entire text of the precautionary care and treatment instructions is visible and legible; however, where the label cannot be manipulated so the instructions are visible to the prospective purchaser and legible, the packages must also be prominently, conspicuously and legibly labeled with the required precautionary care and treatment information or such information must appear prominently, conspicuously and legibly on a hang tag attached to the item.

(2) If the item has been initially tested under §1615.4(g)(4) of the Standard after one washing and drying, it shall be prominently, permanently, conspicuously, and legibly labeled with instructions to wash before wearing.

(3) [Reserved]

(4) Where any fabric or related material intended or promoted for use in children's sleepwear is sold or intended for sale to the ultimate consumer for the purpose of conversion into children's sleepwear, each bolt, roll, or other unit shall be labeled with the information required by this section. Each item of fabric or related material sold to an ultimate consumer must be accompanied by a label, as prescribed by this section, that can by normal household methods be permanently affixed by the ultimate consumer to any item of children's sleepwear made from such fabric or related material.

(5) Where items required to be labeled in accordance with paragraphs (b)(2), (3), and (4) of this section are marketed at retail in packages, and the required label is not readily visible to prospective purchasers, the packages must also be prominently, conspicuously, and legibly labeled with the required information.

(6) Samples, swatches, or specimens used to promote or effect the sale of items subject to the Standard shall be labeled in accordance with this section with the information required by this section, except that such information may appear on accompanying promotional materials attached to fabric samples, swatches, or specimens used to promote the sale of fabrics to garment manufacturers. This paragraph (b)(6) of this section shall not apply, however, to samples, swatches, or specimens prominently, permanently, conspicuously, truthfully, and legibly labeled with the statement "Flammable. Sample only. Not for use or resale. Does not meet Standard for the Flammability of Children's Sleepwear, DOC FF 3–71."

(7) The information required on labels by this section shall be set forth separately from any other information appearing on the same label. Other information, representations, or disclosures not required by this action but placed on the same label with information required by this section, or placed on other labels elsewhere on the item, shall not interfere with the information required by this section. No person, other than the ultimate consumer, shall remove or mutilate, or cause or participate in the removal or mutilation of, any label required by this section to be affixed to any item.

(8) Every manufacturer, importer, or other person (such as a converter) initially introducing items subject to the Standard into commerce shall assign to each item a unit identification (number, letter or date, or combination, thereof) sufficient to identify and relate to the fabric production unit or

garment production unit of which the item is a part. Such unit identification shall be designated in such a way as to indicate that it is a production unit identification under the Standard. The letters "GPU" and "FPU" may be used to designate a garment production unit identification and fabric production unit identification respectively, at the option of the labeler.

(i) Where fabrics required to be labeled or stamped in accordance with this section are marketed at retail in packages and the required label or stamp is not readily visible to the prospective purchaser, the packages must also be prominently, conspicuously, and legibly labeled with the information required by this section.

(ii) Where garments required to be labeled or stamped in accordance with paragraph (b)(8) of this section are marketed at retail in packages and the required label or stamp is not readily visible to the prospective purchasers:

(A) The packages must also be prominently, conspicuously, and legibly labeled with the information required by this section; or

(B) There must be a garment style identification that is prominent, conspicuous, and legible and readily visible to the prospective purchaser, either on a label or hang tag attached to the garments or on the garment packages. A style is a garment design or grouping, preselected by the manufacturer. A style may be composed of garments that form all or part of one or more GPU's and the style may include any number of garments the manufacturer chooses. Style identification means any numbers, letters, or combination thereof that are sufficient to identify the garments of the style and may include information such as color, season or size. If this option B is selected, in any recall of noncomplying items from a particular GPU:

(*1*) The garment manufacturer must recall the entire style(s) from all customers who purchased garments of the style(s) of which the GPU is part. However, retailers may elect to return only garments from the particular GPU necessitating the recall rather than the entire style(s) being recalled; and

(*2*) Within 48 hours of a written request, the garment manufacturer must supply to the Commission any samples in its possession of garments from the GPU, as requested. As required of all persons subject to this section, the garment manufacturer must also, within the time requested, supply to the Commission the names of any customers who purchased during a specified period of time, garments from the GPU (or the style(s) of which the GPU is a part) and supply access to all records required under the Standard and this section.

(iii) Each garment subject to the Standard shall bear a label with minimum dimensions of 1.3 centimeters (0.5 inch) by 1.9 centimeters (0.75 inch) containing the appropriate garment production unit identification for that garment in letters which are clear, conspicuous, and legible and in a color which contrasts with the background of the label, or shall have such information stamped on the garment itself in letters which are clear, conspicuous, and legible and in a color which contrasts with the background, and at least 2.54 centimeters (1 inch) in every direction from any other information. The stamp or label containing the garment production unit identification must be of such construction, and affixed to the garment in such a manner as to remain on or attached to the garment and legible and visible throughout its intended period of use.

(iv) The fabric production unit identification shall appear in letters at least 0.4 centimeters (one-sixth of an inch) in height against a contrasting background on each label that relates to such fabric and is required by the Textile Fiber Products Identification Act (15 U.S.C. 70–70k) and the regulations thereunder (16 CFR 303.1 through 303.45), or by the Wool Products Labeling Act of 1939 (15 U.S.C. 68–68j) and the regulations thereunder (16 CFR 300.1 through 300.35). When the information required by the Textile Fiber Product Identification Act or by the Wool Products Labeling Act of 1939 appears on an invoice used in lieu of labeling, the fabric production unit identification required by this section may be placed clearly, conspicuously, and legibly on the same invoice in lieu of labeling.

(c)–(d) [Reserved]

(e) *Records—manufacturers, importers, or other persons initially introducing items into commerce*—(1) *General.* Every manufacturer, importer, or other person (such as a converter) initially introducing into commerce items subject to the Standard, irrespective of whether guaranties are issued under paragraph (f) of this section, shall maintain written and physical records as hereinafter specified. The records required must establish a line of continuity through the process of manufacture of each production unit of articles of children's sleepwear, or fabrics or related materials intended or promoted for use in children's sleepwear, to the sale and delivery of the finished items and from the specific finished item to the manufacturing records. Such records shall show with respect to such items:

(i) Details, description, and identification of any and all sampling plans engaged in pursuant to the requirements of the Standard. Such records must be sufficient to demonstrate compliance with such sampling plan(s) and must relate the sampling plan(s) to the actual items produced, marketed, or handled. This requirement is not limited by other provisions of paragraph (e) of this section.

(ii) Garment production units or fabric production units of all garments or fabrics marketed or handled. The records must relate to an appropriate production unit identification on or affixed to the item itself in accordance with paragraph (b)(8) of this section, and the production unit identification must relate to the garment production unit or fabric production unit.

(iii) Test results and details of all tests performed, both prototype and production, including char lengths of each specimen tested, average char length of the samples required to be tested, details of the sampling procedure employed, name and signature of persons conducting tests, date of tests, and all other records necessary to demonstrate compliance with the test procedures and sampling plan specified by the standard or authorized alternate sampling plan.

(iv) Disposition of all failing or rejected items. Such records must demonstrate that the items were retested or reworked and retested in accordance with the Standard prior to sale or distribution and that such retested or reworked and retested items comply with the Standard, or otherwise show the disposition of such items.

(v) Fiber content and manufacturing specifications relating the same to prototype and production testing and to the production units to which applicable.

(vi) Data and test results relied on as a basis for inclusion of different colors or different print patterns of the same fabric as a single fabric or garment production unit under § 1615.4(b) of the Standard.

(vii) Data and test results relied on as a basis for reduced laundering of fabric or garments during test procedures under § 1615.4(g)(4) of the Standard and any guaranties issued or received relating to laundering as well as details of the laundering procedure utilized.

(viii) Identification, composition, and details of application of any flame retardant treatments employed. All prototype and production records shall relate to such information.

(ix) Date and quantity of each sale or delivery of items subject to the Standard (except the date of sale to an ultimate consumer) and the name and address of the purchaser or recipient (except an ultimate consumer). The items involved in each such sale or delivery shall be identified by production unit or by style. A style is a garment design or grouping, preselected by the manufacturer. A style may be composed of garments that form all or part of one or more garment production units and the style may include any number of garments that form all or part of one or more garment production units and the style may include any number of garments the manufacturer chooses. If a person subject to the requirements of § 1615.31(e) maintains sales records which identify the items sold or delivered by style, and if recall of one or more production units subject to the Standard is required, that person in recalling such production units shall notify all purchasers of items of the style in which such production unit or units were manufactured. Retailers may elect to return all items of the style involved, or all items of the production unit or units subject to recall.

(2) *Fabrics.* In addition to the information specified in paragraph (e)(1) of this section the written and physical records maintained with respect to each fabric production unit shall include (i) finished fabric samples sufficient to repeat the fabric sampling procedure required by § 1615.4 (b) through (e) of the Standard for each production unit marketed or handled; and (ii) records to relate the samples to the actual fabric production unit. Upon written request of any duly authorized employee or agent of the Commission, samples sufficient for the sampling and testing of any production unit in accordance with § 1615.4 (b) through (e) of the Standard shall be furnished from these records within the time specified in that written request.

(3) *Garments—prototype testing.* In addition to the records specified in paragraph (e)(1) of this section, the following written and physical records shall be maintained with respect to the garment prototype testing required by the Standard:

(i) Specification, fiber content, and details of construction on all seams, fabrics, threads, stitches, and trims used in each garment style or type upon which prototype testing was performed, relating the same to such garment style or type and to all production units to which such prototype testing is applicable.

(ii) Samples sufficient to repeat the prototype tests required by § 1615.4 (b) through (e) of the Standard for all fabrics, seams, threads, stitches, and trims used in such prototype testing, relating such samples to the records required by paragraph (e) of this section including the information required by paragraph (e)(3)(i) of this section. Upon written request of any duly authorized employee or agent of the Commission, samples sufficient for the testing of any prototype specimens identical to those specimens that were actually tested pursuant to the Standard shall be furnished from these records within the time specified in that written request.

(iii) A complete untested garment from each style or type of garment marketed or handled.

(iv) Remains of all physical specimens tested in accordance with the prototype testing required by § 1615.4 (b) through (e) of the Standard, relating such samples to the records required by paragraph (c) of this section including information required by paragraph (e)(3)(i) of this section.

(4) *Garments—production testing.* In addition to the records required by paragraph (e)(1) of this section, written and physical records shall be maintained and shall show with respect to each garment production unit:

(i) Source and fabric production unit identification of all fabrics subject to testing used in each garment production unit.

(ii) Identification and appropriate reference to all prototype records and prototype tests applicable to each production unit.

(iii) Any guaranty relied upon to demonstrate that the fabric utilized in such garments meets the laundering requirements of the Standard.

(iv) Data sufficient to show that tested samples were selected from the production unit at random from regular production.

(v) Written data that will enable the Commission to obtain and test garments under any applicable compliance market sampling plan.

(5) *Record retention requirements.* The records required by paragraph (e) of this section shall be maintained for 3 years, except that records relating to prototype testing shall be maintained for as long as they are relied upon as demonstrating compliance with the prototype testing requirements of the Standard and shall be retained for 3 years thereafter.

(f) *Tests for guaranty purposes.* Reasonable and representative tests for the purpose of issuing a guaranty under section 8 of the Flammable Fabrics Act (15 U.S.C. 1197) for items subject to the Standard shall be those tests performed pursuant to any sampling plan or authorized alternative sampling plan engaged in pursuant to the requirements of the Standard.

(g) *Compliance with this section.* No person subject to the Flammable Fabrics Act shall manufacture, import, distribute, or otherwise market or handle any item subject to the Standard, including samples, swatches, or specimens used to promote or effect the sale thereof, which is not in compliance with this section.

[40 FR 59903, Dec. 30, 1975, as amended at 43 FR 4855 Feb. 6, 1978; 49 FR 3064, Jan. 24, 1984; 61 FR 1116, Jan. 16, 1996]

§ 1615.32 Method for establishment and use of alternate laundering procedures under section 4(g)(4)(ii) of the standard.

(a) *Scope.* (1) Section 1615.4(g)(4)(ii) of the Standard for the Flammability of Children's Sleepwear in sizes 0–6X (16 CFR 1615.4(g)(4)(ii)) requires that all fabrics and certain garments subject to the standard be tested for flammability as produced (or after one washing and drying) and after the items have been washed and dried 50 times in machines, using the procedure specified in AATCC Test Method 124–1996.[6] This section also provides that items may be laundered a different number of times under another washing and drying procedure if the Commission finds that such an alternate laundering procedure is equivalent to the procedure specified in the standard.

(2) This rule provides the procedures to be followed by persons seeking Commission approval for alternate laundering procedures. It also provides the criteria the Commission will use in evaluating the applications.

(3) The alternate laundering procedures provided for in this section apply only to procedures under section 4(g)(4)(ii) of the standard and shall not be used for determining whether different colors or different print patterns of the same fabric may be included in a single fabric or garment production unit.

(4) As used in this section, fabric means fabric or related material promoted or intended for use in children's sleepwear made to identical specifications and containing the same identity while in production.

(b) *Application procedure.* (1) Applicants seeking approval for use of an alternate laundering procedure under § 1615.4(g)(4)(ii) of the standard must submit the following information in writing to the Assistant Executive Director for Compliance, Consumer Product Safety Commission, Washington, DC 20207:

(i) A detailed description of the proposed alternate laundering procedure, and a 6 in. by 6 in. swatch of the fabric or garment for which the procedure is proposed.

(ii) Upon request of the Commission staff, any other information concerning the procedure and/or any machine used in connection with it.

(iii) With regard to each fabric or garment for which an alternate laundering procedure is sought, test data comparing twenty test specimens washed and dried by the proposed alternate laundering procedure and twenty specimens tested in accordance with the 50-wash and dry cycle procedure required in section 4(g)(4)(ii) of the standard. (For purposes of applications, similar fabrics or garments of different finishes shall be considered as different fabrics or garments and therefore separate test results must be submitted). Each group of twenty specimens upon which these data are based must be cut for testing, half in the machine direction and half in the cross machine direction. Where the applicant manufactures the fabric or garments in more than one plant, the data described in this paragraph must be submitted separately for the fabric or garments of each plant for which the proposed alternate laundering procedure is intended to be used. Subsequent applications for use of the same procedure for additional fabrics and garments may incorporate portions of the original application by reference, as appropriate.

[6] AATCC Test Method 124–1996 "Appearance of Fabrics after Repeated Home Laundering," Technical Manual of the American Association of Textile Chemists and Colorists, vol. 73, 1997, which is incorporated by reference. Copies of this document are available from the American Association of Textile Chemists and Colorists, P.O. Box 12215, Research Triangle Park, North Carolina 27709. This document is also available for inspection at the National Archives and Records Administration (NARA). For information on the availability of this material at NARA, call 202–741–6030, or go to: *http://www.archives.gov/federal_register/code_of_federal_regulations/ibr_locations.html*. This incorporation by reference was approved by the Director of the Federal Register in accordance with 5 U.S.C. 552(a) and 1 CFR part 51.

(2) Applications shall be certified by the chief executive officer of the applicant or the official to whom the duty to certify has been delegated in writing. The Commission's Assistant Executive Director for Compliance must be notified in writing of any such delegation.

(c) *Use of alternate laundering procedure.* (1) The applicant may begin to use the alternate laundering procedure 30 days after the application is received by the Assistant Executive Director for Compliance unless notified to the contrary. The Assistant Executive Director for Compliance will normally furnish an applicant with written notice of approval within 30 days. The applicant may be notified that a longer time is needed for evaluation of the application, and in the discretion of the Assistant Executive Director for Compliance, may be authorized to use the alternate laundering procedure pending the final decision. The notice of approval shall be kept by the applicant with other written records required to be maintained in connection with the use of an alternate laundering procedure. So the applicants may ascertain that the application has been received and when the 30-day period has elapsed, it is suggested that applications be sent by certified mail, return receipt requested.

(2) As provided in detail in §1615.32(e), applicants must immediately discontinue use of an alternate procedure, and must immediately notify the Assistant Executive Director for Compliance if there are test failures during revalidation testing.

(d) *Revalidation testing.* (1) In order to assure a continued satisfactory correlation between the alternate laundering procedure and the laundering procedure of the standard, applicants shall perform all the testing described in paragraph (b)(1)(iii) of this section for fabrics or garments from current production at least once for every three-month period during which any of the fabric or garments are produced.

(2) If following initial approval, four successive comparisons of the alternate and the 50-cycle methods as described in paragraph (d)(1) of this section, consistently show acceptable results under the criteria specified by paragraph (f) of this section, the Commission will deem such comparisons to be sufficient demonstration of the equivalence of the alternate laundering procedure with the 50 launderings required in the standard and further revalidation testing will not be required.

(3) Records of revalidation testing need not be submitted to the Assistant Executive Director for Compliance. However such records must be maintained in accordance with paragraph (h) of this section.

(e) *Revalidation testing failures.* (1) If revalidation testing for any fabric or garment does not meet the criteria of §1615.32(f), the applicant must immediately discontinue use of the alternate laundering procedure for the fabric or garment and must immediately notify the Assistant Executive Director for Compliance in writing of the failure to meet the criteria. Also, the testing from the production unit from which the non-correlating samples were taken and the testing from subsequent production units (if any) must be repeated immediately using the laundering procedure prescribed in the standard. These repeat tests shall then be the tests applicable to such production unit(s) and the tests previously performed on the production unit(s) shall be considered invalid.

(2) When use of an alternate laundering procedure for a particular fabric or garment has been discontinued because of a failure to meet the criteria of §1615.32(f), the alternate laundering procedure shall not be used again unless a new application for approval is submitted to the Assistant Executive Director for Compliance and that officer approves the application in writing. In addition to the other information required for applications, the additional application should give facts or reasons showing why the applicant believes the procedure should be considered reliable with the fabric or garments involved, in view of previous failure.

(f) *Commission criteria for evaluating applications.* (1) The Assistant Executive Director for Compliance will approve the alternate laundering procedure as equivalent to the laundering procedure specified in §1615.4(g)(4)(ii) of the standard if testing from 20 specimens laundered by the proposed alternate procedure yields as many or more char lengths in excess of five inches as does testing from the twenty specimens laundered by the 50-laundering cycle method prescribed in the standard.

(2) If the alternate laundering procedure yields fewer char lengths in excess of five inches than does the 50-wash and dry cycle, then the Assistant Executive Director for Compliance will not consider the alternate procedure to be equivalent, with the following exception: If the number of five-inch chars from the alternate procedure is within one of the number of five-inch chars obtained from the 50-cycle procedure, the applicant may repeat the original test with new specimens and if the combined results of both tests show the count of chars exceeding five inches from the alternate is equal to, or greater than, the count from the 50-wash cycle procedure, the Assistant Executive Director for Compliance will approve the alternate laundering procedure.

(g) *Commission testing for compliance.* (1) For the purpose of determining compliance with the standard, the Commission will rely on testing employing the laundering procedure now prescribed in section 4(g)(4)(ii) of the standard.

(2) The Commission may verify equivalency of any procedure submitted by independent testing and evaluation, by or on behalf of the Commission.

(h) *Recordkeeping.* The applicant must maintain a record of all applications filed with the Commission and of all equivalency tests for as long as the procedures to which they relate are in use and for three years thereafter.

[42 FR 55891, Oct. 20, 1977, as amended at 65 FR 12927, Mar. 10, 2000; 65 FR 19818, Apr. 12, 2000]

§ 1615.35 Use of alternate apparatus, procedures, or criteria for testing under the standard.

(a) The Standard for the Flammability of Children's Sleepwear: Sizes 0 through 6X (the Standard) requires every manufacturer, importer, and other person (such as a converter) initially introducing items subject to the Standard into commerce to group items into production units, and to test samples from each production unit. See 16 CFR 1615.4 (b), (c) and (d). The Standard prescribes an apparatus and procedure for performing tests of fabric and garments subject to its provisions. See 16 CFR 1615.4 (a), (f), and (g). The Standard prescribes pass/fail criteria at 16 CFR 1615.3(b).

(b)(1) By issuance of this § 1615.35, the Commission gives its approval to any person or firm desiring to use test apparatus or procedures other than those prescribed by the Standard for purposes of compliance with the Standard, if that person or firm has data or other information to demonstrate that a test utilizing such alternate apparatus or procedures is as stringent as, or more stringent than, a test utilizing the apparatus and procedures specified in the Standard. The Commission considers a test utilizing alternate apparatus or procedures to be "as stringent as, or more stringent than" a test utilizing the apparatus and procedures specified in the standard if, when testing identical specimens, a test utilizing alternate apparatus or procedures yields failing results as often as, or more often than, a test utilizing the apparatus and procedures specified in the Standard.

(2) The data or information required by this paragraph (b) of this section as a condition to the Commission's approval of the use of alternate test apparatus or procedures must be in the possession of the person or firm desiring to use such alternate apparatus or procedures before the alternate apparatus or procedures may be used for purposes of compliance with the Standard.

(3) The information required by this paragraph (b) of this section must be retained by the person or firm using the alternate test apparatus or procedure for as long as that apparatus or procedure is used for purposes of compliance with the Standard, and for a period of one year thereafter.

(c) Written application to the Commission is not required for approval of alternate test apparatus or procedure, and the Commission will not act on any individual written application for approval of alternate test apparatus or procedure.

(d) Use of any alternate test apparatus or procedure without the data or information required by paragraph (b), of this section, may result in violation of the Standard and section 3 of the Flammable Fabrics Act (15 U.S.C. 1192).

(e) The Commission will test fabrics and garments subject to the Standard for compliance with the requirements of the Standard using the apparatus and procedures set forth in the Standard. The Commission will consider any failing results from compliance testing as evidence of a violation of the Standard and section 3 of the Flammable Fabrics Act (15 U.S.C 1192).

(Reporting requirements contained in paragraph (d) were approved by the Office of Management and Budget under control number 3041–0027)

[48 FR 21315, May 12, 1983]

§ 1615.36 Use of alternate apparatus or procedures for tests for guaranty purposes.

(a) Section 8(a) of the Flammable Fabrics Act (FFA, 15 U.S.C. 1197(a)) provides that no person shall be subject to criminal prosecution under section 7 of the FFA (15 U.S.C. 1196) for a violation of section 3 of the FFA (15 U.S.C. 1192) if that person establishes a guaranty received in good faith which meets all requirements set forth in section 8 of the FFA. One of those requirements is that the guaranty must be based upon "reasonable and representative tests" in accordance with the applicable standard.

(b) Section 1615.31(f) of the regulations implementing the Standard for the Flammability of Children's Sleepwear: Sizes 0 through 6X (the Standard) provides that for purposes of supporting guaranties issued in accordance with section 8 of the FFA for items subject to the Standard, "reasonable and representative tests" are tests "performed pursuant to any sampling plan or authorized alternative sampling plan engaged in pursuant to the requirements of the Standard."

(c) At §1615.35, the Commission has set forth conditions under which the Commission will approve the use of test apparatus or procedures other than those prescribed in the Standard for purposes of demonstrating compliance with the requirements of the Standard. Any person or firm meeting the requirements of §1615.35 for use of alternate test apparatus or procedure for compliance with the Standard may also use such alternate test apparatus or procedures under the same conditions for purposes of conducting "reasonable and representative tests" to support guaranties of items subject to the Standard, following any sampling plan prescribed by the Standard or any approved alternate sampling plan.

(d) The Commission will test fabrics and garments subject to the Standard for compliance with the Standard using the apparatus and procedures set forth in the Standard. The Commission will consider any failing results from compliance testing as evidence that the person or firm using alternate test apparatus or procedures has furnished a false guaranty in violation of section 8(b) of the FFA (15 U.S.C. 1197(b)).

[48 FR 21316, May 12, 1983]

Subpart C—Interpretations and Policies

AUTHORITY: Secs. 1–17, 67 Stat. 111–115, as amended, 81 Stat. 568–74; 15 U.S.C. 1191–1204.

§ 1615.61 [Reserved]

§ 1615.62 Policy and interpretation relative to items in inventory or as to recordkeeping requirements.

(a) The Standard for the Flammability of Children's Sleepwear: Sizes 0 through 6X (FF 3–71) (subpart A of this part) was published in the FEDERAL REGISTER on July 29, 1971, at 36 FR 14062 et seq., and amended in the FEDERAL REGISTER of July 21, 1972 (37 FR 14624). The Notice of Standard provided at 36 FR 14063 that "Items in inventory or with the trade on the effective date of the Standard are exempt. All concerned parties shall be required to maintain records that these items offered for sale after the effective date of the Standard are eligible for the exemption."

(b) The Children's Sleepwear Standard was amended on July 21, 1972, at 37 FR 14624 et seq. to incorporate a sleepwear sampling plan therein and to make certain nonsubstantive technical corrections as to the test equipment. The effective date remained the same. In issuance of such amendment the Notice of Amendment specified at 37 FR 14625 that "It is emphasized that the only substantive change made to the standard involves the amendment necessary to include the sampling plan."

(c) The Notice of Amendment did not repeat the language in the original 1971 Notice of Standard relative to items in inventory or as to recordkeeping requirements.

(d) Questions have arisen under this standard as to the application of the standard to goods manufactured outside the United States prior to the effective date of the standard on July 29, 1972, as to whether a person claiming the exemption specified in the standard must maintain records showing eligibility for exemption from the standard.

(e) In the Commission's view, the provisions of the July 29, 1971, Notice of Standard as to exemption of items of children's sleepwear in inventory or with the trade on the effective date of the standard and as to the necessity of maintenance of records to show eligibility for such exemption are in full force and effect.

NOTE: This policy was published by the Federal Trade Commission on January 31, 1973 (38 FR 3014). It continues in effect.

§ 1615.63 Policy regarding garment production unit identification.

No provision of § 1615.31(b)(8) prohibits placement of a garment production unit identification on a label containing other information. Provided, however, that when the garment production unit identification appears on a label containing other information, provisions of § 1615.31(b)(7) require that the garment production unit identification must be set forth separately from any other information appearing on the same label, and that information not required by the applicable enforcement regulation § 1615.31, but placed on the same label with the garment production unit identification, shall not interfere with the garment production unit identification.

§ 1615.64 Policy to clarify scope of the standard.

(a) The Standard for Flammability of Children's Sleepwear: Size 0 Through 6X (16 CFR part 1615) is applicable to any item of children's sleepwear in sizes 0 through 6X.

(1) The term *item* is defined in the Standard at § 1615.1(d) to mean "any product of children's sleepwear, or any fabric or related material intended or promoted for use in children's sleepwear."

(2) The term *children's sleepwear* is defined in the Standard at § 1615.1(a) to mean "any product of wearing apparel up to and including size 6X, such as nightgowns, pajamas, or similar or related items, such as robes, intended to be worn primarily for sleeping or activities relating to sleeping. Diapers and underwear are excluded from the definition."

(b) The Commission makes the following statement of policy regarding (1) the phrase "intended or promoted" as used in the definition of "item" in § 1615.1(d), and (2) the phrase "intended to be worn primarily for sleeping or activities related to sleeping" as used in the definition of "children's sleepwear" in § 1615.1(a).

(c) For enforcement purposes, the meaning of these phrases will be interpreted by the Commission in accordance with the following principles:

(1) *Sleepwear fabrics and related materials*. Whether fabric or related material is "intended or promoted" for use in children's sleepwear depends on the facts and circumstances in each case. Relevant factors include:

(i) The nature of the fabric and its suitability for use in children's sleepwear;

(ii) The extent to which the fabric or a comparable fabric has been sold to manufacturers of children's sleepwear for use in the manufacture of children's sleepwear garments; and

(iii) The likelihood that the fabric will be used primarily for children's sleepwear in a substantial number of cases.

(2) *Sleepwear garments*. Whether a product of wearing apparel is "intended to be worn primarily for sleeping or activities related to sleeping" depends on

the facts and circumstances present in each case. Relevant factors include:

(i) The nature of the product and its suitability for use by children for sleeping or activities related to sleeping;

(ii) The manner in which the product is distributed and promoted; and

(iii) The likelihood that the product will be used by children primarily for sleeping or activities related to sleeping in a substantial number of cases.

(3) The factors set forth in this policy statement are guidelines only, and are not elements of the definition of the term "children's sleepwear" in §1615.1(a) of the Standard. For this reason, a particular fabric or garment may meet the definition of "children's sleepwear" set forth in the Standard, even though all factors listed in this policy statement are not present.

(d) Retailers, distributors, and wholesalers, as well as manufacturers, importers, and other persons (such as converters) introducing a fabric or garment into commerce which does not meet the requirements of the flammability standards for children's sleepwear, have an obligation not to promote or sell such fabric or garment for use as an item of children's sleepwear. Also, retailers, distributors, and wholesalers are advised not to advertise, promote, or sell as an item of children's sleepwear any item which a manufacturer, importer, or other person (such as a converter) introducing the item into commerce has indicated by label, invoice, or, otherwise, does not meet the requirements of the children's sleepwear flammability standards and is not intended or suitable for use as sleepwear. "Infant garments" as defined by §1615.1(c) and "tight-fitting" garments as defined by §1615.1(o) are exempt from the standard which requires flame resistance. They may be marketed as sleepwear for purposes of this section. Additionally, retailers are advised:

(1) To segregate, by placement in different parts of a department or store, fabrics and garments covered by the children's sleepwear standards from all fabrics and garments that are beyond the scope of the children's sleepwear standards but which resemble items of children's sleepwear;

(2) To utilize store display signs indicating the distinction between types of fabrics and garments, for example by indicating which are sleepwear items and which are not; and

(3) To avoid the advertisement or promotion of a fabric or garment that does not comply with the children's sleepwear flammability standard in a manner that may cause the item to be viewed by the consumer as an item of children's sleepwear.

(Sec. 5, Pub.L. 90–189, 81 Stat. 569, 15 U.S.C. 1194; sec. 30(b), Pub.L. 92–573, 86 Stat. 1231, 15 U.S.C. 2079(b); 5 U.S.C. 553)

[49 FR 10250, Mar. 20, 1984, as amended at 64 FR 2832, Jan. 19, 1999; 64 FR 34533, June 28, 1999]

PART 1616—STANDARD FOR THE FLAMMABILITY OF CHILDREN'S SLEEPWEAR: SIZES 7 THROUGH 14 (FF 5–74)

Subpart A—The Standard

Subpart B—Rules and Regulations

Subpart C—Interpretations and Policies

SOURCE: 40 FR 59917, Dec. 30, 1975, unless otherwise noted.

Subpart A—The Standard

AUTHORITY: Sec. 429, Pub. L. 105–276; Sec. 4, 67 Stat. 112, as amended, 81 Stat. 569–570; 15 U.S.C. 1193.

§ 1616.1 Scope and application.

(a) This Standard provides a test method to determine the flammability of children's sleepwear, sizes 7 through 14 and fabric or related material intended or promoted for use in such children's sleepwear.

(b) All sleepwear items as defined in § 1616.2(c), are subject to the requirements of this Standard.

(c) Children's sleepwear items which meet all the requirements of the Standard for the Flammability of Children's Sleepwear: Sizes 0 through 6X (FF 3–71) (subpart A of part 1615 of this chapter) are in compliance with this Standard. FF 3–71 was issued July 29, 1971 (36 FR 14062), and amended July 21, 1972 (37 FR 14624).

(d) As used in this Standard, *pass* and *fail* refer to the test criteria for specimens while *accept* and *reject* refer to the acceptance or rejection of a production unit under the sampling plan.

(e) The flammability standards for clothing textiles and vinyl plastic film, parts 1610 and 1611 of this chapter, are superseded by this part 1616 insofar as they apply to items defined in § 1616.2(c).

§ 1616.2 Definitions.

In addition to the definitions given in section 2 of the Flammable Fabrics Act, as amended (15 U.S.C. 1191), the following definitions apply for purposes of this Standard:

(a) Children's sleepwear means any product of wearing apparel size 7 through 14, such as nightgowns, pajamas, or similar or related items, such as robes, intended to be worn primarily for sleeping or activities related to sleeping, except:

(1) Diapers and underwear; and

(2) "Tight-fitting garments" as defined by section 1616.2(m), below.

(b) *Sizes 7 through 14* means the sizes defined as 7 through 14 in Department of Commerce Voluntary Product Standards PS 54–72 and PS 36–70, previously identified as Commercial Standards, CS 153–48, "Body Measurements for the Sizing of Girls' Apparel" and CS 155–50, "Body Measurements for the Sizing of Boys' Apparel", respectively.[1]

(c) *Item* means any product of children's sleepwear or any fabric of related material intended or promoted for use in children's sleepwear.

(d) *Trim* means decorative materials, such as ribbons, laces, embroidery, or ornaments. This definition does not include (1) individual pieces less than 2 inches in their longest dimension, provided that such pieces do not constitute or cover in aggregate a total of more than 20 square inches of the item or (2) functional materials (findings), such as zippers, buttons or elastic bands, used in the construction of garments.

(e) *Test criteria* means the average char length and the maximum char length which a sample of specimen may exhibit in order to pass an individual test.

(f) *Char length* means the distance from the original lower edge of the specimen exposed to the flame in accordance with the procedure specified in § 1616.5 *Test procedure* to the end of the tear or void in the charred, burned, or damaged area, the tear being made in accordance with the procedure specified in § 1615.5(c)(2) *Specimen burning and evaluation*.

(g) *Afterglow* means the continuation of glowing of parts of a specimen after flaming has ceased.

(h) *Fabric piece* (piece) means a continuous, unseamed length of fabric, one or more of which make up a unit.

(i) *Fabric production unit* (unit) means any quantity of finished fabric up to 4,600 linear m. (5,000 linear yds.) for Normal Sampling or 9,200 linear m. (10,000 linear yds.) for Reduced Sampling which has a specific identity that remains unchanged throughout the unit except for color or print pattern as specified in § 1616.4(a). For purposes of this definition, finished fabric means

[1] Copies available from the National Technical Information Service, 5285 Port Royal Street, Springfield VA 22151. The ordering number for PS 54–72 (CS 153–48), on girls' apparel sizing, is COM 73–50603; the ordering number for PS 36–70 (CS 155–50), on boys' apparel sizing, is PB 86125648.

fabric in its final form after completing its last processing step as a fabric except for slitting.

(j) *Garment production unit* (unit) means any quantity of finished garments up to 500 dozen which have a specific identity that remains unchanged throughout the unit except for size, trim, findings, color, and print patterns as specified in § 1616.4(a).

(k) *Sample* means five test specimens.

(l) *Specimen* means an 8.9±0.5 × 25.4±0.5 cm. (3.5±0.2 × 10±0.2 in.) section of fabric. For garment testing, the specimen will include a seam or trim.

(m) Tight-fitting garment means a garment which:

(1)(i) In each of the sizes listed below does not exceed the maximum dimension specified below for the chest, waist, seat, upper arm, thigh, wrist, or ankle:

	Chest	Waist	Seat	Upper arm	Thigh	Wrist	Ankle
Size 7 Boys [1]							
Maximum dimension:							
Centimeters	63.5	58.4	66	18.7	37.2	13.0	18.7
(inches)	(25)	(23)	(26)	(7⅜)	(14⅝)	(5⅛)	(7⅜)
Size 7 Girls							
Maximum dimension:							
Centimeters	63.5	58.4	67.3	18.7	38.7	13.0	18.7
(inches)	(25)	(23)	(26½)	(7⅜)	(15¼)	(5⅛)	(7⅜)
Size 8 Boys [1]							
Maximum dimension:							
Centimeters	66	59.7	67.3	19.4	38.4	13.3	19.1
(inches)	(26)	(23½)	(26½)	(7⅝)	(15⅛)	(5¼)	(7½)
Size 8 Girls							
Maximum dimension:							
Centimeters	66	59.7	71.1	19.4	41.3	13.3	19.1
(inches)	(26)	(23½)	(28)	(7⅝)	(16¼)	(5¼)	(7½)
Size 9 Boys [1]							
Maximum dimension:							
Centimeters	68.6	61.0	69.2	20	39.7	13.7	19.4
(inches)	(27)	(24)	(27¼)	(7⅞)	(15⅝)	(5⅜)	(7⅝)
Size 9 Girls							
Maximum dimension:							
Centimeters	68.6	61.0	73.7	20	42.6	13.7	19.4
(inches)	(27)	(24)	(29)	(7⅞)	(16¾)	(5⅜)	(7⅝)
Size 10 Boys [1]							
Maximum dimension:							
Centimeters	71.1	62.2	71.1	20.6	41.0	14	19.7
(inches)	(28)	(24½)	(28)	(8⅛)	(16⅛)	(5½)	(7¾)
Size 10 Girls							
Maximum dimension:							
Centimeters	71.1	62.2	76.2	20.6	43.8	14	19.7
(inches)	(28)	(24½)	(30)	(8⅛)	(17¼)	(5½)	(7¾)
Size 11 Boys [1]							
Maximum dimension:							
Centimeters	73.7	63.5	73.7	21	42.2	14.3	20
(inches)	(29)	(25)	(29)	(8¼)	(16⅝)	(5⅝)	(7⅞)
Size 11 Girls							
Maximum dimension:							
Centimeters	73.7	63.5	78.7	21	45.1	14.3	20
(inches)	(29)	(25)	(31)	(8¼)	(17¾)	(5⅝)	(7⅞)
Size 12 Boys [1]							
Maximum dimension:							
Centimeters	76.2	64.8	76.2	21.6	43.5	14.6	20.3
(inches)	(30)	(25½)	(30)	(8½)	(17⅛)	(5¾)	(8)
Size 12 Girls							
Maximum dimension:							
Centimeters	76.2	64.8	81.3	21.6	46.7	14.6	20.3
(inches)	(30)	(25½)	(32)	(8½)	(18½)	(5¾)	(8)

	Chest	Waist	Seat	Upper arm	Thigh	Wrist	Ankle
Size 13 Boys [1]							
Maximum dimension:							
Centimeters	78.7	66	78.7	22.2	44.8	14.9	20.6
(inches)	(31)	(26)	(31)	(8¾)	(17⅝)	(5⅞)	(8⅛)
Size 13 Girls							
Maximum dimension:							
Centimeters	78.7	66	83.8	22.2	47.6	14.9	20.6
(inches)	(31)	(26)	(33)	(8¾)	(18¾)	(5⅞)	(8⅛)
Size 14 Boys [1]							
Maximum dimension:							
Centimeters	81.3	67.3	81.3	22.9	46	15.2	21
(inches)	(32)	(26½)	(32)	(9)	(18⅛)	(6)	(8¼)
Size 14 Girls							
Maximum dimension:							
Centimeters	81.3	67.3	86.4	22.9	49.5	15.2	21
(inches)	(32)	(26½)	(34)	(9)	(19½)	(6)	(8¼)

[1] Garments not explicitly labeled and promoted for wear by girls must not exceed these maximum dimensions.

(ii) Note: Measure the dimensions on the front of the garment. Lay garment, right side out, on a flat, horizontal surface. Smooth out wrinkles. Measure distances as specified below and multiply them by two. Measurements should be equal to or less than the maximum dimensions given in the standards.

(A) Chest—measure distance from arm pit to arm pit (A to B) as in Diagram 1.

(B) Waist—See Diagram 1. *One-piece garment*, measure at the narrowest location between arm pits and crotch (C to D). *Two-piece garment*, measure width at both the bottom/sweep of the upper piece (C to D) and, as in Diagram 3, the top of the lower piece (C to D).

(C) Wrist—measure the width of the end of the sleeve (E to F), if intended to extend to the wrist, as in Diagram 1.

(D) Upper arm—draw a straight line from waist/sweep D through arm pit B to G. Measure down the sleeve fold from G to H. Refer to table below for G to H distances for each size. Measure the upper arm of the garment (perpendicular to the fold) from H to I as shown in Diagram 1.

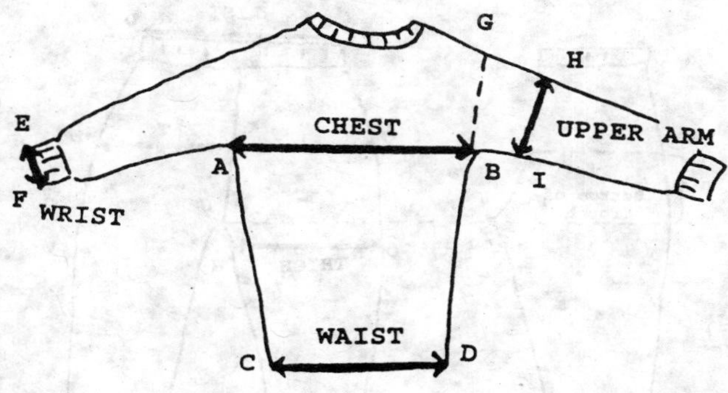

Diagram 1

DISTANCE FROM SHOULDER (G) TO (H) FOR UPPER ARM MEASUREMENT FOR SIZES 7 THROUGH 14

7	8	9	10	11	12	13	14
11.4 cm 4½″	11.7 cm 4⅝″	11.9 cm 4¾″	12.5 cm 4⅞″	12.8 cm 5″	13.1 cm 5⅛″	13.7 cm 5⅜″	14.2 cm 5⅝″

(E) Seat—Fold the front of the pant in half to find the bottom of the crotch at J as in Diagram 2. The crotch seam and inseam intersect at J. Mark point K on the crotch seam at 4 inches above and perpendicular to the bottom of the crotch. Unfold the garment as in Diagram 3. Measure the seat from L to M through K as shown.

(F) Thigh—measure from the bottom of the crotch (J) 1 inch down the inseam to N as in Diagram 2. Unfold the garment and measure the thigh from the inseam at N to O as shown in Diagram 3.

(G) Ankle—measure the width of the end of the leg (P to Q), if intended to extend to the ankle, as in Diagram 3.

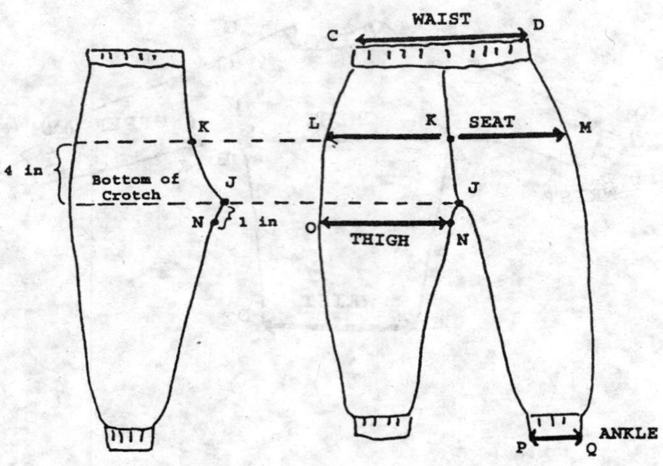

Diagram 2 Diagram 3

(2) Has no item of fabric, ornamentation or trim, such as lace, appliques, or ribbon, which extends more than 6 millimeters (¼ inch) from the point of attachment to the outer surface of the garment;

(3) Has sleeves which do not exceed the maximum dimension for the upper arm at any point between the upper arm and the wrist, and which diminish in width gradually from the top of the shoulder (point G in Diagram 1) to the wrist;

(4) Has legs which do not exceed the maximum dimension for the thigh at any point between the thigh and the ankle, and which diminish gradually in width between the thigh and the ankle;

(5) In the case of a one-piece garment, has a width which does not exceed the maximum dimension for the chest at any point between the chest and the waist and which diminishes gradually from the chest to the waist; and has a width which does not exceed the maximum dimension for the seat at any point between the seat and the waist and which diminishes gradually from the seat to the waist;

(6) In the case of a two-piece garment, has an upper piece with a width which does not exceed the maximum distance for the chest at any point between the chest and the bottom of that piece and which diminishes gradually from the chest to the bottom of that piece; in the case of an upper piece with fastenings, has the lowest fastening within 15 centimeters (6 inches) of the bottom of that piece;

(7) In the case of a two-piece garment, has a lower piece with a width which does not exceed the maximum dimension for the seat at any point between the seat and the top of the lower piece and which diminishes gradually from the seat to the top of that piece;

(8) Complies with all applicable requirements of the Standard for the Flammability of Clothing Textiles (16 CFR part 1610) and the Standard for the

Flammability of Vinyl Plastic Film (16 CFR part 1611); and

(9) Bears a label stating the size of the garment; for example "Size 7." If the label is not visible to the consumer when the garment is offered for sale at retail, the garment size must appear legibly on the package of the garment.

Effective date: These amendments shall become effective on January 1, 1997, and shall be applicable to garments which are introduced into commerce on or after that date.

(10)(i) *Hangtags.* Bears a hangtag as shown following this paragraph stating "For child's safety, garment should fit snugly. This garment is not flame resistant. Loose-fitting garment is more likely to catch fire." The hangtag must measure 1½″ × 6¼″. The text must be enclosed in a text box that measures 1″ × 5¾″ and must be in 18 point Arial/Helvetica font. The hangtag must have a yellow background and black lettering. The color yellow must meet the specifications for Standard Safety Yellow (Hue 5.OY; Value/Chroma 8.0/12) as described in American National Standard ANSI Z535.1–1998, Safety Color Code, p.6, under Munsell Notation.[2] One side of the hangtag must display only this message. The reverse side of the hangtag may display sizing information, but otherwise must be blank. The text must not be obscured by the hole provided for attaching the hangtag to the garment. The hangtag must be prominently displayed on the garment.

For child's safety, garment should fit snugly.
This garment is not flame resistant.
Loose-fitting garment is more likely to catch fire.

(ii) *Packages.* If the garments are sold in packages, the package must have a label as shown following this paragraph with the same language that would appear on the hangtag. The label must have a text box that measures ¾ × 3¾. The text must be 11 point Arial/Helvetica in black lettering against a yellow background. The packages must be prominently, conspicuously, and legibly labeled with the required message. The package label may be adhesive.

For child's safety, garment should fit snugly.
This garment is not flame resistant.
Loose-fitting garment is more likely to catch fire.

[2] ANSI Z535.1–1998, Standard for Safety Color Code, p.6, published by National Electrical Manufacturers Association is incorporated by reference. Copies of this document are available from the National Electrical Manufacturers Association, 1300 N. 17th Street, Suite 1847, Rossylyn, Virginia 22209. This document is also available for inspection at the National Archives and Records Administration (NARA). For information on the availability of this material at NARA, call 202–741–6030, or go to: *http://www.archives.gov/federal_register/code_of_federal_regulations/ibr_locations.html.* The incorporation by reference was approved by the Director of the Federal Register in accordance with 5 U.S.C. 552(a) and 1 CFR part 51.

(11) Bears a label as shown following this paragraph stating "Wear Snug-fitting, Not Flame Resistant." The text must be printed on the front of the sizing label located on the center back of the garment and must be immediately below the size designation. The text must be a minimum of 5 point sans serif font in all capital letters and must be set apart from other label text by a line border. The text must contrast with the background color of the label. The label must not be covered by any other label or tag.

WEAR SNUG-FITTING NOT FLAME RESISTANT

Example in 10 pt Arial font

[40 FR 59917, Dec. 30, 1975, as amended at 50 FR 53307, Dec. 31, 1985; 61 FR 47646, Sept. 9, 1996; 64 FR 2841, Jan. 19, 1999; 64 FR 34535, June 28, 1999; 64 FR 48705, Sept. 8, 1999; 64 FR 61021, Nov. 9, 1999]

§ 1616.3 General requirements.

(a) *Summary of test method.* Conditioned specimens are suspended one at a time vertically in holders in a prescribed cabinet and subjected to a standard flame along their bottom edges for a specified time under controlled conditions. The char lengths are recorded.

(b) *Test criteria.* The test criteria when the testing is done in accordance with § 1616.4 *Sampling and acceptance procedures* and § 1616.5 *Test procedures* are:

(1) *Average char length.* The average char length of five specimens shall not exceed 17.8 cm. (7.0 in.).

(2) *Full-specimen burn.* No individual specimen shall have a char length of 25.4±0.5 cm. (10±0.2 in.).

(c) Details of the number of specimens which must meet the above test criteria for unit acceptance is specified in § 1616.4.

§ 1616.4 Sampling and acceptance procedures.

(a) *General.* (1) The test criteria of § 1616.3(b) shall be used in conjunction with the following fabric and garment sampling plan. The Consumer Product Safety Commission may consider and approve other sampling plans that provide at least the equivalent level of fire safety to the consumer, provided such alternate sampling plans have operating characteristics such that the probability of unit acceptance at any percentage defective does not exceed the corresponding probability of unit acceptance of the following sampling plan in the region of the latter's operating characteristic curves that lies between 5 and 95 percent acceptance probability. Alternate sampling plans approved for one manufacturer may be used by other manufacturers without prior Consumer Product Safety Commission approval.

(2) Different colors or different print patterns of the same fabric may be included in a single fabric or garment production unit, provided such colors or print patterns demonstrate char lengths that are not significantly different from each other as determined by previous testing of at least three samples from each color or print pattern to be included in the unit.

(3) Garments with different trim and findings may be included in a single garment production unit provided the other garment characteristics are identical except for size, color, and print pattern.

(4) For fabrics whose flammability characteristics are not dependent on chemical additives or chemical reactants to polymer, fiber, yarns, or fabrics, the laundering requirement of § 1616.5(c)(4) is met on subsequent fabric production units if results of testing an initial fabric production unit demonstrate acceptability according to the

requirements of paragraph (b) of this section, *Normal sampling*, both before and after the appropriate laundering.

(5) If the fabric has been shown to meet the laundering requirement, § 1616.5(c)(4), the garments produced from that fabric are not required to be laundered prior to testing.

(6) Each sample (five specimens), for Fabric Sampling shall be selected so that two specimens are in one fabric direction (machine or cross-machine) and three specimens are in the other fabric direction, except for the additional sample selected after a failure, in which case all five specimens shall be selected in the fabric direction in which the specimen failure occurred.

(7) Fabric samples may be selected from fabric as outlined in paragraph (b) of this section, *Fabric sampling* or, for verification purposes, from randomly selected garments.

(8) Multi-layer fabrics shall be tested with a hem of approximately 2.5 cm. (1 in.) sewn at the bottom edge of the specimen with a suitable thread and stitch. The specimen shall include each of the components over its entire length. Garments manufactured from multi-layer fabrics shall be tested with the edge finish which is used in the garment at the bottom edge of the specimen.

(b) *Fabric sampling*. A fabric production unit (unit) is either accepted or rejected in accordance with the following plan:

(1) *Normal sampling*. Select one sample from the beginning of the first fabric piece (piece) in the unit and one sample from the end of the last piece in the unit, or select a sample from each end of the piece if the unit is made up of only one piece. Test the two selected samples. If both samples meet all the test criteria of § 1616.3(b), accept the unit. If either or both of the samples fail the 17.8 cm. (7.0 in.) average char length criterion, § 1616.3(b)(1), reject the unit. If two or more of the individual specimens, from the 10 selected specimens, fail the 25.4 cm. (10 in.) char length criterion, § 1616.3(b)(2), reject the unit. If only one individual specimen, from the 10 selected specimens, fails the 25.4 cm. (10 in.) char length criterion, § 1616.3(b)(2), select five additional specimens from the same end of the piece in which the failure occurred, all five to be taken in the fabric direction in which the specimen failure occurred. If this additional sample passes all the test criteria, accept the unit. If this additional sample fails any part of the test criteria, reject the unit.

(2) *Reduced sampling*. (i) The level of sampling required for fabric acceptance may be reduced provided the preceding 15 units of the fabric have all been accepted using the Normal Sampling Plan.

(ii) The reduced Sampling Plan shall be the same as for Normal Sampling except that the quantity of fabric in the unit may be increased to 9,200 linear m. (10,000 linear yds.)

(iii) Select and test two samples in the same manner as in Normal Sampling. Accept or reject the unit on the same basis as with Normal Sampling.

(iv) Reduced Sampling shall be discontinued and Normal Sampling resumed if a unit is rejected.

(3) *Tightened sampling*. Tightened sampling shall be used when a unit is rejected under the Normal Sampling Plan. The Tightened Sampling shall be the same as Normal Sampling except that one additional sample shall be selected and cut from a middle piece in the unit. If the unit is made up of less than two pieces, the unit shall be divided into at least two pieces. The division shall be such that the pieces produced by the division shall not be smaller than 92 linear m. (100 linear yds.) or greater than 2,300 linear m. (2,500 linear yds.). If the unit is made up of two pieces, the additional sample shall be selected from the interior end of one of the pieces. Test the three selected samples. If all three selected samples meet all the test criteria of § 1616.3(b), accept the unit. If one or more of the three selected samples fail the 17.8 cm. (7.0 in.) average char length criterion, § 1616.3(b)(1), reject the unit. If two or more of the individual specimens, from the 15 selected specimens, fail the 25.4 cm. (10 in.) char length criterion, § 1616.3(b)(2), reject the unit. If only one individual specimen, from the 15 selected specimens, fails the 25.4 cm. (10 in.) char length criterion, § 1616.3(b)(2), select five additional specimens from the same end of

the same piece in which the failure occurred, all five to be taken in the fabric direction in which the specimen failure occurred. If this additional sample passes all the test criteria, accept the unit. If this additional sample fails any part of the test criteria, reject the unit. Tightened Sampling may be discontinued and Normal Sampling resumed after five consecutive units have all been accepted using Tightened Sampling. If Tightened Sampling remains in effect for 15 consecutive units, production of the specific fabric in Tightened Sampling must be discontinued until that part of the process or component which is causing failure has been identified and the quality of the end product has been improved.

(4) *Disposition of rejected units*. (i) The piece or pieces which have failed and resulted in the initial rejection of the unit may not be retested, used, or promoted for use in children's sleepwear as defined in §§1616.2(a) and 1615.1(a) of the (Standard for the Flammability of Children's Sleepwear: Sizes 0 through 6X) (FF 3–71) (subpart A of part 1615 of this chapter) except after reworking to improve the flammability characteristics and subsequent retesting and acceptance in accordance with the procedures in *Tightened Sampling*.

(ii) The remainder of a rejected unit, after removing the piece or pieces, the failure of which resulted in unit rejection, may be accepted if the following test plan is successfully concluded at all required locations. The required locations are those adjacent to each such failed piece. (Required locations exist on both sides of the "Middle Piece" tested in Tightened Sampling if failure of that piece resulted in unit rejection). Failure of a piece shall be deemed to have resulted in unit rejection if unit rejection occurred and a sample or specimen from the piece failed any test criterion of §1616.3(b).

(iii) The unit should contain at least 15 pieces for disposition testing after removing the failing pieces. If necessary for this purpose, the unit shall be demarcated into at least 15 approximately equal length pieces unless such division results in pieces shorter than 92 linear m. (100 linear yds.). In this latter case, the unit shall be demarcated into roughly equal length pieces of approximately 92 linear m. (100 linear yds.) each. If such a division results in five pieces or less in the unit for each failing piece after removing the failing pieces, only the individual pieces retest procedure [described in paragraph (b)(4)(vi) of this section] may be used.

(iv) Select and cut a sample from each end of each adjoining piece beginning adjacent to the piece which failed. Test the two samples from the piece. If both samples meet all the test criteria of §1616.3(b), the piece is acceptable. If one or both of the two selected samples fail the 17.8 cm. (7.0 in.) average char length criterion, §1616.3(b)(1), the piece is unacceptable. If two or more of the individual specimens, from the 10 selected specimens, fail the 25.4 cm. (10 in.) char length criterion, §1616.3(b)(2), the piece is unacceptable. If only one individual specimen, from the 10 selected specimens, fails the 25.4 cm. (10 in.) char length criterion, §1616.3(b)(2), select five additional specimens from the same end of the piece in which the failure occurred, all five to be taken in the fabric direction in which the specimen failure occurred. If this additional sample passes all the test criteria, the piece is acceptable. If this additional sample fails any part of the test criteria, the piece is unacceptable.

(v) Continue testing adjoining pieces until a piece has been found acceptable. Then continue testing adjoining pieces until three successive adjoining pieces, not including the first acceptable piece, have been found acceptable or until five such pieces, not including the first acceptable piece, have been tested, whichever occurs sooner. Unless three successive adjoining pieces have been found acceptable among five such pieces, testing shall be stopped and the entire unit rejected without further testing. If three successive pieces have been found acceptable among five such pieces, accept the three successive acceptable pieces and the remaining pieces in the unit.

(vi)(A) Alternately, individual pieces from a rejected unit containing three or more pieces may be tested and accepted or rejected on a piece by piece basis according to the following plan, after removing the piece or pieces, the failure of which resulted in unit rejection.

(B) Select four samples (two from each end) from the piece. Test the four selected samples. If all four samples meet all the test criteria of § 1616.3(b), accept the piece. If one or more of the samples fail the 17.8 cm. (7.0 in.) average char length criterion, § 1616.3(b)(1), reject the piece. If two or more of the individual specimens, from the 20 selected specimens, fail the 25.4 cm. (10 in.) char length criterion, § 1616.3(b)(2), reject the piece. If only one individual specimen, from the 20 selected specimens, fails the 25.4 cm. (10 in.) char length criterion, § 1613.3(b)(2), select two additional samples from the same end of the piece in which the failure occurred. If these additional two samples meet all the test criteria of § 1616.3(b), accept the piece. If one or both of the two additional samples fail any part of the test criteria, reject the piece.

(vii) The pieces of a unit rejected after retesting may not be retested, used, or promoted for use in children's sleepwear as defined in §§ 1616.2(a) and 1615.1(a) of the Standard for the Flammability of Children's Sleepwear: Sizes 0 through 6X (FF 3–71) (subpart A of part 1615 of this chapter) except after reworking to improve the flammability characteristics, and subsequent retesting in accordance with the procedures set forth in *Tightened Sampling.*

(5) *Records.* Written and physical records related to all tests performed under this Standard must be maintained by the manufacturer, importer, or other persons initially introducing items into commerce which are subject to this Standard, beginning on the effective date of the Standard. Such records shall include results of all tests, sizes of all units, and the disposition of all rejected pieces and units. Rules and regulations regarding recordkeeping may be established by the Consumer Product Safety Commission.

(c) *Garment sampling.* (1)(i) The Garment Sampling Plan is made up of two parts: (A) Prototype Testing and (B) Production Testing. Prior to production, prototypes must be tested to assure that the design characteristics of the garment are acceptable. Garment production units (units) are then accepted or rejected on an individual unit basis.

(ii) Edge finishes such as hems, except in multi-layer fabrics, and binding are excluded from testing except that when trim is used on an edge the trim must be subjected to prototype testing. Seams attaching bindings are excluded from testing.

(2) *Prototype testing.* Pre-production prototype testing of each seam and trim specification to be included in each garment in a garment production unit shall be conducted to assure that garment specifications meet the flammability requirements of the Standard prior to production.

(i) *Seams.* Make three samples (15 specimens) using the longest seam type and three samples using each other seam type 10 inches or longer that is to be included in the garment. For purposes of recordkeeping, prior to testing, assign each specimen to one of the three samples. Test each set of three samples and accept or reject each seam design in accordance with the following plan:

(A) If all three samples meet all the test criteria of § 1616.3(b), accept the seam design. If one or more of the three samples fail the 17.8 cm. (7.0 in.) average char length criterion, § 1616.3(b)(1), reject the seam design. If three or more of the individual specimens from the 15 selected specimens fail the 25.4 cm. (10 in.) char length criterion, § 1616.3(b)(2), reject the seam design. If only one of the individual specimens from the 15 selected specimens fails the 25.4 cm. (10 in.) char length criterion, § 1616.3(b)(2), accept the seam design.

(B) If two of the individual specimens; from the 15 selected specimens, fail the 25.4 cm. (10 in.) char length criterion, § 1616.3(b)(2), select three more samples (15 specimens) and retest. If all three additional samples meet all the test criteria of § 1616.3(b), accept the seam design. If one or more of the three additional samples fail the 17.8 cm. (7.0 in.) average char length criterion, § 1616.3(b)(1), reject the seam design. If two or more of the individual specimens, from the 15 selected additional specimens, fail the 25.4 cm. (10 in.) char length criterion, § 1616.3(b)(2), reject the seam design. If only one of the individual specimens, from the 15 selected additional specimens, fails the 25.4 cm. (10 in.) char length criterion, § 1616.3(b)(2), accept the seam design.

(ii) *Trim.* (A) Make three samples (15 specimens) from each type of trim to be included in the garment. For trim used only in a horizontal configuration on the garment, specimens shall be prepared by sewing or attaching the trim horizontally to the bottom edge of an appropriate section of untrimmed fabric. Sleeve and necking trim may not be tested in this manner. Where more than one row of trim is used on the garment, specimens shall be prepared with the same configuration (same number of rows and spacing between rows up to the limit of the specimen size) as the garment. For trim used in other than a horizontal configuration, specimens shall be prepared by sewing or attaching the trim to the center of the vertical axis of an appropriate section of untrimmed fabric, beginning the sewing or attachment at the lower edge of each specimen. For either configuration, the sewing or attachment shall be made in the manner in which the trim is attached in the garment.

(B) Sewing or otherwise attaching the trim shall be done with thread or fastening material of the same composition and size to be used for this purpose in the garment and using the same stitching or seamtype. Trim used in the horizontal configuration shall be sewn or fastened the entire width (smaller dimension) of the specimen. Trim used in other than the horizontal configuration shall be sewn or fastened the entire length (longer dimension) of the specimen. Prior to testing, assign each specimen to one of the three samples. Test the sets of three samples and accept or reject the type of trim and design on the same basis as seam design. A type of trim and design accepted when tested in a vertical configuration, may be used in a horizontal configuration without further testing.

(3) *Production testing.* A unit is either accepted or rejected according to the following plan:

(i) *Normal sampling.* (A) From each unit, select at random sufficient garments and cut three samples (15 specimens) from the longest seam type. No more than five specimens may be cut from a single garment. Prior to testing, assign each specimen to one of the three samples. All specimens cut from a single garment must be included in the same sample. Test the three selected samples. If all three samples meet all the test criteria of § 1616.3(b), accept the unit. If one or more of the three samples fail the 17.8 cm. (7.0 in.) average char length criterion, § 1616.3(b)(1), reject the unit. If four or more of the individual specimens, from the 15 selected specimens, fail the 25.4 cm. (10 in.) char length criterion, § 1616.3(b)(2), reject the unit. If three or less of the individual specimens, from the 15 selected specimens, fail the 25.4 cm. (10 in.) char length criterion, § 1616.3(b)(2), accept the unit.

(B) If the garment under test does not have a seam at least 10 inches long in the largest size in which it is produced, the following selection and testing procedure shall be followed:

(*1*) Select and cut specimens 8.9 cm. (3.5 in.) wide by the maximum available seam length, with the seam in the center of the specimen and extending the entire specimen length. Cut three samples (15 specimens). These specimens shall be placed in specimen holders so that the bottom edge is even with the bottom edge of the specimen holder and the seam begins in the center of the bottom edge. Prior to testing, assign each specimen to one of the three samples. All specimens cut from a single garment must be included in the same sample.

(*2*) Test the three samples. If all three samples pass the 17.8 cm. (7.0 in.) average char length criterion, § 1616.3(b)(1), and if three or fewer individual specimens fail by charring the entire specimen length, accept the unit. If the unit is not accepted in the above test, three samples (15 specimens) of the longest seam type shall be made using fabric and thread from production inventory and sewn on production machines by production operators. The individual fabric sections prior to sewing must be no larger than 20.3 × 63.3 cm. (8 × 25 in.) and must be selected from more than one area of the base fabric. Test the three prepared samples. Accept or reject the unit as described previously in this subsection.

(ii) *Reduced sampling.* (A) The level of sampling required for garment acceptance may be reduced provided the previous 15 units of the garments have all been accepted using the Normal Sampling Plan. The Reduced Sampling Plan shall be the same as for Normal Sampling except that the quantity of garments under test may be increased to up to two production units containing garments which have the same specific identity except for size, trim, findings, color, and print patterns as specified in paragraph (a) of this section.

(B) Select and test three samples in the same manner as in Normal Sampling. Accept or reject both units on the same basis as with Normal Sampling. Reduced Sampling shall be discontinued and Normal Sampling resumed if a unit is rejected.

(4) *Disposition of rejected units.* Rejected units shall not be retested, used, or promoted for use in children's sleepwear as defined in §§ 1616.2(a) and 1615.1(a) of the Standard for the Flammability of Children's Sleepwear: Sizes 0 through 6X (FF 3–71) (subpart A of part 1615 of this chapter) except after reworking to improve the flammability characteristics and subsequent retesting in accordance with the procedures set forth in *Garment production testing* [Paragraph (c)(3) of this section].

(5) *Records.* Written and physical records related to all tests performed under this Standard must be maintained by the manufacturer, importer, or other persons initially introducing items into commerce which are subject to this Standard, beginning on the effective date of this Standard. Such records shall include results of all tests, sizes of all units, and the disposition of all rejected pieces and units. Rules and regulations regarding recordkeeping may be established by the Consumer Product Safety Commission.

(d) *Compliance market sampling plan.* Sampling plans for use in market testing of items covered by this Standard may be issued by the Consumer Product Safety Commission. Such plans shall define noncompliance of a production unit to exist only when it is shown, with a high level of statistical confidence, those production units represented by tested items which fail such plans will, in fact, fail this Standards. Production units found to be noncomplying under the provisions of paragraph (d) of this section, shall be deemed not to conform to this Standard. The Consumer Product Safety Commission may publish such plans in the FEDERAL REGISTER.

(Sec. 30(d), (15 U.S.C. 2079(b)), 86 Stat. 1231)

[40 FR 59917, Dec. 30, 1975, as amended at 43 FR 4855, Feb. 6, 1978]

§ 1616.5 Test procedure.

(a) *Apparatus.* The following test apparatus shall be used for the test. Alternate test apparatus may be used only with prior approval of the Consumer Product Safety Commission.

(1) *Test chamber.* The test chamber shall be a steel cabinet with inside dimensions of 32.9 cm. (12 15/16 in.) wide, 32.9 cm. (12 15/16 in.) deep and 76.2 cm. (30 in.) high. It shall have a frame which permits the suspension of the specimen holder over the center of the base of the cabinet at such a height that the bottom of the specimen is 1.7 cm. (3/4 in.) above the highest point of the barrel of the gas burner specified in paragraph (a)(3) of this section, *Burner* and perpendicular to the front of the cabinet. The front of the cabinet shall be a close-fitting door with a transparent insert to permit observation of the entire test. The cabinet floor may be covered with a piece of asbestos paper, whose length and width are approximately 2.5 cm. (1 in.) less than the cabinet floor dimensions. The cabinet to be used in this test method is illustrated in Figure 1 and detailed in Engineering Drawings, Numbers 1 through 7.

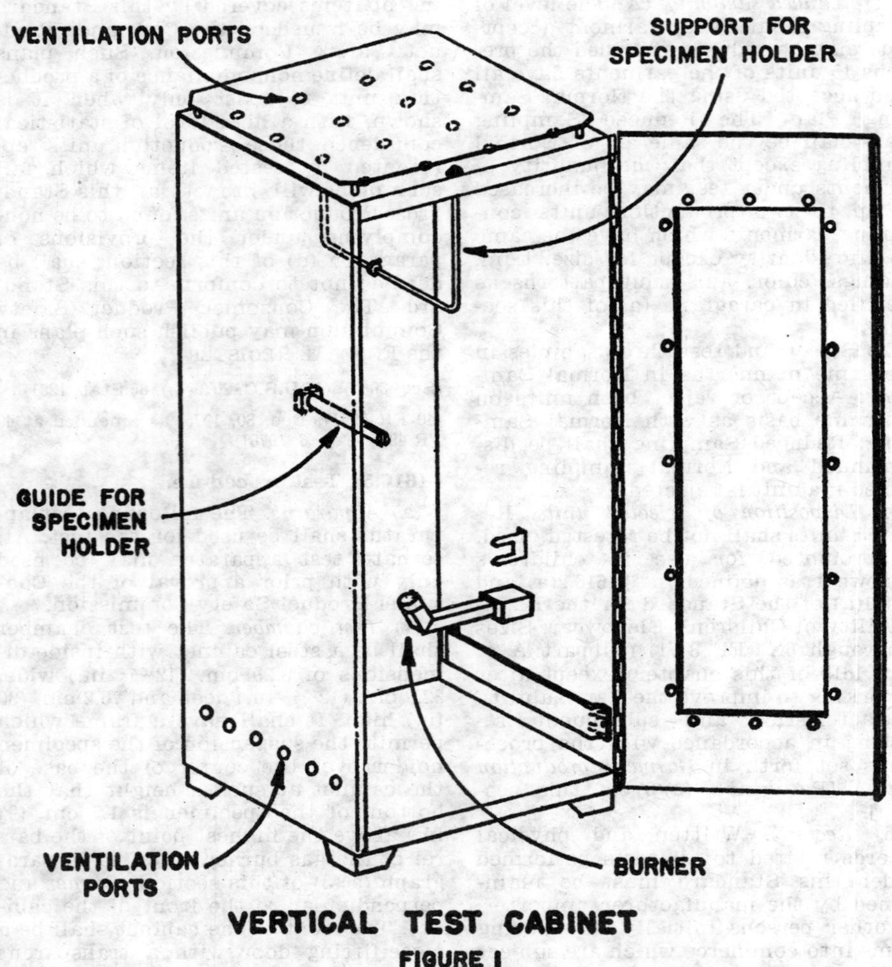

VERTICAL TEST CABINET

FIGURE I

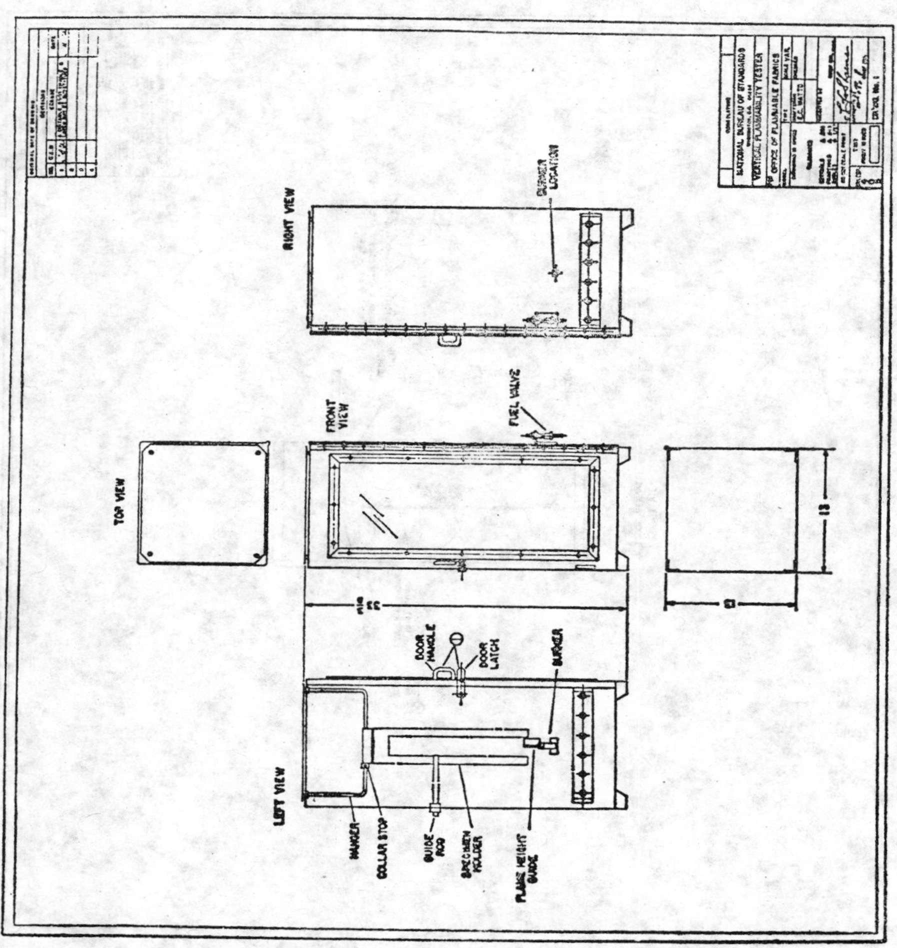
TOP VIEW
FRONT VIEW
RIGHT VIEW
LEFT VIEW
FUEL VALVE
BURNER LOCATION
DOOR HANDLE
DOOR LATCH
BURNER
HANGER
COLLAR STOP
GUIDE ROD
SPECIMEN HOLDER
FLAME HEIGHT GUIDE
13
NATIONAL BUREAU OF STANDARDS
VERTICAL FLAMMABILITY TESTER
OFFICE OF FLAMMABLE FABRICS

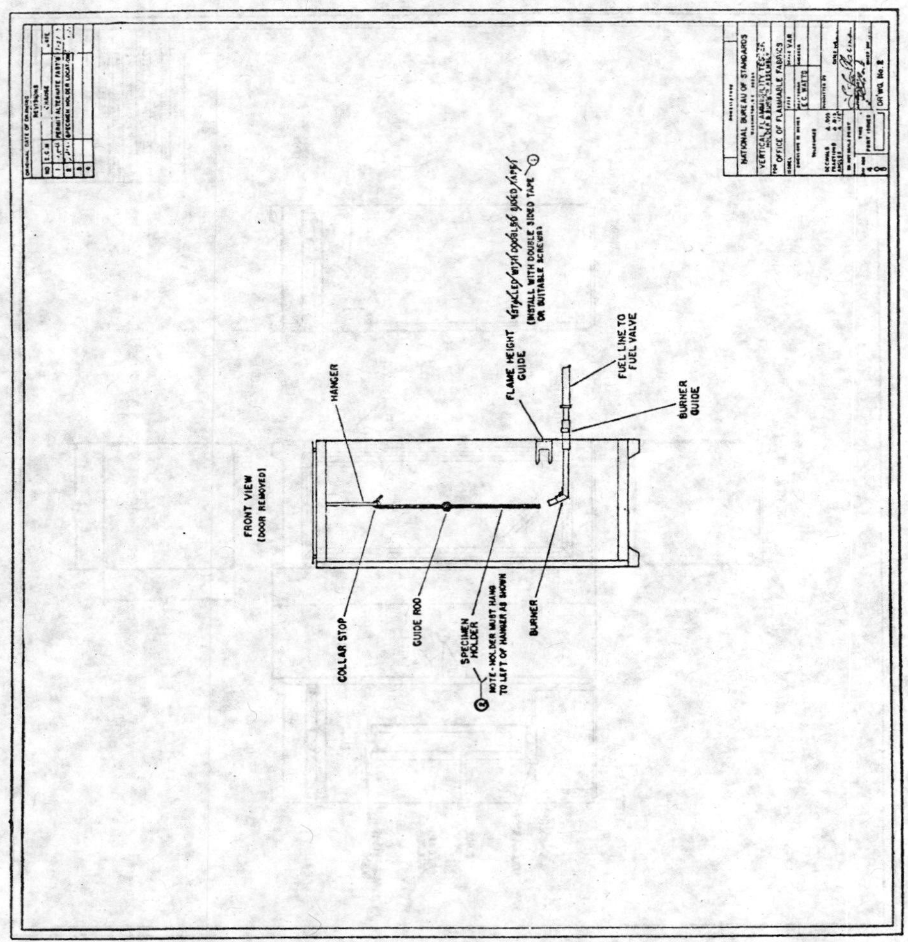
FRONT VIEW
(DOOR REMOVED)
HANGER
COLLAR STOP
GUIDE ROD
SPECIMEN HOLDER
NOTE - HOLDER MUST HANG TO LEFT OF HANGER AS SHOWN
BURNER
FLAME HEIGHT GUIDE
(INSTALL WITH DOUBLE SIDED TAPE OR SUITABLE SCREWS)
BURNER GUIDE
FUEL LINE TO FUEL VALVE
NATIONAL BUREAU OF STANDARDS
OFFICE OF FLAMMABLE FABRICS
DR'WG. No. 8

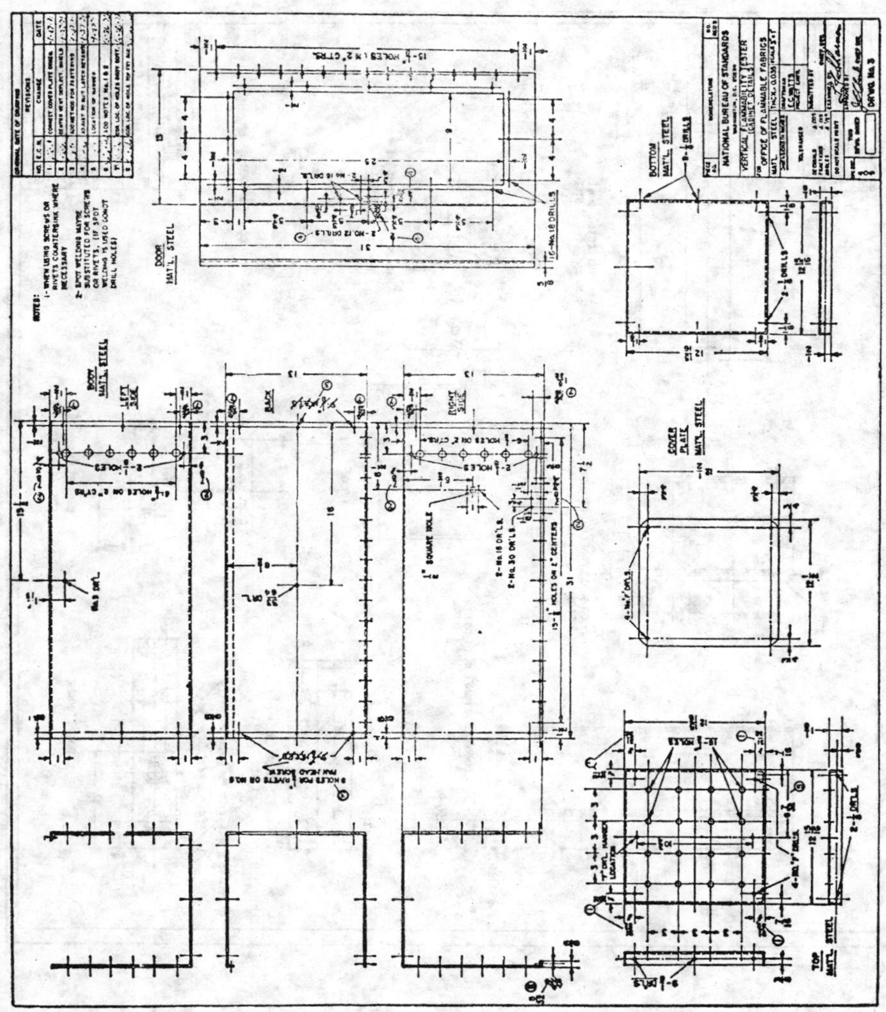
NATIONAL BUREAU OF STANDARDS
VERTICAL FLAMMABILITY TESTER
OFFICE OF FLAMMABLE FABRICS
DOOR MAT'L STEEL
BOTTOM MAT'L STEEL
BODY MAT'L STEEL
COVER PLATE MAT'L STEEL
TOP MAT'L STEEL

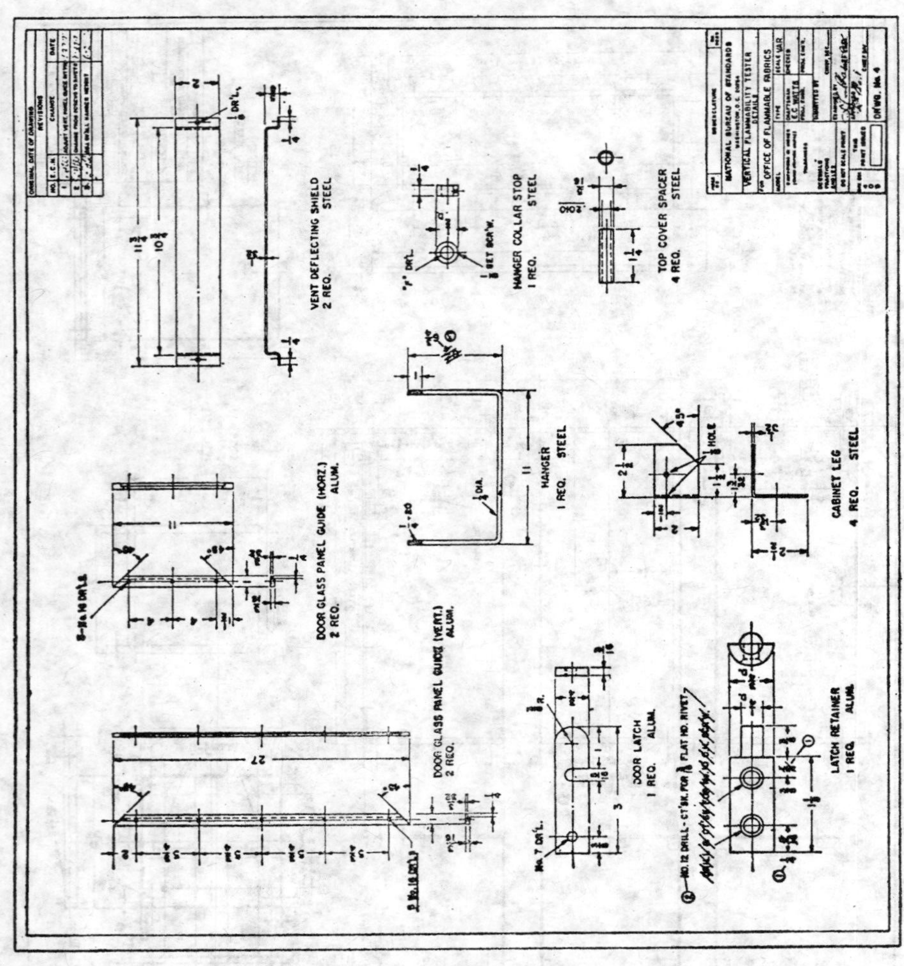
VENT DEFLECTING SHIELD
2 REQ. STEEL
HANGER COLLAR STOP
1 REQ. STEEL
TOP COVER SPACER
4 REQ. STEEL
DOOR GLASS PANEL GUIDE (HORZ.)
2 REQ. ALUM.
HANGER
1 REQ. STEEL
CABINET LEG
4 REQ. STEEL
DOOR GLASS PANEL GUIDE (VERT.)
2 REQ. ALUM.
DOOR LATCH
1 REQ. ALUM.
LATCH RETAINER
1 REQ. ALUM.
NATIONAL BUREAU OF STANDARDS
VERTICAL FLAMMABILITY TESTER
DETAILS
OFFICE OF FLAMMABLE FABRICS
DR'WG. No. 4

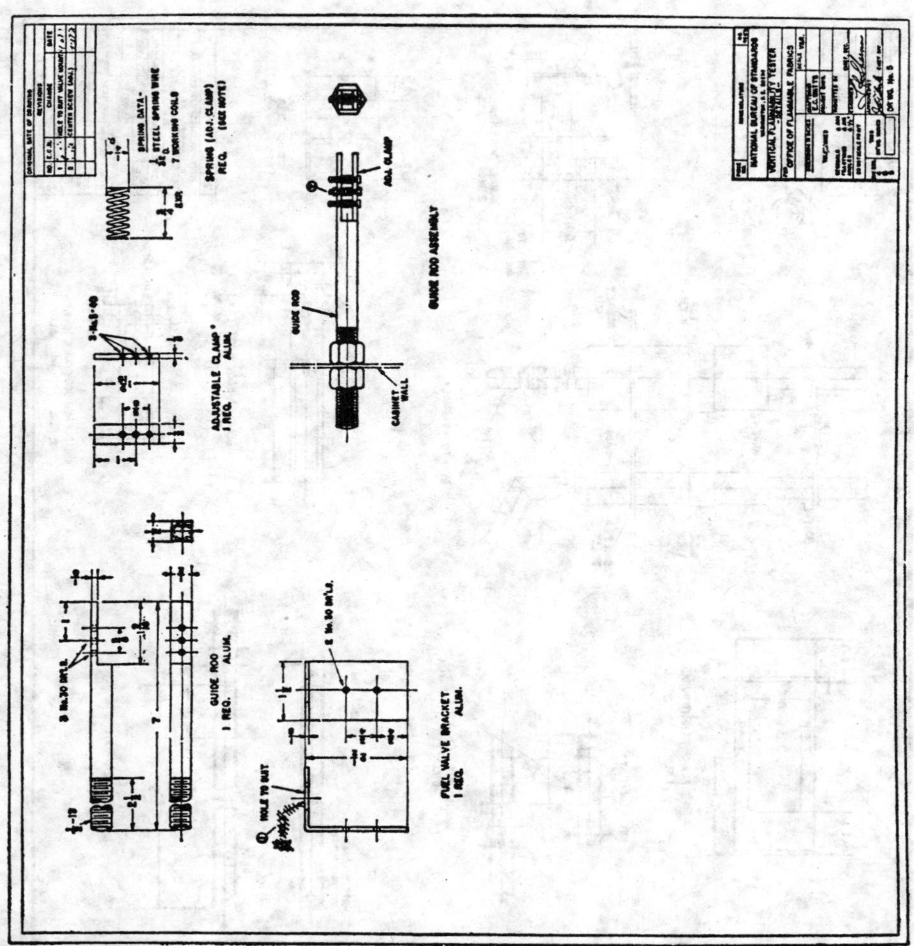

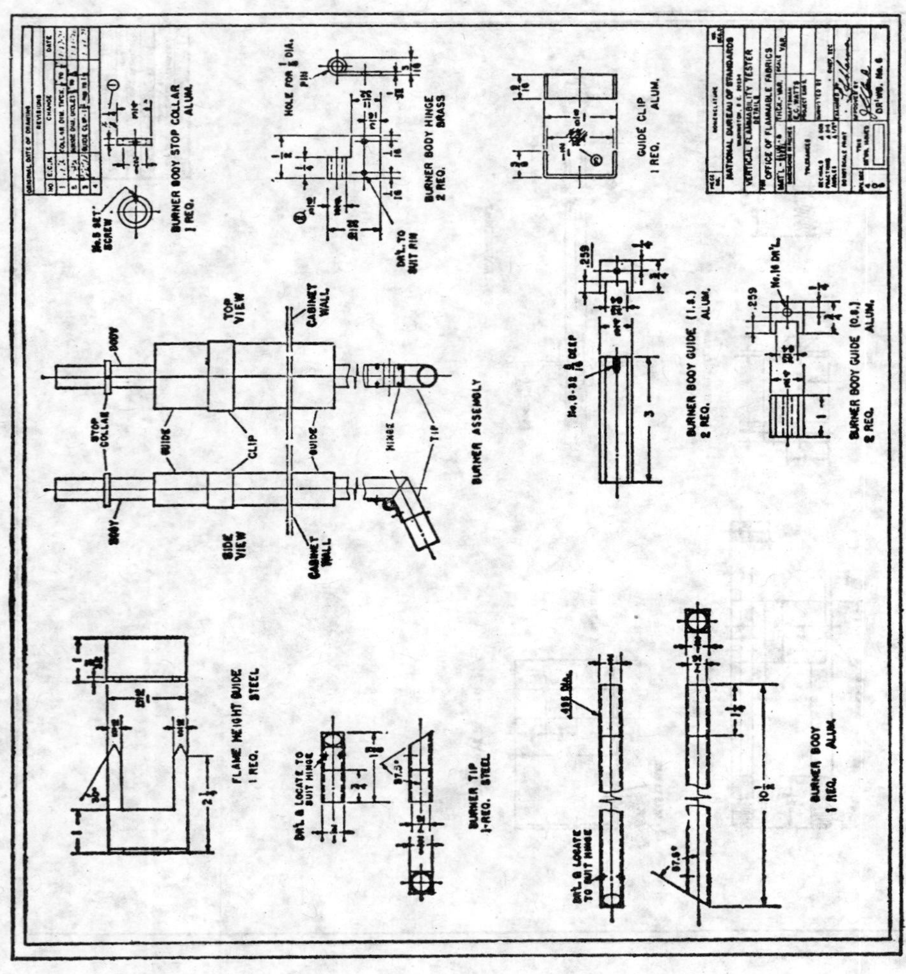
BURNER BODY STOP COLLAR
1 REQ. ALUM.
BURNER BODY HINGE
2 REQ. BRASS
GUIDE CLIP
1 REQ. ALUM.
TOP VIEW
SIDE VIEW
STOP COLLAR
BODY
GUIDE
CLIP
HINGE
TIP
CABINET WALL
BURNER ASSEMBLY
BURNER BODY GUIDE (I.G.)
2 REQ. ALUM.
BURNER BODY GUIDE (O.G.)
2 REQ. ALUM.
FLAME HEIGHT GUIDE
1 REQ. STEEL
BURNER TIP
1-REQ. STEEL
BURNER BODY
1 REQ. ALUM.
NATIONAL BUREAU OF STANDARDS
VERTICAL FLAMMABILITY TESTER
OFFICE OF FLAMMABLE FABRICS

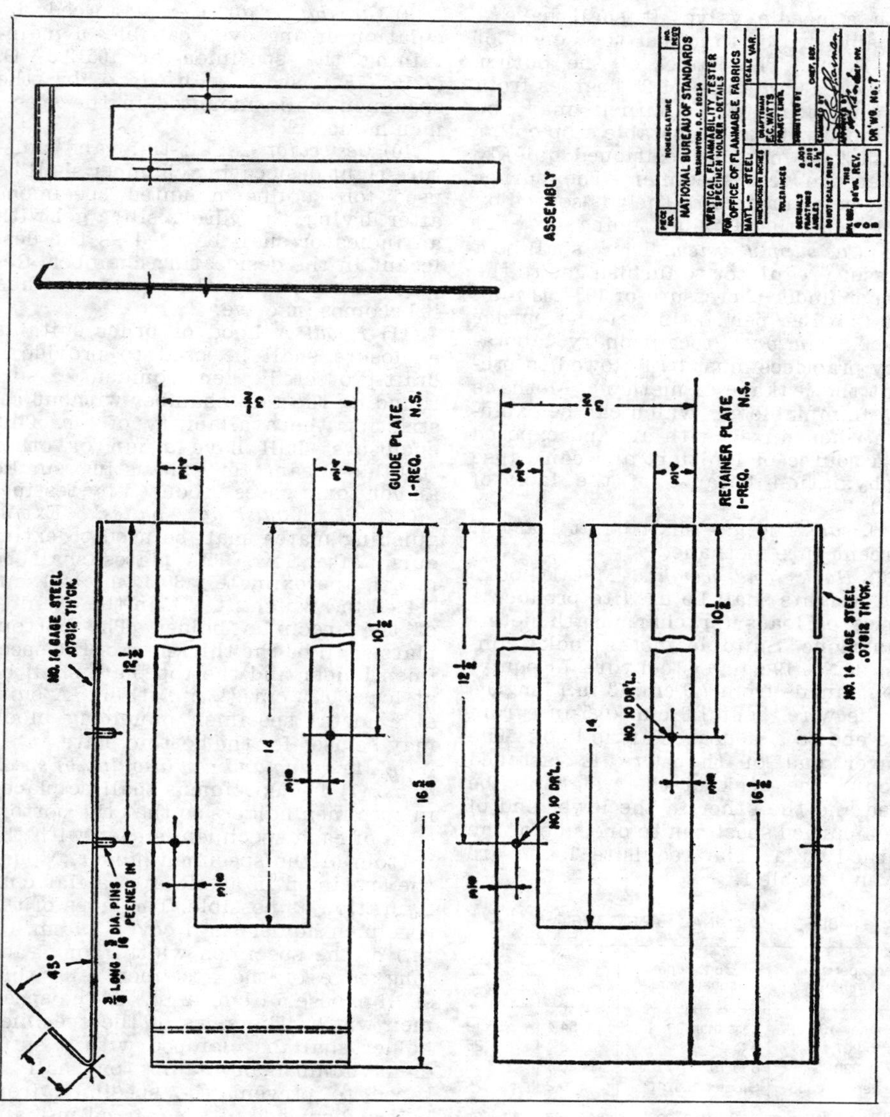

(2) *Specimen holder*. The specimen holder to be used in this test method is detailed in Engineering Drawing Number 7. It is designed to permit suspension of the specimen in a fixed vertical position and to prevent curling of the specimen when the flame is applied. The specimen shall be fixed between the plates, which shall be held together with side clamps.

(3) *Burner*. The burner shall be the same as that illustrated in Figure 1 and detailed in Engineering Drawing Number 6. It shall have a tube of 1.1 cm. (0.43 in.) inside diameter. The input line to the burner shall be equipped

with a needle valve. It shall have a variable orifice to adjust the height of the flame. The barrel of the burner shall be at an angle of 25 degrees from the vertical. The burner may be equipped with an adjustable stop collar so that it may be positioned quickly under the test specimen. The burner shall be connected to the gas source by rubber or other flexible tubing.

(4) *Gas supply system.* There shall be a pressure regulator to furnish gas to the burner under a pressure of 103–259 mm. Hg. (2–5 lbs. per sq. in.) at the burner inlet. (*Caution.* Precautionary laboratory practices must be followed to prevent the leakage of methane. Methane is a flammable gas which can be explosive when mixed with air and exposed to a source of ignition, and can cause asphyxiation because of the lack of air.)

(5) *Gas.* The gas shall be at least 97 percent pure methane.

(6) *Hooks and weights.* Metal hooks and weights shall be used to produce a series of loads for char length determinations. Suitable metal hooks consist of No. 19 gauge steel wire, or equivalent, made from 7.6 cm. (3 in.) lengths of the wire, bent 1.3 cm. (0.5 in.) from one end to a 45-degree angle hook. The longer end of the wire is fastened around the neck of the weight to be used and the other in the lower end of each burned specimen to one side of the burned area. The requisite loads are given in table 1.

TABLE 1—ORIGINAL FABRIC WEIGHT [1]

Grams per square meter	Ounces per square yard	Loads	
		Grams	Pounds
Less than 101	Less than 3	54.4	0.12
101 to 207	3 to 6	113.4	.25
207 to 338	6 to 10	226.8	.50
Greater than 338	Greater than 10	340.2	.75

[1] Weight of the original fabric, containing no seams or trim, is calculated from the weight of a specimen which has been conditioned for at least 8 hr at 21±1.1 °C (70±2 °F) and 65±2 pct relative humidity. Shorter conditioning times may be used if the change in weight of a specimen in successive weighings made at intervals of not less than 2 hr does not exceed 0.2 pct of the weight of the specimen.

(7) *Stopwatch.* A stopwatch or similar timing device shall be used to measure time to 0.1 second.

(8) *Scale.* A linear scale graduated in mm. or 0.1-inch divisions shall be used to measure char length.

(9) *Circulating air oven.* A forced circulation drying oven capable of maintaining the specimen at 105±2.8 °C. (221±5 °F.), shall be used to dry the specimen while mounted in the specimen holders. [3]

(10) *Desiccator.* An air-tight and moisture-tight desiccating chamber shall be used for cooling mounted specimens after drying. Anhydrous silica gel with an indicator shall be used as the desiccant in the desiccating chamber. Replace or reactivate the desiccant when it becomes inactive.

(11) *Hood.* A hood or other suitable enclosure shall be used to provide a draft-protected environment surrounding the test chamber without restricting the availability of air. This enclosure shall have a fan or other suitable means for exhausting smoke and/or toxic gases produced by testing.

(12) *Extinguishing plates.* Extinguishing plates shall be used to extinguish afterglow. The plates shall be metal, approximately 35.6 cm. × 5.1 cm. (14 × 2 in.) which fit within the opening of the specimen holder. The bottom plate shall be the thickness of the specimen holder and the top plate shall be at least 0.32 cm. (1/8 in.) thick. A suitable metal specimen mounting block may be used for the bottom plate.

(b) *Mounting and conditioning of specimens.* (1) The specimens shall be placed in specimen holders so that the bottom edge of each specimen is even with the bottom of the specimen holder. Mount the specimen in as close to a flat configuration as possible. The sides of the specimen holder shall cover 1.9 cm. (3/4 in.) of the specimen width along each long edge of the specimen, and thus shall expose 5.1 cm. (2 in.) of the specimen width. The sides of the specimen holder shall be clamped with a sufficient number of clamps or shall be taped to prevent the specimen from being displaced during handling and testing. The specimens may be taped in the holders if the clamps fail to hold

[3] Procedure 1(1.1.1) of ASTM D 2654–71 "Standard Methods of Test for moisture content and moisture regain of textile material," describes a satisfactory oven (1972 Book of ASTM Standards, part 24, published by the American Society for Testing and Materials, 1916 Race Street, Philadelphia, Pa. 19103).

them. Place the mounted specimens in the drying oven in a manner that will permit free circulation of air at 105 °C. (221 °F.) around them for 30 minutes.[4]

(2) Remove the mounted specimens from the oven and place them in the desiccator for 30 minutes to cool. No more than five specimens shall be placed in a desiccator at one time. Specimens shall remain in the desiccator no more than 60 minutes.

(c) *Testing*—(1) *Burner adjustment*. With the hood fan turned off, use the needle valve to adjust the flame height of the burner to 3.8 cm. (1½ in.) above the highest point of the barrel of the burner. A suitable height indicator is shown in Engineering Drawing Number 6 and Figure 1.

(2) *Specimen burning and evaluation*. (i) One at a time, the mounted specimens shall be removed from the desiccator and suspended in the cabinet for testing. The cabinet door shall be closed and the burner flame impinged on the bottom edge of the specimen for 3.0±0.2 seconds.[5] Flame impingement is accomplished by moving the burner under the specimen for this length of time, and then removing it.

(ii) When flaming has ceased, remove the specimen from the cabinet, except for specimens which exhibit afterglow. If afterglow is evident, the specimen shall be removed from the cabinet 1 minute after the burner flame is impinged on the specimen if no flaming exists at that time. Upon removal from the cabinet, the afterglow shall be promptly extinguished. The afterglow shall be extinguished by placing the specimen while still in the specimen holder on the bottom extinguishing plate and immediately covering it with the top plate until all evidence of afterglow has ceased. After removing the specimen from the cabinet and, if appropriate, extinguishing afterglow, remove it from the holder and place it on a flat clean surface. Fold the specimen lengthwise along a line through the highest peak of the charred or melted area; crease the specimen firmly by hand. Unfold the specimen and insert the hook with the correct weight as shown in table 1 in the specimen on one side of the charred area 6.4 mm. (¼ in.) from the lower edge. Tear the specimen by grasping the other lower corner of the fabric and gently raising the specimen and weight clear of the supporting surface.[6] Measure the char length as the distance from the end of the tear to the original lower edge of the specimen exposed to the flame. After testing each specimen, vent the hood and cabinet to remove the smoke and/or toxic gases.

(3) *Report*. Report the value of char length, in centimeters (or inches), for each specimen, as well as the average char length for each set of five specimens.

(4) *Laundering*. (i) The procedures described under §§ 1616.4 Sampling and acceptance procedures, 1616.5(b) Conditioning and mounting of specimens, and 1616.5(c) Testing shall be carried out on finished items (as produced or after one washing and drying) and after they have been washed and dried 50 times in accordance with sections 8.2.2, 8.2.3, and 8.3.1(A) of AATCC Test Method 124–1996 "Appearance of Fabrics after Repeated Home Laundering," Technical Manual of the American Association of Textile Chemists and Colorists, vol. 73, 1997, which is incorporated by reference. Copies of this document are available from the American Association of Textile Chemists and Colorists, P.O. Box 12215, Research Triangle Park, North Carolina 27709. This document is also available for inspection at the National Archives and Records Administration (NARA). For information on the availability of this material at NARA, call 202–741–6030, or

[4] If the specimens are moist when received, permit them to air dry in laboratory conditions prior to placement in the oven. A satisfactory preconditioning procedure may be found in ASTM D 1776–67, "Conditioning Textiles and Textile Products for Testing". (1972 Book of ASTM Standards, part 24, published by the American Society for Testing and Materials, 1916 Race Street, Philadelphia Pennsylvania 19103.)

[5] If more than 30 seconds elapse between removal of a specimen from the desiccator and the initial flame impingement, that specimen shall be reconditioned prior to testing.

[6] A figure showing how this is done is given in AATCC Test method 34–1969, "Fire Resistance of Textile Fabrics," Technical Manual of the American Association of Textile Chemists and Colorists, Vol. 46, 1970, published by AATCC, P.O. Box 12215, Research Triangle Park, North Carolina 27709.

go to: *http://www.archives.gov/federal_register/code_of_federal_regulations/ibr_locations.html*. This incorporation by reference was approved by the Director of the Federal Register in accordance with 5 U.S.C. 552(a) and 1 CFR part 51. Items which do not withstand 50 launderings shall be tested at the end of their useful service life with prior approval of the Consumer Product Safety Commission.

(ii) Washing shall be performed in accordance with sections 8.2.2 and 8.2.3 of AATCC Test Method 124–1996, using wash temperature V (60° ±3 °C, 140° ±5 °F) specified in Table II of that method, and the water level, agitator speed, washing time, spin speed and final spin cycle specified for "Normal/Cotton Sturdy" in Table III. A maximum washer load shall be 3.64 Kg (8 pounds) and may consist of any combination of test samples and dummy pieces. Drying shall be performed in accordance with section 8.3.1(A) of that test method, Tumble Dry, using the exhaust temperature (66° ±5 °C, 150° ±10 °F) and cool down time of 10 minutes specified in the "Durable Press" conditions of Table IV. Alternatively, a different number of times under another washing and drying procedure may be specified and used, if that procedure has previously been found to be equivalent by the Consumer Product Safety Commission. Such laundering is not required of items which are not intended to be laundered, as determined by the Consumer Product Safety Commission.

(iii) Items which are not susceptible to being laundered and are labeled "dry-clean only" shall be dry-cleaned by a procedure which has previously been found to be acceptable by the Consumer Product Safety Commission.

(iv) For the purpose of the issuance of a guarantee under section 8 of the act, finished sleepwear garments to be tested according to § 1616.4(c) *Garment sampling*, need not be laundered or dry-cleaned provided all fabrics used in making the garments (except trim) have been guaranteed by the fabric producer to be acceptable when tested according to § 1616.4(b) *Fabric sampling*.

[40 FR 59917, Dec. 30, 1975; 41 FR 1061, Jan. 6, 1976, as amended at 46 FR 63252, Dec. 31, 1981; 64 FR 34538, June 28, 1999; 64 FR 61021, Nov. 9, 1999; 65 FR 12928, Mar. 10, 2000]

§ 1616.6 Labeling requirements.

(a) All items of children's sleepwear shall be labeled with precautionary instructions to protect the items from agents or treatments which are known to cause significant deterioration of their flame resistance. If the item has been initially tested under § 1616.5(c)(4) *Laundering*, after one washing and drying, it shall be labeled with instructions to wash before wearing. Such labels shall be permanent and otherwise in accordance with rules and regulations established by the Consumer Product Safety Commission.

(b) [Reserved]

[40 FR 59917, Dec. 30, 1975, as amended at 61 FR 1117, Jan. 16, 1996]

Subpart B—Rules and Regulations

AUTHORITY: Sec. 5, 67 Stat. 112–13, as amended 81 Stat. 571; 15 U.S.C. 1194.

§ 1616.31 Labeling, recordkeeping, retail display and guaranties.

(a) *Definitions*. For the purpose of this section, the following definitions apply:

(1) *Standard* means the Standard for the Flammability of Children's Sleepwear: Sizes 7 through 14 (FF 5–74) (subpart A of part 1616 of this chapter) promulgated by the Consumer Product Safety Commission in the FEDERAL REGISTER of May 1, 1974 (39 FR 15214), and amended in the FEDERAL REGISTER of March 21, 1975 (40 FR 12811) (correction notice published for technical reasons on March 27, 1975, 40 FR 13547).

(2) *Children's sleepwear* means "children's sleepwear" as defined in § 1616.2(a) of the Standard, that is, "any product of wearing apparel size 7 through 14, such as nightgowns, pajamas, or similar or related items, such as robes, intended to be worn primarily for sleeping or activities related to sleeping. Diapers and underwear are excluded from this definition."

(3) *Item* means "item" as defined in § 1616.2(c) of the Standard, that is, "any product of children's sleepwear or any fabric or related material intended or promoted for use in children's sleepwear."

(4) *Market or handle* means any one or more of the transactions set forth in section 3 of the Flammable Fabrics Act (15 U.S.C. 1192).

(5) The definition of terms set forth in § 1616.2 of the Standard shall also apply to this section.

(b) *Labeling.* (1) Where any agent or treatment is known to cause deterioration of flame resistance or otherwise causes an item to be less flame resistant, such item shall be prominently, permanently, conspicuously, and legibly labeled with precautionary care and treatment instructions to protect the item from such agent or treatment; Provided:

(i) Where items required to be labeled in accordance with this paragraph are marketed at retail in packages, and the required label is not readily visible to the prospective purchaser, the packages must also be prominently, conspicuously, and legibly labeled with the required information, and

(ii) Where items are required to be labeled in accordance with this paragraph, the precautionary care and treatment instructions may appear on the reverse side of the permanent label if

(A) The precautionary care and treatment instructions are legible, prominent and conspicuous, and

(B) The phrase "Care Instructions On Reverse" or the equivalent appears permanently, prominently, conspicuously, and legibly on the side of the permanent label that is visible to the prospective purchaser when the item is marketed at retail, and

(C) The item which is so labeled is marketed at retail in such a manner that the prospective purchaser is able to manipulate the label so the entire text of the precautionary care and treatment instructions is visible and legible; however, where the label cannot be manipulated so the instructions are visible to the prospective purchaser and legible, the package must also be prominently, conspicuously and legibly labeled with the required precautionary care and treatment information or such information must appear prominently, conspicuously and legibly on a hang tag attached to the item.

(2) If the item has been initially tested under § 1616.5(c)(4) of the Standard after one washing and drying, it shall be prominently, permanently, conspicuously and legibly labeled with instructions to wash before wearing.

(3) Where any fabric or related material intended or promoted for use in children's sleepwear subject to the Standard is sold or intended for sale to the ultimate consumer for the purpose of conversion into children's sleepwear, each bolt, roll, or other unit shall be labeled with the information required by this section. Each item or fabric or related material sold to an ultimate consumer must be accompanied by a label, as prescribed by this section, which can by normal household methods be permanently affixed by the ultimate consumer to any item of children's sleepwear made from such fabric or related material.

(4)(i) Where items required to be labeled in accordance with paragraphs (b)(2), and/or, (b)(3) of this section and fabrics required to be labeled or stamped in accordance with paragraph (b)(7) of this section are marketed at retail in packages, and the required label or stamp is not readily visible to the prospective purchaser, the packages must also be prominently, conspicuously, and legibly labeled with the required information.

(ii) Where garments required to be labeled or stamped in accordance with paragraph (b)(7) of this section are marketed at retail in packages, and the required label or stamp is not readily visible to the prospective purchaser:

(A) The packages must also be prominently, conspicuously, and legibly labeled with the information required by paragraph (b)(7) of this section; or

(B) There must be a garment style identification that is prominent, conspicuous, and legible and readily visible to the prospective purchaser, either on a label or hang tag attached to the garment design or on the garment packages. A style is a garment design or grouping, preselected by the manufacturer. A style may be composed of garments that form all or part of one or more GPU's and the style may include any number of garments the manufacturer chooses. Style identification means any numbers, letters, or combination thereof that are sufficient to identify the garments of the style and may include information such as color, season or size. If this option B is selected, in any recall of noncomplying items from a particular GPU.

(*1*) The garment manufacturer must recall the entire style(s) from all customers who purchased garments of the style(s) of which the GPU is part. However, retailers may elect to return only garments from the particular GPU necessitating the recall rather than the entire style(s) or portions of style(s) being recalled; and

(*2*) Within 48 hours of a written request, the garment manufacturer must supply to the Commission any samples in its possession of garments from the GPU, as requested. As required of all persons subject to this section, the garment manufacturer must also, within the time requested, supply to the Commission the names of any customers who purchased during a specified period of time, garments from the GPU (or the style(s) of which the GPU is a part) and supply access to all records required under the Standard and this section.

(5) Samples, swatches, or specimens used to promote or effect the sale of items subject to the Standard shall be labeled in accordance with this section with the information required by this section: Except that such information may appear on accompanying promotional materials attached to fabric samples, swatches or specimens used to promote the sale of fabrics to garment manufacturers. This requirement shall not apply, however, to samples, swatches, or specimens prominently, permanently, conspicuously, truthfully and legibly labeled: "Flammable, Sample only. Not for use or resale. Does not meet Standard for the Flammability of Children's Sleepwear; Sizes 7 through 14 (FF 5–74)."

(6) [Reserved]

(7) Every manufacturer, importer, or other person (such as a converter) initially introducing items subject to the Standard into commerce shall assign to each item a unit identification (number, letter or date, or combination thereof) sufficient to identify and relate to the fabric production unit or garment production unit of which the item is a part. Such unit identification shall be designated in such a way as to indicate that it is a production unit under the Standard. The letters "GPU" and "FPU" may be used to designate a garment production unit identification and fabric production unit identification, respectively, at the option of the labeler. In addition to the requirements prescribed by this paragraph (b)(7), the requirements prescribed by paragraph (b)(4) of this section must be met for items marketed at retail in packages.

(i) Each garment subject to the Standard shall bear a label with minimum dimension of 1.3 centimeters (0.5 inch) by 1.9 centimeters (0.75 inch) containing the appropriate garment production unit identification for that garment in letters which are clear, conspicuous, and legible, and in a color which contrasts with the background of the label, or shall have such information stamped on the garment itself in letters which are clear, conspicuous, and legible, and in a color which contrasts with the background, and at least 2.54 centimeters (1 inch) in every direction from any other information. The stamp or label containing the garment production unit identification must be of such construction, and affixed to the garment in such a manner, as to remain on or attached to the garment, and legible and visible throughout its intended period of use.

(ii) The fabric production unit identification shall appear in letters at least 0.4 centimeter (one-sixth of an inch) in height against a contrasting background on each label that relates to such fabric and is required by the Textile Fiber Products Identification Act (15 U.S.C. 70–70k) and the regulations thereunder (16 CFR 303.1 through 303.45) or by the Wool Products Labeling Act of 1939 (15 U.S.C. 68–68j) and the regulations thereunder (16 CFR 300.1 through 300.35). When the information required by the Textile Fiber Products Identification Act or by the Wool Products Labeling Act of 1939 appears on an invoice used in lieu of labeling, the fabric production unit identification required by this section may be placed clearly, conspicuously, and legibly on the same invoice in lieu of labeling.

(8) All items complying with the Standard and manufactured on or after May 1, 1975, through May 1, 1978, shall bear a label which states "Flame-resistant. U.S. Standard FF 5–74." The label must be prominent, conspicuous, and legible and readily visible at the point of sale to ultimate consumers. The label statement may be attached to the item itself, on a hang tag attached to the item, or on a package enclosing the item. The label need not be affixed permanently. The letters of the label must be at least 0.4 centimeter (one-sixth of an inch) in height and in a color which contrasts with the background of the label.

(c) [Reserved]

(d) *Records—manufacturers, importers, or other persons initially introducing items into commerce*—(1) *General.* Every manufacturer, importer, or other person (such as a converter) initially introducing into commerce items subject to the Standard, irrespective of whether guaranties are issued under paragraph (e) of this section, shall maintain written and physical records as hereinafter specified. The records required must establish a line of continuity through the process of manufacture of each production unit of articles of children's sleepwear, or fabrics or related materials intended or promoted for use in children's sleepwear, to the sale and delivery of the finished items and from the specific finished item to the manufacturing records. Such records shall show with respect to such items:

(i) Details, description and identification of any and all sampling plans engaged in pursuant to the requirements of the Standard. Such records must be sufficient to demonstrate compliance with such sampling plan(s) and must relate the sampling plan(s) to the actual items produced, marketed, or handled. This requirement is not limited by other provisions of this paragraph (d).

(ii) Garment production units or fabric production units of all garments or fabrics marketed or handled. The records must relate to an appropriate production unit identification on or affixed to the item itself in accordance with paragraph (b)(7) of this section, and the production unit identification must relate to the garment production unit or fabric production unit.

(iii) Test results and details of all tests performed, both prototype and production, including char lengths of each specimen tested, average char lengths of the samples required to be tested, details of the sampling procedure employed, name and signature of person conducting tests, date of tests, and all other records necessary to demonstrate compliance with the test procedures and sampling plan specified by the Standard or authorized alternate sampling plan.

(iv) Disposition of all failing or rejected items. Such records must demonstrate that the items were retested or reworked and retested in accordance with the Standard prior to sale or distribution and that such retested or reworked and retested items comply with the Standard, or otherwise show the disposition of such items.

(v) Fiber content and manufacturing specifications relating the same to prototype and production testing and to the production units to which applicable.

(vi) Data and test results relied on as a basis for inclusion of different colors or different print patterns of the same fabric as a single fabric or garment production unit under § 1616.4(a)(2) of the Standard.

(vii) Data and test results relied on as a basis for reduced laundering of fabric or garments during test procedures under § 1616.5(c)(4) of the Standard and any quantities issued or received relating to laundering as well as details of the laundering procedure utilized.

(viii) Identification, composition, and details of application of any flame retardant treatments employed. All prototype and production records shall relate to such information.

(ix) Date and quantity of each sale or delivery of items subject to the Standard (except the date of sale to an ultimate consumer) and the name and address of the purchaser or recipient (except an ultimate consumer). The items involved in each sale or delivery shall be identified by production unit or by style. A style is a garment design or grouping, preselected by the manufacturer. A style may be composed of garments that form all or part of one or more garment production units and the style may include any number of garments the manufacturer chooses. If a person subject to the requirements of paragraph (d) of this section maintains sales records which identify the items sold or delivered by style, and if recall of one or more production units subject to the Standard is required, that person in recalling such production units shall notify all purchasers of items of the style in which such production unit or units were manufactured. Retailers may elect to return all items of the style involved, or all items of the production units subject to recall.

(2) *Fabrics.* In addition to the information specified in paragraph (d)(1) of this section, the written and physical records maintained with respect to each fabric production unit shall include (i) finished fabric samples sufficient to repeat the fabric sampling procedure required by §1616.4 of the Standard for each production unit marketed or handled; and (ii) records to relate the samples to the actual fabric production unit. Upon written request of any duly authorized employee or agent of the Commission, samples sufficient for the sampling and testing of any production unit in accordance with the Standard shall be furnished from these records within the time specified in the written request.

(3) *Garments—prototype testing.* In addition to the records specified in paragraph (d)(1) of this section, the following written and physical records shall be maintained with respect to the garment prototype testing required by the Standard:

(i) Specification, fiber content, and details of construction on all seams, fabrics, threads, stitches, and trims used in each garment style or type upon which prototype testing was performed, relating the same to such garment style or type and to all production units to which such prototype testing is applicable.

(ii) Samples sufficient to repeat the prototype tests required by §1616.4 of the Standard for all fabrics, seams, threads, stitches, and trims used in such prototype testing, relating such samples to the records, required by this paragraph (d), including the information required by paragraph (d)(3)(i) of this section. Upon written request of any duly authorized employee or agent of the Commission, samples sufficient for the testing of any prototype specimens identical to those specimens that were actually tested pursuant to the Standard shall be furnished from these records within the time specified in that written request.

(iii) A complete untested garment from each style or type of garment marketed or handled.

(iv) Remains of all physical specimens tested in accordance with the prototype testing required by §1616.4 of the Standard, relating such samples to the records required by this paragraph (d), including information required by paragraph (d)(3)(i) of this section.

(4) *Garments—production testing.* In addition to the records required by paragraph (d)(1) of this section, written and physical records shall be maintained and shall show with respect to each garment production unit:

(i) Source and fabric production unit identification of all fabrics subject to testing used in each garment production unit.

(ii) Identification and appropriate reference to all prototype records and prototype tests applicable to each production unit.

(iii) Any guaranty relied upon to demonstrate that the fabric utilized in such garments meets the laundering requirements of the Standard.

(iv) Data sufficient to show that tested samples were selected from the production unit at random from regular production.

(v) Written data that will enable the Commission to obtain and test garments under any applicable compliance market sampling plan.

(5) *Record retention requirements.* The records required by this paragraph (d) shall be maintained for 3 years, except that records relating to prototype testing shall be maintained for as long as they are relied upon as demonstrating compliance with the prototype testing requirements of the Standard and shall be retained for 3 years thereafter.

(e) *Tests for guaranty purposes.* Reasonable and representative tests for the purpose of issuing a guaranty under section 8 of the Flammable Fabrics Act (15 U.S.C. 1197) for items subject to the Standard shall be those tests performed pursuant to any sampling plan or authorized alternative sampling plan engaged in pursuant to the requirements of the Standard.

(f) *Compliance with this section.* No person subject to the Flammable Fabrics Act shall manufacture, import, distribute, or otherwise market or handle any item subject to the Standard, including samples, swatches, or specimens used to promote or effect the sale thereof, which is not in compliance with this section.

[40 FR 59917, Dec. 30, 1975, as amended at 49 FR 3064, Jan. 24, 1984; 61 FR 1117, Jan. 16, 1996]

§1616.32 Method for establishment and use of alternate laundering procedures under section 5(c)(4)(ii) of the standard.

(a) *Scope.* (1) Section 1616.5(c)(4)(ii) of the Standard for the Flammability of Children's Sleepwear in sizes 7–14 (16 CFR 1616.5(c)(4)(ii)) requires that all fabrics and certain garments subject to the standard be tested for flammability as produced (or after one washing and drying) and after the items have been washed and dried 50 times in machines, using the procedure specified in AATCC Test Method 124–1996.[7] This section also provides that items may be laundered a different number of times under another washing and drying procedure if the Commission finds that such an alternate laundering procedure is equivalent to the procedure specified in the standard.

(2) This rule provides the procedures to be followed by persons seeking Commission approval for alternate laundering procedures. It also provides the criteria the Commission will use in evaluating the applications.

(3) The alternate laundering procedures provided for in this section apply only to procedures under section 5(c)(4)(ii) of the standard and shall not be used for determining whether different colors or different print patterns of the same fabric may be included in a single fabric or garment production unit.

(4) As used in this section, fabric means fabric or related material promoted or intended for use in children's sleepwear made to identical specifications and containing the same identity while in production.

(b) *Application procedure.* (1) Applicants seeking approval for use of an alternate laundering procedure under §1616.5(c)(4)(ii) of the standard must submit the following information in writing to the Assistant Executive Director for Compliance, Consumer Product Safety Commission, Washington, DC 20207:

(i) A detailed description of the proposed alternate laundering procedure, and a 6 in. by 6 in. swatch of the fabric or garment for which the procedure is proposed,

(ii) Upon request of the Commission staff, any other information concerning the procedure and/or any machine used in connection with it,

(iii) With regard to each fabric or garment for which an alternate laundering procedure is sought, test data comparing twenty test specimens washed and dried by the proposed alternate laundering procedure and twenty specimens tested in accordance with the 50-wash and dry cycle procedure required in section 5(c)(4)(ii) of the standard. (For purposes of applications, similar fabrics or garments of different finishes shall be considered as different fabrics or garments and therefore separate test results must be submitted). Each group of twenty specimens upon which these data are based must be cut

[7] AATCC Test Method 124–1996 "Appearance of Fabrics after Repeated Home Laundering," Technical Manual of the American Association of Textile Chemists and Colorists, Vol. 73, 1997, which is incorporated by reference. Copies of this document are available from the American Association of Textile Chemists and Colorists, P.O. Box 12215, Research Triangle Park, North Carolina 27709. This document is also available for inspection at the National Archives and Records Administration (NARA). For information on the availability of this material at NARA, call 202–741–6030, or go to: *http://www.archives.gov/federal_register/code_of_federal_regulations/ibr_locations.html.* This incorporation by reference was approved by the Director of the Federal Register in accordance with 5 U.S.C. 552(a) and 1 CFR part 51.

for testing, half in the machine direction and half in the cross machine direction. Where the applicant manufactures the fabric or garments in more than one plant, the data described in this paragraph must be submitted separately for the fabric or garments of each plant for which the proposed alternate laundering procedure is intended to be used. Subsequent applications for use of the same procedure for additional fabrics and garments may incorporate portions of the original application by reference, as appropriate.

(2) Applications shall be certified by the chief executive officer of the applicant or the official to whom the duty to certify has been delegated in writing. The Commission's Assistant Executive Director for Compliance must be notified in writing of any such delegation.

(c) *Use of alternate laundering procedure.* (1) The applicant may begin to use the alternate laundering procedure 30 days after the application is received by the Assistant Executive Director for Compliance unless notified to the contrary. The Assistant Executive Director for Compliance will normally furnish an applicant with written notice of approval within 30 days. The applicant may be notified that a longer time is needed for evaluation of the application, and in the discretion of the Assistant Executive Director for Compliance, may be authorized to use the alternate laundering procedure pending the final decision. The notice of approval shall be kept by the applicant with other written records required to be maintained in connection with the use of an alternate laundering procedure. So that the applicants may ascertain that the application has been received when the 30-day period has elapsed, it is suggested that applications be sent by certified mail, return receipt requested.

(2) As provided in detail in §1616.32(e), applicants must immediately discontinue use of an alternate procedure, and must immediately notify the Assistant Executive Director for Compliance if there are test failures during revalidation testing.

(d) *Revalidation testing.* (1) In order to assure a continued satisfactory correlation between the alternate laundering procedure and the laundering procedure of the standard, applicants shall perform all the testing described in paragraph (b)(1)(iii) of this section for fabrics or garments from current production at least once for every three-month period during which any of the fabric or garments are produced.

(2) If following initial approval, four successive comparisons of the alternate and the 50-cycle methods as described in paragraph (d)(1) of this section consistently show acceptable results under the criteria specified by paragraph (f) of this section, the Commission will deem such comparisons to be sufficient demonstration of the equivalence of the alternate laundering procedure with the 50 launderings required in the standard and further revalidation testing will not be required.

(3) Records of revalidation testing need not be submitted to the Assistant Executive Director for Compliance. However such records must be maintained in accordance with paragraph (h) of this section.

(e) *Revalidation testing failures.* (1) If revalidation testing for any fabric or garment does not meet the criteria of §1616.32(f), the applicant must immediately discontinue use of the alternate laundering procedure for the fabric or garment and must immediately notify the Assistant Executive Director for Compliance in writing of the failure to meet the criteria. Also the testing from the production unit from which the non-correlating samples were taken and the testing from subsequent production units (if any) must be repeated immediately using the laundering procedure prescribed in the standard. These repeat tests shall then be the tests applicable to such production unit(s) and those tests previously performed on the production unit(s) shall be considered invalid.

(2) When use of an alternate laundering procedure for a particular fabric or garment has been discontinued because of a failure to meet the criteria of §1616.32(f), the alternate laundering procedure shall not be used again unless a new application for approval is submitted to the Assistant Executive Director for Compliance and that officer approves the application in writing. In addition to the other information

required for applications, the additional application should give facts or reasons showing why the applicant believes the procedure should be considered reliable with the fabric or garments involved, in view of the previous failure.

(f) *Commission criteria for evaluating applications.* (1) The Assistant Executive Director for Compliance will approve the alternate laundering procedure as equivalent to the laundering procedure specified in § 1616.5(c)(4)(ii) of the standard if testing from 20 specimens laundered by the proposed alternate procedure yields as many or more char lengths in excess of five inches as does testing from the twenty specimens laundered by the 50-laundering cycle method prescribed in the standard.

(2) If the alternate laundering procedure yields fewer char lengths in excess of five inches than does the 50-wash and dry cycle, then the Assistant Executive Director for Compliance will not consider the alternate procedure to be equivalent, with the following exception: If the number of five-inch chars from the alternate procedure is within one of the number of five-inch chars obtained from the 50-cycle procedure, the applicant may repeat the original test with new specimens and if the combined results of both tests show the count of chars exceeding five inches from the alternate is equal to, or greater than, the count from the 50-wash cycle procedure, the Assistant Executive Director for Compliance will approve the alternate laundering procedure.

(g) *Commission testing for compliance.* (1) For the purpose of determining compliance with the standard, the Commission will rely on testing employing the laundering procedure now prescribed by § 1616.5(c)(4)(ii) of the standard. (15 U.S.C. 1193, 1194; 15 U.S.C. 2079(b)).

(2) The Commission may verify equivalency of any procedure submitted by independent testing and evaluation, by or on behalf of the Commission.

(h) *Recordkeeping.* The applicant must maintain a record of all applications filed with the Commission and of all equivalency tests for as long as the procedures to which they relate are in use and for three years thereafter.

[42 FR 55892, Oct. 20, 1977, as amended at 65 FR 12928, Mar. 10, 2000]

§ 1616.35 Use of alternate apparatus, procedures, or criteria for testing under the standard.

(a) The Standard for the Flammability of Children's Sleepwear: Sizes 7 through 14 (the Standard) requires every manufacturer, importer, and other person (such as a converter) initially introducing items subject to the Standard into commerce to group items into production units, and to test samples from each production unit. See 16 CFR 1616.4. The Standard prescribes an apparatus and procedure for performing tests of fabric and garments subject to its provisions. See 16 CFR 1616.5. The Standard prescribes pass/fail criteria at 16 CFR 1616.3(b).

(b) Section 1616.5(a) states that alternate test apparatus may be used by persons or firms required to perform testing under the Standard "only with prior approval" of the Commission.

(c)(1) By issuance of this § 1616.35, the Commission gives its approval to any person or firm desiring to use test apparatus or procedures other than those prescribed by the Standard for purposes of compliance with the Standard, if that person or firm has data or other information to demonstrate that a test utilizing such alternate apparatus or procedure is as stringent as, or more stringent than, a test utilizing the apparatus and procedure specified in the Standard. The Commission considers a test utilizing alternate apparatus or procedures to be "as stringent as, or more stringent than" a test utilizing the apparatus and procedures specified in the standard, if when testing identical specimens, a test utilizing alternative apparatus or procedures yields failing results as often as, or more often than, a test utilizing the apparatus and procedures specified in the standard.

(2) The data or information required by this paragraph (c) of this section as a condition to the Commission's approval of the use of alternate test apparatus or procedures must be in the possession of the person or firm desiring

to use such alternate apparatus or procedures before the alternate apparatus or procedures may be used for purposes of compliance with the standard.

(3) The information required by this paragraph (c) of this section must be retained by the person or firm using the alternate test apparatus or procedures for as long as that apparatus or procedure is used for purposes of compliance with the standard, and for a period of one year there after.

(d) Written application to the Commission is not required for approval of alternate test apparatus or procedures, and the Commission will not act on any individual written application for approval of alternate test apparatus or procedures.

(e) Use of any alternate test apparatus or procedures without the data or information required by paragraph (c), of this section, may result in violation of the Standard and section 3 of the Flammable Fabrics Act (15 U.S.C. 1192).

(f) The Commission will test fabrics and garments subject to the standard for compliance with the requirements of the standard using the apparatus and procedures set forth in the standard. The Commission will consider any failing results from compliance testing as evidence of a violation of the standard and section 3 of the Flammable Fabrics Act (15 U.S.C. 1192).

(Reporting requirements contained in paragraph (c) were approved by the Office of Management and Budget under control number 3041–0027)

(Sec. 5, Pub. L. 90–189, 81 Stat. 569, 15 U.S.C. 1194; Sec. 30(b), Pub. L. 92–573, 86 Stat. 1231, 15 U.S.C. 2079(b))

[48 FR 21316, May 12, 1983]

§ 1616.36 Use of alternate apparatus or procedures for tests for guaranty purposes.

(a) Section 8(a) of the Flammable Fabrics Act (FFA, 15 U.S.C. 1197(a)) provides that no person shall be subject to criminal prosecution under section 7 of the FFA (15 U.S.C. 1196) for a violation of section 3 of the FFA (15 U.S.C. 1192) if that person establishes a guaranty received in good faith which meets all requirements set forth in section 8 of the FFA. One of those requirements is that the guaranty must be based upon "reasonable and representative tests" in accordance with the applicable standard.

(b) Section 1616.31(e) of the regulations implementing the Standard for the Flammability of Children's Sleepwear: Sizes 7 through 14 (the Standard) provides that for purposes of supporting guaranties issued in accordance with section 8 of the FFA for items subject to the Standard, "reasonable and representative tests" are tests "performed pursuant to any sampling plan or authorized alternative sampling plan engaged in pursuant to the requirements of the Standard."

(c) At § 1616.35, the Commission has set forth conditions under which the Commission will approve the use of test apparatus or procedures other than those prescribed in the Standard for purposes of demonstrating compliance with the requirements of the Standard. Any person or firm meeting the requirements of § 1616.35 for use of alternate test apparatus or procedure for compliance with the Standard may also use such alternate test apparatus or procedure under the same conditions for purposes of conducting "reasonable and representative tests" to support guaranties of items subject to the Standard, following any sampling plan prescribed by the Standard or any approved alternate sampling plan.

(d) The Commission will test fabrics and garments subject to the Standard for compliance with the Standard using the apparatus and procedures set forth in the Standard. The Commission will consider any failing results from compliance testing as evidence that the person or firm using alternate test apparatus or procedures has furnished a false guaranty in violation of section 8(b) of the FFA (15 U.S.C. 1197(b)).

(Sec. 5, Pub. L. 90–189, 81 Stat. 569, 15 U.S.C. 1194; Sec. 30(b), Pub. L. 92–573, 86 Stat. 1231, 15 U.S.C. 2079(b))

[48 FR 21316, May 12, 1983]

Subpart C—Interpretations and Policies

AUTHORITY: Secs. 1–17, 67 Stat. 111–15, as amended, 81 Stat. 568–74; 15 U.S.C. 1191–1204.

§ 1616.61 Enforcement policy.

(a) It is the policy of the Consumer Product Safety Commission that all items of children's sleepwear in sizes 7 through 14 (including garments and fabric or related material intended or promoted for use in such children's sleepwear) are subject to the Standard FF 5–74 (subpart A of this part) unless the manufacturing process has ended before May 1, 1975. The manufacturing process is deemed to end, for the purposes of the Standard, at the time the item is completely assembled, all functional materials have been affixed, and labeling of a permanent nature has been stamped, sewn, or otherwise permanently affixed to the item. Affixing of temporary price or promotional information or the packaging of items of sleepwear (including garments and fabrics or related material intended or promoted for use in such sleepwear) does not affect the date on which the manufacturing process is deemed to end.

(b) All items of children's sleepwear in sizes 7 through 14 (including garments and fabric or related material intended or promoted for use in such children's sleepwear) which are in inventory or with the trade on the effective date of Standard FF 5–74 are exempt from the requirements of the Standard. For domestically-made items of children's sleepwear in sizes 7 through 14 to be considered "in inventory or with the trade" on the effective date of the Standard, the manufacturing process must have ended prior to May 1, 1975. For foreign-made items of children's sleepwear in sizes 7 through 14 to be considered "in inventory or with the trade" on the effective date of the Standard, the manufacturing process must have ended and the goods must have been entered into the United States before May 1, 1975.

§ 1616.62 Policy regarding retail display requirements for items.

For purposes of the retail display and identification requirements of § 1616.31(c), and for those purposes only, any item which was manufactured before May 1, 1975, and for which a retailer has documentary evidence of compliance with all sampling and testing requirements of the Standard (FF 5–74) (subpart A of this part), will be deemed to be a complying item notwithstanding the absence of an affirmative label to indicate compliance with the Standard as required by § 1616.6(b) of the Standard and § 1616.31(b)(8), or the absence of a garment production unit identification or style identification which meets all requirements of § 1616.31(b) (4) and (7), provided that such an item complies with all other labeling requirements of § 1616.31(b).

§ 1616.63 Policy regarding garment production unit identification.

No provision of 16 CFR 1616.31(b)(7) prohibits placement of a garment production unit identification on a label containing other information. Provided, however, that when the garment production unit identification appears on a label containing other information, provisions of § 1616.31(b)(6) require that the garment production unit identification must be set forth separately from any other information appearing on the same label, and that information not required by the applicable enforcement regulation (§ 1616.31), but placed on the same label with the garment production unit identification, shall not interfere with the garment production unit identification.

§ 1616.64 Policy regarding recordkeeping requirements.

No provision of the Standard for the Flammability of Children's Sleepwear: Sizes 7 through 14 (FF 5–74) (subpart A of this part) or of the enforcement regulations at § 1616.31 prohibits the utilization of fabric which was manufactured before May 1, 1975, and which was not manufactured in production units, in the manufacture of children's sleepwear garments which are subject to the Standard. When such fabric is utilized in the manufacture of such garments, the inability of the garment manufacturer to record the fabric production unit identification of such fabric does not constitute a violation of § 1616.31(d)(4)(i).

§ 1616.65 Policy scope of the standard.

(a) The Standard for the Flammability of Children's Sleepwear: Sizes 7 through 14 (16 CFR part 1616) is applicable to any item of children's sleepwear in sizes 7 through 14.

(1) The term *item* is defined in the Standard at § 1616.2(c) to mean "any product of children's sleepwear or any fabric or related material intended or promoted for use in children's sleepwear."

(2) The term *children's sleepwear* is defined in the Standard at § 1616.2(a) to mean "any product of wearing apparel size 7 through 14, such as nightgowns, pajamas, or similar or related items, such as robes, intended to be worn primarily for sleeping or activities related to sleeping. Underwear and diapers are excluded from this definition."

(b) The Commission makes the following statement of policy regarding (1) the phrase "intended or promoted" as used in the definition of "item" in § 1616.2(c), and (2) the phrase "intended to be worn primarily for sleeping or activities related to sleeping" as used in the definition of "children's sleepwear" in § 1616.2(a).

(c) For enforcement purposes, the meaning of these phrases will be interpreted by the Commission in accordance with the following principles:

(1) *Sleepwear fabrics and related materials.* Whether fabric or related material is "intended or promoted" for use in children's sleepwear depends on the facts and circumstances in each case. Relevant factors include:

(i) The nature of the fabric and its suitability for use in children's sleepwear.

(ii) The extent to which the fabric or a comparable fabric has been sold to manufacturers of children's sleepwear for use in the manufacture of children's sleepwear garments; and

(iii) The likelihood that the fabric will be used primarily for children's sleepwear in a substantial number of cases.

(2) *Sleepwear garments.* Whether a product of wearing apparel is "intended to be worn primarily for sleeping or activities related to sleeping" depends on the facts and circumstances present in each case. Relevant factors include:

(i) The nature of the product and its suitability for use by children for sleeping or activities related to sleeping;

(ii) The manner in which the product is distributed and promoted; and

(iii) The likelihood that the product will be used by children primarily for sleeping or activities related to sleeping in a substantial number of cases.

(3) The factors set forth in this policy statement are guidelines only, and are not elements of the definition of the term "children's sleepwear" in § 1616.2(a) of the Standard. For this reason, a particular fabric or garment may meet the definition of "children's sleepwear" set forth in the Standard, even though all factors listed in this policy statement are not present.

(d) Retailers, distributors, and wholesalers, as well as manufacturers, importers, and other persons (such as converters) introducing a fabric or garment into commerce which does not meet the requirements of the flammability standards for children's sleepwear, have an obligation not to promote or sell such fabric or garment for use as an item of children's sleepwear. Also, retailers, distributors, and wholesalers are advised not to advertise, promote, or sell as an item of children's sleepwear any item which a manufacturer, importer, or other person (such as a converter) introducing the item into commerce has indicated by label, invoice, or, otherwise, does not meet the requirements of the children's sleepwear flammability standards and is not intended or suitable for use as sleepwear. "Tight-fitting" garments as defined by § 1616.2(m) are exempt from the standard which requires flame resistance. They may be marketed as sleepwear for purposes of this section. Additionally, retailers are advised:

(1) To segregate, by placement in different parts of a department or store, fabrics and garments covered by the children's sleepwear standards from all fabrics and garments that are beyond the scope of the children's sleepwear standards but which resemble items of children's sleepwear.

(2) To utilize store display sign indicating the distinction between types of fabrics and garments, for example by indicating which are sleepwear items and which are not; and

(3) To avoid the advertisement or promotion of a fabric or garment that

does not comply with the children's sleepwear flammability standards in a manner that may cause the item to be viewed by the consumer as an item of children's sleepwear.

(Sec. 5 Pub. L. 90–189, 81 Stat. 569, 15 U.S.C. 1194; Sec. 30(b), Pub. L. 92–573, 86 Stat. 1231. 15 U.S.C. 2079(b); 5 U.S.C. 553)

[49 FR 10251, Mar. 20, 1984, as amended at 64 FR 2833, Jan. 19, 1999]

PART 1630—STANDARD FOR THE SURFACE FLAMMABILITY OF CARPETS AND RUGS (FF 1–70)

Subpart A—The Standard

Subpart B—Rules and Regulations

Subpart C—Washing Procedures

Subpart D—Interpretations and Policies

SOURCE: 40 FR 59931, Dec. 30, 1975, unless otherwise noted.

Subpart A—The Standard

AUTHORITY: Sec. 4, 67 Stat. 112, as amended, 81 Stat. 569–70; 15 U.S.C. 1193.

§ 1630.1 Definitions.

In addition to the definitions given in section 2 of the Flammable Fabrics Act, as amended (Sec. 1, 81 Stat. 568; 15 U.S.C. 1191), and the procedures under that act for setting standards (part 1607 of this chapter), the following definitions apply for the purposes of this Standard:

(a) *Acceptance Criterion* means that at least seven out of eight individual specimens of a given carpet or rug shall meet the test criterion as defined in this Standard.

(b) *Test Criterion* means the basis for judging whether or not a single specimen of carpet or rug has passed the test, i.e., the charred portion of a tested specimen shall not extend to within 2.54 cm. (1.0 in.) of the edge of the hole in the flattening frame at any point.

(c) *Carpet* means any type of finished product made in whole or in part of fabric or related material and intended for use or which may reasonably be expected to be used as a floor covering which is exposed to traffic in homes, offices, or other places of assembly or accommodation, and which may or may not be fastened to the floor by mechanical means such as nails, tacks, barbs, staples, adhesives, and which has one dimension greater than 1.83 m. (6 ft.) and a surface area greater than 2.23 $m.^2$ (24 sq. ft.). Products such as "carpet squares", with one dimension less than 1.83 m. (6 ft.) and a surface area less than 2.23 $m.^2$ (24 sq. ft.), but intended to be assembled upon installation into assemblies which may have one dimension greater than 1.83 m. (6 ft.) and a surface area greater than 2.23 $m.^2$ (24 sq. ft.), are included in this definition. Mats, hides with natural or synthetic fibers, and other similar products in the above, defined dimensions are included in this definition, but resilient floor coverings such as linoleum, asphalt tile and vinyl tile are not.

(d) *Rug* means the same as carpet and shall be accepted as interchangeable with carpet.

(e) *Traffic Surface* means a surface of a carpet or rug which is intended to be walked upon.

(f) *Timed Burning Tablet* (pill) means a methenamine tablet, flat, with a nominal heat of combustion value of 7180 calories/gram, a mass of 150 mg ±5mg and a nominal diameter of 6mm.

(g) *Fire-Retardant Treatment* means any process to which a carpet or rug has been exposed which significantly decreases the flammability of that carpet or rug and enables it to meet the acceptance criterion of this Standard.

[40 FR 59931, Dec. 30, 1975, as amended at 72 FR 60767, Oct. 26, 2007]

§ 1630.2 Scope and application.

(a) This Standard provides a test method to determine the surface flammability of carpets and rugs when exposed to a standard small source of ignition under carefully prescribed draft-protected conditions. It is applicable to all types of carpets and rugs used as floor covering materials regardless of their method of fabrication or whether they are made of natural or synthetic fibers or films, or combinations of or substitutes for these.

(b) One of a kind, carpet or rug, such as an antique, an Oriental, or a hide, may be excluded from testing under this Standard pursuant to conditions established by the Consumer Product Safety Commission.

§ 1630.3 General requirements.

(a) *Summary of test method.* This method involves the exposure of each of eight conditioned, replicate specimens of a given carpet or rug to a standard igniting source in a draft-protected environment, and measurement of the proximity of the charred portion to the edge of the hole in the prescribed flattening frame.

(b) *Test criterion.* A specimen passes the test if the charred portion does not extend to within 2.54 cm. (1.0 in.) of the edge of the hole in the flattening frame at any point.

(c) *Acceptance criterion.* At least seven of the eight specimens shall meet the test criterion in order to conform with this Standard.

§ 1630.4 Test procedure.

(a) *Apparatus*—(1) *Test chamber.* The test chamber shall consist of an open top hollow cube made of noncombustible material[1] with inside dimensions 30.48 × 40.48 × 30.48 cm. (12 × 12 × 12 in.) and a minimum of 6.35 (¼ in.) wall thickness. The flat bottom of the box shall be made of the same material as the sides and shall be easily removable. The sides shall be fastened together with screws or brackets and taped to prevent air leakage into the box during use.

NOTE: A minimum of two chambers and two extra bottoms is suggested for efficient operation.

(2) *Flattening frame.* A steel plate, 22.86 × 22.86 cm. (9 × 9 in.), 6.35 mm. (¼ in.) thick with a 20.32 cm. (8 in.) diameter hole in its center is required to hold the carpet or rug flat during the course of the test. It is recommended that one be provided for each test chamber.

(3) *Standard igniting source.* A methenamine tablet, flat, with a nominal heat of combustion value of 7180 calories/gram, a mass of 150 mg ±5 mg and a nominal diameter of 6mm. These tablets shall be stored in a desiccator over a desiccant for 24 hours prior to use. (Small quantities of absorbed water may cause the tablets to fracture when first ignited. If a major fracture occurs, any results from that test shall be ignored, and it shall be repeated.)

(4) *Test specimens.* Each test specimen shall be a 22.86 × 22.86 cm. (9 × 9 in.) section of the carpet or rug to be tested. Eight specimens are required.

(5) *Circulating air oven.* A forced circulation drying oven capable of removing the moisture from the specimens when maintained at 105 °C. (221 °F.) for 2 hours.[2]

(6) *Desiccating cabinet.* An airtight and moisture tight cabinet capable of holding the floor covering specimens horizontally without contacting each other during the cooling period following drying, and containing silica gel desiccant.

(7) *Gloves.* Nonhygroscopic gloves (such as rubber polyethylene) for handling the sample after drying, and raising the pile on specimens prior to testing.

(8) *Hood.* A hood capable of being closed and having its draft turned off during each test and capable of rapidly removing the products of combustion

[1] 6.35 mm (¼ in.) cement asbestos board is a suitable material.

[2] Option 1 of ASTM D 2654–67T, "Methods of Test for Amount of Moisture in Textile Materials," describes a satisfactory oven. ("1969 Book of ASTM Standards," part 24, published by the American Society for Testing and Materials, 1916 Race Street, Philadelphia, Pa. 19103.)

following each test. The front or sides of the hood should be transparent to permit observation of the tests in progress.

(9) *Mirror*. A small mirror mounted above each test chamber at an angle to permit observation of the specimen from outside of the hood.

(10) *Vacuum cleaner*. A vacuum cleaner to remove all loose material from each specimen prior to conditioning. All surfaces of the vacuum cleaner contacting the specimen shall be flat and smooth.

(b) *Sampling*—(1)(i) *Selection of samples*. Select a sample of the material representative of the lot and large enough to permit cutting eight test specimens 22.86 × 22.86 cm. (9 × 9 in.), free from creases, fold marks, delaminations, or other distortions. The test specimens should contain the most flammable parts of the traffic surface at their centers. The most flammable area may be determined on the basis of experience or through pretesting.

(ii) If the carpet or rug has had a fire-retardant treatment, or is made of fibers which have had a fire-retardant treatment, the selected sample or oversized specimens thereof shall be washed, prior to cutting of test specimens after they have been washed and dried either 10 times in accordance with sections 8.2.2, 8.2.3, and 8.3.1(A) of AATCC Test Method 124–1996 "Appearance of Fabrics after Repeated Home Laundering," using wash temperature V (60° ±3 °C, 140° ±5 °F) specified in Table II of that method, and the water level, agitator speed, washing time, spin speed and final spin cycle specified for "Normal/Cotton Sturdy" in Table III, and drying shall be performed in accordance with section 8.3.1(A) of that test method, Tumble Dry, maximum load 3.64 Kg (8 pounds), using the exhaust temperature (66° ±5 °C, 150° ±10 °F) and cool down time of 10 minutes specified in the "Durable Press" conditions of Table IV; or such number of times by another washing and drying procedure which the Consumer Product Safety Commission has determined to be equivalent of AATCC Test Method 124–1996. Alternatively, the selected sample or oversized specimens thereof may be washed, drycleaned, or shampooed 10 times, prior to cutting of test specimens, in such manner as the manufacturer or other interested party shall previously have established to the satisfaction of the Consumer Product Safety Commission is normally used for that type of carpet or rug in service.

(iii) AATCC Test Method 124–1996 "Appearance of Fabrics after Repeated Home Laundering," is found in Technical Manual of the American Association of Textile Chemists and Colorists, vol. 73, 1997, which is incorporated by reference. Copies of this document are available from the American Association of Textile Chemists and Colorists, P.O. Box 12215, Research Triangle Park, North Carolina 27709. This document is also available for inspection at the National Archives and Records Administration (NARA). For information on the availability of this material at NARA, call 202–741–6030, or go to: *http://www.archives.gov/federal_register/code_of_federal_regulations/ibr_locations.html*. This incorporation by reference was approved by the Director of the Federal Register in accordance with 5 U.S.C. 552(a) and 1 CFR part 51.

(2) *Cutting*. Cut eight 22.86±0.64 cm. (9±¼ in.) square specimens of each carpet or rug to be tested to comply with paragraph (b)(1) of this section.

(c) *Conditioning*. (1) Clean each specimen with the vacuum cleaner until it is free of all loose ends left during the manufacturing process and from any material that may have been worked into the pile during handling. Care must be exercised to avoid "fuzzing" of the pile yarn.

(2) Place the specimens in the drying oven in a manner that will permit free circulation of the air at 105 °C. (221 °F.) around them for 2 hours.[3] Remove the specimens from the oven with gloved hands and place them horizontally in

[3] If the specimens are moist when received, permit them to air-dry at laboratory conditions prior to placement in the oven. A satisfactory preconditioning procedure may be found in ASTM D 1776–67, "Conditioning Textiles and Textile Products for Testing." ("1969 Book of ASTM Standards", part 24, published by the American Society for Testing and Materials, 1916 Race Street, Philadelphia, Pa. 19103.)

the desiccator with traffic surface up and free from contact with each other until cooled to room temperature, but in no instance less than 1 hour.

(d) *Testing.* (1) Place the test chamber in the draft-protected environment (hood with draft off) with its bottom in place. Wearing gloves, remove a test specimen from the desiccator and brush its surface with a gloved hand in such a manner as to raise its pile. Place the specimen on the center of the floor of the test chamber, traffic surface up, exercising care that the specimen is horizontal and flat. Place the flattening frame on the specimen and position a methenamine tablet on one of its flat sides in the center of the 20.32 cm. (8 in.) hole.

(2) Ignite the tablet by touching a lighted match or an equivalent igniting source carefully to its top. If more than 2 minutes elapse between the removal of the specimen from the desiccator and the ignition of the tablet, the conditioning must be repeated.

(3) Continue each test until one of the following conditions occurs:

(i) The last vestige of flame or glow disappears. (This is frequently accompanied by a final puff of smoke.)

(ii) The flaming or smoldering has approached within 2.54 cm. (1.0 in.) of the edge of the hole in the flattening frame at any point.

(4) When all combustion has ceased, ventilate the hood and measure the shortest distance between the edge of the hole in the flattening frame and the charred area. Record the distance measured for each specimen.

(5) Remove the specimen from the chamber and remove any burn residue from the floor of the chamber. Before proceeding to the next test, the floor must be cooled to normal room temperature or replaced with one that is at normal room temperature.

(e) *Report.* The number of specimens of the eight tested in which the charred area does not extend to within 2.54 cm. (1.0 in.) of the edge of the hole in the flattening frame shall be reported.

(f) *Interpretation of results.* If the charred area does not extend to within 2.54 cm. (1.0 in.) of the edge of the hole in the flattening frame at any point for at least seven of the eight specimens, the carpet or rug meets the acceptance criterion.

[40 FR 59931, Dec. 30, 1975, as amended at 65 FR 12932, Mar. 10, 2000; 72 FR 60767, Oct. 26, 2007]

§ 1630.5 Labeling.

If the carpet or rug has had a fire-retardant treatment or is made of fibers which have had a fire-retardant treatment, it shall be labeled with the letter "T" pursuant to conditions established by the Consumer Product Safety Commission.

Subpart B—Rules and Regulations

§ 1630.31 Reasonable and representative tests and recordkeeping requirements.

EXPLANATION: Section 8 of the act, among other things, provides that no person shall be subject to criminal prosecution under section 7 of the act for a violation of section 3 of the act if such person establishes a guaranty received in good faith signed by and containing the name and address of the person by whom the product, fabric, or related material guaranteed was manufactured, or from whom it was received; to the effect that reasonable and representative tests made in accordance with applicable flammability standards show that the product, fabric, or related material covered by the guaranty conforms with such standards.

While a person establishing a guaranty received in good faith would not be subject to criminal prosecution under section 7 of the act, he and/or the merchandise involved, would nevertheless remain subject to the administrative processes of the Consumer Product Safety Commission under section 5 of the act as well as injunction and condemnation procedures under section 6 thereof. A guarantor derives no immunity of any kind, civil or criminal, from the issuance of his own guaranty or performance of the reasonable and representative tests prescribed by this section.

The furnishing of guaranties is not mandatory under the act. The purpose of this section is to establish minimum requirements for reasonable and representative tests upon which guaranties may be based. The section does not have any legal effect beyond that specified in section 8 of the act.

(a) For the purposes of this section the following definitions apply:

(1) *Standard* means the standards in subpart A of this part.

(2) *Test* means a test as prescribed by the Standard.

(3) *Acceptance criterion* means "acceptance criterion" as defined in the Standard.

(4) *Test criterion* means "test criterion" as defined in the Standard.

(5) *Carpet* and *rug* mean "carpet" and "rug" as defined in the Standard.

(6) *Quality of machine-made carpets or rugs* means any line of carpets or rugs, essentially machine-made, which are substantially alike in all respects, including, as applicable, constructional units (needles, pitch, rows, shot, stitches, and weight), dye class, dyestuff, dyeing application method, gage, pile levels, pile height, average pile thickness, pile weight, pile yarn, total thickness, total weight, tufts, tuft length, tuft bind, warp yarn, filler yarn, yarn ends per needle, loop length, backing, back coating, primary backing, secondary backing, backing thickness, backing fabric count, backing warp and filler yarns, including stuffer and dead frame yards, backing weight, fiber and/or other materials content, and fire-retardant treatment received including the specifications and quantity of chemicals used.

(7) *Quality of handmade or hide carpets or rugs* means any line of carpets or rugs which are essentially handmade and/or are essentially hides and which are alike in all respects, including those specified in paragraph (a)(6) of this section, where applicable, except that such carpets or rugs may vary where unavoidable and/or may vary because of natural variations in hides of the same type, so long as such variations do not affect flammability.

(b) The tests set forth in paragraphs (c), (d), (e), and (f) of this section are reasonable and representative tests with regard to any carpets or rugs or qualities thereof to which they apply, except, however, that any test of any quality, whenever performed, which does not show a meeting of the acceptance criterion of the Standard shall be considered the reasonable and representative test for that quality and no guaranty with respect thereto shall be issued after the performance of such test. Immediately before conditioning and testing, each carpet or rug specimen tested pursuant to this section shall be in the form in which the carpet or rug or quality thereof which it represents is sold or offered for sale to the ultimate consumer.

(c) Reasonable and representative tests with respect to any quality of machine-made carpets or rugs are (1) at least one test performed upon commencement of production, importation, or other receipt thereof, (2) at least one test performed after production, importation, or other receipt of the first 25,000 linear yards of the quality, and (3) at least one test after production, importation, or other receipt of every 50,000 linear yards of the quality thereafter. Except, however, that tests need be performed only after production, importation, or receipt of each additional 100,000 linear yards of the quality, so long as all 24 specimens required to be tested in a complete series of three required tests immediately preceding any given test (eight out of eight specimens in each of the three preceding tests) meet the test criterion, rather than seven out of eight specimens, as permitted under the acceptance criterion of the Standard.

(d) Reasonable and representative tests with respect to any quality of handmade or hide carpets or rugs are at least one test performed upon the commencement of production, importation, or other receipt thereof and at least one test after production, importation, or other receipt of every 10,000 square yards of the quality thereafter.

(e) Reasonable and representative tests of a one-of-a-kind carpet or rug, machine-made, handmade, or hide, is one test thereof or one test of an identical representative sample.

(f) Guaranties for carpets or rugs in inventory upon the effective date of the Standard may be issued in the same manner as other guaranties are issued. Reasonable and representative tests with respect to qualities of such carpets or rugs are at least one test performed upon approximately the first linear yard and one test thereafter for each 25,000 linear yards of a quality of machine-made carpets or rugs and at least one test performed upon approximately the first square yard and thereafter for each 10,000 square yards of a category of handmade or hide carpets or rugs, in the order of the production, importation, or receipt by the guarantor of that quality.

(g) Any person issuing a guaranty for one or more carpets or rugs or qualities thereof based on reasonable and representative tests, shall maintain the following records for a period of 3 years from the date the tests were performed, or in the case of paragraph (h) of this section, the date the guaranties were furnished. These records must be maintained in the United States by a person subject to section 3 of the act:

(1) All identifying numbers, symbols, etc., manufacturing specifications including all other information described in paragraph (a)(6) of this section, as applicable, and source of products or raw materials used therein.

(2) A physical sample of each carpet or rug or quality thereof covered by the guaranty at least 6 inches by 6 inches in size (36 square inches).

(3) The original or a copy of the report of each test performed for purposes of the guaranty (whether or not such report shows a meeting of the acceptance criterion) which shall disclose the date of the test, the results, and sufficient information to clearly identify the carpet or rug tested.

(4) A record applicable to each test in paragraph (g)(3) of this section showing the approximate yardage at which it was performed. Records otherwise required to be maintained in linear yards may be maintained in square yards on the basis of 4 square yards equals 1 linear yard.

(h) Persons furnishing guaranties based on guaranties received by them shall maintain records showing the guaranty received and identification of the carpet or rug or quality thereof guaranteed in turn by them.

(i) Any person furnishing a carpet or rug guaranty under section 8(a) of the act who neglects or refuses to maintain and preserve the records prescribed in this section shall be deemed to have furnished a false guaranty under the provisions of section 8(b) of the act.

(Sec. 5, 67 Stat. 112, as amended, 81 Stat. 570, 15 U.S.C. 1194; sec. 8, 67 Stat. 114, as amended, 81 Stat. 572, 15 U.S.C. 1197)

§ 1630.32 Carpets and rugs with fire-retardant treatment.

(a) For the purposes of this section the following definitions apply:

(1) *Carpet* and *rug* mean "carpet" and "rug" as defined in § 1630.31(c).

(2) *Fire-retardant treatment* means "fire-retardant treatment" as defined in the standard of subpart A of this part.

(b) If a carpet or rug or small carpet or rug is manufactured, imported, or otherwise marketed or handled which has had a fire-retardant treatment or is made of fibers which have had a fire-retardant treatment, the letter "T" shall be set forth legibly and conspicuously, and shall appear at all times, on each label and/or invoice relating thereto pursuant to the requirements of the Textile Fiber Products Identification Act, 15 U.S.C. 70, et seq., and the rules and regulations thereunder, whether or not such letter "T" appears elsewhere on said product. Samples, pieces, rolls, or squares used to promote or effect the sale of such carpet or rug are subject to the aforementioned requirements. As provided in the applicable portions of the aforesaid act and the rules and regulations thereunder, where a carpet or rug or a small carpet or rug; which has had a fire-retardant treatment or is made of fibers which have had a fire-retardant treatment, is sold to an ultimate consumer and was either custom made or commercially installed for such consumer, the labeling required by this section shall not apply with respect to the carpet or rug if an invoice or other paper relating thereto, containing the letter "T", legibly and conspicuously written, is delivered to the consumer in due course of business.

(c) No person subject to the Flammable Fabrics Act shall manufacture, import, distribute, or otherwise market or handle any carpet or rug or small carpet or rug, including samples, swatches, or specimens used to promote or effect the sale thereof, which is not in compliance with this section.

(Sec. 5 of the Act, 67 Stat. 112, as amended by 81 Stat. 570, 15 U.S.C. 1194)

Subpart C—Washing Procedures

AUTHORITY: Secs. 4, 5, 67 Stat. 112, as amended, 81 Stat. 569–570; 15 U.S.C. 1193, 1194.

§ 1630.61 Hide carpets and rugs—alternative washing procedure.

(a) The Standard for the Surface Flammability of Carpets and Rugs (FF 1–70) at § 1630.4(b)(1)(ii) provides that if a carpet or rug has had a fire-retardant treatment, or is made of fibers which have had a fire-retardant treatment, the sample or oversized specimens thereof selected for testing under the standard shall be washed prior to the cutting of test specimens either 10 times under the washing and drying procedure prescribed in Method 124–1996 of the American Association of Textile Chemists and Colorists or such number of times under such other washing and drying procedure as shall previously have been found to be equivalent by the Consumer Product Safety Commission. AATCC Test Method 124–1996 "Appearance of Fabrics after Repeated Home Laundering," is found in Technical Manual of the American Association of Textile Chemists and Colorists, vol. 73, 1997, which is incorporated by reference. Copies of this document are available from the American Association of Textile Chemists and Colorists, P.O. Box 12215, Research Triangle Park, North Carolina 27709. This document is also available for inspection at the National Archives and Records Administration (NARA). For information on the availability of this material at NARA, call 202–741–6030, or go to: *http://www.archives.gov/federal_register/code_of_federal_regulations/ibr_locations.html.* This incorporation by reference was approved by the Director of the Federal Register in accordance with 5 U.S.C. 552(a) and 1 CFR part 51. Alternatively the selected sample or oversized specimens thereof may be washed, dry-cleaned, or shampooed 10 times, prior to the cutting of test specimens, in such manner as the manufacturer or other interested party has previously established to the satisfaction of the Consumer Product Safety Commission is normally used for that type of carpet or rug in service.

(b) On February 10, 1972 (37 FR 3010) the Federal Trade Commission published in the FEDERAL REGISTER a notice of approval of an alternative washing procedure under FF 1–70 for testing the flammability of shearling and hide rugs that (1) consist of natural wool or hair attached to the hide with no synthetic fibers and (2) have been treated with a fire-retardant finish. The notice of approval was corrected on March 17, 1972 (37 FR 5676). This approval is continued in effect by the Consumer Product Safety Commission pursuant to section 30(e) of the Consumer Product Safety Act (15 U.S.C. 2079(e)).

(c) Any hide carpet or rug for which such alternative procedure is utilized must be labeled with a conspicuous, legible and permanent label containing the following statement:

DO NOT WASH OR DRY CLEAN

This rug has been treated with a flame retardant. To keep rug attractive and clean use the following methods:

To eliminate loose dirt or dust, vacuum or shake pelt outdoors.

For spot cleaning, use water dampened cloth and rub lightly in one direction.

DO NOT USE DETERGENTS OR OTHER STAIN REMOVERS

(d) The alternative procedure is as follows: The test specimens shall be cut to size 9″ × 9″ before the procedure is initiated.

(1) Shake specimen vigorously to remove any loose fibers, dust and possible accumulated debris.

(2) Place specimen on a solid flat surface and anchor or hold firmly while conducting the test.

(3) Select an operating applicator consisting of a rod at least 2″ in diameter and 9″ long composed of nonabsorbant material such as glass or plastic.

(4) Select sufficient cloth to form at least five layers when wrapped around the operating applicator. The cloth shall be of the type known as "Crockmeter Test Cloth" as specified in Note 8.3 of AATCC Test Method 8–1969.

(5) Immerse cloth in water (100 °F.) until thoroughly wetted.

(6) Manually wring out the cloth to remove all excess water and wrap around the operating applicator.

(7) Immediately with light pressure, stroke entire surface of specimen with the wrapped operating applicator in one direction only along the natural "lay" of the hair structure for ten complete strokes.

(8) Place test specimen in a circulating drying oven maintained at 212 °F. until dry.

(9) Repeat the above procedure 10 times using a fresh or clean cloth each time.

(10) After 10 successive cycles of washing and drying the dried specimens shall be subjected to the testing procedures (pill test) as outlined in FF 1–70.

(e) This washing procedure and labeling provision are subject to revision or revocation should it be determined that such procedure is inadequate to fully protect the public.

[40 FR 59931, Dec. 30, 1975, as amended at 65 FR 12933, Mar. 10, 2000]

§ 1630.62 Wool flokati carpets and rugs—alternative washing procedure.

(a) The Standard for the Surface Flammability of Carpets and Rugs (FF 1–70) at § 1630.4(b)(1)(ii) provides that if a carpet or rug has had a fire-retardant treatment, or is made of fibers which have had a fire-retardant treatment, the sample or oversized specimens thereof selected for testing under the standard shall be washed prior to the cutting of test specimens either 10 times under the washing and drying procedure prescribed in Method 124–1996 of the American Association of Textile Chemists and Colorists or such number of times under such other washing and drying procedure as shall previously have been found to be equivalent by the Consumer Product Safety Commission. AATCC Test Method 124–1996 ''Appearance of Fabrics after Repeated Home Laundering,'' is found in Technical Manual of the American Association of Textile Chemists and Colorists, vol. 73, 1997, which is incorporated by reference. Copies of this document are available from the American Association of Textile Chemists and Colorists, P.O. Box 12215, Research Triangle Park, North Carolina 27709. This document is also available for inspection at the National Archives and Records Administration (NARA). For information on the availability of this material at NARA, call 202–741–6030, or go to: *http://www.archives.gov/federal_register/code_of_federal_regulations/ibr_locations.html*. This incorporation by reference was approved by the Director of the Federal Register in accordance with 5 U.S.C. 552(a) and 1 CFR part 51. Alternatively the selected sample or oversized specimens thereof may be washed, dry-cleaned, or shampooed 10 times, prior to the cutting of test specimens, in such manner as the manufacturer or other interested party has previously established to the satisfaction of the Consumer Product Safety Commission is normally used for that type of carpet or rug in service.

(b) On September 7, 1972 (37 FR 18122) the Federal Trade Commission published in the FEDERAL REGISTER a notice of approval of an alternative washing procedure under FF 1–70 for testing the flammability of wool flokati carpets and rugs. This approval is continued in effect by the Consumer Product Safety Commission pursuant to section 30(e) of the Consumer Product Safety Act (15 U.S.C. 2079(e)).

(c) Any wool flokati carpet or rug for which such alternative procedure is utilized must be labeled with a conspicuous, legible and permanent label containing the following statement:

DO NOT WASH IN HOME MACHINE OR DRY CLEAN—AVOID RUBBING OR BRUSHING WHILE DAMP

This flokati carpet or rug has been treated with a flame retardant. To maintain this flame retardant and to keep the carpet attractive and clean, use the following methods.

1. Vacuum (using suction head without rotating brush) or shake the rug (depending upon size) to remove loose dirt.

2. Home laundering: Place in bath tub or other suitable receptacle in solution of home detergent and lukewarm water (approximately 105 °F.) . Immerse face down and gently knead back of rug to remove soil. Rinse in lukewarm water (approximately 105 °F.) until detergent is removed. Rug may then be rinsed again in cool water to improve appearance of face if desired. Line dry. Shake while damp to restore surface and fluff up fibers.

3. Spot cleaning: Remove greasy stains with a household grease remover. Remove soluble stains with lukewarm water (approximately 105 °F.) and detergent by immersing spot in a pan and kneading the back of rug. Rinse thoroughly in lukewarm water. Line or floor dry. Shake while damp to restore surface and fluff up fibers.

4. Commercial cleaning: Use Roll-A-Jet equipment (or equivalent) with water not exceeding 105 °F. Avoid use of excessive pressure or reciprocating brushes. Drying temperatures should not exceed 200 °F.

(d) The alternative procedure is as follows:

(1) Cut test specimens to an oversize of 12″×12″ before the procedure is initiated.

(2) Vacuum specimens or shake vigorously to remove any loose fibers, dust or possible accumulated debris.

(3) Place individual specimen face down in a shallow pan which has been filled to a depth of 2″ with a wash solution of 1.1 grams of AATCC (American Association of Textile Chemists and Colorists) Standard Detergent as specified in AATCC Method 124–1996 (or equivalent) per liter of water preheated to 105 °F. Knead the back of the specimen with hand for 1 minute. Water level and temperature should be maintained for each specimen.

(4) Thoroughly rinse specimen face down with warm water at 105 °F. for 1 minute under a faucet with strong pressure.

(5) Remove excess liquor by use of a wringer, hydroextractor or gentle hand squeezing and dry in circulating air oven at 200 °F. until dry.

(6) Repeat the above procedure 10 times using fresh detergent and fresh water for each set of eight specimens.

(7) Subject the dry specimens to the test procedures in FF 1–70.

(e) This washing procedure and labeling provisions are subject to revocation should it be determined that such procedure is inadequate to fully protect the public.

[40 FR 59931, Dec. 30, 1975, as amended at 65 FR 12933, Mar. 10, 2000]

§ 1630.63 Suspension of washing requirements for carpets and rugs with alumina trihydrate in the backing.

(a)(1) The Standard for the Surface Flammability of Carpets and Rugs (FF 1–70) at § 1630.4(b)(1)(ii) provides that if a carpet or rug has had a fire-retardant treatment, or is made of fibers which have had a fire-retardant treatment, the sample or oversized specimens thereof selected for testing under the standard shall be washed prior to the cutting of test specimens either 10 times under the washing and drying procedure prescribed in Method 124–1996 of the American Association of Textile Chemists and Colorists or such number of times under such other washing and drying procedure as shall previously have been found to be equivalent by the Consumer Product Safety Commission. AATCC Test Method 124–1996 "Appearance of Fabrics after Repeated Home Laundering," is found in Technical Manual of the American Association of Textile Chemists and Colorists, vol. 73, 1997, which is incorporated by reference. Copies of this document are available from the American Association of Textile Chemists and Colorists, P.O. Box 12215, Research Triangle Park, North Carolina 27709. This document is also available for inspection at the National Archives and Records Administration (NARA). For information on the availability of this material at NARA, call 202–741–6030, or go to: *http://www.archives.gov/federal_register/code_of_federal_regulations/ibr_locations.html.* This incorporation by reference was approved by the Director of the Federal Register in accordance with 5 U.S.C. 552(a) and 1 CFR part 51. Alternatively the selected sample or oversized specimens thereof may be washed, dry-cleaned, or shampooed 10 times, prior to the cutting of test specimens, in such manner as the manufacturer or other interested party has previously established to the satisfaction of the Consumer Product Safety Commission is normally used for that type of carpet or rug in service.

(2) Section 1630.5 of the Standard provides that if a carpet or rug has had a fire-retardant treatment or is made of fibers which have had a fire-retardant treatment, it shall be labeled with the letter "T."

(b) On April 10, 1972, the Federal Trade Commission, which then had responsibility for enforcement of the Flammable Fabrics Act, announced that the use of alumina trihydrate in adhesives, foams, or latexes in carpet backings or elsewhere in the backings will be considered as a fire-retardant treatment. Therefore, the provisions of §§ 1630.4(b)(1)(ii) and 1630.5 of the Standard apply to carpets with alumina trihydrate in the backings. This interpretation continues in effect.

(c) On May 19, 1972, the Federal Trade Commission published a notice in the FEDERAL REGISTER (37 FR 10104) temporarily suspending the washing requirements under FF 1–70 for carpets and rugs containing alumina trihydrate in the backing. This temporary suspension was extended a number of times. On March 28, 1973 the Federal Trade Commission proposed in the FEDERAL REGISTER (38 FR 8101) an alternative laundering procedure for such carpets and rugs and gave notice that the suspension of the laundering requirement was extended until the completion of the proceeding to establish an alternative laundering procedure. The suspension continues in effect.

[40 FR 59931, Dec. 30, 1975, as amended at 65 FR 12933, Mar. 10, 2000]

Subpart D—Interpretations and Policies

§ 1630.81 Policy on recall of noncomplying carpets and rugs.

(a) *Purpose.* The purpose of this section is to state the policy of the Commission concerning recall of carpets and rugs which are subject to and fail to comply with the Standard for the Surface Flammability of Carpets and Rugs (FF 1–70) (16 CFR part 1630, subpart A). In this policy statement, the Commission reaffirms that provisions of the Flammable Fabrics Act (FFA) authorize recall of any product which fails to comply with an applicable flammability standard issued under that Act. Additionally, this policy statement announces general principles which will be followed by the Commission in exercising the authority contained in the FFA to require recall of carpets and rugs from various levels of distribution, including carpets and rugs in the possession of the ultimate consumer.

(b) *Recall from distributors and retailers.* The Commission will exercise the authority contained in the FFA to order recall of carpets and rugs which fail to comply with the Standard for the Surface Flammability for Carpets and Rugs and which are in the possession of any distributor, retailer, or other person or firm in the chain of distribution, where the facts, including the number and pattern of test failures, indicate that such action is necessary and appropriate.

(c) *Recall from consumers.* (1) In cases involving carpets and rugs distributed in commerce by a domestic manufacturer, or imported into the United States, after July 11, 1978, the Commission will exercise the authority contained in the FFA to order recall of carpets and rugs which fail to comply with the Standard for the Surface Flammability of Carpets and Rugs and which are in the possession of ultimate purchasers, including installed carpet, where the facts, including the number and pattern of test failures, indicate that such action is necessary and appropriate.

(2) The Commission may exercise the authority of section 15 of the Consumer Product Safety Act (15 U.S.C. 2064) to order the repair, replacement, or repurchase of any carpets or rugs in the possession of ultimate purchasers, including installed carpet, if such carpets and rugs present a ‘‘substantial product hazard’’ as that term is used in the Consumer Product Safety Act in any case involving carpets or rugs which were distributed in commerce by a domestic manufacturer or imported into the United States, on or before July 11, 1978, or any time thereafter.

(Sec. 5, 15 U.S.C. 1194, 67 Stat. 112, June 30, 1953; sec. 5, 15 U.S.C. 45(b), 38 Stat. 719, Sept. 26, 1914; sec. 15, 15 U.S.C. 2064, 86 Stat. 1221, Oct. 27, 1972)

[44 FR 2169, Jan. 10, 1979]

PART 1631—STANDARD FOR THE SURFACE FLAMMABILITY OF SMALL CARPETS AND RUGS (FF 2–70)

Subpart A—The Standard

Subpart B—Rules and Regulations

Subpart C—Washing Procedures

SOURCE: 40 FR 59935, Dec. 30, 1975, unless otherwise noted.

Subpart A—The Standard

AUTHORITY: Sec. 4, 67 Stat. 112, as amended, 81 Stat. 569–70; 15 U.S.C. 1193.

§ 1631.1 Definitions.

In addition to the definitions given in section 2 of the Flammable Fabrics Act, as amended (sec. 1, 81 Stat. 568; 15 U.S.C. 1191), and the procedures under that act for setting standards (part 1607 of this chapter), the following definitions apply for the purposes of this Standard:

(a) *Acceptance Criterion* means that at least seven out of eight individual specimens of a small carpet or rug shall meet the test criterion as defined in this Standard.

(b) *Test Criterion* means the basis for judging whether or not a single specimen of small carpet or rug has passed the test, i.e., the charred portion of a tested specimen shall not extend to within 2.54 cm. (1.0 in.) of the edge of the hole in the flattening frame at any point.

(c) *Small Carpet* means any type of finished product made in whole or in part of fabric or related material and intended for use or which may reasonably be expected to be used as a floor covering which is exposed to traffic in homes, offices, or other places of assembly or accommodation, and which may or may not be fastened to the floor by mechanical means such as nails, tacks, barbs, staples, adhesives, and which has no dimension greater than 1.83 m. (6 ft.) and an area not greater than 2.23 $m.^2$ (24 sq. ft.). Products such as "Carpet Squares" with dimensions smaller than these but intended to be assembled, upon installation, into assemblies which may have dimensions greater than these, are excluded from this definition. They are, however, included in the Standard for the surface flammability of carpets and rugs (FF 1–70) (subpart A of part 1630 of this chapter). Mats, hides with natural or synthetic fibers, and other similar products are included in this definition if they are within the defined dimensions, but resilient floor coverings such as linoleum, asphalt tile and vinyl tile are not.

(d) *Small Rug* means, for the purposes of this Standard, the same as small carpet and shall be accepted as interchangeable with small carpet.

(e) *Traffic Surface* means a surface of a small carpet or rug which is intended to be walked upon.

(f) *Timed Burning Tablet* (pill) means a methenamine tablet, flat, with a nominal heat of combustion value of 7180 calories/gram, a mass of 150 mg ±5mg and a nominal diameter of 6mm.

(g) *Fire-Retardant Treatment* means any process to which a small carpet or rug has been exposed which significantly decreases the flammability of that small carpet or rug and enables it to meet the acceptance criterion of this Standard.

[40 FR 59935, Dec. 30, 1975, as amended at 72 FR 60767, Oct. 26, 2007]

§ 1631.2 Scope and application.

(a) This Standard provides a test method to determine the surface flammability of small carpets and rugs when exposed to a standard small source of ignition under carefully prescribed draft-protected conditions. It is applicable to all types of small carpets and rugs used as floor covering materials regardless of their method of fabrication or whether they are made of natural or synthetic fibers or films, or combinations of, or substitutes for these.

(b) One of a kind small carpet or rug, such as an antique, an Oriental or a hide, may be excluded from testing under this Standard pursuant to conditions established by the Consumer Product Safety Commission.

§ 1631.3 General requirements.

(a) *Summary of test method.* This method involves the exposure of each of eight conditioned, replicate specimens of a small carpet or rug to a standard igniting source in a draft-protected environment and measurement of the proximity of the charred portion to the edge of the hole in the prescribed flattening frame.

(b) *Test criterion.* A specimen passes the test if the charred portion does not extend to within 2.54 cm. (1.0 in.) of the edge of the hole in the flattening frame at any point.

(c) *Acceptance criterion.* At least seven of the eight specimens shall meet the test criterion in order to conform with this Standard.

§ 1631.4 Test procedure.

(a) *Apparatus*—(1) *Test chamber.* The test chamber shall consist of an open top hollow cube made of noncombustible material[1] with inside dimensions 30.48 × 30.48 × 30.48 cm. (12 × 12 × 12 in.) and a minimum of 6.35 mm. (¼ in.) wall thickness. The flat bottom of the box shall be made of the same material as the sides and shall be easily removable. The sides shall be fastened together with screws or brackets and taped to prevent air leakage into the box during use.

NOTE: A minimum of two chambers and two extra bottoms is suggested for efficient operation.

(2) *Flattening frame.* A steel plate, 22.86 × 22.86 cm. (9 × 9 in.) 6.35 mm. (¼ in.) thick with a 20.32 cm. (8 in.) diameter hole in its center is required to hold the specimen flat during the course of the test. It is recommended that one be provided for each test chamber.

(3) *Standard igniting source.* A methenamine tablet, flat, with a nominal heat of combustion value of 7180 calories/gram, a mass of 150 mg ±5 mg and a nominal diameter of 6mm. These tablets shall be stored in a desiccator over a desiccant for 24 hours prior to use. (Small quantities of absorbed water may cause the tablets to fracture when first ignited. If a major fracture occurs, any results from that test shall be ignored, and it shall be repeated.)

(4) *Test specimens.* Each test specimen shall be a 22.86 × 22.86 cm. (9 × 9 in.) section of the small carpet or rug to be tested. Eight specimens are required.

(5) *Circulating air oven.* A forced circulation drying oven capable of removing the moisture from the specimens when maintained at 105 °C. (221 °F.) for 2 hours.[2]

(6) *Desiccating cabinet.* An airtight and moisture tight cabinet capable of holding the floor covering specimens horizontally without contacting each other during the cooling period following drying, and containing silica gel desiccant.

(7) *Gloves.* Nonhygroscopic gloves (such as rubber or polyethylene) for handling the sample after drying and raising the pile on specimens prior to testing.

(8) *Hood.* A hood capable of being closed and having its draft turned off during each test and capable of rapidly removing the products of combustion following each test. The front or sides of the hood should be transparent to permit observation of the tests in progress.

(9) *Mirror.* A small mirror mounted above each test chamber at an angle to permit observation of the specimen from outside the hood.

(10) *Vacuum cleaner.* A vacuum cleaner to remove all loose material from each specimen prior to conditioning. All surfaces of the vacuum cleaner contacting the specimen shall be flat and smooth.

(b) *Sampling*—(1) *Selection of samples.* (i) Select a sample of the material representative of the lot and large enough to permit cutting eight test specimens 22.86 × 22.86 cm. (9 × 9 in.) free from creases, fold marks, delaminations or other distortions. The representative sample of material may require the use of more than one small carpet or rug. The test specimens should contain the most flammable parts of the traffic surface at their centers. The most flammable area may be determined on the basis of experience or through pretesting.

---

[1] 6.35 mm. (¼ in.) cement asbestos board is a suitable material.

[2] Option 1 of ASTM D 2654–67T, "Methods of Test for Amount of Moisture in Textile Materials," describes a satisfactory oven. ("1969 Book of ASTM Standards," part 24, published by the American Society for Testing and Materials, 1916 Race Street, Philadelphia, PA 19103.)

(ii) If the carpet or rug has had a fire-retardant treatment, or is made of fibers which have had a fire-retardant treatment, the selected sample or oversized specimens thereof shall be washed, prior to cutting of test specimens after they have been washed and dried either 10 times in accordance with sections 8.2.2, 8.2.3, and 8.3.1(A) of AATCC Test Method 124–1996 "Appearance of Fabrics after Repeated Home Laundering," using wash temperature V (60° ±3 °C, 140° ±5 °F) specified in Table II of that method, and the water level, agitator speed, washing time, spin speed and final spin cycle specified for "Normal/Cotton Sturdy" in Table III, and drying shall be performed in accordance with section 8.3.1(A) of that test method, Tumble Dry, maximum load 3.64 Kg (8 pounds), using the exhaust temperature (66° ±5 °C, 150° ±10 °F) and cool down time of 10 minutes specified in the "Durable Press" conditions of Table IV; or such number of times by another washing and drying procedure which the Consumer Product Safety Commission has determined to be equivalent of AATCC Test Method 124–1996. Alternatively, the selected sample or oversized specimens thereof may be washed, drycleaned, or shampooed 10 times, prior to cutting of test specimens, in such manner as the manufacturer or other interested party shall previously have established to the satisfaction of the Consumer Product Safety Commission is normally used for that type of carpet or rug in service.

(iii) AATCC Test Method 124–1996 "Appearance of Fabrics after Repeated Home Laundering," is found in Technical Manual of the American Association of Textile Chemists and Colorists, vol. 73, 1997, which is incorporated by reference. Copies of this document are available from the American Association of Textile Chemists and Colorists, P.O. Box 12215, Research Triangle Park, North Carolina 27709. This document is also available for inspection at the National Archives and Records Administration (NARA). For information on the availability of this material at NARA, call 202–741–6030, or go to: *http://www.archives.gov/federal_register/code_of_federal_regulations/ibr_locations.html.* This incorporation by reference was approved by the Director of the Federal Register in accordance with 5 U.S.C. 552(a) and 1 CFR part 51.

(2) *Cutting.* Cut eight 22.86±0.64 cm. (9±¼ in.) square specimens of each small carpet or rug to be tested to comply with paragraph (b)(1) of this section.

(c) *Conditioning.* (1) Clean each specimen with the vacuum cleaner until it is free of all loose ends left during the manufacturing process and from any material that may have been worked into the pile during handling.[3] Care must be exercised to avoid "fuzzing" of the pile yarn.

(2) Place the specimens in a drying oven in a manner that will permit free circulation of the air at 105 °C. (221 °F.) around them for 2 hours.[4] Remove the specimens from the oven with gloved hands and place them horizontally in the desiccator with traffic surface up and free from contact with each other until cooled to room temperature, but in no instance less than 1 hour.

(d) *Testing.* (1) Place the test chamber in the draft-protected environment (hood with draft off) with its bottom in place. Wearing gloves, remove a test specimen from the desiccator and brush its traffic surface with a gloved hand in such a manner as to raise its pile. Place the specimen on the center of the floor of the test chamber, traffic surface up, exercising care that the specimen is horizontal and flat. Place the flattening frame on the specimen and position a methenamine tablet on one of its flat sides in the center of the 20.32 cm. (8 in.) hole.

(2) Ignite the tablet by touching a lighted match or an equivalent igniting source carefully to its top. If more

[3] The vacuum cleaning described is not intended to simulate the effects of repeated vacuum cleaning in service.

[4] If the specimens are moist when received, permit them to air-dry at laboratory conditions prior to placement in the oven. A satisfactory preconditioning procedure may be found in ASTM D 1776–67, "Conditioning Textiles and Textile Products for Testing." ("1969 Book of ASTM Standards," part 24, published by the American Society for Testing and Materials, 1916 Race Street, Philadelphia, Pa. 19103.)

than 2 minutes elapse between the removal of the specimen from the desiccator and the ignition of the tablet, the conditioning must be repeated.

(3) Continue each test until one of the following conditions occurs:

(i) The last vestige of flame or glow disappears. (This is frequently accompanied by a final puff of smoke.)

(ii) The flaming or smoldering has approached within 2.54 cm. (1.0 in.) of the edge of the hole in the flattening frame at any point.

(4) When all combustion has ceased, ventilate the hood and measure the shortest distance between the edge of the hole in the flattening frame and the charred area. Record the distance measured for each specimen.

(5) Remove the specimen from the chamber and remove any burn residue from the floor of the chamber. Before proceeding to the next test, the floor must be cooled to normal room temperature or replaced with one that is at normal room temperature.

(e) *Report.* The number of specimens of the eight tested in which the charred area does not extend to within 2.54 cm. (1.0 in.) of the edge of the hole in the flattening frame shall be reported.

(f) *Interpretation of results.* If the charred area does not extend to within 2.54 cm. (1.0 in.) of the edge of the hole in the flattening frame at any point for at least seven of the eight specimens, the small carpet or rug meets the acceptance criterion.

[40 FR 59935, Dec. 30, 1975, as amended at 65 FR 12934, Mar. 10, 2000; 72 FR 60767, Oct. 26, 2007]

§ 1631.5 Labeling requirements.

(a) If a small carpet or rug does not meet the acceptance criterion, it shall, prior to its introduction into commerce, be permanently labeled, pursuant to rules and regulations established by the Consumer Product Safety Commission with the following statement: FLAMMABLE (FAILS U.S. DEPARTMENT OF COMMERCE STANDARD FF 2–70): SHOULD NOT BE USED NEAR SOURCES OF IGNITION.

(b) If a small carpet or rug has had a fire-retardant treatment or is made of fibers which have had a fire-retardant treatment, it shall be labeled with the letter "T" pursuant to rules and regulations established by the Consumer Product Safety Commission.

Subpart B—Rules and Regulations

AUTHORITY: Sec. 5, 67 Stat. 112, as amended, 81 Stat. 570; 15 U.S.C. 1194.

§ 1631.31 Reasonable and representative tests and recordkeeping requirements.

EXPLANATION: Section 8 of the act, among other things, provides that no person shall be subject to criminal prosecution under section 7 of the act for a violation of section 3 of the act if such person establishes a guaranty received in good faith signed by and containing the name and address of the person by whom the product, fabric, or related material guaranteed was manufactured, or from whom it was received, to the effect that reasonable and representative tests made in accordance with applicable flammability standards show that the product, fabric, or related material covered by the guaranty conforms with such standards.

While a person establishing a guaranty received in good faith would not be subject to criminal prosecution under section 7 of the act, he, and/or the merchandise involved, would nevertheless remain subject to the administrative processes of the Consumer Product Safety Commission under section 5 of the act as well as injunction and condemnation procedures under section 6 thereof. A guarantor derives no immunity of any kind, civil or criminal, from the issuance of his own guaranty or performance of the reasonable and representative tests prescribed by this section.

The furnishing of guaranties is not mandatory under the act. The purpose of this section is to establish minimum requirements for reasonable and representative tests upon which guaranties may be based. The section does not have any legal effect beyond that specified in section 8 of the act.

(a) For the purposes of this section the following definitions apply:

(1) *Standard* means the Standard in subpart A of this part.

(2) *Test* means a test as prescribed by the Standard.

(3) *Acceptance criterion* means "acceptance criterion" as defined in the Standard.

(4) *Test criterion* means "test criterion" as defined in the Standard.

(5) *Carpet* and *rug* mean "carpet" and "rug" as defined in the Standard.

(6) *Quality of machine-made carpets or rugs* means any line of carpets or rugs, essentially machine-made, which are

substantially alike in all respects, including, as applicable, constructional units (needles, pitch, rows, shot, stitches, and weight), dye class, dyestuff, dyeing application method, gage, pile levels, pile height, average pile thickness, pile weight, pile yarn, total thickness, total weight, tufts, tuft length, tuft bind, warp yarn, filler yarn, yarn ends per needle, loop length, backing, back coating, primary backing, secondary backing, backing thickness, backing fabric count, backing warp and filler yarns, including stuffer and dead frame yarns, backing weight, fiber and/or other materials content, and fire retardant treatment received including the specifications and quantity of chemicals used.

(7) *Quality of handmade or hide carpets or rugs* means any line of carpets or rugs which are essentially handmade and/or are essentially hides and which are alike in all respects, including those specified in paragraph (a)(6) of this section, where applicable, except that such carpets or rugs may vary where unavoidable and/or may vary because of natural variations in hides of the same type, so long as such variations do not affect flammability.

(b) The tests set forth in paragraphs (c), (d), (e), and (f) of this section are reasonable and representative tests with regard to any carpets or rugs or qualities thereof to which they apply, except, however, that any test of any quality, whenever performed, which does not show a meeting of the acceptance criterion of the Standard shall be considered the reasonable and representative test for that quality and no guaranty with respect thereto shall be issued after the performance of such test. Immediately before conditioning and testing, each carpet or rug specimen tested pursuant to this section shall be in the form in which the carpet or rug or quality thereof which it represents is sold or offered for sale to the ultimate consumer.

(c) Reasonable and representative tests with respect to any quality of machine-made carpets or rugs are (1) at least one test performed upon commencement of production, importation, or other receipt thereof, (2) at least one test performed after production, importation, or other receipt of the first 25,000 linear yards of the quality, and (3) at least one test after production, importation, or other receipt of every 50,000 linear yards of the quality thereafter. Except, however, that tests need be performed only after production, importation, or receipt of each additional 100,000 linear yards of the quality, so long as all 24 specimens required to be tested in a complete series of three required tests immediately preceding any given test (eight out of eight specimens in each of the three preceding tests) meet the test criterion, rather than seven out of eight specimens, as permitted under the acceptance criterion of the Standard.

(d) Reasonable and representative tests with respect to any quality of handmade or hide carpets or rugs are at least one test performed upon the commencement of production, importation, or other receipt thereof and at least one test after production, importation, or other receipt of every 10,000 square yards of the quality thereafter.

(e) Reasonable and representative tests of a one-of-a-kind carpet or rug, machine made, handmade, or hide, is one test thereof or one test of an identical representative sample.

(f) Guaranties for carpets or rugs in inventory upon the effective date of the Standard may be issued in the same manner as other guaranties are issued. Reasonable and representative tests with respect to qualities or such carpets or rugs are at least one test performed upon approximately the first linear yard and one test thereafter for each 25,000 linear yards of a quality of machine-made carpets or rugs and at least one test performed upon approximately the first square yard and thereafter for each 10,000 square yards of a category of hand-made or hide carpets or rugs, in the order of the production, importation, or receipt by the guarantor of that quality.

(g) Any person issuing a guaranty for one or more carpets or rugs or qualities thereof based on reasonable and representative tests, shall maintain the following records for a period of 3 years from the date the tests were performed, or in the case of paragraph (h) of this section, the date the guaranties were furnished. These records must be maintained in the United States by a person subject to section 3 of the act:

(1) All identifying numbers, symbols, etc., manufacturing specifications including all other information described in paragraph (a)(6) of this section, as applicable, and source of products or raw materials used therein.

(2) A physical sample of each carpet or rug or quality thereof covered by the guaranty at least 6 inches by 6 inches in size (36 square inches).

(3) The original or a copy of the report of each test performed for purposes of the guaranty (whether or not such report shows a meeting of the acceptance criterion) which shall disclose the date of the test, the results, and sufficient information to clearly identify the carpet or rug tested.

(4) A record applicable to each test in paragraph (g)(3) of this section showing the approximate yardage at which it was performed. Records otherwise required to be maintained in linear yards may be maintained in square yards on the basis of 4 square yards equals 1 linear yard.

(h) Persons furnishing guaranties based on guaranties received by them shall maintain records showing the guaranty received and identification of the carpet or rug or quality thereof guaranteed in turn by them.

(i) Any person furnishing a carpet or rug guaranty under section 8(a) of the act who neglects or refuses to maintain and preserve the records prescribed in this section shall be deemed to have furnished a false guaranty under the provisions of section 8(b) of the act.

(Sec. 5 of the Act, 67 Stat. 112, as amended by 81 Stat. 570, 15 U.S.C. 1194; sec. 8 of the Act, 67 Stat. 114, as amended by 81 Stat. 572, 15 U.S.C. 1197)

§ 1631.32 Reasonable and representative tests and recordkeeping requirements—additional requirements.

(a) Persons issuing guaranties under section 8(a) of the act for small carpets and rugs subject to FF 2–70 shall be subject to all of the requirements of § 1631.31 except as provided in paragraph (b) of this section.

(b) In lieu of performing tests and maintaining records on the basis of linear yards or square yards as provided in § 1631.31 persons furnishing warranties for small carpets and rugs subject to FF 2–70 shall perform tests and maintain records on the basis of units of carpets or rugs, with "unit" being defined as a single carpet or rug, or on the basis of square yards. At least one test shall be performed upon commencement of production, importation, or other receipt of such small carpet or rug and every 25,000 units or square yards thereafter.

(Sec. 5 of the Act, 67 Stat. 112, as amended by 81 Stat. 570, 15 U.S.C. 1194; sec. 8 of the Act, 67 Stat. 114, as amended by 81 Stat. 572, 15 U.S.C. 1197)

§ 1631.33 Carpets and rugs with fire-retardant treatment.

(a) For the purposes of this section the following definitions apply:

(1) *Small carpet* and *small rug* means "small carpet" and "small rug" as defined in § 1631.1(c).

(2) *Fire-retardant treatment* means "fire-retardant treatment" as defined in the Standard in subpart A of this part.

(b) If a carpet or rug or small carpet or rug is manufactured, imported, or otherwise marketed or handled which has had a fire-retardant treatment or is made of fibers which have had a fire-retardant treatment, the letter "T" shall be set forth legibly and conspicuously, and shall appear at all times, on each label and/or invoice relating thereto pursuant to the requirements of the Textile Fiber Products Identification Act, 15 U.S.C. section 70, et seq., and the rules and regulations thereunder, whether or not such letter "T" appears elsewhere on said product. Samples, pieces, rolls, or squares used to promote or effect the sale of such carpet or rug are subject to the aforementioned requirements. As provided in the applicable portions of the aforesaid Act and the rules and regulations thereunder, where a carpet or rug or a small carpet or rug which has had a fire-retardant treatment or is made of fibers which have had a fire-retardant treatment, is sold to an ultimate consumer and was either custom made or commercially installed for such consumer, the labeling required by this section shall not apply with respect to the carpet or rug if an invoice or other paper relating thereto, containing the letter "T", legibly and conspicuously written, is delivered to the consumer in due course of business.

(c) No person subject to the Flammable Fabrics Act shall manufacture, import, distribute, or otherwise market or handle any carpet or rug or small carpet or rug, including samples, swatches, or specimens used to promote or effect the sale thereof, which is not in compliance with this section.

§ 1631.34 Small carpets and rugs not meeting acceptance criterion.

(a) If any small carpet or rug as defined in the Standard for the Surface Flammability of Small Carpets and Rugs (pill test) FF 2–70, is manufactured, imported, or otherwise marketed or handled and does not meet the acceptance criterion of such standard, it shall, prior to its introduction into commerce, be legibly and conspicuously labeled with a permanent label which sets forth the following statement:

"FLAMMABLE (FAILS U.S. DEPARTMENT OF COMMERCE STANDARD FF 2–70): SHOULD NOT BE USED NEAR SOURCES OF IGNITION."

The required cautionary statement may be set out on or affixed to the small carpet or rug on the same label as the fiber content label required to be affixed under the Textile Fiber Products Identification Act, if said label is permanent, or said statement shall be set forth on a separate permanent label on or affixed to the small carpet or rug in immediate proximity to the said required label under the Textile Fiber Products Identification Act. A label on the front of a small carpet or rug shall be considered to be in immediate proximity to a label on the back, provided they are directly opposite each other and are in immediate proximity to the edge of the small carpet or rug.

(b) Such cautionary statements shall also appear in a conspicuous manner in all advertisements in which said small carpets or rugs are being offered for sale through direct mail, telephone solicitation, or under any other circumstances where the consumer, in the ordinary course of dealing, will not have an opportunity to inspect the label before receiving the merchandise. The phrase "Flammable—Read The Label" shall conspicuously appear in all other advertisements of small carpets or rugs which do not meet the acceptance criterion of the standard.

(c) The information required by this section shall be set forth separately from any other information, representations, or disclosures appearing on the same label or elsewhere on the small carpet or rug, and any such other information, representations, or disclosures shall in no way interfere with, minimize, detract from, or conflict with the information required by this section.

(d) Samples, swatches, or specimens used to promote or effect the sale of small carpets or rugs shall be labeled with the information required by this section, in addition to the label required to be affixed to the small carpets or rugs.

(e) Where small carpets or rugs are marketed at retail in packages, and the labeling information required by this section is not readily visible to prospective purchasers, the packages must also be prominently, conspicuously, and legibly labeled with the information required by this section.

(f) No person, other than the ultimate consumer, shall remove, mutilate, or cause or participate in the removal or mutilation of any affixed labeling information required by this section.

(g) No person subject to the Flammable Fabrics Act shall manufacture, import, distribute, or otherwise market or handle any small carpet or rug, including samples, swatches, or specimens used to promote or effect the sale thereof, which is not in compliance with this section.

Subpart C—Washing Procedures

AUTHORITY: Secs. 4, 5, 67 Stat. 112, as amended, 81 Stat. 569–70; 15 U.S.C. 1193, 1194.

§ 1631.61 Hide carpets and rugs—alternative washing procedure.

(a) The Standard for the Surface Flammability of Carpets and Rugs (FF 1–70) at § 1630.4(b)(1)(ii) provides that if a carpet or rug has had a fire-retardant treatment, or is made of fibers which have had a fire-retardant treatment, the sample or oversized specimens thereof selected for testing under the standard shall be washed prior to the cutting of test specimens either 10 times under the washing and drying procedure prescribed in Method 124–1996 of the American Association of Textile Chemists and Colorists or such number of times under such other washing and drying procedure as shall previously have been found to be equivalent by the Consumer Product Safety Commission. AATCC Test Method 124–1996 "Appearance of Fabrics after Repeated Home Laundering," is found in Technical Manual of the American Association of Textile Chemists and Colorists, vol. 73, 1997, which is incorporated by reference. Copies of this document are available from the American Association of Textile Chemists and Colorists, P.O. Box 12215, Research Triangle Park, North Carolina 27709. This document is also available for inspection at the National Archives and Records Administration (NARA). For information on the availability of this material at NARA, call 202–741–6030, or go to: *http://www.archives.gov/federal_register/code_of_federal_regulations/ibr_locations.html.* This incorporation by reference was approved by the Director of the Federal Register in accordance with 5 U.S.C. 552(a) and 1 CFR part 51. Alternatively the selected sample or oversized specimens thereof may be washed, dry-cleaned, or shampooed 10 times, prior to the cutting of test specimens, in such manner as the manufacturer or other interested party has previously established to the satisfaction of the Consumer Product Safety Commission is normally used for that type of carpet or rug in service.

(b) On February 10, 1972 (37 FR 3010) the Federal Trade Commission published in the FEDERAL REGISTER a notice of approval of an alternative washing procedure under FF 2–70 for testing the flammability of shearling and hide rugs that (1) consist of natural wool or hair attached to the hide with no synthetic fibers and (2) have been treated with a fire-retardant finish. The notice of approval was corrected on March 17, 1972 (37 FR 5676). This approval is continued in effect by the Consumer Product Safety Commission pursuant to section 30(e) of the Consumer Product Safety Act (15 U.S.C. 2079(e)).

(c) Any hide carpet or rug for which such alternative procedure is utilized must be labeled with a conspicuous, legible and permanent label containing the following statement:

DO NOT WASH OR DRY CLEAN

This rug has been treated with a flame retardant. To keep rug attractive and clean use the following methods:

To eliminate loose dirt or dust, vacuum or shake pelt outdoors.

For spot cleaning, use water dampened cloth and rub lightly in one direction.

DO NOT USE DETERGENTS OR OTHER STAIN REMOVERS

(d) The alternative procedure is as follows: The test specimens shall be cut to size 9″ × 9″ before the procedure is initiated.

(1) Shake specimen vigorously to remove any loose fibers, dust and possible accumulated debris.

(2) Place specimen on a solid flat surface and anchor or hold firmly while conducting the test.

(3) Select an operating applicator consisting of a rod at least 2″ in diameter and 9″ long composed of nonabsorbent material such as glass or plastic.

(4) Select sufficient cloth to form at least five layers when wrapped around the operating applicator. The cloth shall be of the type known as "Crockmeter Test Cloth" as specified in Note 8.3 of AATCC Test Method 8–1969.

(5) Immerse cloth in water (100 °F.) until thoroughly wetted.

(6) Manually wring out the cloth to remove all excess water and wrap around the operating applicator.

(7) Immediately, with light pressure, stroke entire surface of specimen with the wrapped operating applicator in one direction only along the natural "lay" of the hair structure for ten complete strokes.

(8) Place test specimen in a circulating drying oven maintained at 212 °F. until dry.

(9) Repeat the above procedure 10 times using a fresh or clean cloth each time.

(10) After 10 successive cycles of washing and drying the dried specimens shall be subjected to the testing procedures (pill test) as outlined in FF 2–70.

(e) This washing procedure and labeling provision are subject to revision or revocation should it be determined that such procedure is inadequate to fully protect the public.

[40 FR 59935, Dec. 30, 1975, as amended at 65 FR 12934, Mar. 10, 2000]

§ 1631.62 Wool flokati carpets and rugs—alternative washing procedure.

(a) The Standard for the Surface Flammability of Carpets and Rugs (FF 1–70) at § 1630.4(b)(1)(ii) provides that if a carpet or rug has had a fire-retardant treatment, or is made of fibers which have had a fire-retardant treatment, the sample or oversized specimens thereof selected for testing under the standard shall be washed prior to the cutting of test specimens either 10 times under the washing and drying procedure prescribed in Method 124–1996 of the American Association of Textile Chemists and Colorists or such number of times under such other washing and drying procedure as shall previously have been found to be equivalent by the Consumer Product Safety Commission. AATCC Test Method 124–1996 ‘‘Appearance of Fabrics after Repeated Home Laundering,’’ is found in Technical Manual of the American Association of Textile Chemists and Colorists, vol. 73, 1997, which is incorporated by reference. Copies of this document are available from the American Association of Textile Chemists and Colorists, P.O. Box 12215, Research Triangle Park, North Carolina 27709. This document is also available for inspection at the National Archives and Records Administration (NARA). For information on the availability of this material at NARA, call 202–741–6030, or go to: *http://www.archives.gov/federal_register/code_of_federal_regulations/ibr_locations.html*. This incorporation by reference was approved by the Director of the Federal Register in accordance with 5 U.S.C. 552(a) and 1 CFR part 51. Alternatively the selected sample or oversized specimens thereof may be washed, dry-cleaned, or shampooed 10 times, prior to the cutting of test specimens, in such manner as the manufacturer or other interested party has previously established to the satisfaction of the Consumer Product Safety Commission is normally used for that type of carpet or rug in service.

(b) On September 7, 1972 (37 FR 18122) the Federal Trade Commission published in the FEDERAL REGISTER a notice of approval of an alternative washing procedure under FF 2–70 for testing the flammability of wool flokati carpets and rugs. This approval is continued in effect by the Consumer Product Safety Commission pursuant to section 30(e) of the Consumer Product Safety Act (15 U.S.C. 2079(e)).

(c) Any wool flokati carpet or rug for which such alternative procedure is utilized must be labeled with a conspicuous, legible and permanent label containing the following statement:

Do Not Wash in Home Machine or Dry Clean—Avoid Rubbing or Brushing While Damp

This Flokati carpet or rug has been treated with a flame retardant. To maintain this flame retardant and to keep the carpet attractive and clean, use the following methods.

1. Vacuum (using suction head without rotating brush) or shake the rug (depending upon size) to remove loose dirt.

2. Home laundering: Place in bath tub or other suitable receptacle in solution of home detergent and lukewarm water (approximately 105 °F.). Immerse face down and gently knead back of rug to remove soil. Rinse in lukewarm water (approximately 105 °F.) until detergent is removed. Rug may then be rinsed again in cool water to improve appearance of face if desired. Line dry. Shake while damp to restore surface and fluff up fibers.

3. Spot cleaning: Remove greasy stains with a household grease remover. Remove soluble stains with lukewarm water (approximately 105 °F.) and detergent by immersing spot in a pan and kneading the back of rug. Rinse thoroughly in lukewarm water. Line or floor dry. Shake while damp to restore surface and fluff up fibers.

4. Commercial cleaning: Use Roll-A-Jet equipment (or equivalent) with water not exceeding 105 °F. Avoid use of excessive pressure or reciprocating brushes. Drying temperatures should not exceed 200 °F.

(d) The alternative procedure is as follows:

(1) Cut test specimens to an oversize 12″ × 12″ before the procedure is initiated.

(2) Vacuum specimens or shake vigorously to remove any loose fibers, dust or possible accumulated debris.

(3) Place individual specimen face down in a shallow pan which has been filled to a depth of 2'' with a wash solution of 1.1 grams of AATCC (American Association of Textile Chemists and Colorists) Standard Detergent as specified in AATCC Method 124–1996 (or equivalent) per liter of water preheated to 105 °F. Knead the back of the specimen with hand for 1 minute. Water level and temperature should be maintained for each specimen.

(4) Thoroughly rinse specimen face down with warm water at 105 °F. for 1 minute under a faucet with strong pressure.

(5) Remove excess liquor by use of a wringer, hydroextractor or gentle hand squeezing and dry in circulating air oven at 200 °F. until dry.

(6) Repeat the above procedure 10 times using fresh detergent and fresh water for each set of eight specimens.

(7) Subject the dry specimens to the test procedures in FF 2–70.

(e) This washing procedure and labeling provisions are subject to revocation should it be determined that such procedure is inadequate to fully protect the public.

[40 FR 59935, Dec. 30, 1975, as amended at 65 FR 12934, Mar. 10, 2000]

PART 1632—STANDARD FOR THE FLAMMABILITY OF MATTRESSES AND MATTRESS PADS (FF 4–72, AMENDED)

Subpart A—The Standard

Subpart B—Rules and Regulations

Subpart C—Interpretations and Policies

AUTHORITY: 15 U.S.C. 1193, 1194; 15 U.S.C. 2079(b).

SOURCE: 49 FR 39796, Oct. 10, 1984, unless otherwise noted.

Subpart A—The Standard

§ 1632.1 Definitions.

In addition to the definitions given in section 2 of the Flammable Fabrics Act as amended (15 U.S.C. 1191), the following definitions apply for the purpose of the standard.

(a) *Mattress* means a ticking filled with a resilient material used alone or in combination with other products intended or promoted for sleeping upon.

(1) This definition includes, but is not limited to, adult mattresses, youth mattresses, crib mattresses including portable crib mattresses, bunk bed mattresses, futons, water beds and air mattresses which contain upholstery material between the ticking and the mattress core, and any detachable mattresses used in any item of upholstered furniture such as convertible sofa bed mattresses, corner group mattresses, day bed mattresses, roll-a-way bed mattresses, high risers, and trundle bed mattresses. See § 1632.8 Glossary of terms, for definitions of these items.

(2) This definition excludes sleeping bags, pillows, mattress foundations, liquid and gaseous filled tickings such as water beds and air mattresses which do not contain upholstery material between the ticking and the mattress core, upholstered furniture which does not contain a detachable mattress such as chaise lounges, drop-arm love seats, press-back lounges, push-back sofas, sleep lounges, sofa beds (including jackknife sofa beds), sofa lounges (including glide-outs), studio couches and studio divans (including twin studio divans and studio beds), and juvenile product pads such as car bed pads, carriage pads, basket pads, infant carrier and lounge pads, dressing table pads, stroller pads, crib bumpers, and playpen pads. See § 1632.8 Glossary of terms, for definitions of these items.

(b) *Mattress Pad* means a thin, flat mat or cushion, and/or ticking filled with resilient material for use on top of a mattress. This definition includes, but is not limited to, absorbent mattress pads, flat decubitus pads, and convoluted foam pads which are totally enclosed in ticking. This definition excludes convoluted foam pads which are not totally encased in ticking.

(c) *Ticking* means the outermost layer of fabric or related material that encloses the core and upholstery materials of a mattress or mattress pad. A mattress ticking may consist of several layers of fabric or related materials quilted together.

(d) *Core* means the main support system that may be present in a mattress, such as springs, foam, hair block, water bladder, air bladder, or resilient filling.

(e) *Upholstery material* means all material, either loose or attached, between the mattress or mattress pad ticking and the core of a mattress, if a core is present.

(f) *Tape edge* (edge) means the seam or border edge of a mattress or mattress pad.

(g) *Quilted* means stitched with thread or by fusion through the ticking and one or more layers of upholstery material.

(h) *Tufted* means buttoned or laced through the ticking and upholstery material and/or core, or having the ticking and upholstery material and/or core drawn together at intervals by any other method which produces a series of depressions on the surface.

(i) *Manufacturer* means an individual plant or factory at which mattresses and/or mattress pads are produced or assembled.

(j) *Mattress prototype* means mattresses of a particular design, sharing all materials and methods of assembly, but excluding differences in mattress size. If it has been shown as a result of prototype qualification testing that an upholstery material or core will not reduce the ignition resistance of the mattress prototype, substitution of another material for such material shall not be deemed a difference in materials for prototype definition. (See §1632.31(c)(4) for records required to demonstrate that a change of materials has not reduced ignition resistance of a mattress prototype.) If it is determined or suspected that a material has influenced the ignition resistance of the mattress prototype, a change in that material, excluding an increase in thickness, shall be deemed a difference in materials for purposes of prototype definition unless it is previously shown to the satisfaction of the Consumer Product Safety Commission that such change will not reduce the ignition resistance of the mattress prototype. Ticking materials may be substituted in accordance with §1632.6. Tape edge materials may be substituted in accordance with §1632.7.

(k) *Mattress pad prototype* means mattress pads of a particular design, sharing all materials and methods of assembly, but excluding differences in mattress pad size. A change in existing material, except an increase in thickness, shall be deemed a difference in materials for purposes of prototype definition unless it is previously shown to the satisfaction of the Consumer Product Safety Commission that such change will not reduce the ignition resistance of the mattress pad prototype. Ticking materials may be substituted in accordance with §1632.6. Tape edge materials may be substituted in accordance with §1632.7.

(l) *Surface* means one side of a mattress or mattress pad which is intended for sleeping upon and which can be tested.

§ 1632.2 Purpose, scope, and applicability.

(a) *Purpose.* (1) This standard prescribes requirements for testing of prototype designs of mattresses and mattress pads before the sale in commerce or the introduction in commerce of any mattress or mattress pad which is subject to the standard. The standard prescribes a test to determine the ignition resistance of a mattress or a mattress pad when exposed to a lighted cigarette.

(2) The standard sets forth a test at §1632.6 which may be used to classify ticking materials for resistance to cigarette ignition.

(3) The standard sets forth a test at §1632.7 which may be used to demonstrate that the substitution of tape

edge materials will not reduce the ignition resistance of a mattress prototype or a mattress pad prototype.

(b) *Scope.* (1) All mattresses, as defined in §1632.1(a), and all mattress pads, as defined in §1632.1(b), manufactured or imported after the effective date of this amendment are subject to the requirements of the standard as amended.

(2) All mattresses, as defined in §1632.1(a), and all mattress pads, as defined in §1632.1(b), manufactured or imported after June 22, 1973, and before the effective date of this amendment are subject to those requirements of the Standard for the Flammability of Mattresses (and Mattress Pads) (16 CFR part 1632) which were in effect before the effective date of this amendment.

(3) Manufacturers or importers desiring to use the ticking substitution procedure provided in §1632.6 may classify the ticking being used on each mattress prototype before or after the effective date of this amendment using the test procedure set forth in that section.

(4) One-of-a-kind mattresses and mattress pads may be excluded from testing under this standard in accordance with rules established by the Consumer Product Safety Commission. (See §1632.31(f): exemption for mattresses and mattress pads prescribed by a physician.)

(c) *Applicability.* (1) The requirements for prototype testing prescribed by this standard are applicable to each "manufacturer" (as that term is defined in §1632.1(i)) of mattresses or mattress pads subject to the standard which are manufactured for sale in commerce. The requirements of this standard for prototype testing are also applicable to all other persons or firms initially introducing mattresses or mattress pads into commerce, including importers; each such firm shall be deemed to be a "manufacturer" for purposes of this standard.

(2) The test at §1632.6 for classification of ticking materials may be used by manufacturers of mattresses or mattress pads and by manufacturers of ticking materials. The test at §1632.7 may be used by manufacturers of mattresses to demonstrate that substitution of tape edge materials will not reduce ignition resistance of a mattress prototype or a mattress pad prototype. Use of the tests in §§1632.6 and 1632.7 is optional.

§ 1632.3 General requirements.

(a) *Summary of test method.* The method measures the ignition resistance of a mattress or mattress pad by exposing the surface to lighted cigarettes in a draft-protected environment. The surfaces to be tested include smooth, tape edge, and quilted or tufted locations, if they exist on the mattress or mattress pad surface. A two-sheet test is also conducted on similar surface locations. In the latter test, the burning cigarettes are placed between the sheets.

(b) *Test criterion.* When testing the mattress or mattress pad surface in accordance with the testing procedure set forth in §1632.4 *Mattress test procedure*, individual cigarette test locations pass the test if the char length is not more than 2 inches (5.1 cm) in any direction from the nearest point of the cigarette. In the interest of safety, the test operator should discontinue the test and record a failure before reaching the 2 inch char length if an obvious ignition has occurred.

(c) *Pre-market testing.* Each manufacturer required to perform prototype testing by the standard shall perform the testing required by the standard with acceptable results before selling in commerce or introducing in commerce any mattress or mattress pad which is subject to the standard.

(d) *Specimen selection and qualification.* (1) Each manufacturer required to perform prototype testing by the standard shall construct or select enough units of each proposed mattress prototype or proposed mattress pad prototype to provide six surfaces for testing. A minimum of three mattresses or mattress pads are required if both sides can be tested; six mattresses or mattress pads are required if only one side can be tested. Test each of the six surfaces according to §1632.4(d). If all the cigarette test locations on all six mattress surfaces yield passing results using the criterion specified in §1632.3(b), accept the mattress prototype. If all six surfaces of a mattress pad yield passing results using the criterion in § 1632.3(b), and all other applicable requirements prescribed by § 1632.5 are met, accept the mattress pad prototype. If one or more of the cigarette test locations on any of the six surfaces fail to meet the test criterion of § 1632.3(b), reject the mattress prototype or the mattress pad prototype.

(2) Prototype qualification testing may be repeated after action has been taken to improve the resistance of the mattress prototype or the mattress pad prototype to cigarette ignition by changes in design, construction methods, materials selection, or other means. When prototype qualification is repeated after rejection of a prototype, such qualification testing shall be conducted in the same manner as original qualification testing.

(3) Each mattress prototype and each mattress pad prototype must be accepted in prototype qualification before any mattress or mattress pad manufactured in accordance with such mattress prototype or mattress pad prototype is sold in commerce or introduced in commerce. Any manufacturer required to perform testing by the standard may rely on prototype tests performed before the effective date of this amended standard, provided that such tests were conducted in accordance with all requirements of §§ 1632.1(i), 1632.3(d), and 1632.4, and yield passing results when the test criterion of § 1632.3(b) is applied. If the ticking classification test at § 1632.6 is to be used when relying on prototype tests performed before the effective date of the standard, the ticking currently used on that mattress prototype must be classified before substitution of ticking using § 1632.6.

(4) Rejected prototype mattresses or prototype mattress pads shall not be retested, offered for sale, sold, or promoted for use as a mattress (as defined in § 1632.1(a)) or for use as a mattress pad (as defined in § 1632.1(b)) except after reworking to improve the resistance to ignition by cigarettes, and subsequent retesting and acceptance of the mattress prototype (as defined in § 1632.1(j)) or the mattress pad prototype (as defined in § 1632.1(k)).

§ 1632.4 Mattress test procedure.

(a) *Apparatus and Test Materials*—(1) Testroom. The testroom shall be large enough to accommodate a full-scale mattress in a horizontal position and to allow for free movement of personnel and air around the test mattress. The test area shall be draft-protected and equipped with a suitable system for exhausting smoke and/or noxious gases produced by testing. The testroom atmospheric conditions shall be greater than 18 °C (65 °F) and at less than 55 percent relative humidity.

(i) The room shall be equipped with a support system (e.g. platform, bench) upon which a mattress may be placed flat in a horizontal position at a reasonable height for making observations.

(ii) If thin flexible mattresses or mattress pads are being testing the room shall also be equipped with a glass fiberboard test surface. The glass fiberboard shall be approximately 1 inch (2.5 cm) thick and have a thermal conductivity of 0.30±0.05 cal (g) / hr cm^2 °C/cm (0.24±0.04 Btu/hr ft^2 °F/in) at 23.9 °C (75 °F). [1]

(2) *Ignition source*. The ignition source shall be a Standard Reference Material cigarette (SRM 1196), available for purchase from the National Institute of Standards and Technology, 100 Bureau Drive, Gaithersburg, MD 20899.

(3) *Fire extinguisher*. A pressurized water fire extinguisher, or other suitable fire extinguishing equipment, shall be immediately available.

(4) *Water bottle*. A water bottle fitted with a spray nozzle shall be used to extinguish the ignited portions of the mattress.

(5) *Scale*. A linear scale graduated in millimeters, 0.1 inch, or 1/16 inch divisions shall be used to measure char length.

(6) *Sheets or Sheeting Material*. White, 100 percent cotton sheets or sheeting material shall be used. It shall not be

[1] Glass fiberboard that meets Federal Specification HH-I-558B is acceptable. Under this specification, the board must be Form A, Class 1, and plain faced. Copies of the specifications may be obtained from the Business Service Centers of the General Services Administration Regional Offices.

treated with a chemical finish which imparts a characteristic such as permanent press or flame resistance. It shall have 120–210 threads per square inch and fabric weight of 3.7±0.8 oz/yd^2 (125±28 gm/m^2). The size of the sheet or sheeting material shall be appropriate for the mattress being tested.

(7) *Other apparatus*. In addition to the above, a thermometer, a relative humidity measuring instrument, a thin rod, straight pins, a knife or scissors, and tongs are required to carry out the testing.

(b) *Test Preparation*—(1) *Mattress samples*. The mattress shall be removed from any packaging prior to conditioning. The mattress surface shall be divided laterally into two sections (see fig. 1), one section for the bare mattress tests and the other for the two-sheet tests.

(2) *Sheets or sheeting material*. The sheets or sheeting material shall be laundered once before use in an automatic home washer using the hot water setting and longest normal cycle with the manufacturer's recommended quantity of a commercial detergent, and dried in an automatic home tumble dryer.

(i) The sheet shall be cut across the width into two equal parts after washing.

(ii) Sheeting material shall be cut in lengths to cover ½ of a mattress as described in §1632.4(d)(3).

(3) *Cigarettes*. Unopened packages of cigarettes shall be selected for each series of tests. The cigarettes shall be removed from packaging prior to conditioning.

(c) *Conditioning*. The mattresses, laundered sheets or sheeting material, and loose cigarettes shall be conditioned in air at a temperature greater than 18 °C (65 °F) and a relative humidity less than 55 percent for at least 48 continuous hours prior to test. The mattresses, laundered sheets or sheeting material, and cigarettes shall be supported in a suitable manner to permit free movement of air around them during conditioning. The mattress meets this conditioning requirement if the mattress and/or all its component materials, except the metallic core, if present, have been exposed only to the above temperature and humidity conditions for at least 48 continuous hours prior to testing the mattress.

(d) *Testing*—(1) General. Mattress specimens shall be tested in a testroom with atmospheric conditions of a temperature greater than 18 °C (65 °F) and a relative humidity less than 55 percent. If the test is not performed in the conditioning room, at least one lit cigarette shall be placed on the mattress surface within 10 minutes of removal from the conditioning room. The other side of the mattress shall be tested immediately after completion of the first side.

(i) At least 18 cigarettes shall be burned on each mattress test surface, 9 in the bare mattress tests and 9 in the 2-sheet tests. If three or more mattress surface locations (smooth surface, tape edge, quilted, or tufted areas) exist in the particular mattress surface under test, three cigarettes shall be burned on each different surface location. If only two mattress surface locations exist in the particular mattress surface under test (tape edge and smooth surface), four cigarettes shall be burned on the smooth surface and five cigarettes shall be burned on the tape edge.

(ii) Light and place one cigarette at a time on the mattress surface. (If previous experience with a similar type of mattress has indicated that ignition is not likely, the number of cigarettes which may be lighted and placed on the mattress at one time is left to the test operator's judgment. The number of cigarettes must be carefully considered because a smoldering or burning mattress is extremely hazardous and difficult to extinguish.) The cigarettes must be positioned no less than 6 inches apart on the mattress surface. Each cigarette used as an ignition source shall be well lighted but not burned more than 4 mm (0.16 inch) when placed on the mattress. (Fire extinguishing equipment must be readily available at all times.)

(iii) If a cigarette extinguishes before burning its full length on any mattress surface location, pops out of position when tested on a tuft, or rolls off a test location, the test must be repeated with a freshly lit cigarette on a different portion of the same type of location on the mattress surface until either: the number of cigarettes specified in § 1632.4(d)(1)(i) have burned their full lengths; the number of cigarettes specified in § 1632.4(d)(1)(i) have extinguished before burning their full lengths; or failure has occurred according to § 1632.3(b) *Test criterion*.

(2) *Bare mattress tests*—(i) *Smooth surface*. Each burning cigarette shall be placed directly on a smooth surface location on the test surface on the half reserved for bare mattress tests. The cigarettes should burn their full lengths on a smooth surface without burning across a tuft, or stitching of a quilted area. However, if this is not possible because of mattress design, then the cigarettes shall be positioned on the mattress in a manner which will allow as much of the butt ends as possible to burn on smooth surfaces. Report results for each cigarette as pass or fail as defined in the test criterion (see § 1632.3(b)). CAUTION: Even under the most carefully observed conditions, smoldering combustion can progress to the point where it cannot be readily extinguished. It is imperative that a test be discontinued as soon as ignition has definitely occurred. Immediately wet the exposed area with a water spray (from water bottle), cut around the burning material with a knife or scissors and pull the material out of the mattress with tongs. Make sure that all charred or burned material is removed. Ventilate the room.

(ii) *Tape edge*. Each burning cigarette shall be placed in the depression between the mattress top surface and the tape edge, parallel to the tape edge of the half of the test surface reserved for bare mattress tests. If there is only a seam or no depression at the edge, support the cigarettes in place along the edge and parallel to the edge with straight pins. Three straight pins may be inserted through the edge at a 45° angle such that one pin supports the cigarette at the burned end, one at the center, and one at the butt. The heads of the pins must be below the upper surface of the cigarette (see fig. 2). Report results for each cigarette as pass or fail as defined in the test criterion (see § 1632.3(b)).

MATTRESS PREPARATION

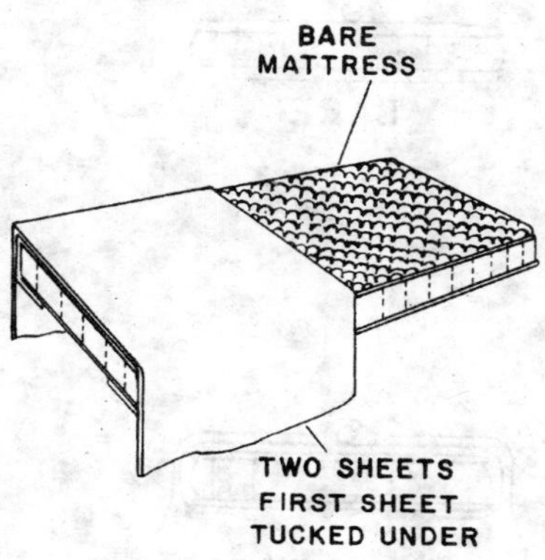

FIGURE 1

CIGARETTE LOCATION

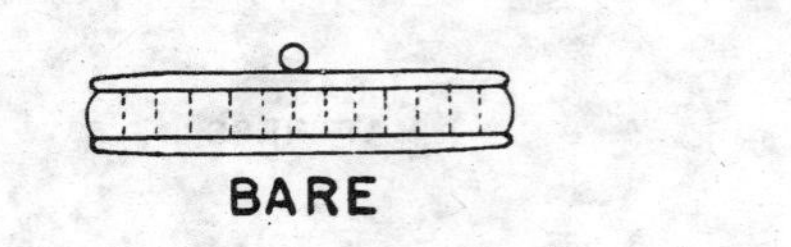

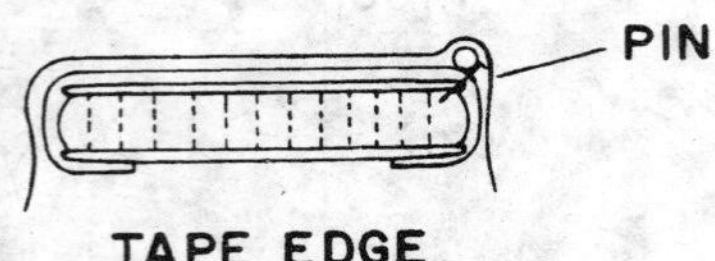

FIGURE 2

(iii) *Quilted location.* If quilting exists on the test surface, each burning cigarette shall be placed on quilted locations of the test surface. The cigarettes shall be positioned directly over the thread or in the depression created by the quilting process on the half of the test surface reserved for bare mattress tests. If the quilt design is such that the cigarettes cannot burn their full lengths over the thread or depression, then the cigarettes shall be positioned in a manner which will allow as much of the butt ends as possible to burn on the thread or depression. Report results for each cigarette as pass or fail as defined in the test criterion (see §1632.3(b)).

(iv) *Tufted location.* If tufting exists on the test surface, each burning cigarette shall be placed on tufted locations of the test surface. The cigarettes shall be positioned so that they burn down into the depression caused by the tufts and so that the butt ends of the cigarettes burn out over the buttons or laces used in the tufts or the depressions made by the tufts on the half of the test surface reserved for bare mattress tests. Report results for each cigarette as pass or fail as defined in the test criterion (see §1632.3(b)).

(3) *Two-sheet tests.* Spread a section of sheet or sheeting material smoothly over the mattress surface which has been reserved for the two-sheet test and tuck under the mattress. Care must be taken that hems or any other portion of the sheet which is more than one fabric thickness, is neither directly under nor directly over the test cigarette in the two-sheet test.

(i) *Smooth surfaces.* Each burning cigarette shall be placed directly on the sheet covered mattress in a smooth surface location as defined in the bare mattress test. Immediately cover the first sheet and the burning cigarette loosely with a second, or top sheet (see fig. 2). Do not raise or lift the top sheet during testing unless obvious ignition has occurred or until the cigarette has burned out. Whether a cigarette has extinguished may be determined by holding the hand near the surface of the top sheet over the test location. If no heat is felt or smoke observed, the cigarette has burned out. If ignition occurs, immediately remove the sheets and cigarette and follow the cautionary procedures outlined in the bare mattress test. Report results for each cigarette as pass or fail as defined in the test criterion (see §1632.3(b)).

(ii) *Tape edge.* (A) Each burning cigarette shall be placed in the depression between the top surface and the tape edge on top of the sheet, and immediately covered with a second sheet. It is important the air space be eliminated, as much as possible, between the mattress and the bottom sheet at the test location before testing. Depress the bottom sheet into the depression using a thin rod or other suitable instrument.

(B) In most cases, the cigarettes will remain in place throughout the test. However, if the cigarettes show a marked tendency to roll off the tape edge location, they may be supported with straight pins. Three straight pins may be inserted through the bottom sheet and tape at a 45° angle such that one pin supports the cigarette at the burning end, one at the center, and one at the butt. The heads of the pins must be below the upper surface of the cigarette (see fig. 2). Report results for each cigarette as pass or fail as defined in the test criterion (see § 1632.3(b)).

(iii) *Quilted locations.* If quilting exists on the test surface, each burning cigarette shall be placed in a depression caused by quilting, directly over the thread and on the bottom sheet, and immediately covered with the top sheet. It is important that the air space be eliminated, as much as possible, between the mattress and the bottom sheet at the test location before testing. Depress the bottom sheet into the depression using a thin rod or other suitable instrument. If the quilt design is such that the cigarettes cannot burn their full lengths over the thread or depression, then the cigarettes shall be positioned in a manner which will allow as much of the butt ends as possible to burn on the thread or depresssion. Report results for each cigarette as pass or fail as defined in the test criterion (see § 1632.3(b)).

(iv) *Tufted locations.* If tufting exists on the test surface, each burning cigarette shall be placed in the depression caused by tufting, directly over the tuft and on the bottom sheet, and immediately covered with the top sheet. It is important that the air space be eliminated, as much as possible, between the mattress and the bottom sheet at the test location before testing. Depress the bottom sheet into the depression using a thin rod or other suitable instrument. The cigarettes shall be positioned so that they burn down into the depression caused by the tuft and so that the butt ends of the cigarettes burn out over the buttons or laces, if used in the tufts. Report results for each cigarette as pass or fail as defined in the test criterion (see § 1632.3(b)).

(e) *Records.* Records of all prototype test results, and the disposition of rejected prototypes shall be maintained by the person or firm required to perform testing by the standard in accordance with § 1632.31(c).

[49 FR 39796, Oct. 10, 1984, as amended at 76 FR 59023, Sept. 23, 2011]

§ 1632.5 Mattress pad test procedure.

(a) *Testing.* All mattress pads shall be tested, in the condition in which they are intended to be sold, according to § 1632.4 Mattress test procedure, using the glass fiberboard substrate.

(b) *Flame resistant mattress pads.* The following additional requirements shall be applicable to mattress pads which contain a chemical fire retardant.

(1) These mattress pads shall be tested in accordance with § 1632.4 Mattress test procedure after they have been washed and dried 10 times as described in § 1632.5(b)(2).

(i) Such laundering is not required of mattress pads which are intended for one time use and/or are not intended to be laundered, as determined by the Consumer Product Safety Commission.

(ii) Mattress pads which are not susceptible to being laundered and are labeled "dryclean only" shall be drycleaned by a procedure which has previously been found acceptable by the Consumer Product Safety Commission.

(2) *Laundering procedure.* (i) Washing shall be performed in accordance with sections 8.2.2 and 8.2.3 of AATCC Test Method 124–1996, using wash temperature V (60° ±3 °C, 140° ±5 °F) specified in Table II of that method, and the water level, agitator speed, washing time, spin speed and final spin cycle specified for "Normal/Cotton Sturdy" in Table III.

(ii) Drying shall be performed in accordance with section 8.3.1(A) of AATCC Test Method 124–1996 "Appearance of Fabrics after Repeated Home Laundering," Tumble Dry, using the exhaust temperature (66° ±5 °C, 150° ±10 °F) and cool down time of 10 minutes specified in the "Durable Press" conditions of Table IV.

(iii) Maximum washer load shall be 3.64 Kg (8 pounds) and may consist of any combination of test samples and dummy pieces.

(iv) AATCC Test Method 124–1996 "Appearance of Fabrics after Repeated Home Laundering," is found in Technical Manual of the American Association of Textile Chemists and Colorists, vol. 73, 1997, which is incorporated by reference. Copies of this document are available from the American Association of Textile Chemists and Colorists, P.O. Box 12215, Research Triangle Park, North Carolina 27709. This document is also available for inspection at the National Archives and Records Administration (NARA). For information on the availability of this material at NARA, call 202–741–6030, or go to: *http://www.archives.gov/federal_register/code_of_federal_regulations/ibr_locations.html.* This incorporation by reference was approved by the Director of the Federal Register in accordance with 5 U.S.C. 552(a) and 1 CFR part 51.

(v) A different number of wash and dry cycles using another procedure may be specified and used, if that procedure has previously been found to be equivalent by the Consumer Product Safety Commission.

(3) *Labeling*—(i) *Treatment label.* If a mattress pad contains a chemical fire retardant, it shall be labeled with the letter "T" pursuant to rules and regulations established by the Consumer Product Safety Commission.

(ii) *Care label.* All mattress pads which contain a chemical fire retardant treatment shall be labeled with precautionary instructions to protect the pads from agents or treatments which are known to cause deterioration of their flame resistance. Such labels shall be permanent and otherwise in accordance with rules and regulations established by the Consumer Product Safety Commission in §1632.31(b).

(iii) *Exception.* One time use products as defined in §1632.5(b)(1)(i) are not subject to these labeling requirements.

[49 FR 39796, Oct. 10, 1984, as amended at 65 FR 12938, Mar. 10, 2000]

§1632.6 Ticking substitution procedure.

(a) This procedure may be used to verify acceptable equivalency if a mattress or mattress pad manufacturer wishes to change the ticking used on a particular mattress or mattress pad prototype without conducting a prototype test as specified in §1632.4 or §1632.5. The procedure includes a ticking classification test that may be used by a ticking, mattress or mattress pad manufacturer or by a distributor of ticking.

(b) *Definitions.* For the purpose of this section the following definitions apply in addition to those in §1632.1.

(1) *Mattress ticking prototype.* Means a ticking of a specific construction, color, or combination of colors or color pattern, weave pattern design, finish application, fiber content, and weight per unit area. With respect to film-coated ticking, a mattress ticking prototype means in addition to the factors listed above, a given method of application, chemical formula, and thickness of application of film coating. With respect to a quilted ticking, a mattress ticking prototype means the combination of a specific ticking as described above; a specific filling, thickness, density, and chemical composition; a specific thread; a specific method of quilting; and a specific backing fabric construction, weave, finish, fiber content, and weight.

(2) *Mattress pad ticking prototype* (i) Means a ticking of a specific construction, color, or combination of colors or color pattern, weave pattern design, finish application, fiber content, and weight per unit area. With respect to film-coated ticking, a mattress pad ticking prototype means in addition to the factors listed above, a given method of application, chemical formula, and thickness of application of film coating.

(ii) Quilted ticking is excluded from this definition. Therefore, the following procedures may not be used to substitute quilted ticking used on or as a mattress pad.

(c) *Scope and application.* (1) This procedure provides an independent evaluation of the cigarette ignition characteristics of ticking and for the classification of ticking into one of three performance classes. Class A represents tickings evaluated as acting as barriers against cigarette ignition; Class B represents tickings evaluated as having no effect on cigarette ignition; and Class

C represents tickings evaluated as having the potential, in some manner, to act as a contributor to cigarette ignition.

(2) Substitution of any ticking which has been evaluated as Class A using the procedure in this § 1632.6 for any other ticking material shall not be a "difference in materials" as that phrase is used in §§ 1632.1 (j) and (k). Consequently, any ticking material evaluated as Class A under this test procedure may be used on any qualified mattress prototype or on any qualified mattress pad prototype without conducting new prototype tests.

(3) Substitution of any ticking which has been evaluated as Class B using the procedure in this § 1632.6 for the ticking material used on any mattress prototype or on any mattress pad prototype which was qualified in prototype testing with a testing material evaluated as Class B or a Class C shall not be a "difference in materials" as that phrase is used in §§ 1632.1 (j) and (k). Consequently, any ticking material evaluated as Class B under this test procedure may be used on any mattress or mattress pad which wa qualified in prototype testing with a Class B or Class C ticking material without conducting new prototype tests. However, if Class B ticking material is to be used on any mattress or mattress pad which was qualified in prototype testing with a Class A ticking material, the mattress prototype or mattress pad prototype must be requalified, using a Class B ticking.

(4) A ticking material which has been evaluated as Class C using the procedure in this § 1632.6 may be used only on a mattress or mattress pad which was qualified in prototype testing with that particular Class C ticking material. Consequently, a ticking material evaluated as Class C under this test procedure may not be used on any mattress or mattress pad which was qualified in prototype testing using another Class C ticking material, or a Class A or Class B ticking material, without conducting new prototype tests.

(d) *General requirements.* (1) This procedure is a ticking prototype performance classification test. Ticking not classified according to this procedure may be used on mattresses or mattress pads if the mattress prototype or mattress pad prototype has been qualified utilizing the unclassified ticking in question.

(2) *Test criterion.* (i) Cigarette—An individual cigarette test location passes the test if the char length is not more than 1 inch (2.54 cm) in any direction from the nearest point of the cigarette, and the cotton felt is not ignited.

CAUTION: In the interest of safety, the test operator should discontinue the test and record a failure before reaching the 1 inch (2.54 cm) char length if, in his opinion, an obvious ignition has occurred.

(ii) Test Specimen—An individual test specimen passes the test if all three cigarette test locations meet the cigarette test criterion of this paragraph.

(3) *Specimen selection.* Three specimens shall be used for each ticking prototype classification test, with each specimen measuring no less than 20 inches by 20 inches (50.8 cm × 50.8 cm) square. The three specimens shall be selected from any fabric piece taken from a ticking prototype. The specimens shall be representative of the ticking prototype.

(4) *Ticking classification.* A ticking prototype is classified as Class A, Class B, or Class C, in accordance with the following schedules.

(i) Class A—A ticking prototype is classified as Class A when three specimens, tested in accordance with § 1632.6(e), meet the test criterion in § 1632.6(d)(2) when the ticking is tested directly over the cotton felt on the test box.

(ii) Class B—A ticking prototype is classified as Class B when three specimens, tested according to § 1632.6(e), meet the test criterion in § 1632.6(d)(2) when the ticking is tested on a ¼ inch ±1⁄32 inch (6.3 mm ±.8 mm) thick urethane foam pad covering the cotton felt on the test box.

(iii) Class C—A ticking prototype is classified as Class C when any specimen tested according to § 1632.6(e), fails to meet the test criterion in § 1632.6(d)(2) when the ticking is tested on a ¼ inch ±1⁄32 inch (6.3 mm ±.8 mm) thick urethane foam pad covering the cotton felt on the test box.

(e) *Test procedure*—(1) *Apparatus*. For the purpose of this section the following apparatus and materials are required in addition to that which is listed in § 1632.4 (a) and (b).

(i) *Sheet and sheeting material*. Test covers made from sheets or sheeting material shall not be less than 12 inches by 12 inches (30.48 cm by 30.48 cm) square.

(ii) *Template*. Designed to allow for a one inch marking around the placement of the cigarette (see figure 3). Use of this template is optional.

(iii) *Stapler or masking tape* or other means of attachment to secure fabric to test box.

(iv) *Mounting box*. A 6 inch deep, 12 inch square plywood box. The box contains two ½ inch in diameter ventilation holes. (See figure 4.)

(v) *Cotton felt*. (A) The cotton felt shall be a thoroughly-garnetted mixture of all new material consisting of not less than 67% linters and of not more than 33% clean picker blend or equivalent binder and not more than 5% non-cellulosic total content. The felt shall not be bleached, moistened or chemically treated in any way.

(B) The felt may be re-used repeatedly after completion of each test by removing all of the smoldering, charred, heat-discolored fibers, or fibers exposed to water as a result of extinguishing the cotton ignited by previous test.

(vi) *Urethane foam*. The urethane foam shall have a density of 1.2 to 1.5 pounds per cubic foot, an indention load deflection of 22 to 35 pounds, with each test specimen measuring no less than 12 inches by 12 inches (30.48 cm by 30.48 cm) square, having a thickness of ¼ inch ±1⁄32 inch (6.3 mm ±.8 mm). The foam shall not be treated with a flame retardant chemical.

(2) *Conditioning*. The test specimens, cigarettes, laundered sheets or sheeting material, foam and felt shall be conditioned as described in § 1632.4(c).

(3) *Specimen preparation*. (i) Place 907.2±4 grams (two pounds) of cotton felt in the test box, allowing the felt to protrude above the opening of the box to a height of up to 3 inches (7.62 cm) at the crown.

(ii) For the first part of this test, place a 12 inches by 12 inches (30.48 cm by 30.48 cm) square urethane foam pad on top of the cotton felt. Stretch the ticking specimen over the foam pad and fasten it to the sides of the test box using a stapler or tape. Be careful to avoid wrinkles in the fabric and have sufficient tautness to assure firm contact between the fabric and the filling materials in the test box.

(4) *Testing*. (i) Ticking specimens shall be tested in a testroom with atmospheric conditions of a temperature greater than 18 °C (65 °F) and a relative humidity less than 55%.

(ii) Three cigarettes shall be burned on each ticking specimen, with no more than one cigarette burning at any time. At least one cigarette shall be placed on the most prominent part of the color and weave pattern design in the ticking. If the ticking is quilted, one cigarette shall be placed over the thread or in the depression created by the quilting process. Each cigarette must be positioned no less than two inches (5.08 cm) from any other cigarette or the edge of the box.

(iii) Light and place one cigarette on the test specimen. Immediately cover the burning cigarette with a sheet test cover. The cigarette shall be well lighted but not burned more than 4 mm (0.16 inch) when placed on the test specimen. The cigarette may be supported by three straight pins such that one pin supports the cigarette at the burning end, one at the center and one at the butt. The heads of the pins must be below the upper surface of the cigarette. Upon completion of the three cigarette burns and removal of the fabric and foam specimens, remove all of the char or heat discoloration on the cotton felt as stated in § 1632.6(e)(v)(B). Fresh new felt shall be added to replace the discarded fibers in the amount necessary to maintain the full 907.2±4 grams (two pounds) of felt for each test.

(iv) If the cigarette extinguishes before burning its full length, the test must be repeated with a freshly lit cigarette on a different portion of the ticking specimen until either three cigarettes have burned their full lengths or three cigarettes have extinguished. Report result for each cigarette as pass or fail as defined in Test

Criterion § 1632.6(d)(2). An obvious ignition is recorded as a failure.

(v) If ignition occurs with any of the three cigarette burns on the ticking specimen, terminate testing of that specimen and classify according to § 1632.6(d)(4).

(vi) If all cigarette test locations meet the Test Criterion in § 1632.6(d)(2), repeat procedure outlined in § 1632.6(e)(4)(iii) for the second part of the test with new ticking specimens that will be retested directly over the cotton felt, without the urethane foam pad. Remove the urethane foam pad and charred or heat discolored area from the cotton felt as specified in § 1632.6(e)(v)(B) prior to testing. Record the test results as pass or fail as defined in *Test Criterion* § 1632.6(d)(2) and classify according to § 1632.6(d)(4).

(5) *Records*. Records of any ticking classification test results relied upon by the mattress or mattress pad manufacturer or importer shall be maintained in accordance with rules and regulations established by the Consumer Product Safety Commission in § 1632.31(c). As provided by § 1632.31(c)(6), manufacturers or importers of mattresses or mattress pads may rely on a certification of compliance with this section of the standard provided by the ticking manufacturer or distributor; however, if a mattress or mattress pad fails to comply with the standard, the mattress or mattress pad manufacturer or importer must assume full responsibility under the standard. The Commission has no authority under this standard to compel ticking manufacturers or distributors to comply with this section or to establish, maintain and provide upon request, the records specified in § 1632.31(c).

FIGURE 3

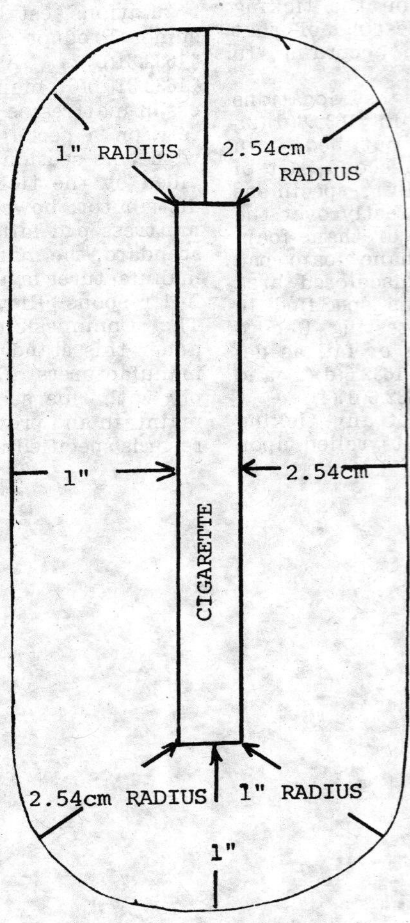

1 INCH (2.54cm) TEMPLATE

TOLERANCES + 1/32" - 0"

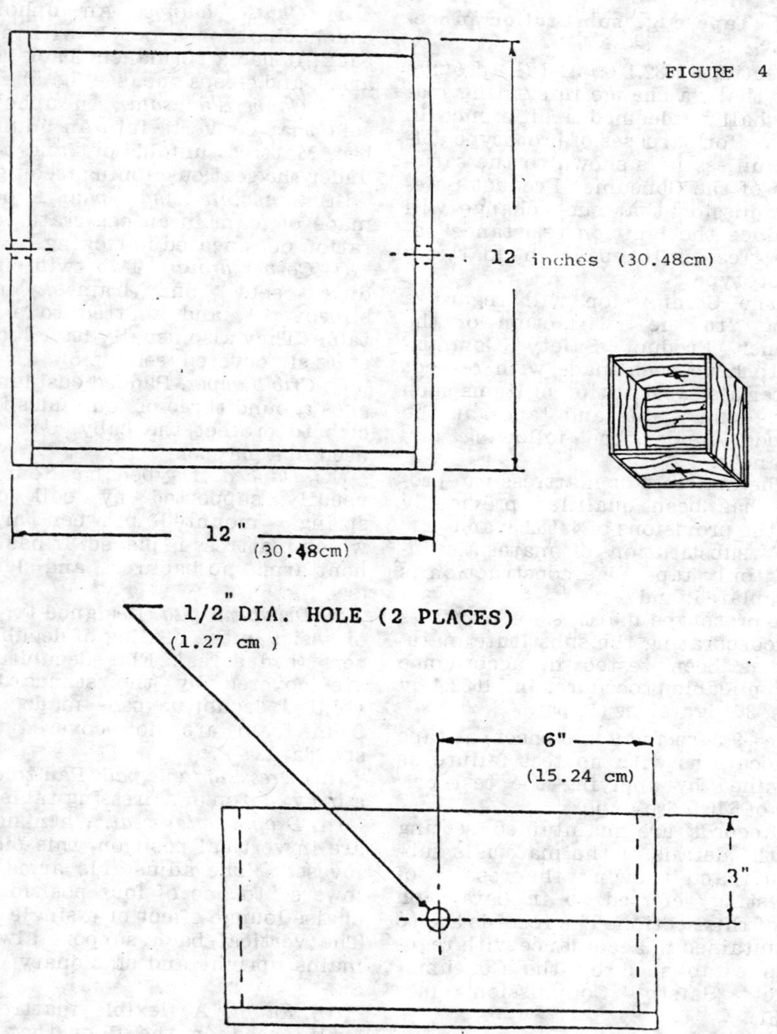

TEST BOX

MATERIAL 1/2" PLYWOOD

TOLERANCES + 1/32 " - 0"

§ 1632.7 Tape edge substitution procedure.

(a) Sections 1632.1 (j) and (k) provide in part that "a change in existing material shall be deemed a difference in materials for purposes of prototype definition unless it is shown to the satisfaction of the Consumer Product Safety Commission that such change will not reduce the ignition resistance" of the mattress prototype or the mattress pad prototype.

(b) The Commission will regard a showing "to the satisfaction of the Consumer Product Safety Commission" to have been made with respect to materials substitution of items such as flange materials and tapes at the tape edge under the following circumstances:

(1) The mattress or mattress pad prototype has been qualified previously under the provisions of § 1632.3; and

(2) A substitution of materials involving only tape edge construction is contemplated; and

(3) A prototype mattress or mattress pad incorporating the substitute materials has been tested in accordance with applicable procedures in § 1632.4 by placing 36 cigarettes (18 per surface—9 bare and 9 two-sheet) at tape edge locations with no test failure as determined by applying the test criterion of § 1632.3(b); and

(4) Records are maintained setting forth the details of the materials substitution and showing the results of the testing referred to in paragraph (b)(3) of this section. The records are to be maintained in accordance with regulations established by the Consumer Product Safety Commission (see § 1632.31).

§ 1632.8 Glossary of terms.

(a) *Absorbent pads.* Pad used on top of mattress. Designed to absorb urine thereby reducing skin irritation, can be one time use.

(b) *Basket pad.* Cushion for use in an infant basket.

(c) *Bunk beds.* A tier of beds, usually two or three, in a high frame complete with mattresses (see fig. 5).

(d) *Car bed.* Portable bed used to carry a baby in an automobile.

(e) *Carriage pad.* Cushion to go into a baby carriage.

(f) *Chaise lounge.* An upholstered couch chair or a couch with a chair back. It has a permanent back rest, no arms, and sleeps one (see fig. 5).

(g) *Convertible sofa.* An upholstered sofa that converts into an adult sized bed. Mattress unfolds out and up from under the seat cushioning (see fig. 5).

(h) *Convoluted foam pad.* A bed pad made of foam in an egg-crate configuration not encased in ticking.

(i) *Corner groups.* Two twin size bedding sets on frames, usually slipcovered, and abutted to a corner table. They also usually have loose bolsters slipcovered (see fig. 5).

(j) *Crib bumper.* Padded cushion which goes around three or four sides inside a crib to protect the baby. Can also be used in a playpen.

(k) *Daybed.* Daybed has foundation, usually supported by coil or flat springs, mounted between arms on which mattress is placed. It has permanent arms, no backrest, and sleeps one (see fig. 5).

(l) *Decubitus pad.* Designed to prevent or assist in the healing of decubitus ulcers (bed sores). Flat decubitus pads are covered by the standard. Convoluted decubitus pads made entirely from foam are not covered by the standard.

(m) *Dressing table pad.* Pad to cushion a baby on top of a dressing table.

(n) *Drop-arm loveseat.* When side arms are in vertical position, this piece is a loveseat. The adjustable arms can be lowered to one of four positions for a chaise lounge effect or a single sleeper. The vertical back support always remains upright and stationary (see fig. 5).

(o) *Futon.* A flexible mattress generally used on the floor that can be folded or rolled up for storage. It usually consists of resilient material covered by ticking.

(p) *High riser.* This is a frame of sofa seating height with two equal size mattresses without a backrest. The frame slides out with the lower bed and rises to form a double or two single beds (see fig. 5).

(q) *Infant carrier and lounge pad.* Pad to cushion a baby in an infant carrier.

(r) *Mattress foundation.* Consists of any surface such as foam, box springs or other, upon which a mattress is placed to lend it support for use in sleeping upon.

(s) *Pillow.* Cloth bag filled with resilient material such as feathers, down, sponge rubber, urethane, or fiber used as the support for the head of a person.

(t) *Playpen pad.* Cushion used on the bottom of a playpen.

(u) *Portable crib.* Smaller size than a conventional crib. Can usually be converted into a playpen.

(v) *Press-back lounges.* Longer and wider than conventional sofa beds. When the lounge seat is pressed lightly, it levels off to form, with the seat, a flat sleeping surface. The seat slopes, in the sitting position, for added comfort (see fig. 5).

(w) *Push-back sofa.* When pressure is exerted on the back of the sofa, it becomes a bed. When the back is lifted, it becomes a sofa again. Styled in tight or loose cushions (see fig. 5).

(x) *Roll-away-bed.* Portable bed which has frame which folds in half with the mattress for compact storage.

(y) *Sleep lounge.* Upholstered seating section is mounted on a sturdy frame. May have bolster pillows along the wall as backrests or may have attached headrests (see fig. 5).

(z) *Stroller pad.* Cushion used in a baby stroller.

(aa) *Sofa bed.* These are pieces in which the back of the sofa swings down flat with the seat to form the sleeping surface. All upholstered. Some sofa beds have bedding boxes for storage of bedding. There are two types: the one-piece, where the back and seat are upholstered as a unit, supplying an unbroken sleeping surface; and the two-piece, where back and seat are upholstered separately (see fig. 5).

(bb) *Sofa lounge*—(includes glideouts). Upholstered seating section is mounted on springs and in a special frame that permit it to be pulled out for sleeping. Has upholstered backrest bedding box that is hinged. Glideouts are single sleepers with sloping seats and backrests. Seat pulls out from beneath back and evens up to supply level sleeping surface (see fig. 5).

(cc) *Studio couch.* Consists of upholstered seating section on upholstered foundation. Many types convert to twin beds (see fig. 5).

(dd) *Studio divan.* Twin size upholstered seating section with foundation is mounted on metal bed frame. Has no arms or backrest, and sleeps one (see fig. 5).

(ee) *Trundle bed.* A low bed which is rolled under a larger bed. In some lines, the lower bed springs up to form a double or two single beds as in a high riser (see fig. 5).

(ff) *Twin studio divan.* Frames which glide out (but not up) and use seat cushions, in addition to upholstered foundation to sleep two. Has neither arms nor back rest (see fig. 5).

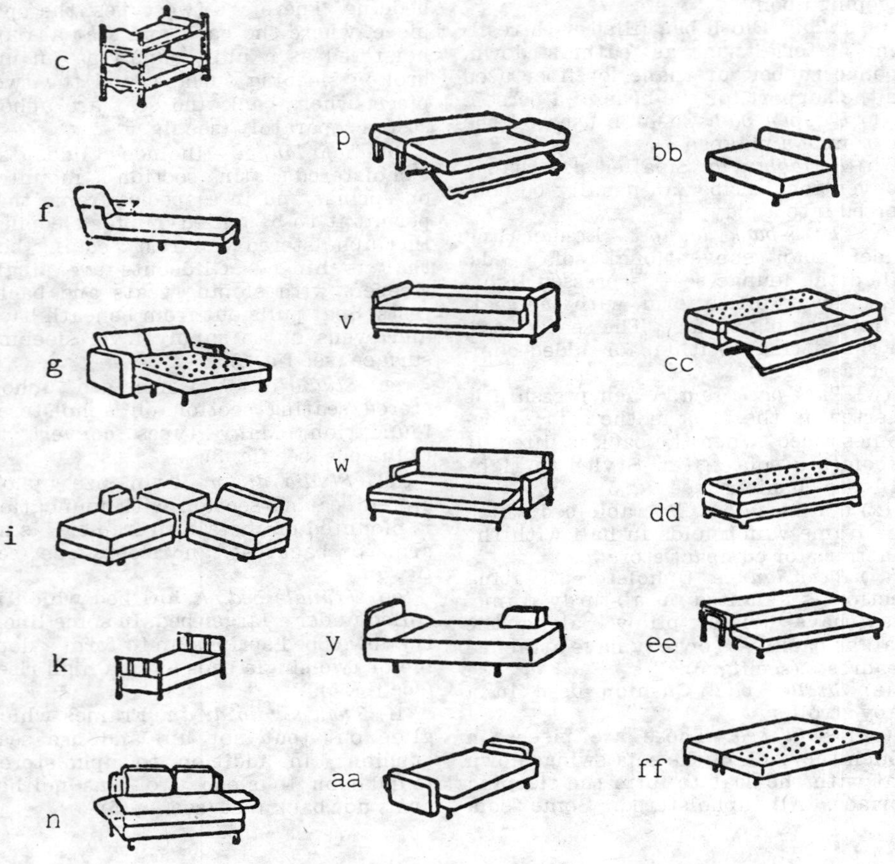

Figure 5

Effective date: The amended standard shall become effective on April 10, 1985. As required by section 4(b) of the Flammable Fabrics Act (15 U.S.C. 1193(b)), mattresses and mattress pads which are in inventory or with the trade on the effective date of the amended standard are exempt from its requirements, but must comply with all applicable requirements of the original standard.

Subpart B—Rules and Regulations

§ 1632.31 Mattresses/mattress pads—labeling, recordkeeping, guaranties and "one of a kind" exemption.

(a) *Definitions.* For the purposes of this section, the following definitions apply:

(1) *Standard for the Flammability of Mattresses* or *Standard* means the Standard for the Flammability of Mattresses and Mattress Pads (FF 4–72, amended), (16 CFR part 1632, subpart A).

(2) The definition of terms set forth in the § 1632.1 of the Standard shall also apply to this section.

(b) *Labeling.* (1) All mattress pads which contain a chemical fire retardant shall be labeled with precautionary instructions to protect the pads from agents or treatments which are known to cause deterioration of their flame resistance. Such labels shall be permanent, prominent, conspicuous, and legible.

(2) If a mattress pad contains a chemical fire retardant, it shall be prominently, conspicuously, and legibly labeled with the letter "T".

(3) Each mattress or mattress pad subject to the Standard shall bear a permanent, accessible, and legible label containing the month and year of manufacture and the location of the manufacturer. (See § 1632.1(i) of the Amended Standard.)

(4) The information required on labels by this section shall be set forth separately from any other information appearing on such label. Other information, representations, or disclosures, appearing on labels required by this section or elsewhere on the item, shall not interfere with, minimize, detract from, or conflict with the required information.

(5) No person, other than the ultimate consumer, shall remove or mutilate, or cause or participate in the removal or mutilation of, any label required by this section to be affixed to any item.

(6) Products intended for one time use (see § 1632.5(b)(1)(i)) are not subject to the requirements of paragraphs (1) and (2) of this § 1632.31(b).

(c) *Records—manufacturers, importers, or persons initially introducing items into commerce.* Every manufacturer, importer, or other person initially introducing into commerce mattresses or mattress pads subject to the standard, irrespective of whether guarantees are issued relative thereto, shall maintain the records hereinafter specified.

(1) Manufacturing specifications and description of each mattress or mattress pad prototype with an assigned prototype identification number.

(2) Test results and details of each prototype test performed in accordance with § 1632.4 or § 1632.5, including prototype identification number, ticking classification if known, test room condition, cigarette locations, number of relights for each location, whether each cigarette location passed or failed, name and signature of person conducting the test and date of test. These records shall include a certification by the person overseeing the testing as to the test results and that the test was carried out in accordance with the Standard.

(3) Photograph (color or black and white) of the bare surface of each mattress or mattress pad tested, in accordance with § 1632.4 or § 1632.5, with the prototype identification number of the mattress or mattress pad and a clear designation as to which part of the mattress or mattress pad was sheeted and which part was tested bare.

(4) Records to support any determination that a particular material, other than the ticking or tape edge material used in a mattress or mattress pad prototype, did not influence the ignition resistance of the prototype and could be substituted by another material. Such record should include photographs or physical specimens.

(5) Manufacturing specifications and description of any new ticking or tape edge material substituted in accordance with § 1632.6 or § 1632.7, with the identification number of the prototype involved.

(6) The test results and details of any ticking classification test conducted in accordance with § 1632.6, including the ticking classification (A, B, or C), the test room condition, the number of relights, whether each cigarette location passed or failed, the name and signature of the person conducting the test and the date of the test, *or* a certification from the ticking supplier. The certification should state the ticking classification and that the ticking was tested in accordance with § 1632.6.

(7) The test results and details of any test of tape edge materials conducted in accordance with § 1632.7, including prototype identification number, test room condition, number of relights, whether each cigarette passed or failed, name and signature of person conducting the test and date of test. The record shall include a certification by the person overseeing the testing as to

the test results and that the test was carried out in accordance with § 1632.7.

(8) Photograph (color or black and white) of the bare surface of each mattress or mattress pad tested in accordance with § 1632.7, with the prototype identification number of the mattress or mattress pad and a clear designation as to which part of the mattress or mattress pad was sheeted and which part was tested bare.

(9) Details of any approved alternate laundering procedure used in laundering mattress pads required by the Standard to be laundered during testing.

(10) Identification, composition, and details of the application of any flame retardant treatments employed relative to mattress pads or mattress pad components.

(11) Disposition of all failing or rejected prototype mattress or mattress pads. Such records must demonstrate that the items were retested and reworked in accordance with the Standard prior to sale or distribution and that such retested or reworked mattresses or mattress pads comply with the Standard, or must otherwise show the disposition of such items.

(12) The records required by this paragraph shall be maintained for as long as the prototype is in production, the ticking is being used on the mattresses or mattress pad prototype, and/or the tape edge material is being used on the mattress or mattress pad prototype, and shall be retained for 3 years thereafter.

(d) *Tests for guaranty purposes.* Reasonable and representative tests for the purpose of issuing a guaranty under section 8 of the Act for mattress or mattress pads subject to the Standard shall be those prototype and substitution tests performed, pursuant to the requirements of the Standard.

(e) *Compliance with this section.* No person subject to the Flammable Fabrics Act shall manufacture for sale, import, distribute, or otherwise market or handle any mattress or mattress pad which is not in compliance with § 1632.31.

(f) *"One of a kind" exemption for physician prescribed mattresses and mattress pads.* (1) A mattress or mattress pad manufactured in accordance with a physician's written prescription or manufactured in accordance with other comparable written medical therapeutic specification, to be used in connection with the treatment or management of a named individual's physical illiness or injury, shall be considered a "one of a kind mattress" and shall be exempt from testing under the Standard pursuant to § 1632.2(b)(4) thereof: Provided, that the mattress bears a permanent, conspicuous and legible label which states:

> WARNING: This mattress or mattress pad may be subject to ignition and hazardous smoldering from cigarettes. It was manufactured in accordance with a physician's prescription and has not been tested under the Federal Standard for the Flammability of Mattresses (FF 4–72).

Such labeling must be attached to the mattress or mattress pad so as to remain on or affixed thereto for the useful life of the mattress or mattress pad. The label must be at least 40 square inches (250 sq. cm) with no linear dimension less than 5 inches (12.5 cm). The letters in the word "WARNING" shall be no less than 0.5 inch (1.27 cm) in height and all letters on the label shall be in a color which contrasts with the background of the label. The warning statement which appears on the label must also be conspicuously displayed on the invoice or other sales papers that accompany the mattress in commerce from the manufacturer to the final point of sale to a consumer.

(2) The manfacturer of a mattress or mattress pad exempted from testing under this paragraph shall, in lieu of the records required to be kept by paragraph (c) of this section, retain a copy of the written prescription or other comparable written medical therapeutic specification for such mattress or mattress pad during a period of three years, measured from the date of manufacture.

(3) For purposes of this regulation the term *physician* shall mean a physician, chiropractor or osteopath licensed or otherwise permitted to practice by any State of the United States.

Subpart C—Interpretations and Policies

§§ 1632.61–1632.62 [Reserved]

§ 1632.63 Policy clarification on renovation of mattress.

(a) Section 3 of the Flammable Fabrics Act (15 U.S.C. 1192) prohibits, among other things, the "manufacture for sale" of any product which fails to conform to an applicable standard issued under the act. The standard for the Flammability of Mattresses, as amended (FF 4–72) (subpart A of this part), issued pursuant to the act, provides that, with certain exceptions, mattress must be tested according to a prescribed method. The standard does not exempt renovation; nor does it specifically refer to renovation.

(b) The purpose of this document is to inform the public that mattresses renovated for sale are considered by the Commission to be mattresses manufactured for sale and, therefore, subject to the requirements of the Mattress Standard. The Commission believes that this policy clarification will better protect the public against the unreasonable risk of fires leading to death, personal injury or significant property damage, and assure that purchasers of renovated mattresses receive the same protection under the Flammable Fabrics Act as purchasers of new mattresses.

(c) For purposes of this document, mattress renovation includes a wide range of operations. Replacing the ticking or batting, stripping a mattress to its springs, rebuilding a mattress, or replacing components with new or recycled materials, are all part of the process of renovation. Any one, or any combination of one or more, of these steps in mattress renovation is considered to be mattress manufacture.

(d) If the person who renovates the mattress intends to retain the renovated mattress for his or her own use, or if a customer or a renovator merely hires the services of the renovator and intends to take back the renovated mattress for his or her own use, "manufacture for sale" has not occurred and such a renovated mattress is not subject to the mattress standard.

(e) However, if a renovated mattress is sold or intended for sale, either by the renovator or the owner of the mattress who hires the services of the renovator, such a transaction is considered to be "manufacture for sale".

(f) Accordingly, mattress renovation is considered by the Commission to be "manufacture for sale" and, therefore, subject to the Mattress Standard, when renovated mattresses are sold or intended for sale by a renovator or the customer of the renovator.

(g) A renovator who believes that certain mattresses are entitled to one-of-a-kind exemption, may present relevant facts to the Commission and petition for an exemption. Renovators are expected to comply with all the testing requirements of the Mattress Standard until an exemption is approved.

PART 1633—STANDARD FOR THE FLAMMABILITY (OPEN FLAME) OF MATTRESS SETS

Subpart A—The Standard

Subpart B—Rules and Regulations

SCREWS), IN RELATION TO, PORTABLE FRAME ALLOWING BURNER HEIGHT ADJUSTMENT

FIGURE 7 TO PART 1633—ELEMENTS OF PROPANE FLOW CONTROL FOR EACH BURNER

FIGURE 8 TO PART 1633—JIG FOR SETTING MATTRESSES AND FOUNDATION SIDES IN SAME PLANE

FIGURE 9 TO PART 1633—BURNER PLACEMENTS ON MATTRESS/FOUNDATION

FIGURE 10 TO PART 1633—JIG FOR SETTING BURNERS AT PROPER DISTANCES FROM MATTRESS/FOUNDATION

FIGURE 11 TO PART 1633—DIAGRAMS FOR GLOSSARY OF TERMS

FIGURE 12 TO PART 1633—LABELS FOR DOMESTIC MATTRESS WITH FOUNDATION

FIGURE 13 TO PART 1633—LABELS FOR IMPORTED MATTRESS WITH FOUNDATION

FIGURE 14 TO PART 1633—LABEL FOR DOMESTIC MATTRESS ALONE AND WITH FOUNDATION

FIGURE 15 TO PART 1633—LABEL FOR IMPORTED MATTRESS ALONE AND WITH FOUNDATION

FIGURE 16 TO PART 1633—LABEL FOR DOMESTIC MATTRESS ONLY

FIGURE 17 TO PART 1633—LABEL FOR IMPORTED MATTRESS ONLY

AUTHORITY: 15 U.S.C. 1193, 1194

SOURCE: 71 FR 13498, Mar. 15, 2006, unless otherwise noted.

Subpart A—The Standard

§ 1633.1 Purpose, scope and applicability.

(a) *Purpose.* This part 1633 establishes flammability requirements that all mattress sets must meet before sale or introduction into commerce. The purpose of the standard is to reduce deaths and injuries associated with mattress fires by limiting the size of the fire generated by a mattress set during a thirty minute test.

(b) *Scope.* (1) All mattress sets, as defined in §1633.2(c), manufactured, imported, or renovated on or after the effective date of this standard are subject to the requirements of the standard.

(2) One-of-a-kind mattress sets may be exempted from testing under this standard in accordance with §1633.13(c).

(c) *Applicability.* The requirements of this part 1633 shall apply to each "manufacturer" (as that term is defined in §1633.2(k)) of mattress sets which are manufactured for sale in commerce.

§ 1633.2 Definitions.

In addition to the definitions given in section 2 of the Flammable Fabrics Act as amended (15 U.S.C. 1191), the following definitions apply for purposes of this part 1633.

(a) *Mattress* means a resilient material or combination of materials enclosed by a ticking (used alone or in combination with other products) intended or promoted for sleeping upon. This includes mattresses that have undergone renovation as defined in paragraph (d) of this section.

(1) This term includes, but is not limited to, adult mattresses, youth mattresses, crib mattresses (including portable crib mattresses), bunk bed mattresses, futons, flip chairs without a permanent back or arms, sleeper chairs, and water beds or air mattresses if they contain upholstery material between the ticking and the mattress core. Mattresses used in or as part of upholstered furniture are also included; examples are convertible sofa bed mattresses, corner group mattresses, day bed mattresses, roll-away bed mattresses, high risers, and trundle bed mattresses. See §1633.9 Glossary of terms, for definitions of these items.

(2) This term excludes mattress pads, mattress toppers (items with resilient filling, with or without ticking, intended to be used with or on top of a mattress), sleeping bags, pillows, liquid and gaseous filled tickings, such as water beds and air mattresses that contain no upholstery material between the ticking and the mattress core, upholstered furniture which does not contain a mattress, and juvenile product pads such as car bed pads, carriage pads, basket pads, infant carrier and lounge pads, dressing table pads, stroller pads, crib bumpers, and playpen pads. See §1633.9 Glossary of terms, for definitions of these items.

(b) *Foundation* means a ticking covered structure used to support a mattress or sleep surface. The structure may include constructed frames, foam, box springs, or other materials, used alone or in combination.

(c) *Mattress set* means either a mattress and foundation labeled by the manufacturer for sale as a set, or a mattress labeled by the manufacturer for sale without any foundation.

(d) *Renovation* means altering an existing mattress set for the purpose of resale.

(1) This term includes any one, or any combination of the following: replacing the ticking or batting, stripping a mattress to its springs, rebuilding a mattress, or replacing components with new or recycled materials.

(2) This term excludes alterations if the person who renovates the mattress intends to retain the renovated mattress for his or her own use, or if a customer or a renovator merely hires the services of the renovator and intends to take back the renovated mattress for his or her own use.

(e) *Ticking* means the outermost layer of fabric or related material of a mattress or foundation. It does not include any other layers of fabric or related materials quilted together with, or otherwise attached to, the outermost layer of fabric or related material.

(f) *Upholstery material* means all material, either loose or attached, between the mattress ticking and the core of a mattress.

(g) *Edge* means the seamed, unseamed or taped border edge of a mattress or foundation that joins the top and/or bottom with the side panels.

(h) *Tape edge* means an edge made by using binding tape to encase and finish raw edges.

(i) *Binding tape* means a fabric strip used in the construction of some edges.

(j) *Seam thread* means the thread used to form stitches in construction features, seams, and tape edges.

(k) *Manufacturer* means an individual plant or factory at which mattress sets are manufactured or assembled. For purposes of this part 1633, importers and renovators are considered manufacturers.

(l) *Prototype* means a specific design of mattress set that serves as a model for production units intended to be introduced into commerce and is the same as the production units with respect to materials, components, design and methods of assembly. A mattress intended for sale with a foundation(s) shall be considered a separate and distinct prototype from a mattress intended for sale without a foundation.

(m) *Prototype developer* means a third party that develops a prototype for use by a manufacturer. Such prototypes may be qualified by either the prototype developer or by the manufacturer.

(n) *Qualified prototype* means a prototype that has been tested in accordance with § 1633.4(a) and meets the criteria stated in § 1633.3(b).

(o) *Confirmed prototype* means a prototype that is part of a pooling arrangement and is the same as a qualified prototype with respect to materials, components, design and methods of assembly and has been tested in accordance with § 1633.5(a)(3) and meets the criteria stated in § 1633.3(b).

(p) *Subordinate prototype* means a mattress set that is based on a qualified or confirmed prototype and is the same as the qualified or confirmed prototype, except as permitted by § 1633.4(b). A subordinate prototype is considered to be represented by a qualified or confirmed prototype and need not be tested in accordance with § 1633.4(a) or § 1633.5(a)(3).

(q) *Prototype pooling* means a cooperative arrangement—whereby one or more manufacturers build mattress sets based on a qualified prototype produced by another manufacturer or prototype developer. A manufacturer who relies on another manufacturer's or prototype developer's qualified prototype must perform a confirmation test on the mattress set it manufactures.

(r) *Confirmation test* means a pre-market test conducted by a manufacturer who is relying on a qualified prototype produced by another manufacturer or prototype developer. A confirmation test must be conducted in accordance with the procedures set forth in § 1633.7 and meet the criteria in § 1633.3(b).

(s) *Production lot* means any quantity of finished mattress sets that are produced in production intervals defined by the manufacturer, and are intended to replicate a specific qualified, confirmed or subordinate prototype that complies with this part 1633.

(t) *Specimen* means a mattress set tested under this regulation.

(u) *Twin size* means any mattress with the dimensions 38 inches (in) (965 millimeters) × 74.5 in. (1892 mm); all dimensions may vary by ±½ in. (±13 mm).

(v) *Core* means the main support system that may be present in a mattress, such as springs, foam, water bladder, air bladder, or resilient filling.

§ 1633.3 General requirements.

(a) *Summary of test method.* The test method set forth in § 1633.7 measures the flammability (fire test response characteristics) of a mattress specimen by exposing the specimen to a specified flaming ignition source and allowing it to burn freely under well-ventilated, controlled environmental conditions. The flaming ignition source shall be a pair of propane burners. These burners impose differing fluxes for differing times on the top and sides of the specimen. During and after this exposure, measurements shall be made of the time-dependent heat release rate from the specimen, quantifying the energy generated by the fire. The rate of heat release must be measured by means of oxygen consumption calorimetry.

(b) *Test criteria.* (1) When testing the mattress set in accordance with the test procedure set forth in § 1633.7, the specimen shall comply with both of the following criteria:

(i) The peak rate of heat release shall not exceed 200 kilowatts (''kW'') at any time within the 30 minute test; and

(ii) The total heat release shall not exceed 15 megajoules (''MJ'') for the first 10 minutes of the test.

(2) In the interest of safety, the test operator should discontinue the test and record a failure if a fire develops to such a size as to require suppression for the safety of the facility.

(c) *Testing of mattress sets.* Mattresses labeled for sale with a foundation shall be tested with such foundation. Mattresses labeled for sale without a foundation shall be tested alone.

(d) *Compliance with this standard.* Each mattress set manufactured, imported, or renovated on or after the effective date of the standard shall meet the test criteria specified in paragraph (b) of this section and otherwise comply with all applicable requirements of this part 1633.

§ 1633.4 Prototype testing requirements.

(a) Except as otherwise provided in paragraph (b) of this section, each manufacturer shall cause three specimens of each prototype to be tested according to § 1633.7 and obtain passing test results according to § 1633.3(b) before selling or introducing into commerce any mattress set based on that prototype, unless the manufacturer complies with the prototype pooling and confirmation testing requirements in § 1633.5.

(b) Notwithstanding the requirements of paragraph (a) of this section, a manufacturer may sell or introduce into commerce a mattress set that has not been tested according to § 1633.7 if that mattress set differs from a qualified or confirmed prototype only with respect to:

(1) Mattress/foundation length and width, not depth (*e.g.*, twin, queen, king);

(2) Ticking, unless the ticking of the qualified prototype has characteristics (such as chemical treatment or special fiber composition) designed to improve performance on the test prescribed in this part; and/or

(3) Any component, material, design or method of assembly, so long as the manufacturer can demonstrate on an objectively reasonable basis that such differences will not cause the mattress set to exceed the test criteria specified in § 1633.3(b).

(c) All tests must be conducted on specimens that are no smaller than a twin size, unless the largest size mattress set produced is smaller than a twin size, in which case the largest size must be tested.

(d)(1) If each of the three specimens meets both the criteria specified in § 1633.3(b), the prototype shall be qualified. If any one (1) specimen fails to meet the test criteria of § 1633.3(b), the prototype is not qualified.

(2) Any manufacturer may produce a mattress set for sale in reliance on prototype tests performed before the effective date of this Standard, provided:

(i) The manufacturer has documentation showing that such tests were conducted in accordance with all requirements of this section and § 1633.7 and yielded passing results according to the test criteria of § 1633.3(b);

(ii) Any tests conducted more than 30 days after publication of this standard in the FEDERAL REGISTER must comply with the recordkeeping requirements in § 1633.11;

(iii) Such mattress sets may be used for prototype pooling only if the manufacturer complies with applicable recordkeeping requirements in § 1633.11; and

(iv) Such mattress sets may serve as the basis for a subordinate prototype only if the manufacturer has all records required by § 1633.11.

§ 1633.5 Prototype pooling and confirmation testing requirements.

(a) *Prototype pooling.* One or more manufacturers may rely on a qualified prototype produced by another manufacturer or prototype developer provided that:

(1) The prototype meets the requirements of § 1633.4;

(2) The mattress sets being produced are the same as the qualified prototype with respect to materials, components, design and methods of assembly; and

(3) The manufacturer producing mattress sets in reliance on a qualified prototype has performed a confirmation test on at least one (1) Specimen of the mattress set it produces in accordance with § 1633.7. The tested specimen must meet the criteria under § 1633.3(b) before any mattress sets based on the qualified prototype may be sold or introduced into commerce.

(b) *Confirmation test failure.* (1) If the confirmation test specimen fails to meet the criteria of § 1633.3(b), the manufacturer thereof shall not sell any mattress set based on the same qualified prototype until that manufacturer takes corrective measures, tests a new specimen, and the new specimen meets the criteria of § 1633.3(b).

(2) If a confirmation test specimen fails to meet the criteria of § 1633.3(b), the manufacturer thereof must notify the manufacturer of the prototype of the test failure.

§ 1633.6 Quality assurance requirements.

(a) *Quality assurance.* Each manufacturer shall implement a quality assurance program to ensure that mattress sets manufactured for sale are the same as the qualified and/or confirmed prototype on which they are based with respect to materials, components, design and methods of assembly, except as permitted by § 1633.4(b). At a minimum these procedures shall include:

(1) Controls, including incoming inspection procedures, of all mattress set materials, components and methods of assembly to ensure that they are the same as those used in the prototype on which they are based;

(2) Designation of a production lot that is represented by the prototype; and

(3) Inspection of mattress sets produced for sale sufficient to demonstrate that they are the same as the prototype on which they are based with respect to materials, components, design and methods of assembly.

(b) *Production testing.* Manufacturers are encouraged to conduct, as part of the quality assurance program, random testing of mattress sets being produced for sale according to the requirements of §§ 1633.3 and 1633.7.

(c) *Failure of mattress sets produced for sale to meet flammability standard*—(1) *Sale of mattress sets.* If any test performed for quality assurance yields results which indicate that any mattress set of a production lot does not meet the criteria of § 1633.3(b), or if a manufacturer obtains test results or other evidence that a component or material or construction/assembly process used could negatively affect the test performance of the mattress set as set forth in § 1633.3(b), the manufacturer shall cease production and distribution in commerce of such mattress sets until corrective action is taken.

(2) *Corrective action.* A manufacturer must take corrective action when any mattress set manufactured or imported for sale fails to meet the flammability test criteria set forth in § 1633.3(b).

§ 1633.7 Mattress test procedure.

(a) *Apparatus and test materials*—(1) *Calorimetry.* The rate of heat release must be measured by means of oxygen consumption calorimetry. The calibration should follow generally accepted practices for calibration. The calorimetry system shall be calibrated at a minimum of two (2) calibration points—at 75 kW and 200 kW.

(2) *Test area.* The test area must have either Test Configuration A or B. The

test area conditions shall be maintained at a temperature greater than 15 °C (59 °F) and less than 27 °C (80.6 °F) and a relative humidity less than 75 percent.

(i) *Test configuration A. (an open calorimeter (or furniture calorimeter)).* In this configuration, the specimen to be tested is placed under the center of an open furniture calorimeter. Figure 1 of this part shows the test assembly atop a bed frame and catch surface. The specimen shall be placed under an open hood which captures the entire smoke plume and is instrumented for heat release rate measurements. The area surrounding the test specimen in an open calorimeter layout shall be sufficiently large that there are no heat re-radiation effects from any nearby materials or objects. The air flow to the test specimen should be symmetrical from all sides. The air flow to the calorimeter hood shall be sufficient to ensure that the entire fire plume is captured, even at peak burning. Skirts may be placed on the hood periphery to help assure this plume capture, if necessary, though they must not be of such an excessive length as to cause the incoming flow to disturb the burning process. Skirts must also not heat up to the point that they contribute significant re-radiation to the test specimen. The air supply to the hood shall be sufficient that the fire is not in any way limited or affected by the available air supply. The fire plume should not enter the hood exhaust duct. Brief (seconds) flickers of flame that occupy only a minor fraction of the hood exhaust duct inlet cross-section are acceptable since they do not signify appreciable suppression of flames.

(ii) *Test configuration B.* The test room shall have dimensions 10 ft. by 12 ft. by 8 ft. (3048 mm × 3658 mm × 2438 mm) high. The specimen is placed within the burn room. All smoke exiting from the room is caught by a hood system instrumented for heat release rate measurements. The room shall have no openings permitting air infiltration other than a doorway opening 38 in ±0.25 in by 80 in ±0.25 in (965 mm ±6.4 mm × 2032 mm ±6.4 mm) located as indicated in Figure 2 of this part and other small openings as necessary to make measurements. The test room shall be constructed of wood or metal studs and shall be lined with fire-rated wallboard or calcium silicate board. An exhaust hood shall be positioned outside of the doorway so as to collect all of the combustion gases. There shall be no obstructions in the air supply to the set-up.

(3) *Location of test specimen.* The location of the test specimen is shown in Figure 2 of this part. The angled placement is intended to minimize the interaction of flames on the side surfaces of the test specimen with the room walls. One corner of the test specimen shall be 13 centimeters (cm) to 17 cm from the wall and the other corner shall be 25 cm to 30 cm from the wall. The test room shall contain no other furnishings or combustible materials except for the test specimen.

(4) *Bed frame.* (i) *Frame dimensions.* The specimen shall be supported around its perimeter by the bed frame with a flat surface and no edges extending up from the surface (i.e., the angle is configured down). For twin size mattresses, the specimen shall be placed on top of a welded bed frame 1.90 m by 0.99 m (75 in by 39 in) made from 40 mm (1.50 in) steel angle. If testing a size other than twin, the test frame shall similarly match the dimensions of the specimen.

(ii) *Frame height.* The frame shall be 115 mm (4.5 in) high, except if adjustments are necessary to accommodate the required burner position in paragraph (h)(2)(ii) of this section. The height of the test frame shall also be adjusted, as necessary, so that the burner is no less than 25mm (1 in) above the supporting surface.

(iii) *Frame crosspieces.* The frame shall be completely open under the foundation except for two crosspieces, 25 mm wide (1 in) at the ⅓ length points, except when sagging of the specimen between the crosspieces exceeds 19 mm (¾ in) below the test frame. Minimal additional crosspieces shall then be added to prevent sagging of the specimen.

(5) *Catch pan.* The bed frame feet shall rest on a surface of either calcium silicate board or fiber cement board, 13 mm (0.5 in) thick, 2.11 m by 1.19 m (83 in by 47 in). The board serves

as a catch surface for any flaming melt/drip material falling from the bed assembly and may be the location of a pool fire that consumes such materials. This surface must be cleaned between tests to avoid build-up of combustible residues. Lining this surface with aluminum foil to facilitate cleaning is not recommended since this might increase fire intensity via reflected radiation.

(6) *Ignition source*—(i) *General*. The ignition source shall consist of two T-shaped burners as shown in Figures 3 and 4 of this part. One burner impinges flames on the top surface of the mattress. The second burner impinges flames on the side of the mattress and on the side of the foundation. Each of the burners shall be constructed from stainless steel tubing (12.7 mm diameter with 0.89 ±0.5 mm wall thickness; 0.50 in diameter with 0.035 ±0.002 in wall). Each burner shall incorporate a stand-off foot to set its distance from the test specimen surface (Figure 5 of this part). Both burners shall be mounted with a mechanical pivot point but the side burner is locked in place to prevent movement about this pivot in normal usage. The top burner, however, is free to rotate about its pivot during a burner exposure and is lightly weighted so as to exert a downward force on the mattress top through its stand-off foot so that the burner follows a receding top surface on the test specimen (Figure 6 of this part). The combination of burner stand-off distance and propane gas flow rate to the burners determines the heat flux they impose on the surface of the test specimen so that both of these parameters are tightly controlled.

(ii) *Top surface burner*. The T head of the top surface burner (horizontal burner, Figure 3 of this part) shall be 305 ±2 mm (12 ±0.08 in) long with gas tight plugs in each end. Each side of the T shall contain 17 holes equally spaced over a 135 mm length (8.5 mm ±0.1 mm apart; 0.333 ±0.005 in). The holes on each side shall begin 8.5 mm (0.33 in) from the centerline of the burner head. The holes shall be 1.45 mm to 1.53 mm (0.058 in to 0.061 in) in diameter (which corresponds to Grade 10 machining practice with a well formed #53 drill bit). The holes shall point 5° out of the plane of the diagram in Figure 3. This broadens the width of the heat flux profile imposed on the surface of the test specimen.

(iii) *Side surface burner*. The T head of the side surface burner (vertical burner) shall be constructed similarly to the top surface burner, as shown in Figure 4 of this part, except that its overall length shall be 254 ±2 mm (10 ±0.08 in). Each side of the burner head shall contain 14 holes spaced evenly over a 110 mm length (8.5 mm ±0.1 mm apart; 0.333 ±0.005 in). The holes shall be 1.45 mm to 1.53 mm (0.058 in to 0.061 in) in diameter (which corresponds to Grade 10 machining practice with a well formed #53 drill bit). The holes shall point 5° out of the plane of the diagram in Figure 4.

(iv) *Burner stand-off*. The burner stand-off on each burner shall consist of a collar fixed by a set screw onto the inlet tube of the burner head (Figure 5 of this part). The collar shall hold a 3 mm diameter stainless steel rod having a 12.7 mm by 51 mm by (2–2.5 mm) thick (0.5 in by 2 in by (0.08–0.10 in) thick) stainless steel pad welded on its end with its face (and long axis) parallel to the T head of the burner. The foot pad shall be displaced about 10 mm to 12 mm from the longitudinal centerline of the burner head so that it does not rest on the test specimen in an area of peak heat flux.

(v) *Burner inlet lines*. A short section (9.5 mm outer diameter ("OD"), about 80 mm long; ⅜ in OD, about 3.2 in long) of copper tubing shall be placed in the inlet gas line just before the burner to facilitate making the burner nominally parallel to the test specimen surface (by a procedure described below). The copper tube on the top surface burner should be protected from excessive heat and surface oxidation by wrapping it with a suitable layer of high temperature insulation to protect the equipment. Both copper tubes are to be bent by hand in the burner alignment process. They must be replaced if they become work-hardened or crimped in any way. The gas inlet lines (12.7 mm OD stainless steel tubing; 0.50 in) serve as arms leading back to the pivot points and beyond, as shown in Figure 6 of this part. The length to the pivot for the top burner shall be approximately 1000 mm (40 in).

(vi) *Burner frame*. Figure 6 of this part shows the frame that holds the burners and their pivots, which are adjustable vertically in height. All adjustments (burner height, burner arm length from the pivot point, counterweight positions along the burner arm) are facilitated by the use of knobs or thumbscrews as the set screws. The three point footprint of the burner frame, with the two forward points on wheels, facilitates burner movement and burner stability when stationary.

(vii) *Arms*. The metal arms attached to the burners shall be attached to a separate gas control console by flexible, reinforced plastic tubing.[1] The gas control console is mounted separately so as to facilitate its safe placement outside of the test room throughout the test procedure. The propane gas lines running between the console and the burner assembly must be anchored on the assembly before running to the burner inlet arms. A 1.5 m ±25 mm (58 in ±1 in) length of flexible, reinforced tubing between the anchor point and the end of each burner inlet allows free movement of the top burner about its pivot point. The top burner arm shall have a pair of moveable cylindrical counterweights that are used, as described below, to adjust the downward force on the stand-off foot.

(viii) *Burner head*. Each burner head shall have a separate pilot light consisting of a 3 mm OD (⅛ in OD) copper tube with an independently-controlled supply of propane gas. The tube terminates within 10 mm of the center of the burner head. Care must be taken to set the pilot flame size small enough so as not to heat the test specimen before the timed burner exposure is begun.

(ix) *Flow control system*. Each burner shall have a flow control system of the type shown in Figure 7 of this part. Propane gas from a source such as a bottle is reduced in pressure to approximately 140 ±5 kilopascals ("kPa") (20 ±1 pounds per square inch gage ("psig")) and fed to the system shown in Figure 7 of this part. The gas flow to the burner is delivered in a square-wave manner (constant flow with rapid onset and termination) by means of the solenoid valve upstream of the flowmeter. An interval timer (accurate to ±0.2 s) determines the burner flame duration. The pilot light assures that the burner will ignite when the solenoid valve opens.[2] The gas flow shall be set using a rotameter type of flowmeter, with a 150 mm scale, calibrated for propane. When calibrating the flowmeter, take into account that the flow resistance of the burner holes causes a finite pressure increase in the flowmeter above ambient. (If a calibration at one atmosphere is provided by the manufacturer, the flowmeter reading, at the internal pressure existing in the meter, required to get the flow rates listed below must be corrected, typically by the square root of the absolute pressure ratio. This calls for measuring the actual pressure in the flow meters when set near the correct flow values. A value roughly in the range of 1 kPa to 3 kPa—5 in to 15 in of water—can be expected.) See information on calibration in paragraph (b) of this section.

(x) *Gas flow rate*. Use propane gas: The propane shall be minimum 99% pure (often described by suppliers as CP or "chemically pure" grade, but this designation should not be relied on since the actual purity may vary by supplier). Each burner has a specific propane gas flow rate set with its respective, calibrated flowmeter. The gas flow rate to the top burner is 12.9 liters per minute ("L/min") ±0.1 L/min at a pressure of 101 ±5 kPa (standard atmospheric pressure) and a temperature of 22 ±3 °C. The gas flow rate to the side burner is 6.6 ±0.05 L/min at a pressure of 101 ±5 kPa (standard atmospheric pressure) and a temperature of 22 ±3 °C. The total heat release rate of the burners is 27 kW.

(b) *Calibration of Propane Flowmeters*—(1) *Preparation*. Once the assembly of the burner is completed and all the connecting points are checked for gas leakage, the most critical task is ensuring the exact flow rates of propane

[1] Fiber-reinforced plastic tubing (6 mm ID by 9.5 mm OD; 0.25 inch ID by 0.4 inch OD) made of PVC should be used.

[2] If the side burner, or more commonly one half of the side burner, fails to ignite quickly, adjust the position of the igniter, bearing in mind that propane is heavier than air. The best burner behavior test assessment is done against an inert surface (to spread the gas as it would during an actual test).

into the top and side burners, as described in the test protocol. The gas flow rates are specified at 12.9 Liters per minute (LPM) ±0.1 LPM and 6.6 LPM ±0.05 LPM for the top and side burners (Burners 1 and 2), respectively, at a pressure of 101 ±5 kiloPascal (kPa) (standard atmospheric pressure) and a temperature of 22 ±3 °C. The rotameters that are installed in the control box of the burner assembly need to be calibrated for accurate measurement of these flow rates.

(i) The most practical and accurate method of measuring and calibrating the flow rate of gases (including propane) is use of a diaphragm test meter (also called a dry test meter). A diaphragm test meter functions based on positive displacement of a fixed volume of gas per rotation and its reading is therefore independent of the type of the gas being used. The gas pressure and temperature, however, can have significant impact on the measurement of flow rate.

(ii) The gas pressure downstream of the rotameters that are installed in the control box of the burner assembly should be maintained near atmospheric pressure (only a few millimeters of water above atmosphere). Therefore, the best location to place the diaphragm test meter for gas flow calibration is right downstream of the control box. The pressure at the propane tank must be set at 20 ±1 pounds per square inch gage (psig).

(2) *Calibration Procedure.* Install the diaphragm test meter (DTM) downstream of the control box in the line for the top burner. Check all connecting points for gas leakage. Open the main valve on the propane tank and set a pressure of 20 ±0.5 psig. Set the timers in the control box for 999 seconds (or the maximum range possible). Record the barometric pressure. Turn the "Burner 1" switch to ON and ignite the top burner. Allow the gas to flow for 2–3 minutes until the DTM is stabilized. Record the pressure and temperature in the DTM. Use a stopwatch to record at least one minute worth of complete rotations while counting the number of rotations.[3] Calculate the propane gas flow rate using the recorded time and number of rotations (total flow in that time). Use the pressure and temperature readings to convert to standard conditions. Repeat this measurement for two additional meter setting to allow for calibrating the flowmeter throughout the range of interest. Plot the flow versus meter reading, fit a best line (possibly quadratic) through these points to find the meter setting for a flow of 12.9 LPM at the above "standard conditions." Repeat this procedure for "Burner 2" using three meter readings to find the setting that gives a flow rate of 6.6 LPM at the standard conditions. After completion of the calibration, re-set the timers to 70 and 50 seconds.

(c) *Conditioning.* Remove the specimens from any packaging prior to conditioning. Specimens shall be conditioned in air at a temperature greater than 18 °C (65 °F) and less than 25 °C (77 °F) and a relative humidity less than 55 percent for at least 48 continuous hours prior to test. Specimens shall be supported in a manner to permit free movement of air around them during conditioning.

(d) *Test preparation*—(1) *General.* Horizontal air flow at a distance of 0.5 m (20 in) on all sides of the test specimen at the mattress top height shall be no more than 0.5 m/s. If there is any visual evidence that the burner flames are disturbed by drafts during their exposure durations, the burner regions must be enclosed on two or more sides by at least a triple layer of screen wire. The screens shall be at least 25 cm tall. The screen(s) for the top burner shall sit on the mattress top and shall be wide enough to extend beyond the area of the burner impingement. All screens shall be far enough away (typically 30 cm or more) from the burner tubes so as not to interfere or interact with flame spread during the burner exposure. The screen for the side burner will require a separate support from below. All screens shall be removed at

[3] With a diaphragm test meter well-sized to this application, this should be more than five rotations. A one liter per rotation meter will require 10 to 15 rotations for the flow measurements and greater than the minimum of one minute recording time specified here.

the end of the 70 second exposure interval.

(2) *Specimen.* Remove the test specimen from the conditioning room immediately before it is to be tested. Testing shall begin within 20 minutes after removal from the conditioning area. Be sure the test frame is approximately centered on the catch surface. Carefully center the foundation on top of the test frame to eliminate any gaps between the bottom periphery of the foundation and the inside edges of the test frame. If the mattress is to be tested alone, place it similarly. A mattress tested with its foundation should be centered longitudinally and laterally on the foundation. Carefully center them on the bed frame and on each other. The mattress shall be centered on top of the foundation (see Figure 1 of this part). However, in order to keep the heat flux exposure the same for the sides of the two components, if the mattress is 1 cm to 2 cm narrower than the foundation, the mattress shall be shifted so that the side to be exposed is in the same plane as the foundation. Refer to Figure 8 of this part. A product having an intended sleep surface on only one side shall be tested with the sleeping side up so that the sleeping surface is exposed to the propane burner.

(e) *Burner flow rate/flow timer confirmation.* Just prior to moving the burner adjacent to the test specimen, briefly ignite each burner at the same time, and check that the propane flow to that burner is set at the appropriate level on its flowmeter to provide the flows listed in §1633.7(a)(6)(x). Check that the timers for the burner exposures are set to 70 seconds for the top burner and 50 seconds for the side burner. For a new burner assembly, check the accuracy of the gas flow timers against a stop watch at these standard time settings. Set pilot flows to a level that will not cause them to impinge on sample surfaces.

(f) *Location of the gas burners.* The general layout for the room configuration is shown in Figure 2 of this part. Place the burner heads so that they are within 300 mm (1 ft) of the mid-length of the mattress. If there are unique construction features (e.g., handles, zippers) within the burner placement zone, the burner shall impinge on this feature. For a quilted mattress top the stand-off foot pad must alight on a high, flat area between dimples or quilting thread runs. The same is to be true for the side burner if that surface is quilted. If a specimen design presents a conflict in placement such that both burners cannot be placed between local depressions in the surface, the top burner shall be placed at the highest flat surface.

(g) *Burner set-up.* The burners shall be placed in relation to the mattress and foundation surfaces in the manner shown in Figure 9 of this part, i.e., at the nominal spacings shown there and with the burner tubes nominally parallel[4] to the mattress surfaces on which they impinge. Since the heat flux levels seen by the test specimen surfaces depend on burner spacing, as well as gas flow rate, care must be taken with the set-up process.

(h) *Burner alignment procedure*—(1) *Preparation.* Complete the following before starting the alignment procedure:

(i) Check that the pivot point for the mattress top burner feed tube and the two metal plates around it are clean and well-lubricated so as to allow smooth, free movement.

(ii) Set the two burners such that the 5° out-of-plane angling of the flame jets makes the jets on the two burners point slightly *toward* each other.

(iii) Check the burner stand-off feet for straightness and perpendicularity between foot pad and support rod and to see that they are clean of residue from a previous test.

(iv) Have at hand the following items to assist in burner set-up: The jig, shown in Figure 10 of this part, for setting the stand-off feet at their proper distances from the front of the burner tube; a 3 mm thick piece of flat stock (any material) to assist in checking the parallelness of the burners to the mattress surfaces; and a 24 gage stainless steel sheet metal platen that is 30 mm (12 in) wide, 610 mm (24 in) long and has

[4] The top burner will tend to be tangential to the mattress surface at the burner midlength; this orientation will not necessarily be parallel to the overall average mattress surface orientation nor will it necessarily be horizontal. This is a result of the shape of the mattress top surface.

a sharp, precise 90° bend 355 mm (14 in) from one 30 mm wide end or another dimension that meets the requirements for a specific sample.

(2) *Alignment.* (i) Place the burner assembly adjacent to the test specimen. Place the sheet metal platen on the mattress with the shorter side on top. The location shall be within 30 cm (1 ft) of the longitudinal center of the mattress. The intended location of the stand-off foot of the top burner shall not be in a dimple or crease caused by the quilting of the mattress top. Press the platen laterally inward from the edge of the mattress so that its side makes contact with either the top and bottom edge or the vertical side of the mattress.[5] Use a sufficient length of duct tape (platen to mattress top) to assure that the platen stays firmly against the surfaces of the mattress.

(ii) With both burner arms horizontal (pinned in this position), fully retract the stand-off feet of both burners and, if necessary, the pilot tubes as well.[6] (Neither is to protrude past the front face of the burner tubes at this point.) Move the burner assembly forward (perpendicular to the mattress) until the vertical burner lightly contacts the sheet metal platen. Adjust the height of the vertical burner on its vertical support column so as to center the tube on the crevice between the mattress and the foundation. (This holds also for pillow top mattress tops, i.e., ignore the crevice between the pillow top and the main body of the mattress.)[7] Adjust the height of the horizontal burner until it sits lightly on top of the sheet metal platen. Its burner arm should then be horizontal.

(iii) Move the horizontal burner in/out (loosen the thumb screw near the pivot point) until the outer end of the burner tube is 13 mm to 19 mm (½ in to ¾ in) from the corner bend in the platen (this is facilitated by putting a pair of lines on the top of the platen 13 mm and 19 mm from the bend and parallel to it). Tighten the thumb screw.

(iv) Make the horizontal burner parallel to the top of the platen (within 3 mm (⅛ inch) over the burner tube length); when properly parallel, it should not be possible to insert the 3 mm flat stock under either burner end by bending the copper tube section appropriately. Note: After the platen is removed (in paragraph (h)(2)(vii) of this section), the burner tube may not be horizontal; this is normal. For mattress/foundation combinations having nominally flat, vertical sides, the similar adjustment for the vertical burner is intended to make that burner parallel to the sides and vertical. Variations in the shape of mattresses and foundations can cause the platen section on the side to be non-flat and/or non-vertical. If the platen is flat and vertical, make the vertical burner parallel to the side of the platen (±3 mm) by bending its copper tube section as needed. If not, make the side burner parallel to the mattress/foundation sides by the best visual estimate after the platen has been removed.

(v) Move the burner assembly perpendicularly back away from the mattress about 30 cm (1 ft). Set the two stand-off feet to their respective distances using the jig designed for this purpose. Install the jig *fully* onto the burner tube (on the *same side* of the tube as the stand-off foot), with its side edges parallel to the burner feed arm,

---

[5] Mattresses having a convex side are treated separately since the platen cannot be placed in the above manner. Use the platen only to set the top burner parallelness. Set the in/out distance of the top burner to the specification in paragraph (h)(1)(iii). Set the side burner so that it is approximately (visually) parallel to the flat side surface of the foundation below the mattress/foundation crevice once its foot is in contact with the materials in the crevice area. The burner will not be vertical in this case. If the foundation side is also non-flat, set the side burner vertical (±3 mm, as above) using a bubble level as a reference. The side surface convexities will then bring the bowed out sections of the specimen closer to the burner tube than the stand-off foot.

[6] The pilot tubes can normally be left with their ends just behind the plane of the front of the burner tube. This way they will not interfere with positioning of the tube but their flame will readily ignite the burner tubes.

[7] For tests of the mattress alone, set the center of the side burner at the lower edge of the mattress OR the top (upper tip) of the side burner 25 mm (1 in) below the top edge of the mattress, whichever is lower. This prevents inappropriate (excessive) exposure of the top surface of the mattress to the side burner.

at about the position where one end of the foot will be. Loosen the set screw and slide the foot out to the point where it is flush with the bottom end of the jig. Tighten the set screw. Make sure the long axis of the foot is parallel to the burner tube. It is essential to use the correct side of the spacer jig with each burner. Double check this. The jig must be clearly marked.

(vi) Set the downward force of the horizontal burner. Remove the retainer pin near the pivot. While holding the burner feed arm horizontal using a spring scale[8] hooked onto the thumbscrew holding the stand-off foot, move the small and/or large weights on the feed tube appropriately so that the spring scale reads 170 g to 225 g (6 oz to 8 oz).

(vii) Remove the sheet metal platen (and tape holding it).

(viii) Hold the horizontal burner up while sliding the burner assembly forward until the vertical burner stand-off foot just touches the mattress and/or the foundation, then release the horizontal burner. The outer end of the burner tube should extend at least 6 mm to 12 mm (¼ in to ½ in) out beyond the uppermost corner/edge of the mattress so that the burner flames will hit the edge. (For a pillow top mattress, this means the outer edge of the pillow top portion and the distance may then be greater than 6 mm to 12 mm.) If this is not the case, move the burner assembly (perpendicular to the mattress side)—not the horizontal burner alone—until it is.[9] Finally, move the vertical burner tube until its stand-off foot just touches the side of the mattress and/or the foundation. (Use the set screw near the vertical burner pivot.)

(ix) Make sure all thumbscrews are adequately tightened. Care must be taken, once this set-up is achieved, to avoid bumping the burner assembly or disturbing the flexible lines that bring propane to it.

(x) If there is *any* indication of flow disturbances in the test facility which cause the burner flames or pilot flames to move around, place screens around the burners so as to minimize these disturbances.[10] These screens (and any holders) must be far enough away from the burners (about 30 cm or more for the top, less for the side) so that they do not interact with the flames growing on the specimen surfaces. For the top surface burner, at least a triple layer of window screen approximately 30 cm high sitting vertically on the mattress top (Figure 9 of this part) has proved satisfactory. For the side burner at least a triple layer of screen approximately 15 cm wide, formed into a square-bottom U-shape and held from below the burner has proved satisfactory. Individual laboratories will have to experiment with the best arrangement for suppressing flow disturbances in their facility.

(i) *Running the test.* (1) Charge the hose line to be used for fire suppression with water.

(2) *Burner Preparation.* (i) Turn AC power on; set propane pressure to 20 psig at bottle; set timers to 70 s (top burner) and 50 s (side burner); with burner assembly well-removed from test specimen, ignite burners and check that, WHEN BOTH ARE ON AT THE SAME TIME, the flowmeters are set to the values that give the requisite propane gas flow rates to each burner. Turn off burners. Set pilot tubes just behind front surface of burners; set pilot flow valves for approximately 2 cm flames. Turn off pilots.

[8] An acceptable spring scale has a calibrated spring mounted within a holder and hooks on each end.

[9] The foot should depress the surface it first contacts by no more than 1 mm to 2 mm. This is best seen up close, not from the rear of the burner assembly. However, if a protruding edge is the first item contacted, compress it until the foot is in the plane of the mattress/foundation vertical sides. The intent here is that the burner be spaced a fixed distance from the vertical mattress/foundation sides, not from an incidental protrusion. Similarly, if there is a wide crevice in this area which would allow the foot to move inward and thereby place the burners too close to the vertical mattress/foundation sides, it will be necessary to use the spacer jig (rather than the stand-off foot) above or below this crevice to set the proper burner spacing. Compress the mattress/foundation surface 1 mm to 2 mm when using the jig for this purpose.

[10] The goal here is to keep the burner flames impinging on a fixed area of the specimen surface rather than wandering back and forth over a larger area.

(ii) Position burner on test specimen and remove sheet metal platen.

(iii) Place screens around both burners.

(3) *Start pilots*. Open pilot ball valves one at a time and ignite pilots with hand-held flame; adjust flame size if necessary being very careful to avoid a jet flame that could prematurely ignite the test specimen (Note that after a long interval between tests the low pilot flow rate will require a long time to displace air in the line and achieve the steady-state flame size.)

(4) *Start recording systems*. With the calorimetry system fully operational, after instrument zeroes and spans, start the video lights and video camera and data logging systems two minutes before burner ignition (or, if not using video, take a picture of the setup).

(5) *Initiate test*. Start test exposure by simultaneously turning on power to both timers (timers will turn off burners at appropriate times). Also start a 30 minute timer of the test duration. Check/adjust propane flow rates (DO THIS ESSENTIAL TASK IMMEDIATELY. Experience shows the flow will not remain the same from test-to-test in spite of fixed valve positions so adjustment is essential.) If not using video, one photo must be taken within the first 45 seconds of starting the burners.

(6) *End of burner exposure*. When the burners go out (after 70 seconds for the longer exposure), carefully lift the top burner tube away from the specimen surface, producing as little disturbance as possible to the specimen. Turn off power to both timers. Remove all screens. Turn off pilots at their ball valves. Remove the burner assembly from the specimen area to facilitate the video camera view of the full side of the specimen. In the case of the room-based configurations, remove the burner assembly from the room to protect it.

(j) *Video Recording/Photographs*. Place a video or still frame camera so as to have (when the lens is zoomed out) just slightly more than a full-length view of the side of the test specimen being ignited, including a view of the flame impingement area while the burner assembly is present. The view must also include the catch pan so that it is clear whether any melt pool fire in this pan participates significantly in the growth of fire on the test specimen. The camera shall include a measure of elapsed time to the nearest 1 second for video and 1 minute for still frame within its recorded field of view (preferably built into the camera). For the room-based configuration, the required full-length view of the sample may require an appropriately placed window, sealed with heat resistant glass, in one of the room walls. Place the camera at a height just sufficient to give a view of the top of the specimen while remaining under any smoke layer that may develop in the room. The specimen shall be brightly lit so that the image does not lose detail to over-exposed flames. This will require a pair or more of 1 kW photo flood lights illuminating the viewed side of the specimen. The lights may need to shine into the room from the outside via sealed windows.

(k) *Cessation of Test*. (1) The heat release rate shall be recorded and video/photographs taken until either 30 minutes has elapsed since the start of the burner exposure or a fire develops of such size as to require suppression for the safety of the facility.

(2) Note the time and nature of any unusual behavior that is not fully within the view of the video camera. This is most easily done by narration to a camcorder.

(3) Run the heat release rate system and datalogger until the fire has been fully out for several minutes to allow the system zero to be recorded.

(l) *Use of alternate apparatus*. Mattress sets may be tested using test apparatus that differs from that described in this section if the manufacturer obtains and provides to the Commission data demonstrating that tests using the alternate apparatus during the procedures specified in this section yield failing results as often as, or more often than, tests using the apparatus specified in the standard. The manufacturer shall provide the supporting data to the Office of Compliance, Recalls & Compliance Division,

U.S. Consumer Product Safety Commission, 4330 East West Highway, Bethesda, Maryland 20814. Staff will review the data and determine whether the alternate apparatus may be used.

[71 FR 13498, Mar. 15, 2006, as amended at 73 FR 6842, Feb. 6, 2008]

§ 1633.8 Findings.

(a) *General.* In order to issue a flammability standard under the FFA, the FFA requires the Commission to make certain findings and to include these in the regulation, 15 U.S.C. 1193(j)(2). These findings are discussed in this section.

(b) *Voluntary standards.* No findings concerning compliance with and adequacy of a voluntary standard are necessary because no relevant voluntary standard addressing the risk of injury that is addressed by this regulation has been adopted and implemented.

(c) *Relationship of benefits to costs.* The Commission estimates the potential total lifetime benefits of a mattress that complies with this standard to range from $45 to $57 per mattress set (based on a 10 year mattress life and a 3% discount rate). The Commission estimates total resource costs of the standard to range from $8 to $22 per mattress. This yields net benefits of $23 to $50 per mattress set. The Commission estimates that aggregate lifetime benefits associated with all mattresses produced the first year the standard becomes effective range from $1,024 to $1,307 million, and that aggregate resource costs associated with these mattresses range from $175 to $511 million, yielding net benefits of about $514 to $1,132 million. Accordingly, the Commission finds that the benefits from the regulation bear a reasonable relationship to its costs.

(d) *Least burdensome requirement.* The Commission considered the following alternatives: alternative maximum peak heat release rate and test duration, alternative total heat released in the first 10 minutes of the test, mandatory production testing, a longer effective date, taking no action, relying on a voluntary standard, and requiring labeling alone (without any performance requirements). The alternatives of taking no action, relying on a voluntary standard (if one existed), and requiring labeling alone are unlikely to adequately reduce the risk. Requiring a criterion of 25 MJ total heat release during the first 10 minutes of the test instead of 15 MJ would likely reduce the estimated benefits (deaths and injuries reduced) without having much effect on costs. Both options of increasing the duration of the test from 30 minutes to 60 minutes and decreasing the peak rate of heat release from 200 kW to 150 kW would likely increase costs significantly without substantial increase in benefits. Requiring production testing would also likely increase costs. Therefore, the Commission finds that an open flame standard for mattresses with the testing requirements and criteria that are specified in the Commission rule is the least burdensome requirement that would prevent or adequately reduce the risk of injury for which the regulation is being promulgated.

§ 1633.9 Glossary of terms.

(a) *Absorbent pad.* Pad used on top of mattress. Designed to absorb moisture/body fluids thereby reducing skin irritation, can be one time use.

(b) *Basket pad.* Cushion for use in an infant basket.

(c) *Bunk beds.* A tier of beds, usually two or three, in a high frame complete with mattresses (see Figure 11 of this part).

(d) *Car bed.* Portable bed used to carry a baby in an automobile.

(e) *Carriage pad.* Cushion to go into a baby carriage.

(f) *Chaise lounge.* An upholstered couch chair or a couch with a chair back. It has a permanent back rest, no arms, and sleeps one (see Figure 11).

(g) *Convertible sofa.* An upholstered sofa that converts into an adult sized bed. Mattress unfolds out and up from under the seat cushioning (see Figure 11).

(h) *Corner groups.* Two twin size bedding sets on frames, usually slipcovered, and abutted to a corner table. They also usually have loose bolsters slipcovered (see Figure 11).

(i) *Crib bumper.* Padded cushion which goes around three or four sides inside a crib to protect the baby. Can also be used in a playpen.

(j) *Daybed.* Daybed has foundation, usually supported by coil or flat springs, mounted between arms on which mattress is placed. It has permanent arms, no backrest, and sleeps one (see Figure 11).

(k) *Dressing table pad.* Pad to cushion a baby on top of a dressing table.

(l) *Drop-arm loveseat.* When side arms are in vertical position, this piece is a loveseat. The adjustable arms can be lowered to one of four positions for a chaise lounge effect or a single sleeper. The vertical back support always remains upright and stationary (see Figure 11).

(m) *Futon.* A flexible mattress generally used on the floor that can be folded or rolled up for storage. It usually consists of resilient material covered by ticking.

(n) *High riser.* This is a frame of sofa seating height with two equal size mattresses without a backrest. The frame slides out with the lower mattress and rises to form a double or two single beds (see Figure 11).

(o) *Infant carrier and lounge pad.* Pad to cushion a baby in an infant carrier.

(p) *Mattress foundation.* This is a ticking covered structure used to support a mattress or sleep surface. The structure may include constructed frames, foam, box springs or other materials used alone or in combination.

(q) *Murphy bed.* A style of sleep system where the mattress and foundation are fastened to the wall and provide a means to retract or rotate the bed assembly into the wall to release more floor area for other uses.

(r) *Pillow.* Cloth bag filled with resilient material such as feathers, down, sponge rubber, urethane, or fiber used as the support for the head of a person.

(s) *Playpen pad.* Cushion used on the bottom of a playpen.

(t) *Portable crib.* Smaller size than a conventional crib. Can usually be converted into a playpen.

(u) *Quilted* means stitched with thread or by fusion through the ticking and one or more layers of material.

(v) *Roll-away-bed.* Portable bed which has frame that folds with the mattress for compact storage.

(w) *Sleep lounge.* Upholstered seating section which is mounted on a frame. May have bolster pillows along the wall as backrests or may have attached headrests (see Figure 11).

(x) *Stroller pad.* Cushion used in a baby stroller.

(y) *Sofa bed.* These are pieces in which the back of the sofa swings down flat with the seat to form the sleeping surface. Some sofa beds have bedding boxes for storage of bedding. There are two types: the one-piece, where the back and seat are upholstered as a unit, supplying an unbroken sleeping surface; and the two-piece, where back and seat are upholstered separately (see Figure 11 of this part).

(z) *Sofa lounge*—(includes glideouts). Upholstered seating section is mounted on springs and in a frame that permit it to be pulled out for sleeping. Has upholstered backrest bedding box that is hinged. Glideouts are single sleepers with sloping seats and backrests. Seat pulls out from beneath back and evens up to supply level sleeping surface (see Figure 11).

(aa) *Studio couch.* Consists of upholstered seating section on upholstered foundation. Many types convert to twin beds (see Figure 11).

(bb) *Studio divan.* Twin size upholstered seating section with foundation is mounted on metal bed frame. Has no arms or backrest, and sleeps one (see Figure 11 of this part).

(cc) *Trundle bed.* A low bed which is rolled under a larger bed. In some lines, the lower bed springs up to form a double or two single beds as in a high riser (see Figure 11).

(dd) *Tufted* means buttoned or laced through the ticking and upholstery material and/or core, or having the ticking and loft material and/or core drawn together at intervals by any other method which produces a series of depressions on the surface.

(ee) *Twin studio divan.* Frames which glide out (but not up) and use seat cushions, in addition to upholstered foundation to sleep two. Has neither arms nor back rest (see Figure 11).

(ff) *Flip or sleeper chair.* Chair that unfolds to be used for sleeping, typically has several connecting fabric covered, solid foam core segments.

Subpart B—Rules and Regulations

§ 1633.10 Definitions.

(a) *Standard* means the Standard for the Flammability (Open-Flame) of Mattress Sets (16 CFR part 1633, subpart A).

(b) The definition of terms set forth in the § 1633.2 of the Standard shall also apply to this section.

§ 1633.11 Records.

(a) *Test and manufacturing records C general.* Every manufacturer and any other person initially introducing into commerce mattress sets subject to the standard, irrespective of whether guarantees are issued relative thereto, shall maintain the following records in English at a location in the United States:

(1) Test results and details of each test performed by or for that manufacturer (including failures), whether for qualification, confirmation, or production, in accordance with § 1633.7. Details shall include: name and complete physical address of test facility, type of test room, test room conditions, time that sample spent out of conditioning area before starting test, prototype or production identification number, and test data including the peak rate of heat release, total heat release in first 10 minutes, a graphic depiction of the peak rate of heat release and total heat release over time. These records shall include the name and signature of person conducting the test, the date of the test, and a certification by the person overseeing the testing as to the test results and that the test was carried out in accordance with the Standard. For confirmation tests, the identification number must be that of the prototype tested.

(2) Video and/or a minimum of eight photographs of the testing of each mattress set, in accordance with § 1633.7 (one taken before the test starts, one taken within 45 seconds of the start of the test, and the remaining six taken at five minute intervals, starting at 5 minutes and ending at 30 minutes), with the prototype identification number or production lot identification number of the mattress set, date and time of test, and name and location of testing facility clearly displayed.

(b) *Prototype records.* In addition to the records specified in paragraph (a) of this section, the following records shall be maintained for each qualified, confirmed and subordinate prototype:

(1) Unique identification number for the qualified or confirmed prototype and a list of the unique identification numbers of each subordinate prototype based on the qualified or confirmed prototype. Subordinate prototypes that differ from each other only be length or width may share the same identification number.

(2) A detailed description of all materials, components, and methods of assembly for each qualified, confirmed and subordinate prototype. Such description shall include the specifications of all materials and components, and the name and complete physical address of each material and component supplier.

(3) A list of which models and production lots of mattress sets are represented by each qualified, confirmed and/or subordinate prototype identification number.

(4) For subordinate prototypes, the prototype identification number of the qualified or confirmed prototype on which the mattress set is based, and, at a minimum, the manufacturing specifications and a description of the materials substituted, photographs or physical specimens of the substituted materials, and documentation based on objectively reasonable criteria that the change in any component, material, or method of assembly will not cause the subordinate prototype to exceed the test criteria specified in § 1633.3(b).

(5) Identification, composition, and details of the application of any flame retardant treatments and/or inherently flame resistant fibers or other materials employed in mattress components.

(c) *Pooling confirmation test records.* In addition to the test and prototype records specified in paragraphs (a) and (b) of this section, the following records shall be maintained:

(1) The prototype identification number assigned by the qualified prototype manufacturer;

(2) Name and complete physical address of the qualified prototype manufacturer;

(3) Copy of qualified prototype test records, and records required by paragraph (b)(2) of this section; and

(4) In the case of imported mattress sets, the importer shall be responsible for maintaining the records specified in paragraph (b) of this section for confirmation testing that has been performed with respect to mattress sets produced by each foreign manufacturing facility whose mattress sets that importer is importing.

(d) *Quality assurance records.* In addition to the records required by paragraph (a) of this section, the following quality assurance records shall be maintained:

(1) A written copy of the manufacturer's quality assurance procedures;

(2) Records of any production tests performed. Production test records must be maintained and shall include, in addition to the requirements of paragraph (a) of this section, an assigned production lot identification number and the identification number of the qualified, confirmed or subordinate prototype associated with the specimen tested;

(3) For each qualified, confirmed and subordinate prototype, the number of mattress sets in each production lot based on that prototype;

(4) The start and end dates of production of that lot; and

(5) Component, material and assembly records. Every manufacturer conducting tests and/or technical evaluations of components and materials and/or methods of assembly must maintain detailed records of such tests and evaluations.

(e) *Record retention requirements.* The records required under this Section shall be maintained by the manufacturer (including importers) for as long as mattress sets based on the prototype in question are in production and shall be retained for 3 years thereafter. Records shall be available upon the request of Commission staff.

(f) Record location requirements. (1) For mattress sets produced in the United States, all records required by this section must be maintained at the plant or factory at which the mattress sets are manufactured or assembled.

(2) For mattress sets produced outside of the United States, a copy of all records required by this section must be maintained at a U.S. location, which must be identified on the mattress set label as specified in § 1633.12(a).

§ 1633.12 Labeling.

(a) Each mattress set subject to the Standard shall bear a permanent, conspicuous, and legible label(s) containing the following information (and no other information) in English:

(1) Name of the manufacturer, or for imported mattress sets, the name of the foreign manufacturer and importer;

(2)(i) For mattress sets produced in the United States, the complete physical address of the manufacturer.

(ii) For imported mattress sets, the complete address of the foreign manufacturer, including country, and the complete physical address of the importer or the United States location where the required records are maintained if different from the importer;

(3) Month and year of manufacture;

(4) Model identification;

(5) Prototype identification number for the mattress set;

(6) A certification that the mattress complies with this standard.

(i) For mattresses intended to be sold without a foundation, a certification stating "This mattress meets the requirements of 16 CFR part 1633 (federal flammability (open flame) standard for mattresses) when used without a foundation"; or

(ii) For mattresses intended to be sold with a foundation, a certification stating "This mattress meets the requirements of 16 CFR part 1633 (federal flammability (open flame) standard for mattresses) when used with foundation <*ID*>." Such foundation(s) shall be clearly identified by a simple and distinct name and/or number on the mattress label; or

(iii) For mattresses intended to be sold both alone and with a foundation, a certification stating "This mattress meets the requirements of 16 CFR part 1633 (federal flammability (open flame) standard for mattresses) when used without a foundation or with foundation(s) <*ID*>.".Such foundation(s) shall be clearly identified by a simple and distinct name and/or number on the mattress label; and

(7) A statement identifying whether the manufacturer intends the mattress to be sold alone or with a foundation.

(i) For mattresses intended to be sold without a foundation, the label shall state "THIS MATTRESS IS INTENDED TO BE USED WITHOUT A FOUNDATION." See Figures 16 and 17 of this part; or

(ii) For mattresses intended to be sold with a foundation, the label shall state "THIS MATTRESS IS INTENDED TO BE USED WITH FOUNDATION(S): <*Foundation ID*>." See Figures 12 and 13 of this part; or

(iii) For mattresses intended to be sold both alone and with a foundation, the label shall state "THIS MATTRESS IS INTENDED TO BE USED WITHOUT A FOUNDATION OR WITH FOUNDATION(S): <*Foundation ID*>." See Figures 14 and 15 of this part.

(b) The mattress label required in paragraph (a) of this section must measure 2¾″ in width and the length can increase as needed for varying information. The label must be white with black text. The label text shall comply with the following format requirements:

(1) All information specified in paragraphs (a)(1) through (6) of this section must be in 6-point font or larger with mixed uppercase and lowercase letters. The text must be left justified and begin ¼″ from left edge of label. See Figure 12–17 of this part.

(2) The statement specified in paragraph (a)(7)(i) of this section must be in 10-point Arial/Helvetica font or larger, uppercase letters with the words "*WITHOUT* A FOUNDATION" bolded and the word "*WITHOUT*" in italics. The text shall be centered in a text box with the width measuring 2½″ and the length increasing as needed. See Figures 16 and 17 of this part.

(3) The statement specified in paragraph (a)(7)(ii) of this section must be in 10-point Arial/Helvetica font or larger in uppercase letters. The foundation identifier should be in 12-point font or larger, bolded, and underlined. The text shall be centered in a text box with the width measuring 2½″ and the length increasing as needed. See Figures 12 and 13 of this part.

(4) The statement specified in paragraph (a)(7)(iii) of this section must be in 10-point or larger Arial/Helvetica font, uppercase letters with the words "*WITHOUT* A FOUNDATION OR" bolded and the word "*WITHOUT*" in italics. The foundation identifier should be in 12-point font or larger, bolded, and underlined. The text shall be centered in a text box with the width measuring 2½″ and the length increasing as needed. See Figures 14 and 15 of this part.

(c) The foundation label required in paragraph (a) of this section must measure 2¾″ in width and the length can increase as needed for varying information. The label must be white with black text. The label shall contain the following:

(1) The information specified in paragraphs (a)(1) through (5) of this section; and

(2) The words "Foundation ID:" followed by a distinct name and/or number that corresponds to the name and/or number used on the mattress. This text must be in 10-point or larger bold Arial/Helvetica font, and the foundation identifier must be underlined. See Figures 12 through 15 of this part.

(d) The statements specified in paragraphs (a)(6)(i) through (iii) and (a)(7)(i) through (iii) of this section may be translated into any other language and printed on the reverse (blank) side of the label.

(e) No person, other than the ultimate consumer, shall remove or mutilate, or cause or participate in the removal or mutilation of, any label required by this section to be affixed to any item.

[71 FR 13498, Mar. 15, 2006, as amended at 73 FR 6843, Feb. 6, 2008]

§ 1633.13 Tests for guaranty purposes, compliance with this section, and "one of a kind" exemption.

(a) *Tests for guaranty purposes.* Reasonable and representative tests for the purpose of issuing a guaranty under section 8 of the Flammable Fabrics Act, 15 U.S.C. 1197, for mattress sets subject to the Standard shall be the tests performed to show compliance with the Standard.

(b) *Compliance with this section.* No person subject to the Flammable Fabrics Act shall manufacture for sale, import, distribute, or otherwise market or handle any mattress set which is not in compliance with the provisions under Subpart B.

(c) *"One of a kind" exemption for physician prescribed mattresses.* (1)(i) A mattress set manufactured in accordance with a physician's written prescription or manufactured in accordance with other comparable written medical therapeutic specification, to be used in connection with the treatment or management of a named individual's physical illness or injury, shall be considered a "one of a kind mattress" and shall be exempt from testing under the Standard pursuant to § 1633.7 thereof: Provided, that the mattress set bears a permanent, conspicuous and legible label which states:

WARNING: This mattress set may be subject to a large fire if exposed to an open flame. It was manufactured in accordance with a physician's prescription and has not been tested under the Federal Standard for the Flammability (Open-Flame) of Mattress Sets (16 CFR part 1633).

(ii) Such labeling must be attached to the mattress set so as to remain on or affixed thereto for the useful life of the mattress set. The label must be at least 40 square inches (250 sq. cm) with no linear dimension less than 5 inches (12.5 cm). The letters in the word "WARNING" shall be no less than 0.5 inch (1.27 cm) in height and all letters on the label shall be in a color which contrasts with the background of the label. The warning statement which appears on the label must also be conspicuously displayed on the invoice or other sales papers that accompany the mattress set in commerce from the manufacturer to the final point of sale to a consumer.

(2) The manufacturer of a mattress set exempted from testing under this paragraph (c) shall, in lieu of the records required to be kept by § 1633.10, retain a copy of the written prescription or other comparable written medical therapeutic specification for such mattress set during a period of three years, measured from the date of manufacture.

(3) For purposes of this regulation the term physician shall mean a physician, chiropractor or osteopath licensed or otherwise permitted to practice by any State of the United States.

FIGURE 1 TO PART 1633—TEST ASSEMBLY, SHOWN IN FURNITURE CALORIMETER (CONFIGURATION A)

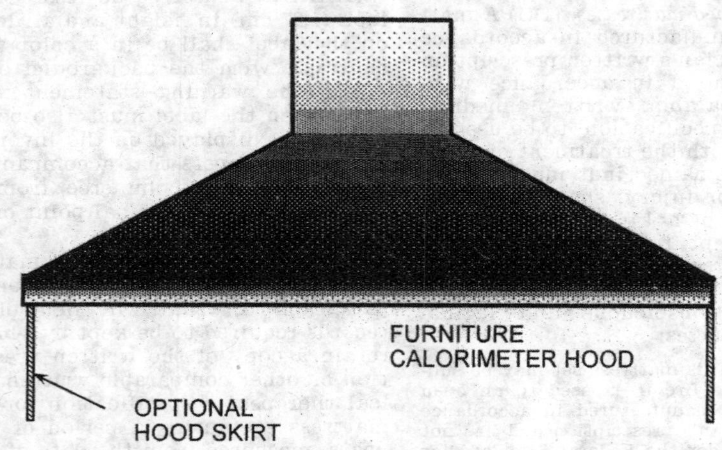

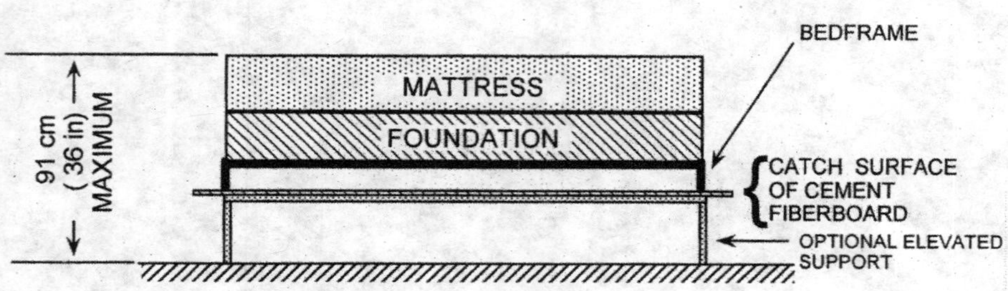

FIGURE 1. TEST ASSEMBLY, SHOWN IN FURNITURE CALORIMETER. (CONFIGURATION A.)

FIGURE 2 TO PART 1633—TEST ARRANGEMENT IN 3.05M × 3.66M (10 FT × 12 FT) ROOM (CONFIGURATION B)

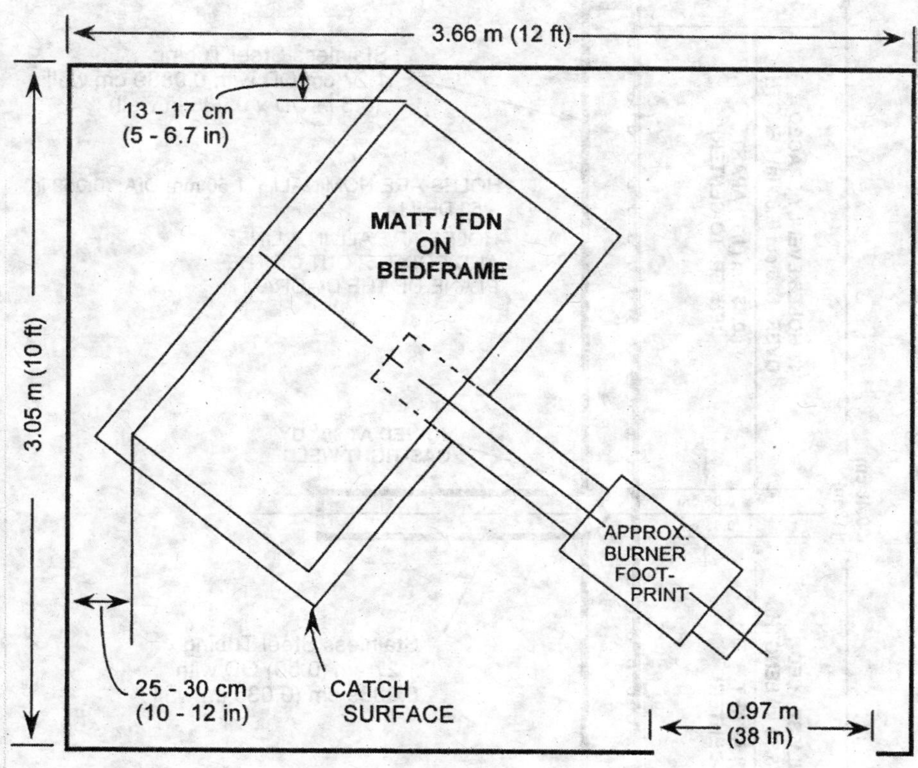

FIGURE 2. TEST ARRANGEMENT IN 3.05m X 3.66 m (10 ft x 12 ft) ROOM; CONFIGURATION B.

FIGURE 3 TO PART 1633—DETAILS OF HORIZONTAL BURNER HEAD

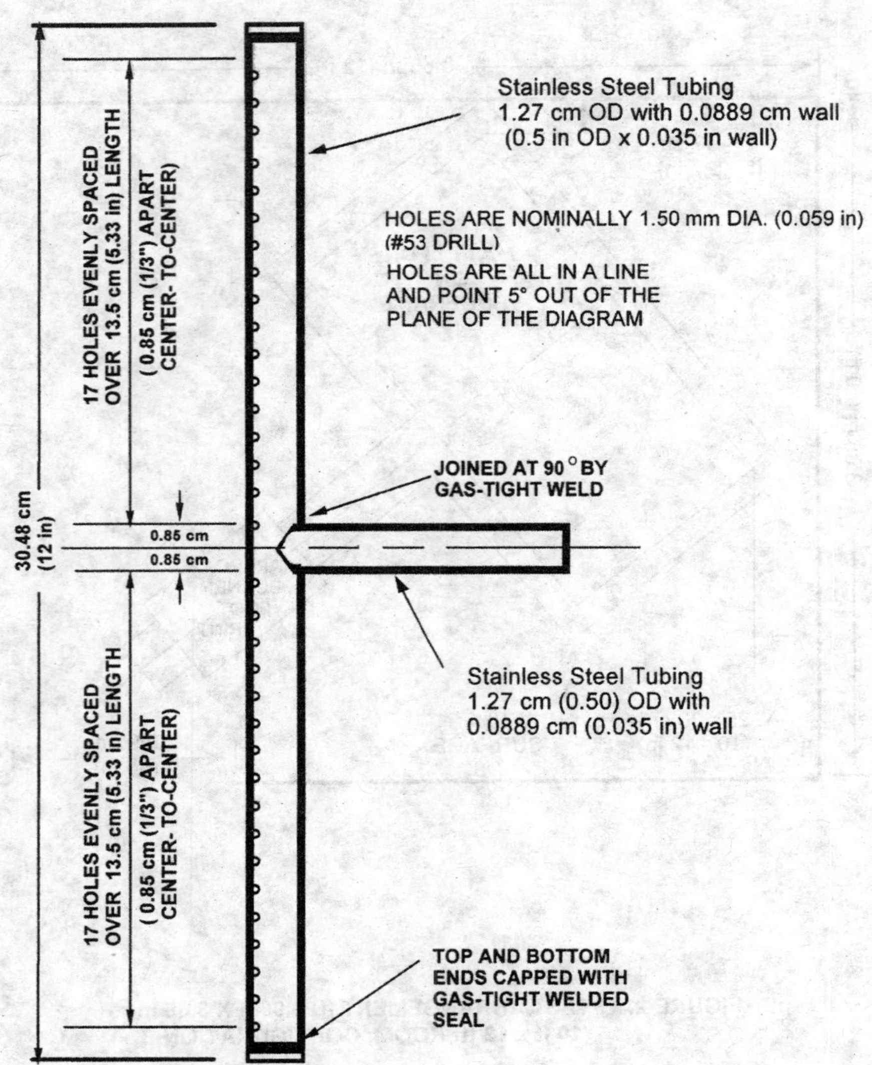

FIGURE 3. DETAILS OF HORIZONTAL BURNER HEAD.

FIGURE 4 TO PART 1633—DETAILS OF VERTICAL BURNER HEAD

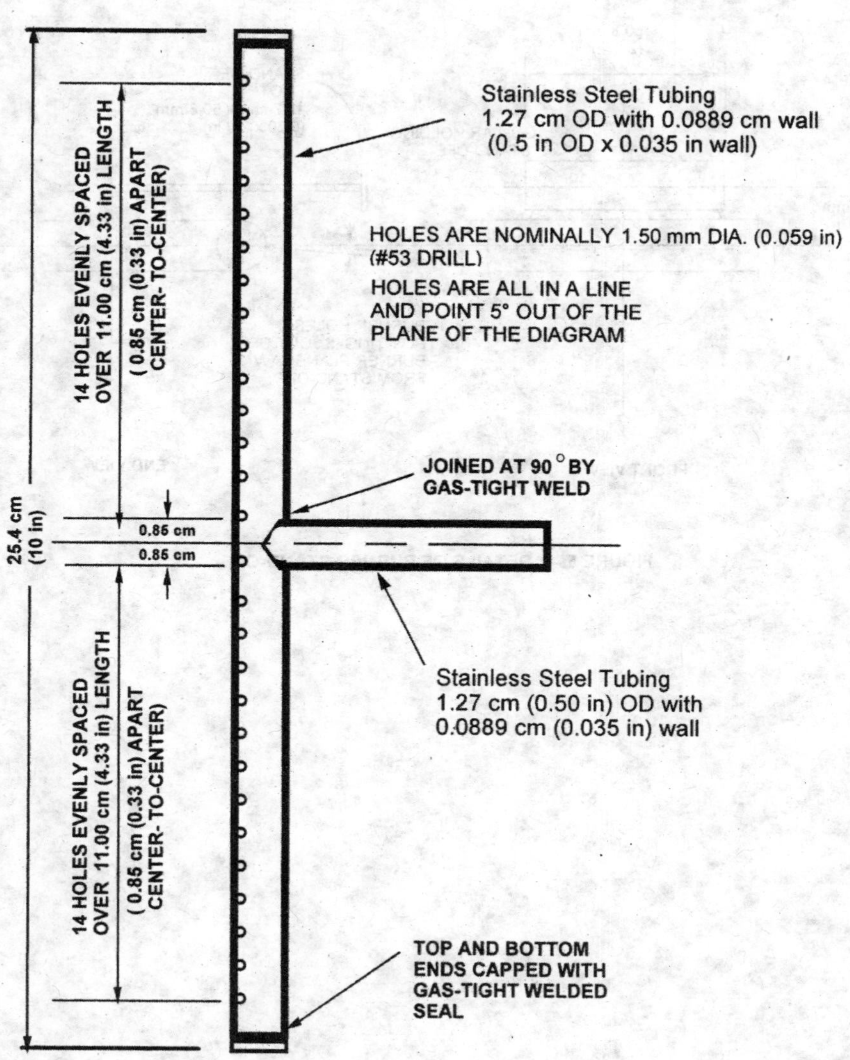

FIGURE 4. DETAILS OF VERTICAL BURNER HEAD.

FIGURE 5 TO PART 1633—DETAILS OF BURNER STAND-OFF

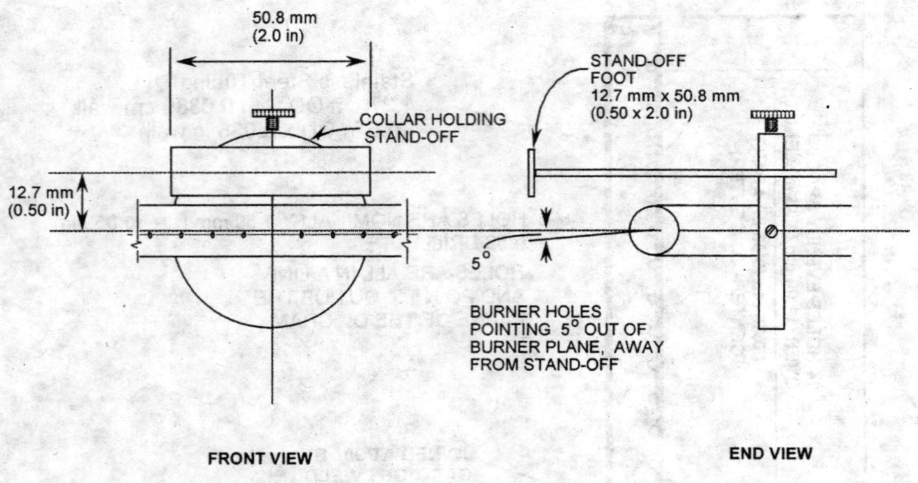

FIGURE 5. DETAILS OF BURNER STAND-OFF

FIGURE 6 TO PART 1633—BURNER ASSEMBLY SHOWING ARMS AND PIVOTS (SHOULDER SCREWS), IN RELATION TO, PORTABLE FRAME ALLOWING BURNER HEIGHT ADJUSTMENT

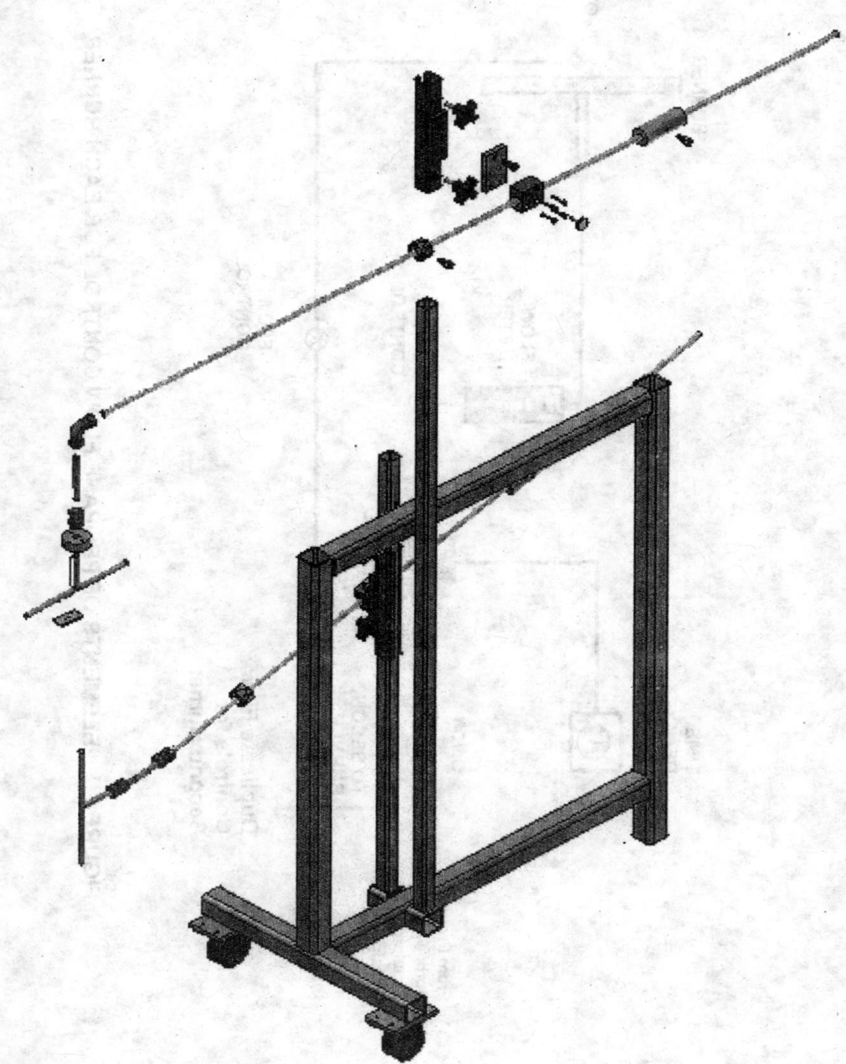

FIGURE 6. BURNER ASSEMBLY* SHOWING ARMS AND PIVOTS (Shoulder Screws), IN RELATION TO, PORTABLE FRAME ALLOWING BURNER HEIGHT ADJUSTMENT.

*Note that the feed tube for the side burner will be horizontal when the side burner pivot is locked in place, as is usual during a test exposure.

FIGURE 7 TO PART 1633—ELEMENTS OF PROPANE FLOW CONTROL FOR EACH BURNER

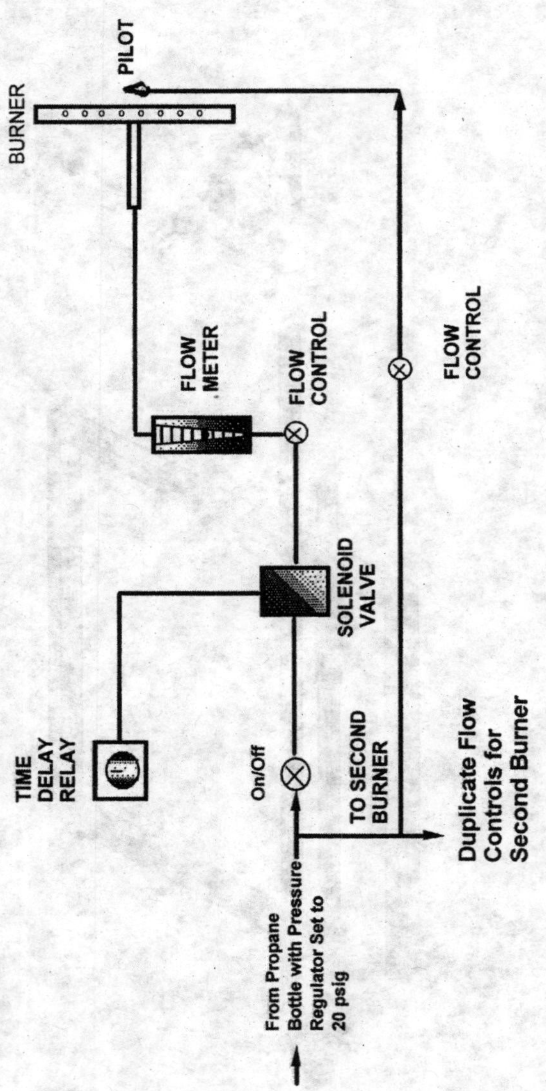

FIGURE 7. ELEMENTS OF PROPANE FLOW CONTROL FOR EACH BURNER

FIGURE 8 TO PART 1633—JIG FOR SETTING MATTRESSES AND FOUNDATION SIDES IN SAME PLANE

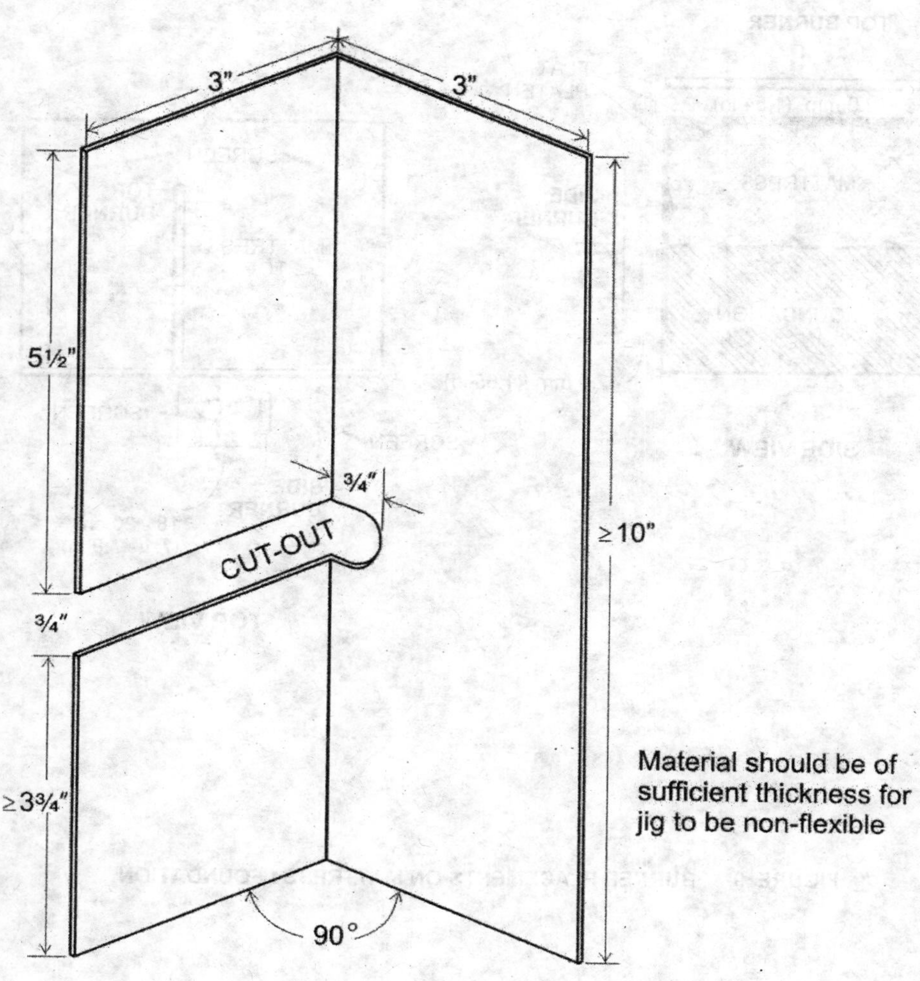

FIGURE 8 JIG FOR SETTING MATTRESS AND FOUNDATION SIDES IN SAME PLANE

FIGURE 9 TO PART 1633—BURNER PLACEMENTS ON MATTRESS/FOUNDATION

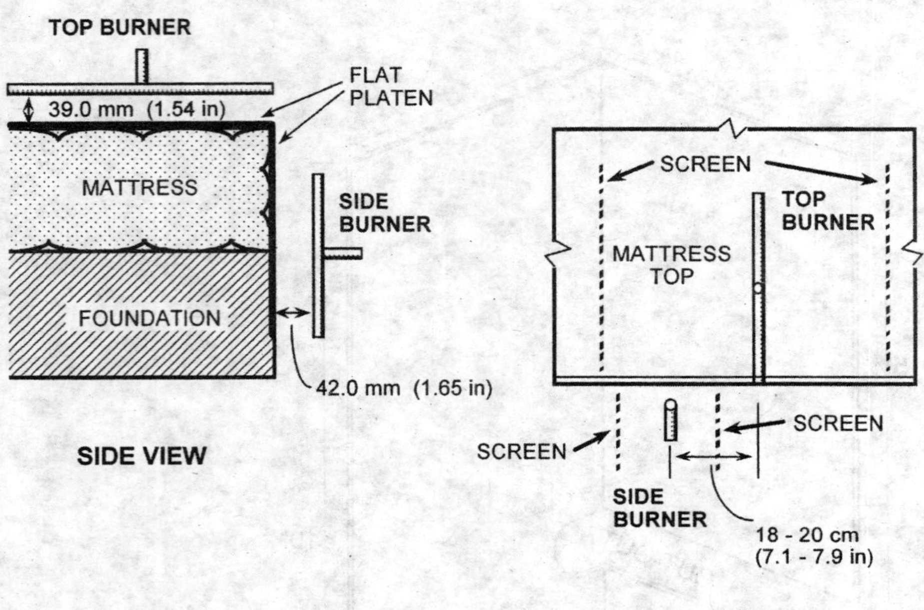

FIGURE 9. BURNER PLACEMENTS ON MATTRESS / FOUNDATION

FIGURE 10 TO PART 1633—JIG FOR SETTING BURNERS AT PROPER DISTANCES FROM MATTRESS/FOUNDATION

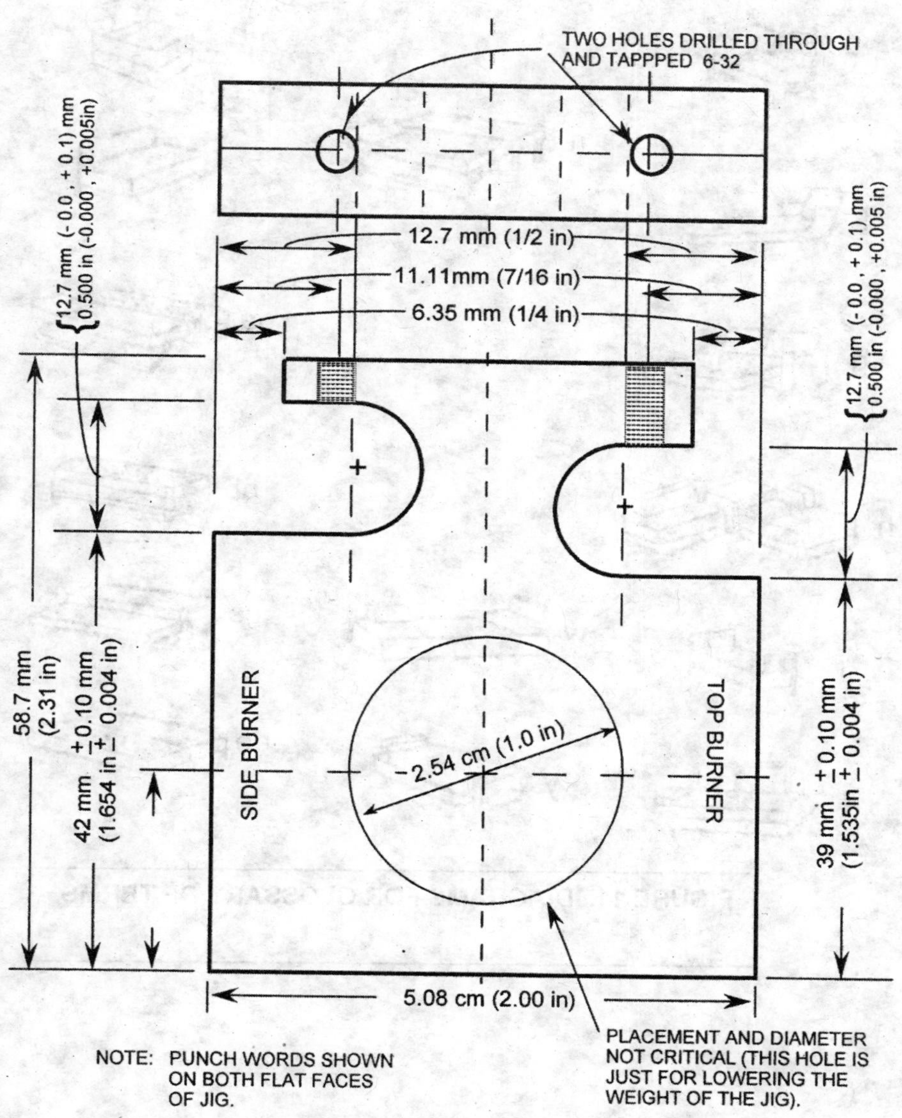

FIGURE 10. JIG FOR SETTING BURNERS AT PROPER DISTANCES FROM MATTRESS / FOUNDATION

FIGURE 11 TO PART 1633—DIAGRAMS FOR GLOSSARY OF TERMS

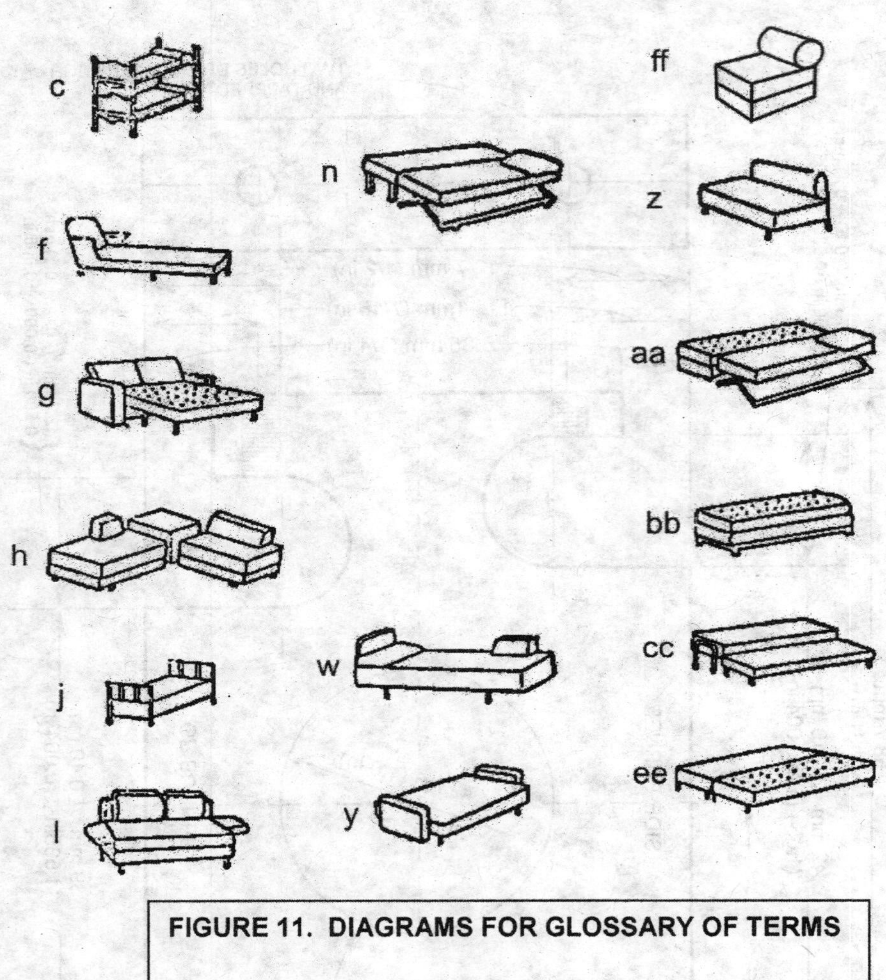

FIGURE 11. DIAGRAMS FOR GLOSSARY OF TERMS

FIGURE 12 TO PART 1633—LABELS FOR DOMESTIC MATTRESS WITH FOUNDATION

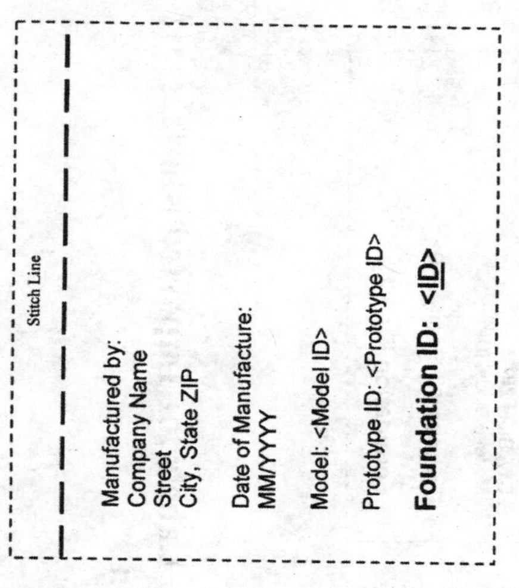

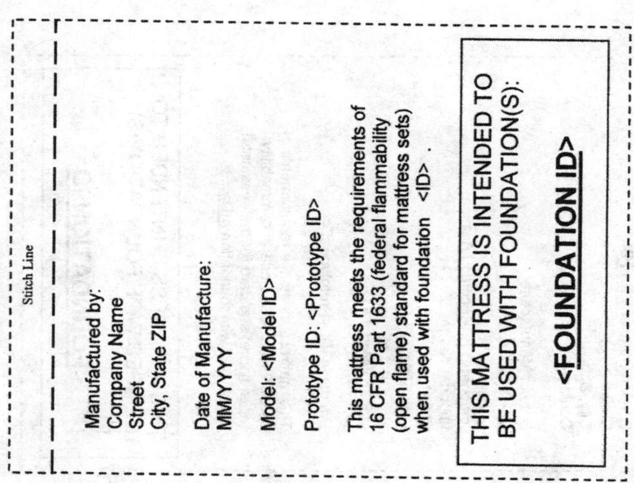

Figure 12. Labels for Domestic Mattress w/ Foundation

FIGURE 13 TO PART 1633—LABELS FOR IMPORTED MATTRESS WITH FOUNDATION

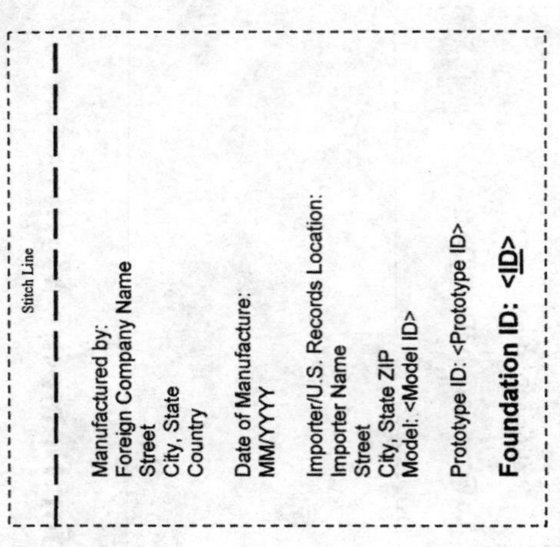

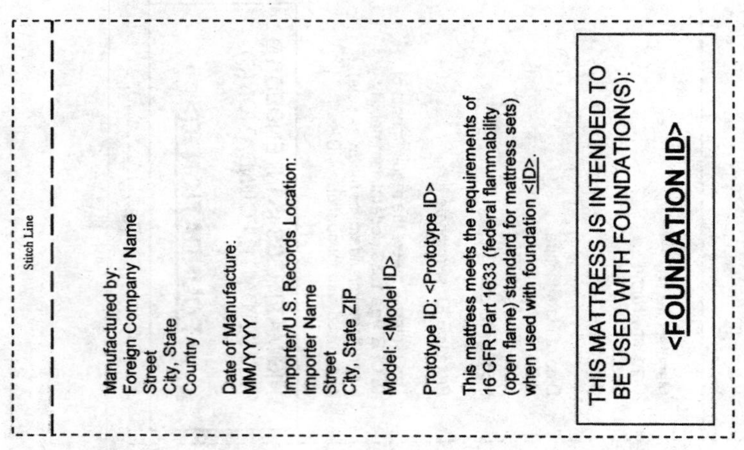

Figure 13. Labels for Imported Mattress w/ Foundation

FIGURES 14 AND 15 TO PART 1633—LABEL FOR DOMESTIC MATTRESS ALONE AND WITH FOUNDATION AND LABEL FOR IMPORTED MATTRESS ALONE AND WITH FOUNDATION

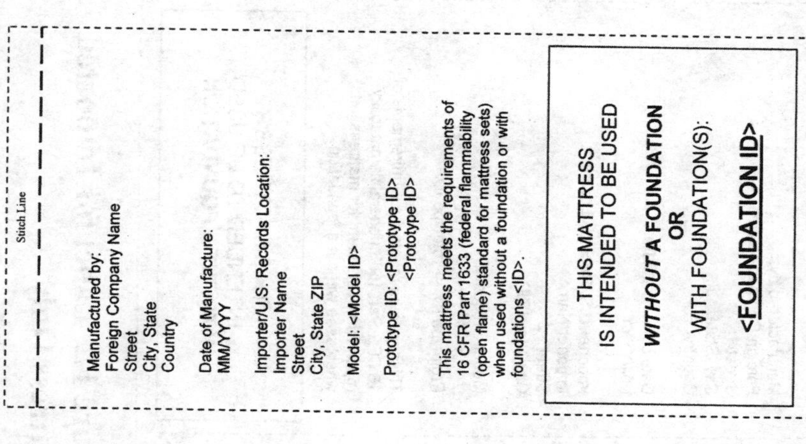

Figure 15. Label for Imported Mattress Alone and w/ Foundation

Stitch Line

Manufactured by:
Company Name
Street
City, State

Date of Manufacture:
MM/YYYY

Model: <Model ID>

Prototype ID: <Prototype ID>
<Prototype ID>

This mattress meets the requirements of 16 CFR Part 1633 (federal flammability (open flame) standard for mattress sets) when used without a foundation or with foundations <ID>.

THIS MATTRESS
IS INTENDED TO BE USED
WITHOUT **A FOUNDATION**
OR
WITH FOUNDATION(S):
<FOUNDATION ID>

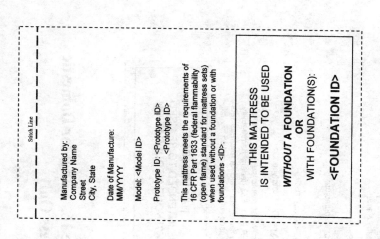

Figure 14. Label for Domestic Mattress Alone and w/ Foundation

FIGURES 16 AND 17 TO PART 1633—LABEL FOR DOMESTIC MATTRESS ONLY AND LABEL FOR IMPORTED MATTRESS ONLY

Stitch Line
Manufactured by:
Company Name
Street
City, State
Date of Manufacture:
MM/YYYY
Model: <Model ID>
Prototype ID: <Prototype ID>
This mattress meets the requirements of 16 CFR Part 1633 (federal flammability (open flame) standard for mattress sets) when used without a foundation.
THIS MATTRESS IS INTENDED TO BE USED *WITHOUT* A FOUNDATION

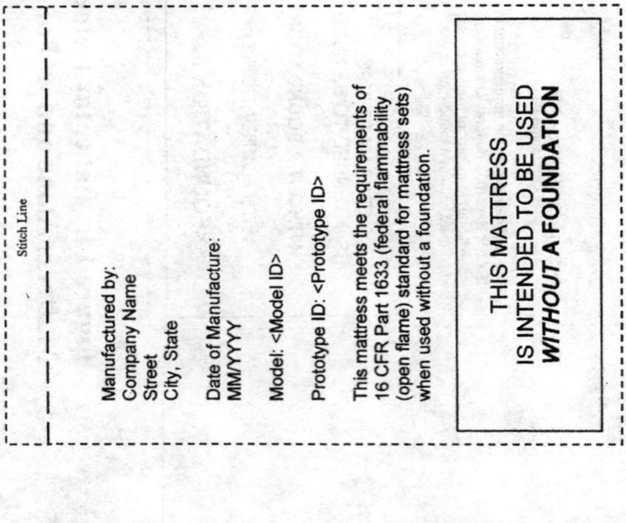

Figure 16. Label for Domestic Mattress Only

Stitch Line
Manufactured by:
Foreign Company Name
Street
City, State
Country
Date of Manufacture:
MM/YYYY
Importer/U.S. Records Location:
Importer Name
Street
City, State ZIP
Model: <Model ID>
Prototype ID: <Prototype ID>
This mattress meets the requirements of 16 CFR Part 1633 (federal flammability (open flame) standard for mattress sets) when used without a foundation.
THIS MATTRESS IS INTENDED TO BE USED *WITHOUT* A FOUNDATION

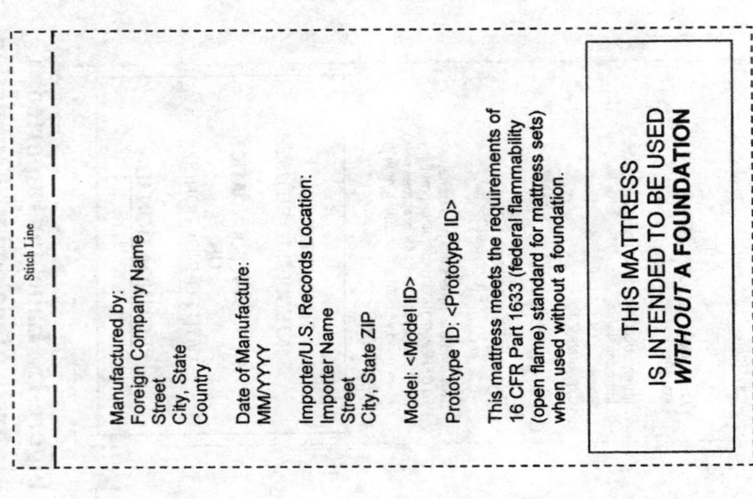

Figure 17. Label for Imported Mattress Only

SUBCHAPTER E—POISON PREVENTION PACKAGING ACT OF 1970 REGULATIONS

PART 1700—POISON PREVENTION PACKAGING

AUTHORITY: 15 U.S.C. 1471–76. Secs. 1700.1 and 1700.14 also issued under 15 U.S.C. 2079(a).

SOURCE: 38 FR 21247, Aug. 7, 1973, unless otherwise noted.

§ 1700.1 Definitions.

(a) As used in this part:

(1) *Act* means the Poison Prevention Packaging Act of 1970 (Pub. L. 91–601, 84 Stat. 1670–74; 15 U.S.C. 1471–75), enacted December 30, 1970.

(2) *Commission* means the Consumer Product Safety Commission established by section 4 of the Consumer Product Safety Act (86 Stat. 1210; 15 U.S.C. 2053).

(3) *Dietary supplement* means any vitamin and/or mineral preparation offered in tablet, capsule, wafer, or other similar uniform unit form; in powder, granule, flake, or liquid form; or in the physical form of a conventional food but which is not a conventional food; and which purports or is represented to be for special dietary use by humans to supplement their diets by increasing the total dietary intake of one or more of the essential vitamins and/or minerals.

(b) Except for the definition of "Secretary," which is obsolete, the definitions given in section 2 of the act are applicable to this part and are repeated herein for convenience as follows:

(1) [Reserved]

(2) *Household substance* means any substance which is customarily produced or distributed for sale for consumption or use, or customarily stored, by individuals in or about the household and which is:

(i) A hazardous substance as that term is defined in section 2(f) of the Federal Hazardous Substances Act (15 U.S.C. 1261(f));

(ii) A food, drug, or cosmetic as those terms are defined in section 201 of the Federal Food, Drug, and Cosmetic Act (21 U.S.C. 321); or

(iii) A substance intended for use as fuel when stored in a portable container and used in the heating, cooking, or refrigeration system of a house.

(3) *Package* means the immediate container or wrapping in which any household substance is contained for consumption, use, or storage by individuals in or about the household and, for purposes of section 4(a)(2) of the act, also means any outer container or wrapping used in the retail display of any such substance to consumers. "Package" does not include:

(i) Any shipping container or wrapping used solely for the transportation of any household substance in bulk or in quantity to manufacturers, packers, or processors, or to wholesale or retail distributors thereof; or

(ii) Any shipping container or outer wrapping used by retailers to ship or deliver any household substance to consumers unless it is the only such container or wrapping.

(4) *Special packaging* means packaging that is designed or constructed to be significantly difficult for children under 5 years of age to open or obtain a toxic or harmful amount of the substance contained therein within a reasonable time and not difficult for normal adults to use properly, but does not mean packaging which all such children cannot open or obtain a toxic or harmful amount within a reasonable time.

(5) *Labeling* means all labels and other written, printed, or graphic matter upon any household substance or

its package, or accompanying such substance.

(Pub. L. 92–573, sec. 30(a), 86 Stat. 1231; (15 U.S.C. 2079(a)))

[38 FR 21247, Aug. 7, 1973, as amended at 41 FR 22266, June 2, 1976; 48 FR 57480, Dec. 30, 1983]

§ 1700.2 Authority.

Authority under the Poison Prevention Packaging Act of 1970 is vested in the Consumer Product Safety Commission by section 30(a) of the Consumer Product Safety Act (15 U.S.C. 2079(a)).

§ 1700.3 Establishment of standards for special packaging.

(a) Pursuant to section 3 of the act, the Commission, after consultation with the technical advisory committee provided for by section 6 of the act, may establish by regulation standards for the special packaging of any household substance if the Commission finds:

(1) That the degree or nature of the hazard to children in the availability of such substance, by reason of its packaging, is such that special packaging is required to protect children from serious personal injury or serious illness resulting from handling, using, or ingesting such substance; and

(2) That the special packaging to be required by such standard is technically feasible, practicable, and appropriate for such substance.

(b) In establishing such a standard, the Commission shall consider:

(1) The reasonableness of such standard;

(2) Available scientific, medical, and engineering data concerning special packaging and concerning childhood accidental ingestions, illness, and injury caused by household substances;

(3) The manufacturing practices of industries affected by the act; and

(4) The nature and use of the household substance.

(c) In the process of establishing such a standard, the Commission shall publish its findings and reasons therefor and shall cite the sections of the act that authorize its action.

(d) In establishing such standards, the Commission shall not prescribe specific packaging designs, product content, package quantity, or labeling except for labeling under section 4(a)(2) of the act. Regarding a household substance for which special packaging is required by regulation, the Commission can prohibit the packaging of such substance in a package which the Commission determines is unnecessarily attractive to children.

(e) Promulgations pursuant to section 3 of the act shall be in accordance with section 5 of the act as to procedure.

§ 1700.4 Effective date of standards.

(a) The FR document promulgating a regulation establishing a child protection packaging standard shall indicate the standard's effective date. Section 9 of the act specifies that the effective date shall not be sooner than 180 days or later than 1 year from the date the standard is promulgated in the FEDERAL REGISTER unless the Commission, for good cause found, determines that an earlier effective date is in the public interest and publishes in the FEDERAL REGISTER the reason for such finding, in which case such earlier effective date shall apply.

(b) Upon becoming effective, a child protection packaging standard shall apply only to household substances packaged on and after its effective date.

§ 1700.5 Noncomplying package requirements.

To make household substances that are subject to requirements for special packaging readily available to elderly or handicapped persons who are unable to use those substances in special packaging, section 4(a) of the act authorizes manufacturers and packers to package such substances in noncomplying packaging of a single size provided that complying packaging is also supplied and the noncomplying packages are conspicuously labeled to indicate that they should not be used in households where young children are present. The purpose of this § 1700.5 is to implement section 4(a) of the act by prescribing requirements for the labeling of noncomplying packages.

(a) *Labeling statement.* (1) The statement "This Package for Households Without Young Children" shall appear conspicuously, and in accordance with all of the requirements of paragraph (a) of this section, on the package of any household substance subject to the special packaging requirements of this part 1700 that is supplied in noncomplying packaging under section 4(a) of the act, unless the package bears the substitute labeling statement in accordance with all of the requirements of paragraph (b) of this section.

(2) The statement required by paragraph (a)(1) of this section shall appear on the principal display panel of the immediate container as well as on the principal display panel of any outer container or wrapping used in the retail display of the substance. If a package bears more than one principal display panel, the required statement shall appear on each principal display panel of the immediate container as well as on each principal display panel of any outer container or wrapping used in the retail display of the substance. The principal display panel is the part of the labeling most likely to be displayed, presented, shown, or examined.

(3) The required labeling statement shall appear within the borderline of a square or rectangle on the principal display panel in conspicuous and easily legible capital letters, shall be in distinct contrast, by typography, layout, color, or embossing, to other matter on the package, and shall appear in lines generally parallel to the base on which the package rests as it is designed to be displayed.

(4) The declaration shall be in letters in type size established in relationship to the area of the principal display panel of the package and shall be uniform for all packages of substantially the same size by complying with the following type-size specifications:

(i) Not less than 1/16 inch in height on packages the principal display panel of which has an area of 7 square inches or less.

(ii) Not less than 3/32 inch in height on packages the principal display panel of which has an area of more than 7 but not more than 15 square inches.

(iii) Not less than 1/8 inch in height on packages the principal display panel of which has an area of more than 15 but not more than 25 square inches.

(iv) Not less than 3/16 inch in height on packages the principal display panel of which has an area of more than 25 but not more than 100 square inches.

(v) Not less than 1/4 inch in height on packages the principal display panel of which has an area of more than 100 square inches.

(5)(i) For the purpose of obtaining uniform type size for the required statement for all packages of substantially the same size, the area of the principal display panel is the area of the side or surface that bears the principal display panel, which shall be:

(A) In the case of a rectangular package where one entire side properly can be considered to be the principal display panel, the product of the height times the width of that side.

(B) In the case of a cylindrical or nearly cylindrical container, 40 percent of the product of the height of the container times the circumference.

(C) In the case of any other shape of container, 40 percent of the total surface of the container; however, if such container presents an obvious principal display (such as the top of a triangular or circular package), the area shall consist of the entire area of such obvious principal display panel.

(ii) In determining the area of the principal display panel exclude tops, bottoms, flanges at the tops and bottoms of cans, and shoulders and necks of bottles or jars. In the case of cylindrical or nearly cylindrical containers, the labeling statement required by this section to appear on the principal display panel shall appear within that 40 percent of the circumference most likely to be displayed, presented, shown, or examined.

(b) *Substitute labeling statement.* If the area of the principal display panel, as determined in accordance with paragraph (a)(5) of this section, is too small to accommodate the statement required by paragraph (a)(1) using the type size required by paragraph (a)(4), the substitute statement "Package Not Child-Resistant" may be used. This substitute statement must comply with all of the requirements for size, placement, and conspicuousness prescribed by paragraph (a) of this section.

[40 FR 4650, Jan. 31, 1975]

§ 1700.14 Substances requiring special packaging.

(a) *Substances.* The Commission has determined that the degree or nature of the hazard to children in the availability of the following substances, by reason of their packaging, is such that special packaging meeting the requirements of § 1700.20(a) is required to protect children from serious personal injury or serious illness resulting from handling, using, or ingesting such substances, and the special packaging herein required is technically feasible, practicable, and appropriate for these substances:

(1) *Aspirin.* Any aspirin-containing preparation for human use in a dosage form intended for oral administration shall be packaged in accordance with the provisions of § 1700.15 (a), (b), and (c), except the following:

(i) Effervescent tablets containing aspirin, other than those intended for pediatric use, provided the dry tablet contains not more than 15 percent aspirin and has an oral LD–50 in rats of 5 grams or more per kilogram of body weight.

(ii) Unflavored aspirin-containing preparations in powder form (other than those intended for pediatric use) that are packaged in unit doses providing not more than 15.4 grains of aspirin per unit dose and that contain no other substance subject to the provisions of this section.

(2) *Furniture polish.* Nonemulsion type liquid furniture polishes containing 10 percent or more of mineral seal oil and/or other petroleum distillates and having a viscosity of less than 100 Saybolt universal seconds at 100 °F., other than those packaged in pressurized spray containers, shall be packaged in accordance with the provisions of § 1700.15 (a), (b), and (d).

(3) *Methyl salicylate.* Liquid preparations containing more than 5 percent by weight of methyl salicylate, other than those packaged in pressurized spray containers, shall be packaged in accordance with the provisions of § 1700.15 (a), (b), and (c).

(4) *Controlled drugs.* Any preparation for human use that consists in whole or in part of any substance subject to control under the Comprehensive Drug Abuse Prevention and Control Act of 1970 (21 U.S.C. 801 et seq.) and that is in a dosage form intended for oral administration shall be packaged in accordance with the provisions of § 1700.15 (a), (b), and (c).

(5) *Sodium and/or potassium hydroxide.* Household substances in dry forms such as granules, powder, and flakes, containing 10 percent or more by weight of free or chemically unneutralized sodium and/or potassium hydroxide, and all other household substances containing 2 percent or more by weight of free or chemically unneutralized sodium and/or potassium hydroxide, shall be packaged in accordance with the provisions of § 1700.15 (a) and (b).

(6) *Turpentine.* Household substances in liquid form containing 10 percent or more by weight of turpentine shall be packaged in accordance with the provisions of § 1700.15 (a) and (b).

(7) *Kindling and/or illuminating preparations.* Prepackaged liquid kindling and/or illuminating preparations, such as cigarette lighter fuel, charcoal lighter fuel, camping equipment fuel, torch fuel, and fuel for decorative or functional lanterns, which contain 10 percent or more by weight of petroleum distillates and have a viscosity of less than 100 Saybolt universal seconds at 100 °F., shall be packaged in accordance with the provisions of § 1700.15 (a) and (b).

(8) *Methyl alcohol (methanol).* Household substances in liquid form containing 4 percent or more by weight of methyl alcohol (methanol), other than those packaged in pressurized spray containers, shall be packaged in accordance with the provisions of § 1700.15 (a) and (b).

(9) *Sulfuric acid.* Household substances containing 10 percent or more by weight of sulfuric acid, except such substances in wet-cell storage batteries, shall be packaged in accordance with the provisions of § 1700.15 (a) and (b).

(10) *Prescription drugs.* Any drug for human use that is in a dosage form intended for oral administration and that is required by Federal law to be dispensed only by or upon an oral or written prescription of a practitioner licensed by law to administer such drug shall be packaged in accordance with

the provisions of § 1700.15 (a), (b), and (c), except for the following:

(i) Sublingual dosage forms of nitroglycerin.

(ii) Sublingual and chewable forms of isosorbide dinitrate in dosage strengths of 10 milligrams or less.

(iii) Erythromycin ethylsuccinate granules for oral suspension and oral suspensions in packages containing not more than 8 grams of the equivalent of erythromycin.

(iv) Cyclically administered oral contraceptives in manufacturers' mnemonic (memory-aid) dispenser packages that rely solely upon the activity of one or more progestogen or estrogen substances.

(v) Anhydrous cholestyramine in powder form.

(vi) All unit dose forms of potassium supplements, including individually-wrapped effervescent tablets, unit dose vials of liquid potassium, and powdered potassium in unit-dose packets, containing not more than 50 milliequivalents of potassium per unit dose.

(vii) Sodium fluoride drug preparations including liquid and tablet forms, containing not more than 110 milligrams of sodium fluoride (the equivalent of 50 mg of elemental fluoride) per package or not more than a concentration of 0.5 percent elemental fluoride on a weight-to-volume basis for liquids or a weight-to-weight basis for non-liquids and containing no other substances subject to this § 1700.14(a)(10).

(viii) Betamethasone tablets packaged in manufacturers' dispenser packages, containing no more than 12.6 milligrams betamethasone.

(ix) Pancrelipase preparations in tablet, capsule, or powder form and containing no other substances subject to this § 1700.14(a)(10).

(x) Prednisone in tablet form, when dispensed in packages containing no more than 105 mg. of the drug, and containing no other substances subject to this § 1700.14(a)(10).

(xi)–(xii) [Reserved]

(xiii) Mebendazole in tablet form in packages containing not more than 600 mg. of the drug, and containing no other substance subject to the provisions of this section.

(xiv) Methylprednisolone in tablet form in packages containing not more than 84 mg of the drug and containing no other substance subject to the provisions of this section.

(xv) Colestipol in powder form in packages containing not more than 5 grams of the drug and containing no other substance subject to the provisions of this section.

(xvi) Erythromycin ethylsuccinate tablets in packages containing no more than the equivalent of 16 grams erythromycin.

(xvii) Conjugated Estrogens Tablets, U.S.P., when dispensed in mnemonic packages containing not more than 32.0 mg of the drug and containing no other substances subject to this § 1700.14(a)(10).

(xviii) Norethindrone Acetate Tablets, U.S.P., when dispensed in mnemonic packages containing not more than 50 mg of the drug and containing no other substances subject to this § 1700.14(a)(10).

(xix) Medroxyprogesterone acetate tablets.

(xx) Sacrosidase (sucrase) preparations in a solution of glycerol and water.

(xxi) Hormone Replacement Therapy Products that rely solely upon the activity of one or more progestogen or estrogen substances.

(xxii) Colesevelam hydrochloride in powder form in packages containing not more than 3.75 grams of the drug.

(xxiii) Sevelamer carbonate in powder form in packages containing not more than 2.4 grams of the drug.

(11) *Ethylene glycol.* Household substances in liquid form containing 10 percent or more by weight of ethylene glycol packaged on or after June 1, 1974, except those articles exempted by 16 CFR 1500.83, shall be packaged in accordance with the provisions of § 1700.15 (a) and (b).

(12) *Iron-containing drugs.* With the exception of: (i) Animal feeds used as vehicles for the administration of drugs, and (ii) those preparations in which iron is present solely as a colorant, noninjectable animal and human drugs providing iron for therapeutic or prophylactic purposes, and containing a total amount of elemental iron, from any source, in a single package, equivalent to 250 mg or more elemental iron in a concentration of 0.025

percent or more on a weight to volume basis for liquids and 0.025 percent or more on a weight to volume basis for liquids and 0.05 percent or more on a weight-to-weight basis for nonliquids (e.g., powders, granules, tablets, capsules, wafers, gels, viscous products, such as pastes and ointments, etc.) shall be packaged in accordance with the provisions of § 1700.15 (a), (b), and (c).

(13) *Dietary supplements containing iron.* Dietary supplements, as defined in § 1700.1(a)(3), that contain an equivalent of 250 mg or more of elemental iron, from any source, in a single package in concentrations of 0.025 percent or more on a weight-to-volume basis for liquids and 0.05 percent or more on a weight-to-weight basis for nonliquids (e.g., powders, granules, tablets, capsules, wafers, gels, viscous products, such as pastes and ointments, etc.) shall be packaged in accordance with the provisions of § 1700.15 (a), (b), and (c), except for the following:

(i) Preparations in which iron is present solely as a colorant; and

(ii) Powdered preparations with no more than the equivalent of 0.12 percent weight-to-weight elemental iron.

(14) [Reserved]

(15) *Solvents for paint or other similar surface-coating material.* Prepackaged liquid solvents (such as removers, thinners, brush cleaners, etc.) for paints or other similar surface-coating materials (such as varnishes and lacquers), that contain 10 percent or more by weight of benzene (also known as benzol), toluene (also known as toluol), xylene (also known as xylol), petroleum distillates (such as gasoline, kerosene, mineral seal oil, mineral spirits, naphtha, and Stoddard solvent, etc.), or combinations thereof, and that have a viscosity of less than 100 Saybolt universal seconds at 100 °F., shall be packaged in accordance with the provisions of § 1700.15 (a) and (b).

(16) *Acetaminophen.* Preparations for human use in a dosage form intended for oral administration and containing in a single package a total of more than one gram acetaminophen shall be packaged in accordance with the provisions of § 1700.15 (a), (b), and (c), except the following—

(i) Effervescent tablets or granules containing acetaminophen, provided the dry tablet or granules contain less than 15 percent acetaminophen, the tablet or granules have an oral LD–50 of 5 grams or greater per kilogram of body weight, and the tablet or granules contain no other substance subject to the provisions of this section.

(ii) Unflavored acetaminophen-containing preparations in powder form (other than those intended for pediatric use) that are packaged in unit doses providing not more than 13 grains of acetaminophen per unit dose and that contain no other substance subject to this § 1700.14(a).

(17) *Diphenhydramine.* Preparations for human use in a dosage form intended for oral administration and containing more than the equivalent of 66 mg diphenhydramine base in a single package shall be packaged in accordance with the provisions of § 1700.15 (a), (b), and (c), if packaged on or after February 11, 1985.

(18) *Glue removers containing acetonitrile.* Household glue removers in a liquid form containing more than 500 mg of acetonitrile in a single container.

(19) *Permanent wave neutralizers containing sodium bromate or potassium bromate.* Home permanent wave neutralizers, in a liquid form, containing in single container more than 600 mg of sodium bromate or more than 50 mg of potassium bromate.

(20) *Ibuprofen.* Ibuprofen preparations for human use in a dosage form intended for oral administration and containing one gram (1,000 mg) or more of ibuprofen in a single package shall be packaged in accordance with the provisions of § 1700.15 (a), (b), and (c).

(21) *Loperamide.* Preparations for human use in a dosage form intended for oral administration and containing more than 0.045 mg of loperamide in a single package (i.e., retail unit) shall be packaged in accordance with the provisions of § 1700.15 (a), (b), and (c).

(22) *Mouthwash.* Except as provided in the following sentence, mouthwash preparations for human use and containing 3 g or more of ethanol in a single package shall be packaged in accordance with the provisions of § 1700.15 (a), (b), and (c). Mouthwash products with nonremovable pump dispensers

that contain at least 7% on a weight-to-weight basis of mint or cinnamon flavoring oils, that dispense no more than 0.03 grams of absolute ethanol per pump actuation, and that contain less than 15 grams of ethanol in a single unit are exempt from this requirement. The term "mouthwash" includes liquid products that are variously called mouthwashes, mouthrinses, oral antiseptics, gargles, fluoride rinses, anti-plaque rinses, and breath fresheners. It does not include throat sprays or aerosol breath fresheners.

(23) *Lidocaine*. Products containing more than 5.0 mg of lidocaine in a single package (i.e., retail unit) shall be packaged in accordance with the provisions of § 1700.15 (a) and (b).

(24) *Dibucaine*. Products containing more than 0.5 mg of dibucaine in a single package (i.e., retail unit) shall be packaged in accordance with the provisions of § 1700.15 (a) and (b).

(25) *Naproxen*. Naproxen preparations for human use and containing the equivalent of 250 mg or more of naproxen in a single retail package shall be packaged in accordance with the provisions of § 1700.15 (a), (b), and (c).

(26) *Ketoprofen*. Ketoprofen preparations for human use and containing more than 50 mg of ketoprofen in a single retail package shall be packaged in accordance with the provisions of § 1700.15 (a), (b) and (c).

(27) *Fluoride*. Household substances containing more than the equivalent of 50 milligrams of elemental fluoride per package and more than the equivalent of 0.5 percent elemental fluoride on a weight-to-volume basis for liquids or a weight-to-weight basis for non-liquids shall be packaged in accordance with the provisions of § 1700.15(a), (b) and (c).

(28) *Minoxidil*. Minoxidil preparations for human use and containing more than 14 mg of minoxidil in a single retail package shall be packaged in accordance with the provisions of § 1700.15(a), (b) and (c). Any applicator packaged with the minoxidil preparation and which it is reasonable to expect may be used to replace the original closure shall also comply with the provisions of § 1700.15(a), (b) and (c).

(29)*Methacrylic acid*. Except as provided in the following sentence, liquid household products containing more than 5 percent methacrylic acid (weight-to-volume) in a single retail package shall be packaged in accordance with the provisions of § 1700.15(a),(b) and (c). Methacrylic acid products applied by an absorbent material contained inside a dispenser (such as a pen-like marker) are exempt from this requirement provided that: (i) the methacrylic acid is contained by the absorbent material so that no free liquid is within the device, and (ii) under any reasonably foreseeable conditions of use the methacrylic acid will emerge only through the tip of the device.

(30) *Over-the-Counter Drug Products*. (i) Any over-the-counter (OTC) drug product in a dosage form intended for oral administration that contains any active ingredient that was previously available for oral administration only by prescription, and thus was required by paragraph (a)(10) of this section to be in special packaging, shall be packaged in accordance with the provisions of § 1700.15(a),(b), and (c). This requirement applies whether or not the amount of that active ingredient in the OTC drug product is different from the amount of that active ingredient in the prescription drug product. This requirement does not apply if the OTC drug product contains only active ingredients of any oral drug product or products approved for OTC marketing based on an application for OTC marketing submitted to the Food and Drug Administration (FDA) by any entity before January 29, 2002. Notwithstanding the foregoing, any special packaging requirement under this § 1700.14 otherwise applicable to an OTC drug product remains in effect.

(ii) For purposes of this paragraph (30), *active ingredient* means any component that is intended to furnish pharmacological activity or other direct effect in the diagnosis, cure, mitigation, treatment, or prevention of disease or to affect the structure or any function of the body of humans; and *drug product* means a finished dosage form, for example, tablet, capsule, or solution, that contains a drug substance (active ingredient), generally, but not necessarily, in association with one or more other ingredients. (These terms are intended to have the meanings assigned to them in the regulations of the Food and Drug Administration appearing at 21 CFR 201.66 (2001) and 21 CFR 314.3 (2000), respectively.)

(31) *Hazardous substances containing low-viscosity hydrocarbons*. All prepackaged nonemulsion-type liquid household chemical products that are hazardous substances as defined in the Federal Hazardous Substances Act (FHSA) (15 U.S.C. 1261(f)), and that contain 10 percent or more hydrocarbons by weight and have a viscosity of less than 100 SUS at 100 °F, shall be packaged in accordance with the provisions of §1700.15(a), (b), and (c), except for the following:

(i) Products in packages in which the only non-child-resistant access to the contents is by a spray device (*e.g.*, aerosols, or pump-or trigger-actuated sprays where the pump or trigger mechanism has either a child-resistant or permanent attachment to the package).

(ii) Writing markers and ballpoint pens exempted from labeling requirements under the FHSA by 16 CFR 1500.83.

(iii) Products from which the liquid cannot flow freely, including but not limited to paint markers and battery terminal cleaners. For purposes of this requirement, hydrocarbons are defined as substances that consist solely of carbon and hydrogen. For products that contain multiple hydrocarbons, the total percentage of hydrocarbons in the product is the sum of the percentages by weight of the individual hydrocarbon components.

(32) *Drugs and cosmetics containing low-viscosity hydrocarbons*. All prepackaged nonemulsion-type liquid household chemical products that are drugs or cosmetics as defined in the Federal Food, Drug, and Cosmetics Act (FDCA) (21 U.S.C. 321(a)), and that contain 10 percent or more hydrocarbons by weight and have a viscosity of less than 100 SUS at 100 °F, shall be packaged in accordance with the provisions of §1700.15(a), (b), and (c), except for the following:

(i) Products in packages in which the only non-child-resistant access to the contents is by a spray device (*e.g.*, aerosols, or pump-or trigger-actuated sprays where the pump or trigger mechanism has either a child-resistant or permanent attachment to the package).

(ii) Products from which the liquid cannot flow freely, including but not limited to makeup removal pads. For the purposes of this requirement, hydrocarbons are defined as substances that consist solely of carbon and hydrogen. For products that contain multiple hydrocarbons, the total percentage of hydrocarbons in the product is the sum of the percentages by weight of the individual hydrocarbon components.

(b) *Sample packages*. (1) The manufacturer or packer of any of the substances listed under paragraph (a) of this section as substances requiring special packaging shall provide the Commission with a sample of each type of special packaging, as well as the labeling for each size product that will be packaged in special packaging and the labeling for any noncomplying package. Sample packages and labeling should be sent to the Consumer Product Safety Commission, Office of Compliance, 4330 East West Highway, Washington, DC 20207.

(2) Sample packages should be submitted without contents when such contents are unnecessary for demonstrating the effectiveness of the packaging.

(3) Any sample packages containing drugs listed under paragraph (a) of this section shall be sent by registered mail.

(4) As used in paragraph (b)(1) of this section, the term *manufacturer or packer* does not include pharmacists and other individuals who dispense, at the retail or user level, drugs listed under paragraph (a) of this section as requiring special packaging.

(c) *Applicability*. Special packaging standards for drugs listed under paragraph (a) of this section shall be in addition to any packaging requirements of the Federal Food, Drug, and Cosmetic Act or regulations promulgated thereunder or of any official compendia recognized by that act.

(Pub. L. 91–601, secs. 2(4), 3, 5, 85 Stat. 1670–72; 15 U.S.C. 1471(4), 1472, 1474; Pub. L. 92–573, 86 Stat. 1231; 15 U.S.C. 2079(a))

[38 FR 21247, Aug. 7, 1973]

EDITORIAL NOTE: For FEDERAL REGISTER citations affecting § 1700.14, see the List of CFR Sections Affected, which appears in the Finding Aids section of the printed volume and at *www.fdsys.gov*.

EFFECTIVE DATE NOTE: At 77 FR 73294, Dec. 10, 2012, § 1700.14 was amended by adding paragraph (a)(33), effective Dec. 10, 2013. For the convenience of the user, the added text is set forth as follows:

§ 1700.14 Substances requiring special packaging.

(a) * * *

(33) *Imidazolines.* Any over-the-counter or prescription product containing the equivalent of 0.08 milligrams or more of an imidazoline (tetrahydrozoline, naphazoline, oxymetazoline, or xylometazoline) in a single package, must be packaged in accordance with the provisions of § 1700.15(a), (b), and (c).

* * * * *

§ 1700.15 Poison prevention packaging standards.

To protect children from serious personal injury or serious illness resulting from handling, using, or ingesting household substances, the Commission has determined that packaging designed and constructed to meet the following standards shall be regarded as "special packaging" within the meaning of section 2(4) of the act. Specific application of these standards to substances requiring special packaging is in accordance with § 1700.14.

(a) *General requirements.* The special packaging must continue to function with the effectiveness specifications set forth in paragraph (b) of this section when in actual contact with the substance contained therein. This requirement may be satisfied by appropriate scientific evaluation of the compatibility of the substance with the special packaging to determine that the chemical and physical characteristics of the substance will not compromise or interfere with the proper functioning of the special packaging. The special packaging must also continue to function with the effectiveness specifications set forth in paragraph (b) of this section for the number of openings and closings customary for its size and contents. This requirement may be satisfied by appropriate technical evaluation based on physical wear and stress factors, force required for activation, and other such relevant factors which establish that, for the duration of normal use, the effectiveness specifications of the packaging would not be expected to lessen.

(b) *Effectiveness specifications.* Special packaging, tested by the method described in § 1700.20, shall meet the following specifications:

(1) Child-resistant effectiveness of not less than 85 percent without a demonstration and not less than 80 percent after a demonstration of the proper means of opening such special packaging. In the case of unit packaging, child-resistant effectiveness of not less than 80 percent.

(2) *Ease of adult opening*—(i) *Senior-adult test.* Except for products specified in paragraph (b)(2)(ii) of this section, special packaging shall have a senior adult use effectiveness (SAUE) of not less than 90% for the senior-adult panel test of § 1700.20(a)(3).

(ii) *Younger-adult test*—(A) *When applicable.* Products that must be in aerosol form and products that require metal containers, under the criteria specified below, shall have an effectiveness of not less than 90% for the younger-adult test of § 1700.20(a)(4). The senior-adult panel test of § 1700.20(a)(3) does not apply to these products. For the purposes of this paragraph, metal containers are those that have both a metal package and a recloseable metal closure, and aerosol products are self-contained pressurized products.

(B) *Determination of need for metal or aerosol container*—(*1*) *Criteria.* A product will be deemed to require metal containers or aerosol form only if:

(*i*) No other packaging type would comply with other state or Federal regulations,

(*ii*) No other packaging can reasonably be used for the product's intended application,

(*iii*) No other packaging or closure material would be compatible with the substance,

(*iv*) No other suitable packaging type would provide adequate shelf-life for the product's intended use, or

(*v*) Any other reason clearly demonstrates that such packaging is required.

(*2*) *Presumption.* In the absence of convincing evidence to the contrary, a product shall be presumed not to require a metal container if the product, or another product of identical composition, has previously been marketed in packaging using either a nonmetal package or a nonmetal closure.

(*3*) *Justification*. A manufacturer or packager of a product that is in a metal container or aerosol form that the manufacturer or packager contends is not required to comply with the SAUE requirements of §1700.20(a)(3) shall provide, if requested by the Commission's staff, a written explanation of why the product must have a metal container or be an aerosol. Manufacturers and packagers who wish to do so voluntarily may submit to the Commission's Office of Compliance a rationale for why their product must be in metal containers or be an aerosol. In such cases, the staff will reply to the manufacturer or packager, if requested, stating the staff's views on the adequacy of the rationale.

(c) *Reuse of special packaging*. Special packaging for substances subject to the provisions of this paragraph shall not be reused.

(d) *Restricted flow*. Special packaging subject to the provisions of this paragraph shall be special packaging from which the flow of liquid is so restricted that not more than 2 milliliters of the contents can be obtained when the inverted, opened container is taken or squeezed once or when the container is otherwise activated once.

(Secs. 2(4), 3, 5, 84 Stat. 1670–72; 15 U.S.C. 1471(4), 1472, 1474)

[38 FR 21247, Aug. 7, 1973, as amended at 60 FR 37734, July 21, 1995]

§ 1700.20 Testing procedure for special packaging.

(a) *Test protocols*—(1) *General requirements*—(i) *Requirements for packaging*. As specified in §1700.15(b), special packaging is required to meet the child test requirements and the applicable adult test requirements of this §1700.20.

(ii) *Condition of packages to be tested*—(A) *Tamper-resistant feature*. Any tamper-resistant feature of the package to be tested shall be removed prior to testing unless it is part of the package's child-resistant design. Where a package is supplied to the consumer in an outer package that is not part of the package's child-resistant design, one of the following situations applies:

(*1*) In the child test, the package is removed from the outer package, and the outer package is not given to the child.

(*2*) In both the adult tests, if the outer package bears instructions for how to open or properly resecure the package, the package shall be given to the test subject in the outer package. The time required to remove the package from the outer package is not counted in the times allowed for attempting to open and, if appropriate, reclose the package.

(*3*) In both the adult tests, if the outer package does not bear any instructions relevant to the test, the package will be removed from the outer package, and the outer package will not be given to the test subject.

(B) *Reclosable packages—adult tests*. In both the adult tests, reclosable packages, if assembled by the testing agency, shall be properly secured at least 72 hours prior to beginning the test to allow the materials (e.g., the closure liner) to "take a set." If assembled by the testing agency, torque-dependent closures shall be secured at the same on-torque as applied on the packaging line. Application torques must be recorded in the test report. All packages shall be handled so that no damage or jarring will occur during storage or transportation. The packages shall not be exposed to extreme conditions of heat or cold. The packages shall be tested at room temperature.

(2) *Child test*—(i) *Test subjects*—(A) *Selection criteria*. Use from 1 to 4 groups of 50 children, as required under the sequential testing criteria in table 1. No more than 20% of the children in each group shall be tested at or obtained from any given site. Each group of children shall be randomly selected as to age, subject to the limitations set forth below. Thirty percent of the children in each group shall be of age 42–44 months, 40% of the children in each group shall be of age 45–48 months, and 30% of the children in each group shall be of age 49–51 months. The children's ages in months shall be calculated as follows:

(*1*) Arrange the birth date and test date by the numerical designations for month, day, and year (e.g., test date: 8/3/1990; birth date: 6/23/1986).

(*2*) Subtract the month, day, and year numbers for the birth date from the respective numbers for the test date. This may result in negative numbers for the months or days. (e.g.,

$$\begin{array}{r} 8 / 03 / 1990 \\ -6 / 23 / 1986 \\ \hline 2 \; -20 \quad 4 \end{array}$$

(*3*) Multiply the difference in years by 12 to obtain the number of months in the difference in years, and add this value to the number of months that was obtained when the birth date was subtracted from the test date (i.e., 4 × 12 = 48; 48 + 2 = 50). This figure either will remain the same or be adjusted up or down by 1 month, depending on the number of days obtained in the subtraction of the birth date from the test date.

(*4*) If the number of days obtained by subtracting the days in the birth date from the days in the test date is +16 or more, 1 month is added to the number of months obtained above. If the number of days is −16 or less, subtract 1 month. If the number of days is between −15 and +15 inclusive, no change is made in the number of months. Thus, for the example given above, the number of days is −20, and the number of months is therefore 50 − 1 = 49 months.

(B) *Gender distribution*. The difference between the number of boys and the number of girls in each age range shall not exceed 10% of the number of children in that range. The children selected should have no obvious or overt physical or mental handicap. A parent or guardian of each child shall read and sign a consent form prior to the child's participation. (The Commission staff will not disregard the results of tests performed by other parties simply because informed consent for children is not obtained.)

(ii) *Test failures*. A test failure shall be any child who opens the special packaging or gains access to its contents. In the case of unit packaging, however, a test failure shall be any child who opens or gains access to the number of individual units which constitute the amount that may produce serious personal injury or serious illness, or a child who opens or gains access to more than 8 individual units, whichever number is lower, during the full 10 minutes of testing. The number of units that a child opens or gains access to is interpreted as the individual units from which the product has been or can be removed in whole or in part. The determination of the amount of a substance that may produce serious personal injury or serious illness shall be based on a 25-pound (11.4 kg) child. Manufacturers or packagers intending to use unit packaging for a substance requiring special packaging are requested to submit such toxicological data to the Commission's Office of Compliance.

(iii) *Sequential test*. The sequential test is initially conducted using 50 children, and, depending on the results, the criteria in table 1 determine whether the package is either child-resistant or not child-resistant or whether further testing is required. Further testing is required if the results are inconclusive and involves the use of one or more additional groups of 50 children each, up to a maximum of 200 children. No individual shall administer the test to more than 30% of the children tested in each group. Table 1 gives the acceptance (pass), continue testing, and rejection (fail) criteria to be used for the first 5 minutes and the full 10 minutes of the children's test. If the test continues past the initial 50-child panel, the package openings shown in table 1 are cumulative.

TABLE 1—NUMBER OF OPENINGS: ACCEPTANCE (PASS), CONTINUE TESTING, AND REJECTION (FAIL) CRITERIA FOR THE FIRST 5 MINUTES AND THE FULL 10 MINUTES OF THE CHILDREN'S PROTOCOL TEST

Test panel	Cumulative number of children	Package openings					
		First 5 minutes			Full 10 minutes		
		Pass	Continue	Fail	Pass	Continue	Fail
1	50	0–3	4–10	11+	0–5	6–14	15+
2	100	4–10	11–18	19+	6–15	16–24	25+
3	150	11–18	19–25	26+	16–25	26–34	35+
4	200	19–30	....	31+	26–40	....	41+

(iv) *Test procedures.* The children shall be divided into groups of two. The testing shall be done in a location that is familiar to the children, for example, their customary nursery school or regular kindergarten. No child shall test more than two special packages. When more than one special package is being tested, each package shall be of a different ASTM type and they shall be presented to the paired children in random order. This order shall be recorded. The children shall be tested by the procedure incorporated in the following test instructions:

STANDARDIZED CHILD TEST INSTRUCTIONS

1. Reclosable packages, if assembled by the testing agency, shall be properly secured at least 72 hours prior to the opening described in instruction number 3 to allow the materials (e.g., the closure liner) to "take a set." Application torques must be recorded in the test report.

2. All packages shall be handled so that no damage or jarring will occur during storage or transportation. The packages shall not be exposed to extreme conditions of heat or cold. The packages shall be tested at room temperature.

3. Reclosable packages shall be opened and properly resecured one time (or more if appropriate), by the testing agency or other adult prior to testing. The opening and resecuring shall not be done in the presence of the children. (In the adult-resecuring test, the tester must not open and resecure the package prior to the test.) If multiple openings/resecurings are to be used, each of four (4) testers shall open and properly resecure one fourth of the packages once and then shall open and properly resecure each package a second, third, fourth, through tenth (or other specified number) time, in the same sequence as the first opening and resecuring. The packages shall not be opened and resecured again prior to testing. The name of each tester and the package numbers that he/she opens and resecures shall be recorded and reported. It is not necessary for the testers to protocol test the packages that they opened and resecured.

4. The children shall have no overt physical or mental handicaps. No child with a permanent or temporary illness, injury, or handicap that would interfere with his/her effective participation shall be included in the test.

5. The testing shall take place in a well-lighted location that is familiar to the children and that is isolated from all distractions.

6. The tester, or another adult, shall escort a pair of children to the test area. The tester shall seat the two children so that there is no visual barrier between the children and the tester.

7. The tester shall talk to the children to make them feel at ease.

8. The children shall not be given the impression that they are in a race or contest. They are not to be told that the test is a game or that it is fun. They are not to be offered a reward.

9. The tester shall record all data prior to, or after, the test so that full attention can be on the children during the test period.

10. The tester shall use a stopwatch(s) or other timing devices to time the number of seconds it takes the child to open the package and to time the 5-minute test periods.

11. To begin the test, the tester shall hand the children identical packages and say, "PLEASE TRY TO OPEN THIS FOR ME."

12. If a child refuses to participate after the test has started, the tester shall reassure the child and gently encourage the child to try. If the child continues to refuse, the tester shall ask the child to hold the package in his/her lap until the other child is finished. This pair of children shall not be eliminated from the results unless the refusing child disrupts the participation of the other child.

13. Each child shall be given up to 5 minutes to open his/her package. The tester shall watch the children at all times during the test. The tester shall minimize conversation with the children as long as they continue to attempt to open their packages. The tester shall not discourage the children verbally or with facial expressions. If a child

gets frustrated or bored and stops trying to open his/her package, the tester shall reassure the child and gently encourage the child to keep trying (e.g., "please try to open the package").

14. The children shall be allowed freedom of movement to work on their packages as long as the tester can watch both children (e.g., they can stand up, get down on the floor, or bang or pry the package).

15. If a child is endangering himself or others at any time, the test shall be stopped and the pair of children eliminated from the final results.

16. The children shall be allowed to talk to each other about opening the packages and shall be allowed to watch each other try to open the packages.

17. A child shall not be allowed to try to open the other child's package.

18. If a child opens his/her package, the tester shall say, "THANK YOU," take the package from the child and put it out of the child's reach. The child shall not be asked to open the package a second time.

19. At the end of the 5-minute period, the tester shall demonstrate how to open the package if either child has not opened his or her package. A separate "demo" package shall be used for the demonstration.

20. Prior to beginning the demonstration, the tester shall ask the children to set their packages aside. The children shall not be allowed to continue to try to open their packages during the demonstration period.

21. The tester shall say, "WATCH ME OPEN MY PACKAGE."

22. Once the tester gets the children's full attention, the tester shall hold the demo package approximately two feet from the children and open the package at a normal speed as if the tester were going to use the contents. There shall be no exaggerated opening movements.

23. The tester shall not discuss or describe how to open the package.

24. To begin the second 5-minute period, the tester shall say, "NOW YOU TRY TO OPEN YOUR PACKAGES."

25. If one or both children have not used their teeth to try to open their packages during the first 5 minutes, the tester shall say immediately before beginning the second 5-minute period, "YOU CAN USE YOUR TEETH IF YOU WANT TO." This is the only statement that the tester shall make about using teeth.

26. The test shall continue for an additional 5 minutes or until both children have opened their packages, whichever comes first.

27. At the end of the test period, the tester shall say, "THANK YOU FOR HELPING." If children were told that they could use their teeth, the tester shall say, "I KNOW I TOLD YOU THAT YOU COULD USE YOUR TEETH TODAY, BUT YOU SHOULD NOT PUT THINGS LIKE THIS IN YOUR MOUTH AGAIN" In addition, the tester shall say, "NEVER OPEN PACKAGES LIKE THIS WHEN YOU ARE BY YOURSELF. THIS KIND OF PACKAGE MIGHT HAVE SOMETHING IN IT THAT WOULD MAKE YOU SICK."

28. The children shall be escorted back to their classroom or other supervised area by the tester or another adult.

29. If the children are to participate in a second test, the tester shall have them stand up and stretch for a short time before beginning the second test. The tester shall take care that the children do not disrupt other tests in progress.

(3) *Senior-adult panel*—(i) *Test subjects.* Use a group of 100 senior adults. Not more than 24% of the senior adults tested shall be obtained from or tested at any one site. Each group of senior adults shall be randomly selected as to age, subject to the limitations set forth below. Twenty-five percent of the participants shall be 50–54 years of age, 25% of participants shall be 55–59 years of age, and 50% of the participants shall be 60–70 years old. Seventy percent of the participants of ages 50–59 and ages 60–70 shall be female (17 or 18 females shall be apportioned to the 50–54 year age group). No individual tester shall administer the test to more than 35% of the senior adults tested. The adults selected should have no obvious or overt physical or mental disability.

(ii) *Screening procedures.* Participants who are unable to open the packaging being tested in the first 5-minute time period, are given a screening test. The screening tests for this purpose shall use two packages with conventional (not child-resistant (CR) or "special") closures. One closure shall be a plastic snap closure and the other a CT plastic closure. Each closure shall have a diameter of 28 mm±18%, and the CT closures shall have been resecured 72 hours before testing at 10 inch-pounds of torque. The containers for both the snap- and CT-type closures shall be round plastic containers, in sizes of 2 ounce±½ ounce for the CT-type closure and 8 drams±4 drams for the snap-type closure. Persons who cannot open and close both of the screening packages in 1-minute screening tests shall not be counted as participants in the senior-adult panel.

(iii) *SAUE.* The senior adult use effectiveness (SAUE) is the percentage of adults who both opened the package in the first (5-minute) test period and opened and (if appropriate) properly resecured the package in the 1-minute test period.

(iv) *Test procedures.* The senior adults shall be tested individually, rather than in groups of two or more. The senior adults shall receive only such printed instructions on how to open and properly secure the special packaging as will appear on or accompany the package as it is delivered to the consumer. The senior-adult panel is tested according to the procedure incorporated in the following senior-adult panel test instructions:

TEST INSTRUCTIONS FOR SENIOR TEST

The following test instructions are used for all senior tests. If non-reclosable packages are being tested, the commands to close the package are eliminated.

1. No adult with a permanent or temporary illness, injury, or disability that would interfere with his/her effective participation shall be included in the test.

2. Each adult shall read and sign a consent form prior to participating. Any appropriate language from the consent form may be used to recruit potential participants. The form shall include the basic elements of informed consent as defined in 16 CFR 1028.116. Examples of the forms used by the Commission staff for testing are shown at §1700.20(d). Before beginning the test, the tester shall say, "PLEASE READ AND SIGN THIS CONSENT FORM." If an adult cannot read the consent form for any reason (forgot glasses, illiterate, etc.), he/she shall not participate in the test.

3. Each adult shall participate individually and not in the presence of other participants or onlookers.

4. The tests shall be conducted in well-lighted and distraction-free areas.

5. Records shall be filled in before or after the test, so that the tester's full attention is on the participant during the test period. Recording the test times to open and resecure the package are the only exceptions.

6. To begin the first 5-minute test period, the tester says, "I AM GOING TO ASK YOU TO OPEN AND PROPERLY CLOSE THESE TWO IDENTICAL PACKAGES ACCORDING TO THE INSTRUCTIONS FOUND ON THE CAP." (Specify other instruction locations if appropriate.)

7. The first package is handed to the participant by the tester, who says, "PLEASE OPEN THIS PACKAGE ACCORDING TO THE INSTRUCTIONS ON THE CAP." (Specify other instruction locations if appropriate.) If the package contains product, the tester shall say, "PLEASE EMPTY THE (PILLS, TABLETS, CONTENTS, etc.) INTO THIS CONTAINER." After the participant opens the package, the tester says, "PLEASE CLOSE THE PACKAGE PROPERLY, ACCORDING TO THE INSTRUCTIONS ON THE CAP." (Specify other instruction locations if appropriate)

8. Participants are allowed up to 5 minutes to read the instructions and open and close the package. The tester uses a stopwatch(s) or other timing device to time the opening and resecuring times. The elapsed times in seconds to open the package and to close the package are recorded on the data sheet as two separate times.

9. After 5 minutes, or when the participant has opened and closed the package, whichever comes first, the tester shall take all test materials from the participant. The participant may remove and replace the closure more than once if the participant initiates these actions. If the participant does not open the package and stops trying to open it before the end of the 5-minute period, the tester shall say, "ARE YOU FINISHED WITH THAT PACKAGE, OR WOULD YOU LIKE TO TRY AGAIN?" If the participant indicates that he/she is finished or cannot open the package and does not wish to continue trying, skip to Instruction 13.

10. To begin the second test period, the tester shall give the participant another, but identical, package and say, "THIS IS AN IDENTICAL PACKAGE. PLEASE OPEN IT ACCORDING TO THE INSTRUCTIONS ON THE CAP." (Specify other instruction locations if appropriate.) If the package contains product, the tester shall say, "PLEASE EMPTY THE (PILLS, TABLETS, CONTENTS, etc.) INTO THIS CONTAINER." After the participant opens the package, the tester says, "PLEASE CLOSE THE PACKAGE PROPERLY, ACCORDING TO THE INSTRUCTIONS ON THE CAP." (Specify other instruction locations if appropriate.)

11. The participants are allowed up to 1 minute (60 full seconds) to open and close the package. The elapsed times in seconds to open and to close the package are recorded on the data sheet as two separate times. The time that elapses between the opening of the package and the end of the instruction to close the package is not counted as part of the 1-minute test time.

12. After the 1-minute test, or when the participant has opened and finished closing the package, whichever comes first, the tester shall take all the test materials from the participant. The participant shall not be allowed to handle the package again. If the participant does not open the package and stops trying to open it before the end of the 1-minute period, the tester shall say, "ARE YOU FINISHED WITH THAT PACKAGE, OR WOULD YOU LIKE TO TRY AGAIN?" If the participant indicates that he/she is finished

or cannot open the package and does not wish to continue trying, this shall be counted as a failure of the 1-minute test.

13. Participants who do not open the package in the first 5-minute test period are asked to open and close two non-child-resistant screening packages. The participants are given a 1-minute test period for each package. The tester shall give the participant a package and say, "PLEASE OPEN AND PROPERLY CLOSE THIS PACKAGE." The tester records the time for opening and closing, or 61 seconds, whichever is less, on the data sheet. The tester then gives the participant the second package and says, "PLEASE OPEN AND PROPERLY CLOSE THIS PACKAGE." The time to open and resecure, or 61 seconds, whichever is less, shall be recorded on the data sheet.

14. Participants who cannot open and resecure both of the non-child-resistant screening packages are not counted as part of the 100-seniors panel. Additional participants are selected and tested.

15. No adult may participate in more than two tests per sitting. If a person participates in two tests, the packages tested shall not be the same ASTM type of package.

16. If more adults in a sex or age group are tested than are necessary to determine SAUE, the last person(s) tested shall be eliminated from that group.

(4) *Younger-adult panel.* (i) One hundred adults, age 18 to 45 inclusive, with no overt physical or mental handicaps, and 70% of whom are female, shall comprise the test panel for younger adults. Not more than 35% of adults shall be obtained or tested at any one site. No individual tester shall administer the test to more than 35% of the adults tested. The adults shall be tested individually, rather than in groups of two or more. The adults shall receive only such printed instructions on how to open and properly resecure the special packaging as will appear on the package as it is delivered to the consumer. Five minutes shall be allowed to complete the opening and, if appropriate, the resecuring process.

(ii) Records shall be kept of the number of adults unable to open and of the number of the other adults tested who fail to properly resecure the special packaging. The number of adults who successfully open the special packaging and then properly resecure the special packaging (if resecuring is appropriate) is the percent of adult-use effectiveness of the special packaging. In the case of unit packaging, the percent of adult-use effectiveness shall be the number of adults who successfully open a single (unit) package.

(b) The standards published as regulations issued for the purpose of designating particular substances as being subject to the requirements for special packaging under the act will stipulate the percent of child-resistant effectiveness and adult-use effectiveness required for each and, where appropriate, will include any other conditions deemed necessary and provided for in the act.

(c) It is recommended that manufacturers of special packaging, or producers of substances subject to regulations issued pursuant to the act, submit to the Commission summaries of data resulting from tests conducted in accordance with this protocol.

(d) *Recommendations.* The following instructions and procedures, while not required, are used by the Commission's staff and are recommended for use where appropriate.

(1) *Report format for child test.*

A. IDENTIFICATION

1. Close-up color photographs(s) clearly identifying the package and showing the opening instructions on the closure.

2. Product name and the number of tablets or capsules in the package.

3. Product manufacturer.

4. Closure model (trade name—e.g., "KLIK & SNAP").

5. Closure size (e.g., 28 mm).

6. Closure manufacturer.

7. Closure material and color(s) (e.g., white polypropylene).

8. Closure liner material.

9. TAC seal material.

10. Opening instructions (quote exactly, e.g., "WHILE PUSHING, DOWN, TURN RIGHT"). Commas are used to separate words that are on different lines.

11. Symbols, numbers, and letters found inside the closure.

12. Package model.

13. Package material and color.

14. Net contents.

15. Symbols, numbers, and letters on the bottom of the package.

16. Other product identification, e.g., EPA Registration Number.

B. PROCEDURES

1. Describe all procedures for preparing the test packages.

2. Describe the testing procedures.

3. Describe all instructions given to the children.

4. Define an individual package failure.

C. RESULTS

1. Openings in each 5-minute period and total openings for males and for females in each age group.
2. Opening methods (e.g., normal opening, teeth, etc.).
3. Mean opening times and standard deviation for each 5-minute test period.
4. The percentage of packages tested at each site as a percentage of total packages.
5. The percentage of packages tested by each tester as a percentage of total packages.
6. Child-resistant effectiveness for the first 5-minute period and for the total test period.

(2) *Standardized adult-resecuring test instructions.* CPSC will use the adult-resecuring test where an objective determination (e.g., visual or mechanical) that a package is properly resecured cannot be made. The adult-resecuring test is performed as follows:

ADULT-RESECURING PROCEDURE

1. After the adult participant in either the senior-adult test of 16 CFR 1700.20(a)(3) or the younger-adult test of 16 CFR 1700.20(a)(4) has resecured the package, or at the end of the test period (whichever comes first), the tester shall take the package and place it out of reach. The adult participant shall not be allowed to handle the package again.
2. The packages that have been opened and appear to be resecured by adults shall be tested by children according to the child-test procedures to determine if the packages have been properly resecured. The packages are given to the children without being opened or resecured again for any purpose.
3. Using the results of the adult tests and the tests of apparently-resecured packaging by children, the adult use effectiveness is calculated as follows:

a. *Adult use effectiveness.*

1. The number of adult opening and resecuring failures, plus the number of packages that were opened by the children during the full 10-minute test that exceeds 20% of the apparently-resecured packages, equals the total number of failures.
2. The total number of packages tested by adults (which is 100) minus the total number of failures equals the percent adult-use effectiveness.

(3) *Report format for adult-resecuring test.*

A. IDENTIFICATION

1. Close-up color photograph(s) clearly identifying the package and showing the top of the closure.
2. Product name and the number of tablets or capsules in the package.
3. Product manufacturer.
4. Closure model (trade name).
5. Closure size (e.g., 28 mm).
6. Closure manufacturer.
7. Closure material and color(s) (e.g., white polypropylene)
8. Closure liner material.
9. Symbols, numbers, and letters found inside the closure.
10. TAC seal material.
11. Opening instructions (Quote exactly, e.g., "WHILE PUSHING, DOWN, TURN RIGHT"). Commas are used to separate words that are on different lines.
12. Package model.
13. Package material and color.
14. Net contents.
15. Symbols, numbers, and letters on the bottom of the package.
16. Other product identification, e.g., EPA Registration Number.

B. PROCEDURES

1. Describe all procedures for preparing the test packages.
2. Describe the testing procedures in detail.
3. Describe all instructions given to participants.
4. Define an individual package failure and the procedures for determining a failure.

C. RESULTS

ADULT TEST

1. Total packages opened and total packages resecured; packages opened by males and by females; and packages resecured by males and by females.
2. Mean opening times and standard deviation for total openings, total openings by females, and total openings by males.
3. Mean resecuring times and standard deviation for total resecurings, total resecurings by females and total resecurings by males.
4. The percentage of packages tested at each site as a percentage of total packages.
5. The percentage of packages tested by each tester as a percentage of total packages.
6. Methods of opening (e.g., normal opening, pried closure off, etc.)

CHILD TEST

1. Openings in each 5-minute period, and total openings, for males and females in each age group.
2. Opening methods.
3. Mean opening times and standard deviation for each 5-minute test period.
4. The percentage of packages tested at each site as a percentage of total packages.
5. The percentage of packages tested by each tester as a percentage of total packages.

(4) Consent forms. The Commission uses the following consent forms for senior-adult testing reclosable and unit-dose packaging, respectively.

1. *Reclosable packages.*

[Testing Organization's Letterhead]

CHILD-RESISTANT PACKAGE TESTING

The U.S. Consumer Product Safety Commission is responsible for testing child-resistant packages to make sure they protect young children from medicines and dangerous household products. With the help of people like you, manufacturers are able to improve the packages we use, keeping the contents safe from children but easier for the rest of us to open.

Effective child-resistant packages have prevented thousands of poisonings since the Poison Prevention Act was passed in 1970. The use of child-resistant packages on prescription medicines alone may have saved the lives of over 350 children since 1974.

As part of this program, we are testing a child-resistant package to determine if it can be opened and properly closed by an adult who is between 50 and 70 years of age. You may or may not be familiar with the packages we are testing. Take your time, and please do not feel that you are being tested—we are testing the package, not you.

Description of the Test

1. I will give you a package and ask you to read the instructions and open and properly close the package.
2. I will then give you an identical package, and ask you to open and properly close it.
3. I may ask you to open some other types of packages.
4. The packages may be empty or they may contain a product.
5. I will ask you whether you think the child-resistant package was easy or hard to use.

CONSENT FORM FOR CHILD-RESISTANT PACKAGE TESTING

The Consumer Product Safety Commission has been using contractors to test child-resistant packages for many years with no injuries to anyone, although it is possible that a minor injury could happen.

I agree to test a child-resistant package. I understand that I can change my mind at any time. I am between the ages of 50 and 70, inclusive.

Birthdate ____________
Signature ____________
Date ____________
Zip Code ____________

Office Use

Site: ____________
Sample Number: ____________
Test Number: ____________
Package Number: ____________

2. *Unit-dose packages.*

[Testing Organization's Letterhead]

UNIT DOSE CHILD-RESISTANT PACKAGE TESTING

The U.S. Consumer Product Safety Commission is responsible for testing child-resistant packages to make sure they protect young children from medicines and dangerous household products. With the help of people like you, manufacturers are able to improve the packages we use, keeping the contents safe from children but easier for the rest of us to open.

Effective child-resistant packages have prevented thousands of poisonings since the Poison Prevention Act was passed in 1970.

The use of child-resistant packages on prescription medicines alone may have saved the lives of over 350 children since 1974.

As part of this program, we are testing a child-resistant package to determine if it can be opened by an adult who is between 50 and 70 years of age. You may or may not be familiar with the packages we are testing. Take your time, and please do not feel that you are being tested—we are testing the package, not you.

Description of the Test

1. I will give you a package and ask you to read the instructions, open one unit, and remove the contents.
2. I will then give you an identical package, and ask you to open one unit and remove the contents.
3. I may ask you to open some other types of packages.
4. I will ask you whether you think the child-resistant package was easy or hard to use.

CONSENT FORM FOR CHILD-RESISTANT PACKAGE TESTING

The Consumer Product Safety Commission has been using contractors to test child-resistant packages for many years with no injuries to anyone, although it is possible that a minor injury could happen.

I agree to test a child-resistant package. I understand that I can change my mind at any time. I am between the ages of 50 and 70, inclusive.

Birthdate ____________
Signature ____________
Date ____________
Zip Code ____________

Office Use

Site: ____________
Sample Number: ____________
Test Number: ____________
Package Number: ____________

[38 FR 21247, Aug. 7, 1973, as amended at 60 FR 37735, 37738, July 22, 1995]

PART 1701—STATEMENTS OF POLICY AND INTERPRETATION

§ 1701.1 Special packaging for substances subject to a standard that are distributed to pharmacies to be dispensed pursuant to an order of a licensed medical practitioner.

(a) In order to assist manufacturers of prescription drugs in discharging their responsibilities under the act concerning such drugs that are distributed to pharmacies, the Consumer Product Safety Commission has codified this statement of its policy concerning which prescription drug packages supplied by manufacturers to pharmacies must comply with the "special" (child-resistant) packaging requirements contained in 16 CFR 1700.15.

(b) Manufacturers of prescription drugs may package such drugs for distribution to pharmacies in different types of packages, depending on whether the manufacturer intends that the package will be the one in which the drug is ultimately given to the consumer or whether it is intended that the pharmacist will repackage the drug before it is dispensed to the consumer. If the drug is supplied in a bulk package from which individual prescriptions are intended to be repackaged by the pharmacist, the manufacturer need not utilize special packaging. However, the Commission interprets the provision of the act as requiring that all prescription drugs subject to a special packaging standard that are distributed to pharmacies shall be in special packaging if the immediate package in which the drugs are distributed by the manufacturer is intended to be the package in which the drugs are dispensed to the consumer. Examples of such packages include mnemonic dispensing devices; dropper bottles; packages with "tear off" labels; packages which incorporate ancillary instructions for consumer handling, storage, or use on permanently affixed portions of their labels; and products intended to be reconstituted in their original containers. The Commission believes that this interpretation is necessary in order to insure that the pharmacist will actually dispense the drug in the proper package. If the pharmacist receives a request from the consumer or an order from the prescribing medical practitioner for conventional (noncomplying) packaging, section 4(b) of the act permits the pharmacist to convert the package to conventional packaging or repackage the drug in conventional packaging.

(c) Manufacturers should also note that section 4(a) of the act (which allows a product to be marketed in noncomplying packaging of a single size under certain circumstances) does not apply to prescription drugs subject to section 4(b) of the act. Thus, since the section 4(a) single-size exemption for over-the-counter drugs and other household substances does not apply to prescription drugs, every unit of a prescription drug subject to a special packaging standard which is distributed to a pharmacy in a package intended by the manufacturer to be dispensed to a consumer shall be in special packaging.

(d) Nothing in this statement of policy and interpretation should be interpreted as relieving the pharmacist of the responsibility of insuring that all prescription drugs subject to a special packaging standard are dispensed to the consumer in special packaging unless otherwise ordered by the prescribing practitioner or otherwise requested by the consumer.

(Secs. 2–4, Pub. L. 91–601, 84 Stat. 1670, 1671 (15 U.S.C. 1471–1473); sec. 701(a), 52 Stat. 1055 (21 U.S.C. 371(a)))

[43 FR 11980 Mar. 23, 1978]

§ 1701.3 Applicability of special packaging requirements to hazardous substances in large size containers.

The special packaging requirements of the PPPA apply to "household substances" for which the Commission has determined there is a need for special packaging, as provided in section 3 of the act (15 U.S.C. 1472). At section 2(2) of the act (15 U.S.C. 1471) (restated at 16

CFR 1700.1(b)(2)), the term *household substance* is defined as "any substance which is customarily produced or distributed for sale for consumption or use, or customarily stored, by individuals in or about the household * * *." The Commission has issued requirements for special packaging for certain hazardous substances at 16 CFR 1700.14(a). Unless otherwise indicated in the requirements for specific hazardous substances, the Commission interprets the term "household substance" as only applying to these hazardous substances when packaged in containers with a capacity of less than 5 gallons. As a result, unless otherwise specified, the hazardous substances at 16 CFR 1700.14(a) are not required to be in special packaging when packaged in containers of 5 gallons or more.

(Secs. 2, 5, 7, 9, Pub. L. 91–601; 94 Stat. 1670–1674 (15 U.S.C. 1471, 1474, 1476, 1478); sec. 30(a), Pub. L. 92–573, 86 Stat. 1231 (15 U.S.C. 2079(a)) [43 FR 53712, Nov. 17, 1978]

PART 1702—PETITIONS FOR EXEMPTIONS FROM POISON PREVENTION PACKAGING ACT REQUIREMENTS; PETITION PROCEDURES AND REQUIREMENTS

Sec.

AUTHORITY: 15 U.S.C. 1471(4), 1472, 1474, 1269(a), 2079(a); 21 U.S.C. 371(a).

SOURCE: 45 FR 13064, Feb. 28, 1980, unless otherwise noted.

§ 1702.1 Purpose and policy.

(a) Section 1700.14(a) of part 1700 lists household substances the Consumer Product Safety Commission requires, under section 3(a)(1) of the Poison Prevention Packaging Act of 1970, 15 U.S.C. 1472, to be contained in special packaging to protect children from serious personal injury or serious illness resulting from handling, using, or ingesting such substances. There may be occasions, however, when the Commission determines that a particular substance should be exempt from special packaging requirements.

(b) The Commission may, either on its own initiative or upon the petition of any interested person, amend the regulation at § 1700.14(a) by exempting a substance or category of substances from special packaging requirements. The purpose of these rules is to provide procedures and requirements for submitting petitions for exemption from special packaging requirements.

§ 1702.2 Procedural requirements and recommendations.

(a) *Requirements.* To be considered a petition for exemption from special packaging requirements under this part a document filed under this part must:

(1) Be mailed to the Office of the Secretary, Consumer Product Safety Commission, Washington, D.C. 20207, or delivered to the Office of the Secretary, Consumer Product Safety Commission, 4330 East West Highway, Bethesda, MD 20814,

(2) Be written in the English language,

(3) Contain the name and address of the petitioner,

(4) Contain an explicit request for exemption from special packaging requirements,

(5) Identify the category of substances under § 1700.14(a) from which the exemption is sought, and

(6) Identify the particular substance for which the exemption is sought.

(b) *Failure to meet requirements.* Where a submission fails to meet all of the requirements of paragraph (a) of this section, the Office of the Secretary shall notify the person submitting it, describe the deficiency, and explain that the petition may be resubmitted when the deficiency is corrected.

(c) *Procedural recommendations.* The following are procedural recommendations to help the Commission in its consideration of petitions. The Commission requests, but does not require, that petitions filed under this part:

(1) Be typewritten,

(2) Include the word "petition" in a heading preceding the text,

(3) Include the telephone number of the petitioner, and

(4) Be accompanied by at least five (5) copies of the petition.

[45 FR 13064, Feb. 28, 1980, as amended at 62 FR 46668, Sept. 4, 1997]

§ 1702.3 Substantive requirements.

(a) A petition filed under this part shall include the information required by this part, or a satisfactory explanation for the absence of the information. As provided by § 1702.4, a petition which is not complete may be closed. To be considered complete, a petition shall include the following:

(1) A statement of the justification for the exemption in accordance with § 1702.7,

(2) All reasonably available human experience data, reasonably available relevant experimental data (both human and animal), product and packaging specifications, labeling, and marketing history, in accordance with §§ 1702.8 through 1702.14,

(b) As used in this regulation, "reasonably available" information is data in the petitioner's possession; data that has previously been generated by the petitioner, and data that is obtainable from such sources as: Reports from Poison Control Centers; reports of adverse reactions that have been submitted to the petitioner; the medical, pharmacological, and toxicological literature; and information required by the FDA for an Investigational Exemption for a New Drug (IND) or a New Drug Application (NDA).

§ 1702.4 Petitions with insufficient or incomplete information.

If a petition is submitted that is not complete and does not explain the reason for the absence of the information, the Commission shall afford the petitioner a reasonable opportunity to provide additional information. If the required information is not submitted to the Commission, or if the petitioner does not satisfactorily explain the absence of the information within a reasonable time, the petition shall be closed if insufficient or incomplete information has been submitted to enable the Commission to evaluate the merits of the exemption request.

§ 1702.5 Failure to supply adverse information.

Failure to obtain and provide the Commission with all reasonably available information that the petitioner knows is unfavorable or could reasonably expect to be unfavorable to the petition shall result in the denial of the petition.

§ 1702.6 Trade secrets and other confidential information.

Where a petition contains material that the petitioner believes should be exempt from public disclosure under the Freedom of Information Act, 5 U.S.C. 552, the petitioner shall comply with the requirements of 16 CFR part 1015, the Commission's regulation under the Freedom of Information Act concerning requests for treatment as exempt material. The Commission shall act upon any request for treatment as exempt material in accordance with the provisions of 16 CFR part 1015.

§ 1702.7 Justification for the exemption.

The justification for the exemption, required under § 1702.3, shall explain the reason for the exemption based on one or more of the following grounds:

(a) If the justification is based on a lack of need for special packaging to protect young children from serious injury or illness from the substance, the justification shall state how the lack of toxicity and lack of adverse human experience for the substance clearly supports granting the exemption.

(b) If the exemption is requested because special packaging is not technologically feasible, practicable, or appropriate for the substance, the justification shall explain why.

(c) If the exemption is requested because special packaging is incompatible with the particular substance, the justification shall explain why.

§ 1702.8 Human experience data.

Human experience data constitutes the primary criterion used by the Commission in evaluating petitions for exemptions. Petitions shall therefore include a compilation of all reasonably available reports pertaining to human use of the particular substance, including the product brand as well as generic equivalents and involving adverse reports of personal injury, illness, and significant allergenicity. Such information in children is of particular importance in evaluating exemption requests. However, similar data in adults shall also be submitted if available. Human experience data may be obtained from such sources as:

(a) Reports from Poison Control Centers,

(b) Reports of adverse reactions relative to the product that have been submitted to the company by physicians, hospitals, consumers, and other sources,

(c) Extensive searches of the medical, pharmacological, and toxicological literature, and

(d) For drugs, where the human experience data submitted is based on data required by FDA to be compiled for an Investigational Exemption for a New Drug (IND), 21 CFR part 312, or a New Drug Application (NDA), 21 CFR part 314, a summary of the relevant data should be provided. The entire NDA and IND material need not be submitted.

§ 1702.9 Relevant experimental data.

Experimental data are generated in both animals and humans in controlled situations in order to evaluate the biological effects of a substance. Certain toxicological effects cannot generally be evaluated in human beings. This is especially true of those substances which are not normally intended to be used in or on the human body or animal body. Therefore, the Commission considers experimental data obtained in animal studies to be an important supplement to such data as may exist from any experimental studies conducted in humans. The minimum toxicological evaluation necessary for a particular household substance is proportional to the expected exposure of man to that substance. Household substances which are not expected, in normal use, to contact man are subject to less extensive studies than those substances, such as drugs, which are designed to be used in or on man. The Commission has, therefore, separated the requirements of this section into three subsections. Section 1702.9(a) lists minimum acute animal toxicity data which shall be submitted, if reasonably available, for all petitions; § 1702.9(b) lists those additional data which shall be submitted, if reasonably available, for drug products and all other household substances which are normally intended to be used in or on the human body; and § 1702.9(c) lists those additional data which shall be submitted, if reasonably available, by petitioners requesting exemption for substances not intended for use in or on the human or animal body. The Commission emphasizes that, while not absolutely necessary, the types of data outlined in § 1702.9(c) may greatly expedite the Commission's evaluation of a particular exemption request.

(a) *General criteria applicable to all petitions.* (1) Each petition for an exemption under this part shall include all reasonably available relevant experimental data relating to the petition regardless of whether such data are unfavorable to the petitioner's request. As used in this part, the term "relevant experimental data" includes, but is not limited to, all data, including animal and human studies revealing the nature and degree of the hazard associated with the particular substance. Generally, the hazard associated with the particular substance involves the risk of injury arising from the acute accidental ingestion of a product. Where a hazard different from the risk of injury arising from accidental ingestion is known to exist (e.g., potential for significant allergenicity, dermal or opthalmic injury from handling or using the product), the petitioner shall also submit all reasonably available relevant experimental data evaluating the nature and degree of any additional hazard(s).

(2) All animal studies submitted in support of exemption requests should be performed in conformity with good pharmacological and toxicological practice which includes, as a minimum, complete descriptions of protocols used in experimental animal studies, and signed laboratory reports which include the following basic information:

(i) An exact description of materials tested;

(ii) A description of test animals employed in studies, including number, age, weight, sex and nutritional state of animals;

(iii) Dosage level(s) and number of animals tested per dosage level;

(iv) Basis upon which dosage was administered (e.g., as salt or base);

(v) Route of administration and dosage volume; and

(vi) Appendices containing all raw data and any additional data generated subsequent to the completion of the original study (e.g., results of histopathological examinations, if performed).

(3) Each petition shall include all reasonably available reports of Median Lethal Dosage (LD50) studies and shall include all raw data obtained in such studies. These studies should normally be conducted in both adult and weanling animals of the same species. The oral route of administration should be followed for studies involving substances subject to regulations promulgated under the Poison Prevention Packaging Act of 1970. Where a percutaneous toxicity hazard exists, the petition shall include reasonably available studies using the percutaneous route of administration. Sufficient dosage levels as well as adequate numbers of test animals per dosage level should be used to give statistical reliability to determined LD50 values.

(4) In view of the fact that LD50 values in themselves do not necessarily reflect a true estimate of the overall toxic potential of a substance, LD50 determinations should, where an LD50 value may be calculated, include:

(i) The LD50 value with 95 percent confidence limits;

(ii) A slope determination for the dose response curve, including 95 percent confidence limits; and

(iii) A description of the statistical method employed in the analysis of such data (with proper citation) as well as the statistical analysis itself.

(5) The Commission shall disregard any data which do not fulfill the strict requirements of the statistical method used in their analyses. Modifications of accepted statistical methods which have been published in the literature are acceptable to the Commission provided that a copy of the published work is submitted.

(6) Acute toxicity studies submitted with petitions should have at least a seven day observation period of test animals. Good pharmacological practice provides that test animals are observed closely for several hours following test substance administration and less frequently on subsequent test days. Succumbing animals should be necropsied as soon as practicable following death, while surviving animals should be necropsied, and gross pathological alterations noted, at the end of the observation period. Documentation of non-lethal effects occurring during these observation periods should be submitted in conjunction with acute toxicity laboratory reports. Documentation of any lethal effects occurring at high dosage levels, including mode of death (e.g., cardiac arrest/respiratory arrest), and time of death should be submitted in conjunction with acute toxicity laboratory reports. Reports of gross necropsies performed upon surviving animals should be submitted, as well as results of necropsies performed upon animals succumbing to the test substance, provided that such animals are examined prior to the onset of autolysis. Results of microscopic examinations, when indicated by the nature or results of an acute toxicity study, shall also be submitted.

(b) *Additional data criteria for petitions involving substances normally used in or on the human or animal body.* (1) Petitioners submitting exemption requests for substances normally used on or taken into the human body or animal body shall, in addition to the requirements of paragraph (a) of this section submit the following data, where reasonably available:

(i) Summary laboratory reports of data obtained in subacute and chronic animal studies where the data pertain to the absorption, distribution, metabolism and excretion of substances in question;

(ii) A median lethal dosage (LD50) determination conducted in one additional species. Of the two LD50 determinations required for persons submitting exemption requests under this part, one should be conducted in a nonrodent species;

(iii) Summary reports of data obtained in human studies designed to measure the absorption, distribution, metabolism, and excretion of substances in question; and

(iv) Data indicating, insofar as is known, the mechanism of action of the substance in question and the mechanism by which expected toxicological effects occur. If these mechanisms are unknown, the petition should state this.

(2) Petitioners submitting exemption requests for substances normally used on or taken into the human or animal body shall, in addition to the requirements of paragraphs (a) and (b)(1) of this section, submit an evaluation of the pharmacology and toxicology of the substance in question based on reasonably available medical and scientific literature. The evaluation should be a comprehensive one, and should include proper literature citations. To the extent possible, information submitted by the petitioner justifying an exemption based on the medical and scientific literature will be evaluated under the criteria specified in §1702.9(a) for evaluating experimental data. In certain cases where the experimental data specified by §1702.9 (a) and (b) are unavailable, the medical and scientific literature may justify granting an exemption, particularly where the pharmacology and toxicology of the substance is well documented in the literature.

(c) *Optional data criteria for petitions involving substances not used in or on the human or animal body.* The following types of data, although often not generated for household substances not normally used in or on the human or animal body, may be available to a petitioner and should, where reasonably available, be submitted.

(1) Summary laboratory reports of data obtained in subacute and chronic animal studies where such data pertain to the absorption, distribution, metabolism, and excretion of the substance in question;

(2) Results of median lethal dosage (LD50) studies conducted in additional species of animals; and

(3) Any additional experimental studies relevant to the exemption request which would provide the Commission with additional means of assessing the hazards to children of the product for which exemption is sought.

§ 1702.10 Human experimental data involving the testing of human subjects.

Any human experimental data submitted with a petition requesting an exemption under this part shall include a statement establishing that adequate measures have been taken to ensure against psychological or physical injury to the subject of the human studies. The Commission considers its regulations concerning the protection of human subjects (16 CFR part 1028) to be an example of measures that are adequate to ensure against psychological or physical injury to human subjects.

§ 1702.11 Product specifications.

Each petition for an exemption shall include:

(a) A complete quantitative formula for the product, including inert ingredients, diluents, and solvents. (Petitioners should refer to §1702.6 for information regarding trade secrets.)

(b) A listing of all physical forms or dosage forms (whichever is appropriate) in which the product is available.

§ 1702.12 Packaging specifications.

Each petition for an exemption shall include the following information for each form of the product for which an exemption is sought:

(a) A description of the packaging currently in use including the name of the manufacturer of the package and all specifications for the package,

(b) A complete packaging description including any carton or wrapping in which the product is offered to the consumer,

(c) A description of each size in which the product is offered, including physical form, color and flavoring, and

(d) An empty sample of each type and size of package petitioned for exemption and, in the case of drugs, a designation of those packages intended to be used in dispensing the product to the consumer for household use.

§ 1702.13 Labeling and packaging samples.

Each petition for an exemption under this part shall include a sample of the label and complete packaging for each size in which each form of the product for which an exemption is sought is packaged. This shall include the immediate container labeling, any package inserts, and other carton or wrapping labeling in which the product is offered to the consumer. In the case of drugs, each petition shall be accompanied by labeling on the outer carton or wrapping in which the product is offered to the retailer, as well as samples of the promotional and advertising information for the product.

§ 1702.14 Marketing history.

Each petition for an exemption under this part shall include a statement of the marketing history of the substance for which an exemption is requested. The marketing history dates from the year in which each form of the product was introduced onto the market. The marketing history shall include the total number of units of each form or strength and package size of the product distributed since the product was introduced onto the market. In the case of prescription drugs, the average prescription size for the product should also be indicated, if known.

§ 1702.15 Petitions alleging the incompatibility of child resistant packaging with the particular substance petitioned for exemption.

(a) Where the petition for an exemption is based upon an allegation that the applicable special packaging standard is incompatible with the particular substance or would seriously and adversely compromise the utility or stability of a substance, the petitioner shall submit adequate evidence to support the allegation.

(b) If the allegation of incompatibility is based upon the fact that package choice is limited by a new drug application filed with the FDA, the petition shall state the limitation of package choice and a description of a time schedule to revise the NDA in order to allow additional package choice.

(c) If the allegation of incompatibility is based upon the fact that the shelf life of the product limits package choice, the petition shall outline the particular limitation and shall include a description of a time schedule to reestablish shelf-life data.

§ 1702.16 Petitions requesting an exemption for a drug or a new drug.

(a) Where the petition requests an exemption for a drug, as defined in section 201(g)(1) of the Federal Food, Drug, and Cosmetic Act (21 U.S.C. 321(g)(1), the petitioner shall include those reports required to be filed under the Food and Drug Administration's Adverse Reaction Reporting Program.

(b) [Reserved]

[45 FR 13064, Feb. 28, 1980, as amended at 66 FR 40115, Aug. 2, 2001]

§ 1702.17 Granting petitions.

Where the Commission determines that reasonable grounds for an exemption are presented by the petition, the Commission shall publish, in the FEDERAL REGISTER, a proposed amendment to the listing of substances requiring special packaging under § 1700.14(a). "Reasonable grounds" for publishing a proposed exemption are information and data sufficient to support the conclusion that:

(a) The degree or nature of the hazard to children in the availability of the substance, by reason of its packaging, is such that special packaging is not required to protect children from serious personal injury or serious illness resulting from handling, using, or ingesting the substance, or

(b) Special packaging is not technically feasible, practicable, or appropriate for the subject substance, or

(c) Special packaging is incompatible with the particular substance.

§ 1702.18 Denying petitions.

Where the Commission determines that reasonable grounds for an exemption are not presented by the petition, the petition shall be denied, and the petitioner notified in writing of the denial, including a brief statement of the reasons therefor.

§ 1702.19 Effect of filing petition.

The filing of a petition for exemption under this part 1702 shall not have the effect of staying the regulation from which the exemption is sought. Therefore, substances subject to special packaging standards shall be considered in violation of the law unless packaged in special packaging during the Commission's consideration of a petition.

SUBCHAPTER F—REFRIGERATOR SAFETY ACT REGULATIONS

PART 1750—STANDARD FOR DEVICES TO PERMIT THE OPENING OF HOUSEHOLD REFRIGERATOR DOORS FROM THE INSIDE

AUTHORITY: Pub. L. 84–930, sec. 3, 70 Stat. 953 (15 U.S.C. 1213).

SOURCE: 38 FR 34729, Dec. 18, 1973, unless otherwise noted.

§ 1750.1 Definitions.

As used in this part:

(a) *Act* means the Refrigerator Safety Act (Pub. L. 84–930, 70 Stat. 953; 15 U.S.C. 1211–14), enacted August 2, 1956.

(b) *Commission* means the Consumer Product Safety Commission established by the Consumer Product Safety Act (Pub. L. 92–573, sec. 4, 86 Stat. 1210; 15 U.S.C. 2053).

(c) *Device* means the mechanism or the means provided for enabling the doors of household refrigerators to be opened from the inside.

(d) *Effective date* means the date under the provisions of the act after which all household refrigerators manufactured and introduced or delivered for introduction into interstate commerce must comply with this standard. This date is October 30, 1958.

(e) *Household refrigerator* means a cabinet or any part of a cabinet designed for the storage of food at temperatures above 0 °C. (32 °F.), having a source of refrigeration, and intended for household use.

(f) *Opened* as applied to a refrigerator door means to effect release of the latching mechanism so that a trapped child would have to apply little or no further effort in order to escape.

(g) *Shelving* means any shelf, basket, drawer, or baffle which can be readily removed from the refrigerator without the use of tools.

§ 1750.2 Transfer of functions.

Effective May 14, 1973, section 30(c) of the Consumer Product Safety Act (86 Stat. 1231; 15 U.S.C. 2079(c)) transferred functions under the Refrigerator Safety Act from the Secretary of Commerce and the Federal Trade Commission to the Consumer Product Safety Commission.

§ 1750.3 Scope and application.

This standard shall apply to devices furnished with household refrigerators manufactured and introduced or delivered for introduction into interstate commerce after the effective date (October 30, 1958) which enable such refrigerators to be opened from the inside. The requirements of this standard shall apply to household refrigerators in their normal operating position only. The releasing feature(s) of the device shall be accessible from all spaces which (a) are bounded by interior walls or shelving, (b) are directly accessible when the exterior hinged door(s) is (are) opened, and (c) have a minimum dimension of 20.3 centimeters (8 inches) or more and a volume of 56.6 cubic decimeters (2 cubic feet) or more either with all shelving in place or as the result of the removal or the rearrangement of any or all of the shelving.

§ 1750.4 General requirements.

Household refrigerators shall be equipped with a device enabling the doors thereof to be opened easily from the inside, either by the application of an outwardly directed force to the inside of the door or by the rotation of a knob similar to a conventional doorknob. The device shall not render the refrigerator unsatisfactory for the preservation of food under any or all normal conditions of use.

§ 1750.5 Detailed requirements.

(a) *Releasing forces*. As determined by the tests prescribed by § 1750.6, the device:

(1) Shall permit the refrigerator door to be opened on the application of a force equivalent to one which, if directed perpendicularly to the plane of

the door and applied anywhere along the latch edge of the inside of the closed door, shall not exceed 66.7 newtons (15 pounds);

(2) Shall permit the refrigerator door to be opened on the application of clockwise or counterclockwise turning moment of not more than 0.57 newton-meter (5 inch-pounds) to a knob on the door through an angle of rotation of 45° ±15° in either direction; or

(3) Shall function automatically to permit the door to be opened with a force of 66.7 newtons (15 pounds) or less applied as described in paragraph (a)(1) of this section whenever space(s) exist(s) or is (are) created with dimensions and volumes exceeding the dimensions and volumes imposed by §1750.3.

(b) *Description and location of knob(s).* The knob(s) shall resemble a conventional doorknob in shape and size and shall be mounted near the latch side of the door extending into the cabinet at least 6.3 millimeters (¼ inch) beyond any inner door surface within a 15.2-centimeter (6-inch) radius of the knob center. The knob(s) shall be mounted in such a manner that there is a minimum of 19.0-millimeter (¾-inch) clearance between the inner periphery of the knob(s) and adjacent inner door surfaces. The knob(s) shall be located so as to provide the accessibility required by §1750.3.

(c) *Wear.* The device shall comply with the requirements of paragraph (a) of this section after 300,000 cycles of operation of the door as determined by the tests prescribed by §1750.6.

(d) *Protection against adverse effects from spillage, cleaning, defrosting, and condensation.* Devices shall be designed so that spillage of foods or beverages, cleaning or defrosting in accordance with manufacturer's recommendations, or normal condensation will not so adversely affect the operation of the device as to result in its failure to meet the requirements of paragraph (a) of this section, as determined by the tests prescribed by §1750.6.

(e) *Devices which permit door to be opened as a result of forces or turning moments applied to movable components inside the refrigerator.* Those components of a device upon which the safety features of the device depend shall not break, crack, permanently deform, nor show other visible damage when subjected to forces and moments specified in the tests under §1750.6(c). The requirements of paragraph (a) of this section shall be satisfied after the device has been subjected to the tests under §1750.6(c).

(f) *Power supply.* The device shall operate in accordance with the requirements of this standard with the electric, gas, or other fuel supply either on or off.

§ 1750.6 Tests.

It is the intent of this standard that where tests are not specified, the general and detailed requirements shall be checked by inspection, simple measurement, and by consideration of pertinent standard commercial practices. Compliance with the requirements of §1750.5 (a), (c), (d), and (e) shall be checked with the aid of the following tests:

(a) *Test for releasing force on door.* The force measurements shall be made by means of a force gage with a calibrated accuracy within ±1.3 newtons (±0.3 pound) when measuring a force of 66.7 newtons (15 pounds). The dial of the gage shall be graduated with finest divisions not exceeding 0.9 newton (0.2 pound), and the full-scale range shall not exceed 133.4 newtons (30 pounds). Measurements shall be made at three points on the door near the inside latch edge—one point near the top of the interior space created by removal of all shelving, one point near the bottom, and one point midway between these two points. The requirements of §1750.5(a)(1) shall be satisfied.

(b) *Test for knob torque.* The measurement of the turning moment required to operate the knob release shall be made with a torque gage adapted for attachment to the knob or knob shaft. The gage shall have a calibrated accuracy within ±0.011 newton-meter (0.10 inch-pound) when measuring a moment of 0.57 newton-meter (5 inch-pounds). The finest graduations on the dial of the gage shall correspond to a moment increment not greater than 0.011 newton-meter (0.10 inch-pound) and the full-scale range shall not exceed 1.13 newton-meters (10 inch-pounds) in each direction from the null reading. The turning moment shall be applied so as to rotate the knob the full amount required for release, in both a clockwise and a counterclockwise direction. The angle of rotation required for release shall be checked by means of an angle gage adapted to measure the angle of rotation about the longitudinal axis of the knob shaft. The gage shall have a calibrated accuracy within ±1° at an angle of 45° and the finest divisions shall not exceed 1°. The requirements of § 1750.5(a)(2) shall be satisfied.

(c) *Tests for strength of device components which affect the safety features of the device.* (1) The tests prescribed by paragraph (c)(2) of this section shall apply only to devices which permit the door to be opened as a result of forces or turning moments applied to movable components inside the refrigerator.

(2) A turning moment of 2.26 newton-meters (20 inch-pounds) shall be applied for 50 successive operations in a clockwise direction, followed by 50 successive similar operations in a counterclockwise direction, to components designed to permit the door to be opened as a result of the application of a turning moment to them. The turning moment shall be applied to the outer periphery of the component provided. The gage used for registering the moment applied shall have a calibrated accuracy within ±0.044 newton-meter (±0.4 inch-pound) when measuring a moment of 2.26 newton-meters (20 inch-pounds). The finest graduations on the dial of the gage shall correspond to a moment increment not greater than 0.044 newton-meter (0.4 inch-pound) and the full-scale range of the gage shall not exceed 4.52 newton-meters (40 inch-pounds) in each direction from the null reading. The turning moment applied in each operation shall be applied for a period of time sufficient for the component to come to rest after completing the extent of movement for which designed. A pushing force of 89.0 newtons (20 pounds) shall be applied for 50 successive operations, followed, if applicable, by 50 successive similar operations with a pulling force, to components designed to permit the door to be opened as a result of the application of a force to them. Areas which may be, in service, subjected to pushing or pulling forces which create maximum stresses (for example, points on the outer periphery of components designed to transmit a turning moment, or unsupported portions of members or areas designed for transmitting a force) shall be subjected to test. The gage used for registering the force applied shall have a calibrated accuracy within ±1.8 newtons (±0.4 pound) when measuring a force of 89.0 newtons (20 pounds). The finest graduations on the dial of the gage shall correspond to a force not in excess of 1.8 newtons (0.4 pound) and the full-scale range shall not exceed 177.9 newtons (40 pounds).

(3) Upon being subjected to the tests prescribed by paragraph (c)(2) of this section, no device component on which the safety features of the device depend shall break, crack, permanently deform, or show other visible damage. The device must satisfy the requirements of § 1750.5(a) after being subjected to the tests in paragraph (c)(2).

(d) *Simulated use test.* Tests shall be conducted on the completely assembled refrigerator in its normal operating position to determine that the release device complies with the requirements of § 1750.5 during and after the 300,000 cycles of door operation and following exposure to spillage of foods and beverages, to cleaning and defrosting in accordance with the manufacturer's recommendations, and to condensation. The equipment provided for operating the door shall open the door sufficiently on each cycle to assure a complete cycle of operation for the latch mechanism.

§ 1750.7 Provision for changes in the standard.

(a) Section 5 of the act provides for the possibility of changes in the commercial standard first established pursuant to section 3 of the act and allows a period of 1 year and 90 days for compliance with such changes after they are published.

(b) Any person wishing to propose a change in this standard shall submit to the Secretary, Consumer Product Safety Commission, Washington, D.C. 20207, the proposed change. Before a change is recommended, the Consumer Product Safety Commission shall secure advice and consultation from public or private sources including particularly the household refrigerator manufacturing industry and the Division of Maternal and Child Health, Health Resources and Services Administration, Public Health Service, Department of Health and Human Services. The Commission shall then take such action as it deems appropriate.

[38 FR 34729, Dec. 18, 1973, as amended at 51 FR 10, Jan. 2, 1986; 52 FR 406, Jan. 6, 1987]

FINDING AIDS

A list of CFR titles, subtitles, chapters, subchapters and parts and an alphabetical list of agencies publishing in the CFR are included in the CFR Index and Finding Aids volume to the Code of Federal Regulations which is published separately and revised annually.

Table of CFR Titles and Chapters

(Revised as of January 1, 2013)

Title 1—General Provisions

I Administrative Committee of the Federal Register (Parts 1—49)
II Office of the Federal Register (Parts 50—299)
III Administrative Conference of the United States (Parts 300—399)
IV Miscellaneous Agencies (Parts 400—500)

Title 2—Grants and Agreements

SUBTITLE A—OFFICE OF MANAGEMENT AND BUDGET GUIDANCE FOR GRANTS AND AGREEMENTS

I Office of Management and Budget Governmentwide Guidance for Grants and Agreements (Parts 2—199)
II Office of Management and Budget Circulars and Guidance (200—299)

SUBTITLE B—FEDERAL AGENCY REGULATIONS FOR GRANTS AND AGREEMENTS

III Department of Health and Human Services (Parts 300— 399)
IV Department of Agriculture (Parts 400—499)
VI Department of State (Parts 600—699)
VII Agency for International Development (Parts 700—799)
VIII Department of Veterans Affairs (Parts 800—899)
IX Department of Energy (Parts 900—999)
XI Department of Defense (Parts 1100—1199)
XII Department of Transportation (Parts 1200—1299)
XIII Department of Commerce (Parts 1300—1399)
XIV Department of the Interior (Parts 1400—1499)
XV Environmental Protection Agency (Parts 1500—1599)
XVIII National Aeronautics and Space Administration (Parts 1800—1899)
XX United States Nuclear Regulatory Commission (Parts 2000—2099)
XXII Corporation for National and Community Service (Parts 2200—2299)
XXIII Social Security Administration (Parts 2300—2399)
XXIV Housing and Urban Development (Parts 2400—2499)
XXV National Science Foundation (Parts 2500—2599)
XXVI National Archives and Records Administration (Parts 2600—2699)
XXVII Small Business Administration (Parts 2700—2799)
XXVIII Department of Justice (Parts 2800—2899)

Title 2—Grants and Agreements—Continued

Chap.	
XXX	Department of Homeland Security (Parts 3000—3099)
XXXI	Institute of Museum and Library Services (Parts 3100—3199)
XXXII	National Endowment for the Arts (Parts 3200—3299)
XXXIII	National Endowment for the Humanities (Parts 3300—3399)
XXXIV	Department of Education (Parts 3400—3499)
XXXV	Export-Import Bank of the United States (Parts 3500—3599)
XXXVII	Peace Corps (Parts 3700—3799)
LVIII	Election Assistance Commission (Parts 5800—5899)

Title 3—The President

I	Executive Office of the President (Parts 100—199)

Title 4—Accounts

I	Government Accountability Office (Parts 1—199)
II	Recovery Accountability and Transparency Board (Parts 200—299)

Title 5—Administrative Personnel

I	Office of Personnel Management (Parts 1—1199)
II	Merit Systems Protection Board (Parts 1200—1299)
III	Office of Management and Budget (Parts 1300—1399)
V	The International Organizations Employees Loyalty Board (Parts 1500—1599)
VI	Federal Retirement Thrift Investment Board (Parts 1600—1699)
VIII	Office of Special Counsel (Parts 1800—1899)
IX	Appalachian Regional Commission (Parts 1900—1999)
XI	Armed Forces Retirement Home (Parts 2100—2199)
XIV	Federal Labor Relations Authority, General Counsel of the Federal Labor Relations Authority and Federal Service Impasses Panel (Parts 2400—2499)
XV	Office of Administration, Executive Office of the President (Parts 2500—2599)
XVI	Office of Government Ethics (Parts 2600—2699)
XXI	Department of the Treasury (Parts 3100—3199)
XXII	Federal Deposit Insurance Corporation (Parts 3200—3299)
XXIII	Department of Energy (Parts 3300—3399)
XXIV	Federal Energy Regulatory Commission (Parts 3400—3499)
XXV	Department of the Interior (Parts 3500—3599)
XXVI	Department of Defense (Parts 3600— 3699)
XXVIII	Department of Justice (Parts 3800—3899)
XXIX	Federal Communications Commission (Parts 3900—3999)
XXX	Farm Credit System Insurance Corporation (Parts 4000—4099)
XXXI	Farm Credit Administration (Parts 4100—4199)

Title 5—Administrative Personnel—Continued

Chap.

LXXXIII Special Inspector General for Afghanistan Reconstruction (Parts 9300—9399)

LXXXIV Bureau of Consumer Financial Protection (Parts 9400—9499)

XCVII Department of Homeland Security Human Resources Management System (Department of Homeland Security—Office of Personnel Management) (Parts 9700—9799)

XCVII Council of the Inspectors General on Integrity and Efficiency (Parts 9800—9899)

Title 6—Domestic Security

I Department of Homeland Security, Office of the Secretary (Parts 1—99)

Title 7—Agriculture

SUBTITLE A—OFFICE OF THE SECRETARY OF AGRICULTURE (PARTS 0—26)

SUBTITLE B—REGULATIONS OF THE DEPARTMENT OF AGRICULTURE

I Agricultural Marketing Service (Standards, Inspections, Marketing Practices), Department of Agriculture (Parts 27—209)

II Food and Nutrition Service, Department of Agriculture (Parts 210—299)

III Animal and Plant Health Inspection Service, Department of Agriculture (Parts 300—399)

IV Federal Crop Insurance Corporation, Department of Agriculture (Parts 400—499)

V Agricultural Research Service, Department of Agriculture (Parts 500—599)

VI Natural Resources Conservation Service, Department of Agriculture (Parts 600—699)

VII Farm Service Agency, Department of Agriculture (Parts 700—799)

VIII Grain Inspection, Packers and Stockyards Administration (Federal Grain Inspection Service), Department of Agriculture (Parts 800—899)

IX Agricultural Marketing Service (Marketing Agreements and Orders; Fruits, Vegetables, Nuts), Department of Agriculture (Parts 900—999)

X Agricultural Marketing Service (Marketing Agreements and Orders; Milk), Department of Agriculture (Parts 1000—1199)

XI Agricultural Marketing Service (Marketing Agreements and Orders; Miscellaneous Commodities), Department of Agriculture (Parts 1200—1299)

XIV Commodity Credit Corporation, Department of Agriculture (Parts 1400—1499)

XV Foreign Agricultural Service, Department of Agriculture (Parts 1500—1599)

XVI Rural Telephone Bank, Department of Agriculture (Parts 1600—1699)

Title 7—Agriculture—Continued

Title 8—Aliens and Nationality

Title 9—Animals and Animal Products

Title 9—Animals and Animal Products—Continued

Chap.

II	Grain Inspection, Packers and Stockyards Administration (Packers and Stockyards Programs), Department of Agriculture (Parts 200—299)
III	Food Safety and Inspection Service, Department of Agriculture (Parts 300—599)

Title 10—Energy

I	Nuclear Regulatory Commission (Parts 0—199)
II	Department of Energy (Parts 200—699)
III	Department of Energy (Parts 700—999)
X	Department of Energy (General Provisions) (Parts 1000—1099)
XIII	Nuclear Waste Technical Review Board (Parts 1300—1399)
XVII	Defense Nuclear Facilities Safety Board (Parts 1700—1799)
XVIII	Northeast Interstate Low-Level Radioactive Waste Commission (Parts 1800—1899)

Title 11—Federal Elections

I	Federal Election Commission (Parts 1—9099)
II	Election Assistance Commission (Parts 9400—9499)

Title 12—Banks and Banking

I	Comptroller of the Currency, Department of the Treasury (Parts 1—199)
II	Federal Reserve System (Parts 200—299)
III	Federal Deposit Insurance Corporation (Parts 300—399)
IV	Export-Import Bank of the United States (Parts 400—499)
V	Office of Thrift Supervision, Department of the Treasury (Parts 500—599)
VI	Farm Credit Administration (Parts 600—699)
VII	National Credit Union Administration (Parts 700—799)
VIII	Federal Financing Bank (Parts 800—899)
IX	Federal Housing Finance Board (Parts 900—999)
X	Bureau of Consumer Financial Protection (Parts 1000—1099)
XI	Federal Financial Institutions Examination Council (Parts 1100—1199)
XII	Federal Housing Finance Agency (Parts 1200—1299)
XIII	Financial Stability Oversight Council (Parts 1300—1399)
XIV	Farm Credit System Insurance Corporation (Parts 1400—1499)
XV	Department of the Treasury (Parts 1500—1599)
XVI	Office of Financial Research (Parts 1600—1699)
XVII	Office of Federal Housing Enterprise Oversight, Department of Housing and Urban Development (Parts 1700—1799)
XVIII	Community Development Financial Institutions Fund, Department of the Treasury (Parts 1800—1899)

Title 13—Business Credit and Assistance

Chap.	
I	Small Business Administration (Parts 1—199)
III	Economic Development Administration, Department of Commerce (Parts 300—399)
IV	Emergency Steel Guarantee Loan Board (Parts 400—499)
V	Emergency Oil and Gas Guaranteed Loan Board (Parts 500—599)

Title 14—Aeronautics and Space

I	Federal Aviation Administration, Department of Transportation (Parts 1—199)
II	Office of the Secretary, Department of Transportation (Aviation Proceedings) (Parts 200—399)
III	Commercial Space Transportation, Federal Aviation Administration, Department of Transportation (Parts 400—1199)
V	National Aeronautics and Space Administration (Parts 1200—1299)
VI	Air Transportation System Stabilization (Parts 1300—1399)

Title 15—Commerce and Foreign Trade

	SUBTITLE A—OFFICE OF THE SECRETARY OF COMMERCE (PARTS 0—29)
	SUBTITLE B—REGULATIONS RELATING TO COMMERCE AND FOREIGN TRADE
I	Bureau of the Census, Department of Commerce (Parts 30—199)
II	National Institute of Standards and Technology, Department of Commerce (Parts 200—299)
III	International Trade Administration, Department of Commerce (Parts 300—399)
IV	Foreign-Trade Zones Board, Department of Commerce (Parts 400—499)
VII	Bureau of Industry and Security, Department of Commerce (Parts 700—799)
VIII	Bureau of Economic Analysis, Department of Commerce (Parts 800—899)
IX	National Oceanic and Atmospheric Administration, Department of Commerce (Parts 900—999)
XI	Technology Administration, Department of Commerce (Parts 1100—1199)
XIII	East-West Foreign Trade Board (Parts 1300—1399)
XIV	Minority Business Development Agency (Parts 1400—1499)
	SUBTITLE C—REGULATIONS RELATING TO FOREIGN TRADE AGREEMENTS
XX	Office of the United States Trade Representative (Parts 2000—2099)
	SUBTITLE D—REGULATIONS RELATING TO TELECOMMUNICATIONS AND INFORMATION
XXIII	National Telecommunications and Information Administration, Department of Commerce (Parts 2300—2399)

Title 16—Commercial Practices

Chap.

I Federal Trade Commission (Parts 0—999)

II Consumer Product Safety Commission (Parts 1000—1799)

Title 17—Commodity and Securities Exchanges

I Commodity Futures Trading Commission (Parts 1—199)

II Securities and Exchange Commission (Parts 200—399)

IV Department of the Treasury (Parts 400—499)

Title 18—Conservation of Power and Water Resources

I Federal Energy Regulatory Commission, Department of Energy (Parts 1—399)

III Delaware River Basin Commission (Parts 400—499)

VI Water Resources Council (Parts 700—799)

VIII Susquehanna River Basin Commission (Parts 800—899)

XIII Tennessee Valley Authority (Parts 1300—1399)

Title 19—Customs Duties

I U.S. Customs and Border Protection, Department of Homeland Security; Department of the Treasury (Parts 0—199)

II United States International Trade Commission (Parts 200—299)

III International Trade Administration, Department of Commerce (Parts 300—399)

IV U.S. Immigration and Customs Enforcement, Department of Homeland Security (Parts 400—599)

Title 20—Employees' Benefits

I Office of Workers' Compensation Programs, Department of Labor (Parts 1—199)

II Railroad Retirement Board (Parts 200—399)

III Social Security Administration (Parts 400—499)

IV Employees' Compensation Appeals Board, Department of Labor (Parts 500—599)

V Employment and Training Administration, Department of Labor (Parts 600—699)

VI Office of Workers' Compensation Programs, Department of Labor (Parts 700—799)

VII Benefits Review Board, Department of Labor (Parts 800—899)

VIII Joint Board for the Enrollment of Actuaries (Parts 900—999)

IX Office of the Assistant Secretary for Veterans' Employment and Training Service, Department of Labor (Parts 1000—1099)

Title 21—Food and Drugs

Chap.

I Food and Drug Administration, Department of Health and Human Services (Parts 1—1299)

II Drug Enforcement Administration, Department of Justice (Parts 1300—1399)

III Office of National Drug Control Policy (Parts 1400—1499)

Title 22—Foreign Relations

I Department of State (Parts 1—199)

II Agency for International Development (Parts 200—299)

III Peace Corps (Parts 300—399)

IV International Joint Commission, United States and Canada (Parts 400—499)

V Broadcasting Board of Governors (Parts 500—599)

VII Overseas Private Investment Corporation (Parts 700—799)

IX Foreign Service Grievance Board (Parts 900—999)

X Inter-American Foundation (Parts 1000—1099)

XI International Boundary and Water Commission, United States and Mexico, United States Section (Parts 1100—1199)

XII United States International Development Cooperation Agency (Parts 1200—1299)

XIII Millennium Challenge Corporation (Parts 1300—1399)

XIV Foreign Service Labor Relations Board; Federal Labor Relations Authority; General Counsel of the Federal Labor Relations Authority; and the Foreign Service Impasse Disputes Panel (Parts 1400—1499)

XV African Development Foundation (Parts 1500—1599)

XVI Japan-United States Friendship Commission (Parts 1600—1699)

XVII United States Institute of Peace (Parts 1700—1799)

Title 23—Highways

I Federal Highway Administration, Department of Transportation (Parts 1—999)

II National Highway Traffic Safety Administration and Federal Highway Administration, Department of Transportation (Parts 1200—1299)

III National Highway Traffic Safety Administration, Department of Transportation (Parts 1300—1399)

Title 24—Housing and Urban Development

SUBTITLE A—OFFICE OF THE SECRETARY, DEPARTMENT OF HOUSING AND URBAN DEVELOPMENT (PARTS 0—99)

SUBTITLE B—REGULATIONS RELATING TO HOUSING AND URBAN DEVELOPMENT

I Office of Assistant Secretary for Equal Opportunity, Department of Housing and Urban Development (Parts 100—199)

Title 24—Housing and Urban Development—Continued

Chap.

II Office of Assistant Secretary for Housing-Federal Housing Commissioner, Department of Housing and Urban Development (Parts 200—299)

III Government National Mortgage Association, Department of Housing and Urban Development (Parts 300—399)

IV Office of Housing and Office of Multifamily Housing Assistance Restructuring, Department of Housing and Urban Development (Parts 400—499)

V Office of Assistant Secretary for Community Planning and Development, Department of Housing and Urban Development (Parts 500—599)

VI Office of Assistant Secretary for Community Planning and Development, Department of Housing and Urban Development (Parts 600—699) [Reserved]

VII Office of the Secretary, Department of Housing and Urban Development (Housing Assistance Programs and Public and Indian Housing Programs) (Parts 700—799)

VIII Office of the Assistant Secretary for Housing—Federal Housing Commissioner, Department of Housing and Urban Development (Section 8 Housing Assistance Programs, Section 202 Direct Loan Program, Section 202 Supportive Housing for the Elderly Program and Section 811 Supportive Housing for Persons With Disabilities Program) (Parts 800—899)

IX Office of Assistant Secretary for Public and Indian Housing, Department of Housing and Urban Development (Parts 900—1699)

X Office of Assistant Secretary for Housing—Federal Housing Commissioner, Department of Housing and Urban Development (Interstate Land Sales Registration Program) (Parts 1700—1799)

XII Office of Inspector General, Department of Housing and Urban Development (Parts 2000—2099)

XV Emergency Mortgage Insurance and Loan Programs, Department of Housing and Urban Development (Parts 2700—2799)

XX Office of Assistant Secretary for Housing—Federal Housing Commissioner, Department of Housing and Urban Development (Parts 3200—3899)

XXIV Board of Directors of the HOPE for Homeowners Program (Parts 4000—4099)

XXV Neighborhood Reinvestment Corporation (Parts 4100—4199)

Title 25—Indians

I Bureau of Indian Affairs, Department of the Interior (Parts 1—299)

II Indian Arts and Crafts Board, Department of the Interior (Parts 300—399)

III National Indian Gaming Commission, Department of the Interior (Parts 500—599)

IV Office of Navajo and Hopi Indian Relocation (Parts 700—799)

V Bureau of Indian Affairs, Department of the Interior, and Indian Health Service, Department of Health and Human Services (Part 900)

Title 29—Labor—Continued

Title 30—Mineral Resources

Title 31—Money and Finance: Treasury

Title 32—National Defense

Title 32—National Defense—Continued

Chap.

Chap.	
V	Department of the Army (Parts 400—699)
VI	Department of the Navy (Parts 700—799)
VII	Department of the Air Force (Parts 800—1099)
	SUBTITLE B—OTHER REGULATIONS RELATING TO NATIONAL DEFENSE
XII	Defense Logistics Agency (Parts 1200—1299)
XVI	Selective Service System (Parts 1600—1699)
XVII	Office of the Director of National Intelligence (Parts 1700—1799)
XVIII	National Counterintelligence Center (Parts 1800—1899)
XIX	Central Intelligence Agency (Parts 1900—1999)
XX	Information Security Oversight Office, National Archives and Records Administration (Parts 2000—2099)
XXI	National Security Council (Parts 2100—2199)
XXIV	Office of Science and Technology Policy (Parts 2400—2499)
XXVII	Office for Micronesian Status Negotiations (Parts 2700—2799)
XXVIII	Office of the Vice President of the United States (Parts 2800—2899)

Title 33—Navigation and Navigable Waters

Chap.	
I	Coast Guard, Department of Homeland Security (Parts 1—199)
II	Corps of Engineers, Department of the Army (Parts 200—399)
IV	Saint Lawrence Seaway Development Corporation, Department of Transportation (Parts 400—499)

Title 34—Education

Chap.	
	SUBTITLE A—OFFICE OF THE SECRETARY, DEPARTMENT OF EDUCATION (PARTS 1—99)
	SUBTITLE B—REGULATIONS OF THE OFFICES OF THE DEPARTMENT OF EDUCATION
I	Office for Civil Rights, Department of Education (Parts 100—199)
II	Office of Elementary and Secondary Education, Department of Education (Parts 200—299)
III	Office of Special Education and Rehabilitative Services, Department of Education (Parts 300—399)
IV	Office of Vocational and Adult Education, Department of Education (Parts 400—499)
V	Office of Bilingual Education and Minority Languages Affairs, Department of Education (Parts 500—599)
VI	Office of Postsecondary Education, Department of Education (Parts 600—699)
VII	Office of Educational Research and Improvement, Department of Education [Reserved]
XI	National Institute for Literacy (Parts 1100—1199)
	SUBTITLE C—REGULATIONS RELATING TO EDUCATION
XII	National Council on Disability (Parts 1200—1299)

Title 35 [Reserved]

Chap.

Title 36—Parks, Forests, and Public Property

I National Park Service, Department of the Interior (Parts 1—199)

II Forest Service, Department of Agriculture (Parts 200—299)

III Corps of Engineers, Department of the Army (Parts 300—399)

IV American Battle Monuments Commission (Parts 400—499)

V Smithsonian Institution (Parts 500—599)

VI [Reserved]

VII Library of Congress (Parts 700—799)

VIII Advisory Council on Historic Preservation (Parts 800—899)

IX Pennsylvania Avenue Development Corporation (Parts 900—999)

X Presidio Trust (Parts 1000—1099)

XI Architectural and Transportation Barriers Compliance Board (Parts 1100—1199)

XII National Archives and Records Administration (Parts 1200—1299)

XV Oklahoma City National Memorial Trust (Parts 1500—1599)

XVI Morris K. Udall Scholarship and Excellence in National Environmental Policy Foundation (Parts 1600—1699)

Title 37—Patents, Trademarks, and Copyrights

I United States Patent and Trademark Office, Department of Commerce (Parts 1—199)

II Copyright Office, Library of Congress (Parts 200—299)

III Copyright Royalty Board, Library of Congress (Parts 300—399)

IV Assistant Secretary for Technology Policy, Department of Commerce (Parts 400—499)

V Under Secretary for Technology, Department of Commerce (Parts 500—599)

Title 38—Pensions, Bonuses, and Veterans' Relief

I Department of Veterans Affairs (Parts 0—199)

II Armed Forces Retirement Home (Parts 200—299)

Title 39—Postal Service

I United States Postal Service (Parts 1—999)

III Postal Regulatory Commission (Parts 3000—3099)

Title 40—Protection of Environment

I Environmental Protection Agency (Parts 1—1099)

IV Environmental Protection Agency and Department of Justice (Parts 1400—1499)

V Council on Environmental Quality (Parts 1500—1599)

Chap.

VI Chemical Safety and Hazard Investigation Board (Parts 1600—1699)

VII Environmental Protection Agency and Department of Defense; Uniform National Discharge Standards for Vessels of the Armed Forces (Parts 1700—1799)

Title 41—Public Contracts and Property Management

SUBTITLE A—FEDERAL PROCUREMENT REGULATIONS SYSTEM [NOTE]

SUBTITLE B—OTHER PROVISIONS RELATING TO PUBLIC CONTRACTS

50 Public Contracts, Department of Labor (Parts 50-1—50-999)

51 Committee for Purchase From People Who Are Blind or Severely Disabled (Parts 51-1—51-99)

60 Office of Federal Contract Compliance Programs, Equal Employment Opportunity, Department of Labor (Parts 60-1—60-999)

61 Office of the Assistant Secretary for Veterans' Employment and Training Service, Department of Labor (Parts 61-1—61-999)

62—100 [Reserved]

SUBTITLE C—FEDERAL PROPERTY MANAGEMENT REGULATIONS SYSTEM

101 Federal Property Management Regulations (Parts 101-1—101-99)

102 Federal Management Regulation (Parts 102-1—102-299)

103—104 [Reserved]

105 General Services Administration (Parts 105-1—105-999)

109 Department of Energy Property Management Regulations (Parts 109-1—109-99)

114 Department of the Interior (Parts 114-1—114-99)

115 Environmental Protection Agency (Parts 115-1—115-99)

128 Department of Justice (Parts 128-1—128-99)

129—200 [Reserved]

SUBTITLE D—OTHER PROVISIONS RELATING TO PROPERTY MANAGEMENT [RESERVED]

SUBTITLE E—FEDERAL INFORMATION RESOURCES MANAGEMENT REGULATIONS SYSTEM [RESERVED]

SUBTITLE F—FEDERAL TRAVEL REGULATION SYSTEM

300 General (Parts 300-1—300-99)

301 Temporary Duty (TDY) Travel Allowances (Parts 301-1—301-99)

302 Relocation Allowances (Parts 302-1—302-99)

303 Payment of Expenses Connected with the Death of Certain Employees (Part 303-1—303-99)

304 Payment of Travel Expenses from a Non-Federal Source (Parts 304-1—304-99)

Title 42—Public Health

I Public Health Service, Department of Health and Human Services (Parts 1—199)

Title 42—Public Health—Continued

Chap.

IV Centers for Medicare & Medicaid Services, Department of Health and Human Services (Parts 400—599)

V Office of Inspector General-Health Care, Department of Health and Human Services (Parts 1000—1999)

Title 43—Public Lands: Interior

SUBTITLE A—OFFICE OF THE SECRETARY OF THE INTERIOR (PARTS 1—199)

SUBTITLE B—REGULATIONS RELATING TO PUBLIC LANDS

I Bureau of Reclamation, Department of the Interior (Parts 400—999)

II Bureau of Land Management, Department of the Interior (Parts 1000—9999)

III Utah Reclamation Mitigation and Conservation Commission (Parts 10000—10099)

Title 44—Emergency Management and Assistance

I Federal Emergency Management Agency, Department of Homeland Security (Parts 0—399)

IV Department of Commerce and Department of Transportation (Parts 400—499)

Title 45—Public Welfare

SUBTITLE A—DEPARTMENT OF HEALTH AND HUMAN SERVICES (PARTS 1—199)

SUBTITLE B—REGULATIONS RELATING TO PUBLIC WELFARE

II Office of Family Assistance (Assistance Programs), Administration for Children and Families, Department of Health and Human Services (Parts 200—299)

III Office of Child Support Enforcement (Child Support Enforcement Program), Administration for Children and Families, Department of Health and Human Services (Parts 300—399)

IV Office of Refugee Resettlement, Administration for Children and Families, Department of Health and Human Services (Parts 400—499)

V Foreign Claims Settlement Commission of the United States, Department of Justice (Parts 500—599)

VI National Science Foundation (Parts 600—699)

VII Commission on Civil Rights (Parts 700—799)

VIII Office of Personnel Management (Parts 800—899) [Reserved]

X Office of Community Services, Administration for Children and Families, Department of Health and Human Services (Parts 1000—1099)

XI National Foundation on the Arts and the Humanities (Parts 1100—1199)

XII Corporation for National and Community Service (Parts 1200—1299)

Title 45—Public Welfare—Continued

Chap.	
XIII	Office of Human Development Services, Department of Health and Human Services (Parts 1300—1399)
XVI	Legal Services Corporation (Parts 1600—1699)
XVII	National Commission on Libraries and Information Science (Parts 1700—1799)
XVIII	Harry S. Truman Scholarship Foundation (Parts 1800—1899)
XXI	Commission on Fine Arts (Parts 2100—2199)
XXIII	Arctic Research Commission (Part 2301)
XXIV	James Madison Memorial Fellowship Foundation (Parts 2400—2499)
XXV	Corporation for National and Community Service (Parts 2500—2599)

Title 46—Shipping

I	Coast Guard, Department of Homeland Security (Parts 1—199)
II	Maritime Administration, Department of Transportation (Parts 200—399)
III	Coast Guard (Great Lakes Pilotage), Department of Homeland Security (Parts 400—499)
IV	Federal Maritime Commission (Parts 500—599)

Title 47—Telecommunication

I	Federal Communications Commission (Parts 0—199)
II	Office of Science and Technology Policy and National Security Council (Parts 200—299)
III	National Telecommunications and Information Administration, Department of Commerce (Parts 300—399)
IV	National Telecommunications and Information Administration, Department of Commerce, and National Highway Traffic Safety Administration, Department of Transportation (Parts 400—499)

Title 48—Federal Acquisition Regulations System

1	Federal Acquisition Regulation (Parts 1—99)
2	Defense Acquisition Regulations System, Department of Defense (Parts 200—299)
3	Health and Human Services (Parts 300—399)
4	Department of Agriculture (Parts 400—499)
5	General Services Administration (Parts 500—599)
6	Department of State (Parts 600—699)
7	Agency for International Development (Parts 700—799)
8	Department of Veterans Affairs (Parts 800—899)
9	Department of Energy (Parts 900—999)
10	Department of the Treasury (Parts 1000—1099)
12	Department of Transportation (Parts 1200—1299)

Chap.

13 Department of Commerce (Parts 1300—1399)

14 Department of the Interior (Parts 1400—1499)

15 Environmental Protection Agency (Parts 1500—1599)

16 Office of Personnel Management, Federal Employees Health Benefits Acquisition Regulation (Parts 1600—1699)

17 Office of Personnel Management (Parts 1700—1799)

18 National Aeronautics and Space Administration (Parts 1800—1899)

19 Broadcasting Board of Governors (Parts 1900—1999)

20 Nuclear Regulatory Commission (Parts 2000—2099)

21 Office of Personnel Management, Federal Employees Group Life Insurance Federal Acquisition Regulation (Parts 2100—2199)

23 Social Security Administration (Parts 2300—2399)

24 Department of Housing and Urban Development (Parts 2400—2499)

25 National Science Foundation (Parts 2500—2599)

28 Department of Justice (Parts 2800—2899)

29 Department of Labor (Parts 2900—2999)

30 Department of Homeland Security, Homeland Security Acquisition Regulation (HSAR) (Parts 3000—3099)

34 Department of Education Acquisition Regulation (Parts 3400—3499)

51 Department of the Army Acquisition Regulations (Parts 5100—5199)

52 Department of the Navy Acquisition Regulations (Parts 5200—5299)

53 Department of the Air Force Federal Acquisition Regulation Supplement [Reserved]

54 Defense Logistics Agency, Department of Defense (Parts 5400—5499)

57 African Development Foundation (Parts 5700—5799)

61 Civilian Board of Contract Appeals, General Services Administration (Parts 6100—6199)

63 Department of Transportation Board of Contract Appeals (Parts 6300—6399)

99 Cost Accounting Standards Board, Office of Federal Procurement Policy, Office of Management and Budget (Parts 9900—9999)

Title 49—Transportation

SUBTITLE A—OFFICE OF THE SECRETARY OF TRANSPORTATION (PARTS 1—99)

SUBTITLE B—OTHER REGULATIONS RELATING TO TRANSPORTATION

I Pipeline and Hazardous Materials Safety Administration, Department of Transportation (Parts 100—199)

II Federal Railroad Administration, Department of Transportation (Parts 200—299)

Title 49—Transportation—Continued

Title 50—Wildlife and Fisheries

Alphabetical List of Agencies Appearing in the CFR
(Revised as of January 1, 2013)

Agency	CFR Title, Subtitle or Chapter
Administrative Committee of the Federal Register	1, I
Administrative Conference of the United States	1, III
Advisory Council on Historic Preservation	36, VIII
Advocacy and Outreach, Office of	7, XXV
Afghanistan Reconstruction, Special Inspector General for	22, LXXXIII
African Development Foundation	22, XV
Federal Acquisition Regulation	48, 57
Agency for International Development	2, VII; 22, II
Federal Acquisition Regulation	48, 7
Agricultural Marketing Service	7, I, IX, X, XI
Agricultural Research Service	7, V
Agriculture Department	2, IV; 5, LXXIII
Advocacy and Outreach, Office of	7, XXV
Agricultural Marketing Service	7, I, IX, X, XI
Agricultural Research Service	7, V
Animal and Plant Health Inspection Service	7, III; 9, I
Chief Financial Officer, Office of	7, XXX
Commodity Credit Corporation	7, XIV
Economic Research Service	7, XXXVII
Energy Policy and New Uses, Office of	2, IX; 7, XXIX
Environmental Quality, Office of	7, XXXI
Farm Service Agency	7, VII, XVIII
Federal Acquisition Regulation	48, 4
Federal Crop Insurance Corporation	7, IV
Food and Nutrition Service	7, II
Food Safety and Inspection Service	9, III
Foreign Agricultural Service	7, XV
Forest Service	36, II
Grain Inspection, Packers and Stockyards Administration	7, VIII; 9, II
Information Resources Management, Office of	7, XXVII
Inspector General, Office of	7, XXVI
National Agricultural Library	7, XLI
National Agricultural Statistics Service	7, XXXVI
National Institute of Food and Agriculture	7, XXXIV
Natural Resources Conservation Service	7, VI
Operations, Office of	7, XXVIII
Procurement and Property Management, Office of	7, XXXII
Rural Business-Cooperative Service	7, XVIII, XLII, L
Rural Development Administration	7, XLII
Rural Housing Service	7, XVIII, XXXV, L
Rural Telephone Bank	7, XVI
Rural Utilities Service	7, XVII, XVIII, XLII, L
Secretary of Agriculture, Office of	7, Subtitle A
Transportation, Office of	7, XXXIII
World Agricultural Outlook Board	7, XXXVIII
Air Force Department	32, VII
Federal Acquisition Regulation Supplement	48, 53
Air Transportation Stabilization Board	14, VI
Alcohol and Tobacco Tax and Trade Bureau	27, I
Alcohol, Tobacco, Firearms, and Explosives, Bureau of	27, II
AMTRAK	49, VII
American Battle Monuments Commission	36, IV
American Indians, Office of the Special Trustee	25, VII

Agency	CFR Title, Subtitle or Chapter
Animal and Plant Health Inspection Service	7, III; 9, I
Appalachian Regional Commission	5, IX
Architectural and Transportation Barriers Compliance Board	36, XI
Arctic Research Commission	45, XXIII
Armed Forces Retirement Home	5, XI
Army Department	32, V
Engineers, Corps of	33, II; 36, III
Federal Acquisition Regulation	48, 51
Bilingual Education and Minority Languages Affairs, Office of	34, V
Blind or Severely Disabled, Committee for Purchase from People Who Are	41, 51
Broadcasting Board of Governors	22, V
Federal Acquisition Regulation	48, 19
Bureau of Ocean Energy Management, Regulation, and Enforcement	30, II
Census Bureau	15, I
Centers for Medicare & Medicaid Services	42, IV
Central Intelligence Agency	32, XIX
Chemical Safety and Hazardous Investigation Board	40, VI
Chief Financial Officer, Office of	7, XXX
Child Support Enforcement, Office of	45, III
Children and Families, Administration for	45, II, III, IV, X
Civil Rights, Commission on	5, LXVIII; 45, VII
Civil Rights, Office for	34, I
Council of the Inspectors General on Integrity and Efficiency	5, XCVIII
Court Services and Offender Supervision Agency for the District of Columbia	5, LXX
Coast Guard	33, I; 46, I; 49, IV
Coast Guard (Great Lakes Pilotage)	46, III
Commerce Department	2, XIII; 44, IV; 50, VI
Census Bureau	15, I
Economic Affairs, Under Secretary	37, V
Economic Analysis, Bureau of	15, VIII
Economic Development Administration	13, III
Emergency Management and Assistance	44, IV
Federal Acquisition Regulation	48, 13
Foreign-Trade Zones Board	15, IV
Industry and Security, Bureau of	15, VII
International Trade Administration	15, III; 19, III
National Institute of Standards and Technology	15, II
National Marine Fisheries Service	50, II, IV
National Oceanic and Atmospheric Administration	15, IX; 50, II, III, IV, VI
National Telecommunications and Information Administration	15, XXIII; 47, III, IV
National Weather Service	15, IX
Patent and Trademark Office, United States	37, I
Productivity, Technology and Innovation, Assistant Secretary for	37, IV
Secretary of Commerce, Office of	15, Subtitle A
Technology, Under Secretary for	37, V
Technology Administration	15, XI
Technology Policy, Assistant Secretary for	37, IV
Commercial Space Transportation	14, III
Commodity Credit Corporation	7, XIV
Commodity Futures Trading Commission	5, XLI; 17, I
Community Planning and Development, Office of Assistant Secretary for	24, V, VI
Community Services, Office of	45, X
Comptroller of the Currency	12, I
Construction Industry Collective Bargaining Commission	29, IX
Consumer Financial Protection Bureau	5, LXXXIV; 12, X
Consumer Product Safety Commission	5, LXXI; 16, II
Copyright Office	37, II
Copyright Royalty Board	37, III
Corporation for National and Community Service	2, XXII; 45, XII, XXV
Cost Accounting Standards Board	48, 99
Council on Environmental Quality	40, V

Agency	CFR Title, Subtitle or Chapter
Court Services and Offender Supervision Agency for the District of Columbia	5, LXX; 28, VIII
Customs and Border Protection	19, I
Defense Contract Audit Agency	32, I
Defense Department	2, XI; 5, XXVI; 32, Subtitle A; 40, VII
Advanced Research Projects Agency	32, I
Air Force Department	32, VII
Army Department	32, V; 33, II; 36, III, 48, 51
Defense Acquisition Regulations System	48, 2
Defense Intelligence Agency	32, I
Defense Logistics Agency	32, I, XII; 48, 54
Engineers, Corps of	33, II; 36, III
National Imagery and Mapping Agency	32, I
Navy Department	32, VI; 48, 52
Secretary of Defense, Office of	2, XI; 32, I
Defense Contract Audit Agency	32, I
Defense Intelligence Agency	32, I
Defense Logistics Agency	32, XII; 48, 54
Defense Nuclear Facilities Safety Board	10, XVII
Delaware River Basin Commission	18, III
District of Columbia, Court Services and Offender Supervision Agency for the	5, LXX; 28, VIII
Drug Enforcement Administration	21, II
East-West Foreign Trade Board	15, XIII
Economic Affairs, Under Secretary	37, V
Economic Analysis, Bureau of	15, VIII
Economic Development Administration	13, III
Economic Research Service	7, XXXVII
Education, Department of	2, XXXIV; 5, LIII
Bilingual Education and Minority Languages Affairs, Office of	34, V
Civil Rights, Office for	34, I
Educational Research and Improvement, Office of	34, VII
Elementary and Secondary Education, Office of	34, II
Federal Acquisition Regulation	48, 34
Postsecondary Education, Office of	34, VI
Secretary of Education, Office of	34, Subtitle A
Special Education and Rehabilitative Services, Office of	34, III
Vocational and Adult Education, Office of	34, IV
Educational Research and Improvement, Office of	34, VII
Election Assistance Commission	2, LVIII; 11, II
Elementary and Secondary Education, Office of	34, II
Emergency Oil and Gas Guaranteed Loan Board	13, V
Emergency Steel Guarantee Loan Board	13, IV
Employee Benefits Security Administration	29, XXV
Employees' Compensation Appeals Board	20, IV
Employees Loyalty Board	5, V
Employment and Training Administration	20, V
Employment Standards Administration	20, VI
Endangered Species Committee	50, IV
Energy, Department of	2, IX; 5, XXIII; 10, II, III, X
Federal Acquisition Regulation	48, 9
Federal Energy Regulatory Commission	5, XXIV; 18, I
Property Management Regulations	41, 109
Energy, Office of	7, XXIX
Engineers, Corps of	33, II; 36, III
Engraving and Printing, Bureau of	31, VI
Environmental Protection Agency	2, XV; 5, LIV; 40, I, IV, VII
Federal Acquisition Regulation	48, 15
Property Management Regulations	41, 115
Environmental Quality, Office of	7, XXXI
Equal Employment Opportunity Commission	5, LXII; 29, XIV
Equal Opportunity, Office of Assistant Secretary for	24, I

Agency	CFR Title, Subtitle or Chapter
Executive Office of the President	3, I
Administration, Office of	5, XV
Environmental Quality, Council on	40, V
Management and Budget, Office of	2, Subtitle A; 5, III, LXXVII; 14, VI; 48, 99
National Drug Control Policy, Office of	21, III
National Security Council	32, XXI; 47, 2
Presidential Documents	3
Science and Technology Policy, Office of	32, XXIV; 47, II
Trade Representative, Office of the United States	15, XX
Export-Import Bank of the United States	2, XXXV; 5, LII; 12, IV
Family Assistance, Office of	45, II
Farm Credit Administration	5, XXXI; 12, VI
Farm Credit System Insurance Corporation	5, XXX; 12, XIV
Farm Service Agency	7, VII, XVIII
Federal Acquisition Regulation	48, 1
Federal Aviation Administration	14, I
Commercial Space Transportation	14, III
Federal Claims Collection Standards	31, IX
Federal Communications Commission	5, XXIX; 47, I
Federal Contract Compliance Programs, Office of	41, 60
Federal Crop Insurance Corporation	7, IV
Federal Deposit Insurance Corporation	5, XXII; 12, III
Federal Election Commission	5, XXXVII; 11, I
Federal Emergency Management Agency	44, I
Federal Employees Group Life Insurance Federal Acquisition Regulation	48, 21
Federal Employees Health Benefits Acquisition Regulation	48, 16
Federal Energy Regulatory Commission	5, XXIV; 18, I
Federal Financial Institutions Examination Council	12, XI
Federal Financing Bank	12, VIII
Federal Highway Administration	23, I, II
Federal Home Loan Mortgage Corporation	1, IV
Federal Housing Enterprise Oversight Office	12, XVII
Federal Housing Finance Agency	5, LXXX; 12, XII
Federal Housing Finance Board	12, IX
Federal Labor Relations Authority	5, XIV, XLIX; 22, XIV
Federal Law Enforcement Training Center	31, VII
Federal Management Regulation	41, 102
Federal Maritime Commission	46, IV
Federal Mediation and Conciliation Service	29, XII
Federal Mine Safety and Health Review Commission	5, LXXIV; 29, XXVII
Federal Motor Carrier Safety Administration	49, III
Federal Prison Industries, Inc.	28, III
Federal Procurement Policy Office	48, 99
Federal Property Management Regulations	41, 101
Federal Railroad Administration	49, II
Federal Register, Administrative Committee of	1, I
Federal Register, Office of	1, II
Federal Reserve System	12, II
Board of Governors	5, LVIII
Federal Retirement Thrift Investment Board	5, VI, LXXVI
Federal Service Impasses Panel	5, XIV
Federal Trade Commission	5, XLVII; 16, I
Federal Transit Administration	49, VI
Federal Travel Regulation System	41, Subtitle F
Financial Crimes Enforcement Network	31, X
Financial Research Office	12, XVI
Financial Stability Oversight Council	12, XIII
Fine Arts, Commission on	45, XXI
Fiscal Service	31, II
Fish and Wildlife Service, United States	50, I, IV
Food and Drug Administration	21, I
Food and Nutrition Service	7, II
Food Safety and Inspection Service	9, III
Foreign Agricultural Service	7, XV
Foreign Assets Control, Office of	31, V

Agency	CFR Title, Subtitle or Chapter
Foreign Claims Settlement Commission of the United States	45, V
Foreign Service Grievance Board	22, IX
Foreign Service Impasse Disputes Panel	22, XIV
Foreign Service Labor Relations Board	22, XIV
Foreign-Trade Zones Board	15, IV
Forest Service	36, II
General Services Administration	5, LVII; 41, 105
Contract Appeals, Board of	48, 61
Federal Acquisition Regulation	48, 5
Federal Management Regulation	41, 102
Federal Property Management Regulations	41, 101
Federal Travel Regulation System	41, Subtitle F
General	41, 300
Payment From a Non-Federal Source for Travel Expenses	41, 304
Payment of Expenses Connected With the Death of Certain Employees	41, 303
Relocation Allowances	41, 302
Temporary Duty (TDY) Travel Allowances	41, 301
Geological Survey	30, IV
Government Accountability Office	4, I
Government Ethics, Office of	5, XVI
Government National Mortgage Association	24, III
Grain Inspection, Packers and Stockyards Administration	7, VIII; 9, II
Harry S. Truman Scholarship Foundation	45, XVIII
Health and Human Services, Department of	2, III; 5, XLV; 45, Subtitle A,
Centers for Medicare & Medicaid Services	42, IV
Child Support Enforcement, Office of	45, III
Children and Families, Administration for	45, II, III, IV, X
Community Services, Office of	45, X
Family Assistance, Office of	45, II
Federal Acquisition Regulation	48, 3
Food and Drug Administration	21, I
Human Development Services, Office of	45, XIII
Indian Health Service	25, V
Inspector General (Health Care), Office of	42, V
Public Health Service	42, I
Refugee Resettlement, Office of	45, IV
Homeland Security, Department of	2, XXX; 6, I; 8, I
Coast Guard	33, I; 46, I; 49, IV
Coast Guard (Great Lakes Pilotage)	46, III
Customs and Border Protection	19, I
Federal Emergency Management Agency	44, I
Human Resources Management and Labor Relations Systems	5, XCVII
Immigration and Customs Enforcement Bureau	19, IV
Transportation Security Administration	49, XII
HOPE for Homeowners Program, Board of Directors of	24, XXIV
Housing and Urban Development, Department of	2, XXIV; 5, LXV; 24, Subtitle B
Community Planning and Development, Office of Assistant Secretary for	24, V, VI
Equal Opportunity, Office of Assistant Secretary for	24, I
Federal Acquisition Regulation	48, 24
Federal Housing Enterprise Oversight, Office of	12, XVII
Government National Mortgage Association	24, III
Housing—Federal Housing Commissioner, Office of Assistant Secretary for	24, II, VIII, X, XX
Housing, Office of, and Multifamily Housing Assistance Restructuring, Office of	24, IV
Inspector General, Office of	24, XII
Public and Indian Housing, Office of Assistant Secretary for	24, IX
Secretary, Office of	24, Subtitle A, VII
Housing—Federal Housing Commissioner, Office of Assistant Secretary for	24, II, VIII, X, XX
Housing, Office of, and Multifamily Housing Assistance Restructuring, Office of	24, IV

Agency	CFR Title, Subtitle or Chapter
Property Management Regulations	41, 128
Labor Department	5, XLII
Employee Benefits Security Administration	29, XXV
Employees' Compensation Appeals Board	20, IV
Employment and Training Administration	20, V
Employment Standards Administration	20, VI
Federal Acquisition Regulation	48, 29
Federal Contract Compliance Programs, Office of	41, 60
Federal Procurement Regulations System	41, 50
Labor-Management Standards, Office of	29, II, IV
Mine Safety and Health Administration	30, I
Occupational Safety and Health Administration	29, XVII
Office of Workers' Compensation Programs	20, VII
Public Contracts	41, 50
Secretary of Labor, Office of	29, Subtitle A
Veterans' Employment and Training Service, Office of the Assistant Secretary for	41, 61; 20, IX
Wage and Hour Division	29, V
Workers' Compensation Programs, Office of	20, I
Labor-Management Standards, Office of	29, II, IV
Land Management, Bureau of	43, II
Legal Services Corporation	45, XVI
Library of Congress	36, VII
Copyright Office	37, II
Copyright Royalty Board	37, III
Local Television Loan Guarantee Board	7, XX
Management and Budget, Office of	5, III, LXXVII; 14, VI; 48, 99
Marine Mammal Commission	50, V
Maritime Administration	46, II
Merit Systems Protection Board	5, II, LXIV
Micronesian Status Negotiations, Office for	32, XXVII
Millennium Challenge Corporation	22, XIII
Mine Safety and Health Administration	30, I
Minority Business Development Agency	15, XIV
Miscellaneous Agencies	1, IV
Monetary Offices	31, I
Morris K. Udall Scholarship and Excellence in National Environmental Policy Foundation	36, XVI
Museum and Library Services, Institute of	2, XXXI
National Aeronautics and Space Administration	2, XVIII; 5, LIX; 14, V
Federal Acquisition Regulation	48, 18
National Agricultural Library	7, XLI
National Agricultural Statistics Service	7, XXXVI
National and Community Service, Corporation for	2, XXII; 45, XII, XXV
National Archives and Records Administration	2, XXVI; 5, LXVI; 36, XII
Information Security Oversight Office	32, XX
National Capital Planning Commission	1, IV
National Commission for Employment Policy	1, IV
National Commission on Libraries and Information Science	45, XVII
National Council on Disability	34, XII
National Counterintelligence Center	32, XVIII
National Credit Union Administration	12, VII
National Crime Prevention and Privacy Compact Council	28, IX
National Drug Control Policy, Office of	21, III
National Endowment for the Arts	2, XXXII
National Endowment for the Humanities	2, XXXIII
National Foundation on the Arts and the Humanities	45, XI
National Highway Traffic Safety Administration	23, II, III; 47, VI; 49, V
National Imagery and Mapping Agency	32, I
National Indian Gaming Commission	25, III
National Institute for Literacy	34, XI
National Institute of Food and Agriculture	7, XXXIV
National Institute of Standards and Technology	15, II
National Intelligence, Office of Director of	32, XVII
National Labor Relations Board	5, LXI; 29, I

Agency	CFR Title, Subtitle or Chapter
National Marine Fisheries Service	50, II, IV
National Mediation Board	29, X
National Oceanic and Atmospheric Administration	15, IX; 50, II, III, IV, VI
National Park Service	36, I
National Railroad Adjustment Board	29, III
National Railroad Passenger Corporation (AMTRAK)	49, VII
National Science Foundation	2, XXV; 5, XLIII; 45, VI
Federal Acquisition Regulation	48, 25
National Security Council	32, XXI
National Security Council and Office of Science and Technology Policy	47, II
National Telecommunications and Information Administration	15, XXIII; 47, III, IV
National Transportation Safety Board	49, VIII
Natural Resources Conservation Service	7, VI
Natural Resource Revenue, Office of	30, XII
Navajo and Hopi Indian Relocation, Office of	25, IV
Navy Department	32, VI
Federal Acquisition Regulation	48, 52
Neighborhood Reinvestment Corporation	24, XXV
Northeast Interstate Low-Level Radioactive Waste Commission	10, XVIII
Nuclear Regulatory Commission	2, XX; 5, XLVIII; 10, I
Federal Acquisition Regulation	48, 20
Occupational Safety and Health Administration	29, XVII
Occupational Safety and Health Review Commission	29, XX
Ocean Energy Management, Bureau of	30, V
Offices of Independent Counsel	28, VI
Office of Workers' Compensation Programs	20, VII
Oklahoma City National Memorial Trust	36, XV
Operations Office	7, XXVIII
Overseas Private Investment Corporation	5, XXXIII; 22, VII
Patent and Trademark Office, United States	37, I
Payment From a Non-Federal Source for Travel Expenses	41, 304
Payment of Expenses Connected With the Death of Certain Employees	41, 303
Peace Corps	2, XXXVII; 22, III
Pennsylvania Avenue Development Corporation	36, IX
Pension Benefit Guaranty Corporation	29, XL
Personnel Management, Office of	5, I, XXXV; 45, VIII
Human Resources Management and Labor Relations Systems, Department of Homeland Security	5, XCVII
Federal Acquisition Regulation	48, 17
Federal Employees Group Life Insurance Federal Acquisition Regulation	48, 21
Federal Employees Health Benefits Acquisition Regulation	48, 16
Pipeline and Hazardous Materials Safety Administration	49, I
Postal Regulatory Commission	5, XLVI; 39, III
Postal Service, United States	5, LX; 39, I
Postsecondary Education, Office of	34, VI
President's Commission on White House Fellowships	1, IV
Presidential Documents	3
Presidio Trust	36, X
Prisons, Bureau of	28, V
Procurement and Property Management, Office of	7, XXXII
Productivity, Technology and Innovation, Assistant Secretary	37, IV
Public Contracts, Department of Labor	41, 50
Public and Indian Housing, Office of Assistant Secretary for	24, IX
Public Health Service	42, I
Railroad Retirement Board	20, II
Reclamation, Bureau of	43, I
Recovery Accountability and Transparency Board	4, II
Refugee Resettlement, Office of	45, IV
Relocation Allowances	41, 302
Research and Innovative Technology Administration	49, XI
Rural Business-Cooperative Service	7, XVIII, XLII, L

Agency	CFR Title, Subtitle or Chapter
Rural Development Administration	7, XLII
Rural Housing Service	7, XVIII, XXXV, L
Rural Telephone Bank	7, XVI
Rural Utilities Service	7, XVII, XVIII, XLII, L
Saint Lawrence Seaway Development Corporation	33, IV
Science and Technology Policy, Office of	32, XXIV
Science and Technology Policy, Office of, and National Security Council	47, II
Secret Service	31, IV
Securities and Exchange Commission	5, XXXIV; 17, II
Selective Service System	32, XVI
Small Business Administration	2, XXVII; 13, I
Smithsonian Institution	36, V
Social Security Administration	2, XXIII; 20, III; 48, 23
Soldiers' and Airmen's Home, United States	5, XI
Special Counsel, Office of	5, VIII
Special Education and Rehabilitative Services, Office of	34, III
State Department	2, VI; 22, I; 28, XI
Federal Acquisition Regulation	48, 6
Surface Mining Reclamation and Enforcement, Office of	30, VII
Surface Transportation Board	49, X
Susquehanna River Basin Commission	18, VIII
Technology Administration	15, XI
Technology Policy, Assistant Secretary for	37, IV
Technology, Under Secretary for	37, V
Tennessee Valley Authority	5, LXIX; 18, XIII
Thrift Supervision Office, Department of the Treasury	12, V
Trade Representative, United States, Office of	15, XX
Transportation, Department of	2, XII; 5, L
Commercial Space Transportation	14, III
Contract Appeals, Board of	48, 63
Emergency Management and Assistance	44, IV
Federal Acquisition Regulation	48, 12
Federal Aviation Administration	14, I
Federal Highway Administration	23, I, II
Federal Motor Carrier Safety Administration	49, III
Federal Railroad Administration	49, II
Federal Transit Administration	49, VI
Maritime Administration	46, II
National Highway Traffic Safety Administration	23, II, III; 47, IV; 49, V
Pipeline and Hazardous Materials Safety Administration	49, I
Saint Lawrence Seaway Development Corporation	33, IV
Secretary of Transportation, Office of	14, II; 49, Subtitle A
Surface Transportation Board	49, X
Transportation Statistics Bureau	49, XI
Transportation, Office of	7, XXXIII
Transportation Security Administration	49, XII
Transportation Statistics Bureau	49, XI
Travel Allowances, Temporary Duty (TDY)	41, 301
Treasury Department	5, XXI; 12, XV; 17, IV; 31, IX
Alcohol and Tobacco Tax and Trade Bureau	27, I
Community Development Financial Institutions Fund	12, XVIII
Comptroller of the Currency	12, I
Customs and Border Protection	19, I
Engraving and Printing, Bureau of	31, VI
Federal Acquisition Regulation	48, 10
Federal Claims Collection Standards	31, IX
Federal Law Enforcement Training Center	31, VII
Financial Crimes Enforcement Network	31, X
Fiscal Service	31, II
Foreign Assets Control, Office of	31, V
Internal Revenue Service	26, I
Investment Security, Office of	31, VIII
Monetary Offices	31, I
Secret Service	31, IV
Secretary of the Treasury, Office of	31, Subtitle A

Agency	CFR Title, Subtitle or Chapter
Thrift Supervision, Office of	12, V
Truman, Harry S. Scholarship Foundation	45, XVIII
United States and Canada, International Joint Commission	22, IV
United States and Mexico, International Boundary and Water Commission, United States Section	22, XI
Utah Reclamation Mitigation and Conservation Commission	43, III
Veterans Affairs Department	2, VIII; 38, I
Federal Acquisition Regulation	48, 8
Veterans' Employment and Training Service, Office of the Assistant Secretary for	41, 61; 20, IX
Vice President of the United States, Office of	32, XXVIII
Vocational and Adult Education, Office of	34, IV
Wage and Hour Division	29, V
Water Resources Council	18, VI
Workers' Compensation Programs, Office of	20, I
World Agricultural Outlook Board	7, XXXVIII
World Agricultural Outlook Board	7, XXXVIII

List of CFR Sections Affected

All changes in this volume of the Code of Federal Regulations (CFR) that were made by documents published in the FEDERAL REGISTER since January 1, 2008 are enumerated in the following list. Entries indicate the nature of the changes effected. Page numbers refer to FEDERAL REGISTER pages. The user should consult the entries for chapters, parts and subparts as well as sections for revisions.

For changes to this volume of the CFR prior to this listing, consult the annual edition of the monthly List of CFR Sections Affected (LSA). The LSA is available at *www.fdsys.gov*. For changes to this volume of the CFR prior to 2001, see the "List of CFR Sections Affected, 1949–1963, 1964–1972, 1973–1985, and 1986–2000" published in 11 separate volumes. The "List of CFR Sections Affected 1986–2000" is available at *www.fdsys.gov*.

2008

16 CFR

73 FR Page

Chapter II

1101 Authority citation revised....72334
1101.1 (b)(1) amended....72334
1101.2 Revised....72334
1101.12 (h) added....72335
1101.21 (a) amended....72335
1101.22 (a)(1), (2) and (b)(2) amended....72335
1101.23 Heading and (c) revised; introductory text, (a) and (b) amended....72335
1101.25 (a) and (b) amended; (c) revised....72335
1101.31 (a) amended....72335
1101.41 (a) revised....72335
1101.43 Revised....72335
1101.61 (b)(4) added....72335
1101.62 (a)(2) revised....72335
1101.71 (b)(1) and (2) amended....72335
1110 Added....68331
1303 Authority citation revised....77493
1303.1 (a) introductory text and (c) revised; (d) added; eff. 8–14–09....77493
1303.2 (b)(2) revised; eff. 8–14–09....77493
1420 Added; eff. 4–13–09....67386
1500.18 (a)(16)(i) introductory text revised....77495
1500.20 Added; eff. 2–10–09....67736

16 CFR—Continued

73 FR Page

Chapter II—Continued

(e)(3) table and footnotes corrected....71545
1500.86 (a)(9) added....77495
1610 Revised....15640
1610.5 (a)(1)(vii) correctly amended....62187
1610.6 (a)(3)(v) correctly amended; (b)(1)(ii) correctly revised....62187
1610 Figure 6 correctly revised....62188
Figure 9 correctly revised....62189
1633.7 (a)(6)(v) through (ix) correctly redesignated as (a)(6)(vi) through (x); (a)(6)(iv) partially redesignated as new (a)(6)(v); new (a)(6)(v) heading added; (a)(4)(i), (ii), (iii), new (6)(vii) footnote 1, new (ix), (b)(1)(ii), (d)(1), (2), (e), (f), (h)(1)(iv), (2)(i), (iv), (viii) and (i)(2)(i) correctly amended....6843
1633.12 (a)(6)(iii) and (d) correctly amended....6843

2009

16 CFR

74 FR Page

Chapter II

1119 Added; interim....45106
1130 Added; eff. 6–28–10....68676
1500 Authority citation revised....6993, 10480

16 CFR—Continued

74 FR Page

Chapter II—Continued

1500.83 (a)(35) introductory text and (i) revised 27249
1500.87 Added 39540
1500.88 Added; interim 6993
1500.89 Added 10480
1500.90 Added 10480
1500.91 Added 43041

2010

16 CFR

75 FR Page

Chapter II

1102 Added; eff. 1–10–11 76867
1115.23—1115.29 (Subpart C) Added 3368
1119 Revised 15998
1130.16 (b)(3) corrected 7551
1200 Added 63077
1215 Policy statement 31688
Added 31698
Technical correction 33683
1215.2 (b)(2)(i) corrected 51178
1216 Added 35273
Policy statement 35282
1216.2 (b)(11)(i) and (21)(i) corrected 51178
1219 Added; eff. 6–28–11 81786
Policy statement 81789
1220 Added; eff. 6–28–11 81787
Policy statement 81789
1420 Policy statement 52616
1450 Added 21987
1500 Authority citation revised 81788
1500.18 (a)(6) introductory text amended 35282
(a)(13) and (14) removed; eff. 6–28–11 81788
1500.83 (a)(2), (3), (4) and (18) introductory text revised 49380
1500.86 (a)(4) introductory text revised 35282
1500.88 Revised 3158
1508 Removed; eff. 6–28–11 81789
1509 Removed; eff. 6–28–11 81789
1512 Stay of enforcement extended 34360
1611 Policy statement 42311
1630 Policy statement 42315
1631 Policy statement 42315
1632 Policy statement 72944
1633 Policy statement 72944

2011

16 CFR

76 FR Page

Chapter II

Policy statement 46598, 49286
1107 Added; eff. 2–8–13 69541
1109 Added 69580
1120 Added 37640
1120.2 (c) added 42507
1120.3 (b) added 42507
1217 Added 22028
Policy statement 22030
1217.2 (c)(6)(iii), (iv) and (7) correctly added 27882
1303 Policy statement 18645
1450.2 Removed 62607
1450.3 Added 47438
1500 Policy statement 44463
1512.2 (b) and (d) revised; (g) added 27888
1512.4 (b) and (i) revised 27888
1512.6 (a) and (c) revised 27888
1512.12 (b) revised 27888
1512.15 (a) and (b) revised 27888
1512.18 (k)(1)(i) and (n)(2)(vii) revised 27888
1610 Policy statement 22608
1632.4 (a)(2) revised 59023
1700.14 (a)(10)(xxii) and (xxiii) added 43851

2012

16 CFR

77 FR Page

Chapter II

Policy statement 10358
1101.25 (a) and (b) corrected; CFR correction 61513
1107.21 (f) added; eff. 2-8-13 72219
1107.26 (a)(4) added; eff. 2-8-13 72219
1112 Added 31084
1130.3 (a)(2) amended 9524
1130.5 (a) and (f) amended 9524
1130.6 Revised 9524
1130.7 Removed; redesignated from 1130.8 9525
1130.8 Redesignated as new 1130.7; redesignated from 1130.9; (d) and (e) added 9525
1130.9 Redesignated as 1130.8 9525
1130 Figure 1 revised 9525
Figure 2 revised 9526
1215 Authority citation revised 45246
1215.2 Revised 45246
1219 Authority citation revised 45246
1219.2 Revised 45246

16 CFR—Continued

77 FR Page

Chapter II—Continued

1221 Added; eff. 2-28-13 52228
1223 Added; eff. 5-7-13 66713
1224 Added 12197
1420.1 Amended 12200
1420.3 (a) revised 12200
1450 Policy statement 30886
1500.3 (c)(1) introductory text, (c)(2) introductory text, (i), (3) and (4) revised; (c)(1)(iii) added; eff. 1-9-13 73293

16 CFR—Continued

77 FR Page

Chapter II—Continued

1500.40 Introductory text revised; eff. 1-9-13 73294
1500.41 Introductory text amended; eff. 1-9-13 73294
1500.42 Introductory text added; (a)(1) amended; (c) revised; eff. 1-9-13 73294
1500.232 Added; eff. 1-9-13 73288
1700.14 (a)(33) added 73301

○